Introduction to Accounting

All Internet Resources are updated every two weeks by Ph.D.-granted professors around the world, as well as a team of full-time technical support staff.

You can always rely on Prentice Hall's PHLIP/CW to provide you and your students with the services you need!

"Syllabus Manager":

- ❏ Allows instructors to construct on-line syllabi tailored to assignments and events for their classes, and linked to specific modules on the Web site and other on-line content
- ❏ Provides students with quick access to course materials by using a calendar feature found on the navigation bar

"Faculty Resources/Lounge" includes:

- ❏ Password- protected site
- ❏ Downloads of on-line supplements Archive of teaching resources created by other faculty using this text
- ❏ Chat room for faculty use only
- ❏ Teaching tools for the "Current Events"
- ❏ PHAS General Ledger

"Study Guide" includes:

- ❏ Separate multiple choice, fill-in-the-blank, and essay practice tests for each chapter
- ❏ "Hints" for each problem
- ❏ Immediate feedback on tests with total score, and an explanation provided for each incorrect answer
- ❏ Ability to e-mail results to faculty member or other designated individual
- ❏ All questions created specifically for the Web site; no duplication of questions taken from text, test bank, or print study guide

Companion Website

Chapter 1: Introduction to Business in the United States

Objectives

After studying this chapter, you should be able to:

1. Describe the four factors of production.

2. Explain the basic concepts of capitalism and how they relate to the profit motive.

3. Explain the basic issues in the debate over whether businesses have a social responsibility.

4. Distinguish among the three basic forms of business organization - the proprietorship, the partnership, and the corporation - and describe the advantages and disadvantages of each.

5. Distinguish among the three major types of business activities and define hybrid type businesses.

6. Explain the basic need for international business trade and the complications involved in this activity.

7. Describe the SEC's authority over accounting reporting standards and describe the current standard-setting process in the United States.

8. Explain the purpose of an independent financial audit.

Introduction
to Accounting

when

Introduction to Accounting
A User Perspective

Kumen H. Jones
Arizona State University, Retired

Michael L. Werner
University of Miami

Katherene P. Terrell
University of Central Oklahoma

Robert L. Terrell
University of Central Oklahoma

Prentice Hall, Upper Saddle River, New Jersey 07458

Executive Editor: Debbie Hoffman
Assistant Editor: Kasey Sheehan
Senior Editorial Assistant: Jane Avery
Editor-in-Chief: PJ Boardman
Executive Marketing Manager: Beth Toland
Production Editor: Marc Oliver
Managing Editor: Sondra Greenfield
Senior Manufacturing Supervisor: Paul Smolenski
Senior Manufacturing/Prepress Manager: Vincent Scelta
Cover Design: Steve Frim
Design Manager: Patricia Smythe
Interior Design: Carlisle Communications
Cover Illustration/Photo: Jerry McDaniel
Composition: Carlisle Communications

Library of Congress Cataloging-in-Publication Data

Introduction to accounting : a user perspective / Kumen H. Jones . . . [et al.].
    p.   cm.
   Includes bibliographical references and index.
   ISBN 0-13-065475-2
   1. Accounting.   2. Accounting—United States.   I. Jones, Kumen H.
HF5635.I654   2000
657—dc21   99–33622
                                                    CIP

Prentice-Hall International (UK) Limited, London
Prentice-Hall of Australia Pty. Limited, Sydney
Prentice-Hall Canada, Inc., Toronto
Prentice-Hall Hispanoamericana, S.A., Mexico
Prentice-Hall of India Private Limited, New Delhi
Prentice-Hall of Japan, Inc., Tokyo
Pearson Education Asia Pte. Ltd., Singapore
Editora Prentice-Hall do Brasil, Ltda., Rio Janeiro

Printed in the United States of America

10 9 8 7 6 5 4 3 2 1

*Our families are our strength
and give meaning to our lives.
We dedicate this book to them.*

*To my wife Mary Ann and my children
Richard and Kim, Thomas and Teresa, Francis and Rachelle,
Brian and Jessica, Stephen and Lindsay, and Cameron
. . . Kumen Jones*

*To my daughters Jessica and Amanda
. . . Michael Werner*

*To our sons Robert and Jonathon
. . . Katherene and Robert Terrell*

*Special Thanks to
George R. Violette, University of Southern Maine
for his contributions*

Contents

CHAPTER   2 *Economic Decision Making*   *F-43*

CHAPTER 5 *Tools of the Trade, Part II*
Income Statement and Statement of Owners' Equity   *F-141*

CHAPTER 6 *Keeping Score: Bases of Economic Measurement*   *F-183*

CHAPTER   7   *Accumulating Accounting Data*   *F-223*

CHAPTER 10 *The Balance Sheet and Income Statement: A Closer Look* *F-373*

INTRODUCTION TO MANAGEMENT ACCOUNTING: A USER PERSPECTIVE   M-1

CHAPTER   1   *Management Accounting: Its Environment and Future*   *M-3*

CHAPTER   2   *Classifying Costs*   *M-19*

CHAPTER 3 *Determining Costs of Products* M-69

CHAPTER 8 *The Operating Budget* M-265

CHAPTER   9   *Standard Costing*   *M-325*

CHAPTER   10   *Evaluating Performance*   *M-377*

Preface

*A*s we enter the twenty-first century, we who are involved in accounting education at the collegiate level have reassessed the way we prepare our students for the business world. Technology changes more quickly than most of us can comprehend, complicating accounting education. Yet one constant remains: Business people must be prepared to perform tasks that only people can perform—in particular, communicating, thinking, and making decisions. Decision making is *the* critical skill in today's business world, and *Introduction to Accounting: A User Perspective*, helps students to better use accounting information and improve their decision-making skills.

This text provides an introduction to financial accounting and management accounting within the context of business and business decisions. Readers will explore accounting information's role in the decision-making process, and learn how to use accounting information found in various external and internal accounting reports. Seeing how accounting information can be used to make better business decisions will benefit all students, regardless of their major course of study or chosen career.

We agree with the recommendations made by the Accounting Education Change Commission in its *Position Statement No. Two: The First Course in Accounting*. We believe the course should be a broad introduction *to* accounting, rather than introductory accounting as it has traditionally been taught, and it should be taught from the perspective of the user, not the preparer. It should emphasize *what* accounting information is, *why* it is important, and *how* it is used by economic decision makers, both external and internal.

As you work with this text, you will find it focuses heavily on the uses of accounting information rather than the preparation of the information. This, however, is only one characteristic which distinguishes *Introduction to Accounting: A User Perspective*, from other texts you may have used in the past.

SUPPORT FOR THE INTERACTIVE CLASSROOM

We believe this text provides tools to actively involve students in their learning processes. The conversational tone of the text, its user perspective, and the logical presentation of topics all contribute to the ability of this text to meet that goal. However, several features are particularly important in developing a classroom atmosphere in which students share ideas, ask questions, and relate their learning to the world around them.

Throughout each chapter of the text, you will find Discussion Questions (DQs) that challenge students to reach beyond the surface of the written text to determine answers. Far from typical review questions, for which the students can scan a few pages of the text to locate an answer, many of the DQs provide relevant learning by relating students' personal experiences to the knowledge they gain through the text.

The DQs provide a variety of classroom experiences:

- Many DQs provide the basis for lively classroom discussions, requiring students to think about issues and formulate or defend their opinions.
- Some DQs are springboards for group assignments (in or out of the classroom) to put cooperative learning into practice.
- DQs may be assigned as individual writing assignments to allow students to practice and develop their writing skills.
- Combining individually written DQ responses with follow-up group discussions leading to group consensus can spark lively debate!
- Having students keep a journal of their responses to all DQs (regardless if they are used in another way) encourages solitary pondering of accounting concepts.

The DQs comprise a critically important part of the text's pedagogy designed to emphasize important points that students may skim across in their initial reading. Even if they are not formally part of the required work for your course, students will gain a greater understanding of the concepts discussed when they take time to consider each question as part of the text.

- Students get enthused about accounting when working with real companies. Chapter F1 and its appendix provide students with information to use library and Internet resources to research companies, and introduce students to annual reports and Form 10-K.
- We included the 1997 Gap Inc. annual report with our text and use it to demonstrate financial analysis in Chapter F12. We added an annual report project to further involve students in the business world that begins in Chapter F1 and continues through Chapter F12.
- Financial Reporting Cases, at the end of Chapters F1 to F6 and Chapters F8 to F12, encourage students to use the Internet and the PHLIP Web site to link to real businesses and explore their financial statements. Three Accounting Cycle Cases are featured in Chapter F7.
- Including real-world situations presents a real challenge in presenting management accounting concepts because (a) many companies modify and tailor management accounting concepts to their individual needs, and (b) management accounting concepts often involve proprietary company policies and processes, so many companies guard their application of these concepts. When possible, however, we have tried to include as many real-world examples as possible in Chapters M1 through M10.

Adventures into *real* information about *real* companies always raises student interest! In addition to these features which help to foster an open, interactive environment in the classroom, a major distinction of this text is its total separation of the *use* of accounting information and its preparation.

SEPARATION OF ACCOUNTING AND BOOKKEEPING

With the exception of Chapter F-7, the text approaches accounting totally from the user perspective. These chapters contain no bookkeeping. Is this an indication we believe that a knowledge of bookkeeping skills is unnecessary? On the contrary, bookkeeping is the nuts and bolts that holds our accounting systems together. What we have learned, though, is that bookkeeping procedures without a conceptual understanding of the uses of accounting information are meaningless. Beginning accounting students cannot digest the use of financial statements, the role of accounting information, the world of business, and the details of bookkeeping simultaneously. Once students have a basic knowledge of the other topics, however, learning details of the recording process becomes effective and efficient.

Separating accounting and bookkeeping makes both subjects easier to grasp and more enjoyable to learn. This approach also allows instructors and institutions to select an appropriate time and degree of bookkeeping coverage for their program. Some schools choose to have all students learn basic recording procedures; others may only require accounting majors to acquire these skills.

To facilitate the separation of accounting and bookkeeping, we introduce the accounting cycle in Chapter F7 and complete its coverage in appendices to Chapters F8, F9, F10, M2, M3, and M9. We placed the accounting cycle coverage in Chapter F7 because this is the point when students have enough basic knowledge of the use of accounting information to be ready for accounting procedures. Some schools leave this material until the end of the semester, some opt to cover the material at the beginning of the second semester, or in a separate course for accounting majors. For this reason, no references are made to Chapter F7 in the remaining chapters except in the appendices.

Chapter F7 and the appendices in Chapter F8 through F10 cover the complete accounting cycle from analyzing transactions through post-closing trial balance, including debits and credits, journals, general ledgers, worksheets, and financial statement preparation. Chapter F7 contains a number of long problems and three Accounting Cycle Cases that are condensed practice sets. The PHLIP Web site for this text contains the PH General Ledger program to allow students to complete the long problems and Accounting Cycle Cases on realistic general ledger software.

Management accounting, by its nature, has less bookkeeping procedure than financial accounting. In chapters M2, M3, and M9, however, we have included appendices that cover the bookkeeping procedures required to record the topics presented.

In addition to the decision to focus on the uses of accounting information rather than the details of accounting procedures in this text, we have made several other deliberate and important choices about topical coverage many real-world examples as we could. In addition to these features which help to foster an open, interactive environment in the classroom, a major distinction of this text is its total separation of the use of accounting and its preparation.

TOPICS COVERED

We carefully considered the inclusion or exclusion of topics from this text consistent with our pedagogical goals of building foundations that support effective student learning. Because our focus introduces students to accounting information and its uses in decision making, we could not simply follow the traditional coverage of topics. As we considered individual topics, we continually explored whether their inclusion would enhance a student's ability to interpret and use accounting information throughout his or her personal and professional life. Based on our own experiences in industry and conversations we have had with both operations and accounting managers from many companies, we believe that *Introduction to Accounting: A User Perspective*, covers those financial accounting and management accounting topics that every accounting student should leave the course understanding well. In short, we sought quality of learning, not quantity of minutiae.

In the financial accounting portion of the text, for example, we cover the calculations of only two depreciation methods—straight line and double declining balance. By limiting the coverage of detailed depreciation calculations, we have the opportunity to focus on the concepts of cost allocation, expense recognition, financial statement differences between the two methods, and the distinction between gains and revenues, and losses and expenses. Students will not only know how to calculate depreciation expense, but also understand *why* they are calculating it and how to use those calculations in making business decisions. In the chapter, students learn how to properly interpret gains and losses. Most of them are surprised to find out that two companies buying identical assets for the same price can sell them later for the same amount and have different results—one company can have a gain and the other experience a loss.

Another example of building foundations to learning in the area of financial accounting is the introduction to the concept of the cost of borrowing. Instead of sending students straight to the present value tables, we take time to measure the cost of borrowing—an important foundation for intermediate accounting and learning how to account for interest costs in long-term liabilities.

In our coverage of the separation of a mixed cost into its variable and fixed components in the management accounting portion of the text, we discuss regression analysis, but do not include any calculations using this method. By limiting the coverage of detailed calculations, we have the opportunity to focus on the concept of cost separation without losing students in computations.

Another example in the management accounting portion is the introduction to the operating budget. Instead of sending students straight into the preparation of the budgets included in the operating budget, we present all the budgets conceptually first, and then walk them through budget preparation.

We also include some topics that traditional books omit. Chapter F1 includes discussions of each major type of business organization. As we discuss various topics, students learn to view the financial statements of each type of organization throughout the book. Chapter F1 and its appendix introduce students to library and Internet research on real companies and start students on a term quest to apply accounting concepts to at least one publicly traded firm. We pay particular attention to students' understanding of the difference between *reality* and the *measurement of reality* and the need to find both the *reality of cash* and the *reality of performance*.

Chapter M7 includes not only information on how to budget for capital expenditures, but where capital budgeting fits in a company's overall planning and control process. This chapter also discusses frankly some of the dysfunctional management behavior caused by inappropriate use of the capital budgeting process. Likewise, Chapter M8 includes a forthright discussion of appropriate and inappropriate uses of the operating budget.

From our classroom experience with this text, we believe that the content is appropriate for college sophomores to embrace and take forward to additional courses. The carefully chosen sequence of topics helps to make them more understandable by establishing firm conceptual foundations.

SEQUENCE OF COVERAGE

To effectively present the user perspective, we developed a logical flow of topics so that each chapter builds on what the student has already learned. Students can easily understand how the topics fit together logically and how they are used together to make good decisions. Moreover, students can see that accounting and the information it provides is not merely something that exists unto itself, but rather it is something developed in response to the needs of economic decision makers.

If you could read the entire text before using it in your classroom, you would have a very clear picture of the experience awaiting your students. However, even a short tour through the material covered in each chapter will show you how we have structured our presentation of the topics to maximize student learning.

Chapter F1 provides a brief overview of business and the role of accounting in the business world, setting the stage for the introduction of accounting information. In the appendix, we provide students with information about public reporting of accounting information and research sources. Without the world of business, there would be no need for accounting information or the accounting profession.

Chapter F2 presents an introduction to economic decision making. Because the stated purpose of financial accounting information is to provide information to be used in making decisions, we believe an understanding of the decision-making process is not only appropriate, but essential. We explore the characteristics crucial to making accounting information useful in that process.

Chapter F3 introduces the balance sheet as the first of several financial tools developed to present accounting information in a useful form. In this chapter we focus on how equity financing affects businesses and how its results are reflected on balance sheets.

Chapter F4 continues the exploration of the balance sheet, this time examining the impact of debt financing. We present notes and bonds as financing options for businesses and introduce the cost of borrowing.

Chapter F5 presents the income statement and statement of owners' equity as additional financial tools. Now that students have been introduced to the first three financial statements used by economic decision makers, they can see how the statements relate to one another.

Chapter F6 compares the cash basis and accrual basis of accounting. Basic knowledge of the cash basis is important for two reasons. First, students should realize that accrual accounting is *one* basis of measurement and not *the* measurement basis. Second, understanding the weaknesses of cash basis accounting makes the logic of accrual accounting much easier to grasp. By the time students finish this chapter, they hunger to have a method of organizing and recording accounting data.

Chapter F7 introduces the eight steps of the accounting cycle using the teaching example in Chapter F6. We discuss the chronology of the accounting cycle and then walk students through each step. The end-of-chapter materials provide students with ample opportunity to practice the skills demonstrated in the chapter. This chapter can be bypassed and used at a later time.

Chapter F8 explores issues surrounding the acquisition, depreciation, and disposal of long-lived tangible assets under accrual accounting. As previously mentioned, this chapter examines effects of depreciation method choice, using straight line and double declining balance as examples. We also show students how to properly interpret gains and losses. The appendix demonstrates how to record the acquisition, depreciation, and disposal of assets.

Chapter F9 explores another challenging issue arising from the use of accrual basis accounting—merchandise inventory and inventory cost flow methods. Students learn how to calculate amounts under LIFO, FIFO, and average cost methods for both periodic and perpetual inventory systems. More important, they learn how the choice of method affects the accounting information provided on income statements and balance sheets. This chapter has two appendices. The first appendix involves inventory purchasing issues and presents a discussion of freight terms and cash discounts and how they alter the cost of purchasing. The second appendix presents the accounting cycle for periodic inventory systems and perpetual inventory systems including all recording, adjusting, and closing entries.

Chapter F10 returns to the balance sheet and income statement, taking a closer look at the way these two financial statements are organized. We explore the information provided in a classified balance sheet and an expanded multistep income statement in detail.

Chapter F11 introduces the statement of cash flows as another financial tool. After using the information provided by the other three financial statements, prepared under accrual accounting, students see the need to refocus their attention on cash. With an understanding of the purpose of the statement of cash flows in hand, students find its creation using both the direct and indirect methods easy to understand. More important, students learn how to read and interpret the information provided on the statement of cash flows.

Chapter F12 explains the importance of gathering various types of information to make the results of financial statement analysis most useful. Ratio analysis is the featured technique; information from the Gap Inc. annual report illustrates the computations, comparisons, and analyses throughout the chapter.

Chapter M1 provides a brief overview of the environment and future of management accounting. We have included not only a description of how management accounting compares and contrasts with financial accounting, but also the historical forces that have led to the development of management accounting techniques. Further, we discuss the state of management accounting today and what kinds of management accounting information will be needed in the future.

Chapter M2 presents an introduction to various cost classifications used in management accounting situations. We cover the concepts of cost objects, direct and indirect costs, and product and period costs. Students are introduced to the differences in product cost for a merchandiser and a manufacturer and learn the components of the costs included in each of the three types of inventory in a manufacturing operation. Finally, we explore the calculation of cost of goods manufactured and cost of goods sold for a manufacturer and cost of services for a service type firm. The chapter appendix presents the journal entries associated with the information presented in the chapter.

Chapter M3 introduces students to how manufacturers determine the cost of manufactured product. We present the documents used to help control the costs of manufactured products and cover how overhead costs are allocated to products using both traditional overhead allocation and activity-based costing. We walk students through the steps required to determine the cost of manufactured product using job order and process costing. The chapter appendix presents the journal entries associated with process costing and job order costing.

Chapter M4 explores the subject of cost behavior. We explain the differences between fixed costs and variable costs, and how to classify costs by cost behavior. We also cover the concept of the relevant range and its effect on cost behavior information. We then present the characteristics of a mixed cost and discuss how to separate a mixed cost into its fixed and variable components using the engineering approach, the scatter graph, the high-low method, and regression analysis.

Chapter M5 extends the topic introduced in Chapter M4 by using cost behavior information to make business decisions. In this chapter we present the functional income statement and contribution income statement and the differences between them. We cover the calculation of per unit amounts for sales, variable cost, and contribution margin, as well as the contribution margin ratio and its importance as a management tool. We present the contribution margin income statement for a merchandiser and introduce the concept of cost-volume-profit analysis, which we use to determine the amount of sales required to break even or to earn a targeted profit in both single-product and multiple-product situations. Finally, we use CVP to perform sensitivity analysis to changes in selling price, variable cost, and fixed cost.

Chapter M6 presents the topic of isolating and using relevant cost information in decision making. Included is a discussion of the characteristics of relevant and irrelevant costs, and a consideration of qualitative factors that should be considered when making business decisions. The specific decision situations covered in the chapter are equipment replacement, whether to accept or reject a special order, and the effects of fixed costs and opportunity costs on a make or buy decision.

Chapter M7 provides an in-depth look at the capital budget. The overall business planning process is discussed and where the capital budget fits in that process. The four shared characteristics of all capital projects are presented, as well as the cost of capital and the concept of scarce resources. Students learn how to identify the information relevant to the capital budgeting decision. We present four techniques used to evaluate proposed capital projects including net present value, internal rate of return, payback, and accounting rate of return. There is an appendix to this chapter which presents the concept of the time value of money and all the calculations students need to compute net present values and internal rates of return.

Chapter M8 presents the operating budget, its benefits, preparation, and uses. First, we introduce and discuss all the budgets included in the operating budget from a conceptual standpoint. Then we present various approaches to budgeting, including perpetual, incremental, zero-based, top-down, bottom-up, imposed, and participative approaches. Next we discuss and stress the importance of the sales forecast in the budgeting process. Finally, we walk students through the preparation of all the budgets, and then discuss appropriate and inappropriate uses of the operating budget in the management process.

Chapter M9 presents the procedures involved in standard costing. We explore what standard costing is and why it can be an effective tool for managers. We cover management by exception, ideal and practical standards, and the weaknesses of standard costing. We compare standard costing, actual costing, and normal costing and introduce students to methods used to set standards for a manufacturing company. Finally, we walk students through the calculations of standard cost variances for direct material, direct labor, variable manufacturing overhead, and fixed manufacturing overhead. The chapter appendix presents the journal entries used to record all the procedures described in the chapter.

Chapter M10 introduces students to various methods of evaluating performance. We discuss centralized and decentralized management styles, business segments, and the problems associated with determining segment costs. We also present the segment income statement and how it is used to evaluate segment performance. We introduce students to return on investment and residual income as methods used to evaluate performance. We also discuss some nonfinancial performance measures including quality, customer satisfaction, employee morale, employee safety, efficiency, and just-in-time.

OTHER IMPORTANT FEATURES OF THIS TEXT

In addition to the Discussion Questions and the inclusion of the Gap Inc. annual report, discussed in detail above, our text offers other features that will enhance the learning process.

- Learning Objectives—Previewing each chapter with these objectives allows students to see what direction the chapter is taking, which makes the journey through the material a bit easier.
- Marginal Glossary—Students often find the process of learning accounting terminology to be a challenge. As each new key word is introduced in the text, it is shown in bold and also defined in the margin. This feature offers students an easy way to review the key terms and locate their introduction in the text.
- Summary—This concise summary of each chapter provides an overview of the main points, but is in no way a substitute for reading the chapter.
- Key Terms—At the end of each chapter, a list of the new key words directs students to the page on which the key word or phrase was introduced.
- Review the Facts—Students can use these basic, definitional questions to review the key points of each chapter. The questions are in a sequence reflecting the coverage of topics in the chapter.
- Apply What You Have Learned—Our end-of-chapter assignment materials include a mix of traditional types of homework problems and innovative assignments requiring critical thinking and writing. Many of the requirements can be used as the basis for classroom discussions. You will find matching problems, short essay questions, and calculations. Assignments dealing

directly with the use of financial statements are also included. Many of these applications also work well as group assignments.

- Glossary of Accounting Terms—An alphabetical listing of important accounting terms, including all of the key terms plus additional terms, defines the terms and lists the page on which the term first appears.

SUPPLEMENTS FOR USE BY THE INSTRUCTOR

Additional support for your efforts in the classroom is provided by our group of supplements.

Instructor's Resource Manual

    Financial Instructor's Resource Manual, 0-13-012549-0
    Management Instructor's Resource Manual, 0-13-182411-2

This comprehensive resource includes *chapter overviews* that identify the chapter concepts, explains the chapter rationale and philosophy, and reviews the significant topics and points of the chapter. Also included are *chapter outlines* organized by objectives, *lecture suggestions, teaching tips,* various *chapter quizzes, transparency masters, group activities* derived from the textbook Discussion Questions (DQs) as well as the *Solutions to the DQs, communication exercises,* and *suggested readings.*

Solutions Manual and Transparencies

    Financial Solutions Manual, 0-13-012547-4
    Financial Transparencies, 0-13-012552-0
    Management Solutions Manual, 0-13-182429-5
    Management Transparencies, 0-13-961898-8

Solutions are provided for all the end-of-chapter assignments. The Solutions Manual is also available in acetate form and on disk to adopters.

Test Item File

    Financial Test Item File, 0-13-012548-2
    Management Test Item File, 0-13-182437-6

The Test Item File includes test items that can be used as quiz and/or exam material. Each chapter contains multiple-choice questions (both conceptual and quantitative), problems, exercises, and critical thinking problems. Each question will identify the difficulty level, page reference, the corresponding learning objective(s), and the category classification according to Bloom's Taxonomy.

Prentice Hall Test Manager by Engineering Software Associates Inc.

    Financial Prentice Hall Test Manager by Engineering Software Associates Inc., 0-13-012540-7
    Management Prentice Hall Test Manager by Engineering Software Associates Inc., 0-13-236480-8

This easy-to-use computerized testing program can create exams, evaluate, and track student results. The PH Test Manager also provides on-line testing capabilities. Test items are drawn from the Test Item File.

PH Professor: A Classroom Presentation on PowerPoint

    Financial PH Professor: A Classroom Presentation on PowerPoint, 0-13-012551-2
    Management PH Professor: A Classroom Presentation on PowerPoint, 0-13-014590-4

PowerPoint presentations are available for each chapter of the text. Each presentation allows instructors to offer a more interactive presentation using colorful graphics, outlines of chapter material, additional examples, and graphical explanations of difficult topics. Instructors have the flexibility to add slides and/or modify the existing slides to meet the course needs.

Each presentation can also be downloaded from our Web site at www.prenhall.com/phbusiness.

PHLIP/CW (Prentice Hall's Learning on the Internet Partnership) offers the most expansive internet-based support available. Our Web site provides a wealth of resources for students and faculty, which include:

- Student Study Hall
- Hotlinks to in-text companies
- Learning Assessment sections
- On-line tutorial assistance
- Practice tests w/immediate grading and feedback
- Faculty lounge
- On-line study guide
- Downloadable supplement
- Distance Learning capabilities

We believe that the instructor and student can have a rich and wonderful experience as they discover how accounting fits into the big picture of business and relates to their life, regardless of their chosen career. We have devised homework and classroom materials to stimulate robust and invigorating interchanges between instructor and student as together they grapple with accounting issues.

ACKNOWLEDGMENTS

No project this large takes place in a vacuum. This project would not have happened without the resounding support and encouragement from a number of people, the faith in the concept's value from Prentice Hall, and the suggestions for improvements from our colleagues.

We thank executive editors Annie Todd and Debbie Hoffman for their patience, determination, and faith in the project. They were always there for us. We also thank Prentice Hall team members PJ Boardman, Jim Boyd, Stephen Deitmer, Jane Avery, Elisa Adams, Charlotte Morrissey, Natacha St. Hill Moore, Marc Oliver, Beth Toland, and Kasey Sheehan for their help and contributions.

Our colleagues keep us on our toes, and this book is enriched by their intellectual contributions and friendship. Martha Doran, San Diego State University, good friend and teacher, shared her wisdom with us about learning and teaching, and our students are better off because of it. Many other colleagues tested our ideas, were brave enough to offer constructive criticism, and gave us friendship through the difficult times. They include: Gary J. Weber and Kay C. Carnes, Gonzaga University; Connie D. Weaver, University of Texas-Austin; Juan M. Rodriguez, Elizabeth Dreike Almer, Paul Munter, Frank Collins, Oscar J. Holzmann, Olga Quintana, Thomas R. Robinson, and the other faculty members at the University of Miami; Richard E. Flaherty, Harriet Maccracken, Patrick B. McKenzie, and Karen Gieger, Arizona State University; Lorren H. Beavers, Charles R. Pursifull, Mary F. Sheets, Bambi A. Hora, Thomas K. Miller, Ura Lee Denson, David J. Harris, Joan Stone, Karen Price, and Jane Calvert, University of Central Oklahoma; Alfonso R. Oddo, Niagara University; Marilyn T. Zarzeski, University of Central Florida; Joanne Sheridan, Montana State University-Billings; Ellene Ormiston and Charles Lewis, Mesa Community College; Allison L. Drews-Bryan, Clemson University; and George R. Violette, University of Southern Maine.

Several other groups deserve special thanks and recognition for their valuable work:

Reviewers for the *Introduction to Financial Accounting, A User Perspective:*

Gerald Ashley	Grossmont College
Sheila Bradford	Tulsa Community College
Carol E. Buchl	Northern Michigan University
Mary D. Maury	St. John's University
Mary Ann M. Prater	Clemson University
John C. Robison	California Polytechnic State University-San Luis Obispo
Sheldon R. Smith	Brigham Young University-Hawaii

Reviewers for the *Introduction to Management Accounting, A User Perspective:*

Jeffrey J. Archambault	Clarkson University
Lorren H. Beavers	University of Central Oklahoma
Roger K. Doost	Clemson University
Cherie L. Francisco	Simpson College
Jessica J. Frazier	Eastern Kentucky University
Edward S. Goodhart	Shippensburg University
Bambi A. Hora	University of Central Oklahoma
Steven D. Hunter	Western Baptist College
Thomas A. Jones	
Raymond L. Larson	Appalachian State University
Mary D. Maury	St. John's University
Alfonso R. Oddo	Niagara University
Charles J. Pineno	Clarion University
Joanne Sheridan	Montana State University-Billings
Sheldon R. Smith	Brigham Young University-Hawaii
Patricia M. Sommerville	Saint Mary's University
Caroly Streuly	
Marilyn T. Zarzeski	University of Central Florida

Supplements Authors:

Barry Nab Dahl	Lake Superior College	PowerPoint Presentation
Karen P. Schoenebeck	Wichita State University	Companion Web site
Diane L. Tanner	University of North Florida	Instructor's Manual
Mary F. Sheets	University of Central Oklahoma	Test Item File
Bambi A. Hora	University of Central Oklahoma	Test Item File
Thomas K. Miller	University of Central Oklahoma	IMA Solutions Manual

Thanks also for contributions made by Charles R. Pursifull, Lorren H. Beavers, and Ura Lee Denson to the Test Item File and the Solutions Manuals.

Thanks go to our students, who are the reason for the work and who become our living laboratory. Special thanks to Stacie R. Mayes and Jason R. Earhart who critiqued this manuscript from the student's perspective. Finally, we thank our families who abide with us through this process.

Kumen H. Jones
Michael L. Werner
Katherene P. Terrell
Robert L. Terrell

Introduction to Financial Accounting

A User Perspective

Chapter 1

Introduction to Business in the United States

You have completed enough credit hours to graduate from the state university. While you are intelligent and creative, you spent enough time working through college to finish with a B− average; this semester the recruiters seem to prefer B+ and A− grade point averages. In addition to your many talents of buying and selling logo products at sporting events, you dabble in pop music. You even managed to save a few dollars from the sporting goods sales. On the popular campus strip, an old roadhouse is for sale. If you cannot find a job, maybe you should create one. Your best friend is in the same predicament, so you put your heads together.

What would it mean to own a business? How should you organize it—by yourself or with your friend? How will you know if you are making money? How much money will it take to get the business going and where will the money come from if it is more than you and your pal have right now? How much can you make and will that be enough to support one or both of you? Should you focus on music, food, and drink, or add logo products to the mix? Will the venture be a success or will it waste what little money you have saved? What to do? Your friend's father wants you both to visit his accountant for advice. What does accounting have to do with this decision?

Accounting touches each of us every day—in both our personal and professional lives. To be used properly, accounting information must be studied in context. Therefore, to better understand accounting for business enterprises and to help answer some of your questions, we must first explore business in its many different forms. ■

> *The business of America is business.*
>
> —Calvin Coolidge
> 30th President of the United States

The word *business* means different things to different people. For some, the word conjures up a dream of excitement and opportunity; for others, it represents a nightmare of greed and exploitation. Whether our view of business is positive or negative, each of us is touched every day by what goes on in the world of business.

Webster's New World Dictionary gives several definitions of business:

> **Busi-ness** (biz′niz) *n.* **1:** One's work or occupation. **2:** A special task or duty. **3:** A matter or affair. **4:** Commerce or trade. **5:** A commercial or industrial establishment.[1]

As you can see, not only do people have different impressions of business, but the word itself has different meanings in different contexts. The last two definitions are particularly relevant for this book. It is important for you to understand that at times *business* is used to describe the entirety of commerce and trade, and at other times it is used to describe an individual company. In fact, in the economic world, and in books about the world of business (including this one), the words *company* and *business* are often used interchangeably. So whenever you see the word *business*, make sure you understand the context in which it is used.

The information in this chapter should provide you with the background necessary to put the accounting concepts presented throughout this text into the proper business context, and to seek information about an individual business entity. After all, accounting information is the key ingredient for making wise business decisions.

LEARNING OBJECTIVES

After completing your work on this chapter, you should be able to do the following:

1. Describe the four factors of production.
2. Explain the basic concepts of capitalism and how they relate to the profit motive.
3. Explain the basic issues in the debate over whether businesses have a social responsibility.
4. Distinguish among the three basic forms of business organization—the proprietorship, the partnership, and the corporation—and describe the advantages and disadvantages of each.
5. Distinguish among the three major types of business activities and define hybrid type businesses.
6. Explain the basic need for international business trade and the complications involved in this activity.
7. Describe the SEC's authority over accounting reporting standards and describe the current standard-setting process in the United States.
8. Explain the purpose of an independent financial audit.

---

[1] *Webster's New World Dictionary* (New York, NY: Prentice Hall, 1989), 59.

WHAT IS BUSINESS?

business Depending on the context, the area of commerce or trade, an individual company, or the process of producing and distributing goods and services.

factors of production The four major items needed to support economic activity: natural resources, labor, capital, and entrepreneurship.

natural resources Land and the materials that come from the land, such as timber, mineral deposits, oil deposits, and water. One of the factors of production.

Essentially, **business** is the process of producing goods and services and then distributing them to those who desire or need them. This process sounds simple enough, but it is actually quite complex and few people ever gain a complete understanding of all its aspects.

Although we cannot present an in-depth study of the many aspects of business, we must talk about a few basics at the outset to present accounting in its proper context. We begin with the factors of production.

Factors of Production

The **factors of production** are the key ingredients needed to support economic activity (see Exhibit 1–1). Economists classify the factors of production into four categories:

1. **Natural resources**—land and the materials that come from the land, such as timber, mineral deposits, oil deposits, and water.

Exhibit 1–1
Factors of Production

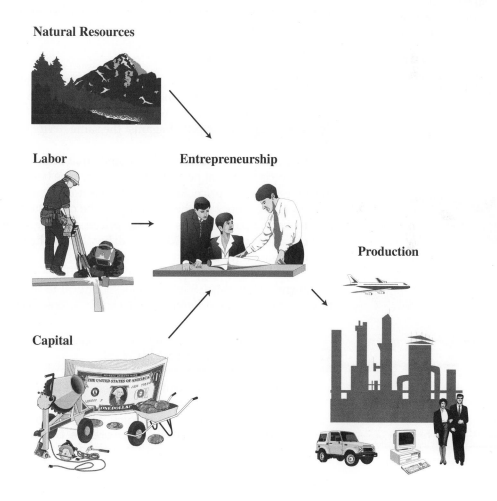

Natural Resources

Labor

Entrepreneurship

Production

Capital

labor The mental and physical efforts of all workers performing tasks required to produce and sell goods and services. This factor of production is also called the human resource factor.

capital A factor of production that includes the buildings, machinery, and tools used to produce goods and services. Also, sometimes used to refer to the money used to buy those items.

entrepreneurship The factor of production that brings the other three factors—natural resources, labor, and capital—together to form a business.

market economy A type of economy in which all or most of the factors of production are privately owned and that relies on competition in the marketplace to determine the most efficient way to allocate the economy's resources.

2. **Labor**—the mental and physical efforts of all workers, regardless of their skill or education, who perform the tasks required to produce and sell goods and services. Labor is sometimes called the human resource factor.
3. **Capital**—the buildings, machinery, and tools used to produce goods and services. The word *capital* has many meanings. Sometimes it refers to the money that buys the buildings, machinery, and tools used in production. Because this double usage can be confusing, be careful to note the context in which the word *capital* is being used.
4. **Entrepreneurship**—the activity that brings the first three factors together to form a business. *Entrepreneurs* accept the opportunities and risks of starting and running businesses. They acquire the capital, assemble the labor force, and utilize available natural resources to produce and sell goods and services.

The way these four factors of production combine to produce goods and services depends on the type of economic system that organizes a society.

In a *planned economy,* a strong, centralized government controls all or most of the natural resources, labor, and capital used to produce goods and services, replacing the entrepreneur. In contrast, a **market economy** relies on competition in the marketplace to determine the most efficient way to allocate the economy's resources. The United States conducts business within the capitalistic economic system, also known as the free enterprise, free market, or private enterprise system.

The Profit Motive

The *profit motive* stimulates a person to do something when the benefit derived from doing it is greater than the sacrifice required to do it. A rational person desires to derive the greatest benefit with the least amount of sacrifice. When this natural desire in one person is pitted against the same desire in another person, competition results.

To illustrate the profit motive, assume that Martin needs a new pair of shoes. Because he is a rational person, Martin desires the best pair of shoes he can buy for the lowest possible price. Roy owns a shoe store. Being a rational person, Roy desires to sell his shoes for the highest price he can. Martin goes to Roy's shoe store and looks at a pair of shoes Roy has priced at $100. Assuming he likes the shoes and can afford to pay $100, Martin will buy them if he feels they provide him with the most benefit for the least sacrifice.

Now, add one other ingredient to the situation—competition. Enter Ellen, who also owns a shoe store. She sells shoes identical to the pair Martin is considering buying at Roy's. The difference is that she is selling them for $90.

Discussion Questions

1-1. What do you think caused Roy and Ellen to establish different selling prices for an identical pair of shoes?
1-2. Assuming Martin decides to buy the shoes, what do you think will determine where he buys them?

In this example, Martin's self-interest pits the self-interests of Roy and Ellen against each other because Martin's desire to pay the lowest price possible for the shoes will make Roy and Ellen compete for his business. If Roy loses enough sales to Ellen because she is selling shoes for less than he is, he will be forced to lower his selling price. In fact, he may want to reduce his selling price for the shoes Martin liked to $85 to attract sales away from Ellen. She will then be forced to lower her selling price. No one makes Roy and Ellen lower their prices; the force comes from competition in the market.

There comes a point, of course, below which the selling price cannot go. If Roy and Ellen pay $55 for the shoes they buy for resale, they obviously cannot sell those shoes for less than $55, unless they are willing to accept a loss. **Profit** is the excess of benefit over sacrifice. Thus, if Martin buys the shoes from Roy for $100, Roy's gross profit can be calculated as:

profit The excess of benefit over sacrifice. A less formal name for net income or net profit.

Amount received from Martin (BENEFIT)	$100
Less what Roy paid for the shoes (SACRIFICE)	55
Equals GROSS PROFIT on the sale of shoes	$ 45

gross margin or **gross profit** The excess of benefit received over the sacrifice made to complete a sale. Gross profit considers only the cost of the item sold; it does not consider the other costs of operations.

The $45 profit that Roy earned is called **gross margin** or **gross profit.** However, it does not represent his actual profit from operating the shoe store. In addition to the cost of the merchandise he buys to sell, he has other costs such as rent on the store, utilities, and wages paid to employees. All these items must be taken into account before he can calculate his *net profit* or *net income.*

If Roy does not earn a sufficient profit on the shoe store business, he will close it and go into another line of work. The same, of course, holds true for Ellen. In a capitalistic economy, businesses that do not earn profits cease to exist.

Profits Versus Social Responsibility

Some people believe that profit connotes greed. These individuals believe that U.S. business should strike a balance between profit and social responsibility. On the other side of this issue are those who believe that business has no obligation beyond earning profits and no social responsibility.

We live in a society that seems to measure success by whether someone "beats" someone else. This situation is described as a zero-sum game, meaning that for every winner, there must be a loser. The following quotation from Vince Lombardi, legendary coach of the Green Bay Packers, seems to more accurately capture the workings of our world than the quotation by sportswriter Grantland Rice.

Winning is not everything, it is the only thing!

—Vince Lombardi

It matters not whether you win or lose, but how you play the game.

—Grantland Rice

In recent years, however, society has renewed its concern over how the game of business is played. An increasing number of investors, creditors, and other economic decision makers have become interested not only in improving "the bottom line" (making money), but also in improving the way companies conduct themselves as citizens in the community. In other words, we can view business as a win-win situation.

Social Responsibility in Business Today

A growing number of U.S. consumers refuse to do business with companies they believe are insensitive to social and environmental concerns. In response to this concern, a great many U.S. companies make a concerted effort to communicate a commitment to responsible and ethical business practices.

stakeholder Anyone who is affected by the way a company conducts its business.

Each business affects its community with the decisions it makes and the manner in which it conducts its affairs. Any entity or individual affected by the way a company conducts its business becomes a **stakeholder** in that business and gains a vested interest in the way a company is run. A business must determine its responsibilities to each of its stakeholders. The first step in determining responsibility usually involves listing the identity of all the firm's stakeholders. Many companies include a section in the annual report about social responsibility to improve investor confidence in the company's good citizenship. The era when a company could conduct its business without regard to anything but making a profit is very likely gone forever. Many investors, both individuals and companies, will not invest in alcohol or tobacco companies, or in companies known to pollute the environment. So the marketplace eventually affects companies that are not socially responsible because certain investors will not invest their money in them.

Discussion Questions

1–3. Make a list of those to whom you think a chemical manufacturing company owes responsibility. What are the specific responsibilities it has to each of these stakeholders? How do you think the company could best go about fulfilling each of those responsibilities?

1–4. Make a list of those to whom you think a retail clothing company owes a responsibility. What are the stakes that each group has? How can the company fulfill each responsibility?

1–5. Can you think of any companies that have fulfilled the responsibilities you outlined in your answers to question 1–3 or 1–4 and yet managed to remain profitable?

FORMS OF BUSINESS ORGANIZATION

There are three forms of business organization in the United States: sole proprietorships, partnerships, and corporations. Each has certain advantages and disadvantages for the firm's owners.

Sole Proprietorships

sole proprietorship An unincorporated business that is owned by one individual. Also called a proprietorship.

A **sole proprietorship,** or proprietorship, is an unincorporated business that is owned by a single individual. A common misconception about this form of business is that it is always small. While the majority of sole proprietorships are small, the classification suggests nothing about the size of the business, only that it has a single owner.

Advantages of Sole Proprietorships

1. **Easy and inexpensive to set up.** There are no special legal requirements associated with starting a sole proprietorship. All a person must do is decide what kind of business he or she wants to establish and obtain the necessary licenses and permits, and that person is in business.

2. **No sharing of profits.** A single owner shares profits only with the government in the form of taxes. Whatever the business earns after taxes belongs solely to the owner.

3. **Total control.** The desire for control probably inspires more people to start their own business than any other reason. The sole proprietor answers to no one when making decisions about how to run the business (as long as they are legal). A sole proprietor has the independence to determine the quantity and quality of business effort.
4. **Few government regulations.** As long as the owner pays his or her taxes and does not engage in illegal activities, a proprietorship is reasonably free of government regulation.
5. **No special income taxes.** From a legal standpoint, a sole proprietorship is simply an extension of its owner. Therefore, a proprietorship pays no separate income tax. The earnings of the company are considered the earnings of the owner and become a part of his or her personal taxable income.
6. **Easy and inexpensive to dissolve.** Sole proprietors can end their business as easily as they can start them. If the owner decides to shut the company down, all he or she must do is notify the appropriate licensing agents of the state and local governments and pay off remaining debts.

Disadvantages of Sole Proprietorships

1. **Unlimited liability.** From a legal standpoint, a sole proprietorship is simply an extension of its owner so all business obligations become the owner's legal obligations. Therefore, if the company fails to pay its debts, the creditors can sue the owner for the owner's personal property, including his or her house, car, boat, or other holdings.
2. **Limited access to capital or money.** All businesses must have money and assets to operate, which is often referred to as capital. The amount of capital available to a sole proprietorship is limited to the amount of personal assets the owner can contribute to the business or the amount the owner can borrow on a personal loan. Remember that legally a proprietorship is not distinguished from its owner; therefore, when the business borrows money, the owner borrows money.
3. **Limited management expertise.** No one is an expert in everything. Many proprietorships fail because the owner lacks skills or expertise in areas critical to the survival of the company.
4. **Personal time commitment.** Running a business is hard work, and a sole proprietor works very long hours—probably longer hours than if he or she were employed. Most sole proprietors consider the time well spent because it benefits them personally. But without a doubt, it takes a tremendous amount of time to run your own business.
5. **Limited life.** Unless the company is sold to another entity or is passed on to the owner's heirs, the life of the business cannot exceed the life of the owner.

Notwithstanding the disadvantages of proprietorship, many people dream of owning their own business, and nearly 71 percent of companies in the United States are sole proprietorships. Because most of them are small businesses, only about 6 percent of all business revenues come from this form of business.

Partnerships

partnership A business form similar to a proprietorship, but having two or more owners.

Think of a **partnership** as a proprietorship with two or more owners who all share in the risks and profits of the business. A common misconception is that all partnerships are small businesses. In fact, some partnerships are quite large. Most large public accounting firms, for instance, are partnerships, and some of them have as many as 1,500 partners and 20,000 employees.

Advantages of Partnerships

1. **Easy to form.** From a legal standpoint, partners can form a partnership almost as easily as a proprietorship. Partners should commit the ownership and profit-sharing structure of the partnership into a formal partnership agreement, signed by each partner, to clarify their consensus about these issues. A well-written partnership agreement helps to resolve conflicts or problems in the future. Once the partners obtain the appropriate licenses and permits, a partnership is in business.

2. **Increased management expertise.** Partners often form partnerships because each has skills in a critical area of business that complement the others. Combining those areas of expertise into a partnership enhances the business's chances of success.

3. **Access to more capital (money, property, or other assets).** Having more than one person involved in the ownership of the business usually increases access to capital. In fact, many partnerships form to combine one partner's special expertise with another's capital.

4. **Few government regulations.** Government subjects partnerships to relatively few regulations. As long as each partner pays his or her individual taxes and the partnership does not engage in illegal activities, government does not interfere.

5. **No special income taxes.** A partnership is not legally separate from its owners and therefore does not pay separate income taxes. Rather, the partnership tax return allocates the partnership profits, according to the partnership profit-sharing agreement, among the partners. Each partner includes his or her share of the profits on the personal tax return as personal income.

6. **Greater business continuity.** Because more people are involved, partnerships tend to have longer lives than do sole proprietorships. When a partner dies or withdraws from the partnership, the legal life of the partnership ends. The heirs do not inherit the right to be partners in the firm. For all practical purposes, however, the business generally need not stop its operations. The partnership agreement may allow the remaining partner or partners to either continue with one less partner or admit another partner to the firm.

Disadvantages of Partnerships

1. **Unlimited liability.** Because partnerships are legally no different from their owners, the partners are personally liable for all obligations of the business. In fact, in most instances, each partner is personally liable for the total obligations of the partnership. Therefore, if any partner makes a decision that obligates the partnership, all the other partners become liable, even if they knew nothing about the decision.

2. **Sharing of profits.** When a partnership is formed, the partners prepare an agreement that outlines how to divide company profits. The profit-sharing arrangement usually considers the amount of capital each partner invests in the partnership, how much time each partner commits on a regular basis, and any special expertise a partner may contribute. Regardless of whether the agreement is fair and equitable, once a partnership has been formed, partners will share profits with each other.

3. **Potential conflicts between partners.** Suppose one partner wants the company to begin selling a new product and another partner disagrees. If the two partners have equal power, they have entered into gridlock. The bases for conflicts among partners range from personal habits to overall business philosophy, and there may be no other way to resolve them but to dissolve the partnership.

4. **Difficulty in dissolving.** Ending a partnership severs personal and professional ties and can be a devastating emotional experience. If individuals forming a partnership are wise, they will include specific provisions for dissolution in the original partnership agreement when all the partners have positive attitudes toward one another. You might think of this as the business version of a prenuptial agreement: The parties forming the business agree on how the business "marriage" will end.

While there are advantages to the partnership form of business, many people believe the disadvantages outweigh them. Only about 1 percent of all businesses in the United States are partnerships, and they account for just about 4 percent of all business revenues.

Separate Entity Assumption

From a record-keeping and accounting standpoint, proprietorships, partnerships, and corporations are considered to be completely separate from their owners. This view reflects the **separate entity assumption** that economic activity can be identified with a particular economic entity whether it is an individual, proprietorship, corporation, or even a division of a business. However, from a legal standpoint, the corporation is the only form of business considered to be a separate legal entity from its owners.

Corporations

Chief Justice John Marshall of the United States Supreme Court made this statement in 1819:

> A corporation is an artificial being, invisible, intangible, and existing only in contemplation of law.

This ruling changed the course of business in the United States forever. As a separate legal entity, a **corporation** has many of the rights and obligations of a person, including the right to enter into contracts and the right to buy, own, and sell property. The law requires a corporation to discharge its obligations lawfully, and creditors can sue for recovery if it does not. A corporation can be taken to court if it breaks the law, and it is obligated to pay taxes like any other person. In addition to the legal obligations of corporations, the moral obligation of corporations to be socially responsible has been a topic of widespread discussion in recent years. The fact that corporations are separate legal entities leads to several distinct advantages and disadvantages.

Advantages of Corporations

1. **Limited liability.** Because a corporation is a separate legal entity from its stockholders, the owners are not personally liable for the corporation's obligations. With limited liability, a **stockholder** (or *shareholder*) limits his or her losses to the amount of his or her investment and not everything else he or she owns.

2. **Greater access to capital.** By dividing the ownership of the firm into relatively low-cost shares of stock, corporations can attract a great number of investors. Some corporations in the United States have more than a million different stockholders.
3. **Easy transferability of ownership.** Because ownership shares in corporations usually cost less than $100, individual investors buy and sell shares much more easily than they could trade an ownership interest in a proprietorship or partnership. Freely traded stock requires no approval or

permission for trading, unlike the approval required to accept a partner into a business.

4. **Continuity of life.** Because a corporation is legally separate and distinct from its owner or owners, it continues to exist even when a complete change in ownership occurs. The transfer of shares of stock has no effect on a corporation.

5. **Greater management expertise.** The stockholders (owners) of the corporation elect a *board of directors* who have the ultimate responsibility of managing the firm. The board of directors, in turn, hires professional managers to run the day-to-day operations.

Disadvantages of Corporations

1. **Greater tax burden.** All businesses, regardless of form, must pay property taxes and payroll taxes. In addition to these taxes, corporations must pay a federal income tax, and in many states also pay state and local income taxes. The board of directors distributes part of the firm's after-tax profit to the shareholders as dividends. The stockholders report dividends as personal income and pay personal income taxes on them. This practice is referred to as *double taxation,* and it has been the subject of fierce debate for many years in the United States.

2. **Greater government regulation.** Government subjects corporations to significantly more control than either sole proprietorships or partnerships. Many corporations file reports with both federal and state regulatory bodies. Filing these reports costs time and money.

3. **Absentee ownership.** In almost all proprietorships and in most partnerships, the owners manage their business according to their wishes. In most corporations, few stockholders (owners) participate in the day-to-day operations of the business. The board of directors hires professional managers to operate the company on behalf of the owners. Professional managers sometimes operate the company in their own interests, rather than the owners' interest.

Although corporations represent a small percentage of the total number of businesses in the United States, corporations transact approximately six times as much business as all proprietorships and partnerships combined. Corporations also control the majority of business resources in the United States. Exhibit 1–2 summarizes the advantages and disadvantages of the three forms of business.

Other Business Forms

Evolutionary changes in business have prompted the creation of new forms of business organizations that combine characteristics of partnerships and corporations. A *limited partnership* consists of at least one general partner and one or more limited partners. The general partners have unlimited liability and operate the partnership. The limited partners enjoy limited liability (like corporate stockholders), but are precluded from a decision-making role in the organization. A *limited liability partnership (LLP)* limits the liability of a general partner to his or her own negligence or misconduct, or the conduct of persons he or she controls. In a regular partnership, each partner is liable for all partnership debts and the conduct of all partners and employees. In a *limited liability corporation (LLC),* stockholders enjoy the limited liability status of a corporation but are taxed as partners in a partnership, thus avoiding double taxation.

Exhibit 1-2
Advantages and Disadvantages of the Three Forms of Business Organization

Business Form	Advantages	Disadvantages
Proprietorship	1. Easy and inexpensive to set up. 2. No sharing of profits. 3. Owner has total control. 4. Few government regulations. 5. No special income taxes. 6. Easy and inexpensive to dissolve.	1. Unlimited liability. 2. Limited access to capital. 3. Limited management expertise. 4. Personal time commitment. 5. Limited life.
Partnership	1. Easy to form. 2. Increased management expertise. 3. Access to more capital. 4. Few government regulations. 5. No special income taxes. 6. Greater business continuity.	1. Unlimited liability. 2. Sharing of profits. 3. Potential conflicts between partners. 4. Difficulty in dissolving.
Corporation	1. Limited liability. 2. Greater access to capital. 3. Easy transferability of ownership. 4. Continuity of life. 5. Greater management expertise.	1. Greater tax burden. 2. Greater government regulation. 3. Absentee ownership.

Discussion Question

1-6. Imagine that you have the opportunity to start a company. Would you prefer to be an owner (or part owner) of a proprietorship, partnership, or corporation? Cite specific reasons for your choice.

TYPES OF BUSINESSES

We can classify companies in the United States not only according to organizational form (proprietorship, partnership, or corporation), but also according to the type of business activity in which they engage. The three broad classifications are manufacturing, merchandising, and service. Although a single company can be involved in all three of these business activities, usually one of the three constitutes the company's major interest.

Manufacturing Companies

manufacturing The business activity that converts purchased raw materials into some tangible, physical product.

A **manufacturing** company purchases raw materials and converts them into some tangible, physical product. Raw materials consist of both unprocessed natural resources (one of the factors of production) and completely finished products manufactured by others. For example, a company that manufactures household appliances purchases many items, such as coils and generators used in the production of refrigerators. These coils and generators—raw materials to the refrigerator manufacturer—are manufactured finished products for another company.

Merchandising Companies

merchandising The business activity involving the selling of finished goods produced by other businesses.

Like a manufacturer, a **merchandising** company sells tangible, physical products, called merchandise, as its major business activity. Instead of manufacturing the product it sells, a merchandising company buys it in a finished form.

There are two kinds of merchandisers:

- *Wholesale merchandiser.* A wholesaler buys its product from the manufacturer (or another wholesaler) and then sells that product to another business that eventually sells it to the final consumer. Examples of wholesale merchandisers are A. L. Lewis, a well-known grocery wholesaler, and W. W. Grainger, a major wholesale merchandiser of tools. These names may be unfamiliar to you because, as a consumer, you most often deal directly with a retailer rather than with a wholesaler. Wholesalers provide a valuable service to retailers by making the retailers' purchasing convenient and cost effective.
- *Retail merchandiser.* A retailer buys its product from a wholesaler or manufacturer and sells the product to the final consumer. Major national retailers are Sears, Wal-Mart, the Gap, and Kmart. Other retail chains focus on specific regions of the country such as Target and Rose's. Still other successful retailers have one location, such as gift shops and specialty stores.

Service Companies

service A business activity that does not deal with tangible products, but rather provides some sort of service as its major operation.

A **service** company does not deal in tangible products, but performs a service as its major business activity. Doctors, lawyers, and accountants provide services instead of products. Service providers perform work for consumers and other businesses. Computer service centers, plumbers, auto mechanics, janitorial services, and copier repairmen frequently provide services to businesses.

Hybrid Companies

hybrid companies Those companies involved in more than one type of activity (manufacturing, merchandising, service).

Some businesses participate in more than one type of activity. These are known as **hybrid companies.** For example, General Motors Corporation manufactures automobiles and trucks and is therefore classified as a manufacturer. In recent years, however, GM has become involved in activities that are classified as services. GM created General Motors Acceptance Corporation (GMAC) to provide financing for customers purchasing GM cars and trucks. Even more recently, it issued credit cards (Visa and MasterCard).

In the near future, we can expect the distinction among manufacturing, merchandising, and service companies to become more blurred. As the struggle for survival in the global marketplace becomes even more intense, many companies find it beneficial to involve themselves in a wide variety of business activities.

Discussion Question

1–7. In what type of business activity (manufacturing, merchandising, or service) would you like to be involved? Describe in detail the type of operation that most interests you. What characteristics of this type of business do you find appealing?

U.S. businesses cannot produce all the goods and services demanded in the U.S. marketplace. On the other hand, certain items produced in the United States either have no U.S. market or are produced in greater quantities than can be sold here. These situations are the forces that drive international business. Ford Motor Company sold an average of 5.8 million cars per year during the last five years. Of these cars, 41.7 percent were sold outside the United States. Clearly, international trade is important to the financial health of Ford, as it is to many other firms.

Foreign producers bring into the United States goods called *imports*. When U.S. producers sell goods outside the United States, they are called *exports*. Most countries' economic health depends upon the importing and exporting of goods; however, conducting business across national borders causes economic and political complications.

Economic Complications

Complications can arise when a business located in one country does business with a firm located in another country with a different economic system. Another complication results from the use of different currencies by different countries: for example, the United States uses dollars, Europe uses the euro and Japan uses yen. When companies in two different countries transact business, their contract establishes the currency they will use. One or both companies then must translate its funds into the specified currency. *Translation* means converting or exchanging the currency of one country (yen, for example) into its equivalent in another country's currency (dollars, for example).

Political Complications

Politics play an important role in international trade. Even countries with the same economic system experience difficulties in economic dealings with each other because each country seeks to protect its own self-interest by exporting a larger quantity of products than it imports. As an extreme example, assume that all of France's merchandisers decide to import all English products to sell in France, because English imports cost less than French-produced merchandise. Before long, all the French manufacturing companies close, all the French jobs disappear, and an essential part of France's economic base ceases to exist. To provide protection for their own economic bases and to prevent this kind of scenario, countries create trade agreements among themselves.

Trade agreements are formal treaties between two or more countries that are designed to control the relationship between imports and exports. These agreements generally establish quotas and/or tariffs on imported products. *Quotas* limit the quantities of particular items that can be imported. For example, a limit may be placed on the number of cars that Japan can bring into and sell in the United States. *Tariffs* are taxes that raise the price of imported products to about the same as similar domestic products.

Trade agreements can take years to negotiate due to their complexity. Shortly after World War II, 92 countries signed the General Agreement on Tariffs and Trade (GATT). President Clinton renegotiated this agreement in 1994. Other recent treaties are the United States–Canada Free Trade Pact of 1989, which eliminated most trade barriers between those two countries, and the North American Free Trade Agreement (NAFTA) signed by the United States, Canada, and Mexico in 1993. Countries frequently break treaty terms, so compliance essentially depends on the good faith of the treaty members.

Business is about making decisions—decisions about what business form to take (proprietorship, partnership, corporation), decisions about what type of business activity to engage in (manufacturing, merchandising, service), and decisions about whether to engage in international business. Accounting information, in one form or another, plays a significant role in all these decisions.

This is an accounting text. Its emphasis, however, is not so much on how accounting information is prepared as on how accounting information is used. To illustrate the relationship between accounting and business decisions, let us return to the example involving Roy, Martin, and Ellen.

Remember that Roy paid $55 for the pair of shoes he later sold to Martin for $100. We calculated the gross profit on the sale of these shoes as:

Amount received from Martin (BENEFIT)	$100
Less what Roy paid for the shoes (SACRIFICE)	55
Equals GROSS PROFIT on the sale of shoes	$ 45

We pointed out that the $45 does not represent Roy's real profit because he has other costs associated with his shoe store that must be considered before he can calculate his real profit. The function of accounting is to provide information to Roy, Ellen, and the shoe manufacturers so they can make sound business decisions.

Discussion Questions

1–8. If rent and other costs associated with his shoe store amount to $3,000 a month, how many pairs of shoes must Roy sell at $100 a pair before he earns a profit?

1–9. What should Roy do if his competitor, Ellen, begins to take sales away by selling identical pairs of shoes for $90?

1–10. What if Roy finds out he can buy the identical pair of shoes from a manufacturer in Mexico for only $40 instead of the $55 he is paying the U.S. manufacturer?

1–11. What should the U.S. shoe manufacturer do if it begins to lose sales to the Mexican shoe manufacturer that is selling these identical shoes at the cheaper price?

We live in the information age. Advances in computer and telecommunication technology give us access to a great deal of information about almost any interesting subject. Not only do we have access to more information, but we can also obtain it almost instantly. Every advance, however, has its price. We sometimes find ourselves in "information overload." Trying to find the optimal amount of information specific to your needs sometimes feels like standing on the beach trying to catch the incoming tide in your mouth. It is easy to drown in all the information available to you.

Authority over Accounting Reporting Standards

The purpose of this book is to provide you with the tools, knowledge, and skills you need to sift through and use the accounting information available to you.

generally accepted accounting principles (GAAP) Guidelines for presentation of financial accounting information designed to serve external decision makers' need for consistent and comparable information.

Securities and Exchange Commission (SEC) The government agency empowered to regulate the buying and selling of stocks and bonds and to establish accounting rules, standards, and procedures and the form and content of published financial reporting.

Members of the accounting profession have developed over time a set of standards to be used for financial reporting known as **generally accepted accounting principles (GAAP).** GAAP provide assurance to outsiders that the information available in a given decision situation was prepared in accordance with some well-defined set of rules and guidelines.

The only companies required by law to follow GAAP are publicly traded companies—those whose stocks or bonds are traded on an organized exchange. The **Securities and Exchange Commission (SEC)** regulates these companies. Companies not subject to SEC regulation may use whatever accounting principles they desire, unless external financial statement users demand that GAAP be followed. For instance, banks and other lending institutions prefer to see financial results prepared under GAAP rules and often require all borrowers to adhere to GAAP. Any nonregulated company that needs to be audited will likely follow GAAP reporting standards.

Discussion Question

1–12. Why do you think a company would be opposed to adopting GAAP?

The Securities and Exchange Commission (SEC)

After the stock market crash in 1929, Congress decided to protect investors and financial statement users by creating the Securities and Exchange Commission with the explicit authority to mandate for publicly traded companies:

> the items or details to be shown in the balance sheet and earning statement, and the methods to be followed in the preparation of accounts, in the appraisal or valuation of assets and liabilities, in the determination of depreciation and depletion, . . . and in the preparation . . . of consolidated balance sheets or income accounts.

Securities Act of 1933, Section 19

The SEC was given the authority to establish (1) the rules, standards, and procedures used to account for transactions and events and (2) the form and content of published financial reporting.

Many thought the creation of the SEC meant that the government would establish accounting rules and standards. In 1938, the SEC decided to allow the accounting profession to establish standards of accounting, as long as there was "substantial authoritative support" for those standards (ASR 4, subparagraph 101). The SEC viewed its principal objective as overseeing adequate disclosure in financial reporting.

The decision to leave the setting of accounting standards to the accounting profession was a profoundly important one. Instead of accounting being rigidly controlled by government bureaucracy, the profession, in the private sector, was allowed to develop standards from an evolutionary perspective that recognizes the changing environment of business. For over 50 years, a series of professional committees and boards, currently the **Financial Accounting Standards Board (FASB),** have determined the accounting standards.

Financial Accounting Standards Board (FASB) The organization that is principally responsible for establishing accounting guidelines and rules in the United States at the present time.

Discussion Questions

1-13. What are the pros and cons of having accounting rules established by the federal government?

1-14. What are the pros and cons of having accounting rules established by the accounting profession?

1-15. If the choice were yours, would you prefer to have accounting standards determined by a government agency or the accounting profession? Explain your decision.

Financial Accounting Standards Board (FASB)

The express mission of the Financial Accounting Standards Board (FASB) is

> to establish and improve standards of financial accounting and reporting for the guidance and education of the public, including issuers, auditors, and users of financial information.[2]

The FASB's structure and operating methods have given it wide acceptance in both the accounting profession and the business community. The FASB is an independent body comprised of seven full-time members, who are required to resign from their employment during their FASB service. Not all members are accountants. Members come from diverse backgrounds, though they must know accounting, finance, and business in general. This diversity gives the FASB a broad perspective of the public interest in matters of financial accounting and reporting.

Early on, the FASB established a conceptual framework of accounting from which to approach the process of setting standards. The framework establishes the objectives of financial reporting and the qualitative characteristics of useful accounting information, and defines accounting elements, assumptions, principles, and constraints (see Exhibit 1–3). We will present the basics of the conceptual framework throughout this text, beginning with Chapter 2.

Discussion Question

1-16. If FASB members are not required to be accountants, from what other professional backgrounds are members likely to be drawn?

The Standards-Setting Process Today

From its beginning, the FASB employed a due process approach to setting standards. A due process approach focuses on the protection of individual rights. From

---

[2]*Handbook of Accounting and Auditing,* 2nd ed., eds. Robert S. Kay and D. Gerald Searfoss (Boston: Warren, Gorham & Lamont, 1989), 46–48.

Exhibit 1-3
Conceptual Framework
of Accounting

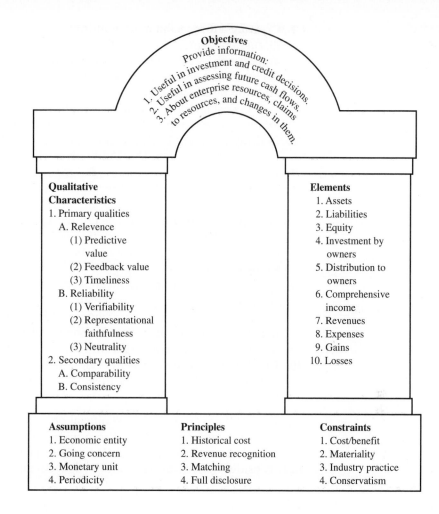

Objectives
Provide information:
1. Useful in investment and credit decisions.
2. Useful in assessing future cash flows.
3. About enterprise resources, claims to resources, and changes in them.

Qualitative Characteristics
1. Primary qualities
  A. Relevence
    (1) Predictive value
    (2) Feedback value
    (3) Timeliness
  B. Reliability
    (1) Verifiability
    (2) Representational faithfulness
    (3) Neutrality
2. Secondary qualities
  A. Comparability
  B. Consistency

Elements
1. Assets
2. Liabilities
3. Equity
4. Investment by owners
5. Distribution to owners
6. Comprehensive income
7. Revenues
8. Expenses
9. Gains
10. Losses

Assumptions
1. Economic entity
2. Going concern
3. Monetary unit
4. Periodicity

Principles
1. Historical cost
2. Revenue recognition
3. Matching
4. Full disclosure

Constraints
1. Cost/benefit
2. Materiality
3. Industry practice
4. Conservatism

the time the FASB identifies an issue that may require a new (or revised) standard to the time a standard is set, interested parties have an opportunity to express their opinions on the matter to FASB.

Under the guidance of the FASB, setting standards follows a ten-step circular process emphasizing due process:

1. **Identifying issues.** The FASB, the American Institute of Certified Public Accountants (AICPA), public accounting firms, business organizations, and the U.S. Congress identify accounting issues and problems. The FASB attempts to treat seriously all issues these parties raise.
2. **Setting an agenda.** The FASB selects issues to be reviewed in the standard-setting process. In considering an issue, the FASB takes account of its own resources, the perceived urgency of the matter, and any interrelationship with other projects already under consideration.
3. **Appointing a task force.** Once an item has been placed on the agenda, FASB appoints a task force to see the project through to its conclusion—either the creation of a new standard or the elimination of the project. Task forces usually include FASB members and outside experts in related areas with diverse views to obtain as many different perspectives as possible.

4. **Creating a discussion memorandum.** The appointed task force prepares a discussion memorandum, which defines the problem, explains the issues, describes the scope of the project, and includes several alternative solutions. All interested parties may respond to the memorandum.
5. **Holding public hearings.** The FASB holds public hearings on major projects under consideration and announces the hearings in the financial press, inviting interested parties to make an oral presentation of their views.
6. **Inviting comment letters.** Those unable to attend the public hearings may write comment letters. The FASB considers every letter.
7. **Deliberating.** After considering the comments from the public hearings, comment letters, FASB's technical staff, and the task force, the FASB decides whether to issue an exposure draft or drop the issue.
8. **Writing an exposure draft.** The FASB prepares a draft version of the proposed standard and exposes it to public comment for at least 60 days. Comments received at this stage often bring about significant changes in the exposure draft.
9. **Issuing a Statement of Financial Accounting Standards.** After a proposed standard goes through the first eight steps of the process, FASB members vote whether to issue a new standard. When a majority of the seven members approves the new rule, a new *Statement of Financial Accounting Standards (SFAS)* becomes part of GAAP.
10. **Conducting a postenactment review.** Because financial accounting and reporting are dynamic areas, the FASB constantly reconsiders, refines, or amends the standards.

The FASB has issued over 133 official pronouncements establishing standards that constitute generally accepted accounting principles. Professional accountants use GAAP in preparing and evaluating financial statements. Auditors must carefully consider GAAP during an audit engagement.

OUTSIDE ASSURANCE ON FINANCIAL STATEMENTS

What Exactly Is an Audit?

audit Examination by an independent CPA of enough of a company's records to determine whether the financial statements have been prepared in accordance with GAAP and demonstrate a fair representation of the company's financial status.

Financial statement users rely on an audit report to assure them that they can believe what they read in the financial statements. During an **audit,** the auditor examines the client's financial statements, with the internal control structure and supporting documentation, to determine whether the financial statements present a fair picture of the client's financial condition and have been prepared in accordance with GAAP. To examine all the client's records would be cost prohibitive—and the cost would outweigh the benefit derived. Statistical theory provides auditors with methods of sampling that allow the auditor to test the records and determine the probability that the records verify the fairness of the financial statement numbers. An auditor does not prepare the financial statements—the company's management prepares them and the auditor has no authority to make changes in the statements without the client's consent.

Generally accepted accounting principles were developed to establish *comparability* among the financial statements of different companies. These principles are also intended to maintain *consistency* in the way companies account for events and transactions from year to year. The audit was developed as a mechanism to provide assurance to external parties that the financial statements they use to make economic decisions have been prepared in accordance with established standards.

Discussion Questions

1-17. Describe how you would decide which and how many records to examine to determine whether your social club's treasurer's report portrays a fair picture of the club's financial activity for the past year.

1-18. How might your answer change to question 1-17 if you were to look at your local Wal-Mart's records for one week?

Auditing standards require auditors to have an extensive knowledge of the economy, the relevant industry, and the client's business. Auditors make inquiries of company personnel and conduct numerous audit procedures, because they must achieve a reasonable assurance that there are no material misstatements in those financial statements. "Reasonable assurance" is what a rational person would consider sufficient. In an accounting context, something is *material* when it would influence the judgment of a reasonable person. A "material misstatement" would change a reasonable person's decision about a company's financial condition.

Who Performs Audits?

Only licensed certified public accountants (CPAs) perform independent audits of U.S. businesses, but not all CPAs are auditors. Auditing is a highly specialized accounting function governed by a set of standards called *generally accepted auditing standards (GAAS)*. The AICPA details the procedures that CPAs must follow during audits through pronouncements called Statements on Auditing Standards (SAS).

Auditors walk a curious tightrope in our society. Lawyers have one responsibility: to represent their clients who pay them to fulfill that responsibility. Doctors have one responsibility: to care for their patients who pay them to fulfill that responsibility. Auditors, on the other hand, have a dual responsibility: They are responsible to the clients who pay them, but they also have a responsibility to all the users of audited financial statements. Auditors must be independent of the entity they are auditing and objective in their assessment of the financial statements' fairness. It is a difficult balancing act, and auditors face a rising level of litigation from statement users who relied on financial statements and then suffered losses. If found guilty of professional negligence, auditors must pay damages to victims. Most CPAs take their responsibility very seriously.

Discussion Question

1-19. What potential problems do you think can arise from the auditor's dual responsibility?

The Audit Opinion

At the conclusion of an audit, the auditor issues an *opinion* as to the fairness of the financial statement presentation. GAAS allows the CPA to issue several different opinions, depending on the findings of the audit. Most firms receive an *unqualified opinion*, in which the CPA states that the financial statements "present fairly, in all material respects, the financial position . . . and the results of operations and its cash flows . . . in conformity with generally accepted accounting principles." Also called a *clean opinion*, a firm seeks to have this opinion given to its statements. A financial statement user should be concerned about financial statements that do not contain an unqualified opinion.

Auditors may issue several other opinions. If the auditor cannot render an opinion because the company did not provide enough evidence or allow enough performance of audit tests, he or she issues a *disclaimer of opinion*. The financial statement user has no assurance from the auditor of fairness or conformity with GAAP with a disclaimer of opinion. Auditors have the option to issue a *qualified opinion* in which they state an exception to general fairness of presentation or conformity with GAAP. Readers should carefully consider the exception(s) the auditor raises. The most devastating opinion an auditor renders is the *adverse opinion*, in which the auditor clearly states that the financial statements are not fairly presented or do not conform with GAAP. Readers should not rely on such financial statements. An informed financial statement user examines the audit opinion before reading the financial statements to determine the auditor's level of assurance.

Discussion Question

1–20. Find the audit opinion in the annual report of the Gap contained in Appendix A beginning on page F-497. Who are the auditors? What type of opinion did the auditors issue?

Now that we have discussed generally accepted accounting principles and outside assurance, we can look more deeply into the financial accounting information available to external decision makers. Two major forms of financial reporting are the annual report and Form 10-K. For a discussion of these two important types of financial reporting, see the appendix to this chapter.

SUMMARY

Business has several different meanings, but in the context of this book, it means either commerce or trade as a whole or a specific company involved in commerce or trade. All economic activity revolves around the four factors of production: natural resources, labor, capital, and entrepreneurship. In a market economy, most of the factors of production are privately owned.

Capitalism, the market economy within which U.S. business operates, depends on each participant's concern about his or her self-interests to create competition. This system relies on the profit motive and its resulting competition to allocate resources and force businesses to operate efficiently. Modern U.S. business practice balances the profit motive with a business' social responsibility to its stakeholders.

The three basic forms of business organization are the proprietorship (one owner), the partnership (two or more owners), and the corporation (a legal entity separate from its owners). Most business activity can be categorized as either manufacturing, merchandising, or service. Hybrid businesses are those that conduct more than one of these types of activities. Most U.S. companies see the world as a global economy, and many engage in international trade.

In response to the users' need for comparable and consistent financial information, accountants developed, over time, standards called generally accepted accounting principles (GAAP). The Securities and Exchange Commission (SEC) has the legal authority to regulate accounting practice; however, it delegated that authority to the accounting profession. Currently, the Financial Accounting Standards Board (FASB), created in 1973, establishes GAAP in the United States. The FASB emphasizes a due process approach, whereby all parties affected by the standards have an opportunity to express their opinions on proposed standards.

External users of financial statements require some form of outside assurance that the financial statements are fairly presented and are prepared according to GAAP. The most stringent form of outside assurance is the audit, in which independent CPAs examine enough of a company's records to determine whether the company's financial statements fairly present the company's economic position and are prepared in accordance with GAAP. At the conclusion of the audit, the auditor issues an audit opinion.

APPENDIX

After completing your work on this appendix, you should be able to do the following:

9. Describe the information found in a typical annual report and Form 10-K.

10. Gather information about a company and obtain an annual report.

CORPORATE REPORTING AND THE ANNUAL REPORT

financial reporting
Financial disclosures provided to economic decision makers that include both quantitative and qualitative information.

The two major consumers of corporate financial reports in the United States today are shareholders and regulators. Indeed, corporate America must regularly answer to these two groups. Two important components of **financial reporting** are the *annual report,* which was developed to meet the demands of stockholders, and *Form 10-K,* which is required by the Securities and Exchange Commission (SEC). The annual report, the most comprehensive presentation of financial reporting to stockholders, contains not only a company's financial statements but also other information designed to assist economic decision makers to predict the future and timing of cash flows. American corporations that sell their stocks or bonds to the public must report to the Securities and Exchange Commission on Form 10-K, a comprehensive annual report that includes financial statements and an array of additional financial and nonfinancial information.

How to Get an Annual Report

Firms prepare annual reports to communicate important information from the corporation to its owners, the shareholders. Thus, if you own shares of stock in a corporation, you will automatically receive a copy of its annual report.

How should you go about getting an annual report if you are not a shareholder? You have three primary sources for information: the Internet, *The Wall Street Journal* Annual Report Service, and the library.

- Most companies maintain a Web site on the Internet. Frequently, the Web includes the annual report, or the financial statement data from the annual report. Web site visitors can often download or print the annual report or complete a request on the home page to receive a copy.

How do you find the address of the company? Trial and error often results in the correct address. Try the company name to start. Examples are:

Company Name	Internet Address
Gap Inc.	www.gap.com
Sears	www.sears.com
Hallmark	www.hallmark.com
JCPenney	www.jcpenney.com

If that is unsuccessful, use a search engine such as Yahoo!, Lycos, or AltaVista for businesses.

- *The Wall Street Journal* provides an Annual Report Service for selected companies. The report service will send a copy of an annual report for any company with a cloverleaf printed beside its ticker symbol on the stock pages. Call 1-800-654-2582 to request any number of reports.
- Many libraries provide computers with CD-ROM capabilities. Among the most popular CD-ROM products offering company information are
  - Infotrac: contains company profiles, investment reports, and article citations.
  - Proquest: the CD-ROM version of ABI/Inform, the premier source of business articles. Contains citations and the full text of articles, including photos and graphical images.
  - Moody's: Provides full-text annual reports of U.S. and international operations.

On-line systems that search databases provide access to extensive information. Among the most widely used databases containing company information are

- DIALOG: Provides access to over 400 databases covering a wide range of topics, not all of which are business related. Available information includes annual reports and articles (both full text and citations).
- LEXIS/NEXIS: Contains full text of all SEC-required filings (such as Form 10-K) and various business articles and newsletters.

Do not hesitate to ask a company for its annual report. Corporations know that public image can be a crucial factor in a company's success or failure. Generally, corporations gladly honor requests for annual reports and will promptly send them. If you cannot order an annual report over the Internet, locate the corporate headquarters address, phone number, or fax number on the Web site or other library reference source to phone or fax your request to the public relations department.

Information Provided in Annual Reports

Many annual reports contain much the same information, mainly because the SEC requires that most of it be included. The table of contents for the Gap Inc.'s annual report, as follows, represents most of the information found in a modern annual report. An asterisk indicates that the SEC requires the information.

Financial Highlights
Letter to Shareholders
*Our Divisions
Employees/Community
Key Financial Statistics
*Ten-Year Selected Financial Data
Management's Discussion and Analysis

*Management's Report on Financial Information
*Independent Auditors' Report
*Consolidated Statement of Earnings
*Consolidated Balance Sheet
*Consolidated Statement of Cash Flows
*Consolidated Statement of Shareholders' Equity
*Notes to Consolidated Financial Statements
Quantitative and Qualitative Disclosures about Market Risk
*Directors
*Corporate Officers
*Divisional Officers
*Corporate Information

Discussion Question

1–21. What other information would you want to know about the Gap Inc.? Would you feel comfortable to call, e-mail, or write to the company with a specific question? Where can you find the addresses and phone number for the Gap in the annual report?

FORM 10-K

Form 10-K looks different from an annual report. Gone are the glossy pages and color photos, but a reader browsing through the Form 10-K will quickly realize that some of the information is the same as that given in the annual report, which is not surprising. After all, the SEC regulates disclosures in both documents. Exhibit 1–4

Exhibit 1–4
Outline of Contents of Form 10-K

Part I
Item 1. Business
Item 2. Properties
Item 3. Legal Proceedings
Item 4. Submission of Matters to a Vote of Security Holders

Part II
Item 5. Market for the Company's Common Equity and Related Stockholder Matters
Item 6. Selected Financial Data
Item 7. Management's Discussion and Analysis of Financial Condition and Results of Operations
Item 8. Financial Statements and Supplementary Data
Item 9. Changes in and Disagreements with Accountants on Accounting and Financial Disclosure

Part III
Item 10. Directors and Executive Officers of the Company
Item 11. Executive Compensation
Item 12. Security Ownership of Certain Beneficial Owners and Management
Item 13. Certain Relationships and Related Transactions

Part IV
Item 14. Exhibits, Financial Statement Schedules and Reports on Form 8-K

lists the contents of the 10-K. To save companies expense, the annual report may be "included by reference" in the Form 10-K to avoid duplication of effort for items contained in both reports.

The SEC prescribes the contents of Form 10-K in *Regulation S-X* and *Regulation S-K*, as revised in 1982. Those revisions created the SEC's *Integrated Disclosure System*, which simplified and improved the quality of disclosures and reduced the cost to the public companies. The Forms 10-K filed with the SEC are available on the Internet through the EDGAR Web site.

GATHERING ADDITIONAL INFORMATION ABOUT A COMPANY

Financial information and an annual report may not satisfy all your information needs for a particular company. If you are considering the Gap as a stock or bond investment, or as a prospective supplier, customer, or employer, you may need to learn when the Gap Inc. was incorporated and in what state, how the business was started, how it grew into the company it is today, and what are its current projects. (If you apply for a job, you should go to the interview with some knowledge of the company's history, employment practices, and goals. You can ask more relevant questions and impress the interviewer with your industriousness.)

Detailed information about companies is easy to find in the information age. The same sources listed for you in the How to Get an Annual Report section can help you locate information. The Internet becomes a valuable source two ways:

1. The company's Web site usually contains current press releases about company accomplishments, problems, financial results, and other important news.
2. You can conduct a search for news about the company with any of the search engines.

Remember to carefully consider the source of information on the Internet. Almost anyone can put information on the Web, so the value of what you find there may be questionable.

Libraries generally have a wide variety of resources available, including handbooks and periodicals. Examples are as follows:

1. *Hoover's Handbook of American Business* offers two pages of information about each of the companies it profiles. Most of the information it provides about the Gap Inc. (Exhibit 1–5 on pages F-27–F-28) is not available in the company's annual report, and background details provided in the sections titled "Overview" and "When" are particularly relevant to potential employees.
2. *Standard and Poor's Stock Reports* details recent news about companies. This loose-leaf publication is updated monthly and contains various types of information. Exhibit 1–6 shows a recent entry for the Gap Inc.
3. *Moody's Industrial Manual* offers extensive company histories and more detailed financial information than can be found in *Hoover's Handbook of American Business* and *Standard and Poor's Stock Reports*.

Periodical indexes help you to find articles about the company. Usually available in hardback or CD-ROM, the *Business Periodicals Index* or the *Wall Street Journal Index* can be most helpful in locating information about a particular company. The most trustworthy sources for information in the press are the *The Wall Street Journal, Business Week, Fortune*, and *Forbes*.

Exhibit 1-5

Gap Inc. Entry in *Hoover's Handbook of American Business.* Courtesy of Hoover's Online (www.hoovers.com).

THE GAP, INC.

OVERVIEW

From infancy to affluence, the Gap has got you (or your body) covered. Based in San Francisco, the vertically integrated clothing company operates about 1,900 retail outlets under the names babyGap, Banana Republic, Gap, GapKids, and Old Navy. Almost all of the Gap's merchandise is private label.

Though the company has experienced record sales and earnings, its newest chain, Old Navy, is the Gap's main source of growth. Old Navy has quickly expanded to almost 200 locations. The units resemble upscale warehouses, with concrete floors and exposed pipes, and offer casual apparel at low prices. The Banana Republic division, which offers upscale

clothing and accessories for the over-30 crowd, has introduced a shoe line as well as personal care products with success.

The company's Gap stores are lagging behind its other chains, in part because they strayed from the tried-and-true classics male customers had come to expect (jeans, T-shirts, and khakis) in favor of trendier styles. The chain is trying to recapture this market and update its image through a new advertising campaign pitching Gap's "Easy Fit Jeans." Gap stores have also introduced high-end items such as perfume and skin products.

Founders Donald and Doris Fisher own 24% of the company.

WHEN

In 1969 Donald Fisher and his wife, Doris, opened a small store near what is now San Francisco State University. The couple named their store the Gap (after "the generation gap") and concentrated on selling Levi's jeans. The couple opened a second store in San Jose eight months later, and by the end of 1970 there were six Gap stores. In the beginning the Fishers catered almost exclusively to teenagers, but in the 1970s they expanded into active wear that would appeal to a larger spectrum of customers. Nevertheless, by the early 1980s the Gap was still dependent upon its largely teenage customer base.

In a 1983 effort to revamp the company's image, Fisher hired Mickey Drexler, a former president of Ann Taylor who had a spotless track record in the apparel industry, as the Gap's new president. Drexler immediately overhauled the motley clothing lines to concentrate on sturdy, brightly colored cotton clothing. He also consolidated the stores' many private clothing labels into the Gap brand. As a final touch Drexler ripped out the stores' circular clothing racks and installed white shelving where the clothes could be neatly stacked and displayed.

Also in 1983 the company bought Banana Republic, a unique chain of stores that sold safari clothing in a jungle decor. The company expanded the chain, which enjoyed tremendous success in the mid-1980s; however, after the novelty of the stores wore off in the late 1980s, sales went into a slump. Drexler responded by introducing a broader range of clothes (including higher-priced leather items) and playing down the jungle image. By 1990 Banana Republic was again profitable.

The retailer opened its first GapKids in 1985 after Drexler couldn't find clothing that he liked for his son. During the late 1980s and early 1990s, the Gap continued to grow rapidly, opening its first stores in Canada and the UK. In 1990 it introduced babyGap in 25 GapKids stores, featuring miniature versions of its GapKids line. The company announced in 1991 it would no longer sell Levi's (which had fallen to less than 2% of total sales) and would go completely private label.

The Gap's earnings fell in fiscal 1993 because of Gap division losses brought on by low margins and high rents. It shuffled management positions and titles as part of a streamlining effort. The company rebounded in 1994, concentrating more on improving profit margins than increasing sales. That year the Gap launched Old Navy Clothing Co., which by 1996 accounted for 16% of sales.

In 1995 the company launched a line of body and bath products at Banana Republic, which that year opened its first two stores outside the US, in Canada's Edmonton and Toronto.

During 1996 the company opened 203 new stores. The Gap also teamed up with the NBA to offer kid's clothes featuring the New York Knick's, Los Angeles Laker's, and Chicago Bull's logos, making it the first major retailer allowed to use team logos on its own clothes.

In 1997 Robert Fisher (the founders' son) became the new president of the Gap division (including babyGap and GapKids), and was charged with turning around the segment's sales decline.

Exhibit 1-5 (Continued)
Gap Inc. Entry in *Hoover's Handbook of American Business*

WHO

Chairman: Donald G. Fisher, age 68, $1,845,360 pay
President and CEO: Millard S. "Mickey" Drexler, age 52, $3,130,385 pay
EVP; President, The Gap, GapKids: Robert J. Fisher, age 42, $1,478,440 pay
EVP and Chief Administrative Officer: John B. Wilson, age 37, $1,194,848 pay
Division EVP Stores, GapKids: Ronald G. Franks
Division EVP Stores: Dennis R. Parodi
Division EVP Stores and Operations, Old Navy: Kevin M. Lonergan
SVP Finance and CFO: Warren R. Hashagen Jr., age 46, $486,660 pay
SVP and Chief Information Officer: Dennis M. Connors
SVP Strategic Planning and Business Development: Charles K. Crovitz
SVP Offshore Sourcing; Managing Director, Gap International Sourcing: James P. Cunningham
SVP and General Counsel: Anne B. Gust, age 39
SVP Distribution: George A. Joseph
SVP Real Estate: Steven B. Kaplan
SVP Personal Care: Gary L. McNatton
SVP Sourcing and Logistics: Stanley P. Raggio
SVP Human Resources: Adrienne M. Johns
VP Human Resources: Susan L. Cooper
CEO, Banana Republic: Jeanne Jackson
President, International: William S. Fisher
Auditors: Deloitte & Touche LLP

WHERE

HQ: One Harrison St., San Francisco, CA 94105
Phone: 650-952-4400 **Fax:** 650-427-2795
Web site: http://www.gap.com

Stores

	No.
US	1,666
Canada	109
UK	71
France	18
Japan	11
Germany	8
Total	**1,883**

WHAT

Stores

	No.
The Gap	947
GapKids	491
Banana Republic	229
Old Navy Clothing	199
babyGap	17
Total	**1,883**

KEY COMPETITORS

Benetton	J. C. Penney	NIKE
Bugle Boy	L.A. Gear	Nordstrom
Calvin Klein	Lands' End	OshKosh B'Gosh
Dayton Hudson	Levi Strauss	Polo
Dillard's	The Limited	Reebok
Edison Brothers	L.L. Bean	Sears
Esprit de Corp.	Luxottica	Spiegel
Federated	May	TJX
Guess?	Mercantile Stores	Toys "R" Us
Gymboree	Nautica	VF
J. Crew	Enterprises	

HOW MUCH

NYSE symbol: GPS FYE: January 31	Annual Growth	1988	1989	1990	1991	1992	1993	1994	1995	1996	1997
Sales ($ mil.)	19.5%	1,062	1,252	1,587	1,934	2,519	2,960	3,296	3,723	4,395	5,284
Net income ($ mil.)	23.1%	70	74	98	145	230	211	258	320	354	453
Income as % of sales	—	6.6%	5.9%	6.2%	7.5%	9.1%	7.1%	7.8%	8.6%	8.1%	8.6%
Earnings per share ($)	22.9%	0.25	0.26	0.35	0.51	0.81	0.74	0.89	1.10	1.23	1.60
Stock price - FY high ($)	—	9.73	5.42	7.69	10.69	29.69	28.13	21.44	24.69	25.50	36.50
Stock price - FY low ($)	—	2.00	2.33	4.41	4.88	10.00	14.06	12.75	14.44	14.88	23.19
Stock price - FY close ($)	31.5%	2.44	4.63	5.84	10.63	26.63	17.25	21.13	16.25	23.56	28.75
P/E - high	—	39	21	22	21	37	38	24	22	21	23
P/E - low	—	8	9	13	10	12	19	14	13	12	14
Dividends per share ($)	17.6%	0.07	0.07	0.09	0.11	0.15	0.16	0.19	0.23	0.24	0.30
Book value per share ($)	22.8%	0.95	0.93	1.20	1.65	2.38	3.08	3.88	4.75	5.70	6.03
Employees	17.3%	15,700	19,800	23,000	26,000	32,000	39,000	44,000	55,000	60,000	66,000

STOCK PRICE HISTORY
HIGH/LOW/CLOSE

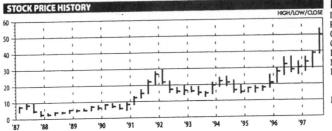

1997 FISCAL YEAR-END

Debt ratio: 0.0%
Return on equity: 27.4%
Cash (mil.): $486
Current ratio: 1.72
Long-term debt (mil.): $0
No. of shares (mil.): 275
Dividends
  Yield: 1.0%
  Payout: 18.8%
Market value (mil.): $7,892

Exhibit 1–6

Gap Inc. Entry in *Standard and Poor's Stock Reports,* November 1998. Source: From *Standard & Poor's Stock Reports,* October 31, 1998. Reprinted by permission of Standard & Poor, New York, NY.

STANDARD &POOR'S STOCK REPORTS

Gap (The)

943
NYSE Symbol **GPS**
In S&P 500

31-OCT-98 **Industry:** Retail (Specialty-Apparel)

Summary: This specialty apparel retailer operates The Gap Stores, Banana Republic, and Old Navy Clothing Co., offering casual clothing to upper, moderate and value-oriented market segments.

S&P Opinion: Hold (★★★)

Recent Price • 60⅛ | 52 Wk Range • 68-32⅞ | Yield • 0.3% | 12-Mo. P/E • 37.6

Quantitative Evaluations

Outlook (1 Lowest—5 Highest)
• **2+**

Fair Value
• **57⅞**

Risk
• **Average**

Earn./Div. Rank
• **A+**

Technical Eval.
• **Bullish** since 2/97

Rel. Strength Rank (1 Lowest—99 Highest)
• **76**

Insider Activity
• **Neutral**

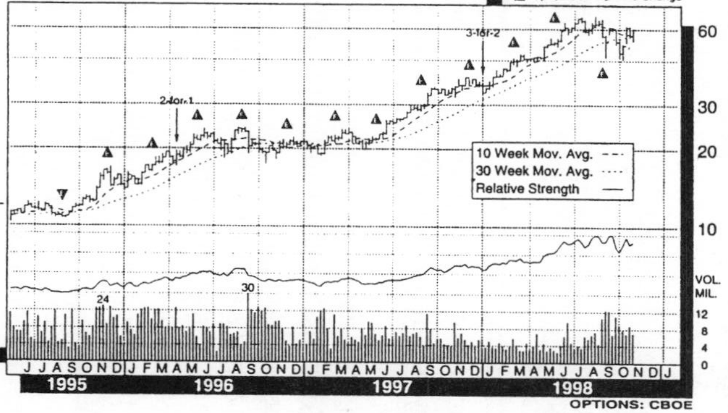

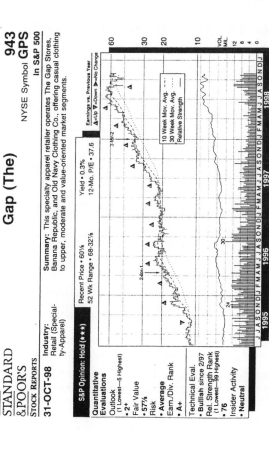

OPTIONS: CBOE

Overview - 26-OCT-98

Same-store sales should advance in the 15% range in FY 99 (Jan.), and with a 16% increase in square footage and strong sales gains at Old Navy stores, total sales could increase 27%. Gross margins should widen, with improved inventory management resulting in a better mix of fashion and basic merchandise. This should boost margins overall. Expense ratios should increase, reflecting higher depreciation charges from new larger stores. Operating income should increase significantly. The aggressive rollout of Old Navy Clothing Co. value priced stores enhances the company's earnings prospects. However, since Old Navy operates with lower margins, as it contributes a larger portion of Gap's business it will lower overall company gross margins. International expansion should also aid long-term growth. The company has taken on a moderate amount of long term debt (about 32% of equity) to fund its $700 million capital expenditure program, adding some 300 to 350 units, and its 30 million common share repurchase program, of which it has completed about half.

Valuation - 26-OCT-98

The shares of this fast growing, well managed retailer should be held for capital appreciation. The premium valuation is justified, given Gap's strong consumer franchise and healthy financial performance. However, with a slowdown in consumer spending anticipated over the next few months and difficult comparisons in the first half of FY 00, we would not add to positions at this time. The company's aggressive expansion, a new Banana Republic catalog and expansion of its Gap on-line business continue to bode well for future earnings gains. We believe the company's core growth rate is about 16% to 19%.

Key Stock Statistics

S&P EPS Est. 1999	1.85	Tang. Bk. Value/Share	3.94
P/E on S&P Est. 1999	32.5	Beta	0.81
S&P EPS Est. 2000	2.15	Shareholders	6,800
Dividend Rate/Share	0.20	Market cap. (B)	$ 23.2
Shs. outstg. (M)	386.3	Inst. holdings	48%
Avg. daily vol. (M)	1.495		

Value of $10,000 invested 5 years ago: $ 57,689

Fiscal Year Ending Jan. 31

	1999	1998	1997	1996	1995	1994
Revenues (Million $)						
1Q	1,720	1,231	1,113	848.7	752.0	643.6
2Q	1,905	1,345	1,120	868.5	773.1	693.2
3Q	—	1,766	1,383	1,156	988.4	898.7
4Q	—	2,165	1,668	1,522	1,210	1,060
Yr.	—	6,508	5,284	4,395	3,723	3,296
Earnings Per Share ($)						
1Q	**0.34**	**0.20**	**0.19**	0.12	0.15	0.10
2Q	**0.34**	**0.17**	**0.15**	0.07	0.10	0.07
3Q	**E0.51**	**0.40**	**0.32**	0.27	0.21	0.18
4Q	**E0.65**	**0.53**	**0.41**	0.36	0.27	0.25
Yr.	**E1.85**	**1.30**	**1.06**	**0.83**	**0.74**	**0.60**

Next earnings report expected: mid November

Dividend Data (Dividends have been paid since 1976.)

Amount ($)	Date Decl.	Ex-Div. Date	Stock of Record	Payment Date
3-for-2	Nov. 24	Dec. 23	Dec. 08	Dec. 22 '97
0.050	Feb. 24	Mar. 04	Mar. 06	Mar. 16 '98
0.050	May. 19	Jun. 03	Jun. 05	Jun. 15 '98
0.050	Sep. 09	Sep. 17	Sep. 21	Oct. 01 '98

STANDARD &POOR'S STOCK REPORTS

The Gap, Inc.

943
31-OCT-98

Business Summary - 26-OCT-98

The Gap, Inc. is synonymous with casual clothing for women, men and children, sold through its Gap, GapKids, babyGap, Banana Republic and Old Navy Clothing Co. concepts. Since its inception in 1969, the company has built retail concepts into brand names. At August 1, 1998, it operated 2,272 stores (1,068 Gap, 271 Banana Republic, 601 GapKids and 332 Old Navy stores).

The Gap format is the company's original concept, started in 1969 in San Francisco. At that time, jeans dominated the stores. The company still emphasizes denim clothing but khakis and other casual staples are now important product categories. With higher margins than staple items, the merchandising mix has shifted toward the addition of fashion items, such as skirts and dresses, and accessories. Complementary product lines, such as shoes and personal care products, have also been added to the store assortment.

Banana Republic was acquired in 1983, with two stores and a mail order catalog. The company expanded its merchandise to feature trendy travel and safari clothing and accessories in a theatrical environment, including jeeps and banana trees. By 1988, the safari look was stale. The catalog was discontinued, and Banana developed a new merchandising strategy offering high quality sophisticated sportswear for men and women.

Targeting low-income customers, The Old Navy Clothing Co. is Gap's fastest growing division. Almost double the size of Gap stores, at 15,000 sq. ft., these stores sell clothing for the entire family. In an attempt to make shopping more fun and to differentiate these stores from others, old cars and gumball machines have been added to the merchandise display. Many Old Navy units also have a place to grab a snack or sit down to eat a light meal.

GapKids was introduced in 1986 to provide parents and gift-givers well-designed clothing for children from two to twelve. The babyGap line of newborn, infant and toddler clothing is available in virtually all GapKids stores.

Gap has moved across the Atlantic with stores in the U.K. and France, and also operates in Japan. Ninety-one stores are located in Canada.

The Gap, Inc. continually tests new products and new product categories in its stores. The company has its own product development and design teams. Gap employs more than 1,000 suppliers located domestically and overseas to manufacture goods to the company's specifications.

Per Share Data ($) (Year Ended Jan. 31)	1998	1997	1996	1995	1994	1993	1992	1991	1990	1989
Tangible Bk. Val.	4.03	4.02	3.80	3.17	2.59	2.05	1.59	1.05	0.76	0.66
Cash Flow	1.96	1.57	1.27	1.12	0.87	0.71	0.70	0.46	0.32	0.24
Earnings	1.30	1.07	0.82	0.73	0.59	0.49	0.54	0.34	0.23	0.17
Dividends	0.20	0.20	0.16	0.15	0.13	0.11	0.10	0.07	0.06	0.04
Payout Ratio	15%	19%	20%	21%	21%	22%	19%	22%	24%	25%
Cal. Yrs.	1997	1996	1995	1994	1993	1992	1991	1990	1989	1988
Prices - High	$38\frac{5}{8}$	$24\frac{3}{8}$	17	$16\frac{1}{2}$	$19\frac{3}{4}$	$19\frac{3}{4}$	$18\frac{3}{4}$	6	$5\frac{1}{8}$	$3\frac{1}{2}$
- Low	$18\frac{5}{8}$	14	$9\frac{7}{8}$	$9\frac{5}{8}$	$9\frac{3}{8}$	$9\frac{3}{8}$	$5\frac{1}{2}$	$3\frac{1}{4}$	3	$1\frac{9}{16}$
P/E Ratio - High	30	23	21	22	40	40	35	18	22	21
- Low	14	13	12	13	19	19	10	10	13	9
Income Statement Analysis (Million $)										
Revs.	6,508	5,284	4,395	3,723	3,296	2,960	2,519	1,934	1,587	1,252
Oper. Inc.	1,121	944	767	687	547	438	444	290	214	167
Depr.	270	215	197	168	122	94.2	70.1	51.3	37.9	31.4
Int. Exp.	Nil	NA	NA	NA	0.8	3.8	3.5	1.4	2.8	3.4
Pretax Inc.	854	749	585	529	425	340	371	237	163	126
Eff. Tax Rate	38%	39%	40%	40%	39%	38%	38%	39%	40%	41%
Net Inc.	534	453	354	320	258	211	230	145	98.0	74.0
Balance Sheet & Other Fin. Data (Million $)										
Cash	913	622	669	588	544	243	193	67.0	39.0	46.0
Curr. Assets	1,831	1,329	1,280	1,056	956	691	566	365	317	258
Total Assets	3,338	2,627	2,343	2,004	1,763	1,379	1,147	777	579	481
Curr. Liab.	992	775	552	500	462	335	330	264	187	152
LT Debt	496	Nil	Nil	Nil	75.0	75.0	77.5	5.0	17.5	20.0
Common Eqty.	1,584	1,654	1,640	1,375	1,126	888	678	466	338	276
Total Cap.	2,080	1,654	1,640	1,375	1,201	963	755	471	355	296
Cap. Exp.	466	372	302	233	223	211	245	208	93.0	67.0
Cash Flow	804	668	551	488	380	305	300	196	136	106
Curr. Ratio	1.8	1.7	2.3	2.1	2.1	2.1	1.7	1.4	1.7	1.7
% LT Debt of Cap.	23.8	Nil	Nil	Nil	6.2	7.8	10.3	1.1	4.9	6.7
% Net Inc.of Revs.	8.2	8.6	8.1	8.6	7.8	7.1	9.1	7.5	6.2	5.9
% Ret. on Assets	17.9	18.2	16.3	17.0	16.4	16.6	23.8	21.3	18.4	16.4
% Ret. on Equity	33.0	27.5	23.5	25.6	25.6	26.8	40.1	35.9	31.8	27.3

Data as orig. reptd.; bef. results of disc. opers. and/or spec. items. Per share data adj. for stk. divs. as of ex-div. date. Bold denotes diluted EPS (FASB 128). E-Estimated. NA-Not Available. NM-Not Meaningful. NR-Not Ranked.

Office—One Harrison St., San Francisco, CA 94105. **Tel**—(415) 952-4400. **Website**—http://www.gap.com **Chrmn**—D. G. Fisher. **Pres & CEO**—M. S. Drexler. **EVP & COO**— R. J. Fisher. **SVP, CFO & Investor Contact**—Warren R. Hashagen. **Secy**—Anne B. Gust. **Dirs**—A. D. P. Bellamy, J. G. Bowes, M. S. Drexler, D. F. Fisher, D. G. Fisher, R. J. Fisher, L. J. Fjeldstad, W. A. Hasler, J. M. Lillie, C. R. Schwab, B. Walker Jr., S. S. Zyman. **Transfer Agent & Registrar**—Harris Trust Co. of California, Chicago. **Incorporated**—in California in 1969. **Empl**— 81,000. **S&P Analyst:** Karen J. Sack, CFA

SUMMARY TO APPENDIX

Two major consumers of corporate financial reports are stockholders and government regulators, most notably the Securities and Exchange Commission (SEC). The most comprehensive presentation of financial reporting to stockholders is the annual report. The SEC has specific disclosure requirements for information provided in the annual report and the Form 10-K, required annually for publicly traded companies. The SEC prescribes the rules for the form and content of the financial statements and other information included in the 10-K under Regulations S-X and S-K. The SEC's Integrated Disclosure System encourages companies to eliminate duplication between the annual report and Form 10-K through "incorporation by reference."

You can gather information about publicly traded companies on the Internet, in the library, or from news sources.

KEY TERMS

audit   F-20
business   F-5
capital   F-6
corporation   F-11
entrepreneurship   F-6
factors of production   F-5
Financial Accounting Standards
   Board (FASB)   F-17
financial reporting   F-23
generally accepted accounting
   principles (GAAP)   F-17
gross margin or gross profit   F-7
hybrid companies   F-14
labor   F-6

manufacturing   F-13
market economy   F-6
merchandising   F-14
natural resources   F-5
partnership   F-9
profit   F-7
Securities and Exchange
   Commission (SEC)   F-17
separate entity assumption   F-11
service   F-14
sole proprietorship   F-8
stakeholder   F-8
stockholder   F-11

REVIEW THE FACTS

A. What are the four factors of production? Define each.
B. Describe the primary difference between a planned economy and a market economy.
C. Explain what is meant by the profit motive.
D. Define gross profit (or gross margin) and net profit.
E. Explain the meaning of stakeholder.
F. Name the three basic forms of business organization and describe several advantages and disadvantages of each.
G. Describe the separate entity concept.
H. Name and describe the three major classifications of business activity. What is a hybrid company?
I. Define quotas and tariffs. Explain the purpose of each.
J. Describe the relationship between business and accounting.
K. Broadly define GAAP. Which companies must adhere to GAAP?
L. Explain the role of the SEC in the regulation of accounting practice.
M. What is the name and abbreviation for the current accounting standards-setting group?

N. Describe the ten-step process used by FASB to set standards.
O. Describe comparability and consistency and how they relate to corporate reporting.
P. What is the purpose of an audit and who can perform independent audits?
Q. Explain "reasonable assurance" and "material misstatements."
R. Describe an auditor's dual responsibility and identify the standards by which auditors are governed.
S. Name and describe the four types of audit report an auditor can issue.
T. Distinguish between financial reporting and financial statements.
*U. Identify the two major documents created as a result of the financial reporting process.
*V. What is the primary purpose of the SEC's Integrated Disclosure System?
*W. Identify three items not required by the SEC, but commonly found in corporate annual reports; describe what can be learned from each.
*X. Why are corporations generally cooperative when individuals request their annual reports?
*Y. How can learning about a company before interviewing for a job there be helpful?

*Includes material found in this chapter's appendix.

APPLY WHAT YOU HAVE LEARNED

LO 1 & 2:   Terminology

1–22. Presented below are items relating to some of the concepts presented in this chapter, followed by the definitions of those items in scrambled order.

a. Entrepreneurship	**e.** Factors of production
b. Labor	**f.** Natural resources
c. Planned economy	**g.** Capital
d. Capitalism	**h.** Profit motive

1. _____ The human resource factor.
2. _____ Land and materials that come from land.
3. _____ The factor of production that brings all the other factors of production together.
4. _____ The motivation to do something when the benefits exceed the sacrifice of doing it.
5. _____ A type of market economy.
6. _____ The four major items needed to support economic activity.
7. _____ Buildings, machinery, tools, and money used to produce goods and services.
8. _____ A strong, centralized government controls all or most of the factors of production.

REQUIRED:
Match the letter next to each item on the list with the appropriate definition. Note that each letter will be used only once.

LO 2:   Business Terminology

1–23. Presented below are items relating to some of the concepts presented in this chapter, followed by the definitions of those items in scrambled order.

a. Hybrid company	f. Manufacturing company
b. Wholesaler	g. Merchandising company
c. Imports	h. Retailer
d. Exports	i. Translation
e. Tariffs	j. Quota

1. _____ Goods sold outside the country in which they were produced.
2. _____ A business that converts purchased raw materials into some tangible, physical product.
3. _____ A company involved in more than one type of business activity.
4. _____ A type of business operated by either a wholesaler or a retailer.
5. _____ A quantity limitation placed on imported goods.
6. _____ A business known as a middleman.
7. _____ The conversion of the currency of one country into its equivalent in another country's currency.
8. _____ Taxes that raise the price of imported products.
9. _____ A business that sells products to the final consumer.
10. _____ Goods brought into a country that were produced in another country.

REQUIRED:

Match the letter next to each item on the list with the appropriate definition. Note that each letter will be used only once.

LO 2:   Computation of Gross Profit and Net Profit

1–24. Larry Melman owns and operates a retail clothing store. Last month clothing sales totaled $5,200. Melman paid $2,800 for the clothing sold last month. He also paid rent of $300 and wages to employees totaling $900.

REQUIRED:
a. Calculate the gross profit on sales for last month. What is the percentage of gross profit to sales?
b. Identify the expenses incurred during the month and explain whether they should be used to compute gross profit or net profit.
c. Calculate the net profit for last month.
d. If Larry always has the same percentage of gross profit, how much must he sell each month to cover expenses of $1,200?

LO 2:   Computation of Gross Profit and Net Profit

1–25. Zippo Marks sells fine imported cigars. During the month of December, Zippo sold 3,000 cigars at a total price of $15,000. Zippo paid $9,000 for the cigars that he sold in December.

REQUIRED:
a. Determine the gross margin for Zippo in December.
b. How would your answer differ if Zippo had paid $6,000 for the cigars?
c. List the expenses you would expect Zippo to have each month to run his store.

LO 2:   Computation of Gross Profit and Net Profit

1–26. Grouchy Marks owns and operates a retail hardware store. In June his sales were $18,000. The items sold cost Mr. Marks $12,600. Mr. Marks spent $1,000 for store rent, $300 for utilities expense, and $1,500 for employee wages.

REQUIRED:

a. Calculate the gross profit on sales for June. What is the percentage of gross profit to sales?
b. Identify the expenses incurred during the month and explain whether they should be used to compute gross profit or net profit.
c. Calculate the net profit for June.
d. If Mr. Marks always has the same percentage of gross profit, and his July expenses will be the same as his June expenses, how much must he sell in July to cover his expenses?

LO 2: Computation of Gross Profit and Net Profit

1–27. In August, Mary bought 24 quilts for $100 each.

REQUIRED:

a. If Mary sells the quilts for $150 each, what is her gross profit for each quilt?
b. If she sells all of the quilts in August, what is her total gross profit?
c. If Mary rents an office for $200 and pays utilities expense of $75, advertising expense of $150, and bank charges of $15, calculate her net income for August.
d. If she pays the expenses in part c. for August, how many quilts must she sell to make a net profit of $500?

LO 2 & 4: Computation of Gross Profit and Net Profit for Different Business Forms

1–28. The Computer Center of America manufactures and sells computers. During the month of October the center produced and sold 1,000 computers. The sale of the computers generated $1,000,000. The Center spent $300,000 for the parts to build the computers and paid $200,000 for the labor to assemble the computers. The center also paid $100,000 for all other costs (overhead) necessary to construct the computers. The Center spent $50,000 on other operating expenses.

REQUIRED:

a. What type of business does the Center operate (i.e., manufacturing, merchandising, or service)?
b. Calculate the gross profit for the month of October.
c. Calculate the net profit for the month of October.

LO 4 & 5: Stockholder vs. Stakeholder

1–29. Explain the concept behind the term *stakeholder,* and contrast it with the definition of the term *stockholder.*

LO 4: Forms of Business Organization

1–30. Presented below are the three basic forms of business in the United States, followed by some of the advantages relating to those forms of business:

    a. Sole proprietorship   b. Partnership   c. Corporation

    1. _____ Owner has total control
    2. _____ Greater business continuity
    3. _____ Easy transfer of ownership

4. _____ Limited liability
5. _____ Greater access to capital
6. _____ Easy and inexpensive to establish
7. _____ Few government regulations
8. _____ Easy to dissolve
9. _____ No special income taxes
10. _____ No sharing of profits
11. _____ Greater management expertise

REQUIRED:
Match the letter next to each form of business with the appropriate advantage. Note that each letter will be used more than once and it is possible that a particular advantage applies to more than one of the business forms.

LO 4: Forms of Business Organization

1–31. Presented below are the three basic forms of business in the United States, followed by some of the disadvantages relating to those forms of business:

    a. Sole proprietorship   **b.** Partnership   **c.** Corporation

1. _____ Usually has less access to capital than the other two forms
2. _____ Greater tax burden
3. _____ Limited management expertise
4. _____ Unlimited liability
5. _____ Absentee ownership
6. _____ Must share profits
7. _____ Greater government regulation
8. _____ Often difficult to dissolve
9. _____ Potential ownership conflicts

REQUIRED:
Match the letter next to each form of business with the appropriate disadvantage. Note that each letter will be used more than once and it is possible that a particular disadvantage applies to more than one of the business forms.

LO 4: Forms of Businesses

1–32. Professor Sharyll Plato is opening a publishing company to publish and distribute accounting textbooks throughout the United States. She feels this will be a successful venture because the textbooks will be based upon a revolutionary new format of accounting education. Plato has extended an invitation to all her students to invest in her new business. She is offering shares of stock for a mere $10 each.

REQUIRED:
a. What form of business is Professor Plato proposing?
b. Briefly explain four advantages of doing business in this form.

LO 5: Distinguishing among Types of Businesses

1–33. Phil Jackson owns and operates a jewelry store. During the past month, he sold a necklace to a customer for $2,500. Phil paid $1,800 for the necklace.

REQUIRED:
a. What type of business does Phil own (manufacturer, wholesaler, retailer, etc.)? Explain how you determined your response.

b. Calculate Phil's gross margin on the sale of the necklace.

c. Identify four costs besides the $1,800 cost of the necklace that Phil might incur in the operation of his jewelry store.

d. If Phil's operating costs are $900 per month, what is his net income for the month?

LO 5: Types of Businesses

1–34. This chapter discusses five types of business in the United States, namely

1. Manufacturer
2. Wholesale merchandiser
3. Retail merchandiser
4. Service
5. Hybrid

REQUIRED:

a. Explain in your own words the characteristics of each type of business.

b. Discuss how each of these five types of business is different from the other four.

c. Give two examples of each type of business (do not use any examples given in the chapter) and explain how you determined your answers.

LO 7: Reporting Standards

1–35. Following are the ten steps in the standards-setting process used by the Financial Accounting Standards Board.

1. Identifying issues
2. Setting an agenda
3. Appointing a task force
4. Creating a discussion memorandum
5. Holding public hearings
6. Inviting comment letters
7. Deliberating
8. Writing an exposure draft
9. Issuing a Statement of Financial Accounting Standards
10. Conducting a postenactment review

REQUIRED:

a. Explain in your own words what happens in each of the ten steps of the standards-setting process.

b. What is meant by a "due process approach" to setting accounting standards?

LO 7: Reporting Standards

1–36. Generally accepted accounting principles have been developed over time to aid in comparability among the financial statements of different companies. They are also intended to maintain consistency in the way a firm accounts for transactions and events from period to period.

An audit is intended to provide some assurance to external parties that the financial statements examined are reasonably presented.

REQUIRED:

a. What determines whether a company in the United States is required to prepare its financial statements according to GAAP?

b. Why are some companies forced to adhere to GAAP even though they are not required by law to do so?

c. Identify a specific decision made by an external decision maker, and explain:

   (1) Why comparability of the accounting information used is important and how GAAP supports comparability.

   (2) Why consistency of the accounting information used is important and how GAAP supports consistency.

LO 7 & 9: Reporting Standards

*1–37. Presented below are some of the items discussed in this chapter, followed by the definitions of those items in scrambled order.

a. Financial reporting	**d.** Annual report
b. Financial statements	**e.** SEC Form 10-K
c. SEC Integrated Disclosure System	**f.** Notes to financial statements

1. _____ One of its objectives is to simplify and improve the quality of disclosures provided to investors and other users of financial information.

2. _____ Disclosures provided to economic decision makers that include not only quantitative information but also descriptive information.

3. _____ Intended to provide important information that should be considered by financial statement users when reading financial statements.

4. _____ Its content is prescribed by the SEC.

5. _____ As presented in the annual report, there are balance sheets for two years and statements of income, cash flows, and stockholders' equity for three years.

6. _____ Originally intended to be used only by stockholders but now is broadly used by a variety of other economic decision makers.

REQUIRED:

Match the letter next to each item on the list with the appropriate definition. Each letter will be used only once.

LO 8: Financial Reporting

1–38. Presented below are some items related to the issue of outside assurance discussed in this chapter, followed by the definitions of those items in scrambled order.

a. Audit	**d.** Qualified opinion
b. Unqualified opinion	**e.** Disclaimer
c. Adverse opinion	

1. _____ Caused by a material uncertainty the auditor does not feel can be adequately communicated, or by the placing of a significant restriction on the auditor as to what records may be examined.

2. _____ The process of examining a company's records to determine whether the financial statements have been prepared in accordance with GAAP standards.

3. _____ Rendered when there are departures from GAAP so pervasive that a reasonable person cannot rely on the financial statements.

4. _____ Unofficially referred to as a "clean" opinion.

5. _____ An auditor states an exception in the audit report.

REQUIRED:
Match the letter next to each item with the appropriate definition. Each letter will be used only once.

LO 8: Financial Reporting

1–39. Your uncle who owns a small business knows that you are taking a course in accounting. He tells you that his banker is requiring him to provide an audited set of financial statements for the last fiscal year. He does not understand why the bank is making this request and he asks you why they would want an audit of his financial statements. How do you respond to his question?

LO 9: Annual Reports

*1–40. Listed below are the items required by the SEC to be included in the annual report, along with some items not required but normally included:

1. _____ Audited financial statements
2. _____ The principal market in which the securities of the firm are traded
3. _____ Industry segment disclosures for the last three fiscal years
4. _____ The management report
5. _____ Offer to provide a free copy of Form 10-K to shareholders upon written request, unless the annual report complies with Form 10-K disclosure requirements
6. _____ Report on corporate citizenship
7. _____ Management's discussion and analysis of financial condition and results of operations
8. _____ Five-year selected financial data
9. _____ Brief description of the business
10. _____ Letter to the stockholders
11. _____ Identification of directors and executive officers, with the principal occupation and employer of each
12. _____ High and low market prices of the company's common stock for each quarter of the two most recent fiscal years and dividends paid on common stock during those years

REQUIRED:
Identify each of the items as either required (R) or optional (O).

LO 9: Annual Reports

*1–41. Describe the basic information one would expect to find in an annual report of a publicly traded company.

LO 11: Annual Reports

*1–42. Use the information contained in the 1997 annual report of the Gap, which is reproduced in the text starting on page F-497 to answer the following:

REQUIRED:
a. What is the name of the CPA firm who audited the financial statements?
b. What type of opinion was rendered by the firm?
c. Which paragraph of the audit report identifies the party responsible for the financial statements?

d. Which paragraph of the audit report identifies who is responsible for the audit of the financial statements?

e. Which paragraph of the audit report actually reports the expression of an opinion?

LO 9: Annual Reports

*1–43. Use the information contained in the 1997 annual report of the Gap, which is reproduced in the text starting on page F-497 to answer the following:

REQUIRED:

a. List the title of each financial statement included in the annual report.

b. The assets, liabilities, and stockholders' equity are listed in which of the financial statements?

c. The sales, cost of goods sold, and the operating expenses are reported in which financial statement?

LO 9: Annual Reports

*1–44. Use the information contained in the 1997 annual report of the Gap, which is reproduced in the text starting on page F-497 to answer the following:

REQUIRED:

a. Who wrote the letter to the stockholders? In your opinion, what were the three most important messages in the letter?

b. What are the divisions of the Gap? For each division, list the following information:

(1) Name

(2) Major markets

(3) Distinction in the marketplace

(4) Goals for the current year

c. How does the information in parts a and b help a potential investor, creditor, or employee?

FINANCIAL REPORTING CASES

Comprehensive

1–45. The Buckle sells clothing to young people in upscale malls around the nation. Known for its fashion sense, The Buckle has little debt, high profits, and a successful marketing strategy. In its 1996 annual report, The Buckle made no mention of community service work or social responsibility.

REQUIRED:

a. What conclusions might you draw about The Buckle's social responsibility if you read its annual report?

b. List three questions you would ask The Buckle's president about the company's social responsibility if he came to the store where you were shopping.

c. What advice would you give the president?

Comprehensive

1–46. The following is the opening section of the 1996 letter to shareholders from M. Anthony Burns, Chairman, President, and Chief Executive Officer of Ryder System, Inc.

Letter to Shareholders

The world in which our company operates has changed in many ways.

Our markets have changed. Some have grown, some have slowed, and all have become more competitive and demanding.

Our customers have changed. Many long-time customers now require new and different services, and the ways in which we relate to and serve our customers are not like they were only a few years ago. In many cases, the customers themselves are different or are in different parts of the world.

At the same time, in the face of all this change, we are eager to increase the value of the company to customers, employees and shareholders alike.

So, for Ryder, 1996 was a year of major decisions.

We launched the most sweeping restructuring of operations in the company's history, eliminated 2450 positions—including 2100 we announced in the fourth quarter, identified nearly 200 facilities and properties for disposal, sold our consumer truck rental business, put our automotive carrier business up for review and waged war on unnecessary costs and inefficiency.

We dramatically altered the shape of the company. We moved more than 80% of corporate staff positions into our business units, which are the engines of Ryder's future growth— Transportation Services, Integrated Logistics and Public Transportation Services. In addition, we combined management of Ryder International and Ryder Integrated Logistics in order to focus more sharply on high-margin, knowledge-based, global, integrated logistics opportunities.

Excluding Automotive Carriers, Ryder is now composed of three streamlined, contractually based, market-focused business units, responsible and accountable for the ambitious goals we have set for them. We have equipped and positioned them for success, and we will accept no less. We are single-minded in our campaign to reduce cost, increase margins and enhance shareholder value, and we are impatient in our dedication to deliver these results quickly. And, we reduced our capital spending $800 million to $1.3 billion, emphasizing investment in higher-return contractual business.

Our transformation was not without cost.

We took a pretax charge of $215 million in the fourth quarter of 1996 to cover the cost of the program, which should be completed by the end of 1997. As a result, full year pretax operating earnings of $204.2 million, before the gain on the sale of our consumer truck rental business, restructuring and other charges and the early extinguishment of debt at a premium, were reduced to a net loss of $41.3 million, or $0.51 a share.

REQUIRED:

a. Summarize the main points of the CEO's message.

b. How do you believe that a CEO should give bad news to stockholders? Why?

Comprehensive

1–47. The following is an excerpt from the 1997 letter to the stockholders from William V. Stephenson, Chairman, President, and CEO of First Brands Corporation.

Local Heroes

First Brands Corporation and our employees pitched in again during fiscal 1997 to improve our communities and the lives of others. Our largest corporate project was the 1997 GLAD Bag-A-Thon, America's largest litter cleanup program, which was conducted in conjunction with Keep America Beautiful, Inc. Twenty-seven million pounds of litter and recyclables were collected by more than a million volunteers in 96 cities using donated GLAD trash bags. Our United Way campaigns were also very successful in generating strong employee and Corporate pledges during the year. But when it comes to helping others, we don't just reach for our wallets in this company. Our local heroes are just as likely to reach for hammers, paint brushes, and computers to give freely of our time and talents. We repair homes for the needy and teach skills to the unemployed. We are big brothers and big sisters, coaches, and scout leaders. First Brands enthusiastically supports volunteerism among our employees.

REQUIRED:

a. In what types of community projects does First Brands Corporation participate?

b. What does this tell you about the culture of this company?

c. Is this the type of company in which you would seek a career? Why?

ANNUAL REPORT PROJECT

Comprehensive

During the term of this course, you will participate in an annual report project either as an individual or a group member. With this project, you will learn everything you can about one company using its annual report, the Internet, the press, stock market results, and contact with company officials. Each chapter contains a section of the project that correlates with the chapter material. You will accumulate these sections throughout the semester, and prepare a well-organized project folder for final submission. Your professors may require a short oral presentation of your findings at the end of the semester. By the end of the project, you will decide if this company is a good stock or bond investment, vendor, customer, or employment prospect.

To save yourself time and trouble, use word-processing software to generate this report so that you can update and rewrite with a minimum of effort. Be sure each group member has a hard copy *and* a disc copy of any group work at all times!

1–48. Select a publicly traded company that interests you as an investment or employment prospect.

REQUIRED:

a. Determine how to obtain an annual report for this company, as explained in this chapter. Within 48 hours of this assignment, have a copy of the annual report either in your hand or in the mail from the company or *The Wall Street Journal*. Each member of a group should secure his or her own copy of the report.

b. From a second source, obtain a copy of the printed glossy annual report for your professor. (For group projects, the professor only needs one copy of the annual report.) Give the second copy to your professor as soon as you receive it.

c. Individually, prepare a detailed listing of the annual report to become familiar with its contents. List each page, including the outside front cover, inside front cover, inside back cover, and outside back cover. For each page listed, write a brief list of the information contained on that page. For example:

Page 2	President's letter to the stockholders
Page 24	Consolidated Balance Sheet
Inside Back Cover	Corporate information including:
	Corporate address, Web site, and phone number
	Ticker symbol
	Annual meeting date
	Dividend payment dates

d. Hand in one copy of this assignment to the professor, keep one copy to use as a quick reference, and keep a clean copy for your final project folder.

Chapter 2

Economic Decision Making

Good fortune has come your way. After several weeks of interviewing, you have received job offers from three firms. The offers differ greatly which leaves you in quite a quandary. You have made this list of the offers:

1. Large national firm, $12 per hour starting wage, life and health insurance paid by the company, a two-week paid vacation each year, and potential for rapid advancement.
2. Small local firm, $20 per hour starting wage, life and health insurance available but you must pay the premiums, a two-week paid vacation each year, stock options and pension plan benefits, and potential for partnership within 10 years.
3. Regional firm, $15 per hour starting wage, full life and health insurance benefits, one-week paid vacation, good pension plan, and moderate advancement potential.

Will you consider the short run or the long run for this decision? Which offer provides you with the most today and which one the most over the next five years? What is the real economic value of the benefits? Aside from the monetary considerations, do you like the work you will perform in each position and the people with whom you will work? How do you organize your thoughts to make this decision?

Regardless of the form of organization or the business activity, success in the world of business—sometimes even survival—depends on making wise economic decisions. A key ingredient is an understanding of the decision-making process itself. Because economic decision making relies heavily on accounting information, it is crucial for that information to be useful to economic decision makers.

Life is a never-ending sequence of decisions, some very complex and others relatively simple. Because we cannot

know the future, we strive to reduce uncertainty in any decision by collecting as much information as possible. We designed this chapter to help you learn a logical decision-making
process. ■

LEARNING OBJECTIVES

After completing your work on this chapter, you should be able to do the following:

1. Explain the concepts of extrinsic and intrinsic rewards, sacrifices, and opportunity costs as they pertain to routine and nonroutine decision situations.
2. Use a general problem-solving model to make decisions.
3. Explain the importance of creativity and the role of values and ethics in the decision-making process.
4. Describe the advantages and disadvantages of individual and group decision making.
5. Describe the two types of economic decision makers and explain the basic differences between management accounting and financial accounting.
6. List the three questions all economic decision makers attempt to answer and explain why these questions are so important.
7. Describe the importance of cash as a measure of business success or failure.
8. Define accounting information and distinguish it from accounting data.
9. Describe the qualitative characteristics of useful accounting information and apply them in decision-making situations.

WHAT IS DECISION MAKING?

Decision making is the process of identifying alternative courses of action and selecting an appropriate alternative in a given decision situation. This definition presents two important parts:

1. *Identifying alternative courses of action* does not mean that an ideal solution exists or can be identified.
2. *Selecting an appropriate alternative* implies that there may be a number of appropriate alternatives and that inappropriate alternatives are to be evaluated and rejected. Thus, judgment is fundamental to decision making.

Choice is implicit in our definition of decision making. We may not like the alternatives available to us, but we are seldom left without choices.

Rewards and Sacrifices: The Trade-off

In general, the aim of all decisions is to obtain some type of reward, either economic or personal. Reward requires sacrifice. When you made the decision to attend college, for example, you certainly desired a reward. What was the sacrifice?

Discussion Questions

2–1. What reward or rewards do you hope to obtain by attending college?

2–2. What sacrifices are you personally making to attend college?

Think of some things you cannot do because you are attending college. Some sacrifices cannot be measured in dollars (such as loss of sleep, lack of home-cooked meals, and loss of leisure time). Some, however, can be measured. Suppose that instead of attending college you could work full time and earn $15,000 a year. Attending college, therefore, costs you that $15,000, in addition to what you pay for tuition and books. We call the $15,000 an opportunity cost of making the decision to attend college. An **opportunity cost** is the reward we forego because we choose a particular alternative instead of another. Most decisions include opportunity costs.

Decision makers want the reward or benefit from a decision to be greater than the sacrifice or cost required to attain it (see Exhibit 2–1). Examining the relationship between rewards and sacrifices is known as **cost/benefit analysis.** In a condition of absolute certainty, in which the outcome of a decision is known without doubt, cost/benefit analysis provides a certain outcome. Unfortunately, absolute certainty rarely, if ever, exists.

In examples that accountants use to describe the trade-off between rewards and sacrifices, money is usually the reward. Money is an *extrinsic reward*, meaning that it comes from outside ourselves and is a tangible object we can acquire. An *intrinsic reward* is one that comes from inside ourselves. When you accomplish a difficult task, the intrinsic reward comes from the sense of satisfaction you feel. An old adage says, "The best things in life are free." Not so! Anything worth having requires sacrifice.

opportunity cost The benefit or benefits forgone by not selecting a particular alternative. Once an alternative is selected in a decision situation, the benefits of all rejected alternatives become part of the opportunity cost of the alternative selected.

cost/benefit analysis Deals with the trade-off between the rewards of selecting a given alternative and the sacrifices required to obtain those rewards.

Exhibit 2–1
Cost versus Benefit

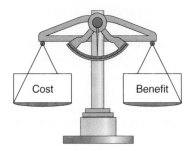

Discussion Questions

2–3. What is the one thing you desire most from life? What sacrifices must you make to obtain it?

2–4. What sacrifice does a business owner make when purchasing machinery for the production plant?

2–5. What benefit does the owner derive from the sacrifice to purchase the machinery?

Coping with Uncertainty and Risk

Uncertainty in any given decision situation increases the chances of making the wrong choice. The higher the degree of uncertainty, the greater the *risk*. Good decision making does not try to eliminate uncertainty, which is impossible, but rather tries to cope with it. Financial decision makers recognize the relationship between uncertainty and reward called the **risk/reward trade-off.** The risk/reward trade-off indicates that the higher the risk, the higher the reward required to induce the decision maker to take that risk. For example, banks set interest rates based upon the credit risk of each borrower. The higher the risk of default on a loan, the higher the interest rate charged by the bank.

risk/reward trade-off The relationship between uncertainty and reward. It indicates that the higher the risk, the higher the reward required to induce the risk taking.

How do you cope with uncertainty? You compile as much relevant information as you can in a given decision situation, thereby reducing the amount of risk involved and increasing your level of comfort in making the decision. This is a valuable strategy no matter what type of decision you face.

Discussion Question

2–6. List the factors you would use to judge the credit risk of a customer if you were a bank loan officer. Tell how each would help to reduce your uncertainty about the customer's risk of default.

Routine and Nonroutine Decisions

We make some decisions so frequently that our choice is automatic or routine. We need to solve such recurring problems only once, and our decision then becomes a rule or standard. Whenever the situation recurs, such as choosing the route to drive from home to work, we implement the rule.

Not all *routine decisions* arise in simple situations. Landing a jet aircraft at a busy airport with 300 people on board may be routine, but it is still complex. Whether a decision is routine depends not on its complexity, but rather on whether the situation recurs.

When we face a new and unfamiliar circumstance, we make a *nonroutine decision*. Whether intricate or simple, an unfamiliar problem is considered nonroutine by its infrequency—not by its complexity.

It is important that we learn to identify which type of decision we face. Routine problems have rule-based solutions. If we apply routine decision rules to nonroutine situations, we can create worse problems by applying the wrong solution.

Discussion Questions

2–7. Think of a decision you consider routine. Can you remember the first time you had to make that particular decision? How did you go about making it?

2–8. Can you think of a nonroutine decision you faced? How did you go about making that decision?

2–9. Describe a situation in which you (or someone else) applied a decision rule developed for a routine decision to a nonroutine situation and experienced unexpected results.

HOW WE MAKE DECISIONS

critical thinking An examination of the way we think to help improve the quality of our decision-making process.

The quality of our decisions is directly related to the way we process information. **Critical thinking,** therefore, improves the quality of the decisions we make, because it helps us examine the way we think.

Information-Processing Styles

Psychological researchers sought to find out how people use their brains to process information. They identified two general information-processing styles—the *intuitive style* and the *systematic style* (see Exhibit 2–2).[1]

Intuitive thinkers prefer to solve problems by looking at the overall situation, exploring many possible solutions, and making a decision based on their hunches or gut reaction. Intuitive thinkers prefer nonroutine situations. They enjoy a rapidly changing environment, dealing with broad issues, and general policy options; they are "big-picture" people.

Conversely, systematic thinkers prefer to solve problems by careful analysis, breaking the problem into component parts. They prefer working in a slower-paced environment that allows them to think methodically; they are "detail" people.

Exhibit 2–2
Information-Processing Styles

Style	Intuitive	Systematic
Approach	Hunches	Methodical
Individual	"Big Picture"	"Detail"

Each style has advantages and disadvantages and can be effective in different situations. Everyone uses both styles to some degree, but all of us favor one style over the other. For example, some investment analysts use primarily an intuitive style and others tend to use a systematic style. The job of a Wall Street investment analyst is to pick good stocks—stocks that will go up in price rather than down. Some analysts systematically study extensive data about a company, carefully sifting the numbers through a computer and analyzing statistics before making a decision. Other analysts do a little computer work, but mainly rely on their intuition. Some of the most successful investors on Wall Street claim to "feel" what is going to happen to the price of a particular stock. While intuition can neither be learned nor taught, systematic thinking can be both learned and taught. Reasoned decision makers follow the same thought process that systematic thinkers employ to make decisions.

Discussion Questions

2–10. To which careers do you think people using the intuitive style are most attracted?

2–11. To which careers do you think people using the systematic style are most attracted?

---

[1]Weston H. Agor, "Managing Brain Skills: The Last Frontier," *Personnel Administrator* (October 1987): 55–56.

2-12. Which of the two information-processing styles do you believe you use most often?

2-13. What kinds of problems could arise when you are forced to work with someone using a different information-processing style?

Reasoned Decision Making

Reasoned decision making, also called cognitive or rational decision making, involves considering various aspects of a situation before deciding on a course of action. This approach to decision making can be used with both intuitive and systematic information processing. Systematic thinkers will feel comfortable with this approach, and intuitive thinkers will become more disciplined thinkers, which may improve their intuitive skills.

Reasoned decision making can be described as a seven-step process (see Exhibit 2–3):

Step 1   Determine the real decision to be made.

The key to successful, reasoned decision making is identifying the real problem, which frequently becomes the most difficult task in the decision process. Too often, we concentrate on a symptom of the problem and not on the problem itself. Firms sometimes hire consultants to identify the real decision and correctly define it as either a routine or nonroutine decision.

Step 2   Identify alternative courses of action.

To appropriately identify alternative courses of action, determine whether the situation is routine or nonroutine. If the decision is routine, apply the appropriate decision rule and skip steps 2, 3, and 4 of this decision model. For nonroutine decisions, some alternatives will emerge quickly, but they often treat symptoms, not problems. Developing plausible alternatives usually requires creative thinking or stepping outside comfortable thinking—learning to be open to more alternative solutions. Sherlock Holmes, the great master sleuth, offered this explanation as to why Dr. Watson had been unable to unravel a particular mystery:

Once again, Watson, you have confused the impossible with the improbable.

To be creative in decision making, you eliminate only impossible potential solutions and consider everything else, however improbable. Fictional characters can always make correct decisions, but real life is more difficult. Because creative decision making is an important topic, following this presentation of the decision-making process, we will discuss it in greater detail.

Step 3   Analyze each alternative critically.

Critical analysis of each decision alternative requires us to trace the alternatives into the future and consider the possible outcomes of each. Completely accurate assessment is impossible because there are too

Exhibit 2-3
The Seven-Step Decision Model

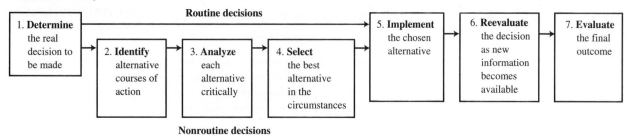

many variables. Instead, you must select a few critical factors such as cost, completion time, and risk and see how each alternative affects those factors.

Step 4 Select the best alternative in the circumstances.

Russell Ackoff, a noted scholar in the field of problem solving, identified three types of alternatives available in any given decision situation:

- those that will resolve the problem,
- those that will solve the problem, and
- those that will dissolve the problem.[2]

Resolving a problem means finding an acceptable alternative. Solving a problem means finding the absolutely best solution. Dissolving a problem means changing the circumstances that caused the problem, thereby not only eliminating the problem but also ensuring that it will not happen again. Ideally, the results of a decision-making process will produce an alternative that dissolves the problem, but realistically, that occurs only occasionally. In fact, Ackoff suggests that most decisions merely resolve problems by finding acceptable, stopgap solutions. For this reason, one decision may create the need to make other decisions.

Step 5 Implement the chosen alternative.

cognitive dissonance
The hesitation that sets in after an alternative has been chosen, but before it has been implemented. In common language, having "second thoughts."

Decision makers sometimes suffer from **cognitive dissonance**,[3] or "second thoughts." Regardless how methodical and analytical your approach to making the decision, you still feel you have not considered everything. To overcome second thoughts, you must find the courage to implement the chosen alternative.

Step 6 Reevaluate the decision as new information becomes available.

After overcoming second thoughts, decision makers become very committed to their decision. In fact, most of us will go out of our way to avoid new information after implementing a decision. Why? Because it puts us back in the position of questioning the soundness of our decision, which can make us extremely uncomfortable. It may sound odd, but to make

---

[2]Russell L. Ackoff, "The Art and Science of Mess Management," *Interfaces 11*, No. 1 (February 1981): 20–21.

[3]Leon Festinger, *A Theory of Cognitive Dissonance* (Stanford, Calif: Stanford University Press, 1975).

tough decisions well, you must become comfortable with being uncomfortable. You must not fear continuing to analyze your decision in the light of new and better information, even after you implement the decision.

Step 7   Evaluate the final outcome.

It may be a long time before you can determine whether your decision was a good one, and others, over whom you have no control, may influence the outcome. Nevertheless, evaluation is an important step in the process if you are to continue refining your decision-making skills.

This basic decision model is not the only correct way to make decisions; however, it does offer you a reasoned, cognitive approach to decision making.

Discussion Questions

2-14. Think back to your decision to choose the college you now attend. If you had used this decision model, would you have made the same choice? Explain.

2-15. Think again about your decision to attend your particular college. At what point will you be able to apply step 7 to your decision-making process?

Creative Decision Making

The second step of the decision-making model stressed the importance of being creative in identifying possible courses of action. Going beyond the obvious alternatives reduces your chances of overlooking the best possible solution.

Anyone can become a more creative decision maker. Sidney J. Parnes, a professor of creative studies at Buffalo State University, states that creativity increases when the problem solver progresses from "what is" (awareness of the facts surrounding the present situation), to "what might be" (free-thinking consideration of many possible alternatives), to "what can be" (elimination of impossible and unacceptable alternatives), to "what will be" (choice of the best alternative in the circumstances), and finally to an action that creates a new "what is."[4] Our seven-step decision model coincides nicely with Parnes' philosophy.

When faced with his company's extinction, Stan Clark searched for creative alternatives to save his fledgling business. His number one product suddenly became illegal for the majority of his customers (what is). To remain open, he had to change his image and his product mix immediately (what might be). In the creative process, he chose to change his marketing focus from music and drink to food and fun (what can be). In the process, he decided to consider one more option. Customers frequently purchased the shirts his waitstaff wore in place of uniforms, but he needed to emphasize their sale. He hated to do this because, after all, he was in the entertainment business, not the clothing business. But the situation made him rethink his position and actively merchandise the T-shirts (what will be). Not only did Stan save the business, but today his company sells more T-shirts than any other organization except Hard Rock Cafe. Although the successful restaurant business is still located in Stillwater, Oklahoma, Eskimo Joe's clothes are sold worldwide through catalog and Internet sales (new what is).

---

[4]Sidney J. Parnes, "Learning Creative Behavior," *The Futurist* (August 1984): 30.

Discussion Questions

2-16. Think of a daily irritation that you currently endure. Use Professor Parnes' creative process to create at least three feasible alternatives under "what might be."

2-17. If you could change one other "what is" into a new "what is," what would it be? How would you do it?

PERSONAL VALUES AND DECISION MAKING

Personal values influence our decisions—both personal and business—because each of us examines critically what we find important to ourselves. Seldom do two people hold the same personal values.

Ethics and Personal Values

ethics A system of standards of conduct and moral judgment.

People with differing personal values can agree on standards of conduct or moral judgment, called **ethics,** within which a group of people or society can operate. There are two very different approaches to ethics. The first approach is *virtues ethics,* or character ethics. Virtues ethics, also called classical ethics because it is derived from the teachings of Socrates, Plato, and Aristotle, comes from within a person. It requires you to contemplate what kind of person you want to be. Once you have identified the virtues and character traits required to be that kind of person, they determine your reaction to any situation. The second approach is *rules ethics,* or quandary ethics. This approach, also called modern ethics, traces its roots to organized religion. It imposes rules that dictate how to react to a given problem.

Virtues ethics presumes that the virtues and character traits the individual identifies as desirable will include respect for others. It can lead to disastrous results if a person confuses ethics with selfishness. Successful application of rules ethics depends upon the individual's ability to apply the appropriate rule in a given situation and society's acceptance of the rules and those who establish them.

An inability to apply the appropriate rule or a loss of respect for the rules (or rule makers) leads to moral confusion and uncertainty.

One truth that most businesspeople have discovered is that "good ethics is good business." Ethical companies that hire ethical management eventually rise above less ethical firms. Businesspeople constantly face ethical dilemmas. Should a U.S. running-shoe manufacturer open a plant in Southeast Asia, where workers are paid only 50 cents an hour? We might argue that the company is exploiting those workers. On the other hand, 50 cents an hour might be double the going wage rate in that country, providing employment for those who otherwise have no jobs. It is a tough decision, without any clear-cut "right" answer.

Discussion Questions

2-18. Agree or disagree with the statement, "Good ethics is good business." Explain your position.

2-19. Do U.S. companies exploit workers in other countries when they pay them less than U.S. minimum wage?

2-20. Should a U.S. company follow U.S. labor laws or less stringent local labor laws?

2-21. Do you believe it is ethical to buy products manufactured by a U.S. company in a foreign country with less restrictive labor laws than the United States? What is your responsibility as a consumer to determine whether products are made under fair labor practices?

INDIVIDUAL VERSUS GROUP DECISION MAKING

Thus far we have discussed the problems in decision making caused by uncertainty, different information-processing styles, routine versus nonroutine decision situations, the need for creativity, and the influence of personal values on the decision-making process. We now consider individual decision making versus group decision making. If two heads are better than one, does involving more people in the decision process improve the chances of making the right decision? Not always.

Individual decision making has some distinct advantages over group decision making. First, you do not spend a lot of time organizing meetings. Second, you do not have to consider others' comments and suggestions that you know will not work. Finally, compromise is unnecessary because you are a committee of one. However, your decision will be only as good as your individual judgment and grasp of the circumstances. That becomes the most significant drawback to making decisions by yourself. When we make important, nonroutine decisions by ourselves, most of us need to bounce the decision off someone else.

Groups bring a greater knowledge base to the decision-making process simply because more people are involved. Viewing the problem from various perspectives usually generates more alternative solutions. Groups also tend to be confident that the decision alternative chosen to solve the problem is a reasonable solution.

On the surface, it would seem that group decision making is superior to individual decision making; however, some serious problems are associated with working in groups.

- *Similarity of information-processing styles.* If all members of the group are intuitive types, the group may have many grandiose ideas but wind up short on specifics. If all members are systematic types, the group may never get past deciding on a seating arrangement at the first meeting. Ideally, the group should be a mix of the two types. But they must be able to work together, utilizing the best aspects of each style, or the group can become paralyzed.

- *Domineering members.* The quality of group decision making usually suffers when some members of the group feel compelled to cave in to other members simply because those other members talk louder and longer.
- *Social pressure.* The pressure to conform to the views of other members of the group, coupled with the natural desire to not look foolish, can stifle an individual's creative contributions.
- *Goal replacement.* The goal of the group should always be to accomplish the purpose for which it was formed. Secondary considerations, such as winning an argument, proving a point, or taking revenge on a fellow group member sometimes become more important to some members of the group.
- *Differing personal values.* Each member of the group will bring a different set of personal values to the process. From time to time, those values may conflict, making resolution difficult or impossible.
- *Unequal effort.* For a group to succeed, all members must do their share of the work. Slackers reduce the quality of work and negatively affect the morale of the other group members.
- *Groupthink.* Many people consider groupthink to be the most dangerous threat to good group decision making. Group members may ignore their own sound judgments in evaluating alternatives to allow the group to achieve consensus. A group member may not feel good about the decision being made but thinks everyone else in the group does, and so he or she goes along with the decision. Remember, the fact that everybody agrees on an alternative does not mean it is a good or even an acceptable alternative.

Discussion Questions

2-22. Which of the potential problems of group decision making have you encountered in groups at work or in school? How has the group resolved the problems?

2-23. If you were the instructor of this course, what policies would you institute to make certain all members of assigned groups worked for the common good of the group?

ECONOMIC DECISION MAKING

Economic decision making, in this book, refers to the process of making business decisions involving money. All economic decisions of any consequence require the use of some sort of accounting information, often in the form of financial reports. Anyone using accounting information to make economic decisions must understand the business and economic environment in which accounting information is generated, and they must also be willing to devote the necessary time and energy to make sense of the accounting reports.

Economic decision makers are either internal or external. **Internal decision makers** are individuals within a company who make decisions on behalf of the company, while **external decision makers** are individuals or organizations outside a company who make decisions that affect the company.

Internal Decision Makers

Internal decision makers decide whether the company should sell a particular product, whether it should enter a certain market, and whether it should hire or fire employees. Note that in all these matters, the responsible internal decision maker makes the decision not for himself or herself, but rather *for* the company.

Depending on their position within the company, internal decision makers may have access to much, or even all, of the company's financial information. They do not have complete information, however, because all decisions relate to the future and always involve unknowns.

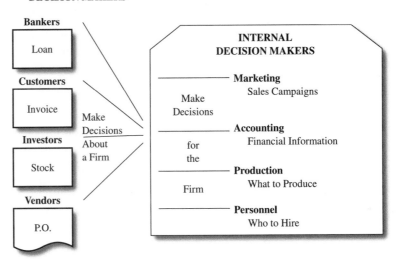

External Decision Makers

External decision makers make decisions *about* a company. External decision makers decide whether to invest in the company, whether to sell to or buy from the company, and whether to lend money to the company.

Unlike internal decision makers, external decision makers have limited financial information on which to base their decisions about the company. In fact, they have only the information the company gives them—which in most cases is not all the information the company possesses.

Discussion Questions

2-24. Identify a particular company (large or small). Who do you think are considered internal and external economic decision makers of the company?

2-25. For what reasons do you think a company would withhold certain financial information from external parties?

2-26. Is it ethical for a company to limit the information available to internal decision makers? External decision makers?

management accounting The branch of accounting developed to meet the informational needs of internal decision makers.

financial accounting The branch of accounting developed to meet the informational needs of external decision makers.

cash flow The movement of cash in and out of a company.

The decisions made by internal and external decision makers are similar in some ways, but so different in other ways that the accounting profession developed two separate branches of accounting to meet the needs of the two categories of users. **Management accounting** generates information for use by internal decision makers, whereas **financial accounting** generates information for use by external parties.

What All Economic Decision Makers Want To Know

Although internal and external parties face different decision situations, both attempt to predict the future, as do all decision makers. Specifically, all economic decision makers attempt to predict future **cash flow**—the movement of cash in and out of a company. So one of the major objectives of financial reporting is to provide helpful information to those trying to predict cash flows.

> Thus, financial reporting should provide information to help investors, creditors, and others assess the amounts, timing, and uncertainty of prospective net cash inflows to the related enterprise.
>
> —Statement of Financial Accounting Concepts #1, Financial Accounting Standards Board, 1986, p. 40

net cash flow The difference between cash inflows and cash outflows; it can be either positive or negative.

The difference between cash inflows and cash outflows is **net cash flow.** Positive net cash flow indicates that the amount of cash flowing into the company exceeds the amount flowing out of the company during a particular period. For example, a company that collects $1,000,000 during a period when it pays out $950,000 has a positive cash flow of $50,000. Negative net cash flow indicates that the amount of cash flowing out of the company exceeds the amount flowing into the company during a particular period (see Exhibit 2–4).

Exhibit 2–4
Cash Flow

Cash inflow	–	Cash outflow	=	Positive net cash flow
$1,000,000	–	$950,000	=	$50,000
Cash inflow	–	Cash outflow	=	Negative net cash flow
$ 500,000	–	$575,000	=	– $75,000

All economic decisions involve attempts to predict the future of cash flows by searching for the answers to the following three questions:

1. *Will I be paid?*
   This question refers to the *uncertainty* of cash flows.
2. *When will I be paid?*
   This question refers to the *timing* of cash flows.
3. *How much will I be paid?*
   This question refers to the *amounts* of cash flows.

The answer to each question contains two parts: return *on* investment and return *of* investment. Return on investment consists of the earnings and profits an investment returns to the investor. Return of investment is the ultimate return of the principal invested. Exhibit 2–5 shows the conceptual link between the three major questions posed by economic decision makers and the resulting cash flows using the following example. Assume you wish to invest in a $1,000 certificate of deposit (CD) at your bank, which will earn 10 percent interest per year, payable every three months, over the course of two years. If you invest in this CD, you must hold it for two years, after which the bank will return your $1,000.

Exhibit 2–5
Three Big Questions for Economic Decision Makers

Questions	Concepts	Cash Outcome	
		Return *on* Investment	Return *of* Investment
1. Will I be paid?	Uncertainty	Interest	CD maturity
2. When will I be paid?	Timing	Quarterly	2 years
3. How much will I be paid?	Amount	$25 per quarter	$1,000
		Total of $200	

Before you make this economic decision, you must attempt to answer the three questions:

1. *Will you be paid?* Because it is impossible to know the future, making an economic decision always involves risk. However, assuming the economy does not collapse and the bank stays in business, you will be paid both your return on investment and your return of investment.
2. *When will you be paid?* You will receive an interest payment every three months for two years (return on investment), and then you will receive your initial $1,000 investment back (return of investment).
3. *How much will you be paid?* The return on your investment is the interest you receive quarterly $25 ($1,000 × 10 percent × 3/12), and the return of your investment is the $1,000 the bank gives you back. The total received in interest in two years is $200 (8 × $25).

Initial Investment		$1,000
Return on Investment	$ 200	
Return of Investment	1,000	
Total Return		1,200
Profit on Investment		$ 200

We can answer these questions easily for the insured certificate of deposit. In the vast majority of economic decision situations, the answers to the three questions we asked are much less certain. We will show you how to use accounting information to answer them in various economic decision situations throughout this text.

Discussion Questions

2-27. Describe how to apply the seven-step decision model to the example of the certificate of deposit.

2-28. Assume that you are a lender with three customers who wish to borrow $10,000. You can lend to only one of them. What information would you require each of them to present for you to answer the three questions? How would you make your decision?

Cash Is the "Ball" of Business

If business were any game such as baseball, football, or soccer, then cash would be the ball. To be successful, the players must keep their eye on the ball. Because the business game is so complex, businesspeople easily become distracted and lose sight of (the ball) cash. Various measures of performance such as gross profit, net income, net worth, and equity help those in business to make economic decisions. These are important measures of financial performance, but they are not cash! Never allow yourself to become so focused on any of them that you lose sight of cash, because when a company runs out of cash, it dies. Only cash pays the bills that keeps the company in business. The secret to becoming a street-smart user of accounting information is learning to balance the complexity of business with the simple rule of keeping your eye on cash flow.

ACCOUNTING INFORMATION

The accounting profession's definition of accounting is as follows:

> Accounting is a service activity. Its function is to provide quantitative information, primarily financial in nature, about economic entities that is intended to be useful in making economic decisions.
>
> —Statement of the Accounting Principles Board #4, 1970, p. 6

A company or a person generates accounting data with every business transaction. You generate a number of transactions each month when you pay your rent, buy groceries, make car payments, lend money to a friend, and so on. In fact, the volume of business accounting data can be staggering.

Data versus Information

accounting information Raw data concerning transactions that have been transformed into financial numbers that can be used by economic decision makers.

information Data that have been transformed so that they are useful in the decision-making process.

Accounting data and **accounting information** are not interchangeable terms. Data are the raw results of transactions: data become **information** only when they are put into some useful form. Consider this example:

Carol Brown, vice president of sales for Balloo Industries, noticed that the recent gasoline expense for the sales staff's company cars was extremely high and she suspected that salespersons were using the company cars for personal trips. Knowing that sales personnel were required to keep detailed odometer records, she notified Jack Parsons, the sales supervisor, of her concerns. He agreed to prepare a report to provide her with the necessary information to determine if the expense was proper.

The report compiled by Mr. Parsons consisted of five columns of data:

1. salesperson's name;
2. make and model of that salesperson's company car;
3. date the car was issued to the salesperson;
4. odometer reading on the date of issue; and
5. odometer reading at time of most recent maintenance.

Ms. Brown quickly concluded that it contained little useful information. She told Parsons that she was trying to determine if any members of the sales force were using company cars for personal activities. Mr. Parsons retreated to his office to try again.

In his second attempt, Parsons included the previous five columns plus four additional columns:

6. sales region covered;
7. how long the salesperson had been with the company;
8. total sales generated by the salesperson this year; and
9. current odometer reading of the vehicle.

Was Ms. Brown pleased with the second version? No! Mr. Parsons had provided additional data, but no additional information.

Discussion Question

2-29. Evaluate the usefulness to Ms. Brown of each column (1–9) of Parsons' data. What information could Parsons have provided Ms. Brown to help her make a determination?

Clearly, the correct data items must be gathered and converted into useful information before they are of any help to economic decision makers. Suppose you consider investing in Safeway stock. You call your broker and she tells you the stock is currently selling at $30 per share. Do you want to buy it? Although your broker has given you a datum (singular form of data), this datum provides insufficient information upon which to base a buying decision. You need to know something about the company's current and historic earnings, the stock price behavior over the past year, the grocery industry's prospects, and so on. That is why brokerage firms such as Merrill Lynch, Morgan Stanley, and Dean Witter have research departments that extract such data and synthesize them into useful information for their clients.

Useful Accounting Information

The user of accounting information has the obligation to understand the business and be willing to study the information. The information provider has an obligation to present it in such a way that economic decision makers can make sense of it. As business and economic activities have become more complex, however, the accounting profession has responded with increasingly complex rules, many of which are difficult for nonaccountants to comprehend. But FASB's Conceptual Framework of Accounting defines certain characteristics that accounting information must possess to be considered useful for decision making. If the accounting profession does not provide the information users need or does not prepare it in a way that makes sense, users must demand a change. Users and preparers must be mindful of the benefits provided by information, and the costs incurred to secure it (the cost/benefit analysis), and of its ultimate ability to make a difference in the decision (the **materiality** test).

materiality Something that will influence the judgment of a reasonable person.

Two parties decide what accounting information is useful and what is not. One is the users and the second is the accounting profession through FASB. FASB focuses on the *qualitative characteristics* of useful accounting information—those qualities it must possess to be useful, whether it is financial or management accounting information.

QUALITATIVE CHARACTERISTICS OF ACCOUNTING INFORMATION

The two primary qualities that distinguish useful accounting information are **relevance** and **reliability**. If either of these qualities is missing, accounting information will not be useful.

relevance One of the two primary qualitative characteristics of useful accounting information. It means the information must have a bearing on a particular decision situation.

reliability One of the two primary qualitative characteristics of useful accounting information. It means the information must be reasonably accurate.

timeliness A primary characteristic of relevance. To be useful, accounting information must be provided in time to influence a particular decision.

predictive value A primary characteristic of relevance. To be useful, accounting must provide information to decision makers that can be used to predict the future and timing of cash flows.

feedback value A primary characteristic of relevance. To be useful, accounting must provide decision makers with information that allows them to assess the progress of an investment.

verifiability A primary characteristic of reliability. Information is considered verifiable if several individuals, working independently, would arrive at similar conclusions using the same data.

representational faithfulness A primary characteristic of reliability. To be useful, accounting information must reasonably report what actually happened.

neutrality A primary characteristic of reliability. To be useful, accounting information must be free of bias.

Relevance

To be considered relevant, accounting information must have a bearing on the particular decision situation. In other words, does it make a difference to decision makers? The accuracy of the information is not important if the content does not matter to the decision being made.

Relevant accounting information possesses at least two characteristics:

- **Timeliness.** If information providers delay making information available until every number is perfectly accurate, it may be too late to be of any value. This does not mean that accuracy does not matter. But if accounting information is not timely, it has no value.

Timeliness alone, however, is not enough. To be relevant, accounting information must also possess at least one of the following characteristics:

- **Predictive Value.** Before economic decision makers commit resources to one alternative instead of another, they must satisfy themselves that a reasonable expectation of a return on investment and a return of investment exists. Accounting information that helps reduce the uncertainty of that expectation has predictive value.

or

- **Feedback Value.** After making an investment decision, the decision maker must have information to assess the progress of that investment. Recall the seven-step decision model. Step 6 is a reevaluation of the decision as new information becomes available, and step 7 is an evaluation of the final outcome of the decision. If accounting information provides input for those evaluations, it has feedback value.

Reliability

To be considered reliable, accounting information must possess three qualities:

- **Verifiability.** We consider accounting information verifiable if several qualified persons, working independently of one another, would arrive at similar conclusions using the same data. For example, if we asked several people to determine the amount of Michael Simpson's wages this year, they should all come to the same conclusion: A simple review of payroll records should provide verifiable information for the amount.
- **Representational Faithfulness.** There must be agreement between what the accounting information says and what really happened. If a company's accounting information reports sales revenue of $1,000 and the company really had sales revenue of $1,000, the accounting information is representationally faithful. However, if a company's accounting information reports sales revenue of $1,000 and the company really had sales revenue of only $800, then the accounting information lacks representational faithfulness.
- **Neutrality.** To be useful, accounting information must be free of bias, which means accountants should not omit details simply because the information is unpleasant. We have stressed how difficult it is to make good decisions. The problem becomes even worse when information is suppressed or slanted, either positively or negatively. The need to remain neutral is one of the most difficult challenges facing the accounting profession.

Discussion Questions

2-30. Recall the seven-step decision model. How would the absence of relevance and reliability affect steps 3 and 4?

2-31. Do you think these qualities apply to information other than financial information? Explain.

Comparability and Consistency

Two secondary qualities of useful accounting information are comparability and consistency. Economic decision makers evaluate alternatives. Accounting information for one alternative must therefore be comparable to accounting information for the others. For example, assume you intend to make an investment in one of two companies. If each company uses different accounting methods, you would find it very difficult to make a useful comparison.

Now consider the concept of consistency. Imagine how difficult it would be to assess the progress of an investment if, through the years, different accounting treatments were applied to similar events such as income recognition or valuation of assets. Consistency in the application of measurement methods over periods of time increases the usefulness of the accounting information provided about a company or an investment alternative.

Comparability is a quality of information from different entities or alternatives. Consistency describes information from the same source over time. Comparability and consistency often have similar effects on the decision-making process. Their presence increases the decision maker's confidence in his or her decision. The absence of these qualities decreases decision maker's confidence or confounds the decision maker's ability to make a decision.

Discussion Question

2-32. Think back to the seven-step decision model. How would the absence of comparability and consistency affect steps 4 and 6?

The following story reflects the frustration of us who live in the information age:

To fulfill his lifelong dream, a man bought a balloon, filled it with hot air, and set out on a journey from Philadelphia to Pittsburgh. The trip was everything he had imagined it might be, but eventually he drifted into a thunderstorm that threw him off course. Before long, he was hopelessly lost, his balloon began to lose air, and he landed in the branches of a huge tree.

Sitting in his balloon basket, hanging in a tree, without the slightest idea where he was, he spotted a woman walking along the road below.

"Pardon me," said the man, "can you tell me where I am?"

"Certainly," replied the woman, "you are in a basket, in a tree."

After reflecting for a moment the man said, "You must be a data specialist!"

"Why yes, I am," she said, "but how did you know?"

"Because," he answered, "your information is totally accurate and absolutely worthless."

To avoid the pitfalls in the previous story, as you work your way through this book, you should develop your ability to determine what information you need, how to get it, and how to become confident that you have quality information to help you make good decisions.

DECISION MAKERS AND UNDERSTANDABILITY

Now that you know the qualities required to make accounting information useful, you can appreciate the fact that, as a decision maker and user of accounting information, you must evaluate the qualities of available information to assess its usefulness. You must also recognize that the information you receive from accountants constitutes only a part of the information you need to make sound economic decisions. It is an important part, to be sure, but only a part. The reports generated from accounting information can be thought of as the tools of the accounting trade. As financial tools are introduced and discussed throughout the rest of this text, keep in mind that each has its limitations and imperfections. After working with the material provided here, however, you should be able to use each financial tool to its fullest potential.

SUMMARY

The aim of all decisions is to obtain some type of reward, either extrinsic or intrinsic, at a cost. Good decisions are made when a reasonable balance is found between the sacrifice and the reward in the context of uncertainty.

Routine decisions are recurring, whereas nonroutine decisions are those that must be made in new and unfamiliar circumstances. The two general information-processing styles are the intuitive style and the systematic style. Each has advantages over the other.

A good decision maker establishes a cognitive approach to the decision process similar to the seven-step model for making decisions. A creative thinker has the ability to consider alternatives that are not readily apparent. Personal values influence the decisions we make and our system of ethics. Good ethics is good business. The two general approaches to ethics are virtues ethics and rules ethics.

Both individual and group decision making have distinct advantages and disadvantages, and all of us participate in both kinds of decision making in our lives.

Economic decisions are those involving business transactions. Internal decision makers are individuals within a company who have access to most of the company's financial information and who make decisions on behalf of the organization. External decision makers are individuals or organizations outside a company who have access to the limited information provided to them by the company and who make decisions about the organization. Management accounting information is prepared for use by internal parties, and financial accounting information is prepared for use by external parties (but is also used by internal parties).

Both internal and external parties attempt to predict the future and timing of cash flows. Essentially, they are all trying to determine whether they will be paid, when they will be paid, and how much they will be paid. Cash flow becomes an important criterion to evaluate business success or failure, with other accounting measures of performance.

Accounting information is a key ingredient of good decision making. Business activity produces data. These data are of no value to decision makers until they are put into a useful form and become information. Accounting information must possess certain qualitative characteristics: (1) relevance, including timeliness and either predictive value or feedback value; and (2) reliability, including verifiability, representational faithfulness, and neutrality. Useful accounting information should also possess comparability and consistency and be understandable to economic decision makers.

KEY TERMS

accounting information   F-57
cash flow   F-55
cognitive dissonance   F-49
cost/benefit analysis   F-45
critical thinking   F-47
ethics   F-51
external decision makers   F-54
feedback value   F-59
financial accounting   F-55
information   F-57
internal decision makers   F-54
management accounting   F-55

materiality   F-59
net cash flow   F-55
neutrality   F-60
opportunity cost   F-45
predictive value   F-59
relevance   F-59
reliability   F-59
representational faithfulness   F-60
risk/reward trade-off   F-46
timeliness   F-59
verifiability   F-59

REVIEW THE FACTS

A. Provide two examples of rewards and sacrifices that may be involved when a decision is being made.
B. What is an opportunity cost?
C. Define *cost/benefit analysis.*
D. Describe the difference between an extrinsic reward and an intrinsic reward.
E. How are risk and reward related?
F. What is the difference between routine and nonroutine decisions?
G. Describe the two major information-processing styles.
H. Explain the term *reasoned decision making.*
I. Describe the seven steps of the decision model presented in this chapter.
J. What is creative decision making and why is it important?
K. What is the role of personal values in the decision-making process?
L. Name and describe the two different approaches to ethics.
M. Describe the advantages and disadvantages of both individual and group decision making.
N. What is economic decision making?
O. Name the two broad categories of economic decision makers, and explain the differences between them.
P. What are the two major branches of accounting and how do they differ?
Q. List the three major questions asked by economic decision makers.
R. What is accounting information?
S. Explain the difference between data and information.
T. Name the two primary qualitative characteristics of useful accounting information.
U. What characteristics are necessary for accounting information to be relevant?
V. List the characteristics necessary for accounting information to be reliable.
W. Explain the difference between the primary and secondary qualities of useful accounting information.
X. What are the secondary qualities of useful accounting information?
Y. Explain the responsibility of both the accounting profession and the user for the understandability of accounting information.

LO 1, 2, & 3:   Decision Making

2–33. Jackie Nichols sent you a letter today. She heard a lot of good things about you, and she wants you to quit school immediately and come to work for her. Your salary would be only $12,000 per year, but you are sure you would find the work very rewarding. If you continue in school and earn your accounting degree in three years, you are almost guaranteed a job with a starting salary of $29,000 per year. You can only make one choice, to work for Jackie or to continue in school (assume no raises in either job in the near future).

REQUIRED:

Analyze your alternatives, using as many of the decision-making tools presented in the chapter as you think apply.

LO 1, 2, & 3:   Decision Making

2–34. Presented below are items relating to concepts discussed in this chapter, followed by the definitions of those items in scrambled order:

    a. Cost/benefit analysis
    b. Ethics
    c. Intuitive information-processing style
    d. Opportunity cost
    e. Systematic information-processing style
    f. Risk
    g. Uncertainty
    h. Reward

    1. _____ Decisions are made after breaking a problem into parts and methodically evaluating each part.
    2. _____ Decisions are based on hunches after considering the big picture and brainstorming.
    3. _____ The probability that an alternative selected will yield unsatisfactory results.
    4. _____ The rewards of selecting a given alternative in relation to the sacrifices required to obtain those rewards.
    5. _____ The benefit forgone by not selecting a particular alternative.
    6. _____ The aim of all decision making.
    7. _____ A system of standards of conduct and moral judgment.
    8. _____ Lack of complete information about the future.

REQUIRED:

Match the letter next to each item with the appropriate definition. Each letter will be used only once.

LO 1:   Intrinsic vs. Extrinsic Rewards

2–35. You have decided to go into business for yourself as a rehabilitation therapist. List the extrinsic rewards and intrinsic rewards associated with this decision.

LO 1: Intrinsic vs. Extrinsic Rewards

2–36. Fred Payne, a college senior, has just gotten a part-time job working with developmentally challenged children making $10 per hour. Fred has always wanted to work with such children and thinks he may pursue this work as a career.

REQUIRED:
a. From the facts given in the problem, what would you consider to be the extrinsic and intrinsic rewards Fred will receive from his new job?
b. Which do you think will be more valuable to Fred, the extrinsic rewards or the intrinsic rewards? Explain your reasoning.

LO 1: Routine vs. Nonroutine Decisions

2–37. Some situations occur routinely in business, and management has standard operating procedures to apply when they happen. Below are a number of situations.

1. _____ An employee calls in sick.
2. _____ An employee makes a mistake in adding his travel claim.
3. _____ You discover that five dollars is missing from the petty cash fund.
4. _____ You discover that the petty cash fund and the petty cashier are missing.
5. _____ A vendor bills you for 25 items and you only received 24.
6. _____ A vendor bills you for 25 items that you neither ordered nor received.
7. _____ Your delivery person taps the bumper of a car while parking.
8. _____ Your delivery person totals the van in a one-vehicle accident.
9. _____ Your delivery person totals the van in a fatality accident.
10. _____ Your building loses its roof in a tornado.
11. _____ Your building suffers extensive hail damage in a storm.
12. _____ An employee fails to return from lunch.

REQUIRED:
Identify whether these situations should invoke a routine (R) or nonroutine (N) decision.

LO 2: Intuitive vs. Systematic Information Processing

2–38. Briefly describe the intuitive and the systematic information-processing styles. Include in your answer ways in which these two styles are similar and ways in which they differ.

LO 2: Intuitive vs. Systematic Information Processing

2–39. Most people have a predominate style of processing information that is either systematic or intuitive. In a given situation, you may prefer to have one style of thinker over another.

1. _____ You need a designer for your dream home.
2. _____ You need a contractor to build a warehouse.
3. _____ You need an engineer to plan a highway system in a wilderness area.
4. _____ You need an engineer to design a five-mile expansion bridge.
5. _____ Two employees have a serious, ongoing conflict. You need to refer them to a mediator.

6. _____ Your business has serious financial problems that must be solved within one week. You need to hire a consultant.
7. _____ You are a systematic thinker and you need a partner.
8. _____ You need an advertising consultant to promote a new product.

REQUIRED:

Identify whether you prefer to have an intuitive (I) thinker or a systematic (S) thinker in each of these situations and state your reasons why.

LO 2: Application of Seven-Step Decision Model

2–40. Kathy Stumpe is in trouble! She has been in Paris on business for the past week. This morning she was supposed to fly to New York for a very important dinner meeting. Unfortunately, Kathy overslept and missed her flight. As she hurries to shower and get dressed, she is trying to decide what to do next. "If only I had not slept through my alarm," she says to herself over and over. "That's the real problem."

REQUIRED:

a. Do you think Kathy has determined her real problem? If not, help her identify it.
b. Now that the real problem has been determined, identify two alternative courses of action Kathy might take to solve her problem. Then analyze each of them critically.

LO 2: Application of Seven-Step Decision Model

2–41. You are presented with the responsibility of choosing the new copy machine for your office. Using the seven-step decision model, describe how you would approach this decision.

LO 2: Application of Seven-Step Decision Model

2–42. Upon graduation from college, you receive three different job offers. Identify the various factors that you might consider to make your decision and illustrate how you would apply the seven-step decision-making model.

LO 2: Application of Seven-Step Decision Model

2–43. Your employer offers two different types of retirement plans to all eligible employees. You may select only one of the plans for participation. Plan A requires you to contribute 10% of your monthly salary, which your employer matches equally. You may not withdraw or borrow from the plan until you reach age 60. Plan B requires you to contribute 10% of your salary, but is matched by your employer with an additional 5%. This plan allows you to borrow against the balance at any time without penalty.

REQUIRED:

Using the seven-step decision model, discuss how you would choose between the plans assuming:
a. You are a single individual 23 years of age.
b. You are a married individual 40 years of age with two teenage children.

LO 2:   Application of Seven-Step Decision Model

2–44. As the chief lending officer for the bank, you received loan requests from three different clients for $150,000 each. You may only make one of the loans. The following information is available to you:

1. The first applicant is 21 years old and needs the loan for four years of Harvard Medical School.
2. The second applicant is a 45-year-old businessman who wants to start his own manufacturing business. He needs the loan for equipment and start-up expenses.
3. The third applicant is a 30-year-old dental school graduate who wishes to start her own practice. She needs the loan for equipment and operating expenses.

REQUIRED:

a. Use the seven-step decision model to decide who should receive the loan.
b. Assume that the interest rate you can assess ranges between 8% and 12%. Using the concepts of risk and uncertainty, how would you assign interest rates to each candidate's loan assuming that person was chosen.

LO 2:   Application of Seven-Step Decision Model

2–45. Now that you have graduated from college and accepted a new position, you are ready to start investing in the stock market. After your preliminary research you have decided that you will invest in pharmaceutical companies, airlines, and computer technology companies.

REQUIRED:

a. List 10 pieces of information that you would like to have for each company in each of the three industries. Be specific and make sure the information that you request is relevant to your decision. Remember that the 10 pieces of information should allow you to make comparisons of each company within the industries.
b. Now that you have your list of 10 pieces of relevant information, where do you think you might look to find this information?

LO 2:   Application of Seven-Step Decision Model

2–46. Compare and contrast the seven-step decision model presented in this chapter with the process outlined in Chapter 1 that demonstrates how the Financial Accounting Standards Board approaches the problem of standard setting. Do you think that the FASB follows the seven-step decision model?

LO 2 & 3:   Application of Seven-Step Decision Model

2–47. The semester break is approaching and Seth Dunlevy, a college student, is trying to decide how he will spend the week. He has narrowed his options to these three:

Option 1: He can go to Vail, Colorado, and ski for the week (he is an avid skier). He estimates the total cost of the trip (airfare, lodging, food, and lift tickets) to be $700. If he selects this option, he will have to cut the last day of classes before the break. He will also have to take time off from his job at Irene's Burger Barn.

He earns $10 per hour and could work as many as 60 hours over the break.

Option 2: He can drive to his parents' home for the week. They live only 140 miles from Seth's school, so he would not have to leave until after his last class. This option requires no out-of-pocket cost because he will be staying at his parents' home and his dad offered to pay for the gas. He would, however, have to take time off from work, just as in Option 1.

Option 3: He can remain at school for the week and devote his time to studying and working at Irene's Burger Barn.

The final decision as to how to spend semester break must be Seth's. He has, however, come to you for advice because he believes you are a person of sound judgment.

REQUIRED:

a. Tell Seth what you think are the most important factors he needs to consider when making his decision. These factors may or may not involve money. Identify the factor you consider to be most important, and explain why you think it is crucial.

b. Prepare an analysis for Seth of what you perceive to be the potential benefits and costs of each of his three alternatives. Although economic benefits and costs are always important, do not restrict yourself to money considerations for either benefits or costs.

c. Assume Seth decides to go skiing in Vail over semester break (Option 1). This decision was made on November 15 and semester break is the last two weeks in December. Identify three pieces of new information Seth might receive before he leaves on his ski trip and explain how each of them might cause him to rethink his decision.

LO 3:   Personal Values and Ethics

2–48. The chapter states that the most important influences on the decisions we make are the personal values we hold.

REQUIRED:

a. Explain in your own words the relationship between personal values and ethics.

b. How do you think that a person's values and ethics change over time? What will cause a person's values and ethics to change?

LO 3:   Personal Values and Ethics

2–49. Charles Rickman, an employee of Failsafe, Inc., has been away on business in Bedford Falls, Pennsylvania, for the past two weeks. Bedford Falls happens to be his hometown, and Charles stayed the entire two weeks with his mother. Wilbur Parker (Charles' boyhood pal) owns the local motel and offered to provide Charles with receipts for a two-week stay at the motel. Charles could submit the receipts and be reimbursed by his company. Failsafe would not be out anything, because the company reimburses employees for out-of-town lodging.

REQUIRED:

a. Explain how Charles would approach this decision situation under virtues ethics.

b. Explain how Charles would approach this decision situation under rules ethics.

c. Which approach do you think would serve Charles better in all such decision situations? Explain your reasoning.

LO 3: Personal Values and Ethics

2–50. You have been working as a staff accountant for Fox Manufacturing Company for the past six months. Your boss needs you to increase the current year's profit by $25,000. He explains how you can accomplish this request. Based on your knowledge, you believe his request is not proper.

REQUIRED:
a. Using the concept of virtues ethics, how would you respond in this situation?
b. How would you apply rules ethics in this situation, and would that change your overall response?
c. Assuming that the method your boss wishes you to use to increase profits is legal, how do you reconcile his request with your personal values?

LO 4: Group Decision Making

2–51. Listed below are the disadvantages of group decision making as presented in the chapter, followed by the definitions of those disadvantages in scrambled order:

    a. Different information-processing styles
    b. Domineering members of the group
    c. Social pressure
    d. Goal replacement
    e. Differing personal values
    f. Unequal effort
    g. Groupthink

    1. _____ Some members of the group may not work as hard as others.
    2. _____ Not everyone believes the same way.
    3. _____ The group may contain both intuitive types and systematic types.
    4. _____ The natural desire to not look foolish may stifle a group member's creative contribution.
    5. _____ Group members are often tempted to ignore their own judgment to achieve consensus.
    6. _____ Winning an argument, proving a point, or taking revenge can become more important than accomplishing the task at hand.
    7. _____ The work of the group suffers simply because some members can talk louder and longer than others.

REQUIRED:
Match the letter next to each disadvantage with the appropriate definition. Each letter will be used only once.

LO 4: Group Decision Making

2–52. Explain in your own words the advantages and disadvantages of group decision making in relation to individual decision making.

LO 5 & 6: Economic Decision Making

2–53. Tommy Hoag is a commercial artist who paints various types of signs for other businesses. He received a $15,000 order from Bill Bates, Inc. for

1,500 signs to be displayed in Bates' retail outlets. This is a very large job for Tommy's new business. He has concerns because he estimates it will take him a month working full time to complete the signs and Bates proposes to pay him the full contract amount 30 days after he delivers the signs. These are Bates' standard payment terms. Tommy did a small job for Bates last year ($1,500) and received payment 50 days after completing the work.

Tommy estimates the materials (sign board, paint, brushes, etc.) will cost $9,500, which he can buy on 30-day terms from Long's Art Supply Company.

Having taken the accounting course in which you are now enrolled, Tommy remembers that any economic decision entails attempting to answer the following three questions:

- Will I be paid?
- When will I be paid?
- How much will I be paid?

REQUIRED:
a. If Tommy can satisfy himself as to the first question (Will I be paid?), what are the answers to the other two questions? Remember the last question (How much?) has two parts.
b. The problem states that Tommy has concerns. What do you think is troubling him about the order from Bill Bates, Inc.?
c. Based on your answer to the previous requirement, identify three things Tommy could do to solve his dilemma.

LO 5 & 6:   Economic Decision Making

2–54. Jon Smythe is a trained automobile engine mechanic. He has received a $25,000 contract from David Watts and Company to repair 25 automobile engines for Watts' taxi cabs. Jon has concerns about the terms of the contract. He estimates it will take him a month working full time to complete the engines and Watts will pay him 30 days after he completes the engines. These are Watts' standard payment terms, and Watts has paid Jon on average after 40 days in the past.

Jon estimates the parts will cost $13,000, which he can buy on a 30-day charge from Sam's Auto Supply Company. Jon has the normal questions of any economic decision:

- Will I be paid?
- When will I be paid?
- How much will I be paid?

REQUIRED:
a. Jon believes that Watts will pay him based on their prior dealings. What are the answers to the other two questions? Remember the last question (How much?) has two parts.
b. The problem states that Jon is concerned about the contract terms. Why do you think he is concerned?
c. Based on your answer to the previous requirement, identify three things Jon could do to lessen his concerns.

LO 5 & 6:   Economic Decision Making

2–55. Rob Schwinn is a manufacturer of quality furniture who specializes in high-quality wooden tables and chairs. He received a $50,000 contract from Dillon Corporation to build 100 upholstered sofas, to be sold in Dillon's stores. Rob believes he needs two months to complete the sofas. He must purchase an industrial sewing machine for the fabric work on the sofas at a cost of $10,000 for the machine and training, which will equal the profit that he will make on this contract. Dillon has agreed to pay Rob Schwinn 30 days after delivery of the sofas.

Rob knows that he can buy the sewing machine on a 90-day plan from Dan's Sewing Machine Company. Rob knows that any economic decision entails attempting to answer the following three questions:

- Will I be paid?
- When will I be paid?
- How much will I be paid?

REQUIRED:

a. Assuming Rob can satisfy himself as to the first question (Will I be paid?), what are the answers to the other two questions? Remember the last question (How much?) has two parts.

b. List the pros and cons of Rob accepting this contract.

LO 7: Cash Concepts

2–56. Interpret the following statement: "Cash is the 'ball' of business."

LO 7, 8, & 9: Qualitative Characteristics of Accounting Information

2–57. Presented below are the qualitative characteristics of useful accounting information as discussed in the chapter, followed by definitions of those items in scrambled order.

a. Relevance
b. Timeliness
c. Predictive value
d. Feedback value
e. Reliability

f. Verifiability
g. Representational faithfulness
h. Neutrality
i. Comparability
j. Consistency

1. _____ The same measurement application methods are used over time.
2. _____ The accounting information is free of bias.
3. _____ The information provides input to evaluate a previously made decision.
4. _____ The information allows the evaluation of one alternative against another alternative.
5. _____ In assessing the information, qualified persons working independently would arrive at similar conclusions.
6. _____ The information helps reduce the uncertainty of the future.
7. _____ The information has a bearing on a particular decision situation.
8. _____ The information is available soon enough to be of value.
9. _____ The information can be dependable.
10. _____ There must be agreement between what the information says and what really happened.

REQUIRED:

Match the letter next to each item with the appropriate definition. Each letter will be used only once.

LO 7, 8, & 9:   Chapter Concepts

2–58. Presented below are items relating to the concepts discussed in this chapter, followed by the definitions of those items in scrambled order:

a. Cash flow
b. Comparability
c. Data
d. Financial accounting

e. Information
f. Management accounting
g. Net cash flow
h. Economic decision making

1. _____ The raw results of transactions and events
2. _____ A branch of accounting developed to meet the information needs of internal decision makers
3. _____ Data transformed so they are useful in the decision-making process
4. _____ The movement of cash in and out of a company
5. _____ Any decision involving money
6. _____ Reports generated for one entity may be compared with reports generated for other entities
7. _____ The difference between the cash coming into a company and the cash going out of a company
8. _____ A branch of accounting developed to meet the information needs of external decision makers

REQUIRED:

Match the letter next to each item with the appropriate definition. Each letter will be used only once.

LO 13:   Qualitative Characteristics of Accounting Information

2–59. Emma Peel is the chief accountant of Venture Company. She is trying to decide whether to extend credit to Freed Company, a new customer. Venture does most of its business on credit, but is very strict in granting credit terms. Frank Freed, the owner and president of Freed Company, has sent the following items for Emma to examine as she performs her evaluation.

1. All company bank statements for the past seven years (a total of 84 bank statements)
2. A detailed analysis showing the amount of sales the company expects to have in the coming year and its estimated profit
3. Another, less detailed analysis outlining projected company growth over the next 20 years
4. A biographical sketch of each of the company's officers and a description of the function each performs in the company
5. Ten letters of reference from close friends and relatives of the company's officers
6. A report of the company's credit history prepared by company employees on Freed Company letterhead
7. A letter signed by all company officers expressing their willingness to personally guarantee the credit Venture extends to Freed. (You may assume this is a legally binding document.)

REQUIRED:

a. As she evaluates Freed Company's application for credit, is Emma Peel an internal decision maker or an external decision maker? Explain your reasoning.

b. Analyze each item Freed sent in light of the primary qualitative characteristics of relevance (including timeliness, predictive value, and feedback value) and reliability (including verifiability, representational faithfulness, and neutrality). Explain how each item either possesses or does not possess these characteristics.

LO 9: Qualitative Characteristics of Accounting Information

2–60. You are in the market for a used car. You notice a promising advertisement in the local newspaper and make an appointment to meet with the seller, whose name is Chet. During your meeting you obtain the following information:

1. The car is a 1996 model.
2. Chet said he has used the car only for commuting to and from work.
3. You notice the car has out-of-state license tags.
4. The odometer reading is 65,319 miles.
5. Chet reports that he has had the oil changed every 3,000 miles since he bought the car new.
6. Chet says this is the greatest car he has ever owned.
7. The glove box contains a maintenance record prepared by a licensed mechanic.

REQUIRED:
a. Evaluate each item from the list above in terms of its relevance (specifically, predictive value and timeliness) to your decision about whether to buy Chet's car.
b. Evaluate each item from the list above in terms of its reliability (verifiability, representational faithfulness, and neutrality) for deciding whether to buy Chet's car.

LO 9: Qualitative Characteristics of Accounting Information

2–61. The chapter states that to be useful, accounting information must possess the primary qualitative characteristics of relevance (timeliness and predictive value or feedback value) and reliability (verifiability, representational faithfulness, and neutrality). These characteristics are also applicable to other types of information.

Suppose that prior to taking your midterm exam in this course, your instructor gives you two options:

Option 1: One week before the midterm exam you will be given a rough idea of what is going to be on the exam.

or

Option 2: On the day following the exam, you will be given a copy of the actual midterm exam with an answer key.

Assume further that you have two goals:

Goal 1: To prepare for the midterm exam.
Goal 2: To evaluate your performance on the midterm exam.

REQUIRED:
Within the context of each of your two goals, evaluate both options using the primary qualitative characteristics. Be sure to explain how the primary characteristics are present or absent and how such presence or absence affects you as a rational decision maker.

LO 9:   Qualitative Characteristics of Accounting Information

2–62. Suppose you are about to buy a new car. The car you want is a Nissan Maxima. You have $30,000 in the bank, ready to spend on the new car. You obtain the following items of information:

1. On your first visit to Quality Nissan, a salesperson casually tells you that the price of a new Nissan Maxima is $25,500.
2. A friend tells you he heard that someone was selling a three-year-old Maxima for $18,000.
3. Another friend just bought a new Chevy pickup truck for $22,000.
4. The sticker price of a Maxima with the options you want is $26,800.
5. A Nissan dealer in the area is advertising a new Maxima with the options you want for $26,200.
6. A friend tells you she heard that someone bought a new Maxima a couple months ago for around $24,000.

Assume that you are about to visit a Nissan dealership and your goal is to buy a new Maxima for the best price. You intend to use the previous information to evaluate whether or not the price you get is a good deal.

REQUIRED:
a. Evaluate each item from the list above in terms of its relevance (feedback value, predictive value, and timeliness). Explain how the presence or absence of the characteristics affects your ability to use the information to determine if you are getting a good deal.
b. Evaluate each item from the list above in terms of its reliability (verifiability, representational faithfulness, and neutrality). Explain how the presence or absence of these characteristics affects your ability to use the information to determine if you are getting a good deal.

LO 9:   Qualitative Characteristics of Accounting Information

2–63. Exactly two weeks from today you must take the midterm exam for this class. You feel you are in trouble because you cannot seem to grasp exactly how you should prepare for the exam. As you are walking across campus, you see the following notice pinned to a bulletin board:

I CAN HELP!!!

I GUARANTEE AN "A" OR "B"

WILL TUTOR FOR $15 PER HOUR

Qualifications:

1. Got an "A" in the course myself.
2. Have outlines of all chapters of the text.
3. Have over 120 satisfied customers from previous semesters.
4. Know the Professor personally.
5. Know the authors of the text personally.
6. Working on a graduate degree in History.

CALL BILL AUSTIN AT 555-5555

REQUIRED:
Evaluate each of Bill's claimed qualifications in relation to the primary characteristics of:

a. Relevance (including timeliness and predictive value or feedback value).
b. Reliability (including verifiability, representational faithfulness, and neutrality).

FINANCIAL REPORTING CASES

2–64. Look at the Gap's annual report to answer the following questions.

 a. List the divisions of the Gap and the primary market of each division.
 b. What factors should the Gap Inc. consider before adding a new division?
 c. For what reasons would the Gap sell or close a division? What factors should management consider to make such a decision?

(For the next two cases, visit the PHLIP Web site for this text at www.prenhall.com/jones)/

2–65. JCPenney operated profitably the Thrift Drug store chain for 28 years. Penney's purchased Kerr Drug in 1995 and Fay's in 1996. In February 1997, Penney's completed the purchase of Eckerd Drug to have the fourth-largest drug store chain in the United States. (For more information on JCPenney, visit the PHLIP Web site and click on the JCPenney link.)

REQUIRED:
a. Why would a mall-centered retail department store acquire large chains of pharmacies?
b. Why do you think JCPenney operates all of the drug stores under the Eckerd name instead of the JCPenney name?

Challenge question: How much did the Eckerd acquisition cost JCPenney?

2–66. The Limited is a major mall competitor of JCPenney and the Gap. Visit its Web site by clicking on The Limited's link at the PHLIP Web site to find its annual report information.

REQUIRED:
a. List the divisions of The Limited and describe the market of each division.
b. Which of its divisions do you believe are the most successful?
c. What factors do you believe The Limited uses to assess the success of a division?
d. Did you know that all the divisions were owned by The Limited? Why do you think The Limited does not advertise the common ownership of the divisions?

ANNUAL REPORT PROJECT

You now have your annual report and have prepared an index of its contents. Your annual report project will contain the following sections.

 I. General Information
 II. SWOT Analysis
 III. Capital Structure
 IV. Assets

2–67. Section I contains the following subsections.
   A. Record the Internet address of your company.
   B. Identify the company's industry.
   C. Identify the Standard Industrial Classification (SIC) code of your company. You can find SIC codes in several ways:
      1. Sometimes the annual report contains the SIC. Look in general information often at the end of the annual report.
      2. The front page of the SEC form 10-Q contains the SIC. If your company sent you the 10-Q, check there.
      3. If you did not receive the 10-Q, try the Internet address of the firm. Look on the Web site, or e-mail the company for the information.
      4. If all these fail, go tp the library and consult a reference librarian to find a reference publication that will give you this information.
   D. Identify the stock exchange(s) where your company's stock trades.
   E. Record the ticker symbol of the company.
   F. Find the auditor's report and record the name of the auditing firm.
   G. Read the president's (or CEO's) message and prepare a brief summary of this message.
   H. Read any other promotional or informational material about the company. This information usually relates the firm's views on social responsibility, marketing strategy, direction for the future, environmental issues, and so on. Write a brief summary of this information provided in the annual report.

REQUIRED:
Complete section I of your project. Turn in one copy to your instructor and retain a clean copy for your final project folder. For group projects, divide the parts equitably among the group members.

Chapter 3

Tools of the Trade, Part I
The Balance Sheet:
Initial Financing—
Investments by Owners

*B*otany was your favorite nonmajor course in college. You were fortunate to have Dr. Bidlack for an honors section, and he required a project to complete the course. Known for his unusual use of plant substances for practical home applications, you isolated a resin in petunia seeds that resists all dirt and moisture. You added this to paint, repainted a tag on the front of your car, and found that nothing stuck to it—not even road tar or mud. Could these be the seeds of your success?

Your best friend is a marketing major and would love to sell this to the paint industry for use in automotive vehicles and house paints. Dr. Bidlack could lend a lot of expertise. If you form a company for this endeavor, should it be a partnership or a corporation? How much money will it take to get started and where do you get it? Your banker asked you for a financial statement, and you have no earthly idea what he wants. Where do you start?

Financial statements should be thought of as tools for solving economic problems. Like all tools, the accounting profession developed these statements in response to specific needs. If these financial tools are adequate and properly used, they will produce satisfactory results. If they are inadequate or improperly used, they will not produce good results and disaster may result. In this chapter, we will discuss only one financial statement—the balance sheet. There are several other kinds of financial statements, and we will discuss them as we proceed through this text. ■

After completing your work on this chapter, you should be able to do the following:

1. Identify and explain the accounting elements contained in the balance sheet.
2. Demonstrate how the balance sheet provides information about the financial position of a business.
3. Compare and contrast the balance sheets of proprietorships, partnerships, and corporations.
4. Describe the basic organizational structure of a corporation.
5. Differentiate between common stock and preferred (preference) stock.
6. Describe the components of stockholders' equity and explain the meaning of treasury stock.
7. Identify what information is available on a corporate balance sheet and what information is not available.
8. Explain the basic process operating in the primary and secondary stock markets.

THE FIRST TOOL: INTRODUCTION TO THE BALANCE SHEET

balance sheet A financial statement providing information about an entity's present condition. Reports what a company possesses (assets) and who has claim to those possessions (liabilities and owners' equity).

In Chapter 2, we defined the problems facing those who make economic decisions. As decision makers evaluate alternative investment opportunities, they try to determine whether they will be paid, and if so, when the payment will occur and how much it will be. This evaluation begins with an assessment of an investment's present condition and past performance. Remember that the present and the past are useful only if they have predictive value. Over time, accountants developed financial tools to convey information about the present condition and past performance of an entity. The financial tool that focuses on the present condition of a business is the **balance sheet.**

Discussion Questions

3-1. Your uncle's will stipulates that you and your cousin Terry (with whom you have always competed) will inherit the two businesses he owned. You get first choice, and you may ask ten questions to determine the present condition of each company. Lawyers for the estate will provide the answers. List your ten questions.

3-2. You are locked in a room that has no windows and only one door. To get out of the room, you must request one tool and explain how you will use it to get through the door. You may not request a key or any lock-picking equipment. Choose the one tool you request and describe its features. Then explain in detail how you will use it to get out of the room.

The Accounting Elements

The conceptual framework of accounting (Exhibit 1–4) lists ten *accounting elements* as shown in Exhibit 3–1. We can classify the results of every economic transaction or event experienced by a company into one or more accounting elements. In this

Exhibit 3–1
Accounting Elements

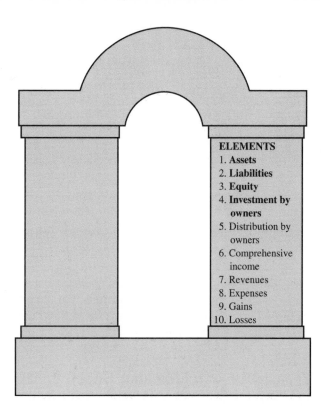

ELEMENTS
1. **Assets**
2. **Liabilities**
3. **Equity**
4. **Investment by owners**
5. Distribution by owners
6. Comprehensive income
7. Revenues
8. Expenses
9. Gains
10. Losses

assets An accounting element that is one of the three components of a balance sheet. Assets are probable future economic benefits controlled by an entity as a result of previous transactions or events—that is, what a company has.

liabilities An accounting element that is one of the three components of a balance sheet. Liabilities are probable future sacrifices of assets arising from present obligations of an entity as a result of past transactions or events—that is, what a company owes.

equity An accounting element that is one of the three components of a balance sheet. Equity is the residual interest in the assets of an entity that remains after deducting liabilities.

investments by owners That part of owners' equity generated by the receipt of cash (or other assets) from the owners.

chapter, we will discuss four accounting elements that make up the balance sheet. We will present the other accounting elements later in the text. As we discuss these elements, we will give both the actual FASB definition in italics and a less technical explanation in roman type.

The three accounting elements that are major components of a balance sheet are:

1. **Assets.** *Probable future economic benefits obtained or controlled by a particular entity as a result of past transactions or events.* Assets are the things a company owns or controls (such as leased assets). Cash is the item most easily identified as an asset.

2. **Liabilities.** *Probable future sacrifices of economic benefits arising from present obligations of a particular entity to transfer assets or provide services to other entities in the future as a result of past transactions or events.* Liabilities are the debts a company owes. A company may have an obligation to transfer assets to someone to pay off a debt, or to provide services when the company received payment in advance. Liabilities arise from past transactions, not events that might occur in the future. An entity must, however, settle or pay liabilities some time in the future.

3. **Equity.** *The residual interest in the assets of an entity that remains after deducting its liabilities.* Equity is the ownership interest in a company. It is the difference between its assets and its liabilities on those assets. The result represents the portion of the assets that the owner(s) own free and clear. Consequently, some people refer to equity as net assets.

   The present financial position of an entity can be captured in these three elements: assets, liabilities, and equity. Equity in a company comes from two sources:

   a. **Investments by owners.** This accounting element represents the amount invested by the owner(s) of the company. It represents "seed money" put into the company to get it started or to finance its expansion.

Exhibit 3–2
Accounting Equation

If you buy an automobile by paying $3,000 in cash and borrowing $5,000 from the bank, both you and the bank have a claim against the car.

$$\text{Assets} = \text{Liabilities} + \text{Equity}$$
$$\text{Car} = \text{Bank Loan} + \text{Equity}$$
$$\$8,000 = \$5,000 + \$3,000$$

By rearranging the equation to

$$\text{Assets} - \text{Liabilities} = \text{Equity}$$
$$\$8,000 - \$5,000 = \$3,000$$

you can see that in this situation, you have a car worth $8,000, the bank has a $5,000 claim against the car, and you have a $3,000 equity in the automobile.

earned equity The total amount a company has earned since its beginning, less any amounts distributed to the owner(s). In a corporation, this amount is called retained earnings.

b. **Earned equity.** This is the total amount a company has earned since it was first started, less any amounts that have been taken out by the owner(s). Earned equity comes from the profitable operation of the company over time.

Organization of the Balance Sheet

A constant relationship exists among the three main elements on the balance sheet (assets, liabilities, and equity). Logically, the assets of a company must be owned by someone. Therefore, the company's assets will be equal to the claims that are made on those assets—creditors' claims (liabilities) or the owners' claims (equity). In most cases, both creditors and owners share claims on the assets (see Exhibit 3–2). This relationship can be stated as an equation:

$$\text{ASSETS} = \text{LIABILITIES} + \text{EQUITY}$$

We call this equation the *accounting equation,* but we could easily call it the business equation because it sums up the reality of business. Accounting uses this equation to measure that reality. Because the equation has all the properties of a mathematical equation, we can rearrange it as:

$$\text{ASSETS} - \text{LIABILITIES} = \text{EQUITY}$$

This presentation of the equation shows equity for what it is: the owners' residual interest in the company. We usually use the phrase *owners' equity* instead of the word *equity.* Thus, the accounting equation is usually presented as:

$$\text{ASSETS} = \text{LIABILITIES} + \text{OWNERS' EQUITY}$$

To understand the balance sheet, you must understand the meaning of the equation. The term *balance sheet* comes from the need to keep both sides of the equation in balance. The financial statement's formal name is the *statement of financial position* or *statement of financial condition,* both of which describe the true purpose of the statement. Common usage in the business world, however, remains the *balance sheet.*

Balance sheets are presented in two different forms, the account form or the report form. The account form places assets on the left side of the page and the liabilities and equity on the right. As you can see in Exhibit 3–3, the story told by the balance sheet is

$$\text{ASSETS} = \text{LIABILITIES} + \text{OWNERS' EQUITY}$$

The same information can be placed on the page in a vertical format called the report form (Exhibit 3–4).

Exhibit 3–3
Account Form of the
Balance Sheet

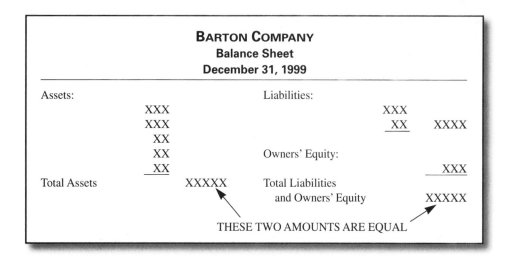

Exhibit 3–4
Report Form of the
Balance Sheet

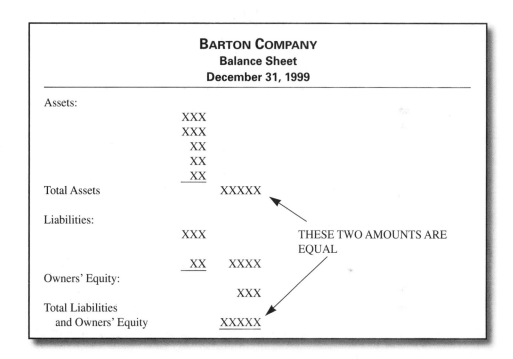

Note that the balance sheet is a "financial snapshot" of a company. Like any snapshot, it only shows what existed on the day it was taken. It is not a valid representation of the day before it was taken, nor the day after. What it says is that on the day the financial snapshot was taken, these are the assets the company possessed and here is who had claim to those assets.

STARTING A BUSINESS—INVESTMENTS BY OWNERS

Laura wants to begin the operation of her new company. What does she need to do? Starting out BIG may require many things—hiring a secretary and/or other employees, getting a company car, or renting office space. Even if she plans to

Exhibit 3–5
Balance Sheet for a
Proprietorship

LAURA'S BUSINESS
Balance Sheet
January 1, 1999

Assets:		Liabilities:	$ 0
Cash	$10,000		
		Owner's Equity:	
		Laura, Capital	10,000
		Total Liabilities and	
Total Assets	$10,000	Owners' Equity	$10,000

begin as a one-person operation, she has many things to consider, such as having stationery and/or business cards printed and insurance to protect the company in case of lawsuits.

Even the smallest company has start-up costs. Therefore, Laura's new operation needs cash! Normally, the entrepreneur's first task in starting a new company is obtaining the cash to get underway. The owner is the most logical source for this initial funding. As we develop the balance sheet in this chapter, we will assume that the new company will be initially financed with cash from owners.

Recall the three major forms of business organization in Chapter 1: proprietorships, partnerships, and corporations. Each form requires a slightly different presentation of the initial financing of a new company.

Balance Sheet for a Proprietorship

A proprietorship, a business entity with only one owner, keeps track of only one owner's equity. If Laura's proprietorship began operations on January 1, 1999, with an owner's investment of $10,000 cash, her company's first balance sheet would look like Exhibit 3–5.

Notice that the business (accounting) equation still holds true:

$$\text{ASSETS} = \text{LIABILITIES} + \text{OWNERS' EQUITY}$$
$$\$10,000 = \quad 0 \quad + \$10,000$$

We use a capital account to represent the owner's claim to the assets held by a sole proprietorship. In a proprietorship, there is only one owner; therefore, there will be only one capital account.

Balance Sheet for a Partnership

Partnerships, you recall, are organized like proprietorships, except that they have more than one owner. Assume that two partners, Laura and Stephanie, start the new company. If Laura invests $6,000 and Stephanie invests $4,000 to begin operations, the partnership's first balance sheet would look like Exhibit 3–6.

Compare the balance sheet for this partnership with that for the proprietorship (Exhibit 3–5). Notice that the total assets, $10,000 in cash, are the same. Total owners' equity ($10,000) is also the same. The only difference is that we must keep track of each partner's claim to the assets in a separate capital account.

In our example, one partner—Laura—provided 60 percent of the beginning capital ($6,000/$10,000 = 60 percent) and the other partner—Stephanie—provided 40 percent of the initial capital ($4,000/$10,000 = 40 percent). The proportional size

Exhibit 3–6
Balance Sheet for a
Partnership

LAURA AND STEPHANIE'S BUSINESS
Balance Sheet
January 1, 1999

Assets:		Liabilities:		$ 0
Cash	$10,000			
		Owners' Equity:		
		Laura, Capital	$6,000	
		Stephanie, Capital	4,000	
		Total Owners' Equity		10,000
Total Assets	$10,000	Total Liabilities and		
		Owners' Equity		$10,000

of a partner's initial investment is generally reflected by the proportional size of the beginning balance in the partner's capital account.

Partners can construct partnership agreements that are simple or complex, but as long as the partners agree and understand clearly how their claims to the assets of the company (their capital balances) are being calculated, they can adopt any rules.

Balance Sheet for a Corporation

A corporation is a legal entity separate and apart from its owners. That characteristic sets it apart from proprietorships and partnerships. With very few exceptions, such as national banks (which are incorporated under federal law), incorporators create the corporate entity by obtaining a *corporate charter* from one of the 50 states. This charter is a legal contract between the state and the corporation allowing the firm to conduct business.

To form a corporation, states require the *incorporators* to submit a formal application for the corporate charter and file it with the appropriate state agency. The application, called the *articles of incorporation,* generally must include (1) basic information about the corporation and its purpose; (2) details concerning the types of stock to be issued; and (3) the names of the individuals responsible for the corporation.

If the state agency approves the application, it issues a charter that entitles the corporation to begin operations. The incorporators then meet to formulate the corporate *bylaws*. These bylaws serve as basic rules for management to use in conducting the corporation's business. Next, the incorporators raise capital by issuing stock, thereby exchanging ownership interests in the corporation for cash. Once stock has been issued, the corporation has stockholders who elect a board of directors. The directors meet to appoint a president and such other officers as they deem necessary to manage the company.

CORPORATE ORGANIZATIONAL STRUCTURE

In the preceding section, we referred to several groups of people within the structure of the corporate form. Because these groups are critical to the successful operation of a corporation, we will now discuss each of them in greater detail.

The Stockholders

The stockholders (or *shareholders*) own the corporation. Shareholders provide cash or other assets to the corporation in exchange for ownership shares in the company. In most corporations, the stockholders are not involved in the daily management of the company, unless they have been elected to the board of directors or have been appointed as officers or managers.

When stockholders invest in the corporation they receive a *stock certificate*, a legal document providing evidence of ownership and containing the provisions of the stock ownership agreement. The stockholders usually meet once a year to elect members of the board of directors and conduct other business important to the corporation.

Board of Directors

The board of directors has ultimate responsibility for managing the corporation. In practice, however, most boards restrict themselves to formulating very broad corporate policy and appointing officers to conduct the corporation's daily operations. The board serves as a link between the stockholders and the officers of the company. If the officers are not managing the corporation in the best interests of the stockholders, the board of directors, acting on behalf of the stockholders, can replace the officers. The board of directors elects a chairperson who can also serve as the corporate president.

Corporate Officers

A corporation's *chief executive officer (CEO)* normally is the corporate president (and sometimes concurrently the chairperson of the board of directors). The CEO is responsible for all activities of the company. In addition to the president, most corporations have one or more vice presidents who are responsible for specific functions of the company, such as marketing, finance, and production. Many corporations name a *chief financial officer (CFO)*, who directs the corporation's fi-

Exhibit 3–7
An Example of
Corporate Structure

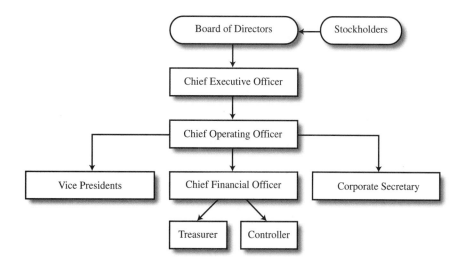

nancial affairs, and a *chief operating officer (COO)*, who may work closely with the president to direct the daily operations of the company.

Other corporate officer positions include the *controller*, who is responsible for all accounting functions; the *treasurer*, who is responsible for managing the company's cash; and the *corporate secretary*, who maintains the minutes of the board of directors' and stockholders' meetings and may also represent the company in legal proceedings.

Exhibit 3–7 illustrates the relationship among the various groups in the corporate structure.

Very small corporations with only a few stockholders operate more like sole proprietorships and partnerships. The CEO may be the chairperson of the board of directors, president, sole stockholder, and may empty the trash cans at the end of the day. Any business may assume the corporate form providing it meets certain legal requirements of the state in which it operates. Although we may focus on larger, publicly held corporations in annual report projects, the concepts apply to corporations of any size.

Discussion Questions

3–3. In his book *Short-Term America*, Michael Jacobs reports that "nearly 80 percent of the chief executives of U.S. companies also serve as chairman of the board" (1991, p. 82). In light of our discussion of the functions of corporate officers and the board of directors, express your views concerning this information. Does this dual role present any conflict of interest? Support your view with specific reasons.

3–4. Jacobs also reports that the practice of having a CEO serve as board chairperson "is used by only 30 percent of British firms, 11 percent of Japanese companies, and never in Germany" (1991, p. 82). Why do you think there is such a difference in this practice between the United States and other countries? Does this new information affect your response to Discussion Question 3–3?

CORPORATE CAPITAL STRUCTURE

authorized shares The maximum number of shares of stock a corporation has been given permission to issue under its corporate charter.

issued shares Stock that has been distributed to the owners of the corporation in exchange for cash or other assets.

outstanding shares Shares of stock actually held by shareholders. The number may be different than that for issued shares because a corporation may reacquire its own stock (treasury stock).

treasury stock Corporate stock that has been issued and then reacquired by the corporation.

contributed capital Total amount invested in a corporation by its shareholders. Also called paid-in capital.

paid-in capital The portion of stockholders' equity representing amounts invested by the owners of the corporation. Consists of common stock, preferred stock, and amounts received in excess of the par values of those stocks. Also called contributed capital.

retained earnings The sum of all earnings of a corporation since inception minus the amount of dividends declared.

dividends A distribution of earnings from a corporation to its owners. Dividends are most commonly distributed in the form of cash.

common stock A share of ownership in a corporation. Each share represents one vote in the election of the board of directors and other pertinent corporate matters.

As part of the formal application to create a corporation, the incorporators must include details of their plans to sell shares of stock. They request the authority to issue (sell) a certain number of shares of stock. **Authorized shares** are the maximum number of shares that can legally be issued under the corporate charter. The shares do not exist until they are issued, however, and ownership in the corporation is based on issued, not authorized, shares. **Issued shares** refer to the number of shares of stock already distributed to stockholders in exchange for cash or other assets. **Outstanding shares** refer to shares of stock currently being held by stockholders. In many instances, issued shares and outstanding shares will be the same number. Occasionally, however, a corporation reacquires shares of stock it has previously issued. This reacquired stock, called **treasury stock,** will cause the numbers of issued shares and outstanding shares to be different. For example, assume a corporation issued 100,000 shares of its stock and then later reacquired 2,000 of those shares. The company still has 100,000 shares issued but now has only 98,000 outstanding shares. The cash paid to reacquire the treasury stock is deducted from both cash and total stockholders' equity to keep the accounting equation in balance.

The equity of a corporation is called *stockholders' equity* (instead of owner's equity as in a proprietorship). In the corporate form, the equity of the stockholders is the excess of assets over liabilities, just as it is for proprietorships and partnerships. There are, however, some differences in the way equity items are classified on the balance sheet.

In the corporate form, the owners' capital accounts are replaced by common stock accounts. Most state corporation laws require stockholders' equity to be divided into the portion invested by the owners and the portion earned by the company and retained in the corporation. Amounts received by the corporation in exchange for shares of stock are called **contributed capital** or **paid-in capital.** A classification called **retained earnings** is used to reflect earnings kept in the company and not distributed to the owners in the form of **dividends.** Total stockholders' equity is a combination of contributed capital and retained earnings.

Because most corporations have many shareholders, some into the thousands or millions, the individual ownership interests of each shareholder are not disclosed on the face of the balance sheet. Instead, only totals of the ownership interests represented by each class of stock are shown. The two basic classes of stock are common stock and preferred stock.

Common Stock

Common stock is the voting stock of the corporation. Each share of common stock represents an equal share in the ownership of the corporation; therefore, the stockholders' equity portion of a corporate balance sheet will show information about common stock.

Common stock may or may not have a par value. **Par value** is an arbitrary dollar amount placed on the stock by the incorporators at the time they make application for the corporate charter. To protect investors and creditors, states once required a par value to set the legal limits of liability for stockholders. If you recall, corporations protect stockholders' assets from the liabilities of the corporation through limited liability. Therefore, if a stock had a par value of $10 and the corporation issued it at $8, the stockholder had a potential liability to creditors of $2 if the corporation defaulted on the loan and closed the business. Par value has nothing to do with the market value of the stock. All 50 states have removed the par value requirement. So why do we discuss par value if it is no longer required? Because most of the large corporations in the United States were formed before the

Exhibit 3–8

Par Value versus Market Value for Common Stock of Some Major U.S. Corporations (August 21, 1998)

	Par Value	Market Value (August 21, 1998)
GM	$10.00	65 1/8
IBM	$ 1.25	127 7/8
GE	$ .16	89 5/8
Mobil Oil	$ 1.00	73 1/2
Philip Morris	$ 1.00	43 3/4
Chevron	$ 3.00	80 3/16
Chrysler	$ 1.00	55 1/2
Boeing	$ 5.00	36 3/8
PepsiCo	$ .01	32 1/2

par value (for stocks) An arbitrary amount assigned to each share of stock by the incorporators at the time of incorporation.

par value stock Stock with a par value printed on the stock certificate (see *par value*).

additional paid-in capital The amount in excess of the stock's par value received by the corporation when par value stock is issued.

requirement was eliminated, so the stocks carry a par value. Also, many incorporators elect to issue **par value stock** in newly formed corporations.

Most corporations set the par value of their stock considerably below its actual value because most states do not allow stock to be sold for less than its par value (see Exhibit 3–8 for a comparison of par and market values for some major corporations' stocks). It is not unusual to see par values of $1 per share or even lower. Pfizer Inc., for example, has a par value on its stock of five cents ($0.05) per share.

To see what issuing par value common stock involves, assume that Laura selected the corporate form for her new company and the Laura Corporation began operations on January 1, 1999, by issuing (selling) 2,000 shares of its $1 par value stock for $5 per share. The business receives a total of $10,000 cash, so assets increase by that amount. The transaction also affects the other side of the accounting equation in stockholders' equity. Most states stipulate that only the par value of the stock multiplied by the number of shares issued can be classified as common stock. In the case of Laura Corporation, that would be $2,000 (2,000 shares × $1 par value). We classify the remaining $8,000 ($10,000 cash received less the $2,000 classified as common stock) on the balance sheet as **additional paid-in capital** or some similarly descriptive title. A balance sheet prepared immediately after the sale of the stock would look like Exhibit 3–9.

Exhibit 3–9

Balance Sheet for a Corporation That Issued Par Value Common Stock

LAURA CORPORATION
Balance Sheet
January 1, 1999

Assets:		Liabilities:		$ 0
Cash	$10,000			
		Shareholders' Equity:		
		Common Stock	$2,000	
		Additional Paid-in Capital	8,000	
		Total Shareholders' Equity		10,000
		Total Liabilities and		
Total Assets	$10,000	Shareholders' Equity		$10,000

Understand what this balance sheet can and cannot tell you. The $2,000 shown as common stock is the par value of the common stock multiplied by the number of shares issued by the corporation. Combining that amount with the $8,000 additional paid-in capital tells you that the corporation received a total of $10,000 in return for the 1,000 shares of common stock it issued. What is the value of those shares of common stock today? The answer to that question cannot be found on the balance sheet. Amounts shown on the corporate financial statements are intended to provide information about the results of past activities of the corporation—not the current market values of stock already issued to shareholders.

Discussion Question

3–5. If the balance sheet of a corporation does not show the current market value of the shares of stock, where do you think an investor could find this information?

No-Par Stock

no-par stock Stock that has no par value assigned to it.

Stock that does not have a par value is known as **no-par stock.** Choosing to issue no-par stock instead of stock with a par value has no effect on the market value of the shares. Procter and Gamble's stock has no par value and was selling for over $60 per share in 1998. No-par stock is considered by many to have at least two distinct advantages over par value stock:

- Accounting for stock transactions is less complicated for no-par stock than it is for par value stock.
- No-par stock prevents confusion as to the amount received from the sale of the stock. The relevant information is what shareholders were willing to pay for the stock, and an arbitrary par value may mislead some investors.

If the Laura Corporation's common stock in the previous example had been no-par stock, the entire $10,000 proceeds from the sale of the stock would be classified as common stock and the balance sheet immediately after the sale would look like Exhibit 3–10. Like Exhibit 3–9, this balance sheet can tell us how much was received from the sale of stock, but it does not tell us about the current market value of the stock.

Exhibit 3–10
Balance Sheet for a Corporation That Issued No-Par Common Stock

LAURA CORPORATION
Balance Sheet
January 1, 1999

Assets:		Liabilities:		$ 0
Cash	$10,000			
		Shareholders' Equity:		
		Common Stock	$10,000	
		Total Shareholders' Equity		10,000
		Total Liabilities and		
Total Assets	$10,000	Shareholders' Equity		$10,000

Discussion Questions

3–6. If you were setting up a new corporation, would you establish a par value for your common stock? Why or why not?

3–7. Michael Jacobs reports in *Short-Term America*, "Twenty-five years ago, shares of companies traded on the New York Stock Exchange were held an average of eight years; by 1987, the average holding period had declined to a little more than a year" (1991, p. 60). Some experts believe we are no longer a nation of investors, but rather a nation of speculators. What do you think that statement means? What influence do you think this shorter-term ownership is having on the way companies are run in the United States?

Regardless of whether the stock has a par value, investors buy a lot of common stock. When they do so, they should accept the risk willingly in exchange for the rewards they may earn. The major risks of common stock investments are:

1. risk of loss of investment; and
2. risk of no dividends, small dividends, or unstable dividends.

The rewards that investors seek with common stock are:

1. increase in market price of common stock (capital appreciation);
2. increase in or steady growth in the amount of dividends paid; and
3. a voice in the direction of the company.

Investors who buy common stocks seek different opportunities and accept different risks from those who buy preferred stocks.

Preferred Stock

preferred (preference) stock A share of ownership in a corporation that has preference over common stock as to dividends and as to assets upon liquidation of the corporation. Usually nonvoting stock.

Preferred stock, also referred to as preference stock, has certain preference features over common stock. Although preferred shareholders do not have voting rights, they receive other types of benefits, outlined in the stock agreement. Two benefits of ownership normally found in preferred stock agreements are:

- Owners of preferred stock must receive a dividend before any dividend is paid to owners of common stock.
- In the event of a corporation's liquidation, preferred shareholders receive a distribution of assets before any assets can be distributed to common shareholders. Liquidation refers to the process of going out of business: The corporation is shut down, all assets are sold, and all liabilities are settled.

Preferred stock usually carries a par value. Although par value has little meaning for common stock, the par value of preferred stock is important because dividends are usually stated as a percentage of par value. For example, if a corporation issued 8 percent preferred stock with a par value of $100 per share, the annual dividend would be $8 per share ($100 × 8% = $8). Most corporations must offer a reasonable dividend to encourage investors to buy their preferred stock. Because the dividends are stated as a percentage of par, most preferred stock has a par value of $50 to $100. The market value of preferred stock is normally much closer to the par value of preferred shares. Investors in preferred stock tend to be conservative investors. They frequently buy preferred stock to earn a guaranteed rate of return through the stated dividend. Assume that Jason desires an 8% rate of return and is willing to invest $1,000. If he finds a $100 acceptable preferred stock paying an 8% dividend, he would probably be willing to pay par value for the stock. The preferred stock's market value fluctuates more with the dividend rate than any other measure.

To illustrate how preferred stock is issued, let us assume that Laura Corporation, in addition to the common stock it issued as described in our previous discussion, issued (sold) 50 shares of $100 par value preferred stock for $105 per share on January 1, 1999. Then the total amount the business received from the sale of stock would be $15,250 (50 shares of preferred stock × $105 = $5,250 + $10,000 from the sale of the common stock). Under the laws of most states, only the par value of the preferred stock multiplied by the number of shares issued would be classified as preferred stock (50 shares × $100 par value = $5,000). The remaining $250 of the proceeds would be classified as additional paid-in capital. A balance sheet prepared immediately after the sale of the two classes of stock would look like Exhibit 3–11.

Exhibit 3–11
Balance Sheet for a Corporation That Issued Preferred and Common Stock

LAURA CORPORATION **Balance Sheet** **January 1, 1999**			
Assets:		Liabilities:	$ 0
Cash	$15,250	Shareholders' Equity:	
		Preferred Stock	$5,000
		Additional Paid-in	
		Capital—Preferred Stock	250
		Common Stock	2,000
		Additional Paid-in	
		Capital—Common Stock	8,000
		Total Shareholders' Equity	15,250
		Total Liabilities and	
Total Assets	$15,250	Shareholders' Equity	$15,250

Again, the balance sheet reveals the amounts received for issuing each class of stock ($10,000 for common and $5,250 for preferred), but the current market value of the stock is not shown.

The following information is a portion of the December 31, 1999, balance sheet of Earhart Supply, Inc. Look at it carefully, and then try to answer the following questions.

Common stock, $100 par value, authorized

10,000 shares; issued 5,000 shares $500,000
Additional paid-in capital............533,000

1. What was the total amount the corporation received for the sale of its stock?
2. What was the average selling price per share?
3. If the corporation wanted to sell all the stock it could possibly sell, how many more shares could it offer for sale?
4. If all the stock mentioned in question 3 were sold, how much money would the corporation receive?

Try to reason through each question, using what you have learned about stock from reading this chapter, before you look at the answers. Do not give up too easily!

Here are the answers.

1. In total, the corporation received $1,033,000 for its stock. That is the total of the par value and the additional paid-in capital ($500,000 + $533,000).
2. If the corporation received a total of $1,033,000 from the sale of its stock, the average selling price was $206.60.

($1,033,000 / 5,000 shares = $206.60 per share)

3. The corporation has been authorized to sell up to 10,000 shares. If 5,000 shares have already been issued, an additional 5,000 shares could be sold.
4. Based solely on the information provided, there is no way to determine the current market value of the stock. If the stock is traded on a public stock exchange, the current selling price is common knowledge. Business publications such as *The Wall Street Journal* and the business sections of many daily newspapers publish stock prices daily. We will provide more information about the trading of stock in the rest of this chapter.

THE STOCK MARKET

In Chapter 1, we discussed the regulation of stock sales by the Securities and Exchange Commission. Not only does the SEC regulate stock transactions, but most states also have a state securities commission to regulate transfers of stock for small companies with few investors. Most small companies trade privately. Corporations do not have to register with the SEC unless they have a large number of shareholders. Most state securities commissions regulate corporations that have more than 25 shareholders.

Public trading occurs on the *stock market*, consisting of a number of exchanges including the New York Stock Exchange (NYSE), the American Stock Exchange (AMEX), and regional stock exchanges such as the Midwest Stock Exchange in Chicago and the Pacific Stock Exchange in Los Angeles and San Francisco. The NASDAQ (National Association of Securities Dealers' Automated Quotations) stock exchange prides itself on its ability to attract and support the growth of many of the most successful and innovative U.S. companies, including Microsoft, MCI, Apple Computer, and Intel. In 1993, *Fortune* magazine reported that 65 of the nation's 100 fastest-growing companies chose to be listed with NASDAQ rather than with the older, more established stock exchanges. The trend continues today because of NASDAQ's aggressive competition for listings and savvy marketing. By 1998, the staid NYSE took lessons from NASDAQ and began to court new companies, having learned that the investment world would not automatically come through its doors.

A *stock exchange* is an organization created to provide a place where interested buyers and sellers of shares of stock can get together. As recently as 1980, the U.S. stock market (encompassing all the national and regional exchanges) accounted for better than half the stock trading in the world. By 1990, that figure was down to just over 34 percent, and the trend toward worldwide exchanges outside the United States is expected to continue into the next century. Already, stock exchanges in Tokyo, London, and several other foreign cities are as important to world stock trading as exchanges in the United States.

Primary and Secondary Markets

When a corporation (such as Laura Corporation) desires to raise additional capital (money) by selling shares of stock, it makes what is referred to as a *stock offering*. A stock offering gives investors the opportunity to purchase ownership shares in the company. When a company offers stock to the general public for the first time, it is called an *initial public offering (IPO)*. The company announces the offering in such business publications as *The Wall Street Journal,* outlining the number of shares being offered and the anticipated selling price. If investors are interested in purchasing shares, the company can sell its stock and raise the money it needs.

Although a company can market its stock directly to the public, most offerings are made through investment bankers. **Investment bankers,** also called **underwriters,** act as intermediaries between the company issuing the shares of stock and the investors who ultimately purchase those shares. An investment banker purchases all the shares of stock being offered, then resells the shares to other investors (for a higher price). Some well-known investment banking firms are Merrill Lynch, Salomon Brothers, and Morgan Stanley.

What we have just described is known as the **primary stock market.** Primary means first or initial in this instance, not main or most important. Earlier in the chapter we illustrated the issuing (sale) of stock for Laura Corporation and how the sale of that stock was reflected on the company's balance sheet. That illustration showed the primary or initial sale of the stock.

After a company has initially sold shares of its stock, all further sales of those shares take place in the **secondary stock market.** The company itself receives no money from the sale of its stock in the secondary market. It needs to be notified, of course, when shares of its stock are sold by one investor to another, because it must know to whom it should send dividend payments. But the company itself is not directly involved in the trading of its stock in the secondary market.

The daily reports we hear about fluctuations in the overall stock market and in the Dow Jones Industrial Average refer to the trading of previously issued shares of stock in the secondary stock market. Whether you someday own a corporation, work for one, or invest your money in one, you will find that a basic understanding of corporate structure and the operation of the stock market is quite valuable.

How Stock Prices Are Quoted

Stock market exchanges report the results of trading each day that the market is open. Reports differ depending upon the source, but often contain the following information:

- ticker symbol for each stock (an abbreviation of the company name)
- dividends
- price earnings ratio
- number of shares traded during the day
- closing price for the day
- change from the closing price of the previous trading day

At the close of the week, stock reports often indicate additional information such as the high and low price for the year.

The following depicts a typical daily stock market report:

		PE	Sales Hds	Last	Chg.
Catepillr	1.20	10	23013	45 7/8	+3 7/8
Dole	.40	18	1070	43 7/8	+3/8
Dow Ch	3.48	11	15051	79 3/16	+1 3/16
EKodak	1.76		20687	79 5/8	+5/8
Gannett	.80	18	11214	58 7/8	− 1/8
GaylordE	.60	28	314	26 3/4	− 7/16

investment bankers Intermediaries between the corporation issuing stock and the investors who ultimately purchase the shares. Also called *underwriters.*

underwriters Professionals in the field of investment banking. Also called *investment bankers.*

primary stock market The business activity involved in the initial issue of stock from a corporation.

secondary stock market The business activity focusing on trades of stock among investors subsequent to the initial issue.

Remember to identify the information contained in each column by referring to a legend in the report. For this report the columns (left to right) represent:

Ticker symbol
Annual dividend per share
PE = the price earning ratio
Sales Hds = the number of shares sold, expressed in hundreds
Last = the closing price sold
Chg. = the change in the closing price from the prior trading day

As an example, the third listing is for Dow Chemical. It pays an annual dividend of $3.48 per common share. The current PE ratio is 11, indicating that the price is 11 times the current earnings per share. During this trading day, traders exchanged 1,505,100 shares (15,051 × 100) of Dow's stock. The closing price was $79.1875 (79 3/16 × $1.00). Stocks are quoted as dollars and fractions of dollars, in quarters ($0.25), eights ($0.125), and sixteenths ($0.0625). Dow's stock closed $1.1875 higher than the previous day. Therefore, yesterday the stock closed at $78. Analysts watch these statistics carefully to understand the market's reaction to this stock as economic information becomes available to investors.

Government Influence on the Stock Market

The SEC regulates reporting and trading of securities. Despite its influence, the SEC cannot prevent fluctuations in the stock market, such as the crash of October 19, 1987, when the Dow Jones Industrial Average fell 508 points, or 22.3 percent of its value, in one day. To prevent another drop of this magnitude, the stock exchanges created "circuit breakers" so that, in the future, trading would be halted when the market dropped more than a certain percentage. Fortunately, investors shrugged off the 1987 crash and started buying stocks again almost immediately. Within a few months, the Dow Jones Industrial Average had recovered all its losses, and by 1994, it had nearly doubled in value.

When companies issue stock, the lead investment bank often puts an ad, such as the one in Exhibit 3–12, in *The Wall Street Journal* and other papers to alert potential investors to the offering. This particular ad indicates that William Blair & Company is the lead underwriter for 2,185,000 shares of Tessco Technologies stock, priced at $12 per share. The other securities firms helping to distribute the shares are also listed in the ad. Note that the ad's disclaimer directs interested investors to contact one of the brokers listed to obtain a prospectus, the legal document describing the offering in detail.

In addition to its authority to regulate the buying and selling of corporate stock, the SEC has the power to regulate the buying and selling of corporate bonds. Selling corporate bonds is a highly sophisticated form of borrowing. It is one of the major topics addressed in the next chapter.

SUMMARY

The balance sheet is a financial tool that provides information about the present financial position of an entity. This financial statement shows the relationship of three accounting elements: assets, liabilities, and owners' equity. This relationship is known as the accounting equation or business equation:

ASSETS = LIABILITIES + OWNERS' EQUITY

*This is not an offer to sell nor a solicitation of offers to buy any of these securities.
This offer is made only by the Prospectus.*

September 28, 1994

2,185,000 Shares

TESSCO TECHNOLOGIES

Common Stock

Price $12 Per Share

---

*Copies of the Prospectus may be obtained within any State from any
Underwriter who may lawfully offer these securities within such State.*

William Blair & Company

Alex. Brown & Sons Incorporated	Dean Witter Reynolds Inc.	Dillon, Read & Co. Inc.
Donaldson, Lufkin & Jenrette Securities Corporation	A.G. Edwards & Sons, Inc.	Hambrecht & Quist Incorporated
Montgomery Securities	Oppenheimer & Co., Inc.	PaineWebber Incorporated
Prudential Securities Incorporated		Robertson, Stephens & Company
Salomon Brothers Inc	Smith Barney Inc.	Wertheim Schroder & Co. Incorporated
Robert W. Baird & Co. Incorporated	George K. Baum & Company	J.C. Bradford & Co.
The Chicago Corporation	Cowen & Company	Crowell, Weedon & Co.
Ferris, Baker Watts Incorporated	First of Michigan Corporation	Gabelli & Company, Inc.
Hanifen, Imhoff Inc.	Janney Montgomery Scott Inc.	Kemper Securities, Inc.
C.L. King & Associates, Inc.		Ladenburg, Thalmann & Co. Inc.
Legg Mason Wood Walker Incorporated	McDonald & Company Securities, Inc.	Mesirow Financial, Inc.
Morgan Keegan & Company, Inc.	Needham & Company, Inc.	The Ohio Company
Pennsylvania Merchant Group Ltd		Raymond James & Associates, Inc.
The Robinson-Humphrey Company, Inc.	Sutro & Co. Incorporated	Tucker Anthony Incorporated
Unterberg Harris	Wessels, Arnold & Henderson	Wheat First Butcher Singer

Basically, assets are what the company owns, liabilities are what the company owes to outsiders, and owners' equity is what is left when liabilities are subtracted from assets—the residual interest claims of the owners. Regardless of the type of business, the balance sheet shows the relationship among the company's assets, liabilities, and owners' equity.

Generally, the owner(s) of a new company must acquire first the cash needed to begin operations. Most often, this cash comes from the owner or owners of the company. The balance sheet for each type of business organization presents the results of this investment by owners in a slightly different way. Proprietorships have a single capital account, representing the ownership interest of the sole proprietor. Partnerships generally show a separate capital account for each partner, because their levels of ownership interest may vary. Corporations are legal entities owned by many stockholders; therefore, ownership interests are shown in common stock and additional paid-in capital accounts.

Because it is a separate legal entity, a corporation has a more complex organizational structure than either of the other two business forms. Corporate stockholders elect a board of directors to oversee the management of the corporation. The board, however, usually restricts itself to setting broad corporate policy; it appoints officers to conduct the daily affairs of the corporation. Corporate officers normally consist of a chief executive officer (usually the president), one or more vice presidents, a controller, a treasurer, and a corporate secretary.

Corporations may issue both common stock and preferred stock. Common stock is voting stock, and the common shareholders are the residual owners of the business. Common stock may have a par value, or it may be no-par stock. Preferred (preference) stock is usually nonvoting stock that enjoys two preferences over common stock: Dividends (which are usually based on some percentage of the par value) are paid first to preferred shareholders, and preferred shareholders have prior claim to net assets if the corporation is liquidated.

Corporate capital (stockholders' equity) is classified by source: paid-in (contributed) capital and earned capital (retained earnings). Paid-in capital represents the cash or other assets acquired by the company from the owners, generally through the sale of stock. Retained earnings represents the amount of earnings held in the business rather than distributed to the owners in the form of dividends. For a number of reasons, a corporation might reacquire shares of stock it previously issued. Reacquired stock is known as treasury stock. Treasury stock is still considered issued stock, but is no longer considered outstanding; it is shown on the balance sheet as a reduction of stockholders' equity.

The balance sheet is a representation of the financial position of the business on a particular date. The current market value of the corporation's stock cannot be determined from its balance sheet. Rather, the balance sheet provides information about how much was received by the corporation for the stock when it was originally issued.

Corporations initially issue stock in the primary stock market, either to individuals or to an investment banker (or underwriter), who resells the stock to individual investors. Secondary stock market activity includes all subsequent trading of the shares of stock. Although the corporation does not receive money from trades in the secondary market, since these trades determine the market value of the stock, they are certainly important to the corporation. Activity in both the primary and secondary stock markets is regulated by the Securities and Exchange Commission (SEC).

KEY TERMS

additional paid-in capital   F-87
assets   F-79
authorized shares   F-86
balance sheet   F-78
common stock   F-86
contributed capital   F-86
dividends   F-86
earned equity   F-80
equity   F-79
investment bankers   F-92
investments by owners   F-79
issued shares   F-86

liabilities   F-79
no-par stock   F-88
outstanding shares   F-86
paid-in capital   F-86
par value (for stocks)   F-87
par value stock   F-87
preferred (preference) stock   F-89
primary stock market   F-92
retained earnings   F-86
secondary stock market   F-92
treasury stock   F-86
underwriters   F-92

REVIEW THE FACTS

A. List and define the three accounting elements that are components of the balance sheet.
B. Describe the two sources from which a company builds equity.
C. State the business or accounting equation.
D. What is a more formal and descriptive name for the balance sheet?
E. Name and describe the two formats of the balance sheet.
F. How does the balance sheet for a proprietorship differ from that for a partnership?
G. In what ways does a stockholder of a corporation differ from a partner in a partnership?
H. Explain the differences among authorized, issued, and outstanding shares of stock.
I. Define treasury stock.
J. Name and describe the two major components of stockholders' equity.
K. What are the two major classes of stock and how do they differ?
L. What is meant by the par value of stock and what significance does it have?
M. Explain what a stock exchange and a stock offering are.
N. What is the role of underwriters or investment bankers?
O. Distinguish between the primary stock market and the secondary stock market.
P. What type of organization is the SEC and what is its function?

APPLY WHAT YOU HAVE LEARNED

LO 1: Accounting Equation

3–8. a. Write the basic accounting equation.
b. Define each element of the equation in your own words.
c. Provide examples of each element of the basic accounting equation.

LO 1: Accounting Equation

3–9. Presented below is a list of three accounting elements, followed by partial definitions of those items in scrambled order:

a. Assets   b. Liabilities   c. Equity

1. _____ Debts of the company
2. _____ Probable future economic benefits
3. _____ "Things" of value a company has
4. _____ The residual interest in the assets of an entity that remains after deducting its liabilities
5. _____ Probable future sacrifices of economic benefits
6. _____ What the company owes
7. _____ What the company has less what it owes
8. _____ The owner's interest in the company

REQUIRED:
For each partial definition, identify the element (a, b, or c) to which it refers.

LO 1: Accounting Equation

3–10. Presented below is a list of three accounting elements, followed by list of items in scrambled order:

    a. Assets   **b.** Liabilities   **c.** Equity

  1. _____ Cash
  2. _____ Additional paid-in capital
  3. _____ Bonds payable
  4. _____ Land
  5. _____ Common stock
  6. _____ Retained earnings
  7. _____ Notes payable
  8. _____ Withdrawals
  9. _____ Partners' capital
10. _____ Preferred stock

REQUIRED:
For each item in the list, identify the element (a, b, or c) to which it refers.

LO 1: Balance Sheet Terminology and Format

3–11. Examine the following balance sheet:

KAREN BEAN ENTERPRISES
Balance Sheet
For the Year Ended December 31, 2000

Assets		Liabilities and Owner's Equity	
Land	$120,000	Cash	$ 20,000
Less: Note Payable	20,000	Common Stock, $10 Par Value	40,000
		Additional Paid-in Capital	50,000
		Retained Earnings	10,000
Total Assets	$100,000	Total Liabilities and Owner's Equity	$120,000

REQUIRED:
  a. List the errors in the balance sheet.
  b. Prepare a corrected balance sheet.

LO 1: Balance Sheet Terminology and Format

3–12. Examine the following balance sheet:

L. STALLWORTH, INC.
Balance Sheet
November 31, 1999

Assets		Liabilities and Owner's Equity	
Cash	$50,000	Note Payable	$20,000
Treasury Stock	20,000	Stallworth, Capital, $10 Par Value	40,000
		Retained Earnings	10,000
Total Assets	$70,000	Total Liabilities and Owner's Equity	$70,000

REQUIRED:
  a. List the errors in the balance sheet.
  b. Prepare a corrected balance sheet.

LO 1: Balance Sheet Terminology and Format

3–13. Examine the following balance sheet:

SWEET CORPORATION
Balance Sheet
For the Year Ended December 31, 2000

Assets		Liabilities and Owner's Equity	
Cash	$120,000	Note Payable	$30,000
Sweet Capital	20,000		
Barnes Capital	40,000	Retained Earnings	30,000
Total Assets	$180,000	Total Liabilities and Owner's Equity	$60,000

REQUIRED:

a. List the errors in the balance sheet.
b. Prepare a corrected balance sheet.

LO 2: Financial Position

3–14. The following balance sheet of Gerner Enterprises was compiled shortly after Gerner started his business:

GERNER ENTERPRISES
Balance Sheet
October 1, 1999

Assets		Liabilities and Owner's Equity	
Cash	$100,000	Note Payable—Union Bank	$ 50,000
Land	50,000	Graham Gerner, Capital	100,000
Total Assets	$150,000	Total Liabilities and Equity	$150,000

REQUIRED:

a. Write a description of what Gerner did financially to start his business based on the information provided in the balance sheet.
b. What type of business organization is Gerner Enterprises?

LO 2: Financial Position

3–15. The following balance sheet of Susan Dick and Associates was compiled at the end of its first year of operations:

SUSAN DICK AND ASSOCIATES
Balance Sheet
December 31, 2000

Assets		Liabilities and Owner's Equity	
Cash	$40,000	Note Payable—Central Bank	$10,000
Land	20,000	Susan Dick, Capital	25,000
		Julie Pham, Capital	25,000
Total Assets	$60,000	Total Liabilities and Equity	$60,000

REQUIRED:

a. Write a description of what this balance sheet tells you about the financial position of the company.
b. What type of business organization is Susan Dick and Associates?

c. From the information provided, can you determine how much profit the company made in the first year?

d. From the information provided, can you determine how profits are split?

LO 2: Financial Position

3–16. The balance sheet below was compiled for Quynh Vu Enterprises at the end of its first year of operations:

QUYNH VU ENTERPRISES
Balance Sheet
December 31, 1999

Assets		Liabilities and Stockholder's Equity	
Cash	$120,000	Note Payable—Sooner Bank	$ 20,000
		Common Stock, $10 Par Value	40,000
		Additional Paid-in Capital	50,000
		Retained Earnings	10,000
Total Assets	$120,000	Total Liabilities and Stockholder's Equity	$120,000

REQUIRED:

a. Write a description of what this balance sheet tells you about the financial position of the company.

b. What type of business organization is Quynh Vu Enterprises?

c. From the information provided, can you determine how much profit the company made in its first year?

d. How many stockholders does Quynh Vu Enterprises have?

e. How many shares of stock did Quynh Vu Enterprises sell and what was the selling price?

LO 3: Balance Sheets for Different Types of Business Organizations

3–17. On January 2, 1999, Randy Peoples started an appliance repair business.

REQUIRED:

a. Prepare a balance sheet as of January 2, 1999, assuming Randy's company is a sole proprietorship named Randy Peoples Enterprises and that he invested $5,000 cash in the operation.

b. Now assume that the business organized on January 2, 1999, was a partnership started by Randy and his brother, Sandy, which they have named R&S Enterprises. Randy invested $2,000 and Sandy invested $3,000. Prepare a balance sheet as of January 2, 1999, for the partnership to reflect the partners' investment.

c. Now assume that the business organized on January 2, 1999, was a corporation started by Randy and his brother Sandy, which they have named R&S Enterprises, Inc. Randy invested $2,000 and received 200 shares of common stock. Sandy invested $3,000 and received 300 shares of common stock. The common stock has a par value of $2 per share. Prepare a balance sheet as of January 2, 1999, for the company to reflect the stockholders' investment.

d. Assume the same facts as in requirement c, except that the common stock is no-par stock. Prepare a balance sheet as of January 2, 1999, for the company to reflect the stockholders' investment.

e. Explain why Randy might want to form a partnership rather than a sole proprietorship.

LO 3: Types of Business Organizations

3–18. On June 2, 2000, Arthur Johnson started a manufacturing business.

REQUIRED:
a. Prepare a balance sheet as of June 2, 2000, assuming Arthur's company is a sole proprietorship named Arthur Johnson Enterprises and that he invested $50,000 cash in the operation.
b. Now assume that the business organized on June 2, 2000, was a partnership started by Arthur and his friend Charles Smith, which they have named A&C Enterprises. Arthur invested $50,000 and Charles invested $30,000. Prepare a balance sheet as of June 2, 2000, for the partnership to reflect the partners' investment.
c. Now assume that the business organized on June 2, 2000, was a corporation started by Arthur and his friend Charles, which they have named A&C Enterprises, Inc. Arthur invested $50,000 and received 5,000 shares of common stock. Charles invested $30,000 and received 3,000 shares of common stock. The common stock has a par value of $1 per share. Prepare a balance sheet as of June 2, 2000, for the company to reflect the stockholders' investment.
d. Assume the same facts as in requirement c, except that the common stock is no-par stock. Prepare a balance sheet as of June 2, 2000, for the company to reflect the stockholders' investment.
e. Explain how the balance sheet describes the financial position of the business entity.

LO 3: Types of Business Organizations

3–19. On July 1, 2000, Fred Berfel started a retail business.

REQUIRED:
a. Prepare a balance sheet as of July 1, 2000, assuming Fred's company is a sole proprietorship named Fred Berfel Enterprises and that he invested $90,000 cash in the operation.
b. Now assume that the business organized on July 1, 2000, was a partnership started by Fred and his father Dan, which they have named F&D Enterprises. Fred invested $40,000 and Dan invested $50,000. Prepare a balance sheet as of July 1, 2000, for the partnership to reflect the partners' investment.
c. Now assume that the business organized on July 1, 2000, was a corporation started by Fred and his father Dan, which they have named F&D Enterprises, Inc. Fred invested $40,000 and received 4,000 shares of common stock. Dan invested $50,000 and received 5,000 shares of common stock. The common stock has a par value of $2 per share. Prepare a balance sheet as of July 1, 2000, for the company to reflect the stockholders' investment.
d. Assume the same facts as in requirement c, except that the common stock is no-par stock. Prepare a balance sheet as of July 1, 2000, for the company to reflect the stockholders' investment.
e. Describe the advantages of forming a corporation over a partnership.

LO 3: Types of Business Organizations

3–20. On March 1, 2000, Sandy Sanders started a business.

REQUIRED:

a. Prepare a balance sheet as of March 1, 2000, assuming Sandy's company is a sole proprietorship named Sandy Sanders Enterprises and that he invested $40,000 cash in the operation and a piece of land valued at $5,000.

b. Now assume that the business organized on March 1, 2000, was a partnership started by Sandy and his brother Darryl, which they have named S&D Enterprises. Sandy invested $40,000 cash and a piece of land valued at $10,000, and Darryl invested $30,000 cash. Prepare a balance sheet as of March 1, 2000, for the partnership to reflect the partners' investment.

c. Now assume that the business organized on March 1, 2000, was a corporation started by Sandy and his other brother Darryl, which they have named S&D Enterprises, Inc. Sandy invested $40,000 cash and the piece of land valued at $10,000 and received 5,000 shares of common stock. Darryl invested $30,000 cash and received 3,000 shares of common stock. The common stock has a par value of $1 per share. Prepare a balance sheet as of March 1, 2000, for the company to reflect the stockholders' investment.

d. Assume the same facts as in requirement c, except that the common stock is no-par stock. Prepare a balance sheet as of March 1, 2000, for the company to reflect the stockholders' investment.

e. Describe the advantages of forming a corporation rather than a partnership.

LO 3: Types of Business Organizations

3–21. The chapter discusses the balance sheet presentations for each of the three forms of business organization. Discuss the similarities and differences in the balance sheets of proprietorships, partnerships, and corporations.

LO 4: Terminology of the Corporate Business Form

3–22. Presented below is a list of items relating to the corporate form of business, followed by definitions of those items in scrambled order:

a. Incorporators   f. Board of directors
b. Charter   g. Corporate officers
c. Bylaws   h. Par value
d. Stockholders   i. Additional paid-in capital
e. Stock certificate   i. Market value

1. _____ An arbitrary value placed on either common stock or preferred stock at the time a corporation is formed
2. _____ The group of men and women who have the ultimate responsibility for managing a corporation
3. _____ The owners of a corporation
4. _____ Any amount received by a corporation when it issues stock that is greater than the par value of the stock issued
5. _____ The formal document that legally allows a corporation to begin operations
6. _____ The group of men and women who manage the day-to-day operations of a corporation
7. _____ The person or persons who submit a formal application with the appropriate government agencies to form a corporation
8. _____ A legal document providing evidence of ownership in a corporation
9. _____ Rules established to conduct the business of a corporation
10. _____ The amount at which common stock sells

REQUIRED:

Match the letter next to each item on the list with the appropriate definition. Each letter will be used only once.

LO 4: Terminology of the Corporate Form of Organization

3–23. a. Identify the various officers of a corporation and describe their individual duties.

b. Explain the difference between authorized shares, issued shares, outstanding shares, and treasury stock.

LO 4: Terminology of the Corporate Form of Organization

3–24. The balance sheet of Ramona Rahill, Inc. contains the following information in its equity section:

Stockholders' Equity:

Common Stock, $5 Par Value, 1,000,000 shares authorized, 800,000 shares issued and outstanding	$ 4,000,000
Additional Paid-in Capital	4,800,000
Retained Earnings	2,000,000
Total Stockholders' Equity	$10,800,000

REQUIRED:

a. How many shares of stock could Rahill issue if the board of directors desired to do so?

b. What is the average price at which Rahill sold its stock?

c. If the board of directors declared a $1.25 per share dividend, how much cash would be required to issue the dividend?

d. If Rahill has distributed $3,500,000 to shareholders since its formation, how much profit has the corporation earned since its formation?

LO 4: Terminology of the Corporate Form of Organization

3–25. The following is an excerpt from the equity section of the balance sheet of Juliette Richard Corporation:

Stockholders' Equity:

Common Stock, $10 Par Value, 1,000,000 shares authorized, 800,000 shares issued and 750,000 shares outstanding	$ 8,000,000
Additional Paid-in Capital	8,000,000
Retained Earnings	9,500,000
	$25,500,000
Less: Treasury Stock (at cost)	4,100,000
Total Stockholders' Equity	$21,400,000

REQUIRED:

a. How many shares of stock could Richard Corporation sell if the board of directors desired to do so?

b. What is the average price at which Richard Corporation sold its stock?

c. If the board of directors declared a $2 per share dividend, how much cash would be required to issue the dividend?

d. If Richard has distributed $5,500,000 to shareholders since its formation, how much profit has the corporation earned since its formation?

e. What was the average cost per share of the treasury stock?

f. If the board of directors wished to raise $5,000,000, how much would it have to sell stock for if all available shares were sold?

LO 4: Terminology of the Corporate Form of Organization

3–26. The following is an excerpt from the equity section of the balance sheet of David Luza Corporation:

Stockholders' Equity:

Common Stock, $10 Par Value, 1,000,000 shares authorized and issued, 950,000 shares outstanding	$10,000,000
Additional Paid-in Capital	8,000,000
Retained Earnings	9,500,000
	$27,500,000
Less: Treasury Stock (at cost)	2,500,000
Total Stockholders' Equity	$25,000,000

REQUIRED:

a. How many shares of stock could the corporation sell if the board of directors desired to do so?

b. What is the average price at which the corporation sold its stock?

c. If the board of directors declared a $1.50 per share dividend, how much cash would be required to issue the dividend?

d. If Luza has earned $9,500,000 since its formation, how much profit has the corporation distributed to stockholders in the form of dividends since its formation?

e. What was the average cost per share of the treasury stock?

f. If the current market price of the stock is $60 per share, how much cash could the board of directors raise if it sold all available shares?

LO 5: Differences between Common and Preferred Stock

3–27. A corporation with both preferred stockholders and common stockholders is in the process of liquidating its assets. Identify the group of stockholders who will receive a distribution and explain why.

LO 5: Differences between Common and Preferred Stock

3–28. Assume you have $20,000 to invest and you are trying to decide between investing in the preferred stock of Alpha Company and the common stock of Alpha Company.

REQUIRED:

a. List and briefly explain at least two reasons why you would invest in the preferred stock rather than the common stock of Alpha Company.

b. List and briefly explain at least two reasons why you would invest in the common stock rather than the preferred stock of Alpha Company.

LO 5: Differences between Common and Preferred Stock

3–29. For each characteristic listed below, determine if the characteristic applies to common stock (C), preferred stock (P), both (B), or neither (N).

1. _____ Often has a par value.
2. _____ Must have a par value.
3. _____ Can legally pay a dividend.
4. _____ Pays a pre-established dividend amount.
5. _____ Usually has voting rights.
6. _____ Usually does not have voting rights.
7. _____ Has preference in dividends.

8. _____ Has preference in liquidation.
9. _____ Is preferred by all investors.
10. _____ Represents the residual ownership in the corporation.

LO 5: Differences between Common and Preferred Stock

3–30. Discuss the characteristics of investors who invest in

    a. Common stock
    b. Preferred stock

Include in your discussion willingness to take risk, desire for current income, and desire for capital appreciation in addition to other factors.

LO 5, 6, & 8: Stock Issuances

3–31. Klauss Corporation began operations in 1972 by issuing 20,000 shares of its no-par common stock for $5 per share. The following details provide information about the company's stock in the years since that time.

    1. In 1992, the company issued an additional 50,000 shares of common stock for $15 per share.
    2. Klauss Corporation stock is traded on the New York Stock Exchange (NYSE). During an average year, about 25,000 shares of its common stock are sold by one set of investors to another.
    3. On December 31, 1997, Klauss Corporation common stock was quoted on the NYSE at $38 per share.
    4. On December 31, 1999, Klauss Corporation common stock was quoted on the NYSE at $55 per share.

REQUIRED:

a. Which of the stock transactions described above involved the primary stock market and which ones involved the secondary stock market?
b. How much money has Klauss Corporation received in total from the sales of its common stock since it was incorporated in 1972?
c. When Klauss Corporation prepares its balance sheet as of December 31, 1999, what dollar amount will it show in the owners' equity section for common stock?
d. What, if anything, can you infer about Klauss Corporation's performance during 1999 from the price of its common stock on December 31, 1997, and December 31, 1999?

LO 5, 6, & 8: Stock Issuances

3–32. Shiner Corporation began operations in 1988 by issuing 35,000 shares of its common stock for $10 per share. The following details provide information about the company's stock in the years since that time.

    1. In 1992, the company issued an additional 80,000 shares of common stock for $15 per share.
    2. Shiner Corporation stock is traded on the American Stock Exchange (AMEX). During an average year, about 40,000 shares of its common stock are sold by one set of investors to another.
    3. On December 31, 1998, Shiner Corporation common stock was quoted on the AMEX at $79 per share.
    4. On December 31, 1999, Shiner Corporation common stock was quoted on the AMEX at $45 per share.

REQUIRED:

a. Which of the stock transactions described above involved the primary stock market and which ones involved the secondary stock market?

b. How much money has Shiner Corporation received in total from the sales of its common stock since it was incorporated in 1988?

c. When Shiner Corporation prepares its balance sheet as of December 31, 1999, what dollar amount will it show in the owners' equity section for common stock?

d. What, if anything, can you infer about Shiner Corporation's performance during 1999 from the price of its common stock on December 31, 1998, and December 31, 1999?

LO 5, 6, & 8:   Stock Issuances

3–33. La Forge Corporation began operations in January, 1992, by issuing 90,000 shares of its no-par common stock for $25 per share and 10,000 shares of its $100 par value 6% preferred stock. The following details provide information about the company's stock in the years since that time.

1. In January, 1993, the company issued an additional 50,000 shares of common stock for $35 per share and 5,000 shares of preferred stock for $150 per share.

2. La Forge Corporation stock is traded on the New York Stock Exchange (NYSE). During an average year, about 100,000 shares of its common stock and 6,000 shares of preferred stock are sold by one set of investors to another.

3. On December 31, 1999, La Forge Corporation common stock was quoted on the NYSE at $55 per share. The preferred stock was quoted at $135 per share.

4. On December 31, 2000, La Forge Corporation common stock was quoted on the NYSE at $65 per share. The preferred stock was quoted at $150 per share.

REQUIRED:

a. Which of the stock transactions described above involved the primary stock market and which ones involved the secondary stock market?

b. How much money has La Forge Corporation received in total from the sales of its stock since it was incorporated in 1992?

c. When La Forge Corporation prepares its balance sheet as of December 31, 2000, what dollar amount will it show in the owners' equity section for common stock and for preferred stock?

d. What is the market value of LaForge's stock on December 31, 1999, and December 31, 2000?

e. How much has LaForge Corporation earned in profits since incorporation?

f. How much has LaForge Corporation paid in dividends to common shareholders and preferred shareholders since incorporation?

LO 5, 6, & 8:   Stock Issuances

3–34. Bennett Corporation began operations in 1979 by issuing 40,000 shares of its no-par common stock for $10 per share. The following details provide information about the company's stock in the years since that time.

1. In 1992, the company issued an additional 70,000 shares of common stock for $15 per share.

2. Bennett Corporation stock is traded on the New York Stock Exchange (NYSE). During an average year, about 50,000 shares of its common stock are sold by one set of investors to another.
3. On January 1, 1995, Bennett Corporation repurchased 10,000 shares of common stock at $20 per share.
4. On December 31, 1997, Bennett Corporation common stock was quoted on the NYSE at $56 per share.
5. On December 31, 1998, Bennett Corporation common stock was quoted on the NYSE at $35 per share.

REQUIRED:
a. Which of the stock transactions described above involved the primary stock market and which ones involved the secondary stock market?
b. How much money has Bennett Corporation received in total from the sales of its common stock since it was incorporated in 1979?
c. When Bennett Corporation prepares its balance sheet as of December 31, 1998, what dollar amount will it show in the owners' equity section for common stock?
d. What, if anything, can you infer about Bennett Corporation's performance during 1998 from the price of its common stock on December 31, 1997, and December 31, 1998.

LO 5 & 6:   Stock Issuances

3–35. Gaylord Corporation began operations on July 10, 1999, by issuing 10,000 shares of $5 par value common stock and 2,000 shares of $100 par value preferred stock. The common stock sold for $10 per share and the preferred stock sold for $130 per share.

REQUIRED:
Prepare a balance sheet for Gaylord Corporation at July 10, 1999, immediately after the common stock and preferred stock were issued.

LO 5 & 6:   Stock Issuances

3–36. Sheets Corporation began operations on May 5, 1999, by issuing 150,000 shares of $2 par value common stock and 25,000 shares of $100 par value preferred stock. The common stock sold for $10 per share and the preferred stock sold for $150 per share.

REQUIRED:
Prepare a balance sheet for Sheets Corporation at May 5, 1999, immediately after the common stock and preferred stock were issued.

LO 5 & 6:   Stock Issuance

3–37. Mayes Corporation began operations on April 15, 1999, by issuing 200,000 shares of no-par value common stock and 20,000 shares of $50 par value preferred stock. The common stock sold for $25 per share and the preferred stock sold for $125 per share.

REQUIRED:
Prepare a balance sheet for Mayes Corporation at April 15, 1999, immediately after the common stock and preferred stock were issued.

LO 7:   Balance Sheet Information

3–38. The questions below are based on this selected information from the balance sheet of G. Garretson, Inc.

(Dollars in millions)

	December 31	
	1999	**1998**
Common Stock, $0.60 par value; 900,000,000 shares authorized; issued at Dec. 31: 1999—671,242,137; 1998—669,847,961	$ 403	$ 402
Additional Paid-in Capital	4,418	4,342

REQUIRED:

a. What was the average selling price of the stock that had been issued as of December 31, 1998?
b. The par value of the outstanding shares of common stock as of December 31, 1999, is shown as $403 million, which is actually a rounded amount. What is the exact par value of the common stock outstanding as of that date?
c. How many shares of common stock were issued during 1999?
d. How many shares would Garretson be allowed to issue during 2000?

FINANCIAL REPORTING CASES

Comprehensive

3–39. Look at the Gap's annual report to answer the following questions.

REQUIRED:

a. What types of stock are reported on the balance sheet?
b. For each type of stock listed, identify the number of shares authorized, the number issued, and the number outstanding for each year presented on the balance sheet.
c. Why might the Gap issue preferred stock?
d. Write the accounting equation for the Gap for both years presented in the balance sheet.

Comprehensive

3–40. Go to the PHLIP Web site for this book to find the link to The Pep Boys and answer the following questions.

REQUIRED:

a. What types of stock are reported on the balance sheet?
b. For each type of stock listed, identify the number of shares authorized, the number issued, and the number outstanding for each year presented on the balance sheet.
c. What is the total cost of the shares held in the treasury?
d. Write the accounting equation for The Pep Boys for both years presented in the balance sheet.

Comprehensive

3–41. Go to the PHLIP Web site for this book to find the link to The Buckle and find its annual report information.

REQUIRED:

a. What types of stock are reported on the balance sheet?
b. For each type of stock listed, identify the number of shares authorized, the number issued, and the number outstanding for each year presented on the balance sheet.
c. How much long-term liabilities are reported for each year on the balance sheet?
d. Write the accounting equation for The Buckle for both years presented in the balance sheet.

ANNUAL REPORT PROJECT

You are now ready to complete Section III (Capital Structure) of the Annual Report Project. Section II (SWOT Analysis) of the Annual Report Project will be completed after Chapters 5 and 6.

3–42. Section III contains the following information:

A. List of the total liabilities (be sure you have included all the liabilities both current and long term) and the total stockholders' equity for each year presented in your balance sheet.
B. Comment on how the mix of liabilities and equity relates to or impacts your company. (Hint: Look at the text of the managements' discussion and analysis or read the footnotes for information on how the debt may be used.)
C. List the number of shares of outstanding stock (common and preferred) for each year shown in the report.
D. Does the company have any treasury stock? If so, list the number of shares presented for each year and describe why you think the company acquired it. (Hint: Check the managements' discussion and analysis and read the footnote for capital stock for reasons for acquisition.)
E. List the stock market prices quoted in the annual report.

REQUIRED:
Complete Section III of your project. Turn in one copy to your instructor and retain a clean copy for your final project folder. For group projects, divide the parts equitably among the group members.

Chapter 4

The Balance Sheet (Continued): Additional Financing— Borrowing from Others

Your small business has done very well. It has generated enough income for you and your spouse to finally have your dream home—with an appropriate mortgage. Yesterday, an employee brought you an idea that may revolutionize your product and give you at least a five-year lead on the competition. That is the good news. The bad news is that it will require at least $5,000,000. After checking with the controller, you discover that you have a $210,000 cash reserve. What are the risks involved in this venture? How should you raise the money? Should you borrow from one bank, issue bonds, or issue more common stock? Which costs the least? What should you do?

Businesses often need more funding than is available through investments by their owners. Additional cash to support day-to-day operations or expansion of the business is often acquired through borrowing. Results of borrowing are reflected on a company's balance sheet.

No matter what organizational form companies take (proprietorship, partnership, corporation), or the type of business (service, merchandise, manufacturing), all companies have one thing in common: Each must obtain capital (money) to support operations. In the long run, a company must finance its activities with the profits from its operations. We call this **internal financing.** However, either when starting out or in a time of expansion, almost all companies find it necessary to obtain capital from sources other than the profits, which is **external financing.** ■

The two external sources of capital are equity financing and debt financing. **Equity financing** offers ownership interest in the company in exchange for the needed cash. Most businesses begin their operations using cash invested by the owners. Chapter 3 illustrated the impact of this initial financing on the balance sheets of proprietorships, partnerships, and corporations. In many cases, however, the owners need more cash than they can raise to get the operation started. Almost all companies, at one time or another, need additional funds from outsiders. To obtain these funds, companies can sell more ownership shares or they can borrow funds. Borrowing funds for business operations is **debt financing.**

> *Neither a borrower nor a lender be!*
> —William Shakespeare

Although Shakespeare's advice may serve you well in your personal life, many companies could not survive without borrowing. Borrowing and lending have become an integral part of today's business world. In this chapter, you will learn about several different approaches to debt financing. As you will see, financial institutions function as primary lenders. The bond market also serves as a source of debt financing. Companies borrow funds for various reasons. The need for external funding does not indicate a weakness. On the contrary, a company often needs funds because it is growing even faster than expected.

LEARNING OBJECTIVES

After completing your work on this chapter, you should be able to do the following:

1. Describe how banks earn profits.
2. Explain the effects on a company's balance sheet when funds are borrowed from a bank.
3. Distinguish among notes, mortgages, and bonds.
4. Calculate interest payments for notes and bonds.
5. Explain the functions of underwriters in the process of issuing bonds.
6. Describe the effect of market interest rates on bond selling prices.
7. Contrast the operations of the primary and secondary bond markets.
8. Compare and contrast two investment alternatives—equity investment and debt investment.

The financing requirements of companies fall into two general categories. A company needs short-term financing to run its day-to-day operations and long-term financing to achieve its long-range goals. From a financial market perspective, **short-term financing** is any financing that must be repaid within five years. **Long-term financing** has a repayment period that extends past five years. These definitions do not correspond to the accounting definition of short-term and long-term liabilities, which we will consider in Chapter 10. Several sources provide these two types of financing to businesses.

The commercial banking industry has changed dramatically in the past two decades. Banks used to be hometown businesses that served a small town or neighborhood. Savings and loan associations, credit unions, and thrifts provided a narrow range of services to limited customer groups. Today, the banking industry includes all these types of financial institutions that serve a broad range of customers. Large banking institutions, operating nationally or regionally, have replaced many neighborhood banks. Financial institutions meet the needs of individuals and companies, creating both consumer and commercial borrowing.

consumer borrowing
Loans obtained by individuals to buy homes, cars, or other personal property.

commercial borrowing
The process that businesses go through to obtain financing.

Banks base the classification of a loan on its purpose, not its amount. If the purpose of the loan is personal, to pay for such items as homes, cars, vacations, school tuition, and other personal needs, the loan is classified as **consumer borrowing.** When a company negotiates a loan to finance day-to-day operations or achieve long-term goals, the loan is classified as **commercial borrowing.**

Several distinct types of financial institutions serve consumer and commercial borrowing needs. Some originated to satisfy the need for consumer loans, while others began to meet the financing needs of businesses, though the distinction between consumer lenders and commercial lenders has become somewhat blurred over the past several years.

- *Savings and Loan Associations (S&Ls) and Mutual Savings Banks (MSBs).* Savings and loan associations were formed primarily to lend money for home mortgages. Over time, S&Ls began lending money for other consumer items. In the 1980s, many S&Ls ventured into other lending arrangements, such as real estate speculation, in which many S&Ls lost a great deal of money. Mutual savings banks are somewhat different from S&Ls in that they are owned by their depositors and any profits earned are divided proportionately among those depositors. Like S&Ls, MSBs began as consumer lending institutions (particularly for home mortgages), but over time broadened the focus into other activities. Like S&Ls, many MSBs also experienced financial difficulties in the 1980s.
- *Credit Unions (CUs).* A company, labor union, or professional group typically forms a credit union. A credit union accepts deposits from and lends money to only its members. To become a credit union member, a person must meet a specific set of qualifications such as working for a particular employer or belonging to the organization that formed the credit union. Traditionally, CUs have concentrated on short-term consumer loans (financing cars and stereos, for example) and savings deposits for their members. In recent years, most credit unions have added checking services. Credit unions continue to focus lending activities on members' consumer purchases rather than financing business activities.
- *Commercial Banks.* A commercial bank is what comes to mind when most people think of a bank. As the name implies, commercial banks are heavily involved in commercial lending. In fact, although banks have ventured into the area of consumer lending, these institutions primarily lend to businesses, for commercial purposes. There are roughly 13,000 commercial banks in the United States today. Exhibit 4–1 is a list of the 10 largest.

This book deals primarily with business and how accounting information is used in making business decisions. Therefore, when we refer to "the bank," we mean a commercial bank.

	1997 Revenues (in $ millions)	1997 Profits (in $ millions)
Citicorp	$34,697	$3,591
Chase Manhattan	30,381	3,708
BankAmerica	23,583	3,210
NationsBank	21,735	3,077
J. P. Morgan	17,701	1,465
First Union Corp.	14,329	1,896
Banc One	13,219	1,306
Bankers Trust	12,176	866
First Chicago NBD	10,098	1,525
Wells Fargo	9,608	1,155

How Banks Earn Profits

Think back to our discussion of Roy and his shoe store in Chapter 1. To stay in business, Roy must be profitable. He must sell shoes for enough money to recover what the shoes cost him, plus pay all other expenses associated with running his store. Whatever is left after all those costs have been covered is his profit. A bank is a business also, and to stay in business, a bank must be profitable. The majority of a bank's income comes from the interest paid on loans by borrowers.

interest The cost to the borrower of using someone else's money. Also, what can be earned by lending money to someone else.

Interest represents rent paid to use borrowed money. The bank rents money from its depositors and then in turn rents it out to borrowers. Logic dictates that the rent the bank pays (interest expense) must be less than the rent it receives (interest revenue) if it is to be profitable. For example, you open a savings account at the bank by depositing $100. The bank agrees to pay you five percent (5%) annual interest on the amount you have deposited. If you leave the $100 in the bank for a full year, you will earn $5 interest.

Assume that nine other people did exactly as you did and opened savings accounts at the bank by depositing $100 each. The bank agreed to pay each depositor five percent annual interest on the deposits. The bank now has $1,000 ($100 × 10 depositors), and the interest the bank must pay on this $1,000 is $50 ($5 to each of the 10 depositors).

The bank can now lend the $1,000 to a borrower. Obviously, it must charge something greater than five percent interest on the loan(s) it makes with the $1,000, or it will lose on the exchange. Assume that the bank lends the $1,000 to someone for one year and that person agrees to pay the bank nine percent (9%) annual interest on the loan.

At the end of the year, the person who borrowed the $1,000 repays the loan, plus $90 interest ($1,000 × 9%). After the bank adds $5 to the account of each of the ten depositors, it has earned a gross profit of $40, calculated as follows:

Interest the bank received on the loan	$90
Less the interest paid to the 10 depositors	50
Equals gross profit on the loan	$40

Although this process seems simple enough, there are a number of possible complications. Two complications immediately come to mind.

default Failure to repay a loan as agreed.

1. The person who borrowed the $1,000 may fail to repay the loan. Failure to repay is known as a **default** on the loan.
2. One or more of the 10 depositors may decide to not leave their $100 deposit in the bank for the full year.

Discussion Questions

4-1. In addition to the two complications described in the text, what other factors may complicate the process whereby banks earn their profits by making loans?

4-2. What steps would you suggest to the bank to overcome the two complications listed in the text plus the ones you thought of in your response to Discussion Question 4-1?

By the way, the $40 profit we calculated for the bank on the loan does not constitute the bank's real profit. As was the case with Roy selling a pair of shoes to Martin in Chapter 1, the profit we just calculated represents gross profit (see Exhibit 4–2). All other costs involved in running the bank must be deducted before the net profit (real profit) can be calculated.

Exhibit 4–2
How Banks Earn Profits

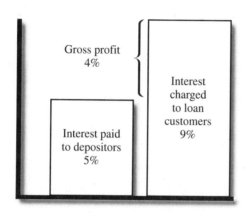

Notes Payable

note payable An agreement between a lender and a borrower that creates a liability for the borrower.

If a company needs to borrow funds for only a short time (usually five years or less), a bank may lend it money and require it to sign a note payable. A **note payable** is a written agreement or debt instrument between a lender and a borrower that creates a liability for the borrower to repay both principal and interest. The judgment of the lending officer and the bank's policies determine the amount of money lent and the term (length) of the loan. Borrowing funds by signing a note payable adds to the assets of the company, but at the same time creates a liability. Building upon the example introduced in the previous chapter, we illustrate the effects of borrowing funds in Exhibit 4–3.

The balance sheet information indicates that the company borrowed $1,000 by signing a note payable. This transaction provided the company with $1,000 additional cash, so total assets rose to $11,000. Because the additional asset amount is claimed by someone external to the business (probably a bank), it counts as a liability. Notice that the business equation still holds true:

$$\text{ASSETS} = \text{LIABILITIES} + \text{OWNERS' EQUITY}$$
$$\$11,000 = \quad \$1,000 \quad + \$10,000$$

promissory note A legal promise to repay a loan.

collateral Something of value that will be forfeited if a borrower fails to make payments as agreed.

A note payable generally requires the signing of a **promissory note,** a legal "promise to repay." In addition, the lender may require the use of collateral to secure the loan. **Collateral** is something of value that is forfeited to the lender if the borrower fails to make payments as agreed. For example, if you borrow money from BankAmerica to buy a new car, the car generally serves as collateral. If you

LAURA CORPORATION
Balance Sheet
January 1, 1999

Assets:		Liabilities:		
		Notes Payable	$1,000	
Cash	$11,000	Total Liabilities		$1,000
		Shareholders' Equity:		
		Common Stock	$2,000	
		Additional Paid-in Capital	8,000	
		Total Shareholders' Equity		10,000
		Total Liabilities and		
Total Assets	$11,000	Shareholders' Equity		$11,000

fail to make the payments, the bank may repossess the car and sell it to get its money back.

By offering collateral, companies may be able to borrow more funds for a greater length of time. This type of larger, longer-term debt that identifies a specific item as collateral is a **mortgage.** For instance, a company can mortgage a piece of property it owns by allowing it to serve as collateral for a loan. In this case, the lender (bank) has the right to seize the property if the borrower defaults.

mortgage A document that states the agreement between a lender and a borrower who has secured the loan by offering something of value as collateral.

The Cost of Borrowing

The difference between what one borrows and what one repays is the cost of borrowing or interest. The cost of borrowing money can be determined using information about the note payable. You should become familiar with the terminology used when funds are borrowed. Here's an example:

> Boston Brothers borrowed $5,000 on January 2, 1999, by signing an eight percent, three-year note. The lender requires annual interest payments to be made on the anniversary of the note.

The rate of interest is always stated as an annual percentage. Therefore, eight percent (8%) refers to the amount of interest the lender requires for a full year, regardless of the loan terms. Interest is based on the amount borrowed, the **principal.** The formula to determine the annual interest amount is:

principal In the case of notes and mortgages, the amount of funds actually borrowed.

$$\text{Principal} \times \text{Rate} = \text{Annual Interest}$$

In our example of the Boston Brothers' note, the amount of interest due each year is calculated as:

$$\text{Principal} \times \text{Rate} = \text{Annual Interest}$$
$$\$5,000 \times .08 = \$400$$

Notice that for purposes of calculations, the percentage rates can be converted to decimals. The note terms require the following schedule of payments:

Date	Interest Payments	Principal Payments	Total Payments
January 1, 2000	$ 400		$ 400
January 1, 2001	400		400
January 1, 2002	400	$5,000	5,400
Totals	$1,200	$5,000	$6,200

Remember that the difference between what is borrowed and what is paid back represents the cost of borrowing:

Amount received from the loan	$5,000	
Amount repaid	6,200	
Cost of borrowing (interest)	$1,200	for the three-year period

The term (length of time between borrowing and repaying) of notes payable varies. If Boston Brothers needed to borrow the funds from the bank for only a short time, the note may have been described as a

$$\text{\$5,000, 8\%, 3-month note}$$

This terminology suggests that the $5,000 must be repaid three months from the day the funds were borrowed. On that day, Boston Brothers would pay the lender the principal ($5,000) and the interest due. Recall that interest rates are stated in annual terms, so eight percent indicates the amount of interest that would be due if the funds were held for one year. If the funds are held for three months, only a portion of the year's interest would be due.

Now we can use a formula that considers the length of time the funds are held:

$$\text{Principal} \times \text{Rate} \times \text{Time} = \text{Interest}$$
$$P \times R \times T = I$$

The calculation to determine the interest owed by the Boston Brothers is:

$$P \times R \times T = I$$
$$\$5,000 \times .08 \times 3/12 = \$100$$

Because the interest rate is annual, the time factor in the calculation is a fraction of the year. If the funds are borrowed for three months, time is represented by 3/12, indicating three of the 12 months in a year. If, however, the note read:

$$\text{\$5,000, 8\%, 90-day note}$$

the time factor represents the number of days involved as a proportion of the number of days in a year. When this method is used, the previous calculation could be presented as:

$$\$5,000 \times .08 \times 90/365 = \$98.63$$

Banks have a choice whether to use 365 days or 360 days (often called the business year). With the advent of personal computers and financial calculators, banks typically use 365 days. When the note specifies months, use the monthly calculation approach. When the note specifies days, use the actual number of days. For example, how many days span the time from December 4 to March 4 in a non–leap year? (Do not count the first day because interest begins on that day.)

December (31 days minus 4 days)	27
January	31
February (non–leap year)	28
March	4
Total days	90

In this case the three-month period equals 90 days. What if we measure March 4 to June 4?

March (31 days minus 4 days)	27
April	30
May	31
June	4
Total days	92

Remember that not all three-month intervals contain the same number of days.

Discussion Questions

4-3. In the example given in the text of the Boston Brothers' three-month loan, what is the lender's return of investment and return on investment?

Note: The next two Discussion Questions require that you go to the business section of your local newspaper and look up current interest rates.

4-4. List the different rates a local bank is paying on various certificates of deposit (CDs). Explain why the bank is offering these various rates.

4-5. What are the current rates banks are charging for mortgages in your area? What are the current credit card rates? Why are there differences between these two rates?

Effective Interest Rate

Lenders write loan terms to conform to the specific needs of the lender or the borrower. Therefore, not all terms are the same for each customer or for all loans made to one customer. Look at the following loan information:

> Boston Brothers deposited $9,000 as the proceeds (cash received) of a $10,000 discounted loan due one year from today.

discounted note A loan arrangement in which the bank deducts the interest from the proceeds of the loan.

The lender deducted the 10 percent interest on the loan in advance. We call this arrangement whereby a bank deducts the full interest in advance a **discounted note.** What are the implications of such an action? Return to our analysis model for the cost of borrowing:

Amount received from the loan	$ 9,000
Amount repaid	10,000
Cost of borrowing (interest)	$ 1,000

We used the following formula to calculate the interest for an annual loan:

$$P \times R = I$$

By rearranging the equation, we can solve for the interest rate (R). The principal of the loan should be considered the amount received in the loan process.

$$R = \frac{I}{P} = \frac{\$1,000}{\$9,000} = 11.11\%$$

effective interest rate The rate of interest actually earned by a lender. This amount will be different from the nominal interest rate if a bond is bought at a discount or premium, or a note is discounted. Also called *yield rate* or *market interest rate.*

As you can see, the **effective interest rate** is not the 10 percent quoted by the bank, but 11.11 percent. The act of discounting the note—deducting the interest from the proceeds—effectively increases the true interest paid on the borrowing. Is the bank lying about the interest? No, because each lender must indicate clearly the true cost of borrowing, the annual percentage rate (APR), on the face of the note. The bank will disclose the true (effective) interest rate of 11.11 percent. The business community understands the implications of a discounted note and the fact that it increases the effective interest rate of the loan.

Interest costs are an important factor in the decision whether or not to borrow funds. Businesspersons in various capacities (CEOs, regional managers, store managers) frequently face financing decisions. We began our discussion of how companies are financed by saying that companies require both short-term financing to run day-to-day operations and long-term financing to achieve long-range

Discussion Questions

4–6. Banks frequently require a borrower to maintain a compensating balance. If the bank agrees to loan a business $100,000 but requires the borrower to keep no less than $30,000 (the compensating balance) in its checking account at all times, how much of the loan can the business utilize? On how much of the loan does the business pay interest? How might this affect the effective interest rate of the loan?

4–7. A credit card company offers to grant you $1,000 of credit at an APR of 21% in a special offer for first-time credit card holders. It also requires that you deposit $500 in a savings account paying 5%, from which you may not make withdrawals as long as there is a balance on the credit card. Comment on the effective interest rate on the credit card assuming that your balance is the full $1,000.

---

goals. The coordination of short-term activities with short-term financing and long-term activities with long-term financing is called *matching maturities.* Good cash management relies on matching maturities to effectively manage the cash inflows and outflows. While the use of collateral may allow a company to secure financing for a longer term, the commercial banks discussed in the previous section are ideally suited to provide short-term financing. According to the Federal Reserve Board, in the last quarter of 1998, the total dollar amount of commercial and industrial loans outstanding from banks was $913.2 billion, most due within five years.

Although no law prevents banks from lending money to companies for long periods of time, a couple of factors may make this type of lending arrangement infeasible for most banks. First, many companies are looking for financing for as long as 40 years, and most banks are not interested in making loans of that duration because the depositors will not commit to leave their deposits for such a long time. Second, and perhaps more importantly, the amount of money required for long-term financing in many large companies is more than a single bank can accommodate. Even very large banks are unwilling or unable to address the borrowing needs of these large companies. For this reason, another source of financing is available for corporations.

BORROWING BY ISSUING BONDS

bond An interest-bearing debt instrument that allows corporations to borrow large amounts of funds for long periods of time and creates a liability for the borrower.

debenture An unsecured bond payable.

A **bond** is a type of note payable, usually a $1,000 interest-bearing debt instrument. The main differences between a bond and a note payable to a bank are the length of time the debt will be outstanding and the amount of money borrowed. Notes payable are usually up to five years in duration and are limited to the amount of money a single lender can lend to one customer. Bonds payable can have a term of 40 years. One type of bond is a **debenture** bond, a bond with no collateral pledged for it. Corporations sell bonds to (borrow money from) many different parties so the total amount borrowed can exceed what one bank could lend.

The Bond Market Association estimates that U.S. corporations will owe $2.348 trillion at the end of 1998 (see Exhibit 4–4). U.S. businesses use bonds as a major source of external financing and typically have millions or billions of dollars in

Exhibit 4–4
Growth of Corporate
Bonds

*Source: The Bond
Market Association*

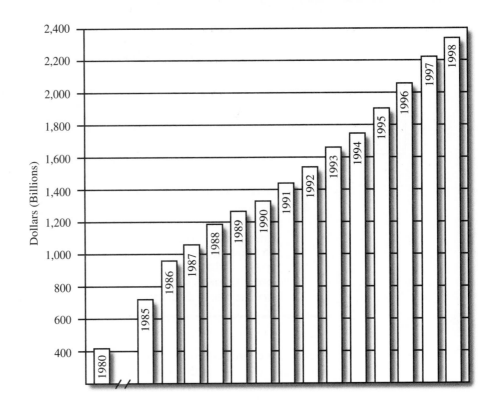

par value (for bonds) The
amount that must be paid back
upon maturity of a bond. Also
called *face value* or *maturity
value.*

nominal interest rate The
interest rate set by the issuers
of bonds, stated as a
percentage of the par value of
the bonds. Also called the
contract rate, coupon rate, or
stated rate.

indenture The legal
agreement made between a
bond issuer and a bondholder
that states repayment terms
and other details.

selling price The amount
received when bonds are
issued or sold. This amount is
affected by the difference
between the nominal interest
rate and the market rate.
Selling price is usually stated
as a percentage of the bond's
par value. Also called the
market price.

long-term debt on their balance sheets. For example, AT&T Corp. had long-term bonds outstanding of $7.67 billion as of December 31, 1997.

Bonds are issued in a set denomination, generally $1,000 for each bond. **Par value** represents the principal of the loan and is also called the *face value* or the *maturity value.* The par value of such bonds is $1,000, indicating that when the borrower pays back the debt, $1,000 will be repaid.

The **nominal interest rate** governs the amount of annual interest paid on a bond and is always a percentage of the par value of the bond. In other words, it is the rate of interest that the issuing company (borrower) has agreed to pay on the face value of the bond. The nominal rate is also called the *contract rate, coupon rate,* or *stated rate,* and these terms are used interchangeably.

The SEC regulates bond issuances. Each bond issue provides information such as the par value and the nominal interest rate in its bond **indenture.** This legal document details the agreement between the company issuing the bonds (the borrower) and the buyers of the bonds (the lenders), including the timing of the interest payments and repayment (retirement) of the bonds.

In contrast to the nominal interest rate, which is set at the time bonds are issued and remains constant, the effective interest rate fluctuates with market conditions. The effective interest rate denotes the actual interest rate that the bondholder will earn over the life of the bond. Unlike the nominal rate, which is determined by the issuing company, the effective rate is determined by the financial markets and may cause a bond to sell for more or less than its par value. The effective rate is also called the *yield rate* or *market interest rate;* these terms are used interchangeably.

The **selling price** is the amount for which a bond actually sells and is also called the *market price.* As we stated, it is determined by the effective or market interest rate. If the effective interest rate and the nominal interest rate are the same, a bond is said to be selling at par or 100, meaning at 100 percent of its face or par value. Bonds may sell for less than par value. For instance, a selling price of 95 means the bond is selling at 95 percent of its par value. This situation occurs when the stated rate is less than the market rate. If you think about it, you will realize why, if you are trying to sell a bond that pays a rate lower than the market rate, you will be forced to lower the price. Only by lowering the price will you attract the investors (buyers) you need.

If Yoko Industries issues one thousand $1,000, 12 percent, 10-year bonds at 95 (to yield 12.92 percent), the bonds sell below par because the market wants a 12.92 percent rate of return on investment and the bonds only pay a 12 percent return on investment.

Bond proceeds (1,000 bonds × $1,000 × .95)		$ 950,000
Amount repaid:		
Maturity value ($1,000 × 1,000)	$1,000,000	
Interest paid ($1,000,000 × 12% × 10 years)	1,200,000	2,200,000
Total cost of borrowing for 10 years		$1,250,000

As you can see, the total cost of borrowing for 10 years exceeds the cash payments for interest. Therefore, the yield rate of interest is higher than the 12 percent nominal rate. Because bonds exceed more than one year of life, the effective rate of interest must be computed using present value techniques, which you will study in future courses.

Bonds may also sell for more than their par value. This happens when a bond's stated rate of interest is more than the market interest rate. A bond with a sale price of 106 is selling for 106 percent of its par value. If Yoko Industries issues one thousand $1,000, 12 percent, 10-year bonds at 104 (to yield 11.31 percent), the bonds sell above par because the market only requires an 11.31 percent rate of return on investment and the bonds will pay a 12 percent cash return on investment.

Bond proceeds (1,000 bonds × $1,000 × 1.04)		$1,040,000
Amount repaid:		
Maturity value ($1,000 × 1,000)	$1,000,000	
Interest paid ($1,000,000 × 12% × 10 years)	1,200,000	2,200,000
Total cost of borrowing for 10 years		$1,160,000

The total cost of borrowing for 10 years is less than the cash interest paid indicating that the bonds yield less than the cash interest paid. The market interest rate required is less than the nominal rate.

Discussion Questions

4–8. If Keri Corporation sells 1,000, 10-year, 9% $1,000 bonds at 98, what are the proceeds of the bond issue?

4–9. Describe the total cost of borrowing over the life of the bonds. What is the annual cash payment for interest? Is the effective interest rate more than 9% or less than 9%? How can you determine this?

4–10. How would your answers to 4-9 change if the bonds sold at 103?

Issuing Bonds Sold at Par

To illustrate the impact of issuing bonds at par value, assume Laura Corporation issued $300,000 worth of 10-year, eight percent bonds on January 1, 1999. From Exhibit 4–3, we know that Laura Corporation sold $10,000 worth of common stock

Exhibit 4–5

Balance Sheet for a Corporation That Has Issued Both Stock and Bonds and Borrowed from a Bank

---

LAURA CORPORATION
Balance Sheet
January 1, 1999

Assets:		Liabilities:		
		Notes Payable	$ 1,000	
		Bonds Payable	300,000	
Cash	$311,000	Total Liabilities		$301,000
		Shareholders' Equity:		
		Common Stock	$ 2,000	
		Additional Paid-in Capital	8,000	
		Total Shareholders' Equity		10,000
		Total Liabilities and		
Total Assets	$311,000	Shareholders' Equity		$311,000

---

and borrowed $1,000 from the bank. Exhibit 4–5 shows results of all three of these activities.

On January 1, 1999 (the day the bonds were sold), Laura Corporation records the sale of the bonds. Assets (cash) increase by $300,000, and liabilities (bonds payable) increase by the same amount. The business equation remains in balance:

ASSETS = LIABILITIES + OWNERS' EQUITY
$311,000 = $301,000 + $10,000

As stated earlier, most bonds are issued in denominations of $1,000; Laura sold 300 of these $1,000 bonds, agreeing to pay eight percent of the par value per year in interest. Therefore, the nominal rate on the bonds is eight percent. If other opportunities for investors offer eight percent per year for using their money, the market interest rate is said to be eight percent. When the market interest rate and the nominal interest rate are the same, investors are generally indifferent between buying the bonds and choosing other investment opportunities. This indifference results in these bonds being sold at par or 100, meaning 100 percent of their par value.

Interest payments on corporate bonds are generally paid semiannually (twice each year). In the case of Laura Corporation, interest will be paid each June 30 and December 31. As we did for the examples of notes payable, we can calculate the annual interest due on the corporate bonds issued by Laura Corporation:

$300,000 × .08 = $24,000

This indicates that $24,000 is the annual interest the corporation owes to its bondholders. If interest payments are made every six months, Laura Corporation will send a total of $12,000 to its bondholders on each interest payment date. The semiannual interest payments are to be made throughout the 10-year life of the bonds. At the end of 10 years, Laura Corporation must pay back the principal amount borrowed, $300,000. For Laura Corporation, the cost of borrowing is calculated as follows:

Bond proceeds (300 bonds × $1,000 × 1.00)		$300,000
Amount repaid:		
Maturity value ($1,000 × 300)	$300,000	
Interest paid ($300,000 × 8% × 10 years)	240,000	540,000
Total cost of borrowing for 10 years		$240,000

In this case, the cost of borrowing equals the interest paid because the bonds sold at par.

Corporate bonds, as we noted earlier, were developed to accommodate companies' long-term financing needs. Bonds also facilitate borrowing larger sums of money than any single lender is either willing or able to handle. If businesses are to have access to large sums of money, there must be some mechanism for bringing together companies that want to issue bonds and investors who are interested in buying them. That mechanism is the bond market, and it is similar to the stock market.

Initial Offerings—The Primary Bond Market

Like stocks, there is both a primary and a secondary bond market. The initial sale of bonds by the issuing corporation occurs in the primary bond market. Most corporations do not attempt to handle the details of the actual sale of their bonds to individual investors. For this reason, most corporations with large bond offerings hire an intermediary investment banker, or a group of such bankers called a **syndicate**, to sell large bond offerings to the public. The bankers, serving as underwriters, buy all the bonds available in the offering and then resell them to interested investors at a higher price. The underwriters' basic fee is known as the spread—the difference between the price paid to the issuer and the price at which securities are sold to the public. Underwriters typically charge a fee of one percent of the total amount of bonds issued.

syndicate   A group of underwriters working together to get a large bond issue sold to the public.

Underwriting is a primary source of income for investment banking firms. Exhibit 4–6 contains a list of the major underwriters. Many of the firms' names are probably familiar to you.

Exhibit 4–6
Top Global Underwriters of Debt and Equity (in $billions for 1997)

Source: Securities Data Company, Inc.

	Amount Underwritten	1997 Market Share
Merrill Lynch & Co., Inc.	$208.1	16.1%
Salomon Smith Barney	167.0	12.9%
Morgan Stanley Dean Witter	139.5	10.8%
Goldman, Sachs & Co.	137.3	10.6%
Lehman Brothers Inc.	121.0	9.4%
J. P. Morgan & Co. Inc.	104.0	8.0%
Credit Suisse First Boston	67.7	5.2%
Bear, Stearns & Co. Inc.	57.5	4.4%
Donaldson, Lufkin & Jenrette	46.0	3.6%
Chase Manhattan Corporation	33.1	2.6%
Top 10	$1081.3	83.6%
Industry total	$1293.0	83.6%

The underwriter assists the corporation in completing all the necessary steps for a successful bond issue. One of the most important steps in the process is preparing the prospectus. The **prospectus** provides important information to prospective buyers of the bonds, including information about the issuing corporation and about the bond issue itself. The preliminary prospectus is just one of the documents that must be filed with the Securities and Exchange Commission. It contains no selling price

prospectus   A description of an upcoming bond issue that is provided as information for potential investors.

Corporations issue bond certificates to their bondholders just as they issue stock certificated to their stockholders. The bond certificate serves as evidence of the investment made by those who purchase the bonds. a bond certificate looks very much like the stock certificate in Chapter 3.
Four by Five, Inc.

information and no offering date. While the SEC is reviewing the documents filed by the corporation, no sale of the bonds may take place.

The final selling price results from the negotiations between the underwriter and the corporation and is determined at the very last minute, often just one day prior to offering the bonds for sale. A crucial meeting takes place after the SEC grants approval to the corporation to issue the bonds, at which the corporate officials and the underwriter settle the selling price of the bonds to the underwriter. Investors in the open market determine how much they are willing to pay for the bonds based upon their calculations of the present value of the bonds at their desired rate of return. Bond selling prices are stated in relation to their par value. That is, if a bond sells below its par value, it is said to be selling at a **discount.** Bonds with prices above par value are said to be selling at a **premium.** Most underwriters hope to be able to sell bonds for par value or at only a slight discount. Psychologically, it is easier to sell a bond that is priced at or below par value than it is to sell one at a premium. For this reason, new issues are rarely sold at a premium.

When the bonds are ready to be sold to the public, the underwriter makes a bond offering, which is similar to the stock offering discussed in Chapter 3. The offering is announced in business publications, such as *The Wall Street Journal*, and in major newspapers across the country. The announcement includes information about the number of bonds being offered, the denomination of each bond, the interest rate being offered, the term of the bonds, and other features of the bonds. If the underwriter has negotiated well, investors will buy all the bonds within a few days, and the risk originally taken by the underwriter will be quickly eliminated. At that point, the agreement is between the issuing corporation and the investors. Any subsequent trades are part of the secondary bond market.

discount   If a bond's selling price is below its par value, the bond is being sold at a discount.

premium   If a bond's selling price is above its par value, the bond is being sold at a premium.

Interest Rates and the Secondary Bond Market

Once the bonds have been issued, those who purchased them are free to sell the bonds to other investors. After a company initially sells its bonds, it receives no money when those bonds are resold. It needs to be notified, of course, when the bonds pass from one investor to another, because it must know to whom it should send the interest payments and who should receive the repayment amount when the bonds are retired (repaid).

During the life of a bond (20, 30, or 40 years), the investment may be traded many times. Remember that the corporation fixed the coupon rate or interest rate prior to the original sale of the bonds. However, the market rate of interest—what investors expect as a return on their investments—fluctuates considerably. For this reason, during the life of a bond, its price on the secondary market may fluctuate considerably as well.

Market pressure and competing opportunities for investors affect the price of a bond selling in the secondary bond market. Remember that the interest payment made by the corporation is the coupon rate, and is unaffected by the current selling price of the bond.

Business publications offer daily information about bonds traded in the secondary market. In the first column, we find the stated interest rate and year of maturity. The current yield indicates the effective interest rate. The third column is the volume of trading. Notice how each bond's price at the end of the business day (close) determines whether the current yield is above or below the stated interest rate, because the price is above or below 100. When a bond sells at 100, its stated rate is equal to its current yield. When a bond sells below 100, its stated rate is below the desired market rate. The net change column indicates the change in price from the previous day.

Bonds	Cur Yld	Vol	Close	Net Chg.
NCNB 8⅜99	8.4	4	99⅝	...
NJBTI 7¼11	8.2	5	88⅜	...
NMed 12⅛95	12.1	50	100⁹⁄₃₂	−¹⁄₁₆
Navstr 9s04	9.6	22	94	+1
NETelTel 6⅜08	7.9	5	81	−1½
NETelTel 8⅝01	8.5	32	102	−1¼
NETelTel 6¼97	6.6	10	94½	−1
NYTel 3⅜96	3.6	5	94½	+⅛
NYTel 4⅞06	6.6	8	73½	+¼
NYTel 7¾06	8.3	5	93¾	...
NYTel 7⅜11	8.4	3	88¼	+⅛
NYTel 7⅞17	8.7	19	90¾	−1
NYTel 6½00	7.4	10	87⅞	+⅞
NYTel 7¼24	8.5	20	85⅜	

Discussion Question

4-11. If you wish to earn 10% on a bond investment, does it matter whether you buy a bond at a discount price or a bond at a premium price if the yield is 10%? Explain your answer.

The bond market receives much less attention from the media than the stock market. Nevertheless, it plays a significant role in the way corporations finance their long-term capital needs. As Exhibit 4–7 shows, businesses use both internal and external financing to support their operations. The two types of external financing provide investment opportunities for those with excess funds. From an investor's point of view, the stock market and the bond market offer two distinctly different types of investment that we can compare.

Exhibit 4–7
Financing a Business

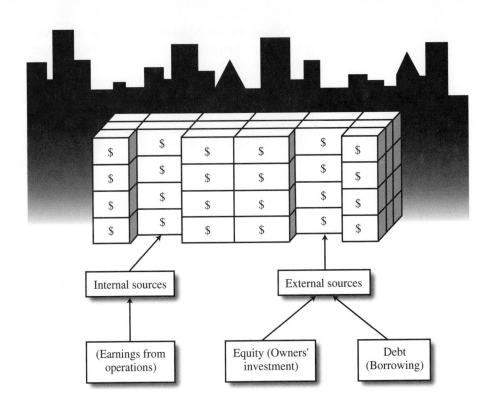

EQUITY AND DEBT INVESTMENTS COMPARED

We presented equity and debt financing in this and the preceding chapter from the standpoint of the company receiving the proceeds from the sale of stocks and bonds. We will now look at the same subject from the standpoint of the investor. Consider the following:

> Charlene's Aunt Tillie recently passed away and left Charlene $1,000,000. After all the inheritance taxes were paid, Charlene received $750,000. Upon mature reflection, she decides to blow $250,000 on cars, world cruises, and other such extravagant items. She plans to invest the remaining $500,000 on January 2, 2000, and has narrowed the list of possible investments to the following two. Both alternatives involve Weatherman Corporation, a large company with an impressive track record over the past 35 years.

- Charlene can purchase shares of Weatherman's no-par common stock. On January 2, 2000, the stock will be selling for about $50 per share, so Charlene would be able to purchase 10,000 shares. Weatherman has a million shares of common stock outstanding, so Charlene would own only one percent of the company.
- Charlene can purchase 500 of Weatherman's $1,000, five-year, eight percent bonds. Weatherman pays interest semiannually on June 30 and December 31. The bonds will be issued on January 2, 2000, and will mature on December 31, 2004. The first interest payment will be made on June 30, 2000.

Does it make more sense for Charlene to buy stock in Weatherman (equity investment) or to buy the company's corporate bonds (debt investment)? Before we can decide that question, we need to ask how the two investment alternatives answer the three questions that should be posed by all economic decision makers:

1. Will I be paid?
2. When will I be paid?
3. How much will I be paid?

Remember that inherent in these three questions is a consideration of return on the investment and return of the investment.

Equity Investments

Question 1: Will Charlene Be Paid?   There is no way to answer this question with absolute certainty; it is dependent on how Weatherman performs in the future. If it is a solid company with a good market for its products and/or services, if the economy is (and stays) strong, and if the industry is (and stays) healthy, she will probably receive both a return on and a return of her investment. Charlene should be aware, however, that with only a one percent ownership interest, she will be able to exert little influence on how the company is run.

Question 2: When Will Charlene Be Paid?   We cannot answer this question with absolute certainty either. Payment on a stock investment is of two types. First, Charlene may receive a periodic dividend on each share of stock she owns. Remember, however, that corporations are not required to pay dividends. Weatherman may or may not pay dividends to its stockholders. Second, Charlene can sell her stock in the secondary stock market, if other investors are willing to buy Weatherman common stock. In any event, the company itself is under no obligation to return Charlene's $500,000. She has contributed that amount to the company and must find some third party to buy her shares if she desires to sell them.

Question 3: How Much Will Charlene Be Paid?   Like the first two questions, this one cannot be answered with absolute certainty. To answer it at all, we need to explain the two components of return on investment for an equity investment.

a. *Dividends.* The dividend component is easy to understand. Charlene pays $50 for each of the 10,000 shares she buys. If Weatherman currently pays an annual dividend of $1.50 per share, and has a stable earnings record, Charlene anticipates receiving $15,000 (10,000 shares × $1.50) per year. This constitutes a part of the return on her $500,000 investment.

b. *Stock Appreciation.* In most instances, stock appreciation represents the greater part of return on investment. If Weatherman performs well in the future, the price of each share of its common stock will go up in the secondary stock market. The stock appreciates in value because as the company posts profits, more and more investors will desire to own shares of its stock. They will, in effect, bid up the price. For example, suppose Weatherman posts record profits and the stock's price rises to $125 per share. If Charlene sells her 10,000 shares, she will have earned a return on investment of $75 per share, or a total of $750,000, calculated as follows:

	Per Share	Total
What Charlene sold the stock for	$125	$1,250,000
What Charlene paid for the stock	50	500,000
Charlene's return on investment	$ 75	$ 750,000

Note that when Charlene sold the stock, she received not only a return on her investment, but also a return of her investment. Also note that we talked about "stock appreciation" and "sale" as if they had already happened. But as Charlene ponders whether or not to buy Weatherman's common stock, she has no way of knowing for sure whether the corporation will perform well enough to drive the stock price to the level we used (or even whether the company will be profitable at all). Charlene also faces the risk that the stock price could fall below the current $50 per share.

In the final analysis, the equity investment alternative yields rather vague answers to the three questions. Now let us see how the debt investment alternative answers the same three questions.

Debt Investments

Question 1: Will Charlene Be Paid?
The answer to this first question is essentially the same for the debt investment alternative as it was for the equity investment alternative. That is, it is dependent on how Weatherman performs in the future. Again, if it is a solid company with a good market for its products and/or services, if the economy is (and stays) strong, and if the industry is (and stays) healthy, Charlene will probably receive both a return on and a return of her investment.

As a creditor of the company rather than a stockholder, Charlene will have absolutely no voice in how Weatherman conducts its business, as long as it makes the periodic interest payments on the bonds and accumulates a sufficient amount of cash to retire the bonds when they mature.

Charlene must also consider that by law the investors who purchase the bonds will be paid the periodic interest *before* any dividends are paid to the investors who purchase the shares of common stock.

Question 2: When Will Charlene Be Paid?
Assuming Weatherman performs well enough to make the interest payments on the bonds and retire them upon maturity, the answer to this question of when Charlene will be paid is absolutely certain. Charlene will be paid interest every June 30 and December 31 throughout the life of the bonds. On December 31, 2004, in addition to the final interest payment, Charlene will receive her initial investment back.

Question 3: How Much Will Charlene Be Paid?
The answer to this question, too, is absolutely certain assuming Weatherman performs well enough to meet the financial obligations created by issuing the bonds. Over the life of the bonds, Charlene will earn a return on her investment of $200,000 ($20,000 $\times$ 10 semiannual interest payments). On December 31, 2004, she will receive $500,000, which represents the return of her investment.

In the final analysis, if Charlene satisfies herself as to Question 1, the answers to the last two questions are very certain for the debt investment alternative.

Which Is Better, Equity Investment or Debt Investment?

Take a few minutes to ponder the way the two investment alternatives answered the three questions. If you were advising Charlene, which investment would you suggest she make? If you were the one with the $500,000 to invest, which alternative would you choose?

On the surface, it appears to be no contest. Although the answer to Question 1 was essentially the same for both alternatives, the debt investment alternative is much more certain in its answers to Questions 2 and 3 than is the equity investment alternative. So why would Charlene (or anyone, for that matter) even consider the equity investment as an alternative? The one-word answer to that question is POTENTIAL!

Although risk is associated with any investment, equity investments are inherently riskier than debt investments. With the additional risk, however, comes the potential for greater reward.

Assume that the following events happen during the five-year period of Charlene's two investment alternatives in Weatherman Corporation. The company earns net income each year of $10 million for the next five years. If Charlene chooses the bond alternative, she will receive $20,000 interest every six months for five years and then will receive her $500,000 back. But what if Weatherman's net income turns out to be $100 million each year for the next five years, or even $1 billion each year? How will that affect Charlene's return if she purchases the bonds? The answer is that it does not matter how profitable Weatherman is, Charlene will only receive $20,000 every six months, plus the return of her $500,000 when the bonds mature after five years.

If Charlene chooses to buy the 10,000 shares of stock, however, the return on her $500,000 investment will be very different if Weatherman earns $1 billion profit each year than if the company earns $10 million or $100 million each year. For one thing, the more profitable the company is, the higher its dividends are likely to be. For another, the market price of Weatherman's stock in the stock market will almost certainly increase as the company's profits increase, thereby increasing Charlene's return. In other words, the potential associated with the equity investment alternative is theoretically unlimited.

Whether a person chooses an equity investment or a debt investment depends on how that person feels about the trade-off between the amount of risk involved and the potential reward. The real key to evaluating any investment alternative is reducing the uncertainty surrounding the question: Will I be paid? In attempting to predict an alternative's future cash flow potential, economic decision makers must consider the past performance and present condition of that alternative. Most big-name public companies have issued both debt and equity—they need both sources of funds to grow and prosper. But a few are so successful that they can grow rapidly without any debt financing. One example is Microsoft, the big software developer. Between 1992 and 1998, the company's sales rose from $2.8 billion to $14.5 billion. Its long-term debt is $0.

In Chapters 3 and 4 we introduced you to the balance sheet, a financial tool that provides information about the present condition of a company. Chapter 5 will introduce you to two additional financial tools—the income statement and the statement of owners' equity.

SUMMARY

Companies often need more funds than they can get from their owners. The other major source of external financing is debt financing, or borrowing. Banks earn their profits by charging borrowers interest. Therefore, at agreed-upon intervals or when the loan is repaid, the company will pay interest in addition to the original amount borrowed.

If a company makes a bank loan, it incurs a liability—commonly called notes payable—and it receives cash. Loans from commercial banks usually meet companies' needs for short-term financing (five years or less).

A company may be required to provide collateral for its loan. If a particular asset is identified as collateral in the loan agreement, the note is generally referred to as a mortgage. Bank loans are generally suitable only for short-term financing; if a company needs long-term financing (up to 40 years or more), the alternative is to issue bonds. Bonds are similar to notes payable in that (1) both are liabilities and (2) both require repayment of the borrowed amount plus interest. Bonds are issued in set denominations, generally $1,000, and are sold to many different investors. Corporations can issue bonds for very large amounts.

Regardless of the type of borrowing involved, the amount of interest being charged can be calculated using the formula Principal × Rate × Time = Interest. In this calculation, *principal* refers to the amount owed, *rate* refers to the annual interest rate, and *time* reflects how much of the year is being considered in this particular borrowing situation.

Most corporations do not have the expertise necessary to tend to all the details involved in issuing bonds. Documents must be filed with regulatory agencies, and the actual transactions of issuing bonds to a large number of investors may be quite involved. For this reason, corporations usually use underwriters, or investment bankers, who for a fee assist the corporation to prepare the bond issue. The underwriters assume all the risk of the debt issuance by buying the entire bond issue. They then immediately resell the bonds to individual investors.

The face value or par value of a bond is the principal amount that must be repaid (generally in denominations of $1,000). If a bond is said to be selling at par, it is sold for $1,000. To entice investors, bond issuers usually have to sell their bonds at a discount (below par value) when the market rate of interest is higher than the rate paid on the bond.

The buying and selling of bonds is the focus of the bond market. Like the stock market, the bond market consists of activity in both a primary and secondary market. The activity of the primary bond market is centered around the initial issuance of corporate bonds. In the secondary bond market, the debt investments are traded. If the market rate of interest is lower than the nominal rate, investors will pay a premium (a sale price above par value) for the bonds. Conversely, if the market rate of interest (the return available to investors through other investments) is higher than the rate paid by a bond, that bond will sell below its par value (at a discount).

Activity in the bond market is similar to activity in the stock market, even though these two markets represent the activity of investors with regard to two different investment alternatives. Investors may purchase bonds (make a debt investment) or purchase stock (make an equity investment). Each type of investment has its own advantages and disadvantages. Debt investment and equity investment were compared in light of the three questions asked by economic decision makers:

1. Will I be paid?
2. When will I be paid?
3. How much will I be paid?

KEY TERMS

bond F-117	discounted note F-116
collateral F-113	effective interest rate F-116
commercial borrowing F-111	equity financing F-110
consumer borrowing F-111	external financing F-110
debt financing F-110	indenture F-118
debenture F-117	interest F-112
default 000	internal financing F-110
discount F-122	long-term financing F-110

REVIEW THE FACTS

A. Explain the difference between internal and external financing.

B. What are the two major sources of external financing?

C. Contrast consumer borrowing and commercial borrowing.

D. What are the three major types of financial institutions providing financing in the United States today?

E. What is interest?

F. Describe the effects of borrowing on the balance sheet of a business.

G. Explain the formula used to determine the amount of interest owed for a particular time period.

H. What is collateral? How can it help a borrower?

I. What is a mortgage, and how is it different from a note payable?

J. Why are bonds sometimes necessary to meet the borrowing needs of businesses?

K. Explain the terms *par value* and *stated rate* as they pertain to bonds.

L. How do the nominal rate and the market rate of bonds differ?

M. What is the relationship between the selling price of a bond and its face value?

N. What is the primary function of underwriters?

O. Explain what causes a bond to sell for either a premium or a discount.

P. How do the primary and secondary bond markets differ?

Q. Explain the calculation used to determine the annual effective interest rate earned by an investor.

R. On what basis do investors choose between equity investments and debt investments?

APPLY WHAT YOU HAVE LEARNED

LO 1:   Effect of Interest on Banks

4–12. a. Explain in your own words how banks make a profit when you borrow money to buy a new car.

b. Distinguish between consumer lending and borrowing and commercial lending and borrowing.

LO 1:   Comparison of Financial Institutions

4–13. Compare and contrast savings and loan associations, mutual banks, credit unions, and commercial banks.

LO 1:   Effect of Interest on Banks

4–14. Bill Walters decided to buy a new boat. The boat will cost $15,000 and Bill plans to borrow 80% of the purchase price from his bank.

a. If the bank charges Bill 9% interest, how much interest will the bank earn in the first year of the loan?

b. If Bill makes a $2,000 principal payment at the end of year one and the bank continues to charge 9% interest, how much interest will the bank earn for the second year of the loan?

LO 1: Effect of Interest On Banks

4–15. Ted Bandy decided to buy a new car to be used in his business. The car will cost $20,000 and Ted plans to borrow 70% of the purchase price from his bank.

a. If the bank charges Ted 10% interest, how much interest will the bank earn in the first year of the loan?

b. If Ted makes a $3,000 principal payment at the end of year one and the bank continues to charge 10% interest, how much interest will the bank earn for the second year of the loan?

LO 1: Effect of Interest on Banks and the Borrower

4–16. Susan Ryan decided to buy a new computer to be used in her business. The computer will cost $10,000 and Susan plans to borrow 75% of the purchase price from her bank.

a. If the bank charges Susan 12% interest, how much interest will the bank earn in the first year of the loan?

b. If Susan makes a $2,000 principal payment at the end of year one and the bank continues to charge 12% interest, how much interest will the bank earn for the second year of the loan?

c. If Susan makes a $4,000 principal payment at the end of year one, how much interest will she save in year two?

LO 2: Effect of Borrowing on the Balance Sheet

4–17. Fred and Ethel formed F&E Enterprises, Inc. on January 2, 1999. Fred invested $20,000 and received 2,000 shares of common stock. Ethel invested $10,000 and received 1,000 shares of common stock. The common stock has a par value of $5 per share. A balance sheet prepared immediately after the corporation was formed was as follows:

F&E ENTERPRISES, INC.
Balance Sheet
January 2, 1999

Assets:		Liabilities:	$ -0-
Cash	$30,000	Stockholders' Equity:	
		Common Stock	$15,000
		Additional Paid-in Capital	15,000
		Total Stockholders' Equity	$30,000
		Total Liabilities and	
Total Assets	$30,000	Stockholders' Equity	$30,000

On January 3, 1999, F&E Enterprises borrowed $20,000 from the 2nd National Bank by signing a one-year, 8% note. The principal and interest on the note must be paid to the bank on January 2, 2000.

REQUIRED:

a. Prepare a balance sheet for F&E Enterprises, Inc. at January 3, 1999, to reflect the $20,000 note payable.

b. Calculate the amount of interest F&E Enterprises must pay on January 2, 2000.

c. Think about the three questions all economic decision makers are trying to answer (Will I be paid? When? How much?). Assuming 2nd National Bank has satisfied itself as to the first question, how would the bank answer the second and third questions regarding the loan to F&E?

LO 2: Effect of Borrowing on the Balance Sheet

4–18. Assume the same facts as in the preceding application question, except that the note is for three months rather than one year, so it must be repaid on April 2, 1999.

REQUIRED:

a. Prepare a balance sheet for F&E Enterprises, Inc. at January 3, 1999, to reflect the $20,000 note payable.

b. Calculate the amount of interest F&E Enterprises must pay on April 2, 1999.

c. If the note were for 90 days instead of three months, what would be the due date? How much interest would be due the bank on the due date?

d. Think about the three questions all economic decision makers are trying to answer (Will I be paid? When? How much?). Assuming 2nd National Bank has satisfied itself as to the first question, how would the bank answer the second and third questions regarding the loan to F&E?

LO 2: Effect of Borrowing on the Balance Sheet

4–19. Refer to the opening balance sheet of F&E Enterprises in application problem 4–17.

On January 3, 1999, F&E Enterprises sold 100 of its $1,000, five-year, 10% bonds. Interest is to be paid semiannually on July 2 and January 2. The bonds mature (must be repaid) on January 2, 2004.

REQUIRED:

a. Prepare a balance sheet for F&E Enterprises, Inc. at January 3, 1999, to reflect the sale of the bonds, assuming they sold at their par value.

b. Calculate the amount of interest F&E must pay each July 2 and January 2.

c. How much would F&E Enterprises, Inc. have received from the sale of the bonds on January 3, 1999, assuming they sold at 98 (a discount)?

d. How much would F&E Enterprises, Inc. have received from the sale of the bonds on January 3, 1999, assuming they sold at 103 (a premium)?

LO 3: Terminology

4–20. Presented below are some items related to notes payable and bonds payable, followed by definitions of those items in scrambled order.

a. Interest	**f.** Premium
b. Nominal interest rate	**g.** Principal
c. Effective interest rate	**h.** Defaulting
d. Maturity value	**i.** Note payable
e. Discount	**j.** Bonds payable

1. _____ The amount above par value for which a bond is sold
2. _____ The amount of funds actually borrowed
3. _____ The rate of interest actually earned by a bondholder
4. _____ Failing to repay a loan as agreed

5. _____ Liabilities that allow corporations to borrow large amounts of money for long periods of time
6. _____ The cost of using someone else's money
7. _____ The amount below par value for which a bond is sold
8. _____ An agreement between a lender (usually a bank) and borrower that creates a liability for the borrower
9. _____ The interest rate set by the issuers of bonds, stated as a percentage of the par value of the bonds
10. _____ The amount that is payable at the end of a borrowing arrangement

REQUIRED:

Match the letter next to each item on the list with the appropriate definition. Each letter will be used only once.

LO 3: Bonds vs. Notes

4–21. The two main instruments of debt financing are bonds and notes. Explain under what circumstances each instrument is generally used.

LO 3: Terminology

4–22. Presented below are two definitions of items related to interest on bonds payable, followed by a list of terms used to describe bond interest.

a. The rate of interest actually earned by the bondholder
b. The interest rate set by the issuer of the bond, stated as a percentage of the par value of the bond

1. _____ Nominal interest rate
2. _____ Effective interest rate
3. _____ Stated interest rate
4. _____ Coupon rate
5. _____ The interest rate printed on the actual bond
6. _____ Market interest rate
7. _____ Contract rate
8. _____ Yield rate

REQUIRED:

For each of the eight items above, indicate to which definition (a or b) it refers.

LO 3: Notes vs. Bonds

4–23. Miller Company needs to borrow funds to modernize their plant facility. Miller decided to issue $50 million worth of 30-year bonds in the primary bond market. Explain why Miller Company would rather issue bonds than borrow money at the bank.

LO 3 & 4: Due Dates

4–24. The Weaver Company borrowed $20,000 at the bank. The note was a 90-day, 8% note. Calculate the due date of the note assuming the note was signed on the following dates:

a. March 3
b. April 20
c. July 19
d. October 5

LO 3 & 4:   Due Dates

4–25. The Schwartz Company borrowed $8,000 at the bank. The note was a 120-day, 7% note. Calculate the due date of the note assuming the note was signed on the following dates:

    a. March 7   **c.** May 5

    b. April 19   **d.** August 10

LO 3 & 4:   Due Dates

4–26. The Davis Company borrowed $5,000 at the bank. The note was a 60-day, 7% note. Calculate the due date of the note assuming the note was signed on the following dates:

    a. April 3   **c.** June 5

    b. May 19   **d.** July 10

LO 3 & 4:   Computation of Effective Interest Rates

4–27. The Commerce Bank discounted a $20,000 loan to the Gaily Company for a period of 120 days. The loan was signed on April 25. Answer the following questions.

    a. What is the due date of the loan?

    b. What is the total of the loan proceeds the bank should receive as repayment?

    c. Compute the effective interest rate for the bank.

LO 3 & 4:   Computation of Effective Interest Rates

4–28. The Commerce Bank discounted a $20,000, 10% loan to the Gaily Company for a period of 120 days. The loan was signed on April 25. Answer the following questions.

    a. What is the due date of the loan?

    b. What is the net amount of loan proceeds that Gaily will deposit to its account?

    c. What is the total amount the bank should receive as repayment?

    d. Compute the effective interest rate for the bank.

LO 3 & 4:   Computation of Effective Interest Rates

4–29. The Union Bank discounted a $50,000, 8% loan to the Irvin Company for a period of 90 days. The loan was signed on May 5. Answer the following questions.

    a. What is the due date of the loan?

    b. What is the net amount of loan proceeds that Irvin will deposit to its account?

    c. What is the total amount the bank should receive as repayment?

    d. Compute the effective interest rate for the bank.

LO 3 & 4:   Computation of Effective Interest Rates

4–30. The Hennings Bank discounted a $10,000, 12% loan to the Lett Company for a period of 180 days. The loan was signed on March 19. Answer the following questions.

    a. What is the due date of the loan?

    b. What is the net amount of loan proceeds that Hennings will deposit to its account?

c. What is the total amount the bank should receive as repayment?

d. Compute the effective interest rate for the bank.

LO 4: Return on Investment

4–31. Assume that a company sells 6,500 five-year, $1,000 bonds paying 8% interest at 96.

REQUIRED:

a. How much cash will the company selling the bonds receive from the sale?

b. How much total cash will the bond buyers receive each year as interest?

c. Determine the return on investment and the return of investment for each $1,000 bond over its life.

d. Is the effective (market) interest rate less than, equal to, or greater than 8%? How can you determine this?

LO 4: Return on Investment

4–32. Assume a company sells 2,500 five-year, $1,000 bonds paying 12% interest at 103.

REQUIRED:

a. How much cash will the company selling the bonds receive from the sale?

b. How much total cash will the bond buyers receive each year as interest?

c. Determine the return on investment and the return of investment for each $1,000 bond over its life.

d. Is the effective (market) interest rate less than, equal to, or greater than 12%? How can you determine this?

LO 4: Calculation of Interest (Return on Investment)

4–33. Assume that an investor pays $950 for a five-year, $1,000 bond paying 9% interest.

REQUIRED:

a. How much cash will the investor receive each year as interest?

b. Calculate the return on investment and the return of investment for the $1,000 bond.

c. Is the effective (market) interest rate less than, equal to, or greater than 9%? How can you determine this?

LO 4: Calculation of Interest (Return on Investment)

4–34. Assume an investor pays $1,040 for a five-year, $1,000 bond paying 8% interest.

REQUIRED:

a. How much cash will the person buying the bond receive each year as interest?

b. Calculate the return on investment and the return of investment over the life of the bond.

c. Is the effective (market) interest rate less than, equal to, or greater than 8%? How can you determine this?

LO 4: Computation of Interest

4–35. Alto, Inc. borrowed $10,000 on July 1, 2000, by signing a 10% note at ABC Bank due December 31, 2000.

REQUIRED:
a. Determine the total amount Alto will have to pay (principal and interest) on December 31, 2000.
b. How much interest will ABC Bank earn on this note?
c. How will the answer to part b differ if the note was signed on October 1, 2000?

LO 4: Computation of Interest and Principal

4–36. The Leverett Company borrows $20,000 in the year 2001, to finance a piece of equipment. Calculate the interest and principal they would pay to the bank for the year 2001 if the loan is due December 31, 2001, and:

a. the loan is at 12%, signed on January 2, 2001.
b. the loan is at 10%, signed on January 2, 2001.
c. the loan is at 12%, signed on April 1, 2001.
d. the loan is at 9%, signed on September 1, 2001.

LO 4: Computation of Interest and Principal

4–37. The Habiger Company borrows $100,000 to purchase a building. Calculate the interest they would pay to the bank for the year 2001 if the loan is due December 31, 2001, and:

a. the loan is at 6%, signed on January 2, 2001.
b. the loan is at 8%, signed on January 2, 2001.
c. the loan is at 6%, signed on April 1, 2001.
d. the loan is at 8%, signed on September 1, 2001.

LO 5: Underwriters

4–38. Describe the function of underwriters and explain why they are important to the financial markets.

LO 5: Matching

4–39. Presented below are some items related to underwriters and bonds payable, followed by definitions of those items in scrambled order.

a. syndicate   d. premium
b. prospectus   e. spread
c. discount   f. Bear, Stearns & Co., Inc.

1. _____ Difference between price paid to the issuer and the price at which securities are sold to the public
2. _____ A group of underwriters working together to get a large bond issue sold to the public
3. _____ A description of a bond issue that provides information to potential investors
4. _____ Bond selling price is below its par value
5. _____ Bond selling price is above par value
6. _____ A global underwriter

LO 6:   Effect of Market Interest on Bond Selling Prices

4–40. Explain how an increase in the market rate of interest will impact a new issuance of bonds in terms of the selling price of the bonds.

LO 6:   Effect of Market Interest on Bond Selling Prices

4–41. Explain how a decrease in the market rate of interest will impact a new issuance of bonds in terms of the selling price of the bonds.

LO 6 & 7:   Effect of Market Interest on Bond Selling Prices

4–42. King Corporation has decided to sell bonds. King Corporation is prepared to issue 5,000 bonds with a par value of $1,000 paying interest of 6%. If the market rate of interest is currently 8%, answer the following questions:

   a. Would you expect the bonds to sell for par value, a premium, or a discount?
   b. Will these bonds sell in the primary or secondary bond market?

LO 6 & 7:   Effect of Market Interest on Bond Selling Prices

4–43. Tamara Corporation has decided to sell bonds. Tamara Corporation is prepared to issue 9,000 bonds with a par value of $1,000 paying interest of 8%. If the market rate of interest is currently 7%, answer the following questions:

   a. Would you expect the bonds to sell for par value, a premium, or a discount? Explain.
   b. Will these bonds sell in the primary or secondary bond market?

LO 6 & 7:   Effect of Market Interest on Bond Selling Prices

4–44. Gadfly Corporation has decided to sell bonds. Gadfly Corporation is prepared to issue 7,000 bonds with a par value of $1,000 paying interest of 5%. If the market rate of interest is currently 5%, answer the following questions:

   a. Would you expect the bonds to sell for par value, a premium, or a discount? Explain.
   b. Will these bonds sell in the primary or secondary bond market?

LO 8:   Equity vs. Debt

4–45. Edie Bennett formed Bennett Engines, Inc. on January 2, 1999. Edie invested $24,000 and received 1,200 shares of common stock. The common stock has a par value of $1 per share. On January 3, 1999, Bennett Engines, Inc. borrowed $12,000 from Miami National Bank by signing a one-year, 9% note. The principal and interest on the note must be paid to the bank on January 2, 2000.

REQUIRED:
   a. Prepare a balance sheet as of January 2, 1999, immediately following Edie's investment of $24,000.

b. Prepare a balance sheet as of January 3, 1999, that reflects both Edie's investment of $24,000 and the $12,000 borrowed from the bank.

c. Calculate the amount of interest Bennett Engines, Inc. must pay on January 3, 2000.

d. Assume that the note was for six months rather than one year, so it must be repaid on July 3, 1999. Calculate the amount of interest Bennett Engines, Inc. must pay on July 3, 1999.

LO 8:   Equity vs. Debt

4–46. Teddy Stowers formed Stowers Public Relations, Inc. on January 2, 1999. Teddy invested $30,000 cash and received 3,000 shares of common stock. The common stock has a par value of $5 per share. On January 3, 1999, Stowers Public Relations, Inc. sold 100 of its $1,000, five-year, 9% bonds at par. Interest is to be paid semiannually on June 2 and January 2. The bonds mature (must be repaid) on January 2, 2004.

a. Prepare a balance sheet for Stowers Public Relations, Inc. at January 2, 1999, to reflect Stowers' investment of $30,000.

b. Prepare a balance sheet for Stowers Public Relations, Inc. at January 3, 1999, to reflect both Stowers' investment of $30,000 and the sale of the bonds, assuming they sold at their par value.

c. Calculate the amount of interest Stowers Public Relations, Inc. must pay each June 2 and January 2.

d. How much would Stowers Public Relations, Inc. have received from the sale of the bonds on January 3, 1999, if they had sold at 99 (a discount)?

e. How much would Stowers Public Relations, Inc. have received from the sale of the bonds on January 3, 1999, if they had sold at 105 (a premium)?

LO 8:   Equity vs. Debt

4–47. Gloria's Corporation had the following balance sheet at December 31, 1999:

GLORIA'S CORPORATION
Balance Sheet
December 31, 1999

Assets:		Liabilities and Stockholders' Equity:	
		Liabilities	$ -0-
Cash	$200,000	Stockholders' Equity:	
		Common Stock	$200,000
		Total Liabilities and	
Total Assets	$200,000	Stockholders' Equity	$200,000

On January 2, 2000, Gloria's Corporation issued $300,000 worth of 10-year, 10% bonds at their par value.

REQUIRED:

Prepare a new balance sheet for Gloria's Corporation reflecting the sale of the bonds on January 2, 2000.

LO 8:   Equity vs. Debt

4–48. Chapters 3 and 4 of the text discuss two very different forms of financing available to corporations: debt and equity.

REQUIRED:
a. Explain why a corporation would prefer to issue bonds rather than shares of common stock.
b. Explain why an investor would prefer to purchase shares of a company's common stock rather than a company's corporate bonds.

LO 7 & 8:   Equity vs. Debt

4–49. Define nominal interest rates and market interest rates for a bond, and briefly explain how these rates affect a bond's selling price.

LO 7 & 8:   Equity vs. Debt

4–50. Ed Furgol has $20,000 to invest. His options are as follows:

Option 1: Big Company's five-year, $1,000 par value, 8% bonds, which are selling for 98 on the secondary bond market.

Option 2: Little Company's initial offering of no-par common stock, which is selling for $20 per share. Although there is no formal requirement to pay dividends, it is anticipated that Little Company will pay an annual dividend of $0.80 per share on its common stock.

REQUIRED:
a. How many of the Big Company bonds can Ed buy with his money?
b. How much cash will Ed receive from Big Company each year if he buys the bonds?
c. What will Ed's return on investment and return of investment be for the bonds if he holds them until maturity?
d. How many shares of Little Company's common stock can Ed purchase with his $20,000?
e. Assuming Little does pay the anticipated annual dividend on its common stock, how much will Ed receive each year if he invests his $20,000 in the stock?
f. Based on your answer to part e, what is the effective rate of return Ed would earn on his investment in Little's stock?

LO 7 & 8:   Equity vs. Debt

4–51. Joshua Pak has $50,000 to invest. His options are as follows:

Option 1: Grand Oil Company's five-year, $1,000 par value, 12% bonds, which are selling for 103 on the secondary bond market.

Option 2: Little Giant Oil Company's initial offering of common stock, which is selling for $75 per share. Although there is no formal requirement to pay dividends, it is anticipated that Little Giant will pay an annual dividend of $2 per share on its common stock.

REQUIRED:
a. How many of the Grand Oil bonds can Joshua buy with his money?
b. How much cash will Joshua receive from Grand Oil each year if he buys the bonds?

c. What will Joshua's return on investment and return of investment be for the bonds if he holds them until maturity?

d. How many shares of Little Giant's common stock can Joshua purchase with his $50,000?

e. Assuming Little Giant does pay the anticipated annual dividend on its common stock, how much will Joshua receive each year if he invests his $50,000 in the stock?

f. Based on your answer to part e, what is the effective rate of return Joshua would earn on his investment in Little Giant's stock?

FINANCIAL REPORTING CASES

Comprehensive

4–52. In its 1997 annual report, Southwest Airlines Co. reported total long-term liabilities of $628,106,000. Of that amount, $100,000,000 represented 7 3/8% debentures due in 2027. On the balance sheet date, the bonds were worth $105,660,000 on the secondary bond market.

REQUIRED:

a. What is a debenture?

b. How do you explain the difference between the balance sheet value and the bond market value of these bonds?

Comprehensive

4–53. First Brands Corporation, multinational producer and marketer of such products as Glad® plastic products, STP® Oil Treatment, and Scoop Away® cat litter, included the following in its 1997 annual report Notes to Consolidated Financial Statements:

Principal payments dues on long-term debt (including current maturities) will require the following future payments: $2,811,000 in fiscal 1998, $3,747,000 in fiscal 1999, $6,149,000 in fiscal 2000, $7,033,000 in fiscal 2001, $12,313,000 in fiscal 2002, and $351,225,000 thereafter.

a. What does the term *fiscal 2000* mean?

b. Why would First Brands include this information in the annual report?

c. What information does this provide the annual report readers?

d. If you were loaning First Brands money on a short-term basis, in which year would you prefer to schedule the loan repayment?

Comprehensive

4–54. Claire's Stores, Inc. operates fashion accessories stores in malls throughout the United States, Canada, Japan, the Caribbean, England, Scotland, and Wales. The following information was taken from its 1997 annual report:

Current Liabilities	$ 42,866,000
Other Liabilities	5,473,000
Total Stockholders' Equity	194,512,000

a. How much are total assets?

b. Claire's has no long-term debt. Consider the nature of its business and the concept of matching maturities. Why might Claire's have no long-term debt?

c. How would you rate the risk of investment for Claire's? (Go to the PHLIP Web site to link to Claire's Web site if you need additional information to answer these questions.)

ANNUAL REPORT PROJECT

4–55. You can now complete Section VI of the project. The information you develop in this part of the report may be helpful in preparing other sections of the project. In this section of the project report, you will obtain (a) financial and operating information about the company during a period subsequent to the date of the annual report, (b) industry information, and (c) secondary stock market data. In this section of the project (VI), you should obtain the following:

a. Current press releases. Using the Internet, locate the company's Web page. Select and print three press releases that pertain to your company which were issued after the annual report date. In addition to the Web page, you may use other financial news services available on the Internet, such as CNN financial news (cnnfn), *Fortune, Forbes,* and *The Wall Street Journal* (free service).

b. Industry information. Find the SIC (Standard Industry Classification) code(s) for your company, located on the cover page of the form 10-Q. Using the SIC code, go to *Moody's, Standard and Poor's, Robert Morris & Associates,* or some other industry reporting service and list your company's major industries and major competitors.

c. Secondary stock activity. Using *The Wall Street Journal* or the Internet, record the following weekly market activity for the company's stock for each week included in your term:

(1) Weekly trading volume

(2) Closing price on each Friday

(3) Net change for the week

REQUIRED:

Complete Section VI of your report. Make a copy for your instructor and keep a copy for your final report.

Chapter 5

Tools of the Trade, Part II
Income Statement and
Statement of Owners' Equity

Your father comes to you for some help with a problem. He learned recently that he will retire early in a few months. Being an active person who wants to keep working, he investigated several businesses which are for sale. He narrowed his list to a few that he finds interesting, but needs help making his final decision. The sellers were to give him balance sheets and income statements from each business, but when you examine them, you find that one seller gave him three sets of year-end statements, one seller only gave him last year's tax return, and another seller gave him a balance sheet and income statement that is two years old. You now understand the balance sheet, but wonder exactly what the income statements can tell you. What does an income statement predict and how well does it predict the future? You wish to give your father sound advice, so you need to understand these income statements.

Accounting information, in the form of financial statements, provides a major source of information to economic decision makers. In Chapters 3 and 4, you encountered the first financial tool—the balance sheet. This financial statement provides information that helps economic decision makers evaluate the present condition of a company. The balance sheet tells what the company owns (assets), what it owes (liabilities), and what claim the owners have to the remaining resources (owners' equity). This picture of the financial position of a company is an important item of information. It is not, however, enough information to support the decision-making process. ■

To make wise decisions, economic decision makers must gather all the information they need to assess the future timing and amounts of cash flows. Accurate prediction of the future performance of a company depends on high-quality assessment of both the present condition *and* the past performance of the firm.

To assess the past performance of a company, decision makers rely on another financial tool—the income statement. The income statement provides information about the business activities of a company during a particular period.

In addition to the income statement, in this chapter we introduce you to one other financial tool—the statement of owners' equity. This third financial statement provides a bridge between the information provided by the income statement and that provided by the balance sheet.

By the time you finish this chapter, you will have explored three financial statements. Remember that these are tools for economic decision makers. Their importance lies in their usefulness and contribution to the decision-making process.

LEARNING OBJECTIVES

After completing your work on this chapter, you should be able to do the following:

1. Describe how the income statement provides information about the past performance of a business.
2. Distinguish between single-step and multistep income statements.
3. Explain the impact of net income or net loss on owners' equity.
4. Construct statements of capital for proprietorships and partnerships.
5. Identify the differences between statements of stockholders' equity and statements of retained earnings for corporations and construct the statement of stockholders' equity.
6. Compare and contrast the impact of drawings on statements of capital and the impact of dividends on statements of stockholders' equity and statements of retained earnings.
7. Explain why dividends are paid and under what circumstances they can be paid.
8. Describe in your own words the articulation of income statements, balance sheets, and statements of owners' equity.

INTRODUCTION TO THE INCOME STATEMENT

income statement A financial statement providing information about an entity's past performance. Its purpose is to measure the results of the entity's operations for some specific time period. Also called the *statement of earnings* or the *statement of results of operations.*

The **income statement** is a financial tool that provides information about a company's past performance. Recall that the balance sheet, the financial tool we studied in detail, lists assets, liabilities, and owners' equity—three accounting elements described by the FASB in the *Statements of Financial Accounting Concepts.* The income statement also includes accounting elements (see Exhibit 5–1). The italicized definitions in the following list are provided by the FASB. A less formal definition of each element follows the words of the FASB.

1. **Revenues.** *Inflows of assets to an entity from delivering or producing goods, rendering services, or carrying out other activities.* Revenue represents what a company's customers pay for its goods or services. Revenues are the reward of doing business.

Exhibit 5–1
Accounting Elements

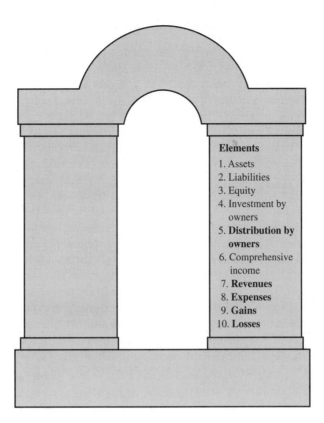

Elements
1. Assets
2. Liabilities
3. Equity
4. Investment by owners
5. **Distribution by owners**
6. Comprehensive income
7. **Revenues**
8. **Expenses**
9. **Gains**
10. **Losses**

revenues An accounting element representing the inflows of assets as a result of an entity's ongoing major or central operations. These are the rewards of doing business.

expenses An accounting element representing the outflow of assets resulting from an entity's ongoing major or central operations. These are the sacrifices required to attain the rewards (revenues) of doing business.

2. **Expenses.** *Outflows or other using up of assets from delivering or producing goods, rendering services, or carrying out other activities.* Expenses are the sacrifices required to attain revenues.

The difference between the rewards (revenues) and the sacrifices (expenses) for a given period of activity is the net reward of doing business, which we call **net income.** Accountants also call net income *earnings, net earnings,* or *net profit.* If the expenses for the period are greater than the revenues for the period, the result is a **net loss.** The relationship between revenues, expenses, and either net income or net loss can be represented by the following equation:

REVENUES − EXPENSES = NET INCOME (OR NET LOSS)

You should memorize the income statement equation and fix its meaning in your mind because we will deal with it over and over again.

Discussion Questions

5-1. Identify the transactions in your personal finances during the last month. Which transactions resulted in revenues and which resulted in expenses?

5-2. Use the equation given in the text and your responses to Discussion Question 5–1 to determine whether you had a net income or a net loss for the month.

net income The amount of profit that remains after all costs have been considered. The net reward of doing business for a specific time period. Also called *earnings, profit,* or *net earnings.*

net loss The difference between revenues and expenses of a period in which expenses are greater than revenues.

period Length of time (usually a month, quarter, or year) for which activity is being reported on an income statement.

Construction of the Income Statement

The basic format of an income statement is shown in Exhibit 5–2. The heading must include the name of the business, the name of the statement, and the **period** for which activity is being reported. You may know that economists use the terms *stock* to describe a quantity at a given point in time and *flow* to describe a quantity over a period of time. A balance sheet provides stock information and its heading includes the precise date for which the information is presented. If the balance sheet is a "snapshot" of a business at a particular point in time, then the income statement, which provides flow information, is something of a "home video" of a company for a period of time (usually a month, quarter, or year). For that reason, the income statement heading identifies the period of time described. The income statement indicates that during this specific time period, the company earned so much revenue, incurred so much expense, and produced either a net income or a net loss. Accountants produce income statements annually, quarterly, monthly, or for some other interval that provides useful accounting information.

The income statement's formal name is the *statement of results of operations*, which is a far better description of its function than income statement. It is also sometimes called the *statement of earnings.* However, most companies use the informal title, "Income Statement." The authors of *Accounting Trends and Techniques*[1] report that of 600 companies surveyed, over half used *income* as a key word in the headings of their 1996 financial statements—though when the financial statements showed a net loss, the title "Statement of Operations" was frequently chosen.

Exhibit 5–2
Basic Format of the
Income Statement

LAURA'S BUSINESS		
Income Statement		
For the Year Ending December 31, 1999		
Revenues:		
	XXX	
	XX	
	XX	
Total Revenues		XXXX
Expenses:		
	XX	
	XX	
	XX	
	X	
	X	
Total Expenses		(XXX)
Net Income		XX

Notice that the basic format of the income statement illustrated in Exhibit 5–2 suggests that a company may have more than one type of revenue. Revenues comprise earned inflows of the company arising from primary operations or incidental company activities. A business may be a service organization that produces service revenues or professional fees such as a law firm, lawn service company, or accounting firm. If a business is involved in merchandising or manufacturing, its major revenue will be sales of tangible products.

---

[1] *Accounting Trends and Techniques* (AICPA, 1997), 281.

Discussion Question

5–3. Which of the following companies earn revenues primarily from manufacturing products, reselling products, or providing services?

a. General Motors

b. Exxon

c. Wal-Mart

d. Taco Bell

e. Prudential Insurance

f. B. Dalton Bookstores

In addition to the revenues from its major operations, a company may produce revenues through other activities. For example, it may rent out portions of the office building it owns to produce rent revenue. If the company has invested some of its cash in certificates of deposit, it earns interest revenue.

The income statement format in Exhibit 5–2 also allows for several different types of expenses. Expenses are the outflows of the company that allow the firm to produce revenue. Expenses take many different forms, such as salaries or wages expense for employees, or rent expense for the sales office. If a company maintains vehicles, the income statement may show fuel expense and/or maintenance expense. These are just a few examples of the numerous expenses a company faces.

cost of goods sold The cost of the product sold as the primary business activity of a company. Also called *cost of products sold* or *cost of sales*.

Merchandisers and manufacturers sell goods to generate primary revenues. Costs associated with these goods make up the expense called the **cost of goods sold,** or *cost of sales,* or *cost of products sold.* For many companies, cost of goods sold comprises the major expense of doing business.

Discussion Questions

5–4. Some items could be in either the revenue or the expense category (e.g., interest, rent). If you were in charge of keeping track of a company's revenues and expenses, describe how you would know whether "rent" or "interest" was a revenue or an expense.

5–5. Think of a fast-food restaurant, such as Taco Bell. List the costs you think the restaurant incurs in its day-to-day operations. Which of these costs do you think should be included in the cost of goods sold and which ones are other expenses? Explain.

single-step income statement A format of the income statement that gathers all revenues into "total revenues" and all expenses into "total expenses." Net income is calculated as a subtraction of total expenses from total revenues.

Single-Step Format of the Income Statement

In the basic form of the income statement, all revenues are added to provide "total revenues," and all expenses are added to create "total expenses." This format is called the **single-step income statement,** because in one step, total expenses are subtracted from total revenues to determine net income (or net loss).

We can use Laura's Business to illustrate the single-step format of the income statement. Assume that Laura's Business had $2,690 in sales revenue and $990 in rent revenue during 1999. Also assume that during the period the company spent

Exhibit 5–3
Single-Step Format of
the Income Statement

LAURA'S BUSINESS
Income Statement
For the Year Ending December 31, 1999

Revenues:		
Sales	$2,690	
Rent Revenue	990	
Total Revenues		$3,680
Expenses:		
Cost of Goods Sold	$ 955	
Wages Expense	675	
Utilities Expense	310	
Interest Expense	120	
Total Expenses		(2,060)
Net Income		$1,620

$955 for cost of goods sold, $675 for wages, $310 for utilities, and $120 for interest payments. Based on that information, the company's 1999 income statement, prepared in a single-step format, would be as shown in Exhibit 5–3.

Unlike the balance sheet, the income statement is not directly affected by the type of business organization involved. Income statements for proprietorships, partnerships, and corporations all take the same general form. The only difference is in the name of the company included in the heading of the statement. Companies do, however, have the option of using either of the basic formats—the single-step format we have been discussing or the multistep format.

multistep income statement
An income statement format that highlights gross margin and operating income.

gross margin An item shown on a multistep income statement, calculated as: Sales − Cost of Goods Sold. Also called *gross profit.*

operating income Income produced by the major business activity of the company. An item shown on the multistep income statement. Also called *income from operations.*

sales revenue The revenue generated from the sale of a tangible product as a major business activity. Also called *sales.*

Multistep Format of the Income Statement

The **multistep income statement** provides two items of information not presented in income statements using the single-step format: (1) **gross margin** or *gross profit* and (2) **operating income** or *income from operations.*

Choice of format does not change the bottom line, or net income. However, the information provided within the income statement differs from one format to another. The single-step income statement format sums all revenues to form "total revenues" and all expenses to form "total expenses." No special treatment is given to any specific revenue or expense. In contrast, the multistep format highlights the relationships among various items of accounting information.

Gross margin is one piece of information not shown on a single-step income statement. This item highlights the relationship between sales revenue and cost of goods sold. Recall that **sales revenue** is the revenue produced by the primary activity of the firm, which for a merchandiser or manufacturer comes from selling tangible units of product. Cost of goods sold is the cost of the tangible units of product sold and is very often the largest expense relating to sales. The difference between sales revenue and cost of goods sold is the gross margin or gross profit. For example, sales of running shoes is the revenue produced by Nike, Inc. Cost of goods sold is the cost of the shoes to Nike. The difference between these amounts represents Nike's gross margin.

Nike, Inc. sells millions of pairs of running shoes each year. The cost of every piece of material you see in a shoe is included in Nike's cost of goods sold. For 1998, Nike reported sales of $9.55 billion and cost of goods sold totaling $6.07 billion. The company's 1998 gross margin, therefore, was $3.48 billion.

Discussion Questions

5–6. For Nike, Inc., what specific costs do you think are included in the cost of goods sold related to the running shoes?

5–7. Identify two additional manufacturing or merchandising companies. For each company, describe the source of its sales revenues and the components of its costs of goods sold.

A merchandiser or manufacturer cannot possibly be profitable unless it sells its product for more than what it paid for that product. Gross margin represents how much more a company received from the sale of its products than what the products cost the company. It also represents the amount available from sales to cover all other expenses the company incurs. For example, assume Kearns Company (a merchandiser) sells its product for $30 per unit. Each unit of product costs Kearns $24. If the company sold 5,000 units of product in January, it would have a gross margin of $30,000, calculated as follows:

Sales (5,000 × $30)	$150,000
LESS: Cost of goods sold (5,000 × $24)	120,000
Gross margin	$ 30,000

This $30,000 represents the amount Kearns has to cover all the company's other January expenses. Assuming the company had no revenues other than sales, if those other expenses were less than $30,000, the company had a net income for the month; if they were greater than $30,000, the company experienced a net loss.

Economic decision makers frequently use gross margin as one measure to evaluate the performance of a manufacturing or merchandising company. Examining gross margin allows financial statement readers to quickly see the relationship among revenue produced by selling product, the cost of the product, and all the other expenses the company incurs. Gross margins tend to be similar among firms in the same industry but vary widely from one industry to another.

Discussion Question

5-8. Consider the following simplified multistep income statement for Kanaly Company:

Sales (1,000 units)	$ 375,000
LESS: Cost of Goods Sold	380,000
Gross Margin	$(5,000)
LESS: Other Expenses	32,000
Net Income (Loss)	$(37,000)

a. What can you learn about Kanaly Company from its gross margin?

b. How many units must the company sell to earn a net profit?

c. At what unit selling price would Kanaly earn a $5,000 net profit?

In addition to highlighting the relationship between sales and cost of goods sold, the multistep income statement separates income generated by the ongoing major activity of the firm from the revenues and expenses produced by other business activities. Operating income or income from operations denotes the results of the merchandising or manufacturing activity that is the company's primary business activity. This income can be expected to continue, but some of the revenues and expenses associated with secondary activities of the company may not be repeated. When economic decision makers are attempting to use the past performance of a company as presented on the income statement to predict the future, operating income may be more useful than final net income as an indicator of performance. Therefore, multistep income statements, which show both net income and operating income, may prove more useful to users of accounting information than single-step income statements, which show only net income.

Exhibit 5–4 depicts Laura's income statement for 1999 in the multistep format. As you can see, the net income reported is the same as that shown in Exhibit 5–3, using the single-step format. Notice, though, that the multistep format makes two

Exhibit 5–4
Multistep Format of the Income Statement

LAURA'S BUSINESS
Income Statement
For the Year Ending December 31, 1999

Sales	$2,690	
LESS: Cost of Goods Sold	955	
Gross Margin		$ 1,735
Wages Expense	$ 675	
Utilities Expense	310	
Total Operating Expenses		(985)
Operating Income		$ 750
Other Revenues:		
Rent Revenue		990
Other Expenses:		
Interest Expense		(120)
Net Income		$ 1,620

important stops before arriving at the bottom line: gross margin and operating income (thus the term *multistep*).

Net Income as an Increase in Owners' Equity

Owners' equity has four components:

1. Contributions by owners
2. Revenues
3. Expenses
4. Distributions to owners

Contributions by owners and revenues increase owners' equity, while expenses and distributions to owners decrease owners' equity. Positive net income increases the owners' interest in the business because the revenue increase exceeds the expense decrease. Net losses (negative net income) decrease owners' equity. Revenues and expenses make up earned equity, one of two sources of owners' equity. Earned equity is directly affected by net income because each revenue is an asset received (increasing earned equity), and each expense is an asset sacrificed (decreasing earned equity). A net profit, therefore, increases earned equity, whereas a net loss decreases earned equity.

If a company's earned equity increases, it follows that its owners' equity also increases. Net income, or net profit, is thus a particular period's addition to the owners' equity in the company and links the information on the income statement with the information on the balance sheet. This link is logical when you realize that the past performance of a company is at least partially responsible for the present condition of that company.

INTRODUCTION TO THE STATEMENT OF OWNERS' EQUITY

statement of owners' equity The financial statement that reports activity in the capital accounts of proprietorships and partnerships and in the stockholders' equity accounts of corporations. The statement of owners' equity serves as a bridge between the income statement and the balance sheet. Also called statement of partners' capital for a partnership.

statement of capital
A statement of owner's equity for a proprietorship.

Some companies prepare only an income statement and balance sheet. A third financial statement, however, connects the income statement with the balance sheet. The **statement of owners' equity** shows how the owners' equity, as reported on the balance sheet, moved from its balance at the beginning of the period to its balance at the end of the period. Although the specifics of the statement vary according to the organizational form of the company, the basic format of this financial statement is shown in Exhibit 5–5. Notice that the format contains the four components of equity.

Proprietorships—Statement of Capital

Earned equity goes by various names, depending on the form of the business. Proprietorships and partnerships usually make no distinction between the equity from owners' investment and earned equity. Because both forms of business legally are considered to be extensions of the owner or owners, the two types of equity are added together under the title "owners' equity" or "owners' capital." The statement of owner's equity for a sole proprietorship is generally called the **statement of capital**. Exhibit 5–6 shows the format of a proprietor's statement of capital that indicates the changes in capital arising from the four components of capital.

You will notice from the heading that the statement of owner's equity represents a flow, the changes in equity during a particular time period. The beginning balance used in Exhibit 5–6 is actually the ending balance from the previous period. The net income amount is drawn directly from the income statement. The amount of distributions to owners reduces the equity, and the ending balance is

Exhibit 5–5
Basic Format of the
Statement of Owner's
Equity

> **LAURA'S BUSINESS**
> **Statement of Owner's Equity**
> **For the Year Ending December 31, 1999**
>
> | | | |
> |---|---:|---:|
> | Beginning Owner's Equity | | $XXX |
> | ADD: Contributions by Owner | $XXX | |
> | Net Income | XXX | XXX |
> | DEDUCT: Distributions to Owner | | XXX |
> | Laura, Capital, December 31, 1999 | | $XXX |

Exhibit 5–6
Statement of Owner's
Equity (Capital) for a
Proprietorship

> **LAURA'S BUSINESS**
> **Statement of Capital**
> **For the Year Ending December 31, 1999**
>
> | | | |
> |---|---:|---:|
> | Laura, Capital, January 1, 1999 | | $XXX |
> | ADD: Contributions by Owner | $XXX | |
> | Net Income | XXX | XXX |
> | DEDUCT: Distributions to Owner | | XXX |
> | Laura, Capital, December 31, 1999 | | $XXX |

Exhibit 5–7
Statement of Owner's
Equity (Capital) for a
Proprietorship

> **LAURA'S BUSINESS**
> **Statement of Capital**
> **For the Year Ending December 31, 1999**
>
> | | | |
> |---|---:|---:|
> | Laura, Capital, January 1, 1999 | | $ 0 |
> | ADD: Contributions by Owner | $10,000 | |
> | Net Income | 1,620 | 11,620 |
> | DEDUCT: Distributions to Owner | | 0 |
> | Laura, Capital, December 31, 1999 | | $11,620 |

calculated as shown. This ending balance appears not only on the statement of capital but also in the owners' equity section of the balance sheet. Earlier we referred to the statement of owners' equity as a bridge statement because it uses the net income figure from the income statement for the period and shows the calculation of the ending owners' equity amount that appears on the balance sheet.

Examine the statement of capital for Laura's Business in Exhibit 5–7. Laura had no previous balance for equity because her business began during the current year and she made no withdrawals.

Partnerships—Statement of Capital

statement of partners' capital A statement of owners' equity for a partnership.

A similar statement produced for a partnership would follow the same general outline but might be designated a **statement of partners' capital.** Of course, there would be a capital balance for each partner, and the net income for the period

Exhibit 5–8
Statement of Owners'
Equity (Capital) for a
Partnership

LAURA AND STEPHANIE'S BUSINESS
Statement of Partners' Capital
For the Year Ending December 31, 1999

Laura, Capital, January 1, 1999	$ 0	
ADD: Laura's Contribution	6,000	
Net Income	972	
Laura, Capital, December 31, 1999		$ 6,972
Stephanie, Capital, January 1, 1999	$ 0	
ADD: Stephanie's Contribution	4,000	
Net Income	648	
Stephanie, Capital, December 31, 1999		4,648
Total Partners' Capital, December 31, 1999		$11,620

($1,620) would be shared by the partners according to the rules stated in their partnership agreement. Using Laura and Stephanie's Business for our example, Exhibit 5–8 shows a statement of capital for this type of business form.

Exhibit 5–8 assumes that the partners, Laura and Stephanie, have agreed to share the net income in the same proportion as their initial investments. Thus, Laura's capital balance is increased by 60 percent of the total net income for the period, and Stephanie's capital balance is increased by 40 percent of the net income.

Corporations—Statement of Stockholders' Equity

Because a corporation is a legal entity separate from its owner or owners, keeping the equity from owners' investment and the earned equity separate is a legal requirement. In corporations, you will recall, the investment by owners is called *contributed capital* and earned equity is called *retained earnings*. A statement providing information about a corporation would use a format similar to that shown in Exhibit 5–9.

Exhibit 5–9
Statement of Owners' (Stockholders') Equity for a Corporation

LAURA CORPORATION					
Statement of Stockholders' Equity					
For the Year Ending December 31, 1999					
	Common Stock	**Additional Paid-in Capital**	**Retained Earnings**	**Treasury Stock**	**Total Stockholders' Equity**
Balance, January 1	$XXXX	$XXXX	$XXXX	$(XXX)	$XXXX
Stock Issued	XXXX	XXXX			XXXX
Net Income			XXXX		XXXX
Treasury Stock Transactions				XXX	XXX
Dividend Distributions			(XXX)		(XXX)
Balance, December 31	$XXXX	$XXXX	$XXXX	$(XXX)	$XXXX

LAURA CORPORATION
Statement of Stockholders' Equity
For the Year Ending December 31, 1999

	Common Stock	Additional Paid-in Capital	Retained Earnings	Total Stockholders' Equity
Balance, January 1	$ 0	$ 0	$ 0	$ 0
Stock Issued	2,000	8,000		
Net Income			1,620	1,620
Balance, December 31	$2,000	$8,000	$1,620	$11,620

Exhibit 5–10 presents the Laura Corporation's statement of stockholders' equity for 1999. Note that the beginning balances are the previous period's ending balances, which in Laura Corporation's case is zero, because this is the company's first year of operation. The net income figure comes directly from the income statement, and the ending balance is calculated as shown. Also notice that the statement of stockholders' equity reflects activity in both types of total owners' equity—contributed capital and earned equity. Common stock and additional paid-in capital are components of contributed capital, and retained earnings represents the earned equity portion of stockholders' equity. Treasury stock is a deduction from total stockholders' equity. It is not part of either contributed capital or earned equity. The five totals at the bottom of the statement of stockholders' equity would all be shown in the stockholders' equity section of the balance sheet prepared at the end of the period.

Laura Corporation issued all of the existing stock during 1999, so the activity is reported in the contributed capital section (common stock and additional paid-in capital) of the statement of stockholders' equity. The activity in retained earnings is not affected by such changes in the contributed capital sections. The amount of retained earnings is increased by net income each period or decreased by net loss and decreased by dividend distributions to stockholders. Thus, if the beginning balance of retained earnings is zero, as it is in Exhibit 5–10, we might assume that this statement describes activity during the first year of operations for the company.

Exhibit 5–11 outlines the differences among owners' equity for the three business forms as we examined them for Laura's business activities.

Exhibit 5–11
Owners' Equity by Business Organizational Form

Organizational Form	Proprietorship	Partnership	Corporation
Name of Statement	Statement of Capital	Statement of Partners' Capital	Statement of Stockholders' Equity
Statement Section	Capital	Partners' Capital	Contributed Capital and Retained Earnings
Equity Account Titles	Laura, Capital	Laura, Capital Stephanie, Capital	Common Stock Additional Paid-in Capital Retained Earnings

Discussion Question

5-9. How would it be possible for Laura Corporation to have a zero balance in retained earnings on January 1, 1999, if 1999 were not the company's first year of business? Is there any other financial statement information that might confirm that this was the first year of operations?

DISTRIBUTIONS TO OWNERS

With time, if the operations of a company are successful, owners' equity will increase. Eventually, the owner, or owners, will expect some type of distribution of this equity. Distributions to owners is another accounting element shown in Exhibit 5–1. Just as net income increases owners' equity, distributions to owners decrease owners' equity.

Do not interpret these distributions as some sort of salary paid to the owners. Distributions are not considered expenses of the company and thus are not shown on the income statement. Rather, distributions to owners represent a return on the investment they made. We handle distributions to owners in different ways, depending on the organizational form of the company. However, in each case, these distributions reduce total owners' equity.

Drawings—Proprietorships and Partnerships

In the case of a proprietorship, little beyond common sense restricts the owner from taking funds out of the company. If the cash is available and is not needed to cover future business expenses, the owner may take it for his or her personal use. In this case, the distributions to the owner are called **drawings** or *withdrawals*. If Laura chose to take $500 in cash from her proprietorship, the drawing would be reflected on the statement of capital as shown in Exhibit 5–12.

Partnership agreements may state explicitly when and in what amounts partners may take withdrawals, or they may leave it to the discretion of the partners. Clearly, the partnership must have sufficient cash to support the actions of its owners. When thinking of making a withdrawal of cash from the company, a partner must consider the impact of this action on his or her capital account. Partners may take withdrawals that are disproportionate to the profit-sharing arrangement. Frequently, partners agree to allow one partner to take larger withdrawals because

drawings Distributions to the owners of proprietorships and partnerships. Also called *withdrawals*.

Exhibit 5–12
Distributions to Owners in a Proprietorship: Drawings

LAURA'S BUSINESS
Statement of Capital
For the Year Ending December 31, 1999

Laura, Capital, January 1, 1999	$ 0
ADD: Contributions by Owner	10,000
Net Income	1,620
	$11,620
DEDUCT: Drawings	500
Laura, Capital, December 31, 1999	$11,120

of an unusual personal need. Another partner may decide to not take normal withdrawals but to leave the capital in the business. The timing and amount of partners' withdrawals can become a common source of partnership conflict, however, and can lead to the dissolution of a partnership.

Using the partnership of Laura and Stephanie, we can examine the impact of a withdrawal made by only one of the partners. Assume that Stephanie finds herself in a personal cash bind. Since the partnership agreement does not restrict withdrawals and sufficient cash is on hand, she decides to withdraw $500. This action reduces Stephanie's capital account and the total amount of owners' equity, but it has no impact on Laura's capital balance. Exhibit 5–13 shows the resulting statement of capital for the partnership.

Exhibit 5–13
Distributions to Owners
in a Partnership:
Drawings

LAURA AND STEPHANIE'S BUSINESS		
Statement of Partners' Capital		
For the Year Ending December 31, 1999		
Laura, Capital, January 1, 1999	$ 0	
ADD: Laura's Contribution	6,000	
Net Income	972	
Laura, Capital, December 31, 1999		$ 6,972
Stephanie, Capital, January 1, 1999	$ 0	
ADD: Stephanie's Contribution	4,000	
Net Income	648	
	$4,648	
DEDUCT: Drawings	500	
Stephanie, Capital, December 31, 1999		4,148
Total Owners' Equity, December 31, 1999		$11,120

Distributions to Owners—Corporate Form

Owners of corporations (shareholders) have much less control over when and in what amount they receive a distribution than do owners of a proprietorship or partnership. This is particularly true in large corporations. Distributions to owners of a corporation are called *dividends*. By law, dividend distributions to shareholders must be proportionate to the number of shares they own. Although not legally required to do so, virtually all corporations pay dividends at some point in their existence.

Why do corporations pay dividends if they are not legally required to do so? In the long run, investors (those who buy the corporation's stock) demand this distribution. A number of factors cause a company's stock to either go up or go down in value, but probably the most important factor is whether or not the company is profitable. Profitability becomes most meaningful to shareholders when demonstrated by the payment of dividends. A profitable corporation periodically pays a dividend to stockholders (usually every three months) as a demonstration of its ability and willingness to reward the stockholders for investing in the company.

If a corporation sustains losses or lacks the free cash flow to pay dividends, investors and potential investors may become dissatisfied with the return on their investment. This dissatisfaction may translate into a decline in demand for the company's stock, which will result in a fall in the stock's price. When this situation occurs, the corporation may find it difficult to obtain funds necessary to support its operations. Opportunities for both major types of external funding—issuing stock and borrowing funds—may disappear. Eventually, if enough people lose faith in the company, it will run out of cash and cease to exist.

Communication is a powerful tool. Some successful companies resist the pressure to pay dividends in order to reinvest profits in research and development, and they clearly communicate this strategy to the stockholders. Microsoft is one such company. Investors have accepted Microsoft's reinvestment policy as a wise business strategy, and the company's stock price has not suffered. Ben and Jerry's is another successful company that does not pay dividends on its stock. By publicizing the corporate philosophy of using profits to keep the company healthy and growing, Ben and Jerry's has avoided any misinterpretation of its actions. Shareholders are well aware of the company's business strategy and have demonstrated their confidence in it by holding the stocks.

stock dividend A dividend paid in the corporation's own stock.

The board of directors makes all decisions associated with the corporation's dividend policy. The policy includes whether or not to pay a dividend, the type of dividend to be paid, and when the dividend will be paid. The board of directors can also choose to distribute additional shares of the firm's stock as a dividend, called a **stock dividend.** It is, however, much more common for companies to distribute cash dividends. Of the 600 companies surveyed by *Accounting Trends and Techniques,* 74 percent issued a cash dividend in 1996.[2]

Cash Dividends on Common Stock   A cash payment is what comes to mind when we hear the word *dividend.* To be able to pay a cash dividend, a corporation must possess two things: sufficient retained earnings and sufficient cash.

1. *Sufficient Retained Earnings.* Dividends are distributions of earnings; however, corporations are not restricted to the current year's earnings to cover the distribution. Although it may be desirable for a company to declare dividends from the current year's earnings, dividends are actually declared from retained earnings. Remember, net income is only this period's addition to retained earnings; thus, it is not necessary that current net income be greater than the dividend amount. The legal requirement is that the retained earnings balance exceeds the amount of the dividend.

Exhibit 5–14 shows how retained earnings increase over time and how they are affected by net income, losses, and dividends.

Exhibit 5–14
How Retained Earnings Are Created

	1997	1998	1999	2000	2001
Beginning Balance	$ -0-	$ 800	$1,300	$ 700	$1,150
Net Income (Loss)	800	1,000	(100)	950	400
Dividends	-0-	(500)	(500)	(500)	(500)
Ending Balance	$800	$1,300	$ 700	$1,150	$1,050

Note two things as you look at Exhibit 5–14. First, the ending balance of one period (in this case, a year) becomes the beginning balance of the next period. Second, the payment of dividends is not directly related to profits in a given period. In 1999, this company paid dividends even though it experienced a net loss for the year, and in 2001, it paid out more in dividends than it earned for the year. This company appears to have adopted a policy of paying $500 per year in total

---

[2]*Accounting Trends and Techniques,* 413.

dividends, regardless of its net income or loss for a particular year. This policy is perfectly acceptable, as long as the company has both sufficient retained earnings and sufficient cash each year to cover the dividend amount.

2. *Sufficient Cash.* Retained earnings is not cash. The only item on the balance sheet that represents cash is the cash account. Retained earnings is the sum of all profits earned by the corporation since its inception minus all dividends declared. Except by extraordinary coincidence, the amount of retained earnings and the amount of cash on hand at a given time differ. In fact, the amount of cash and the amount of retained earnings are unrelated amounts. A corporation must make certain it has sufficient cash to pay the dividend. A company may feel it so important to pay a regular cash dividend that it will borrow short-term cash if it has insufficient cash to cover its regular dividend amount.

The Laura Corporation has sufficient retained earnings and sufficient cash to pay a dividend to its shareholders. Recall that the corporation has 2,000 shares of $1 par value common stock outstanding. If the corporation declared a $0.25 per share dividend, the total dividend amount would be $500. Dividends reduce retained earnings and total stockholders' equity. The Laura Corporation's statement of stockholders' equity after the payment of a $500 dividend is shown in Exhibit 5–15.

Exhibit 5–15
Distribution to Owners in a Corporation: Dividends

	Common Stock	Additional Paid-in Capital	Retained Earnings	Total Stockholders' Equity

LAURA CORPORATION
Statement of Stockholders' Equity
For the Year Ending December 31, 1999

	Common Stock	Additional Paid-in Capital	Retained Earnings	Total Stockholders' Equity
Balance, January 1	$ 0	$ 0	$ 0	$ 0
Stock Issued	2,000	8,000		10,000
Net Income			1,620	1,620
Dividends			(500)	(500)
Balance, December 31	$2,000	$8,000	$1,120	$11,120

Notice that the contributed capital section reflects the issuance of stock, but the income and dividend activity affect only the retained earnings section. Both net income and dividends change the balance in retained earnings, but neither affects any portion of contributed capital.

statement of retained earnings A corporate financial statement that shows the changes in retained earnings during a particular period.

Statement of Retained Earnings If a corporation has not issued stock or engaged in any other activity that would affect contributed capital, it may issue a **statement of retained earnings** instead of the more comprehensive statement of stockholders' equity. A statement of retained earnings is similar in form to the statement of capital for proprietorships and partnerships. Exhibit 5–16 contains a statement of retained earnings for Laura Corporation.

Exhibit 5–16
Statement of Retained
Earnings for a
Corporation

LAURA CORPORATION
Statement of Retained Earnings
For the Year Ending December 31, 1999

Retained Earnings, January 1, 1999	$ 0
ADD: Net Income	1,620
	$1,620
DEDUCT: Dividends	500
Retained Earnings, December 31, 1999	$1,120

This simpler statement is an acceptable substitute for the statement of stockholders' equity only if no changes have been made in a corporation's contributed capital. However, because most corporations are frequently involved in activities affecting their stock accounts or other parts of their contributed capital, corporations use the statement of stockholders' equity more often than the statement of retained earnings. Of the 600 companies surveyed in *Accounting Trends and Techniques*, 84 percent used the statement of stockholders' equity in 1996.[3] Only eight percent of the corporations presented a statement of retained earnings. The remaining group chose to not present either form of this "bridge statement," but placed a schedule in the notes to the financial statements.

Dividend Dates The ownership shares of most large corporations are held by many different people, and these shares of stock change hands constantly. Because their shares of stock are widely traded, most corporations do not know exactly who their stockholders are on any given day. For this reason, most corporations do not declare and pay a dividend on the same day.

Three important dates are associated with the payment of a cash dividend:

date of declaration The date upon which a corporation announces plans to distribute a dividend. At this point, the corporation becomes legally obligated to make the distribution: A liability is created.

date of record Owners of the shares of stock on this day are the ones who will receive the dividend announced on the date of declaration.

date of payment The date a corporate dividend is actually paid. The payment date is generally announced on the date of declaration.

1. **Date of Declaration.** As stated earlier, the board of directors decides whether and when a cash dividend is to be paid. The day the board votes to pay a dividend is the date of declaration. The date of declaration marks the creation of a legal liability for the corporation.
2. **Date of Record.** The date of record may follow the date of declaration by several weeks. Whoever owns shares of stock on the date of record will receive the dividend. Every time a company's stock changes hands, the company is notified, though that notification may take several days or even weeks, especially in large corporations.
3. **Date of Payment.** The date the dividend is actually paid is the date of payment. The corporation pays the dividend to whoever owned shares of stock on the date of record, even though some of those people may have sold their shares of stock between the date of record and the date of payment. The payment of the cash dividend removes the liability for the dividend from the company's records.

Generally, on the date the board of directors declares a dividend, the date of record and the date of payment are announced as shown in Exhibit 5–17.

---

[3] *Accounting Trends and Techniques*, 413.

Exhibit 5–17
Example of Dividends
Reported in the
Business Press

*Source: The Daily
Oklahoman*

Dividends Reported September 17, 1998

Company	Period	Amount	Record Date	Payable Date
ABC Bancorp.	Q	.10	9-30	10-23
Acadiana Bncshrs	Q	.11	9-30	10-15
Autodesk Inc	Q	.06	10-9	10-23
Bk of the Ozarks	Q	.06	10-9	10-16
Bedford Bncshrs	Q	.08	9-30	10-11
Bindley West	Q	.02	9-22	9-30
Brill China	S	.04	10-8	10-30
CBL & Assoc	Q	.465	9-28	10-1
CIM Hi Yld Secs	M	.625	9-25	10-5
Clayton Homes	Q	.02	9-23	10-14
G&L Realty	Q	.39	9-30	10-15
GSFB Bncp	Q	.075	9-30	10-20
State Street	Q	.13	10-1	10-15
Summit Prop	Q	.4075	10-12	11-16
Wesco Fincl	Q	.285	11-4	12-9

Discussion Questions

Assume today is September 17, 1998, and use the information in Exhibit 5–17 to answer Discussion Questions 5–10 through 5–13.

5-10. If you own 100 shares of Autodesk Inc. stock, how much is the next dividend you expect to receive and when would you expect to receive it?

5-11. If you are wondering whether to sell your shares of Clayton Homes stock in the next few weeks, what data should you consider?

5-12. If you own 200 shares of State Street stock, how much would you expect to receive in dividends during the next year?

5-13. Which of the stocks listed has a dividend rate per share nearest to that of CBL & Associates?

5-14. As you listened to a broadcast of consumer news on public radio, you heard an angry consumer advocate, Ms. Sheila Long, accuse large corporations of taking advantage of the small stockholder. As part of her angry attack, Ms. Long cited the following example:

Mega-Millions, Incorporated pays only $0.60 per share dividend each year on its common stock, even though its retained earnings balance is now in excess of $6 billion.

She then went on to accuse Mega-Millions of hoarding profits. How would you respond to Ms. Long's accusation if you were the spokesperson for Mega-Millions, Incorporated?

Cash Dividends on Preferred Stock The procedures associated with the payment of dividends on preferred stock are exactly the same as those for common stock. The distinctions between these two classes of stock are based on the preference features of preferred stock. If a corporation has preferred stock and elects to pay dividends, the preferred stockholders receive their dividend before the common stockholders can be paid.

ARTICULATION

articulation The links among the financial statements.

Earlier in this chapter, we referred to the link between income and owners' equity. We call this link the **articulation** (or connection) of the financial statements. The three financial statements discussed thus far are definitely linked. Articulation is an important concept to understand. The income statement tells the story of the company's earnings activity for this period, and the balance sheet presents a picture of the company's current financial position. The third statement we introduced, the statement of owners' equity, provides a bridge between the other two. Let us look closer at how these three tools fit together.

Financial Statements of a Proprietorship

For a proprietorship, the set of these statements would look like that shown in Exhibit 5–18, which visually presents articulation. The arrows connecting items from the three financial statements show the relationships that should always exist. Net income is calculated on the income statement and used on the statement of capital. The ending balance shown on the statement of capital is used on the balance sheet. The following accounting equation shows that this important relationship still holds true.

$$A = L + OE$$
$$\$12,120 = \$1,000 + \$11,120$$

Exhibit 5–18 illustrates each of the three statements in a very simplistic form. Notice that Laura's Business has only one asset—cash—the assumption being that all activities recorded in these three statements involved cash. If only accounting statements really were so simple! Make sure you know how to use the information provided on this simple set of statements before we move on to investigate more complex sets of statements. Also, be sure you can explain in your own words how the information provided on each statement is affected by the information shown on the others.

Discussion Question

5-15. If a clerk in Laura's Business decided to slip the cash from a sale into his pocket and not record the sale, how would each of the statements in Exhibit 5–18 be affected?

Financial Statements of a Partnership

By now it should be clear that the formats of the financial statements of partnerships are only slightly different from those for proprietorships. To provide a com-

Exhibit 5–18
Income Statement,
Statement of Capital,
and Balance Sheet for a
Proprietorship

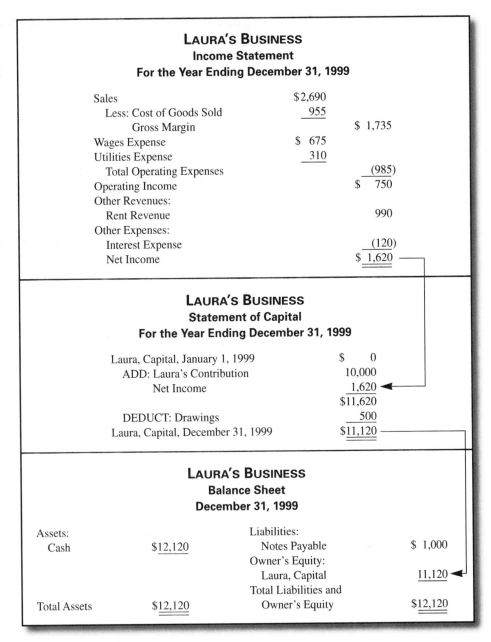

LAURA'S BUSINESS
Income Statement
For the Year Ending December 31, 1999

Sales	$2,690	
Less: Cost of Goods Sold	955	
Gross Margin		$ 1,735
Wages Expense	$ 675	
Utilities Expense	310	
Total Operating Expenses		(985)
Operating Income		$ 750
Other Revenues:		
Rent Revenue		990
Other Expenses:		
Interest Expense		(120)
Net Income		$ 1,620

LAURA'S BUSINESS
Statement of Capital
For the Year Ending December 31, 1999

Laura, Capital, January 1, 1999	$ 0
ADD: Laura's Contribution	10,000
Net Income	1,620
	$11,620
DEDUCT: Drawings	500
Laura, Capital, December 31, 1999	$11,120

LAURA'S BUSINESS
Balance Sheet
December 31, 1999

Assets:		Liabilities:	
Cash	$12,120	Notes Payable	$ 1,000
		Owner's Equity:	
		Laura, Capital	11,120
		Total Liabilities and	
Total Assets	$12,120	Owner's Equity	$12,120

plete set of examples, however, we present the articulated statements of Laura and Stephanie's partnership in Exhibit 5–19.

Again, the arrows show the articulation between statements. The major difference between this set of statements and the set prepared for a proprietorship (Exhibit 5–18) is that these provide information about the activity in each partner's capital account and the statement of owners' equity has a different name.

As we explained in Chapter 1, not all partnerships are small organizations. The KPMG Peat Marwick LLP, for example, is one of the largest accounting firms in the

Exhibit 5–19
Income Statement, Statement of Partners' Capital, and Balance Sheet for a Partnership

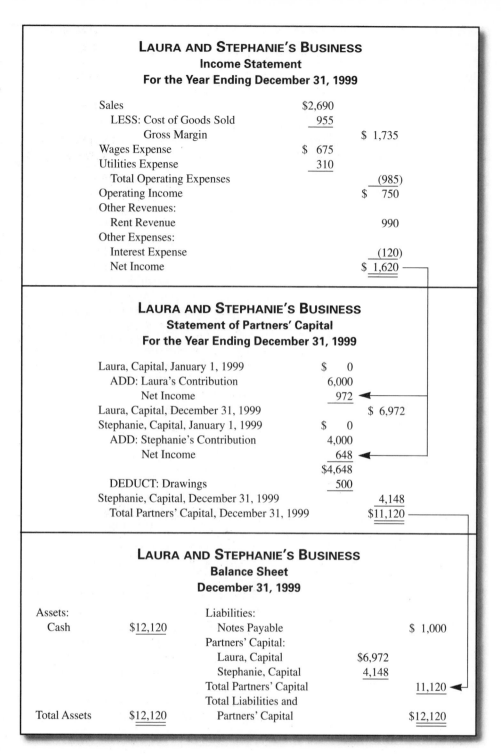

LAURA AND STEPHANIE'S BUSINESS
Income Statement
For the Year Ending December 31, 1999

Sales	$2,690	
LESS: Cost of Goods Sold	955	
Gross Margin		$ 1,735
Wages Expense	$ 675	
Utilities Expense	310	
Total Operating Expenses		(985)
Operating Income		$ 750
Other Revenues:		
Rent Revenue		990
Other Expenses:		
Interest Expense		(120)
Net Income		$ 1,620

LAURA AND STEPHANIE'S BUSINESS
Statement of Partners' Capital
For the Year Ending December 31, 1999

Laura, Capital, January 1, 1999	$ 0	
ADD: Laura's Contribution	6,000	
Net Income	972	
Laura, Capital, December 31, 1999		$ 6,972
Stephanie, Capital, January 1, 1999	$ 0	
ADD: Stephanie's Contribution	4,000	
Net Income	648	
	$4,648	
DEDUCT: Drawings	500	
Stephanie, Capital, December 31, 1999		4,148
Total Partners' Capital, December 31, 1999		$11,120

LAURA AND STEPHANIE'S BUSINESS
Balance Sheet
December 31, 1999

Assets:		Liabilities:		
Cash	$12,120	Notes Payable		$ 1,000
		Partners' Capital:		
		Laura, Capital	$6,972	
		Stephanie, Capital	4,148	
		Total Partners' Capital		11,120
		Total Liabilities and		
Total Assets	$12,120	Partners' Capital		$12,120

United States; it has more than 1,600 partners. With an organizational structure of that size, the financial statements of KPMG Peat Marwick LLP could not possibly offer details of each partner's holdings. Instead, figures are presented in terms of average amounts "per partner."

Exhibit 5–20
Income Statement,
Statement of
Stockholders' Equity,
and Balance Sheet for a
Corporation

LAURA CORPORATION
Income Statement
For the Year Ending December 31, 1999

Sales	$2,690	
LESS: Cost of Goods Sold	955	
Gross Margin		$ 1,735
Wages Expense	$ 675	
Utilities Expense	310	
Total Operating Expenses		(985)
Operating Income		$ 750
Other Revenues: Rent Revenue		990
Other Expenses: Interest Expense		(120)
Net Income		$ 1,620

LAURA CORPORATION
Statement of Stockholders' Equity
For the Year Ending December 31, 1999

	Common Stock	Additional Paid-in Capital	Retained Earnings	Total Stockholders' Equity
Balance, January 1	$ 0	$ 0	$ 0	$ 0
Stock Issued	2,000	8,000		10,000
Net Income			1,620	1,620
Dividends			(500)	(500)
Balance, December 31	$2,000	$8,000	$1,120	$11,120

LAURA CORPORATION
Balance Sheet
December 31, 1999

Assets:		Liabilities:		
Cash	$12,120	Notes Payable		$ 1,000
		Shareholders' Equity:		
		Common Stock	$ 2,000	
		Additional Paid-in Capital	8,000	
		Total Contributed Capital	$10,000	
		Retained Earnings	1,120	
		Total Shareholders' Equity		11,120
		Total Liabilities and		
Total Assets	$12,120	Shareholders' Equity		$12,120

Financial Statements of a Corporation

Financial statements providing information about corporate activities differ from those based on the activities of proprietorships or partnerships. Income statements for the three business forms generally use the same format. The differences occur in the other two financial statements. To illustrate these differences, examine Exhibit 5–20, which shows the full set of three financial statements for Laura Corporation.

LAURA CORPORATION
Income Statement
For the Year Ending December 31, 1999

Sales	$2,690	
LESS: Cost of Goods Sold	955	
Gross Margin		$ 1,735
Wages Expense	$ 675	
Utilities Expense	310	
Total Operating Expenses		(985)
Operating Income		$ 750
Other Revenues: Rent Revenue		990
Other Expenses: Interest Expense		(120)
Net Income		$ 1,620

LAURA CORPORATION
Statement of Retained Earnings
For the Year Ending December 31, 1999

Retained Earnings, January 1, 1999	$ 0
ADD: Net Income	1,620
	1,620
DEDUCT: Dividends	500
Retained Earnings, December 31, 1999	$1,120

LAURA CORPORATION
Balance Sheet
December 31, 1999

Assets:		Liabilities:		
Cash	$12,120	Notes Payable		$ 1,000
		Shareholders' Equity:		
		Common Stock	$ 2,000	
		Additional Paid-in Capital	8,000	
		Total Contributed Capital	$10,000	
		Retained Earnings	1,120	
		Total Shareholders' Equity		11,120
		Total Liabilities and		
Total Assets	$12,120	Shareholders' Equity		$12,120

Once again, the arrows demonstrate the articulation of these corporate statements. As you can see, the income statement is exactly like that in Exhibits 5–18 and 5–19, because the form of business organization does not affect that statement. The information from the income statement is used on the statement of stockholders' equity in Exhibit 5–20. Note that the balance sheet, although different from that for a proprietorship or partnership, still reflects the ending balance shown on the statement of stockholders' equity.

Exhibit 5–21 completes our demonstration of articulation. Here Laura Corporation uses a statement of retained earnings instead of the statement of stockholders' equity. Note that the same relationships among the statements hold true.

Discussion Question

5-16. The balance sheet for the corporate form of business is a bit more detailed than that for the proprietorship. Comparing the two, what can you learn from the corporate balance sheet that you would not know from looking at the proprietorship's balance sheet?

Now that you have been introduced to the first three major financial statements and have seen how they fit together, you may be wondering when you can begin using them to make economic decisions and predict future cash flows. The more you know, the better you can utilize the financial statements, so we must first discuss how we measure the items included in them. Chapter 6 introduces and discusses two different measurement bases. After you complete your work on that chapter, you will be better prepared to use the income statement, statement of owners' equity, and balance sheet to predict future cash flows.

SUMMARY

The income statement is a financial statement providing information about the past performance of a company during a particular period of time. It consists of information about the rewards (revenues) and sacrifices (expenses) of doing business. The income statement shows the result of subtracting expenses from revenues. If revenues are greater than expenses, the result is net income; if expenses are larger than revenues for the period, the result is net loss.

Income statements may be prepared following either the single-step or multistep format. In the single-step income statement format, all revenues are gathered to form "total revenues." Then all expenses are listed and totaled to form "total expenses." In one step, expenses are subtracted from revenues, and the resulting net income or net loss is presented. The multistep format begins with one special revenue—sales. From that revenue, cost of goods sold is subtracted to determine gross margin. All remaining operating expenses are then subtracted to determine income from operations. Any other revenues or expenses are then presented to arrive at the final "net income" or "loss." The bottom line (net income or loss) of the two formats of income statements is the same, but the presentation of the revenues and expenses for the period is different.

Regardless of the income statement format chosen, net income results in an increase in owners' equity, and net losses result in a decrease in owners' equity. The effect of net income or net loss on owners' equity is shown on the statement of owners' equity. This financial statement shows the beginning balance in owners' equity at a particular point in time and how that balance was affected during the period to arrive at the ending balance.

The statement of owners' equity will take one of several forms, depending on the organizational form of the company. The owners' equity sections of proprietorships and partnerships consist of capital accounts for each owner. Therefore, we call a proprietorship statement a statement of capital and a partnership statement a statement of partners' capital.

Corporations prepare statements of stockholders' equity. These statements can show changes in all parts of owners' equity—stock accounts, additional paid-in capital accounts, and retained earnings. Net income or loss affects retained earnings, and if this portion of stockholders' equity is the only one having activity during the period, a corporation may simply prepare a statement of retained earnings.

In addition to net income or net loss, another item that affects the balance of owners' equity is distributions to owners. For proprietorships and partnerships, these distributions are called drawings or withdrawals. In a corporate setting, distributions to owners are called dividends, and cause a reduction of retained earnings. Both dividends and drawings reduce total owners' equity.

Dividends are paid to provide investors a return on their investment and also to indicate the corporation's financial well-being. Two criteria must be met before a corporation can pay a dividend: (1) sufficient cash must be available to actually make the payment; and (2) the corporation's balance in retained earnings must exceed the dividend amount.

The income statement, statement of owners' equity, and balance sheet are all connected. The way in which these three financial statements fit together is known as articulation. The net income (or net loss) reported on the income statement is shown as an increase (or decrease) to owners' equity on the statement of capital, statement of stockholders' equity, or statement of retained earnings. The ending balance shown on this bridge statement is reported on the balance sheet. Articulation exists among the financial statements of a company, regardless of its form of business organization.

KEY TERMS

articulation   F-159
cost of goods sold   F-145
date of declaration   F-157
date of payment   F-157
date of record   F-157
drawings   F-153
expenses   F-144
gross margin   F-146
income statement   F-143
multistep income statement   F-146
net income   F-144

net loss   F-144
operating income   F-146
period   F-144
revenues   F-143
sales revenue   F-146
single-step income statement   F-145
statement of capital   F-149
statement of owners' equity   F-149
statement of partners' capital   F-150
statement of retained earnings   F-156
stock dividend   F-155

REVIEW THE FACTS

A. Name and define in your own words the accounting elements used to determine net income.
B. What is the primary expense associated with the products sold by merchandisers and manufacturers?
C. Name the two formats of the income statement and describe the differences between them.
D. What item is responsible for the primary increase in the capital account?
E. What is the difference between a statement of stockholders' equity and a statement of retained earnings?
F. What is the effect of owners' drawings, and on what financial statement is this information reported?
G. Under what circumstances is a corporation able to pay a dividend?
H. How is a corporation's financial position affected by the payment of a dividend?
I. Explain the following terms: date of declaration, date of record, and date of payment.
J. Describe the meaning of articulation as it is used in accounting.

APPLY WHAT YOU HAVE LEARNED

LO 1: Terminology

5–17. Presented below is a list of items relating to the concepts discussed in this chapter, followed by definitions and examples of those items in scrambled order:

a. Assets
b. Liabilities
c. Equity
d. Revenues
e. Expenses

1. _____ Debts of the company
2. _____ Sales
3. _____ Probable future economic benefits
4. _____ Inflows of assets from delivering or producing goods, rendering services, or other activities
5. _____ "Things" of value a company has
6. _____ The residual interest in the assets of an entity that remains after deducting its liabilities.
7. _____ Probable future sacrifices of economic benefits
8. _____ Outflows or other using up of assets from delivering or producing goods, rendering services, or carrying out other activities
9. _____ Costs that have no future value
10. _____ What the company owes
11. _____ What the company has less what it owes
12. _____ The owner's interest in the company

REQUIRED:
Match the letter next to each item on the list with the appropriate definition.

LO 1: Income Statement Terminology

5–18. Define the following terms in your own words:

a. Revenue
b. Expense
c. Net income
d. Net loss
e. Profit
f. Earnings

LO 1 & 2: Terminology

5–19. Presented below is a list of items relating to the concepts discussed in this chapter, followed by definitions of those items in scrambled order:

a. Revenues
b. Expenses
c. Income statement
d. Statement of owners' equity
e. Dividends
f. Drawings
g. Date of declaration
h. Date of record
i. Date of payment
j. Articulation

1. _____ The date distributions of earnings to owners of a corporation are actually paid
2. _____ Inflows of assets from delivering or producing goods, rendering services, or other activities
3. _____ Distribution of earnings to the owners of a corporation
4. _____ The link between the income statement and the balance sheet

5. _____ A bridge statement showing how the income statement and balance sheet are related

6. _____ Distribution of earnings to the owners of proprietorships and partnerships

7. _____ Outflows or other using up of assets from delivering or producing goods, rendering services, or carrying out other activities

8. _____ The date a corporation announces it will make a distribution of earnings to its owners

9. _____ A financial tool providing information about an entity's past performance

10. _____ Whoever owns shares of stock on this date will receive the distribution of earnings previously declared

REQUIRED:

Match the letter next to each item on the list with the appropriate definition. Each letter will be used only once.

LO 2: Income Statement Preparation

5–20. Phil Brock and Company had $75,985 in sales revenue during 2001. In addition to the regular sales revenue, Brock rented out a small building it owned and received $4,800 for the year. Cost of goods sold for the year totaled $31,812. Other expenses for the year were as follows:

Rent	$10,500
Utilities	2,195
Advertising	4,265
Wages	12,619
Interest	996

REQUIRED:

a. Prepare a 2001 income statement for Phil Brock and Company using a single-step format.

b. Prepare a 2001 income statement for Phil Brock and Company using a multistep format.

LO 2: Income Statement Preparation

5–21. Sam Sosa and Company had $245,000 in sales revenue during 1999. In addition, Sosa had interest revenue of $7,600 for the year. Cost of goods sold for the year totaled $102,000. Other expenses for the year were:

Rent	$24,000
Wages	13,500
Advertising	2,200
Utilities	2,900

REQUIRED:

a. Prepare a 1999 income statement for Sam Sosa and Company using a single-step format.

b. Prepare a 1999 income statement for Sam Sosa and Company using a multistep format.

LO 2: Income Statement Preparation

5–22. Pipkin's Camera and Video, Inc. had sales revenue of $770,000 during 2000. Expenses for the year were:

Wages	$ 72,000
Rent	64,000
Advertising	16,400
Cost of goods sold	550,000
Utilities	13,600

REQUIRED:

a. Prepare a 2000 income statement for Pipkin's Camera and Video, Inc. using a single-step format.

b. Prepare a 2000 income statement for Pipkin's Camera and Video, Inc. using a multistep format.

LO 2: Income Statement Preparation

5–23. The following information is taken from the accounting records of Albert's Baseball Card Shop for 1999:

Sales	$650,000
Wages	220,000
Store rent	39,000
Interest expense	42,000
Advertising	28,200
Electricity	6,800
Telephone	1,400
Cost of goods sold	420,000
Rent revenue	18,000

REQUIRED:

a. Prepare a 1999 income statement for Albert's Baseball Card Shop using a single-step format.

b. Prepare a 1999 income statement for Albert's Baseball Card Shop using a multistep format.

c. If you were the owner of the company, which format of income statement would you prefer to use? Why?

LO 2: Income Statement Preparation

5–24. The following information is taken from the accounting records of Bea's Pet Shop for 2000:

Sales	$830,000
Cost of goods sold	440,000
Wages	280,000
Utilities	34,000
Rent	28,000
Advertising	22,000
Interest revenue	5,000

REQUIRED:

a. Prepare a 2000 income statement for Bea's Pet Shop using a single-step format.

b. Prepare a 2000 income statement for Bea's Pet Shop using a multistep format.

LO 3: Impact of Net Income on Owners' Equity

5–25. Refer to Bea's Pet Shop in 5–24.

REQUIRED:

a. Prepare the statement of capital for Bea's Pet Shop for 2000 assuming that it operates as the sole proprietorship of Beatrice Wilson who had a beginning capital balance of $10,000 and withdrew $20,000 during 2000.

b. Prepare the statement of retained earnings for Bea's Pet Shop for 2000 assuming that Bea is the sole stockholder, the beginning retained earnings balance is $21,000, and Bea paid a dividend of $12,000.

LO 3: Impact of Net Income on Owners' Equity

5–26. The Alvin Smith Company reported the following information in the records for 2000:

Sales	$250,000
Cost of goods sold	120,000
Salaries	70,000
Utilities	4,000
Rent	3,000
Advertising	1,000
Interest expense	2,000

REQUIRED:

a. Prepare the income statement for the Alvin Smith Company for the year of 2000, using the multistep format.

b. Explain how the result determined in part a will affect the owner's equity for the year assuming that the company is a sole proprietorship.

LO 3: Impact of Net Income on Owners' Equity

5–27. Refer to the Alvin Smith Company in 5–26.

REQUIRED:

a. Prepare the statement of capital for Alvin Smith Company assuming it operates as the sole proprietorship of Alvin Smith, Sr., who had a beginning capital balance of $50,000.

b. Prepare the statement of partners' capital for Alvin Smith Company assuming it operates as a partnership between Alvin Smith, Sr., and Al Smith, Jr.

	Alvin Smith, Sr.	Al Smith, Jr.
Partners share of profits	60%	40%
Beginning capital balance	$50,000	$5,000
Withdrawals	$20,000	$20,000

LO 3: Impact of Net Income on Owner's Equity

5–28. The Ben Jones Company reported the following information in the records for 2000:

Sales	$530,000
Cost of goods sold	220,000
Wages	160,000
Utilities	74,000
Rent	8,000
Advertising	11,000
Interest revenue	3,000

REQUIRED:

a. Prepare the income statement for the Ben Jones Company for the year 2000, using the single-step format.
b. Explain how the result determined in part a will affect the owner's equity for the year assuming that the company is a sole proprietorship.
c. Explain how the result determined in part a will affect the equity if the company is a corporation. (What account will be affected?)

LO 3: Impact of Net Income on Owners' Equity

5–29. Refer to the Ben Jones Company in 5–28.

REQUIRED:

a. Prepare the statement of capital for Ben Jones Company assuming it operates as the sole proprietorship of Ben Jones who had a beginning capital balance of $50,000.
b. Prepare the statement of partners' capital for Ben Jones Company assuming it operates as a partnership between Ben Stiller and Kathy Jones.

	Ben Stiller	Kathy Jones
Partners' share of profits	35%	65%
Beginning capital balance	$15,000	$45,000
Withdrawals	$12,000	$25,000
Additional capital contributions	$ 5,000	$ 0

LO 3: Impact of Net Income on Retained Earnings

5–30. The Carl Smythe Company reported the following information in its records for 1999:

Net loss	$ 5,000
Sales	85,000
Beginning balance—Retained Earnings	26,000
Cost of sales	55,000
Expenses	35,000
Dividends	2,000

REQUIRED:

a. What is the balance of Retained Earnings at the end of 1999?
b. Prepare a single-step income statement for 1999.
c. Prepare the statement of retained earnings for 1999.

LO 4, 5, & 6: Preparation of a Statement of Equity

5–31. Pfister Company was organized on January 3, 1998. Although many companies are not profitable in their first year, Pfister experienced a modest net income of $9,500 in 1998.

REQUIRED:

a. Prepare a statement of capital for Pfister Company for the year ending December 31, 1998, assuming Ken Pfister began the company as a sole proprietorship by investing $20,000 of his own money.
b. Prepare a statement of partners' capital for Pfister Company for the year ending December 31, 1998, assuming Kendra Pfister, Stephanie Winters, and Harriet Higgins began the company as a partnership. The three partners have agreed to share any income or loss in the same proportion as their initial investments, which were as follows:

Pfister	$ 6,000
Winters	4,000
Higgins	2,000
Total	$12,000

c. Prepare a statement of stockholders' equity for Pfister Company for the year ending December 31, 1998, assuming Kendra Pfister, Stephanie Winters, and Harriet Higgins organized the company as a corporation. The corporate charter authorized 50,000 shares of $2 par value common stock. The following shares were issued on January 3, 1998 (all at $10 per share):

500 shares to Pfister	$ 5,000
300 shares to Winters	3,000
200 shares to Higgins	2,000
Total	$10,000

LO 4, 5, & 6:   Preparation of Statement of Equity

5–32. This problem is a continuation of problem 5–31. It is now December 31, 1999, and it is time to prepare the statement of owners' equity for Pfister Company. Net income for the year ending December 31, 1999, was $18,000, and there were no additional owner investments during the year.

REQUIRED:

a. Prepare a statement of capital for Pfister Company for the year ending December 31, 1999, assuming the business was a proprietorship and that Pfister took drawings totaling $8,000 during 1996.

b. Prepare a statement of partners' capital for Pfister Company for the year ending December 31, 1999, assuming the partnership form. Recall from the previous problem that the partners share income in the same proportion as their initial investment. Drawings by the three partners during 1999 were as follows:

Pfister	$4,000
Winters	2,500
Higgins	1,500
Total	$8,000

c. Prepare a statement of stockholders' equity for Pfister Company for the year ending December 31, 1999, assuming the corporate form. Recall from the previous problem that 1,000 shares of common stock were issued at the time of incorporation. Dividends paid during the year were $6.00 per share.

d. Prepare a statement of retained earnings for Pfister Company, assuming the same information given in part c.

LO 4, 5, & 6:   Preparation of a Statement of Equity

5–33. Modell Company was organized on January 3, 2000. Many companies are not profitable in their first year, and Modell experienced a modest net loss of $4,500 in 2000.

REQUIRED:

a. Prepare a statement of capital for Modell Company for the year ending December 31, 2000, assuming Art Modell began the company as a sole proprietorship by investing $50,000 of his own money. During 2000, Modell withdrew $5,000.

b. Prepare a statement of partners' capital for Modell Company for the year ending December 31, 2000, assuming Art Modell, Sally Weber, and Hillary Hager began the company as a partnership. The three partners have agreed to share any income or loss in the same proportion as their initial investments, which were as follows:

Modell	$ 5,000
Weber	4,000
Hager	1,000
Total	$10,000

c. Prepare a statement of stockholders' equity for Modell Company for the year ending December 31, 2000, assuming Modell, Weber, and Hager organized the company as a corporation. The corporate charter authorized 100,000 shares of $5 par value common stock. The following shares were issued on January 3, 2000 (all at $10 per share):

500 shares to Modell	$ 5,000
400 shares to Weber	4,000
100 shares to Hager	1,000
Total	$10,000

LO 4, 5, & 6: Preparation of a Statement of Equity

5–34. This problem is a continuation of problem 5–33. It is now December 31, 2001, and it is time to prepare the statement of owners' equity for Modell Company. Net income for the year ending December 31, 2001, was $54,000, and there were no additional owner investments during the year.

REQUIRED:

a. Prepare a statement of capital for Modell Company for the year ending December 31, 2001, assuming the business was a proprietorship and that Modell took drawings totaling $18,000 during 2001.

b. Prepare a statement of partners' capital for Modell Company for the year ending December 31, 2001, assuming the partnership form. Recall from the previous problem that the partners share income in the same proportion as their initial investment. Drawings by the three partners during 2001 were as follows:

Modell	$ 8,000
Weber	5,000
Hager	5,000
Total	$18,000

c. Prepare a statement of stockholders' equity for Modell Company for the year ending December 31, 2001, assuming Modell Company took the corporate form. Recall from the previous problem that 1,000 shares of common stock were issued at the time of incorporation. Dividends paid during the year were $3.00 per share.

d. Prepare a statement of retained earnings for Modell Company, assuming the same information given in part c.

LO 5 & 8:   Identification of Business Type

5–35. Use the following set of financial statements to meet the requirements.

BONITA HERNANDEZ COMPANY
Income Statement
For the Year Ending December 31, 2000

Sales		$88,722
LESS: Cost of Goods Sold		41,912
Gross Margin		$46,810
Rent	$17,500	
Wages	14,408	
Advertising	7,345	
Utilities	1,640	
Total Operating Expenses		(40,893)
Operating Income		$ 5,917
Other Revenues: Rent Revenue		2,700
Other Expenses: Interest Expense		(1,166)
Net Income		$ 7,451

BONITA HERNANDEZ COMPANY
Statement of Capital
For the Year Ending December 31, 2000

Hernandez, Capital, January 1, 2000	$33,806
ADD: Net Income	7,451
	$41,257
DEDUCT: Drawings	9,000
Hernandez, Capital, December 31, 1995	$32,257

BONITA HERNANDEZ COMPANY
Balance Sheet
December 31, 2000

Assets:		Liabilities:	
Cash	$57,257	Notes Payable	$25,000
		Owner's Equity:	
		Hernandez, Capital	32,257
		Total Liabilities and	
Total Assets	$57,257	Owner's Equity	$57,257

REQUIRED:

a. Is Hernandez a sole proprietorship, a partnership, or a corporation? Explain how you arrived at your answer.

b. Is Hernandez Company's income statement in the single-step or multistep format? Explain how you determined your answer.

c. Explain the term *articulation,* and describe how the financial statements of Hernandez Company articulate.

LO 5 & 8: Identification of Business Type

5–36. Use the following set of financial statements to meet the requirements below:

THE CHRISTOPHER WYONT COMPANY
Income Statement
For the Year Ending December 31, 1999

Sales		$688,250
LESS: Cost of Goods Sold		422,745
Gross Margin		$265,505
Rent	$ 38,456	
Wages	112,144	
Advertising	7,345	
Utilities	24,000	
Total Operating Expenses		(181,945)
Operating Income		$ 83,560
Other Revenues: Rent Revenue		24,600
Other Expenses: Interest Expense		(3,246)
Net Income		$ 104,914

THE CHRISTOPHER WYONT COMPANY
Statement of Capital
For the Year Ending December 31, 1999

Wyont, Capital, January 1, 1999	$388,560
ADD: Net Income	104,914
	$493,474
DEDUCT: Drawings	38,000
Wyont, Capital, December 31, 1999	$455,474

THE CHRISTOPHER WYONT COMPANY
Balance Sheet
December 31, 1999

Assets:		Liabilities:	
Cash	$705,474	Notes Payable	$250,000
		Owner's Equity:	
		Wyont, Capital	455,474
		Total Liabilities and	
Total Assets	$705,474	Owner's Equity	$705,474

REQUIRED:
a. Is The Christopher Wyont Company a sole proprietorship, a partnership, or a corporation? Explain how you arrived at your answer.
b. Prepare a single-step income statement for The Christopher Wyont Company.
c. Explain the term *articulation,* and describe how the financial statements of The Christopher Wyont Company articulate.

LO 6: Statement of Stockholders' Equity vs. Statement of Retained Earnings

5–37. The Wynn Corporation had the following information available for 1999:

Common Stock ($1 par value, 100,000 shares	
issued and outstanding)	$100,000
Net income for 1999	10,000
Dividends for 1999	5,000
Retained earnings at January 1, 1999	250,000
Additional paid-in capital	50,000

REQUIRED:

a. Prepare a statement of stockholders' equity for 1999 for the Wynn Corporation. No stock transactions occurred during 1999.

b. Prepare a statement of retained earnings for 1999 for the Wynn Corporation.

c. Explain the difference between the two statements.

LO 6: Statement of Stockholders' Equity vs. Statement of Retained Earnings

5–38. The Bishop Corporation had the following information available at the end of 1999:

Common Stock, January 1, 1999 ($5 par value,	
50,000 shares authorized)	$125,000
Net income for 1999	20,000
Dividends for 1999	10,000
Retained earnings at January 1, 1999	70,000
Additional paid-in capital, January 1, 1999	150,000
Sale of additional 5,000 shares of stock	75,000

REQUIRED:

a. Prepare a statement of stockholders' equity for 1999 for the Bishop Corporation.

b. Prepare a statement of retained earnings for 1999 for the Bishop Corporation.

c. Explain the difference between the two statements. Considering the transactions that occurred this year, which statement would be most informative to the user?

LO 6: Statement of Stockholders' Equity vs. Statement of Retained Earnings

5–39. The Rook Corporation had the following information available for 2000:

Common Stock, January 1, 2000 (No par value,	
50,000 shares authorized, 25,000 shares	
issued and outstanding)	$175,000
Net loss for 2000	35,000
Dividends for 2000	10,000
Retained earnings at January 1, 2000	197,000
Sale of 10,000 shares of no-par stock during 2000	100,000

REQUIRED:

a. Prepare a statement of stockholders' equity for 2000 for the Rook Corporation.

b. Prepare a statement of retained earnings for 2000 for the Rook Corporation.

c. Explain the difference between the two statements. Considering the transactions that occurred this year, which statement would be most informative to the user?

LO 6: Statement of Stockholders' Equity vs. Statement of Retained Earnings

5–40. The Einstein Corporation had the following information available for 2001:

Common Stock, January 1, 2001 ($10 par value, 150,000 shares authorized, 25,000 shares issued and outstanding)	$250,000
Net income for 2001	55,000
Dividends for 2001	25,000
Retained earnings at January 1, 2001	160,000
Additional paid-in capital, January 1, 2001	75,000
Sale of 10,000 shares on March 10	150,000
Repurchase of 5,000 shares on November 6	50,000

REQUIRED:

Prepare a statement of stockholders' equity for 2001 for the Einstein Corporation.

LO 7: Dividend Terminology

5–41. The Simpson Company decided to pay a cash dividend to its stockholders. This dividend is the first that has ever been paid and the board of directors questions the proper procedure.

REQUIRED:

Explain the procedure for the payment of cash dividends by explaining what happens on the three important dates that control the payment of dividends.

LO 7: Dividends

5–42. The board of directors of McCormick Corporation is trying to decide whether or not to issue a cash dividend for the current year.

REQUIRED:

Identify and discuss the various business and legal issues that the board of directors must consider when setting the corporate dividend policy.

Comprehensive

5–43. The Cronin Corporation has paid a quarterly divided for each of the past 45 quarters. The current quarter posted a $150,000 loss, which is not unusual for the second quarter each year. Cronin is in an unfortunate position of having only $25,000 in cash reserves more than required to operate during the next 45 days.

REQUIRED:

a. List at least three alternatives that Cronin has in this situation.

b. Select the best of your alternatives and indicate how this will help the company in this dilemma.

Comprehensive

5–44. The Michelle Miller Company began on January 15, 1998, when Ms. Miller contributed $10,000 to a business account. During 1998 she contributed another $10,000 on June 1 and $15,000 on September 30. Ms. Miller withdrew $5,000 on December 20. The following is a summary of the remaining receipts and expenditures for the year of 1998:

Receipts:

Sales	$235,000
Inventory loan from bank	50,000

Expenditures:

Inventory	140,000
Repayment of loan	40,000
Selling expenses	37,000
Operating expenses	39,000
Interest expense	2,000

REQUIRED:

a. Prepare a multistep income statement for the year of 1998 for Michelle Miller Company.

b. Prepare a statement of capital for Michelle Miller Company for the year of 1998.

Comprehensive

5–45. The Gan Manufacturing Company began on March 10, 2000, when LiLi Gan contributed $16,000 and MiMi Gan contributed $8,000. During the year, LiLi contributed an additional $5,000 and MiMi contributed an additional $2,000. The partnership agreement requires that profits be divided two-thirds to LiLi and one-third to MiMi and that losses be divided equally. Because the partnership agreement also requires that any withdrawals be equal, each partner withdrew $4,000 in December.

REQUIRED:

a. Prepare a statement of partners' capital assuming that the net profit for the year was $6,000.

b. Prepare a statement of partners' capital assuming that the net loss for the year was $8,000.

Comprehensive

5–46. Pezant, Inc. began operations during 2001. During the year, the corporation issued 30,000 shares of $10 par value stock on the following dates for the indicated amounts:

Date	Number of Shares	Price per Share
March 19	10,000	$15
May 16	15,000	$16
November 6	5,000	$20

The corporation earned a net profit of $5,600 during 2001 and declared a modest $0.10 per share dividend on December 1 to shareholders of record on December 15, and paid the dividend on December 30.

REQUIRED:

Prepare a statement of stockholders' equity for 2001.

FINANCIAL REPORTING CASES

Comprehensive

5–47. Presented below are the consolidated statements of stockholders' equity for Southwest Airlines Co. for the years of 1995, 1996, and 1997:

SOUTHWEST AIRLINES CO.
Consolidated Statement of Stockholders' Equity

Years Ended December 31, 1997, 1996, and 1995

(in thousands except per share amounts)	Common Stock	Capital in Excess of Par Value	Retained Earnings	Total
Balance at December 31, 1994	$143,256	$151,746	$943,704	$1,238,706
Issuance of common stock upon exercise of executive stock options and pursuant to Employee stock option and purchase plans (Note 7)	777	9,907	—	10,684
Tax benefit of options exercised	—	1,051	—	1,051
Cash dividends, $.02667 per share	—	—	(5,749)	(5,749)
Net income—1995	—	—	182,626	182,626
Balance at December 31, 1995	144,033	162,704	1,120,581	1,427,318
Issuance of common stock upon exercise of executive stock options and pursuant to Employee stock option and purchase plans (Note 7)	1,079	14,513	—	15,592
Tax benefit of options exercised	—	4,433	—	4,433
Cash dividends, $.02932 per share	—	—	(6,368)	(6,368)
Net income—1996	—	—	207,337	207,337
Balance at December 31, 1996	145,112	181,650	1,321,550	1,648,312
Three-for-two stock split (Note 6)	73,578	(73,578)	—	—
Issuance of common stock upon exercise of executive stock options and pursuant to Employee stock option and purchase plans (Note 7)	2,517	37,818	—	40,335
Tax benefit of options exercised	—	9,806	—	9,806
Cash dividends, $.0331 per share	—	—	(7,207)	(7,207)
Net income—1997	—	—	317,772	317,772
Balance at December 31, 1997	$221,207	$155,696	$1,632,115	$2,009,018

a. What caused the changes in the common stock account in each of the three years? Did Southwest Airlines sell additional shares of stock to the public?

b. List the amount of net income for each year and the amount paid in dividends each year.

c. What percentage of net income did Southwest pay in dividends for each year?

d. What would you guess to be Southwest Airlines dividend policy? For more information go to the PHLIP Web site for this book at www.prenhall.com/jones and find the Southwest Airlines link.

Comprehensive

5–48. Following are the comparative income statements for Claire's Stores, Inc. and Subsidiaries for fiscal years ended 1995, 1996, and 1997:

CLAIRE'S STORES, INC. AND SUBSIDIARIES
Consolidated Statements of Income

	Fiscal Year Ended		
	February 1, 1997	**February 3, 1996**	**January 28, 1995**
Net sales	$440,184,000	$344,881,000	$301,435,000
Cost of sales, occupancy and buying expenses	208,016,000	157,857,000	139,092,000
Gross profit	232,168,000	187,024,000	162,343,000
Other expenses:			
Selling, general and administrative	147,087,000	124,461,000	110,887,000
Depreciation and amortization	15,759,000	14,969,000	13,882,000
Interest (income), net	(2,961,000)	(2,015,000)	(901,000)
	159,885,000	137,415,000	123,868,000
Income before income taxes	72,283,000	49,609,000	38,475,000
Income taxes	27,153,000	18,694,000	14,620,000
Net income	$45,130,000	$30,915,000	$23,855,000
Net income per share	$.95	$.66	$.51

a. Are the income statements presented in single-step or multistep format?

b. What is the total dollar increase in gross profit from FY 1995 to FY 1997?

c. What is the percentage of gross profit in relationship to net sales for each of the three years?

d. What is the percentage of cost of sales, occupancy, and buying expenses in relationship to net sales for each of the three years?

e. What is the percentage of net income in relationship to net sales for the three year period.

f. Summarize your opinion of Claire's earnings performance for the last three years and its potential as an investment. (For more information, go to the PHLIP Web site for this book at www.prenhall.com/jones and find the link to Claire's Website.

Comprehensive

5–49. Following are the comparative income statements for the Coca-Cola Company and Subsidiaries for fiscal years ended 1995, 1996, and 1997.

THE COCA-COLA COMPANY AND SUBSIDIARIES
Consolidated Statements of Income

Year Ended December 31. (in millions except per share data)	1997	1996	1995
Net Operating Revenues	$18,868	$18,673	$18,127
Cost of goods sold	6,015	6,738	6,940
Gross Profit	12,853	11,935	11,187
Selling, administrative and general expenses	7,852	8,020	7,161
Operating Income	5,001	3,915	4,026
Interest income	211	238	245
Interest expense	258	286	272
Equity income	155	211	169
Other income-net	583	87	86
Gains on issuances of stock by equity investees	363	431	74
Income before Income Taxes	6,055	4,596	4,328
Income taxes	1,926	1,104	1,342
Net Income	$ 4,129	$ 3,492	$ 2,986
Basic Net Income per Share	$ 1.67	$ 1.40	$ 1.18
Diluted Net Income per Share	$ 1.64	$ 1.38	$ 1.17
Average Shares Outstanding	2,477	2,494	2,525
Dilutive effect of stock options	38	29	24
Average Shares Outstanding Assuming Dilution	2,515	2,523	2,549

See Notes to Consolidated Financial Statements.

   a. Are the income statements presented in single-step or multistep format?

   b. What is the total dollar increase in gross profit from FY 1995 to FY 1997?

   c. What is the percentage of gross profit in relationship to net sales for each of the three years?

   d. What is the percentage of cost of sales, occupancy, and buying expenses in relationship to net sales for each of the three years?

   e. What is the percentage of net income in relationship to net sales for the three-year period?

   f. Summarize your opinion of Coke's earnings performance for the last three years and its potential as an investment.

   g. Go to the PHLIP Web site for this book at www.prenhall.com/jones and find the link to Coke's Web site. Find a statement about Coke's dividend policy.

5–50. You can now begin your work on Section II of the annual report project. Section II involves the preparation of a SWOT analysis for your selected company. The acronym SWOT stands for strengths, weaknesses, opportunities, and threats. This section of the report should include an analysis of each of these four elements. The strengths and weaknesses of the company should be viewed from an internal perspective, and the opportunities and threats are viewed from an external perspective. You will focus on the external opportunities and threats in Chapter 6 and the internal strengths and weaknesses in this chapter. This part of your project is very interesting and informative. It should improve your ability to come to an overall conclusion about your company at the end of the project.

For this assignment, analyze the internal strengths and weaknesses of your company using the following outline:

I. List the specific strengths and weaknesses in your company in the areas of:
   A. Corporate Structure
      1. Does the structure improve decision making?
      2. Does the structure fit the current business environment?
   B. Corporate Culture
      1. What are the beliefs, values, and expectations of the personnel?
      2. Is the corporate mission clear to employees, customers, and the community?
      3. Is the corporate mission consistent with the corporate beliefs and values?
      4. Is the mission carried out well?
   C. Corporate Resources—How strong or weak are the following resources?
      1. Human resources
      2. Financial resources
      3. Management information system
      4. Manufacturing
      5. Research and development
      6. Marketing
      7. Distinctive competencies (Something this company is known for doing very well.)

Information gathered for the Section I may provide you with some good insight into your findings for the SWOT analysis. The press releases and articles published about your company and its industry will be helpful in finding the necessary information. A major source of information for this part of the project may be found in the Management's Discussion and Analysis of your company's annual report.

II. After listing the attributes of your company, write at least a two-paragraph summary of your analysis of the internal environment of the company.

Turn this assignment in to your professor and keep a copy for your final report.

Chapter 6

Keeping Score: Bases of Economic Measurement

You and three friends are having a philosophical debate about the measure of wealth and income. Charlie asserts that cash is the only measure of wealth because it has a guaranteed value. Valerie insists that cash is a poor measure of wealth because many people own property and other assets that, in the long run, are more valuable than cash. Mandy lets everyone know that the only thing cash is good for is spending.

They continue to discuss income and the conversation follows a somewhat predictable pattern. Charlie states that all he wants is the highest salary possible from his job. He does not care about fringe benefits—he will buy his own benefits. Valerie claims the higher the fringe benefits, the better the income because her company can purchase her benefits (such as health insurance and retirement plans) at a much cheaper price than she can privately. Mandy wants her salary directly deposited to her credit card account.

As you listen to your friends, you wonder about the use of cash as the final measurement. On payday, you have a lot of cash—the day after you have a lot less. Is it fair to measure your wealth or income only on paydays? Do paydays tell the whole story? By the same token, would it be fair to only measure your wealth or income on the day before payday? What about the stack of bills you have on your desk the day before payday? How do unpaid bills and cash fit together? Would financial statements help? If so, how do we measure all this information? ■

Thus far we have explored the development of three financial tools—the income statement, the statement of owners' equity, and the balance sheet. Each of these statements provides accounting information designed to assist in the decision-making process. Economic decision makers rely heavily on the information contained in the financial statements provided by companies.

All three of the financial statements examined thus far are composed of measurements of economic activity. Before decision makers can use this accounting information with confidence, however, they must answer one basic question: From what perspective have the measurements been made? Unless decision makers know what basis of economic measurement was used to prepare the financial statements, the information provided will be of little value to them.

The two general bases of economic measurement are the cash basis and the accrual basis. It is important to understand the distinctions between them. In this chapter, we consider these two approaches to measuring revenue and expense for a particular time period.

LEARNING OBJECTIVES

After completing your work on this chapter, you should be able to do the following:

1. Explain the difference between reality and the measurement of reality.
2. Apply the criteria for revenue and expense recognition under the cash basis of accounting to determine periodic net income.
3. Determine periodic net income applying the rules of revenue and expense recognition required by accrual accounting.
4. Explain the concept of matching and describe how it relates to depreciation.
5. Describe the difference between accruals and deferrals and provide examples of each.
6. Contrast the cash basis and accrual basis of economic measurement, describing the relative strengths and weaknesses of each.

REALITY VERSUS THE MEASUREMENT OF REALITY

A firm performs the following four functions:

1. it operates to produce revenues,
2. it invests resources to enable it to operate,
3. it finances its operations and investments from internal and external sources, and
4. it makes decisions.

These activities constitute the reality of conducting business. Reality happens every moment of the business day. To keep records of business transactions, the firm's officers must measure the reality of each event. But remember this: *No matter how accurately the measurement of reality reflects that reality, it is not the reality.*

To illustrate this concept, think of a person giving testimony in court. A court reporter records the exact words uttered by the witness and the transcript accurately measures the reality of the words spoken. If Rob reads the trial transcript and

Keri hears the testimony in court, could Rob and Keri draw different conclusions about the substance of the testimony?

Discussion Questions

6-1. What is the difference between the transcript testimony and the actual testimony?

6-2. Is there any other measurement of the testimony that might better reflect the reality of the testimony?

Errors in measurement create more distortion between reality and the measurement of reality. Assume Laura's Business purchased some office supplies and wrote a check for $480. In recording the check in the check register, the accountant read the amount of the check incorrectly and entered $48. After the $48 was deducted, the check register indicated a balance of $1,127. However, the fact that the accountant entered the wrong amount for the check in no way changes the reality of how much money was spent and how much actually remains in the company's checking account.

Discussion Questions

6-3. Assuming the accountant made no other errors in the check register, what is the actual cash balance in Laura's checking account?

6-4. In what ways could this incorrect measurement of reality have an effect on reality? Explain.

We can easily grasp the concept that errors may cause differences between reality and the measurement of reality. Many people, however, find it difficult to understand that sometimes perfectly legitimate differences exist between reality and its measure. This discrepancy can best be demonstrated in the measurement of the revenues and expenses to be reported in the income statement of a company for a particular time period.

The Problems of Periodic Measurement

periodicity The assumption that the economic activities of an entity can be traced to some specific time period and results of those activities can be reported for any arbitrary time period chosen.

Most discrepancies between reality and its measurement occur when earnings activities are measured for a specific period of time (Exhibit 6–1). An accounting assumption of the conceptual framework, called **periodicity,** states that the economic activities of an entity can be traced to some specific time period and the results of those activities can be reported for any arbitrary time period. The assumption is often easier to understand than the practice of determining which revenues and which expenses should be included in the earnings (net income) of a particular period (month, quarter, or year). In fact, the only final measure of net income for a company is a comparison between revenues and expenses over the entire life of that company.

Exhibit 6–1
Periodic Measurement

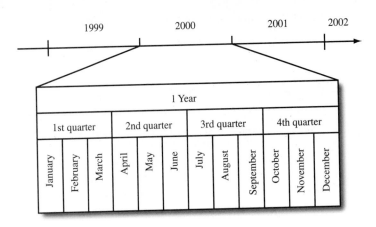

Discussion Question

6–5. Checker Business Systems sells computer equipment to small businesses. During 1999, the sales activity was as follows:

February: Sold $6,000 of equipment on account. The customers paid in full on March 15.

March: Sold $4,500 of equipment on account. Customers paid in full on April 15.

Describe the impact of different periodic measurements by determining how much should be included in each period if the business activity is measured

a. each month,
b. each quarter,
c. each year.

In some ways, determining net income in the fifteenth century was easier and more precise than it is today. In the era of Christopher Columbus, if an entrepreneur planned to sail to the New World and bring back goods to sell, the net income for that particular venture could be measured. The entrepreneur began with a sum of money. With those funds, he bought a ship and supplies and hired men to help with the expedition. The group would set sail, gather treasures and commodities from the New World, return, and sell the goods. Then the entrepreneur paid the workers, sold the ship, and counted the money. If the ending money exceeded the beginning funds, the difference was a net income. If the beginning money exceeded the ending funds, the entrepreneur suffered a loss on the venture.

In today's world, it is unrealistic to expect a company to stop operations and sell off all its assets to determine its "true" net income. So although lifetime income is the only precise measurement of an operation's success or failure, users of accounting information demand current information every year, or quarter, or month. Only the need to artificially break the company's operations into various time periods requires us to make decisions about when revenues and expenses should be reported.

Revenue and Expense Recognition

recognition The process of recording an event in your records and reporting it on your financial statements.

In accounting, the term **recognition** has a very specific meaning. It refers to the process of (1) *recording* in the books and (2) *reporting* on the financial statements.

The problem of when to recognize an item applies to all the accounting elements we have discussed so far, as well as to the ones we have yet to discuss. The greatest difficulties, however, occur in deciding when to recognize revenues and expenses.

When should a revenue be recognized? When should an expense be recognized? These are two difficult questions, for which there are no perfect answers. The accounting establishment had to set criteria to determine when to recognize accounting elements, particularly revenues and expenses. Over time, the accounting profession developed several different recognition systems, each attempting to find some rational basis for the measurement of revenue and expense in a particular time period.

Those of you who have taken another accounting class may have learned a particular set of criteria for revenue and expense recognition. Do not forget what you learned, but temporarily slide those criteria to the back of your mind, because what you learned is one set of criteria, but not the only set of criteria.

Discussion Questions

6–6. Revenue is defined as the reward of doing business. At what point in the cycle of sales, from the customer's order point to the seller's delivery to the customer, do you think it should be recognized as revenue? Explain.

6–7. If an expense is defined as the sacrifice necessary to obtain a revenue, at what point do you think it should be recognized? Explain.

Bases of Economic Measurement

There are two basic approaches to recording economic activity. Each presents a different measurement of reality. Each depicts a different, but important, version of the measurement of revenues, expenses, assets, liabilities, and owners' equity.

We will use a single set of data to illustrate the two bases of measurement. Consider the following information concerning McCumber Company (a proprietorship) for January 2000:

1. Gertie McCumber started the company on January 2 by investing $200,000.
2. McCumber Company borrowed $100,000 from the Friendly Bank on January 2 by signing a one-year, 12 percent note payable. Although the $100,000 does not have to be repaid until January 2, 2001, the interest charge must be paid each month, beginning on February 2, 2000.
3. The company purchased a vehicle on January 2 for $14,000 cash. Gertie estimates that the vehicle will fill the company's needs for four years, after which she estimates she can sell it for $2,000.
4. The company paid cash for $75,000 of merchandise inventory on January 8.
5. On January 15, the company sold merchandise that cost $42,000 for a total selling price of $78,000 and collected the cash the same day.
6. On January 22, the company sold merchandise that cost $15,000 for a total selling price of $32,000 on account (a credit sale). The terms of the sale were 30 days, meaning McCumber can expect to receive payment by February 21.

7. Cash payments for operating expenses in January totaled $22,500.
8. Besides the bank loan, the only amounts owed by the company at the end of the month were:
   a. $2,000 to company employees for work performed in January. They will be paid on February 3.
   b. A $700 utility bill that was received on January 26 and will be paid on February 15.

This information is the reality of what happened in the McCumber Company during January 2000. The measurement of that reality will be different, depending on the basis of accounting used to recognize the transactions. Remember, both treatments we will show are based on exactly the same reality—they are simply different methods of measuring that reality.

CASH BASIS OF ECONOMIC MEASUREMENT

cash basis accounting A basis of accounting in which cash is the major criterion used in measuring revenue and expense for a given income statement period. Revenue is recognized when the associated cash is received, and expense is recognized when the associated cash is paid.

The first approach to measuring economic activity is **cash basis accounting**—the simpler of the two bases. Everyone understands what cash is and can readily grasp the measurement criterion of this method. Its greatest strength, however, lies in the fact that it keeps the user's eye on the ball. As its name implies, the cash basis has only one measurement criterion: CASH!

Under cash basis accounting, we recognize economic activity only when the associated cash is received or paid. Consequently, we recognize a revenue only when the company receives the associated cash as a result of the earnings process. But not all cash received by a firm is revenue because cash received from company owners increases contributed capital and cash received from lenders increases liabilities.

Similarly, we do not recognize all cash paid out as an expense in cash basis accounting. When a company pays a dividend to its owners, we recognize the expenditure not as a company expense, but as a distribution of profits or a return on the owners' original investment. As discussed in Chapter 5, we report these transactions on the statement of owners' equity and/or on the balance sheet, but not on the income statement.

Cash Basis Revenue Recognition

The cash basis has two criteria for revenue recognition:

1. Cash must be received, or *realized*, in the transaction. In accounting terminology, **realization** occurs.
2. The receipt of cash must relate to delivering or producing goods, rendering services, or other business activities.

realization Actual receipt of cash or payment of cash. Once cash has been collected or a transaction is complete, it is considered to be realized.

If a transaction meets both these requirements, we recognize it as a revenue for cash basis accounting and report it on the income statement.

Cash Basis Expense Recognition

The cash basis has two criteria for expense recognition:

1. Cash must be paid in the transaction.
2. The disbursement must relate to delivering or producing goods, rendering services, or conducting other business activities.

If a transaction meets both these requirements, we recognize it as an expense for cash basis accounting and report it on the income statement.

Cash Basis Financial Statements

In preparing the income statement, statement of capital, and balance sheet using the cash basis, we first isolate the events and transactions involving cash. From our example of the McCumber Company, only the following meet that requirement:

1. Gertie McCumber started the company on January 2 by investing $200,000.
2. McCumber Company borrowed $100,000 from the Friendly Bank on January 2 by signing a one-year, 12 percent note payable. Although the $100,000 does not have to be repaid until January 2, 2001, the interest charge must be paid each month, beginning on February 2, 2000.
3. The company purchased a vehicle on January 2 for $14,000 cash. Gertie estimates that the vehicle will fill the company's needs for four years, after which she estimates she can sell it for $2,000.
4. The company paid cash for $75,000 of merchandise inventory on January 8.
5. On January 15, the company sold merchandise inventory that cost $42,000 for a total selling price of $78,000 and collected the cash the same day.
7. Cash payments for operating expenses in January totaled $22,500.

We record these transactions in McCumber's books and report them on one or more of the financial statements: the income statement, statement of owner's equity, or balance sheet.

To determine which of the cash transactions should be reported on the cash basis income statement, we must determine which relate directly to McCumber's major or central operation (which appears to be the buying and selling of some product). Transactions 3, 4, 5, and 7 meet the second criterion. The cash basis income statement for the month of January 2000, based on those transactions, is shown in Exhibit 6–2.

Exhibit 6–2
Cash Basis Income Statement

MCCUMBER COMPANY
Income Statement
For the Month Ended January 31, 2000

Sales Revenue	$78,000	
Cost of Goods Sold	75,000	
Gross Margin		$ 3,000
Expenses:		
Cost of Vehicle	$14,000	
Cash Operating Expenses	22,500	
Total Operating Expenses		(36,500)
Net Loss		$(33,500)

Consider the following items from Exhibit 6–2:

- *Sales Revenue.* Because McCumber received only $78,000 in cash from sales in the month of January, only that amount meets both cash basis revenue recognition criteria.
- *Cost of Goods Sold.* McCumber paid $75,000 in cash for merchandise inventory during January. Because the $75,000 was paid, we recognize this amount as the cost of goods sold.
- *Expenses.* We recognize the cash expenses of $22,500 plus the entire $14,000 for the vehicle purchased as expenses in January, because both are part of McCumber's revenue producing activities for January. Other expenses will be recognized as the cash is paid by the company.

Transaction 1 reflects an inflow of cash, so the cash basis of measurement requires that it be recognized. This transaction represents an investment by the owner, Gertie McCumber. The owner's investment increases her capital account, while the net loss determined in Exhibit 6–2 decreases it. Exhibit 6–3 is the statement of owner's equity prepared using the cash basis of measurement.

Exhibit 6–3
Cash Basis Statement of Owner's Equity

McCUMBER COMPANY
Statement of Owner's Equity
For the Month Ended January 31, 2000

G. McCumber, Capital, January 1, 2000	$ 0
Investment by Owner	200,000
Net Loss	(33,500)
G. McCumber, Capital, January 31, 2000	$166,500

The remaining cash transaction of the McCumber Company during January 2000 is transaction 2, the $100,000 bank loan. Borrowing money creates a liability that would appear on the balance sheet. Exhibit 6–4 shows McCumber Company's balance sheet at January 31, 2000, under cash basis accounting.

Cash transactions consist of the following:

Transaction Number	Receipts	Expenditures
1	$200,000	
2	100,000	
3		$ 14,000
4		75,000
5	78,000	
7		22,500
Total	$378,000	$111,500

Therefore, the balance of cash is $378,000 minus $111,500, or $266,500.

Exhibit 6–4
Cash Basis Balance Sheet

McCUMBER COMPANY
Balance Sheet
January 31, 2000

Assets:		Liabilities:	
Cash	$266,500	Note Payable	$100,000
		Owner's Equity:	
		G. McCumber, Capital	166,500
Total Assets	$266,500	Total Liabilities and Owner's Equity	$266,500

Notice the articulation of the McCumber Company financial statements. The net loss from the income statement articulates to the statement of owner's equity, and the ending balance in the capital account from the statement of owner's equity articulates to the balance sheet. The cash amount showing on the balance sheet is simply the $200,000 the owner invested in the company plus the $100,000 borrowed from the bank less the $33,500 net loss for the month of January.

Discussion Questions

6-8. Assume for a moment that you are McCumber's loan officer at the bank. How would you evaluate the income statement and balance sheet presented in Exhibits 6-2 and 6-4 in terms of the primary qualitative characteristic of relevance, including predictive value and feedback value? (Hint: See Chapter 2.)

6-9. If your response to Discussion Question 6-8 led you to the conclusion that there is a problem in terms of predictive value and feedback value, what item or items do you believe caused the problem? How do you think the company could account for the item or items to better relate costs to the revenues they generate?

Strengths and Weaknesses of Cash Basis Accounting

Besides its relative simplicity, the greatest strength of the cash basis of accounting is its objectivity. Cash basis accounting presents the *reality of cash,* an important reality in conducting a business. Cash basis accounting requires less subjective judgment than the other measurement basis. The cash basis has an Achilles' heel that prevents it from being the perfect measurement basis, however. Management can easily manipulate revenues and expenses reported in a particular income statement period simply by speeding up or delaying the receipt of revenues or the payment of amounts owed on expenses. The greatest weakness of the cash basis is that it makes no attempt to recognize expenses in the same period as the revenues they helped generate, offering a poor measurement of the *reality of performance.* This problem makes the cash basis income statement difficult to use either for predicting future profitability or for assessing past performance in cases where the company does not always receive cash at the point of sale or pay for expenses when it receives the goods and services.

Discussion Question

6-10. Provide two examples of situations in which your checkbook balance did not provide relevant information.

ACCRUAL BASIS OF ECONOMIC MEASUREMENT

accrual basis accounting
A method of accounting in which revenues are recognized when they are earned, regardless of when the associated cash is collected. The expenses incurred in generating the revenue are recognized when the benefit is derived rather than when the associated cash is paid.

The second basis of economic measurement is **accrual basis accounting.** The accrual basis does not rely on the receipt or payment of cash to determine when revenues and expenses should be recognized. The key to understanding accrual basis accounting is to understand the word **accrue.** To accrue means

To come into being as a legally enforceable claim.

Essentially, in accrual basis accounting, sales, purchases, and all other business transactions are recognized whenever a legally enforceable claim to the associated cash is established. The main focus of accrual accounting is determining when a legally enforceable claim to cash has been established between the parties involved in the transaction.

Accrual Basis Revenue Recognition

accrue As used in accounting, to come into being as a legally enforceable claim.

Accrual accounting has two criteria required to recognize revenue:

1. Revenue must be earned; that is, the earning process must be substantially complete.
2. There must be a legally enforceable claim to receive the asset traded for the revenue. When a legally enforceable claim exists, the cash or other asset becomes a realizable asset such as an account **receivable.** In the cash basis, the cash receipt had to be *realized.* In the accrual, it must only be *realizable.*

receivable Money due to an entity from an enforceable claim.

Both criteria must be met to recognize revenue.

Three possible relationships can exist between the timing of the cash movement and the recognition of the revenue.

1. *Cash is received* **at the time** *the revenue is earned.* When you pay cash for a pair of Gap jeans, the Gap recognizes revenue at the point of sale. Delivery of the jeans constitutes completion of the earning process and your payment of cash realizes receipt of cash. Both criteria are met because the revenue is earned and realized.
2. *Cash is received* **after** *the revenue has been earned.* When you go to Office Depot to buy supplies for your office and Office Depot allows you to pay next month on a 30-day charge, Office Depot will receive your cash after the revenue has been earned. Delivery of the supplies completes the earning process and your signing of the invoice gives the store an enforceable claim to your cash.
3. *Cash is received* **before** *the revenue has been earned.* If you subscribe to *Fortune* magazine for one year, you pay the subscription at the beginning of the year. *Fortune* realizes your cash but has not yet earned it. The earning process will not be complete until *Fortune* delivers all twelve issues to you.

Because revenue must be earned before it can be recognized, the timing of the cash receipt is irrelevant. When the earning process is substantially complete **and** an enforceable claim exists to receive the cash, then the revenue is recognized. In Examples 1 and 2, the revenue is recorded in the books and shown on the financial statements at the time the sale is made. The fact that in Example 2 the company did not receive cash at that time does not affect recognition of the revenue. In Example 3, the receipt of cash does not cause revenue to be recognized because, under accrual accounting, the revenue is not recognized until it is earned (when the publisher sends the magazines to the customer).

Identifying the point in time when a revenue is earned is not always a simple matter. Accountants try to answer three questions in determining when revenue has been earned and therefore should be recognized. To emphasize that these questions are in no way related to the three examples, we are using letters to list them.

a. *Has* **title** *(legal ownership) to whatever was sold been transferred to the customer?* If the answer to this question is yes, revenue should be recognized. This question can be applied more easily to the sale of tangible products than to the sale of services. Services must be substantially complete to recognize revenue.
b. *Has an exchange taken place?* Each party to the exchange gives the other party something of value—goods and services in exchange for cash or receivables. In other words, has the customer taken receipt of whatever he or she purchased? If the answer to this question is yes, the revenue will likely be recognized.

c. *Is the earnings process virtually complete?* This is the toughest of the three questions to answer and applies better to the sale of services than it does to the sale of tangible products. Let us say that you have contracted with Bill Austin to remodel your kitchen. It is a two-week job, and at the end of the second week, Bill has completed everything but changing the lamp over the dinette area. He ordered the lamp two months ago, but the supplier backordered it. It should arrive within another week. Has Bill substantially completed the work? Probably yes. He can recognize the revenue because the job is "virtually" complete.

It is not necessary for all three questions to be answered "yes" for revenue to be recognized. In most cases, a positive answer to any one of them is persuasive evidence that revenue has been earned and should be recognized.

Discussion Questions

6-11. On Saturday morning, you finally decide which model of Dell computer to buy. The salesperson has agreed to have all the software you need installed and have the machine delivered to you by Tuesday afternoon. Because you purchased your last computer at Image Technologies, the store has agreed to extend credit to you as an established customer. You have 30 days to pay for your new computer. As of Monday,
   a. has title passed?
   b. has an exchange taken place?
   c. is the earnings process complete?

6-12. When should Image Technologies recognize revenue
   a. under the cash basis?
   b. under the accrual basis?

Accrual Basis Expense Recognition

Under accrual accounting, there is only one criterion for expense recognition: A firm recognizes an expense when it receives the benefit from the expense. Like revenue recognition, expense recognition under accrual accounting is unrelated to the movement of cash.

Again, there are three possible relationships between the timing of the cash movement and the recognition of an expense.

1. *Cash is paid **at the time** the expense is incurred.* If a company holds a Christmas party and pays for the food when the caterer delivers it, the company receives the benefit of the expense at the same time it transfers the cash to the vendor.

2. *Cash is paid **after** the expense has been incurred.* A public utility cannot immediately exchange electricity for cash and must bill its customers on a monthly basis. When a firm receives and pays an electric bill, it expends the cash after the receipt of the electric service.

3. *Cash is paid **before** the expense has been incurred.* All insurance contracts require cash in advance to issue the policy and keep it in force. The policy expires or the expense occurs for each day as time passes during the policy's time span.

Discussion Question

6–13. Why would insurance companies require policies to be paid in advance?

If the one criterion for expense recognition is receiving the benefit from the expense, how do we know when the expense benefits the firm? For the most part, the key to expense recognition under accrual accounting is revenue recognition. Remember that to be useful for predicting future profitability and cash flow, an income statement should measure revenues for a specific period of time and the expenses required to obtain those revenues. Thus, accrual accounting attempts to capture the relationship between revenues and expenses. This relationship is referred to as matching.

The Matching Principle

matching principle
Accounting principle that relates the expenses to the revenues of a particular income statement period. Once it is determined in which period a revenue should be recognized, the expenses that helped to generate the revenue are matched to that same period.

The **matching principle** requires that we match revenue with the cost of producing that revenue (expenses). Therefore, the first step in the accrual matching process requires us to determine in which income statement period to recognize a particular revenue. The second step demands that we determine which expenses helped to generate that revenue. Consequently, we recognize both the revenue and expense in that same financial statement period. This approach makes the income statement for that time period more reflective of true earnings results, and therefore more relevant for predicting future potential. Accrual accounting attempts to portray the *reality of performance*. Do not be misled. It can be very difficult to determine which expenses are responsible for generating which revenue, so we exercise a significant amount of judgment in recognizing expenses under the accrual basis of accounting.

Two possible relationships exist between revenues and expenses that determine when to recognize expenses:

1. *Direct cause and effect.* When a direct link can be found between an expense and the revenue it helps generate, we can easily apply the matching principle. If State Farm Insurance Company pays a 10 percent sales commission to its salespersons, and a salesperson makes a sale of $1,000, the company incurs a $100 expense. Once State Farm determines in which income statement period to recognize the $1,000 revenue, it recognizes the $100 in that same period.

2. *No direct cause and effect.* When no direct cause and effect exists, a firm has two possible expense recognition treatments:

   a. ALLOCATION TO THE PERIODS BENEFITED. If a purchased item provides a discernible benefit to future income statement periods and the periods can be reasonably estimated, the item is recorded as an asset when purchased. (Remember that an asset has a probable future benefit to the entity.) The cost of that item is then systematically converted to expense in the periods benefited. For example, when we pay a two-year premium for insurance coverage, a benefit to future periods exists. Further, we can clearly estimate which of those future periods benefit from the policy—the next 24 months. As time passes during the two years, we allocate the cost of the insurance coverage to expense.

   b. IMMEDIATE RECOGNITION. Two situations make immediately recording the expense the most appropriate course of action.

1. If a purchased item has no discernible future benefit, or the periods benefited cannot be reasonably estimated, we immediately recognize the cost of the item as an expense. Honda's television advertising, intended to increase sales of the Civic, provides Honda with immediate benefits and some lasting benefits such as name recognition. Television ads purchased and presented to the public in one period probably benefit future periods, but we cannot reasonably estimate how many periods and how much benefit in each of those periods. Thus, we usually recognize the cost of television advertising as an expense in the periods when the ads are presented to consumers.

2. When the amount of an expenditure, which provides future benefits, is not material, we immediately recognize it as an expense because allocation of the cost over several periods provides us with no additional useful information. As an example, if IBM purchases a $10 stapler that can last five years, the recognition of $2 per year for five years versus $10 in the year of purchase is immaterial to IBM's income statement in any of those years. In addition, the record-keeping cost of recording the stapler as an asset on the balance sheet and then allocating $2 per year as an expense on the income statement for five years far outweighs the benefit of doing so. Therefore, we use the cost/benefit assumption to recognize the $10 cost as an immediate expense.

When a firm acquires assets that will benefit the company for more than one accounting period, the cost is recorded as an asset (unexpired cost) on the balance sheet. As time passes, the cost is transferred to expense on the income statement. We call this form of "allocation to the periods benefited" **depreciation.** Depreciation is applied to a variety of long-lived assets such as machinery, buildings, and equipment. One asset that has a long life but is not depreciated is land.

depreciation The systematic and rational conversion of a long-lived asset's cost from asset to expense in the income statement periods benefited.

Accounting Depreciation

Accounting depreciation is a systematic and rational allocation of the cost of a long-lived item from asset to expense. Under cash basis accounting, McCumber Company's purchase of a $14,000 vehicle resulted in a $14,000 expense because that amount of cash was spent. Did the company use all the benefits of that vehicle in that year, or does the asset still have a future benefit? Clearly the vehicle has not been used up all in a single year, nor has the company received all the benefit from it. The accrual basis of measurement takes the position that the $14,000 cash payment represents an asset because it has probable future benefit to McCumber. Over time, McCumber will convert the cost of the vehicle from asset to expense as it derives the benefit from the use of the vehicle. The resulting expense is called **depreciation expense.**

depreciation expense The amount of cost associated with a long-lived asset converted to expense in a given income statement period.

Do not confuse the accounting term *depreciation* with the common usage of depreciation. Common usage of *depreciation* involves the loss of market value. Accounting depreciation is the systematic allocation of cost to expense for long-lived assets. This allocation requires two highly subjective estimates: (1) the useful life of the asset and (2) the residual value of the asset.

The useful life of an asset is the length of time the asset will be of use to the company (not the length of time the asset will exist). Notice that in the case of the McCumber Company, Gertie McCumber feels that the vehicle will fill the company's needs for four years, which is not the same as saying the vehicle will last four years. There is an important distinction.

If the estimated useful life of an asset is less than the physical life of that asset, it follows that the asset will probably be sold at the end of its useful life. The estimated amount for which the asset can be sold at the end of its useful life is known as its **residual value,** *salvage value,* or *scrap value.*

In calculating depreciation, we subtract the estimated residual value from the asset cost to arrive at the **depreciable base.** Gertie McCumber Company recorded the $14,000 cost of the vehicle and estimated that at the end of its four-year useful life, the vehicle could be sold for $2,000. The depreciable amount is $12,000 ($14,000 − $2,000). In one sense, McCumber's true vehicle cost is $12,000, because the company expects to recoup $2,000 of the purchase price when the vehicle is sold.

Once the useful life and residual value of the asset have been estimated, a company must select a depreciation method. Members of the accounting profession have developed several over the years. The simplest method is **straight-line depreciation,** and we will use it to demonstrate how to calculate depreciation.

The straight-line approach allocates an equal amount of depreciation expense to each period of the asset's estimated useful life. The amount of expense is calculated by dividing the estimated useful life of the asset into the depreciable amount of the asset. In the case of McCumber's vehicle, the expense amount equals $3,000 per year ($12,000/4). Each year of the four-year estimated useful life, McCumber will transfer $3,000 of the asset "vehicle" on the balance sheet into the expense "depreciation" on the income statement, until the entire depreciable base has been recognized as expense.

The depreciation process is one example of the matching principal at work. Because the timing of cash receipts and payments does not always coincide with the proper recognition of revenues and expenses, we have to explore other needed adjustments.

residual value   The estimated value of an asset when it has reached the end of its useful life. Also called *salvage* or *scrap value.*

depreciable base   The total amount of depreciation expense that is allowed to be claimed for an asset during its useful life. The depreciable base is the cost of the asset less its residual value.

straight-line depreciation A method of calculating periodic depreciation. The depreciable base of an asset is divided by its estimated useful life. The result is the amount of depreciation expense to be recognized in each year of the item's estimated useful life: (Cost − Residual Value)/N = Annual Depreciation Expense.

Discussion Question

6–14. Recall the scenario, introduced in Discussion Question 6–11, involving your purchase of a computer from Image Technologies. If the computer is to be used in the business you operate from your home, how should the purchase be treated
   a. under the cash basis?
   b. under the accrual basis?

Accruals and Deferrals

Because accrual accounting attempts to recognize revenues in the income statement period they are earned, and to match the expenses that generated the revenue to the same income statement period, adjustments must be made each period to ensure that these guidelines have been followed. The adjustment process takes place at the end of the financial statement period, but before the financial statements can be prepared. This process involves reviewing the financial records to be sure that all items that should be recognized in the current period have been recorded, and that no items that should be recognized in future periods appear in the current period's records.

The two basic types of **adjustments** that are necessary are accruals and deferrals.

adjustments   Changes made in recorded amounts of revenues and expenses in order to follow the guidelines of accrual accounting.

accruals   Adjustments made to record items that should be included on the income statement, but have not yet been recorded.

1. **Accruals** are adjustments made to recognize items that should be included in the income statement period but have not yet been recorded. Accrual adjustments recognize revenue or expense *before* the associated cash is received or paid. There are two types of accruals:

accrued revenues
Revenues appropriately recognized under accrual accounting in one income statement period although the associated cash will be received in a later income statement period.

accrued expenses
Expenses appropriately recognized under accrual accounting in one income statement period although the associated cash will be paid in a later income statement period.

deferrals   Situations in which cash is either received or paid, but the income statement effect is delayed until some later period. Deferred revenues are recorded as liabilities, and deferred expenses are recorded as assets.

deferred revenues
Revenues created when cash is received before the revenue is earned. Because the cash received has not yet been earned, an obligation is created and a liability is recorded. Later, when the cash is deemed to have been earned, it will be recognized as a revenue.

deferred expenses
Expenses created when cash is paid before any benefit is received. Because the benefit to be derived is in the future, the item is recorded as an asset. Later, when the benefit is received from the item, it will be recognized as an expense.

a. **Accrued revenues** are revenues that are considered to be earned during the financial statement period, because they met the revenue recognition criteria, but that have not yet been recognized. Consider Warner Management Consulting Services, Inc. For regular clients, the company sends bills on the second day of each month for work done during the previous month. Warner has a legal claim at the end of December to services it provided in that month. Revenues recognized (recorded) should include the amount earned in December, even though the clients will not be billed until January 2 of the next year.

b. **Accrued expenses** are expenses that are deemed to have been incurred during the financial statement period but that have not yet been recognized. Assume Pellum Company pays its employees every two weeks for work performed in the previous two weeks. If part of the two-week pay period is in 1999 and part is in 2000, Pellum must make an adjustment at the end of 1999 to recognize the portion of wages expense incurred during that period.

2. **Deferrals** are postponements of the recognition of revenue or expense even though the cash has been received or paid. Deferrals are adjustments of revenues for which the cash has been collected but not yet earned, and of expenses for which cash has been paid but no benefit has yet been received.

a. **Deferred revenues** are created when cash is received before it is earned. For example, Chad's Lawn Service provides lawn care to many Miami families. On June 1, the Bidlack family sends Chad's $450 for the cost of three months' lawn service. As of June 1, Chad's Lawn Service has not earned any revenue, even though it has received cash. In fact, receipt of unearned cash creates a liability. The company owes the Bidlack family either three months of lawn service or a cash refund. The key here is who has legal claim to the cash. Because Chad's Lawn Service has no legal claim to the cash, it cannot account for it as earned revenue. By the time the month ends in June, however, Chad earns one month's fees and recognizes $150 as revenue. The remaining $300, representing two month's fees, remains a deferred revenue. This amount represents a liability for Chad's Lawn Service and will remain so until the company either performs the services required to attain a legal claim to the cash, or returns the cash to the Bidlack family.

b. **Deferred expenses** are created when cash is paid before an expense has been incurred. On January 2, 1999, Crockett Cookie Company purchased a three-year insurance policy for $2,400. By December 31, 1999, one-third of the insurance coverage has expired (one-third of the benefit has been received). Financial statements prepared for 1999 should reflect the fact that one-third of the cost of the policy ($800) is an expense for that year. The remaining portion of the policy, two years' worth of coverage, is an asset providing future benefits to the company. Even though the entire $2,400 was spent in 1999, two-thirds of the cost is a deferred expense, an asset that will be recognized as an expense in future periods.

The adjusting process preserves the integrity of accrual basis accounting. Keep in mind the following:

1. Accruals occur in situations when the cash flow has not yet taken place, but the revenue or expense should be recognized.
2. Deferrals are necessary in cases when the cash flow has already taken place, but the associated revenue or expense should not yet be recognized. The type of adjustments necessary to reflect the guidelines of accrual accounting depends on the way the item is originally recorded. Understand, too, that the

original transaction (the receipt or payment of cash) is not an adjustment, but rather it creates a situation in which an adjustment will be necessary later.

Whether they reflect expenses or revenues, accruals and deferrals will always possess the following three characteristics:

1. *A revenue item or an expense item will always be affected.* The whole purpose of the adjustment process is to make certain that revenues and expenses associated with a given financial statement period are recognized in that period. Clearly, adjustments will always affect the income statement.
2. *An asset item or a liability item will always be affected.* Accruals and deferrals require the adjustment or recognition of an asset or liability. Thus, the balance sheet will also be affected by the adjustment process.
3. *Cash is never affected by accruals or deferrals.* Remember, adjustments are made to properly recognize accounting elements. It is assumed that inflows and outflows of cash were properly recorded at the time they occurred.

Accrual Basis Financial Statements

Let us revisit the transactions of the McCumber Company for the month of January 2000. For your convenience, the descriptions of the company's transactions are restated here.

1. Gertie McCumber started the company on January 2 by investing $200,000.
2. McCumber Company borrowed $100,000 from the Friendly Bank on January 2 by signing a one-year, 12 percent note payable. Although the $100,000 does not have to be repaid until January 2, 2000, the interest charge must be paid each month, beginning on February 2, 2000.
3. The company purchased a vehicle on January 2 for $14,000 cash. Gertie estimates that the vehicle will fill the company's needs for four years, after which she estimates she can sell it for $2,000.
4. The company paid cash for $75,000 of merchandise inventory on January 8.
5. On January 15, the company sold merchandise that cost $42,000 for a total selling price of $78,000 and collected the cash the same day.
6. On January 22, the company sold merchandise that cost $15,000 for a total selling price of $32,000 on account (a credit sale). The terms of the sale were 30 days, meaning McCumber can expect to receive payment by February 21.
7. Cash payments for operating expenses in January totaled $22,500.
8. Besides the bank loan, the only amounts owed by the company at the end of the month were:
   a. $2,000 to company employees for work performed in January. They will be paid on February 3.
   b. A $700 utility bill that was received on January 26 and will be paid on February 15.

All eight transactions will affect the income statement and/or the balance sheet and statement of owners' equity under the accrual basis of accounting. The income statement for January 2000 looks like Exhibit 6–5.

Most of the items on this income statement differ from those on the income statement prepared under the cash basis (Exhibit 6–2). Look closely at each item:

- *Sales Revenue.* Under the accrual basis, we recognize revenue when it is earned and is either realized or it has an enforceable claim to receive the cash. McCumber made two sales during January; one was received in cash and the other created an enforceable account receivable. We recognize both as sales revenue for January of $110,000 ($78,000 cash sale + $32,000 credit sale).

Exhibit 6–5
Accrual Basis Income
Statement

McCumber Company
Income Statement
For the Month Ended January 31, 2000

Sales Revenue	$110,000	
Cost of Goods Sold	57,000	
Gross Margin		$53,000
Expenses:		
Cash Operating Expenses	$ 22,500	
Wages Expense	2,000	
Utilities Expense	700	
Interest Expense	1,000	
Depreciation Expense	250	
Total Operating Expenses		(26,450)
Net Income		$26,550

- *Cost of Goods Sold.* Accrual accounting attempts to match all expenses to the same income statement period as the revenues they help generate. Cost of goods sold directly relates to the sales made in January because it is the cost of those items sold in January. The inventory sold cost $57,000 ($42,000 + $15,000). McCumber purchased $75,000 of inventory and sold $57,000, leaving $18,000 of merchandise inventory on hand. We will discuss this remaining inventory when we talk about the balance sheet.
- *Cash Operating Expenses.* Under the accrual basis measurement, expenses paid in cash this period to support operations during this period (with no future benefits) are considered to be expenses for this period.
- *Wages Expense of $2,000.* Because employees earned wages during January, McCumber has a legal liability at January 31 for this amount. Because McCumber derived the benefit from the employees' work in January, we recognize the expense in January, regardless of when McCumber pays the employees.
- *Utilities Expense of $700.* Because McCumber received the bill in January, it represents utilities purchased and used during January. In that case, the expense should be recognized in January.
- *Interest Expense of $1,000.* When McCumber borrows money from the bank, interest accrues from the first day of the loan. Because the company had the $100,000 throughout the month of January, the interest cost for the month should be recognized as a January expense. The amount is calculated using the formula explained in Chapter 4:

$$\text{Principal} \times \text{Rate} \times \text{Time} = \text{Interest}$$
$$\$100{,}000 \times 12\% \times 1/12 = \$1{,}000$$

- *Depreciation Expense of $250.* Accrual accounting depreciates the cost of long-lived assets over the period useful to the entity. Using straight-line depreciation, depreciation equals ($14,000 − $2,000)/4 = $3,000 per year. Because McCumber's financial statements depict only the month of January 2000, the amount of depreciation expense would be only $250 ($3,000/12) for the month.

Discussion Questions

6-15. Reexamine each item on McCumber Company's accrual basis income statement. Identify the items that result from the adjustment process.

6-16. Consider the following statement as it relates to the accrual basis of economic measurement: "Net income is an opinion, cash is a fact." What do you think this means?

Now that we have discussed the effect of accrual accounting on the income statement, we can see how this system affects the statement of owners' equity. The $200,000 investment by the owner is treated just as it was under the cash basis. However, the results presented on the income statement under accrual accounting differ, so the statement of owner's equity (Exhibit 6–6) also differs from the cash basis statement in Exhibit 6–3.

Exhibit 6-6
Accrual Basis
Statement of Owner's
Equity

MCCUMBER COMPANY
Statement of Owner's Equity
For the Month Ended January 31, 2000

G. McCumber, Capital, January 1, 2000	$ 0
Investment by Owner	200,000
Net Income	26,550
G. McCumber, Capital, January 31, 2000	$226,550

Exhibit 6–7 illustrates the accrual basis balance sheet for McCumber Company at January 31, 2000. Note that the items we discussed for the income statement also have an effect on the balance sheet. Many items on this balance sheet differ from

Exhibit 6-7
Accrual Basis Balance
Sheet

MCCUMBER COMPANY
Balance Sheet
January 31, 2000

Assets:			Liabilities:	
Cash		$266,500	Accounts Payable	$ 700
Accounts Receivable		32,000	Wages Payable	2,000
Inventory		18,000	Interest Payable	1,000
Vehicle	$14,000		Note Payable	100,000
Less: Accumulated			Total Liabilities	$103,700
Depreciation	(250)		Owner's Equity:	
Vehicle, Net		13,750	G. McCumber, Capital	226,550
			Total Liabilities	
Total Assets		$330,250	and Owner's Equity	$330,250

those on the balance sheet prepared under the cash basis (Exhibit 6–4). We will discuss each item on the statement:

- *Cash of $266,500.* The cash amount results from the cash transactions. Method of measurement does not change cash.
- *Accounts Receivable of $32,000.* Transaction 6 created the account receivable. McCumber recognized the sale because an exchange took place and title to the merchandise inventory passed to the customer, creating an enforceable claim to $32,000 in February. The claim provides McCumber with a probable future benefit or an asset. It will remain classified as an asset until the customer pays McCumber the cash.
- *Inventory of $18,000.* The remaining amount of merchandise inventory not sold has probable future benefit to McCumber. It will remain classified as an asset until it is sold.
- *Vehicle of $14,000.* The original cost of the vehicle remains on the balance sheet until McCumber sells or disposes of the asset.
- *Accumulated Depreciation of $250.* To alert users that a portion of the original vehicle cost was converted to expense, we deduct an amount called **accumulated depreciation** from the asset cost to derive a **book value** of $13,750. The accumulated depreciation amount grows until it reaches the depreciable base; likewise, the book value declines until it reaches the residual value.
- *Accounts Payable of $700.* As McCumber uses utilities during the month, it accrues a legal liability to pay the utility company. When McCumber receives the bill, it can measure the amount of the liability. McCumber recognizes the utilities expense, and the corresponding liability that requires the future sacrifice of assets (cash) in the future. It will remain classified as a liability until McCumber pays the bill.
- *Wages Payable of $2,000.* McCumber owes its employees for wages at the balance sheet date. We recognize the expense and the liability during the adjustment process.
- *Interest Payable of $1,000.* McCumber owes the bank at the balance sheet for the interest accrued during January. We recognize the expense and the liability during the adjustment process.
- *Note Payable of $100,000.* McCumber Company owes Friendly Bank for the loan borrowed in January.
- *Capital of $226,550.* The ending capital balance shown on the accrual basis statement of capital articulates to the accrual basis balance sheet. The accrual basis and cash basis statements differ because of the difference in accrual basis and cash basis net income.

accumulated depreciation
The total amount of cost that has been systematically converted to expense since a long-lived asset was first purchased.

book value The original cost of a long-lived asset less its accumulated depreciation.

Strengths and Weaknesses of Accrual Basis Accounting

The strength of the accrual basis is that it attempts to match revenues and the expenses incurred in generating those revenues. Accrual basis accounting income statements present the *reality of performance* and balance sheets include all assets and liabilities of the firm. Economic decision makers use accrual basis income statements to assess the past performance of a company, the resources of the company, and the existing claims against those resources.

Accrual accounting turns the focus of the reader away from cash. An accrual basis income statement provides decision makers with no information about cash inflows or outflows. Because revenue and expense recognition under the accrual basis are totally unrelated to the receipt or payment of cash, net income or loss does not represent an increase or decrease in cash for the period covered by the income statement. The accounting profession addressed this weakness in accrual accounting by adding the statement of cash flows to required financial statements. By using the accrual basis income statement and the statement of cash flows, readers see both the *reality of performance* and the *reality of cash*. We will look closely at the statement of cash flows in Chapter 11 after we visit other accounting issues necessary to understand the preparation and use of that statement.

COMPARING THE TWO BASES OF ECONOMIC MEASUREMENT

Exhibits 6–8 and 6–9 illustrate two sets of financial statements for the McCumber Company. The first set depicts the cash basis of economic measurement, and the second set depicts the accrual basis.

Each set demonstrates the articulation of financial statements. The net loss presented on the cash basis income statement results in a reduction of the owner's capital account. The accrual basis income statement shows a net income of $26,550, which increases the owner's capital account. In both sets of statements, the ending

Exhibit 6–8
Set of Financial Statements Prepared Using the Cash Basis of Economic Measurement

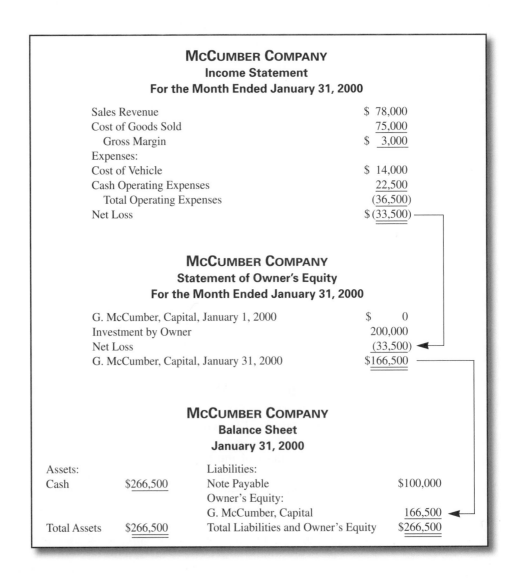

McCUMBER COMPANY
Income Statement
For the Month Ended January 31, 2000

Sales Revenue	$ 78,000
Cost of Goods Sold	75,000
Gross Margin	$ 3,000
Expenses:	
Cost of Vehicle	$ 14,000
Cash Operating Expenses	22,500
Total Operating Expenses	(36,500)
Net Loss	$ (33,500)

McCUMBER COMPANY
Statement of Owner's Equity
For the Month Ended January 31, 2000

G. McCumber, Capital, January 1, 2000	$ 0
Investment by Owner	200,000
Net Loss	(33,500)
G. McCumber, Capital, January 31, 2000	$166,500

McCUMBER COMPANY
Balance Sheet
January 31, 2000

Assets:		Liabilities:	
Cash	$266,500	Note Payable	$100,000
		Owner's Equity:	
		G. McCumber, Capital	166,500
Total Assets	$266,500	Total Liabilities and Owner's Equity	$266,500

Exhibit 6-9
Set of Financial Statements Prepared Using the Accrual Basis of Economic Measurement

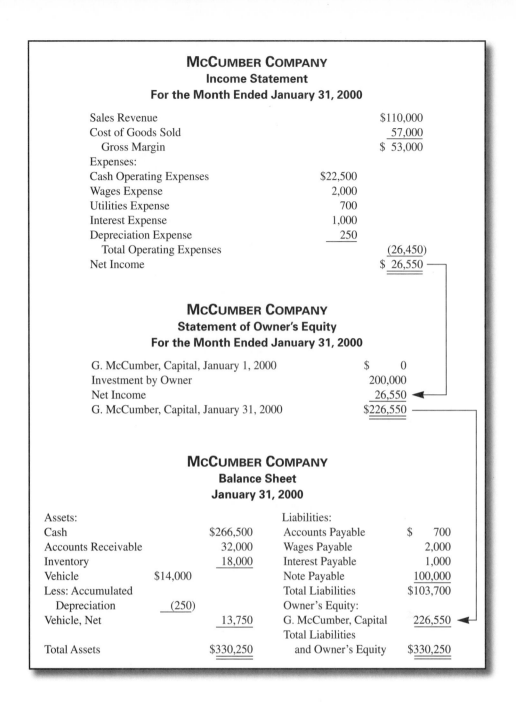

McCumber Company
Income Statement
For the Month Ended January 31, 2000

Sales Revenue		$110,000
Cost of Goods Sold		57,000
Gross Margin		$ 53,000
Expenses:		
Cash Operating Expenses	$22,500	
Wages Expense	2,000	
Utilities Expense	700	
Interest Expense	1,000	
Depreciation Expense	250	
Total Operating Expenses		(26,450)
Net Income		$ 26,550

McCumber Company
Statement of Owner's Equity
For the Month Ended January 31, 2000

G. McCumber, Capital, January 1, 2000	$ 0
Investment by Owner	200,000
Net Income	26,550
G. McCumber, Capital, January 31, 2000	$226,550

McCumber Company
Balance Sheet
January 31, 2000

Assets:			Liabilities:	
Cash		$266,500	Accounts Payable	$ 700
Accounts Receivable		32,000	Wages Payable	2,000
Inventory		18,000	Interest Payable	1,000
Vehicle	$14,000		Note Payable	100,000
Less: Accumulated			Total Liabilities	$103,700
Depreciation	(250)		Owner's Equity:	
Vehicle, Net		13,750	G. McCumber, Capital	226,550
			Total Liabilities	
Total Assets		$330,250	and Owner's Equity	$330,250

balance in the capital account, shown on the statement of owner's equity, transfers to the balance sheet.

Remember that we prepared both sets of statements using exactly the same transactions and events. The differences are caused, not by the reality of what happened in McCumber Company during January 2000, but by the different measurement criteria used by the cash and accrual bases of accounting.

Discussion Questions

6-17. Which of the two sets of financial statements do you think more closely relates the measurement of reality to reality? In other words, which set do you think is the better presentation of what actually happened during January 2000? Explain.

6-18. Which of the two sets of financial statements do you think better reflects McCumber Company's future profit potential? Explain.

So, which of the bases is better? The answer depends on the type of information you need for your decision. Each has strengths and weaknesses in relation to the other, and each is appropriate for certain entities in certain situations.

An economic decision maker incurs difficulty when trying to compare two companies that use different bases of measurement, especially if the decision maker is not aware of the basis used. Anticipating this difficulty, FASB requires that accountants use the accrual basis to be in accordance with generally accepted accounting principles (GAAP) or indicate that the statements were prepared using some other economic basis.

You may have found that accumulation of the information to prepare the financial statements was complicated. This process becomes much easier with an accounting system to properly capture the data. Chapter 7 introduces the basics of the accounting cycle to help us accumulate and organize transactions into meaningful information.

SUMMARY

A firm performs four functions: It operates to produce revenues, invests in productive resources, finances those investments, and makes decisions. Such activities constitute the reality of business transactions and events. Accountants attempt to measure that reality in the accounting records and reports. The measurement of reality may not precisely reflect reality because of the basis selected to recognize revenues and expenses in a particular time period. This chapter presents two distinct bases: the cash basis and the accrual basis.

The cash basis of accounting recognizes revenues and expenses when realized—when the cash associated with revenue is received, and when the cash associated with an expense is paid. Periodic net income (or loss) under the cash basis is simply the difference between revenues received and expenses paid.

Under accrual accounting, revenue is recognized when it is both earned and realizable (when the company has a legal claim to the associated cash). Expenses are recognized when their benefit is deemed to have been received, regardless of when the associated cash is paid. Further, accrual accounting utilizes the matching principle to recognize expenses in the same income statement period as the revenues they helped generate.

The matching principle provides the foundation for accrual accounting's treatment of long-lived assets. The cost of a long-lived asset represents an asset because it provides the company with future benefits. The asset cost is systematically converted from asset to expense in the income statement periods benefited by the conversion process called depreciation.

In addition to depreciation, we record accrual and deferral adjustments in the accounting records to ensure that accrual accounting's revenue and expense recognition guidelines have been met before we prepare the financial statements. Accruals are adjustments made prior to any cash inflow or outflow to record earned but unreceived revenues and incurred but unpaid expenses. Deferrals are adjustments made for situations when the cash flow has already occurred to record unearned revenues and unexpired expenses.

Accrual accounting presents the best measurement of the reality of performance, making the income statement and balance sheet more useful as predictive and feedback tools than financial statements prepared under the cash basis. The cash basis presents the best measurement of the reality of cash by keeping the financial statement user's eye on cash. Recognizing this problem, GAAP require both the accrual basis to provide the *reality of performance,* and the inclusion of the statement of cash flows to provide the *reality of cash.*

KEY TERMS

accrual basis accounting   F-191
accruals   F-196
accrue   F-192
accrued expenses   F-197
accrued revenues   F-197
accumulated depreciation   F-201
adjustments   F-196
book value   F-201
cash basis accounting   F-188
deferrals   F-197
deferred expenses   F-197

deferred revenues   F-197
depreciable base   F-196
depreciation   F-195
depreciation expense   F-195
matching principle   F-194
periodicity   F-185
realization   F-188
receivable   F-192
recognition   F-187
residual value   F-196
straight-line depreciation   F-196

REVIEW THE FACTS

A. Explain the difference between reality and the measurement of reality, and provide an example of each.
B. How does periodic measurement create complications?
C. In accounting, what does it mean for an item to be "recognized"?
D. In accounting, what does it mean for an item to be "realized"?
E. Under the cash basis of measurement, when does revenue recognition occur?
F. Under the cash basis, when are expenses recognized?
G. What is the greatest strength of the cash basis?
H. What is the greatest weakness of the cash basis?
I. Under the accrual basis of measurement, when does revenue recognition occur?
J. Under the accrual basis, when are expenses recognized?
K. Explain the concept of matching.
L. What is depreciation and why is it necessary in accrual accounting?
M. Compare and contrast accruals and deferrals.
N. What is the greatest strength of the accrual basis?
O. What is the greatest weakness of the accrual basis?
P. Explain the difference between the reality of cash and the reality of performance.

LO 1 & 2: Terminology

6–19. Presented below is a list of items relating to the concepts discussed in this chapter, followed by definitions of those items in scrambled order:

a. Cash basis revenues
b. Accrual basis expenses
c. Immediate recognition
d. Matching principle
e. Title passes to customer
f. Depreciation
g. No direct cause and effect between costs and revenues
h. Cash basis expenses
i. Residual value
j. Accrual basis revenues

1. _____ The amount of the cost of a long-lived asset that is never allocated to the periods benefited
2. _____ Recognized when cash associated with a sale is received
3. _____ The situation that causes costs to be either recognized immediately as an expense or allocated to the income statement periods supposed benefited
4. _____ One of three evidences that revenue has been earned under accrual accounting
5. _____ Recognized when the cash associated with a cost is paid
6. _____ Recognized when there is a legal claim to the cash associated with a sale
7. _____ An attempt to recognize expenses in the same income statement period as the revenues they generate
8. _____ Recognized when the benefit is received rather than when the cash is paid
9. _____ The process of converting the cost of a long-lived item from asset to expense
10. _____ The treatment for costs when no future benefit can be determined or allocation to future periods serves no useful purpose

REQUIRED:
Match the letter next to each item on the list with the appropriate definition. Each letter will be used only once.

LO 1 & 2: Cash Basis Measurement

6–20. Katie Bales Company began operation on January 2, 1999. During its first month of operation, the company had the following transactions:
- Purchased $35,000 of merchandise inventory on January 2. The amount due is payable on February 2.
- Paid January office rent of $3,000 on January 3.
- Purchased $10,000 of merchandise inventory on January 5. Paid cash at the time of purchase.
- Sold inventory that cost $18,000 for $30,000 to a customer on January 10 and received the cash on that date.
- Sold inventory that cost $5,000 for $9,000 to a customer on January 20. The sale was on account and the customer has until February 20 to pay.
- Paid cash expenses during January of $7,500.
- Received bills for utilities, advertising, and phone service totaling $1,500. All these bills were for services received in January. They will all be paid the first week in February.

REQUIRED:

a. Prepare a January 1999 multistep income statement for Katie Bales Company using the cash basis of accounting.

b. Do you think the income statement you prepared for the previous requirement provides a good measure of the reality of the company's performance during January? Explain your reasoning.

LO 3: Accrual Basis Measurement

6–21. Katie Bales Company began operation on January 2, 1999. During its first month of operation, the company had the same seven transactions as noted in problem 6–20.

REQUIRED:

a. Prepare a January 1999 multistep income statement for Katie Bales Company using the accrual basis of accounting.

b. Do you think the income statement you prepared for the previous requirement provides a good measure of the reality of the company's performance during January? Explain your reasoning.

LO 1 & 2: Cash Basis Measurement

6–22. Snow and Ice Company began operation on June 1, 1999. During its first month of operation, the company had the following transactions:

- Purchased $40,000 of merchandise inventory on June 1. The amount due is payable on August 1.
- Paid June office rent of $2,000 on June 3.
- Purchased $20,000 of merchandise inventory on June 4. Paid cash at the time of purchase.
- Sold inventory that cost $30,000 for $42,000 to a customer on June 10 and received the cash on that date.
- Sold inventory that cost $10,000 for $14,000 to a customer on June 20. The sale was on account and the customer has until July 20 to pay.
- Paid cash expenses during June of $9,500.
- Received bills for utilities, advertising, and phone service totaling $3,500. All these bills were for services received in June. They will all be paid the first week in July.

REQUIRED:

a. Prepare a June 1999 multistep income statement for Snow and Ice Company using the cash basis of accounting.

b. Do you think the income statement you prepared for the previous requirement provides a good measure of the reality of the company's performance during June? Explain your reasoning.

LO 3: Accrual Basis Measurement

6–23. Snow and Ice Company began operation on June 1, 1999. During its first month of operation, the company had the same seven transactions as noted in problem 6–22.

REQUIRED:

a. Prepare a June 1999 multistep income statement for Snow and Ice Company using the accrual basis of accounting.

b. Do you think the income statement you prepared for the previous requirement provides a good measure of the reality of the company's performance during June? Explain your reasoning.

LO 2 & 3:   Cash vs. Accrual

6–24. Roger Webb and Company began operation on January 2, 2001. During its first month of operation, the company had the following transactions:
- Paid January office rent of $2,000 on January 2.
- Purchased $25,000 of merchandise inventory on January 5. The amount due is payable on February 5.
- Purchased $15,000 of merchandise inventory on January 8. Paid cash at the time of purchase.
- Sold merchandise that cost $12,000 for $18,000 to a customer on January 16 and received the cash on that date.
- Sold merchandise that cost $9,000 for $13,500 to a customer on January 26. The sale was on account and the customer has until February 26 to pay.
- Paid February office rent of $2,000 on January 31.

REQUIRED:
a. Prepare a January 2001 multistep income statement for Roger Webb and Company using the cash basis of accounting.
b. Prepare a January 2001 multistep income statement for Roger Webb and Company using the accrual basis of accounting.
c. Explain in your own words what caused the differences between the income statement prepared under the cash basis and the one prepared under the accrual basis.
d. Which of the two income statement presentations do you think:
  (1) provides better information as to cash flow for the month of January?
  (2) provides better information as to what Webb earned during the month of January?
  (3) better reflects Webb's ability to generate future earnings and cash flow?

LO 2, 3 & 4:   Cash vs. Accrual

6–25. This is a continuation of the Roger Webb and Company problem begun in 6–24. During February 2001, the company had the following transactions:
- Sold all the merchandise inventory it had on hand at the beginning of February for $28,500 cash on February 2.
- On February 5, the company paid the $25,000 it owed for the merchandise inventory it purchased on January 5.
- Purchased $20,000 of merchandise inventory on February 11. Paid cash at the time of purchase.
- Sold the merchandise that cost $20,000 it had purchased on February 11 for $30,000 to a customer on February 21 and received the cash on that date.
- On February 26, Webb collected the $13,500 from the sale of January 26.

REQUIRED:
a. Prepare a February 2001 multistep income statement for Roger Webb and Company using the cash basis of accounting.
b. Prepare a February 2001 multistep income statement for Roger Webb and Company using the accrual basis of accounting.

c. Explain in your own words what caused the differences between the income statement prepared under the cash basis and the one prepared under the accrual basis.

d. Which of the two income statement presentations do you think:

(1) provides better information as to cash flow for the month of February?

(2) provides better information as to what Webb earned during the month of February?

(3) better reflects Webb's ability to generate future earnings and cash flow?

LO 2, 3, & 4:   Cash vs. Accrual

6–26. During the months of January and February 2001, Roger Webb and Company (which began operations on January 2, 2001) had the following transactions:

- Paid January office rent of $2,000 on January 2.
- Purchased $25,000 of merchandise inventory on January 5. The amount due is payable in February.
- Purchased $15,000 of merchandise inventory on January 8. Paid cash at the time of purchase.
- Sold merchandise that cost $12,000 for $18,000 to a customer on January 16 and received the cash on that date.
- Sold merchandise that cost $9,000 for $13,500 to a customer on January 26. The sale was on account and the customer has until February 26 to pay.
- Paid February office rent of $2,000 on January 31.
- Sold all the merchandise inventory it had on hand at the beginning of February for $28,500 cash on February 2.
- On February 5, the company paid the $25,000 it owed for the merchandise inventory it purchased on January 5.
- Purchased $20,000 of merchandise inventory on February 11. Paid cash at the time of purchase.
- Sold the merchandise that cost $20,000 it had purchased on February 11 for $30,000 to a customer on February 21 and received the cash on that date.
- On February 26, Webb collected the $13,500 from the sale of January 26.

REQUIRED:

a. Prepare a multistep income statement for Roger Webb and Company using the cash basis of accounting for the two-month period ending February 28, 2001.

b. Prepare a multistep income statement for Roger Webb and Company using the accrual basis of accounting for the two-month period ending February 28, 2001.

c. Explain in your own words what caused the differences between the income statement prepared under the cash basis and the one prepared under the accrual basis.

LO 2, 3, & 4:   Cash vs. Accrual

6–27. Arley Safer and Company began operation on August 2, 2000. During its first month of operation, the company had the following transactions:

- Paid August office rent of $3,000 on August 2.
- Purchased $35,000 of merchandise inventory on August 5. The amount due is payable on September 5.

- Purchased $25,000 of merchandise inventory on August 8. Paid cash at the time of purchase.
- Sold merchandise that cost $22,000 for $33,000 to a customer on August 16 and received the cash on that date.
- Sold merchandise that cost $10,000 for $15,000 to a customer on August 26. The sale was on account and the customer has until September 26 to pay.
- Paid September office rent of $3,000 on August 31.

REQUIRED:

a. Prepare an August 2000 multistep income statement for Arley Safer and Company using the cash basis of accounting.

b. Prepare an August 2000 multistep income statement for Arley Safer and Company using the accrual basis of accounting.

c. Explain in your own words what caused the differences between the income statement prepared under the cash basis and the one prepared under the accrual basis.

d. Which of the two income statement presentations do you think:
   (1) provides better information as to cash flow for the month of August?
   (2) provides better information as to what Arley Safer earned during the month of August?
   (3) better reflects Arley Safer's ability to generate future earnings and cash flow?

LO 2, 3, & 4: Cash vs. Accrual

6–28. This is a continuation of the Arley Safer and Company problem begun in 6–27. During the month of September 2000, the company had the following transactions:

- Sold all the merchandise inventory it had on hand at the beginning of September for $42,000 cash on September 2.
- On September 5, the company paid the $35,000 it owed for the merchandise inventory it purchased on August 5.
- Purchased $30,000 of merchandise inventory on September 11. Paid cash at the time of purchase.
- Sold merchandise that cost $30,000 it had purchased on September 11 for $45,000 to a customer on September 21 and received the cash on that date.
- On September 26, Arley Safer and Company collected the $15,000 from the sale of August 26.

REQUIRED:

a. Prepare a September 2000 multistep income statement for Arley Safer and Company using the cash basis of accounting.

b. Prepare a September 2000 multistep income statement for Arley Safer and Company using the accrual basis of accounting.

c. Explain in your own words what caused the differences between the income statement prepared under the cash basis and the one prepared under the accrual basis.

d. Which of the two income statement presentations do you think:
   (1) provides better information as to cash flow for the month of September?
   (2) provides better information as to what Arley Safer and Company earned during the month of September?
   (3) better reflects Arley Safer and Company's ability to generate future earnings and cash flow?

LO 2, 3, & 4:   Cash vs. Accrual

6–29. During the months of August and September 2000, Arley Safer and Company (which began operations on August 2, 2000) had the following transactions:

- Paid August office rent of $3,000 on August 2.
- Purchased $35,000 of merchandise inventory on August 5. The amount due is payable on September 5.
- Purchased $25,000 of merchandise inventory on August 8. Paid cash at the time of purchase.
- Sold merchandise that cost $22,000 for $33,000 to a customer on August 16 and received the cash on that date.
- Sold merchandise that cost $10,000 for $15,000 to a customer on August 26. The sale was on account and the customer has until September 26 to pay.
- Paid September office rent of $3,000 on August 31.
- Sold all the merchandise inventory it had on hand at the beginning of September for $42,000 cash on September 2.
- On September 5, the company paid the $35,000 it owed for the merchandise inventory it purchased on August 5.
- Purchased $30,000 of merchandise inventory on September 11. Paid cash at the time of purchase.
- Sold merchandise that cost $30,000 it had purchased on September 11 for $45,000 to a customer on September 21 and received the cash on that date.
- On September 26, Arley Safer and Company collected the $15,000 from the sale of August 26.

REQUIRED:

a. Prepare a multistep income statement for Arley Safer and Company using the cash basis of accounting for the two-month period ending September 30, 2000.

b. Prepare a multistep income statement for Arley Safer and Company using the accrual basis of accounting for the two-month period ending September 30, 2000.

c. Explain in your own words what caused the differences between the income statement prepared under the cash basis and the one prepared under the accrual basis.

LO 4:   The Matching Principle

6–30. Linda Leonard, Inc. purchased inventory in December 2001 for $65,000 cash. It sold merchandise that cost $25,000 in December and the remainder in January 2002.

REQUIRED:

a. Calculate how much of the $65,000 of merchandise appears in Cost of Goods Sold in December 2001 and January 2002 if Leonard uses the cash basis of accounting.

b. Calculate how much of the $65,000 of merchandise appears in Cost of Goods Sold in December 2001 and January 2002 if Leonard uses the accrual basis of accounting.

LO 4:   The Matching Principle

6–31. Chrisco, Inc. purchased $100,000 of merchandise inventory on December 15, 2000 on a 30-day account. It sold merchandise that cost $35,000 in December and the remainder in January 2001.

REQUIRED:

a. On what date should Chrisco pay for the merchandise?
b. Calculate how much of the $100,000 of merchandise appears in Cost of Goods Sold in December 2000 and how much appears on the balance sheet in Merchandise Inventory on December 31, 2000, if Chrisco uses the cash basis of accounting.
c. Calculate how much of the $100,000 of merchandise appears in Cost of Goods Sold in December 2000 and how much appears on the balance sheet in Merchandise Inventory on December 31, 2000, if Chrisco uses the accrual basis of accounting.

LO 4:   The Matching Principle

6–32. Karen Price, Inc. purchased $150,000 of merchandise inventory on December 5, 1999, on a special 90-day account. It sold merchandise that cost $55,000 in December and $70,000 in January 2000.

REQUIRED:

a. On what date should Price pay for the merchandise?
b. Calculate how much of the $150,000 of merchandise appears in Cost of Goods Sold in December 1999 and how much appears on the balance sheet in Merchandise Inventory on December 31, 1999, if Price uses the cash basis of accounting.
c. Calculate how much of the $150,000 of merchandise appears in Cost of Goods Sold in January 2000 and how much appears on the balance sheet in Merchandise Inventory on January 31, 2000, if Price uses the cash basis of accounting.
d. Calculate how much of the $150,000 of merchandise appears in Cost of Goods Sold in December 1999 and how much appears on the balance sheet in Merchandise Inventory on December 31, 1999, if Price uses the accrual basis of accounting.
e. Calculate how much of the $150,000 of merchandise appears in Cost of Goods Sold in January 2000 and how much appears on the balance sheet in Merchandise Inventory on January 31, 2000, if Price uses the accrual basis of accounting.

LO 4:   The Matching Principle

6–33. Geoffrey Corporation purchased a two-year insurance policy on May 1, 1999, by paying $4,800 on that date.

REQUIRED:

a. Indicate how Geoffrey will list information concerning this policy on its December 31, 1999, income statement and balance sheet under the cash basis.
b. Indicate how Geoffrey will list information concerning this policy on its December 31, 1999, income statement and balance sheet under the accrual basis.
c. Indicate how Geoffrey will list information concerning this policy on its December 31, 2000, income statement and balance sheet under the cash basis.

d. Indicate how Geoffrey will list information concerning this policy on its December 31, 2000, income statement and balance sheet under the accrual basis.

LO 4: The Matching Principle

6–34. Kazu & Liu paid their landlord $10,000 for five months' rent on November 1, 2000. The partnership has a calendar year end.

REQUIRED:

a. Indicate how Kazu & Liu will list information concerning this rental on its December 31, 2000, income statement and balance sheet under the cash basis.

b. Indicate how Kazu & Liu will list information concerning this rental on its December 31, 2000, income statement and balance sheet under the accrual basis.

c. Indicate how Kazu & Liu will list information concerning this rental on its December 31, 2001, income statement and balance sheet under the cash basis.

d. Indicate how Kazu & Liu will list information concerning this rental on its December 31, 2001, income statement and balance sheet under the accrual basis.

LO 4: The Matching Principle

6–35. Regina's Closet paid her landlord $1,600 for the first and last months' rent on March 1, 2000, when she opened her business. The lease on her shop is for one year.

REQUIRED:

a. Indicate how Regina's Closet will list information concerning this rental on her March 31, 2000, income statement and balance sheet under the cash basis.

b. Indicate how Regina's Closet will list information concerning this rental on her March 31, 2000, income statement and balance sheet under the accrual basis.

LO 4: The Matching Principle

6–36. Lechleiter Real Estate Company collected $10,000 from Kazu & Liu for five months' rent on November 1, 2000. Lechleiter operates on a February 28 year end.

REQUIRED:

a. How much rental income will Lechleiter recognize in its February 28, 2001, income statement under the cash basis? How will this affect the February 28, 2001, balance sheet?

b. How much rental income will Lechleiter recognize in its February 28, 2001, income statement under the accrual basis? How will this affect the February 28, 2001, balance sheet?

c. How much rental income will Lechleiter recognize in its February 28, 2002, income statement under the cash basis? How will this affect the February 28, 2002, balance sheet?

d. How much rental income will Lechleiter recognize in its February 28, 2002, income statement under the accrual basis? How will this affect the February 28, 2002, balance sheet?

LO 4: The Matching Principle

6-37. Gaylon Garretson paid her accountant, Shannon Davis, $675 for three months' services in advance on December 16, 1999. By the end of December, Davis had completed the December services.

REQUIRED:
 a. How much should Davis report as income for 1999 under the cash basis? How will this affect Davis' December 31, 1999, balance sheet?
 b. How much should Davis report as income for 2000 under the accrual basis? How will this affect Davis' January 31, 2000, balance sheet?
 c. How should Garretson report this payment on her income statement and balance sheet for December 31, 1999, under the cash basis?
 d. How should Garretson report this payment on her income statement and balance sheet for December 31, 1999, under the accrual basis?

LO 4: The Matching Principle

6-38. Dylan Hillhouse borrowed $10,000 for three months from First Fidelity Bank on November 1, 2000. Because Dylan was a recent graduate, the bank deducted the interest from the proceeds and deposited $9,700 to Dylan's bank account.

REQUIRED:
 a. How much interest income should the bank report for 2000 for this loan if it uses the cash basis of accounting?
 b. How much interest income should the bank report for 2000 for this loan if it uses the accrual basis of accounting?
 c. How much interest expense should Dylan report for 2000 for this loan if he uses the cash basis of accounting?
 d. How much interest expense should Dylan report for 2000 for this loan if he uses the accrual basis of accounting?

LO 4: The Matching Principle

6-39. Frank Dolf Imports Company purchased with cash $200,000 of merchandise inventory in 2000, its first year of operations. In addition, Frank paid $10,000 to package and label the entire inventory with his private label. It cost him $12,000 to ship the items sold to his customers. Frank sold 75% of the inventory by year end.

REQUIRED:
 a. List the expenses Frank would show on his income statement for 2000 under the cash basis of accounting. How would this information affect the December 31, 2000, balance sheet?
 b. List the expenses Frank would show on his income statement for 2000 under the accrual basis of accounting. How would this information affect the December 31, 2000, balance sheet?

LO 4: The Matching Principle

6-40. Perry Dennis borrowed $15,000 for his business at 9% interest from the Nations Bank on June 1, 1999, due on May 31, 2000. Interest is payable on the due date of the note.

REQUIRED:

  a. How much interest will Dennis owe the bank when he pays the note on May 31, 2000?

  b. How will Dennis report this event on his income statement and balance sheet for calendar year 1999 if he uses the cash basis of accounting?

  c. How will Dennis report this event on his income statement and balance sheet for calendar year 1999 if he uses the accrual basis of accounting?

LO 4: The Matching Principle and Depreciation

6–41. Tiffany's Toppers bought a commercial stitching machine on July 1, 2000, for $25,000. She estimates this machine will be useful for five years and will have no residual value because there is little market for used stitching machines.

REQUIRED:

  a. Assuming Tiffany uses the cash basis of accounting, how much will she recognize as expense for the stitching machine in 2000, 2001, and 2002?

  b. Assuming Tiffany uses the accrual basis of accounting, how much will she recognize as expense for the stitching machine in 2000, 2001, and 2002?

  c. Assuming Tiffany uses the cash basis of accounting, how will she report this on her ending balance sheets for 2000, 2001, and 2002?

  d. Assuming Tiffany uses the accrual basis of accounting, how will she report this on her ending balance sheets for 2000, 2001, and 2002?

LO 4: The Matching Principle and Depreciation

6–42. Christine's Delivery Service purchased a van on October 1, 1999, to deliver parcels for local merchants. Christine estimates that the van will last four years and can be sold for $2,000 at the end of the fourth year.

REQUIRED:

  a. For accrual basis accounting, how much will Christine recognize as depreciation expense for the calendar years of 1999, 2002, and 2004 if the cost of the van was

  (1) $26,000?

  (2) $34,000?

  b. What will be the balance of Accumulated Depreciation on December 31, 1999, 2002, and 2003 if the cost of the van was

  (1) $26,000?

  (2) $34,000?

LO 4: The Matching Principle and Depreciation

6–43. Pitman Photo purchased a racing boat for $300,000 on March 31, 2000, to enter into sporting events as a method of advertising. The owner believes that the boat can last 10 years (unless it is wrecked). He knows, however, that to remain competitive, he will need to replace the boat after five years. If he keeps the boat five years, the residual value will be 50% of cost; and if he keeps it 10 years, the residual value will be 15% of cost.

REQUIRED:

a. For accrual basis accounting, how much will Pitman recognize as depreciation expense for the calendar years of 2000, 2002, and 2004 if he plans to keep the boat
   (1) 5 years?
   (2) 10 years?
b. What will be the balance of Accumulated Depreciation on December 31, 2000, 2002, and 2004 if he plans to keep the boat
   (1) 5 years?
   (2) 10 years?

LO 5: Accruals and Deferrals

6–44. Explain the difference between a deferred expense and an accrued expense. A simple definition of these items will not suffice. You should concentrate on what these items really mean. Include in your answer at least one example of a deferred expense and one example of an accrued expense.

LO 5: Accruals and Deferrals

6–45. Explain why accruals and deferrals are necessary under accrual basis accounting but not under cash basis accounting. Your answer should include a discussion of accruals and deferrals as they apply to both revenues and expenses.

LO 5: Accruals and Deferrals

6–46. The Pratt Company reported sales of $200,000 for the year ended December 31, 2001. Sales were reported on the accrual basis. The accounts receivable at December 31, 2000, were $25,000 and at December 31, 2001, the receivables were $12,000.

REQUIRED:

Calculate the amount Pratt collected from customers for 2001.

LO 5: Accruals and Deferrals

6–47. The Foskin Company reported accounts receivable of $35,000 at December 31, 2000, and $48,000 at December 31, 2001. Cash collections from customers were $196,000 for the year.

REQUIRED:

Calculate the amount of sales reported on the accrual basis for the calendar year 2001.

LO 5: Accruals and Deferrals

6–48. The Frazier Corporation purchases all merchandise for resale on account. The balance of Accounts Payable at December 31, 2001, was $34,000 and the balance at December 31, 2002, was $29,000. Frazier paid $245,000 for merchandise purchases during the year. Frazier uses the accrual basis of accounting.

REQUIRED:

Determine the amount of merchandise purchases for the year of 2002.

LO 5: Accruals and Deferrals

6–49. The Tyson Corporation purchases all merchandise for resale on account. The balance of Accounts Payable at December 31, 2002, is $96,000 and the balance at December 31, 2003, is $120,000. Tyson paid $365,000 for merchandise purchases during the year.

REQUIRED:

Determine the amount of merchandise purchases on the accrual basis for the year 2003.

LO 6: Cash vs. Accrual

6–50. Academy, Inc. sold some merchandise inventory for cash during the current month. Unfortunately, the company's accounting clerk simply slipped the cash from the sale into his pocket and did not record the sale. Academy uses accrual accounting.

REQUIRED:

a. Explain how each of the following financial statements would be affected by the accounting clerk's behavior. Avoid using one-word responses such as *understated* and *overstated*. You should approach this requirement as if you were explaining the effects to someone with no knowledge of accounting or financial statements.
  (1) Income statement
  (2) Statement of stockholders' equity
  (3) Balance sheet
b. Briefly explain how your answer would differ if Academy used the cash basis of accounting.

LO 6: Cash vs. Accrual

6–51. The bookkeeper for Ajax Corporation mistakenly recorded a disbursement for equipment as if the payment had been for repairs and maintenance expense.

REQUIRED:

a. Explain how each of the following financial statements would be affected by the bookkeeper's error. Avoid using one-word responses such as *understated* and *overstated*. You should approach this requirement as if you were explaining the effects to someone with no knowledge of accounting or financial statements.
  (1) Income statement
  (2) Statement of stockholders' equity
  (3) Balance sheet
b. Briefly explain how your answer would differ if Ajax used the cash basis of accounting.

LO 6: Cash vs. Accrual

6–52. The bookkeeper for Lisa Miller Corporation mistakenly recorded a disbursement for advertising expense as if the payment had been for a parcel of land.

REQUIRED:

a. Explain how each of the following financial statements would be affected by the bookkeeper's error. Avoid using one-word responses such as *understated* and *overstated.* You should approach this requirement as if you were explaining the effects to someone with no knowledge of accounting or financial statements.

    (1) Income statement
    (2) Statement of stockholders' equity
    (3) Balance sheet

b. Briefly explain how your answer would differ if Miller used the cash basis of accounting.

LO 6: Cash vs. Accrual

6–53. The bookkeeper for Elmendorf Corporation mistakenly recorded a disbursement for rent expense as if the payment had been for an insurance expense.

REQUIRED:

a. Explain how each of the following financial statements would be affected by the bookkeeper's error. Avoid using one-word responses such as *understated* and *overstated.* You should approach this requirement as if you were explaining the effects to someone with no knowledge of accounting or financial statements.

    (1) Income statement
    (2) Statement of stockholders' equity
    (3) Balance sheet

b. Briefly explain how your answer would differ if Elmendorf used the cash basis of accounting.

LO 6: Cash vs. Accrual Revenue Recognition

6–54. Guthrie Corporation uses the accrual basis of accounting. Guthrie recognizes revenue at the time it sells product or delivers a service. The entity engages in the following activities during August.

    1. Collects $5,000 from customers for the sale of merchandise in the month of August.
    2. Collects $10,000 from customers for the sale of merchandise in the month of July.
    3. Collects $4,000 from customers for merchandise to be ordered and delivered in September.

REQUIRED:

a. Calculate the amount of revenue to be recognized in August.
b. Calculate the amount of revenue to be recognized in August if the company were on a cash basis.

LO 6: Cash vs. Accrual Revenue Recognition

6–55. Clinton Corporation uses the accrual basis of accounting. Clinton recognizes revenue at the time it sells product or delivers a service. The entity engages in the following activities during November.

    1. Collects $10,000 from customers for the sale of merchandise in the month of October.
    2. Collects $18,000 from customers for the sale of merchandise in the month of November.
    3. Collects $12,000 from customers for merchandise to be ordered and delivered in December and January.

REQUIRED:

a. Calculate the amount of revenue to be recognized in November.

b. Calculate the amount of revenue to be recognized in November if the company were on a cash basis.

LO 6: Cash vs. Accrual Expense Recognition

6–56. Gore Corporation uses the accrual basis of accounting. Gore recognizes expenses in accordance with the matching principle. The entity engaged in the following activities during July:

1. Paid $20,000 to suppliers for office supplies used in the month of July.
2. Paid $22,000 for radio and television advertising that aired in June.
3. Paid $6,000 for insurance expense that covers the months of July, August, and September.

REQUIRED:

a. Calculate the amount of expense to be recognized in the month of July.

b. Calculate the amount of expense to be recognized in July if the company were on a cash basis.

LO 6: Cash vs. Accrual Expense Recognition

6–57. Tipper Corporation uses the accrual basis of accounting. Tipper recognizes expenses in accordance with the matching principle. The entity engaged in the following activities during December.

1. Paid $8,000 to suppliers for office equipment rental in the month of December.
2. Paid $32,000 for radio and television advertising that aired in November.
3. Paid $8,000 for insurance expense that covers the months of December through March.

REQUIRED:

a. Calculate the amount of expense to be recognized in December.

b. Calculate the amount of expense to be recognized in December if the company were on a cash basis.

LO 6: Cash vs. Accrual Determination of Net Income

6–58. The following represent transactions entered into by the Murphy Company in January:

1. Purchased $10,000 of merchandise for resale paying cash.
2. Paid $2,000 for office rent for January and February.
3. Ordered $15,000 worth of merchandise to sell.
4. Paid $3,000 for a piece of office furniture that will last five years with no residual value.
5. Received and paid for merchandise ordered in transaction 3.
6. Sold merchandise that cost $2,000 for $6,000.
7. Paid one month's salary of $3,500.
8. Sold merchandise on credit for $20,000 that cost $7,000. Payment was received in February.
9. Purchased advertising for January on credit for $2,000 agreeing to pay for it in February.

REQUIRED:

a. Determine the net income or net loss for the month of January on a cash basis.

b. Determine the net income or net loss for the month of January on the accrual basis.

LO 6:   Cash vs. Accrual Determination of Net Income

6–59. The Sheets Corporation entered into the following transactions during February:
1. Purchased $56,000 of merchandise for cash.
2. Paid $3,600 for office rent for January and February.
3. Ordered $45,000 worth of merchandise to sell.
4. Paid $5,400 for a computer for the accounting department. The computer should last three years with no residual value.
5. Received the merchandise ordered in transaction 3. Payment is due to the vendor on March 10.
6. Sold merchandise that cost $24,000 for $38,000.
7. Paid weekly salaries of $4,500 for the first three weeks. The last week's salary will be paid March 1.
8. Sold merchandise on credit for $80,000 that cost $45,000. Payment was received in February.
9. Paid advertising for January of $12,000. February's ads were $8,000 and will be paid by March 15.

REQUIRED:
a. Determine February's net income or net loss on the cash basis.
b. Determine February's net income or net loss on the accrual basis.

LO 6:   Cash vs. Accrual Determination of Net Income

6–60. Arnell Johnson Enterprises completed the following transactions in November.
1. Purchased $100,000 of merchandise for resale with cash.
2. Paid $12,000 for office rent for the next 12 months.
3. Ordered $85,000 worth of merchandise for resale on a 30-day account.
4. Purchased a delivery van for $25,000 that should last five years.
5. Received the merchandise ordered in transaction 3.
6. Sold merchandise that cost $72,000 for $106,000.
7. Paid one month's salaries of $13,500.
8. Sold merchandise on credit for $72,000 that cost $54,000. Payment was received in December.
9. Purchased advertising for November on credit for $9,000 agreeing to pay for it in December.

REQUIRED:
a. Determine the net income or net loss for the month of November on a cash basis.
b. Determine the net income or net loss for the month of November on the accrual basis.

FINANCIAL REPORTING CASES

Comprehensive

6–61. Visit the PHLIP Web site for this book at *www.prenhall.com/jones* to find the CMI Corporation link. Look up the current copy of the annual report and find the footnotes section. The first footnote should contain a description of business and a summary of the significant accounting policies.

REQUIRED:
Does CMI report on a cash or accrual basis? Write a two-page summary of the important accounting issues discussed in the first footnote.

Comprehensive

6–62. Tour Disney World by visiting the Walt Disney Corporation Web site. (Go to the PHLIP Web site for this book at *www.prenhall.com/jones* for the link to Disney.) Locate the footnote section in the current annual report. The first footnote should contain a description of business and a summary of the significant accounting policies.

REQUIRED:
Does Disney use the cash basis or accrual basis of accounting? Write a two-page summary of the important accounting issues discussed in the first footnote.

Comprehensive

6–63. Visit the Coca-Cola Corporation Web site by finding the link on the PHLIP Web site for this book at *www.prenhall.com/jones*. Look up the current annual report and go to the footnotes section. Footnote 1 should describe the business and summarize the significant accounting policies.

REQUIRED:
Does Coca-Cola use the cash or accrual basis of accounting? Write a two-page summary of the important issues discussed in the first footnote.

ANNUAL REPORT PROJECT

6–64. After this assignment, you will be able to complete Section II of the annual report project. In Chapter 5 you completed the strengths and weaknesses section of the SWOT analysis and now you can focus on the opportunities and threats facing your company. The opportunities and threats are viewed from an external perspective.

Use the following outline to complete your company's analysis.

I. List the specific opportunities and threats in the external environment in the areas of:
   A. Industry Environment—What specific problems or opportunities exist for your company with the following groups?
   1. Customers
   2. Suppliers
   3. Competitors
   4. Substitute products or services

B. Macroenvironment—What specific problems or opportunities exist for your company in the following areas?
1. Economic
2. Social (changes in societal trends and attitudes)
3. Political/Legal
4. Technology
5. Globalization
6. Demographics

Information gathered for the previous section may provide you with some good insight into your findings for the SWOT analysis. The press releases and articles published about your company and its industry will be helpful in finding the necessary information. You can find a major source of information for this part of the project in the Management's Discussion and Analysis section of your company's annual report.

II. After listing the attributes of your company, write at least a two-paragraph summary of your analysis of the external environment of the company.

III. Write the conclusion of your overall SWOT analysis of your company.

Turn this in to your professor and keep a copy for your final report.

Chapter 7

Accumulating Accounting Data

Your mother recently retired, or tried to retire. The only problem was that her former clients continued to call her with small jobs. Because she could not say no, her retirement has turned into a new job as a consultant. Mom always worked for someone else and never kept records beyond weekly expense reports. At the end of the year she realized that she would soon need to prepare her tax return for the IRS and account to Social Security for the amount of her earnings. She is not sure what to report to either agency. You try to explain to her about expenses and net income but she is confused. When you ask to see her books, her response is, "What books?" Sounds like she could use your help.

Although financial statement users often do not care how the numbers got to the financial statements, the better a user understands the accounting process, the more he or she can understand the implications of those numbers. When we understand how the accounting system interprets the revenue recognition and the expense recognition principles, we understand the meaning of the income and expense numbers on the income statement. When we comprehend the checks and balances inherent in the accounting system, we can appreciate the need for internal control to protect those checks and balances. When we grasp the concept of financial statement articulation, we notice when something is not right with a set of financial statements. ■

So where do we begin? We will walk through each step of the accounting process, learning how to apply the accounting equation in each decision-making situation. We will apply the concepts discussed in Chapter 6 about revenue and expense recognition, accruals, and deferrals. We will exercise the financial statement concepts from Chapters 3, 4, and 5. In essence, we will utilize the decision-making skills we discussed in Chapter 2, applying accounting principles within an accounting system that transforms events and data into valuable accounting information.

LEARNING OBJECTIVES

After completing your work on this chapter, you should be able to do the following:

1. Identify the eight steps of the accounting cycle.
2. Distinguish between debits and credits and apply them to the accounting equation.
3. Describe accounts, journals, ledgers, and worksheets.
4. Record transactions in journals and post them to the general ledger.
5. Prepare trial balances and worksheets.
6. Prepare adjusting journal entries and reconcile a bank account.
7. Prepare financial statements from a worksheet.
8. Prepare closing journal entries.
9. Prepare a post-closing trial balance.

THE ACCOUNTING CYCLE

You may have found it frustrating to prepare financial statements from the transactions in Chapter 6 because you had no way of easily accumulating the number you needed for each item on the financial statements. Humans figured this out as early as ancient Roman times and developed a system to ease the frustration. We call this system the accounting cycle.

accounting cycle The sequence of steps repeated in each accounting period to enable the firm to analyze, record, classify, and summarize the transactions into financial statements.

The **accounting cycle** is the sequence of steps repeated in each accounting period to enable the firm to analyze, record, classify, and summarize the transactions into financial statements. The steps are:

Step 1: Analyzing Transactions

Step 2: Journalizing Transactions

Step 3: Posting Transactions to the General Ledger

Step 4: Preparing the Trial Balance (or Worksheet)

Step 5: Adjusting the Accounts and Reconciling the Bank Statement

Step 6: Preparing Financial Statements

Step 7: Preparing and Posting Closing Entries

Step 8: Preparing the Post-Closing Trial Balance

The accounting process is a cycle because some events occur daily, some monthly, and some annually (see Exhibit 7–1). At the end of the annual cycle, the process begins anew.

Exhibit 7–1
The Accounting Cycle:
A Dynamic System

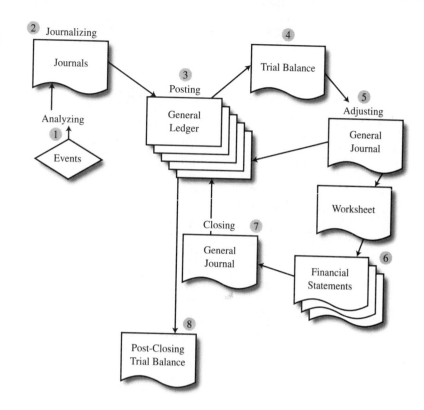

We will look at what happens in each step of the cycle and then learn how to apply each step of the cycle to the McCumber Company transactions we viewed in Chapter 6.

Step 1: Analyzing Transactions

Analyzing transactions, the most important step in the accounting cycle, consists of two parts (see Exhibit 7–2). The first is deciding when a transaction occurs. The simple answer is that a transaction occurs when an accounting element changes. For example, if a customer pays the company, cash increases and accounts receivable decreases. Assets both increase and decrease, and a transaction occurs. What if a company orders merchandise that the vendor will deliver in three weeks? Has

Exhibit 7–2
Analyzing Transactions

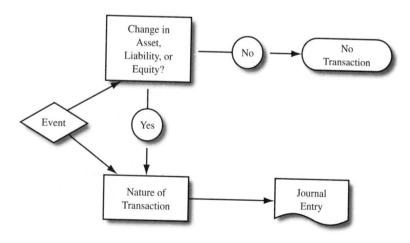

a transaction occurred? No. Neither assets, nor liabilities, nor equity has changed. When will this transaction occur? The transaction will occur when title to the merchandise passes from the vendor to the buyer during the shipping process. At that moment, the company will have new assets and a new liability.

The second part of analyzing transactions is identifying the nature of the transaction. If we correctly determine that a transaction occurs but misinterpret the transaction, we introduce an error into the accounting system. If we classify the merchandise purchase on credit as a long-term asset and reduce cash by the amount, we have created errors in four accounts—inventory, long-term assets, accounts payable, and cash are either overstated or understated. As you can see, knowing when to record a transaction and how to record the transaction are critical to maintaining the integrity of the accounting records. We make the decision about transactions as frequently as we journalize transactions.

Discussion Questions

7-1. With the many "accounting for dummies" software packages on the market, why do we need accountants?

7-2. What is the difference between a bookkeeper and an accountant?

Step 2: Journalizing Transactions

journal A book of original entry in which is kept a chronological record of an entity's transactions.

Journalizing transactions is the act of recording accounting transactions into a journal. A **journal** is a book of original entry where we record a chronology of the business entity's transactions. In the days of pen and ink, the accountant or bookkeeper kept the journal in a book. Today, with computerization, a journal may be a listing of transactions on a computer printout or a file in the computer. Regardless of form, the journal lists transactions in order of occurrence. Employees, management, and auditors frequently use the journal's chronological listing of transactions to trace transactions and answer inquiries. For this reason, we record transactions formally into journals daily, weekly, or sometimes monthly for small businesses. Large companies use on-line, real-time processing techniques that create the journals as the transactions occur. Sophisticated cash register systems often create journals simultaneously as the cashier scans the items sold.

special journal A book of original entry designed to record a specific type of transaction.

general journal A book of original entry in which is recorded all transactions not otherwise recorded in a special journal.

Businesses use a number of journals to capture details. The most common forms are sales journals, cash receipt journals, cash payment journals, purchases journals, and the general journal. All except the general journal are called **special journals,** which record a specific type of transaction such as sales. The sales journal, for instance, contains a record of the firm's sales to its customers but no other type of transaction. We use the **general journal** to record all transactions that cannot be recorded in a special journal. If a firm has no special journals, it records all transactions in the general journal (see Exhibit 7–3). Why do we have special journals? Special journals save a great deal of time when a firm experiences many similar transactions during a period. The reason for this will become obvious when we discuss posting to the general ledger, the next step in the accounting cycle.

Journals have many uses in the business operation, but the long lists of data contained in them lack the quality of information. The next step in the cycle helps us to produce usable information.

Exhibit 7–3
Journalizing
Transactions

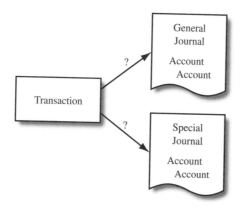

Step 3: Posting Transactions to the General Ledger

With the journals full of difficult to use data, we need a method of sorting or classifying the data into usable information. The information we desire is the amount of sales we made, the amount of cash or inventory we have, how much we owe for purchases, and so on. Each of the accounting elements provides us with information about the financial statements, so the elements become the classification system for accounting records.

We sort transactions into the increases and decreases for each accounting element. Each accounting element has an **account**, which contains the history of all increases and decreases in the accounting element. A **chart of accounts** is a list of all the accounts used by a business entity. The chart of accounts lists each account with its account number (particularly important in computerized systems) in the order of assets, liabilities, equity, revenue, and expense accounts. To be systematic, charts of account normally appear in balance sheet and income statement order. The chart of accounts becomes a reference tool to accountants and expands as needed to record new types of transactions. Each business entity should tailor its chart of accounts to its business activities.

The entire group of accounts makes up the **general ledger.** Each account is a page or a file in the general ledger. At the end of a month or a week, the accounting system posts the journal transactions to the general ledger (see Exhibit 7–4). In a computerized system, the software actually re-sorts the transactions from a date order to an account number order and accumulates like account numbers in each account. Then we have a record of what happened to each account as a result of

account   A record that contains the history of all increases and decreases of an accounting element.

chart of accounts   A list of all the accounts used by a business entity. The list usually contains the name of the account and the account number.

general ledger   A book of final entry which includes a page for each account in the chart of accounts.

Exhibit 7–4
Posting to the
General Ledger

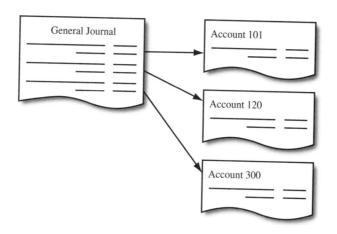

Exhibit 7–5
Preparing the Trial
Balance

General Ledger

these transactions. We add all increases and subtract all decreases to the previous balance of the account to arrive at a new account balance. We use the general ledger account balances to prepare financial statements after two additional steps in the accounting cycle.

Step 4: Preparing the Trial Balance (or Worksheet)

Each time we post a month's or a week's transactions from the journals, we need to make sure that the accounting equation remains in balance. To accomplish this, we prepare a trial balance. A **trial balance** is a listing of each general ledger account balance to verify that the general ledger, and therefore the accounting equation, is in balance (see Exhibit 7–5). Accounting software packages often print a trial balance after each processing session. Others automatically check to be sure that the system is in balance and alert the operator if it is out of balance.

Frequently, accountants use a **worksheet** to aid in the preparation of the financial statements. Most firms prepare monthly financial statements and follow this step each time financial statements are prepared. (Some firms prepare financial statements weekly, quarterly, or semiannually.) The first two columns of the ten-column worksheet are the trial balance as of the balance sheet date. The worksheet allows the accountant to examine the accounts, adjust the accounts, and gather the data to prepare the financial statements. We will examine the details of worksheet preparation of a trial balance and a worksheet as we apply these concepts.

trial balance The listing of the general ledger account balances which proves that the general ledger and, therefore, the accounting equation are in balance.

worksheet A tool used by the accountant to accumulate the necessary information used to prepare the financial statements.

Step 5: Adjusting the Accounts and Reconciling the Bank Statement

At the end of an accounting period, prior to the preparation of financial statements, accountants review the accounts to properly match the expenses of the period with the revenues that they helped to produce and to make sure that the assets, liabilities, and equity accounts are properly stated (see Exhibit 7–6). The adjustment process may involve entries to defer or accrue revenues or expenses as we discussed in Chapter 6. The adjustment process requires the application of the following steps:

Exhibit 7–6
Adjusting the Accounts
and Reconciling the
Bank Statement

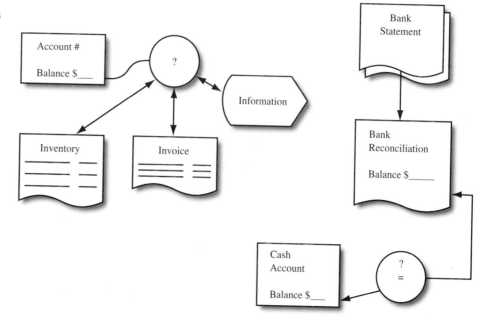

1. Identification of any accounts requiring adjustment
2. Determination of the correct balance in each account requiring adjustment
3. Preparation of the necessary adjusting entry or entries to bring the accounts into agreement with the balances determined in the previous step

   Another major step in the adjusting process is reconciling the bank statement. Because most transactions ultimately result in the receipt or the payment of cash, it is important to reconcile the bank statement as part of the firm's internal control structure. Since cash represents the most liquid and easily transported of the firm's assets, the use of a checking account by a business entity requires the implementation of some important internal controls. For example, only designated persons should have the authority to sign checks, and the person designated to reconcile the bank account should have no other duties involving the receipt or disbursement of funds. We will prepare a bank reconciliation as we apply these concepts later in the chapter.

Step 6: Preparing Financial Statements

When the accountant is satisfied that the bank accounts are reconciled and the accounts listed on the worksheet represent fair amounts, he or she will prepare the financial statements (see Exhibit 7–7). The accountant should verify that the financial statements articulate. Specifically, the net income or net loss figure for the period must agree with the net income or net loss on the statement of owners' equity or the statement of retained earnings.

Discussion Question

7-3. How often should a company prepare its financial statements?

Exhibit 7–7
Preparation of the
Financial Statements

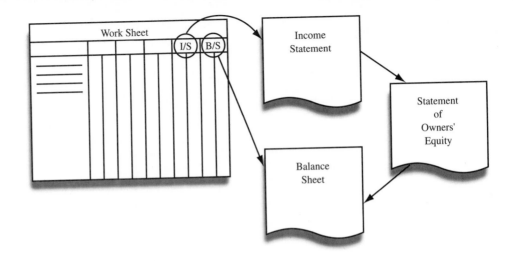

Step 7: Preparing and Posting Closing Entries

At the end of each fiscal year, after the accounting staff adjusts all the accounts and the auditors have finished the audit, we close the books. The closing process resets the temporary accounts to zero and moves the net income to the appropriate equity accounts (see Exhibit 7–8). **Temporary (or nominal) accounts** are all revenue,

Exhibit 7–8
Closing the
Temporary Accounts

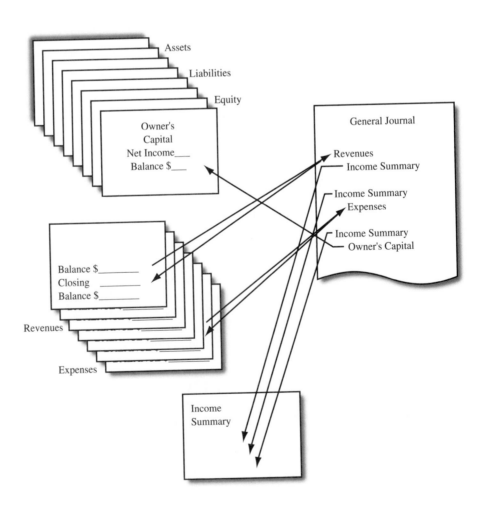

expense, gain, and loss accounts that are part of net income plus the owner withdrawals and dividend accounts. We do not close permanent accounts in this process. **Permanent (or real) accounts** include asset, liability, and equity accounts, except for owner withdrawals and dividend accounts. The closing entries zero the temporary accounts much like a trip switch on an automobile odometer. The odometer (like permanent accounts) continues to record miles, but we reset the trip switch (like temporary accounts) to zero before each event (like a new fiscal year). Each year we reset the temporary accounts to zero to accumulate the current year's net income. At the end of the year we close the net income into the equity accounts and start over again. We make four closing entries:

1. Close the revenue accounts to Income Summary.
2. Close the expense accounts to Income Summary.
3. Close the Withdrawals accounts to Owner's or Partner's Capital accounts or Dividends accounts to Retained Earnings.
4. Close Income Summary to Owner's or Partner's Capital accounts or Retained Earnings.

Step 8: Preparing the Post-Closing Trial Balance

After we prepare the closing entries and post them to the general ledger, only the balance sheet accounts should have a balance remaining. In addition, any owner withdrawal or dividend accounts should have a zero balance. We prepare a **post-closing trial balance** after the closing entries to prove that the closing entries zeroed the temporary accounts (see Exhibit 7–9). In a computerized system, this step is crucial to verify the integrity of the closing process and that the accounting equation remains in balance.

Before we apply the steps of the accounting cycle to the McCumber Company, we need to discuss several topics necessary to begin the data accumulation.

Exhibit 7–9
Post-Closing
Trial Balance

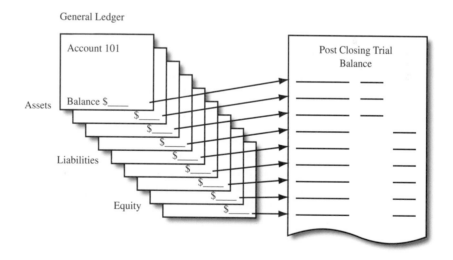

Debits and Credits

An **accounting system** gathers data from source transactions to create the books and records that transform the data into a manageable format that will eventually produce useful information in the form of financial statements. The accounting system bases its process on the basic accounting equation:

$$\text{Assets} = \text{Liabilities} + \text{Equity}$$

As we know from mathematics, a change in one side of the equation requires a change in the other side to keep the equation in balance. This concept is the origin of the term *double-entry bookkeeping*.

When Friar Luca Pacioli published the first accounting text in 1494 in Venice, he stressed the importance of a balanced accounting equation. His *Summa de Arithmetica, Geometria, Proportioni et Proportionalita* was written in Latin. In Latin, *debere* means "left" and *credere* means "right." Thus,

Assets = Liabilities + Equity

Left = Right

Debit (*Debere*) = Credit (*Credere*)

When our accounting system is in balance, the debits equal the credits; left equals right.

We assign a normal balance to each account depending upon which side of the equation it normally resides. Therefore, assets have normal debit balances and liabilities and equity accounts have normal credit balances. An account's **normal balance** defines the type of entry that increases the account; debits increase debit balance accounts and credits decrease debit balance accounts.

normal balance The balance of the account derived from the type of entry (debit or credit) that increases the account.

Assets = Liabilities + Equity

Normal Balance: Debit = Credit + Credit

We also learned in Chapter 5 about the four components of equity. We can expand the accounting equation to include these components of equity as follows:

Assets = Liabilities + Owners' Contributions − Owners' Withdrawals + Revenues − Expenses

Debit = Credit + Credit − Debit + Credit − Debit

With the expanded equation we can identify the normal balances of revenues, expenses, and owners' withdrawals. Therefore, a **debit**:

debit A term that means the left side of a general ledger account.

1. Increases assets
2. Decreases liabilities
3. Decreases owners' equity
   a. Decreases owner's or partner's capital and capital stock accounts
   b. Increases owner's or partner's withdrawal accounts or the dividend account
   c. Decreases revenues or gains
   d. Increases expenses or losses

credit A term that means the right side of a general ledger account.

A **credit**:

1. Decreases assets
2. Increases liabilities
3. Increases owners' equity
   a. Increases owner's or partner's capital or capital stock accounts
   b. Decreases owner's or partner's withdrawal accounts or the dividend account
   c. Increases revenues or gains
   d. Decreases expenses or losses

The Account

Each account contains a summary of its activity during the year. It includes the following important information:

1. Account name and number
2. Date of each transaction
3. Beginning balance

Exhibit 7–10
The Account Form

Account Name Cash in Bank					Account Number 101	
2000		Post			Balance	
Date	Description	Ref.	Debit	Credit	Debit	Credit
Dec 1	Beginning Balance				34,589.26	
31		CR34	54,197.75		88,787.01	
31		CD57		56,110.68	32,676.33	

4. Each posting from journals including the date, reference, and amount
5. Ending balance

A typical account might look like that shown in Exhibit 7–10.

When you read the account, you learn that on December 1, 2000, this company began with $34,589.26 in the bank. It collected $54,197.75 recorded on page 34 of the Cash Receipts Journal and paid out $56,110.68 recorded on page 57 of the Cash Payments Journal. At month's end, the company had $32,676.33 in the bank. Notice that there are no dollar signs in the general ledger. Dollar signs appear in financial statements and reports, such as a trial balance, but not on journals, ledgers, or worksheets.

For discussion purposes, we often use an abbreviated account form called the T-account. The **T-account** represents the general ledger account with only two columns. The balance appears after a horizontal line. We use this form to save time when analyzing an account. Exhibit 7–11 contains the T-account version of the cash account illustrated in Exhibit 7–10.

T-account An account form that represents the general ledger account with only two columns.

Exhibit 7–11
T-Account

Cash in Bank 101

2000				
12-1	34,589.26			
12-31	54,197.75	56,110.68	12-31	
	32,676.33			

The Journal Entry

For simplicity, we will utilize only the General Journal in this chapter. Proper general journal entries contain the pertinent details of the transaction in an easy-to-read format. Exhibit 7–12 illustrates a general journal page that contains a journal entry.

Discussion Questions

7-4. From the entry made into the General Journal, describe what happened with this transaction.

7-5. Where will this entry be posted in the General Ledger?

7-6. Can each journal entry have only one debit and one credit?

Exhibit 7-12
The General Journal

General Journal			Page 423	
Date **2001**	**Description**	**Post Ref.**	**Debit**	**Credit**
Jan 24	Account Receivable	110	23,425.00	
	Sales	401		23,425.00
	To record the sale of 1500 units to			
	John George, Inc. Terms 2/10, n 30			

The journal entry provides us with the following information:

1. The date of the transaction
2. The accounts affected by the transaction
3. A description of the transaction with any important details
4. The amounts of the debit or credit to each account

compound journal entry
Any entry recorded in the general journal that contains more than two accounts.

Notice that the debit equals the credit. Journal entries with more than two accounts are called **compound journal entries.** Regardless of the number of accounts involved, the total debits must equal the total credits for each transaction or the system will be out of balance. Now that we know what to do and how to do it, we can apply the accounting cycle to actual transactions.

ACCOUNTING CYCLE APPLICATION

To illustrate the accounting cycle, we will use the McCumber Company proprietorship accrual-basis transactions for January, 2000, that you examined in Chapter 6. We have reproduced those here for your convenience.

1. Gertie McCumber started the company on January 2 by investing $200,000.
2. McCumber Company borrowed $100,000 from the Friendly Bank on January 2 by signing a one-year, 12 percent note payable. Although the $100,000 does not have to be repaid until January 2, 2001, the interest charge must be paid each month, beginning on February 2, 2000.
3. The company purchased a vehicle on January 2 for $14,000 cash. Gertie estimates that the vehicle will fill the company's needs for four years, after which she estimates she can sell it for $2,000.
4. The company paid cash for $75,000 of merchandise inventory on January 8.
5. On January 15, the company sold merchandise that cost $42,000 for a total selling price of $78,000 and collected the cash the same day.
6. On January 22, the company sold merchandise that cost $15,000 for a total selling price of $32,000 on account (a credit sale). The terms of the sale were 30 days, meaning McCumber can expect to receive payment by February 21.
7. Cash payments for operating expenses in January totaled $22,500.

8. Besides the bank loan, the only amounts owed by the company at the end of the month were:
   a. $2,000 to company employees for work performed in January. They will be paid on February 3.
   b. A $700 utility bill that was received on January 26 and will be paid on February 15.

The first seven transactions should be recorded in the first two steps of the accounting cycle, analyzing and journalizing transactions. We analyzed these entries in Chapter 6 and now know how to properly record them in the general journal.

Steps 1 & 2–Analyzing and Journalizing Transactions

We would normally begin by examining the chart of accounts. McCumber's chart of accounts is as follows:

101	Cash in Bank
110	Accounts Receivable
120	Inventory
150	Automotive Equipment
155	Accumulated Depreciation
200	Accounts Payable
210	Wages Payable
220	Interest Payable
250	Notes Payable
300	Gertie McCumber, Capital
310	Gertie McCumber, Withdrawals
400	Sales
500	Cost of Goods Sold
600	Operating Expenses
620	Wages Expense
640	Utilities Expense
660	Interest Expense
680	Depreciation Expense

We have recorded each of transactions 1 through 7 on the general journal beginning with page 1.

After examining the general journal on the following page you might notice the following items:

1. Dates—We write the name of the month only at the top of each page, unless it changes in the middle of the page. All entries are in chronological order.
2. Account titles—We write all debits first in one journal entry and then the credits. Write debits on the margin and indent the credits five spaces.
3. Posting references—Nothing is written in this column. We write the account number in this column as we post to the general ledger in Step 3. This clues the bookkeeper as to whether the item is posted.
4. Debit and credit amounts—Since this problem is in whole dollars, we omitted the cents. There are no dollar signs because this is a journal.
5. Explanations—A complete explanation follows each journal entry so that the reader can understand the analysis of the transaction.
6. Compound entry—The January 22 journal entry is similar to the two entries on January 15. To save time writing two explanations, the January 22 entry combined the separate entries of January 15. Either way is acceptable in a general journal because the sale of merchandise involves all four accounts, but it may be thought of as two separate transactions or one complex transaction. A compound journal entry has more than one debit or credit.

General Journal — Page 1

Date 2000		Description	Post Ref.	Debit	Credit
Jan	1	Cash in Bank		200,000	
		McCumber, Capital			200,000
		To record the owner's capital			
		contribution.			
	2	Cash in Bank		100,000	
		Notes Payable			100,000
		To record loan from Friendly Bank			
		due January 2, 2001 with 12%			
		interest payable monthly.			
		Automotive Equipment		14,000	
		Cash in Bank			14,000
		To record the purchase of a vehicle, 4-			
		year useful life, $2,000 residual			
		value.			

General Journal — Page 2

Date 2000		Description	Post Ref.	Debit	Credit
Jan	8	Inventory		75,000	
		Cash in Bank			75,000
		To record the purchase of inventory.			
	15	Cash in Bank		78,000	
		Sales			78,000
		To record sales that cost $42,000.			
		Cost of Goods Sold		42,000	
		Inventory			42,000
		To record the cost of the previous sale.			
	22	Accounts Receivable		32,000	
		Cost of Goods Sold		15,000	
		Sales			32,000
		Inventory			15,000
		To record a sale terms net 30 that cost			
		$15,000.			
	31	Operating Expenses		22,500	
		Cash in Bank			22,500
		To record the payment of cash			
		operating expenses.			

Assuming that these transactions represent all transactions for the month of January, we can now post these to the general ledger in Step 3.

Step 3–Posting to the General Ledger

Although time consuming, the posting process presents no serious challenge. Posting requires attention to detail in the following procedures:

1. Post to the general ledger each entry in the order that it appears in the general journal.
2. Record the date as the same date as the entry in the general journal.
3. There is no need to write any description unless you wish to indicate a special notation.
4. For the posting reference on the general ledger, use the page number of the journal page, such as GJ1 or GJ2.
5. Record the amount of the entry in the correct debit or credit column.
6. Place the general ledger account number in the posting reference column of the general journal.

Exhibit 7–13 shows the postings of the first two general journal entries. Then Exhibit 7–14 presents the final appearance of the general journal pages 1 and 2 and the general ledger accounts for each account that has a balance after the monthly transactions.

Now that we have posted the general ledger, we can prepare the trial balance.

Step 4–Preparing the Trial Balance

To prepare the trial balance, simply list in order each general ledger account and its account balance. Put each debit balance in the debit column and each credit balance in the credit column. Total each column and verify that the debits equal the credits. The trial balance appears in Exhibit 7–15 on page F-241.

Because the debits equal the credits in the trial balance, our general ledger balances.

Discussion Questions

7-7. If the debits equal the credits, does this mean that the general ledger is correct? If not, what can be wrong?

7-8. If the debits do not equal the credits, what are the most likely causes of the imbalance?

When we want to prepare financial statements, we prepare a worksheet. The worksheet has five pairs of columns; each pair contains a debit and a credit column. To complete the worksheet, we use the following steps.

1. Place a heading on the worksheet that includes the company name, the title "Worksheet," and the period covered by the worksheet.

Exhibit 7–13
The Posting Process

General Journal			Page 1		

Date 2000		Description	Post Ref.	Debit	Credit
Jan	1	Cash in Bank	101	200,000	
		McCumber, Capital	300		200,000
		To record the owner's capital			
		contribution.			
	2	Cash in Bank	101	100,000	
		Notes Payable	250		100,000
		To record loan from Friendly Bank			
		due January 2, 2001 with 12%			
		interest payable monthly.			

Account Name Cash in Bank   **Account Number** 101

2000		Post			Balance	
Date	Description	Ref.	Debit	Credit	Debit	Credit
Jan 1		GJ1	200,000		200,000	
2		GJ1	100,000		300,000	

Account Name Notes Payable   **Account Number** 250

2000		Post			Balance	
Date	Description	Ref.	Debit	Credit	Debit	Credit
Jan 2		GJ1		100,000		100,000

Account Name McCumber, Capital   **Account Number** 300

2000		Post			Balance	
Date	Description	Ref.	Debit	Credit	Debit	Credit
Jan 1		GJ1		200,000		200,000

Exhibit 7–14
After the Posting
Process

General Journal — Page 1

Date 2000		Description	Post Ref.	Debit	Credit
Jan	1	Cash in Bank	101	200,000	
		McCumber, Capital	300		200,000
		To record the owner's capital			
		contribution.			
	2	Cash in Bank	101	100,000	
		Notes Payable	250		100,000
		To record loan from Friendly Bank			
		due January 2, 2001 with 12%			
		interest payable monthly.			
		Automotive Equipment	150	14,000	
		Cash in Bank	101		14,000
		To record the purchase of a vehicle, 4-			
		year useful life, $2,000 residual			
		value.			

General Journal — Page 2

Date 2000		Description	Post Ref.	Debit	Credit
Jan	8	Inventory	120	75,000	
		Cash in Bank	101		75,000
		To record the purchase of inventory.			
	15	Cash in Bank	101	78,000	
		Sales	400		78,000
		To record sales that cost $42,000.			
		Cost of Goods Sold	500	42,000	
		Inventory	120		42,000
		To record the cost of the previous sale.			
	22	Accounts Receivable	110	32,000	
		Cost of Goods Sold	500	15,000	
		Sales	400		32,000
		Inventory	120		15,000
		To record a sale terms net 30 that cost			
		$15,000.			
	31	Operating Expenses	600	22,500	
		Cash in Bank	101		22,500
		To record the payment of cash			
		operating expenses.			

Exhibit 7-14
Continued

Account Name *Cash in Bank*   **Account Number** *101*

2000		Post			Balance	
Date	Description	Ref.	Debit	Credit	Debit	Credit
Jan 1		GJ1	200,000		200,000	
2		GJ1	100,000		300,000	
		GJ1		14,000	286,000	
8		GJ2		75,000	211,000	
15		GJ2	78,000		289,000	
31		GJ2		22,500	266,500	

Account Name *Accounts Receivable*   **Account Number** *110*

2000		Post			Balance	
Date	Description	Ref.	Debit	Credit	Debit	Credit
Jan 22		GJ2	32,000		32,000	

Account Name *Inventory*   **Account Number** *120*

2000		Post			Balance	
Date	Description	Ref.	Debit	Credit	Debit	Credit
Jan 8		GJ2	75,000		75,000	
15		GJ2		42,000	33,000	
22		GJ2		15,000	18,000	

Account Name *Automotive Equipment*   **Account Number** *150*

2000		Post			Balance	
Date	Description	Ref.	Debit	Credit	Debit	Credit
Jan 2		GJ1	14,000		14,000	

Account Name *Notes Payable*   **Account Number** *250*

2000		Post			Balance	
Date	Description	Ref.	Debit	Credit	Debit	Credit
Jan 2		GJ1		100,000		100,000

Exhibit 7-14
Continued

Account Name McCumber, Capital   **Account Number** 300

| 2000 | | Post | | | Balance | |
Date	Description	Ref.	Debit	Credit	Debit	Credit
Jan 1		GJ1		200,000		200,000

Account Name Sales   **Account Number** 400

| 2000 | | Post | | | Balance | |
Date	Description	Ref.	Debit	Credit	Debit	Credit
Jan 15		GJ2		78,000		78,000
22		GJ2		32,000		110,000

Account Name Cost of Goods Sold   **Account Number** 500

| 2000 | | Post | | | Balance | |
Date	Description	Ref.	Debit	Credit	Debit	Credit
Jan 15		GJ2	42,000		42,000	
22		GJ2	15,000		57,000	

Account Name Operating Expenses   **Account Number** 600

| 2000 | | Post | | | Balance | |
Date	Description	Ref.	Debit	Credit	Debit	Credit
Jan 31		GJ2	22,500		22,500	

Exhibit 7-15
The Trial Balance

McCumber Company
Trial Balance
January 31, 2000

	Account	Debit	Credit
101	Cash in Bank	$266,500	
110	Accounts Receivable	32,000	
120	Inventory	18,000	
150	Automotive Equipment	14,000	
250	Notes Payable		$100,000
300	McCumber Capital		200,000
400	Sales		110,000
500	Cost of Goods Sold	57,000	
600	Operating Expenses	22,500	
	Totals	$410,000	$410,000

2. Head the columns with the titles:
   a. Account
   b. Trial Balance (followed by the date of the trial balance)
   c. Adjustments
   d. Adjusted Trial Balance
   e. Income Statement
   f. Balance Sheet
3. Place the trial balance amounts in the trial balance columns after the account name. It is easiest to list the accounts in the general ledger order and include accounts without balances that might be used in the worksheet. Verify that the trial balance balances.
4. Examine each account, using additional information you have available, to determine if any adjusting journal entries should be made (see Step 5). Write the adjustments in its columns, then add the two columns down to verify that the debits equal the credits.
5. After completing all adjustments, add the first four columns across to create an adjusted trial balance. Verify that the adjusted trial balance balances.
6. Place each amount listed on the adjusted trial balance in the appropriate income statement or balance sheet columns. Total the four columns. The amounts will not balance, but what you should find is that each set of columns is off by the same amount. That amount is net income. See Exhibit 7–16 for the completed worksheet.

Step 5–Adjusting the Accounts and Reconciling the Bank Statement

We examine each account to see whether the balance is reasonable and to determine whether any accrual, deferral, or correcting entry is needed. Cash normally appears first in the chart of accounts. The best way to examine the cash account is to reconcile the bank statement. Each month the bank sends a statement that lists the beginning and ending account balance according to the bank's records. It also lists each check that cleared and each deposit the bank received. Remember that the bank refers to debits and credits from the bank's perspective. The bank's debits and credits are the opposite of the company's debits and credits. How is this possible? Because our bank account has a debit balance, but our bank account is a liability to the bank and a liability has a credit balance. On February 5, 2000, McCumber received the following bank statement from Valley National Bank.

Exhibit 7–17 contains a standard bank reconciliation format. We will use it to reconcile McCumber's bank account and verify our cash balance.

Reconciling a bank statement uses the following process:

1. Record the bank statement's ending balance on the appropriate line.
2. Record any deposits recorded in the books that have not been included in the bank statement. These deposits should be at the end of the month. If you find other deposits missing, notify the bank at once. Most banks require that you notify them within 10 days of the bank statement date of any errors. Beyond that time, the bank assumes that the statement is correct.
3. Look at the list of checks that cleared the bank on the bank statement. List any checks that were written through the end of the month but did not appear on the bank statement. Those are outstanding checks.
4. Compute the corrected bank balance. Write the balance per the general ledger on the appropriate line. If that balance agrees with the book balance, the reconciliation is complete.

Exhibit 7-16
The Worksheet

McCumber Company
Worksheet
For the Month Ended January 31, 2000

#	Account Name	Trial Balance Debit	Trial Balance Credit	Adjustments Debit	Adjustments Credit	Adjusted Trial Balance Debit	Adjusted Trial Balance Credit	Income Statement Debit	Income Statement Credit	Balance Sheet Debit	Balance Sheet Credit
101	Cash in Bank	266,500				266,500				266,500	
110	Accounts Receivable	32,000				32,000				32,000	
120	Inventory	18,000				18,000				18,000	
150	Automotive Equipment	14,000				14,000				14,000	
155	Accumulated Depreciation				250		250				250
200	Accounts Payable				700		700				700
210	Wages Payable				2,000		2,000				2,000
220	Interest Payable				1,000		1,000				1,000
250	Notes Payable		100,000				100,000				100,000
300	McCumber Capital		200,000				200,000				200,000
400	Sales		110,000				110,000		110,000		
500	Cost of Goods Sold	57,000				57,000		57,000			
600	Operating Expense	22,500				22,500		22,500			
620	Wage Expenses			2,000		2,000		2,000			
640	Utilities Expense			700		700		700			
660	Interest Expense			1,000		1,000		1,000			
680	Depreciation Expense			250		250		250			
	Totals	410,000	410,000	3,950	3,950	413,950	413,950	83,450	110,000	330,500	303,950
	Net Income							26,550			26,550
								110,000	110,000	330,500	330,500

Valley National Bank

Account Name: McCumber Company 500 North Mulberry Street Fargo, North Dakota	**Account Number:** 3489432 **Date:** January 31, 2000

Previous statement balance 12–31–99	$ 0.00
3 Deposits or other credits totaling	378,000.00
2 Checks or other debits totaling	89,000.00
Current balance as of statement date 01–31–00	$ 289,000.00

Account Transactions

Date	Debits	Credits	Description
01/02		200,000.00	Deposit
01/02		100,000.00	Deposit Loan Proceeds
01/17		78,000.00	Deposit

Checks

Date	Check #	Amount	Date	Check #	Amount
01/05	1001	14,000.00	01/19	1002	75,000.00

Exhibit 7–17
Standard Bank
Reconciliation Format

COMPANY NAME
Bank Reconciliation
Date

Balance per Bank Statement $_____
Add: Deposits in Transit

_____   _____
_____   _____   _____

Deduct: Checks Outstanding
#____ _____   #____ _____
#____ _____   #____ _____
#____ _____   #____ _____   _____

Corrected Bank Balance $_____

Balance per Books $_____
Add: _____
_____
_____

Deduct: Service Charges $ _____
_____
_____   _____

Corrected Book Balance $_____

5. If the corrected bank balance and the book balance do not agree, you must look for the difference. This process can be simple or aggravating. Following are the most likely errors that occur and help with how to spot them:

   a. Bank service charges—Banks charge for many services and do not notify the firm of the charges except with the bank statement. These include check printing charges, monthly service fees, overdraft charges, and special service fees.

   b. Checks or deposits recorded incorrectly in the journals—Transposed check amounts, such as recording $275 as $257, will cause an error in the cash account. Transposition errors are always evenly divisible by nine. For example, if the check was recorded as $257 instead of $275 the difference is $18, evenly divisible by nine. When the difference between the corrected bank balance and the book balance is divisible by nine, look for a transposition error.

   c. Other deductions by the bank—Banks deduct checks returned from the firm's deposits and other items that may not be included in the bookkeeping records.

   d. If the balances still do not agree, the next step is to check the bank's encoding of the check or deposit amount against the amount of the deposit or check. The bank's encoding is in the bottom, right-hand corner of the check or deposit slip. Banks seldom make errors, but can on occasion.

McCumber's bank reconciliation has only one reconciling item. The bank statement includes all deposits for the month but omits the final check written on January 31. Because the account is so large, the bank did not deduct a service charge for the month.

McCUMBER COMPANY
Bank Reconciliation
January 31, 2000

Balance per Bank Statement		$289,000
Add: Deposits in Transit		-0-
Deduct: Checks Outstanding		
#1003	$22,500	22,500
Corrected Bank Balance		$266,500
Balance per Books		$266,500
Deduct: Service Charges $-0-		-0-
Corrected Book Balance		$266,500

Now that the Cash in Bank balance is verified, we can proceed down the list of accounts looking for possible adjustments.

1. Accounts Receivable traces to the last sale of the month and appears to be correct. With complicated activity, we would compare the A/R balance to a listing prepared by an accounts receivable clerk to verify accuracy.

2. Inventory consists of the unsold items that we purchased on January 8. Normally, we could compare this to a computer-generated inventory listing or to a physical count of the inventory.

3. The company still owns the vehicle listed in the Automotive Equipment account. However, since it was used this month, depreciation should be recorded in an adjusting journal entry. The depreciation expense equals $250 for the month computed as

   Cost $14,000 − Residual Value $2,000 = Depreciable Base $12,000
   $12,000 / 48 months = $250 per month

4. Item 8 in McCumber's information tells us that McCumber owes employees $2,000 and a utility provider $700 at month end in addition to the bank loan. This information requires us to make three adjusting journal entries for the wages, the utilities, and the loan interest. To compute the loan interest

$$\text{Interest} = \text{Principal } \$100,000 \times \text{Rate } 12\% \times \text{Time } 1/12 = \$1,000$$

5. Notes Payable and McCumber's capital are correctly stated, as are Sales, Cost of Sales, and Operating Expenses. Sales can normally be verified from a sales journal or listing. We usually check the cost of goods sold percentage to determine whether the cost of sales amount seems reasonable.

We can prepare the four required journal entries in Exhibit 7–18.

The final step is to post these to the general ledger accounts. After posting the adjusting entries, the general ledger will agree with the worksheet in Exhibit 7–16.

Exhibit 7–18
Adjusting Journal Entries

General Journal			Page 3		
Date 2000		Description	Post Ref.	Debit	Credit
Jan	31	Depreciation Expense	680	250	
		Accumulated Depreciation	155		250
		To record depreciation on vehicle.			
		($12,000 / 48 = $250)			
		Wage Expense	620	2,000	
		Wages Payable	210		2,000
		To accrue wages owed on 1-31-00.			
		Utilities Expense	640	700	
		Accounts Payable	200		700
		To accrue utility bill due 2-15-00.			
		Interest Expense	660	1,000	
		Interest Payable	220		1,000
		To accrue one month's interest.			
		($100,000 x 12% x 1/12 = $1,000)			

Step 6–Preparing Financial Statements

We have all the information we need from the worksheet to prepare the income statement, statement of owner's equity, and balance sheet. Exhibit 7–19 contains the completed financial statements.

Compare the financial statements in Exhibit 7–19 to the accrual-basis statements in Chapter 6 (page F-198), and you will see that they are identical.

Exhibit 7–19
McCumber Financial
Statements
January 31, 2000

McCUMBER COMPANY
Income Statement
For the Month Ended January 31, 2000

Sales Revenue		$110,000
Cost of Goods Sold		57,000
Gross Margin		$ 53,000
Expenses:		
Cash Operating Expenses	$22,500	
Wages Expense	2,000	
Utilities Expense	700	
Interest Expense	1,000	
Depreciation Expense	250	
Total Operating Expenses		26,450
Net Income		$26,550

McCUMBER COMPANY
Statement of Owner's Equity
For the Month Ended January 31, 2000

G. McCumber, Capital, January 1, 2000	$ 0
Investment by Owner	200,000
Net Income	26,550
G. McCumber, Capital, January 31, 2000	$226,550

McCUMBER COMPANY
Balance Sheet
January 31, 2000

Assets:			Liabilities:		
Cash		$266,500	Accounts Payable		$ 700
Accounts Receivable		32,000	Wages Payable		2,000
Inventory		18,000	Interest Payable		1,000
Vehicle	$14,000		Note Payable		100,000
Less: Accumulated			Total Liabilities		$103,700
Depreciation	(250)				
Vehicle, Net		13,750	Owner's Equity:		
			G. McCumber, Capital		226,550
			Total Liabilities		
Total Assets		$330,250	and Owner's Equity		$330,250

Step 7–Closing the Accounts

For the sake of simplicity, assume that McCumber decided to have a January 31 year end. Many companies choose a fiscal year that differs from the calendar year but coincides with the end of the normal business cycle for the industry. This simplifies inventory taking and year-end accounting procedures. To close McCumber's books, we will attempt to zero the temporary or nominal accounts and close them to income summary. We can review the four normal closing entries for a sole proprietorship:

1. Close the revenue and gain accounts to Income Summary.
2. Close the expense and loss accounts to Income Summary.

3. Close the Withdrawals account to the owner's capital account.
4. Close the Income Summary account to the owner's capital account.

From the worksheet we can tell that there is one revenue account and seven expense accounts to close. The owner made no withdrawals during this period. Therefore, we must make only three closing entries as follows:

Date 2000		Description	Post Ref.	Debit	Credit
Jan	31	Sales	400	110,00	
		Income Summary	800		110,000
		To close the revenue account.			
		Income Summary	800	83,450	
		Cost of Goods Sold	500		57,000
		Operating Expenses	600		22,500
		Wage Expense	620		2,000
		Utilities Expense	640		700
		Interest Expense	660		1,000
		Depreciation Expense	680		250
		To close the expense accounts.			
		Income Summary	800	26,550	
		McCumber, Capital	300		26,550
		To close the Income Summary account.			

General Journal — Page 4

The posting process is the same as in Step 3. After posting the closing entries, the general ledger appears as follows:

Account Name Cash in Bank   **Account Number** 101

2000		Post			Balance	
Date	Description	Ref.	Debit	Credit	Debit	Credit
Jan 1		GJ1	200,000		200,000	
2		GJ1	100,000		300,000	
		GJ1		14,000	286,000	
8		GJ2		75,000	211,000	
15		GJ2	78,000		289,000	
31		GJ2		22,500	266,500	

Account Name *Accounts Receivable*   **Account Number** *110*

| 2000 | | Post | | | Balance | |
Date	Description	Ref.	Debit	Credit	Debit	Credit
Jan 22		GJ2	32,000		32,000	

Account Name *Inventory*   **Account Number** *120*

| 2000 | | Post | | | Balance | |
Date	Description	Ref.	Debit	Credit	Debit	Credit
Jan 8		GJ2	75,000		75,000	
15		GJ2		42,000	33,000	
22		GJ2		15,000	18,000	

Account Name *Automotive Equipment*   **Account Number** *150*

| 2000 | | Post | | | Balance | |
Date	Description	Ref.	Debit	Credit	Debit	Credit
Jan 2		GJ1	14,000		14,000	

Account Name *Accumulated Depreciation*   **Account Number** *155*

| 2000 | | Post | | | Balance | |
Date	Description	Ref.	Debit	Credit	Debit	Credit
Jan 31		GJ3		250		250

Account Name *Accounts Payable*   **Account Number** *200*

| 2000 | | Post | | | Balance | |
Date	Description	Ref.	Debit	Credit	Debit	Credit
Jan 31		GJ3		700		700

Account Name *Wages Payable*   **Account Number** *210*

| 2000 | | Post | | | Balance | |
Date	Description	Ref.	Debit	Credit	Debit	Credit
Jan 31		GJ3		2,000		2,000

Account Name *Interest Payable* **Account Number** 220

| 2000 | | Post | | | Balance | |
Date	Description	Ref.	Debit	Credit	Debit	Credit
Jan 31		GJ3		1,000		1,000

Account Name *Notes Payable* **Account Number** 250

| 2000 | | Post | | | Balance | |
Date	Description	Ref.	Debit	Credit	Debit	Credit
Jan 2		GJ1		100,000		100,000

Account Name *McCumber, Capital* **Account Number** 300

| 2000 | | Post | | | Balance | |
Date	Description	Ref.	Debit	Credit	Debit	Credit
Jan 1		GJ1		200,000		200,000
31	To close income summary	GJ4		26,550		226,550

Account Name *Sales* **Account Number** 400

| 2000 | | Post | | | Balance | |
Date	Description	Ref.	Debit	Credit	Debit	Credit
Jan 15		GJ2		78,000		78,000
22		GJ2		32,000		110,000
31	To close	GJ4	110,000			0

Account Name *Cost of Goods Sold* **Account Number** 500

| 2000 | | Post | | | Balance | |
Date	Description	Ref.	Debit	Credit	Debit	Credit
Jan 15		GJ2	42,000		42,000	
22		GJ2	15,000		57,000	
31	To close	GJ4		57,000	0	

Account Name *Operating Expenses* **Account Number** 600

| 2000 | | Post | | | Balance | |
Date	Description	Ref.	Debit	Credit	Debit	Credit
Jan 31		GJ2	22,500		22,500	
31	To close	GJ4		22,500	0	

Account Name _Wage Expense_   **Account Number** _620_

| 2000 | | Post | | | Balance | |
Date	Description	Ref.	Debit	Credit	Debit	Credit
Jan 31		GJ3	2,000		2,000	
31	To close	GJ4		2,000	0	

Account Name _Utilities Expense_   **Account Number** _640_

| 2000 | | Post | | | Balance | |
Date	Description	Ref.	Debit	Credit	Debit	Credit
Jan 31		GJ3	700		700	
31	To close	GJ4		700	0	

Account Name _Interest Expense_   **Account Number** _660_

| 2000 | | Post | | | Balance | |
Date	Description	Ref.	Debit	Credit	Debit	Credit
Jan 31		GJ3	1,000		1,000	
31	To close	GJ4		1,000	0	

Account Name _Depreciation Expense_   **Account Number** _680_

| 2000 | | Post | | | Balance | |
Date	Description	Ref.	Debit	Credit	Debit	Credit
Jan 31		GJ3	250		250	
31	To close	GJ4		250	0	

Account Name _Income Summary_   **Account Number** _800_

| 2000 | | Post | | | Balance | |
Date	Description	Ref.	Debit	Credit	Debit	Credit
Jan 31	To close revenues	GJ4		110,000		110,000
	To close expenses	GJ4	83,450			26,550
	To close account	GJ4	26,550			0

Step 8–Preparing the Post-Closing Trial Balance

We have reached the final step in the process. By preparing the post-closing trial balance, we verify that each temporary account is closed and the general ledger remains in balance. The post-closing trial balance becomes the opening balances for the new fiscal year. Exhibit 7–20 contains McCumber's post-closing trial balance at January 31, 2000.

Exhibit 7–20
Post-Closing Trial
Balance

	Account	Debit	Credit
	McCumber Company **Post-Closing Trial Balance** **January 31, 2000**		
101	Cash in Bank	$266,500	
110	Accounts Receivable	32,000	
120	Inventory	18,000	
150	Automotive Equipment	14,000	
155	Accumulated Depreciation		$ 250
200	Accounts Payable		700
210	Wages Payable		2,000
220	Interest Payable		1,000
250	Notes Payable		100,000
300	McCumber, Capital		226,550
	Total	$330,500	$330,500

So far we have examined how accountants measure reality and accumulate data to provide meaningful information to financial decision makers. Chapters 8 and 9 explore areas in which we allow flexibility in the recognition of revenues and expenses. These variations reduce the comparability of financial statement information between companies. Therefore, to be an informed user, you should understand the variations and their influence on the financial statements.

SUMMARY

The accounting cycle is an eight-step process of accumulating accounting data and transforming it into useful accounting information.

1. Analyzing transactions requires deciding when a transaction occurs and determining which accounts it affects. Analysis occurs at least daily.
2. Journalizing transactions records the transaction chronologically in a journal, a book of original entry. The proper journal for each entry depends on the unique accounting system the company employs. Some systems have only a general journal and others have special journals to record similar transactions. Journalizing occurs at least monthly.
3. Posting transactions transfers the journal information to the general ledger, sorted by account. Each account indicates the beginning and ending balance and all transactions recorded during the period for that account. Posting occurs at least monthly in most systems.
4. Preparing a trial balance proves that the general ledger (and the accounting equation) is in balance. We prepare a worksheet to aid in the preparation of financial statements. A trial balance should be prepared each time we post journals to the general ledger and worksheets are prepared as often as the firm prepares financial statements.
5. Adjusting the accounts records all accruals, deferrals, and corrections necessary to provide quality accounting information. We adjust accounts as often as we prepare financial statements.

6. Preparing the financial statements represents the final step in the transformation of data into information. Most firms prepare financial statements at least monthly for internal users and quarterly for external users.
7. Closing the temporary (nominal) accounts occurs one time each year after the final adjustments are made to the accounts. We close the temporary accounts to owner's equity, partner's equity, or to retained earnings.
8. Preparing the post-closing trial balance ensures that all temporary accounts were properly closed and that the permanent (real) accounts left in the general ledger are in balance. This occurs annually after the closing entries. The post-closing trial balance amounts become the opening balances for the new fiscal year.

The accounting system records transactions as either debits or credits. Debit means left and credit means right, referring to the sides of the accounting equation. Debits must always equal credits in each transaction, each journal, and the general ledger to keep the equation in balance. Debits increase assets and expenses, and decrease liabilities, equity, and revenue. Credits increase liabilities, equity, and revenues and decrease assets and expenses.

KEY TERMS

account   F-227
accounting cycle   F-224
accounting system   F-231
chart of accounts   F-227
compound journal entry   F-234
credit   F-232
debit   F-232
general journal   F-226
general ledger   F-227

journal   F-226
normal balance   F-232
permanent (or real) accounts   F-231
post-closing trial balance   F-231
special journal   F-226
T-account   F-233
temporary (or nominal) accounts   F-231
trial balance   F-228
worksheet   F-228

REVIEW THE FACTS

A. List the eight steps in the accounting cycle.
B. Distinguish between debits and credits and explain how they relate to the accounting equation.
C. Describe the differences between an account, a journal, a ledger, and a worksheet.
D. Explain the purposes of the general journal and special journals.
E. List the important elements of a general journal entry.
F. Describe how to post general journal entries to the general ledger.
G. Describe the purpose of the trial balance and the worksheet.
H. Describe at least four causes of a trial balance failing to balance.
I. Explain how a worksheet aids in the preparation of the financial statements. Include as part of your answer a description of the worksheet's five pairs of columns.
J. What is the purpose of the closing entries?
K. Describe the contents of the post-closing trial balance and explain its purpose.

LO 1: Terminology

7–9. Presented below is a list of items relating to the concepts discussed in this chapter, followed by definitions of those items in scrambled order.

a. Accounting cycle
b. General Journal
c. General Ledger
d. Trial Balance
e. Debit

f. Credit
g. Account
h. Chart of Accounts
i. Posting
j. Journalizing

1. _____ A collection of all the accounts of a business entity
2. _____ The left side of an account
3. _____ The series of steps repeated each accounting period to enable a business entity to record, classify, and summarize financial information
4. _____ A book of original entry
5. _____ A device used to sort accounting data into similar groupings
6. _____ The process of recording into the general ledger from a journal
7. _____ The process of recording transactions into the book of original entry
8. _____ A listing to prove the equality of debits and credits
9. _____ The complete list of the account titles used by an entity
10. _____ The right side of an account

REQUIRED:

Match the letter next to each item on the list with the appropriate definition. Each letter will be used only once.

LO 1: The Accounting Cycle

7–10. Identify and list in order of occurrence the steps of the accounting cycle.

LO 1: The Accounting Cycle

7–11. Define the following terms.

a. Journal
b. Ledger
c. Posting
d. Trial balance
e. Adjusting entries
f. Closing entries

LO 2: Normal Account Balances

7–12. Examine the following accounts.

1. _____ Cash
2. _____ Accounts Payable
3. _____ Smith, Capital Account
4. _____ Revenues
5. _____ Prepaid Insurance
6. _____ Merchandise Inventory
7. _____ Rent Expense
8. _____ Income Tax Expense

9. _____ Income Taxes Payable
10. _____ Common Stock

REQUIRED:

Indicate whether the normal balance of each account is a debit (DR) or credit (CR) in the space provided.

LO 2: Permanent or Temporary Accounts

7-13. Examine the following accounts.

1. _____ Cash
2. _____ Accounts Payable
3. _____ Smith, Capital Account
4. _____ Revenues
5. _____ Prepaid Insurance
6. _____ Merchandise Inventory
7. _____ Rent Expense
8. _____ Income Tax Expense
9. _____ Income Taxes Payable
10. _____ Common Stock

REQUIRED:

Indicate whether the type of account is permanent (P) or temporary (T) in the space provided.

LO 2: Normal Account Balances

7-14. Examine the following accounts.

1. _____ Accounts Receivable
2. _____ Notes Payable
3. _____ Jones, Drawing Account
4. _____ Sales
5. _____ Prepaid Rent
6. _____ Supplies Inventory
7. _____ Insurance Expense
8. _____ Income Tax Expense
9. _____ Wages Payable
10. _____ Retained Earnings

REQUIRED:

Indicate whether the normal balance of each account is a debit (DR) or credit (CR) in the space provided.

LO 2: Permanent or Temporary Accounts

7-15. Examine the following accounts.

1. _____ Accounts Receivable
2. _____ Notes Payable
3. _____ Jones, Drawing Account
4. _____ Sales
5. _____ Prepaid Rent
6. _____ Supplies Inventory
7. _____ Insurance Expense
8. _____ Income Tax Expense
9. _____ Wages Payable
10. _____ Retained Earnings

REQUIRED:

Indicate whether the type of account is permanent (P) or temporary (T) in the space provided.

LO 2: Account Classification

7–16. Examine the following accounts.

1. _____ Prepaid Taxes
2. _____ Advertising Expense
3. _____ Retained Earnings
4. _____ Depreciation Expense
5. _____ Rent Revenue
6. _____ Automotive Equipment
7. _____ Allowance for Doubtful Accounts
8. _____ Truck Expense
9. _____ Gasoline Expense
10. _____ Common Stock

REQUIRED:

Indicate the classification of each of the accounts listed above.

a. Asset
b. Liability
c. Revenue

d. Expense
e. Equity
f. Contra Asset

LO 2: Account Classification

7–17. Examine the following accounts.

1. _____ Cash
2. _____ Accounts Payable
3. _____ Smith, Capital Account
4. _____ Revenues
5. _____ Prepaid Insurance
6. _____ Merchandise Inventory
7. _____ Rent Expense
8. _____ Income Tax Expense
9. _____ Income Taxes Payable
10. _____ Preferred Stock

REQUIRED:

Indicate the classification of each of the accounts listed above.

a. Asset
b. Liability
c. Revenue

d. Expense
e. Equity
f. Contra Asset

LO 2: Account Classification

7–18. You are presented with the following accounts.

1. _____ Accounts Receivable
2. _____ Notes Payable
3. _____ Jones, Drawing Account
4. _____ Sales
5. _____ Prepaid Rent
6. _____ Supplies Inventory

7. _____ Insurance Expense
8. _____ Income Tax Expense
9. _____ Wages Payable
10. _____ Additional Paid-in Capital

REQUIRED:
Indicate the classification of each of the accounts listed above.

a. Asset   d. Expense
b. Liability   e. Equity
c. Revenue   f. Contra Asset

LO 2 & 3: Normal Account Balances

7–19. Examine the following accounts.

1. _____ Prepaid Taxes
2. _____ Advertising Expense
3. _____ Retained Earnings
4. _____ Depreciation Expense
5. _____ Rent Revenue
6. _____ Automotive Equipment
7. _____ Allowance for Doubtful Accounts
8. _____ Truck Expense
9. _____ Gasoline Expense
10. _____ Common Stock

REQUIRED:
Indicate whether the normal balance of each account is a debit (DR) or credit (CR) in the space provided.

LO 2 & 3: Transaction Analysis

7–20. On May 1, Bill Simon started a computer repair business. Simon opened a bank account for the business by depositing $7,000. He paid two months' rent in advance totaling $400. On May 3, Simon purchased computer repair supplies for $700 and three computers at a total cost of $4,500. Simon hired a student helper, agreeing to pay the helper $1,000 per month of which he paid $500 on May 15 and May 31. On May 25, Simon paid $200 for a newspaper advertisement to announce the opening of the business. Bill earned $3,500 in July of which he collected $2,800 in cash.

REQUIRED:
Prepare journal entries to record these transactions.

LO 2 & 3: Transaction Analysis

7–21. On July 1, Katy Tener began the KT Travel Agency and deposited $10,000 in a company bank account. She paid $500 for one month's rent. On July 5 she purchased office supplies for $700 and three desks at a total cost of $1,500. Katy hired a travel consultant, agreeing to pay her $20 per hour. The consultant worked 100 hours in July which Katy will pay on August 1. Katy paid $100 on July 29 for a newspaper advertisement to announce the opening of the business. Katy booked a cruise for her first customer and received a check from the cruise line for $800 on July 22. On July 31, she borrowed $12,000 from the bank for two years at 9%.

REQUIRED:

Prepare journal entries to record these transactions.

LO 4: Transaction Analysis

7-22. On December 1, 2001, Jogina Sisemore, CPA, opened a practice. She contributed $5,000 to a company bank account and paid office rent for three months in advance, totaling $900. On December 2 she purchased a desk for cash of $500 and bought $1,200 worth of office supplies on account. Jogina also borrowed $1,500 from the First State Bank for three years at 6% to purchase computer equipment from a local dealer.

REQUIRED:

Prepare journal entries to record these transactions.

LO 4: Recording Transactions

7-23. The transactions for September, 2001, for Tom Miller's Two Mile High Flight School are as follows:

Sept. 1	Deposited $125,000 in a business bank account from personal funds.
1	Purchased an airplane for $80,000.
2	Purchased fuel for the airplane costing $1,500.
2	Paid $260 for a newspaper advertisement.
2	Paid rent on an airplane hangar for six months in advance totaling $3,000.
5	Collected $100 for a new student's first lesson.
5	Purchased a desk for $200.
5	Borrowed $10,000 from the bank for two years at 8%.
6	Purchased office supplies for $450.
8	Collected $100 for the second lesson of our student.
12	Withdrew $1,000 for personal living expenses.
15	Paid the yellow pages advertising bill of $800.
20	Ordered $1,000 of repair parts for the airplane.
23	Received the parts ordered on the 20th, paying cash.
29	Paid the utility bill received for $150.

REQUIRED:

Record each of the above transactions in a general journal.

LO 4: Recording Transactions

7-24. The Ace Termite Company transactions for October, 2001, are as follows:

Oct. 1	Proprietor Helen Laws deposited $35,000 in a business bank account from her personal savings account.
1	Purchased a truck for $18,000.
1	Borrowed $8,000 from the bank using the truck as collateral. Interest of 9% will be paid monthly on the first day of each month.
2	Purchased spraying equipment for the truck costing $3,500 including $400 of chemicals.
2	Paid $600 for a newspaper advertisement to run each week in October.

2   Paid rent on an office for six months in advance totaling $6000.

5   Collected $75 for spraying a new residence .

5   Purchased a desk for $100 at a garage sale.

5   Billed a customer $150 for spraying the lawn.

6   Purchased office supplies for $200.

8   Collected $100 for a termite inspection.

9   Collected the $150 from the customer on the 5th.

12   Withdrew $500 for personal living expenses.

15   Paid the yellow pages advertising bill of $300.

20   Ordered $1,000 of chemicals.

23   Received the chemicals ordered on the 20th with payment due in 10 days.

28   Collected $2,300 in termite inspections for a loan company and billed an apartment complex $1,200 for spraying 40 units.

29   Paid the utility bill on the office for $135.

REQUIRED:

Record each of the above transactions in a general journal.

LO 4:   Recording Transactions

7–25. The transactions for December, 2001, for Brad Sanders Auto Repair Shop are as follows:

Dec. 1   Deposited $45,000 in a business bank account from his personal checking account.

1   Purchased a wrecker for $30,000.

1   Borrowed $25,000 at 8% interest from the bank to pay for the wrecker, using it as collateral. Interest is payable monthly on the first day of the month and a semiannual principal payment of $5,000 is due the first day of June and December each year.

2   Purchased shop equipment costing $12,500.

2   Paid $360 for a newspaper advertisement to announce the opening of his business.

2   Paid rent on garage and office for six months in advance totaling $8,100.

5   Signed a contract to perform maintenance service on all auto equipment for a car rental shop.

5   Purchased a desk and chair for $250.

5   Billed a customer $250 for auto repairs.

6   Purchased office supplies for $250.

8   Billed the rental agency $2,500 for work performed.

10   Collected the $250 from the customer on the 5th.

12   Withdrew $500 for personal living expenses.

15   Paid the telephone bill of $300.

21   Paid the local parts distributor $600 for parts used on jobs and ordered $1,300 of parts for inventory.

25   Received the parts ordered on the 21st and paid cash on delivery.

29   Paid the office and shop electric bill of $320.

31   Billed the rental agency $3,600 for services that used $680 of parts.

REQUIRED:

Record each of the above transactions in a general journal.

LO 4: Posting Transactions

7–26. Refer to problem 7–21.

REQUIRED:
a. Prepare a chart of accounts for the KT Travel Agency.
b. Post the transactions in the general ledger.
c. Prepare a trial balance after completion of the posting process.

LO 4: Posting Transactions

7–27. Refer to problem 7–22.

REQUIRED:
a. Prepare a chart of accounts for Jogina Sisemore, CPA.
b. Post the transactions to the general ledger.
c. Prepare a trial balance after completion of the posting process.

LO 4: Posting Transactions

7–28. Refer to problem 7–23.

REQUIRED:
a. Prepare a chart of accounts for the Two Mile High Flight School.
b. Post the transactions to the general ledger.
c. Prepare a trial balance after completion of the posting process.

LO 6: Adjusting Entries

7–29. The Arnold Ziffel Company had the following accrual information available at the end of the year 2002.

   a. Unpaid wages to employees were $2,500.
   b. Interest due on a loan to the bank was $1,000.
   c. Sales taxes collected during December and unpaid to the state were $3,000.
   d. A customer owed one year's interest on a note to Ziffel for $4,000.
   e. One of Ziffel's renters failed to pay the December rent of $5,000 because she was out of the country. She will pay this amount when she returns on January 10.

REQUIRED:
Prepare the appropriate general journal entries with explanations to record the above adjustments.

LO 6: Adjusting Entries

7–30. The Pat Haney Corporation had the following information available at the end of the year 2002.

   a. The accountant completed the 2002 depreciation schedule which showed the depreciation expense as $10,520. The Depreciation Expense account has a balance of $8,500.
   b. Commissions for December of $22,000 will be paid to Haney's sales staff on January 5. The Commissions Payable account has a zero balance.
   c. Haney's Accounts Receivable account shows $64,500. After the accountant completed an analysis, he discovered that it should be

$68,400. The difference is a sale made on December 31 that was not recorded.

d. A good customer borrowed $20,000 on July 1 for one year at 12% interest. The principal and interest will be paid on June 30, 2003.

e. On July 1, Haney paid $14,000 in rent for one year on a temporary warehouse. The accountant recorded this payment as rent expense.

REQUIRED:

Prepare the appropriate general journal entries with explanations to record the above adjustments.

LO 6: Adjusting Entries

7–31. The Buttram Company has the following information available at year end.

a. Wages earned by employee but not paid at year end is $4,000.

b. A two-year insurance policy was paid for on October 1 for $2,000. The Insurance Expense account's balance is $2,000.

c. Service Fee Income earned but not collected at year end is $14,000. Accounts Receivable has a zero balance.

d. Real estate taxes unpaid at year end are $3,900.

e. Interest owed to the bank but not paid at year end is $2,200.

REQUIRED:

Prepare the appropriate general journal entries with explanations to record the above adjustments.

LO 6: Adjusting Entries—Prepaid Items

7–32. The Koch Company's trial balance at June 30, its year end, has the following balances before adjustments.

Unearned Rental Income	$7,200
Prepaid Rent Expense	3,600
Prepaid Insurance	4,800
Supplies Inventory	1,200

a. On May 1, the company paid the rent expense for one year in the amount of $3,600.

b. On April 1, the company collected rental income in advance for the following 24 months in the amount of $14,400.

c. On June 1, the company paid for its business umbrella insurance policy for the next two years in the amount of $4,200.

d. At year end, the physical count of the supplies inventory indicated that $295 of supplies were on hand.

REQUIRED:

Prepare the appropriate adjusting entries with explanations to record the above information.

LO 6: Adjusting Entries—Prepaid Items

7–33. The Earhart Company's trial balance at June 30, its year end, has the following balances before adjustments.

Unearned Rental Income	$7,200
Prepaid Rent	3,600
Insurance Expense	4,800
Supplies Inventory	200

a. On October 1, the company paid the rent expense of $3,600 for one year's rent in advance.

b. On March 1, the company collected rental income of $600 per month in advance, for the following 24 months.

c. On May 1, the company paid for a catastrophe insurance policy for the next two years at a rate of $2,400 per year. This was the only policy in force.

d. On June 30, the physical count of the supplies inventory on hand was $400.

REQUIRED:

Prepare the appropriate adjusting entries with explanations to record the above adjustments.

LO 6: Adjusting Entries—Prepaid Items

7–34. In 2001, the *Fare of the Hearty Cooking* magazine sold 1,000 annual subscriptions to its monthly magazine for $16 each. It also sold 500 two-year subscriptions for $25 each and 250 two-year subscriptions for $32 each.

REQUIRED:

a. Prepare the appropriate adjusting entries with explanations to record the adjustments necessary at the end of years 1 and 2 if the subscriptions were all sold at the beginning of 2001 and were originally recorded as income.

b. Prepare the appropriate adjusting entries with explanations to record the adjustments necessary at the end of years 1 and 2 if the subscriptions were all sold at the beginning of 2001 and were originally recorded as a liability.

LO 6: Adjusting Entries—Depreciation

7–35. At the beginning of the year the Smeltzer Company purchased a copy machine for $2,000. The firm believed the machine would have an estimated useful life of six years and a salvage value of $200. The firm also purchased a delivery van costing $28,000 with an estimated useful life of four years and a salvage value of $4,000. The company decided to use straight-line depreciation for both assets.

REQUIRED:

a. Prepare the appropriate adjusting entries with explanations to record the depreciation expense at the end of year 1.

b. Prepare the appropriate adjusting entries with explanations to record the depreciation adjustment at the end of year 1 if the Accumulated Depreciation account had a balance of $4,500 at the end of year 1 and these were the only depreciable assets the company owned.

LO 6: Adjusting Entries—Depreciation

7–36. At the beginning of the year the Walsh Company purchased a copy machine for $3,000. The firm believed the machine would have an estimated useful life of four years and a salvage value of $200. The firm also purchased a tractor costing $56,000 with an estimated useful life of six years and a salvage value of $2,000. The company decided to use straight-line depreciation for both assets.

REQUIRED:
a. Prepare the appropriate adjusting entries with explanations to record the depreciation adjustment at the end of year 1 assuming that the company recorded no depreciation in the first year.
b. Prepare the appropriate adjusting entries with explanations to record the depreciation adjustment at the end of year 1 if the Accumulated Depreciation account has a balance of $10,800 and these are the only depreciable assets the company owns.

LO 6:   Adjusting Entries—Depreciation

7–37. At the start of the year the Marshall Corporation purchased a piece of equipment for $36,000. The firm believed the machine would have an estimated useful life of five years and a salvage value of $6,000. The firm also purchased a building costing $200,000 with an estimated useful life of 40 years and no residual value. The company uses straight-line depreciation.

REQUIRED:
a. Prepare the appropriate adjusting entries with explanations to record the depreciation adjustment at the end of year 1 if the company did not record any depreciation.
b. Prepare the appropriate adjusting entries with explanations to record the depreciation adjustment at the end of year 1 assuming that the Accumulated Depreciation account had a balance of $30,000 and these are the only depreciable assets the company owns.

LO 6:   Adjusting Entries

7–38. At the beginning of the year the Lynn Hughes Company purchased a computer for $3,000. The firm believed the computer would last three years with a residual value of $200. The firm also purchased a truck costing $56,000 with an estimated useful life of four years and a salvage value of $6,000. The company uses straight-line depreciation for both assets. At year end, the general ledger contains the following accounts and balances:

Office Equipment	$ 2,800 Debit
Accumulated Depreciation	200 Debit
Automotive Equipment	56,000 Debit
Accumulated Depreciation	14,000 Credit
Depreciation Expense	14,000 Debit

REQUIRED:
Prepare the appropriate adjusting entries with explanations to record the depreciation adjustment at the end of year 1.

LO 6:   Adjustments from Trial Balance Accounts with Supplemental Information

7–39. The following is a partial trial balance for the Denton Company as of December 31, 2002.

THE DENTON COMPANY
Partial Trial Balance
December 31, 2002

	Debit	Credit
Prepaid Insurance	$12,000	
Prepaid Rent Expense	18,000	
Interest Receivable	-0-	
Wages Payable		$10,000
Unearned Fee Income		36,000
Interest Income		12,000

Additional information includes the following:

    a. The insurance policy indicates that on December 31, 2002, seven months remain on the 24-month policy that originally cost $18,000.

    b. Denton has a note receivable with $2,500 of interest due and payable on January 1, 2003.

    c. The books show that two-thirds of the fees paid in advance by a customer on June 30 have now been earned.

    d. The company prepaid rent for nine months on July 1.

    e. The wages payable on December 31 were $7,000. The amount in the Wages Payable account is from December 31, 2001.

REQUIRED:

Record in proper general journal form, the adjustments required by the above information.

LO 6: Adjustments from Trial Balance Accounts with Supplemental Information

    7–40. The following is a partial trial balance for the Reese Company as of December 31, 2003.

THE REESE COMPANY
Partial Trial Balance
December 31, 2003

	Debit	Credit
Prepaid Insurance	$ 6,000	
Prepaid Rent Expense	10,000	
Wages Expense	25,000	
Subscription Income		$72,000
Interest Expense	38,000	

Additional information includes the following:

    a. The company paid a $7,200 premium on a three-year business insurance policy on July 1, 2002.

    b. Reese borrowed $200,000 on January 2 and must pay 12% interest on January 2, 2004, for the entire year of 2003.

    c. The books show that $60,000 of subscriptions have now been earned and the balance is a liability.

    d. The company prepaid 10 months' rent in advance on November 1, 2003, to take advantage of a special discount that reduced the rent to $1,000 per month.

    e. Wages for December 31 of $3,000 will be paid to employees on January 6, 2004.

REQUIRED:

Record in proper general journal form, the adjustments required by the above information.

LO 6: Adjustments from Trial Balance Accounts with Supplemental Information

7–41. The following is a partial trial balance for the Marr Company as of December 31, 2002.

THE MARR COMPANY
Partial Trial Balance
December 31, 2002

	Debit	Credit
Office Supply Expense	$ 36,000	
Cost of Goods Sold	122,000	
Merchandise Inventory	63,000	
Office Supply Inventory	400	
Wages Payable	41,500	
Wage Expense	4,000	

Additional information includes the following:

a. Office supplies on hand at year end were $1,230.

b. The ending merchandise inventory was $61,350. The cost of the goods sold during the year was $122,000.

c. The total payroll cost for the year 2002 was $50,000. At the end of last year, the company owed employees $4,000 for December wages and at December 31, 2002, the company owes employees $4,500 for December wages.

REQUIRED:

Record in proper general journal form, the adjustments required by the above information.

LO 6: Bank Reconciliation

7–42. The Fretz Company showed a cash balance of $2,517 on November 30, 2000. The company received the bank statement for November 2000 that showed a balance of $2,750. The other differences that appear between the company's book balance of cash and the bank statement include:

a. A deposit of $500 that was made on November 30 was not included in the bank statement.

b. Outstanding checks on November 30 were $1,280.

c. Bank service charges imposed by the bank were $35.

d. The bank included a debit memo for an NSF (nonsufficient funds) check totaling $512.

REQUIRED:

a. Prepare a bank reconciliation for the Fretz Company of November 30, 2000.

b. Prepare the general journal entries necessary to adjust the accounts.

LO 6: Bank Reconciliation

7–43. The Coyote Company received the bank statement for October 2000. The following information is available for the bank reconciliation of October 31, 2000:

Balance per general ledger	$7,500
Balance per bank statement	8,250
NSF check from customer returned by the bank	1,000
Outstanding checks total	2,365
Deposits in transit	1,800
Bank charges	60
Credit memo for collection from customer of amount owed on a note	1,245

REQUIRED:

a. Prepare a bank reconciliation for the Coyote Company of October 31, 2000.

b. Prepare the general journal entries necessary to adjust the accounts.

LO 6: Bank Reconciliation

7–44. The Godfrey Company received the bank statement for December 2000. The company showed a cash balance of $1,838 on December 31, 2000, but the bank statement showed a balance of $3,500. The other differences that appear between the company's book balance of cash and the bank statement include:

1. A deposit of $300 that was made on December 31 was not included in the bank statement.
2. Outstanding checks on December 31 were $1,280.
3. Bank service charges imposed by the bank were $28.
4. The bank included a debit memo for credit card discounts totaling $690.
5. Included in the bank statement was a credit memo for $1,400 for the collection of an outstanding account owed by a customer.

REQUIRED:

a. Prepare a bank reconciliation for the Godfrey Company of December 31, 2000.

b. Prepare the general journal entries necessary to adjust the accounts.

LO 6 & 7: Adjustments and the Impact on Financial Statements

7–45. The Wallberg Company has the following account balances at the end of the year:

Prepaid Insurance	$6,000
Rental Income	4,800
Wages Expense	7,660
Taxes Payable	4,398
Interest Income	2,325

The company also has the following information available at the end of the year:
1. $4,000 of the prepaid insurance has now expired.
2. $2,200 of the rental income has not yet been earned.
3. The company must accrue an additional $1,500 of wages expense.

4. The Taxes Payable account is overstated by $398.

5. The company has earned an additional $500 of interest income.

REQUIRED:

a. Prepare the journal entries necessary to adjust the accounts.

b. Use T-accounts to compute and present both the income statement and balance sheet account balances after the adjustments have been prepared.

LO 6 & 7:   Adjustments and the Impact on Financial Statements

7–46. The Mary McHaffie Company has the following account balances at the end of the year:

Insurance Expense	$4,000
Unearned Rental Income	3,800
Wages Payable	5,550
Taxes Expense	4,398
Depreciation Expense	7,625

The company also has the following information available at the end of the year:

1. $1,000 of the Insurance Expense has not yet expired.

2. $1,600 of the Unearned Rental Income has now been earned.

3. The company currently owes employees $1,200 of wages.

4. The company owes an additional $4,900 in real estate taxes.

5. Depreciation expense for the year is a total of $8,743.

REQUIRED:

a. Prepare the journal entries necessary to adjust the accounts.

b. Use T-accounts to compute and present both the income statement and balance sheet account balances after the adjustments have been prepared.

LO 6 & 7:   Adjustments and the Impact on Financial Statements

7–47. The Hale Company has the following account balances at the end of the year:

Insurance Expense	$5,400
Unearned Fee Income	3,525
Wages Payable	3,000
Advertising Expense	9,500
Depreciation Expense	3,850

The company also has the following information available at the end of the year:

1. $3,200 of the Insurance Expense has not yet expired.

2. $1,200 of the Unearned Fee Income was earned in the last month of the year.

3. The company must accrue an additional $1,800 of wages expense.

4. The company paid $1,900 for advertisements that will be shown next month.

5. Depreciation expense for the year is a total of $8,625.

REQUIRED:

a. Prepare the journal entries necessary to adjust the accounts.

b. Use T-accounts to compute and present both the income statement and balance sheet account balances after the adjustments have been prepared.

LO 6 & 7: Adjustments and the Impact on Financial Statements

7–48. The Watson Company has the following account balances at the end of the year:

Supplies Expense	$2,000
Supplies on Hand	230
Unearned Subscription Income	3,758
Prepaid Rent Expense	4,950
Taxes Expense	1,259
Accumulated Depreciation	8,964

The company also has the following information available at the end of the year.

1. $500 of the supplies are still on hand.
2. $1,785 of the Unearned Subscription Income has now been earned.
3. Two months of rent at $850 per month is still prepaid.
4. The Taxes Expense account is overstated by $189.
5. Depreciation expense for the year is a total of $12,326.

REQUIRED:
a. Prepare the general journal entries necessary to adjust the accounts.
b. Use T-accounts to compute and present both the income statement and balance sheet account balances after the adjustments have been prepared.

Comprehensive

7–49. The Alco Home Improvement Center began operations on November 1, 2000. Transactions for the month of November are as follows:

Nov. 1 Herb Alco invested $45,000 in his new venture.
    5 Alco signed a lease on a store and paid six months' rent in advance of $9,450.
    6 Purchased $500 of office supplies from Mott's Office Supply on account.
    8 Purchased $25,000 merchandise for resale from Associated Supply on account.
   10 Paid $100 for the freight bill on the November 8 purchase.
   11 Paid $175 for a radio ad to announce the store opening.
   12 Borrowed $5,000 from First National Bank. Signed a 9%, 90-day note with interest payable on the last day of each month.
   14 Sold merchandise for cash of $4,000 that cost $2,400.
   15 Sold $2,500 merchandise that cost $1,750 on a 30-day account to J. Adams.
   16 Paid freight on sale to Adams of $75.
   17 Sold $3,000 merchandise that cost $1,950 on a 30-day account to A. Bear.
   19 Purchased $10,000 merchandise from the Rider Company on account.
   20 Made cash sales of $20,000 that cost $13,200.
   21 Paid Mott's Office Supply.
   23 Paid Associated Supply for the purchase on the 8th.
   24 Collected payment in full from A. Bear.
   25 Paid Rider Company for the purchase on the 19th.
   25 Received payment in full from J. Adams.
   26 Purchased a forklift to move merchandise for $5,000 cash.

28 Paid utilities for the month of $800.
29 Paid wages for the month of $4,000.
30 Alco withdrew $1,000 for personal living expenses.

REQUIRED:

a. Journalize the transactions for the month of November in the general journal.
b. Open the necessary accounts in the general ledger and post the November transactions to the appropriate accounts in the general ledger.
c. Prepare a trial balance on November 30, 2000.
d. Prepare adjusting entries and complete a worksheet using the following information in addition to that listed in the transactions:

  1. Alco depreciated the forklift for the entire month of November, assuming straight-line depreciation with no residual value and a five-year estimated life.
  2. Alco accrued the interest on the bank loan for 18 days.
  3. Alco incurred payroll tax expense of $900 for the month.

e. Prepare a balance sheet as of November 30, 2000, and a statement of income and a statement of owner's equity for the month ended November 30, 2000.

Comprehensive

7–50. The Baer Distributing Company began operations on December 1, 2000. Transactions for the month of December are as follows:

Dec. 1 Max Baer invested $75,000 in his new venture.
    2 Baer signed a lease on a warehouse and paid six months' rent in advance of $6,000.
    5 Purchased $1,500 of office supplies from Mardel Office Supply on account.
    7 Purchased $15,000 of merchandise for resale from Agape Supply on account.
    9 Paid $200 to the carrier for the freight bill on the December 7 purchase.
  11 Paid the Time Express newspaper $350 for an ad to announce the grand opening of the distribution center.
  11 Borrowed $10,000 from First National Bank. Signed a 10%, 180-day note.
  13 Sold merchandise for cash of $8,200 that cost $6,300.
  14 Sold $5,000 merchandise on account to J. Adair that cost $3,725.
  15 Paid freight on sale to Adair of $175.
  16 Sold $4,000 merchandise on account to J. Bronson that cost $3,050.
  17 Purchased $20,000 merchandise from the Lowe Company on account.
  19 Made cash sales of $10,000 that cost $7,950.
  21 Paid Mardel Office Supply.
  22 Paid Agape Supply for the purchase on the 5th.
  24 Collected payment in full from J. Adair.
  26 Paid Lowe Company for the purchase of the 17th.
  27 Received payment in full from Bronson.
  30 Purchased a used truck to deliver merchandise for $14,000 cash.
  30 Paid utilities for the month of $1,800.
  31 Paid wages for the month of $7,000.
  31 Baer withdrew $1,800 for personal living expenses.

REQUIRED:

a. Journalize the transactions for the month of December in the general journal.

b. Open the necessary accounts in the general ledger and post the December transactions to the appropriate accounts in the general ledger.

c. Prepare a trial balance at December 31, 2000.

d. Prepare adjusting entries and complete a worksheet using the following information in addition to that included in the transactions:

    1. Baer depreciated the truck for the entire month of December, assuming straight-line depreciation with no residual value and a 3-year estimated life.

    2. Baer accrued the interest on the bank loan for 18 days.

    3. Baer incurred payroll tax expense of $1,900 for the month.

e. Prepare a balance sheet as of December 31, 2000, and a statement of income and a statement of owner's equity for the month ended December 31, 2000.

ACCOUNTING CYCLE CASES

These problems contain some concepts covered in Chapters 8, 9, and 10 and the appendices to those chapters.

Sole Proprietorship

7–51. John Robles began his retail clothing business, Fineries, on November 1, 2000, as a sole proprietor. The post-closing trial balance at November 30, 2000, appeared as follows:

FINERIES
Post-Closing Trial Balance
November 30, 2000

	Debits	Credits
Cash	$40,000	
Prepaid Rent	200	
Merchandise Inventory	24,000	
Fixtures	6,000	
Accumulated Depreciation		$ 1,000
Wages Payable		1,500
Robles, Capital		67,700
Totals	$70,200	$70,200

The following transactions occurred in the month of December, 2000.

Dec. 1 Robles invested an additional $100,000 cash in his venture.

    1 Bought store fixtures on account from the Acme Company for $13,600, terms n/30.

    1 Paid six months' rent in advance, $12,000.

    5 Purchased $8,000 of merchandise on account from Triad Company. The invoice date was December 5, terms 2/10, n/60.

    7 Paid for a 36-month contents policy for fire damage at a cost of $1,440.

    8 Purchased merchandise for resale for $25,000 cash.

    9 Returned damaged merchandise to Triad Company and received credit for $1,600.

   10 Sold merchandise to Jean Peoples on account for $12,600. The terms of the sale were 1/10, n/30.

12	Paid the balance due to Triad Company.
15	Cash sales for the first half of the month totaled $27,500.
16	Sold merchandise to Janeal Foster on account for $10,000. The terms of the sale were 1/10, n/30.
16	Paid wages for the first half of the month totaling $5,500, including the balance due from November.
18	Purchased merchandise on account from Kerr Company for $9,500. The invoice date was December 20, and the terms were 2/10, n/30.
20	Purchased office supplies totaling $250.
22	Received merchandise returned by Janeal Foster. Issued a credit memo for $1,500.
22	Received a check from Jean Peoples for her invoice less discount.
25	Received a check from Janeal Foster for payment of invoice less discount.
28	Sold merchandise on account to Paul Larsen, $8,600. The terms were 1/10, n/30.
28	Paid utility bill of $300 for December.
28	Received telephone bill for $100 for the month of December.
28	Paid Kerr Company for the invoice of December 18, less discount.
31	Recorded cash sales for the second half of December totaling $44,900.
31	Paid wages for the second half of December, $4,500.
31	Received a bill for delivery services for December, $250.

REQUIRED:

a. Journalize the transactions for the month of December in the general journal.
b. Open the necessary accounts in the general ledger and post the December transactions to the general ledger.
c. Prepare a trial balance at December 31, 2000.
d. Prepare adjusting entries and complete a worksheet using the following information and that found in the transactions:

1. Robles accrued payroll tax expense of $1,200 for the month.
2. Store fixtures had a six-year life and no salvage value.
3. Ending inventory balance was $14,000.

e. Prepare a balance sheet as of December 31, 2000, a statement of income, and a statement of owner's equity for the month ended December 31, 2000.

Corporation

7–52. Jay Chambless started a retail hardware store, Chambless Home Haven, Inc., on December 1, 2001. The following transactions occurred in the month of December:

Dec. 1	Chambless invested $200,000 cash to purchase 100,000 shares of common stock of Chambless Home Haven, Inc. The stock had a par value of $1 per share, and there were 200,000 shares authorized.
1	Bought store fixtures on account from the Ace Company for $22,000, terms n/30.
1	Paid three months' rent in advance, $9,000.
5	Purchased merchandise on account from Taylor Company for $50,000. The invoice date was December 5, terms 2/10, n/30.

7 Paid for a 12-month contents policy for fire damage at a cost of $1,200.

8 Purchased merchandise for resale for $30,000 cash.

9 Returned damaged merchandise to Taylor Company and received credit for $16,000.

10 Sold merchandise to A.V. Hill on account, $24,000. The terms were 1/10, n/30.

12 Paid the balance due to Taylor Company.

15 Cash sales for the first half of the month totaled $30,000.

16 Sold merchandise to Mel Hays on account $5,000. The terms were 1/10, n/30.

16 Paid wages for the first half of the month totaling $7,000.

18 Purchased merchandise on account from McGee Company for $18,000. The invoice date was December 20, terms 2/10, n/30.

20 Purchased office supplies for cash of $400.

22 Received merchandise returned by Mel Hays. Issued a credit memo for $700.

22 Received a check from A.V. Hill for invoice less discount.

25 Received a check from Mel Hays for payment of invoice less discount.

28 Sold merchandise on account to Dennis Rhodes for $12,600, terms 1/10, n/30.

28 Paid utility bill of $600 for December.

28 Received telephone bill for $200 for the month of December due on January 12.

28 Paid McGee Company for the invoice of December 18, less discount.

31 Recorded cash sales for the second half of December totaling $35,200.

31 Paid wages for the second half of December, $7,500.

31 Received a bill for delivery services for December for $400 due January 10.

31 Chambless declared and paid a $.10 per share cash dividend.

REQUIRED:

a. Journalize the transactions for the month of December in the general journal.

b. Open the necessary accounts in the general ledger and post the December transactions to the appropriate accounts.

c. Prepare a trial balance at December 31, 2001.

d. Prepare adjusting entries and complete a worksheet using the following information:

1. Chambless accrued payroll tax expense of $2,000 for the month.
2. Fixtures are depreciated using the straight-line method over four years and no salvage value.
3. Ending inventory balance is $15,000.
4. The combined corporate tax rate is 40%.

e. Prepare a balance sheet as of December 31, 2000, a statement of income, and a statement of retained earnings for the month ended December 31, 2000.

f. Assume that Chambless selects a calendar year. Prepare the closing entries to close the year.

g. Prepare a post-closing trial balance at December 31, 2001.

Partnership

7–53. The Blues Brothers began a management consulting business on October 1, 2001, called Blues Brothers Consulting. The following transactions occurred in the month of October.

2001

Oct. 1 John Blue invested $6,000 in the partnership for a 60% interest in the business and his brother Art invested $4,000 for a 40% interest in the business.

1 Purchased a computer for $3,000 and a copy machine for $2,000. Each piece of equipment had an expected life of five years with no residual value. The computer was financed with a three-year, 10% interest bank loan that calls for monthly interest payments and annual principal payments on September 30 each year of $1,000.

1 Paid three months' rent in advance, $3,000.

5 Purchased office supplies on account from Spring Company for $700. The invoice date was October 5, terms 2/10, n/30.

6 Paid for a one-year contents policy for fire damage at a cost of $600.

7 Returned damaged merchandise to Spring Company and received credit for $100.

10 Performed consulting services and billed Sam Hall on account, $14,000. The terms were 1/10, n/30.

11 Received $4,000 for cash consulting services performed.

15 Paid for the office supplies purchased from Spring Company on the 5th.

15 Received $2,000 cash for consulting services performed.

15 Billed Gary Suter $5,000 for consulting fees, terms 2/10, n/30.

16 Paid secretary wages for the first half of the month totaling $1,000.

19 Purchased computer supplies on account from Dale Company, $400. The invoice date was October 19, terms 2/10, n/30.

20 Purchased office supplies for cash totaling $400.

20 Received payment from Sam Hall.

25 Received a check from Gary Suter for payment of invoice less discount.

28 Provided services on account to Dan Lee for $1,600. The terms were 1/10, n/30.

28 Paid utility bill of $300 for October.

28 Received telephone bill for $250 for the month of October.

28 Paid Dale Company for the invoice of October 19, less discount.

31 Paid wages for the second half of October, $1,500.

31 Received a bill for fax services for October, $100.

31 John withdrew $1,500 for personal expenses and Art withdrew $1,200.

REQUIRED:

a. Journalize the transactions for the month of October in the general journal.

b. Open the necessary accounts in the general ledger and post the October transactions to the appropriate accounts.

c. Prepare a trial balance at October 31, 2001.

d. Prepare adjusting entries and complete a worksheet using the following information and that listed in the transactions:

1. Accrued payroll tax expense is $300 for the month.
2. Office supplies of $100 were on hand at October 31.
3. There were no computer supplies left at year end.
4. The partnership agreement indicates that the partners share profits and losses equally.

e. Prepare a balance sheet as of October 31, 2001, a statement of income, and a statement of partners' capital for the month ended October 31, 2001.

f. Assume that the Blues Brothers selected October 31 as the year end. Prepare and post the closing entries to close the year.

g. Prepare a post-closing trial balance at October 31, 2001.

Chapter 8

Challenging Issues under Accrual Accounting: Long-Lived Depreciable Assets—A Closer Look

While working your way through college, you spent over two years in a campus copy shop. After learning the business from every angle, you have the opportunity to purchase the shop from Connie, the retiring owner. She recently replaced all the equipment and has maintained it well. Your accountant suggests that you use as rapid a depreciation method as possible. Not wanting to sound ignorant, you let the comment pass. Later, your friend Jon, an accounting major, explained some of the concepts to you but asks you to consider some additional issues. He wants to know how rapidly the technology changes in copiers, how many copies each machine can run economically before it begins to break down, and how many copies the shop runs each year. You vow to find the answers to these questions, but still do not understand all the implications of his issues. What do these issues have to do with the profitability of the copy shop?

Because accrual accounting recognizes revenues in the periods in which they were earned, and it tries to record expenses in the same periods as the revenues they helped earn, it requires more judgment and estimation than cash accounting. One of the best examples of the effects of estimates in accrual accounting is the depreciation of long-lived assets.

In this chapter, we extend our discussion of depreciation by considering several issues that further complicate the depreciation process. First, we consider the impacts of management's estimates of an asset's useful life and its residual value. Second, we examine the effects of management's selection of different depreciation methods. Third, we look at the effects of disposing of assets and how such transactions create a gain or loss. ■

LEARNING OBJECTIVES

After completing your work on this chapter, you should be able to do the following:

1. Explain the process of depreciating long-lived assets as it pertains to accrual accounting.
2. Determine depreciation expense amounts using both straight-line and double-declining-balance depreciation methods.
3. Describe in your own words the effects on the income statement and balance sheet of using different methods of depreciation.
4. Compare gains and losses to revenues and expenses.
5. Calculate a gain or loss on the disposal of a long-lived depreciable asset.
6. Explain the effects on a company's financial statements when management disposes of a depreciable asset.
7. Draw appropriate conclusions when presented with gains or losses on an income statement.
*8. Complete the recording process for long-lived assets and depreciation.

DEPRECIATION

historical cost Total of all costs required to bring an asset to a productive state.

tangible property Property used in a business such as buildings, equipment, machinery, furniture, and fixtures.

As you recall from our discussion in Chapter 6, depreciation is defined as a systematic and reasoned allocation of the cost of a long-lived asset. Over time, the depreciation process transfers the historical cost of the asset from the balance sheet to depreciation expense on the income statement, to more closely match the expenses with the revenues they help produce. We measure **historical cost** as the total costs to bring an asset to a usable state. This includes the invoice price, applicable sales tax, installation costs, cost of insurance while in transit, shipping costs, and cost of training personnel to use the machine. It does not include repairs and maintenance or insurance once the asset becomes productive.

When a firm purchases **tangible property** to be used to produce revenues in more than one income statement period, it recognizes the item as a balance sheet asset that will produce future benefits to the company. Under the matching principle, the company allocates part of the cost of that asset to the period in which it produces revenues through depreciation expense on the income statement. Just how much it recognizes as expense in a given year depends on several factors, including the estimates of useful life and residual value made and the depreciation method used.

The Effect of Estimates

Estimates of the length of the asset's useful life and the amount of its residual value directly affect the amount of depreciation expense recognized each year. For example, assume McMillan & Cox, a consulting firm, purchases a new computer network for $40,000. If management estimates that the computer system has a residual value of $4,000, the asset has a depreciable base of $36,000 (cost less residual value). The amount of depreciation expense recognized each year will be different if the useful life is estimated to be four years rather than three or five years. By the same token, the depreciable base will be different if the residual value is estimated

Exhibit 8-1
McMillan & Cox's New
$40,000 Computer
Network

Option	Details	Depreciable Base	Annual Expense
Decision 1	Residual value: $4,000 Useful life: 4 years	$36,000	$9,000
Decision 2	Residual value: $4,000 Useful life: 5 years	$36,000	$7,200
Decision 3	Residual value: $2,000 Useful life: 4 years	$38,000	$9,500
Decision 4	Residual value: $2,000 Useful life: 5 years	$38,000	$7,600

to be $2,000 rather than $4,000. Exhibit 8–1 shows how different depreciable bases result in different amounts of depreciation expense being recognized each year of the useful life of the machine.

Discussion Questions

8-1. What factors do you think a company should consider in determining the estimated useful life of a long-lived asset?

8-2. How do you think a company would go about determining the estimated residual value of a long-lived asset?

8-3. Consider a long-lived asset with a cost of $30,000. How would net income be affected by using an estimated useful life of six years and an estimated residual value of $6,000 rather than a four-year estimated useful life and a residual value of $5,000? Explain.

The Effect of Different Depreciation Methods

Most companies have more than one depreciable asset, and many firms use more than one depreciation method. As users of the financial accounting information provided by these companies, you should understand the impact of depreciation method choice on financial statements. To illustrate these effects, we will explore in detail the two most commonly used depreciation methods—straight-line depreciation and **double-declining-balance depreciation.**

According to *Accounting Trends and Techniques,* 95 percent of the 600 SEC-registered companies surveyed in 1996 use straight-line depreciation.[1] Straight-line methods of depreciation offer an equal amount of cost allocation every year over the life of the asset. Other methods, collectively called **accelerated depreciation methods,** record a large amount of depreciation expense in the early years of an asset's life and reduce that amount each year. At least 15 percent of the companies surveyed by the authors of *Accounting Trends and Techniques* used some type of accelerated depreciation.[2] (Remember, some companies use more than one type of method.) In addition, the Internal Revenue Service requires that businesses use a prescribed depreciation method called the **Modified Accelerated**

double-declining-balance method An accelerated depreciation method in which depreciation expense is twice the straight-line percentage multiplied by the book value of the asset.

accelerated depreciation methods Those methods that record more depreciation expense in the early years of an asset's life and less in the later years.

---

[1] *Accounting Trends and Techniques,* p. 359.
[2] Ibid.

Exhibit 8–2
Straight-Line
Depreciation versus
Accelerated
Depreciation

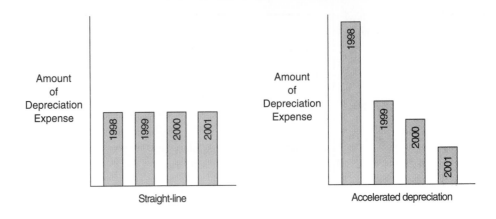

Modified Accelerated Cost Recovery System (MACRS)
Depreciation method taxpayers use to calculate depreciation expense for tax purposes.

Cost Recovery System (MACRS) for tax purposes. MACRS does not conform to GAAP, which therefore requires companies to use two different methods—one for tax purposes and another for financial statement purposes. As the name implies, MACRS is an accelerated depreciation method.

How do companies make the choice between using straight-line depreciation and an accelerated depreciation method? Recall that the matching principle requires us to match expenses with the revenues they help produce. Theoretically, we should use straight-line depreciation for an asset that produces the same amount of revenue in each period of its useful life, and, conversely, an accelerated depreciation method for an asset that produces more revenue in the early years and less as time goes by. However, the choice of depreciation method is more likely to be made on more practical grounds.

When considering the cost/benefit constraint, firms often select straight-line depreciation because it is easy to implement. Another reason is the anticipated effect on the financial statements during the asset's useful life. Exhibit 8–2 contrasts depreciation expense recorded under the straight-line method to the amount recorded if an accelerated method is used. As we explore the consequences of depreciation method choice, you can see the significant impact this decision can have on the accounting information offered to economic decision makers.

To illustrate that impact, we will contrast the results of straight-line depreciation with those of an accelerated depreciation method—the double-declining-balance method, which is the most widely used of the accelerated methods. We will explore the application of this method not simply so you can learn how to use it, but more importantly to demonstrate the impact of the choice of depreciation method on depreciation expense (and therefore on reported net income).

Straight-Line Depreciation

In Chapter 6, we introduced the concept of depreciation with an example of the straight-line method. To review how straight-line depreciation is calculated, assume Beavers Corporation purchased a milling machine on January 2, 1999, for a total price of $300,000. Beavers' management estimates the useful life of this machine to be five years, at the end of which the machine can be sold for an estimated $25,000. For simplicity, we will assume that Beavers owns only this machine.

We compute Beavers' yearly depreciation expense as $55,000:

Cost	$300,000
Less: Residual Value	25,000
Depreciable Base	$275,000
Divided by Useful Life	5
Annual Depreciation	$ 55,000

Exhibit 8–3
Book Value Using Production Method Straight-Line Depreciation

	Book Value Beginning of Year	Current Year's Production	Per Unit Depreciation	Current Year's Depreciation	Book Value End of Year
1999	$300,000	25,000	$2.75	$ 68,750	$231,250
2000	245,000	25,000	2.75	68,750	162,500
2001	190,000	20,000	2.75	55,000	107,500
2002	135,000	20,000	2.75	55,000	52,500
2003	80,000	10,000	2.75	27,500	25,000
Total		100,000		$275,000	

production depreciation method A straight-line depreciation method that uses production activity as the base to assign depreciation expense.

We could also decide that the life of this milling machine might be better measured by the number of units it could produce over its useful life. Instead of time as the straight-line measure, we could use units of production. If the milling machine can produce 100,000 units of hardware, we might measure its depreciation in units of product. This type of straight-line depreciation is called the **production depreciation method.** The production depreciation method is appropriate for many types of assets when the useful life is based not on time passing, but on the amount of usage. For these assets, the quantity used has more to do with length of life and residual value than the passage of time. In our example of the milling machine, if we measured depreciation in terms of units produced, we would calculate it in this manner:

Estimated units of production   100,000 units
Cost per thousand units
$$= \text{Depreciable base/Units}$$
$$= \$275,000/100,000 \text{ units}$$
$$= \$2.75 \text{ per unit printed}$$

If Beavers produces 25,000 units the first year, we recognize $68,750 in depreciation expense. See Exhibit 8–3 for a breakdown of the depreciation over the life of the asset. Notice the difference in depreciation expense in each year is based upon the difference in production from one year to the next.

Discussion Questions

8-4. How would you set the units of production for the following types of assets?

    a. Long-distance truck
    b. Commercial airliner
    c. Milling machine
    d. Cruise ship

8-5. Name five assets that would best be depreciated by the passage of time.

Return to our regular straight-line example based on time. In each of the five years of the asset's useful life, we will transfer $55,000 of the original asset cost from the asset balance on the balance sheet to depreciation expense on the income statement. To see this point, locate Beavers Corporation's income statements and balance sheets for the years 1999 through 2003 in Exhibit 8–4. For ease of interpretation, we held constant most of the items not affected by the depreciation process applied to the machine.

Exhibit 8–4

Beavers Corporation's Financial Statements Using Straight-Line Depreciation

Income Statements

	1999	2000	2001	2002	2003
Sales	$755,000	$755,000	$755,000	$755,000	$755,000
Cost of Goods Sold	422,000	422,000	422,000	422,000	422,000
Gross Margin	$333,000	$333,000	$333,000	$333,000	$333,000
Operating Expenses Other Than Depreciation	(236,000)	(236,000)	(236,000)	(236,000)	(236,000)
Depreciation Expense	(55,000)	(55,000)	(55,000)	(55,000)	(55,000)
Net Income	$ 42,000	$ 42,000	$ 42,000	$ 42,000	$ 42,000

Balance Sheets

	1999	2000	2001	2002	2003
ASSETS:					
Cash	$ 50,000	$ 96,000	$157,000	$213,000	$289,000
Accounts Receivable	206,000	257,000	293,000	334,000	355,000
Inventory	77,000	77,000	77,000	77,000	77,000
Machine	300,000	300,000	300,000	300,000	300,000
LESS: Accumulated Depreciation	(55,000)	(110,000)	(165,000)	(220,000)	(275,000)
Total Assets	$578,000	$620,000	$662,000	$704,000	$746,000
LIABILITIES AND STOCKHOLDERS' EQUITY:					
Accounts Payable	$206,000	$206,000	$206,000	$206,000	$206,000
Notes Payable	170,000	170,000	170,000	170,000	170,000
Common Stock	100,000	100,000	100,000	100,000	100,000
Additional Paid-in Capital	10,000	10,000	10,000	10,000	10,000
Retained Earnings	92,000	134,000	176,000	218,000	260,000
Total Liabilities and Stockholders' Equity	$578,000	$620,000	$662,000	$704,000	$746,000

Note that regardless of what else happened in Beavers' operations for the years 1999 through 2003, the amount of depreciation expense each year did not change. This constant depreciation expense is one of the main characteristics of straight-line depreciation. You should also note the direct correlation between the yearly depreciation expense shown on the income statements and the book value of the machine on the balance sheets. Recall from Chapter 6 that book value is the cost of a long-lived asset less all the depreciation expense recognized since the asset was placed in service (Exhibit 8–5). The total depreciation expense recognized since the asset was put in service is reflected in the balance of accumulated depreciation. Therefore,

$$\text{Book Value} = \text{Cost} - \text{Accumulated Depreciation}$$

Each year, as $55,000 of depreciation expense is recognized, the balance in accumulated depreciation increases by that amount, reducing the book value of the machine by that same $55,000. This example illustrates that straight-line depreciation causes the book value of assets to decline by the same amount each year. The book value at the end of 2003 is $25,000 ($300,000 – $275,000), which is equal to the

Exhibit 8–5
Book Value Using
Straight-Line
Depreciation

	Book Value Beginning of Year	Current Year's Depreciation	Book Value End of Year
1999	$300,000	$ 55,000	$245,000
2000	245,000	55,000	190,000
2001	190,000	55,000	135,000
2002	135,000	55,000	80,000
2003	80,000	55,000	25,000
Total Depreciation		$275,000	

estimated residual value. A total of $275,000 depreciation expense has been recorded, which is the amount of the depreciable base, and is therefore the maximum amount of allowable depreciation expense. At this point, the asset is considered to be fully depreciated.

Discussion Question

8-6. Refer back to Exhibit 8–1, which illustrates McMillan & Cox's four possible sets of estimates relating to its new copy machine. For each decision setting, determine the book value of the asset after three years of depreciation have been recorded.

Obviously, a different estimated useful life or a different estimated residual value would change the amount of yearly depreciation expense. So, too, would the selection of a different method of calculating yearly depreciation expense. To demonstrate how the choice of depreciation method can affect depreciation expense, we explore the most widely used accelerated depreciation method.

Double-Declining-Balance Depreciation

The double-declining-balance method received its name because it calculates depreciation expense at twice the straight-line rate, and it applies the doubled rate to its book value at the beginning of each period.

These are the simple steps to calculating double-declining-balance method each year:

1. Figure the straight-line rate in percentages.
   (100%/N, where N = number of years in the asset's useful life)
2. Double the straight-line percentage.
3. Multiply the doubled percentage by the asset's book value.

As an example, apply this method to Beavers' milling machine for the first year. These steps follow the previous directions:

1. Figure the straight-line percentage.   **100%/5 = 20% (per year)**
2. Double the straight-line percentage.   **20% × 2 = 40% (per year)**
3. Multiply the doubled percentage by the asset's book value.   **40% × $300,000 = $120,000**

Exhibit 8–6

Book Value Using
Double-Declining-
Balance Depreciation

	Book Value Beginning of Year		Double Rate	Current Year's Depreciation	Book Value End of Year
1999	$300,000	×	40%	$120,000	$180,000
2000	180,000	×	40%	72,000	108,000
2001	108,000	×	40%	43,200	64,800
2002	64,800	×	40%	25,920	38,880
2003	38,880			13,880	25,000
Total Depreciation				$275,000	

For 1999, Beavers Corporation would record $120,000 depreciation expense. Step 3 of this process uses the book value of the asset. Note that in the first year of the asset's useful life, before any depreciation has been recorded, the book value of the asset equals the cost of the asset. Though it may seem that the double-declining-balance method ignores the residual value, the maximum we can depreciate using the double-declining-balance method is the same depreciable base used in straight-line depreciation.

Exhibit 8–6 shows how we calculate the yearly depreciation expense for Beavers' $300,000 machine using double-declining-balance depreciation, a $25,000 residual value, and a five-year estimated useful life.

As you examine the calculations in the exhibit, you should note several points. First, the book value of the machine declines each year by the amount of depreciation expense recognized that year, just as with straight-line depreciation.

Second, the final year's depreciation does not equal 40 percent of the book value at the beginning of the year ($38,820 × 40% = $15,552). Because the asset cannot depreciate below its residual value, the amount of depreciation expense in 2003 has been limited to $13,880 ($38,880 – $25,000 = $13,880.) As shown in Exhibit 8–5, total depreciation over the five-year life of the asset is $275,000 for both straight-line and double-declining-balance methods.

Third, depreciation expenses start out high but quickly decrease. This rapid decrease is characteristic of all accelerated depreciation methods and has a profound effect on the financial statements of companies using accelerated depreciation methods. Beavers Corporation's income statements for the years 1999 through 2003 and its balance sheets at the end of each of those years using the double-declining-balance method of calculating depreciation illustrate this point in Exhibit 8–7. Again, many items not affected by the company's choice of depreciation method have been held constant from year to year.

Discussion Questions

8-7. Based on the financial statements of Beavers Corporation presented in Exhibit 8–7, and assuming no dividends were declared during 1999, what was the balance in retained earnings at the beginning of 1999?

8-8. Construct the 1999 statement of retained earnings if Beavers Corporation had not recorded any depreciation on its milling machine.

Exhibit 8–7
Beavers Corporation's Financial Statements Using Double-Declining-Balance Depreciation

Income Statements

	1999	2000	2001	2002	2003
Sales	$755,000	$755,000	$755,000	$755,000	$755,000
Cost of Goods Sold	422,000	422,000	422,000	422,000	422,000
Gross Margin	$333,000	$333,000	$333,000	$333,000	$333,000
Operating Expenses Other Than Depreciation	(236,000)	(236,000)	(236,000)	(236,000)	(236,000)
Depreciation Expense	(120,000)	(72,000)	(43,200)	(25,920)	(13,880)
Net Income (Loss)	$(23,000)	$ 25,000	$ 53,800	$ 71,080	$ 83,120

Balance Sheets

	1999	2000	2001	2002	2003
ASSETS:					
Cash	$ 50,000	$ 96,000	$157,000	$213,000	$289,000
Accounts Receivable	206,000	257,000	293,000	334,000	355,000
Inventory	77,000	77,000	77,000	77,000	77,000
Machine	300,000	300,000	300,000	300,000	300,000
LESS: Accumulated Depreciation	(120,000)	(192,000)	(235,200)	(261,120)	(275,000)
Total Assets	$513,000	$538,000	$591,800	$662,880	$746,000
LIABILITIES AND STOCKHOLDERS' EQUITY:					
Accounts Payable	$206,000	$206,000	$206,000	$206,000	$206,000
Notes Payable	170,000	170,000	170,000	170,000	170,000
Common Stock	100,000	100,000	100,000	100,000	100,000
Additional Paid-in Capital	10,000	10,000	10,000	10,000	10,000
Retained Earnings	27,000	52,000	105,800	176,880	260,000
Total Liabilities and Stockholders' Equity	$513,000	$538,000	$591,800	$662,880	$746,000

Understanding the Impact of Depreciation Method Choice

When you compare Beavers Corporation's income statements and balance sheets prepared using straight-line depreciation (Exhibit 8–4) with those same statements prepared using double-declining-balance depreciation (Exhibit 8–7), you should notice several differences and similarities:

- There are significant differences in the reported depreciation expense in each of the five years.
- There are significant differences in the reported net income in each of the five years.
- *Total* depreciation expense and *total* net income over the five-year period are exactly the same regardless of which depreciation method is used. The differences occur in individual years, not over the total five-year period.
- There are significant differences in the amounts of accumulated depreciation on the balance sheets for years 1999 through 2002. The 2003 balance sheet, however, shows exactly the same amount of accumulated depreciation in both presentations. In fact, the 2003 balance sheets in the two presentations are identical.

Exhibit 8–8

Comparison of Depreciation Expense, Net Income, and Book Value of Beavers' Machine under the Two Depreciation Methods

	Straight-Line			Double-Declining-Balance		
Year	Depreciation Expense	Net Income	Book Value of Machine	Depreciation Expense	Net Income	Book Value of Machine
1999	$ 55,000	$ 42,000	$245,000	$120,000	($ 23,000)	$180,000
2000	$ 55,000	$ 42,000	$190,000	$ 72,000	$ 25,000	$108,000
2001	$ 55,000	$ 42,000	$135,000	$ 43,200	$ 53,800	$ 64,800
2002	$ 55,000	$ 42,000	$ 80,000	$ 25,920	$ 71,080	$ 38,880
2003	$ 55,000	$ 42,000	$ 25,000	$ 13,880	$ 83,120	$ 25,000
Total	$275,000	$210,000		$275,000	$210,000	

Neither the straight-line method nor the double-declining-balance method is better than the other. Exhibit 8–8 depicts how the depreciation method can have a substantial effect on reported net income and on portions of the balance sheet from year to year, but over the life of the asset, the method of depreciation is irrelevant.

Discussion Questions

8-9. Explain why the 2003 balance sheets for Beavers Corporation, using the two different depreciation methods, are identical, while all five income statements and the first four years' balance sheets are different.

8-10. Compare the amount of cash shown on the Beavers Corporation balance sheets using straight-line depreciation and double-declining-balance depreciation for each given year. Explain your findings.

8-11. Assume that Exhibit 8–8 depicts information from two different companies, and you are making an investment decision in 2000 with only the 1999 accounting information. How would you make a decision based on the given information?

DISPOSAL OF DEPRECIABLE ASSETS

Ideally, a firm would use a long-lived asset for exactly the time originally estimated, after which it would sell the asset for exactly the residual value originally estimated. In reality, this situation rarely occurs. The actual useful life of an asset normally differs from its estimated useful life, because a company may dispose of an asset at any time. A company holds an asset as long as it is productive, regardless of how long the company estimated it would hold it at the time of its purchase. Technological advances, competition, market changes, changes in business strategy, and many other factors affect the length of time an asset remains productive. A firm might sell an asset shortly after acquisition because it fails to be useful, or it may use an asset long after it is fully depreciated.

When a firm determines the estimated useful life of an asset, it needs to consider the possibility of both the technological obsolescence and the functional

technological obsolescence Occurs when an asset is no longer compatible with current technology.

functional obsolescence Occurs when an asset can no longer perform the function for which it was purchased.

obsolescence of the asset. **Technological obsolescence** occurs when technology exceeds the asset's current version. **Functional obsolescence** occurs when the firm can no longer use the asset to create revenue. Consider the case of computers. If you have a computer with workable software that fulfills all your needs, it does not matter to you whether it is the most current version of technology. It does not even matter that it may be technologically obsolete; it still is functional. If, however, your professor assigns an Internet assignment, and your computer cannot be connected to the Internet because it lacks the proper capacity to install and run the appropriate software, it has now become functionally obsolete. Functional obsolescence affects the asset's useful life. Both functional and technological obsolescence should be considered in determining the useful life of the asset.

A company has no guarantee that it will receive the estimated residual amount when it sells the asset. Technological obsolescence dramatically reduces the asset's residual value. Functional obsolescence may not reduce the asset's residual value if the asset has current technology. What is no longer functional to one company may still be functional to another company. The decision to keep or dispose of an asset should be based on the needs of the business, not on accounting considerations about depreciation.

As a general rule, disposing of depreciable assets is not an ongoing central activity in a company, it is incidental or peripheral to the major operation of the business. For this reason, we do not consider any increase or decrease in equity from the disposal of depreciable assets as a revenue or expense. Rather, equity changes from the disposition of assets represent the accounting elements reported on the income statement as gains (increases) and losses (decreases).

Gains and Losses—Important Accounting Elements

In *Statement of Financial Accounting Concepts #6*, the FASB defined gains and losses as follows:

gains Net inflows resulting from peripheral activities of a company. An example is the sale of an asset for more than its book value.

losses Net outflows resulting from peripheral activities of a company. An example is the sale of an asset for less than its book value.

1. **Gains.** *Increases in equity from peripheral or incidental transactions of an entity and from all other transactions and other events and circumstances affecting the entity except those that result from revenues or investments by owners.*
2. **Losses.** *Decreases in equity from peripheral or incidental transactions of an entity and from all other transactions and other events and circumstances affecting the entity except those that result from expenses or distributions to owners.*

With this knowledge of gains and losses, we can now expand the four components of capital from Chapter 5 to include them. The four components of capital are

1. Contributions by owners
2. Revenues and gains
3. Expenses and losses
4. Distributions to owners

Why do we distinguish between revenues and gains or between expenses and losses? Remember that an income statement provides information about the past performance of a company so that decision makers can better predict the company's future performance. Because gains and losses are incidental to a company's central operations and are usually one-time events, we cannot depend on them to predict the future success of a company's operations. Therefore, the income statement presents revenues and expenses as components of operating income and presents gains and losses separately. Decision makers can assign different predictive values to operating income (revenue minus expenses) and gains and losses. Gains and losses expand the net income equation from Chapter 5 as follows:

$$\text{REVENUES} + \text{GAINS} - \text{EXPENSES} - \text{LOSSES} = \text{NET INCOME}$$

Exhibit 8-9
Accounting Elements:
Gains and Losses

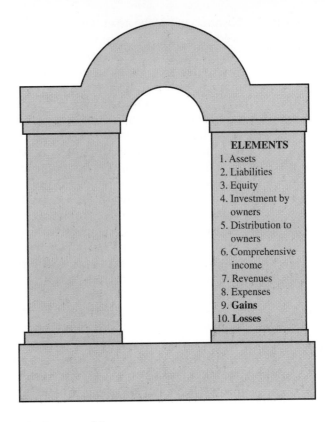

ELEMENTS
1. Assets
2. Liabilities
3. Equity
4. Investment by owners
5. Distribution to owners
6. Comprehensive income
7. Revenues
8. Expenses
9. **Gains**
10. **Losses**

Calculating Gains and Losses

We calculate gains and losses on the disposal of assets by comparing the value received and the value given. The value given consists of the book value of the asset on the date disposed. Depreciation should always be calculated and recorded up to date of disposal before we attempt to calculate any gain or loss.

Asset received − book value of asset given = gain (loss)

Return to the Beavers Corporation and its $300,000 milling machine. Assume Beavers depreciated this machine using the straight-line method over a five-year estimated useful life, with an estimated residual value of $25,000 (Exhibit 8–4).

On January 2, 2004, Beavers decides to sell the machine because it no longer benefits the company's operations. The machine has a $25,000 book value at the end of 2003 ($300,000 cost − $275,000 accumulated depreciation). Although the accounting records indicate a $25,000 book value, that seldom represents the market value. The book value is based on an estimate made five years ago and is irrelevant in the marketplace because buyers pay market value. Market value depends on the condition of the machine, the state of technology, and the selling price of comparable used machines. However, we use the book value to calculate accounting gains and losses.

Gain on Disposal Assume Beavers sells the machine for a cash price of $32,000. Because the company has received more than the book value of the machine, it recognizes a gain.

Asset received − book value of asset given = gain (loss)
$32,000 − $25,000 = $7,000

The $7,000 appears as a gain on the income statement for the year 2004. Exhibit 8–10 shows Beavers' income statements for the years 2003 and 2004 and its balance sheets at the end of each of those years, reflecting a $7,000 gain on the disposal of its machine.

Exhibit 8–10

Beavers Corporation's Financial Statements for 2003 and 2004 Reflecting a Gain on the Sale of Its Machine

BEAVERS CORPORATION

Income Statements

	2003	2004
Sales	$755,000	$941,000
Cost of Goods Sold	422,000	525,000
Gross Margin	$333,000	$416,000
Operating Expenses		
Other Than Depreciation	(236,000)	(319,000)
Depreciation Expense	(55,000)	-0-
Operating Income	$ 42,000	$ 97,000
Gain on Sale of Machine	-0-	7,000
Net Income	$ 42,000	$104,000

Balance Sheets

	2003	2004
ASSETS:		
Cash	$289,000	$225,000
Accounts Receivable	355,000	313,000
Inventory	77,000	172,000
Machine	300,000	-0-
LESS: Accumulated Depreciation	(275,000)	-0-
Total Assets	$746,000	$710,000
LIABILITIES AND STOCKHOLDERS' EQUITY:		
Accounts Payable	$206,000	$216,000
Notes Payable	170,000	20,000
Common Stock	100,000	100,000
Additional Paid-in Capital	10,000	10,000
Retained Earnings	260,000	364,000
Total Liabilities and Stockholders' Equity	$746,000	$710,000

As you examine these financial statements, consider the following points:

- On the income statement for the year 2004, the $7,000 gain is shown in a different place than revenues from Beavers' ongoing major operations.
- The $7,000 gain has exactly the same effect on net income as the revenues from Beavers' ongoing major operations on the income statement for the year 2004.
- Both the cost of the machine ($300,000) and the accumulated depreciation ($275,000) have been removed from the balance sheet at the end of the year 2004.

Discussion Question

8-12. Note that Beavers Corporation's income statements are presented in a multistep format in Exhibit 8–10. What specific items on the income statements are unique to this format and would not appear on a single-step statement?

Loss on Disposal   Assume Beavers sells the machine for a cash price of only $19,000. Because the company received less than the book value of the machine, it recognizes a loss.

$$\text{Asset received} - \text{book value of asset given} = \text{gain (loss)}$$
$$\$19,000 - \$25,000 = \$(6,000)$$

The $6,000 will be reported as a loss on the income statement for the year 2004. Exhibit 8–11 shows Beavers' income statements for the years 2003 and 2004 and its balance sheets at the end of each of those years, reflecting a $6,000 loss on the disposal of its machine.

As you study these financial statements, consider the following points:

- On the income statement for the year 2004, the $6,000 loss is shown in a different place than expenses required to support Beavers' ongoing major operations.
- The $6,000 loss has exactly the same effect on net income as the expenses required to support Beavers' ongoing major operations on the income statement for the year 2004.

Exhibit 8–11
Beavers Corporation's Financial Statements for 2003 and 2004 Reflecting a Loss on the Sale of Its Machine

BEAVERS CORPORATION

Income Statements

	2003	2004
Sales	$755,000	$941,000
Cost of Goods Sold	422,000	525,000
Gross Margin	$333,000	$416,000
Operating Expenses		
Other Than Depreciation	(236,000)	(319,000)
Depreciation Expense	(55,000)	-0-
Operating Income	$ 42,000	$ 97,000
Loss on Sale of Machine	-0-	(6,000)
Net Income	$ 42,000	$ 91,000

Balance Sheets

	2003	2004
ASSETS:		
Cash	$289,000	$212,000
Accounts Receivable	355,000	313,000
Inventory	77,000	172,000
Machine	300,000	-0-
LESS: Accumulated Depreciation	(275,000)	-0-
Total Assets	$746,000	$697,000
LIABILITIES AND STOCKHOLDERS' EQUITY:		
Accounts Payable	$206,000	$216,000
Notes Payable	170,000	20,000
Common Stock	100,000	100,000
Additional Paid-in Capital	10,000	10,000
Retained Earnings	260,000	351,000
Total Liabilities and Stockholders' Equity	$746,000	$697,000

- Both the cost of the machine ($300,000) and the accumulated depreciation ($275,000) have been removed from the balance sheet at the end of the year 2004.

In our examples of both a gain and a loss, we have assumed that Beavers was able to sell its machine for some amount of cash. However, there are times when an asset has no market value and must simply be abandoned. If this were the case with the Beavers machine, it would result in a loss of $25,000 ($0 cash received − $25,000 book value = a $25,000 loss).

Discussion Question

8-13. Look again at Beavers Corporation's income statements and balance sheets in Exhibit 8–11. What items on the financial statements for the year 2004 would be different (and by how much) if Beavers had simply abandoned the machine?

Disposal with No Gain or Loss   Assume now that Beavers sells the machine for a cash price of $25,000. Because the company received exactly the book value of the machine, there is neither a gain nor a loss.

Asset received − book value of asset given = gain (loss)
$25,000 − $25,000 = $0

As Exhibit 8–12 shows, the sale of the machine will not directly affect the income statement for the year 2004, but it will affect the balance sheet.

As you examine these statements, there are two points you should note:

- There is no gain or loss from the disposal of the machine on the income statement for the year 2004.
- Both the cost of the machine ($300,000) and the accumulated depreciation ($275,000) have been removed from the balance sheet at the end of the year 2004.

Thus far you have seen how to calculate gains and losses, and how these elements affect a company's financial statements. We now are ready to see how to properly interpret gains and losses when they are a part of the accounting information made available during the decision-making process.

UNDERSTANDING THE TRUE MEANING OF GAINS AND LOSSES

Assume that two companies have business activities that are identical in almost all respects. The companies have the exact same sales for the year, and all their operating expenses (except depreciation) are the same.

The two companies in this example are Straight Arrow Automotive and Accelerated Automotive. Both companies purchased a fleet of trucks for $228,000 on January 2, 1999. In addition, both companies estimated a useful life of four years and a residual value of $92,000 for the trucks. Because Straight Arrow Automotive uses straight-line depreciation and Accelerated Automotive uses the double-declining-balance method, we expect to see differences in their financial statements. Exhibit 8–13 contains the 1999 income statement and balance sheet for each company.

Exhibit 8–12

Beavers Corporation's Financial Statements for 2003 and 2004 Reflecting the Sale of Its Machine for Book Value

BEAVERS CORPORATION

Income Statements

	2003	2004
Sales	$755,000	$941,000
Cost of Goods Sold	422,000	525,000
Gross Margin	$333,000	$416,000
Operating Expenses		
Other Than Depreciation	(236,000)	(319,000)
Depreciation Expense	(55,000)	-0-
Operating Income	$ 42,000	$ 97,000
Gain (Loss) on Sale of Machine	-0-	-0-
Net Income	$ 42,000	$ 97,000

Balance Sheets

	2003	2004
ASSETS:		
Cash	$289,000	$218,000
Accounts Receivable	355,000	313,000
Inventory	77,000	172,000
Machine	300,000	-0-
LESS: Accumulated Depreciation	(275,000)	-0-
Total Assets	$746,000	$703,000
LIABILITIES AND		
STOCKHOLDERS' EQUITY:		
Accounts Payable	$206,000	$216,000
Notes Payable	170,000	20,000
Common Stock	100,000	100,000
Additional Paid-in Capital	10,000	10,000
Retained Earnings	260,000	357,000
Total Liabilities and Stockholders' Equity	$746,000	$703,000

Discussion Questions

Refer to Exhibit 8–13 to answer the following questions.

8–14. The amount of depreciation expense recorded by each company is given. Provide computations to explain how these amounts were determined.

8–15. The financial statements indicate four items on the income statements that differ between the companies. Six items on the balance sheets differ between the companies. Identify each item and explain the cause of the difference.

8–16. Assuming that no dividends were paid by either company, what was the balance in retained earnings on January 1, 1999, for each company?

Exhibit 8-13
1999 Financial Statements of Straight Arrow Automotive and Accelerated Automotive

Income Statements
For the Year Ending December 31, 1999

	Straight Arrow Automotive		Accelerated Automotive	
Sales	$769,000		$769,000	
LESS: Cost of Goods Sold	295,500		295,500	
Gross Margin		$473,500		$473,500
Wages Expense	$ 67,500		$ 67,500	
Utilities Expense	31,000		31,000	
Depreciation Expense	34,000		114,000	
Total Operating Expenses		(132,500)		(212,500)
Operating Income		$341,000		$261,000
Other Revenues and Expenses:				
Interest Expense		(120,000)		(120,000)
Net Income		$221,000		$141,000

Balance Sheets
December 31, 1999

	Straight Arrow Automotive		Accelerated Automotive	
ASSETS:				
Cash		$226,000		$226,000
Accounts Receivable		198,000		198,000
Inventory		223,000		223,000
Trucks	$228,000		$228,000	
Accumulated Depreciation	(34,000)		(114,000)	
Trucks, Net		194,000		114,000
Total Assests		$841,000		$761,000
LIABILITIES:				
Accounts Payable	$ 22,000		$ 22,000	
Notes Payable	61,000		61,000	
Total Liabilities		$ 83,000		$ 83,000
Owners' Equity:				
Common Stock	$200,000		$200,000	
Additional Paid-in Capital	194,000		194,000	
Contributed Capital	394,000		394,000	
Retained Earnings	364,000		284,000	
Total Shareholders' Equity		758,000		678,000
Total Liabilities				
and Owners' Equity		$841,000		$761,000

8-17. What are the depreciation expense and accumulated depreciation for each company? Are these two items always the same?

8-18. What are the accumulated depreciation and book value of the trucks for each company? Why are Accelerated Automotive's figures the same, but Straight Arrow's figures different?

Income Statements
For the Year Ending December 31, 2000

	Straight Arrow Automotive		Accelerated Automotive	
Sales	$769,000		$769,000	
LESS: Cost of Goods Sold	295,500		295,500	
Gross Margin		$473,500		$473,500
Wages Expense	$ 67,500		$ 67,500	
Utilities Expense	31,000		31,000	
Depreciation Expense	34,000		22,000	
Total Operating Expenses		(132,500)		(120,500)
Operating Income		$341,000		$353,000
Other Revenues and Expenses:				
Interest Expense		(120,000)		(120,000)
Net Income		$221,000		$233,000

Balance Sheets
December 31, 2000

	Straight Arrow Automotive		Accelerated Automotive	
ASSETS:				
Cash		$ 426,000		$426,000
Accounts Receivable		253,000		253,000
Inventory		223,000		223,000
Trucks	$228,000		$228,000	
Accumulated Depreciation	(68,000)		(136,000)	
Trucks, Net		160,000		92,000
Total Assets		$1,062,000		$994,000
LIABILITIES:				
Accounts Payable	$ 22,000		$ 22,000	
Notes Payable	61,000		61,000	
Total Liabilities		$ 83,000		$ 83,000
Owners' Equity:				
Common Stock	$200,000		$200,000	
Additional Paid-in Capital	194,000		194,000	
Contributed Capital	$394,000		$394,000	
Retained Earnings	585,000		517,000	
Total Shareholders' Equity		979,000		911,000
Total Liabilities and Owners' Equity		$1,062,000		$994,000

The impact of the choice of depreciation method becomes even more evident over time. Exhibit 8–14 shows the income statements and balance sheets of Straight Arrow Automotive and Accelerated Automotive at the end of 2000. Again, we have held constant the items that are not affected by the use of different depreciation methods.

Discussion Question

8–19. Provide computations and an explanation to show how Accelerated Automotive's depreciation expense amount of $22,000 was determined (Exhibit 8–14).

Even more profound than the differences occurring on the financial statements as the companies record depreciation, is the effect of an early disposal. Suppose that Straight Arrow Automotive and Accelerated Automotive both decide to sell their trucks on December 31, 2000. All trucks have the identical age, condition, and market value. In exchange for its truck fleet, each company receives $150,000 cash—the market value of the truck fleet on the day of the sale. Because the sale occurs on the last day of the year, both companies must record depreciation for the full year, as reflected in the previous statements.

Discussion Question

8–20. Were the companies wise to sell the fleet? Did they get "a good deal"? What information would help you decide whether the companies made a smart move?

Even though Straight Arrow Automotive and Accelerated Automotive incurred the identical transactions, the financial statement presentation of the results of the sale appears quite different, as shown in Exhibit 8–15.

When both companies made exactly the same transaction, why do the financial statements show different results of the sale? Straight Arrow Automotive recorded a $10,000 loss, but the same activity resulted in a $58,000 gain for Accelerated Automotive. However, both companies paid cash of $228,000 for the trucks and sold them for $150,000 after using the fleet for two years. The moral of the story? Smart financial statement users understand the true meaning of gains or losses on productive, depreciable assets. Remember, gains and losses on depreciable assets represent only the difference between the book value and the market value of assets sold. Do not assume that a gain indicates the sale was "good for business," or that a loss signifies that management made a bad move. In our example, we do not have enough information to determine whether the sale of the trucks for $150,000 was a wise business decision or a poor one. Clearly, though, the sale was no wiser for one company than for the other.

Also note that the retained earnings balance shown by Straight Arrow Automotive and Accelerated Automotive in Exhibit 8–15 is the same—$575,000. If Straight Arrow shows a loss on the sale and Accelerated shows a gain on the sale, how can both show the same retained earnings balance? The answer lies in the fact that both companies transferred the same amount of cost to the income statement over the life of the assets. See Exhibit 8–16 to verify that the same cost of $78,000 was transferred to each income statement—the same amount as the difference between the purchase price of $228,000 and the sale price of $150,000.

Because accelerated depreciation methods transfer costs more rapidly than straight-line methods, firms that employ accelerated depreciation methods have a greater chance of showing gains on the disposal of an asset before the end of its useful life. The earlier the disposition, the more likely the firm is to record a gain.

Exhibit 8–15
Impact of the Sale of Trucks at the End of 2000 on the Financial Statements of Straight Arrow Automotive and Accelerated Automotive

Income Statements
For the Year Ending December 31, 2000

	Straight Arrow Automotive		Accelerated Automotive	
Sales	$769,000		$769,000	
LESS: Cost of Goods Sold	295,500		295,500	
Gross Margin		$473,500		$473,500
Wages Expense	$ 67,500		$ 67,500	
Utilities Expense	31,000		31,000	
Depreciation Expense	34,000		22,000	
Total Operating Expenses		(132,500)		(120,500)
Operating Income		$341,000		$353,000
Other Revenues and Expenses:				
Gain on Sale of Trucks				58,000
Loss on Sale of Trucks		(10,000)		
Interest Expense		(120,000)		(120,000)
Net Income		$211,000		$291,000

Balance Sheets
December 31, 2000

	Straight Arrow Automotive		Accelerated Automotive	
ASSETS:				
Cash	$576,000		$576,000	
Accounts Receivable	253,000		253,000	
Inventory	223,000		223,000	
Totals Assets		$1,052,000		$1,052,000
LIABILITIES:				
Accounts Payable	$ 22,000		$ 22,000	
Notes Payable	61,000		61,000	
Total Liabilities		$ 83,000		$ 83,000
Owners' Equity:				
Common Stock	$200,000		$200,000	
Additional Paid-in Capital	194,000		194,000	
Contributed Capital	$394,000		$394,000	
Retained Earnings	575,000		575,000	
Total Shareholders' Equity		969,000		969,000
Total Liabilities and Owners' Equity		$1,052,000		$1,052,000

Exhibit 8–16
Total Costs Transferred to Expense by Straight Arrow Automotive and Accelerated Automotive

		Straight Arrow Automotive	Accelerated Automotive
1999	Depreciation Expense	$34,000	$114,000
2000	Depreciation Expense	34,000	22,000
2000	Result of Sale (Gain) or Loss	10,000	(58,000)
	TOTAL COST TRANSFERRED	$78,000	$ 78,000

As you can see from our discussion of the items presented in this chapter, the depreciation and disposal of long-lived depreciable assets can have a significant impact on a company's reported net income for a given year during the useful life of an asset. The issues surrounding depreciation are complex, and users of financial statements must have some understanding of them if they hope to be able to use financial statements for predicting a company's future or assessing its past performance.

Many issues besides depreciation have complicating effects under the accrual basis of accounting. We will continue our discussion of these complications in Chapter 9, where we consider issues surrounding the sale of merchandise inventory.

SUMMARY

Depreciation is the process of allocating the cost of long-lived assets to the periods in which they help to earn revenues. When a firm purchases an asset, its historical cost is recorded on the balance sheet. As time passes, the company transfers the cost from an asset on the balance sheet to an expense on the income statement. The recording of depreciation expense accomplishes this transfer. The amount of accumulated depreciation for an asset represents all the depreciation expense related to that asset that has been recognized thus far. We report accumulated depreciation on the balance sheet as a reduction of the asset cost.

GAAP allows several depreciation methods. Straight-line methods allocate cost evenly over the asset life measured either in time or productivity. Accelerated depreciation methods, such as the double-declining-balance method, recognize a greater amount of depreciation expense in the early years of an asset's life and a smaller amount in the later years.

The choice of depreciation methods affects companies' financial statements. In total, over the useful life of an asset, straight-line and double-declining-balance depreciation methods record the same amount of depreciation expense. In any particular period, however, different depreciation methods usually result in different amounts of depreciation expense, which causes a difference in reported net income. Because the amount of depreciation expense affects accumulated depreciation, the balance sheets of companies using different depreciation methods will also be different during most of the asset's life.

Eventually, a company disposes of its depreciable assets, and these transactions usually result in a gain or a loss. Gains increase and losses decrease net income in a manner similar to that of revenues and expenses, but gains and losses do not appear in operating income. Gains and losses result from activities peripheral to the major activity of the company; revenues and expenses are direct results of the company's primary business activity.

An asset's book value is its original cost less the amount of its accumulated depreciation. If an asset sells for more than its book value, the transaction results in a gain. Conversely, selling an asset for less than its book value results in a loss.

If the disposal of an asset results in a gain or loss, that outcome is reported on the income statement. If, however, an asset is sold for exactly its book value, the transaction results in no gain or loss. In any case, when a company disposes of an asset, both the asset and its corresponding accumulated depreciation account are removed from the balance sheet.

Gains and losses on the sale of productive depreciable assets does not indicate that the company has won or lost anything. The cost of using an asset over its life is the difference between its original cost and its final sales price. Gains and losses simply adjust the total depreciation charged to the income statement to total cost of using the asset. Accelerated methods tend to show more gains if an asset is sold in the early years of its life.

APPENDIX—RECORDING LONG-LIVED ASSETS AND DEPRECIATION

After completing Chapter 7, you can look at the journal entries for long-lived assets and depreciation. The recording process for long-lived assets involves three types of entries:

1. Purchase of an asset
2. Annual depreciation
3. Disposal of an asset

To record these types of entries, we need to have four accounts available for use:

1. Long-lived asset
2. Accumulated depreciation (a contra asset account)
3. Depreciation expense
4. Gain (Loss) on the disposal of assets

Remember that debits increase assets, expenses, and losses, and credits increase liabilities, equity, revenues, and gains. All journal entries must contain equal dollar amounts of debits and of credits.

We can examine the journal entries that the Beavers Corporation made to record the transactions for its milling machine. The following illustrates the straight-line example when Beavers sells the asset for $32,000.

Straight-Line Depreciation

1. Purchase of an asset:

1999		Debit	Credit
January 2	Milling Machine	300,000	
	Cash		300,000
	To record the purchase of a milling machine.		

2. Annual Depreciation:

1999		Debit	Credit
December 31	Depreciation Expense	55,000	
	Accumulated Depreciation		55,000
	To record annual depreciation expense.		

This same entry is made each year on December 31 for the years 2000, 2001, 2002, and 2003.

3. Disposal of an asset:

2004		Debit	Credit
January 2	Cash	32,000	
	Accumulated Depreciation	275,000	
	Milling Machine		300,000
	Gain on Sale of Asset		7,000
	To record the sale of the milling machine.		

Before we make the final entry to record the disposal, we must record any expired and unrecorded depreciation. Because the milling machine was last depreciated on December 31, 2003, and is now fully depreciated, no entry is required. The final entry removes the asset and accumulated depreciation accounts from the asset accounts. Because a gain increases equity, a gain creates a credit to balance the journal entry. Look at the following T-accounts to see how the entries affect each account.

	Milling Machine			Accumulated Depreciation	
1-2-99	300,000				
12-31-99				55,000	12-31-99
12-31-00				55,000	12-31-00
12-31-01				55,000	12-31-01
12-31-02				55,000	12-31-02
12-31-03				55,000	12-31-03
	300,000			275,000	
1-2-04		300,000	275,000		
	-0-			-0-	

Notice that the accounts show the history of what happened to this asset. See now how the entries change when Beavers selects the double-declining-balance method of depreciation.

Double-Declining-Balance Depreciation

1. Purchase of an asset:

1999		Debit	Credit
January 2	Milling Machine	300,000	
	Cash		300,000
	To record the purchase of a milling machine.		

2. Annual Depreciation:

1999		Debit	Credit
December 31	Depreciation Expense	120,000	
	Accumulated Depreciation		120,000
	To record annual depreciation expense for 1999.		

2000		Debit	Credit
December 31	Depreciation Expense	72,000	
	Accumulated Depreciation		72,000
	To record annual depreciation expense for 2000.		

2001		Debit	Credit
December 31	Depreciation Expense	43,200	
	Accumulated Depreciation		43,200
	To record annual depreciation expense for 2001.		

2002		Debit	Credit
December 31	Depreciation Expense	25,920	
	Accumulated Depreciation		25,920
	To record annual depreciation expense for 2002.		

2003		Debit	Credit
December 31	Depreciation Expense	13,880	
	Accumulated Depreciation		13,880
	To record annual depreciation expense for 2003.		

A different entry is made each year on December 31 for the years 2000, 2001, 2002, and 2003.

3. Disposal of an asset:

2004		Debit	Credit
January 2	Cash	32,000	
	Accumulated Depreciation	275,000	
	Milling Machine		300,000
	Gain on Sale of Asset		7,000
	To record the sale of the		
	milling machine.		

Notice that the purchase entry is the same regardless of the depreciation method. When the asset has been fully depreciated, the sale entry is also the same. See how these entries affect the individual accounts.

	Milling Machine			**Accumulated Depreciation**	
1-2-99	300,000				
12-31-99				120,000	12-31-99
12-31-00				72,000	12-31-00
12-31-01				43,200	12-31-01
12-31-02				25,920	12-31-02
12-31-03				13,880	12-31-03
	300,000			275,000	
1-2-04		300,000	275,000		
	-0-			-0-	

Recording a Loss

When the asset is fully depreciated, the method of depreciation makes no difference when the asset is sold. How would the final entry change if Beavers received only $19,000 for the machine on January 2, 2004?

2004		Debit	Credit
January 2	Cash	19,000	
	Accumulated Depreciation	275,000	
	Loss on Sale of Asset	6,000	
	Milling Machine		300,000
	To record the sale of the		
	milling machine.		

Because a loss reduces equity, the loss creates a debit entry to the loss account to balance the journal entry.

Sale at Book Value

When a sale occurs for book value, no gain or loss is recognized. Look at the journal entry to record the sale for $25,000.

2004		Debit	Credit
January 2	Cash	25,000	
	Accumulated Depreciation	275,000	
	Milling Machine		300,000
	To record the sale of the		
	milling machine.		

Sale before the End of Asset Life

If we look at the sale of Accelerated Automotive's fleet in the second year of life, we see how the journal entries unfold for an asset that has not been fully depreciated. The entries are the same as for a fully depreciated asset, except that we must be careful to record any unrecognized depreciation from the last time depreciation was recorded to the date of disposal.

1. Purchase of an asset:

1999		Debit	Credit
January 2	Truck Fleet	228,000	
	Cash		228,000
	To record the purchase of a truck fleet.		

2. Annual Depreciation:

1999		Debit	Credit
December 31	Depreciation Expense	120,000	
	Accumulated Depreciation		120,000
	To record the first year's depreciation expense.		

3. Disposal of an asset:
   a. First, bring the asset's depreciation up to date. The fleet was last depreciated on December 31, 1999, one year ago. A full year's depreciation expired since that time, but has not been recorded.

2000		Debit	Credit
December 31	Depreciation Expense	72,000	
	Accumulated Depreciation		72,000
	To record the second year's depreciation expense.		

   b. Second, record the asset disposal in accordance with the terms of the sale.

		Debit	Credit
December 31	Cash	150,000	
	Accumulated Depreciation	192,000	
	Truck Fleet		228,000
	Gain on Sale of Asset		114,000
	To record the sale of the truck fleet.		

SUMMARY TO APPENDIX

Recording transactions for long-lived assets involves four accounts: a long-lived asset, accumulated depreciation, depreciation expense, and a gain or loss on the disposal of the asset. We record the original purchase of the asset as a debit to the asset account. Annual depreciation results in a debit to depreciation expense and a credit to the accumulated depreciation, a contra asset account. When the owner sells an asset, we must first recognize all depreciation up to the date of disposal. When depreciation is current, we debit the asset received (usually cash), debit the accumulated depreciation, credit the asset, and credit gain on sale or debit loss on sale as the balancing item in the journal entry.

KEY TERMS

REVIEW THE FACTS

A. Provide three examples of long-lived depreciable assets.
B. In your own words, describe the depreciation process.
C. What two estimates made by management will affect the amount of depreciation recorded each period?
D. What is the depreciable base of an asset?
E. Explain the two bases we can use for straight-line allocation of the cost of fixed assets.
F. Explain what is meant by an accelerated depreciation method. Theoretically, in what situation is an accelerated depreciation method the appropriate choice?
G. Explain how the amount of depreciation expense is calculated using straight-line depreciation.
H. What is meant by an asset's book value?
I. What does the amount of accumulated depreciation represent?
J. In your own words, describe the process of determining depreciation expense using the double-declining-balance method.
K. Compared to straight-line depreciation, what is the effect of an accelerated depreciation method on the balance sheet? On the income statement?
L. Regardless of what depreciation method is used, at what point is an asset considered "fully depreciated"?
M. On what financial statement do gains and losses appear?
N. What is the difference between a revenue and a gain? A loss and an expense?
O. How is a gain or loss calculated?
P. What effect does the disposal of an asset that results in no gain or loss have on the income statement? On the balance sheet?

APPLY WHAT YOU HAVE LEARNED

LO 1:   Terminology

8–21. Presented below is a list of items relating to the concepts discussed in this chapter, followed by definitions of those items in scrambled order.

a. Accelerated depreciation
b. Book value
c. Gain on sale of asset
d. Losses
e. Estimated useful life

f. Straight-line depreciation
g. Gains
h. Loss on sale of asset
i. Depreciable base
j. Production method

1. _____ A factor determining how much of an asset's cost will be allocated to the periods supposedly benefited.
2. _____ A depreciation method that uses activity instead of time as the basis of allocation.
3. _____ More of the cost of a long-lived asset is converted to expense in the early years of its life than in later years.
4. _____ The cost of a long-lived asset less the estimated residual value.

5. _____ Results when a depreciable asset is sold for more than its book value.
6. _____ An equal amount of a long-lived asset's cost is converted to expense in each year of its useful life.
7. _____ Net inflows resulting from peripheral activities.
8. _____ The cost of a long-lived depreciable asset less its accumulated depreciation.
9. _____ Results when a depreciable asset is sold for less than its book value.
10. _____ Net outflows resulting from peripheral activities.

REQUIRED:
Match the letter next to each item on the list with the appropriate definition. Each letter will be used only once.

LO 1:   Depreciation Process

8–22. Evaluate the following: "The depreciation process is a process designed to value fixed assets on the balance sheet."

LO 2:   Computation of Depreciation Expense—
Straight-Line Method

8–23. Jerry Garcia and Company purchased a lathe for use in its manufacturing operation. The machine cost $150,000, has a five-year estimated useful life, and will be depreciated using the straight-line method. The only thing remaining to be determined before yearly depreciation expense can be calculated is the estimated residual value. The alternatives are
  1. $10,000 estimated residual value
  2. $20,000 estimated residual value
  3. $30,000 estimated residual value

REQUIRED:
a. Calculate the yearly depreciation expense for the new lathe under each of the alternatives given.
b. Which of the three alternatives will result in the highest net income?
c. How long will the new lathe be useful to Garcia and Company?

LO 2:   Computation of Depreciation Expense—
Straight-Line Method

8–24. Jones and Werner Inc. has just purchased a minicomputer for use in its manufacturing operation. The machine cost $75,000, has a four-year estimated useful life, and will be depreciated using the straight-line method. The only thing remaining to be determined before yearly depreciation expense can be calculated is the estimated residual value. The alternatives are
  1. $7,500 estimated residual value
  2. $12,500 estimated residual value
  3. $17,500 estimated residual value

REQUIRED:
a. Calculate the yearly depreciation expense for the new minicomputer under each of the alternatives given.

b. Which of the three alternatives will result in the highest net income? Which of the three alternatives will result in the lowest net income?

c. How long will the new minicomputer be useful to Jones and Werner Inc.?

LO 2: Computation of Depreciation Expense—Straight-Line Method

8–25. Nathan Verner Publishing Company purchased a new printing press for a total installed cost of $700,000. The printing press will be depreciated using the straight-line method, in accordance with corporate policy. Robert Sloan, the corporate controller, is trying to decide on an estimated useful life and an estimated residual value for the asset. The alternatives are

1. A six-year estimated useful life with a $40,000 estimated residual value
2. A five-year estimated useful life with a $100,000 estimated residual value
3. A four-year estimated useful life with a $140,000 estimated residual value

REQUIRED:

a. Calculate the yearly depreciation expense for the new printing press under each of the alternatives given.

b. Which of the three alternatives will result in the lowest yearly net income? Which of the three alternatives will result in the highest yearly net income?

c. What should be the deciding factor in selecting among the three alternatives?

LO 2: Computation of Depreciation Expense—Straight-Line Method

8–26. The Pizzeria Restaurant Company purchased a new walk-in freezer for a total installed cost of $250,000. The walk-in freezer will be depreciated using the straight-line method, in accordance with corporate policy. Jon Noel the corporate controller, is trying to determine an estimated useful life and residual value for the asset. His alternatives are

1. A five-year estimated useful life with a $10,000 estimated residual value
2. A four-year estimated useful life with a $25,000 estimated residual value
3. A three-year estimated useful life with a $50,000 estimated residual value

REQUIRED:

a. Calculate the yearly depreciation expense for the new printing press under each of the alternatives given.

b. Which of the three alternatives will result in the lowest yearly net income? Which of the three alternatives will result in the highest yearly net income?

c. What should be the deciding factor in selecting among the three alternatives?

LO 2: Computation of Double-Declining-Balance Depreciation Expense and Book Value

8–27. Wedtech Company purchased a high-tech assembler on January 2, 2000, for a total cost of $600,000. The assembler has an estimated useful life to the company of five years. Wedtech thinks it can sell the used assembler for $40,000 after five years. The company chose to depreciate the new assembler using the double-declining-balance method.

REQUIRED:

a. Prepare a schedule showing the amount of depreciation expense for each of the five years of the estimated useful life.
b. What will be the book value of the assembler at the end of the five-year estimated useful life?
c. What does book value represent?

LO 2: Computation of Double-Declining-Balance Depreciation Expense and Book Value

8–28. Mothball Company purchased an earthmoving machine on January 2, 2001, for a total cost of $900,000. The earthmover has an estimated useful life to the company of four years. Mothball believes it can sell the used earthmover for $80,000 after four years. The company selected the double-declining-balance method of depreciation.

REQUIRED:

a. Prepare a schedule showing the amount of depreciation expense for each of the four years of the estimated useful life.
b. What will be the book value of the earthmover at the end of the four-year estimated useful life?
c. What does book value represent?

LO 2: Computation of Depreciation Expense—Straight-Line and Double-Declining Balance

8–29. Wanda Company purchased a sophisticated stamping machine on January 2, 2000, for $480,000. The estimated useful life of the stamping machine is six years. Wanda estimates the machine's residual value is $40,000.

REQUIRED:

a. Calculate the yearly depreciation expense for the stamping machine assuming the company uses the straight-line depreciation method.
b. Prepare a schedule showing the amount of depreciation expense for each of the six years of the estimated useful life assuming the company uses the double-declining-balance depreciation method.

LO 2: Computation of Depreciation Expense—Straight-Line and Double-Declining Balance

8–30. WebCo, Inc. purchased a pasteurizing machine on January 2, 1999, for $375,000. The estimated useful life of the machine is four years with a residual value of $45,000.

REQUIRED:

a. Calculate the yearly depreciation expense for the machine assuming the company uses the straight-line depreciation method.
b. Prepare a schedule showing the amount of depreciation expense for each of the four years of the estimated useful life assuming the company uses the double-declining-balance depreciation method.

LO 2 & 5: Computation of Depreciation Expense and Gains or Losses—Production Method

8–31. Knoorfleet Inc. purchased a delivery truck on January 2, 2001, for $70,000. Knoorfleet estimates the estimated useful life of the vehicle is 1,000,000 miles, and the residual value at $10,000. The truck is driven 200,000 miles in 2001; 225,000 miles in 2002; 300,000 miles in 2003; and 275,000 miles in 2004.

REQUIRED:

a. Calculate the yearly depreciation expense for the vehicle assuming the company uses the production depreciation method.

b. Calculate the gain or loss on the sale if Knoorfleet sells the truck at the end of 2004 for $15,000.

c. Calculate the gain or loss on the sale if Knoorfleet sells the truck at the end of 2004 for $5,000.

d. Calculate the gain or loss on the sale if Knoorfleet sells the truck at the end of 2004 for $1,000.

LO 2 & 5: Computation of Depreciation Expense and Gains or Losses—Production Method

8–32. Janek Inc. purchased a printing press on January 2, 2000, for $95,000. Janek estimates the useful life of the press is 2,000,000 pages or five years, after which he can sell the press for $5,000. The press produces 500,000 pages in 2000; 400,000 pages in 2001; 430,000 pages in 2002; 600,000 pages in 2003; and 350,000 pages in 2004.

REQUIRED:

a. Calculate the yearly depreciation expense for the press assuming the company uses the production depreciation method.

b. Calculate the gain or loss on the sale if Janek sells the press at the end of 2004 for $15,000.

c. Calculate the gain or loss on the sale if Janek sells the press at the end of 2004 for $5,000.

d. Calculate the gain or loss on the sale if Janek sells the press at the end of 2004 for $2,000.

LO 2 & 5: Computation of Depreciation Expense and Gains or Losses—Production Method

8–33. Rufus, Inc. purchased a lathe on January 2, 2001, for $200,000. Rufus estimates its useful life as 1,600,000 hours or four years, and its residual value at $4,000. He uses the lathe for 500,000 hours in 2001; 430,000 hours in 2002; 300,000 hours in 2003; and 300,000 hours in 2004.

REQUIRED:

a. Calculate the yearly depreciation expense for the machine assuming the company uses the production depreciation method.

b. Calculate the gain or loss on the sale if Rufus sells the lathe after four years for $12,000.

c. Calculate the gain or loss on the sale if Rufus sells the lathe after four years for $3,000.

d. Calculate the gain or loss on the sale if Rufus sells the lathe after four years for $10,000.

LO 2 & 3: Computation of Depreciation Expense— Straight-Line and Double-Declining Balance

8–34. Pepco Inc. purchased a fleet of delivery trucks on January 2, 2001, for $700,000. The estimated useful life of the fleet is four years, after which Pepco estimates it can sell the entire fleet for $50,000.

REQUIRED:

a. Calculate the yearly depreciation expense for the fleet of vehicles assuming the company uses the straight-line depreciation method.

b. Prepare a schedule showing the amount of depreciation expense for each of the four years of the estimated useful life assuming the company uses the double-declining-balance depreciation method.

c. Address the following questions:
   (1) Double-declining-balance calculates depreciation at twice the straight-line rate. Why is the amount of depreciation expense in 2001 under double-declining-balance not exactly twice the amount under straight-line for 2001?
   (2) Over the four-year estimated useful life of the vehicles, how much depreciation expense will be charged against income using the straight-line method? How much will be charged against income using the double-declining-balance method?
   (3) Discuss the impact on the net income of each method of depreciation in the first two years of life of the asset.

LO 2 & 3: Computation of Depreciation Expense— Straight-Line and Double-Declining-Balance Methods

8–35. Ozzie and Harriet, Inc. purchased a fleet of taxis on January 2, 2001, for $600,000. The corporation estimates the useful life of the vehicles is three years, after which it can sell the entire fleet for $50,000.

REQUIRED:

a. Calculate the yearly depreciation expense for the fleet of vehicles assuming the company uses the straight-line depreciation method.

b. Prepare a schedule showing the amount of depreciation expense for each of the three years of the estimated useful life assuming the company uses the double-declining-balance depreciation method.

c. Address the following questions:
   (1) Double-declining-balance calculates depreciation at twice the straight-line rate. Why is the amount of depreciation expense in 2001 under double-declining-balance not exactly twice the amount under straight-line for 2001?
   (2) Over the three-year estimated useful life of the vehicles, how much depreciation expense will be charged against income using the straight-line method? How much will be charged against income using the double-declining-balance method?
   (3) Discuss the impact on the net income of each method of depreciation in the first two years of life of the asset.

LO 4 & 5: Computation of Gain or Loss

8–36. Cruse Company purchased a machine in January 2000 for $200,000. When originally purchased, the machine had an estimated useful life of five years and an estimated residual value of $25,000. The company uses straight-line depreciation. It is now June 30, 2003, and the company has decided to dispose of the machine.

REQUIRED:
a. Calculate the book value of the machine as of June 30, 2003.
b. Calculate the gain or loss on the sale of the machine assuming Cruse sells it for $102,000.
c. Calculate the gain or loss on the sale of the machine assuming Cruse sells it for $25,000.

LO 4 & 5: Computation of Gain or Loss

8–37. Farr Company purchased a machine in January 2000 and paid $150,000 for it. When originally purchased, the machine had an estimated useful life of four years and an estimated residual value of $10,000. The company uses straight-line depreciation. It is now September 30, 2002, and the company has decided to dispose of the machine.

REQUIRED:
a. Calculate the book value of the machine as of September 30, 2002.
b. Calculate the gain or loss on the sale of the machine assuming Farr sells it for $172,000.
c. Calculate the gain or loss on the sale of the machine assuming Farr sells it for $25,000.

LO 4 & 5: Computation of Gain or Loss

8–38. Simpson Company purchased a machine in January 2001 for $450,000. When originally purchased, the machine had an estimated useful life of 10 years and an estimated residual value of $50,000. The company uses straight-line depreciation. It is now January 2, 2008, and the company has decided to dispose of the machine.

REQUIRED:
a. Calculate the book value of the machine as of December 31, 2007.
b. Calculate the gain or loss on the sale of the machine assuming Simpson sells it for $130,000.
c. Calculate the gain or loss on the sale of the machine assuming Simpson sells it for $30,000.

LO 4, 5, & 6: Impact of Depreciation Methods on Gains and Losses

8–39. Millie and Maude are twins. Each of them has her own company. Three years ago, on the same day, they each purchased copiers for use by their companies. The machines were identical in every way and cost exactly the same amount ($28,000). The machines had the same estimated useful life (five years) and the same estimated residual value ($3,000). The only difference was the depreciation method chosen. Millie chose to depreciate her copier using straight-line based on time, while Maude selected an accelerated depreciation method.

Owing to rapid technological developments in the machines, Millie decided at the end of two years to sell her old machine and buy a new one. Maude decided to do the same thing. In fact, they each received exactly the same amount when they sold their machines ($16,500). Later, while they were having lunch together, Maude mentioned that when she sold her copier, she had a gain of more than $6,000 on the sale. Millie kept quiet, but was confused because she knew she had sold her copier for exactly the same amount as Maude, yet the sale of her copier had resulted in a loss of $1,500.

REQUIRED:
Explain how Millie could have had a loss of $1,500 on the sale of her copier, while Maude had a sizable gain.

LO 4, 5, & 6: Impact of Depreciation Methods on Gains and Losses

8–40. Redd and Fred each ran their own automotive repair shop. Each bought a new piece of equipment costing $10,000 on January 2. The equipment is expected to have a five-year life and no salvage value. Redd used straight-line depreciation and Fred used double-declining-balance depreciation. At the end of three years, each of them sold their machines for $5,500.

REQUIRED:
a. Compute the depreciation for both Redd and Fred through the third year.
b. Compute the gain or loss that each would recognize on the sale of the machine.
c. If the gain or loss is different for each of them, explain why.

LO 4, 5, & 6: Impact of Depreciation Methods on Gains and Losses

8–41. Ethel and Lucy each ran their own cooking school. Each bought a new piece of equipment costing $20,000 on January 2. The equipment is expected to have a five-year life and no salvage value. Ethel used straight-line depreciation and Lucy used double-declining-balance depreciation. At the end of three years, each of them sold their machines for $11,000.

REQUIRED:
a. Compute the depreciation for both Ethel and Lucy through the third year.
b. Compute the gain or loss that each would recognize on the sale of the machine.
c. If the gain or loss is different for each of them, explain why.

LO 4, 5, & 6: Impact of Depreciation Methods on Gains and Losses

8–42. Ricky and Fred each ran their own construction business. Each bought a new piece of equipment costing $40,000 on January 2. The equipment is expected to have a five-year life and no salvage value. Ricky used straight-line depreciation and Fred used double-declining-balance depreciation. At the end of three years, each of them sold their machines for $22,000.

REQUIRED:
a. Compute the depreciation for both Ricky and Fred through the third year.
b. Compute the gain or loss that each would recognize on the sale of the machine.
c. If the gain or loss is different for each of them, explain why.

LO 7:   Meaning of Gains and Losses

8–43. Explain in your own words what a gain or loss on the sale of a piece of equipment means and how the gain or loss relates to depreciation expense.

LO 7:   Comprehensive

8–44. Exhibit 8–7 in the text illustrates Beavers Corporation's financial statements, based on double-declining-balance depreciation. Use the income statements and balance sheets presented in the exhibit as a basis for completing the following requirements.

REQUIRED:
a. Prepare statements of retained earnings for Beavers Corporation as of the end of 1999, 2000, 2001, and 2002.
b. What can you conclude about the dividend policy of Beaver Corporation from the information provided and your response to Requirement a?
c. If no depreciation had been recorded, how would the statements of retained earnings have been different?

LO 7:   Comprehensive

8–45. Barker Company opened for business on January 2, 1999. During its first month of operation, the company had the following transactions.

Jan 2:   Purchased a truck for $10,000 and paid cash. The truck has an estimated useful life of three years. The company estimates the truck's residual value to be $1,000, and uses straight-line depreciation.

Jan 2:   Purchased $40,000 of merchandise inventory on account. Payment in full is due February 2.

Jan 3:   Paid January office rent of $2,500.

Jan 5:   Purchased $15,000 of merchandise inventory and paid cash on that date.

Jan 10: Sold $12,000 of merchandise inventory for $25,000 to a customer and received the cash on that date.

Jan 20: Sold $7,000 of merchandise inventory for $11,000. The sale was on account and the customer has until February 20 to pay.

Jan 24: Paid miscellaneous January operating expenses totaling $8,000.

Jan 31: Received bills for utilities, advertising, and phone service totaling $1,200. All these bills were for services performed in January. They will all be paid the first week in February.

Use the January 1999 income statements for Barker Company prepared under the cash and accrual bases of accounting to complete the following requirements.

REQUIRED:
a. Explain why the Cost of Goods Sold amounts on the two income statements differ?
b. Barker purchased $55,000 of merchandise inventory during January 1999. However, under the accrual basis of accounting, the company properly expensed $19,000 as cost of goods sold for the month. Explain where (if anywhere) the company shows the remaining $36,000 of merchandise inventory?
c. Barker purchased $55,000 of merchandise inventory during January 1999. Under the cash basis of accounting, the company properly expensed $15,000 as cost of goods sold for the month. Explain where (if anywhere) the company shows the remaining $40,000 of merchandise inventory?

d. Both income statements show an expense related to the truck purchased on January 2, 1999. How were the amounts on each income statement determined? Include in your answer what the amounts represent and why the cost of the truck is treated as it is.

e. What will be the book value of the truck on the December 31, 1999, balance sheet under
   (1) cash basis accounting?
   (2) accrual basis accounting?

f. What will be the book value of the truck on the December 31, 2001, balance sheet under
   (1) cash basis accounting?
   (2) accrual basis accounting?

g. Comment generally on why the net income (loss) amounts on the two income statements are so different.

BARKER COMPANY
Income Statement
For the Month Ending January 31, 1999

Cash Basis

Sales	$25,000	
LESS: Cost of Goods Sold	15,000	
Gross Margin		$10,000
Operating Expenses:		
Truck	$10,000	
Rent	2,500	
Miscellaneous Expenses	8,000	
Total Operating Expenses		(20,500)
Net Income (Loss)		$(10,500)

BARKER COMPANY
Income Statement
For the Month Ending January 31, 1999

Accrual Basis

Sales	$36,000	
LESS: Cost of Goods Sold	19,000	
Gross Margin		$17,000
Operating Expenses:		
Rent	$2,500	
Depreciation—Truck	250	
Miscellaneous Expenses	8,000	
Accrued Expenses	1,200	
Total Operating Expenses		(11,950)
Net Income (Loss)		$ 5,050

LO 8:   Recording Assets and Depreciation

*8–46. Cunningham Corporation purchased a new piece of equipment for $60,000 cash. Cunningham estimates the useful life of the equipment at five years with a salvage value of $10,000.

REQUIRED:
a. Prepare the journal entry to record the purchase of the asset.
b. Prepare the journal entries to record the depreciation for the first year of life of the asset.

LO 8:   Recording Assets and Depreciation

*8–47. Buffington, Inc. purchased a new piece of equipment for $560,000. The company paid $125,000 in cash and borrowed the remainder from the bank. Buffington estimates the useful life of the equipment at six years with a salvage value of $60,000.

REQUIRED:
a. Prepare the journal entry to record the purchase of the asset.
b. Prepare the journal entry to record the depreciation for the first year of life of the asset.

LO 8:   Recording Assets and Depreciation

*8–48. Buffington, Inc. purchased a new piece of equipment for $560,000. The company paid $125,000 in cash and borrowed the remainder from the bank. Buffington estimates the useful life of the equipment at six years with a salvage value of $60,000.

REQUIRED:
a. Compute the gain or loss if the company sells the equipment for $86,000 at the end of the fourth year using straight-line depreciation.
b. Prepare the journal entry to record the sale of the equipment.

LO 8:   Recording Assets and Depreciation

*8–49. Malph Corporation purchased a new piece of equipment for $75,000 cash. Malph estimates the useful life of the equipment at seven years with a salvage value of $5,000.

REQUIRED:
a. Prepare the journal entry to record the purchase of the asset.
b. Prepare the journal entry to record the depreciation for the first year of life of the asset.

LO 8:   Recording Assets and Depreciation

*8–50. Dustin Corporation purchased a new piece of equipment for $75,000. The company paid $5,000 in cash and borrowed the remainder from the bank. Dustin estimates the useful life of the equipment at seven years with a salvage value of $12,000.

REQUIRED:
a. Prepare the journal entry to record the purchase of the asset.
b. Prepare the journal entry to record the depreciation for the first year of life of the asset.

LO 8:   Recording Assets and Depreciation

*8–51. Dustin Corporation purchased a new piece of equipment for $75,000. The company paid $5,000 in cash and borrowed the remainder from the bank. Dustin estimates the useful life of the equipment at seven years with a salvage value of $12,000.

REQUIRED:
a. Compute the gain or loss if the company sells the equipment for $8,000 at the end of the fourth year using double-declining-balance depreciation.
b. Prepare the journal entry to record the sale of the equipment.

LO 8: Recording Assets and Depreciation

*8–52. Randall Company purchased a stamping machine on January 2, 2001, for $480,000. The estimated useful life of the stamping machine is five years. The machine has an estimated residual value of $40,000.

REQUIRED:

a. Calculate the yearly depreciation expense for the stamping machine assuming the company uses the straight-line depreciation method.

b. Record the journal entries for the depreciation that would be required each year.

c. Prepare the required journal entries to record the sale of the machine at the end of two years for $200,000.

LO 8: Recording Assets and Depreciation

*8–53. Wooten Company purchased a pasteurizing machine on January 2, 2000, for $375,000. The estimated useful life of the machine is five years. The machine has an estimated residual value of $40,000.

REQUIRED:

a. Calculate the yearly depreciation expense for the machine assuming the company uses the double-declining-balance depreciation method and prepare the journal entries to record depreciation each year.

b. Assuming the machine is sold at the end of 2002 for $50,000, prepare the required entries to record the sale.

c. Assuming the machine is sold at the end of April 2002 for $50,000, prepare the required entries to record the sale.

LO 8: Recording Assets and Depreciation

*8–54. Chesley, Inc. purchased a fleet of delivery trucks on January 2, 2001, for $700,000. The estimated useful life of the vehicles is four years, after which Chesley thinks it will be able to sell the entire fleet for $50,000.

REQUIRED:

a. Calculate the yearly depreciation expense for the fleet of vehicles assuming the company uses the straight-line depreciation method and prepare the journal entries to record the depreciation.

b. Assume the fleet is sold at the end of the life for $70,000. Prepare the journal entries to record the transaction.

c. Assume the fleet is sold on March 31, 2004, for $30,000. Prepare the journal entries to record the transaction.

LO 8: Recording Assets and Depreciation

*8–55. Ricky and Fred each run their own construction business. Each bought a new piece of equipment costing $40,000 on January 2, 2000. The equipment is expected to have a five-year life and no salvage value. Ricky uses straight-line depreciation and Fred uses double-declining-balance depreciation. On June 30, 2003, each of them sold their machines for $22,000.

REQUIRED:

a. Compute the depreciation for both Ricky and Fred through the date of sale.

b. Compute the gain or loss that each would recognize on the sale of the equipment.
  c. Prepare the journal entries necessary to record the purchase, annual depreciation, and sale of Ricky's and Fred's equipment.

FINANCIAL REPORTING CASES

Comprehensive

8–56. Go to the PHLIP Web site for this book at www.prenhall.com/jones and find the CMI Corporation link. Look up the current copy of the annual report and go to the footnotes section. Read footnote 1 and summarize the information presented about Property, Plant, and Equipment. Include in your summary the method or methods used for depreciation and the methods used to record Property, Plant, and Equipment.

Comprehensive

8–57. Go to the PHLIP Web site for this book at www.prenhall.com/jones and find the First Brands Corporation link. Look up the current copy of the annual report and go to the footnotes section. Find information about the Property, Plant, and Equipment in both the first footnote and the footnote about long-lived assets.

REQUIRED:
  a. What type of depreciation method does First Brands employ?
  b. What are the useful lives assigned to the different types of assets by First Brands?
  c. How much depreciation expense did First Brands recognize in the last year? How can you determine this amount?

Comprehensive

8–58. Go to the PHLIP Web site for this book at www.prenhall.com/jones and find the AT&T link. Look up the current copy of the annual report and go to the footnotes section.

REQUIRED:
  a. Determine the type of depreciation methods used for different types of long-lived assets.
  b. How much depreciation did AT&T record for the current year? In how many places did you find the amount of depreciation.

ANNUAL REPORT PROJECT

8–59. You will complete a portion of Section IV of the project. For Property, Plant, and Equipment you should do the following:
  a. List the total of Property, Plant, and Equipment for the three years listed in your company's report.
  b. List the total of Accumulated Depreciation associated with Property, Plant, and Equipment for the three years listed in your company's report.

c. Identify the method or methods of depreciation used by your company.
  d. List the total of all assets for the three years listed in your company's report.
  e. List the total of the current assets for the three years listed in your company's report.
  f. Is your company capital intensive, that is, does it have many more long-term assets than other assets?
  g. Does your company appear to be growing in terms of long-term assets?
  h. In the period presented in the balance sheet, has your company had significant changes in asset structure, such as major purchases of other companies, investments, or discontinued operation?
  i. If your company has acquired long-term assets, how were they financed?
  j. Does your company have major resources it does not report on the balance sheet, such as brand names or significant human resources?

REQUIRED:

Complete this part of Section IV of your report. Make a copy for your instructor and keep a copy for your final report.

Chapter 9

Challenging Issues under Accrual Accounting: Merchandise Inventory and Cost of Goods Sold

Your boss has offered you a promotion to manage the inventory in a new division the company is opening in Denver. You want this opportunity because you love to ski, and you enjoy working with inventory. You will be part of the team that selects the inventory software package and designs the inventory protection system. Part of your compensation package includes a bonus at the end of the year based upon both the gross profit percentage and the net income. How does inventory management relate to gross profit and net income? Your secretary reminds you to be careful about LIFO and FIFO. What is she talking about and how does that tie into profits? Time to find an accounting textbook.

In Chapter 8, we explored one source of variation across companies' financial statements—choice of depreciation method. Remember that GAAP allow companies a choice, among generally accepted accounting principles, because different industries have different operating characteristics. Accounting principles do not specify just one practice that fits all.

To gauge the cost of goods a firm sells, GAAP allow several alternative methods that measure the cost flow of inventory. The way a company accounts for its merchandise inventory purchases and sales can have a direct and significant impact on the firm's reported net income. ■

LEARNING OBJECTIVES

After completing your work on this chapter, you should be able to do the following:

1. Explain goods available for sale (GAFS) and name its components.
2. Describe the relationship between ending inventory and cost of goods sold.
3. Differentiate between the physical flow of merchandise and the cost flow of merchandise.
4. Explain the differences between periodic and perpetual inventory systems.
5. List different inventory cost flow assumptions and contrast how the use of each affects reported net income on the income statement.
6. Calculate cost of goods sold and ending inventory using FIFO, LIFO, and average cost inventory cost flow assumptions.
*7. Calculate cash discounts and invoice due dates, and determine who bears the freight expense from the freight terms.
*8. Complete the recording process for inventory purchases and sales.

TRACKING INVENTORY COSTS

Merchandising Companies

merchandise inventory
The physical units (goods) a company buys to resell as part of its business operation. Also called inventory.

beginning inventory The amount of merchandise inventory (units or dollars) on hand at the beginning of the income statement period.

purchases The amount of merchandise inventory bought during the income statement period.

goods available for sale (GAFS) The total amount of merchandise inventory a company has available to sell in a given income statement period.

cost of goods sold (COGS) The cost of the merchandise inventory no longer on hand, and assumed sold during the period. Also called cost of sales.

ending inventory The amount of inventory (in units or dollars) still on hand at the end of an accounting period.

The tangible products that merchandisers sell are called **merchandise inventory,** or **inventory.** For example, Office Depot sells office equipment, Lazy Boy sells desks and chairs, and Chrysler sells cars and trucks. The product each firm sells is called inventory. However, to customers, these products may be long-lived assets.

When we discuss inventory, we must consider two aspects: the number of units of inventory and the cost of each of those units. To apply the matching principle, we must determine the quantity of units sold and how much expense matches the sales of the period. A mathematical relationship exists between the beginning inventory, the purchases during the period, the cost of goods sold, and the ending inventory.

At the beginning of an income statement period, a firm has an amount of merchandise inventory on hand called **beginning inventory.** During the period, the firm buys additional inventory we call **purchases.** The cost of purchases includes all the costs to bring the item to a saleable state, including freight, packaging, and make-ready costs. A firm can sell only the goods it has on hand during a period, represented by the total of the beginning inventory plus the amount it bought (purchases). We call this total the **goods available for sale (GAFS).** Whether we are referring to the physical count of inventory units or its cost, the following relationship between beginning inventory (BI), purchases (Purch), and goods available for sale (GAFS) holds true:

$$\text{Beginning Inventory} + \text{Purchases} = \text{Goods Available for Sale}$$
$$\text{BI} + \text{Purch} = \text{GAFS}$$

Once a firm has goods to sell, reality dictates that at the end of the period, the merchandise is either gone or still on hand. We recognize the inventory that is gone as an income statement expense of the period called **cost of goods sold (COGS)** or **cost of sales.** The inventory still on hand is the **ending inventory,** a balance sheet asset, because it has probable future economic benefit since it can generate future sales. We can calculate the cost of goods sold (COGS) by subtracting the ending inventory from goods available for sale. Thus, the total amount that we could have sold (GAFS) minus the amount we still had at the end of the period (EI) equals the amount that we sold (COGS):

$$GAFS - EI = COGS$$

Conversely, if we know cost of goods sold, we can determine a company's ending merchandise inventory for a given period. The total amount we could have sold (GAFS) less the amount we did sell (COGS) is the amount we should have left at the end of the period (EI):

$$GAFS - COGS = EI$$

These relationships hold true whether we are considering the quantity of inventory (physical units) or the cost of that inventory.

Discussion Question

9-1. If inventory is gone at the end of a period but was not sold, what could have happened to it?

Exhibit 9–1 shows examples of these relationships in terms of both units and dollar amounts for the Strawn Book Company for one month's operations. The month starts with 200 books on hand; Strawn buys 600 new books, sells 650 books, and has 150 books on hand at the end of the month. This information contains four different data items. We need only three of these items to compute any fourth item. In the first table in the exhibit, we use ending inventory to calculate cost of goods sold, and in the second table, we use cost of goods sold to calculate ending inventory. It is important to learn from these two calculations that the total of ending inventory and cost of goods sold will always equal goods available for sale (in units and in dollars).

Exhibit 9–1
Relationships among BI, Purch, GAFS, EI, and COGS for Strawn Book Company

	Units	Cost	
Beginning Inventory	200	$2,000	BI
+ Purchases	600	6,000	+ Purch
= Goods Available for Sale	800	$8,000	= GAFS
− Ending Inventory	150	1,500	− EI
= Cost of Goods Sold	650	$6,500	= COGS

OR

	Units	Cost	
Beginning Inventory	200	$2,000	BI
+ Purchases	600	6,000	+ Purch
= Goods Available for Sale	800	$8,000	= GAFS
− Cost of Goods Sold	650	6,500	− COGS
= Ending Inventory	150	$1,500	= EI

Discussion Question

9-2. You invite your friends to a party. You check your supplies and find hot dogs, dip, and pretzels. You go to the store to buy soda, chips, hot dog buns, peanuts, and ice cream. Following an enjoyable party, you survey the aftermath and find the pantry and refrigerator bare. The freezer is full of ice cream because everyone forgot to eat it. To figure out how much the party cost you, describe the following:

a. beginning inventory
b. purchases
c. goods available
d. ending inventory
e. "cost" of the party

raw materials inventory
The inventory of raw materials to be transferred into production in a manufacturing company.

work-in-process inventory
The cost of raw materials, labor, and other expenses associated with unfinished units during the process of converting raw materials into finished goods for a manufacturing company.

finished goods inventory
The inventory ready to sell in a manufacturing company. Also called finished goods.

cost of goods manufactured
The cost of converting raw materials into finished goods in a manufacturing firm. The cost is equivalent to purchases in a merchandising firm.

Manufacturing Companies

The inventory that manufacturing companies sell can have different forms—goods ready for retail sale or component parts for other manufacturers. Manufacturers convert raw materials to another form for customers. In the manufacturing process, a manufacturer has three inventories. A manufacturer buys raw materials and keeps these costs in its **raw materials inventory.** While the workers convert the raw materials into the finished product, the material costs and other costs accumulate in the **work-in-process inventory.** The manufacturer calls its final products *finished goods* and records the cost in the **finished goods inventory.** When the manufacturer sells the inventory, the cost of goods sold formula is exactly the same for a manufacturer and a merchandiser except the manufacturer has **cost of goods manufactured** instead of purchases. As you can see, although the same concepts for tracking costs presented for merchandising firms apply to manufacturing firms, manufacturing accounting is complicated. Therefore, we will present manufacturing costs beginning with Chapter 1 of management accounting.

INVENTORY SYSTEMS

A firm selects the type of inventory system it uses to determine the reality of the inventory quantity it has and the measurement of that reality. Over time, businesses have developed two major inventory systems—the periodic and the perpetual methods. Each has advantages and disadvantages in comparison.

Periodic Inventory System

periodic inventory system
An inventory system in which all inventory and cost of goods sold calculations are done at the end of the income statement period.

Under a **periodic inventory system,** the purchases of new inventory are treated as an expense until the end of the period. Unsold goods (ending inventory) become an asset on the balance sheet. We make the cost of goods sold calculations at the end of the income statement period similar to the calculations in Exhibit 9–1. Detailed inventory records are not updated during the period. Companies using this system do not track which products have been sold until the end of period, when the company prepares its financial statements.

The strength of the periodic inventory system is that it involves relatively little additional record keeping. This fact may be important to a firm with 10,000 different inventory items. Its greatest weakness is that it does not provide the company with any day-to-day information about the status of its inventory.

Prior to the computer age, most companies with a moderate volume of inventory employed the periodic inventory system, because keeping detailed inventory records manually was too time consuming. The costs of keeping timely inventory information far outweighed the benefits of the knowledge. However, current computer technology has made the task of keeping daily records of inventory transactions a low-cost and reasonably efficient process. Today's software includes features that automatically reorder inventory when it reaches a preselected level. Scanning devices even automate the record-keeping process. Consequently, the perpetual inventory system has grown in popularity.

Inventory data consists of two components: units and dollar costs. Although many companies now keep detailed information about the quantity of the inventory units, it is not certain that all companies keep perpetual cost information. Keeping cost information requires much more time, expense, and computer storage space. Some companies may keep both the units and dollar costs on the periodic system, and others may keep only the dollar costs on the periodic basis. Therefore, we will consider the accounting treatment of the periodic system to determine cost of goods sold and ending inventory.

Perpetual Inventory System

perpetual inventory system
An inventory system in which both the physical count of inventory units and the cost classification (asset or expense) are updated when a transaction involves inventory.

Under a complete **perpetual inventory system,** both the physical count of inventory units and the cost classification (asset or expense) are updated whenever the transaction involves inventory. A perpetual inventory system considers inventory an asset until it is sold, when it is transferred to the expense cost of goods sold. Each inventory item has its own control report that the system updates daily, weekly, or monthly depending upon the needs of the business. So a business that sells 1,000 different items will have 1,000 control reports, one for each item. If all the units in Exhibit 9–1 were the same inventory item, the control report for the month of June might look like Exhibit 9–2.

This report shows four important facts for this inventory:

1. the beginning balance of 200 units that cost $2,000
2. the total purchases during the month of 600 units that cost $6,000
3. the total sales during the month of 650 units that cost $6,500
4. the ending balance of inventory of 150 units that cost $1,500

Exhibit 9–2
Inventory Control Report under Perpetual Inventory System

Date	Explanation	Purchases Units	Unit Cost	Total Cost	Cost of Goods Sold Units	Unit Cost	Total Cost	Inventory Balance Units	Unit Cost	Total Cost
6-1	Beg. Balance							200	$10	$2,000
6-10	Purchase	400	$10	$4,000				600	$10	$6,000
6-15	Sale				300	$10	$3,000	300	$10	$3,000
6-20	Purchase	200	$10	$2,000				500	$10	$5,000
6-30	Sale				350	$10	$3,500	150	$10	$1,500
	Total	600		$6,000	650		$6,500			

We expect to find the cost of goods sold of $6,500 on the income statement for the period and the ending balance of inventory of $1,500 on the balance sheet for the last day of the period. In addition, we see the history of the purchases and sales for the inventory item. This detail provides marketing managers, purchasing agents, and other company employees valuable information. In this way, accounting data contribute to the efficient operation of the entire business.

Strawn uses a computerized accounting system to generate its inventory control reports automatically. Computerized systems capture purchases and sales data either by keyboard entries or by a scanning device. Retailers use scanners to read bar codes—formally known as Universal Product Codes (UPCs)—printed on the inventory labels. The computer can be programmed to assign a given cost to a given inventory item and thus can perform the necessary calculations to update inventory records. In addition to ringing up the sales price of a book, the computer software simultaneously updates the inventory records by changing the number of physical units on hand and transferring the cost of the book sold from merchandise inventory to cost of goods sold. This technology gives Strawn's employees a timely report to help them determine the number of books sold and the number of books remaining on the shelf without physically counting them.

Discussion Questions

9–3. Assume that a book's inventory control report shows 25 books remaining on the shelf. Just to make sure, the bookstore manager goes over to the shelf, counts the remaining books, and finds there are only 22. What might explain the discrepancy?

9–4. If you were the manager responsible for inventory, how often would you count the items to verify the inventory control records? Are there any events that might encourage you to perform a physical count?

The Necessity of a Physical Inventory Count

Regardless of whether a firm chooses a periodic or perpetual inventory system, it must conduct physical counts of its inventory at least annually to satisfy Internal Revenue Service regulations and auditors' requirements. The nature of the inventory determines the most cost-effective frequency for physical inventory counts. Normally, the higher the number of different items and the lower the cost per unit, the less frequently the company physically counts. Consider the case of a grocery store or variety store that contains thousands of different items with relatively low cost per item. Contrast this with a car dealership. A cost-benefit analysis would tell you that one person could count the cars on the lot in an hour, and if there were a discrepancy of one vehicle, the dollar value would be substantial. A whole team of employees would have to work eight or 10 hours to count the items in a grocery store, and the dollar value of missing items might be less than the dollar cost of the employees' wages to count.

Beyond the need to satisfy external parties' requirements, why would a company conduct a physical count? If the company maintains a periodic inventory system, the physical count is mandatory to determine the amount of both the ending inventory and, consequently, the cost of goods sold. Does this mean that a firm with a perpetual inventory system can omit the physical count? The accounting system generates the amount of ending inventory, called **book inventory**. Book inventory may or may not coincide with the merchandise inventory actually on hand

book inventory The amount of ending inventory (units and dollars) resulting from transactions recorded by a perpetual inventory system.

Exhibit 9–3
Adjusted Record of
Ending Inventory after
Physical Count

	Per Books		Per Physical Count	
	Units	Cost	Units	Cost
Beginning Inventory, January 1	200	$2,000	200	$2,000
+ Purchases	600	6,000	600	6,000
= Goods Available for Sale	800	$8,000	800	$8,000
− Ending Inventory, January 31	150	1,500	130	1,300
= Cost of Goods Sold	650	$6,500	670	$6,700

at the end of the period. Errors in the recording process, shoplifting, and employee theft can occur to cause the book inventory to differ from the actual inventory. In addition, inventory can be intentionally or accidentally damaged, discarded, or spoiled. Some inventory actually evaporates over time. The results of a physical inventory help management to pinpoint possible problems to improve the internal control procedures, and physical control of the inventory. Remember that for most merchandising firms, inventory may represent the largest investment in assets. Safeguarding a large asset is critical to the success of the firm.

Results of the physical inventory count take precedence over the book inventory generated by the inventory records. We adjust both the inventory asset and the cost of goods sold for the period for any differences between the physical count and the book inventory so that the periodic count is reflected in the financial statements. To illustrate, assume that Strawn Book Company takes a physical count of books and finds only 130 books on hand instead of 150 that the inventory record shows. Exhibit 9–3 shows the calculation of cost of goods sold and ending inventory based on the physical records and the amounts adjusted for the ending physical count.

In this case, an adjustment of the records is necessary to reflect reality: The amount shown on the balance sheet as ending inventory must be the amount actually on hand. Because we know that cost of goods available for sale ($8,000) will end up as either cost of goods sold or ending inventory, a change in the amount shown as ending inventory will cause a change in the amount shown as cost of goods sold. The cost of goods sold reported as an expense on the income statement for the period is $6,700. The merchandise inventory reported as an asset on the balance sheet is $1,300, which reflects the reality of the number of units actually on hand at the end of the period. With this adjustment of the records, Strawn Book Company's financial statement amounts will more accurately reflect reality.

Discussion Questions

9-5. If careless employees break inventory items and discard them, or dishonest employees steal inventory items, how is a company's income statement affected?

9-6. Which causes companies more losses each year in the United States, employee theft or shoplifting? (Hint: Visit the Web site of the Association of Certified Fraud Examiners. To find the link, go to the PHLIP Web site for this text at www.prenhall.com/jones).

9-7. How can companies guard against shoplifting and employee theft?

The Physical Movement of Inventory (Reality)

A merchandising company purchases goods from a manufacturer or wholesale distributor that delivers the goods to the company's warehouse. A firm's warehouse may not always be a building with four walls and a roof. The natural differences among products causes the warehousing function to differ. Consider the following examples:

1. Corn delivered to a silo
2. Gravel stored in a pit
3. Oil placed in an underground storage tank
4. Cars, trucks, and vans parked on a lot

first in, first out (FIFO) The inventory flow concept based on the assumption that the first units of inventory purchased are the first ones sold.

When a farmer delivers corn to a silo, he deposits the corn in the top of the silo and receives payment from the grain dealer. When the grain dealer sells the corn to a customer, the customer extracts the corn from the bottom of the silo. Silos function because of the law of gravity, so the oldest corn is in the bottom of the silo and the newest corn is in the top of the silo. Therefore, the physical movement of the corn is on a **first-in, first-out (FIFO)** basis. The first corn deposited into the silo is the first corn removed from the silo.

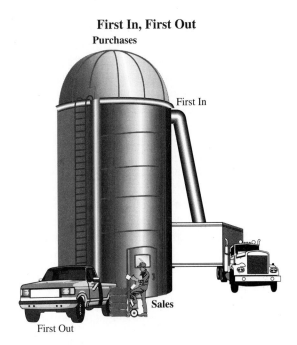

First In, First Out

Purchases

First In

Sales

First Out

last in, first out (LIFO) The inventory flow concept based on the assumption that the last units of inventory purchased are the first ones sold.

Gravel dealers frequently keep the gravel inventory in a pit. When new gravel arrives at the dealer's location, the truck driver dumps the gravel into the pit. When the gravel dealer makes a sale, she removes the gravel from the top of the pit because she cannot access the bottom. The physical movement of the gravel is on a **last-in, first-out (LIFO)** basis. The last gravel deposited into the pit is the first gravel to be removed.

Last In, First Out

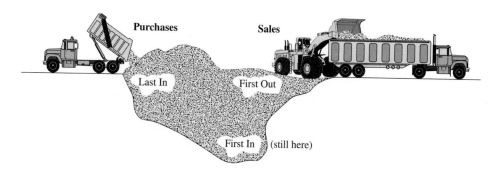

When an oil producer delivers oil to a customer, it frequently delivers the oil to an aboveground storage tank. Because of the physical properties of oil, it blends with other oil when added into a container. So when oil enters a storage tank, it mixes with other oil and loses its unit identity. Therefore, any oil extracted from the tank is a mixture of all oil added to the tank. We might say that extracted oil represents an average of the oil inventory.

Average Cost

Finally, look at a dealer's lot of cars, trucks, and vans. Each vehicle has unique characteristics and a serial number. The dealer places the vehicles wherever there is room and frequently moves the vehicles around the lot. Customers purchase their choice of vehicle, based not on its location, but on its ability to suit their needs. Each customer specifically identifies the vehicle he or she wants. The physical movement of the vehicles is based upon the specific identification of the desired unit.

Discussion Questions

9–8. For what products would it be important that the first units purchased be the first ones sold? Explain.

9–9. Describe five different categories of products for sale in a grocery store. How do stock personnel typically restock the shelves for each of these products? Why?

9–10. If you owned a retail computer store, what reasons would you have for insisting that your employees sell the first Pentium computer received before the ones that arrived at the store later?

The Flow of Inventory Cost (Measurement of Reality)

We have discussed the physical flow of units in and out of inventory. But what about the cost of these units? As a firm purchases inventory, we add its cost to inventory in the accounting records. Likewise, as the firm sells the merchandise, we remove its cost from inventory and transfer it to cost of goods sold. You might suppose that accounting rules require the flow of costs through a company's accounting records to reflect the reality of the way the physical units flow through the company's inventory. However, accounting rules do not require that the cost flow for inventory mirror the flow of physical units. Regardless of how physical units flow through inventory, a company may select any cost flow assumption it chooses. Thus we see another example of how reality and the measurement of reality may differ.

COST FLOW ASSUMPTIONS

When a company purchases one product and sells it before it buys another product, the physical flow of product equals the cost flow of the product. However, when a firm buys many products at different times for different amounts, the physical inventory flow (reality) and the cost flow (measurement of reality) seldom coincide. As you might guess from our discussion of the physical flow of goods, accounting has four basic cost flow assumptions:

1. First in, first out (FIFO)
2. Last in, first out (LIFO)
3. Average cost
4. Specific identification

The most common physical flow of goods is first in, first out (FIFO); however, GAAP do not require that the inventory cost method match the physical flow of inventory. Many firms use more than one cost flow assumption by using different assumptions for different types of inventory. According to the authors of *Accounting Trends & Techniques*, in 1996, 69.5 percent of companies surveyed used the FIFO method, 55 percent used LIFO, and 30 percent used the average cost method to cost all or part of the inventory.[1]

A firm may select any of the inventory costing methods regardless of the way the physical units of merchandise inventory flow through the warehouse. This

---

[1] *Accounting Trends & Techniques*, 51st ed. (Jersey City: AICPA, 1997), 154.

results in another situation in which the difference between reality and the measurement of reality leads to some complexities in accrual accounting. Due to current U.S. tax laws, many firms select the LIFO costing method to reduce taxes, even though it does not match the physical flow of goods. Financial statement users should understand the way in which companies track inventory costs and arrive at the amounts presented on their financial statements, because as you will see, the inventory costing method selected changes the net income and balance sheet assets. To understand these differences, we will explore different cost flow assumptions that take different approaches to measuring the flow of inventory costs through both a periodic and a perpetual inventory system. Because the specific identification method is unique and results in the same valuation regardless of periodic or perpetual system, we will look at this method first.

Specific Identification Cost Flow Assumption

specific identification The method of inventory cost flow that identifies each item sold by a company.

Dobbs Motor Company sells antique automobiles to an exclusive clientele and appropriately uses the **specific identification** method to cost its vehicles. Exhibit 9–4 details the cars in the inventory at the beginning of March, those purchased during the month, and those sold during March.

Exhibit 9–4
Dobbs Motor Company Inventory Transactions for March 2000

Date of Purchase	Description	Cost	Date Sold	Selling Price
10-15-1999	1926 Bentley	$35,000	3-5-2000	$45,000
12-25-1999	1935 Mercedes	42,000		
1-25-2000	1955 Thunderbird	25,000	3-9-2000	38,000
2-10-2000	1935 Model T Ford	24,000	3-18-2000	36,000
3-10-2000	1940 Cadillac	38,000		
3-25-2000	1932 Silver Cloud	80,000		

We can analyze this information to determine Dobbs' sales, cost of goods sold, and gross profit for the month of March as follows:

1. Sales total $119,000. ($45,000 + $38,000 + $36,000)
2. The beginning inventory consisted of the first four cars listed:

1926 Bentley	$ 35,000
1935 Mercedes	42,000
1955 Thunderbird	25,000
1935 Model T Ford	24,000
Total Cost	$126,000

3. Dobbs purchased two cars during March:

1940 Cadillac	$ 38,000
1932 Silver Cloud	80,000
Total Cost	$118,000

4. The cost of goods sold included three cars:

1926 Bentley	$35,000
1955 Thunderbird	25,000
1935 Model T Ford	24,000
Total Cost	$84,000

5. The ending inventory includes three cars:

1935 Mercedes	$ 42,000
1940 Cadillac	38,000
1932 Silver Cloud	80,000
Total Cost	$160,000

6. Summary of information in the format of the income statement:

Sales		$119,000
Cost of Goods Sold:		
Beginning Inventory	$126,000	
Purchases	118,000	
Goods Available for Sale	$244,000	
Ending Inventory	160,000	
Cost of Goods Sold		84,000
Gross Profit		$ 35,000

Because each inventory item is unique, there is no cost determination difference between a periodic system and a perpetual system with a specific identification method. The same is true if each product included in beginning inventory and each item purchased (or made) during the period cost exactly the same amount per unit. LIFO, FIFO, and average cost methods would result in identical measurements of reality. However, the cost of products rarely remains constant because of technological advances, economic conditions, and competition. We will look at the effect on inventory and cost of goods sold caused by changing prices using the periodic and perpetual inventory systems.

COST FLOW ASSUMPTIONS UNDER A PERIODIC SYSTEM

Changes in the cost of inventory items over time cause different cost flow assumptions to result in different amounts for cost of goods sold and ending inventory. To illustrate this in a periodic system, we examine the effect of three different cost flow assumptions on one product sold by the Harwood Equipment Company. Exhibit 9–5 contains the inventory activity for Harwood during September.

We can analyze the information based on our knowledge of inventory cost, cost of goods sold, and gross profit.

1. Harwood sold three units at $1,500 for a total of $4,500.
2. Harwood had a beginning inventory of one unit that cost $800.

Exhibit 9–5
Harwood Equipment Company Inventory Transactions

Date	Transaction	Units	Unit Cost	Unit Selling Price
9-1	Beginning Inventory	1	$ 800	
9-3	Purchase	2	1,025	
9-17	Sale	1		$1,500
9-22	Purchase	1	1,100	
9-26	Purchase	1	1,200	
9-29	Purchase	1	1,450	
9-30	Sale	2		1,500

3. Harwood purchased the following items:

9-3	2 @ $1,025	$2,050
9-22	1 @ $1,100	1,100
9-26	1 @ $1,200	1,200
9-29	1 @ $1,450	1,450
Total purchases		$5,800

4. The goods available for sale is $6,600: Beginning inventory of $800 plus purchases of $5,800.

The goods available for sale will be $6,600 no matter which method we use to determine the cost of goods sold and the ending inventory. In the periodic system, we determine the cost of the units sold and the cost of the ending inventory for the whole period of time.

First-In, First-Out Method (FIFO)

Using the first-in, first-out (FIFO) cost method under a periodic system, we assume that the first units owned were sold, and the last units purchased make up the ending inventory. Harwood had six units to sell during September, sold three, and had three remaining at the end of the month. Using FIFO, we assume that the first three units owned were sold:

Beginning inventory	1 @ $800	$ 800
September 3 purchase	2 @ $1,025	2,050
Cost of units sold		$2,850

Likewise, the ending inventory comes from the last purchases:

September 29	1 @ $1,450	$1,450
September 26	1 @ $1,200	1,200
September 22	1 @ $1,100	1,100
Cost of ending inventory		$3,750

FIFO METHOD (PERIODIC)

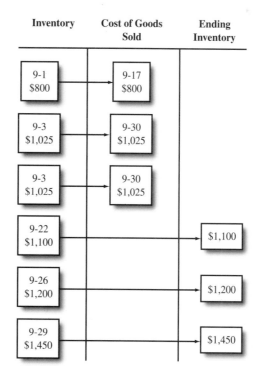

By using the cost of sales calculation, we can determine from an accounting viewpoint which units were sold and which units remain.

	Units	Cost
Beginning inventory	1	$ 800
Purchases	5	5,800
Goods available for sale	6	$6,600
Ending inventory	3	3,750
Cost of goods sold	3	$2,850

Last-In, First-Out Method (LIFO)

Using the last-in, first-out (LIFO) cost method under a periodic system, we assume that the last units owned were sold, and the first units purchased comprise the ending inventory—exactly the opposite of the FIFO method. Harwood had six units to sell during September, sold three, and had three remaining at the end of the month. Under LIFO, we assume that the last three units purchased were sold:

September 29	1 @ $1,450	$1,450
September 26	1 @ $1,200	1,200
September 22	1 @ $1,100	1,100
Cost of units sold		$3,750

Likewise, the ending inventory comes from the first units owned:

Beginning inventory	1 @ $800	$ 800
September 3 purchase	2 @ $1,025	2,050
Cost of ending inventory		$2,850

LIFO METHOD (PERIODIC)

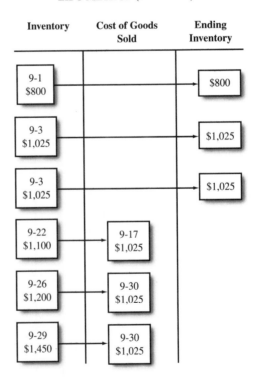

By using the cost of sales calculation we can determine from an accounting viewpoint, which units were sold and which units remain.

	Units	Cost
Beginning inventory	1	$ 800
Purchases	5	5,800
Goods available for sale	6	$6,600
Ending inventory	3	2,850
Cost of goods sold	3	$3,750

Average Cost Method

average cost method The inventory cost flow method that assigns an average cost to the units of inventory on hand at the time of each sale.

Instead of separating the inventory cost into two groups, the **average cost method** assigns the same cost to each inventory unit. Harwood owned six units of inventory that cost $6,600. The average cost method is simple to apply. Divide the cost of goods available for sale by the number of units available to determine the average unit cost.

$$\text{Average cost} = \frac{\text{Total cost of goods available for sale}}{\text{Number of units available for sale}} = \frac{\$6,600}{6} = \$1,100 \text{ per unit}$$

Use the cost of sales calculation to measure the cost of the units sold and the cost of the units remaining from an accounting viewpoint.

AVERAGE COST METHOD (PERIODIC)

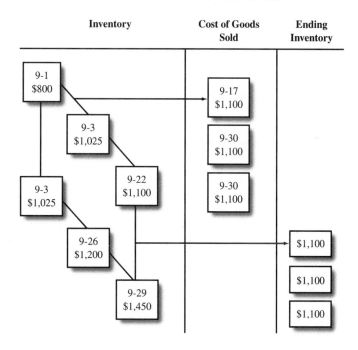

	Units	Cost
Beginning inventory	1	$ 800
Purchases	5	5,800
Goods available for sale	6	$6,600
Ending inventory	3	3,300
Cost of goods sold	3	$3,300

HARWOOD EQUIPMENT COMPANY
Schedule of Gross Profit
For the Month of September, 2000

	FIFO	LIFO	Average Cost
Sales	$4,500	$4,500	$4,500
Cost of Goods Sold:			
Beginning Inventory	$ 800	$ 800	$ 800
Purchases	5,800	5,800	5,800
Goods Available for Sale	$6,600	$6,600	$6,600
Ending Inventory	3,750	2,850	3,300
Cost of Goods Sold	$2,850	$3,750	$3,300
Gross Profit	$1,650	$ 750	$1,200

Comparison of Methods

We stated earlier that the three assumptions produced different results. Exhibit 9–6 indicates these differences in cost of goods sold, ending inventory, and gross profit.

Discussion Questions

9–11. What accounts for the difference in cost of goods sold, ending inventory, and gross profit among the three methods?

9–12. Which units actually were sold in each scenario?

9–13. What would happen to gross profit for each method if the costs were decreasing with each purchase instead of increasing?

As you may have concluded, the differences among methods occur because of the changing prices. As prices rise, LIFO produces the highest cost of sales and the lowest ending inventory. As prices fall, the opposite occurs and FIFO produces the highest cost of sales and the lowest ending inventory. Normally, the average cost method will produce costs in between LIFO and FIFO. Now consider what results when we apply the perpetual method to these three cost methods.

COST FLOW ASSUMPTIONS UNDER A PERPETUAL INVENTORY SYSTEM

Under the periodic system, we applied the cost methods to the entire period. When we utilize a perpetual system, we determine the cost of inventory items sold at the time of each sale. This complicates the decision-making process and produces different results for LIFO and average cost methods. We will use the same information for Harwood Equipment Company for our study of the perpetual system. As we analyzed the information under the periodic system, we were not concerned about the dates of the sales. Under the perpetual system, the date controls the application of the cost flow method.

Consider the Harwood transactions. Which items were sold on September 17 and 30? In reality, the items sold were probably the ones conveniently located in the warehouse. About the only thing you can determine, however, is that the unit sold on September 22 was purchased before September 22. Because the purchase prices of the units varied, we cannot determine the cost of goods sold unless we know which units were sold. The cost allocation methods define the accounting measurement of which items were sold, regardless of which specific products left the warehouse. Our goal remains to separate the $6,600 into cost of goods sold and the ending inventory.

First-In, First-Out Method

The first-in, first-out (FIFO) method in a perpetual system assumes that the first items purchased are the first to be sold, exactly as in the periodic system. The first sale took place on September 17. At that time, Harwood held three units, and the earliest of those was from the beginning inventory, which cost $800. The second sale took place on September 30 when Harwood held five units. The first units acquired were purchased on September 3 for $1,025 each. Therefore, we can separate the cost of sales and ending inventory as follows:

Units sold:

Beginning inventory	1 @ $800	$ 800
September 3 purchase	2 @ $1,025	2,050
Cost of units sold		$2,850

Ending inventory:

September 29	1 @ $1,450	$1,450
September 26	1 @ $1,200	1,200
September 22	1 @ $1,100	1,100
Cost of ending inventory		$3,750

FIFO METHOD (PERPETUAL)

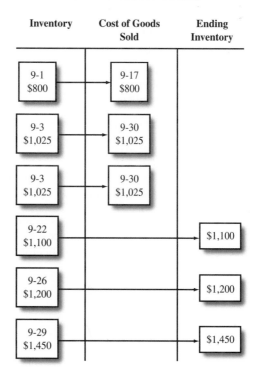

The cost of goods sold calculation will appear as follows:

	Units	Cost
Beginning inventory	1	$ 800
Purchases	5	5,800
Goods available for sale	6	$6,600
Ending inventory	3	3,750
Cost of goods sold	3	$2,850

Discussion Questions

9-14. Compare the cost of goods sold and ending inventory amounts with the FIFO example under the periodic system on page F-330. Is the result of your comparison a coincidence?

9-15. When Harwood makes its next sale of two items, which two will the FIFO method in a perpetual system assume are sold?

We will now turn our attention to the LIFO method in a perpetual system.

Last-In, First-Out Method

The last-in, first-out (LIFO) method under the perpetual system assumes that the last units placed in inventory are the first units sold. In applying this assumption, we assume that the very last item purchased is the one sold. On September 17, Harwood held three units, the most recently purchased on September 3 for $1,025. Under LIFO, we designate the $1,025 unit as sold on September 17. On September 30, Harwood held five units, the last two of which were purchased on September 29 and 26, costing $1,450 and $1,200 respectively. We can separate the cost of goods sold and the ending inventory as follows:

Units sold:

September 29	1 @ $1,450	$1,450
September 26	1 @ $1,200	1,200
September 3	1 @ $1,025	1,025
Cost of units sold		$3,675

Likewise, the ending inventory comes from the first units owned:

Beginning inventory	1 @ $800	$ 800
September 3 purchase	1 @ $1,025	1,025
September 22 purchase	1 @ $1,100	1,100
Cost of ending inventory		$2,925

By using the cost of sales calculation, we can determine from an accounting viewpoint which costs transfer to cost of goods sold on the income statement and which costs remain on the balance sheet in ending inventory.

	Units	Cost
Beginning inventory	1	$ 800
Purchases	5	5,800
Goods available for sale	6	$6,600
Ending inventory	3	2,925
Cost of goods sold	3	$3,675

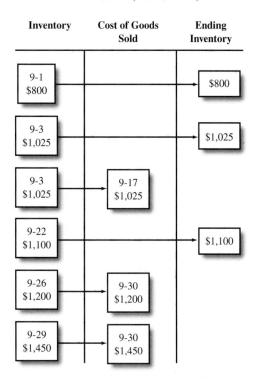

Discussion Questions

9–16. Compare the cost of goods sold and ending inventory amounts with the LIFO example under the periodic system on page F-330. Can you draw a conclusion about LIFO costs under the different inventory systems?

9–17. If Harwood sells two more units before purchasing any more of the item, which two will be assumed sold under LIFO in a perpetual system?

Although the results for LIFO differ for the periodic and the perpetual systems, the methods of determining the costs are relatively simple. This is not as true when we look at the moving average method of costing inventory under the perpetual system.

Moving Average Cost Method

moving average cost method The inventory cost flow method that assigns an average cost to the units of inventory on hand at the time of each sale in a perpetual inventory system.

The **moving average cost method** derives its name from the process that computes a new weighted average cost of all units of inventory on hand each time a new purchase is made. We will carefully build a table in which we can make the calculations for the moving average. Applying average cost logic, we assign all units on hand an average cost and assume that one of the units at that cost was sold. Remember that each time Harwood purchases new units, the average cost changes. The formula to determine the average at any time is:

$$\text{Weighted average cost} = \frac{\text{Total cost of inventory on hand}}{\text{Number of units on hand}}$$

We construct the weighted average table with the following columns:

(A) Number of units for the current transaction
(B) Unit cost for the current transaction
(C) Total cost of the transaction (A × B)
(D) Cumulative cost equals column D from the prior transaction plus C from the current transaction
(E) Cumulative units equal column E from the prior transaction plus A from the current transaction
(F) Average cost equals D divided by E

	Date	Description	(A) **# of** **Units**	(B) **Unit** **Cost**	(C) **Total** **Cost**	(D) **Cumulative** **Cost**	(E) **Cumulative** **Units**	(F) **Average** **Cost**
(1)	9-1	Beginning Inventory	1	$800	$800	$800	1	$800
(2)	9-3	Purchase	2	1,025	2,050	2,850	3	950
(3)	9-17	Sale	<1>	<950>	<950>	1,900	2	950
(4)	9-22	Purchase	1	1,100	1,100	3,000	3	1,000
(5)	9-26	Purchase	1	1,200	1,200	4,200	4	1,050
(6)	9-29	Purchase	1	1,450	1,450	5,650	5	1,130
(7)	9-30	Sale	<2>	<1,130>	<2,260>	3,390	3	1,130

We can examine each line to verify the calculations:

(1) The beginning inventory is one unit at a cost of $800.
(2) After the first purchase of two units for $2,050, apply the formula:

$$\text{Weighted average cost} = \frac{\text{Total cost of inventory on hand}}{\text{Number of units on hand}} \text{ or } \frac{D}{E} = \frac{\$2,850}{3} = \$950$$

(3) Cumulative cost is $800 + $2,050 − $950 = $1,900. Cumulative units are $1 + 2 − 1 = 2$. Apply the formula and the average remains $950 ($1,900 / 2 = $950). Notice that sales do not change the average cost; only purchases change the average cost.
(4) After an additional purchase of one unit for $1,100, apply the formula:

$$\text{Weighted average cost} = \frac{D}{E} = \frac{\$1,900 + \$1,100}{3} = \$1,000$$

(5) After an additional purchase of one unit for $1,200, apply the formula:

$$\text{Weighted average cost} = \frac{D}{E} = \frac{\$3,000 + \$1,200}{4} = \$1,050$$

(6) After an additional purchase of one unit for $1,450, apply the formula:

$$\text{Weighted average cost} = \frac{D}{E} = \frac{\$4,200 + \$1,450}{5} = \$1,130$$

(7) After the sale of two units, the ending inventory results in three units at a total cost of $3,390.

The cost of goods sold calculation will appear as follows:

	Units	Cost
Beginning inventory	1	$ 800
Purchases	5	5,800
Goods available for sale	6	$6,600
Ending inventory	3	3,390
Cost of goods sold	3	$3,210

HARWOOD EQUIPMENT COMPANY
Schedule of Gross Profit
For the Month of September, 2000

	FIFO	LIFO	Average Cost
Sales	$4,500	$4,500	$4,500
Cost of Goods Sold:			
Beginning Inventory	$ 800	$ 800	$ 800
Purchases	5,800	5,800	5,800
Goods Available for Sale	$6,600	$6,600	$6,600
Ending Inventory	3,750	2,925	3,390
Cost of Goods Sold	$2,850	$3,675	$3,210
Gross Profit	$1,650	$825	$1,290

Comparison of Methods

Similar to the periodic system, the three assumptions produced different results. Exhibit 9–7 indicates the differences in cost of goods sold, ending inventory, and gross profit under the perpetual method.

Discussion Questions

9–18. What accounts for the difference in the cost of goods sold, ending inventory, and gross profit among the three methods?

9–19. Which units actually were sold in each scenario?

9–20. What would happen to gross profit for each method if the costs decreased with each purchase instead of increasing?

The comparison of the three methods in a perpetual system produces similar results to the periodic method because FIFO produces the highest gross profit, LIFO the lowest, and the moving average is in between FIFO and LIFO. The opposite is generally true when prices decrease during a period, depending on the timing of the purchases and sales during the period. Remember that FIFO produces the same results in a periodic or perpetual system, which seldom happens with LIFO or average cost methods.

We examined the effects of each method for both periodic and perpetual systems. Now we will look at the effect that inventory assumptions and the inventory system have on financial statements.

The Effects of Inventory Cost Flow Assumption Choice

Assume that Harwood Equipment Company had no other transactions during September except those related to this product and the payment of $200 in warehouse rent. Exhibit 9–8 portrays the August 31, 2000, balance sheet representing the beginning balances, the September income statement, and the resulting balance sheet for September 30, 2000, under all three cost flow assumptions for a periodic inventory system.

HARWOOD EQUIPMENT COMPANY
Income Statement
For the Month Ended September 30, 2000

	FIFO	LIFO	Average Cost
Sales	$4,500	$4,500	$4,500
Cost of Goods Sold	2,850	3,750	3,300
Gross Margin	$1,650	$ 750	$1,200
Operating Expenses:			
Warehouse Rent	200	200	200
Net Income	$1,450	$ 550	$1,000

HARWOOD EQUIPMENT COMPANY
Balance Sheet
August 31, 2000, and September 30, 2000

		FIFO	LIFO	Average Cost
	August 31	**September 30**		
ASSETS:				
Cash	$21,000	$22,300	$22,300	$22,300
Accounts Receivable	1,500	4,500	4,500	4,500
Merchandise Inventory	800	3,750	2,850	3,300
Total Assets	$23,300	$30,550	$29,650	$30,100
LIABILITIES AND STOCKHOLDERS' EQUITY:				
Accounts Payable	$ -0-	$ 5,800	$ 5,800	$ 5,800
Common Stock	15,000	15,000	15,000	15,000
Additional Paid-in Capital	8,000	8,000	8,000	8,000
Retained Earnings	300	1,750	800	1,300
Total Liabilities and Stockholders' Equity	$23,300	$30,550	$29,650	$30,100

Exhibit 9–9 portrays the August 31, 2000, balance sheet representing the beginning balances, the September income statement, and the resulting balance sheet for September 30, 2000, under all three cost flow assumptions for a perpetual inventory system. As you examine Exhibit 9–9, compare it with the results in Exhibit 9–8 for a periodic system.

Discussion Questions

9-21. The financial statements prepared using FIFO in Exhibits 9–8 and 9–9 show Harwood to be more profitable than the financial statements for LIFO or average cost regardless of the inventory system used. Is the company more profitable if it used FIFO instead of LIFO or average cost?

9-22. Did Harwood pay for the purchases of inventory during September? How can you determine this?

Exhibit 9–9

Comparative Financial Statements Using a Perpetual System for FIFO, LIFO, and Average Cost Methods

HARWOOD EQUIPMENT COMPANY
Income Statement
For the Month Ended September 30, 2000

	FIFO	LIFO	Average Cost
Sales	$4,500	$4,500	$4,500
Cost of Goods Sold	2,850	3,675	3,210
Gross Margin	$1,650	$ 825	$1,290
Operating Expenses:			
Warehouse Rent	200	200	200
Net Income	$1,450	$ 625	$1,090

HARWOOD EQUIPMENT COMPANY
Balance Sheet
August 31, 2000, and September 30, 2000

		FIFO	LIFO	Average Cost
ASSETS:	**August 31**		**September 30**	
Cash	$21,000	$22,300	$22,300	$22,300
Accounts Receivable	1,500	4,500	4,500	4,500
Merchandise Inventory	800	3,750	2,925	3,390
Total Assets	$23,300	$30,550	$29,725	$30,190
LIABILITIES AND STOCKHOLDERS' EQUITY:				
Accounts Payable	$ -0-	$ 5,800	$ 5,800	$ 5,800
Common Stock	15,000	15,000	15,000	15,000
Additional Paid-in Capital	8,000	8,000	8,000	8,000
Retained Earnings	300	1,750	925	1,390
Total Liabilities and Stockholders' Equity	$23,300	$30,550	$29,725	$30,190

9-23. Did Harwood's customers pay for their purchases during September? How can you determine this?

9-24. How do you explain the increase in cash from $21,000 to $22,300 from August to September?

Companies may choose from a variety of inventory cost flow assumptions. We have explored three approaches most commonly used in periodic and perpetual inventory systems and have seen how these different cost flow assumptions result in different net profits on the income statements and inventory amounts on the balance sheets. The reality of the sales and delivery of inventory to the customer is the same. What differs is the measurement of that reality. However, the choice of inventory method does not change the ultimate profitability of a company. To illustrate, we will extend our example to October.

Assume that Harwood purchased no additional units in October but sold the remaining three units in October. Further assume that the only expense in October was the warehouse rent of $200.

The cost of goods sold calculation for the *periodic* system is as follows:

	Units	FIFO	LIFO	Average Cost
Beginning inventory	3	$3,750	$2,850	$3,300
Purchases	0	-0-	-0-	-0-
Goods available for sale	3	$3,750	$2,850	$3,300
Ending inventory	0	-0-	-0-	-0-
Cost of goods sold	3	$3,750	$2,850	$3,300

The cost of goods sold calculation for the *perpetual* system is as follows:

	Units	FIFO	LIFO	Average Cost
Beginning inventory	3	$3,750	$2,925	$3,390
Purchases	0	-0-	-0-	-0-
Goods available for sale	3	$3,750	$2,925	$3,390
Ending inventory	0	-0-	-0-	-0-
Cost of goods sold	3	$3,750	$2,925	$3,390

Now we can see the effect that October's activity has on the balance sheet and income statement. Exhibit 9–10 contains the October balance sheets and income statements for all three cost methods under a periodic inventory system.

Exhibit 9–10
Comparative Financial Statements Using a Periodic System for FIFO, LIFO, and Average Cost Methods

HARWOOD EQUIPMENT COMPANY
Income Statement
For the Month Ended October 31, 2000

	FIFO	LIFO	Average Cost
Sales	$4,500	$4,500	$4,500
Cost of Goods Sold	3,750	2,850	3,300
Gross Margin	$ 750	$1,650	$1,200
Operating Expenses:			
Warehouse Rent	200	200	200
Net Income	$ 550	$1,450	$1,000

HARWOOD EQUIPMENT COMPANY
Balance Sheet
October 31, 2000

	FIFO	LIFO	Average Cost
ASSETS:		September 30	
Cash	$20,800	$20,800	$20,800
Accounts Receivable	4,500	4,500	4,500
Merchandise Inventory	-0-	-0-	-0-
Total Assets	$25,300	$25,300	$25,300
LIABILITIES AND STOCKHOLDERS' EQUITY:			
Accounts Payable	$ -0-	$ -0-	$ -0-
Common Stock	15,000	15,000	15,000
Additional Paid-in Capital	8,000	8,000	8,000
Retained Earnings	2,300	2,300	2,300
Total Liabilities and Stockholders' Equity	$25,300	$25,300	$25,300

Exhibit 9–11
Comparative Financial
Statements Using a
Perpetual System for
FIFO, LIFO, and
Average Cost Methods

HARWOOD EQUIPMENT COMPANY
Income Statement
For the Month Ended October 31, 2000

	FIFO	LIFO	Average Cost
Sales	$4,500	$4,500	$4,500
Cost of Goods Sold	3,750	2,925	3,390
Gross Margin	$ 750	$1,575	$1,110
Operating Expenses:			
Warehouse Rent	200	200	200
Net Income	$ 550	$1,375	$ 910

HARWOOD EQUIPMENT COMPANY
Balance Sheet
October 31, 2000

	FIFO	LIFO	Average Cost
ASSETS:			
Cash	$20,800	$20,800	$20,800
Accounts Receivable	4,500	4,500	4,500
Merchandise Inventory	-0-	-0-	-0-
Total Assets	$25,300	$25,300	$25,300
LIABILITIES AND STOCKHOLDERS' EQUITY:			
Accounts Payable	$ -0-	$ -0-	$ -0-
Common Stock	15,000	15,000	15,000
Additional Paid-in Capital	8,000	8,000	8,000
Retained Earnings	2,300	2,300	2,300
Total Liabilities and Stockholders' Equity	$25,300	$25,300	$25,300

Exhibit 9–11 contains the October 31, 2000, balance sheets and income statements under all three cost assumptions in a perpetual system. Note the similarities and differences between the October 31, 2000, financial statements for the periodic and perpetual systems and each of the cost flow assumptions.

Discussion Questions

9–25. Because the balance sheet is affected by the income statement, how can the ending balance sheets at the end of October be identical under all three inventory cost flow methods for both periodic and perpetual systems when the income statements for October were different?

9–26. Compute the total gross profit for September and October for each inventory cost method for both the periodic and perpetual systems? How do they compare?

9–27. Which method (FIFO, LIFO, or average cost) matches the most recent cost to current revenues?

9–28. Which inventory cost method is the best to use? Which inventory system is the best to use?

After examining Harwood Equipment Company's financial statements for two months, you might rightly come to the conclusion that no one method of determining inventory cost flow is better than another. Likewise, the type of inventory system does not change the profit reality over time. From the time a firm buys its first item of inventory to the time it sells its last item of inventory, its total gross profit over time will be equal, regardless of inventory method or system. For one firm, we may conclude that the choice of inventory costing method is relevant in the short term and irrelevant in the long term. It becomes important, however, when comparing the profitability of two firms that use different costing methods.

As was the case with accounting for depreciation of long-lived assets, accounting for the cost of merchandise inventory has a significant impact on a company's reported net income for a given income statement period and for the reported inventory on the balance sheet. Informed financial statement users must have an understanding of the impact of inventory cost flow method choice to utilize the information to the fullest extent possible.

Now that you have an understanding of some of the issues and situations that impact financial statements, we will explore in more detail the construction of the balance sheet and income statement in Chapter 10.

SUMMARY

Merchandise inventory represents the physical units of goods that a company plans to sell. Inventory on hand at the beginning of a given income statement period (beginning inventory) and the inventory bought during the period (purchases) constitute the total amount of goods the company could sell (goods available for sale). Goods available for sale will either remain on hand at the end of the period or be assumed sold.

Accountants developed two types of systems to track inventory costs. The periodic system counts inventory and traces costs only at the end of each income statement period, whereas the perpetual system updates inventory counts and costs each time a sale or purchase is made. Perpetual inventory systems usually make use of computer technology and scanners that read UPC. Even though inventory records are updated often when a perpetual system is in place, physical inventory counts are still necessary. Determining the actual amount of inventory on hand may uncover theft, damage, or spoilage of inventory. Some businesses use a perpetual system to track the number of units in inventory and integrate the counts into automatic purchasing reorder systems, but they may cost the inventory under a periodic system.

In a periodic system using accrual-basis accounting, we use the computation of cost of goods sold to determine the amount of expense on the income statement. The ending inventory is reported on the balance sheet as an asset. Under accrual accounting in a perpetual inventory system, when a company purchases inventory, its cost is considered an asset to the company and is listed as such on the balance sheet. As inventory is sold, its cost is converted from an asset to an expense, which is listed on the income statement as cost of goods sold. It follows, then, that the total cost of goods available for sale will end up either as ending inventory (an asset on the balance sheet) or as cost of goods sold (an expense on the income statement).

The physical flow of inventory may differ from the flow of inventory costs. Several methods have been developed to trace inventory costs as they move from the balance sheet to the income statement. All these methods are cost flow assumptions that prescribe which inventory items are assumed to be the ones sold.

Specific identification relates the exact cost of each unit of inventory to cost of goods sold when the item is sold. Firms that deal in expensive and unique items (such as cars, boats, and luxury items) utilize the specific identification method. The first-in, first-out (FIFO) method assumes that the first units of inventory purchased are the first ones sold. Conversely, the last-in, first-out (LIFO) method assumes that the last units of inventory purchased are the first sold. The average cost method assigns a weighted average cost to the units of inventory.

In a periodic system, we apply the cost assumptions for the entire period. In a perpetual system, we apply FIFO, LIFO, and moving average cost assumptions at the time of each sale, which produces different results than when we apply the assumptions for the entire period. Average cost method under a periodic system calculates one inventory cost for all goods sold and remaining in inventory while the moving average method under a perpetual system recalculates the average each time a new purchase is made.

Companies may choose to use any of these cost flow assumptions. If the price they pay for inventory items varies during the period, the choice will impact both net income and asset values reported on the company's financial statements each year. In the long run, however, choice of inventory cost method makes no difference to one firm. Financial statement users must be aware of the differences that inventory methods make when comparing companies that use different inventory cost methods.

APPENDIX—INVENTORY PURCHASING ISSUES

Two issues arise for firms that purchase merchandise inventory—freight costs and cash discounts. When negotiating purchase terms, buying agents pay particular attention to the freight and payment terms. Careful negotiations can decrease the cost of purchasing merchandise.

Cash Discounts

A firm frequently encourages its customer to pay invoices quickly by offering a cash discount, which improves the firm's cash flow. A company may devise its own credit terms that appeal to its customers; the following represent frequently used payment terms and their meaning.

1. *2/10, net 30 days*—A two percent discount is allowed if paid within 10 days from the invoice date; otherwise payment is due 30 days after the invoice date.
2. *net 30 days*—The net amount is due 30 days after the invoice date with no cash discount.
3. *1/10, EOM, net 60 days*—A one percent discount is allowed if paid within 10 days after the end of the month; otherwise payment is due 60 days from the invoice date.

Return to our example of Harwood Equipment Company. If the purchase on September 3 had terms of 2/10, net 30, Harwood would pay the invoice by September 13 to receive a two percent discount. Payment required by September 13 would be 98 percent of $2,050, or $2,009. The discount of $41 (2% x $2,050) reduces the cost of the purchase to Harwood. Good cash managers take advantage of cash discounts.

Discussion Questions

9–29. When would payment be due by Harwood if the terms were net 30 days? 1/10 EOM, net 60 days?

9–30. What is the annual percentage rate of a two percent discount for payment in 10 days instead of 30 days? One percent discount for 15 days instead of 30 days?

Freight Terms

Freight terms define the point at which title passes between the seller and the purchaser. FOB (free on board) shipping point indicates that the title passes when the merchandise leaves the seller's shipping dock. FOB destination indicates that the title passes when the merchandise arrives at the purchaser's loading dock. Transportation costs transfer to the buyer at the FOB point when the title passes. Therefore, if the terms are FOB shipping point, title passes at the sellers dock and the buyer bears the freight expense. If the terms are FOB destination, the seller owns the goods until delivery and bears the freight expense.

Payment of the freight adds another complication. When the seller arranges for transportation, it contracts either for freight prepaid or freight collect. Shippers such as United Parcel Service contract mostly for prepaid freight, while other common carriers can accommodate either payment method. When the terms are FOB destination and the seller pays the shipper directly, or when the terms are FOB shipping point and the seller sends the goods freight collect, the correct entity pays the expense. However, when the seller ships freight prepaid for FOB shipping point, the seller must bill the buyer for the freight cost. If the seller ships freight collect for FOB destination, the buyer must deduct the freight costs from its accounts payable when it pays the seller.

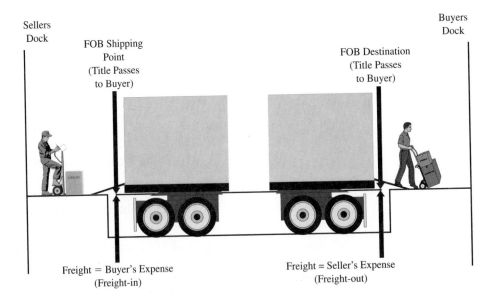

If Harwood buys two units from Taylor Equipment, Inc. on September 3 terms FOB shipping point, freight collect, Harwood will pay the $125 shipping costs directly to the common carrier. If Harwood buys the goods freight collect with terms FOB destination, Harwood will pay the carrier direct and pay its vendor only $1,925 in full payment of the $2,050 invoice amount.

Discussion Question

9-31. If Harwood buys two units from Taylor Equipment on September 3 with terms of 2/10, net 30, FOB shipping point, freight prepaid and the shipping charges are $210, how much will Harwood pay Taylor if it pays on September 3? October 3?

APPENDIX—RECORDING INVENTORY

After completing Chapter 7, you can look at the journal entries required to account for inventory. The recording process differs for periodic and perpetual inventory systems. We will look at the periodic system first.

Periodic Inventory Systems

The recording process for periodic inventory systems involves eight types of entries:

1. Purchase of the inventory
2. Return of defective merchandise
3. Payment of freight charges on purchases
4. Payment of the vendor
5. Recording ending inventory in closing entries
6. Sale of inventory
7. Payment of freight charges on sales
8. Receipt of cash from customer

To record these entries, we will utilize several new accounts:

Asset account:	Inventory or Merchandise Inventory
Expense accounts:	Purchases
	Purchase Discounts
	Purchase Returns and Allowances
	Freight-in (a cost of goods sold expense)
	Freight-out (a selling expense)
Revenue accounts:	Sales
	Sales Returns and Allowances
	Sales Discounts

To apply these concepts, we use the transactions during September 2000 for Harwood Equipment Company with the addition of a few items. In a periodic system, the costs of purchasing merchandise are charged to the previously listed expense accounts for Purchases, Purchase Returns and Allowances, Freight-in, and Purchase Discounts. We ignore the asset account for Inventory until the closing entries for the year.

To record the purchase of two units from Taylor on September 3, terms 2/10, net 30, FOB destination, freight collect:

2000		Debit	Credit
September 3	Purchases	2,050	
	Accounts Payable—Taylor		2,050
	To record purchase of two units,		
	terms 2/10, net 30, FOB destination.		

To record the receipt and payment of a freight bill to Mistletoe Express for $125:
Because this freight is not the expense of Harwood, it will reduce the amount that Harwood must pay to Taylor for the invoice.

		Debit	Credit
September 4	Accounts Payable—Taylor	125	
	Cash		125
	To record the payment of freight collect on FOB destination.		

To record payment of the invoice within the discount period:

		Debit	Credit
September 12	Accounts Payable—Taylor	1,925	
	Purchase Discounts		41
	Cash		1,884
	To record the payment of Taylor's 9-3-2000 invoice.		

The payment to Taylor was for a $2,050 invoice less a two percent discount and freight charges of $125 leaving an amount due of $1,884 ($2,050 − $41 − $125).

To record the sale on September 17 of one unit to Earhart Industries for $1,500, terms 2/10, net 30, FOB shipping point, freight collect:

		Debit	Credit
September 17	Accounts Receivable—Earhart	1,500	
	Sales		1,500
	To record sale to Earhart, 2/10, net 30, FOB shipping point.		

Because Harwood shipped the goods freight collect, the buyer will pay its freight costs. In the periodic system, no recognition occurs for the cost of each sale because the purchases are being recorded as an expense and the income statement computes the cost of goods sold with the cost of sales calculation.

To record the purchase of one unit from Allen Corp., terms 1/15, net 30, FOB shipping point, freight collect (shipping charges were $93):

		Debit	Credit
September 22	Purchases	1,100	
	Accounts Payable—Allen		1,100
	To record purchase from Allen, 1/15, net 30, FOB shipping point.		

To record the payment of the freight to Mistletoe Express:

		Debit	Credit
September 24	Freight-in	93	
	Cash		93
	To record the freight charges on the Allen purchase.		

Because the terms of the purchase were FOB shipping point, Harwood records the freight bill as an expense.

To record the purchase of one unit from the Bostwick Exchange, terms 2/10, net 30, FOB destination, freight prepaid (shipping charges $85):

		Debit	Credit
September 26	Purchases	1,200	
	Accounts Payable—Bostwick		1,200
	To record purchase from Bostwick 2/10, net 30, FOB destination.		

After Harwood received the Bostwick purchase, the inventory control specialist realized that the equipment item was defective. Harwood notified Bostwick and on

September 28, Bostwick issued a credit memorandum to Harwood. Harwood returned the merchandise to Bostwick freight collect.

To record the return of the Bostwick purchase:

		Debit	Credit
September 28	Accounts Payable—Bostwick	1,200	
	Purchases returns and allowances		1,200
	To record the return of defective		
	merchandise to Bostwick.		

To record the purchase of one unit from Allen Corp., terms 1/15, net 30, FOB shipping point, freight collect (shipping costs $115):

		Debit	Credit
September 29	Purchases	1,450	
	Accounts Payable—Allen		1,450
	To record the purchase from Allen,		
	1/15, net 30, FOB shipping point.		

To record the freight expense on the Allen purchase:

		Debit	Credit
September 30	Freight-in	115	
	Cash		115
	To record payment of freight expense		
	on Allen purchase.		

To record the sale of two units to Kiamichi, Inc., terms 1/10, net 30, FOB destination, freight prepaid:

		Debit	Credit
September 30	Accounts Receivable—Kiamichi	3,000	
	Sales		3,000
	To record the sale to Kiamichi, 1/10,		
	net 30, FOB destination.		

To record payment of freight on Kiamichi sale for $146 on September 30:

		Debit	Credit
September 30	Freight-out	146	
	Cash		146
	To record payment of freight on		
	Kiamichi sale.		

Periodic Inventory Closing Entries

We close all revenue and expense accounts (temporary accounts) at the close of each year. Assume that the following revenue and expense accounts appeared on the adjusted trial balance of Harwood Equipment Company at its year end of December 31, 2000:

	Debit	**Credit**
Sales		75,000
Sales Returns and Allowances	1,500	
Sales Discounts	940	
Purchases	48,000	
Purchases Returns and Allowances		2,400
Purchase Discounts		800
Freight-in	2,300	
Warehouse Rent	2,400	
Freight-out	1,950	

In addition, the Inventory account shows a balance of $2,300, which represents the beginning balance on January 1, 2000. In a periodic inventory system, only two closing entries are made to the Inventory account each year. Therefore, the Inventory asset account always carries the beginning inventory amount except for the last day of the fiscal year. The physical count of the inventory on December 31 indicated a $4,550 inventory using the FIFO costing assumption.

The following are the closing entries for Harwood for 2000:

		Debit	Credit
December 31	Sales	75,000	
	Purchase Returns and Allowances	2,400	
	Purchase Discounts	800	
	Income Summary		78,200
	To close the accounts with credit balances.		
December 31	Income Summary	57,090	
	Sales Returns and Allowances		1,500
	Sales Discounts		940
	Purchases		48,000
	Freight-in		2,300
	Warehouse Rent		2,400
	Freight-out		1,950
	To close accounts with debit balances.		
December 31	Income Summary	2,300	
	Inventory		2,300
	To close the beginning inventory amount.		
December 31	Inventory	4,550	
	Income Summary		4,550
	To record the ending inventory amount.		

The periodic system income statement for Harwood Equipment Company for the year 2000 is as follows:

HARWOOD EQUIPMENT COMPANY
Income Statement
For the Year Ended December 31, 2000

Sales				$75,000
Less: Sales Returns & Allowances			$ 1,500	
Sales Discounts			940	2,440
Net Sales				$72,560
Cost of Goods Sold:				
Beginning Inventory			$ 2,300	
Purchases		$48,000		
Less: Returns & Allowances	$2,400			
Discounts	800	(3,200)		
Add: Freight-in		2,300		
Net Purchases			47,100	
Goods Available for Sale			$49,400	
Less: Ending Inventory			4,550	
Cost of Goods Sold				44,850
Gross Profit				$27,710
Operating Expenses:				
Warehouse Rent			$ 2,400	
Freight-out Expense			1,950	4,350
Net Income				$23,360

We now turn our attention to the recording process for the perpetual inventory system.

Perpetual Inventory Systems

The recording process for perpetual inventory systems involves nine types of entries:

1. Purchase of the inventory
2. Return of defective merchandise
3. Payment of freight charges on purchases
4. Payment of the vendor
5. Recording ending inventory in closing entries
6. Sale of inventory
7. Recording of cost of goods sold
8. Payment of freight charges on sales
9. Receipt of cash from customer

To record the entries we will use the following accounts:

Asset account:	Inventory or Merchandise Inventory
Expense accounts:	Cost of Goods Sold
	Freight-out (a selling expense)
Revenue accounts:	Sales
	Sales Returns and Allowances
	Sales Discounts

To introduce these procedures for the perpetual system, we will use the same transactions as we used for the periodic system. In a perpetual system, all inventory costs are debited directly to the asset account, and reductions for returns or discounts are likewise credited directly to the asset account. Each time a unit is sold, we credit the Inventory account for its cost and debit the Cost of Goods Sold expense account.

To record the purchase of two units from Taylor on September 3, terms 2/10, net 30, FOB destination, freight collect:

2000		Debit	Credit
September 3	Inventory	2,050	
	Accounts Payable—Taylor		2,050
	To record purchase of two units,		
	terms 2/10, net 30, FOB destination.		

To record the receipt and payment of a freight bill to Mistletoe Express for $125:
Because this freight is not the expense of Harwood, it will reduce the amount that Harwood must pay to Taylor for the invoice.

		Debit	Credit
September 4	Accounts Payable—Taylor	125	
	Cash		125
	To record the payment of freight		
	collect on FOB destination.		

To record payment of the invoice within the discount period:

		Debit	Credit
September 12	Accounts Payable—Taylor	1,925	
	Inventory		41
	Cash		1,884
	To record the payment of Taylor's		
	9-3-2000 invoice.		

The payment to Taylor was for a $2,050 invoice less a two percent discount and freight charges of $125 leaving an amount due of $1,884 ($2,050 − $41 − $125). Because we debited the Inventory account for the whole amount before the discount on the invoice date, we reduce the Inventory account for the discount to lower the cost of the purchase to $2,009.

To record the sale on September 17 of one unit to Earhart Industries for $1,500, terms 2/10, net 30, FOB shipping point, freight collect:

		Debit	Credit
September 17	Accounts Receivable—Earhart	1,500	
	Sales		1,500
	To record sale to Earhart, 2/10, net 30, FOB shipping point.		

Because Harwood shipped the goods freight collect, the buyer will pay its freight costs. In the perpetual system, we must recognize the cost of each sale, we also make the following entry:

		Debit	Credit
September 17	Cost of Goods Sold	800	
	Inventory		800
	To record the cost of the sale under the FIFO cost assumption.		

To record the purchase of one unit from Allen Corp., terms 1/15, net 30, FOB shipping point, freight collect (shipping charges were $93):

		Debit	Credit
September 22	Inventory	1,100	
	Accounts Payable—Allen		1,100
	To record purchase from Allen, 1/15, net 30, FOB shipping point.		

To record the payment of the freight to Mistletoe Express:

		Debit	Credit
September 24	Inventory	93	
	Cash		93
	To record the freight charges on the Allen purchase.		

Because the terms of the purchase were FOB shipping point, Harwood records the freight bill as a cost of the inventory.

To record the purchase of one unit from the Bostwick Exchange, terms 2/10, net 30, FOB destination, freight prepaid (shipping charges $85):

		Debit	Credit
September 26	Inventory	1,200	
	Accounts Payable—Bostwick		1,200
	To record purchase from Bostwick 2/10, net 30, FOB destination.		

After Harwood received the Bostwick purchase, the inventory control specialist realized that the equipment item was defective. Harwood notified Bostwick and on September 28, Bostwick issued a credit memorandum to Harwood. Harwood returned the merchandise to Bostwick freight collect.

To record the return of the Bostwick purchase:

		Debit	Credit
September 28	Accounts Payable—Bostwick	1,200	
	Inventory		1,200
	To record the return of defective		
	merchandise to Bostwick.		

To record the purchase of one unit from Allen Corp., terms 1/15, net 30, FOB shipping point, freight collect (shipping costs $115):

		Debit	Credit
September 29	Inventory	1,450	
	Accounts Payable—Allen		1,450
	To record the purchase from Allen,		
	1/15, net 30, FOB shipping point.		

To record the freight expense on the Allen purchase:

		Debit	Credit
September 30	Inventory	115	
	Cash		115
	To record payment of freight expense		
	on Allen purchase.		

To record the sale of two units to Kiamichi, Inc., terms 1/10, net 30, FOB destination, freight prepaid:

		Debit	Credit
September 30	Accounts Receivable—Kiamichi	3,000	
	Sales		3,000
	To record the sale to Kiamichi, 1/10,		
	net 30, FOB destination.		

		Debit	Credit
September 30	Cost of Goods Sold	2,009	
	Inventory		2,009
	To record the cost of the sale made		
	to Kiamichi at $2,009.		

To record payment of freight on Kiamichi sale for $146 on September 30:

		Debit	Credit
September 30	Freight-out	146	
	Cash		146
	To record payment of freight on		
	Kiamichi sale.		

Perpetual Inventory Closing Entries

We close all revenue and expense accounts (temporary accounts) at the close of each year. Assume that the following revenue and expense accounts appeared on the adjusted trial balance of Harwood Equipment Company at its year end of December 31, 2000:

	Debit	Credit
Sales		75,000
Sales Returns and Allowances	1,500	
Sales Discounts	940	
Cost of Goods Sold	44,440	
Warehouse Rent	2,400	
Freight-out	1,950	

In addition, the Inventory account shows a balance of $4,960 which represents the ending balance on December 31, 2000. The physical count of the inventory on December 31 indicated a $4,550 inventory using the FIFO costing assumption.

The following are the closing entries for Harwood for 2000:

		Debit	Credit
December 31	Sales	75,000	
	Income Summary		75,000
	To close the accounts with credit		
	balances.		

		Debit	Credit
December 31	Income Summary	48,790	
	Cost of Goods Sold		44,440
	Warehouse Rent		2,400
	Freight-out		1,950
	To close accounts with debit balances.		

		Debit	Credit
December 31	Income Summary	410	
	Inventory		410
	To adjust the ending inventory		
	amount to the physical count.		

The perpetual system income statement for Harwood Equipment Company for the year 2000 is as follows:

HARWOOD EQUIPMENT COMPANY
Income Statement
For the Year Ended December 31, 2000

Sales		$75,000
Less: Sales Returns & Allowances	$1,500	
Sales Discounts	940	2,440
Net Sales		$72,560
Cost of Goods Sold		44,850
Gross Profit		$27,710
Operating Expenses:		
Warehouse Rent	$2,400	
Freight-out Expense	1,950	4,350
Net Income		$23,360

Remember that the FIFO method produces the same results in a periodic or perpetual system. Therefore, both income statements show the same final results in net income—only the presentation of the cost of goods sold section differs.

SUMMARY OF THE APPENDICES

Cash discounts encourage customers to pay invoices ahead of normal credit terms by reducing the amount paid for the invoice. The terms quoted on the invoice indicate the discount period length and the percentage of the discount.

Freight terms define the point that title passes from seller to buyer. When terms are FOB shipping point, title passes when goods leave the sellers shipping dock and the buyer bears the freight expense. When terms are FOB destination, title passes when the goods arrive at the buyers loading dock and the seller bears the freight expense.

Periodic inventory systems record purchases in detailed expense accounts. The inventory asset account carries the beginning inventory all year and closing entries adjust the balance to the ending inventory balance at year end. The Cost of

Goods Sold section of the income statement computes the cost of goods sold using the balances of the Purchases, Purchase Returns and Allowances, Purchase Discounts, and Freight-in accounts. The Freight-out account accumulates freight paid for customers and is considered a selling expense.

Perpetual inventory systems accumulate all inventory costs, including Freight-in reduced by cash discounts and returns or allowances, in the asset Inventory account. As each sale is made, the cost of the sale is transferred to the Cost of Goods Sold account by debiting it and crediting the Inventory account. The only year-end adjustment to inventory reconciles the balance to the physical inventory count.

KEY TERMS

average cost method F-329	last in, first out (LIFO) F-322
beginning inventory F-316	merchandise inventory F-316
book inventory F-320	moving average cost method F-333
cost of goods manufactured F-318	periodic inventory system F-318
cost of goods sold (COGS) F-316	perpetual inventory system F-319
ending inventory F-316	purchases F-316
finished goods inventory F-318	raw materials inventory F-318
first in, first out (FIFO) F-322	specific identification F-325
goods available for sale (GAFS) F-316	work-in-process inventory F-318

REVIEW THE FACTS

A. Define the terms *inventory* and *merchandise inventory*.
B. What two amounts are added to determine goods available for sale (GAFS)?
C. GAFS is allocated to two places in financial statements. Name them.
D. Under accrual accounting, the cost of inventory still on hand at the end of the period is shown on which financial statement?
E. Under accrual accounting, the cost of inventory no longer on hand at the end of the period is shown on which financial statement?
F. Explain the difference between the physical flow of merchandise and the cost flow of merchandise.
G. What are the two types of inventory systems? Explain the differences between them.
H. List three causes of differences between book inventory and the results of a physical inventory count.
I. Why are FIFO, LIFO, and average cost referred to as "assumptions"?
J. Describe in your own words the differences among the FIFO, LIFO, and average cost methods.

APPLY WHAT YOU HAVE LEARNED

LO 1: Terminology

9–32. Presented below is a list of items relating to the concepts presented in this chapter, followed by definitions of those items in scrambled order:

a. Periodic inventory system	**e.** Merchandise inventory
b. Perpetual inventory system	**f.** First-in, first-out method
c. Goods available for sale	**g.** Last-in, first-out method
d. Cost of goods sold	**h.** Average cost method

1. _____ The total amount of merchandise inventory a company can sell during a particular income statement period.
2. _____ All inventory and cost of goods sold calculations are done at the end of the period.
3. _____ Cost of goods sold is determined based on the assumption that the first units acquired are the first ones sold.
4. _____ Updates both the physical count of inventory units and the cost classification of those units when a transaction involves inventory.
5. _____ The physical units of product a company buys and then resells as part of its business operation.
6. _____ Cost of goods sold is based on the assumption that the last units acquired are the first ones sold.
7. _____ Cost of goods sold is determined based on the total cost of inventory units divided by the number of units.
8. _____ The cost of merchandise inventory that has been converted from an asset on the balance sheet to an expense on the income statement.

REQUIRED:
Match the letter next to each item on the list with the appropriate definition. Each letter will be used only once.

LO 1: Elements of Cost of Goods Sold

9–33. Ned Flanders Company began the month of March 2001 with 304 units of product on hand at a total cost of $3,648. During the month, the company purchased an additional 818 units at $30 per unit. Sales for March were 732 units at a total cost of $10,068.

REQUIRED:
From the information provided, complete the following schedule:

		Units	Cost
	Beginning Inventory	_____	$_____
+	Purchases	_____	_____
=	Goods Available for Sale	_____	_____
−	Cost of Goods Sold	_____	_____
=	Ending Inventory	_____	_____

LO 1: Elements of Goods Available for Sale

9–34. Identify the various components of goods available for sale and define each component.

LO 1: Elements of Cost of Goods Sold

9–35. Kenny G. Company began the month of June 2000 with 150 units of product on hand at a total cost of $3,000. During the month, the company purchased an additional 460 units at $40 per unit. Sales for June were 510 units at a total cost of $17,400.

REQUIRED:

From the information provided, complete the following schedule:

		Units	Cost
	Beginning Inventory	___	$___
+	Purchases	___	___
=	Goods Available for Sale	___	___
−	Ending Inventory	___	___
=	Cost of Goods Sold	___	___

LO 1: Elements of Cost of Goods Sold

9–36. Edward Murdoch Company began the month of April 2002 with 452 units of product on hand at a cost of $54 per unit. During the month, the company purchased an additional 1,500 units at a total cost of $40,500. At the end of April, 616 units were still on hand at a cost of $16,632.

REQUIRED:

From the information provided, complete the following schedule:

		Units	Cost
	Beginning Inventory	___	$___
+	Purchases	___	___
=	Goods Available for Sale	___	___
−	Ending Inventory	___	___
=	Cost of Goods Sold	___	___

LO 1: Elements of Cost of Goods Sold

9–37. Vaughan and Miles Company began the month of July 2002 with 412 units of product on hand at a cost of $34 per unit. During the month, the company purchased an additional 1,300 units at a total cost of $22,100. At the end of July, 712 units were still on hand at a cost of $12,104.

REQUIRED:

From the information provided, complete the following schedule:

		Units	Cost
	Beginning Inventory	___	$___
+	Purchases	___	___
=	Goods Available for Sale	___	___
−	Ending Inventory	___	___
=	Cost of Goods Sold	___	___

LO 1: Elements of Cost of Goods Sold

9–38. Paula Cole and Company began the month of February 2000 with 650 units of product on hand at a total cost of $11,050. During the month, the company purchased an additional 1,884 units at $36 per unit. Sales for February were 1,734 units at $64 per unit. The total cost of the units sold was $30,812 and operating expenses totaled $18,900.

REQUIRED:

a. From the information provided, complete the following schedule:

		Units	Cost
	Beginning Inventory	____	$____
+	Purchases	____	____
=	Goods Available for Sale	____	____
−	Ending Inventory	____	____
=	Cost of Goods Sold	____	____

b. Prepare Paula Cole and Company's income statement for the month ended February 28, 2000.

LO 1:   Elements of Cost of Goods Sold

9–39. Bill Mathes and Company began the month of October 2002 with 470 units of product on hand at a total cost of $7,520. During the month, the company purchased an additional 1,244 units at $34 per unit. Sales for October were 1,280 units at $60 per unit. The total cost of the units sold was $21,290 and operating expenses totaled $11,300.

REQUIRED:

a. From the information provided, complete the following schedule:

		Units	Cost
	Beginning Inventory	____	$____
+	Purchases	____	____
=	Goods Available for Sale	____	____
−	Ending Inventory	____	____
=	Cost of Goods Sold	____	____

b. Prepare Bill Mathes and Company's income statement for the month ended October 31, 2002.

LO 2:   Relationship between Cost of Goods Sold and Ending Inventory

9–40. How do changes in the ending inventory affect the cost of goods sold?

LO 3 & 4:   Cost Flow vs. Physical Flow of Goods

9–41. Joan Stone TV Sales and Service began the month of March with two identical TV sets in inventory. During the month, six additional TV sets (identical to the two in beginning inventory) were purchased as follows:

2 on March 9
1 on March 13
3 on March 24

The company sold two of the TV sets on March 12, another one on March 17, and two more on March 28.

REQUIRED:

a. Assuming the company uses a perpetual inventory system and the first-in, first-out cost flow method:
   (1) Which two TV sets were sold on March 12?
   (2) Which one was sold on March 17?

(3) Which two TV sets were sold on March 28?

(4) The cost of which three TV sets will be included in Stone's inventory at the end of March?

b. If the company uses a perpetual inventory system and the last-in, first-out cost flow method, the cost of which three TV sets will be included in Stone's inventory at the end of March?

LO 3 & 4: Cost Flow vs. Physical Flow of Goods

9–42. Pfeiffer's Piano Sales & Service began the month of February with two identical pianos in inventory. During the month, six additional pianos (identical to the two in beginning inventory) were purchased as follows:

2 on February 10
1 on February 20
3 on February 26

The company sold two of the pianos on February 12, another one on February 17, and two more on February 28.

REQUIRED:

a. Assuming the company uses a perpetual inventory system and the first-in, first-out cost flow method:

(1) Which two pianos were sold on February 12?

(2) Which one was sold on February 17?

(3) Which two pianos were sold on February 28?

(4) The cost of which three pianos will be included in Pfeiffer's inventory at the end of February?

b. If the company uses a perpetual inventory system and the last-in, first-out cost flow method, the cost of which three pianos will be included in Pfeiffer's inventory at the end of February?

LO 4: Inventory Cost

9–43. The Springer Company purchased 500 drill presses from the Falcon Machinery Company. Each drill press cost $350. The presses are to be sold for $700 each. Springer paid $1,850 for freight and $260 for insurance while the presses were in transit. Springer Company hired two more salespeople for a cost of $4,000 per month.

REQUIRED:

Calculate the cost of the inventory of drill presses to be recorded in the books and records.

LO 4: Inventory Cost

9–44. The Baker Company acquired 4,000 hand saws from the Snaggletooth Saw Company. Each saw cost $10. The saws are to be sold for $25 each. Baker paid $750 for freight and $250 for insurance while the saws were in transit. Baker Company ran a special newspaper ad costing $800 to advertise the saws.

REQUIRED:

Calculate the cost of the inventory of saws to be recorded in the books and records.

LO 4:   Inventory Cost

9–45. The Winter Company acquired 10,000 cases of wine from the Sonoma Wine Company. Each case of wine cost $130 and contains 12 bottles. The wine will sell for $20 per bottle. Sonoma paid $1,200 for freight and $550 for insurance while the cases were in transit. Winter Company ran a special newspaper ad costing $1,800 to advertise the wine.

REQUIRED:
Calculate the cost of the inventory of wine to be recorded in the books and records.

LO 4:   Inventory Cost

9–46. The Zeus Grocery Store began operations on July 1. The following transactions took place in the month of July.

    a. Cash purchases of merchandise during July were $500,000.
    b. Purchases of merchandise on account during July were $400,000.
    c. The cost of freight to deliver the merchandise was $25,000.
    d. Warehouse costs including taxes, depreciation, and utilities totaled $19,000 for the month.
    e. Zeus returned $22,000 of merchandise purchased in part b to the supplier.
    f. The grocery store manager's salary is $3,000 for the month.

REQUIRED:
Calculate the amount that the Zeus should include in the valuation of its merchandise inventory.

LO 4:   Inventory Cost

9–47. The Michaelangelo Gift Shop began operations on September 1. The following transactions took place in the month of September.

    a. Cash purchases of merchandise during September were $175,000.
    b. Purchases of merchandise on account during September were $225,000.
    c. The cost of freight to deliver the merchandise was $5,000.
    d. Rental expenses including utilities totaled $6,000 for the month.
    e. Michaelangelo returned $13,000 of merchandise purchased in part b to the supplier.
    f. The store manager's salary is $3,000 for the month.
    g. Advertising for the month of September totaled $4,000.

REQUIRED:
Calculate the amount that the Michaelangelo should include in the valuation of its merchandise inventory.

LO 4, 5, & 6:   Periodic Inventory Systems

9–48. The University Bookstore reported the following information for the year 2001, regarding sweatshirts with the school logo.

Date	Units	Unit Cost	Total Cost
Inventory @ January 2, 2001	1,000	$10	$10,000
Purchases:			
January 15	1,500	11	16,500
March 23	1,200	12	14,400
June 10	1,000	13	13,000

August 18	1,100	10	11,000
December 1	1,400	11	15,400
Total Goods Available for Sale	7,200		$80,300

At the end of the year a physical count is taken and there are 1,800 sweatshirts left on December 31, 2001.

REQUIRED:

Use the periodic inventory system and determine the ending inventory and the cost of goods sold using:

a. LIFO cost flow method
b. FIFO cost flow method
c. Weighted average cost flow method

LO 4, 5, & 6:   Periodic Inventory Systems

9–49. The University Bookstore reported the following information for the year 2002, regarding ball caps with the school logo.

Date	Units	Unit Cost	Total Cost
Inventory @ January 2, 2002	500	$10	$ 5,000
Purchases:			
January 23	800	11	8,800
March 14	600	12	7,200
July 5	500	12	6,000
August 10	1,100	10	11,000
December 15	1,200	9	10,800
Total Goods Available for Sale	4,700		$48,800

At the end of the year a physical count is taken and there are 600 ball caps left on December 31, 2002.

REQUIRED:

Use the periodic inventory system and determine the ending inventory and the cost of goods sold using:

a. LIFO cost flow method
b. FIFO cost flow method
c. Weighted average cost flow method

LO 4, 5, & 6:   Periodic Inventory Systems

9–50. The Widget Manufacturing Company reported the following information for the year 2002, regarding widgets :

Date	Units	Unit Cost	Total Cost
Inventory @ January 2, 2002	5,000	$10	$ 50,000
Purchases:			
January 23	8,000	12	96,000
March 14	7,000	13	91,000
July 5	6,000	12	72,000
August 10	11,000	10	110,000
December 15	12,000	9	108,000
Total Goods Available for Sale	49,000		$527,000

At the end of the year a physical count is taken and there are 8,350 widgets left on December 31, 2002.

REQUIRED:

Use the periodic inventory system and determine the ending inventory and the cost of goods sold using:

a. LIFO cost flow method
b. FIFO cost flow method
c. Weighted average cost flow method

LO 4, 5, & 6:   Periodic Inventory Systems

9–51. The Powell Jewelry Manufacturing Company purchases silver by the ounce to manufacture fine jewelry. During the month of August, its first month of operations, Powell acquired the following:

	Quantity	Cost per Ounce	Total Cost
August 1	50 ounces	$35.00	$1,750
August 8	25 ounces	40.00	1,000
August 19	30 ounces	42.00	1,260
August 22	10 ounces	43.00	430
August 30	20 ounces	45.00	900
Total Goods Available for Sale	135 ounces		$5,340

Powell's inventory at the end of August is 27 ounces of silver. Assume a periodic system of inventory.

REQUIRED:

Compute the cost of the inventory at August 31, and the cost of goods sold for the month of August under each of the following cost flow assumptions:

a. FIFO
b. LIFO
c. Weighted average

LO 4, 5, & 6:   Periodic Inventory Systems

9–52. The Reo Rock Company purchases rock by the ton to sell to homebuilders. During the month of June, its first month of operations, Reo purchased the following:

	Quantity (tons)	Cost per Ton	Total Costs
June 1	700	$100	$ 70,000
June 6	250	140	35,000
June 17	300	125	37,500
June 24	150	130	19,500
June 30	200	145	29,000
Total Goods Available for Sale	1,600		$191,000

Reo's inventory at the end of June is 230 tons of rock. Assume a periodic system of inventory.

REQUIRED:

Compute the cost of the inventory at June 30, and the cost of goods sold for the month of August under each of the following cost flow assumptions:

a. FIFO
b. LIFO
c. Weighted average

LO 4, 5, & 6:   Perpetual Inventory Systems

9–53. The Widget Manufacturing Company reported the following information for the year 2002, regarding widgets:

Date	Units	Unit Cost	Total Cost
Inventory @ January 2, 2002	5,000	$10	$ 50,000
Purchases:			
January 23	8,000	12	96,000
March 14	7,000	13	91,000
July 5	6,000	12	72,000
August 10	11,000	10	110,000
December 15	12,000	9	108,000
Total Goods Available for Sale	49,000		$527,000

Sales of widgets occurred in the following manner:

January 28	6,000 units
February 15	3,000 units
July 6	15,000 units
August 12	10,000 units
December 24	6,650 units

At the end of the year a physical count is taken and there are 8,350 widgets left on December 31, 2002.

REQUIRED:

Use the perpetual inventory system and determine the ending inventory and the cost of goods sold using:

a. LIFO cost flow method
b. FIFO cost flow method
c. Average cost flow method

LO 4, 5, & 6:   Perpetual Inventory Systems

9–54. The Powell Gold Mine Company mines silver by the ounce to sell to manufacturers of fine jewelry. During the month of August, its first month of operations, Powell had the following transactions:

		Purchases (ounces)	Cost per Ounce	Total Costs
August 1		50	$35	$1,750
August 3	Sold 40 ounces			
August 8		25	40	1,000
August 11	Sold 20 ounces			
August 19		30	42	1,260
August 20	Sold 18 ounces			
August 22		10	43	430
August 29	Sold 30 ounces			
August 30		20	45	900
Total Goods Available for Sale		135		$5,340

Powell's inventory at the end of August is 27 ounces of silver. Assume a perpetual system of inventory.

REQUIRED:

Compute the cost of the inventory at August 31, and the cost of goods sold for the month of August under each of the following cost flow assumptions:

a. FIFO cost flow method
b. LIFO cost flow method
c. Moving average cost flow method

LO 4, 5, & 6: Periodic Inventory Systems

9–55. The Reo Rock Company purchases rock by the ton to sell to homebuilders. During the month of June, its first month of operations, Reo engaged in the following transactions:

		Purchases (tons)	Cost per Ton	Total Costs
June 1		700	$100	$70,000
June 3	Sold 400 tons			
June 6		250	140	35,000
June 17		300	125	37,500
June 20	Sold 400 tons			
June 24		150	130	19,500
June 26	Sold 570 tons			
June 30		200	145	29,000
Total Goods Available for Sale		1,600		$191,000

Reo's inventory at the end of June is 230 tons of rock. Assume a perpetual system of inventory.

REQUIRED:

Compute the cost of the inventory at June 30, and the cost of goods sold for the month of June under each of the following cost flow assumptions:

a. FIFO cost flow assumption
b. LIFO cost flow assumption
c. Moving average cost flow assumption

LO 5 & 6: Comparison of Cost Flow Assumptions

9–56. Cox Company buys and then resells a single product as its primary business activity. This product is called the Whatzit and is subject to rather severe cost fluctuations. Following is information concerning Cox's inventory activity for the Whatzit product during the month of July 2001:

July 1:	431 units on hand, $3,017
July 2:	Sold 220 units
July 9:	Purchased 500 units @ $11 per unit
July 12:	Purchased 200 units @ $9 per unit
July 16:	Sold 300 units
July 21:	Purchased 150 units @ $6 per unit
July 24:	Purchased 50 units @ $8 per unit
July 29:	Sold 500 units

REQUIRED:

Assuming Cox employs a perpetual inventory system, calculate cost of goods sold (units and cost) for the month of July 2001 and ending inventory (units and cost) at July 31, 2001, using the following:

a. FIFO cost flow assumption
b. LIFO cost flow assumption

c. Moving average cost flow assumption (round all unit cost calculations to the nearest penny)

d. Which of the three methods resulted in the highest cost of goods sold for July? Which one will provide the highest ending inventory value for Cox's balance sheet?

e. How would the differences among the three methods affect Cox's income statement and balance sheet for the month?

LO 5 & 6: Comparison of Cost Flow Assumptions

9–57. Frank Naifeh Company buys and then resells a single product as its primary business activity. Following is information concerning Naifeh's inventory activity for the product during October 2002:

October 1:	216 units on hand @ $4 per unit
October 5:	Sold 80 units
October 7:	Purchased 150 units @ $7 per unit
October 11:	Purchased 100 units @ $11 per unit
October 15:	Sold 200 units
October 21:	Purchased 300 units @ $13 per unit
October 25:	Purchased 50 units @ $18 per unit
October 29:	Sold 350 units

REQUIRED:

a. Assuming Naifeh employs a perpetual inventory system, calculate cost of goods sold (units and cost) for the month of October, using the following:
   (1) FIFO cost flow assumption
   (2) LIFO cost flow assumption
   (3) Moving average cost flow assumption (round all unit cost calculations to the nearest penny)

b. Which of the three methods resulted in the highest cost of goods sold for October? Which one will provide the highest ending inventory value for Naifeh's balance sheet?

c. How would the differences among the three methods affect Naifeh's income statement and balance sheet for the month?

LO 5 & 6: Comparison of Cost Flow Assumptions

9–58. David Harris Company buys and then resells a single product as its primary business activity. Following is information concerning the David Harris Company's inventory activity for the product during August 2002:

August 1:	216 units on hand @ $18 per unit
August 5:	Sold 80 units
August 7:	Purchased 150 units @ $13 per unit
August 11:	Purchased 100 units @ $11 per unit
August 15:	Sold 200 units
August 21:	Purchased 300 units @ $7 per unit
August 25:	Purchased 50 units @ $4 per unit
August 29:	Sold 350 units

REQUIRED:

a. Assuming Harris employs a perpetual inventory system, calculate cost of goods sold (units and cost) for the month of August, using the following:
   (1) FIFO cost flow assumption
   (2) LIFO cost flow assumption

(3) Moving average cost flow assumption (round all unit cost calculations to the nearest penny)

b. Which of the three methods resulted in the highest inventory amount for Harris' August 31 balance sheet?

c. How would the differences among the three methods affect Harris' income statement and balance sheet for the month?

LO 5 & 6: Comparison of Cost Flow Assumptions

9–59. Dennis Lee Company buys and then resells a single product as its primary business activity. Following is information concerning Lee's inventory activity for the product during the month of July 2000:

July 1:	216 units on hand @ $4 per unit
July 5:	Sold 80 units
July 7:	Purchased 150 units @ $4 per unit
July 11:	Purchased 100 units @ $4 per unit
July 15:	Sold 200 units
July 21:	Purchased 300 units @ $4 per unit
July 25:	Purchased 50 units @ $4 per unit
July 29:	Sold 350 units

REQUIRED:

a. Assuming Lee employs a perpetual inventory system, calculate cost of goods sold (units and cost) for the month of July, using the following:
   (1) First-in, first-out method
   (2) Last-in, first-out method
   (3) Moving average cost flow assumption (round all unit cost calculations to the nearest penny)

b. Which of the three methods resulted in the highest cost of goods sold for July?

c. Describe the differences among income statements and balance sheets prepared under the three cost flow assumptions.

LO 5 & 6: Impact of Errors on Financial Statements

9–60. The Rugby Company's records reported the following at the end of the fiscal year:

Beginning Inventory	$ 25,000
Ending Inventory	35,000
Cost of Goods Sold	128,000

The staff completed a physical inventory and found that the inventory was actually $39,500.

REQUIRED:

Determine the impact of the inventory error on each of the financial statements.

LO 5 & 6: Impact of Errors on Financial Statements

9–61. The Owens Company's records reported the following at the end of the fiscal year:

Beginning Inventory	$ 80,000
Ending Inventory	75,000
Cost of Goods Sold	280,000

The staff completed a physical inventory and found that the inventory was actually $68,000.

REQUIRED:
Determine the impact of the inventory error on each of the financial statements.

LO 5 & 6: Impact of Errors on Financial Statements

9–62. The Corning Company's records reported the following at the end of the fiscal year:

Beginning Inventory	$190,000
Ending Inventory	160,000
Cost of Goods Sold	495,000

The staff completed a physical inventory and found that the inventory was actually $168,000.

REQUIRED:
Determine the impact of the inventory error on each of the financial statements.

Comprehensive

9–63. Benny Blades Company and Emeril Behar Company both began their operations on January 2, 2001. Both companies experienced exactly the same reality during 2001: They purchased exactly the same number of units of merchandise inventory during the year at exactly the same cost, and they sold exactly the same number of inventory units at exactly the same selling price during the year. They also purchased exactly the same type and amount of property, plant, and equipment and paid exactly the same amount for those purchases.

At the end of 2001, the two companies prepared income statements for the year. Blades reported net income of $92,000 and Behar reported net income of $55,000.

REQUIRED:
List and discuss all items you can think of that might have caused the reported net income for the two companies to be different. (Note: Do not restrict yourself to items covered in Chapter 9.)

Comprehensive

9–64. Pete Rush and Company is a merchandiser. The company uses a perpetual inventory system, so both the physical count of inventory units and the cost classification (asset or expense) are updated when a transaction involves inventory. The company's accounting records yielded the following schedule for October 2002:

		Units	Cost
	Beginning Inventory, October 1	200	$ 600
+	Purchases during October	1,700	5,100
=	Goods Available for Sale	1,900	$5,700
−	Cost of Goods Sold	1,500	4,500
=	Ending Inventory, October 31	400	$1,200

On October 31, 2002, Rush conducted a physical count of its inventory and discovered there were only 375 units of inventory actually on hand.

REQUIRED:
a. Show Rush's schedule of cost of goods sold and ending inventory as it should be, to reflect the results of the physical inventory count on October 31.

b. Explain in your own words how the company's income statement and balance sheet will be affected by the results of the physical inventory count on October 31.

c. What are some possible causes of the difference between the inventory amounts in Rush's accounting records and the inventory amounts from the physical count?

LO 7: Freight Terms and Cash Discounts

*9–65. The Fallwell Company made the following purchases from the Grode Company in August of the current year:

Aug. 2   Purchased $5,000 of merchandise, terms 1/10, n/30, FOB shipping point. The goods were received on August 8.

Aug. 5   Purchased $2,000 of merchandise, terms 2/10, n/45, FOB shipping point. The goods were received on August 15.

Aug. 10   Purchased $4,000 of merchandise, terms 3/10, n/15, FOB destination. The goods were received on August 18.

REQUIRED:

For each of the listed purchases, answer the following questions.

a. When is the payment due assuming the company takes advantage of the discount?

b. When is the payment due if the company does not take advantage of the discount?

c. What is the amount of the cash discount allowed?

d. Assume the freight charges are $250 on each purchase. Which company is responsible for the freight charges?

e. What is the total amount of inventory costs for the month of August assuming that all discounts were taken?

LO 7: Freight Terms and Cash Discounts

*9–66. The Gruber Company made the following purchases from the Belte Company in May of the current year:

May 2   Purchased $3,000 of merchandise, terms 2/10, n/30, FOB destination point. The goods were received on May 10.

May 10   Purchased $2,800 of merchandise, terms 2/10, n/60, FOB shipping point. The goods were received on May 19.

May 20   Purchased $6,000 of merchandise, terms 3/10, n/20, FOB destination. The goods were received on May 23.

REQUIRED:

For each of the listed purchases, answer the following questions.

a. When is the payment due assuming the company takes advantage of the discount?

b. When is the payment due if the company does not take advantage of the discount?

c. What is the amount of the cash discount allowed?

d. Assume the freight charges are $400 on each purchase. Which company is responsible for the freight charges?

e. What is the total amount of inventory costs for the month of May assuming that all discounts were taken?

LO 7: Freight Terms and Cash Discounts

*9–67. The Payne Company made the following purchases from the Ritz Company in July of the current year:

July 3 Purchased $7,000 of merchandise, terms 2/10, n/15, FOB shipping point. The goods were received on July 9.

July 7 Purchased $1,700 of merchandise, terms 1/10, n/60, FOB shipping point. The goods were received on July 17.

July 20 Purchased $9,000 of merchandise, terms 4/10, n/10, FOB destination. The goods were received on July 23.

REQUIRED:

For each of the listed purchases, answer the following questions.

a. When is the payment due assuming the company takes advantage of the discount?

b. When is the payment due if the company does not take advantage of the discount?

c. What is the amount of the cash discount allowed?

d. Assume the freight charges are $400 on each purchase. Which company is responsible for the freight charges?

e. What is the total amount of inventory costs for the month of July assuming that all discounts were taken?

LO 7: Recording Purchase, Purchase Discounts, and Freight Costs

*9–68. The Fallwell Company made the following purchases from the Grode Company in August of the current year:

Aug. 2 Purchased $5,000 of merchandise, terms 1/10, n/30, FOB shipping point. The goods were received on August 8.

Aug. 5 Purchased $2,000 of merchandise, terms 2/10, n/45, FOB shipping point. The goods were received on August 15.

Aug. 10 Purchased $4,000 of merchandise, terms 3/10, n/15, FOB destination. The goods were received on August 18.

REQUIRED:

a. For each of the listed purchases, prepare the journal entries to record the purchase assuming the discount is taken.

b. For each of the listed purchases, prepare the journal entries to record the purchase and the freight charge assuming the discount is not taken.

LO 7: Recording Purchase, Purchase Discounts, and Freight Costs

*9–69. The Gruber Company made the following purchases from the Belte Company in May of the current year:

May 2 Purchased $3,000 of merchandise, terms 2/10, n/30, FOB destination point. The goods were received on May 10. Paid freight charges of $200 when the goods were received.

May 10 Purchased $2,800 of merchandise, terms 2/10, n/60, FOB shipping point. The goods were received on May 19.

May 20 Purchased $6,000 of merchandise, terms 3/10, n/20, FOB destination. The goods were received on May 23. Paid freight charges of $100 upon receipt of the goods.

REQUIRED:

a. For each of the listed purchases, prepare the journal entries to record the purchase and the freight charge assuming the discount is taken.

b. For each of the listed purchases, prepare the journal entries to record the purchase and the freight charge assuming the discount is not taken.

LO 7:   Recording Purchase, Purchase Discounts, and Freight Costs

*9–70. The Payne Company made the following purchases from the Ritz Company in July of the current year:

July 3	Purchased $7,000 of merchandise, terms 2/10, n/15, FOB shipping point. The goods were received on July 9.
July 7	Purchased $1,700 of merchandise, terms 1/10, n/60, FOB shipping point. The goods were received on July 17.
July 20	Purchased $9,000 of merchandise, terms 4/10, n/10, FOB destination. The goods were received on July 23. Paid freight charges of $50 upon receipt of the goods.

REQUIRED:

a. For each of the listed purchases, prepare the journal entries to record the purchase and the freight charge assuming the discount is taken.

b. For each of the listed purchases, prepare the journal entries to record the purchase and the freight charge assuming the discount is not taken.

LO 8:   Preparation of Journal Entries for a Perpetual Inventory System

*9–71. The Edwards Company has a beginning inventory of $50,000 and completes the following transactions during the month.

Year 2001

June 1	Purchased 1,000 radios for cash from the Barrow Company at a cost of $20 per unit, terms 2/10, n/30.
June 3	Purchased 2,500 clocks on account from the Adams Company at a cost of $10 per unit, terms 1/10, n/30.
June 6	Purchased 3,000 clocks on account from the Adams Company at a cost of $10 per unit, terms 1/10, n/30.
June 12	Paid for the units purchased in the June 3 transaction.
June 17	Paid for the units purchased in the June 6 transaction.
June 25	Paid cash for office supplies costing $2,000.
June 26	Purchased on account a piece of office furniture costing $800.

REQUIRED:

Prepare the general journal entries to record the transactions using the perpetual inventory method.

LO 8:   Preparation of Journal Entries for a Periodic Inventory System

*9–72. The Edwards Company has a beginning inventory of $50,000 and completes the following transactions during the month.

Year 2001

June 1	Purchased 1,000 radios for cash from the Barrow Company at a cost of $20 per unit, terms 2/10, n/30.
June 3	Purchased 2,500 clocks on account from the Adams Company at a cost of $10 per unit, terms 1/10, n/30.
June 6	Purchased 3,000 clocks on account from the Adams Company at a cost of $10 per unit, terms 1/10, n/30.
June 12	Paid for the units purchased in the June 3 transaction.
June 17	Paid for the units purchased in the June 6 transaction.
June 25	Paid cash for office supplies costing $2,000.
June 26	Purchased on account a piece of office furniture costing $800.

REQUIRED:

Prepare the general journal entries to record the transactions using the periodic inventory method.

LO 8:   Entries to Record Ending Inventory—Perpetual Method

*9–73. Refer to Problem 9–61. Assume that at the end of the period the inventory is $45,000.

REQUIRED:

Prepare the entry necessary to adjust the ending inventory to the proper balance.

LO 8:   Entries to Record Ending Inventory—Periodic Method

*9–74. Refer to Problem 9–62. Assume that at the end of the period the inventory is $45,000.

REQUIRED:

Prepare the entries necessary to close the beginning inventory and to create the ending inventory.

LO 8:   Entries to Record a Perpetual Inventory System

*9–75. The Sosa Company maintains a perpetual inventory system. It accepts all purchases FOB destination and returns merchandise at the supplier's expense. The following items represent a summary of the data from the records for April 2001, the first month of operation.

Purchases on account	$490,000
Purchases for cash	160,000
Purchase returns of merchandise for credit	50,000
Cash operating expenses	100,000
Sales on account	850,000
Cash sales	200,000
Cost of goods sold per inventory records	525,000

REQUIRED:

a. Prepare journal entries dated April 30, 2001, to record the purchase, purchase returns, sales, and operating expenses.
b. Prepare the appropriate closing entries.

LO 8: Entries to Record a Periodic Inventory System

*9–76. The Sosa Company maintains a periodic inventory system. It accepts all purchases FOB destination and returns merchandise at the supplier's expense. The following items represent a summary of the data from the records for April 2001, the first month of operation.

Purchases on account	$490,000
Purchases for cash	160,000
Purchase returns of merchandise for credit	50,000
Cash operating expenses	100,000
Sales on account	850,000
Cash sales	200,000
Inventory per physical count on April 30	75,000

REQUIRED:

a. Prepare journal entries dated April 30, 2001, to record the purchase, purchase returns, sales, and operating expenses.

b. Prepare the appropriate closing entries.

LO 8: Entries to Record a Perpetual Inventory System

*9–77. The Alou Company maintains a perpetual inventory system. It accepts all purchases FOB destination and returns merchandise at the supplier's expense. The following items represent a summary of the data from the records for July 2002.

Beginning inventory	$ 85,000
Purchases on account	355,000
Purchases for cash	280,000
Purchase returns of merchandise for credit	80,000
Cash operating expenses	125,000
Sales on account	642,000
Cash sales	258,000
Cost of goods sold per inventory records	475,000

REQUIRED:

a. Prepare journal entries dated July 31, 2002, to record the purchase, purchase returns, sales, and operating expenses.

b. Prepare the appropriate closing entries.

LO 8: Entries to Record a Periodic Inventory System

*9–78. The Alou Company maintains a periodic inventory system. It accepts all purchases FOB destination and returns merchandise at the supplier's expense. The following items represent a summary of the data from the records for July 2002.

Beginning inventory	$ 85,000
Purchases on account	355,000
Purchases for cash	280,000
Purchase returns of merchandise for credit	80,000
Cash operating expenses	125,000
Sales on account	642,000
Cash sales	258,000
Inventory per physical count on July 31	165,000

REQUIRED:

a. Prepare journal entries dated July 31, 2002, to record the purchase, purchase returns, sales, and operating expenses.

b. Prepare the appropriate closing entries.

LO 8: Entries to Record a Perpetual Inventory System

*9–79. The Rose Company maintains a perpetual inventory system. It accepts all purchases FOB destination and returns merchandise at the supplier's expense. The following items represent a summary of the data from the records for August 2001.

Beginning inventory	$ 37,000
Purchases on account	126,000
Purchases for cash	138,000
Purchase returns of merchandise for credit	30,000
Cash operating expenses	103,000
Sales on account	321,000
Cash sales	258,000
Cost of goods sold per inventory records	129,000

REQUIRED:

a. Prepare journal entries dated August 31, 2001, to record the purchase, purchase returns, sales, and operating expenses.

b. Prepare the appropriate closing entries.

LO 8: Entries to Record a Periodic Inventory System

*9–80. The Morgan Company maintains a periodic inventory system. It accepts all purchases FOB destination and returns merchandise at the supplier's expense. The following items represent a summary of the data from the records for September 2002.

Beginning inventory	$ 25,000
Purchases on account	133,000
Purchases for cash	120,000
Purchase returns of merchandise for credit	20,000
Cash operating expenses	195,000
Cash sales	236,000
Inventory per physical count on September 30	75,000

REQUIRED:

a. Prepare journal entries dated September 30, 2002, to record the purchase, purchase returns, sales, and operating expenses.

b. Prepare the appropriate closing entries.

LO 8: Adjusting Entries for Errors in Inventory Systems

*9–81. The Sweiss Company manufactures a product for the computer industry. At the end of the first year of operations the company reported the following information under the perpetual inventory method.

Beginning Inventory	$ -0-
Cost of Goods Sold	295,000
Ending Inventory	88,000

The company determined that the ending inventory was in error and was actually $95,000.

REQUIRED:
a. Prepare the journal entry or entries necessary to correct this discovery.
b. Assume the company uses a periodic system of inventory and prepare the necessary journal entry or entries to correct this discovery.

LO 8: Adjusting Entries for Errors in Inventory Systems

*9–82. The Pippen Company manufactures a product for the automotive industry. At the end of the first year of operations the company reported the following information under the perpetual inventory method.

Beginning Inventory	$ -0-
Cost of Goods Sold	880,000
Ending Inventory	165,000

The company determined that the ending inventory was in error and was actually $148,000.

REQUIRED:
a. Prepare the journal entry or entries necessary to correct this discovery.
b. Assume the company uses a periodic system of inventory and prepare the necessary journal entry or entries to correct this discovery.

LO 8: Adjusting Entries for Errors in Inventory Systems

*9–83. The Dowers Company manufactures seats for the aircraft industry. At the end of the first year of operations the company reported the following information under the perpetual inventory method.

Beginning Inventory	$ -0-
Cost of Goods Sold	996,000
Ending Inventory	287,000

The company determined that the ending inventory was in error and was actually $298,000.

REQUIRED:
a. Prepare the journal entry or entries necessary to correct this discovery.
b. Assume the company uses a periodic system of inventory and prepare the necessary journal entry or entries to correct this discovery.

FINANCIAL REPORTING CASES

Comprehensive

9–84. Visit the PHLIP Web site for this book at www.prenhall.com/jones to find the Pep Boys Corporation link. Look up the current annual report and go to the footnotes section of the annual report. Look at the first footnote and review the section on inventories.

REQUIRED:

Answer the following questions referring to the footnotes and the financial statements.

  a. How are the inventories stated on the balance sheet?
  b. What is the gross profit for the year?
  c. What is the total cost of goods sold for the year?
  d. What is the percentage of gross profit and cost of goods sold in relation to sales for the year?

Comprehensive

9–85. Visit the PHLIP Web site for this book at www.prenhall.com/jones to find the Nortek, Inc. link. Look up the current annual report and go to the footnotes section of the annual report. Look at the first footnote and review the section on inventories. Determine the methods used to value inventories. Look at the financial statements and determine the Cost of Goods Sold and the Gross Profit reported by the company.

REQUIRED:

Prepare a brief summary of the information requested.

Comprehensive

9–86. Tour the Web site of Brown-Forman Corporation by going to the PHLIP Web site for this textbook at www.prenhall.com/jones and connect with the link. Look up the current annual report and go to the footnotes section of the annual report. Look at the first footnote and review the section on inventories.

REQUIRED:

Answer the following questions:

  a. How are the inventories stated on the balance sheet?
  b. How are the warehousing, insurance, and ad valorem taxes associated with the inventories handled?
  c. What is the gross profit for the year?
  d. What is the total cost of goods sold for the year?
  e. What is the percentage of gross profit and cost of goods sold in relation to sales for the year?

ANNUAL REPORT PROJECT

9–87. You may now complete Section IV of the project. For inventories you should do the following:

    a. List the different inventories of your firm, assuming that your firm has inventories.
    b. Identify the method or methods used by your company to value the inventories.
    c. List the total dollar value of inventory for each balance sheet presented in your company's annual report.

    d. Compute the percentage of inventories to total assets for each year of your annual report's balance sheets.

    e. Does your company's inventories appear to be growing as a percentage of total assets?

    f. List the Cost of Goods Sold and the Gross Profit for your company for each income statement appearing in the annual report.

    g. Calculate the percentage of Cost of Goods Sold to Net Sales and the percentage of Gross Profit to Net Sales for each period presented.

    h. Does it appear that the Cost of Goods Sold and Gross Profit percentages have remained relatively stable for the income statements appearing in the report? If not, describe the changes.

REQUIRED:

Complete Section IV of your report. Make a copy for your instructor and keep a copy for your final report.

Chapter 10

The Balance Sheet and Income Statement: A Closer Look

Your brother-in-law, the one you like, just sent you an annual report of a company that he believes will be the next Microsoft in terms of growth and market domination. He wants you to consider getting in on the ground floor and knows that you have a little money set aside that you might want to invest. Although you have only seen a few annual reports, none seemed this complex. The balance sheet contains a lot of "intangible" assets. If these assets are not tangible, what are they, thin air? The income statement has numerous items after operating income. Should you really care about those figures? To top it off, the earnings per share has six different amounts. Which one of them is the right one to use to compute a basic market price? The highest is only $0.45 a share, and your brother-in-law wants you to pay $12 per share for this stock! That is almost 27 times the annual income per share, if you are looking at the right one. Maybe this brother-in-law is a real turkey, just like the other three.

Balance sheets and income statements are generally more complex than the ones we have explored so far. An understanding of the organization of these two financial statements is crucial, particularly when very detailed information is included. Even complex balance sheets and income statements are organized in a manner that serves to clarify rather than complicate the information provided.

In this chapter, to help you to better comprehend the information provided by them, we will explore in further detail the organization of the balance sheet and income statement. After all, the primary purpose of these and other financial statements is to provide information useful to economic decision makers. In addition, understanding the construction of the income statement and balance sheet is necessary to do financial statement analysis, which we will discuss in Chapter 12. ■

LEARNING OBJECTIVES

After completing your work on this chapter, you should be able to do the following:

1. Describe how the balance sheet and income statement were developed as financial statements.
2. Explain the organization and purpose of the classified balance sheet.
3. Explain why recurring and nonrecurring items are presented separately on the income statement.
4. Interpret the net of tax disclosure of extraordinary items, discontinued operations, and accounting changes.
5. Calculate earnings per share and properly disclose it on the income statement.
6. Describe the additional information provided by comparative financial statements.
*7. Complete the recording process for income taxes.

HISTORY AND DEVELOPMENT OF THE BALANCE SHEET AND INCOME STATEMENT

Ever since human beings began living in organized societies, they have kept track of their business affairs by accounting for economic events and transactions, recording them on stone or clay tablets, papyrus, paper, or whatever writing material was available.

Originally, accounting records were kept to assist in conducting a company's operation rather than to report on the operation of a company. Amounts owed to suppliers, for example, were recorded primarily so a company could keep track of what had and had not been paid, without regard for balance sheet presentation. Eventually, however, recordkeeping began for the specific purpose of preparing financial statements. In *A History of Accounting Thought*, Michael Chatfield describes this transition as follows:

> More than most accounting tools, financial statements are the result of cumulative historical influences. Before the Industrial Revolution they were usually prepared as arithmetic checks of ledger balances. Afterward the roles were reversed and it was account books which were reorganized to facilitate statement preparation. As statements became communication devices rather than simple bookkeeping summaries, the journal and ledger evolved from narratives to tabulations of figures from which balances could easily be taken.[1]

Financial statements as we know them are a relatively recent phenomenon. While accounting has been with us since about 5000 B.C., the balance sheet's function as a financial statement only emerged during the Renaissance, around A.D. 1600. For the next several hundred years the balance sheet was the primary output of the accounting process. Accountants developed the income statement in the late

---

[1]Michael Chatfield, *A History of Accounting Thought* (Huntington, NY: R. E. Kriger Publishing Co., 1974), 164.

1800s, but did not consider the information nearly as important as the balance sheet figures. In his landmark work, *Accounting Evolution to 1900*, A. C. Littleton makes the following observation:

> . . . it seems that the primary motive for separate financial statements was to obtain information regarding capital; this was the center of the interest of partners, shareholders, lenders, and the basis of the calculation of early property taxes. Thus balance-sheet data were stressed and refined in various ways, while expense and income data were incidental—in fact, the latter in the seventeenth century were presented merely as a "proof of estate"—to demonstrate by another route the correctness of the balance sheet.[2]

At the beginning of the 20th century, banks served as the chief form of external financing to U.S. companies. For this reason, creditors were the primary audience for whom financial statements were prepared. Creditors looked at a company's ability to repay its debts and at the balance sheet—which focuses on the relationships among assets, liabilities, and owners' equity—to assure themselves.

During the first two decades of the 20th century, U.S. companies changed the methods of financing expansion. Relying less on debt financing and more on equity financing, companies began to borrow less from banks and issue more capital stock. When selling stock became the major source of external financing, stockholders became the primary users of financial statements. Stockholders were interested in the performance of the company and its impact on dividend payments and the value of the company's stock. Stockholders focused on net income, so the income statement came to be considered more important than the balance sheet. Over time even long-term creditors realized that earning power was crucial to debt repayment, so they also began to rely more on the income statement than on the balance sheet.

By the 1930s, it became apparent that the balance sheet and the income statement are best used together. Neither is more important than the other because each provides valuable information for economic decision makers. By learning more about the detailed structure of the balance sheet and income statement, you can make the best use of the information provided by each statement.

ORGANIZATION OF THE BALANCE SHEET

In introducing the balance sheet in Chapter 3, we used this simple equation:

Assets = Liabilities + Owners' Equity

The equation does not distinguish one asset from another or one liability from another. A balance sheet prepared for Louise Eliason and Company at December 31, 2000, using the basic format would look like Exhibit 10–1.

This balance sheet gives economic decision makers little useful information about the financial position of Eliason and Company at December 31, 2000. Even if the company uses the cash basis of accounting (meaning the $1,516,800 of assets is cash), we see no indication of how soon the $851,000 of liabilities must be paid or how much of the $665,800 of stockholders' equity represents contributed capital and how much represents retained earnings.

Why does any of this matter and what difference does it make to those who use the balance sheet? The answer is obvious if you remember that economic decision

---

[2]A. C. Littleton, *Accounting Evolution to 1900* (New York: Russell & Russell, 1966), 153.

Exhibit 10–1
Basic Format
Balance Sheet

LOUISE ELIASON AND COMPANY
Balance Sheet
December 31, 2000

Total Assets	$1,516,800
Liabilities	$851,000
Stockholders' Equity	665,800
Total Liabilities and Stockholders' Equity	$1,516,800

makers are attempting to predict the future and timing of cash flows by looking at the balance sheet. Accountants developed a more detailed balance sheet in response to users need for additional information.

The Classified Balance Sheet

classified balance sheet
A balance sheet showing assets and liabilities categorized into current and long-term items.

A **classified balance sheet** prepared from the same accounting data as Exhibit 10–1 for Louise Eliason and Company at December 31, 2000, would look like Exhibit 10–2. Notice that the assets still total $1,516,800; total liabilities are still $851,000; and stockholders' equity is still $665,800. The only difference in the two balance sheet presentations is the amount of detail disclosed.

As we explain why the classified balance sheet is organized as it is, we will make reference to the Eliason and Company classified balance sheet in Exhibit 10–2.

Discussion Question

10–1. Which of the two balance sheet presentations for Eliason and Company do you think would be more useful in predicting the future and timing of the company's cash flow? Provide three specific examples to support your position.

The accrual accounting basis of measurement creates a need to segregate, or classify, assets on the balance sheet because, under this basis, items besides cash are considered assets. Two classifications of assets are identified on Eliason's balance sheet: current and long-term. **Current assets** are defined as assets that either are cash already or are expected to become cash within one year or one operating cycle, whichever is longer. An **operating cycle** is the length of time it takes for an entity to complete one revenue producing cycle. For a manufacturer, a revenue cycle is the length of time from receiving raw materials, including producing and selling the final product, to collecting cash from its customers. For a merchandiser, the operating cycle is the time it takes from receiving merchandise to collecting the cash from its customers. Most businesses have several operating cycles in one year. Some businesses, such as wineries, timber operations, or long-term construction companies have operating cycles that last as long as five years or more. As you can see from Exhibit 10–2, accounts receivable and inventory are examples of current assets.

current assets Assets that are either cash or will become cash within one year.

operating cycle The length of time it takes for an entity to complete one revenue producing cycle from purchase of goods to collection of cash.

Long-term assets are defined as those assets that are expected to benefit the organization more than one year or that are not anticipated to become cash within one year. Depreciable assets such as buildings, equipment, and vehicles are examples of long-term assets. Because of the way the classified balance sheet is orga-

long-term assets Assets that are expected to benefit the company for longer than one year.

Exhibit 10–2
Classified Balance
Sheet

LOUISE ELIASON AND COMPANY
Balance Sheet
December 31, 2000

ASSETS:

Current Assets:

Cash		$ 100
Accounts Receivable		251,000
Inventory		298,900
Prepaid Expenses		50,000
Total Current Assets		$ 600,000

Long-Term Assets:

Land		$125,000
Plant and Equipment	$1,075,000	
Less: Accumulated Depreciation	(283,200)	
Plant and Equipment, Net		791,800
Total Long-Term Assets		916,800
Total Assets		$1,516,800

LIABILITIES:

Current Liabilities:

Accounts Payable		$ 501,000
Short-Term Note Payable		50,000
Total Current Liabilities		$ 551,000

Long-Term Liabilities:

Bonds Payable		300,000
Total Liabilities		$ 851,000

STOCKHOLDERS' EQUITY:

Common Stock, No Par Value,		
10,000 Shares Issued and Outstanding	$400,000	
Retained Earnings	265,800	
Total Stockholders' Equity		665,800
Total Liabilities and Stockholders' Equity		$1,516,800

nized, users can tell in a quick glance just which assets (and their dollar amount) the company thinks will be turned into cash within the next year (current assets) and which ones are not expected to be converted into cash (long-term assets).

liquidity An item's nearness to cash.

Assets are listed on a classified balance sheet in order of decreasing liquidity. **Liquidity** means nearness to cash. Notice that we always list cash first on the balance sheet because by definition it is the most liquid asset. The farther down you read the asset section of a classified balance sheet, the less likelihood there is that an item will be converted to cash in the near future. In the case of Eliason and Company, current assets total $600,000 and long-term assets total $916,800.

Discussion Questions

10–2. Are there any items listed as current assets on Eliason's December 31, 2000, classified balance sheet (Exhibit 10–2) that you think will never be converted into cash? If there are, why do you think they are classified as current assets?

10–3. Eliason has classified plant and equipment as long-term assets in 2000. Does this mean the company cannot sell one of its buildings in 2001? Explain your reasoning.

investments Assets that represent long-term ownership in subsidiaries, or funds set aside for specific purposes, bond sinking funds, or bonds of other companies.

intangible assets Assets consisting of contractual rights such as patents, copyrights, and trademarks.

amortization The systematic allocation of the cost of intangible assets over the economic life of the asset.

Some firms possess two other classifications of assets—investments and intangibles. **Investments** represent long-term commitments to ownership of other entities (called subsidiaries) or investments in trust funds set aside for a specific purpose, bond sinking funds (money set aside to repay the firm's own bonds payable), or bonds of other corporations. The firm does not intend to utilize these assets within the next year. Their location in the balance sheet indicates how soon the company might convert these investments to cash.

Intangible assets denote company investments in contractual arrangements such as patents, copyrights, trademarks, trade names, and purchased goodwill. These investments provide the firm with future economic benefits. Similar to the way we depreciate long-term assets, we amortize the cost of intangible assets over their economic lives. The **amortization** of intangible assets tries to match the cost of the asset with the periods of time benefited or with the revenue it helps to create.

Discussion Questions

10–4. For what reasons would a company set aside special funds in a long-term account?

10–5. Do intangibles such as copyrights, patents, and trademarks have value? Do companies try to protect the value of such intangibles?

10–6. How would you determine the economic life of an intangible?

When we classify liabilities in liquidity order, we look at how quickly they must be settled. If settlement involves cash, liquidity represents the order of payment. If settlement requires performance, such as delivery of goods or services, liquidity refers to how soon performance is required. Liquidity and priority of claims require that liabilities be listed on the balance sheet before stockholders' equity: If a company goes out of business, obligations to creditors must be paid before funds can be distributed to the owners.

current liabilities Liabilities that must be settled within one year.

long-term liabilities Amounts that are not due for settlement until at least one year from now.

Current liabilities require settlement within one year. Certainly, the suppliers to whom Eliason and Company owes a total of $501,000 (accounts payable) expect repayment within the year, usually within 30 to 60 days. Eliason classifies debts not requiring settlement within the next year as **long-term liabilities.** Because of the way the balance sheet is organized, users know at a quick glance which liabilities are expected to be retired within the next year (current liabilities) and which ones are not (long-term liabilities). This enables them to assess future cash flows. Eliason's current liabilities total $551,000 and long-term liabilities total $300,000.

Exhibit 10–3 illustrates the current and long-term classifications of assets and liabilities.

Exhibit 10–3
Examples of Current and Long-Term Assets and Liabilities

Assets		Liabilities	
Current	**Long-Term**	**Current**	**Long-Term**
• Cash	• Land	• Accounts	• Notes Payable
• Inventory	• Plant	Payable	• Bonds Payable
• Accounts	• Equipment	• Short-Term	• Mortgages
Receivable		Notes Payable	Payable

Discussion Questions

10–7. Provide three examples of current liabilities and three examples of long-term liabilities not shown on the Eliason and Company balance sheet in Exhibit 10–2.

10–8. Eliason shows $600,000 of current assets and $551,000 of current liabilities. Who might be interested in these amounts, and why?

The stockholders' equity section of a classified balance sheet is also separated into two classifications. Because all equity is either contributed by owners or earned, we classify equity into contributed and earned. Preferred stockholders have first priority in paying out dividends and in liquidation. Therefore, the contributed or paid-in section of equity begins with preferred stock, second is common stock, then the remaining paid-in capital accounts. In the case of Eliason and Company, we first list the $400,000 classified as no-par common stock. Because there are no other contributed equity accounts, we list retained earnings next. At December 31, 2000, Eliason and Company had a retained earnings balance of $265,800.

Discussion Questions

10–9. Explain the exact meaning of the $265,800 of retained earnings on Eliason and Company's balance sheet.

10–10. On average, how much did Eliason and Company receive for each share of stock sold?

10–11. What is the total current market value of the Eliason and Company stock?

ORGANIZATION OF THE INCOME STATEMENT

When we introduced the income statement in Chapter 5, we used the following simple equation:

Revenues − Expenses = Net Income

An income statement prepared for Louise Eliason and Company for the year ended December 31, 2000, using this simple format, would look like Exhibit 10–4.

Exhibit 10–4
Basic Format
Income Statement

LOUISE ELIASON AND COMPANY	
Income Statement	
For the Year Ended December 31, 2000	
Revenue	$752,500
Less: Expenses	840,400
Net Loss	$ (87,900)

Exhibit 10–5
Expanded Format
Income Statement

LOUISE ELIASON AND COMPANY
Income Statement
For the Year Ended December 31, 2000

Sales Revenue		$752,500
Less: Cost of Goods Sold		352,800
Gross Profit on Sales		$399,700
Less: Operating Expenses:		
Selling	$60,250	
General and Administrative	96,250	
Total Operating Expenses		156,500
Operating Income		$243,200
Less: Interest Expense		30,650
Income Before Taxes		$212,550
Less: Income Taxes		64,660
Income Before Extraordinary Item		$147,890
Extraordinary Loss (Less: Income Taxes of $87,420)		(235,790)
Net Loss		$ (87,900)

Net income or net loss discloses whether or not a company has been profitable for a given period. Although net income or loss is very important, the net loss for 2000 does not tell Eliason's performance story very well.

Accountants have developed income statement presentation guidelines to furnish a more complete picture of what happened to a business during a particular income statement period. Income statements prepared following these guidelines provide more detail than given in the basic format shown in Exhibit 10–4, as well as important information about the characteristics of the revenues and expenses. Exhibit 10–5 presents an income statement for Eliason and Company for the year ended December 31, 2000, prepared using the expanded format.

Although this income statement bears little resemblance to the one presented earlier in our discussion, revenues still total $752,500; total deductions from revenues still total $840,400; and the net loss is still $87,900. You should be familiar with the beginning of the format because only the last few lines are new.

Discussion Questions

10–12. Is Exhibit 10–5 a single-step or multistep income statement? How can you tell?

10–13. If you were considering some kind of economic involvement with Eliason and Company, which number on the expanded income statement would you consider most reliable in predicting the company's future profitability? Explain.

Recurring and Nonrecurring Items

Besides presenting more detail concerning Eliason and Company's regular revenues and expenses for 2000, the income statement in Exhibit 10–5 shows an extraordinary loss of $235,790, which is separated from the company's regular, recurring revenues and expenses. An extraordinary loss (or gain) is one of the items the accounting profession has determined should be shown separately as a nonrecurring item on the income statement.

A **nonrecurring item** can be broadly defined as any item (either positive or negative) that should not be considered a normal part of continuing operations because it is not expected to recur. We will explore the logic of separating recurring and nonrecurring items on the income statement.

Suppose an event happened to a company during the income statement period that was not expected to recur. Whether the event was good or bad, the company must report its occurrence, even though it is not likely to happen again. If you were attempting to predict the company's ability to generate future profits and cash flows, and the company included this one-time event with revenues and expenses that happen each year, your prediction would not be realistic. Therefore, if nonrecurring items do not represent the ongoing results of a company's operations, we should report them separately from recurring items to protect the integrity of reported earnings.

If the extraordinary loss is truly a nonrecurring item for Eliason, then the net loss of $87,900 for 2000 is not a good predictor of future profitability and cash flow. In fact, the best predictive number on this income statement is probably $147,890 listed as the income before extraordinary item.

In this section, we will more fully explain the presentation and interpretation of information about nonrecurring items on the income statement. Throughout our discussion, we will use the Pursifull, Inc. income statement for the year ended December 31, 2000, presented in Exhibit 10–6.

Exhibit 10–6
Income Statement for Pursifull, Inc. for the Year Ended December 31, 2000

PURSIFULL, INC.
Income Statement
For the Year Ended December 31, 2000

Sales		$858,600
Less: Cost of Goods Sold		456,800
Gross Profit on Sales		$401,800
Less: Operating Expenses:		
Selling	$ 94,450	
General and Administrative	116,050	
Total Operating Expenses		210,500
Operating Income		$191,300
Less: Interest Expense		30,650
Income from Continuing Operations Before Taxes		$160,650
Less: Income Taxes		64,260
Income from Continuing Operations		$ 96,390
Discontinued Operations:		
Income from Discontinued Operations		
(Less: Income Taxes of $47,520)	$ 71,280	
Loss on Disposal of Discontinued Operation		
(Less: Income Taxes of $36,000)	(54,000)	17,280
Income Before Extraordinary Item and Cumulative		
Effect of a Change in Accounting Principle		$113,370
Extraordinary Gain (Less: Income Taxes of $88,000)		132,000
Cumulative Effect of a Change in Accounting		
Principle (Less: Income Taxes of $24,800)		(37,200)
Net Income		$208,470

The first half of Pursifull's income statement reflects results of activities that will probably continue in the future. The income tax amount shown ($64,260) relates only to the ongoing activities of the company and is calculated as:

Income Tax Expense = Income from Continuing Operations Before Tax × Tax Rate
$64,260 = $160,650 × 40%

Notice the item identified as Income from Continuing Operations. The $96,390 represents the net results of Pursifull's ongoing operations, which we assume have a predictive value for future earnings. Information provided on the income statement below this point relates to nonrecurring items. The income from Continuing Operations separates the recurring from nonrecurring activities. Some income statements show the title as Income Before Extraordinary Items. Regardless of the title, nonrecurring items always come after the income tax expense.

There are three general types of nonrecurring items, listed in their order of presentation on the income statement:

1. Discontinued operations
2. Extraordinary items
3. Cumulative effect of changes in accounting principles

Proper classification of items as recurring or nonrecurring is critical to the usefulness of the accounting information. A company might be tempted to treat an item as nonrecurring because it reduces net income or to include an item with recurring revenues when it increases net income. To prevent companies from confusing the users of financial statements this way, the accounting profession restricts the items that may be considered nonrecurring. We will consider the criteria for each of these items after we discuss the income tax effects of these nonrecurring items.

Income Tax Disclosure

On Pursifull's income statement the income tax amount shown in the income from continuing operations section of $64,260 is the amount of tax expense associated with the ongoing, recurring operation of the business. But how should the company disclose the income tax effect of the nonrecurring items shown on the income statement? The nonrecurring events cannot escape income tax consequences, and those consequences must be disclosed.

Since we present nonrecurring items separately from continuing operations, lumping their tax effect with the tax expense shown for continuing operations would distort the information. For example, the net tax effect on Pursifull's income statement is $138,980 ($64,260 + $47,520 − $36,000 + $88,000 − $24,800). If we showed this on the income statement, it would appear as follows:

Income from Continuing Operations Before Taxes	$160,650
Less: Income Taxes	138,980
Income from Continuing Operations	$ 21,670

This example makes it appear that Pursifull, Inc. pays 86.5 percent income tax. On the contrary, we could show two different amounts of income taxes as follows:

Income from Continuing Operations Before Taxes		$160,650
Less: Income Taxes from Continuing Operations	$64,260	
Income Taxes from Nonrecurring Events	96,390	138,980
Income from Continuing Operations		$ 21,670

This financial statement leaves readers to ponder the difference and still distorts the income from continuing operations. To eliminate the distortion and confusion, members of the accounting profession decided that the only tax expense shown on the income statement as a separate line item will be the amount associated with continuing operations. Therefore, the three major types of nonrecurring items included on the income statement are shown "less income tax," or "net of tax."

net of tax The proper presentation format for nonrecurring items shown below income from continuing operations on the income statement.

Net of tax means the amount shown for an item has been adjusted for any income tax effect. To calculate the tax expense, simply multiply the effective tax rate by the amount of the nonrecurring gain or loss. In Pursifull's example, we calculate the amounts as:

Income from Discontinued Operations $118,800 × 40% = $47,520
Disposal of Discontinued Operation $ 90,000 × 40% = $36,000
Extraordinary Gain $220,000 × 40% = $88,000
Cumulative Effect of Accounting Principal Change $ 62,000 × 40% = $24,800

How did we determine the full amount of the nonrecurring item? There are two accurate ways. The first is to simply add the tax to the gain or loss amount. The second is to divide the net of tax amount of gain or loss by the reciprocal of the tax amount or (1 − Tax Rate), in this case 60 percent.

Income from Discontinued Operations = $71,280 + $47,520 = $118,800
or = $71,280/.60 = $118,800

When a business experiences a gain, the total income of the business increases and the Internal Revenue Service will require more taxes. The gain increases the amount of taxes owed, which in turn reduces the amount of the gain (see Exhibit 10–7). When a business experiences a loss, the total income of the business decreases and the Internal Revenue Service will require less taxes. The loss decreases the amount of taxes owed, which in turn reduces the amount of the loss.

Current accounting rules require that on the face of the income statement the tax effect on each of these nonrecurring items, and the amount of that item after the tax effect, be shown. With this information, financial statement users can determine the actual amount of the item before any tax effect.

Now look again at the income statement for Pursifull, Inc. (Exhibit 10–6 on page F-381). Notice that the statement includes examples of the three major types

Exhibit 10–7
Effect of Tax on
Gains and Losses

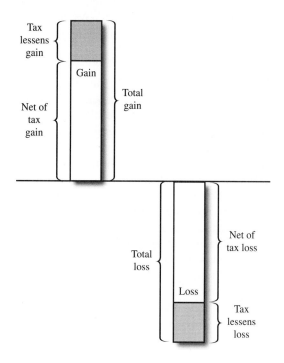

of nonrecurring items, and all receive the same general presentation: Each is shown below the Income from Continuing Operations line, and each is shown "net of tax."

We now explore the criteria for and specific presentation of each of these types of nonrecurring items.

Discontinued Operations

If a company disposes of a major segment of its business, the results of operations for the segment of the company sold and any gain or loss from the actual disposal of the business segment are reported as nonrecurring items on the income statement. A **business segment** may be a portion of an entity representing either a separate major line of business or class of customer. In either case, specific criteria must be met for the **discontinued operations** to qualify as the disposal of a business segment. The part of the business being eliminated is considered a business segment

business segment A portion of the business for which assets, results of operations, and activities can be separately identified.

discontinued operations The disposal of a business segment. One of the nonrecurring items shown net of tax on the income statement.

> provided that its assets, results of operations, and activities can be clearly distinguished, physically and operationally and for financial reporting purposes, from the other assets, results of operations, and activities of the entity.
>
> —*(APB Opinion No. 30,* paragraph 13)

The following examples of situations meeting the criteria for disposal of a business segment will help you understand the application of these criteria.

1. A sale by a diversified company of a major division which represents the company's only activities in the electronics industry . . .
2. A sale by a meat packing company of a 25% interest in a professional football team . . .
3. A sale by a communications company of all its radio stations which represent 30% of gross revenues. The company's remaining activities are three television stations and a publishing company . . .
4. A food distributor disposes of one of its two divisions. One division sells food wholesale primarily to supermarket chains and the other division sells food through its chain of fast food restaurants, some of which are franchised and some of which are company-owned.

> —*(AICPA Accounting Interpretations,* AIN-APB30, #1)

Once a judgment has been made that the discontinued operations should be considered the disposal of a business segment, GAAP require specific disclosures on the income statement. To illustrate, recall Exhibit 10–6, the income statement for Pursifull, Inc. for the year ended December 31, 2000.

Pursifull, Inc. buys and resells toys. Many years ago, Pursifull purchased a company that manufactured hats. Although this portion of the business has always been profitable, current management did not believe that the hat business fit into the corporation's strategic plans and sold it during 2000. Two items presented on Pursifull's 2000 income statement reflect the disposal of the hat operation.

Pursifull reported income from discontinued operations of $71,280. In 2000, prior to being sold, the hat operation had revenues of $220,100 and expenses of $101,300. So its pretax income for the time Pursifull owned it during the year was $118,800 ($220,100 revenues − $101,300 expenses). Income taxes on the results of discontinued operations totaled $45,720, so the amount shown for income from discontinued operations on the income statement is $71,280 ($118,800 − $45,720). Because the hat operation is gone by the end of the year and can no longer be expected to generate income, the results for that part of the business are reported separately, net of tax.

Pursifull also shows a $54,000 loss on the disposal of discontinued operations. When the company sold the hat operation, it incurred a $90,000 pretax loss on the sale. This loss resulted in a reduction of $36,000 in income taxes for the year. The after-tax loss was $54,000 ($90,000 − $36,000).

After we report each component of the results of discontinued operations, we combine the two amounts. We then net the $71,280 income from discontinued operations and the $54,000 loss on disposal of the discontinued operation, which results in a total of $17,280 under discontinued operations, properly reported on Pursifull's income statement for 2000.

Extraordinary Items

extraordinary item A gain or loss that is both unusual in nature and infrequent in occurrence. One of the nonrecurring items shown net of tax on the income statement.

For an event to result in an **extraordinary item** under GAAP, the event must be **both** unusual in nature and infrequent in occurrence. If an event is either unusual in nature or infrequent in occurrence, it qualifies as a special expense reported in the operating expenses or special revenue reported in other revenues and gains segment of the income statement. The statement preparer must exercise judgment in deciding whether to classify the result of an event as an extraordinary item or a special item in continuing operations.

When applying the criterion of "unusual in nature," the accountant must consider the operating environment of the business entity.

> The environment of an entity includes such factors as the characteristics of the industry or industries in which it operates, the geographical location of its operations, and the nature and extent of government regulation. Thus, an event or transaction may be unusual in nature for one entity but not for another because of differences in their respective environments.
>
> —(*APB Opinion No. 30*, paragraph 21)

So, a gain or loss that would be considered unusual for one company might be considered an ordinary event for another company.

Accountants must also consider the operating environment of the entity when applying the criterion of "infrequent in occurrence." To be considered infrequent, an event must not be expected to recur in the foreseeable future.

As you use financial statement information, a basic appreciation of how these criteria are applied will enhance your ability to interpret the impact of extraordinary items. The following events or transactions meet the criteria of both unusual and infrequent and should therefore be presented as extraordinary items on the income statement.

1. A hailstorm destroys a large portion of a tobacco manufacturer's crops in an area where hailstorms are rare.
2. A steel fabricating company sells the only land it owns. The company acquired the land 10 years ago for future expansion but shortly thereafter abandoned all plans for expansion and held the land for appreciation in value instead.
3. A company sells a block of common stock of a publicly traded company. The block of shares, which represents less than 10 percent of the publicly held company, is the only security investment the company has ever made.
4. An earthquake in Texas destroys one of the oil refineries owned by a large multinational oil company.

Discussion Question

10–14. The following examples do not qualify as extraordinary items. For each one, explain specifically what criterion/criteria have not been met.

    a. A citrus grower's Florida crop is damaged by frost. . . .

    b. A company which operates a chain of warehouses sells excess land around one of its warehouses. Normally, when the company buys land for a new warehouse, it buys more land than it needs for the warehouse expecting that the land will appreciate in value. . . .

    c. A large diversified company sells from its portfolio a block of shares which it has acquired for investment purposes. This is the first sale from its portfolio of securities. . . .

    d. A textile manufacturer with only one plant moves to another location. It has not relocated a plant in twenty years and has no plans to do so in the foreseeable future. . . .

            —(AICPA Accounting Interpretations, AIN-APB30, #1)

Because extraordinary items enter the income statement after income from continuing operations, we present them net of tax. Return to the income statement for Pursifull, Inc. (Exhibit 10–6). Pursifull reported an extraordinary gain of $132,000 ($220,000 less income taxes of $88,000). This gain resulted from the city government's purchase of Pursifull's land adjacent to the municipal airport. The government expropriated the land to complete an airport expansion, and Pursifull had no choice but to sell the property to the government. Normally forced sales to government agencies do not create a taxable gain if the citizen or business entity replaces the property with property that costs as much as the proceeds of the sales. Because Pursifull decided not to replace the land, the transaction was taxable.

This type of transaction is both unusual in nature and infrequent in occurrence for Pursifull. Therefore we should report it as an extraordinary item.

Changes in Accounting Principles

One important factor in the usefulness of accounting information is consistency. In Chapter 3 we discussed how the need for this quality discourages companies from changing their accounting methods. However, from time to time, business entities do find it necessary to make changes. In fact, the Financial Accounting Standards Board views changes in accounting principles or standards as part of accounting's natural progression.

Consistent use of accounting principles from one accounting period to another, if pushed too far, can inhibit accounting progress. No change to a preferred accounting method can be made without sacrificing consistency, yet there is no way that accounting can develop without change. Fortunately, it is possible to make the transition from a less preferred to a more preferred method of accounting and still retain the capacity to compare the periods before and after the change if the effects of the change of method are disclosed.

            —(Statement of Accounting Concepts #2, paragraph 122)

cumulative effect of a change in accounting principle Results of adopting a new accounting standard or changing from one acceptable method of accounting to another. One of the nonrecurring items shown net of tax on the income statement.

Disclosure of the effects of these changes results in the third major type of nonrecurring item that is shown on the income statement net of tax: **cumulative effect of a change in accounting principle.** This nonrecurring item can result from either of two scenarios. Bear in mind, however, that in both cases the company must be changing from one acceptable accounting treatment to another acceptable treatment.

The first scenario involves the adoption of a newly required accounting standard. When a company applies a new accounting method required by the implementation of a new FASB standard, net income is often adversely affected. This effect on net income must be reported in the year of implementation of the new rule. However, often the impact of a new standard is actually a cumulative effect, so the presentation represents how the new standard would have affected income if it had been in place throughout the life of the company. When a new standard is implemented, the effect is considered to be a nonrecurring item and is presented net of tax on the income statement just before net income.

The second scenario occurs because a company has many acceptable choices to measure its transactions and events. A company may also choose to change from one acceptable method of accounting for an item to another acceptable method. For instance, in Chapter 8 we discussed two different methods for calculating periodic depreciation expense—straight-line and double-declining-balance—and in Chapter 9 we presented three different methods of accounting for the flow of inventory costs—FIFO, LIFO, and average cost. The choice among these methods can have a significant impact on reported net income for a period. Therefore, changes among these methods require proper presentation of the effect of the change on the income statement. The choice to change accounting methods should be made after careful consideration of all ramifications of such an action. Investors, creditors, the SEC, and IRS take a dim view of companies that change methods more than once.

The required presentation for a cumulative effect of a change in accounting principle is the same whether the change was caused by a new accounting rule or was a discretionary choice. For an illustration of this presentation, return once again to the example of Pursifull, Inc. This company began operation in 1971, and from the beginning it used the FIFO method to account for its inventory transactions. Then in 2000, Pursifull decided to change from the FIFO method to the average cost method. The effect of this change was a significant reduction in the company's cumulative net income. This arises because if we go back to 1971 and calculate the income as if the average cost method were used from 1971 to 2000, cost of goods sold would have been higher for the 30-year period, and therefore, net income would have been lower over that same time span.

The change represents a management decision made in 2000, so the effect must be reported in 2000. But to report the entire amount as an effect on cost of goods sold in 2000 would be misleading to those who use Pursifull's 2000 income statement to try to predict future results. Instead, Pursifull shows the cumulative effect of this change from FIFO to average cost as a nonrecurring item on the 2000 income statement (Exhibit 10–6).

In the 1996 income statements of the 600 companies surveyed by the authors of *Accounting Trends & Techniques*,[3] five companies reported accounting principle changes, 54 reported discontinued operations, and 63 reported extraordinary gain or loss items for a total of 122 nonrecurring events. In 1993, the total was 928 nonrecurring items. Over 50 percent of the 1993 events were due to new FASB requirements.

---

[3]*Accounting Trends & Techniques*, 290, 397, 402.

Exhibit 10–8

Pursifull's Stockholders' Equity Section of the Balance Sheet for December 31, 2000 and 1999

PURSIFULL, INC.
Stockholders' Equity Section
December 31

	2000	1999
Contributed Capital:		
9% Preferred Stock, $100 Par Value		
5,000 authorized, issued and outstanding	$ 500,000	$ 500,000
Common Stock, $10 Par Value, authorized 100,000		
shares, issued and outstanding 90,000 and 85,000	900,000	850,000
Additional Paid-in Capital	450,000	390,000
Total Contributed Capital	$1,850,000	$1,740,000
Retained Earnings	794,050	675,580
Total Stockholders' Equity	$2,644,050	$2,415,580

comprehensive income
The change in equity during a period from nonowner sources.

The FASB continues to change its requirements. In 1997, FASB released *SFAS No. 130* that requires companies to report comprehensive income. **Comprehensive income** measures all changes in equity from nonowner sources. (Owner sources include contributions made by owners and distributions to owners.) In many instances, especially for small companies, comprehensive income may be equal to the income on the income statement. Pursifull's stockholders' equity section appears in Exhibit 10–8.

Discussion Questions

10–15. How much did Pursifull receive from the sale of the stock? How much per share did Pursifull receive on average for the stock sold before 2000? During 2000?

10–16. How much did Pursifull pay in dividends during 2000? If dividends were paid after the sale of the common stock, how much did Pursifull pay per preferred share and per common share?

We can calculate Pursifull's comprehensive income by the following formula:

Comprehensive Income = Ending Equity − Beginning Equity − Owners' Contributions + Owners' Distributions

$208,470 = $2,644,050 − 2,415,580 − 110,000 + 90,000

This figure is equal to net income on the income statement plus several items of unrecognized and/or unrealized income currently included in stockholders' equity. FASB gave firms until 1998 to implement this requirement and a choice of one of three methods to comply with its provisions:

1. A separate statement of comprehensive income
2. A combined statement of income and comprehensive income
3. Special presentation in the statement of stockholders' equity

It appears that many firms will select the third option because that has been the practice in recent years. This issue is beyond the scope of this course, but we include the information because most of the annual reports you may examine will include comprehensive income in one of these places in the financial statements.

Comprehensive Income is an Accounting Element.

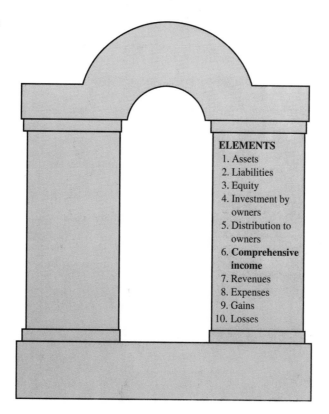

ELEMENTS
1. Assets
2. Liabilities
3. Equity
4. Investment by owners
5. Distribution to owners
6. **Comprehensive income**
7. Revenues
8. Expenses
9. Gains
10. Losses

EARNINGS PER SHARE

earnings per share (EPS)
A calculation indicating how much of a company's total earnings is attributable to each share of common stock.

Many investors and other financial statement users rely on one statistic more than any other to measure a company's performance—earnings per share. To comply with GAAP, income statements must disclose the firm's **earnings per share (EPS),** which reveals how much of a company's total earnings is attributable to each share of common stock. We calculate basic earnings per share with the following formula:

$$\text{Earnings per share} = \frac{\text{Net income} - \text{Preferred dividend requirement}}{\text{Weighted average number of shares of common stock oustanding}}$$

basic earnings per share
A simple calculation of earnings per share based on shares outstanding on the balance sheet date.

convertible securities
Debt or equity securities that can be converted into shares of the company's common stock.

diluted earnings per share
A calculation of earnings per share including all potentially dilutive securities.

GAAP require that two measures of EPS be calculated—basic and diluted. **Basic earnings per share** computes EPS based on the reality of the status of the company on the balance sheet date. If a company has convertible securities on its balance sheet, the current status of the company may change in the future. **Convertible securities** are debt or equity securities that owners may, at their option, convert to common stock. Examples are convertible bonds and convertible preferred stocks. Because these pose a possible dilutive threat to the current and future common stockholders, we must disclose the consequences of having such securities. The dilutive threat arises because the owners of the bonds or preferred stocks may convert these to common stock. The earnings must then be shared among more stockholders and the earnings per share will decrease. **Diluted earnings per share** includes the potential impact of any issued dilutive securities. When we calculate the diluted earnings per share, we modify the formula as if the conversion took place in the beginning of the year. We can illustrate the appropriate changes in the example.

Calculating Earnings per Share

Assume that each share of preferred stock is convertible into six shares of common stock and that Pursifull, Inc. sold the 5,000 shares of new stock on April 1, 2000. We must first compute the weighted average shares of stock outstanding for the year, similar to the way we computed the weighted average cost of inventory. Look at the following computational chart:

Date	(A) Number of Shares Outstanding	(B) Period of Time	(A) × (B)
January 1	85,000	3/12	21,250
April 1	90,000	9/12	67,500
	Weighted average shares		88,750

Now we can calculate basic and diluted earnings per share for Pursifull:

Basic Earnings per Share:

$$\text{EPS} = \frac{\text{Net income} - \text{Preferred dividend requirement}}{\text{Weighted average number of shares of common stock outstanding}}$$

$$= \frac{\$208,470 - (9\% \times \$500,000)}{88,750} = \frac{\$208,470 - \$45,000}{88,750}$$

$$= \$1.84 \text{ per share (rounded)}$$

Diluted Earnings per Share:

$$\text{EPS} = \frac{\text{Net income} - \text{Preferred dividend requirement}}{\text{Weighted average number of shares of common stock outstanding}}$$

$$= \frac{\$208,470 - 0}{88,750 + (6 \times 5,000)} = \frac{\$208,470}{118,750} = \$1.76 \text{ per share (rounded)}$$

To understand the calculation of diluted EPS, look first to the numerator of the equation. If the preferred stock is converted at the beginning of the year, there is no requirement to pay dividends for the year. The denominator changes because, if the preferred stock is converted, there will be an additional 30,000 shares outstanding all year. The result lowers the EPS by $0.08 per share and warns prospective investors that this is the worst-case scenario for the current earnings attributed to one share of stock.

Income Statement Presentation

GAAP require that basic and fully diluted earnings per share be prominently displayed on the income statement for each item on the income statement below income tax expense. Exhibit 10–9 illustrates the proper statement presentation for Pursifull, Inc.

We can look at the calculations of (a) through (f):

Basic EPS	Diluted EPS
(a) $\dfrac{\$96,390 - \$45,000}{88,750} = \$0.58$	$\dfrac{\$96,390}{118,750} = \$0.81$
(b) $\dfrac{\$71,280}{88,750} = \$0.80$	$\dfrac{\$71,280}{118,750} = \$0.60$
(c) $\dfrac{\$(54,000)}{88,750} = \$(0.61)$	$\dfrac{\$(54,000)}{118,750} = \$(0.46)$

PURSIFULL, INC.
Income Statement
For the Year Ended December 31, 2000

			Basic EPS	Diluted EPS	
Sales		$858,600			
Less: Cost of Goods Sold		456,800			
Gross Profit on Sales		$401,800			
Less: Operating Expenses:					
Selling	$ 94,450				
General and Administrative	116,050				
Total Operating Expenses		210,500			
Operating Income		$191,300			
Less: Interest Expense		30,650			
Income from Continuing Operations Before Taxes		$160,650			
Less: Income Taxes		64,260			
Income from Continuing Operations		$96,390	$.58	$.81	(a)
Discontinued Operations:					
Income from Discontinued Operations					
(Less: Income Taxes of $47,520)	$71,280		.80	.60	(b)
Loss on Disposal of Discontinued Operation					
(Less: Income Taxes of $36,000)	(54,000)	17,280	(.61)	(.46)	(c)
Income Before Extraordinary Item and Cumulative					
Effect of a Change in Accounting Principle		$113,370	$.77	$.95	(d)
Extraordinary Gain (Less: Income Taxes of $88,000)		132,000	1.49	1.11	(e)
Cumulative Effect of a Change in Accounting					
Principle (Less: Income Taxes of $24,800)		(37,200)	(.42)	(.31)	(f)
Net Income		$208,470	$1.84	$1.76	

(d) $\dfrac{\$113,370 - \$45,000}{88,750} = \$0.77$ $\qquad$ $\dfrac{\$113,370}{118,750} = \$0.95$

(e) $\dfrac{\$132,000}{88,750} = \$1.49$ $\qquad$ $\dfrac{\$132,000}{118,750} = \$1.11$

(f) $\dfrac{\$(37,200)}{88,750} = \$(0.42)$ $\qquad$ $\dfrac{\$(37,200)}{118,750} = \$(0.31)$

We have applied the EPS formula to each income item, treating that item as the numerator in place of net income. Notice that only the net income from continuing operations, net income before extraordinary items and accounting principle change, and net income subtract the preferred dividends from the numerator in computing basic earnings per share. Mathematically, you should ignore the preferred dividends in all other EPS calculations.

The income statement provides users with a great deal of information with which to predict the future amount and timing of a company's cash flows. Understanding the details of the information provided in an income statement will make you a wiser financial statement user. But one year's information is for a relatively short period of time—too short to be used in making many long-term economic decisions. For this reason, serious analysis of income statement and balance sheet information requires financial statements for more than one accounting period.

COMPARATIVE FINANCIAL STATEMENTS

comparative financial statements Financial statements showing results from two or more consecutive periods.

Comparative financial statements show results for two or more consecutive periods—usually years or quarters. Financial statement analysts use comparative statements to develop a sense of the big picture of the company's performance over time. Comparative statements help the statement user to find trends in the information that improve future income and cash flow predictions. Companies registered with the SEC are required to present at least two years' balance sheets and three years' income statements and cash flow statements plus selected financial information for at least five consecutive years. The Committee on Accounting Procedure described the importance of comparative financial statements this way:

> Such presentation emphasizes the fact that statements for a series of periods are far more significant than those for a single period and that the accounts for one period are but an installment of what is essentially a continuous history.
>
> —*(ARB 43*, Chapter 2, paragraph 1)

To illustrate the presentation of comparative financial statements, we provide the 2000 and 2001 income statements and balance sheets for Norton, Inc. in Exhibit 10–10.

Discussion Questions

10-17. Using the comparative income statements and balance sheets of Norton, Inc. presented in Exhibit 10–10, prepare the company's 2001 statement of retained earnings.

10-18. What specific information that was not apparent from Norton's income statements or balance sheets did the statement of retained earnings you developed for Discussion Question 10–17 provide?

Comparative financial statements enhance the user's ability to analyze a company's past performance and present condition. They also make it possible to perform several analytical techniques, which we will explore in later chapters. Financial statement analysis, in fact, begins with the use of the statement of cash flows—the fourth financial statement, which we introduce in the next chapter.

SUMMARY

Both the balance sheet and income statement are useful tools. By learning more about the construction and organization of these statements, users of balance sheet and income statement information are able to use the information contained in the statements more effectively.

The classified balance sheet separates assets into four major categories: current, long-term, investments, and intangibles. Liabilities on a classified balance sheet are separated into current and long-term. These classifications provide additional information to users of the information.

Income statements often include items that are not part of the company's normal operations and are not expected to recur. Inflows or outflows of this type must be separated from results of activities that are expected to recur as part of the company's

Exhibit 10–10
2001 and 2000 Financial Statements for Norton, Inc.

NORTON, INC.
Income Statements
For the Years Ended December 31, 2001 and 2000
(in thousands)

		2001		2000
Sales		$14,745		$12,908
Less: Cost of Goods Sold		10,213		8,761
Gross Profit on Sales		$ 4,532		$ 4,147
Less: Operating Expenses				
Selling	$1,022		$ 546	
General and Administrative	2,721		2,451	
Total Operating Expenses		3,743		2,997
Operating Income		$ 789		$ 1,150
Less: Interest Expense		172		137
Income Before Taxes		$ 617		$ 1,013
Less: Income Taxes		123		355
Net Income		$ 494		$ 658

NORTON, INC.
Balance Sheets
December 31, 2001 and December 31, 2000
(in thousands)

Assets:		2001		2000
Current Assets:				
Cash		$ 2,240		$1,936
Accounts Receivable		2,340		2,490
Merchandise Inventory		776		693
Prepaid Expenses		200		160
Total Current Assets		$ 5,556		$5,279
Plant and Equipment:				
Buildings	$7,723		$6,423	
Less: Accumulated Depreciation	3,677		3,534	
Buildings, Net		$ 4,046		$2,889
Equipment	$2,687		$2,387	
Less: Accumulated Depreciation	1,564		1,523	
Equipment, Net		1,123		864
Total Plant and Equipment		$ 5,169		$3,753
Total Assets		$10,725		$9,032
Liabilities:				
Current Liabilities:				
Accounts Payable		$ 1,616		$1,080
Notes Payable		2,720		2,920
Total Current Liabilities		$ 4,336		$4,000
Long-Term Liabilities		2,000		1,600
Total Liabilities		$ 6,336		$5,600
Stockholders' Equity:				
Common Stock, No Par Value		$ 3,000		$2,400
Retained Earnings		1,389		1,032
Total Stockholders' Equity		$ 4,389		$3,432
Total Liabilities and Stockholders' Equity		$10,725		$9,032

normal, ongoing operations. Reporting recurring items and nonrecurring items separately offers financial statement users additional useful information. Three major types of nonrecurring items (discontinued operations, extraordinary items, and changes in accounting principles) are presented below income from continuing operations and are shown net of tax. The other most common type of nonrecurring item, one that is unusual or infrequent but not both, is shown within the section of the income statement related to continuing operations, but is identified as a special item.

Comprehensive income represents the change in equity from nonowner sources. GAAP now require that comprehensive income be prominently displayed in the financial statements. GAAP also require that basic and diluted earnings per share be disclosed on the income statement for each item of income from *income from continuing operations* through *net income*. Comparative financial statements, providing information for two or more consecutive periods, offer a clearer view of a company's performance and financial position.

APPENDIX—
RECORDING INCOME TAX EXPENSE

In previous chapters we ignored the effect of income taxes on income statements. Because proprietorships and partnerships have no income taxes, this treatment is proper for them. However, a corporation pays corporate income taxes because it has the legal status of a person. Accounting for income taxes requires two basic entries and requires three new accounts. We will make entries to:

1. Accrue the income tax expense as computed for the income statement.
2. Record the payment of accrued taxes.
3. Record the payment of prepaid or estimated taxes.

To make these entries we will need the following accounts:

1. Expense account—Income Tax Expense
2. Current liability account—Income Taxes Payable
3. Prepaid asset account—Prepaid Income Taxes

We can look at the Pursifull, Inc. example in Exhibit 10–6 on page F-381 and prepare the journal entries to record the expense and the liability. We make the entries to record the expense and liability for the income taxes without regard to the character of the income tax. Remember that the aim of recording and reporting differ. Recording accumulates the reality of measurement of transactions and events (data) while reporting provides information (organized data) to users. In the recording process, we record Pursifull's total income tax expense and liability.

To record income tax expense and liability:

2000		Debit	Credit
December 31	Income Tax Expense	138,980	
	Income Taxes Payable		138,980
	To record the 2000 expense		
	per the income statement.		

($64,260 + $47,520 − $36,000 + $88,000 − $24,800)

Assume that Pursifull paid the resulting liability on March 15, 2001, when the CFO filed the corporate tax return.

To record payment of tax liability:

2001		Debit	Credit
January 15	Income Taxes Payable	138,980	
	Cash		138,980
	To record payment of 2000 income taxes.		

The Internal Revenue Service has requirements for corporations to pay estimated income taxes four times each year, a concept similar to individuals allowing withholding taxes to be taken from each paycheck. This transfers money to the government during the year and prevents the corporations from using the cash for other purposes and being unable to pay the taxes at year end. Assume that on April 15, June 15, September 15, and December 15 Pursifull paid the IRS estimated taxes of $30,000 in anticipation of the 2000 expense and made a final payment on March 15, 2001, when the tax return was filed. Look how the entries would be made:

To record estimated tax payments:

2000		Debit	Credit
April 15	Prepaid Income Taxes	30,000	
	Cash		30,000
	To record estimated income tax payments for 2000.		

The entries for June 15, September 15, and December 15 would be exactly the same.

To record accrual of income tax expense:

December 31	Income Tax Expense	138,980	
	Prepaid Income Taxes		120,000
	Income Taxes Payable		18,980
	To record income tax expense for 2000.		

To record final payment of taxes:

2001			
March 15	Income Taxes Payable	18,980	
	Cash		18,980
	To record payment of the final tax liability for 2000.		

SUMMARY OF APPENDIX

We record income tax expense in the same manner as other expenses. The cash outflow may precede the expense accrual and be recorded as a prepaid expense. The cash outflow may follow the accrual and extinguish the liability. In the recording process, we ignore income statement separation of the income tax expense into recurring and nonrecurring activities and add all the amounts together into one amount.

KEY TERMS

REVIEW THE FACTS

A. What was the original purpose of accounting records?
B. What caused the shift in attention from the balance sheet to the income statement?
C. Explain why a decision maker may prefer a classified balance sheet to one using the simplest possible format.
D. What is the difference between current and long-term assets? Offer two examples of each.
E. In what order are assets presented on a classified balance sheet?
F. Describe investment and intangible assets and provide two examples of each that are not listed in the chapter.
G. Describe the difference between current and long-term liabilities and provide two examples of each.
H. Explain the difference between recurring and nonrecurring items on an income statement. Why are these items reported separately?
I. Identify the three major types of nonrecurring items that are shown net of tax on the income statement.
J. Explain the effect of taxes on both gains and losses.
K. What is a business segment?
L. What criteria must be met for an item to be considered extraordinary?
M. What does the cumulative effect of a change in accounting principle represent?
N. Define comprehensive income.
O. Define earnings per share and distinguish between basic and diluted earnings per share.
P. Describe comparative financial statements and explain their benefits to economic decision makers.

APPLY WHAT YOU HAVE LEARNED

LO 2:   Balance Sheet Terminology

10–19. Presented below are items related to the organization of the classified balance sheet, followed by the definitions of those items in scrambled order.

a. Liquidity
b. Current assets
c. Long-term assets
d. Current liabilities
e. Intangible asset
f. Long-term liabilities

g. Stockholders' equity
h. Total liabilities and
   stockholders' equity
i. Plant and equipment, net
j. Investments

1. _____ Obligations not requiring payment within the next year
2. _____ Items controlled by a company that are not expected to become cash within the next year
3. _____ Describes an item's nearness to cash
4. _____ The owners' residual interest in a corporation
5. _____ Long-lived tangible assets less all the depreciation expense ever recognized on those assets
6. _____ Obligations that must be retired within the next year
7. _____ Equal to total assets
8. _____ Items controlled by a company that are expected to become cash within the next year
9. _____ An investment in a contractual arrangement such as a patent
10. _____ A long-term commitment to ownership of other entities

REQUIRED:
Match the letter next to each item with the appropriate definition. Each letter will be used only once.

LO 2: Balance Sheet Accounts

10–20. **a.** What are investments on a balance sheet and how are they classified?
b. Provide three examples of investments and discuss how they would be classified on the balance sheet.

LO 2: Balance Sheet Accounts

10–21. **a.** Define intangible assets in your own words.
b. Provide three examples of intangible assets and discuss how they would be classified on the balance sheet.
c. What is the term applied to the process of matching the cost of an intangible with the periods of time benefited or with the revenues they help to create?

LO 2: Balance Sheet Accounts

10–22. Presented below are the major sections of the classified balance sheet, followed by a list of items normally shown on the balance sheet.

a. Current assets		**e.** Long-term liabilities	
b. Long-term assets		**f.** Contributed capital	
c. Current liabilities		**g.** Retained earnings	
d. Intangible asset		**h.** Investments	

1. _____ Accounts payable
2. _____ Common stock
3. _____ Franchise
4. _____ Accounts receivable
5. _____ Note payable due within one year
6. _____ Prepaid expenses
7. _____ Preferred stock
8. _____ Note payable due in two years
9. _____ Amounts earned by the company but not yet distributed to the owners of the business
10. _____ Amounts received in excess of par value on the sale of stock

11. _____ Bonds held for the interest to be earned
12. _____ Land
13. _____ Stock of a subsidiary
14. _____ Wages payable
15. _____ Vehicles
16. _____ Copyright
17. _____ Cash
18. _____ Buildings
19. _____ Bonds payable
20. _____ Trade mark

REQUIRED:

Indicate where each item on the list should be shown on the classified balance sheet by placing the letter of the appropriate balance sheet section in the space provided. The letters may be used more than once.

LO 2:   Preparation of Balance Sheet

10–23. The following items relate to the Dana Corporation at December 31, 2002:

Land	$210,000
Cash	14,600
Accounts Receivable	92,300
Accounts Payable	74,000
Common Stock (75,000 Shares Outstanding)	300,000
Bonds Payable	100,000
Additional Paid-in Capital—Common Stock	10,000
Inventory	118,000
Prepaid Expenses	11,200
Taxes Payable	17,000
Short-Term Note Payable	50,000
Buildings and Equipment	400,000
Retained Earnings	?
Wages Payable	35,800

Accumulated Depreciation (which is not reflected in the previous totals) is $142,000 on the Buildings and Equipment.

REQUIRED:

a. What is the par value of Dana Corporation's common stock? Explain how you determined your answer.
b. How much cash did Dana Corporation receive from the sale of its common stock? Explain how you determined your answer.
c. Prepare a classified balance sheet for Dana Corporation at December 31, 2002.

LO 2:   Preparation of Balance Sheet

10–24. The following items relate to Wesnidge and Company at December 31, 2003:

Accounts Payable	$172,000
Common Stock ($2 Par Value)	400,000
Bonds Payable	307,700
Prepaid Expenses	9,800
Taxes Payable	47,000

Short-Term Note Payable	70,000
Buildings and Equipment	875,000
Additional Paid-in Capital—Common Stock	240,000
Land	490,000
Cash	124,200
Accounts Receivable	212,000
Inventory	338,000
Retained Earnings	?
Wages Payable	77,600

Accumulated Depreciation (which is not reflected in the previous totals) is $271,000 on the Buildings and Equipment.

REQUIRED:

a. How many shares of Wesnidge and Company's common stock are outstanding at December 31, 2003? Explain how you determined your answer.

b. How much cash did Wesnidge and Company receive from the sale of its common stock? Explain how you determined your answer.

c. Prepare a classified balance sheet for Wesnidge and Company at December 31, 2003.

LO 2: Preparation of Balance Sheet

10–25. The following items relate to the Janis Marple Company at December 31, 2002:

Accounts Payable	$516,000
Common Stock ($2 Par Value)	800,000
Bonds Payable	923,100
Prepaid Expenses	29,400
Taxes Payable	141,000
Short-Term Note Payable	210,000
Buildings and Equipment	985,000
Additional Paid-in Capital—Common Stock	240,000
Land	690,000
Cash	124,200
Accounts Receivable	212,000
Inventory	338,000
Retained Earnings	?
Wages Payable	132,800

Accumulated Depreciation (which is not reflected in the previous totals) is $385,000 on the Buildings and Equipment.

REQUIRED:

a. How many shares of Marple Company's common stock are outstanding at December 31, 2002? Explain how you determined your answer.

b. How much cash did Marple Company receive from the sale of its common stock? Explain how you determined your answer.

c. Prepare a classified balance sheet for Marple Company at December 31, 2002.

LO 2: Classified Balance Sheet

10–26. Assets on the classified balance sheet are identified as either current or long-term. Liabilities on the classified balance sheet are also identified as either current or long-term.

REQUIRED:

a. What criterion is used to determine whether an asset or liability is classified as current or long-term?

b. Explain in your own words why the following parties would be interested in the separation of current and long-term assets and liabilities on a company's balance sheet:

  (1) Short-term creditors (other businesses from whom the company buys inventory, supplies, etc.)

  (2) Long-term creditors (banks and others from whom the company borrows money on a long-term basis)

  (3) The company's stockholders

  (4) The company's management

LO 2: Classified Balance Sheet

10–27. Stockholders' equity on the classified balance sheet of a corporation is divided into two major categories: contributed capital and retained earnings.

REQUIRED:

a. Explain in your own words what each of the two major categories under stockholders' equity represents.

b. Explain in your own words why the following parties would be interested in the relative amounts of contributed capital and retained earnings in the stockholders' equity section of a company's balance sheet:

  (1) Short-term creditors (other businesses from whom the company buys inventory, supplies, etc.)

  (2) Long-term creditors (banks and others from whom the company borrows money on a long-term basis)

  (3) The company's stockholders

  (4) The company's management

LO 3: Income Statement Terminology

10–28. Presented below are several sections of the multistep income statement, followed by several independent situations or transactions.

a. Sales	d. Discontinued operation
b. Cost of goods sold	e. Extraordinary item
c. Income from continuing operations	f. Change in accounting principle

1. _____ A manufacturing company sells a warehouse with a book value of $20,000 for $20,000.

2. _____ A company changed from the FIFO method to the average cost method of accounting for inventory cost flows.

3. _____ A company sells units of inventory in the normal course of its business operation.

4. _____ A company located in San Francisco, California, experiences a loss from earthquake damage. This loss is determined to be a "special" item.

5. _____ A company disposes of a major segment of its business.

6. _____ A company pays wages, rent, utilities, and so forth.

7. _____ A company located in Columbia, South Carolina, experiences a loss from earthquake damage. This loss is determined to be both unusual in nature and infrequent in occurrence.

8. _____ A company adopts a newly required accounting standard for accounting for postretirement benefits other than pensions. As a result, net income for the year is adversely affected.

REQUIRED:
Indicate where the result of each situation or transaction should be shown on the multistep income statement by placing the letter of the appropriate income statement section in the space provided. The letters may be used more than once. Note: The results of some situations or transactions may not be shown on the income statement. If so, place the letter *n* in the space provided.

LO 3:   Income Statement Terminology

10–29. Presented below are items related to the multistep income statement as discussed in this chapter, followed by the definitions of those items in scrambled order.

a. Gross profit on sales
b. Operating expenses
c. Income from continuing operations
d. Discontinued operation

e. Extraordinary item
f. Change in accounting principle
g. Recurring item
h. Nonrecurring item

1. _____ A material gain or loss that is both unusual in nature and infrequent in occurrence
2. _____ Generally, the difference between normal ongoing revenues and normal ongoing expenses
3. _____ The difference between sales and cost of goods sold
4. _____ Any item that should not be considered a normal part of continuing operations because it is not expected to happen again
5. _____ Sacrifices incurred in the normal day-to-day running of a business
6. _____ Any item considered a normal part of continuing operations because it is expected to happen on an ongoing basis
7. _____ A change from a less preferred to a more preferred method of accounting
8. _____ The disposal of a business segment

REQUIRED:
Match the letter next to each item with the appropriate definition. Each letter will be used only once.

LO 3:   Income Tax Disclosure

10–30. a. What is the purpose of reporting discontinued items, extraordinary gains and losses, and the cumulative effect of changes in accounting principle net of income taxes?
b. Discuss the meaning of the phrase "net of tax" and how this is reported on the income statement.

LO 3:   Discontinued Operations

10–31. On March 1, 2001, the board of directors of the Tabitha Company approved the disposal of a segment of its business. For the period of January 1 through February 28, 2001, the segment had revenues of

$200,000 and expenses of $350,000. The company sold the assets of the segment at a loss of $100,000.

REQUIRED:
Describe how the corporation should report the previous information on the financial statements. Be as specific as possible.

LO 3:   Discontinued Operations

10–32. On July 1, 2002, the board of directors of Elwood Company approved the sale of a segment of its business. For the period of January 1 through June 30, 2002, the segment had revenues of $1,100,000 and expenses of $1,500,000. The company sold the assets of the segment at a gain of $200,000.

REQUIRED:
Describe how the corporation should report the previous information on the financial statements. Be as specific as possible.

LO 3:   Discontinued Operations

10–33. On October 1, 2003, the board of directors of Dodd Company approved the disposal of a segment of its business. For the period of January 1 through September 30, 2003, the segment had revenues of $1,500,000 and expenses of $2,500,000. The company sold the assets of the segment at a gain of $300,000.

REQUIRED:
Describe how the corporation should report the previous information on the financial statements. Be as specific as possible.

LO 4:   Multistep Income Statement

10–34. The following items relate to Kim Cook, Inc., for the year ended December 31, 2002:
- Sales for the year totaled $665,000.
- Cost of goods sold for the year totaled $271,000.
- Regular operating expenses for the year were $145,000.
- Interest expense for the year was $27,000.
- On February 18, 2002, one of Cook's warehouses burned to the ground. The company's loss (after the insurance settlement) was $106,000 before any tax effect. This loss was determined to be both unusual in nature and infrequent in occurrence.
- During 2002, Cook changed the way it depreciated its property, plant, and equipment from an accelerated method to the straight-line method. The cumulative effect of this change was a $93,000 increase in net income before any tax effect.
- Cook's income tax rate is 40% on all items.

REQUIRED:
Prepare Cook's income statement for the year ended December 31, 2002, using the expanded multistep format presented in this chapter.

LO 4: Multistep Income Statement

10–35. The following items relate to Linda Doyle and Company for the year ended December 31, 2003:
- Sales for the year totaled $575,000.
- Cost of goods sold for the year totaled $372,500.
- Regular operating expenses for the year were $121,500.
- Interest expense for the year was $16,000.
- On September 5, 2003, Doyle sold the only land it owned at a pretax gain of $50,000. The land was acquired in 1996 for future expansion, but shortly thereafter the company abandoned all plans for expansion and held the land for appreciation.
- During 2003, Doyle changed the way it accounted for inventory from the FIFO method to the average cost method. The cumulative effect of this change was an $80,000 decrease in net income before any tax effect.
- Doyle's income tax rate is 30% on all items.

REQUIRED:
Prepare Doyle's income statement for the year ended December 31, 2003, using the expanded multistep format presented in this chapter.

LO 4: Multistep Income Statement

10–36. The following items relate to Fred Cole Company for the year ended December 31, 2001:
- Sales for the year totaled $1,075,000.
- Cost of goods sold for the year totaled $667,000.
- Operating expenses for the year were $102,500.
- Interest expense for the year was $43,000.
- On June 30, 2001, Cole sold a major segment of its business at a loss of $95,000 before any tax effects. This segment of the company represented a major line of business that was totally separate from the rest of Cole's operation.
- Prior to being sold, the business segment had sales during 2001 of $150,000, cost of goods sold of $90,000, and operating expenses of $45,000. These amounts are not included in the previous information provided.
- Cole's income tax rate is 40% on all items.

REQUIRED:
Prepare Cole's income statement for the year ended December 31, 2001, using the expanded multistep format presented in this chapter.

LO 4: Multistep Income Statement

10–37. The following items relate to Toni Bradshaw, Inc. for the year ended December 31, 2002:
- Sales for the year totaled $465,000.
- Cost of goods sold for the year totaled $239,000.
- Operating expenses for the year were $113,200.
- Interest expense for the year was $11,000.
- On July 16, 2002, Bradshaw sold a major segment of its business at a gain of $50,000 before any tax effects. This segment of the company represented a major line of business that was totally separate from the rest of Bradshaw's operation.

- Prior to being sold, the business segment had sales during 2002 of $60,000, cost of goods sold of $40,000, and operating expenses of $35,000. These amounts are not included in the previous information provided.
- Bradshaw's income tax rate is 30% on all items.

REQUIRED:

Prepare Bradshaw's income statement for the year ended December 31, 2002, using the expanded multistep format presented in this chapter.

LO 4:   Discussion of Income Statement

10–38. The multistep income statement as presented in this chapter separates recurring items from nonrecurring items. Further, three major types of nonrecurring items are shown on the income statement net of tax.

REQUIRED:

a. Explain in your own words the rationale behind showing recurring and nonrecurring items separately on the multistep income statement.
b. Explain in your own words what the phrase "net of tax" means and why three major types of nonrecurring items are shown in this manner on the income statement.

LO 5:   Earnings Per Share—Simple Capital Structure

10–39. The Jacobs Company reported income after taxes for the year ended December 31, 2002, of $337,600. At the end of the year 2002, the Jacobs Company had the following shares of capital stock outstanding:
Preferred Stock, 5%, $200 par value, nonconvertible, 10,000 issued and outstanding.
Common Stock, $2 par value, 40,000 shares issued and outstanding.

REQUIRED:

Calculate basic earnings per share for 2002.

LO 5:   Earnings Per Share—Simple Capital Structure

10–40. The Schweizer Company reported income after taxes for the year ended December 31, 2002, of $337,600. During the year 2002, the Schweizer Company had the following shares of capital stock outstanding:
Preferred Stock, 5%, $200 par value, nonconvertible, 10,000 issued and outstanding.
Common Stock, $2 par value, 40,000 shares issued and outstanding on January 1, 2002.
Additional 5,000 shares issued April 1, 2002.

REQUIRED:

Calculate basic earnings per share for 2002.

LO 5:   Earnings Per Share—Simple Capital Structure

10–41. The Ward Company reported income after taxes for the year ended December 31, 2002, of $775,200. During the year 2002, the Ward Company had the following shares of capital stock outstanding:
Preferred Stock, 5%, $100 par value, nonconvertible, 20,000 issued and outstanding.

Common Stock, $3 par value, 80,000 shares issued and outstanding on January 1, 2002.

Additional 10,000 shares issued July 1, 2002.

REQUIRED:

Calculate basic earnings per share for 2002.

LO 5: Earnings per Share—Complex Capital Structure

10–42. The Schweizer Company reported income after taxes for the year ended December 31, 2002, of $337,600. During the year 2002, the Schweizer Company had the following shares of capital stock outstanding:

Preferred Stock, 5%, $200 par value, 10,000 issued and outstanding, each share convertible into three shares of common stock.

Common Stock, $2 par value, 40,000 shares issued and outstanding on January 1, 2002.

Additional 5,000 shares issued October 1, 2002.

REQUIRED:

a. Calculate basic earnings per share.
b. Calculate diluted earnings per share.

LO 5: Earnings per Share—Complex Capital Structure

10–43. The Ward Company reported income after taxes for the year ended December 31, 2002, of $775,200. During the year 2002, the Ward Company had the following shares of capital stock outstanding:

Preferred Stock, 5%, $100 par value, convertible, 20,000 issued and outstanding. Each share of preferred stock is convertible into five shares of common stock.

Common Stock, $3 par value, 80,000 shares issued and outstanding on January 1, 2002.

Additional 10,000 shares issued July 1, 2002.

REQUIRED:

a. Calculate basic earnings per share.
b. Calculate diluted earnings per share.

LO 5: Earnings per Share—Complex Capital Structure

10–44. The Ward Company reported income after taxes for the year ended December 31, 2002, of $775,200. During the year 2002, the Ward Company had the following shares of capital stock outstanding:

Preferred Stock, 5%, $100 par value, convertible, 20,000 issued and outstanding. Each share of preferred stock is convertible into five shares of common stock.

Common Stock, $3 par value, 80,000 shares issued and outstanding on January 1, 2002.

Additional 10,000 shares issued April 1, 2002.

Additional 5,000 shares issued October 1, 2002.

REQUIRED:

a. Calculate basic earnings per share.
b. Calculate diluted earnings per share.

LO 7: Income Tax Entries

*10–45. The Hassenfuss Company reports $385,000 of net income subject to a 40% tax rate. The company has paid timely estimated tax payments of $87,000.

REQUIRED:

Prepare the journal entry to record the income tax expense and the remaining liability for the year.

LO 7: Income Tax Entries

*10–46. The Warren Company reports $160,000 of net income before taxes and an extraordinary gain of $10,000. The company is subject to a 30% tax rate. The company has paid timely estimated tax payments of $25,000.

REQUIRED:

Prepare the journal entry or entries to record the income tax expense and the remaining liability for the year.

LO 7: Income Tax Entries

*10–47. The Xena Corporation reports $200,000 of net operating income before taxes and an extraordinary loss of $25,000. The company is also reporting a loss from discontinued operations of $70,000. The company is subject to a 35% tax rate. The company has paid timely estimated tax payments of $10,000.

REQUIRED:

Prepare the journal entry or entries to record the income tax expense and the remaining liability for the year.

FINANCIAL REPORTING CASES

Comprehensive

10–48. Visit the PHLIP Web site for this book at www.prenhall.com/jones for the link to Abercrombie and Fitch. Locate the financial statements and answer the following questions.

REQUIRED:

a. Determine the amount of extraordinary gain or loss incurred by the company. What gave rise to the extraordinary gain or loss?

b. Does the company report any disposals of segments? If so, how much do they report and what segment or segments were disposed?

c. Does the company report a cumulative effect of an accounting change? If so, what is the nature of the change in principle and what is the dollar amount?

d. What is the amount of earnings per share? Does the company report both basic and diluted earnings per share? If so, how much of each?

e. What is the amount of current assets and current liabilities reported by the company? Explain the meaning of these figures.

f. Does the company report comprehensive income on the financial statements? If so, how is it reported (as part of the income statement or as a completely separate statement)?

Comprehensive

10–49. Visit the PHLIP Web site for this book at www.prenhall.com/jones for the link to American Airlines. Locate the financial statements and answer the following questions.

REQUIRED:

a. Determine the amount of extraordinary gain or loss incurred by the company. What gave rise to the extraordinary gain or loss?
b. Does the company report any disposals of segments? If so, how much do they report and what segment or segments were disposed?
c. Does the company report a cumulative effect of an accounting change? If so, what is the nature of the change in principle and what is the dollar amount?
d. What is the amount of earnings per share? Does the company report both basic and diluted earnings per share? If so, how much of each?
e. Does the company report comprehensive income on the financial statements? If so, how is it reported (as part of the income statement or as a completely separate statement)?

Comprehensive

10–50. Go to the PHLIP Web site for this book at www.prenhall.com/jones for the link to Ford Motor Company. Locate the financial statements and answer the following questions.

REQUIRED:

a. Determine the amount of extraordinary gain or loss incurred by the company. What gave rise to the extraordinary gain or loss?
b. Does the company report any disposals of segments? If so, how much do they report and what segment or segments were disposed?
c. Does the company report a cumulative effect of an accounting change? If so, what is the nature of the change in principle and what is the dollar amount?
d. What is the amount of earnings per share? Does the company report both basic and diluted earnings per share? If so, how much of each?
e. What is the amount of retained earnings reported by the company? Explain what this figure represents.
f. Does the company report comprehensive income on the financial statements? If so, how is it reported (as part of the income statement or as a completely separate statement)?

ANNUAL REPORT PROJECT

10–51. At this point in your preparation of the annual report project you will locate information that will help you in the final phase of the report. In this segment you only need to fill in the blanks with the requested information. This information will be used to prepare the required ratios at the end of Chapter 12. By preparing the information at this point, the computations will require minimal time and effort.

From the financial statements in your annual report locate or determine the following items. Remember that you might have to review footnotes if you do not find a particular piece of information.

Current Assets   _____

Current Liabilities   _____

Working Capital (CA-CL)   _____

Quick Assets   _____

Total Assets   _____

Total Liabilities   _____

Net Worth   _____

Sales   _____

Accounts Receivable   _____

Cost of Sales   _____

Inventory   _____

Net Income Before Taxes   _____

Net Income After Taxes   _____

Total Equity   _____

Interest Expense   _____

After you have completed this worksheet you need only retain it to complete the ratios at the end of Chapter 12.

Chapter 11

Tools of the Trade, Part III
The Statement of Cash Flows:
Bringing the Focus Back to Cash

Your business has been growing by leaps and bounds. It seems that your customers cannot get enough of the product and the order department continues to add new employees. Your CPA moans constantly about trying to reduce the taxes on your climbing net income. You added two new inventory warehouses and still have only a week's supply of inventory on hand. At the same time, the controller continually complains about being short of cash. How can such a thriving business be short of cash? You do not know whether the CPA cannot count or someone is stealing cash. Your CPA guarantees that if you read the statement of cash flows, it might answer all of your questions. What is a statement of cash flows?

We have explored three major financial statements: the income statement, the statement of owners' equity, and the balance sheet. We focused on information produced under the accrual basis of measurement. Recall that accrual accounting is affected by a number of items, which we have also discussed:

- Determining when revenue should be recognized under accrual accounting
- Matching expenses to the same income statement period as the revenues they helped generate
- Estimating the useful life and residual value required for depreciation
- Choosing the inventory cost flow assumption (e.g., FIFO, LIFO) and depreciation method (e.g., straight-line or double-declining-balance method). ■

These are just a few of the items that cause net income under accrual accounting to be different from the change in cash.

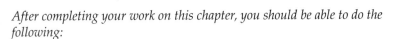

Considering the number of estimates and assumptions necessary to measure accrual accounting, this statement rings true. As we promised in Chapter 6, however, the accounting profession put the eye back on cash by requiring a fourth financial statement tool: the statement of cash flows. When information from this additional source is combined with the information contained in the other three financial statements, decision makers have a more complete picture of a company's financial health.

LEARNING OBJECTIVES

After completing your work on this chapter, you should be able to do the following:

1. Explain the purpose of the statement of cash flows.
2. Describe the three types of activities that can either generate or use cash in any business.
3. Reconcile accrual net income to the change in cash.
4. Determine where a company obtains its financing by examining its statement of cash flows.

BASIC ORGANIZATION OF THE STATEMENT OF CASH FLOWS

statement of cash flows
A financial statement that provides information about the causes of a change in a company's cash balance from the beginning to the end of a specific period.

working capital The difference between current assets and current liabilities.

In its present format, the **statement of cash flows** has existed only since 1988. However, other forms of the statement have been in existence for a very long time. These earlier forms were known by such names as the "statement of source and application of funds" and the "statement of changes in financial position." The earlier versions had similar objectives as today's statement of cash flows but focused on working capital rather than on cash in the analysis. **Working capital** consists of current assets and current liabilities. So although they helped users interpret the impact of accrual accounting procedures, they did not bring the financial statement user's focus firmly back to cash.

Discussion Question

11-1. How do revenue recognition and expense recognition criteria under accrual accounting take the focus off cash?

In addition to providing information about a company's cash receipts and cash payments during a specific period, the statement of cash flows helps investors, creditors, and other external parties to:

1. Assess a company's ability to generate positive future net cash flows
2. Assess a company's need for external financing and its ability to pay its debts and pay dividends
3. Assess a company's overall financial health
4. Reconcile the differences between net income and the change in cash

As you recall from Chapter 6, a firm performs four functions—it operates to generate revenues, invests earnings to support operations, finances operating and investing activities, and makes decisions. To accomplish the disclosure objectives previously listed, we separate the cash inflows and outflows into three categories that conform to the first three functions of a firm:

Operating
Investing
Financing

Exhibit 11–1 contains the basic format of the statement of cash flows.

Exhibit 11–1
Basic Form of the Statement of Cash Flows

Statement of Cash Flows		
For the Year Ended December 31, 2000		
Cash Flows from Operating Activities:		
	$ XXX	
	XX	
Net Cash Provided (Used) by Operating Activities		$XXX
Cash Flows from Investing Activities:		
	$ XX	
	XX	
Net Cash Provided (Used) by Investing Activities		XXX
Cash Flows from Financing Activities:		
	$XXXX	
	XX	
Net Cash Provided (Used) by Financing Activities		XXX
Net Increase (Decrease) in Cash during 2000		$XXX
Beginning Cash Balance, January 1, 2000		XXX
Ending Cash Balance, December 31, 2000		$XXX

Discussion Question

11-2. If you owned a small bookstore, what do you think would be your

    a. operating activities?
    b. investing activities?
    c. financing activities?

Explain your reasons for the classifications you made.

To develop a statement of cash flows, we must identify the business activities that took place during the period and to categorize them as operating, investing, or financing activities. We now describe each type of activity in turn.

Operating Activities

Operating activities are those centered around the company's primary business activities. These activities generate the company's operating revenues and expenses and utilize the company's current assets and current liabilities. Operating cash inflows come from the firm's customers or from interest or dividends the company receives. Some customers pay for sales at the time of sale and others charge their purchases and pay for them later. Operating cash outflows come from the myriad of expenses a company incurs, whether paid for in cash as incurred or paid for later by paying accounts payable or other payables. How do the cash inflows and outflows differ from income measurement? For cash flow purposes, we measure only the cash inflow or outflows, not the revenues and expenses. Thus, we have come full circle back to the cash basis income.

Discussion Question

11-3. Where would you look for the information to determine net cash flow from operations if your business used the cash basis of accounting?

If you think about the items listed in the previous paragraph, you will see they are all items that are reported on the income statement. Therefore, when attempting to determine the cash inflow and cash outflow from operating activities, we start with the income statement for the period. If Troll's Toggery uses the cash basis of accounting, net income for the period will equal the net cash inflow (or outflow) for the period from operating activities. If, however, Troll's uses the accrual basis of accounting, the net income figure must be adjusted for any revenue item that did not provide cash during this income statement period and any expense item that did not use cash during this income statement period. You will discover that to determine the operating activities for the cash flow statement, you will analyze the income statement and the current assets and liabilities for items that represent accruals and deferrals of revenues and expenses. We will illustrate how this works later in the chapter.

Discussion Questions

11-4. Recall the situation in which you owned a small bookstore. If one of your customers placed a large book order on account and had 30 days after she received the books to pay for them, how would the revenue from this credit sale be reported for your company
   a. on a cash basis?
   b. on an accrual basis?

11-5. Continuing this scenario, for your company's statement of cash flows, how would you determine the net cash flow from operations in an accrual basis accounting system?

Investing Activities

investing activities
Business activities related to long-term assets. Examples are the purchase and sale of property, plant, and equipment.

Investing activities provide the resources that support operations. This support may take the form of either investments in assets necessary to the operation or investments outside the company to wisely use any excess funds. When a company invests in noncurrent assets, it uses cash. When it sells these assets, it receives cash inflow.

Companies normally sell these types of assets when they are no longer useful to the firm. However, a company cannot logically sell assets it needs to run its operations because the cash generated through operating activities would eventually cease. An airline could generate cash by selling all its airplanes, but if it did so, it would no longer be able to transport passengers and would go out of business. Instead of selling its property, plant, and equipment to generate cash, a growing and healthy company will likely use cash to acquire additional assets that can generate additional revenues. For this reason, healthy, growing companies frequently experience negative net cash flow from investing activities. In such an instance, negative investing cash flow represents economic health.

A company can use cash to purchase the stock of other companies or lend other companies money. Cash is generated when a company sells equity or debt investments (stocks or bonds of other companies). If you think about the examples of investing activities mentioned in the previous two paragraphs, you will see they all involve items that are reported in the noncurrent asset sections of the balance sheet. The only exceptions are current investments and cash loans made to other entities or individuals. All investments and cash loans, whether current or long term, are considered to be investing activities. Current assets, other than cash, that represent accruals of revenue or deferrals of expenses are classified as operating activities. Therefore, when attempting to determine the cash inflow and cash outflow from investing activities, you must analyze the current and long-term asset section of the balance sheets at both the start and the end of the period. We will demonstrate the process a little later in the chapter.

Financing Activities

financing activities
Business activities, such as the issuance of debt or equity and the payment of dividends, that focus on the external financing of the company.

Because internal financing is accomplished through operating activities, **financing activities** reported on the statement of cash flows deal only with external financing. A company obtains financing cash from two external sources: (1) selling common or preferred stock (equity financing) or (2) borrowing from lenders in the form of loans or issuing corporate bonds (debt financing). A company uses cash for financing activities when it repays loan or bond principal, pays dividends to shareholders, and purchases treasury stock. Notice that we included only the principal on borrowed money. Cash paid for interest expense is an operating cash outflow.

To determine the items that are reported in the financing activities of the cash flow statement we analyze the right side of the balance sheet, primarily the long-term liability or owners' equity section. Most of the current liabilities are involved with the operating activities, except for any liabilities representing cash borrowed from banks or other lenders. Any current liabilities that involve cash borrowed instead of expenses accrued are financing activities. Current liabilities that represent expense accruals or revenue deferrals are part of operating activities. We will demonstrate this analysis process a little later in the chapter.

Exhibit 11–2 summarizes the three types of business activities as they are reported in the statement of cash flows. You should refer to this exhibit often as we discuss the construction and uses of the statement, because every inflow and outflow of cash can be classified as a result of either operating, investing, or financing activities.

Exhibit 11-2
Summary of the Three
Types of Business
Activities Reported on
the Statement of Cash
Flows

Operating Activities (Income Statement Items)

Cash inflows:
From customers as a result of the sale of goods or services.
From interest earned on loans to others.
From dividends received from investment in the stock of other companies.

Cash outflows:
To suppliers for the purchase of inventory.
To employees for salaries and wages.
To governments for taxes.
To creditors for interest on loans.
To others for operating expenses.

Investing Activities (Long-Term Asset Items)

Cash inflows:
From the sale of property, plant, and equipment.
From the sale of investments in debt or equity securities of other companies.
From the collection of monies loaned to others.

Cash outflows:
To purchase property, plant, and equipment.
To purchase debt and equity investments in other companies or loan money to others.

Financing Activities (Long-Term Liability and Owners' Equity Items)

Cash inflows:
From selling shares of common stock or preferred stock.
From selling treasury stock.
From loan proceeds or the sale of corporate bonds.

Cash outflows:
To pay dividends to stockholders.
To reacquire shares of capital stock from stockholders.
To repay principal of loans or redeem corporate bonds.

Before we begin to construct the statement of cash flows, we must recognize that the FASB allows us to use two different methods to present the operating cash flows.

Direct Method versus Indirect Method

The FASB allows two methods of preparing the operating section of the statement of cash flows: the direct method and the indirect method. Both arrive at exactly the same amount of cash flow from operations. The difference lies in how the information is presented.

When the FASB issued *SFAS No. 95*, which created the cash flow statement in its present form, it asked accountants to prepare the operating section under the direct method and include as a supplemental statement a "reconciliation of net income to operating cash flows" called the indirect method. It required that if the direct method were used, the reconciliation be a required supplemental statement, because the reconciliation links (or articulates) the cash flow statement to the income statement. However, if the preparer chose to use the reconciliation in place of the direct method, the preparer did not have to include the direct method but did have to include a supplemental statement indicating the amount of cash paid for interest and taxes.

direct method The format of a statement of cash flows that provides detail about the individual sources and uses of cash associated with operating activities.

indirect method The more widely used format of the statement of cash flows. This approach begins with a reconciliation of accrual net income to the cash provided by or used by operating activities.

The **direct method** uses a series of calculations to determine the amount of cash inflow (from customers, interest earned on loans, dividends received, etc.) and cash outflow (to suppliers, employees, creditors, for taxes and interest, etc.). The **indirect method** is more closely tied to accrual accounting. Unlike the direct method, it does not attempt to provide any detail about the individual sources and uses of cash associated with the operating activities of a company. When the indirect method is used, the operating section begins with the accrual net income for the period. Then adjustments are made for all items included in the calculation of net income that did not either generate or use cash.

Users (including students) find the direct method easier to read, but most preparers find it harder to prepare. Because preparers have to consider the costs and benefits of their work, they soon learn that it is always less work to prepare one statement than two. It did not take long for the indirect method to become the method of choice for most accountants. The detail concerning individual sources and uses of cash provided under the direct method may be useful, but few companies employ the direct approach. *Accounting Trends & Techniques* reports that of the 600 companies it surveyed in 1996, only 11 used the direct method for preparation of the statement's operating section.[1] Because the vast majority of firms use the indirect method, we will concentrate on the indirect method in this chapter, although we will demonstrate how to prepare and read the direct method.

CONSTRUCTION OF THE STATEMENT OF CASH FLOWS

We need three financial statements to prepare a statement of cash flows: two consecutive balance sheets and the income statement that bridges them. We will analyze and account for each change in the balance sheet accounts by utilizing the information contained in the income statement and balance sheets. If you think about it, the sum of all items on the left side of the balance sheet equals the sum of all items on the right side of the balance sheet. If we explain the difference in each account other than cash from the beginning to the end of the year, we have successfully explained the difference in cash from the beginning to the end of the year.

For our example, we will use the information provided by the comparative balance sheets of Pipkin Company for 2001 and 2000 in Exhibit 11–3, and assume Pipkin uses accrual accounting for its income statement in Exhibit 11–4. Be sure you understand that the balances in the asset, liability, and owners' equity accounts at the end of one period become the beginning balances in the next period. Thus, Exhibit 11–3 provides beginning and ending balances for all Pipkin Company's balance sheet accounts for the year 2001—necessary information for the preparation of the company's statement of cash flows for 2001.

There are six logical steps to prepare the cash flow statement:

1. Gather the information needed to prepare the statement:
   a. Comparative, consecutive balance sheets
   b. The income statement for the period between the two balance sheets
   c. Any other information needed about noncash transactions
2. Determine the net change in each account of the balance sheets.
3. Determine the method to use for the operating activities section and complete it.
4. Complete the investing activities section.

---

[1] *Accounting Trends & Techniques*, 495.

Exhibit 11–3
Comparative Balance Sheets for Pipkin Company for 2001 and 2000

PIPKIN COMPANY
Balance Sheets
December 31, 2001, and December 31, 2000
(in thousands)

Assets:		2001		2000
Current Assets:				
Cash		$ 2,800		$ 2,420
Accounts Receivable		2,925		3,112
Merchandise Inventory		970		866
Prepaid Expenses		250		200
Total Current Assets		$ 6,945		$ 6,598
Plant and Equipment:				
Buildings	$9,654		$8,029	
LESS: Accumulated Depreciation	4,597		4,417	
Buildings, Net		$ 5,057		$ 3,612
Equipment	$3,359		$2,984	
LESS: Accumulated Depreciation	1,955		1,904	
Equipment, Net		1,404		1,080
Total Plant and Equipment		$ 6,461		$ 4,692
Total Assets		$13,406		$11,290
Liabilities:				
Current Liabilities:				
Accounts Payable		$ 2,020		$ 1,816
Notes Payable		3,400		2,700
Total Current Liabilities		$ 5,420		$ 4,516
Long-Term Liabilities		2,500		2,000
Total Liabilities		$ 7,920		$ 6,516
Stockholders' Equity:				
Common Stock, No Par Value		$ 3,400		$ 3,000
Retained Earnings		2,086		1,774
Total Stockholders' Equity		$ 5,486		4,774
Total Liabilities and Stockholders' Equity		$13,406		$11,290

5. Complete the financing activities section.
6. Add the operating, investing, and financing activities to derive the net change in cash. Check to see whether it agrees with the balance sheet. If it does not, retrace steps one through five.

Step 1 Gather information:

    a. Balance sheets are in Exhibit 11–3.

    b. Income statement is in Exhibit 11–4.

    c. Additional information was gathered from Pipkin employees:

        (1) During 2001, Pipkin paid cash for a building for a total cost of $1,625,000 and equipment for a total cost of $375,000.

        (2) During 2001, Pipkin paid cash dividends to its stockholders of $137,000.

Exhibit 11–4
Income Statement for
Pipkin Company for
2001

PIPKIN COMPANY
Income Statement
For the Year Ended December 31, 2001
(in thousands)

Sales		$15,158
LESS: Cost of Goods Sold		11,151
Gross Margin		$ 4,007
LESS: Operating Expenses:		
Depreciation—Buildings	$ 180	
Depreciation—Equipment	51	
Other Selling and Administration	3,047	
Total Operating Expenses		3,278
Operating Income		$ 729
LESS: Interest Expense		160
Income Before Taxes		$ 569
Income Taxes		120
Net Income		$ 449

Discussion Questions

Refer to Exhibit 11–3 to answer the following questions:

11-6. What was Pipkin Company's balance in accounts
receivable on January 1, 2001? Did accounts receivable
increase or decrease during 2001?

11-7. What was Pipkin Company's balance in retained earnings
on January 1, 2001? What do you think caused the
increase from the beginning of 2001 to the end of the
year?

Before we tackle the preparation of the statement of cash flows, we should take
a few minutes to review Pipkin's balance sheets and income statement. There are
a few items you should note about the financial statements. First, if you look at the
cash balances on the two balance sheets in Exhibit 11–3, you will see that cash increased from the start of 2001 to the end of 2001 ($2,800 − $2,420 = $380). Note that
the Pipkin Company's financial statements are presented "in thousands" of dollars
so that the $380 increase in cash is really $380,000. What caused the increase? As we
discussed before, the increase was caused by all the cash transactions that caused
all other balance sheet accounts to change, including the net income. Remember
that net income causes the retained earnings account to change. The statement of
cash flows, if properly prepared and analyzed, will disclose exactly what caused
cash to change by the amount it did and will reconcile the net income figure with
that change in cash.

PIPKIN COMPANY

Statement of Cash Flows

For the Year Ended December 31, 2001

(in thousands)

Cash Flows from Operating Activities:	
Net Cash Provided (Used) by Operating Activities	$?
Cash Flows from Investing Activities:	
Net Cash Provided (Used) by Investing Activities	?
Cash Flows from Financing Activities:	
Net Cash Provided (Used) by Financing Activities	?
Net Increase (Decrease) in Cash during 2001	$ 380
Beginning Cash Balance, January 1, 2001	2,420
Ending Cash Balance, December 31, 2001	$2,800

Discussion Question

11–8. Back to the scenario in which you own a small bookstore. . . What cash flows could you receive or pay out in your book business that would not show up in cash basis net income?

Now we have all the necessary information to prepare Pipkin Company's statement of cash flows. This detailed explanation of the construction of this statement is not intended to make you an expert preparer, but rather to help you become a wiser user of this financial tool. Knowing how the amounts on a statement of cash flows were determined will help you to assess their usefulness and impact on your decision-making process.

We begin by creating a format for Pipkin's statement of cash flows in Exhibit 11–5.

Note two items about this format. First, it is divided into the three broad types of activities that can either generate or use cash (operating, investing, and financing). Second, we have already put three amounts into the statement (the $380,000 increase in cash from the end of 2000 to the end of 2001, and the beginning and ending cash balances). If nothing else, accounting is neat and tidy and the cash flow statement epitomizes this fact. The cash flow statement is one of the few accounting reports for which we know the result before we start to prepare it. In the case of Pipkin Company, we determined the change in cash by looking at the comparative balance sheets (Exhibit 11–3). Remember, the more important purpose of the statement of cash flows is not to disclose what the change in cash was, but to disclose what caused the change.

Step 2 Determine the net change in each account on the balance sheet:

See Exhibit 11–6. Notice that the increase (decrease) column adds up exactly like the balance sheet, and the net change in assets must equal the net change in liabilities and equity.

Step 3 Determine the method to use for the operating activities section:

We will first examine the direct method, and then the indirect method to prepare the operating activities section of the cash flow statement.

Exhibit 11–6
Comparative Balance
Sheets for Pipkin
Company for 2001
and 2000

PIPKIN COMPANY
Balance Sheets
December 31, 2001, and December 31, 2000
(in thousands)

Assets:	2001	2000	Increase (Decrease)
Current Assets:			
Cash	$ 2,800	$ 2,420	$ 380
Accounts Receivable	2,925	3,112	(187)
Merchandise Inventory	970	866	104
Prepaid Expenses	250	200	50
Total Current Assets	$ 6,945	$ 6,598	$ 347
Plant Equipment:			
Buildings	$ 9,654	$ 8,029	$1,625
LESS: Accumulated Depreciation	4,597	4,417	180
Buildings, Net	$ 5,057	$ 3,612	$1,445
Equipment	$ 3,359	$ 2,984	$ 375
LESS: Accumulated Depreciation	1,955	1,904	51
Equipment, Net	$ 1,404	$ 1,080	$ 324
Total Plant and Equipment	$ 6,461	$ 4,692	$1,769
Total Assets	$13,406	$11,290	$2,116
Liabilities:			
Current Liabilities:			
Accounts Payable	$ 2,020	$ 1,816	$ 204
Notes Payable	3,400	2,700	700
Total Current Liabilities	$ 5,420	$ 4,516	$ 904
Long-Term Liabilities	2,500	2,000	500
Total Liabilities	$ 7,920	$ 6,516	$1,404
Stockholders' Equity:			
Common Stock, No Par Value	$ 3,400	$ 3,000	$ 400
Retained Earnings	2,086	1,774	312
Total Stockholders' Equity	$ 5,486	$ 4,774	$ 712
Total Liabilities and Stockholders' Equity	$13,406	$11,290	$2,116

Determining Cash Flow from Operating Activities— Direct Method

SFAS No. 95 indicates that the preferred preparation method for the operating section is the direct method, supplemented by the reconciliation schedule. To prepare the direct method, we transform the income statement into a statement of cash receipts and disbursements by reversing the accruals and deferrals used in creating the accrual basis accounting. Does it seem that we are going backwards? We might consider it going forward in a circular pattern. We circle back to the cash view of the business because it presents the reality of cash. If we think of it as reversing the accrual process, it should not be very difficult. To accomplish this feat, we examine the income statement along with the current assets and current liabilities on the comparative balance sheets.

We begin by assembling our information and examining the format that we must use to create the direct method. Exhibit 11–7 contains the basic form for the direct method operating activities.

Exhibit 11-7
Basic Format of Direct
Method Operating
Activities of the Cash
Flow Statement

PIPKIN COMPANY

Statement of Cash Flows

For the Year Ended December 31, 2001

(in thousands)

Cash Flows from Operating Activities:		
Cash Received from Customers		$?
Cash Paid for:		
Merchandise	$?	
Operating Expenses	?	
Interest	?	
Income Taxes	?	
Net Cash Provided (Used) by Operating Activities		$?

We must determine five values to complete the operating section.

1. **Cash received from customers**—To determine the cash that customers paid, we must examine Sales and Accounts Receivable. Sales made during the period increase Accounts Receivable, and cash paid by customers decreases it. We can formulate the following mathematical relationship between sales, cash, and accounts receivable (A/R):

Beginning A/R + Sales − Customers' Cash Payments = Ending A/R

Anytime we know all but one item in an equation, we can solve for the unknown. We know the beginning and ending balances of Accounts Receivable from the comparative balance sheets and sales from the income statement. Therefore we can determine the amount of cash collected from customers as follows:

Beginning A/R + Sales − Customers' Cash Payments = Ending A/R
$3,112 + $15,158 − Customers' Cash Payments = $2,925
Customers' Cash Payments = $3,112 + $15,158 − $2,925
Customers' Cash Payments = $15,345

2. **Cash paid for merchandise**—To determine the cash paid for merchandise, we must look at the relationship between Cost of Goods Sold, Inventory, and Accounts Payable. Purchases of new merchandise increase the Inventory account and the cost of product sold decreases it. Purchases of new merchandise increase the Accounts Payable account, and payment of cash for purchases decreases it. We can establish the following mathematical relationship among Cost of Goods Sold, Inventory, Accounts Payable (A/P), and cash paid for merchandise:

Beginning Inventory + Purchases − Cost of Goods Sold = Ending Inventory

and

Beginning A/P + Purchases − Cash Paid for Merchandise = Ending A/P

By substituting information, we can determine the cash paid for merchandise:

Beginning Inventory + Purchases − Cost of Goods Sold = Ending Inventory

$866 + Purchases − $11,151 = $970
Purchases = $970 − $866 + $11,151
Purchases = $11,255

Beginning A/P + Purchases − Cash Paid for Merchandise = Ending A/P
$1,816 + $11,255 − Cash Paid for Merchandise = $2,020
Cash Paid for Merchandise = $1,816 + $11,255 − $2,020
Cash Paid for Merchandise = $11,051

3. **Cash paid for operating expenses**—To determine the cash paid for operating expenses, we examine the Operating Expenses on the income statement and Prepaid Expenses and Accrued Expenses on the balance sheet. When we incur operating expense, we frequently either pay them in advance (such as insurance or rent) or pay them after the fact (such as supplies, utilities, and wages). Prepaid Expenses is increased by payments of cash and decreased by recognition of the expense on the income statement. Incurring an expense increases Accrued Expenses and payment of the expense decreases the accrued expense account. We could establish the following mathematical relationships among Operating Expenses, Prepaid Expenses (PP Expenses), Accrued Expenses (AE), and cash paid for operating expenses:

Beginning PP Expenses + Cash Paid for Operating Expenses −
Expense Used = Ending PP Expenses

and

Beginning AE + Expense Used − Cash Paid for Operating Expenses = Ending AE

By substituting information from the balance sheet and income statement, we can determine the cash paid for operating expenses. Because Pipkin has no accrued expenses, we need only make the computation for prepaid expenses.

Beginning PP Expenses + Cash Paid for Operating Expenses − Expense Used =
Ending PP Expenses
$200 + Cash Paid for Operating Expenses − $3,047 = $250
Cash Paid for Operating Expenses = $250 − $200 + $3,047
Cash Paid for Operating Expenses = $3,097

4. **Cash paid for interest**—To determine the amount of cash paid for interest, we explore the relationship between Interest Expense and the liability for Accrued Interest. The passage of time without payment triggers interest expense which increases the Accrued Interest account and payment of interest decreases the account. We can formulate the following mathematical relationship among Interest Expense, Accrued Interest Expense, and cash payments for interest:

Beginning Accrued Interest + Interest Expense − Cash Interest Payments
= Ending Accrued Interest
$0 + $160 − Cash Interest Payments = $0
Cash Interest Payments = $160

We can therefore conclude that when there is no beginning and ending balance in the Accrued Expense account, the cash paid equals the expense amount.

5. **Cash paid for income taxes**—To calculate the cash paid for income taxes, we examine the income tax expense and the income taxes payable account. The income taxes payable account is increased by the tax expense for the period and decreased by the cash payments made during the period. We can express the mathematical relationship between the income tax expense, income taxes payable, and the cash paid for income taxes as follows:

Beginning Taxes Payable + Income Tax Expense − Cash Tax Payments
= Ending Taxes Payable
$0 + $120 − Cash Tax Payments = $0
Cash Tax Payments = $120

PIPKIN COMPANY

Statement of Cash Flows

For the Year Ended December 31, 2001

(in thousands)

Cash Flows from Operating Activities:		
Cash Received from Customers		$15,345
Cash Paid for:		
Merchandise	$11,051	
Operating Expenses	3,097	
Interest	160	
Income Taxes	120	14,428
Net Cash Provided (Used) by Operating Activities		$ 917

Similar to the interest expense, Pipkin has no beginning or ending income taxes payable account, so the amount paid in cash for income taxes equals the expense.

Now we can insert our calculations into the format and complete Pipkin's direct method net cash flow from operating activities section of the cash flow statement in Exhibit 11–8.

Discussion Question

11–9. What items from the income statement were included in the direct method operating activities? What items were omitted? Why?

The FASB requires that the reconciliation (indirect method) also be presented when the direct method is employed. We can now turn our attention to the indirect method of presenting cash flow from operations.

Determining Cash Flow from Operating Activities— Indirect Method

The reconciliation method receives its name from its format, which begins with net income and transforms net income into cash flow from operations. We can do this because most items involved in net income, except depreciation and amortization, are either already cash or are expected to eventually become cash. Revenues will eventually become cash inflows, and most expenses (except depreciation and amortization) will eventually become cash outflows. Over the entire life of the company, net income on the cash basis and accrual basis will equal one another. Therefore, we must adjust the net income figure for any differences between the cash and accrual basis of revenue and expense recognition. In addition, some gains and losses recognized on the income statement come from investing and financing activities. We also want to remove those activities from the operating section of the cash flow statement. In summary, we will remove accrual differences, noncash expenses, and nonoperating activities from net income to arrive at cash flow from operations.

PIPKIN COMPANY

Partial Statement of Cash Flows

For the Year Ended December 31, 2001

(in thousands)

Cash Flows from Operating Activities:		
Net Income		$449
Adjustments to Reconcile Net Income		
to Net Cash Provided by Operating Activities:		
Depreciation Expense	$231	
Gain or Loss on Sale of Assets		
Increase in ?	?	
Decrease in ?	?	
Net Cash Provided (Used) by Operating Activities		$?

Discussion Question

11–10. Why is retained earnings not equal to cash?

We will begin our trek through the indirect method by looking at the basic format for the indirect method in Exhibit 11–9.

As we mentioned, we make three basic types of adjustments to net income. We list these in the following order on the cash flow statement:

1. Add back depreciation and amortization.
2. Add back losses or subtract gains on the sale of assets or any other investing and financing event.
3. Add or subtract the adjustments for accrual accounting from current assets and current liabilities that represent operating activities. Remember not to include Notes Receivable, current Marketable Securities, and Notes Payable, because these represent investing and financing activities.

We will utilize information primarily from the income statement, the current assets and current liabilities, and other information pertinent to preparing the report. We need to determine three groups of values:

1. **Depreciation and amortization**—Because depreciation and amortization represent a noncash expenditure of converting the cost of long-lived items (buildings and equipment in Pipkin's case) from asset to expense, the deduction for them on the income statement reduces income but not cash. Therefore, we must add the amount of depreciation and amortization expense for the period to net income. Pipkin's income statement (Exhibit 11–4) had depreciation expense for the year of $231,000 ($180,000 on buildings and $51,000 on equipment) and no amortization expense. Thus, our adjustment is $231,000.

    What if depreciation was included in cost of goods sold or combined with other expenses? Is it possible to determine how much depreciation was expensed? The answer is yes. Provided that no depreciable or amortizable assets were disposed of, we can look at the change in the Accumulated Depreciation accounts or the intangible asset accounts to determine the

Exhibit 11–10
Current Assets and
Current Liabilities
Sections of Balance
Sheets for Pipkin
Company for 2001
and 2000

PIPKIN COMPANY

Partial Balance Sheets

December 31, 2001, and December 31, 2000

Current Assets and Current Liabilities Only

(in thousands)

	2001	2000	Increase (Decrease)
Current Assets:			
Cash	$2,800	$2,420	$380
Accounts Receivable	2,925	3,112	(187)
Merchandise Inventory	970	866	104
Prepaid Expenses	250	200	50
Total Current Assets	$6,945	$6,598	$347
Current Liabilities:			
Accounts Payable	$2,020	$1,816	$204
Notes Payable	3,400	2,700	700
Total Current Liabilities	$5,420	$4,516	$904

amounts. First look on the income statement to determine whether there are any gains or losses on the disposal of assets. Pipkin had none for 2001. Next, look at Exhibit 11–6. The net change in the Accumulated Depreciation accounts for buildings was $180,000 and for equipment $51,000. This amount matches the information we found on the income statement.

2. **Gains or losses on disposal of assets**—The income statement shows no gains or losses on disposal of assets. Another clue would be finding that the amount of long-lived assets decreased on the balance sheet or intangible assets decreased more than the amount of the amortization.

3. **Changes in current assets or current liabilities**—As we saw with the analysis of the direct method, the change in current assets and current liabilities is directly related to the difference between cash and accrual basis statements. We now look at each account, reproduced in Exhibit 11–10.

   a. **Accounts Receivable**—According to Pipkin's balance sheets, Accounts Receivable decreased $187,000 during 2001. If you refer back to our analysis of cash received from customers in the direct method, the cash received was $15,345,000 compared with sales of $15,158,000. The difference is $187,000. The only way Accounts Receivable can decrease is for the customers' payments to exceed current sales. Conversely, the only way Accounts Receivable can increase is for current sales to exceed customers' payments. Therefore, we add decreases in Accounts Receivable and subtract increases in Accounts Receivable to convert from the accrual basis to the cash basis. We must add the $187,000 as an adjustment to net income.

   b. **Merchandise Inventory**—The inventory account increased by $104,000 during 2001 according to Exhibit 11–6. The increase in inventory requires the use of cash resources. When inventory decreases, we use up inventory purchased in previous periods and conserve current cash. As we saw with the direct method, merchandise inventory is linked to accounts payable. However, with the indirect method, we consider each account independently. Therefore, we add decreases and subtract increases in the inventory account to net income. We must subtract Pipkin's increase in the inventory account.

c. **Prepaid Expenses**—Pipkin increased its Prepaid Expenses by $50,000 during 2001. If you refer to the equation for Prepaid Expenses in the direct method, you can see that cash payments generate increases in the account. If the account increases, the cash payments must exceed the amount of the expense. If the account decreases, the cash payments must be less than the amount of the expense. Therefore, we must add decreases and subtract increases in the Prepaid Expenses account. Pipkin's increase in Prepaid Expenses should be subtracted from net income as part of the adjustments.

d. **Accounts Payable**—Pipkin increased its Accounts Payable by $204,000 during 2001. After examining the equation for the account in the direct method section, you can see that purchases increase and cash payments reduce the amount of the Accounts Payable. If the account increases during a period, then the firm purchases more than it pays. Conversely, if the company pays more cash on the liability than it purchases, the account balance will decrease. Therefore, we will add increases and subtract decreases in the account as an adjustment to net income. Notice that increases and decreases in liabilities take the opposite sign of increases and decreases to assets. Pipkin's $204,000 will be added to the net income.

e. **Notes Payable**—Changes in Notes Payable represent financing activities even though it is a current liability.

With these calculations made, we can complete the operating section of the cash flow statement in Exhibit 11–11.

Exhibit 11–11
Basic Format for Pipkin Company's Indirect Method Operating Section of the Statement of Cash Flows

PIPKIN COMPANY		
Partial Statement of Cash Flows		
For the Year Ended December 31, 2001		
(in thousands)		
Cash Flows from Operating Activities:		
Net Income		$449
Adjustments to Reconcile Net Income		
to Net Cash Provided by Operating Activities:		
Depreciation Expense	$231	
Decrease in Accounts Receivable	187	
Increase in Merchandise Inventory	(104)	
Increase in Prepaid Expenses	(50)	
Increase in Accounts Payable	204	468
Net Cash Provided (Used) by Operating Activities		$917

Discussion Questions

11-11. Compare the two amounts of operating activities in Exhibits 11-8 and 11-11. Explain the results.

11-12. How would you use the information given in the direct method? Indirect method? Which do you prefer?

Exhibit 11–12
Long-Term Asset
Section of Balance
Sheets for Pipkin
Company for 2001 and
2000

Plant and Equipment:			
Buildings	$9,654	$8,029	$1,625
LESS: Accumulated Depreciation	4,597	4,417	180
Buildings, Net	$5,057	$3,612	$1,445
Equipment	$3,359	$2,984	$ 375
LESS: Accumulated Depreciation	1,955	1,904	51
Equipment, Net	$1,404	$1,080	$ 324
Total Plant and Equipment	$6,461	$4,692	$1,769

Step 4   Complete the Investing Activities Section:

Determining Cash Flow from Investing Activities

Determining cash flow from investing activities requires analysis of the noncurrent assets plus additional information we collected. Exhibit 11–12 duplicates that section from the company's comparative balance sheets.

The $1,625,000 increase in the building account and the $375,000 increase in the equipment account make us suspect that Pipkin invested in a new building and new equipment. We can verify this information from the additional information we gathered in Step 2 that indicated the $2,000,000 investment was paid by cash. The only other changes in the plant and equipment accounts represent the depreciation for the current year that we examined in the indirect method section on depreciation. Pipkin has two investing activities that we can add to the growing cash flow statement in Exhibit 11–13.

Exhibit 11–13
Partial Statement of
Cash Flows for Pipkin
Company Operating
Activities and Investing
Activities Sections

PIPKIN COMPANY
Partial Statement of Cash Flows
For the Year Ended December 31, 2001
(in thousands)

Cash Flows from Operating Activities:		
Net Income		$449
Adjustments to Reconcile Net Income		
to Net Cash Provided by Operating Activities:		
Depreciation Expense	$231	
Decrease in Accounts Receivable	187	
Increase in Merchandise Inventory	(104)	
Increase in Prepaid Expense	(50)	
Increase in Accounts Payable	204	468
Net Cash Provided by Operating Activities		$917
Cash Flows from Investing Activities:		
Purchase of Building	$(1,625)	
Purchase of Equipment	(375)	
Net Cash Used by Investing Activities		(2,000)

Determining Cash Flow from Financing Activities

By analyzing the liabilities and stockholders' equity sections of the balance sheet, we can determine Pipkin's financing activities. We have duplicated those sections from Pipkin Company's comparative balance sheets in Exhibit 11–14.

Exhibit 11–14
Long-Term Liabilities and Stockholders' Equity Sections of Balance Sheets for Pipkin Company for 2001 and 2000

PIPKIN COMPANY
Partial Balance Sheets
December 31, 2001, and December 31, 2000
Long-Term Liabilities and Stockholders' Equity Only
(in thousands)

	2001	2000	Increase (Decrease)
Notes Payable	$3,400	$2,700	$700
Long-Term Liabilities	2,500	2,000	500
Common Stock, No Par Value	3,400	3,000	400
Retained Earnings	2,086	1,774	312

We must consider the changes in the notes payable from current liabilities, long-term liabilities, and equity accounts. Pipkin increased its Notes Payable by $700,000 and its Long-Term Liabilities by $500,000. In addition, Pipkin sold $400,000 in no-par stock. All of these changes represent cash inflows to the company. But, what about the $312,000 change in Retained Earnings? We can examine the composition of Retained Earnings to see what increases and decreases it by referring back to Exhibit 5–16, the statement of retained earnings. Net income increases Retained Earnings and dividends decrease Retained Earnings. We can generate this formula for Retained Earnings (R/E):

Beginning R/E + Net Income − Dividends = Ending R/E
$1,774,000 + $449,000 − Dividends = $2,086,000
Dividends = $2,086,000 − $1,774,000 − $449,000
Dividends = $137,000

We can verify this calculation with the additional information we gathered in Step 1. The dividends represent a financing cash outflow. We can now complete the statement of cash flow in Exhibit 11–15.

Pipkin Company's statement of cash flows was fairly simple to create because there were relatively few things to consider in its construction. Statements of cash flows for actual companies can be complicated. But whether simple or complex, all statements of cash flows assume the basic format used for Pipkin Company.

Supplemental Schedule

To complete the disclosures for users, the preparer has to include a supplemental schedule that outlines any significant noncash investing and financing activities. Examples of such transactions include trading an asset for a loan or stock, repaying a loan by issuing stock to the creditor, or trading one asset for another. In such transactions, no cash exchanges hands but the transaction may have future cash

Exhibit 11–15
Complete Statement of
Cash Flows for Pipkin
Company

PIPKIN COMPANY

Statement of Cash Flows

For the Year Ended December 31, 2001

(in thousands)

Cash Flows from Operating Activities:		
Net Income		$ 449
Adjustments to Reconcile Net Income		
to Net Cash Provided by Operating Activities:		
Depreciation Expense	$ 231	
Decrease in Accounts Receivable	187	
Increase in Merchandise Inventory	(104)	
Increase in Prepaid Expense	(50)	
Increase in Accounts Payable	204	468
Net Cash Provided by Operating Activities		$ 917
Cash Flows from Investing Activities:		
Purchase of Building	$(1,625)	
Purchase of Equipment	(375)	
Net Cash Used by Investing Activities		(2,000)
Cash Flows from Financing Activities:		
Proceeds from Long-Term Loan	$ 500	
Proceeds from Notes Payable	700	
Proceeds from Sale of Common Stock	400	
Payment of Cash Dividends	(137)	
Net Cash Provided by Financing Activities		1,463
Net Increase in Cash during 2001		$ 380
Beginning Cash Balance, January 1, 2001		2,420
Ending Cash Balance, December 31, 2001		$2,800

consequences. Look at a company that pays off a bond issue with common stock. The issuance of common stock removes the future cash outflow required to repay the bonds because common stocks have no maturity value or required repayment date. The issuance of common stock, however, will increase the amount of dividends required in the future. Both have future cash flow implications.

HOW TO USE THE STATEMENT OF CASH FLOWS

The purpose of the statement of cash flows is to disclose the company's sources and uses of cash during a specific time period. One of the most important things the statement shows is what a company invested in during the period and how that investment was financed. Investments in long-lived productive assets produce revenues and, eventually, cash. Operating and financing activities finance investments. How that investment was financed is presented in both the top section of the statement (operating activities) and the bottom section of the statement (financing activities).

To demonstrate this concept, we have extracted the cash flow totals for the three types of activities from Pipkin's statement of cash flows (Exhibit 11–15):

Net cash provided by operating activities	$ 917,000
Net cash used by investing activities	$(2,000,000)
Net cash provided by financing activities	$ 1,463,000

Pipkin invested $2,000,000 in a building and equipment during 2001. Pipkin made the investment to enhance the way the company conducts its business by either upgrading its manufacturing facilities, allowing entry into new markets, or developing new products. Although we cannot assess whether this investment was good or bad, we can determine how Pipkin financed it.

Pipkin or any company has only two sources of available cash. A company either generates cash internally (from profitable operations) or obtains cash from external sources (borrowing or selling stock). Pipkin generated about 46 percent of the cash required for the investment internally (from operating activities) and the balance from outside sources (financing activities). With that in mind, focus on this important concept: **In the long run, all investments must be financed through operations, because the only renewable source of cash is operations.** A firm can only borrow a finite amount of cash, can only sell a finite amount of stock, and can only sell a few of its assets or it would have none. Operations provide a renewable source of cash limited only by the firm's ability to operate profitably.

Now you can see why the statement of cash flows is an economic decision maker's most valuable tool in determining how a company finances its investments. By carefully examining it, users can obtain insights into many aspects of a company's operations. The statement of cash flows, in combination with the three financial statements introduced earlier in this text (income statement, statement of owners' equity, and balance sheet), provides important information upon which economic decision makers rely. In the next chapter we will explore other methods of analyzing the financial statements to make decisions for and about a company.

SUMMARY

Accountants developed the statement of cash flows to give financial statement users information about the cash flows of companies during a particular period. Information necessary for the development of a statement of cash flows can be found on a company's comparative balance sheets and the income statement of the period. A company may choose whether to calculate operating cash flows by the direct or indirect method.

The statement of cash flows provides information about cash flows used by or provided by three major functions (or activities) of the firm: operating, investing, and financing. Operating cash flows represent cash provided from revenue-producing activities and are similar to cash basis net income. Healthy companies have positive operating cash flows. To compute operating activities cash flow, analyze the income statement, current assets, and current liabilities.

Investing cash flows represent cash inflows and outflows from the long-term assets the firm buys and sells. Typical transactions that are classified as investing activities are the purchase and sale of property, plant, and equipment or long-term investments in other companies. Growing companies normally have negative investing cash flows.

The financing activities section of the statement of cash flows shows what types of external financing the company used to provide funds. Information showing the results of financing activities can be found in the long-term liability section and the owners' equity section of the balance sheet.

The statement of cash flows furnishes valuable information about the cash inflows and outflows of a business during a particular period. It provides an explanation of the changes in cash from the beginning to the end of a period. Therefore, the statement of cash flows can be considered a financial statement analysis tool as well as a financial statement.

KEY TERMS

direct method   F-415
financing activities   F-413
indirect method   F-415
investing activities   F-413

operating activities   F-412
statement of cash flows   F-410
working capital   F-410

REVIEW THE FACTS

A. When did the present format of the statement of cash flows come into existence?
B. What is the main purpose of the statement of cash flows?
C. Name the two methods of preparing the statement of cash flows. Which method is more commonly used by publicly traded companies?
D. What are the three major classifications of activities presented on the statement of cash flows?
E. In what category are the cash flows related to interest and dividends received and interest paid usually reported?
F. Provide examples of an inflow of cash and an outflow of cash for each of the three categories of business activity shown on the statement of cash flows.
G. Distinguish between the direct method and the indirect method of presenting operating cash flows.
H. What is the starting point for calculation of cash flows from operating activities using the indirect method?
I. Where are the items included in operating activities reported in the financial statements?
J. Where are the items included in investing activities reported in the financial statements?
K. Where are the items included in financing activities reported in the financial statements?
L. Which section(s) of the statement of cash flows tells the user how much cash the company used to acquire depreciable assets?
M. Which section(s) of the statement of cash flows tells the user how investments made by the company were financed?

APPLY WHAT YOU HAVE LEARNED

LO 1:   Cash Flow Terminology

11–13. Presented below is a list of items relating to the concepts discussed in this chapter, followed by definitions of those items in scrambled order:

a. Operating activities
b. Indirect method
c. Depreciation expense
d. Comparative financial statements

e. Financing activities
f. Working capital
g. Direct method
h. Investing activities

1. _____ Provides a reconciliation of accrual net income to the cash provided by or used by operating activities
2. _____ Accounting reports providing information from two or more consecutive periods at once

3. _____ Activities centered around the actual day-to-day business transactions of a company
4. _____ Current assets less current liabilities
5. _____ Business activities related to long-term assets
6. _____ Provides detail as to the individual sources and uses of cash associated with operating activities
7. _____ An item that reduces reported net income, but does not require the use of cash
8. _____ Activities such as the issuance of debt or equity and the payment of dividends

REQUIRED:
Match the letter next to each item on the list with the appropriate definition. Each letter will be used only once.

LO 2: Identification of Activities

11–14. Listed below are the three broad types of activities that can either generate or use cash in any business, followed by descriptions of various items.

a. Operating activities   **c.** Financing activities
b. Investing activities

1. _____ Payment of dividends
2. _____ Adjustment for depreciation
3. _____ Purchase of merchandise inventory
4. _____ Purchase of vehicles
5. _____ Repayment of 90-day loans
6. _____ Issuing capital stock
7. _____ Payment of wages to employees
8. _____ Payment of taxes
9. _____ Cash from sale of property and equipment
10. _____ Loans to other companies
11. _____ Adjustments for changes in current asset and current liability items
12. _____ Cash from selling investments in other companies

REQUIRED:
Classify each of the items listed above by placing the letter of the appropriate activity category in the space provided.

LO 2: Identification of Activities

11–15. Listed below are the three broad types of activities that can either generate or use cash in any business, followed by descriptions of various items.

a. Operating activities   **c.** Financing activities
b. Investing activities

1. _____ Amortization expense
2. _____ Depreciation expense
3. _____ Sale of merchandise inventory
4. _____ Sale of treasury stock
5. _____ Repayment of 30-day loans
6. _____ Purchase of one's own stock

7. _____ Payment of rent on office space
8. _____ Payment of insurance on factory equipment
9. _____ Cash from sale of treasury stock
10. _____ Purchase of stock in other companies
11. _____ Cash from the sale of bonds held for investment
12. _____ Cash from the collection of accounts receivable

REQUIRED:

Classify each of the items listed above by placing the letter of the appropriate activity category in the space provided.

LO 2: Identification of Sources and Uses—Indirect Method

11–16. Following are the changes in some of Sam Cagle Company's assets, liabilities, and equities from December 31, 2000, to December 31, 2001:

1. _____ Accounts payable decreased.
2. _____ Property and equipment increased.
3. _____ Accounts receivable increased.
4. _____ Long-term notes payable decreased.
5. _____ Prepaid expenses decreased.
6. _____ Short-term notes payable increased.
7. _____ Taxes payable decreased.
8. _____ Common stock increased.
9. _____ Wages payable increased.
10. _____ Merchandise inventory decreased.

REQUIRED:

Cagle is in the process of preparing the operating activities section of its statement of cash flows for 2001. Some of the items above will be included and others will not. Place the letter *S* in the space next to each item that should be considered a source of cash in the operating activities section, and place the letter *U* in the space next to each item that should be considered a use of cash in the operating activities section. Place the letter *N* next to any item not included in the operating activities section.

LO 4: Operating Activities Section—Indirect Method

11–17. Presented below are partial comparative balance sheets of Jackson Company at December 31, 2002 and 2001:

JACKSON COMPANY
Partial Balance Sheets
December 31, 2002, and December 31, 2001
Current Assets and Current Liabilities Only
(in thousands)

	2002	2001	Increase (Decrease)
Current Assets:			
Cash	$3,400	$2,920	$ 480
Accounts Receivable	1,825	2,212	(387)
Merchandise Inventory	1,170	966	204
Prepaid Expenses	240	270	(30)
Total Current Assets	$6,635	$6,368	$ 267
Current Liabilities:			
Accounts Payable	$2,321	$1,740	$ 581
Notes Payable	3,100	3,300	(200)
Total Current Liabilities	$5,421	$5,040	$ 381

Additional Information: Net income for 2002 was $406,000. Included in the operating expenses for the year was depreciation expense of $175,000.

REQUIRED:
Prepare the operating activities section of Jackson Company's statement of cash flows for 2002.

LO 4: Operating Activities Section—Indirect Method

11–18. Presented below are partial comparative balance sheets of Scotia Company at December 31, 2001 and 2000:

SCOTIA COMPANY
Partial Balance Sheets
December 31, 2001, and December 31, 2000
Current Assets and Current Liabilities Only
(in thousands)

	2001	2000	Increase (Decrease)
Current Assets:			
Cash	$2,110	$2,650	$(540)
Accounts Receivable	1,254	977	277
Merchandise Inventory	730	856	(126)
Prepaid Expenses	127	114	13
Total Current Assets	$4,221	$4,597	$(376)
Current Liabilities:			
Accounts Payable	$1,054	$1,330	$(276)
Notes Payable	2,100	1,750	350
Total Current Liabilities	$3,154	$3,080	$ 74

Additional Information: Net income for 2001 was $86,900. Included in the operating expenses for the year was depreciation expense of $102,000.

REQUIRED:
Prepare the operating activities section of Scotia Company's statement of cash flows for 2001.

LO 4: Operating Activities Section—Indirect Method

11–19. The Powers Corporation worksheet for the preparation of its 2003 statement of cash flows included the following:

	January 1	December 31
Accounts Receivable	$78,000	$71,000
Allowances for Uncollectible Accounts	4,000	2,000
Prepaid Insurance	48,000	36,000
Inventory	56,000	75,000

Powers Corporation reported net income of $450,000 for the year.

REQUIRED:
Prepare the cash flow from operating activities section of Powers Corporation's statement of cash flows.

LO 4: Investing Activities Section

11–20. In preparing its cash flow statement for the year ended December 31, 2003, Mavis Company gathered the following data:

Gain on sale of machinery	$18,000
Proceeds from sale of machinery	60,000
Purchase of Fred, Inc. bonds (face value $100,000)	80,000
Amortization of bond discount	4,000
Dividends declared	75,000
Dividends paid	40,000
Proceeds from the sale of treasury stock	50,000

REQUIRED:

Prepare the cash flow from investing section of the cash flow statement for Mavis Company.

LO 4: Investing Activities Section

11–21. In preparing its cash flow statement for the year ended December 31, 2002, Nash Company gathered the following data:

Loss on sale of machinery	$ 24,000
Proceeds from sale of machinery	40,000
Purchase of Alco, Inc. bonds (face value $800,000)	980,000
Amortization of bond premium	16,000
Dividends declared	95,000
Dividends paid	96,000
Purchase of treasury stock	80,000

REQUIRED:

Prepare the cash flow from investing section of the cash flow statement for Nash Company.

LO 4: Investing Activities Section

11–22. In preparing its cash flow statement for the year ended December 31, 2004, Rambler Company gathered the following data:

Loss on sale of equipment	$ 4,000
Proceeds from sale of equipment	20,000
Purchase of equipment	980,000
Dividends declared	35,000
Dividends paid	28,000
Purchase of treasury stock	60,000

REQUIRED:

Prepare the cash flow from investing section of the cash flow statement for Rambler Company.

LO 4: Financing Activities Section

11–23. In preparing its cash flow statement for the year ended December 31, 2004, Reo Company gathered the following data:

Gain on sale of equipment	$ 4,000
Proceeds from sale of equipment	30,000
Proceeds from sale of common stock	890,000

Dividends declared	35,000
Dividends paid	28,000
Purchase of treasury stock	60,000
Proceeds from bank loan	200,000

REQUIRED:

Prepare the cash flow from financing section of the cash flow statement for Reo Company.

LO 4: Financing Activities Section

11–24. In preparing its cash flow statement for the year ended December 31, 2002, Diamond Company gathered the following data:

Loss on sale of equipment	$ 54,000
Proceeds from sale of equipment	230,000
Proceeds from sale of preferred stock	200,000
Dividends declared	95,000
Dividends paid	80,000
Proceeds from sale of treasury stock	160,000
Proceeds from bank loan	300,000
Repayment of bank loan (interest)	20,000
Repayment of bank loan (principal)	120,000

REQUIRED:

Prepare the cash flow from financing section of the cash flow statement for Diamond Company.

LO 4: Financing Activities Section

11–25. In preparing its cash flow statement for the year ended December 31, 2005, Cirrus Company gathered the following data:

Gain on sale of equipment	$ 27,000
Proceeds from sale of equipment	115,000
Proceeds from sale of preferred stock	100,000
Dividends declared	65,000
Dividends paid	75,000
Proceeds from sale of common stock	500,000
Proceeds from bank loan	300,000
Repayment of bank loan (interest)	100,000
Repayment of bank loan (principal)	400,000

REQUIRED:

Prepare the cash flow from financing section of the cash flow statement for Cirrus Company.

LO 4: Concepts of Cash Flow Statements

11–26. Presented below is Rock Company's statement of cash flows for the year ended December 31, 2002:

ROCK COMPANY
Statement of Cash Flows
For the Year Ended December 31, 2002
(in thousands)

Cash Flows from Operating Activities:		
Net Income		$ 389
Adjustments to Reconcile Net Income		
to Net Cash Provided by Operating Activities:		
Depreciation Expense	$ 131	
Increase in Accounts Receivable	(287)	
Increase in Merchandise Inventory	(104)	
Increase in Prepaid Expense	(70)	
Decrease in Accounts Payable	(4)	(334)
Net Cash Provided by Operating Activities		$ 55
Cash Flows from Investing Activities:		
Purchase of Building	$(1,255)	
Purchase of Equipment	(304)	
Net Cash Used by Investing Activities		(1,559)
Cash Flows from Financing Activities:		
Proceeds from Long-Term Loan	$ 800	
Proceeds from Sale of Common Stock	300	
Payment of Cash Dividends	(100)	
Net Cash Provided by Financing Activities		1,000
Net Decrease in Cash during 2002		$ (504)
Cash Balance, January 1, 2002		1,000
Cash Balance, December 31, 2002		$ 496

REQUIRED:
Respond to the following questions:
  a. For which of the three broad types of activities did Rock use the majority of its cash during 2002?
  b. What does your answer to the previous question tell you about Rock Company?
  c. From which of the three broad types of activities did Rock obtain the majority of its cash during 2002?
  d. Is the activity you identified in the previous requirement an appropriate source of cash in the long run? Explain your reasoning.

LO 4: Concepts of Cash Flow Statements

11–27. Presented below is McDougle Company's statement of cash flows for the year ended December 31, 2002:

MCDOUGLE COMPANY
Statement of Cash Flows
For the Year Ended December 31, 2002
(in thousands)

Cash Flows from Operating Activities:		
Net Income		$ 1,608
Adjustments to Reconcile Net Income		
to Net Cash Provided by Operating Activities:		
Depreciation Expense	$ 218	
Increase in Accounts Receivable	(341)	
Decrease in Merchandise Inventory	81	
Increase in Prepaid Expense	(100)	
Increase in Accounts Payable	154	12
Net Cash Provided by Operating Activities		$ 1,620

Cash Flows from Investing Activities:		
Purchase of Building	$(1,000)	
Purchase of Equipment	(200)	
Net Cash Used by Investing Activities		(1,200)
Cash Flows from Financing Activities:		
Repayment of Long-Term Loan	$ (350)	
Proceeds from Sale of Common Stock	350	
Payment of Cash Dividends	(100)	
Net Cash Used by Financing Activities		(100)
Net Increase in Cash during 2002		$ 320
Cash Balance, January 1, 2002		430
Cash Balance, December 31, 2002		$ 750

REQUIRED:

Respond to the following questions:

a. For which of the three types of activities did McDougle use the majority of its cash during 2003?

b. What does your answer to the previous question tell you about McDougle Company?

c. From which of the three types of activities did McDougle obtain the majority of its cash during 2003?

d. Is the activity you identified in the previous requirement an appropriate source of cash in the long run? Explain your reasoning.

LO 4: Preparation of Cash Flow Statement

11–28. Use the balance sheets, income statement, and the additional information provided below to complete this problem.

HOOPLE COMPANY

Balance Sheets

At December 31, 2003, and December 31, 2002

(in thousands)

	2003		2002	
ASSETS:				
Current Assets:				
Cash		$ 1,618		$1,220
Accounts Receivable		1,925		2,112
Merchandise Inventory		1,070		966
Prepaid Expenses		188		149
Total Current Assets		$ 4,801		$4,447
Plant and Equipment:				
Buildings	$4,818		$3,292	
LESS: Accumulated Depreciation	(361)		(300)	
Buildings, Net		$ 4,457		$2,992
Equipment	$1,434		$1,145	
LESS: Accumulated Depreciation	(141)		(100)	
Equipment, Net		1,293		1,045
Total Plant and Equipment		$ 5,750		$4,037
Total Assets		$10,551		$8,484
LIABILITIES:				
Current Liabilities:				
Accounts Payable		$ 1,818		$1,686
Notes Payable		900		1,100
Total Current Liabilities		$ 2,718		$2,786
Long-Term Liabilities		2,500		2,000
Total Liabilities		$ 5,218		$4,786

STOCKHOLDERS' EQUITY:

Common Stock, No Par Value	$ 3,390	$ 2,041
Retained Earnings	1,943	1,657
Total Stockholders' Equity	$ 5,333	$ 3,698
Total Liabilities and		
Stockholders' Equity	$10,551	$ 8,484

HOOPLE COMPANY
Income Statement
For the Year Ended December 31, 2003
(in thousands)

Net Sales		$11,228
LESS: Cost of Goods Sold		7,751
Gross Profit on Sales		$ 3,477
LESS: Operating Expenses:		
Depreciation—Buildings and Equipment	$ 102	
Other Selling and Administrative	2,667	
Total Expenses		(2,769)
Operating Income		$ 708
LESS: Interest Expense		(168)
Income Before Taxes		$ 540
Income Taxes		(114)
Net Income		$ 426

Additional Information: There were no sales of plant and equipment during the year, and the company paid dividends to stockholders during the year of $140,000.

REQUIRED:
a. Prepare Hoople Company's statement of cash flows for the year ended December 31, 2003, using the direct method for operating activities.
b. In which of the three categories of activities did Hoople use the majority of its cash during 2003?
c. What does your answer to the previous question tell you about Hoople Company?
d. From which of the three types of activities did Hoople obtain the majority of its cash during 2003?
e. Is the activity you identified in the previous requirement an appropriate source of cash in the long run? Explain your reasoning.

LO 4: Preparation of Cash Flow Statement

11–29. Use the Hoople financial statements in 11–28 to complete the following requirements.

REQUIRED:
a. Prepare Hoople Company's statement of cash flows for the year ended December 31, 2003, using the indirect method for operating activities.
b. In which of the three categories of activities did Hoople use the majority of its cash during 2003?
c. What does your answer to the previous question tell you about Hoople Company?
d. From which of the three types of activities did Hoople obtain the majority of its cash during 2003?
e. Is the activity you identified in the previous requirement an appropriate source of cash in the long run? Explain your reasoning.

LO 4: Preparation of Cash Flow Statement

11–30. Use the balance sheets, income statement, and the additional information presented below to complete this problem.

AL MUZNY COMPANY
Balance Sheets
At December 31, 2002, and December 31, 2001
(in thousands)

	2002		2001	
ASSETS:				
Current Assets:				
Cash		$ 529		$ 660
Accounts Receivable		1,006		1,011
Merchandise Inventory		396		452
Prepaid Expenses		38		62
Total Current Assets		$ 1,969		$ 2,185
Plant and Equipment:				
Buildings	$2,000		$1,681	
LESS: Accumulated Depreciation	(176)		(146)	
Buildings, Net		$ 1,824		$ 1,535
Equipment	$ 809		$ 609	
LESS: Accumulated Depreciation	(76)		(61)	
Equipment, Net		733		548
Total Plant and Equipment		$ 2,557		$ 2,083
Total Assets		$ 4,526		$ 4,268
LIABILITIES:				
Current Liabilities:				
Accounts Payable		$ 726		$ 809
Notes Payable		750		600
Total Current Liabilities		$ 1,476		$ 1,409
Long-Term Liabilities		1,500		1,200
Total Liabilities		$ 2,976		$ 2,609
STOCKHOLDERS' EQUITY:				
Common Stock, No Par Value		$ 1,300		$ 1,000
Retained Earnings		250		659
Total Stockholders' Equity		$ 1,550		$1,659
Total Liabilities and				
Stockholders' Equity		$ 4,526		$ 4,268

AL MUZNY COMPANY
Income Statement
For the Year Ended December 31, 2002
(in thousands)

Sales		$ 6,391
LESS: Cost of Goods Sold		4,474
Gross Profit on Sales		$ 1,917
LESS: Operating Expenses:		
Depreciation—Buildings and Equipment	$ 45	
Other Selling and Administrative	2,066	
Total Expenses		2,111
Operating Income		$ (194)
LESS: Interest Expense		145
Income Before Taxes		$ (339)
Income Taxes		-0-
Net Loss		$ (339)

Additional Information: There were no sales of plant and equipment during the year, and the company paid dividends to stockholders during the year of $70,000.

REQUIRED:

a. Prepare Muzny Company's statement of cash flows for the year ended December 31, 2002, using the indirect method for operating activities.
b. In which of the three broad activities did Muzny use the majority of its cash during 2002?
c. What does your answer to the previous question tell you about Muzny Company?
d. In which of the three broad activities did Muzny obtain the majority of its cash during 2002?
e. Is the activity you identified in the previous requirement an appropriate source of cash in the long run? Explain your reasoning.
f. Prepare Muzny Company's statement of retained earnings for 2002.

LO 4:   Preparation of Cash Flow Statement

11–31. Use the Muzny financial statements in 11–30 to complete the following requirements.

REQUIRED:

a. Prepare Muzny Company's statement of cash flows for the year ended December 31, 2002, using the direct method for operating activities.
b. In which of the three broad activities did Muzny use the majority of its cash during 2002?
c. What does your answer to the previous question tell you about Muzny Company?
d. In which of the three broad activities did Muzny obtain the majority of its cash during 2002?
e. Is the activity you identified in the previous requirement an appropriate source of cash in the long run? Explain your reasoning.
f. Prepare Muzny Company's statement of retained earnings for 2002.

LO 4:   Analysis of Cash Flow Information

11–32. Presented below are the totals from the main three sections of Arlene Job and Company's most recent statement of cash flows:

Net cash provided by operating activities	$ 1,812,000
Net cash used by investing activities	$(1,280,000)
Net cash used by financing activities	$ (153,000)

REQUIRED:

a. What do these totals tell you about Job and Company?
b. What additional information would you want to see before you analyze Job and Company's ability to generate positive cash flow in the future?
c. Did Job and Company have a net income or loss for the period? What additional information would you want before trying to predict the company's net income for the next period?

LO 4:   Analysis of Cash Flow Information

11–33. Presented below are the totals from the main three sections of Kay Coleman and Company's most recent statement of cash flows:

Net cash used by operating activities	$ (835,000)
Net cash used by investing activities	$(1,280,000)
Net cash provided by financing activities	$ 2,153,000

REQUIRED:

a. What do these totals tell you about Coleman and Company?

b. What additional information would you want to see before you analyze Coleman and Company's ability to generate positive cash flow in the future?

c. Did Coleman and Company have a net income or loss for the period? What additional information would you want before trying to predict the company's net income for the next period?

LO 4: Analysis of Cash Flow Information

11–34. Presented below are the totals from the main three sections of Carl Faulkner and Company's most recent statement of cash flows:

Net cash used by operating activities	$(1,409,000)
Net cash provided by investing activities	$ 1,980,000
Net cash used by financing activities	$ (303,000)

REQUIRED:

a. What do these totals tell you about Faulkner and Company?

b. What additional information would you want to see before you analyze Faulkner and Company's ability to generate positive cash flow in the future?

LO 4: Discussion

11–35. Remember, tools are developed to solve problems. This chapter is titled "Tools of the Trade, Part III: The Statement of Cash Flows: Bringing the Focus Back to Cash."

REQUIRED:

a. Explain in your own words what caused the focus of financial statements to shift to something other than cash.

b. Describe how the statement of cash flows serves as a tool to bring the focus of economic decision makers back to cash.

LO 4: Discussion—Direct Method vs. Indirect Method

11–36. Compare the two methods for preparing the statement of cash flows, the direct method and the indirect method. Which sections are different and which sections are the same?

LO 4: Depreciation and Purchases of Equipment

11–37. The Skaggs Company is preparing a statement of cash flows for the year ended December 31, 2002. Selected beginning and ending account balances are as follows:

	Beginning	Ending
Machinery	$450,000	$475,500
Accumulated Depreciation—Machinery	95,000	129,000
Loss on sale of machinery		2,000

During the year, the company received $44,500 for a machine that cost $49,500 and purchased other items of equipment.

REQUIRED:

a. Compute the depreciation on machinery for the year.

b. Compute the amount of machinery purchases for the year.

LO 4: Depreciation and Purchases of Equipment

11–38. The Miles Company is preparing a statement of cash flows for the year ended December 31, 2003. Selected beginning and ending account balances are as follows:

	Beginning	Ending
Machinery	$250,000	$280,000
Accumulated Depreciation—Machinery	65,000	89,000
Gain on sale of machinery		2,000

During the year, the company received $50,000 for a machine that cost $65,000 and purchased other items of equipment.

REQUIRED:

a. Compute the depreciation on machinery for the year.

b. Compute the amount of machinery purchases for the year.

LO 4: Depreciation and Purchases of Equipment

11–39. The Bennett Company is preparing a statement of cash flows for the year ended December 31, 2001. Selected beginning and ending account balances are as follows:

	Beginning	Ending
Computers	$300,000	$390,000
Accumulated Depreciation—Computers	165,000	215,000
Gain on sale of computers		12,000

During the year, the company received $20,000 for a computer that cost $40,000 and purchased other items of equipment.

REQUIRED:

a. Compute the depreciation on computers for the year.

b. Compute the amount of computer purchases for the year.

LO 4: Operating Activities—Direct Method

11–40. The Foster Company gathered the following information from its accounting records:

Collections from customers	$450,000
Payments to suppliers	150,000
Payments for income taxes	75,000
Interest received from investments	5,000
Payments to employees	64,000
Payments for interest	85,000
Depreciation expense	50,000

REQUIRED:

Prepare the operating section of the cash flow statement for the Foster Company using the direct method.

LO 4:   Operating Activities—Direct Method

11–41. The Galway Company gathered the following information from its accounting records:

Collections of accounts receivable	$350,000
Cash sales	85,000
Payments to suppliers	260,000
Payments for income taxes	45,000
Interest received from investments	15,000
Payments to employees	95,000
Payments for interest	68,000
Depreciation expense	25,000

REQUIRED:

Prepare the operating section of the cash flow statement for the Galway Company using the direct method.

LO 4:   Operating Activities—Direct Method

11–42. The Porter Company gathered the following information from its accounting records:

Payment for treasury stock	$200,000
Payments for dividends	100,000
Collections of accounts receivable	870,000
Cash sales	385,000
Payments to suppliers on account	738,000
Cash purchases	250,000
Payments for income taxes	245,000
Interest received from investments	95,000
Payments to employees	460,000
Payments for interest	35,000
Depreciation expense	125,000

REQUIRED:

Prepare the operating section of the cash flow statement for the Porter Company using the direct method.

LO 4:   Statement of Cash Flows—Direct Method

11–43. The following information is from the records of the Wolf Company for the year ended December 31, 2001.

- Loaned $2,000 to Jones Company
- Sold Wolf Company stock for cash of $10,000
- Purchased equipment for cash of $20,000
- Cash sales to customers were $95,000
- Sales on account $-0-
- Sold equipment for cash of $4,000
- Paid cash to employees for wages $9,500
- Paid cash for merchandise $29,000
- Paid a $2,000 cash dividend
- Borrowed $6,000 from Friendly National Bank
- Purchased Ford Motor Company stock $5,000

- Received a cash dividend from Ford of $200
- Paid cash for other expenses $8,000
- Made a loan payment to Friendly Bank of $2,200 which included $200 interest

REQUIRED:
Prepare a statement of cash flows for Wolf Company for the year ended December 31, 2001.

LO 4: Statement of Cash Flows—Direct Method

11–44. The following information is from the records of the RoJo Company for the year ended December 31, 2002.

- Purchased equipment for cash of $8,000
- Cash sales to customers were $75,000
- Sold RoJo Company stock for cash of $6,000
- Loaned $1,000 to Jordan Company
- Sales on account $-0-
- Sold equipment for cash of $1,000
- Paid cash to employees for wages $4,500
- Borrowed $5,000 from Peoples National Bank
- Paid cash for merchandise $32,000
- Paid a $500 cash dividend
- Made a loan payment to Peoples Bank of $1,500 which included $100 interest
- Purchased DuPont Company stock $2,000
- Received a cash dividend from DuPont $100
- Paid cash for other expenses $3,000

REQUIRED:
Prepare a statement of cash flows for RoJo Company for the year ended December 31, 2002.

LO 4: Statement of Cash Flows—Direct Method

11–45. The following information is from the records of the Byrd Company for the year ended December 31, 2002.

- Sales on account $-0-
- Paid cash to employees for wages $7,000
- Purchased equipment for cash of $3,000
- Cash sales to customers were $80,000
- Sold Byrd Company stock for cash of $9,000
- Loaned $2,000 to Pippen Company
- Paid cash for merchandise $24,000
- Sold equipment for cash of $2,000
- Borrowed $8,000 from Central National Bank
- Paid a $100 cash dividend
- Made a loan payment to Central Bank of $3,000 which included $500 interest
- Purchased Lucent Company stock $1,000
- Received a cash dividend from Lucent $50
- Paid cash for other expenses $2,000

REQUIRED:
Prepare a statement of cash flows for Byrd Company for the year ended December 31, 2002.

FINANCIAL REPORTING CASES

Comprehensive

11–46. Visit the PHLIP Web site for this book at www.prenhall.com/jones to find the Walt Disney Company link. Find Disney's statement of cash flows to answer the following questions.

REQUIRED:
a. List the total for operating, financing, and investing cash flows for each of the years shown in the report's statement of cash flows.
b. Does the company use the direct or indirect method of preparing the statement of cash flows?
c. Have the operating cash flows been positive?
d. Do the cash flows from operations provide enough cash flow to service the debt of the corporation?

Comprehensive

11–47. Visit the PHLIP Web site for this book at www.prenhall.com/jones to find the Coca-Cola Company link. Find Coke's statement of cash flows to answer the following questions.

REQUIRED:
a. List the total for operating, financing, and investing cash flows for each of the years shown in the report's statement of cash flows.
b. Does the company use the direct or indirect method of preparing the statement of cash flows?
c. Have the operating cash flows been positive?
d. Identify the transactions that affect the cash flow for financing activities.

Comprehensive

11–48. Visit the PHLIP Web site for this book at www.prenhall.com/jones to find the Nortek Company link. Find the statement of cash flows to answer the following questions.

REQUIRED:
a. List the total for operating, financing, and investing cash flows for each of the years shown in the report's statement of cash flows.
b. Does the company use the direct or indirect method of preparing the statement of cash flows?
c. Have the operating cash flows been positive?
d. Identify each of the transactions that affect cash flow from investing activities.

ANNUAL REPORT PROJECT

11–49. After this assignment you will be able to complete Section V of the annual report project. For the section on cash flows you should complete the following requirements.

    a. List the total for operating, investing, and financing cash flows for each of the years shown in the report's statement of cash flows.

    b. Examine the operating cash flows. Have the operating cash flows been positive? Have the operating cash flows increased or decreased in the years presented? Are the operating cash flows sufficient to pay principal and interest on debt and meet other cash requirements?

    c. Examine investing cash flows. For each line presented in the investing section, discuss how the line relates to another part of the annual report. Include the page number where you found the information. The Management Discussion and Analysis may be a very good place to find this information.

    d. Examine the financing cash flows. For each line presented in this section, trace the amount or find a discussion of the amount elsewhere in the report. The statement of stockholders' equity may be an excellent place to look. Document by page reference where you found the information.

    e. What method is used to prepare the cash flow statement, direct or indirect?

Chapter 12

Financial Statement Analysis

Your fledgling business has begun to grow and a major retailer recently approached you wanting to place a very large order. To produce the order and wait for the retailer to pay you will require a substantial amount of cash. (Now you understand all that discussion about the necessity of cash!) Your first meeting with the local bank's loan officer went well; however, she indicated that you must provide her with detailed financial statements so that she could "run the ratios." She further explained that if you passed the ratio tests, the bank would probably make the loan. Your CPA will help you prepare the financial statements, but how will you know whether your business can pass these tests? Should your CPA compute the ratios before you go to the bank? Better yet, are there any banks that do not require these ratio tests?

Financial reporting is an essential source of information for economic decision makers, and financial statements are a central component of financial reporting. In the appendix to Chapter 1, we explored the information provided in the annual report and the SEC's Form 10-K. Gathering and reading this kind of information forms the first step in analyzing the information to make it useful in the decision-making process.

Financial statement analysis is the process of looking beyond the face of the financial statements to gain additional insight into a company. Financial statement analysis involves many different facets including trend analysis and ratio analysis. Your study of the statement of cash flows in Chapter 11 was also a type of financial statement analysis, for the statement of cash flows analyzes what caused the change in cash from one period to the next. ■

trend analysis A technique whereby an analyst tries to determine the amount of changes in key financial amounts over time to see if a pattern of change emerges.

ratio analysis A technique for analyzing the relationship between two items from a company's financial statements for a given period.

In this chapter, we explore two forms of financial statement analysis—trend analysis and ratio analysis—and show you how to use the results in proper combination with other information to make economic decisions. With **trend analysis,** the analyst tries to determine the amount of changes in key financial amounts over time to see if a pattern of change emerges. **Ratio analysis** is a technique for analyzing the relationship between two items from a company's financial statements for a given period. These items may be on the same financial statement, or they may come from different financial statements. The ratios discussed in this chapter are based on items from the balance sheet and the income statement.

LEARNING OBJECTIVES

After completing your work on this chapter, you should be able to do the following:

1. Identify the three major categories of users of financial statement analysis and describe the objectives of each.
2. Gather information to evaluate the political climate and general economic conditions and describe the ways in which each can affect business.
3. Locate sources of information about specific industries.
4. Describe the purpose of trend analysis and ratio analysis and explain the three primary characteristics it helps users evaluate.
5. Calculate financial ratios designed to measure a company's profitability, liquidity, and solvency.
6. Explain the purpose of the Standard Industrial Classification system and specify what an SIC code indicates.
7. Evaluate a company's ratios using a comparison to industry averages.
8. Use ratio values from consecutive time periods to evaluate the profitability, liquidity, and solvency of a business.
9. State the limitations of ratio analysis.

WHO PERFORMS FINANCIAL STATEMENT ANALYSIS AND WHY?

financial statement analysis The process of looking beyond the face of the financial statements to gather more information.

Several different types of economic decision makers perform **financial statement analysis,** and because their objectives vary, their perspectives on the results of that analysis will differ. Our focus in this chapter will be on three types of economic decision makers:

1. Creditors (short-term and long-term)
2. Equity investors (present and potential)
3. Company management

Independent auditors, government agencies, prospective employees, and others also are interested in analyzing a company's financial statements, but we will concentrate on these three important categories of users. First, we examine their objectives, and later in this chapter, we will see how ratio analysis meets their informational needs.

Objectives of Creditors

Creditors lend money to a company on either a short-term or a long-term basis. Do not confuse the concepts of current assets or liabilities with short-term or long-term lending. For financial statement purposes, the "current" designation describes assets or liabilities that are due within one year or one operating cycle, whichever is longer. For lenders, short-term lending is for loans of less than five years and long-term lending is for more than five years.

There are two major types of *short-term creditors*. One group, called trade creditors, provides goods and services to a business and expects payment within whatever time period is customary in the industry (usually between 30 and 60 days). Trade creditors seldom charge interest. Because the credit they extend to a company is essentially an interest-free loan, they analyze a company's financial statements to determine whether that company pays its bills on time and will be able to pay promptly in the future.

Lending institutions offer commercial loans to support the day-to-day operations of a business in exchange for the business signing a short-term note. Unlike trade creditors, banks charge interest. The objectives of these two groups of short-term creditors, however, are quite similar. Both want to be assured of receiving prompt payments from the company.

Long-term creditors also seek assurance of receiving prompt payments, but from a different perspective. These creditors—generally banks and corporate bondholders—lend money to companies for relatively long periods of time. Therefore, in analyzing a company's financial statements, their principal objectives are to determine whether the company will be able to make its periodic interest payments and to repay the loan when required.

When we explore the information resulting from ratio analysis later in the chapter, we will see how it is used by both short-term and long-term creditors. However, creditors are only one class of users of this information.

Objectives of Equity Investors

Equity investors are those who have purchased or might purchase an ownership interest in a company through stock ownership or partnership. Investors expect a return on their investment. Recall from our discussion in Chapter 4 that return on investment for a corporate equity investor has two components:

1. Dividends: the distribution of earnings from a corporation to its owners (stockholders)
2. Stock appreciation: the increase in the selling price of a share of stock in the secondary stock market between the time it is purchased and the time it is sold

When analyzing a company's financial statements, present and potential equity investors want to determine whether the company will be able to distribute dividends in the future and whether its stock will rise in value. Both these future activities depend on the company's ability to generate income and cash in the future. Cash dividends can only be paid if a company has sufficient cash and sufficient retained earnings, both of which depend on future generation of earnings. Further, generation of earnings is widely considered to be the single, most important factor affecting a company's stock appreciation over time.

Both creditors and equity investors are external decision makers who use ratio analysis. However, ratio analysis is also a useful tool for internal decision makers—namely, a company's management.

Objectives of Management

Management is responsible for a company's day-to-day operation. Because they are decision makers they share some objectives of external parties, but because they are internal they also have other, different objectives in performing financial statement analysis.

In the context of this chapter, management has two major objectives in analyzing its own company's financial statements. The first is to put those statements in the best possible light before presenting them to important external parties. This is a natural and legitimate objective, since a company's relationship with creditors and stockholders is vital. However, management's natural desire to analyze the company's financial statements with a view toward favorably impressing external parties can lead to managing the financial statements rather than managing the business.

Discussion Questions

12-1. What do you think the phrase "managing the financial statements rather than managing the business" means?

12-2. Are there any ethical boundaries in managing the financial statements?

Management's second objective in analyzing the company's financial statements is to monitor the overall performance of the business in much the same manner as creditors and investors. The company's financial statements, of course, provide managers with important information for making business decisions, but because managers are internal parties, they can access additional, internally generated information. At times, managers focus on management accounting information when they evaluate their company's performance. Later you will explore the use of management accounting information, but we will limit our discussion in this chapter to publicly available financial accounting information.

Now that you understand the basic objectives of the three primary users of financial statement analysis, we can explore important factors that affect company performance and that should be considered by anyone undertaking financial statement analysis.

GATHERING BACKGROUND INFORMATION—AN IMPORTANT FIRST STEP

In the appendix to Chapter 1, we discussed how to find background information on companies. Anyone who wants to do a thorough analysis of a company's financial statements should consult the sources suggested in that appendix and gather enough background information on the company to put its financial statement information in proper context. The assignment in the Chapter 5 Annual Report Project (p. F-181) helps you analyze a firm's internal environment.

Since businesses do not operate in a vacuum, it is also important to gather background information about a company's external environment. The Financial Accounting Standards Board warns that external factors can seriously affect a company's performance:

Those who use financial information for business and economic decisions need to combine information provided by financial reporting with pertinent information from other sources, for example, information about general economic conditions or expectations, political events and political climate, or industry outlook.

—(FASB, Statement of Concepts #1, para. 22)

Because ratio analysis is based on financial statement information, conclusions drawn from its results should also consider the three factors mentioned in the FASB statement: general economic conditions, political events and political climate, and industry outlook. (A thorough external environment analysis can be found in the Chapter 6 Annual Report Project, p. F-221.)

General Economic Conditions and Expectations

The general economic environment in which a company operates affects its business activity and therefore its financial results. For a company producing goods bought by the general public, bright economic conditions generally enhance sales. For a company manufacturing and selling equipment to other companies, an economy that encourages business growth is an important factor. So first we must consider general economic conditions and expectations when evaluating the performance and overall financial position of a business.

The health of the American economy receives widespread daily news coverage. Popular business periodicals such as *Business Week* and *Fortune* inform their readers about current economic conditions. Statistical data on measures of economic health (e.g., gross national product, producer price index) are available in such books as *The Economic Indicators Handbook.* The U.S. Department of Commerce, in a monthly publication called *Survey of Current Business,* provides data from dozens of general economic and business cycle indicators.

Economic decision makers not only evaluate past performance of businesses: they also attempt to predict future performance. Business periodicals are good sources for information about anticipated changes in economic conditions. Business analysts, economists, and politicians often voice their views on television, on radio, and in print. Remember, though, all of these "expert" predictions of the future of the U.S. economy are, at best, educated guesses. Use this information carefully!

Although general economic conditions certainly affect a company's performance, a company's poor performance should not be excused because the economy is in a recession. Neither should a company's exceptional performance be dismissed as simply the product of a healthy economy. Economic conditions provide one context within which we evaluate the results of business activity. Other external factors must also be considered.

Political Events and Political Climate

Politics is the second external factor mentioned by the FASB. The terms *political events* and *political climate* are closely related yet different terms. A political event is an action that has already taken place, whereas a political climate is a situation that can lead to an action.

Political parties each take credit when the general economy improves and blame each other when it declines. That is the nature of politics. The truth is that both improvement and decline in the general economy result from many interrelated and complex factors. Indeed, the factors affecting the general economy are so complicated and intertwined that no political party can control the economy enough to take credit or blame. Still, there is no question that what goes on in politics, both domestic and foreign, has a significant influence on the general economy as well as on the world of business. The actions taken by Congress and the president on such matters as the amount of government regulation, income taxes, health care, and welfare reform will have an enormous impact on the general economy. And we know that changes in the general economy will affect the level of business activity.

The collapse of the Soviet Union, the reunification of Germany, and other world political events that marked the end of the Cold War had strong repercussions in the U.S. economy in the last decade of the twentieth century. These foreign political events changed the entire defense industry, which created a ripple effect on many other industries and the communities that depend on them. Reduced purchases by the Pentagon of items used for national defense, for example, forced such companies as Motorola, Lockheed, and Rockwell International to make major adjustments in their businesses.

In the United States, the political climate is generally reflected in public opinion. For the past two decades, the public has scrutinized companies' positions on social and environmental issues. The concept of being "politically correct" arose from such public scrutiny. As we discussed in Chapter 1, a wise firm pays close attention to its social responsibility and frequently describes its corporate citizenship in its annual report. A growing number of investors have resolved to invest their money only in companies that have a genuine commitment to responsible behavior. This trend has generated a broader sense of social responsibility in American corporations.

Where, then, can you find accurate, objective information about a company's corporate citizenship? Your library most likely has publications intended to give you this information, but the evaluations you read will reflect the writer's views of corporate social responsibility, which may not coincide with your own. We suggest that instead of naively accepting such appraisals, you carefully consider the perspective of each author.

Thus far we have explored the impact of both economic and political conditions on business activity. In addition to considering these factors when using financial information, the FASB also warns us to consider the outlook for the industry in which the company operates.

Industry Outlook

The third factor to consider when using financial information is the industry in which a company operates, for industry affiliation may define the company's prospects for future growth. As Roy Taub, vice president of Standard and Poor's, once pointed out:

> The industry is the environment in which the company operates and it defines both the opportunities the company may seize and the challenges it must face.

> —(S&P, 1983, p. 2)

Industry opportunities and challenges are key considerations in evaluating a company's outlook. For example, a company in an industry that is facing an overall decline in demand may be powerless to take any action to encourage its own future growth. As we mentioned earlier, cuts in the federal defense budget resulted in reduced demand for such items as military aircraft and tanks, affecting the entire industry producing these goods. Certainly, this type of industry-wide trend touches all companies within the industry.

Government action is not the only force that produces industry-wide effects. Technological change often spurs spectacular growth within an industry. The field of telecommunications, for instance, has undergone a revolution in the past decade. Just a short time ago, the fax machine was an expensive luxury—a form of communication reserved for "big business." Today, most computers come from the factory with internal faxes and many individuals have complete computer systems connected to the Internet.

Often a technological change that opens the doors of opportunity in one industry closes them in another. For example, the development of personal computers has virtually wiped out opportunities for expansion among companies producing typewriters. But remember that each threat produces opportunity. Adaptable companies will change the product mix to seize upon new opportunities and discontinue product lines that no longer have markets. So when considering a company's outlook for the future, it is important to learn what lies ahead for the entire industry and to see how the company has planned to meet any environmental threats.

Discussion Question

12–3. Changes in society, family structures, and the way people behave and interact have had dramatic impact since the 1970s. Cite two examples of such changes, identify industries they have affected, and describe how they did so.

Not only does a company's industry affiliation affect the opportunities it faces, but it may also define the challenges ahead. For example, a few decades ago, companies did not have to consider the environmental impact of their actions. After the establishment of the Environmental Protection Agency, however, many companies were forced to spend significant amounts of money to comply with EPA regulations. These regulations cost some industries more than others. For example, when the EPA banned the use of DDT as a pesticide, companies that manufactured this product either converted to the production of other products or went out of business. The impact of this ban was also felt in agriculture, as farmers who had depended on DDT as their primary pesticide were forced to switch to less effective, sometimes more expensive, products.

The flip side of government regulation is deregulation. When government suddenly discontinues its regulation and frees the market, it has an impact on all companies operating within the deregulated industry. For example, when the federal government deregulated the commercial airline industry in the early 1980s, all airline companies were affected, and many did not survive.

Prior to deregulation, the federal government set standard airfares. All airlines flying passengers from one specific destination to another charged the same fare. Companies competed on amenities—in-flight movies, food, drink, and the like—not on price. The government also required airlines to operate unprofitable flights for the convenience of customers in underpopulated areas. Fares of profitable flights were set high enough to offset the companies' losses from these unprofitable flights.

With deregulation came competition. Forced to make every flight profitable, airlines canceled many routes and began scrambling to attract customers. The result was a price war that forced several legendary carriers such as Pan Am out of business. Deregulation was seen by newer "upstart" companies as an opportunity, but unregulated competition became an environment of survival of the fittest. Many old and new companies failed to survive.

Discussion Questions

12–4. Identify two industries and describe their similarities and differences.

12–5. If you were offered an upper-level management position in two companies—one from each of the industries you identified in your response to Discussion Question 12–4—which would you take? Why?

12–6. If you had $2,000 to invest and your only options were the common stock of two companies—one from each of the industries you identified in your response to Discussion Question 12–4—which would you choose? Explain your reasoning.

Where do you look for information about a particular industry? Several sources are available. *Standard and Poor's Industry Surveys* is composed of numerous sections with various types of information. One section offers recent articles about each industry written by professional business analysts or drawn from business publications. Another good source is the *U.S. Industry & Trade Outlook*, which offers background information and projections for the 10 fastest-growing and 10 slowest-growing industries, 40 service industries, and over 150 manufacturing industries. This book includes references to sources that contain more detailed information about each industry. *Moody's Industry Review* provides comparative statistics on specific industries. These are three good examples available in your library.

Heeding the warning of the FASB, we have explored the importance of background information and suggested how you can gather data on general economic conditions and expectations, political climate and events, and industry outlook. The impact of each of these factors on a company's past performance and its prospects should be considered when doing any type of financial statement analysis, for these impacts provide the context within which financial information should be evaluated.

Now we turn to the heart of this chapter—ratio analysis.

RATIO ANALYSIS: CALCULATING THE RATIOS

Before we compute any ratios, you need to understand that the absolute numbers resulting from the calculations are of little value in themselves. It is the analysis and interpretation of the numbers—the art of ratio analysis—that produces the desired information. To be truly useful to economic decision makers, a company's ratios need to be compared to other information, such as the ratio values for industry averages or the company's ratios in past years. After introducing all the ratios in this section of the chapter, we will make these comparisons and interpret the findings in the next.

Ratio analysis, as we explained at the beginning of the chapter, is a method of analyzing the relationship between two items from a company's financial statements for a given period. You will recall that we said important relationships may exist between two items on the same financial statement or between two items from different financial statements. All the ratios we present here are based on information from the balance sheet and the income statement. Some use items from the same financial statement, while others use one item from each statement.

As we introduce each ratio, we will explore what information it offers and show how it is calculated. The 14 ratios we have selected for presentation are representative ratios only. There are many more ratios than these. The reason we chose these particular 14 ratios is that they are the ratios found in the *Almanac of Business and Industrial Financial Ratios,* which we use later in the chapter to compare the Gap's ratios to industry averages.

One other item needs to be addressed before we begin computing and comparing ratios: There is a lack of consistency among analysts in the way they calculate various ratios. Even when the name of the ratio is the same from one analyst to the next, the financial statement items the two analysts used to calculate that ratio may have been different. This inconsistency often makes it very difficult to compare ratios calculated by different analysts or financial publications. Descriptions of the ratios in this chapter are consistent with those provided in the *Almanac of Business and Industrial Financial Ratios,* a widely used source of financial ratio data, but by no means the only one. Computations of each ratio will be illustrated using the Gap Inc. financial statements presented in the company's 1997 annual report. Be certain you understand how we determined which figures from the Gap's balance sheet and income statement to use for each ratio.

A variety of ratios are computed by decision makers analyzing financial statements. These ratios are used to glean information about a company's past performance and current financial position that will help the decision maker predict future results of business activity. The 14 ratios presented in this chapter are used to measure either profitability, liquidity, or solvency—three characteristics important to those assessing a company's well-being. As each characteristic is described, we will discuss which users are most interested in it and why it is of concern to them.

Measuring Profitability

profitability The ease with which a company generates income.

Profitability is the ease with which a company generates income. If a company generates a high level of income very easily, it is said to have high profitability. All companies must maintain at least a minimum level of profitability to meet their obligations, such as servicing long-term debt and paying dividends to stockholders. **Profitability ratios** measure a firm's past performance and help predict its future profitability level. Present and potential stockholders, and long-term creditors, therefore, use these ratios to evaluate investments. Similarly, managers use them to monitor and evaluate their company's performance.

profitability ratios A set of ratios that measures a firm's past performance and help predict its future profitability level.

Analysts must utilize profitability ratios carefully. Managers have two potential reasons to boost these ratios and make the company appear very profitable. First, they may want to make the company's financial results look more appealing to external decision makers. Second, their own compensation may be directly tied to these profitability ratios, for often managers receive bonuses based on the level of profitability achieved by the company. Do stockholders and creditors also want the company to be profitable? Yes, but profitability ratios are based on short-term results (usually one year), and the only way to boost them is to attain the highest possible profit for any given year. That in itself seems satisfactory, however:

> **A preoccupation with short-term profits is detrimental to the long-term value of a business!**

Stockholders and creditors, then, should generally take a longer-term view of the company's health than can be measured by profitability alone.

As you look at the profitability ratios in this section, focus both on what they should reveal about a company and on how they might encourage shortsighted behavior by management. It is quite common for managers to slant business decisions toward that which makes the ratios "look better" to the decision makers who are using their company's financial statements.

Discussion Question

12–7. Give an example of a management decision that would be made differently depending on whether the decision maker is considering the short-term or long-term well-being of the company. Explain the impact of the two different perspectives on the outcome of the decision.

return on assets ratio
A profitability ratio that measures how efficiently the company uses assets to produce profits.

Return on Assets Ratio

The **return on assets ratio** (sometimes called the return on total assets) measures how efficiently the company uses its assets to produce profits. After all, the reason companies invest in assets is to produce revenue and ultimately profit (net income). Southwest Airlines, for example, invests in aircraft and other assets for the express purpose of producing income. Southwest's creditors (particularly long-term), stockholders, and management are all interested in knowing how efficiently the aircraft and other assets are being used to produce the company's income. The return on assets ratio is one approach to measuring that efficiency. It is computed as follows:

$$\text{Return on assets} = \frac{\text{Net income before taxes}}{\text{Total assets}}$$

The numerator comes from the income statement and represents the total return (pretax) on the company's assets. The denominator is drawn from the balance sheet, and indicates the company's level of investment in assets. We calculate the Gap's return on assets for 1997:

$$\frac{\$854,242}{\$3,337,502} = 0.25595 \text{ or } 25.6\%$$

If a company has a low return on its assets, how would it determine the cause of the problem and improve the situation? The answer to that question lies in the next two profitability ratios we will examine, because they are actually the two components of the return on assets ratio.

profit margin before income tax ratio A profitability ratio that measures the earnings produced from a given level of revenues by comparing net income before income tax to the revenue figure.

Profit Margin Before Income Tax Ratio

The **profit margin before income tax ratio** has the same numerator as the return on assets ratio. The denominator for this ratio is total sales for the period. By comparing net income to sales, we can determine the amount of income produced by a given level of revenue. We calculate the profit margin before income tax as follows:

$$\text{Profit margin before income tax} = \frac{\text{Net income before taxes}}{\text{Sales}}$$

Both components of the profit margin before tax are drawn from the income statement. This ratio indicates the contribution of sales to the overall profitability of the company—it shows how much net income is generated from a dollar of sales. The Gap's profit margin before income taxes for 1997 is:

$$\frac{\$854,242}{\$6,507,825} = 0.13126 \text{ or } 13.1\%$$

Discussion Question

12–8. What situations might cause a company to have a low profit margin before income tax?

Profit margin before income tax is just one component of the return on assets ratio; the second component—total asset turnover—is equally important.

total asset turnover ratio A profitability ratio that indicates the amount of revenues produced for a given level of assets used.

Total Asset Turnover Ratio　The **total asset turnover ratio** shows the amount of sales produced for a given level of assets used. The purpose of this ratio is similar to that of the return on total assets ratio except that it indicates how effectively the company uses its total assets to generate sales rather than net income. Total asset turnover has the same denominator as the return on assets ratio, but the numerator is total sales for the period. We calculate total asset turnover as follows:

$$\text{Total asset turnover} = \frac{\text{Sales}}{\text{Total assets}}$$

The numerator is drawn from the income statement and the denominator from the balance sheet. We calculate the total asset turnover ratio for Gap Inc. in 1997 as:

$$\frac{\$6,507,825}{\$3,337,502} = 1.9499 \text{ or } 1.95 \text{ times}$$

By comparing the sales figure for the period to the total assets used to produce the revenue, we can determine the amount of revenue produced by a given level of asset investment. Our calculation indicates that the Gap produced 1.95 times as many dollars in sales as it had invested in assets.

Now that we have explored both components of the return on assets ratio, we can look more closely at the relationship among the three ratios:

$$\frac{\text{Return on}}{\text{Assets}} = \frac{\text{Profit margin}}{\text{before taxes}} \times \frac{\text{Total asset}}{\text{turnover}}$$

$$\frac{\text{Net income before taxes}}{\text{Total assets}} = \frac{\text{Net income before taxes}}{\text{Sales}} \times \frac{\text{Sales}}{\text{Total assets}}$$

If a company's return on assets is low, both its profit margin before income tax and its total asset turnover should be investigated—separately—to determine the source of the problem. After each component is analyzed, the company will be in a position to focus on areas needing improvement.

Discussion Questions

12–9. Offer two separate suggestions as to how a company can make its total asset turnover ratio higher.

12–10. A company wishing to boost its return on assets ratio could focus its efforts on either component—profit margin before income tax or total asset turnover ratio. Which component do you think would be easier to improve? Explain how you came to your conclusion.

Rather than relying on any single measure of profitability, wise financial statement users turn to several different ratios. We now explore three more profitability ratios.

profit margin after income tax ratio A profitability ratio that measures the earnings produced from a given level of revenues by comparing net income after income tax with the revenue figure.

Profit Margin After Income Tax Ratio As its name suggests, this ratio is only slightly different from the profit margin measure already discussed. The **profit margin after income tax ratio** indicates the amount of after-tax net income generated by a dollar of sales. This difference is subtle, but it may be important in some analyses. The profit margin after income tax is calculated as follows:

$$\text{Profit margin after income tax} = \frac{\text{Net income after taxes}}{\text{Sales}}$$

Both components of this ratio are drawn from the income statement. The calculation of the Gap's profit margin after income tax for 1997 is:

$$\frac{\$533,901}{\$6,507,825} = 0.082 \text{ or } 8.2\%$$

Whether profit margin is computed before or after taxes, the result is a useful measure of profitability. As Dennis E. Logue suggests in the *Handbook of Modern Finance:*

> The profit margin percentage measures a firm's ability to (1) obtain higher prices for its products relative to competitors and (2) control the level of operating costs, or expenses, relative to revenues generated. By holding down costs, a firm increases the profits from a given amount of revenue and thereby improves its profit margin percentage.

Just as profit margin after tax is similar to profit margin before tax, the final two profitability ratios we will examine are also similar to one another.

return on equity ratio A profitability ratio that measures the after-tax net income generated from a given level of investment by a company's owners.

Return on Equity Ratio The **return on equity ratio** demonstrates profitability by comparing a company's after-tax net income to the amount of investment by the company's owners. Equity represents the owners' claims to the assets of the business. Return on equity indicates how much after-tax income was generated for a given level of equity. The return on equity ratio is calculated as follows:

$$\text{Return on equity} = \frac{\text{Net income after taxes}}{\text{Equity}}$$

The numerator of this ratio is drawn from the income statement and the denominator is taken from the balance sheet. The calculation of the Gap's return on equity for 1997 is:

$$\frac{\$533,901}{\$1,583,986} = 0.189 \text{ or } 18.9\%$$

The final profitability ratio we will examine is only slightly different from the return on equity ratio.

return before interest on equity ratio A profitability ratio that measures the level of earnings (before the cost of borrowing) generated from a given level of equity.

Return Before Interest on Equity Ratio As its name suggests, the **return before interest on equity ratio** considers the earnings of the company before interest expense. To calculate net income before interest, we add the interest expense of the period to the after-tax net income. This addition of interest expense to the numerator is the only difference between return before interest on equity and return on equity. The denominator, total shareholders' equity, remains the same.

$$\text{Return before interest on equity} = \frac{\text{Net income after taxes} + \text{Interest expense}}{\text{Equity}}$$

The only problem we have is that the Gap's income statement does not indicate how much interest expense the company paid in 1997. We must look into the Notes to the Financial Statements to find this information. The most logical place to look is the note on debt. Note B on page 33 of the annual report discusses debt financing. The last sentence of the first column contains the information we seek in whole dollars. Notice that the financial statements are in thousands of dollars, so we must convert the $8,399,000 to $8,399 for our equation. The calculation of the Gap's return before interest on equity for 1997 is:

$$\frac{\$533,901 + \$8,399}{\$1,583,986} = 0.34236 \text{ or } 34.2\%$$

By the nature of the calculation, as long as a company has at least some interest expense, its return before interest on equity will be higher than its return on equity.

Discussion Questions

12–11. Can we always find the amount of interest expense for the reporting period in the annual report? Why?

12–12. Name at least three places the interest expense might be found in an annual report.

Measuring Liquidity

An asset's liquidity describes the ease with which it can be converted to cash. A company's liquidity refers to its ability to generate the cash needed to meet its short-term obligations. Clearly, all economic decision makers must consider a firm's liquidity, for if a company cannot meet its current obligations, it may not be around long enough to be profitable in the long run. Short-term creditors and company's management, however, tend to be the information users who pay most careful attention to liquidity.

Over time many ratios have been developed specifically to measure liquidity. The five **liquidity ratios** we have chosen to discuss take different approaches to evaluating a firm's ability to generate sufficient cash to meet its short-term obligations. Several of them consider current assets and current liabilities. Recall that a current asset is one that is either already cash or is expected to become cash within one year, and a current liability is any obligation that must be paid within one year. If we are interested in liquidity, certainly we would expect to find helpful information in these two balance sheet categories.

liquidity ratios A set of ratios developed to measure a firm's ability to generate sufficient cash in the short run to retire short-term liabilities.

current ratio A liquidity ratio that measures a company's ability to meet short-term obligations by comparing current assets to current liabilities.

Current Ratio The **current ratio** is probably the most widely used measure of a company's liquidity. It compares current assets to current liabilities, offering a measure of the company's ability to meet its short-term financial obligations with cash generated from current assets. The current ratio is calculated as follows:

$$\text{Current ratio} = \frac{\text{Current assets}}{\text{Current liabilities}}$$

This ratio indicates the amount of current assets for each dollar of current liabilities. The 1997 current ratio for Gap Inc. is:

$$\frac{\$1,830,947}{\$991,548} = 1.85 \text{ to } 1$$

This figure indicates that Gap Inc. had $1.85 of current assets for every $1.00 of current liabilities at the end of 1997.

Many experts believe that companies should maintain a ratio of $2.00 of current assets to every $1.00 of current liabilities because of the uncertain nature of some of the current assets. For example, some accounts receivable may not be collected, and some inventory may not be salable. Some companies choose to exceed this recommendation and maintain more than twice as many current assets as current liabilities. However, many companies have found that a current ratio lower than 2:1 is adequate. You will learn how to interpret the Gap's current ratio of 1.85 later in this chapter.

Discussion Question

12–13. If Gap Inc. were to borrow money to retire current liabilities, it would have to pay interest on the borrowed funds. What effect (if any) would the additional interest expense have on the following ratios:

    a. profit margin before income tax?
    b. profit margin after income tax?
    c. return on assets?
    d. return on equity?
    e. total asset turnover?

quick ratio or **acid-test ratio** A liquidity ratio that is similar to the current ratio, but a more stringent test of liquidity, because only current assets considered to be highly liquid (quickly converted to cash) are included in the calculation.

Quick Ratio   The **quick ratio,** which is sometimes called the **acid-test ratio,** is similar to the current ratio. It is a more stringent test of liquidity, however, because it considers only current assets that are highly liquid (quickly convertible into cash) in the numerator. Some variation exists as to what assets are included in the quick ratio calculation because the definition of "highly liquid" is quite subjective. We calculate the quick ratio as follows:

$$\text{Quick ratio} = \frac{\text{Cash} + \text{Receivables} + \text{Marketable (Trading) Securities}}{\text{Current liabilities}}$$

In the numerator of our equation, cash is obviously liquid. We also assume accounts receivable and notes receivable will be quickly converted to cash. However, if a company knows that any account receivable or note receivable will not be quickly converted, it should not include that item in the calculation of this ratio. Marketable securities held in a company's trading portfolio is highly liquid and often represents excess cash that the company plans to use in the near future. The denominator of the quick ratio is identical to the one used for the current ratio.

Discussion Question

12–14. Besides the three assets—cash, accounts receivable, and notes receivable—considered in our version of the quick ratio, what other current assets might a company have?

The 1997 quick ratio for Gap Inc. is:

$$\frac{\$913,169 + \$0 + \$0}{\$991,548} = 0.921 \text{ to } 1$$

This figure suggests that Gap Inc. has $0.92 of quick assets for each $1.00 of current liabilities. Note that the Gap's quick ratio (0.921) is lower than its current ratio (1.85). That is as it should be because we have removed assets that are not highly liquid from the numerator, while the denominator remained untouched. Some experts believe that a company should maintain a ratio of $1.00 of quick assets to every $1.00 of current liabilities. As our calculation shows, Gap Inc.'s quick ratio is slightly lower, but current trends find healthy companies pulling the quick ratio as low as .80. Later in the chapter we will see how to interpret results of the quick ratio calculation.

Discussion Question

12–15. How would holding an excessive amount of inventory affect the following ratios:

    a. profit margin before income tax?
    b. profit margin after income tax?
    c. return on assets?
    d. return on equity?
    e. current ratio?
    f. quick ratio?
    g. total asset turnover?

The liquidity ratios we have examined thus far have focused on the proportion of current assets to current liabilities. The next liquidity ratio considers the difference between current assets and current liabilities.

net sales to working capital ratio A ratio used to measure the level of sales generated from a given level of working capital.

Net Sales to Working Capital Ratio Recall that liquidity refers to a company's ability to generate sufficient cash to meet its short-term obligations. Our discussion of the current ratio suggested that to maintain their liquidity, companies should have more current assets than current liabilities. The difference between current assets and current liabilities is called working capital. Some decision makers use working capital to evaluate a company's liquidity. The **net sales to working capital ratio** goes one step further: It indicates the level of sales generated for a given level of working capital, and it is calculated as follows:

$$\text{Net sales to working capital} = \frac{\text{Sales}}{\text{Current assets} - \text{Current liabilities}}$$

This ratio indicates the amount of sales generated for each $1.00 of working capital. The 1997 net sales to working capital ratio for Gap Inc. is:

$$\frac{\$6,507,825}{\$1,830,947 - \$991,548} = 7.75 \text{ to } 1$$

This figure suggests that in 1997 the Gap generated $7.75 in sales for every $1.00 of working capital it had at the end of 1997.

The net sales to working capital ratio is not the only liquidity ratio to focus on the generation of sales. Receivables turnover does, as well.

receivables turnover ratio A liquidity ratio that measures how quickly a company collects its accounts receivable.

Receivables Turnover Ratio

The **receivables turnover ratio** measures the liquidity of accounts receivable. Accounts receivable is the amount a company is owed by its customers, and it is often a sizable current asset. Companies need to convert accounts receivable to cash as quickly as possible because they represent interest-free loans to customers. Most companies routinely sell to their customers on a credit basis. Because all the Gap's sales are cash sales, it has no receivables, which increases the timing of Gap Inc.'s cash flow and shortens its operating cycle.

The receivables turnover ratio indicates how quickly a company collects its receivables. The calculation for receivables turnover is:

$$\text{Receivables turnover} = \frac{\text{Sales}}{\text{Accounts receivable}}$$

The sales figure is drawn from the income statement and accounts receivable is found on the balance sheet. The 1997 receivables turnover ratio for Gap Inc. is:

$$\frac{\$6,507,825}{\$0} = \infty$$

Obviously, the ratio is meaningless when the company has no receivables. Later in the chapter we will see whether this occurrence is common to the industry. If Gap Inc. had receivables and its ratio were six times, we would know that the company turns its receivables over an average of six times per year. A higher number would indicate that a company turns over its receivables more often, suggesting that the company collects cash from its credit customers more quickly. A lower number would suggest that it collects payments from customers more slowly.

The information that a company turns over its accounts receivable six times per year becomes easier to interpret if we extend it to determine the average collection period for its accounts receivable. We can do that by dividing the receivables turnover into 365 (the number of days in a year) to determine the average time it takes the company to collect its receivables:

$$\frac{365}{6} = 60.8 \text{ days}$$

Our calculation shows that it takes a company an average of 60.8 days from the time it makes a credit sale to collect cash from the customer. Is that good or bad? Once again, there is no way to tell from the absolute number. This figure only becomes meaningful when it is compared with a company's results for other years and the average for the industry in which it operates.

The final liquidity ratio we present is quite similar in nature to the receivables turnover.

inventory turnover ratio A liquidity ratio that indicates how long a company holds its inventory.

Inventory Turnover Ratio

Like the receivables turnover ratio, the **inventory turnover ratio** is a measure of the liquidity of one specific asset—in this case, inventory. This ratio indicates the number of times total merchandise inventory is purchased and sold during a period. The calculation of inventory turnover is as follows:

$$\text{Inventory turnover} = \frac{\text{Cost of sales}}{\text{Inventory}}$$

We normally find the cost of sales expense on the income statement, and the inventory asset on the balance sheet. But Gap Inc.'s income statement amount includes the cost of occupancy, which gives us a less than desirable measure of the inventory turnover. Upon further inspection of the annual report, we find Ten-Year Selected Financial Data on pages 20 and 21. This listing of information includes cost of goods sold and occupancy expenses excluding depreciation and amortization for 10 years. That information is closer to what we want, although it still includes some of the occupancy expense. As we discussed, analysts sometimes have to find the information they need in the footnotes and other information. Using the amount shown on pages 20 and 21, the 1997 inventory turnover ratio for the Gap is:

$$\frac{\$3,775,957}{\$733,174} = 5.15 \text{ times}$$

This means Gap Inc. turns its inventory over an average of 5.15 times per year. A higher number would indicate that the Gap turns over its inventory more often, suggesting that the company requires a lower investment in inventory to support its sales.

We find the information that Gap Inc. turns over its inventory 5.15 times per year easier to interpret if we extend it to determine the average number of days Gap Inc. holds its inventory. By dividing the inventory turnover into 365 (the number of days in a year), we can determine the average time the Gap holds inventory between its purchase and its sale.

$$\frac{365}{5.15} = 70.87 \text{ days}$$

Our calculation shows that, on average, 70.87 days pass between the time Gap Inc. purchases inventory and the time it sells that inventory. Is that good or bad? As was the case with receivables turnover, there is no way to tell from the absolute number. This figure only becomes useful when it is compared with the Gap's results for other years and the average for the industry in which the Gap operates. Later in the chapter, when we compare the Gap's ratios with industry averages, we will use the 5.15 figure because the *Almanac of Business and Industrial Financial Ratios* presents data on inventory turnover ratios rather than the average days inventory is held.

Measuring Solvency

solvency A company's ability to meet the obligations created by its long-term debt.

Solvency is the third important characteristic that decision makers use as an indication of companies' financial well-being. **Solvency** is a company's ability to meet the obligations created by its long-term debt. Obligations resulting from debt include both paying back the amount borrowed and paying interest on the debt. A set of **solvency ratios** has been developed to measure firms' solvency. Some of these ratios focus on the overall level of debt a company carries, while others measure a company's ability to make interest payments. A solvency ratio focusing on ability to make interest payments is similar in purpose to a liquidity ratio.

solvency ratios A set of ratios developed to measure a firm's ability to meet its long-term debt obligations.

Solvency ratios are of most interest to stockholders, long-term creditors, and, of course, company management. There are numerous solvency ratios; we will look at three of the ones most widely used.

debt ratio A solvency ratio that indicates what proportion of a company's assets is financed by debt.

Debt Ratio The **debt ratio** measures what proportion of a company's assets is financed by debt. All of a company's assets are claimed by either creditors or owners. This can be demonstrated by looking once again at the accounting (business) equation:

Assets = Liabilities + Owners' Equity
100% = Some % + Some %

Calculation of the debt ratio illustrates the percentage of assets that are supported by debt financing. Creditors and stockholders watch the debt ratio from their individual perspectives and tend to get nervous if they perceive it to be out of balance. The format of the debt ratio may vary somewhat. We will calculate it as follows:

$$\text{Debt ratio} = \frac{\text{Total liabilities}}{\text{Total assets}}$$

Both the items necessary to calculate the debt ratio can be found on the balance sheet. The Gap's 1997 debt ratio is:

$$\frac{\$1,753,516}{\$3,337,502} = 0.52539 \text{ or } 52.54\%$$

This equation would indicate that 52.54 percent of the Gap's assets are supported by debt, leaving 47.46 percent of the company's assets to be claimed by the shareholders. There is no hard-and-fast rule concerning what amount of a company's assets should be financed through debt, although a rule of thumb ranges from 40 to 60 percent debt financing. A company's debt ratio must be evaluated in light of the industry in which the company operates, the maturity of the company (new businesses tend to have more debt relative to equity), and management's philosophy concerning the proper balance between debt financing and equity financing.

Discussion Question

12–16. How did we determine Gap Inc.'s 1997 total liabilities were $1,753.5 million? Provide a calculation to support your answer.

The debt ratio indicates the relationship between the amount of liabilities and the assets held by a company. The next solvency ratio we examine considers a company's liabilities in relation to stockholders' equity.

total liabilities to net worth ratio A solvency ratio indicating the relationship between creditors' claims to a company's assets and the owners' claims to those assets.

Total Liabilities to Net Worth Ratio   Net worth is synonymous with total owners' equity or assets minus liabilities. The **total liabilities to net worth ratio** is a solvency ratio indicating the relationship between creditors' claims to the company's assets (liabilities) and owners' claims to those assets (net worth).

As is obvious from its name, the total liabilities to net worth ratio is calculated as:

$$\text{Total liabilities to net worth} = \frac{\text{Total liabilities}}{\text{Net worth}}$$

Both the items necessary to calculate the total liabilities to net worth ratio can be found on the balance sheet. The numerator is the same as for the debt ratio. The Gap's 1997 total liabilities to net worth ratio is:

$$\frac{\$1,753,516}{\$1,583,986} = 1.107$$

The Gap has $1.11 of debt for every $1 of equity.

Both the debt ratio and total liabilities to net worth ratio focus on the overall debt load carried by a company. The last solvency ratio we will examine indicates a company's ability to meet the obligations associated with its debt.

coverage ratio or **times interest earned ratio** A solvency ratio that provides an indication of a company's ability to make its periodic interest payments.

Coverage Ratio   The **coverage ratio,** also called the **times interest earned ratio,** indicates a company's ability to make its periodic interest payments. It compares the amount of income available for interest payments to the interest requirements. Creditors use this ratio to assess the risk associated with lending money to a business. The formula used to calculate this ratio is:

$$\text{Coverage ratio} = \frac{\text{Earnings before interest expense and income taxes}}{\text{Interest expense}}$$

The numerator consists of earnings before interest and tax expense because this figure represents the amount of earnings available for periodic interest payments. To arrive at this amount, we need to add interest expense to earnings before taxes on the income statement. Interest expense is usually found on the income statement, but we already found the Gap's interest expense in the footnotes to the financial statement. The Gap's 1997 coverage ratio is:

$$\frac{\$854,242 + 8,399}{\$8,399} = 102.7 \text{ times}$$

Some experts believe a coverage ratio of at least four provides an appropriate degree of safety for creditors. This means a company's earnings before interest and taxes should be at least four times as great as its interest expense. The Gap's figure far exceeds that level.

To arrive at a valid assessment of a company's solvency, financial statement users should evaluate ratios that indicate the level of debt carried by the company (debt ratio and total liabilities to net worth) as well as those indicating the company's ability to meet its obligations associated with the debt (coverage ratio). In fact, when evaluating any of the three characteristics indicative of a company's well-being, more than one approach should be considered.

Analysts use ratio analysis to evaluate the company's current levels of profitability, liquidity, and solvency. Ratios can send up red flags that warn management, creditors, and investors of trouble ahead. An unprofitable company becomes illiquid because it cannot generate profits and cash, which eventually leads to insolvency. Insolvency then leads to bankruptcy. When red flags appear, management can initiate corrective action to prevent future troubles. Exhibit 12–1 summarizes the calculations and purpose of the profitability, liquidity, and solvency ratios discussed in this chapter.

Discussion Questions

12–17. Assume you had to decide to invest in one of two companies with no information other than values of four of their financial ratios. Which four would you want to know? Explain the reasons for your choices.

12–18. Martino Company and Patco Corporation are in the same line of business. However, Martino uses straight-line depreciation, whereas Patco uses an accelerated depreciation method. If this is the only difference in the business activity of the two companies, how should their financial ratios compare at the end of their first year of operations? Explain the effect of the difference in depreciation methods on each of the 14 ratios described in this chapter.

Exhibit 12–1
Summary of Key Ratios

Ratio	Calculation	Purpose of Ratio
Profitability Ratios		
1. Return on Assets	$\dfrac{\text{Net income before taxes}}{\text{Total assets}}$	Measures the return earned on investment in assets.
2. Profit Margin Before Income Tax	$\dfrac{\text{Net income before taxes}}{\text{Sales}}$	Measures the pretax earnings produced from a given level of revenues.
3. Total Asset Turnover	$\dfrac{\text{Sales}}{\text{Total assets}}$	Indicates the firm's ability to generate revenues from a given level of assets.
4. Profit Margin After Income Tax	$\dfrac{\text{Net income after taxes}}{\text{Sales}}$	Measures the amount of after-tax net income generated by a dollar of sales.
5. Return on Equity	$\dfrac{\text{Net income after taxes}}{\text{Equity}}$	Measures the after-tax income generated from a given level of equity.
6. Return Before Interest on Equity	$\dfrac{\text{Net income after taxes } + \text{ Interest expense}}{\text{Equity}}$	Measures the return on equity before the cost of borrowing.
Liquidity Ratios		
7. Current Ratio	$\dfrac{\text{Current assets}}{\text{Current liabilities}}$	Indicates a company's ability to meet short-term obligations.
8. Quick Ratio	$\dfrac{\text{Cash } + \text{ Accounts receivable } + \text{ Notes receivable}}{\text{Current liabilities}}$	Measures short-term liquidity more stringently than the current ratio does.
9. Net Sales to Working Capital	$\dfrac{\text{Sales}}{\text{Current assets } - \text{ Current liabilities}}$	Measures the level of sales generated from a given level of working capital.
10. Receivables Turnover	$\dfrac{\text{Sales}}{\text{Accounts receivable}}$	Indicates how quickly a company collects its receivables.
11. Inventory Turnover	$\dfrac{\text{Cost of sales}}{\text{Inventory}}$	Indicates how long a company holds its inventory.
Solvency Ratios		
12. Debt Ratio	$\dfrac{\text{Total liabilities}}{\text{Total assets}}$	Measures the proportion of assets financed by debt.
13. Total Liabilities to Net Worth	$\dfrac{\text{Total liabilities}}{\text{Net worth}}$	Directly compares the amount of debt financing to the amount of equity financing.
14. Coverage Ratio	$\dfrac{\text{Earnings before interest expense and income taxes}}{\text{Interest expense}}$	Indicates a company's ability to make its periodic interest payments.

RATIO ANALYSIS: USING THE RATIOS

We have calculated 14 ratios based on the financial statements included in Gap Inc.'s 1997 annual report. So now, how do we use these ratios to evaluate the profitability, liquidity, and solvency of the business?

Financial ratios are bits of data that become valuable information when used in comparison to prior years' ratios or to industry averages. This kind of interpretation is what we referred to earlier as the "art of ratio analysis." In this section of the chapter, we first do the industry comparison, and then the company analysis.

Before we can proceed to the industry comparison, however, you need to understand the system developed to classify companies into industry groupings.

Standard Industrial Classification System

In the appendix to Chapter 1, we made reference to a variety of publications you can use to find information about different industries and companies. These publications list companies alphabetically, but many of them also group firms by their industry affiliation. In other words, you may find lists in which companies are grouped or identified according to the industry in which they operate. The most widely accepted method for indicating the various industries is known as the Standard Industrial Classification (SIC) system. This system uses four-digit SIC codes to specify the industry in which a company operates.

A multiagency Technical Committee on Industrial Classification, sponsored by the federal Office of Management and Budget, developed the SIC codes, which have attained broad acceptance in financial publications. The Internal Revenue Service (IRS) uses a slightly modified version of these codes for the filing of corporate income tax returns.

Each of the four digits of an SIC code has a specific meaning. The first two digits indicate the major industrial division into which a company has been classified. The SIC separates U.S. industry into 11 major divisions, as shown in Exhibit 12–2. In fact, we can broadly identify a company just by looking at the first digit of its SIC code. If the first digit is a 0, the company's major business pursuit is agriculture, forestry, or fishing. If the first digit is a 1, the company is a member of either the mining division or the construction division.

Exhibit 12–2
The 11 Major Industrial Divisions of the SIC System

01 to 09	Agriculture, Forestry, and Fishing
10 to 14	Mining
15 to 17	Construction
20 to 39	Manufacturing
40 to 49	Transportation, Communications, Electric, Gas, and Sanitary Services
50 to 51	Wholesale Trade
52 to 59	Retail Trade
60 to 67	Finance, Insurance, and Real Estate
70 to 89	Services
91 to 97	Public Administration
99	Nonclassifiable Establishments

Because Gap Inc. operates in the retail sales industry, we will take a closer look at the retail division, indicated by digits 52 to 59. Any company whose SIC code has 52 through 59 as its first two digits is classified as a retailer.

The 11 major industrial divisions are further divided into more specific groups. Exhibit 12–3 lists the 82 major groups indicated by the first two digits of the SIC code. Consider a company that has an SIC code with 56 as the first two digits. We know immediately that the company is a retailer because the first two digits are between 52 and 59. Under the SIC code classifications, Group 56 represents apparel and accessory stores.

Notice several categories are titled nonclassifiable establishments. These categories include operations of the type described and other closely related types "not elsewhere classified." Even with approximately 900 four-digit SIC code categories, the system may not have a classification that clearly identifies a company's activities.

Exhibit 12–3
The 82 Major Groups in the SIC System

Industrial Division A.	Agriculture, Forestry, and Fishing	
	Major Group 01.	Agricultural production—crops
	Major Group 02.	Agriculture production livestock and animal specialties
	Major Group 07.	Agricultural services
	Major Group 08.	Forestry
	Major Group 09.	Fishing, hunting, and trapping
Industrial Division B.	Mining	
	Major Group 10.	Metal mining
	Major Group 12.	Coal mining
	Major Group 13.	Oil and gas extraction
	Major Group 14.	Mining and quarrying of nonmetallic minerals, except fuels
Industrial Division C.	Construction	
	Major Group 15.	Building construction—general contractors and operative builders
	Major Group 16.	Heavy construction other than building construction—contractors
	Major Group 17.	Construction—special trade contractors
Industrial Division D.	Manufacturing	
	Major Group 20.	Food and kindred products
	Major Group 21.	Tobacco products
	Major Group 22.	Textile mill products
	Major Group 23.	Apparel and other finished products made from fabrics and similar materials
	Major Group 24.	Lumber and wood products, except furniture
	Major Group 25.	Furniture and fixtures
	Major Group 26.	Paper and allied products
	Major Group 27.	Printing, publishing, and allied industries
	Major Group 28.	Chemicals and allied products
	Major Group 29.	Petroleum refining and related industries
	Major Group 30.	Rubber and miscellaneous plastics products
	Major Group 31.	Leather and leather products
	Major Group 32.	Stone, clay, glass, and concrete products
	Major Group 33.	Primary metal industries
	Major Group 34.	Fabricated metal products, except machinery and transportation equipment
	Major Group 35.	Industrial and commercial machinery and computer equipment
	Major Group 36.	Electronic and other electrical equipment and components, except computer equipment
	Major Group 37.	Transportation equipment
	Major Group 38.	Measuring, analyzing, and controlling instruments; photographic, medical and optical goods; watches and clocks
	Major Group 39.	Miscellaneous manufacturing industries
Industrial Division E.	Transportation, Communications, Electric, Gas, and Sanitary Services	
	Major Group 40.	Railroad transportation
	Major Group 41.	Local and suburban transit and interurban highway passenger transportation
	Major Group 42.	Motor freight transportation and warehousing
	Major Group 43.	United States Postal Service
	Major Group 44.	Water transportation
	Major Group 45.	Transportation by air
	Major Group 46.	Pipelines, except natural gas
	Major Group 47.	Transportation services
	Major Group 48.	Communications
	Major Group 49.	Electric, gas, and sanitary services

Exhibit 12–3
Continued

Industrial Division F.	Wholesale Trade	
	Major Group 50.	Wholesale trade—durable goods
	Major Group 51.	Wholesale trade—nondurable goods
Industrial Division G.	Retail Trade	
	Major Group 52.	Building materials, hardware, garden supply, and mobile home dealers
	Major Group 53.	General merchandise stores
	Major Group 54.	Food stores
	Major Group 55.	Automotive dealers and gasoline service stations
	Major Group 56.	Apparel and accessory stores
	Major Group 57.	Home furniture, furnishings, and equipment stores
	Major Group 58.	Eating and drinking places
	Major Group 59.	Miscellaneous retail
Industrial Division H.	Finance, Insurance, and Real Estate	
	Major Group 60.	Depository institutions
	Major Group 61.	Nondepository credit institutions
	Major Group 62.	Security and commodity brokers, dealers, exchanges, and services
	Major Group 63.	Insurance carriers
	Major Group 64.	Insurance agents, brokers, and service
	Major Group 65.	Real estate
	Major Group 67.	Holding and other investment offices
Industrial Division I.	Services	
	Major Group 70.	Hotels, rooming houses, camps, and other lodging places
	Major Group 72.	Personal services
	Major Group 73.	Business services
	Major Group 75.	Automotive repair, services, and parking
	Major Group 76.	Miscellaneous repair services
	Major Group 78.	Motion pictures
	Major Group 79.	Amusement and recreation services
	Major Group 80.	Health services
	Major Group 81.	Legal services
	Major Group 82.	Educational services
	Major Group 83.	Social services
	Major Group 84.	Museums, art galleries, and botanical and zoological gardens
	Major Group 86.	Membership organizations
	Major Group 87.	Engineering, accounting, research, management, and related services
	Major Group 88.	Private households
	Major Group 89.	Miscellaneous services
Industrial Division J.	Public Administration	
	Major Group 91.	Executive, legislative, and general government, except finance
	Major Group 92.	Justice, public order, and safety
	Major Group 93.	Public finance, taxation, and monetary policy
	Major Group 94.	Administration of human resource programs
	Major Group 95.	Administration of environmental quality and housing programs
	Major Group 96.	Administration of economic programs
	Major Group 97.	National security and international affairs
Industrial Division K.	Nonclassifiable Establishments	
	Major Group 99.	Nonclassifiable establishments

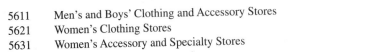

5611	Men's and Boys' Clothing and Accessory Stores
5621	Women's Clothing Stores
5631	Women's Accessory and Specialty Stores
5641	Children's and Infants' Wear Stores
5651	Family Clothing Stores
5661	Shoe Stores
5699	Miscellaneous Apparel and Accessory Stores

If you think about the many different types of apparel stores that exist, you will realize that the information provided by the second digit of the SIC code is not detailed enough to specify the exact industry in which the company operates. It is the third and fourth digits of the code that tell us the specific type clothing that Gap Inc. sells. Exhibit 12–4 is an excerpt from the *Standard Industrial Classification Manual*, which provides a numerical listing of each SIC code and the specific type of operation it indicates. Because Gap Inc. has a variety of stores that cater to a number of customer types, it is classified as 5651, family clothing stores.

Now that you have a basic understanding of the most widely accepted classification system for identifying business activities, we can proceed to gather the information we need to evaluate the ratios we calculated for the Gap.

Industry Comparisons

We will now compare the absolute numbers calculated as the ratio values for Gap Inc. with values for industry averages. There are several sources of information about industry averages. We will, as mentioned earlier, use data gathered from the *Almanac of Business and Industrial Financial Ratios*. For your information, you can also obtain industry averages from two other widely used sources: *Robert Morris Associates' Annual Statement Studies* and Dun & Bradstreet's *Industry Norms and Key Business Ratios*.

Regardless of the source, your first step in making an industry comparison is to determine the industry affiliation of the company being analyzed. That is, you need to determine which SIC code properly identifies the activities of the company. Several business directories mentioned in Chapter 13 provide SIC codes for companies:

- *Ward's Business Directory of U.S. Private and Public Companies*
- *All-In-One Business Contactbook*
- *D & B Million Dollar Directory*
- *Standard and Poor's Register of Corporations, Directors & Executives*

Each of these references lists only one SIC code for Gap Inc. For many firms, especially diversified companies, the references list many different SIC codes. No single SIC code can properly indicate all the operations of a diversified company. However, for purposes of industry comparisons, we need to identify a code that indicates the primary activities of the business. An analysis of the sales in each business segment of a company will help us to determine the sales activities that comprise the largest portion of the business activities. SEC requires that segment sales information be included in the annual report for companies that operate in more than one segment.

Now we can look in the *Almanac of Business and Industrial Financial Ratios* for the data to make an industry comparison of the Gap's ratios. Data in the *Almanac* is compiled from approximately 3.7 million corporate federal income tax returns.

Gathering data from the IRS rather than other publicly available sources of financial information has two distinct advantages: (1) Information about all active corporations is included (other sources include only large or publicly held corporations); and (2) because of substantial penalties for misreporting, corporate data submitted to the IRS are more reliable than that from other sources.

The IRS uses industry groupings which closely follow the SIC codes; however, the IRS classifications are not as specific as the four-digit SIC codes. Generally, a single IRS classification covers several SIC codes. The *Almanac* provides an easy-to-use table of correspondence to identify the IRS classification which properly identifies each SIC code. For our example, the Gap's SIC code, 5651, corresponds to the IRS industry group 5600. This IRS group includes SIC codes from 5611 to 5699.

Information provided in the *Almanac* for each industry is four pages, consisting of two tables. Table I provides an analysis of all companies in the particular industry, regardless of whether they had any net income for the year. Table II provides the same information items as Table I, but it considers only companies that showed a net income for the year. Exhibit 12–5 is a portion of Table II for IRS classification 5600.

Looking down the left-hand column of the exhibit, you will see the 14 key financial ratios we presented earlier in this chapter. They are not in the same order as we covered them and are numbered from 24 to 37. We did not include items 1 through 23 because we are interested only in the ratios (items 24 to 37).

Also included in the portion of Table II reproduced in Exhibit 12–5 are 13 columns of data. Looking at the column headings, we discover that the first column ("Total") provides averages for all companies in the industry. The other columns provide averages for companies of different size within the industry. As we compare Gap Inc.'s ratios to industry averages, we will be interested in the first column and the last column—the first because we want to see how the Gap compares with the entire industry, and the last because Gap Inc. is comparable in size to companies with total assets exceeding $250 million.

Finally, look at Exhibit 12–6. The list of ratios and the two columns of averages were drawn directly from the *Almanac*. The last column shows the 14 key ratios as we calculated them in this chapter. Now at last, we can begin to analyze the Gap's ratios in a context that can give us some insight into how the company compares with its industry.

To best understand Gap Inc. we will use a four-step analysis process. First, we compare the Gap's ratios to the industry statistics. Second, we look for trends in Gap Inc.'s ratios over a five year period. Third, we gather industry information and economic projections to consider the industry environment. Finally, we synthesize all the information to draw our conclusions about the profitability, liquidity, solvency, and investment potential of the company.

Company Analysis—Step 1: Comparing Ratios to the Industry Averages

To organize our study of the Gap, we will first compare its profitability ratios to the industry averages shown in Exhibit 12–7.

The Gap exceeds every industry profitability ratio for the total industry and for companies over $250,000 in assets. Its return on assets is over twice the industry average even though the total asset turnover is only slightly more than the industry. Both the profit margin before tax and after tax are more than two times the industry average. Return on equity is almost three times the industry but the return before interest on equity is only 1.5 times the industry. It seems easy to conclude that in general Gap Inc. outperforms the industry and is highly profitable.

Exhibit 12-5

Table II from *Almanac of Business and Industrial Financial Ratios* for Industry 5600. *Source:* Leo Troy, *Almanac of Business and Industrial Financial Ratios*
© 1998. Reprinted by permission of Prentice Hall, Inc., Paramus, New Jersey.

CORPORATIONS WITH NET INCOME
Retail Trade
5600

Apparel and Accessory Stores

Money Amounts and Size of Assets in Thousands of Dollars

Item Description for Accounting Period 7/94 through 6/95		Total	Zero Assets	Under 100	100 to 250	251 to 500	501 to 1,000	1,001 to 5,000	5,001 to 10,000	10,001 to 25,000	25,001 to 50,000	50,001 to 100,000	100,001 to 250,000	250,001 and over
Number of Enterprises	1	20883	62	7605	7989	2213	1913	888	71	66	13	23	19	19
Selected Financial Ratios (Times to 1)														
Current Ratio	24	1.8	•	3.1	3.2	2.6	2.4	2.0	1.9	2.0	2.0	2.2	2.4	1.6
Quick Ratio	25	0.5	•	0.9	0.8	0.8	0.8	0.6	0.5	0.5	0.4	0.6	0.7	0.5
Net Sales to Working Capital	26	7.2	•	7.0	5.2	4.9	5.4	6.1	5.9	8.1	7.5	6.4	5.4	8.6
Coverage Ratio	27	5.0	6.8	•	14.3	•	4.7	3.7	10.7	5.0	12.0	6.4	4.5	4.4
Total Asset Turnover	28	1.9	•	4.2	3.2	2.4	2.5	2.3	2.5	3.0	2.3	2.0	1.9	1.6
Inventory Turnover	29	6.8	•	7.6	6.0	5.5	5.9	5.5	6.1	7.0	6.8	6.8	6.3	7.3
Receivables Turnover	30	•	•	•	•	•	•	•	•	•	•	•	•	•
Total Liabilities to Net Worth	31	1.1	•	1.8	0.9	0.8	1.0	1.5	1.2	1.5	0.8	1.0	0.9	1.2
Selected Financial Factors (in Percentages)														
Debt Ratio	32	52.9	•	64.0	46.8	45.2	49.2	60.6	53.9	60.4	43.7	49.2	47.5	53.7
Return on Assets	33	11.6	•	33.0	18.6	13.1	9.2	8.1	16.3	12.2	13.8	12.3	10.6	11.1
Return on Equity	34	14.1	•	•	29.0	19.5	12.8	13.2	25.8	22.2	18.0	15.3	10.7	12.0
Return Before Interest on Equity	35	24.6	•	•	35.0	23.9	18.2	20.4	•	30.6	24.6	24.2	20.2	23.9
Profit Margin, Before Income Tax	36	5.0	5.3	7.6	5.4	5.1	2.9	2.6	6.0	3.3	5.6	5.3	4.3	5.3
Profit Margin, After Income Tax	37	3.6	4.0	7.3	4.8	4.4	2.6	2.3	4.8	6.0	4.5	4.0	2.9	3.5

Exhibit 12–6
Key Ratio Comparisons: Total Industry, Companies with Assets Exceeding $250 Million, and Gap Inc.

	Ratio	Total Industry	$250 Million and Over	Gap Inc.
Current Ratio	24	1.8	1.6	1.85
Quick Ratio	25	0.5	0.5	.921
Net Sales to Working Capital	26	7.2	8.6	7.75
Coverage Ratio	27	5.0	4.4	102.7
Total Asset Turnover	28	1.9	1.6	1.95
Inventory Turnover	29	6.8	7.3	5.15
Receivables Turnover	30	*	*	*
Total Liabilities to Net Worth	31	1.1	1.2	1.11
Debt Ratio	32	52.9	53.7	52.54
Return on Assets	33	11.6	11.1	25.6
Return on Equity	34	14.1	12.0	33.7
Return Before Interest on Equity	35	24.6	23.9	34.2
Profit Margin, Before Income Tax	36	5.0	5.3	13.1
Profit Margin, After Income Tax	37	3.6	3.5	8.2

Exhibit 12–7
Profitability Ratios for Gap Inc.

	Ratio	Total Industry	$250 Million and Over	Gap Inc.
Return on Assets	33	11.6	11.1	25.6
Profit Margin, Before Income Tax	36	5.0	5.3	13.1
Total Asset Turnover	28	1.9	1.6	1.95
Profit Margin, After Income Tax	37	3.6	3.5	8.2
Return on Equity	34	14.1	12.0	33.7
Return Before Interest on Equity	35	24.6	23.9	34.2

Discussion Questions

12–19. Gap Inc.'s return on equity is almost three times the industry average but the return on equity before interest is only 1.5 times the industry average. How can this happen?

12–20. Which of the following groups do you think would be interested in Gap Inc.'s return on equity ratio and its return before interest on equity ratio:

a. trade creditors?
b. other short-term creditors (banks)?
c. long-term creditors?
d. stockholders?
e. management?

Explain your reasoning.

Next, we can examine the liquidity ratios in Exhibit 12–8.

Exhibit 12–8
Liquidity Ratios for
Gap Inc.

	Ratio	Total Industry	$250 Million and Over	Gap Inc.
Current Ratio	24	1.8	1.6	1.85
Quick Ratio	25	0.5	0.5	.921
Net Sales to Working Capital	26	7.2	8.6	7.75
Receivables Turnover	30	*	*	*
Inventory Turnover	29	6.8	7.3	5.15

The Gap has a strong current ratio and a quick ratio that is almost twice the industry average. The net sales to working capital is better than the total industry and lags behind the larger companies. Neither Gap Inc. nor the industry appear to have receivables indicating the sales are all for cash or bank credit cards. The Gap's inventory turnover appears to be lower than the industry; however, our cost of sales includes occupancy costs so we do not get a true inventory turnover. We might conclude that the Gap exhibits strong liquidity and a lagging inventory turnover.

Discussion Questions

12–21. Would removing the cost of occupancy from the cost of sales raise or lower the inventory turnover? Why would Gap Inc. have a lower inventory turnover than its competitors?

12–22. Which of the following groups do you think would be interested in the Gap's inventory turnover ratio:

a. trade creditors?

b. other short-term creditors (banks)?

c. long-term creditors?

d. stockholders?

Explain your reasoning.

12–23. Why does the Gap have a higher current and quick ratio than the industry but a lower net sales to working capital ratio?

Finally, we look at Gap Inc.'s solvency ratios in Exhibit 12–9.

The Gap has a slightly lower debt ratio than the industry and about the same liabilities to net worth. Gap Inc.'s coverage ratio is 20 times the industry average and 25 times the average of the larger firms. The large coverage ratio occurs because Gap Inc. incurs little interest expense. Compared to the industry, Gap Inc. has better-than-average solvency ratios.

Exhibit 12–9
Solvency Ratios for
Gap Inc.

	Ratio	Total Industry	$250 Million and Over	Gap Inc.
Debt Ratio	32	52.9	53.7	52.54
Total Liabilities to Net Worth	31	1.1	1.2	1.11
Coverage Ratio	27	5.0	4.4	102.7

Discussion Questions

12-24. If the Gap's coverage ratio were 1.02 instead of 102.7, and you owned some Gap Inc. long-term debt, would you be concerned? Why or why not?

12-25. Which of the following groups might be concerned if Gap Inc.'s total liabilities to net worth ratio and debt ratio were much higher than the industry average:

    a. trade creditors?
    b. other short-term creditors (banks)?
    c. long-term creditors?
    d. stockholders?

    Explain the reason for their concern.

    To further reassure ourselves of Gap Inc.'s position in the industry, we can consult other sources for information. *Moody's Industry Review* lists the rankings of companies in the various industries by several key indicators. *Moody's* provides us with the information in Exhibit 12–10 for retail specialty stores, in which it includes the Gap.

Exhibit 12–10
Gap Inc. Rankings from *Moody's Industry Review* Out of 101 Retail Specialty Stores for 1997.

Item	Gap Inc. Statistic	Rank in Industry
Revenues (in $Millions)	$6,507.82	10
Net Income (in $Millions)	$533.90	2
Operating Profit Margin	13.08%	5
Return on Capital	25.67%	7
Return on Assets	16.00%	6
Inventory Turnover	6.13	13
Working Capital (in $Millions)	$839.40	5
Cash and Securities (in $Millions)	$913.17	1

Source: Moody's Investors Service, Inc., *Moody's Industry Review* © 1998, New York City, New York.

    Notice that the revenues, net income, and working capital items equal the annual report items. Some of the ratios differ from our amounts because *Moody's* uses different formulas to calculate the ratios. If you examine the rank in the industry, the Gap scores very high in all areas but the inventory turnover, which is still in the top 15 percent of the industry. If we have satisfied ourselves that Gap Inc. ranks high in profitability, liquidity, and solvency compared with the industry, now we need to look at what has happened within the Gap in the past five years.

Company Analysis—Step 2: Looking for Company Trends

When we compare the company's ratios to themselves over time, we perform a simple type of trend analysis. Exhibit 12–11 contains the ratios we could compute with information provided in the annual report for the past five years. Notice that we could not compute all the ratios because not all the information necessary was included in the annual report for five years. Beyond what is on the comparative balance sheets and income statements, we used the information provided in the section named "Ten-Year Selected Financial Data" beginning on page 20 of the annual report.

Exhibit 12-11
Trend Analysis of Gap Inc. Financial Ratios for the Past Five Years.

Ratio	1997	1996	1995	1994	1993
Return on Assets	25.60%	48.35%	24.98%	26.41%	24.10%
Profit Margin before Income Taxes	13.13%	24.04%	13.31%	14.22%	12.89%
Total Asset Turnover	1.95	2.02	1.88	1.86	1.87
Profit Margin After Income Tax	8.20%	8.57%	8.06%	8.60%	7.84%
Return on Equity	33.71%	27.37%	21.58%	23.29%	22.94%
Return before Interest on Equity	34.23%	27.54%	21.72%	*	*
Current Ratio	1.85	1.72	1.71	1.39	1.69
Quick Ratio	.525	.639	*	*	*
Net Sales to Working Capital	7.75	9.53	6.03	6.70	6.67
Receivables Turnover	*	*	*	*	*
Inventory Turnover	5.15	5.35	5.48	5.94	6.03
Debt Ratio	52.54%	37.02%	29.99%	31.38%	36.11%
Total Liabilities to Net Worth	1.11	.59	.428	.457	.565
Coverage Ratio	102.71	454.62	258.34	*	*

*The data needed to calculate these ratios are not available in Gap Inc.'s 1997 annual report.

Different users concentrate on different parts of the analysis in Exhibit 12–11, depending on their individual perspective. Short-term creditors, for example, would probably focus their attention on the liquidity ratios. Long-term creditors and stockholders would probably concentrate on the solvency ratios, but they would also pay attention to the profitability ratios. The Gap's management, of course, would be interested in all these ratios.

We can accomplish two objectives with our five-year analysis of Gap Inc.'s ratios, both of which grow out of the industry comparisons we did earlier. First, we can determine whether the Gap's 1997 ratios are representative of the company's performance over the five-year period. Second, we can analyze the ratios to see whether the ratios present any trends.

If we examine Exhibit 12–11, we notice the following:

1. The year 1996 was unusually profitable for the Gap. This profitability caused the return on assets, the profit margins before and after taxes, and the coverage ratio to be unusually high.
2. If we overlook those items in 1996, most of the remaining ratios represent the previous years, except a few which have steadily increased or decreased over time. For example, return on equity, return before interest on equity, current ratio, and net sales to working capital have steadily increased for the past three years.
3. Inventory turnover and the coverage ratio have decreased significantly. The coverage ratio declined because the company borrowed almost $500 million in 1998 to finance a significant expansion which increased its interest expense. The inventory turnover decline may be troublesome. As we saw in the industry comparison, the Gap has a lower inventory turnover than the average. We would want to investigate this decline further to discover whether this is a sign of financial trouble.
4. Because of the expansion, the debt ratio and the total liabilities to net worth ratio increased significantly. Because Gap Inc.'s debt ratio remains below the industry average, we would not be concerned about this increase. Firms

borrow money to finance expansions, and this may be a sign of financial health and growth potential.

Summarizing the five-year ratio analysis, the 1997 ratios reasonably represent the past five years except for the inventory turnover, the debt ratio, and the coverage ratio. We can spot the following trends:

1. The profitability ratios have increased over the five year period. The return on assets, profit margins, and asset turnover have increased between two and six percent over the five-year period. However, the return on equity increased approximately 47 percent during the five-year period. How can this be? Remember that the financial statements link together. Therefore the ratios also have linkage. The return on equity increased dramatically because the Gap used borrowed money to finance its expansion without increasing its owner contributions. This leverages the owners' investment and makes it more profitable to the stockholders. The downside of leverage is that it also increases the risk to the owners.

2. The liquidity ratios, with the exception of inventory turnover, have steadily improved. The current ratio increased 11 percent while the net sales to working capital increased 16 percent. As previously noted, the inventory turnover has steadily declined each year and is below the industry average. This may be an early warning of trouble that management should correct with future purchasing and marketing strategies.

3. The solvency ratios eroded over the five years, but this is not troublesome because the Gap had an unusually conservative debt structure in 1993. At its current levels, Gap Inc. maintains a rather conservative debt ratio.

Discussion Question

12–26. For which ratios is a higher statistic better? For which ratios is a lower statistic better?

Based on the Gap's financial data over the last five years, we can conclude that the company has been highly profitable since 1993 and maintains excellent liquidity and solvency. Yet, the falling inventory turnover signals a change in purchasing performance and/or merchandising strategies. This illustrates the principle that no conclusion should be drawn based on a single ratio value nor should any single ratio value be ignored.

The ratios in this chapter and others you will encounter in the future are interrelated. Any conclusions drawn from ratio analysis must consider the company's overall financial position and performance rather than one aspect alone. Moreover, as we pointed out in the section on gathering background information, you cannot make full use of financial information unless you consider such external factors as general economic conditions and expectations, political events and political climate, and industry outlook.

Company Analysis—Step 3:
Considering the Industry Environment

The industry outlook will normally change frequently. Any sudden change in political or economic forecasts will have a ripple effect in most industries. The Gap participates at the high end of the family clothing business. It will be more subject to economic downturns than Wal-Mart, because Wal-Mart offers basic necessities at low prices and the Gap offers trendy fashion at higher prices. When researching the industry outlook, you cannot find the outlook for SIC 5651 because information sources consider broad groups of related industries for its industry outlooks. Look for the most appropriate industry classification. *U.S. Industry & Trade Outlook '98* (a Standard & Poor's publication) contains Chapter 42 on the retail trade to cover SIC codes 5200 through 5999. It predicts hard times for retailers through the year 2002 with only a two percent average growth rate. Pointing to the excessive square footage per person for retail stores in the United States, it describes the U.S. retail market as "overstored." Standard & Poor's suggests that a successful retailer will have to increase its market share by offering fair prices, creating value for its customers, being convenient for busy shoppers, and emphasizing customer service.

Standard & Poor's produces another publication, *Industry Surveys*, that is more specific to individual groups. It contains weekly and monthly updates in a loose-leaf publication format. In the September 1998 issue (*Monthly Investment Review*, p. 54) S & P discusses that the retail (specialty-apparel) industry has outperformed the total stock market with a stock price increase of 31.2 percent contrasted with the 2.7 percent increase in the S & P 1500 stocks. The companies' stocks, which are classified in this industry, have risen 31.2 percent while their sales during the same time period have increased only 2.4 percent. In light of this contrasting information, investor confidence is surprising. With consumer disposable income increasing in 1998, *Industry Surveys* predicts good short-term results for specialty-apparel retailers but warns that U.S. demographics continue to move toward an older population which spends less of its income on fashion. It suggests that only firms with superior management and moderate debt structures will prosper in the long run.

Industry Surveys focuses on one area in each publication, such as the January 22, 1998, issue that focused on specialty retailing. Specialty stores continue to decline slightly in the market share of clothing sales, losing to discount stores. In addition, mall shopping is declining in popularity, especially among women because they have less time to shop. More consumers are precision shoppers who go after what they want and are less likely to make impulse purchases. Shoppers also want sale prices, with 70 percent buying most of their clothing on sale.

Now that we have all this information, what do we do with it? Look at the important pieces of information for the Gap:

1. Growth in this industry will depend upon value, price, convenience, and service.
2. Short-term sales may be good but long-term growth will depend on the ability to sell to an aging U.S. population.
3. Mall shopping is declining especially among women and most of Gap Inc.'s outlets are located in malls.
4. Discount stores continue to increase their market share.

Armed with this information, we can now draw our conclusions.

Company Analysis—Step 4: Drawing Conclusions

The evaluation process by nature depends on individual perception. Remember that the industry information we gathered is only good for the time period in which we did our research. By the time you read this material it will undoubtedly change. As for the process, however, we might draw the following conclusions:

1. The Gap is an industry leader with strong profitability and liquidity and a moderate solvency picture.

2. If Gap Inc. can maintain its leadership position and hold down its debt, it might be a survivor in the tough competitive industry in which it operates.
3. Part of Gap Inc.'s survival will depend on increasing its inventory turnover ratio to lower its dependence on discounted sales prices to turn inventory.
4. If we choose to invest in a retail apparel stock, the Gap is one to consider.

LIMITATIONS OF RATIO ANALYSIS

Ratio analysis is an excellent tool for gathering additional information about a company, but it does have its limitations.

1. *Attempting to predict the future using past results depends on the predictive value of the information we use.* Changes in the general economy, in the economy of the particular industry being studied, and in the company's management present some of the uncertainties that can cause past results to be an unreliable predictor of the future.
2. *The financial statements used to compute the ratios are based on historical cost.* In a time of rapidly changing prices, comparison between years might be difficult.
3. *Figures from the balance sheet (i.e., assets, liabilities) used to calculate the ratios are year-end numbers.* Because most businesses have their fiscal year-end in the slowest part of the year, the balances in such accounts as receivables, payables, and inventory at year-end may not be representative of the rest of the year. Some analysts suggest using averages (i.e., average current assets for the year). However, even when this approach is taken, the problem is not eliminated, for averages are typically based on year-end numbers from two consecutive years.
4. *Industry peculiarities create difficulty in comparing the ratios of a company in one industry with those of a company in another industry.* Even comparison of companies within an industry may not be reasonable at times because different companies use different accounting methods (e.g., depreciation methods).
5. *Lack of uniformity concerning what is to be included in the numerators and denominators of specific ratios makes comparison to published industry averages extremely difficult.*

Perhaps the greatest single limitation of ratio analysis is that people tend to place too much reliance on the ratios. Financial ratios should not be viewed as a magical checklist in the evaluation process. Ratio analysis only enriches all the other information decision makers should consider when making credit, investment, and similar types of decisions.

SUMMARY

In response to the need to reduce uncertainty in the decision-making process, analysts developed several techniques to assist economic decision makers as they evaluate financial statement information. Creditors (short-term and long-term), equity investors (present and potential), and company management comprise the three major categories of financial statement users. Because their objectives vary, their perspectives on the results of financial statement analysis will differ.

Three external factors—general economic conditions and expectations, political events and political climate, and industry outlook—affect business performance and should be considered when evaluating results of any type of financial statement analysis.

One important method of financial statement analysis is ratio analysis, a technique for analyzing the relationship between two items from a company's financial statements for a given period. We compute ratios by dividing the dollar amount of one item from the financial statements by the dollar amount of the other item from the statements. Another method is trend analysis which looks at one ratio or financial statistic over time to determine if an upward or downward trend exists.

Analysts have developed a great many ratios over time to help economic decision makers assess a company's financial health. Because not all ratios are relevant in a given decision situation, decision makers must take care to select appropriate ratios to analyze. Ratio values, in and of themselves, have very little meaning. They become meaningful only when compared to other relevant information, such as industry averages or the company's ratio values from other years.

We broadly classify financial ratios as profitability ratios, liquidity ratios, and solvency ratios. Profitability ratios attempt to measure the ease with which companies generate income. Liquidity ratios measure a company's ability to generate positive cash flow in the short run to pay off short-term liabilities. Solvency ratios attempt to measure a company's ability to meet the obligations created by its long-term debt. Individual ratios are listed in Exhibit 12–1.

Each of the profitability, liquidity, and solvency ratios provides valuable information for both internal and external decision makers. Ratio analysis does have its limitations. Placing too much reliance on the financial statements and the ratios derived from them without putting the information in the proper political, economic, and industry perspective can lead to poor decisions. Ratio analysis is an important financial analysis tool. As with the other tools we have discussed throughout this book, it must be used wisely and in the proper context.

KEY TERMS

coverage ratio or times interest
   earned ratio   F-464
current ratio   F-459
debt ratio   F-463
financial statement analysis   F-448
inventory turnover ratio   F-462
liquidity ratios   F-459
net sales to working capital ratio   F-461
profit margin after income
   tax ratio   M-458
profit margin before income
   tax ratio   F-456
profitability   F-455

profitability ratios   F-455
quick ratio or acid-test ratio   F-460
ratio analysis   F-448
receivables turnover ratio   F-462
return before interest on
   equity ratio   F-458
return on assets ratio   F-456
return on equity ratio   F-458
solvency   F-463
solvency ratios   F-463
total asset turnover ratio   F-457
total liabilities to net worth ratio   F-464
trend analysis   F-448

REVIEW THE FACTS

  A. What is the purpose of financial statement analysis?
  B. List the three financial statement user groups discussed in the chapter and describe what each group hopes to learn from financial statement analysis.
  C. Describe the three types of external factors the Financial Accounting Standards Board (FASB) warns users of financial information to consider, and explain how each factor can impact a company's performance.

D. From which financial statements are components of the ratios discussed in the chapter drawn?

E. Define profitability.

F. List the six profitability ratios discussed in the chapter. For each one, describe the calculation used and the purpose of the ratio.

G. What are the two component ratios of the return on assets?

H. Define liquidity.

I. List the five liquidity ratios discussed in the chapter. For each one, describe the calculation used and the purpose of the ratio.

J. What is the difference between the current ratio and the quick ratio? What is the purpose in examining both?

K. Define solvency.

L. List the three solvency ratios discussed in the chapter. For each one, describe the calculation used and the purpose of the ratio.

M. How are the debt ratio and total liabilities to net worth related?

N. What information can be gathered from calculating a company's coverage ratio?

O. Briefly describe the purpose and meaning of SIC codes.

P. Describe what additional information can be gleaned from an industry comparison of a company's ratios.

Q. What is the purpose of conducting a comparison among a company's ratio values from several recent years?

R. Describe the six limitations of ratio analysis discussed in the chapter.

APPLY WHAT YOU HAVE LEARNED

LO 1:   Discussion

12–27. Identify the three major categories of financial statement analysis users and describe the basic objectives of each group.

LO 2:   Discussion

12–28. Discuss how one goes about gathering background information on a company.

LO 4:   Matching

12–29. Listed below are items relating to the concepts presented in this chapter, followed by definitions of those items in scrambled order.

a. Financial statement analysis	**h.** Profitability ratios
b. Ratio analysis	**i.** Liquidity
c. Short-term creditors	**j.** Liquidity ratios
d. Long-term creditors	**k.** Solvency
e. Stockholders	**l.** Solvency ratios
f. Management	**m.** Standard Industrial Classification
g. Profitability	

1. _____ Designed to measure a firm's ability to generate sufficient cash to meet its short-term obligations.

2. _____ A method for analyzing the relationship between two items from a company's financial statements for a given period.

3. _____ Designed to measure the ease with which a company generates income.

4. _____ Focus on interest payments and the overall debt load a company carries.
5. _____ A system of four-digit codes to indicate a company's industry.
6. _____ Looking beyond the face of the financial statements to gather additional information.
7. _____ Those who own an equity interest in a corporation.
8. _____ The ease with which an item, such as an asset, can be converted into cash.
9. _____ Trade creditors and lending institutions such as banks.
10. _____ A company's ability to meet the obligations created by its long-term debt.
11. _____ Bondholders and lending institutions such as banks.
12. _____ The ease with which companies generate income.
13. _____ Responsible for a company's day-to-day operations.

REQUIRED:
Match the letter next to each item on the list with the appropriate definition. Each letter will be used only once.

LO 4: Matching

12–30. Listed below are all the ratios discussed in this chapter, followed by explanations of what the ratios are designed to measure in scrambled order.

a. Return on assets	g. Net sales to working capital
b. Profit margin before income tax	h. Debt ratio
	i. Coverage ratio
c. Profit margin after income tax	j. Return on equity
	k. Return before interest on equity
d. Total asset turnover	l. Receivables turnover
e. Current ratio	m. Inventory turnover
f. Quick ratio	n. Total liabilities to net worth

1. _____ Most common ratio used to measure a company's ability to meet short-term obligations.
2. _____ Measures a company's ability to make periodic interest payments.
3. _____ Measures the return earned on investment in assets.
4. _____ A more stringent test of short-term liquidity than the current ratio.
5. _____ Measures the pretax earnings produced from a given level of revenues.
6. _____ Measures the amount of after-tax net income generated by a dollar of sales.
7. _____ Measures the level of sales a company generated using its working capital.
8. _____ Indicates the proportion of assets financed by debt.
9. _____ Measures a company's ability to generate revenues from a given level of assets.
10. _____ Compares the amount of debt financing with the amount of equity financing.
11. _____ Measures how much after-tax income was generated for a given level of equity investment.
12. _____ Indicates how long a company holds its inventory.

13. _____ Measures the return on equity before the cost of borrowing.
14. _____ Measures how quickly a company collects amounts owed to it by its customers.

REQUIRED:
Match the letter next to each item on the list with the appropriate explanation. Each letter will be used only once.

LO 4: Matching

12–31. Listed below are all the ratios discussed in this chapter.

1. _____ Return on assets
2. _____ Debt ratio
3. _____ Profit margin before income tax
4. _____ Quick ratio
5. _____ Total asset turnover
6. _____ Current ratio
7. _____ Net sales to working capital
8. _____ Coverage ratio
9. _____ Return on equity
10. _____ Receivables turnover
11. _____ Return before interest on equity
12. _____ Inventory turnover
13. _____ Total liabilities to net worth
14. _____ Profit margin after income tax

REQUIRED:
Identify each of the 14 ratios as a profitability ratio (P), a liquidity ratio (L), or a solvency ratio (S) by assigning it the appropriate letter.

LO 5: Ratio Computation

12–32. Presented below are partial comparative balance sheets of Mikey Company at December 31, 2002 and 2001:

MIKEY COMPANY
Partial Balance Sheets
December 31, 2002, and December 31, 2001
Current Assets and Current Liabilities Only
(in thousands)

	2002	2001
Current Assets:		
Cash	$3,400	$2,920
Accounts Receivable	1,825	2,212
Merchandise Inventory	1,170	966
Prepaid Expenses	240	270
Total Current Assets	$6,635	$6,368
Current Liabilities:		
Accounts Payable	$2,321	$1,740
Notes Payable	3,100	3,300
Total Current Liabilities	5,421	$5,040

REQUIRED:
a. Calculate Mikey's current ratios for 2002 and 2001.
b. Calculate Mikey's quick ratios for 2002 and 2001.

c. Which financial statement users are most interested in these two sets of ratios? Explain why the ratios are considered important to these users.

d. Assume that the average company in Mikey's industry has a current ratio of 2:1 and a quick ratio of 1.25:1. If you were evaluating Mikey's liquidity, what could you learn by comparing Mikey's ratios to the industry averages?

LO 5: Ratio Computation

12–33. Presented below are partial comparative balance sheets of Harold Company at December 31, 2002 and 2001:

HAROLD COMPANY
Partial Balance Sheets
December 31, 2002, and December 31, 2001
Current Assets and Current Liabilities Only
(in thousands)

	2002	2001
Current Assets:		
Cash	$2,110	$2,650
Accounts Receivable	1,254	977
Merchandise Inventory	730	856
Prepaid Expenses	127	114
Total Current Assets	$4,221	$4,597
Current Liabilities:		
Accounts Payable	$1,054	$1,330
Notes Payable	2,100	1,750
Total Current Liabilities	$3,154	$3,080

REQUIRED:

a. Calculate Harold's current ratios for 2002 and 2001.

b. Calculate Harold's quick ratios for 2002 and 2001.

c. Which financial statement users are most interested in these two sets of ratios? Explain why the ratios are considered important to these users.

d. Assume that the average company in Harold's industry has a current ratio of 2.5:1 and a quick ratio of 1:1. If you were evaluating Harold's liquidity, what could you learn by comparing Harold's ratios to those of the industry averages?

e. What, if anything, could you determine by comparing Harold's current ratio and quick ratio for 2001 with the same ratios for 2002? Explain your reasoning.

LO 8: Liquidity Evaluation

12–34. A five-year comparative analysis of Steven Sagal Company's current ratio and quick ratio is as follows:

	2000	2001	2002	2003	2004
Current ratio	1.24	1.95	2.55	3.68	4.13
Quick ratio	1.20	1.06	0.96	0.77	0.51

REQUIRED:

a. What does this analysis tell you about the overall liquidity of Sagal Company over the five-year period?

b. What does this analysis tell you about what has happened to the composition of Sagal's current assets over the five-year period?

LO 8: Liquidity Evaluation

12–35. A five-year comparative analysis of Carnegie Company's current ratio and quick ratio is as follows:

	2000	2001	2002	2003	2004
Current ratio	4.24	3.95	2.95	2.68	1.93
Quick ratio	0.51	0.86	1.03	1.33	1.68

REQUIRED:

a. What does this analysis tell you about the overall liquidity of Carnegie Company over the five-year period?

b. What does this analysis tell you about what has happened to the composition of Carnegie's current assets over the five-year period?

LO 8: Profitability Evaluation

12–36. A five-year comparative analysis of "Buggsey" Moron Company's profit margin before tax and profit margin after tax is as follows:

	2000	2001	2002	2003	2004
Profit margin before tax	3.68	4.61	6.88	7.96	9.87
Profit margin after tax	2.22	2.95	4.41	5.27	7.09

REQUIRED:

a. What does this analysis indicate about Moron's performance over the five-year period?

b. Which of the following groups would be interested in this analysis? Include in your answer a brief discussion of how you think each of them would interpret this analysis.

    (1) Trade creditors
    (2) Long-term creditors
    (3) Stockholders

LO 8: Profitability Evaluation

12–37. A five-year comparative analysis of Dexter Manley Company's profit margin before tax and profit margin after tax is as follows:

	2000	2001	2002	2003	2004
Profit margin before tax	11.28	9.16	8.48	7.01	5.78
Profit margin after tax	9.33	8.59	6.14	5.72	3.89

REQUIRED:

a. What does this analysis indicate about Manley's performance over the five-year period?

b. Which of the following groups would be interested in this analysis? Include in your answer a brief discussion of how you think each of them would interpret this analysis.

    (1) Trade creditors
    (2) Long-term creditors
    (3) Stockholders

LO 8:   Capital Structure Evaluation

12–38. A five-year comparative analysis of Cibyll Smythe Company's total
liabilities to net worth ratio and debt ratio is as follows:

	2000	2001	2002	2003	2004
Total liabilities to net worth	2.75	2.50	2.25	1.50	1.00
Debt ratio	73.33	71.43	69.23	60.00	50.00

REQUIRED:

a. What does this analysis indicate about Smythe's capital structure over the
five-year period?
b. Which of the following groups would be interested in this analysis? Include
in your answer a brief discussion of how you think each of them would
interpret this analysis.
  (1) Trade creditors
  (2) Long-term creditors
  (3) Stockholders

LO 8:   Capital Structure Evaluation

12–39. A five-year comparative analysis of Peggy Bausch Company's total
liabilities to net worth ratio and debt ratio is as follows:

	2000	2001	2002	2003	2004
Total liabilities to net worth	1.50	1.15	2.65	2.25	1.90
Debt ratio	60.00	53.49	72.60	69.23	65.52

REQUIRED:

a. What does this analysis indicate about Bausch's capital structure over the
five-year period?
b. Which of the following groups would be interested in this analysis? Include
in your answer a brief discussion of how you think each of them would
interpret this analysis.
  (1) Trade creditors
  (2) Long-term creditors
  (3) Stockholders

LO 5:   Ratio Computation

12–40. Presented below are the comparative balance sheets for Whipple
Company at December 31, 2002 and 2001. Also included is Whipple's
income statement for the year ended December 31, 2002.

WHIPPLE COMPANY
Balance Sheets
December 31, 2002, and December 31, 2001
(in thousands)

	2002	2001
ASSETS:		
Current Assets:		
Cash	$ 1,618	$1,220
Accounts Receivable	1,925	2,112
Merchandise Inventory	1,070	966
Prepaid Expenses	188	149
Total Current Assets	$ 4,801	$4,447

Plant and Equipment:		
Buildings, Net	$ 4,457	$2,992
Equipment, Net	1,293	1,045
Total Plant and Equipment	$ 5,750	$4,037
Total Assets	$10,551	$8,484
LIABILITIES:		
Current Liabilities:		
Accounts Payable	$ 1,818	$1,686
Notes Payable	900	1,100
Total Current Liabilities	$ 2,718	$2,786
Long-Term Liabilities	2,500	2,000
Total Liabilities	$ 5,218	$4,786
STOCKHOLDERS' EQUITY:		
Common Stock, No Par Value	$ 3,390	$2,041
Retained Earnings	1,943	1,657
Total Stockholders' Equity	$ 5,333	$3,698
Total Liabilities and Stockholders' Equity	$10,551	$8,484

WHIPPLE COMPANY
Income Statement
For the Year Ended December 31, 2002
(in thousands)

Sales Revenue		$11,228
LESS: Cost of Goods Sold		7,751
Gross Profit on Sales		$ 3,477
LESS: Operating Expenses:		
Depreciation—Buildings and Equipment	$ 102	
Other Selling and Administrative	2,667	
Total Expenses		2,769
Income Before Interest and Taxes		$ 708
LESS: Interest Expense		168
Income Before Taxes		$ 540
Income Taxes		114
Net Income		$ 426

REQUIRED:
Calculate the following ratios for 2002:

1. Return on assets
2. Profit margin before income tax
3. Total asset turnover
4. Profit margin after income tax
5. Return on equity
6. Return before interest on equity
7. Current ratio
8. Quick ratio
9. Net sales to working capital
10. Receivables turnover
11. Inventory turnover
12. Debt ratio
13. Total liabilities to net worth
14. Coverage ratio

LO 5: Ratio Computation

12–41. Presented below are the comparative balance sheets for Earlywine Company at December 31, 2002 and 2001 and the income statements for the years ended December 31, 2002 and 2001.

EARLYWINE COMPANY
Balance Sheets
December 31, 2002, and December 31, 2001
(in thousands)

	2002	2001
ASSETS:		
Current Assets:		
Cash	$1,292	$ 980
Accounts Receivable	1,068	1,112
Merchandise Inventory	970	906
Prepaid Expenses	88	109
Total Current Assets	$3,418	$3,107
Plant and Equipment:		
Buildings, Net	$3,457	$2,442
Equipment, Net	993	945
Total Plant and Equipment	$4,450	$3,387
Total Assets	$7,868	$6,494
LIABILITIES:		
Current Liabilities:		
Accounts Payable	$ 998	$ 786
Notes Payable	600	500
Total Current Liabilities	$1,598	$1,286
Long-Term Liabilities	837	467
Total Liabilities	$2,435	$1,753
STOCKHOLDERS' EQUITY:		
Common Stock, No Par Value	$2,490	$2,000
Retained Earnings	2,943	2,741
Total Stockholders' Equity	$5,433	$4,741
Total Liabilities and Stockholders' Equity	$7,868	$6,494

EARLYWINE COMPANY
Income Statements
For the Years Ended December 31, 2002 and 2001
(in thousands)

	2002	2001
Sales Revenue	$9,228	$8,765
LESS: Cost of Goods Sold	6,751	6,097
Gross Profit on Sales	$2,477	$2,668
LESS: Operating Expenses:		
Depreciation—Buildings and Equipment	$ 80	$ 56
Other Selling and Administrative	1,667	1,442
Total Expenses	$1,747	$1,498
Income Before Interest and Taxes	$ 730	$1,170
LESS: Interest Expense	98	89
Income Before Taxes	$ 632	$1,081
Income Taxes	190	357
Net Income	$ 442	$ 724

REQUIRED:

a. Calculate the following ratios for 2002 and 2001:

   (1) Return on assets
   (2) Profit margin before income tax
   (3) Total asset turnover
   (4) Profit margin after income tax
   (5) Return on equity
   (6) Return before interest on equity
   (7) Current ratio
   (8) Quick ratio
   (9) Net sales to working capital
   (10) Receivables turnover
   (11) Inventory turnover
   (12) Debt ratio
   (13) Total liabilities to net worth
   (14) Coverage ratio

b. Using the ratios you calculated in the previous requirement, complete the following comparison of Earlywine's ratios to those of its entire industry and companies of comparable asset size for 2002.

	Total Industry	Assets Between $5 Million and $10 Million	Earlywine
Current ratio	1.46	1.95	
Quick ratio	0.93	1.11	
Net sales to working capital	6.42	5.78	
Coverage ratio	5.63	5.16	
Total asset turnover	1.76	1.42	
Inventory turnover	5.73	5.47	
Receivables turnover	7.83	6.54	
Total liabilities to net worth	1.94	1.93	
Debt ratio	65.99	65.87	
Return on assets	9.30	10.40	
Return on equity	6.12	5.85	
Return before interest on equity	8.92	9.73	
Profit margin before tax	6.27	5.88	
Profit margin after tax	4.99	4.61	

c. Analyze the industry comparison you completed in the previous requirement as follows:

   (1) Identify any ratios you think do not warrant further analysis. Be sure to explain why any particular ratio is not going to be analyzed further.
   (2) For those ratios you felt deserved further analysis, assess whether Earlywine's ratios are better or worse relative to both the entire industry and companies of comparable asset size.

LO 5:   Ratio Analysis

12–42. Presented below is a comparison of Dirty Harry Company's ratios for the years 2002 through 2006.

	2002	2003	2004	2005	2006
Current ratio	1.77	1.91	2.93	2.41	3.12
Quick ratio	1.40	1.26	1.08	0.94	0.79
Net sales to working capital	10.33	9.89	9.43	7.67	5.19
Coverage ratio	6.90	6.91	5.76	5.24	3.49
Total asset turnover	1.46	1.40	1.17	1.08	0.99
Inventory turnover	8.88	8.24	8.11	6.46	4.45
Receivables turnover	8.93	7.41	6.52	5.87	5.34
Total liabilities to net worth	0.96	1.22	1.97	2.21	2.54
Debt ratio	48.97	54.95	66.33	68.85	71.75
Return on assets	9.28	8.44	8.20	7.68	6.21
Return on equity	8.31	8.06	7.22	6.38	4.77
Return before interest on equity	9.98	9.56	8.80	8.43	5.71
Profit margin before tax	10.00	9.45	8.27	7.78	4.12
Profit margin after tax	8.66	7.90	7.14	6.52	2.28

REQUIRED:

Analyze the five-year company comparison as follows:

  a. Identify any ratios you think do not warrant further analysis. Be sure to explain why any particular ratio is not going to be analyzed further.
  b. For each ratio you felt deserved further analysis, assess whether it has improved or worsened over the five-year period.
  c. Based on your analysis of the five-year company comparison, comment briefly on the trend of Dirty Harry Company's performance over the five-year period.

Applications 12–43 through 12–47 are based on the following comparative financial statements of Ross Atkinson and Company.

ROSS ATKINSON AND COMPANY
Balance Sheets
December 31, 2002, and December 31, 2001
(in thousands)

	2002		2001	
ASSETS:				
Current Assets:				
Cash		$ 2,240		$1,936
Accounts Receivable		2,340		2,490
Merchandise Inventory		776		693
Prepaid Expenses		200		160
Total Current Assets		$ 5,556		$5,279
Plant and Equipment:				
Buildings	$7,723		$6,423	
Less: Accumulated Depreciation	3,677		3,534	
Buildings, Net		$ 4,046		$2,889
Equipment	$2,687		$2,387	
Less: Accumulated Depreciation	1,564		1,523	
Equipment, Net		1,123		864
Total Plant and Equipment		$ 5,169		$3,753
Total Assets		$10,725		$9,032

LIABILITIES:
Current Liabilities:

Accounts Payable	$ 1,616	$1,080
Notes Payable	2,720	2,920
Total Current Liabilities	$ 4,336	$4,000
Long-Term Liabilities	2,000	1,600
Total Liabilities	$ 6,336	$5,600
STOCKHOLDERS' EQUITY:		
Common Stock, No Par Value	$ 3,000	$2,400
Retained Earnings	1,389	1,032
Total Stockholders' Equity	$ 4,389	$3,432
Total Liabilities and Stockholders' Equity	$10,725	$9,032

ROSS ATKINSON AND COMPANY
Income Statements
For the Years Ended December 31, 2002 and 2001
(in thousands)

	2002		2001	
Sales Revenue		$14,745		$12,908
LESS: Cost of Goods Sold		10,213		8,761
Gross Profit on Sales		$ 4,532		$ 4,147
LESS: Operating Expenses:				
Advertising and Sales Commissions	$1,022		$ 546	
General and Administrative	2,721		2,451	
Total Expenses		3,743		2,997
Income Before Interest and Taxes		$ 789		$ 1,150
LESS: Interest Expense		172		137
Income Before Taxes		$ 617		$ 1,013
LESS: Income Taxes		123		355
Net Income		$ 494		$ 658

LO 5: Calculating Ratios

12–43. Using the Atkinson and Company financial statements, calculate the following ratios for 2002 and 2001:

1. Return on assets
2. Profit margin before income tax
3. Total asset turnover
4. Profit margin after income tax
5. Return on equity
6. Return before interest on equity
7. Current ratio
8. Quick ratio
9. Net sales to working capital
10. Receivables turnover
11. Inventory turnover
12. Debt ratio
13. Total liabilities to net worth
14. Coverage ratio

LO 7: Comparing Ratios to Industry Averages

12–44. Presented below is a partially completed comparison of Atkinson's ratios to those of its entire industry and companies of comparable asset size for 2002.

	Total Industry	Assets Between $10 Million and $25 Million	Atkinson
Current ratio	2.24	1.95	
Quick ratio	1.33	1.31	
Net sales to working capital	7.22	9.38	
Coverage ratio	5.43	3.16	
Total asset turnover	1.76	1.42	
Inventory turnover	5.78	5.77	
Receivables turnover	7.83	6.54	
Total liabilities to net worth	2.28	1.94	
Debt ratio	69.51	65.99	
Return on assets	9.30	10.40	
Return on equity	16.12	15.85	
Return before interest on equity	11.11	11.73	
Profit margin before tax	6.67	3.88	
Profit margin after tax	4.49	2.61	

REQUIRED:

a. Complete the industry comparison by calculating each of Atkinson and Company's ratios for 2002 and recording them in the space provided. (Note: If you have completed Application 12–43, you have already done the calculations. Just use the ratios you have already calculated.)

b. Analyze the industry comparison you completed in the previous requirement as follows:

(1) Identify any ratios you think do not warrant further analysis. Be sure to explain why any particular ratio is not going to be analyzed further.

(2) For those ratios you felt deserved further analysis, assess whether Atkinson's ratios are better or worse relative to both the entire industry and companies of comparable asset size.

(3) Based on your analysis of the industry comparison, comment briefly on how you think Atkinson and Company compares to other companies in its industry.

LO 5: Calculating Ratios

12–45. Presented below is a partially completed comparison of Atkinson's ratios for the years 1998 through 2002.

	1998	1999	2000	2001	2002
Current ratio	2.07	2.62	1.79		
Quick ratio	1.00	1.09	1.01		
Net sales to working capital	9.33	8.41	9.97		
Coverage ratio	6.31	5.44	4.48		
Total asset turnover	1.11	1.86	1.34		
Inventory turnover	10.88	11.37	11.81		
Receivables turnover	4.80	4.99	5.10		
Total liabilities to net worth	1.22	1.65	1.61		
Debt ratio	54.95	62.26	61.69		
Return on assets	5.22	6.11	5.34		
Return on equity	10.98	11.62	11.05		
Return before interest on equity	14.48	13.77	15.43		
Profit margin before tax	4.68	4.12	4.44		
Profit margin after tax	3.06	3.16	3.31		

REQUIRED:

a. Complete the five-year company comparison by calculating each of Atkinson's ratios for 2001 and 2002 and recording them in the space provided. (Note: If you have completed Application 12–43 you have already done the calculations. Just use the ratios you have already calculated.)

b. Analyze the five-year company comparison you completed in the previous requirement as follows:

(1) Identify any ratios you think do not warrant further analysis. Be sure to explain why any particular ratio is not going to be analyzed further.

(2) For each ratio you felt deserved further analysis, assess whether it has improved or gotten worse over the five-year period.

(3) Based on your analysis of the five-year company comparison, comment briefly on the trend of Atkinson and Company's performance over the five-year period.

Comprehensive

12–46. This chapter focused on ratio analysis performed on the income statement and the balance sheet. For this reason, the financial statements for Ross Atkinson and Company did not include a statement of cash flows. To assess the company's overall performance in 2002, however, you should also look at its statement of cash flows.

REQUIRED:

a. Using the 2001 and 2002 comparative balance sheets and the income statement for 2002, prepare Atkinson's 2002 statement of cash flows.

b. Which of the three broad activities (operating, investing, and financing) provided Atkinson with the majority of its cash during 2002?

c. Briefly discuss whether the activity you identified in the previous requirement is an appropriate source of cash in the long run.

d. In which of the three broad activities (operating, investing, and financing) did Atkinson use most of its cash during 2002?

e. Briefly discuss what your answer to the previous requirement reveals about Atkinson.

Comprehensive

12–47. This chapter focused on ratio analysis performed on the income statement and the balance sheet. For this reason, the financial statements for Ross Atkinson and Company did not include a statement of stockholders' equity. To assess the company's overall performance in 2002, however, you should also look at the company's statement of stockholders' equity.

REQUIRED:

a. Using the 2001 and 2002 comparative balance sheets and the income statement for 2002, prepare Atkinson's 2002 statement of stockholders' equity.

b. Briefly discuss how the statement of stockholders' equity demonstrates articulation among Atkinson's financial statements.

LO 6: Standard Industrial Classification Code

12–48. Listed below are the 11 numerical divisions of the Standard Industrial Classification system, followed by the various industries in scrambled order.

a. 01 to 09
b. 10 to 14
c. 15 to 17
d. 20 to 39
e. 40 to 49
f. 50 to 51

g. 52 to 59
h. 60 to 67
i. 70 to 89
j. 91 to 97
k. 99

1. _____ Wholesale Trade
2. _____ Construction
3. _____ Public Administration
4. _____ Services
5. _____ Agriculture, Forestry, and Fishing
6. _____ Nonclassifiable Establishments
7. _____ Manufacturing
8. _____ Retail Trade
9. _____ Mining
10. _____ Finance, Insurance, and Real Estate
11. _____ Transportation, Communications, Electric, Gas, and Sanitary Services

REQUIRED:

Match the letter next to each item on the list with the appropriate industry.

LO 9: Limitations of Ratio Analysis

12–49. The chapter discussed several limitations of ratio analysis, namely:

1. Using past results to predict future performance
2. Using historical cost as a basis for ratios
3. Using year-end balances as either the numerator or denominator for many ratios
4. Industry peculiarities
5. Lack of uniformity in defining the numerators and denominators used in calculating ratios
6. Giving too much credence to ratio analysis

REQUIRED:

Explain why each of the six items listed above limit the usefulness of ratio analysis.

Financial Reporting Cases

Comprehensive

12–50. Visit the PHLIP Web site for this book at www.prenhall.com/jones to find the link for two companies in the same industry. Select an industry in which you are interested.

REQUIRED:

a. Calculate the 14 basic ratios presented in the chapter for the most current year for each of the companies.
b. Based on the ratios that you have computed, and the information learned in the chapter, how do these companies compare with each other and the

industry averages on the basis of the ratios that you have computed. Industry averages may be obtained from the sources identified in the text, which are usually found in the reference section of the library.

Comprehensive

12–51. Visit the PHLIP Web site for this book at www.prenhall.com/jones and locate the links for Ford Motor Company and for General Motors Corporation.

REQUIRED:

a. Using the corporations' financial statements, calculate the following ratios for the last year presented. (Assume minority interest is part of stockholders' equity.)

   (1) Return on assets
   (2) Profit margin before income tax
   (3) Total asset turnover
   (4) Profit margin after income tax
   (5) Return on equity
   (6) Return before interest on equity
   (7) Current ratio
   (8) Quick ratio
   (9) Net sales to working capital
   (10) Receivables turnover
   (11) Inventory turnover
   (12) Debt ratio
   (13) Total liabilities to net worth
   (14) Coverage ratio

b. Compare the two companies' profitability, liquidity, and solvency. Determine which of the two you would invest in if you had to select one of them. Explain the reasons for your choice.

Comprehensive

12–52. Visit the PHLIP Web site for this book at www.prenhall.com/jones and locate the link for Ford Motor Company.

REQUIRED:

a. Using the financial statements and the financial summary of Ford Motor Company, complete the following five-year company ratio analysis. If you find it impossible to calculate a particular ratio, put an asterisk (*) where the ratio would go. (Assume any minority interest is part of stockholders' equity.)

   Current ratio
   Quick ratio
   Net sales to working capital
   Coverage ratio
   Total asset turnover
   Inventory turnover
   Receivables turnover
   Total liabilities to net worth
   Debt ratio
   Return on assets
   Return on equity
   Return before interest on equity
   Profit margin before tax
   Profit margin after tax

  b. Analyze the five-year company comparison you completed in the previous requirement as follows:

    (1) Identify any ratios you think do not warrant further analysis. Be sure to explain why any particular ratio is not going to be analyzed further.

    (2) For each ratio you felt deserved further analysis, assess whether it has improved or worsened over the five-year period.

    (3) Based on your analysis of the five-year company comparison, comment briefly on the trend of Ford's performance over the five-year period.

Annual Report Project

12–53. With the work you have done during the term, you can now complete the last two sections of your project. Refer to the work you accomplished on the project in Chapter 10 to compute your company's ratios to complete Part VI.

REQUIRED:

Part VII Summary and Conclusion

  a. Compute the 14 basic ratios presented in Chapter 12 for the last two years and present them in tabular form.

  b. Locate the industry averages for your company's SIC code for the current year and include them in the table prepared in part A. Be sure to find the time period that most closely matches your company's year end.

  c. Evaluate your company's profitability, liquidity, and solvency comparing them to industry averages.

  d. Prepare a summary of your conclusions about your company using all of the information you have gathered during the term. Part of your conclusion should include a recommendation of whether or not to invest in this company.

  e. Assemble your entire report, place in an appropriate folder, and submit it to your professor.

Appendix

Gap Inc.
1997 Annual Report
Financial Information

Ten-Year Selected Financial Data

	Compound Annual Growth Rate			1997 52 weeks	1996 52 weeks
	3-year	5-year	10-year		
OPERATING RESULTS ($000)					
Net sales	21%	17%	20%	$6,507,825	$5,284,381
Cost of goods sold and occupancy expenses, excluding depreciation and amortization	—	—	—	3,775,957	3,093,709
Percentage of net sales	—	—	—	58.0%	58.5%
Depreciation and amortization[a]	—	—	—	$ 245,584	$ 191,457
Operating expenses	—	—	—	1,635,017	1,270,138
Net interest (income) expense	—	—	—	(2,975)	(19,450)
Earnings before income taxes	17	20	21	854,242	748,527
Percentage of net sales	—	—	—	13.1%	14.2%
Income taxes	—	—	—	$ 320,341	$ 295,668
Net earnings	19	20	23	533,901	452,859
Percentage of net sales	—	—	—	8.2%	8.6%
Cash dividends	—	—	—	$ 79,503	$ 83,854
Capital expenditures	—	—	—	483,114	375,838
PER SHARE DATA					
Net earnings–basic[b]	21%	21%	23%	$1.35	$1.09
Net earnings–diluted[c]	21	22	23	1.30	1.06
Cash dividends	—	—	—	.20	.20
Shareholders' equity (book value)[d]	—	—	—	4.03	4.02
FINANCIAL POSITION ($000)					
Property and equipment, net	18%	16%	24%	$1,365,246	$1,135,720
Merchandise inventory	26	15	14	733,174	578,765
Total assets	19	19	23	3,337,502	2,626,927
Working capital	15	19	21	839,399	554,359
Current ratio	—	—	—	1.85:1	1.72:1
Total long-term debt, less current installments	—	—	—	$ 496,044	—
Ratio of long-term debt to shareholders' equity	—	—	—	.31:1	N/A
Shareholders' equity	5	12	19	$1,583,986	$1,654,470
Return on average assets	—	—	—	17.9%	18.2%
Return on average shareholders' equity	—	—	—	33.0%	27.5%
STATISTICS					
Number of stores opened	20%	21%	10%	298	203
Number of stores expanded	—	—	—	98	42
Number of stores closed	—	—	—	22	30
Number of stores open at year-end[e]	12	10	10	2,130	1,854
Net increase in number of stores	—	—	—	15%	10%
Comparable store sales growth (52-week basis)	—	—	—	6%	5%
Sales per square foot (52-week basis)[f]	—	—	—	$463	$441
Square footage of gross store space at year-end	19	19	15	15,312,700	12,645,000
Percentage increase in square feet	—	—	—	21%	14%
Number of employees at year-end	14	16	18	81,000	66,000
Weighted-average number of shares–basic[b]	—	—	—	396,179,975	417,146,631
Weighted-average number of shares–diluted[c]	—	—	—	410,200,758	427,267,220
Number of shares outstanding at year-end, net of treasury stock	—	—	—	393,133,028	411,775,997

(a) Excludes amortization of restricted stock, discounted stock options and discount on long-term debt.
(b) Based on weighted-average number of shares excluding restricted stock.
(c) Based on weighted-average number of shares adjusted for dilutive effect of stock options and restricted stock.
(d) Based on actual number of shares outstanding at year-end.
(e) Includes the conversion of GapKids departments to their own separate stores. Converted stores are not classified as new stores.
(f) Based on weighted-average gross square footage.

1995 53 weeks	1994 52 weeks	1993 52 weeks	1992 52 weeks	1991 52 weeks	1990 52 weeks	1989 53 weeks	1988 52 weeks
$4,395,253	$3,722,940	$3,295,679	$2,960,409	$2,518,893	$1,933,780	$1,586,596	$1,252,097
2,645,736	2,202,133	1,996,929	1,856,102	1,496,156	1,187,644	1,006,647	814,028
60.2%	59.2%	60.6%	62.7%	59.4%	61.4%	63.4%	65.0%
$ 175,719	$ 148,863	$ 124,860	$ 99,451	$ 72,765	$ 53,599	$ 39,589	$ 31,408
1,004,396	853,524	748,193	661,252	575,686	454,180	364,101	277,429
(15,797)	(10,902)	809	3,763	3,523	1,435	2,760	3,416
585,199	529,322	424,888	339,841	370,763	236,922	162,714	125,816
13.3%	14.2%	12.9%	11.5%	14.7%	12.3%	10.3%	10.0%
$ 231,160	$ 209,082	$ 166,464	$ 129,140	$ 140,890	$ 92,400	$ 65,086	$ 51,585
354,039	320,240	258,424	210,701	229,873	144,522	97,628	74,231
8.1%	8.6%	7.8%	7.1%	9.1%	7.5%	6.2%	5.9%
$ 66,993	$ 64,775	$ 53,041	$ 44,106	$ 41,126	$ 29,625	$ 22,857	$ 18,244
309,599	236,616	215,856	213,659	244,323	199,617	94,266	68,153
$ .85	$ .76	$ .62	$ .51	$ .56	$ .36	$.24	$.18
.83	.74	.60	.49	.54	.34	.23	.17
.16	.15	.13	.11	.10	.07	.06	.05
3.80	3.17	2.59	2.05	1.59	1.10	.80	.65
$ 957,752	$ 828,777	$ 740,422	$ 650,368	$ 547,740	$ 383,548	$ 238,103	$ 191,257
482,575	370,638	331,155	365,692	313,899	247,462	243,482	193,268
2,343,068	2,004,244	1,763,117	1,379,248	1,147,414	776,900	579,483	481,148
728,301	555,827	494,194	355,649	235,537	101,518	129,139	106,210
2.32:1	2.11:1	2.07:1	2.06:1	1.71:1	1.39:1	1.69:1	1.70:1
—	—	$ 75,000	$ 75,000	$ 80,000	$ 17,500	$ 20,000	$ 22,000
N/A	N/A	.07:1	.08:1	.12:1	.04:1	.06:1	.08:1
$1,640,473	$1,375,232	$1,126,475	$ 887,839	$ 677,788	$ 465,733	$ 337,972	$ 276,399
16.3%	17.0%	16.4%	16.7%	23.9%	21.3%	18.4%	16.2%
23.5%	25.6%	25.7%	26.9%	40.2%	36.0%	31.8%	27.0%
225	172	108	117	139	152	98	106
55	82	130	94	79	56	7	N/A
53	34	45	26	15	20	38	21
1,680	1,508	1,370	1,307	1,216	1,092	960	900
11%	10%	5%	7%	11%	14%	7%	10%
0%	1%	1%	5%	13%	14%	15%	8%
$425	$444	$463	$489	$481	$438	$389	$328
11,100,200	9,165,900	7,546,300	6,509,200	5,638,400	4,762,300	4,056,600	3,879,300
21%	21%	16%	15%	18%	17%	5%	6%
60,000	55,000	44,000	39,000	32,000	26,000	23,000	20,000
417,718,397	421,644,426	417,905,336	412,629,996	407,007,521	401,965,082	399,847,754	410,942,274
427,752,515	431,619,827	428,937,902	427,068,347	423,687,625	419,978,006	420,619,541	434,112,567
431,621,976	434,294,247	435,746,184	432,555,714	427,570,002	423,792,090	421,654,212	421,576,368

Management's Discussion and Analysis
of Results of Operations and Financial Condition

The information below and elsewhere in this Annual Report contains certain forward-looking statements which reflect the current view of Gap Inc. (the "Company") with respect to future events and financial performance. Wherever used, the words "expect," "plan," "anticipate," "believe" and similar expressions identify forward-looking statements.

Any such forward-looking statements are subject to risks and uncertainties that could cause the Company's actual results of operations to differ materially from historical results or current expectations. Some of these risks include, without limitation, ongoing competitive pressures in the apparel industry, risks associated with challenging international retail environments, changes in the level of consumer spending or preferences in apparel, and/or trade restrictions and political or financial instability in countries where the Company's goods are manufactured and other factors that may be described in the Company's filings with the Securities and Exchange Commission. Future economic and industry trends that could potentially impact revenues and profitability remain difficult to predict.

The Company does not undertake to publicly update or revise its forward-looking statements even if experience or future changes make it clear that any projected results expressed or implied therein will not be realized.

Results of Operations

NET SALES

	Fifty-two Weeks Ended Jan. 31, 1998	Fifty-two Weeks Ended Feb. 1, 1997	Fifty-three Weeks Ended Feb. 3, 1996
Net sales ($000)	$6,507,825	$5,284,381	$4,395,253
Total net sales growth percentage	23	20	18
Comparable store sales growth percentage (52-week basis)	6	5	0
Net sales per average gross square foot (52-week basis)	$463	$441	$425
Square footage of gross store space at year-end (000)	15,313	12,645	11,100
Number of:			
New stores	298	203	225
Expanded stores	98	42	55
Closed stores	22	30	53

The total net sales growth for all years presented was attributable primarily to the increase in retail selling space, both through the opening of new stores (net of stores closed) and the expansion of existing stores. An increase in comparable store sales also contributed to net sales growth in 1997 and 1996.

The increase in net sales per average square foot in 1997 and 1996 was primarily attributable to increases in comparable store sales.

COST OF GOODS SOLD AND OCCUPANCY EXPENSES

Cost of goods sold and occupancy expenses as a percentage of net sales were 61.8 percent in 1997, 62.2 percent in 1996 and 64.2 percent in 1995.

The .4 percentage point decrease in 1997 from 1996 was primarily attributable to a .6 percentage point decrease in occupancy expenses, partially offset by a decrease in merchandise margin. The decrease in occupancy expenses as a percentage of net sales was primarily attributable to leverage achieved through comparable store sales growth.

The 2.0 percentage point decrease in 1996 from 1995 was due to a 1.2 percentage point increase in merchandise margin combined with an .8 percentage point decrease in occupancy expenses as a percentage of net sales. The increase in merchandise margin was driven by increases in initial merchandise markup and in the percentage of merchandise sold at regular price. The decrease in occupancy expenses was primarily attributable to the effect of the growth of the Old Navy division, which carries lower occupancy expenses as a percentage of net sales when compared to other divisions, and leverage achieved through comparable store sales growth.

The Company reviews its inventory levels in order to identify slow-moving merchandise and broken assortments (items no longer in stock in a sufficient range of sizes) and uses markdowns to clear merchandise. Such markdowns may have an adverse impact on earnings, depending upon the extent of the markdown and the amount of inventory affected.

OPERATING EXPENSES

Operating expenses as a percentage of net sales were 25.1 percent for 1997, 24.0 percent for 1996 and 22.9 percent for 1995.

In 1997, the 1.1 percentage point increase was primarily attributable to an .8 percentage point increase in advertising/marketing costs as part of the Company's brand development efforts. An increase in the write-off of leasehold improvements and fixtures associated with the remodeling, relocation and closing of certain stores planned for the next fiscal year accounted for .4 percentage point of the increase.

In 1996, the 1.1 percentage point increase was primarily attributable to a .3 percentage point increase in advertising/marketing costs to support the Company's brands and a .5 percentage point increase in incentive bonus expense.

NET INTEREST INCOME

Net interest income was $3.0, $19.5 and $15.8 million for 1997, 1996 and 1995, respectively. The decrease in 1997 was due to the interest expense related to the long-term debt securities issued during the third quarter, as well as to a decrease in gross average investments. The change in 1996 from 1995 was primarily attributable to an increase in gross average investments.

INCOME TAXES

The effective tax rate was 37.5 percent in 1997 and 39.5 percent in 1996 and 1995. The decrease in the effective tax rate in 1997 was a result of the impact of tax planning initiatives to support changing business needs.

Liquidity and Capital Resources

The following sets forth certain measures of the Company's liquidity:

| | Fiscal Year | | |
	1997	1996	1995
Cash provided by operating activities ($000)	$844,651	$834,953	$489,087
Working capital ($000)	839,399	554,359	728,301
Current ratio	1.85:1	1.72:1	2.32:1

For the fiscal year ended January 31, 1998, the increase in cash provided by operating activities was due to an increase in net earnings offset by investments in merchandise inventory and the timing of payments for income taxes and certain payables. For the fiscal year ended February 1, 1997, the increase in cash provided by operating activities was attributable to an increase in net earnings and the timing of certain year-end payables and accrued expenses.

The Company funds inventory expenditures during normal and peak periods through a combination of cash flows provided by operations and normal trade credit arrangements. The Company's business follows a seasonal pattern, peaking over a total of about ten to twelve weeks during the Back-to-School and Holiday periods. During 1997 and 1996, these periods accounted for approximately 35 and 33 percent, respectively, of the Company's annual sales.

The Company has committed credit facilities totaling $950 million, consisting of an $800 million, 364-day revolving credit facility, and a $150 million, 5-year revolving credit facility through June 30, 2002. These credit facilities provide for the issuance of up to $450 million in letters of credit. The Company has additional uncommitted credit facilities of $300 million for the issuance of letters of credit. At January 31, 1998, the Company had outstanding letters of credit of approximately $498 million.

To provide financial flexibility, the Company issued $500 million of 6.9 percent, 10-year debt securities in fiscal 1997. The proceeds from this issuance are intended to be used for general corporate purposes, including store expansion, brand investment, development of additional distribution channels and repurchases of the Company's common stock pursuant to its ongoing repurchase program.

Capital expenditures, net of construction allowances and dispositions, totaled approximately $450 million in 1997. These expenditures resulted in a net increase in store space of approximately 2.7 million square feet or 21 percent due to the addition of 298 new stores, the expansion of 98 stores and the remodeling of certain stores. Capital expenditures for 1996 and 1995 were $359 million and $291 million, respectively, resulting in a net increase in store space of approximately 1.5 million square feet in 1996 and approximately 1.9 million square feet in 1995.

The increase in capital expenditures in 1997 from 1996 was primarily attributable to the number of stores opened, expanded and remodeled, as well as the expansion of headquarters facilities. The increase in capital expenditures in 1996 from 1995 was primarily attributable to the construction of two distribution centers and a headquarters facility. Expenditures in 1997, 1996 and 1995 also included costs for equipment.

For 1998, the Company expects capital expenditures to total approximately $700 million, net of construction allowances. This represents the addition of 300 to 350 new stores, the expansion of approximately 80 to 90 stores and the remodeling of certain stores, as well as amounts for headquarters facilities, distribution centers and equipment. The Company expects to fund such capital expenditures with cash flow from operations and other sources of financing. Square footage growth is expected to be 18 to 20 percent before store closings. New stores are generally expected to be leased.

In 1997, the Company completed construction of a headquarters facility in San Bruno, California for approximately $60 million. The facility became fully operational in October 1997. To further support its growth, the Company continues to explore alternatives for additional headquarters facilities in San Francisco and San Bruno, California. The Company acquired land in 1997 in San Francisco and in the fourth quarter entered into a purchase contract to acquire additional land in San Bruno.

Also during 1997, the Company commenced construction on a distribution center in Fresno, California for an estimated cost at completion of $60 million. The majority of the expenditures for this facility will be incurred in 1998. The facility is expected to begin operations in early 1999.

On November 24, 1997, the Company's Board of Directors authorized a three-for-two split of its common stock effective December 22, 1997, in the form of a stock dividend for shareholders of record at the close of business on December 8, 1997. Share and per share amounts herein and in the accompanying consolidated financial statements have been restated to reflect the stock split.

In October 1996, the Board of Directors approved a program under which the Company may repurchase up to 45 million shares of its outstanding common stock in the open market over a three-year period. As of January 31, 1998, 28 million shares had been repurchased for $744 million. The program announced in October 1996 follows an earlier 27 million share repurchase program which was completed in November 1996 at a cost of approximately $450 million.

During fiscal 1997, the Company entered into various put option contracts in connection with the share repurchase program to hedge against stock price fluctuations. The Company also continued to enter into foreign exchange forward contracts to reduce exposure to foreign currency exchange risk involved in its commitments to purchase merchandise for foreign operations. Additional information on these contracts and agreements is presented in the Notes to Consolidated Financial Statements (Note E). Quantitative and qualitative disclosures about market risk for financial instruments are presented on page 38.

The Company pursues a diversified global import operations strategy which includes relationships with vendors in over 40 countries. These sourcing operations may be adversely affected by political instability resulting in the disruption of trade from exporting countries, significant fluctuation in the value of the U.S. dollar against foreign currencies, restrictions on the transfer of funds and/or other trade disruptions. The current financial instability in Asia is an example of this instability, which could affect some suppliers adversely. Although to date the instability in Asia has not had a material adverse effect on the Company's ability to import apparel, and therefore on the Company's results of operations and financial condition, no assurances can be given that it will not have such an effect in the future.

The Company is addressing the need to ensure that its operations will not be adversely impacted by software or other system failures related to year 2000. A program office was established in 1997 to coordinate the identification, evaluation and implementation of any necessary changes to computer systems, applications and business processes. The costs associated with this effort are expected to be incurred through 1999 and are not expected to have a material impact on the results of operations, cash flows or financial condition in any given year. However, no assurances can be given that the Company will be able to completely identify or address all year 2000 compliance issues, or that third parties with whom the Company does business will not experience system failures as a result of the year 2000 issues, nor can the Company fully predict the consequences of noncompliance.

Per Share Data

Fiscal	Market Prices				Cash Dividends	
	1997		1996		1997	1996
	High	Low	High	Low		
1st Quarter	$24 1/8	$19 1/16	$20 5/16	$15 7/16	$.05	$.05
2nd Quarter	29 13/16	20 9/16	24 1/16	18 1/8	.05	.05
3rd Quarter	35 3/4	28	24 5/16	17 5/16	.05	.05
4th Quarter	41 1/4	32 15/16	22 5/16	18 9/16	.05	.05
Year					$.20	$.20

The principal markets on which the Company's stock is traded are the New York Stock Exchange and the Pacific Exchange. The number of holders of record of the Company's stock as of March 9, 1998 was 7,108.

Management's Report on Financial Information

Management is responsible for the integrity and consistency of all financial information presented in the Annual Report. The financial statements have been prepared in accordance with generally accepted accounting principles and necessarily include certain amounts based on Management's best estimates and judgments.

In fulfilling its responsibility for the reliability of financial information, Management has established and maintains accounting systems and procedures appropriately supported by internal accounting controls. Such controls include the selection and training of qualified personnel, an organizational structure providing for division of responsibility, communication of requirement for compliance with approved accounting control and business practices and a program of internal audit. The extent of the Company's system of internal accounting control recognizes that the cost should not exceed the benefits derived and that the evaluation of those factors requires estimates and judgments by Management. Although no system can ensure that all errors or irregularities have been eliminated, Management believes that the internal accounting controls in use provide reasonable assurance, at reasonable cost, that assets are safeguarded against loss from unauthorized use or disposition, that transactions are executed in accordance with Management's authorization and that the financial records are reliable for preparing financial statements and maintaining accountability for assets. The financial statements of the Company have been audited by Deloitte & Touche LLP, independent auditors. Their report, which appears below, is based upon their audits conducted in accordance with generally accepted auditing standards.

The Audit and Finance Committee (the "Committee") of the Board of Directors is comprised solely of directors who are not officers or employees of the Company. The Committee is responsible for recommending to the Board of Directors the selection of independent auditors. It meets periodically with Management, the independent auditors and the internal auditors to assure that they are carrying out their responsibilities. The Committee also reviews and monitors the financial, accounting and auditing procedures of the Company in addition to reviewing the Company's financial reports. Deloitte & Touche LLP and the internal auditors have full and free access to the Committee, with and without Management's presence.

Independent Auditors' Report
To the Shareholders and Board of Directors of The Gap, Inc.:

We have audited the accompanying consolidated balance sheets of The Gap, Inc. and subsidiaries as of January 31, 1998 and February 1, 1997, and the related consolidated statements of earnings, shareholders' equity and cash flows for each of the three fiscal years in the period ended January 31, 1998. These financial statements are the responsibility of the Company's management. Our responsibility is to express an opinion on these financial statements based on our audits.

We conducted our audits in accordance with generally accepted auditing standards. Those standards require that we plan and perform the audits to obtain reasonable assurance about whether the consolidated financial statements are free of material misstatement. An audit includes examining, on a test basis, evidence supporting the amounts and disclosures in the financial statements. An audit also includes assessing the accounting principles used and significant estimates made by management, as well as evaluating the overall financial statement presentation. We believe that our audits provide a reasonable basis for our opinion.

In our opinion, such consolidated financial statements present fairly, in all material respects, the financial position of the Company and its subsidiaries as of January 31, 1998 and February 1, 1997, and the results of their operations and their cash flows for each of the three fiscal years in the period ended January 31, 1998 in conformity with generally accepted accounting principles.

Deloitte & Touche LLP

San Francisco, California
February 27, 1998

Consolidated Statements of Earnings

($000 except share and per share amounts)	Fifty-two Weeks Ended January 31, 1998	Percentage to Sales	Fifty-two Weeks Ended February 1, 1997	Percentage to Sales	Fifty-three Weeks Ended February 3, 1996	Percentage to Sales
Net sales	$6,507,825	100.0%	$5,284,381	100.0%	$4,395,253	100.0%
Costs and expenses						
Cost of goods sold and occupancy expenses	4,021,541	61.8	3,285,166	62.2	2,821,455	64.2
Operating expenses	1,635,017	25.1	1,270,138	24.0	1,004,396	22.9
Net interest income	(2,975)	0.0	(19,450)	(0.4)	(15,797)	(0.4)
Earnings before income taxes	854,242	13.1	748,527	14.2	585,199	13.3
Income taxes	320,341	4.9	295,668	5.6	231,160	5.2
Net earnings	$ 533,901	8.2%	$ 452,859	8.6%	$ 354,039	8.1%
Weighted-average number of shares–basic	396,179,975		417,146,631		417,718,397	
Weighted-average number of shares–diluted	410,200,758		427,267,220		427,752,515	
Earnings per share–basic	$1.35		$1.09		$.85	
Earnings per share–diluted	1.30		1.06		.83	

See Notes to Consolidated Financial Statements.

Consolidated Balance Sheets

($000)	January 31, 1998	February 1, 1997
ASSETS		
Current Assets		
Cash and equivalents	$ 913,169	$ 485,644
Short-term investments	—	135,632
Merchandise inventory	733,174	578,765
Prepaid expenses and other current assets	184,604	129,214
Total current assets	1,830,947	1,329,255
Property and Equipment		
Leasehold improvements	846,791	736,608
Furniture and equipment	1,236,450	960,516
Land and buildings	154,136	99,969
Construction-in-progress	66,582	101,520
	2,303,959	1,898,613
Accumulated depreciation and amortization	(938,713)	(762,893)
Property and equipment, net	1,365,246	1,135,720
Long-term investments	—	36,138
Lease rights and other assets	141,309	125,814
Total assets	$ 3,337,502	$ 2,626,927
LIABILITIES AND SHAREHOLDERS' EQUITY		
Current Liabilities		
Notes payable	$ 84,794	$ 40,050
Accounts payable	416,976	351,754
Accrued expenses	389,412	282,494
Income taxes payable	83,597	91,806
Deferred lease credits and other current liabilities	16,769	8,792
Total current liabilities	991,548	774,896
Long-Term Liabilities		
Long-term debt	496,044	—
Deferred lease credits and other liabilities	265,924	197,561
Total long-term liabilities	761,968	197,561
Shareholders' Equity		
Common stock $.05 par value		
Authorized 500,000,000 shares; issued 439,922,841 and 476,796,135 shares; outstanding 393,133,028 and 411,775,997 shares	21,996	23,840
Additional paid-in capital	317,674	434,104
Retained earnings	2,392,750	1,938,352
Foreign currency translation adjustments	(15,230)	(5,187)
Deferred compensation	(38,167)	(47,838)
Treasury stock, at cost	(1,095,037)	(688,801)
Total shareholders' equity	1,583,986	1,654,470
Total liabilities and shareholders' equity	$ 3,337,502	$ 2,626,927

See Notes to Consolidated Financial Statements.

Consolidated Statements of Cash Flows

($000)	Fifty-two Weeks Ended January 31, 1998	Fifty-two Weeks Ended February 1, 1997	Fifty-three Weeks Ended February 3, 1996
CASH FLOWS FROM OPERATING ACTIVITIES			
Net earnings	$533,901	$452,859	$354,039
Adjustments to reconcile net earnings to net cash provided by operating activities:			
Depreciation and amortization[a]	269,706	214,905	197,440
Tax benefit from exercise of stock options by employees and from vesting of restricted stock	23,682	47,348	11,444
Deferred income taxes	(13,706)	(28,897)	(2,477)
Change in operating assets and liabilities:			
Merchandise inventory	(156,091)	(93,800)	(113,021)
Prepaid expenses and other	(44,736)	(16,355)	(15,278)
Accounts payable	63,532	88,532	1,183
Accrued expenses	107,365	87,974	9,427
Income taxes payable	(8,214)	25,706	24,806
Deferred lease credits and other long-term liabilities	69,212	56,681	21,524
Net cash provided by operating activities	844,651	834,953	489,087
CASH FLOWS FROM INVESTING ACTIVITIES			
Net maturity (purchase) of short-term investments	174,709	(11,774)	116,134
Net purchase of long-term investments	(2,939)	(40,120)	(30,370)
Net purchase of property and equipment	(465,843)	(371,833)	(302,260)
Acquisition of lease rights and other assets	(19,779)	(12,206)	(6,623)
Net cash used for investing activities	(313,852)	(435,933)	(223,119)
CASH FLOWS FROM FINANCING ACTIVITIES			
Net increase in notes payable	44,462	18,445	20,787
Net issuance of long-term debt	495,890	—	—
Issuance of common stock	30,653	37,053	17,096
Net purchase of treasury stock	(593,142)	(466,741)	(71,314)
Cash dividends paid	(79,503)	(83,854)	(66,993)
Net cash used for financing activities	(101,640)	(495,097)	(100,424)
Effect of exchange rate changes on cash	(1,634)	2,155	(465)
Net increase (decrease) in cash and equivalents	427,525	(93,922)	165,079
Cash and equivalents at beginning of year	485,644	579,566	414,487
Cash and equivalents at end of year	$913,169	$485,644	$579,566

See Notes to Consolidated Financial Statements.

(a) Includes amortization of restricted stock, discounted stock options and discount on long-term debt.

Consolidated Statements of Shareholders' Equity

($000 except share and per share amounts)	Common Stock	
	Shares	Amount
Balance at January 28, 1995	470,918,331	$23,546
Issuance of common stock pursuant to stock option plans	1,491,558	75
Net issuance of common stock pursuant to management incentive restricted stock plans	1,547,070	77
Tax benefit from exercise of stock options by employees and from vesting of restricted stock		
Foreign currency translation adjustments		
Amortization of restricted stock		
Purchase of treasury stock		
Reissuance of treasury stock		
Net earnings		
Cash dividends ($.16 per share)		
Balance at February 3, 1996	473,956,959	$23,698
Issuance of common stock pursuant to stock option plans	2,386,761	119
Net issuance of common stock pursuant to management incentive restricted stock plans	452,415	23
Tax benefit from exercise of stock options by employees and from vesting of restricted stock		
Foreign currency translation adjustments		
Amortization of restricted stock		
Purchase of treasury stock		
Reissuance of treasury stock		
Net earnings		
Cash dividends ($.20 per share)		
Balance at February 1, 1997	476,796,135	$23,840
Issuance of common stock pursuant to stock option plans[a]	2,848,567	142
Net cancelations of common stock pursuant to management incentive restricted stock plans	(946,861)	(47)
Tax benefit from exercise of stock options by employees and from vesting of restricted stock		
Foreign currency translation adjustments		
Amortization of restricted stock and discounted stock options		
Purchase of treasury stock		
Reissuance of treasury stock		
Retirement of treasury stock	(38,775,000)	(1,939)
Net earnings		
Cash dividends ($.20 per share)		
Balance at January 31, 1998	439,922,841	$21,996

See Notes to Consolidated Financial Statements.
(a) Includes payout of cash for fractional shares resulting from the three-for-two split of common stock effective December 22, 1997.

Additional Paid-in Capital	Retained Earnings	Foreign Currency Translation Adjustments	Deferred Compensation	Treasury Stock		Total
				Shares	Amount	
$282,716	$1,282,301	$ (8,320)	$(54,265)	(36,624,084)	$ (150,746)	$1,375,232
9,591						9,666
19,531			(16,191)			3,417
11,444						11,444
		(751)				(751)
			21,721			21,721
				(6,289,200)	(72,717)	(72,717)
4,012				578,301	1,403	5,415
	354,039					354,039
	(66,993)					(66,993)
$327,294	$1,569,347	$ (9,071)	$(48,735)	(42,334,983)	$ (222,060)	$1,640,473
19,694			(9,648)			10,165
32,799			(12,903)			19,919
47,348						47,348
		3,884				3,884
			23,448			23,448
				(23,284,650)	(468,246)	(468,246)
6,969				599,495	1,505	8,474
	452,859					452,859
	(83,854)					(83,854)
$434,104	$1,938,352	$ (5,187)	$(47,838)	(65,020,138)	$ (688,801)	$1,654,470
47,963			(18,166)			29,939
(10,452)			3,869			(6,630)
23,682						23,682
		(10,043)				(10,043)
			23,968			23,968
				(21,190,300)	(598,149)	(598,149)
7,344				645,625	5,007	12,351
(184,967)				38,775,000	186,906	0
	533,901					533,901
	(79,503)					(79,503)
$317,674	$2,392,750	$(15,230)	$(38,167)	(46,789,813)	$(1,095,037)	$1,583,986

Notes to Consolidated Financial Statements

For the Fifty-two Weeks ended January 31, 1998 (fiscal 1997), the Fifty-two Weeks ended February 1, 1997 (fiscal 1996) and the Fifty-three Weeks ended February 3, 1996 (fiscal 1995).

NOTE A: SUMMARY OF SIGNIFICANT ACCOUNTING POLICIES

Gap Inc. (the "Company") is an international specialty retailer which operates stores selling casual apparel, personal care and other accessories for men, women and children under a variety of brand names including: Gap, GapKids, babyGap, Banana Republic and Old Navy. Its principal markets consist of the United States, Canada, Europe and Asia with the United States being the most significant.

On November 24, 1997, the Company's Board of Directors authorized a three-for-two split of its common stock effective December 22, 1997, in the form of a stock dividend for shareholders of record at the close of business on December 8, 1997. Share and per share amounts in the accompanying consolidated financial statements for all periods have been restated to reflect the stock split.

The consolidated financial statements include the accounts of the Company and its subsidiaries. Intercompany accounts and transactions have been eliminated.

The preparation of financial statements in conformity with generally accepted accounting principles requires Management to make estimates and assumptions that affect the reported amounts of assets and liabilities and disclosure of contingent assets and liabilities at the date of the financial statements and the reported amounts of revenue and expenses during the reporting period. Actual results could differ from those estimates.

Cash and equivalents represent cash and short-term, highly liquid investments with original maturities of three months or less.

Short-term investments include investments with an original maturity of greater than three months and a remaining maturity of less than one year. Long-term investments include investments with an original and remaining maturity of greater than one year. Effective July 1997, the Company's short- and long-term investments, which consist primarily of debt securities, are classified as available for sale and are carried at fair market value. Any unrealized gains or losses computed in marking these securities to market are reported within shareholders' equity. Prior to July 1997, such securities were classified as held to maturity and were carried at amortized cost.

Merchandise inventory is stated at the lower of FIFO (first-in, first-out) cost or market.

Property and equipment are stated at cost. Depreciation and amortization are computed using the straight-line method over the estimated useful lives of the related assets.

Lease rights are recorded at cost and are amortized over 12 years or the lives of the respective leases including option periods, whichever is less.

Costs associated with the opening or remodeling of stores, such as pre-opening rent and payroll, are expensed as incurred. The net book value of fixtures and leasehold improvements for stores scheduled to be closed or expanded within the next fiscal year is charged against current earnings.

Costs associated with the production of advertising, such as writing copy, printing and other costs, are expensed as incurred. Costs associated with communicating advertising that has been produced, such as magazine and billboard space, are expensed when the advertising first takes place. Advertising costs were $175 million, $96 million and $64 million in fiscal 1997, 1996 and 1995, respectively.

Deferred income taxes arise from temporary differences between the tax basis of assets and liabilities and their reported amounts in the consolidated financial statements.

Translation adjustments result from the process of translating foreign subsidiaries' financial statements into U.S. dollars. Balance sheet accounts are translated at exchange rates in effect at the balance sheet date. Income statement accounts are translated at average exchange rates during the year. Resulting translation adjustments are included in shareholders' equity.

The Company accounts for stock-based awards using the intrinsic value-based method under Accounting Principles Board (APB) Opinion No. 25, *Accounting for Stock Issued to Employees*, and has provided pro forma disclosures of net earnings and earnings per share in accordance with the provisions of Statement of Financial Accounting Standards (SFAS) No. 123, *Accounting for Stock-Based Compensation*. Restricted stock and discounted stock options represent deferred compensation and are shown as a reduction of shareholders' equity.

In the fourth quarter of 1997, the Company adopted SFAS No. 128, *Earnings per Share*, which requires dual presentation of basic earnings per share (EPS) and diluted EPS. All prior periods have been restated to conform with the new statement. Basic EPS is computed as net earnings divided by the weighted-average number of common shares outstanding, excluding restricted stock, for the period. Diluted EPS reflects the potential dilution that could occur from common shares issuable through stock-based compensation including stock options, restricted stock and other convertible securities.

The Financial Accounting Standards Board issued SFAS No. 130, *Reporting Comprehensive Income,* which requires that an enterprise report, by major components and as a single total, the change in its net assets during the period from non-owner sources; and SFAS No. 131, *Disclosures About Segments of an Enterprise and Related Information,* which establishes annual and interim reporting standards for an enterprise's operating segments and related disclosures about its products, services, geographic areas and major customers. Adoption of these standards will not impact the Company's consolidated financial position, results of operations or cash flows, and any effect will be limited to the form and content of its disclosures. SFAS No. 130 and SFAS No. 131 are effective for the Company's fiscal years ending after January 31, 1998.

Certain reclassifications have been made to the 1995 and 1996 financial statements to conform with the 1997 financial statements.

NOTE B: DEBT AND OTHER CREDIT ARRANGEMENTS

The Company has committed credit facilities totaling $950 million, consisting of an $800 million, 364-day revolving credit facility, and a $150 million, 5-year revolving credit facility through June 30, 2002. These credit facilities provide for the issuance of up to $450 million in letters of credit. The Company has additional uncommitted credit facilities of $300 million for the issuance of letters of credit. At January 31, 1998, the Company had outstanding letters of credit of $498,256,000.

Borrowings under the Company's credit agreements are subject to the Company not exceeding a certain debt ratio. The Company was in compliance with this debt covenant at January 31, 1998.

During fiscal 1997, the Company issued long-term debt which consists of $500 million of 6.9 percent unsecured notes, due September 15, 2007. Interest on the notes is payable semi-annually. The fair value at January 31, 1998 of the notes was approximately $526 million, based on the current rates at which the Company could borrow funds with similar terms and remaining maturities. The balance of the debt is net of unamortized discount.

Gross interest payments were $8,399,000, $2,800,000 and $2,274,000 in fiscal 1997, 1996 and 1995, respectively.

NOTE C: INCOME TAXES

Income taxes consisted of the following:

($000)	Fifty-two Weeks Ended Jan. 31, 1998	Fifty-two Weeks Ended Feb. 1, 1997	Fifty-three Weeks Ended Feb. 3, 1996
Currently Payable			
Federal	$279,068	$266,063	$176,200
State	33,384	36,167	40,111
Foreign	21,595	22,335	17,348
Total currently payable	334,047	324,565	233,659
Deferred			
Federal	(14,832)	(23,980)	(7,169)
State and foreign	1,126	(4,917)	4,670
Total deferred	(13,706)	(28,897)	(2,499)
Total provision	$320,341	$295,668	$231,160

The foreign component of pretax earnings before eliminations and corporate allocations in fiscal 1997, 1996 and 1995 was $84,487,000, $82,220,000 and $71,545,000, respectively. No provision was made for U.S. income taxes on the undistributed earnings of the foreign subsidiaries as it is the Company's intention to utilize those earnings in the foreign operations for an indefinite period of time or repatriate such earnings only when tax effective to do so. Undistributed earnings of foreign subsidiaries were $218,113,000 at January 31, 1998.

The difference between the effective income tax rate and the United States federal income tax rate is summarized as follows:

	Fifty-two Weeks Ended Jan. 31, 1998	Fifty-two Weeks Ended Feb. 1, 1997	Fifty-three Weeks Ended Feb. 3, 1996
Federal tax rate	35.0%	35.0%	35.0%
State income taxes, less federal benefit	3.2	4.4	5.0
Other	(.7)	.1	(.5)
Effective tax rate	37.5%	39.5%	39.5%

Deferred tax assets (liabilities), reported in other assets in the Consolidated Balance Sheets, consisted of the following at January 31, 1998 and February 1, 1997:

($000)	Jan. 31, 1998	Feb. 1, 1997
Compensation and benefits accruals	$ 31,367	$ 31,640
Scheduled rent	44,451	40,834
Inventory capitalization	28,776	16,459
Nondeductible accruals	20,003	18,705
Other	17,854	24,224
Gross deferred tax assets	142,451	131,862
Depreciation	(9,553)	(13,611)
Other	(6,345)	(5,404)
Gross deferred tax liabilities	(15,898)	(19,015)
Net deferred tax assets	$126,553	$112,847

Income tax payments were $320,744,000, $249,968,000 and $197,802,000 in fiscal 1997, 1996 and 1995, respectively.

NOTE D: LEASES

The Company leases most of its store premises and head-quarters facilities and some of its distribution centers. These leases expire at various dates through 2013.

The aggregate minimum non-cancelable annual lease payments under leases in effect on January 31, 1998 are as follows:

Fiscal Year	($000)
1998	$ 409,607
1999	403,285
2000	387,668
2001	364,270
2002	332,364
Thereafter	1,172,849
Total minimum lease commitment	$3,070,043

Many leases entered into by the Company include options, which are generally exercised, that may extend the lease term beyond the initial commitment period, subject to terms agreed to at lease inception. Some leases also include early termination options which can be exercised under specific conditions. If conditions did not warrant invoking early termination of any leases, and all renewal options were exercised for current lease agreements, the total lease commitment for the Company would be approximately $4.1 billion.

For leases that contain predetermined fixed escalations of the minimum rentals, the Company recognizes the related rental expense on a straight-line basis and records the difference between the recognized rental expense and amounts payable under the leases as deferred lease credits. At January 31, 1998 and February 1, 1997, this liability amounted to $129,981,000 and $110,633,000, respectively.

Cash or rent abatements received upon entering into certain store leases are recognized on a straight-line basis as a reduction to rent expense over the lease term. The unamortized portion is included in deferred lease credits.

Some of the leases relating to stores in operation at January 31, 1998 contain renewal options for periods ranging up to 25 years. Many leases also provide for payment of operating expenses, real estate taxes and for additional rent based on a percentage of sales. No lease directly imposes any restrictions relating to leasing in other locations (other than radius clauses).

Rental expense for all operating leases was as follows:

($000)	Fifty-two Weeks Ended Jan. 31, 1998	Fifty-two Weeks Ended Feb. 1, 1997	Fifty-three Weeks Ended Feb. 3, 1996
Minimum rentals	$391,472	$337,487	$300,171
Contingent rentals	38,657	30,644	22,464
Total	$430,129	$368,131	$322,635

NOTE E: FINANCIAL INSTRUMENTS

Foreign Exchange Forward Contracts

The Company enters into foreign exchange forward contracts to reduce exposure to foreign currency exchange risk. These contracts are primarily designated and effective as hedges of commitments to purchase merchandise for foreign operations. The market value gains and losses on these contracts are deferred and recognized as part of the underlying cost to purchase the merchandise. At January 31, 1998, the Company had contracts maturing at various dates through 1998 to sell the equivalent of $123,230,000 in foreign currencies (20,200,000 British pounds, 46,200,000 Canadian dollars, 62,625,260,078 Italian lire, 1,543,000,000 Japanese yen and 1,234,884,074 Spanish pesetas) at the contracted rates. The deferred gains and losses on the Company's foreign exchange forward contracts at January 31, 1998 are immaterial.

Put Options

At January 31, 1998, the Company had various put option contracts to repurchase up to 3,050,000 shares of its common stock. The contracts have exercise prices ranging from $32.95 to $38.37, with expiration dates extending to the third quarter of fiscal 1998.

Interest Rate Swaps

During fiscal 1997, the Company entered into interest rate swap agreements in order to reduce interest rate risk on a substantial portion of its long-term debt. The swap agreements, which were issued at an aggregate notional amount of $400 million, were settled in September 1997 at an interest rate of 6.7 percent. The gains on the interest rate swaps were deferred and are being amortized to reduce interest expense over the life of the debt.

NOTE F: EMPLOYEE BENEFIT
AND INCENTIVE STOCK COMPENSATION PLANS

Retirement Plans

The Company has a qualified defined contribution retirement plan, called GapShare, which is available to employees who meet certain age and service requirements. This plan permits employees to make contributions up to the maximum limits allowable under the Internal Revenue Code. Under the plan, the Company matches all or a portion of the employee's contributions under a predetermined formula. The Company's contributions vest over a seven-year period. Company contributions to the retirement plan in 1997, 1996 and 1995 were $12,907,000, $11,427,000 and $9,839,000, respectively.

A nonqualified Executive Deferred Compensation Plan was established on January 1, 1994 and a nonqualified Executive Capital Accumulation Plan was established on April 1, 1994. Both plans allow eligible employees to defer compensation up to a maximum amount defined in each plan. The Company does not match employees' contributions.

A Deferred Compensation Plan was established on August 26, 1997 for nonemployee members of the Board of Directors. Under this plan, Board members may elect to defer receipt on a pre-tax basis of eligible compensation received for serving as nonemployee directors of the Company. In exchange for compensation deferred, Board members are granted discounted stock options to purchase shares of the Company's common stock. All options are fully exercisable upon the date granted and expire seven years after grant or one year after retirement from the Board, if earlier. The Company may issue up to 300,000 shares under the plan.

Incentive Stock Compensation Plans

The 1996 Stock Option and Award Plan (the "Plan") was established on March 26, 1996. The Board authorized 41,485,041 shares for issuance under the Plan, which includes shares available under the Management Incentive Restricted Stock Plan ("MIRSP") and an earlier stock option plan established in 1981, both of which were superseded by the Plan. The Plan empowers the Compensation and Stock Option Committee of the Board of Directors to award compensation primarily in the form of nonqualified stock options or restricted stock to key employees. Stock options generally expire ten years from the grant date or one year after the date of retirement, if earlier. Stock options generally vest over a three-year period, with shares becoming exercisable in full on the third anniversary of the grant date. Nonqualified stock options are generally issued at fair market value but may be issued at prices less than the fair market value at the date of grant or at other prices as determined by the Compensation and Stock Option Committee. Total compensation cost for those stock options issued at less than fair market value under the Plan and for the restricted shares issued under MIRSP was $17,170,000, $22,248,000 and $23,743,000 in 1997, 1996 and 1995, respectively.

Employee Stock Purchase Plan

The Company has an Employee Stock Purchase Plan under which all eligible employees may purchase common stock of the Company at 85 percent of the lower of the closing price of the Company's common stock on the grant date or the purchase date on the New York Stock Exchange Composite Transactions Index. Employees pay for their stock purchases through payroll deductions at a rate equal to any whole percentage from 1 percent to 15 percent. There were 645,625 shares issued under the plan during fiscal 1997, 599,495 during 1996 and 578,301 during 1995. All shares were acquired from reissued treasury stock. At January 31, 1998, there were 4,176,579 shares reserved for future subscriptions.

NOTE G: SHAREHOLDERS'
EQUITY AND STOCK OPTIONS

Common and Preferred Stock

The Company is authorized to issue 60,000,000 shares of Class B common stock which is convertible into shares of common stock on a share-for-share basis; transfer of the shares is restricted. In addition, the holders of the Class B common stock have six votes per share on most matters and are entitled to a lower cash dividend. No Class B shares have been issued.

The Board of Directors is authorized to issue 30,000,000 shares of one or more series of preferred stock and to establish at the time of issuance the issue price, dividend rate, redemption price, liquidation value, conversion features and such other terms and conditions of each series (including voting rights) as the Board of Directors deems appropriate, without further action on the part of the shareholders. No preferred shares have been issued.

In October 1996, the Board of Directors approved a share-buyback program under which the Company may repurchase up to 45,000,000 shares of its outstanding stock in the open market over a three-year period. As of January 31, 1998, 28,184,650 shares were repurchased for $743,805,000 under this program.

Stock Options

Under the Company's Stock Option Plans, nonqualified options to purchase common stock are granted to officers, directors and key employees at exercise prices equal to the fair market value of the stock at the date of grant or at other prices as determined by the Compensation and Stock Option Committee of the Board of Directors.

Stock option activity for all employee benefit plans was as follows:

	Shares	Weighted-Average Exercise Price
Balance at January 28, 1995	11,619,816	$10.18
Granted	14,226,600	11.94
Exercised	(1,491,558)	6.48
Canceled	(894,222)	12.27
Balance at February 3, 1996	23,460,636	$11.41
Granted	9,364,110	20.60
Exercised	(2,386,761)	8.30
Canceled	(1,198,608)	14.85
Balance at February 1, 1997	29,239,377	$14.46
Granted	11,392,531	21.62
Exercised	(2,849,034)	10.65
Canceled	(2,559,295)	16.01
Balance at January 31, 1998	35,223,579	$16.97

Outstanding options at January 31, 1998 have expiration dates ranging from March 20, 1998 to January 29, 2008 and represent grants to 2,347 key employees.

At January 31, 1998, the Company reserved 60,083,011 shares of its common stock, including 14,996 treasury shares, for the exercise of stock options. There were 24,859,432 and 32,745,096 shares available for granting of options at January 31, 1998 and February 1, 1997, respectively. Options for 4,299,847 and 4,373,222 shares were exercisable as of January 31, 1998 and February 1, 1997, respectively, and had a weighted-average exercise price of $11.66 and $9.01 for those respective periods.

The Company accounts for its Stock Option and Award Plans in accordance with APB Opinion No. 25, under which no compensation cost has been recognized for stock option awards granted at fair market value. Had compensation cost for the Company's stock-based compensation plans been determined based on the fair value at the grant dates for awards under those plans in accordance with the provisions of SFAS No. 123, *Accounting for Stock-Based Compensation*, the Company's net earnings and earnings per share would have been reduced to the pro forma amounts indicated below. The effects of applying SFAS No. 123 in this pro forma disclosure are not indicative of future amounts. SFAS No. 123 does not apply to awards prior to fiscal year 1995. Additional awards in future years are anticipated.

	Fifty-two Weeks Ended Jan. 31, 1998	Fifty-two Weeks Ended Feb. 1, 1997	Fifty-three Weeks Ended Feb. 3, 1996
Net earnings ($000)			
As reported	$533,901	$452,859	$354,039
Pro forma	507,966	437,232	348,977
Earnings per share			
As reported—basic	$1.35	$1.09	$.85
Pro forma—basic	1.28	1.05	.84
As reported—diluted	1.30	1.06	.83
Pro forma—diluted	1.24	1.02	.82

The weighted-average fair value of the stock options granted during fiscal 1997, 1996 and 1995 was $8.76, $7.47 and $4.18, respectively. The fair value of each option granted is estimated on the date of the grant using the Black-Scholes option-pricing model with the following weighted-average assumptions for grants in 1997: dividend yield of .7 percent; expected price volatility of 31 percent; risk-free interest rates ranging from 5.9 percent to 7.0 percent and expected lives between 3.9 and 5.8 years. The fair value of stock options granted prior to 1997 was based on the following weighted-average assumptions: dividend yield of 1.0 percent; expected price volatility of 30 percent; risk-free interest rates ranging from 5.5 percent to 6.5 percent; and expected lives between 3.6 and 5.8 years.

The following table summarizes information about stock options outstanding at January 31, 1998:

Range of Exercise Prices	Options Outstanding			Options Exercisable	
	Number Outstanding at Jan. 31, 1998	Weighted-Average Remaining Contractual Life (in years)	Weighted-Average Exercise Price	Number Exercisable at Jan. 31, 1998	Weighted-Average Exercise Price
$ 3.86 to $11.29	8,215,077	5.10	$10.12	1,995,467	$ 8.39
11.40 to 13.03	7,454,625	5.75	12.96	210,600	11.79
13.42 to 20.88	10,688,682	8.08	19.13	2,077,095	14.68
20.89 to 39.00	8,865,195	8.66	24.10	16,685	25.79
$ 3.86 to $39.00	35,223,579	7.04	$16.97	4,299,847	$11.66

NOTE H: EARNINGS PER SHARE

Under SFAS No. 128, the Company provides dual presentation of EPS on a basic and diluted basis. The Company's granting of certain stock options and restricted stock resulted in potential dilution of basic EPS. The following summarizes the effects of the assumed issuance of dilutive securities on weighted-average shares for basic EPS.

	Fifty-two Weeks Ended Jan. 31, 1998	Fifty-two Weeks Ended Feb. 1, 1997	Fifty-three Weeks Ended Feb. 3, 1996
Weighted-average number of shares–basic	396,179,975	417,146,631	417,718,397
Incremental shares from assumed issuance of:			
Stock options	10,037,700	5,597,219	1,939,485
Restricted stock	3,983,083	4,523,370	8,094,633
Weighted-average number of shares–diluted	410,200,758	427,267,220	427,752,515

The number of incremental shares from the assumed issuance of stock options and restricted stock is calculated applying the treasury stock method.

Excluded from the above computation of weighted-average shares for diluted EPS were options to purchase 440,063 shares of common stock during fiscal 1997, 5,084,978 during 1996 and 3,087,269 during 1995. Issuance of these securities would have resulted in an antidilutive effect on EPS.

NOTE I: RELATED PARTY TRANSACTIONS

The Company has an agreement with Fisher Development, Inc. (FDI), wholly owned by the brother of the Company's chairman, setting forth the terms under which FDI may act as general contractor in connection with the Company's construction activities. FDI acted as general contractor for 266, 177 and 204 new stores' leasehold improvements and fixtures during fiscal 1997, 1996 and 1995, respectively. In the same respective years, FDI supervised construction of 97, 38 and 54 expansions, as well as remodels of existing stores and headquarters facilities. Total cost of construction was $233,777,000, $111,871,000 and $164,820,000, including profit and overhead costs of $16,845,000, $10,751,000 and $11,753,000 for fiscal 1997, 1996 and 1995, respectively. At January 31, 1998 and February 1, 1997, amounts due to FDI were $10,318,000 and $6,456,000, respectively. The terms and conditions of the agreement with FDI are reviewed annually by the Audit and Finance Committee of the Board of Directors.

NOTE J: QUARTERLY FINANCIAL INFORMATION (UNAUDITED)

Fiscal 1997 Quarter Ended

($000 except per share amounts)	Thirteen Weeks Ended May 3, 1997	Thirteen Weeks Ended Aug. 2, 1997	Thirteen Weeks Ended Nov. 1, 1997	Thirteen Weeks Ended Jan. 31, 1998	Fifty-two Weeks Ended Jan. 31, 1998
Net sales	$1,231,186	$1,345,221	$1,765,939	$2,165,479	$6,507,825
Gross profit	442,060	462,135	721,266	860,823	2,486,284
Net earnings	84,304	69,458	164,523	215,616	533,901
Earnings per share–basic	.21	.17	.42	.55	1.35
Earnings per share–diluted	.20	.17	.40	.53	1.30

Fiscal 1996 Quarter Ended

($000 except per share amounts)	Thirteen Weeks Ended May 4, 1996	Thirteen Weeks Ended Aug. 3, 1996	Thirteen Weeks Ended Nov. 2, 1996	Thirteen Weeks Ended Feb. 1, 1997	Fifty-two Weeks Ended Feb. 1, 1997
Net sales	$1,113,154	$1,120,335	$1,382,996	$1,667,896	$5,284,381
Gross profit	413,840	400,170	545,221	639,984	1,999,215
Net earnings	81,573	65,790	134,310	171,186	452,859
Earnings per share–basic	.19	.16	.32	.42	1.09
Earnings per share–diluted	.19	.15	.32	.41	1.06

Quantitative and Qualitative Disclosures About Market Risk

The table on the right provides information about the Company's market sensitive financial instruments as of January 31, 1998 and constitutes a forward-looking statement. The Company operates in foreign countries which exposes it to market risk associated with foreign currency exchange rate fluctuations. The Company's policy is to hedge substantially all merchandise purchases for foreign operations through foreign exchange forward contracts. These contracts are entered into with large reputable financial institutions, thereby minimizing the risk of credit loss. Further discussion of these contracts appears in the Notes to Consolidated Financial Statements (Note E).

The Company issued unsecured notes payable with a fixed interest rate of 6.9 percent. By entering into the fixed-rate notes, the Company avoided interest rate risk from variable rate fluctuations.

A portion of the Company's fixed-rate short-term borrowings used to finance foreign operations are denominated in foreign currencies. By borrowing and repaying the loans in local currencies, the Company avoided the risk associated with exchange rate fluctuations.

($000)	Average Contract Rate[a]	Notional Amount of Forward Contracts in U.S. Dollars	Fair Value at Jan. 31, 1998[b]
Foreign exchange forward contracts[c]			
British pounds	.60	$33,394	$33,269
Canadian dollars	1.40	32,984	31,757
Italian lire	1,743.25	35,924	35,383
Japanese yen	120.52	12,803	12,266
Spanish pesetas	151.98	8,125	8,112
Total foreign exchange forward contracts		$123,230	$120,787

($000)	Fixed Interest Rate	Carrying Amount in U.S. Dollars	Fair Value at Jan. 31, 1998[d]
Notes payable[e]	6.9%	$496,044	$526,128

(a) Currency per U.S. dollar.

(b) Calculated using spot rates at January 31, 1998.

(c) All contracts mature within one year.

(d) Based on the rates at which the Company could borrow funds with similar terms and remaining maturities at January 31, 1998.

(e) Principal amount $500 million due September 15, 2007.

Glossary of Accounting Terms in IFA

accelerated depreciation methods Those methods that record more depreciation expense in the early years of an asset's life and less in the later years. (p. F-277)

account A record that contains the history of all increases and decreases of an accounting element. (p. F-227)

accounting cycle The sequence of steps repeated in each accounting period to enable the firm to analyze, record, classify, and summarize the transactions into financial statements. (p. F-224)

accounting information Raw data concerning transactions that have been transformed into financial numbers that can be used by economic decision makers. (p. F-57)

accounting system The overall format used to gather data from source transactions to create the books and records which are used to prepare the financial statements of a business entity. (p. F-231)

accrual basis accounting A method of accounting in which revenues are recognized when they are earned, regardless of when the associated cash is collected. The expenses incurred in generating the revenue are recognized when the benefit is derived rather than when the associated cash is paid. (p. F-191)

accruals Adjustments made to record items that should be included on the income statement but have not yet been recorded. (p. F-196)

accrue As used in accounting, to come into being as a legally enforceable claim. (p. F-192)

accrued expenses Expenses appropriately recognized under accrual accounting in one income statement period although the associated cash will be paid in a later income statement period. (p. F-197)

accrued revenues Revenues appropriately recognized under accrual accounting in one income statement period although the associated cash will be received in a later income statement period. (p. F-197)

accumulated depreciation The total amount of cost that has been systematically converted to expense since a long-lived asset was first purchased. (p. F-201)

additional paid-in capital The amount in excess of the stock's par value received by the corporation when par value stock is issued. (p. F-87)

adjustments Changes made in recorded amounts of revenues and expenses in order to follow the guidelines of accrual accounting. (p. F-196)

amortization The systematic allocation of the cost of intangible assets over the economic life of the asset. (p. F-378)

articulation The links among the financial statements. (p. F-159).

assets An accounting element that is one of the three components of a balance sheet. Assets are probable future economic benefits controlled by an entity as a result of previous transactions or events—that is, what a company has. (p. F-79)

audit Examination by an independent CPA of enough of a company's records to determine whether the financial statements have been prepared in accordance with GAAP. (p. F-20)

authorized shares   The maximum number of shares of stock a corporation has been given permission to issue under its corporate chart (p. F-86)

average cost method   The inventory cost flow method that assigns an average cost to the units of inventory on hand at the time of each sale. (p. F-329)

basic earnings per share   A simple calculation of earnings per share based on shares outstanding on the balance sheet date. (p. F-389)

beginning inventory   The amount of merchandise inventory (units or dollars) on hand at the beginning of the income statement period. (p. F-316)

book inventory   The amount of ending inventory (units and dollars) resulting from transactions recorded by a perpetual inventory system. (p. F-320)

book value   The original cost of a long-lived asset less its accumulated depreciation. This item is often shown on the balance sheet. (p. F-201)

bond   An interest-bearing debt instrument that allows corporations to borrow large amounts of funds for long periods of time and creates a liability for the borrower. (p. F-117)

business   Depending on the context, the area of commerce or trade, an individual company, or the process of producing and distributing goods and services. (p. F-5)

business segment   A portion of the business for which assets, results of operations, and activities can be separately identified. (p. F-384)

capital   A factor of production that includes the buildings, machinery, and tools used to produce goods and services. Also, sometimes used to refer to the money used to buy those items. (p. F-6)

cash basis accounting   A basis of accounting in which cash is the major criterion used in measuring revenue and expense for a given income statement period. Revenue is recognized when the associated cash is received, and expense is recognized when the associated cash is paid. (p. F-188)

cash flow   The movement of cash in and out of a company. (p. F-55)

chart of accounts   A list of all the accounts used by a business entity. The list usually contains the name of the account and the account number. (p. F-227)

classified balance sheet   A balance sheet showing assets and liabilities categorized into current and long-term items. (p. F-376)

cognitive dissonance   The hesitation that sets in after an alternative has been chosen, but before it has been implemented. In common language, having "second thoughts." (p. F-49)

collateral   Something of value that will be forfeited if a borrower fails to make payments as agreed. (p. F-113)

commercial borrowing   The process that businesses go through to obtain financing. (p. F-111)

common stock   A share of ownership in a corporation. Each share represents one vote in the election of the board of directors and other pertinent corporate matters. (p. F-86)

comparative financial statement   Financial statements showing results from two or more consecutive periods. (p. F-392)

compound journal entry   Any entry recorded in the general journal that contains more than two accounts. (p. F-234)

comprehensive income   The change in equity during a period from non-owner sources. (p. F-388)

consumer borrowing   Loans obtained by individuals to buy homes, cars, or other personal property. (p. F-111)

contributed capital Total amount invested in a corporation by its shareholders. Also called paid-in capital. (p. F-86)

convertible securities Debt or equity securities that can be converted into shares of the company's common stock. (p. F-389)

corporation One of the three forms of business organization. The only form that is legally considered to be an entity separate from its owners. (p. F-11)

cost/benefit analysis Deals with the trade-off between the rewards of selecting a given alternative and the sacrifices required to obtain those rewards. (p. F-45)

cost of goods manufactured The cost of converting raw materials into finished goods in a manufacturing firm. The cost is equivalent to purchases in a manufacturing firm. (p. F-318)

cost of goods sold The cost of the product sold as the primary business activity of a company. (p. F-145).

cost of goods sold The cost of the merchandise inventory no longer on hand, and assumed sold during the period. Also called cost of sales. (p. F-316)

coverage ratio or times interest earned ratio A solvency ratio that provides an indication of a company's ability to make its periodic interest payments. (p. F-464)

credit A term that means the right side of a general ledger account. (p. F-232)

critical thinking An examination of the way we think to help improve the quality of our decision-making process. (p. F-47)

cumulative effect of a change in accounting principle Results of adopting a new accounting standard or changing from one acceptable method of accounting to another. One of the nonrecurring items shown net of tax on the income statement. (p. F-387)

current assets Assets that are either cash or will become cash within one year. (p. F-376)

current liabilities Liabilities that must be paid within one year. (p. F-378)

current ratio A liquidity ratio that measures a company's ability to meet short-term obligations by comparing current assets to current liabilities. (p. F-459)

date of declaration The date upon which a corporation announces plans to distribute a dividend. At this point, the corporation becomes legally obligated to make the distribution: A liability is created. (p. F-157).

date of payment The date a corporate dividend is actually paid. The payment date is generally announced on the date of declaration. (p. F-157).

date of record Owners of the shares of stock on this day are the ones who will receive the dividend announced on the date of declaration. (p. F-157).

debenture An unsecured bond payable. (p. F-117)

debit A term that means the left side of a general ledger account. (p. F-232)

debt financing Acquiring funds for business operations by borrowing. Debt financing is one type of external financing. (p. F-110)

debt ratio A solvency ratio that indicates what proportion of a company's assets is financed by debt. (p. F-463)

default Failure to repay a loan as agreed. (p. F-112)

deferrals Situations in which cash is either received or paid, but the income statement effect is delayed until some later period. Deferred revenues are recorded as liabilities, and deferred expenses are recorded as assets. (p. F-197)

deferred expenses Expenses created when cash is paid before any benefit is received. Because the benefit to be derived is in the future, the item is recorded as an asset. Later, when the benefit is received from the item, it will be recognized as an expense. (p. F-197)

deferred revenues Revenues created when cash is received before the revenue is earned. Because the cash received has not yet been earned, an obligation is created and a liability is recorded. Later, when the cash is deemed to have been earned, it will be recognized as a revenue. (p. F-197)

depreciable base The total amount of depreciation expense that is allowed to be claimed for an asset during its useful life. The depreciable base is the cost of the asset less its residual value. (p. F-196)

depreciation The systematic and rational conversion of a long-lived asset's cost from asset to expense in the income statement periods benefited. (p. F-195)

depreciation expense The amount of cost associated with a long-lived asset converted to expense in a given income statement period. (p. F-195)

diluted earnings per share A calculation of earnings per share including all potentially dilutive securities. (p. F-389)

direct method The format of a statement of cash flows that provides detail about the individual sources and uses of cash associated with operating activities. (p. F-415)

discontinued operations The disposal of a business segment. One of the nonrecurring items shown net of tax on the income statement. (p. F-384)

discount If a bond's selling price is below its par value, the bond is being sold at a discount. (p. F-122)

discounted note A loan arrangement in which the bank deducts the interest from the proceeds of the loan. (p. F-116).

dividends A distribution of earnings from a corporation to its owners. Dividends are most commonly distributed in the form of cash. (p. F-86)

double-declining-balance method An accelerated depreciation method in which depreciation expense is twice the straight-line percentage multiplied by the book value of the asset. (p. F-277)

drawings Distributions to the owners of proprietorships and partnerships. Also called withdrawals. (p. F-153).

earned equity The total amount a company has earned since its beginning, less any amounts distributed to the owner(s). In a corporation, this amount is called retained earnings. (p. F-80)

earnings per share A calculation indicating how much of a company's total earnings is attributable to each share of common stock. (p. F-389)

effective interest rate The rate of interest actually earned by a lender. This amount will be different from the nominal interest rate if a bond is bought at a discount or premium, or a note is discounted. Also called yield rate or market interest rate. (p. F-116).

ending inventory The amount of inventory (in units or dollars) still on hand at the end of an accounting period. (p. F-316)

entrepreneurship The factor of production that brings the other three factors—natural resources, labor, and capital—together to form a business. (p. F-6)

equity An accounting element that is one of the three components of a balance sheet. Equity is the residual interest in the assets of an entity that remains after deducting liabilities. Also called net assets. (p. F-79)

equity financing Acquiring funds for business operations by giving up ownership interest in the company. For a corporation, this means issuing capital stock. Equity financing is one type of external financing. (p. F-110).

ethics A system of standards of conduct and moral judgment. (p. F-51)

expenses An accounting element representing the outflow of assets resulting from an entity's ongoing major or central operations. These are the sacrifices required to attain the rewards (revenues) of doing business. (p. F-143).

external decision makers Economic decision makers outside a company who make decisions about the company. The accounting information they use to make those decisions is limited to what the company provides them. (p. F-54)

external financing Acquiring funds from outside the company. Equity and debt financing are the two major types of external financing. (p. F-110).

extraordinary item A gain or loss that is both unusual in nature and infrequent in occurrence. One of the nonrecurring items shown net of tax on the income statement. (p. F-385)

factors of production The four major items needed to support economic activity: natural resources, labor, capital, and entrepreneurship. (p. F-5)

feedback value A primary characteristic of relevance. To be useful, accounting must provide decision makers with information that allows them to assess the progress of an investment. (p. F-59)

financial accounting The branch of accounting developed to meet the informational needs of external decision makers. (p. F-55)

Financial Accounting Standards Board (FASB) The organization that is principally responsible for establishing accounting guidelines and rules in the United States at the present time. (p. F-17)

financial reporting Financial disclosures provided to economic decision makers that include both quantitative (numerical) information and qualitative (descriptive) information. (p. F-23)

financial statement analysis The process of looking beyond the face of the financial statements to gather more information. (p. F-448)

financing activities Business activities, such as the issuance of debt or equity and the payment of dividends, that focus on the external financing of the company. (p. F-413)

finished goods inventory The inventory ready to sell in a manufacturing company. Equivalent to the merchandise inventory in a merchandising firm. (p. F-318)

first in, first out (FIFO) The inventory flow concept based on the assumption that the first units of inventory purchased are the first one sold. (p. F-322)

functional obsolescence Occurs when an asset can no longer perform the function for which it is purchased. (p. F-285)

gains Net inflows resulting from peripheral activities of a company. An example is the sale of an asset for more than its book value. (p. F-285)

general journal A book of original entry in which is recorded all transactions not otherwise recorded in a special journal. (p. F-226)

general ledger A book of final entry which contains a page for each account listed in the chart of accounts. (p. F-227)

generally accepted accounting principles (GAAP) Guidelines for presentation of financial accounting information designed to serve external decision makers' need for consistent and comparable information. (p. F-17)

goods available for sale The total amount of merchandise inventory a company has available to sell in a given income statement period. (p. F-316)

gross margin An item shown on a multistep income statement, calculated as: Sales—Cost of Goods Sold. (p. F-146).

gross margin or gross profit The excess of benefit received over the sacrifice made to complete a sale. Gross profit considers only the cost of the item sold; it does not consider the other costs of operations. (p. F-7)

historical cost Total of all costs required to bring an asset to a productive state. (p. F-276)

hybrid companies   Those companies involved in more than one type of activity (manufacturing, merchandising, service). (p. F-14)

income statement   A financial statement providing information about an entity's past performance. Its purpose is to measure the results of the entity's operations for some specific time period. (p. F-142).

indenture   The legal agreement made between a bond issuer and a bondholder that states repayment terms and other details. (p. F-118).

indirect method   The more widely used format of the statement of cash flows. This approach begins with a reconciliation of accrual net income to the cash provided by or used by operating activities. (p. F-415)

information   Data that have been transformed so that they are useful in the decision-making process. (p. F-57)

intangible assets   Assets consisting of contractual rights such as patents, copyrights, and trademarks. (p. F-378)

interest   The cost to the borrower of using someone else's money. Also, what can be earned by lending money to someone else. (p. F-112).

internal decision makers   Economic decision makers within a company who make decisions for the company. They have access to much or all of the accounting information generated within the company. (p. F-54)

internal financing   Providing funds for the operation of a company through the earnings process of that company. (p. F-110).

inventory turnover ratio   A liquidity ratio that indicates how long a company holds its inventory. (p. F-462)

investing activities   Business activities related to long-term assets. Examples are the purchase and sale of property, plant, and equipment. (p. F-413)

investment bankers   Intermediaries between the corporation issuing stock and the investors who ultimately purchase the shares. Also called underwriters. (p. F-92)

investments   Assets that represent long-term ownership in subsidiaries or funds set aside for specific purposes, bond sinking funds or bond of other companies. (p. F-378)

investments by owners   That part of owners' equity generated by the receipt of cash (or other assets) from the owners. (p. F-79)

issued shares   Stock that has been distributed to the owners of the corporation in exchange for cash or other assets. (p. F-86)

journal   A book of original entry in which is kept a chronological record of the transactions of a business entity. (p. F-226)

labor   The mental and physical efforts of all workers performing tasks required to produce and sell goods and services. This factor of production is also called the human resource factor. (p. F-6)

last in, first out (LIFO)   The inventory flow concept based on the assumption that the last units of inventory purchased are the first ones sold. (p. F-322)

liabilities   An accounting element that is one of the three components of a balance sheet. Liabilities are probable future sacrifices of assets arising from present obligations of an entity as a result of past transactions or events— that is, what a company owes. (p. F-79)

liquidity   An item's nearness to cash. (p. F-377)

liquidity ratios   A set of ratios developed to measure a firm's ability to generate sufficient cash in the short run to retire short-term liabilities. (p. F-459)

long-term assets   Assets that are expected to benefit the company for longer than one year. (p. F-376)

long-term financing   Any financing in which repayment extends beyond five years. This type of financing supports the long-range goals of the company. (p. F-110).

long-term liabilities Amounts that are not due for repayment until at least one year from now. (p. F-378)

losses Net outflows resulting from peripheral activities of a company. An example is the sale of an asset for less than its book value. (p. F-285)

management accounting The branch of accounting developed to meet the informational needs of internal decision makers. (p. F-55)

manufacturing The business activity that converts purchased raw materials into some tangible, physical product. (p. F-13)

market economy A type of economy in which all or most of the factors of production are privately owned and that relies on competition in the marketplace to determine the most efficient way to allocate the economy's resources. (p. F-6)

matching principle Accounting principle that relates the expenses to the revenues of a particular income statement period. Once it is determined in which period a revenue should be recognized, the expenses that helped to generate the revenue are matched to that same period. (p. F-194)

materiality Something that will influence the judgment of a reasonable person. (p. F-58)

merchandise inventory The physical units (goods) a company buys to resell as part of its business operation. Also called inventory. (p. F-316)

merchandising The business activity involving the selling of finished goods produced by other businesses. (p. F-14)

Modified Accelerated Cost Recovery System (MACRS) Depreciation method taxpayers use to calculate depreciation expense for tax purposes. (p. F-278)

mortgage A document that states the agreement between a lender and a borrower who has secured the loan by offering something of value as collateral. (p. F-114).

moving average cost method The inventory cost flow method that assigns an average cost to the units of inventory on hand at the time of each sale in a perpetual inventory system. (p. F-333)

multistep income statement An income statement format that highlights gross margin and operating income. (p. F-146).

natural resources Land and the materials that come from the land, such as timber, mineral deposits, oil deposits, and water. One of the factors of production. (p. F-5)

net cash flow The difference between cash inflows and cash outflows; it can be either positive or negative. (p. F-55)

net income The amount of profit that remains after all costs have been considered. The net reward of doing business for a specific time period. (p. F-144).

net loss The difference between revenues and expenses of a period in which expenses are greater than revenues. (p. F-144).

net of tax The proper presentation format for non recurring items shown below income from con tinuing operations on the income statement. (p. F-383)

net sales to working capital ratio A ratio used to measure the level of sales generated from a given level of working capital. (p. F-461)

neutrality A primary characteristic of reliability. To be useful, accounting information must be free of bias. (p. F-59)

nominal interest rate The interest rate set by the issuers of bonds, stated as a percentage of the par value of the bonds. Also called the contract rate, coupon rate, or stated rate. (p. F-118).

nonrecurring item Results of activities that cannot be expected to occur again, and therefore should not be used to predict future performance. (p. F-381)

no-par stock   Stock that has no par value assigned to it. (p. F-88)

normal balance   The balance of the account derived from the type of entry (debit or credit) that increases the account. (p. F-232)

note payable   An agreement between a lender and a borrower that creates a liability for the borrower. (p. F-113).

operating activities   Activities that result in cash inflows and outflows generated from the normal course of business. (p. F-412)

operating cycle   The length of time it takes for an entity to complete one revenue producing cycle from purchase of goods to collection of cash. (p. F-376)

operating income   Income produced by the major business activity of the company. An item shown on the multistep income statement. (p. F-146).

opportunity cost   The benefit or benefits forgone by not selecting a particular alternative. Once an alternative is selected in a decision situation, the benefits of all rejected alternatives become part of the opportunity cost of the alternative selected. (p. F-45)

outstanding shares   Shares of stock actually held by shareholders. The number may be different than that for issued shares because a corporation may reacquire its own stock (treasury stock). (p. F-86)

paid-in capital   The portion of stockholders' equity representing amounts invested by the owners of the corporation. Consists of common stock, preferred stock, and amounts received in excess of the par values of those stocks. Also called contributed capital. (p. F-86)

partnership   A business form similar to a proprietorship, but having two or more owners. (p. F-9)

par value (for bonds)   The amount that must be paid back upon maturity of a

bond. Also called face value or maturity value. (p. F-118).

par value (for stocks)   An arbitrary amount assigned to each share of stock by the incorporators at the time of incorporation. (p. F-87)

par value stock   Stock with a par value printed on the stock certificate (see par value). (p. F-87)

period   Length of time (usually a month, quarter, or year) for which activity is being reported on an income statement. (p. F-144).

periodic inventory system   An inventory system in which all inventory and cost of goods sold calculations are done at the end of the income statement period. (p. F-318)

periodicity   The assumption that the economic activities of an entity can be traced to some specific time period and results of those activities can be reported for any arbitrary time period chosen. (p. F-185)

permanent (or real) accounts   The general ledger accounts that are never closed. The permanent accounts include assets, liabilities, and equity accounts except for owner withdrawals and dividends. (p. F-231)

perpetual inventory system   An inventory system in which both the physical count of inventory units and the cost classification (asset or expense) are updated when a transaction involves inventory. (p. F-319)

post-closing trial balance   A trial balance prepared after all closing entries have been posted which proves that the only accounts remaining in the general ledger are the permanent accounts and that the accounting equation remains in balance. (p. F-231)

predictive value   A primary characteristic of relevance. To be useful, accounting must provide information to decision makers that can be used to predict the future and timing of cash flows. (p. F-59)

preferred (preference) stock   A share of ownership in a corporation that has preference over common stock as to dividends and as to assets upon liquidation of the corporation. Usually nonvoting stock. (p. F-89)

premium If a bond's selling price is above its par value, the bond is being sold at a premium. (p. F-122).

primary stock market The business activity involved in the initial issue of stock from a corporation. (p. F-92)

principal In the case of notes and mortgages, the amount of funds actually borrowed. (p. F-114).

production depreciation method A straight-line depreciation method that uses production activity as the base to assign depreciation expense. (p. F-279)

profit The excess of benefit over sacrifice. A less formal name for net income or net profit. (p. F-7)

profitability The ease with which a company generates income. (p. F-455)

profitability ratios A set of ratios that measure a firm's past performance and help predict its future profitability level. (p. F-455)

profit margin after income tax ratio A profitability ratio that measures the earnings produced from a given level of revenues by comparing net income after income tax to the revenue figure. (p. F-458)

profit margin before income tax ratio A profitability ratio that measures the earnings produced from a given level of revenues by comparing net income before income tax to the revenue figure. (p. F-456)

promissory note A legal promise to repay a loan. (p. F-113).

prospectus A description of an upcoming bond issue that is provided as information for potential investors. (p. F-121).

purchases The amount of merchandise inventory bought during the income statement period. (p. F-316)

quick ratio or acid-test ratio A liquidity ratio that is similar to the current ratio, but a more stringent test of liquidity, because only current assets considered to be highly liquid (quickly converted to cash) are included in the calculation. (p. F-460)

ratio analysis A technique for analyzing the relationship between two items from a company's financial statements for a given period. (p. F-448)

raw materials inventory The inventory of raw materials to be transferred into production in a manufacturing company. (p. F-318)

realization Actual receipt of cash or payment of cash. Once cash has been collected or a transaction is complete, it is considered to be realized. (p. F-188)

receivable Money due to an entity from an enforceable claim. (p. F-192)

receivables turnover ratio A liquidity ratio that measures how quickly a company collects its accounts receivable. (p. F-462)

recognition The process of recording an event in your records and reporting it on your financial statements. (p. F-187)

relevance One of the two primary qualitative characteristics of useful accounting information. It means the information must have a bearing on a particular decision situation. (p. F-59)

reliability One of the two primary qualitative characteristics of useful accounting information. It means the information must be reasonably accurate. (p. F-59)

representational faithfulness A primary characteristic of reliability. To be useful, accounting information must reasonably report what actually happened. (p. F-59)

residual value The estimated value of an asset when it has reached the end of its useful life. Also called salvage or scrap value. (p. F-196)

retained earnings The sum of all earnings of a corporation minus the amount of dividends declared. (p. F-86)

return before interest on equity ratio A profitability ratio that measures the level of earnings (before the cost of borrowing) generated from a given level of equity. (p. F-458)

return on assets ratio   A profitability ratio that measures how efficiently the company uses its assets to produce profits. (p. F-456)

return on equity ratio   A profitability ratio that measures the after-tax net income generated from a given level of investment by a company's owners. (p. F-458)

revenues   An accounting element representing the inflows of assets as a result of an entity's ongoing major or central operations. These are the rewards of doing business. (p. F-143).

risk/reward trade-off   The relationship between uncertainty and reward. It indicates that the higher the risk, the higher the reward required to induce the risk taking. (p. F-46)

sales revenue   The revenue generated from the sale of a tangible product as a major business activity. (p. F-146).

secondary stock market   The business activity focusing on trades of stock among investors subsequent to the initial issue. (p. F-92)

Securities and Exchange Commission (SEC)   The government agency empowered to regulate the buying and selling of stocks and bonds and to establish accounting rules, standards, and procedures, and the form and content of published financial reporting. (p. F-17)

selling price   The amount received when bonds are issued or sold. This amount is affected by the difference between the nominal interest rate and the market rate. Selling price is usually stated as a percentage of the bond's par value. (p. F-118).

separate entity assumption   The assumption that economic activity can be identified with a particular economic entity and that the results of activities for each entity will be recorded separately. (p. F-11)

service   A business activity that does not deal with tangible products, but rather provides some sort of service as its major operation. (p. F-14)

short-term financing   Financing secured to support an operation's day-to-day activities. Repayment is usually required within five years. (p. F-110).

single-step income statement   A format of the income statement that gathers all revenues into "total revenues" and all expenses into "total expenses." Net income is calculated as a subtraction of total expenses from total revenues. (p. F-145).

sole proprietorship   An unincorporated business that is owned by one person. Also called a proprietorship. (p. F-8)

solvency   A company's ability to meet the obligations created by its long-term debt.   (p. F-463)

solvency ratios   A set of ratios developed to measure a firm's ability to meet its long-term debt obligations. (p. F-463)

special journal   A book of original entry designed to record a specific type of transaction. (p. F-226)

specific identification   The method of inventory cost flow that identifies each item sold by a company. (p. F-325)

stakeholder   Anyone who is affected by the way a company conducts its business. (p. F-8)

statement of capital   A statement of owner's equity for a proprietorship. (p. F-149).

statement of cash flows   A financial statement that provides information about the causes of a change in a company's cash balance from the beginning to the end of a specific period. (p. F-410)

statement of owners' equity   The financial statement that reports activity in the capital accounts of proprietorships and partnerships and in the stockholders' equity accounts of corporations. The statement of owners' equity serves as a bridge between the income statement and the balance sheet.

Also called statement of capital. (p. F-149).

statement of partners' capital A statement of owners' equity for a partnership. (p. F-150).

statement of retained earnings A corporate financial statement that shows the changes in retained earnings during a particular period. (p. F-156).

stock dividend A dividend paid in the corporation's own stock. (p. F-155).

stockholder A person who owns shares of stock in a corporation. (p. F-11)

straight-line depreciation A method of calculating periodic depreciation. The depreciable base of an asset is divided by its estimated useful life. The result is the amount of depreciation expense to be recognized in each year of the item's estimated useful life: (Cost - Residual Value)/N = Annual Depreciation Expense. (p. F-196)

syndicate A group of underwriters working together to get a large bond issue sold to the public. (p. F-121).

T-account An account form that represents the general ledger account with only two columns. (p. F-233)

tangible property Property used in a business such as buildings, equipment, machinery, furniture, and fixtures. (p. F-276)

technological obsolescence Occurs when an asset is no longer compatible with current technology. (p. F-285)

temporary (or nominal) accounts The general ledger accounts that are closed to a zero balance at the end of the fiscal year as the net income or net loss is transferred to the appropriate equity account. Temporary accounts include revenues, expenses, gains, losses, owner withdrawal and dividend accounts. (p. F-231)

timeliness A primary characteristic of relevance. To be useful, accounting information must be provided in time to influence a particular decision. (p. F-59)

total asset turnover ratio A profitability ratio that indicates the amount of revenues produced for a given level of assets used. (p. F-457)

total liabilities to net worth ratio A solvency ratio indicating the relationship between creditors' claims to a company's assets and the owners' claim to those assets. (p. F-464)

treasury stock Corporate stock that has been issued and then reacquired by the corporation. (p. F-86)

trend analysis A technique whereby an analyst tries to determine the amount of changes in key financial amounts over time to see if a pattern of change emerges. (p. F-448)

trial balance The listing of the general ledger account balances which proves that the general ledger and therefore, the accounting equation is in balance. (p. F-228)

underwriters Professionals in the field of investment bankers. Also called investment bankers. (p. F-92)

verifiability A primary characteristic of reliability. Information is considered verifiable if several individuals, working independently, would arrive at similar conclusions using the same data. (p. F-59)

working capital The difference between current assets and current liabilities. (p. F-410)

work-in-process inventory The cost of raw materials, labor, and other expenses associated with unfinished units during the process of converting raw materials into finished goods for a manufacturing company. (p. F-318)

worksheet A tool used by the accountant to accumulate the necessary information used to prepare the financial statements. (p. F-228)

Introduction to Management Accounting

A User Perspective

Chapter 1

Management Accounting: Its Environment and Future

*T*imes have changed! During the 1970s and 1980s the United States saw a serious erosion in its position as the world's business leader. Industry after industry in the United States began to suffer from the effects of significant foreign competition. At the time, experts offered any number of reasons to explain what was happening. Low labor costs in foreign countries, excessively high labor costs at home, too much government regulation of U.S. industries, and too little government regulation of U.S. industries were just a few of the explanations offered.

Because the "reasons" given were simplistic, the "solutions" were simplistic. U.S. industries lobbied Congress for tariffs on imported products (essentially a form of tax) to offset the low labor costs in foreign countries. The issue of excessively high labor rates was used by U.S. companies in negotiating labor costs with their employees, either to hold the line on wage increases, or in some instances to actually negotiate lower wage rates. Throughout the 1970s and 1980s, the U.S. government alternatively deregulated and then reregulated some American industries to try and increase U.S. companies' competitiveness globally.

Eventually, as the quick fix, simplistic approaches did not solve the competitiveness problem, managers in the United States began to see that the problem arose from differences in organizational structure and worker productivity between U.S. businesses and their foreign competitors. Consider the following comparison of U.S. and Japanese auto manufacturers in the mid-1980s.[1]

---

[1]John Lee, *Managerial Accounting Changes for the 1990s (Addison Wesley, 1987)*, 14.

Ford
- Produced an average of two engines a day per employee
- Daily production required 777 square feet of plant space

Toyota
- Produced an average of nine engines a day per employee
- Daily production required 454 square feet of plant space

Chrysler
- Had about 500 in-plant classifications

Toyota
- Had 7 in-plant job classifications

A Typical U.S. Auto Plant
- A change from metal-stamping one model to another required 6 hours

Toyota
- The same change required 3–5 minutes

Because of more efficient production techniques, a small Toyota car cost $1,700 less to produce than a comparable U.S. car. This cost difference made it difficult for U.S. automakers to effectively compete against Toyota and the other car companies employing more efficient manufacturing methods.

The automobile industry was by no means alone. By the mid-1980s, U.S. companies in many different industries had realized the need to change business operations to remain competitive. Beginning in the last half of the 1980s and continuing throughout the 1990s, many of those businesses began to take significant steps to increase their competitiveness.

Our focus will be not on the specific changes that managers made but rather on the way these changes have affected their accounting needs and how accounting information has responded. ■

LEARNING OBJECTIVES

After completing your work on this chapter, you should be able to do the following:

1. Describe management accounting and contrast it with financial accounting.
2. Explain major historical developments that have affected management accounting.
3. Discuss what may have led to the stagnation in the development of management accounting.
4. Describe how changes in management accounting affect today's businesses.
5. Explain how businesspeople use management accounting information and skills.

WHAT IS MANAGEMENT ACCOUNTING?

management accounting
The branch of accounting designed to provide information to internal economic decision makers (managers).

managerial accounting
Another name for management accounting.

cost accounting A narrow application of management accounting dealing specifically with procedures designed to determine how much a particular item (usually a unit of manufactured product) costs.

Management accounting is the branch of accounting designed to provide information to the firm's internal economic decision makers, or managers. It is also sometimes called **managerial accounting** or **cost accounting.** Because these three terms are often used interchangeably in accounting literature, confusion can result. Management accounting is

... the process of identification, measurement, accumulation, analysis, preparation, interpretation, and communication of financial information used by management to plan, evaluate, and control ... an organization ...

Statement on Management Accounting (No.1A. IMA, 1981)

Management accounting and managerial accounting mean exactly the same thing. We will use the term *management accounting* throughout our discussions of the subject. However, in references to other writings you may see the term *managerial accounting.*

The third term, *cost accounting,* is a narrow application of management accounting. Cost accounting deals specifically with procedures designed to determine how much a particular item (usually a unit of manufactured product) costs.

CONTRASTING FINANCIAL AND MANAGEMENT ACCOUNTING

Financial accounting provides information to external decision makers—to people outside the company. Management accounting, in contrast, provides information to internal decision makers. Exhibit 1–1 lists only some of the many external and internal users of a company's accounting information.

Exhibit 1–1
External and Internal Decision Makers

External	Internal
• Stockholders (present and potential)	• Marketing managers
• Bankers and other lending institutions	• Salespersons
• Bondholders (present and potential)	• Production managers
• Suppliers	• Production supervisors
• Customers	• Strategic planners
• Competitors	• Company president
	• Engineers

Discussion Questions

1–1. For each of the external parties listed in Exhibit 1–1, suggest one economic decision they might make regarding a company.

1–2. Name two external parties in addition to those listed in Exhibit 1–1, and provide an example of an economic decision each might make regarding a company.

1–3. For each of the internal parties listed in Exhibit 1–1, describe one economic decision they might make regarding their company.

1–4. Name two more internal parties in addition to those listed in Exhibit 1–1, and give an example of an economic decision each might make regarding the company.

Discussion Questions 1–1 through 1–4 highlight the different nature of the decisions made by external and internal parties. If you review your answers to these questions, you will discover that the decisions external parties make focus on the company as a whole, whereas the decisions internal parties make usually center on some *part* of the company. Because people use financial accounting information and management accounting information differently, the nature of the two differs.

Accounting Rules

Financial accounting information must be prepared in accordance with rules known as Generally Accepted Accounting Principles (GAAP). No such rules apply to management accounting. Because management accounting information is prepared for use by those working within the company, its users can question the content, meaning, level of detail, and validity of the accounting information they receive. They can also determine the format of the information. As discussed later, in addition to accountants, managers may also gather and prepare management accounting information. In sum, internal decision makers can generally make certain the information they receive is exactly what they want. External decision makers must accept the financial accounting information they receive, like it or not.

Level of Detail

In contrast to the general-purpose nature of financial accounting information, firms prepare management accounting information to address specific company issues. Therefore, it is often much more detailed than financial accounting information. For example, it may be fine for a potential investor to know that IBM's sales were $82 billion last year, but this information would be nearly useless to the national sales manager for IBM ThinkPads™, the company's line of notebook computers, who needs to know that product's sales numbers for last year.

Discussion Question

1–5. In addition to sales information, what other accounting information would you want if you were the national sales manager for IBM ThinkPads™?

In addition to preparing general-purpose financial statements for the public, a company's accountants also prepare management accounting information for the managers or employees who need it. For a given internal decision, a user may need specific information from a division, product line, product, or department. The company's accountants should be able to customize information to fit the needs of the user.

For example, Motorola, Inc. has a production facility on 52nd Street and McDowell Road in Phoenix, Arizona. This facility requires various types of maintenance, including mowing the lawn and weeding the flower beds outside the buildings. This maintenance costs money. The amount spent for grounds maintenance at this Phoenix facility is totally irrelevant to external parties. The maintenance supervisor at that facility, however, would find that amount quite relevant. Motorola's accountants should be able to customize a report providing the supervisor with pertinent cost information.

Timeliness

Timeliness is important to both financial and management accounting information users. Regardless of whether the user is external or internal, accounting information is useful only if it is available in time to help the decision maker.

Because it has become customary, users of financial accounting information expect that financial results will be available quarterly. However, managers making frequent decisions need information much more often. They need information monthly, weekly, or even daily, so they can make informed decisions. Because of the fast pace of business decision making, sometimes it is better to forfeit precision in favor of speed. Management accountants must strike a balance between information accuracy and timeliness to provide managers with information that is accurate enough to make good decisions, and yet timely enough to make a difference.

Future Orientation

Although financial accounting information should have predictive value, it primarily depicts historical results. In contrast, management accounting has a forward-looking orientation. Management accounting focuses on estimating future revenues, costs, and other measures to forecast future activities and their results. Firms use these forecasts to plan their course of action toward future goals.

As you can see, because of the fundamental differences between the information needs of external and internal parties, financial and management accounting differ. Exhibit 1–2 summarizes the differences we have discussed.

Exhibit 1–2
Contrast of Financial and Management Accounting

Feature	Financial Accounting	Management Accounting
• Principal users	External parties	Internal parties
• Rules and regulations	Governed by GAAP	No rules
• Level of detail	Deals with the company as a whole	Deals with various parts of the company
• Timeliness	Quarterly and annually	As users need
• Orientation	The past	The future

WHERE ACCOUNTING FITS IN A COMPANY

treasurer The corporate officer who is responsible for cash and credit management and for planning activities, such as investment in long-lived property, plant, and equipment.

Exhibit 1–3 presents a typical corporate organizational structure. Note where financial and management accounting fit within a company.

The accounting function centers around the treasurer and the controller. Generally, the **treasurer** is responsible for managing cash and credit and for planning activities, such as investment in long-lived property, plant, and equipment. The **controller** is a company's chief accountant. This person is responsible for preparing accounting reports for both external and internal decision makers.

Exhibit 1–3
Corporate Organization

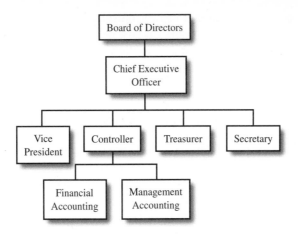

controller A company's chief accountant, who is responsible for the preparation of accounting reports for both external and internal decision makers.

In a large company, such as Sara Lee or Rockwell, the treasurer and controller are both likely to have large staffs reporting to them. At a midsized company, one or two people may perform all the duties of the treasurer and controller. In small firms, one person may perform all the functions.

Discussion Question

1–6. What possible problems may arise when the same accountants prepare reports for both external parties and internal parties?

THE ORIGIN AND EVOLUTION OF MANAGEMENT ACCOUNTING

Accounting and accounting records have existed since the dawn of civilization. Indeed, formal accounting systems have been in use for thousands of years. The need for accounting information for management decision-making purposes, however, did not exist until the early 19th century. Before that time almost all businesses were proprietorships or small partnerships. Businesses had no permanent employees to speak of and no management as we know it today. Management usually consisted of the proprietor or partners and immediate family members. Because businesses had no management, they had no need for management accounting information. Virtually all transactions were between the company and parties outside the company. Transactions with external parties such as suppliers, contract labor, and customers were easy to measure and evaluate: A company was successful if it collected more cash from its customers than it paid to suppliers and contract laborers.

In the hundred years between 1825 and 1925, however, four significant changes took place in business operation and organization: the emergence of permanent employees, the Industrial Revolution, the rise of scientific management, and diversification. These changes altered the nature of management accounting.

Emergence of Permanent Employees

For the most part, businesses had no employees before the 1880s. Businesses purchased labor with a piece rate contract and hired independent contractors to complete all their production functions. A chair manufacturer, for example, purchased wood at a certain price per board foot. Then the company contracted someone to turn the wood into legs, arms, seats, and backs at some specified rate per item. When the pieces were produced and paid for, the company contracted someone else to assemble the chairs, and paid that person some specified amount per chair assembled. Determining the cost of a chair produced was very simple—the sum of the wood cost, the amount paid per component piece (arm, leg, and so on), and the cost of assembling it. The company was not terribly interested in how long it took any of these contractors to complete their tasks, so long as they met the needs of the company.

Then companies began hiring permanent employees to fill the role of the independent contractors. Why the switch to permanent employees happened and whether it was positive or negative has been hotly debated by scholars for over 100 years. From the company's standpoint, moving from a contract system to a wage system gave the firm greater control of the production process and, in fact, created what we now know as the factory. From the laborer's standpoint, the change was likely an exchange of freedom for security.

Discussion Questions

1-7. In what ways do you think hiring permanent employees gives a company greater control of the production process?

1-8. What kinds of freedom do you think permanent employees exchange for security?

When we see the word *factory*, we tend to think of the huge factories of the 20th century. Actually, early factories were still small businesses. Management accounting did not develop because of the size or complexity of the organization. Rather, it developed because the accounting systems then in existence did not provide business people with enough information to determine the cost of a manufactured product.

Discussion Question

1-9. Why do you think the emergence of the factory (even a small one) made it more difficult to determine the cost of a manufactured product?

The Industrial Revolution

Industrial Revolution A term used to describe the transition in the United States from an agricultural-based economy to a manufacturing-based economy.

The **Industrial Revolution** was the 19th-century transition of the United States from an agricultural-based economy to a manufacturing-based economy. From 1825 to 1925 businesses greatly increased their investment in property, plant, and equipment and began to rely more on machines instead of human labor to produce products. As companies grew in size and complexity, owners found it impossible to be in all places at all times. They were forced to create hierarchical levels of management for their organizations. These managers sought needed information to control costs and production processes. Over time, businesses developed methods to measure the conversion of raw materials into units of finished product. These methods were the foundation for present-day management accounting. Their focus was on the effectiveness and efficiency of various internal processes, rather than on the overall profitability of the company.

Scientific Management

scientific management A management philosophy based on the notion that factories were run by machines—some mechanical and some human. Scientific management experts believed they could improve production efficiency by establishing standards of performance for workers.

The scientific management movement began near the end of the 19th century and had a tremendous influence on business management and management accounting. **Scientific management** was a philosophy based on the notion that factories were run by machines—some mechanical and some human. You may think it insensitive to treat employees as nothing more than machines plugged into the production process. Nonetheless, scientific management took this view. Experts in this area believed they could improve production efficiency by establishing standards of performance for workers. In a tool-manufacturing company, for instance, experts conducted time-and-motion studies to set a standard for the time workers should take to convert a given amount of resources into a finished product, such as a hammer.

These standards of performance were quickly adapted to accounting for the purpose of determining how much it *should* cost to manufacture a product. The experts, often engineers, determined how much material, labor, and other resources a business needed to manufacture a single unit of product. This information served as a yardstick to measure whether resources were used efficiently or squandered during the production process. Such standards were the beginning of what is referred to as *standard costing*, one of the most important developments in management accounting. We will discuss standard costing in greater detail in Chapter 9.

Discussion Questions

Assume a company manufactures tables. Scientific management studies show that each tabletop requires 4 square feet of wood, and it takes a worker 45 minutes to convert the wood into a tabletop.

1–10. If the wood costs the company $2 per square foot and the company's workers are paid $10 per hour, how much does each tabletop cost to produce?

1–11. What other costs should be considered in the calculation of the cost to produce the tabletop? Explain.

Diversification

During the first two decades of the 20th century, companies began to diversify. Before this time, virtually all companies undertook only one activity, for example, railroad companies were strictly in the railroad business and steel companies were strictly in the steel business. The primary investment decision for these single-activity companies was whether to expand. The emergence of diversified, multi-activity companies changed the nature of decision making.

Discussion Question

1-12. Why do you think companies began to diversify in the early years of the 20th century?

Owners of diversified companies could not directly manage all the various business operations. Instead, they relied on others to manage operations that they could not personally oversee; and they obtained additional management accounting information from the various parts of the business so they could plan, control, and evaluate performance. Company accountants tailored reports to meet the needs of managers at each level of the organization. Lower-level managers, such as production supervisors, received reports that focused on production efficiencies. Higher-level managers received reports that focused on product profits.

Development Stops (or at least dramatically slows)

Institute of Management Accountants (IMA) A professional association of management accountants comparable to the professional association of financial accountants (American Institute of Certified Public Accountants).

In 1919, the formation of the **Institute of Management Accountants (IMA)**—formerly the National Association of Accountants—signified that management accounting was a recognized branch of the accounting profession separate and distinct from financial accounting. Among other purposes, the IMA provided the same sort of professional status for management accountants as the American Institute of Certified Public Accountants (AICPA) did for financial accountants.

In approximately 1925, however, something curious occurred. For reasons we will discuss, development of new management accounting techniques virtually ceased. Essentially all management accounting tools in use as late as 1985 were already in place by 1925. Certainly the business environment changed between 1925 and 1985. Why then were so few management accounting techniques developed to respond to those changing needs? This question has been the subject of much analysis and debate over the past decade by both accountants and business leaders. In the following section, we examine possible causes of the stagnation in the development of management accounting techniques.

Dominance of Financial Accounting

The growth of publicly held corporations, the stock market crash, and the Great Depression led to the establishment of Generally Accepted Accounting Principles (GAAP) and the Securities and Exchange Commission (SEC). The new rules and regulations governed financial reporting to external parties and required that corporations file audited financial statements with the SEC that were prepared in accordance with GAAP. The rules and regulations led to the design of accounting systems that could provide financial information and reports to outsiders. These financial accounting systems, however, ignored (or at least underrepresented) information managers could use to make decisions about the internal processes of their companies.

Companies could have maintained two systems—one that generated and gathered information to meet external reporting requirements, and another that generated the information managers needed to manage and control the operation of the company. Or, a common system could collect data for both purposes and then customize the information to conform to the informational requests and needs of users. The cost of creating and maintaining a dual-purpose system, however, would have been prohibitive before computers, which is when GAAP and the SEC came into being.

Today, a high percentage of management accountants have a financial accounting background. It stands to reason that those who bring that type of background into a management accounting setting will tend to approach management accounting from a financial accounting perspective.

Consider also the legal environment existing in the 1930s after the creation of the SEC. If a company failed to have an accounting system designed to produce financial accounting information for external parties in accordance with GAAP, there would be serious legal consequences. If a company's accounting system did not produce management accounting information, however, there were no legal consequences. Given this situation, it is not surprising that at that time financial accounting requirements drove the creation and use of accounting information.

Discussion Question

1-13. What possible problems do you think arise when a company's single accounting system is designed to produce financial accounting information? Explain.

Accounting Education

Prior to 1900, colleges did not teach accounting. As a result, no uniform methods for gathering and distributing management accounting information were developed. Accountants gathered and distributed management accounting information as needed to suit management's needs. After the formation of the SEC and the development of GAAP, companies needed accountants trained to provide financial accounting information. In response, colleges began to offer accounting courses that focused on financial accounting information preparation.

As college-trained accountants became available, businesses began to rely on them for more than their expertise in providing information to outsiders. Managers also began to rely on accountants to specify *what* management accounting information should be gathered and *how* it should be presented. In the late 1800s, for instance, owners and company engineers developed product costing methods to make reasonable product cost estimates and better pricing decisions. In the early 1900s, trained accountants adapted established accounting methods of product costing to provide information to managers. In short, managers began relying on product costing methods their accountants learned in school instead of newly developed techniques tailored specifically to the needs of the company.

Focus on Financial Profits

Another possible reason for the slowdown in the development of management accounting is that we usually focus on financial profits in the performance evaluation of managers. Virtually all measures used to evaluate managers in U.S. companies are short-term financial accounting measures. Managers are bright people. In no time they determine how to manipulate the financial results of operations to maximize a short-run performance measure. Think about it. It seems reasonable to expect managers to focus on short-term financial accounting measures if their compensation and career advancement rely on these items.

Bonus programs that motivate key managers to perform better seem reasonable, except that most bonuses are heavily weighted in favor of short-term, not long-term, performance. As John Lee noted in his book *Managerial Accounting Changes for the 1990s:*

Since, at most companies, bonuses for short-term performance are larger than the payments from the long-term incentive program, executives tend to stress short-term strategies to maximize their incomes. For example, at Holiday Inns, the chief executive's 1983 short-term bonus was about $600,000, compared to the annual payout from the long-term incentive program of $46,000. In this type of system, executives have relatively little incentive to concentrate on the long-term health of the company.[2]

These incentives encourage managers to focus on improving financial statement measures rather than on improving productivity and efficiency measures. Preoccupation with financial accounting income has diminished their interest in demanding new management accounting techniques.

The problem of the short-term view is compounded by the mobility of management. In the early part of the century, managers stayed in their jobs longer than they do today. It was not uncommon for a manager to occupy the same position for 10 or even 20 years. For such managers, taking actions that would result in an impressive short-term performance at the expense of the long run made no sense. Today, however, many managers believe they will stay in a particular position for only a few years, so their objective is often to maximize short-term measures and not worry about what will happen in 5 or 10 years.

Lack of Competitive Pressure

Until the 1970s, the lack of competition from outside the country allowed U.S. companies to flourish, despite management's short-run view. Because many industries lacked serious competition, many decisions—even those made without sophisticated accounting information—led to favorable financial results. If satisfactory decisions could be made without sophisticated accounting information, then why would management even recognize that improvements were needed? Even business executives who were aware of the weaknesses in management accounting systems did not believe changes were worth making because they felt they were no worse off than their competition.

By the early 1980s, however, competition from foreign companies with more sophisticated management accounting systems forced U.S. companies to pay more attention to the relevance of the accounting information they were using to make short-term and long-term business decisions.

Who or What Should We Blame?

Which factor or factors should we blame for the slowdown in the development of management accounting techniques—the preoccupation of accountants with financial accounting, formal accounting education, management focus on financial results, or the lack of competition? It is difficult to say, but even if we cannot determine precisely why management accounting development slowed, business leaders and accounting academics now recognize a need for better management accounting information for today's business leaders. Even if we could determine who or what caused the problem, what would be the point? An old adage applies well to the situation in the United States in the mid-1980s:

LET'S FIX PROBLEMS, NOT BLAME.

---

[2]Lee, *Managerial Accounting Changes for the 1990s*, 10.

The first step in solving a problem is to recognize that you have a problem. By the mid-1980s, U.S. companies had certainly recognized that they had a problem, and since then have made great strides toward solving that problem.

CHALLENGES AND TRENDS IN MANAGEMENT ACCOUNTING

As we move toward the 21st century, businesses face many challenges. Global competition is one we have discussed already. Another is a basic consideration of what kind of economy is going to exist in the United States in the future. Many business analysts believe that we are moving away from the traditional manufacturing-based economy toward a service-based economy. If so, management accounting techniques must adapt to such a change.

The Giant Awakes

Although the United States continues to be a world leader in manufacturing, its businesses have lost some of their dominance. The heightened global competition spurred changes in business operations and management accounting in the United States. Like a giant roused from sleep, the United States has fought back to quell competitive threats.

First, businesses began using production and management techniques that were initiated in other countries, most notably Japan and what used to be West Germany. Second, companies became more innovative. Automobile manufacturers in the United States are much more efficient in their production processes than they were a decade ago. In the area of inventory control alone, American auto manufacturers have drastically reduced the level of inventories on hand, thereby reducing their annual inventory holding cost by hundreds of millions of dollars. This reduced cost translates into cars that are cheaper to manufacture.

As businesses examined and reorganized their operations to become more competitive, they also examined the way managers use accounting information to make decisions. Managers and accountants are making or considering many changes in management accounting as a result.

The question really is, what kind of changes must be made in management accounting techniques and procedures to cope with a dynamic business environment? Opinions about which "old" management accounting techniques still apply and what "new" techniques should be developed are sharply divided. Next, we present three alternative perspectives on what is and what should be happening in management accounting to respond to these fundamental changes taking place in business.

Out with the Old, in with the New

The first perspective contends that virtually all the management accounting techniques and practices used before the mid-1980s are obsolete and do not apply to the new business environment. Advocates of this perspective urge businesses to develop entirely new management accounting techniques and to shed past methods. A few of the techniques they categorize as "new" include Just-in-time (JIT) inventory systems, Activity Based Management (ABM), Activity Based Costing (ABC), design for manufacturing (DFM), and Process Value Added (PVA).

Keep the Status Quo

The second perspective does not advocate any change in management accounting methods. Supporters of this view perceive business problems as unrelated to accounting. They believe that as new business practices are developed, management accounting methods of the past can and will provide managers with the information they need to operate their companies. Advocates believe that many of the management accounting techniques developed over the past 10 years are simply variations of traditional techniques that have only been renamed.

Don't Change Just for the Sake of Change

The third perspective lies somewhere between the first two. Those who hold this view believe that there are serious flaws in the management accounting techniques of the past and that some of them probably have no place in the new business environment. They warn, however, not to change just to change. Supporters of this view advocate caution in abandoning old ways and embracing new ones. They believe that many of the techniques developed over the past 15 years lack universal application—they may greatly benefit some companies, some industries, or some circumstances but should not be hailed as cures for all problems facing all businesses.

The debate over the future of management accounting show no signs of waning. No matter what happens over the next several years, you will have begun your business careers before the debate is settled. The majority of firms today still employ traditional management accounting techniques and practices, and they likely will for many years. Some companies, however, have embraced new techniques. We discuss both traditional and new management accounting techniques throughout the following chapters.

CONSUMERS OF MANAGEMENT ACCOUNTING INFORMATION

To make effective decisions, business managers must understand the firm's management accounting system, know whether the information is reliable, and recognize that no system will provide perfect information. Decision making by its very nature is forward-looking, and the future always contains an element of uncertainty. Managers should look for ways to reduce the amount of that uncertainty.

Every decision results in an outcome, and even good decisions can lead to bad outcomes. For example, say that you are about to get in the checkout line at the grocery store. You evaluate the lines leading to open cash registers and, after counting the number of people in line and eyeballing the amount of groceries each customer is about to buy, you select what appears to be the shortest line. Your decision is sound and based on the information available. Well, just as the person ahead of you is about to pay, shopping disaster strikes. That customer does not have an acceptable check guarantee card. You must now wait for the manager to arrive and resolve the problem (a process that seems to take as long as college registration) before the cashier can help you. Quickly you look to see whether you can jump to another line, but it is too late: The other lines are now too long, and you must wait it out. Did you make a poor decision? No, you made the best decision you could with the available information. Your good decision simply led to a poor outcome.

Regardless of your career, at some point you will probably use accounting information to make a decision. If you are studying marketing, you may start as an assistant who helps prepare and implement marketing programs. As you advance in the firm, you may manage a staff of people who handle marketing programs, so you will need the accounting tools to make well-informed decisions. When you are responsible for the well-being of a company, department, division, or management team, you will face decisions that depend on your using management accounting information. The following chapters will teach you to be a careful consumer of accounting information.

SUMMARY

Management accounting is the process of identifying, measuring, and communicating financial information used by managers to plan, evaluate, and control their organization.

Financial accounting, which is intended for use by external parties, is subject to Generally Accepted Accounting Principles (GAAP). No such rules apply to management accounting, which is intended for use by internal parties. The general-purpose financial statements produced by financial accounting focus on past results. Reports produced by management accounting are much more detailed and focus on the future of the organization.

Although accounting and accounting records have existed since the dawn of civilization, the need for accounting information for use by management did not exist prior to the early 19th century. The emergence of permanent employees, the Industrial Revolution, scientific management, and the diversification by businesses all contributed to significant development of management accounting techniques between 1825 and 1925.

Around the year 1925, there was a dramatic slowdown in the development of new management accounting techniques. Some of the contributing factors often cited for this slowdown are the dominance of financial accounting, weaknesses in accounting education, a focus by many companies on short-term financial results, and the lack of competitive pressure on U.S. businesses. However, great strides have been made in the past 15 years toward developing improved management accounting techniques.

American companies face significant competitive challenges as we move toward the 21st century, and the role of management accounting information in helping these companies will be critical.

KEY TERMS

controller M-8
cost accounting M-5
Industrial Revolution M-9
Institute of Management
  Accountants (IMA) M-11

management accounting M-5
managerial accounting M-5
scientific management M-10
treasurer M-7

REVIEW THE FACTS

A. What are the differences among management accounting, managerial accounting, and cost accounting?
B. What is the purpose of management accounting?
C. What are the primary differences between financial accounting and management accounting?

D. Financial accounting information must be prepared in conformity with GAAP. Why are there no such rules for management accounting?
E. List four significant changes in business that led to the development of management accounting.
F. What is the IMA and what is its purpose?
G. Describe four factors that possibly led to the stagnation of management accounting development.
H. Explain the difference between a good decision and a good outcome.
I. Why is an understanding of management accounting an important ingredient of success in your career?

APPLY WHAT YOU HAVE LEARNED

LO 1: Contrast Management Accounting and Financial Accounting

1–14. Following are certain characteristics of either financial accounting information or management accounting information.

1. _____ Must conform to GAAP.
2. _____ Tends to be quite detailed.
3. _____ Generally limited to presenting historical information.
4. _____ Need not conform to a formal set of rules and standards.
5. _____ Information prepared primarily for external users.
6. _____ Tends to include only a limited amount of detail.
7. _____ Information prepared on a quarterly or yearly basis.
8. _____ Information prepared on a monthly, weekly, or daily basis.
9. _____ Information often includes future projections.
10. _____ Information prepared for use by internal parties.

REQUIRED:
Designate each of the characteristics as pertaining to (a) financial accounting information or (b) management accounting information.

LO 1: Describe Management Accounting

1–15. Is management accounting important for not-for-profit organizations as well as for-profit organizations? Explain.

LO 1: Describe Management Accounting

1–16. If you were the manager of a Blockbuster Entertainment Store, what accounting information would you desire to help you do your job better?

LO 3: Stagnation in Development of Management Accounting

1–17. Explain why managers tend to focus on improving short-term financial results.

LO 4: Changes in Management Accounting

1–18. Explain why there has been a renewed emphasis on the development of management accounting in the United States in the last decade.

LO 1: Contrast Management Accounting and Financial Accounting

1–19. Following are examples of users of financial accounting information and users of management accounting information.

1. _____ Sales supervisor
2. _____ Salespersons
3. _____ Wall Street analyst
4. _____ Suppliers
5. _____ Current shareholders
6. _____ Potential shareholders
7. _____ Personnel manager
8. _____ Maintenance supervisor
9. _____ Maintenance worker
10. _____ Loan officer at a company's bank

REQUIRED:

Designate each of the users of accounting information as either (a) external party or (b) internal party.

Chapter 2

Classifying Costs

Suppose for a moment that your boss has asked you to organize a consumer catalog of all the toys in the world. You need to classify the toys in several ways so users of your catalog will be able to find information easily. After thinking about your task for a while, you start a list of toy classifications—toys organized by age or gender of user, by price, or by design. Your initial list of categories may look like the following:

Classification

By Age of User: Toys for infants
Toys for toddlers ages one to three
Toys for children ages three to five
Toys for children ages five to nine
Toys for children ages 10 and older

By Gender of User: Toys designed for girls
Toys designed for boys
Toys for all children

By Price: Toys under $10
Toys for $10 to $50
Toys for $51 to $99
Toys over $100

By Design: Electronic toys vs. nonelectronic toys
Toys with wheels vs. toys without wheels
Breakable vs. unbreakable toys

Your boss now wants you to pick only one or two categories, to make your job easier. You scan your list to see which classifications will be most useful. You realize that the catalog must have each classification to be as useful as possible, because purchasers may need different information for different decisions.

For instance, if purchasers are choosing toys to donate to the annual toy drive for needy children, they may want to focus on price so they can donate several toys. In this case, the price classification would be most helpful. Further, those same purchasers may want to use the gender classification to find toys for all children because they would not know in advance whether the child receiving the toy is a girl or a boy.

If buyers are shopping for a birthday gift intended for a two-year-old relative, they would use the age classification to find appropriate toys. They might also want to use the price category to help them decide how much to spend. As these examples show, even in making just one decision, more than one classification may provide useful information.

Like our hypothetical toy purchasers, managers must have information to make effective planning and controlling decisions. Cost information is one of the key components of financial decision making; but what exactly is a cost? In accounting, a cost is how much we have to give up to get something. Put more formally, a **cost** is the resources forfeited to receive some goods or services. Note that cost is different from price. Price is what we charge; cost is what we pay.

cost The resources forfeited to receive some goods or services.

Business managers classify costs in many different ways because, just like the vast array of toys, there are many types of costs. Each classification can provide managers with useful information. In this chapter, we explore several different cost classifications that managers use to make decisions. ■

LEARNING OBJECTIVES

After completing your work on this chapter, you should be able to do the following:

1. Classify costs by cost objects, and distinguish between direct and indirect costs.
2. Distinguish between product costs and period costs, and contrast their accounting treatment.
3. Explain the differences between product cost for a merchandiser and for a manufacturer.
4. Describe the components of the costs included in each of the three types of inventory in a manufacturing operation.
5. Calculate cost of goods manufactured and cost of goods sold.
6. Describe the components of the cost of services provided by a service firm.

MAJOR COST CLASSIFICATIONS

Businesses incur many different costs as they operate and there are many useful ways to classify these costs. As managers make each internal business decision, they must determine what cost classifications will help them most. We will first identify important cost terms and investigate several cost classifications.

Exhibit 2–1
Common Cost Object Designations

Cost Object	Examples
• Activity	• Repairing equipment, testing manufactured products for quality
• Product	• Paper towels, personal computers, automobiles (These can be either purchased or manufactured products.)
• Service	• Performing surgery, accounting work, legal work
• Project	• Constructing a bridge, designing a house
• Geographic region	• A state, a city, a county
• Department	• Marketing department, accounting department

Assigning Costs to Cost Objects

cost object Any activity or item for which a separate cost measurement is desired.

One of the most useful classifications of cost is by cost object. A **cost object** is any activity or item for which we desire a separate cost measurement. Think of any noun associated with business and you have a potential cost object. Exhibit 2–1 lists some cost objects commonly used by companies.

We identify a cost object to determine the cost of that particular object. Such classification can provide useful information. For example, a manufacturer may need information about the cost of the products it manufactures. In this case, the individual products are the cost objects. All costs associated with a particular product are grouped to determine the full cost of that product. Managers may also want to determine the cost associated with a group of products, such as a fleet of delivery trucks. When we assign costs to cost objects, we classify costs as direct or indirect.

direct cost A cost that can be easily traced to an individual cost object.

indirect cost A cost that supports more than one cost object.

common cost Another name for *indirect cost.*

A cost that is easily traced to individual cost objects is a **direct cost.** Many times, however, a cost may benefit more than one cost object, so tracing that cost to individual cost objects becomes difficult or even impossible. A cost that supports more than one cost object is an **indirect cost.** An indirect cost may also be called a **common cost,** because it is common to more than one cost object.

To illustrate the difference between direct and indirect costs, consider 12 Sears stores in Alabama. Each store has a manager who is responsible for the day-to-day operation of that store. Sears also has a general manager who is responsible for the operation of all stores in the state. If we define each of the 12 stores as cost objects, the salary of each store manager would be considered a direct cost to his or her store. The salary of the general manager is not incurred to support any one of the 12 stores. Rather, it supports all 12 stores. Therefore, the general manager's salary would be considered an indirect cost of each cost object (the individual stores).

Discussion Questions

Assume that instead of defining each individual Sears store as a cost object, we define the entire Sears operation in Alabama as a cost object.

2-1. In this case, would the salaries of the 12 store managers be considered direct or indirect costs? Explain your reasoning.

2-2. Would the salary of the general manager be considered a direct or an indirect cost? Explain your reasoning.

2-3. Why do you think managers at various levels in a company would find it useful to classify costs as direct or indirect?

Product Cost

product cost The cost of the various products a company sells.

When you see inventory on store shelves, you know the store did not get the inventory for free. Rather, each unit of product had some cost. The cost of the various products that a company sells is called **product cost.** More specifically, product costs are the costs associated with making the products available and ready to sell. For a bookstore, such as B. Dalton Booksellers or WaldenBooks, product cost is the cost of the books purchased for resale, the freight to get the books to the store (also known as freight-in), and other costs involved in getting the books ready to sell.

inventoriable cost Another name for *product cost.*

Product costs are also known as **inventoriable costs**—product costs become part of a company's inventory until the goods associated with the costs are sold. Because product held for sale is considered an asset, its cost is shown on the balance sheet (inventory) until the product is actually sold. When the goods are sold, the product cost is converted from an asset on the balance sheet to an expense (cost of goods sold) on the income statement.

For example, when Payless Shoe Source buys shoes to sell, the cost of the shoes is a product cost and is added to inventory on the balance sheet. The cost remains in inventory on the balance sheet until the shoes are sold. When the shoes are sold, the reality of the reduced inventory caused by the sale is reflected in the company's accounting records by reducing inventory on the balance sheet and increasing cost of goods sold on the income statement.

Period Cost

period cost All costs incurred by a company that are not considered product cost. Includes selling and administrative cost.

Period costs are all the costs that a company incurs which are not considered product costs. They include selling and administrative expenses, but not any costs associated with acquiring product or getting it ready to sell.

selling cost The cost of locating customers, attracting customers, convincing customers to buy, and the cost of necessary paperwork to document and record sales.

Selling Cost Selling cost includes the cost of locating customers, attracting them, convincing them to buy, and the cost of necessary paperwork to document and record sales. Examples of selling cost include salaries paid to members of the sales force, sales commissions, and advertising.

Two selling costs are less obvious: the cost of delivering product to customers (also known as freight-out) and the cost of storing merchandise inventory. The reason delivery cost is considered a selling cost is that companies probably would not provide delivery unless it helped sell more product. If customers would buy with or without free delivery, the seller would probably not offer it.

Do not confuse freight-out (period cost) with freight-in (product cost). The key to keeping the two straight is to think about when they are incurred. Freight-in is a cost incurred before the product is ready to sell and is therefore considered a product cost. Freight-out is incurred after the product is ready for sale and is therefore classified as a period cost.

The cost of storing merchandise inventory is also classified as a selling cost, because merchandise in stock enhances its sales potential. Businesses cannot easily sell what they do not have. For example, if you went to your local music shop to buy a compact disc and the salesperson told you, "We don't keep that CD in stock, but we'll be glad to order it for you," then you would probably walk out and find another store that carries a better-stocked inventory of compact discs rather than wait. Because both delivery and merchandise inventory enhance sales, these items are considered selling costs.

administrative cost All costs incurred by a company that are not product costs or selling costs. Includes the cost of accounting, finance, employee relations, and executive functions.

Administrative Cost Administrative cost includes all costs that are not product or selling cost. These costs are typically associated with support functions—areas that offer support to the product and selling areas, such as accounting, finance, human resources, and executive functions.

Generally, period costs are shown as operating expenses (selling and administrative expenses) on the income statement. Most period costs—administrators' salaries, for example—are presented as expenses when the expenditure is made. When long-lived assets that will be used for selling or administrative functions are purchased, a slightly different treatment is necessary. At the time they are purchased, the cost of long-lived assets is shown on the balance sheet. As time passes, the depreciation expense associated with these assets becomes part of selling and administrative expense.

Discussion Questions

Assume that you are using a felt-tip highlighter to mark this book as you read it. Assume further that you purchased the marker at the college bookstore.

2–4. What costs associated with the marker do you think the bookstore would consider to be product costs? Explain your reasoning for each cost you included.

2–5. What costs associated with operating the bookstore do you think would be considered period costs (selling and administrative)? Explain your reasoning for each cost you included.

Comparing Product and Period Costs

The distinction between product cost and period cost is based on whether the cost in question benefits the process of getting products ready for sale (product cost), or the selling and administrative functions (period cost). Let us look at some examples to make sure you understand the distinction. The cost of a factory security guard is a product cost because it benefits the plant. Conversely, the cost of a security guard in the sales office is a selling expense, which is a period cost. Note that the classification depends on the company function that benefits from the cost.

What about the salary of the vice president of manufacturing? Even though vice president of manufacturing may sound like an administrative position, the cost of it benefits the manufacturing function, so it is a product cost. Further, all costs associated with that position, including the depreciation on the vice president's desk, the cost of his or her support personnel, travel costs, and all other costs associated with this position, would be classified as a product cost. Likewise, the vice president of marketing would be an example of selling expense, which is a period cost. The depreciation on a company sales representative's car would be a selling expense, because it benefits the sales area of the company.

Next, we examine how manufacturing, merchandising, and service firms identify their product costs.

PRODUCT COST IDENTIFICATION FOR MERCHANDISING FIRMS

Merchandising firms, whether wholesale or retail, purchase products ready to sell, add a markup, and resell the goods. They generate profits by selling merchandise for a price that is higher than their cost. Wholesalers generally buy products from manufacturers (or other wholesalers) and then sell them to retailers. Retailers buy from manufacturers or the wholesalers and sell their products to the final consumers.

In this section we explore how a merchandising company identifies product costs and how those product costs flow through the balance sheet and income statement.

For a merchandising firm, product cost includes the cost of the merchandise itself, freight costs to obtain the merchandise, and any other costs incurred to get the product ready to sell. Because merchandisers buy goods for resale, often the cost of getting products ready to sell is minor or nonexistent. Product cost does not include any cost incurred after the product is in place and ready to sell.

Product cost is often the most significant of all costs for a merchandiser. It is not uncommon for merchandising companies to have cost of goods sold as high as 80 percent of the selling price of the product sold, indicating of course that they have a gross profit as low as 20 percent. Besides increasing sales, managers are always interested in reducing expenses, which is impossible without an understanding of what items are included in product cost. Efforts to reduce total cost of goods sold may focus on any component of that expense, that is, any component of product cost.

The Flow of Product Cost—Merchandising Company

If you were responsible for the profitability of a product or group of products, not only would you want to know total product cost, but you would also want to know and understand the various components of each product's cost. With this understanding, you could analyze reports detailing these products' cost components and work to isolate costs that could be reduced or eliminated. The diagram in Exhibit 2–2 illustrates the flow of costs in a merchandising operation.

Exhibit 2–2
Flow of Product Costs—
Merchandising
Company

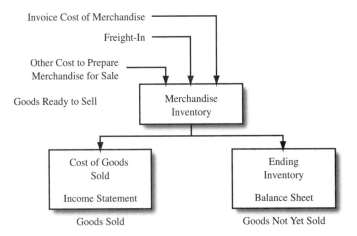

Exhibit 2–2 indicates that as goods are purchased, their cost is classified as merchandise inventory. In fact, all product costs are originally shown like those in Exhibit 2–2, as an asset on the balance sheet. Typically, a merchandising firm has only one inventory classification, which is usually referred to as *merchandise inventory* or, simply, *inventory*. As the units of product are sold, their cost is converted to an expense and shown on the income statement as the cost of goods sold.

Cost of Goods Sold

Exhibit 2–3 is a cost of goods sold schedule for Jason's Supply Company. As the exhibit shows, we add purchases to the inventory on hand at the beginning of the period to arrive at the goods available for sale. Generally, one of two things can

Exhibit 2–3
Cost of Goods Sold
Schedule

JASON'S SUPPLY COMPANY
Cost of Goods Sold Schedule
For the Year Ending December 31, 1998

	Beginning Inventory at January 1, 1998	$ 23,000
+	Purchases during 1998	300,000
=	Goods Available for Sale in 1998	$323,000
−	Ending Inventory at December 31, 1998	(30,000)
=	Cost of Goods Sold for 1998	$293,000

happen to the goods available for sale: They are either sold or remain on hand at the end of the period and are reflected as ending inventory. Thus, when ending inventory is subtracted from the goods available for sale, we can determine the cost associated with the products that have been sold—that is, we can determine the cost of goods sold.

The January 1, 1998, beginning inventory amount shown in Exhibit 2–3 is actually the ending inventory from Jason's balance sheet at December 31, 1997, and the ending inventory amount shown is from Jason's balance sheet at December 31, 1998. The cost of goods sold amount is included as an expense item on the company's income statement for the year ending December 31, 1998.

Discussion Question

2-6. Accounting for the flow of product cost for a merchandiser seems to be a lot of bother. If all merchandise inventory will eventually be sold anyway, why not just record it as an expense (cost of goods sold) on the income statement when it is purchased?

Any company that sells tangible, physical product must sell its product for more than the product costs or it will eventually go bankrupt. This may seem very obvious, and in fact, good business managers are well aware of this necessity. Understanding the need is one thing; making sure it happens is another. Competitive pressures exist in most industries that cause companies to sell their products for less than desired. Managers of these businesses must have a solid understanding of the relationship between the selling price of their products and the cost of those products, or they may actually sell product for less than it costs.

It's like the two guys who bought watermelons for $1 each and were selling them for $0.90 each. Business was certainly brisk because they were underselling all their competition. Finally, one guy turned to the other and said, "Harry, we need to get a bigger truck." Well, a bigger truck would not help. They could never sell enough watermelons to be profitable because they were selling each melon for less than it cost. Without a thorough understanding of the relationship between the cost of a product and the selling price of that product, managers cannot hope to make prudent business decisions.

Virtually all the products that consumers purchase have undergone some manufacturing process. In this section we explore how a manufacturing company identifies product costs and how those product costs flow through the balance sheet and income statement. As in merchandising firms, product cost for a manufacturer includes all costs associated with acquiring the product and getting it ready to sell. For manufacturers, however, getting the product ready to sell is usually an extensive process requiring the use of factory facilities such as production machinery and factory workers.

For a manufacturer, units of product are normally considered cost objects and their cost encompasses three distinct elements. We will introduce them briefly here and then discuss each of them in more detail a bit later. As we present each of the elements, think back to our discussion earlier in the chapter about cost objects and direct versus indirect costs.

direct materials cost The cost of all raw materials that can be traced directly to a unit of manufactured product.

1. **Direct materials cost.** Direct materials cost is the cost of all raw materials that can be traced directly to a single unit of manufactured product, or the cost incurred for only one cost object. Note that direct materials cost is not the cost of all materials used in the manufacture of the product. In most manufacturing operations some materials costs are incurred for multiple cost objects. These costs are indirect materials cost, which we consider a part of manufacturing overhead.

direct labor cost The cost of all production labor that can be traced directly to a unit of manufactured product.

2. **Direct labor cost.** Direct labor cost is the cost of all production labor that can be traced directly to a unit of manufactured product. Note that direct labor cost is not the cost of all labor incurred in the manufacture of product. In most manufacturing operations some labor costs are incurred for multiple cost objects. That type of cost is indirect labor cost, which we consider a part of manufacturing overhead, discussed next.

manufacturing overhead cost All costs associated with the operation of the manufacturing facility besides direct materials cost and direct labor cost. It is composed entirely of indirect manufacturing cost incurred to support multiple cost objects.

3. **Manufacturing overhead cost.** Manufacturing overhead is all the costs associated with the operation of the manufacturing facility other than direct materials cost and direct labor cost. It is composed entirely of indirect manufacturing cost—that is, manufacturing cost incurred to support multiple cost objects. Among others, manufacturing overhead includes indirect materials and indirect labor as discussed in items 1 and 2.

Inventory Classifications

As with merchandising firms, product costs for a manufacturer are inventoriable costs. However, manufacturing companies have not just one, but three types of inventory: raw materials, work in process, and finished goods. Note that these three types of inventory are not the same as the three elements of manufactured product we just introduced. Rather, these inventory classifications specify where manufactured product is at any given time in the production process.

As we discuss the three inventory classifications used by manufacturers, consider the following thoughts. First, our discussion in this chapter is intended to serve only as a broad introduction to the flow of product cost through a manufacturing company. The following chapter deals with specific methods used to accumulate product cost for a manufacturer. Second, there is a difference between reality and the measurement of reality. Reality is physical units of product moving through the production process, separate from our attempt to measure that reality.

raw materials inventory Materials that have been purchased but have not yet entered the production process.

material stores Another name for *raw materials inventory.*

Raw materials inventory, sometimes called **material stores,** consists of materials that have been purchased but have not yet entered the production process. Included in raw materials inventory are those that will eventually be accounted for as either direct or indirect materials. For example, Steelcase, Inc. manufactures metal desks, filing cabinets, and other metal office furniture. Raw materials inventory for Steelcase would consist of the sheet metal, screws, paint, and glue it has on hand with which to make metal office furniture. It would not include any of the material in the office furniture the company has begun to manufacture but has not yet finished, nor would it include the material in the office furniture that has been completed. Until raw materials actually enter the production process, the cost associated with those materials is classified as raw materials inventory on the balance sheet.

work-in-process inventory
Products that have entered the production process but have not yet been completed.

Work-in-process inventory consists of products that have entered the production process but have not yet been completed—those units currently on the production line or in the production process. In our Steelcase example, work-in-process inventory at any given time would consist of the desks, filing cabinets, and other metal office furniture that have been started but are not yet finished. The reality is partially completed desks, filing cabinets, and other metal office furniture. The measurement of reality counts the costs associated with these partially completed units of product and classifies them as work-in-process inventory on the balance sheet. These costs include the cost of the materials associated with these units, the labor cost incurred so far in the production process, and some amount of manufacturing overhead applied to each of the partially completed units of product.

Work-in-process inventory does not include the cost of raw materials that have not yet entered the production process, nor does it include the cost associated with products that have been completed.

finished goods inventory
Products that have been completed and are ready to sell.

As you might imagine, **finished goods inventory** consists of products that have been completed and are ready to sell. With respect to Steelcase, finished goods inventory would be the pieces of metal office furniture completed but not yet sold. Remember, these are real units of finished product: They are reality. They have completed the production process and are sitting in a warehouse somewhere waiting to be sold. The measurement of that reality is a classification of inventory on the balance sheet called finished goods inventory. Included in that amount are all the materials, labor, and manufacturing overhead costs accumulated for those units completed, but not yet sold.

Discussion Question

2-7. Why do you think managers of a manufacturing firm would find it beneficial to separate the amount and cost of inventory items into raw materials, work in process, and finished goods?

If managers in manufacturing businesses are to make prudent production decisions, they must have relevant information. The decisions they must make include how much and what type of materials they need to purchase, how many production workers are needed, what skill level these workers must possess, and whether production capacity is sufficient to produce the product required. The information that managers need to help them make these and many other production decisions includes the amount and cost of raw materials on hand, the composition of the labor force, the capacity and cost of production facilities, and the amount and cost of both work-in-process and finished goods inventory.

Although much of the relevant information managers need to make these decisions is provided by nonaccountants, such as marketing and sales personnel, accountants provide vital information concerning the cost of raw materials, work in process, and finished goods. All three classifications of inventory have one or more of the product cost elements introduced earlier: direct material, direct labor, and manufacturing overhead. We will now discuss each of those elements in more detail.

Direct Material

direct material The raw material that becomes a part of the final product and can be easily traced to the individual units produced.

Direct material is the raw material that becomes part of the final product and can be easily traced to the individual units produced. Obviously, direct materials cost is the cost of these raw materials. Examples of direct materials used in the manufacture of automobiles are sheet metal, plastic, and window glass. In the manufacture of computers, direct materials include circuit boards, cathode ray tubes, and other items. At Steelcase, Inc., direct materials would include the sheet metal used to manufacture the desks, filing cabinets, and other metal office furniture.

Often, the final product of one company is purchased by another to be used as part of its raw material in the manufacturing process. For example, direct materials used in the manufacture of Cessna aircraft include aluminum, wheels, tires, cables, and engines. The tires that Cessna uses as raw materials in the manufacture of its aircraft are the finished product of one of the company's suppliers, Goodyear Tire and Rubber Company.

Discussion Questions

2-8. In addition to the tires supplied by Goodyear, what other finished products do you think Cessna uses in its production of small aircraft? What companies might produce these products?

2-9. Name three additional pairs of manufacturing companies that have a supplier-buyer relationship—that is, the finished product of one company becomes the raw material of another company.

When materials are purchased for use in the manufacture of products, their cost at first is added to raw materials inventory. Once the material has entered the production process (reality), its cost is removed from raw materials inventory and added to work-in-process inventory (measurement of reality). Thus, in our Steelcase example, as sheet metal is purchased, its cost is added to raw materials. Once the metal has been used to make a desk or other piece of office furniture, its cost is removed from raw materials inventory and becomes part of work-in-process inventory.

Direct Labor

direct labor hours The time spent by production workers as they transform raw materials into units of finished products.

Direct labor hours are defined as the time spent by production workers as they transform raw materials into units of finished products. Direct labor costs are the salaries and wages paid to these workers, which can be easily traced to the products the workers produce.

Think about some article of clothing, say a pair of pants, you are wearing at this moment. Certainly there is material in the pants. But how did the pants become pants? Well, you may not know all the steps, but you do know that somewhere, someone sat at a sewing machine and stitched the cut material into a pair of pants. The money paid to that person, whether in Taiwan, Korea, or New Jersey, is considered direct labor, because her or his efforts (and therefore cost) can easily be traced to that single cost object (the pair of pants).

The accounting treatment of direct labor cost may surprise you. In prior chapters, employees' wages were classified as wage expense, salaries expense, or some similar expense. However, direct labor needed to get products ready to sell is a product cost that enhances the value of direct material. Because product costs are inventoriable costs, direct labor cost is added to the value of work-in-process inventory, along with direct material. Why? Because the work of production-line personnel increases the value of material as it is fabricated, assembled, painted, or processed. As a result, the cost of production-line labor should increase the value of inventory, shown as an asset on the balance sheet and ultimately as cost of goods sold on the income statement. In our Steelcase example, then, wages paid to workers who actually make the desks, filing cabinets, and other metal office furniture would be considered direct labor and added to work-in-process inventory.

Thus far we have explored two elements of product costs for a manufacturing firm: direct material and direct labor. Next, we consider the third and last element of manufacturers' product costs—manufacturing overhead.

Manufacturing Overhead

manufacturing overhead All activities involved in the manufacture of products besides direct materials or direct labor.

factory overhead Another name for *manufacturing overhead cost.*

factory burden Another name for *manufacturing overhead cost.*

overhead In a manufacturing company, another name for manufacturing overhead cost; in a service type business, the indirect service cost.

indirect materials Materials consumed in support of multiple cost objects.

Manufacturing overhead is defined as all activities involved in the manufacture of products besides direct materials or direct labor. Manufacturing overhead cost, then, is the cost of these indirect manufacturing activities. It is also referred to as **factory overhead, factory burden,** or simply **overhead.** In recent years, manufacturing companies have begun to call the cost of manufacturing overhead *indirect manufacturing cost,* which is certainly more descriptive than any of its other names. Old habits die hard, however, so we will call it manufacturing overhead because this term has been and remains universally understood in business.

To be considered part of manufacturing overhead, the cost must be associated with the manufacturing facility, not some other aspect of the company such as selling or administrative functions. Manufacturing overhead includes three groups of costs: indirect materials, indirect labor, and other indirect manufacturing costs.

Indirect Material **Indirect materials** are those consumed in a manufacturing facility in support of multiple cost objects. There are two types of indirect material costs in manufacturing. The first is the cost of raw materials so insignificant that the added benefit of physically tracing these materials to individual products is not worth the effort. Examples include glue, rivets, solder, small nails, and caulking. In fact, businesses could physically trace all material cost to their products, but in the case of indirect materials, the effort required to trace the cost outweighs the benefit of the additional information. The second type of indirect material is factory supplies. These are materials used in the manufacturing facility but not incorporated into the product. Examples include paper towels, janitorial supplies, and lubricants for production machinery. The cost of all indirect materials, whether the materials actually become part of manufactured product, is added to the cost of the product as part of manufacturing overhead.

indirect labor The labor incurred in support of multiple cost objects.

Indirect Labor **Indirect labor** is labor incurred in a manufacturing facility in support of multiple cost objects. As was the case with indirect material costs, there are two types of indirect labor in manufacturing. The first is the cost associated with factory workers who are neither on the production line nor directly involved in the manufacturing process. Examples include the cost of materials handlers, production supervisors, plant security personnel, plant janitorial personnel, factory secretarial and clerical personnel, and the vice president of manufacturing. Although the effort of these workers is important to the production process, their labor costs are not easily traceable to products. They are therefore classified as indirect labor.

The second type of indirect labor is the cost of wages paid to direct labor employees when they are doing something other than working on the product they produce. These activities might include setting up equipment for production runs or sweeping up at the end of a shift. The idea is that direct labor should include only the cost of direct labor personnel when they are actually working on the product. The cost of all indirect labor is added to the cost of the product as part of manufacturing overhead.

Some manufacturers in the United States now consider *all* labor as indirect labor. In some types of operations, the direct labor element of a manufactured product is as low as four percent of the total manufacturing cost. If managers believe labor cost is insignificant, they may choose not to separate it into direct and indirect labor cost and may instead classify all labor costs as indirect.

Other Overhead Costs   In addition to indirect material and indirect labor, manufacturing overhead includes other costs associated with the production facility. Examples include depreciation on the factory building, rent paid for production equipment, factory insurance, property taxes for the factory, and telephone service for the factory. All the costs in this category are associated with the operation of the production facility.

We have seen that manufacturing overhead is the sum of all indirect material, indirect labor, and other overhead costs. Manufacturing overhead costs are necessary costs to produce products and enhance the value of the goods being manufactured. Accordingly, as products are being manufactured, manufacturing overhead costs are added to work-in-process inventory.

Discussion Question

2-10. The textbook you are reading was published (manufactured) by Prentice Hall. What costs of manufacturing this book do you think Prentice Hall would include as

   a. direct materials?

   b. direct labor?

   c. manufacturing overhead?

The Flow of Product Cost—Manufacturing Company

In a manufacturing environment, just as in merchandising operations, managers must understand the flow of product costs to successfully control and plan for them. Product cost information is also an essential element of the information needed when making pricing and sales decisions. How could a business price a product if none of its managers knew how much the product cost to produce? Having the information is not enough, though. Managers must also understand the components of product cost and the way these costs will affect the company's assets as reported on the balance sheet and the profits as on the income statement. Exhibit 2–4 shows the flow of product costs through a manufacturing operation.

Exhibit 2–4
The Flow of Product
Costs—Manufacturing
Company

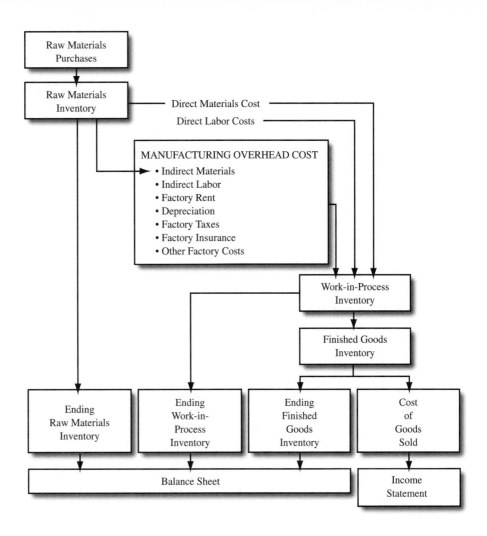

Exhibit 2–4 looks more complicated than it really is. In fact, this exhibit summarizes our entire discussion of product cost identification for a manufacturer. Let us take some time to walk through the diagram.

As raw materials are purchased, they become part of raw materials inventory (a).

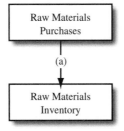

When materials actually enter the production process, their cost is classified as either direct materials (b) or indirect materials (c) depending on the type of material. The cost of any raw materials still on hand at the end of the production period is classified as ending raw materials inventory on the balance sheet at the end of the period (d).

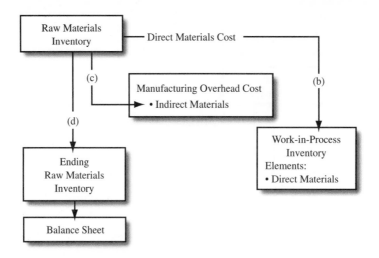

Note that the cost of direct materials is added to work-in-process inventory at this point, whereas the cost of indirect materials is classified as manufacturing overhead. We will return to manufacturing overhead in a moment.

We now have one of the three elements of product cost in work-in-process inventory (direct materials). The next element added is labor. Note that direct labor (e) is added directly to work-in-process inventory, whereas indirect labor (f) is classified as manufacturing overhead.

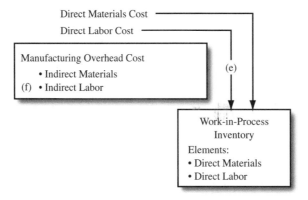

We now have two of the three elements of product cost in work-in-process inventory (direct materials and direct labor). The last element added is manufacturing overhead. In addition to indirect materials and indirect labor (which we classified as manufacturing overhead earlier), all other indirect manufacturing costs are classified as manufacturing overhead (g). The ones we have provided in Exhibit 2–4 are representative only. In reality, the list is almost endless.

Once the manufacturing overhead items and amounts have been accumulated, the cost of manufacturing overhead is added to work in process (h).

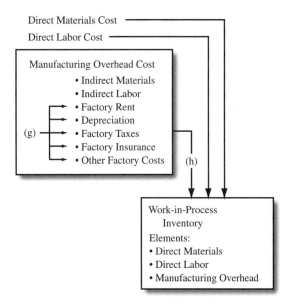

Work-in-process inventory, then, consists of the direct material, direct labor, and manufacturing overhead cost associated with goods that are currently in production. As units are completed, the cost associated with these units is transferred from work-in-process inventory to finished goods inventory (i). The cost of product still in production at the end of the production period is classified as ending work-in-process inventory on the balance sheet at the end of the period (j).

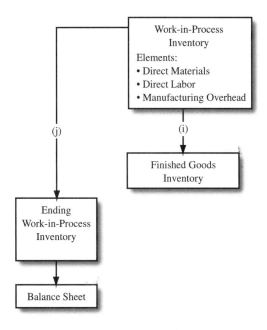

Once finished units of product (and their cost) have been transferred to finished goods inventory, usually only one of two things will happen to the actual units: Either they will be sold by the end of the accounting period or they will not be sold. If they are sold, we transfer the cost associated with them to cost of goods sold (k). We classify the cost of finished product still on hand at the end of the accounting period as ending finished goods inventory on the balance sheet at the end of the period (l).

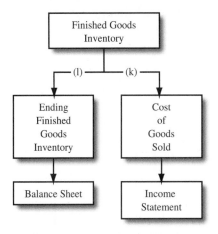

For most manufacturers, inventory is a sizeable asset requiring considerable financial resources. A walk through a manufacturing facility would make you aware of the significance of inventory, because you would be able to see stacks of it sitting there. Raw materials, work in process, and finished goods are all important assets of a manufacturer. Proper measurement of these assets is crucial if managers are to make good decisions about inventory management. For this reason, business people should understand the component costs of each type of inventory.

Cost of Goods Manufactured

We have seen that a manufacturer's product cost consists of direct material, direct labor, and manufacturing overhead. These three product classifications are summarized on the cost of goods manufactured schedule. You will find a typical presentation of this schedule for Lowell Manufacturing, Inc. in Exhibit 2–5.

Exhibit 2–5
Cost of Goods
Manufactured Schedule

LOWELL MANUFACTURING, INC.		
Cost of Goods Manufactured Schedule		
For the Year Ending December 31, 1998		
Direct Materials:		
Beginning Direct Material Inventory	$ 13,000	
+ Purchases during 1998	400,000	
= Materials Available during 1998	$413,000	
− Ending Direct Material Inventory	(20,000)	
= Direct Materials Used during 1998		$ 393,000
Direct Labor during 1998		220,000
Manufacturing Overhead Cost:		
Indirect Materials	$ 5,000	
Indirect Labor	20,000	
Factory Rent	144,000	
Depreciation of Equipment	250,000	
Repairs and Maintenance on Equipment	40,000	
Utilities	39,000	
Property Taxes	15,000	
Total Manufacturing Overhead Cost during 1998		513,000
Manufacturing Cost for Current Period		$1,126,000
+ Beginning Work-in-Process Inventory (1/1/98)		41,000
= Cost of Goods Available to be Finished in 1998		$1,167,000
− Ending Work-in-Process Inventory (12/31/98)		(65,000)
= Cost of Goods Manufactured during 1998		$1,102,000

Although this schedule looks quite involved, it consists of four relatively simple parts.

1. Direct Materials Section. This section is similar in format to the cost of goods sold section of the income statement. In both cases, we deal with costs stored in inventory to determine the cost of the inventory that has been used.

LOWELL MANUFACTURING, INC.
Cost of Goods Manufactured Schedule
Direct Materials Section
For the Year Ending December 31, 1998

Direct Materials:		
Beginning Direct Material Inventory	$ 13,000	
+ Purchases during 1998	400,000	
= Materials Available during 1998	$413,000	
− Ending Direct Material Inventory	(20,000)	
= Direct Materials Used during 1998		$393,000

2. Direct Labor Section. We see that the direct labor section of Lowell Manufacturing's cost of goods manufactured schedule consists of only one line, which is a common way to present this information. Remember, direct labor represents the cost of employees directly involved in the production process.

LOWELL MANUFACTURING, INC.
Cost of Goods Manufactured Schedule
Direct Labor Section
For the Year Ending December 31, 1998

Direct Labor during 1998	$220,000

3. The Manufacturing Overhead Section. This section lists manufacturing overhead costs by functional description. Depending on the level of detail desired, this section can be as short as one line, which depicts total manufacturing overhead. Lowell's cost of goods manufactured schedule provides several lines detailing the various components of manufacturing overhead.

LOWELL MANUFACTURING, INC.
Cost of Goods Manufactured Schedule
Manufacturing Overhead Section
For the Year Ending December 31, 1998

Manufacturing Overhead Cost:		
Indirect Materials	$ 5,000	
Indirect Labor	20,000	
Factory Rent	144,000	
Depreciation of Equipment	250,000	
Repairs and Maintenance on Equipment	40,000	
Utilities	39,000	
Property Taxes	15,000	
Total Manufacturing Overhead Cost during 1998		$513,000

4. Cost Summary and Work-in-Process Section. The last section of the cost of goods manufactured schedule summarizes the current period's product cost and incorporates the beginning and ending work-in-process inventory balances. Note that as in a cost of goods sold schedule, beginning inventory is added and ending inventory is subtracted to arrive at inventory used.

LOWELL MANUFACTURING, INC.
Cost of Goods Manufactured Schedule
Cost Summary and Work-in-Process Section
For the Year Ending December 31, 1998

	Manufacturing Cost for Current Period	$1,126,000
+	Beginning Work-in-Process Inventory (1/1/98)	41,000
=	Cost of Goods Available to be Finished during 1998	$1,167,000
−	Ending Work-in-Process Inventory (12/31/98)	(65,000)
=	Cost of Goods Manufactured during 1998	$1,102,000

Using the information from the cost of goods manufactured schedule, we can prepare a cost of goods sold schedule, such as the one for Lowell Manufacturing, Inc. shown in Exhibit 2–6.

Exhibit 2–6
Cost of Goods Sold
Schedule

LOWELL MANUFACTURING, INC.
Cost of Goods Sold Schedule
For the Year Ending December 31, 1998

	Beginning Finished Goods Inventory	$ 70,000
+	Cost of Goods Manufactured during 1998	1,102,000
=	Goods Available for Sale in 1998	$1,172,000
−	Ending Finished Goods Inventory	(28,000)
=	Cost of Goods Sold for 1998	$1,144,000

PRODUCT COST IDENTIFICATION FOR SERVICE FIRMS

In contrast to both merchandisers and manufacturers, service type businesses such as law firms, health care providers, airlines, and accounting firms do not sell tangible, physical products. Many service firms are huge. For example, Hilton Hotels Corporation is a diversified service company in the hospitality industry. The company reported revenues from hotel and casino services of over $1.6 billion for 1996.

Service companies offer their customers a product just as real as those sold by merchandisers and manufacturers, but service products lack physical substance. Determining the cost of its product is as important for a service company as it is for merchandisers and manufacturers, but the procedures differ because service type businesses have no inventory.

Costs can be accumulated for almost any facet of a service company's operation. To illustrate, let us consider the Marston Medical Clinic. The three doctors at the clinic (Dr. Helen Marston and two of her medical school classmates) perform routine physical exams, examinations in response to specific patient symptoms, immunizations, and minor surgery. Major surgery is performed by the doctors at a local hospital. Any one of these services could be designated as a cost object, and cost could be accumulated for a particular service provided to an individual patient. Likewise, costs can be accumulated for a particular category of procedure, for a department or a particular area of the medical practice, or for each of the three doctors or the five nurses.

The three broad cost classifications included in the cost of services provided are materials, labor, and indirect service cost (sometimes called overhead). The cost classifications for a service firm look almost exactly like the classifications used in costing manufactured products, with some important differences.

Materials

The materials used in performing services are normally incidental supplies. The cost of these materials is relatively insignificant compared to the direct materials used in the production of manufactured products. In the case of Marston Medical Clinic, materials would include items such as tongue depressors, the needles and serum used for immunizations, bandages, and so forth.

Some service companies separate material that is significant enough to trace to individual cost objects from insignificant material that is simply treated as indirect overhead cost. In many cases, however, the materials used in performing a service are actually more like the indirect materials used by a manufacturer. Whereas a manufacturer such as Steelcase might consider glue and screws to be indirect materials, a legal firm would probably consider legal pads, computer discs, and pens as indirect materials, and all costs of materials are treated as indirect (overhead) cost.

Labor

Generally, service businesses are labor intensive, meaning that the largest component of product cost for service organizations is often labor cost. It includes costs of those people who perform part or all the service. In the case of Marston Medical Clinic, labor cost would certainly include the salaries of the three doctors and the five nurses. It would not, however, include the amount paid to the receptionist or bookkeeper. Even though their work is important, these employees do not perform the health care services provided by the clinic. The labor cost of the receptionist and bookkeeper, then, would be considered a period cost.

Overhead or Indirect Service Costs

The overhead costs in a service business are similar to those for a manufacturer. They are costs that are associated specifically with performing the services provided but that cannot easily be traced to one specific cost object. In the case of the Marston Clinic, rent on the clinic building is an indirect cost of providing health care—the building is necessary to provide patient services. However, its cost is hard to trace to one cost object, so it is considered an overhead cost.

Discussion Question

2-11. Airline companies, such as United Airlines, often define the routes they fly as cost objects. Given that definition, consider a specific route from New York to Los Angeles and describe the costs you believe United Airlines would include as

    a. materials
    b. labor
    c. overhead

The Flow of Service Cost—Service Company

Just as managers in manufacturing and merchandising operations must understand the flow of costs associated with products they sell, managers of service type businesses must understand the flow of service costs if they are to control and plan for them. Also, service cost information is an essential element of the information needed when making pricing and sales decisions. Having the information is not enough though. Managers must also understand how these costs will affect the company's assets reported on the balance sheet and profits on the income statement. The flow of costs through a typical service firm is shown in Exhibit 2–7.

Exhibit 2–7
The Flow of Service Costs—Service Company

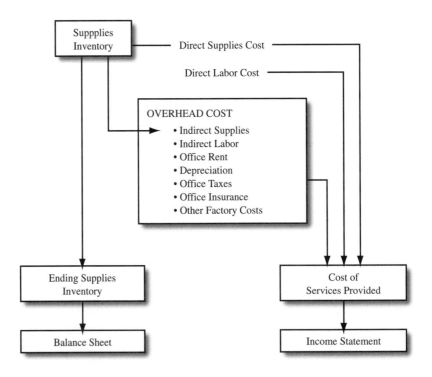

Cost of Services

As Exhibit 2–7 indicates, cost of services has three parts: direct labor, overhead, and supplies. With this in mind, we can easily create a schedule computing the cost of service products. As an example, the schedule in Exhibit 2–8 shows the computation of cost of medical services for Marston Medical Clinic.

Exhibit 2–8
Cost of Services Schedule

MARSTON MEDICAL CLINIC Cost of Services Schedule For the Year Ending December 31, 1998		
Direct Labor Cost		$ 940,000
Overhead Cost:		
Indirect Supplies	$12,000	
Office Rent	24,000	
Depreciation	18,000	
Office Taxes	2,000	
Office Insurance	8,000	
Other Indirect Costs	6,000	
Total Overhead Cost		70,000
Direct Supplies Cost		$ 20,000
Cost of Services Provided		$1,030,000

Exhibit 2–8 shows that the cost of services for Marston Medical Clinic was $1,030,000 for the year ended December 31, 1998. The total cost included the three components of service product cost: direct labor, overhead, and direct supplies.

We have examined how service firms identify product costs and how those costs flow through the firm. We now turn briefly to hybrid firms, which produce both goods and services.

HYBRID FIRMS

hybrid firms Companies that generate revenue from both providing services and selling products.

Some companies, called **hybrid firms,** generate revenue from both providing services and selling products. For example, although the majority of Blockbuster Entertainment's revenue comes from its videotape rental service, the company also generates significant revenue from videotape product sales. In accounting for an operation that combines service and products, companies such as Blockbuster must incorporate techniques used by both service and merchandising firms. A single company, such as General Motors, might actually be a manufacturer (making cars and trucks), a merchandiser (selling floor mats and other accessories to GM dealers), and a service type business (offering GMAC Financing).

MERCHANDISING, MANUFACTURING, AND SERVICE— A COMPARISON

Now that we have explored how merchandising, manufacturing, and service businesses identify their product costs and how those costs flow through each type of operation, we can see how merchandisers, manufacturers, and service businesses present product costs and period costs on their income statements. We begin with a merchandising operation, then we look at a manufacturer and a service business.

JASON'S SUPPLY COMPANY
Cost of Goods Sold Schedule
For the Year Ending December 31, 1998

Beginning Inventory at January 1, 1998	$ 23,000
+ Purchases during 1998	300,000
= Goods Available for Sale in 1998	$323,000
− Ending Inventory at December 31, 1998	(30,000)
= Cost of Goods Sold for 1998	$293,000

JASON'S SUPPLY COMPANY
Income Statement
For the Year Ending December 31, 1998

Sales		$673,000
Cost of Goods Sold		293,000
Gross Profit		$380,000
Operating Expenses:		
Selling Expense	$120,000	
Administrative Expense	80,000	
Total Operating Expenses		200,000
Operating Income		$180,000

Exhibit 2–9 illustrates how a merchandiser reports its product costs and period costs on an income statement. This exhibit shows the 1998 income statement for Jason's Supply Company and includes the cost of goods sold schedule we developed for Jason earlier in the chapter (presented as Exhibit 2–3).

As Exhibit 2–9 indicates, the amount of product cost recognized as expense (cost of goods sold) on Jason's 1998 income statement ($293,000) is calculated in the cost of goods sold schedule. The period cost recognized is the total of the operating expenses ($200,000).

Exhibit 2–10 illustrates how a manufacturer reports its product costs and period costs on an income statement. This exhibit shows the 1998 income statement for Lowell Manufacturing, Inc. and includes the cost of goods manufactured schedule (presented as Exhibit 2–5) and cost of goods sold schedule (presented as Exhibit 2–6) we developed for Lowell earlier in the chapter.

As Exhibit 2–10 indicates, the amount of product cost recognized as expense (cost of goods sold) on Lowell's 1998 income statement ($1,144,000) is calculated in the cost of goods manufactured schedule and the cost of goods sold schedule. The period cost recognized is the total of the operating expenses ($430,000).

Exhibit 2–11 illustrates how a service type company reports its cost of services and period costs on an income statement. This exhibit shows the 1998 income statement for Marston Medical Clinic and includes the cost of services schedule we developed for Marston earlier in the chapter (presented as Exhibit 2–8).

As Exhibit 2–11 indicates, the amount of services cost recognized as expense (cost of services) on Marston's 1998 income statement ($1,030,000) is calculated in the cost of services schedule. The period cost recognized is the total of the operating expenses ($175,000).

Whether the costs are related to products purchased for sale, products manufactured for sale, or services provided, cost information is an important input in the

LOWELL MANUFACTURING, INC.
Cost of Goods Manufactured Schedule
For the Year Ending December 31, 1998

Direct Materials:

Beginning Direct Material Inventory	$ 13,000	
+ Purchases during 1998	400,000	
= Materials Available during 1998	$413,000	
− Ending Direct Material Inventory	(20,000)	
= Direct Materials Used during 1998		$393,000
+ Direct Labor during 1998		220,000
+ Manufacturing Overhead Cost:		
Indirect Materials	$ 5,000	
Indirect Labor	20,000	
Factory Rent	144,000	
Depreciation of Equipment	250,000	
Repairs and Maintenance on Equipment	40,000	
Utilities	39,000	
Property Taxes	15,000	
Total Manufacturing Overhead Cost during 1998		513,000
= Manufacturing Cost for Current Period		$1,126,000
+ Beginning Work-in-Process Inventory (1/1/98)		41,000
= Cost of Goods Available to be Finished		$1,167,000
− Ending Work-in-Process Inventory (12/31/98)		(65,000)
= Cost of Goods Manufactured during 1998		$1,102,000

Cost of Goods Sold Schedule
For the Year Ending December 31, 1998

Beginning Finished Goods Inventory	$ 70,000
+ Cost of Goods Manufactured during 1998	1,102,000
= Goods Available for Sale in 1998	$1,172,000
− Ending Finished Goods Inventory	(28,000)
= Cost of Goods Sold for 1998	$1,144,000

Income Statement
For the Year Ending December 31, 1998

Sales		$1,884,000
Cost of Goods Sold		1,144,000
Gross Profit		$ 740,000
Operating Expenses:		
Selling Expense	$250,000	
Administrative Expense	180,000	
Total Operating Expenses		430,000
Operating Income		$ 310,000

decision-making process. Remember that management accounting information helps internal decision makers plan and control the firm's future. In the chapters that follow, you will see how the cost classifications and cost flows you learned about in this chapter will help you understand and apply management accounting decision-making techniques.

Exhibit 2-11
Cost of Services and
Period Costs on the
Income Statement—
Service Type Company

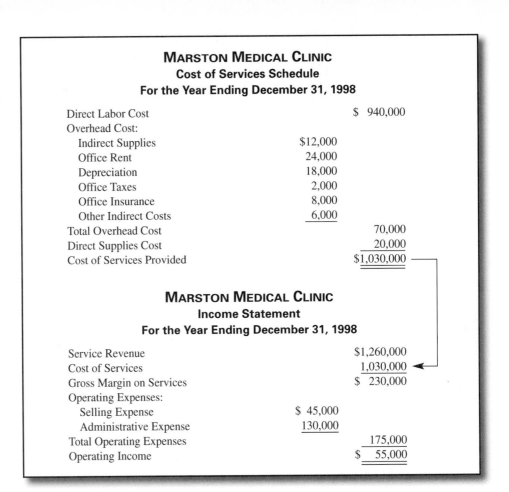

MARSTON MEDICAL CLINIC
Cost of Services Schedule
For the Year Ending December 31, 1998

Direct Labor Cost		$ 940,000
Overhead Cost:		
Indirect Supplies	$12,000	
Office Rent	24,000	
Depreciation	18,000	
Office Taxes	2,000	
Office Insurance	8,000	
Other Indirect Costs	6,000	
Total Overhead Cost		70,000
Direct Supplies Cost		20,000
Cost of Services Provided		$1,030,000

MARSTON MEDICAL CLINIC
Income Statement
For the Year Ending December 31, 1998

Service Revenue		$1,260,000
Cost of Services		1,030,000
Gross Margin on Services		$ 230,000
Operating Expenses:		
Selling Expense	$ 45,000	
Administrative Expense	130,000	
Total Operating Expenses		175,000
Operating Income		$ 55,000

SUMMARY

Businesses incur many different costs as they operate in the modern business world. These costs can be classified in many different ways and managers must determine what cost classifications will be most helpful if they are to make effective planning and control decisions.

Costs can be accumulated by cost object, which is any activity or item for which we desire a separate cost measurement. Some of the costs associated with a cost object can be traced directly to that cost object. These are called direct costs. Other costs incurred to support multiple cost objects are known as indirect costs.

The classification of costs as either product cost or period cost is very important because it determines how costs are reported on a company's income statement. Product cost is the sum of all costs required to make the products available and ready to sell and is reported on the income statement as cost of goods sold. Period costs are all costs a company incurs that are not classified as product cost. Period costs are divided into selling and administrative costs and are reported on the income statement as expenses.

There are significant differences in the way product cost is determined for merchandising companies and for manufacturing companies. For a merchandiser, product cost includes the cost of the merchandise itself and freight costs to obtain the merchandise. For a manufacturer, product cost includes the direct materials, direct labor, and manufacturing overhead required to produce finished units of product.

Manufacturing companies have additional cost classification challenges because they have three distinct types of inventory: raw materials that have been purchased but have not yet entered the production process, work-in-process units that have begun the production process but are not yet complete, and units that have been completed and are ready for sale.

Cost of services performed for a service type business is similar in many ways to product cost for a manufacturer. It includes the cost of materials, labor, and overhead required to perform services.

APPENDIX

This appendix is intended to provide a basic overview of how costs are accumulated in the accounting records of a manufacturer. To keep the example simple, we assume that the factory makes only one product and manufacturing overhead is attributed directly to work in process. The technical aspects of the application of manufacturing overhead to production will be covered in the next chapter.

After completing your work in this appendix, you should be able to record the following types of entries:

1. The purchase of raw material
2. The three main components of manufacturing cost
   a. Direct material
   b. Direct labor
   c. Manufacturing overhead
3. The transfer of the cost of completed units from work in process to finished goods
4. The sale of completed units

The following accounts will be used for the entries in this appendix:

1. Cash
2. Accounts receivable
3. Raw materials inventory
4. Work-in-process inventory
5. Finished goods inventory
6. Accounts payable
7. Sales
8. Cost of goods sold

Recall that debits increase assets, expenses, and losses, while credits increase liabilities, equity, revenues, and gains. The dollar amount of the debits must equal that of the credits in each journal entry.

1. $90,000 of raw material was purchased on account on January 2, 2000:

   2000
   Jan. 2   Raw material inventory   95,000
                  Accounts payable   95,000
              To record the purchase of raw material.

2. a. $70,000 of direct material was transferred to production on January 3, 2000:

   2000
   Jan. 3   Work-in-process inventory   70,000
                  Raw material inventory   70,000
              To record the transfer of direct material
              to production.

2. b. $80,000 of direct labor cost was incurred during January 2000.

2000			
Jan. 31	Work-in-process inventory	80,000	
	Cash		70,000
	To record wages paid for direct labor in January.		

2. c. Paid for various factory overhead items totaling $110,000 during January 2000. To keep the example simple, manufacturing overhead is attributed directly to production. As you will see in the next chapter, manufacturing overhead is generally allocated to production which necessitates the use of more complicated accounting procedures.

2000			
Jan. 31	Work-in-process inventory	110,000	
	Cash		110,000
	To record manufacturing overhead for January.		

After the above entries have been posted, the balance in the work-in-process account is $260,000 as shown in the t-account below.

Work-in-Process

70,000	
80,000	
110,000	
260,000	

3. At January 31, a physical count of the goods in production revealed that $230,000 or all but $30,000 of the goods were completed and transferred to finished goods inventory. The amount transferred from work-in-process to finished must equal the cost of goods manufactured.

2000			
Jan. 31	Finished goods inventory	230,000	
	Work-in-process inventory		230,000
	To transfer completed goods from production to finished goods.		

After the $230,000 is transferred to finished goods, the work-in-process account and finished goods have balances of $30,000 and $260,000, respectively, as shown below.

Work-in-Process

70,000	230,000
80,000	———
110,000	
260,000	230,000
30,000	

Finished Goods

230,000	

4. Goods that cost $210,000 to manufacture were sold on account for $300,000. This transaction is recorded in two parts. First the sale on account is recorded:

2000			
Jan. 31	Accounts receivable	300,000	
	Sales		300,000

Next the reduction in finished goods inventory and increase in cost of goods sold is recorded:

2000
Jan. 31   Cost of goods sold   210,000
              Finished goods   210,000

The following t-accounts depict balances after recording the $300,000 sale.

Work-in-Process

70,000	230,000
80,000	
110,000	
260,000	230,000
30,000	

Finished Goods

| 230,000 | 210,000 |
| 20,000 | |

Accounts Receivable

| 300,000 | |

Sales

| | 300,000 |

Cost of Goods Sold

| 210,000 | |

APPENDIX SUMMARY

Recording basic manufacturing entries involves eight accounts: cash, accounts receivable, accounts payable, raw material, work in process, finished goods, cost of goods sold, and sales. The basic flow through the accounts is depicted in Exhibit 2–A1. The purchase of raw material is recorded with a debit to raw material. Work in process is debited to record the transfer of direct material to production and the incurrence of direct labor and manufacturing overhead costs. When goods are completed, work in process is credited and finished goods is debited for the amount of the cost of the goods manufactured. When the finished goods are sold, separate entries are made to reflect the sale and to reflect the decrease in inventory and increase in cost of goods sold.

KEY TERMS

administrative cost   M-22
common cost   M-21
cost   M-20
cost object   M-21
direct cost   M-21
direct material   M-28
direct materials cost   M-26

direct labor cost   M-26
direct labor hours   M-28
factory burden   M-29
factory overhead   M-29
finished goods inventory   M-27
hybrid firms   M-39
indirect cost   M-21

Exhibit 2–A1
Basic Flow of Costs Through Manufacturing Accounts

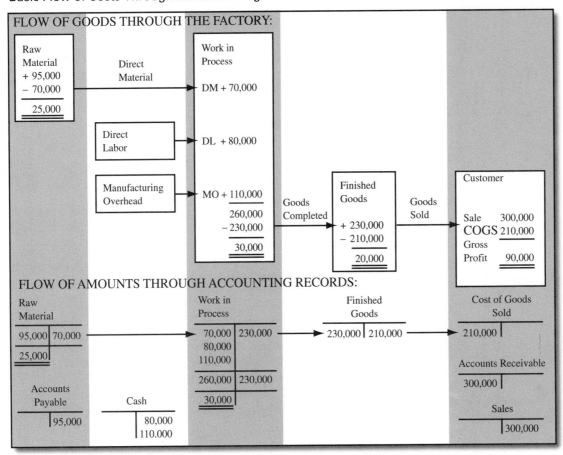

indirect labor   M-29
indirect materials   M-29
inventoriable cost   M-22
manufacturing overhead   M-29
manufacturing overhead cost   M-26
material stores   M-26

overhead   M-29
period cost   M-22
product cost   M-22
raw materials inventory   M-26
selling cost   M-22
work-in-process inventory   M-27

REVIEW THE FACTS

A. What is a cost object?
B. What is the difference between a direct cost and an indirect cost?
C. What is product cost?
D. What is period cost?
E. Why is the cost of delivering merchandise to customers included in selling expense?
F. Why is the cost of storing inventory that is ready to sell included in selling expense?
G. What classification includes costs that are neither product costs nor costs directly associated with selling activities?
H. Why are product costs called inventoriable costs?

I. Describe the difference between the accounting treatment for product costs and period costs.

J. Describe the flow of inventory costs for a merchandising operation as goods are bought and then sold.

K. What are the inventory classifications for a manufacturing type firm?

L. What are the three main cost components included in product cost for a manufacturing type firm?

M. What is the difference between direct material and indirect material?

N. What is the difference between direct labor and indirect labor?

O. In which product cost classification would you most likely find indirect material and indirect labor?

P. With respect to the cost of goods sold section of an income statement, what is the similarity between purchases for a merchandising type company and cost of goods manufactured for a manufacturing type company?

Q. What is included in the cost of services provided for a service type firm?

APPLY WHAT YOU HAVE LEARNED

LO 1: Distinguish between Direct and Indirect Costs

2–12. Brittany operates a small chain of five children's shoe stores called Baby Feet. She employs a store manager and two sales clerks for each store. In addition, she rents office space which houses her office, the personnel department, and the bookkeeping department for the chain.

Brittany has collected the following information regarding the stores and has asked you to determine which costs are direct and which are indirect costs.

REQUIRED:

For each of the following items, indicate which would describe a direct cost (D) for the store at the corner of Elm Street and Main and which would describe an indirect cost (I) for an individual store.

_____ 1. Rent for the office space
_____ 2. Rent for the store
_____ 3. Brittany's salary
_____ 4. The store manager's salary
_____ 5. The company personnel manager's salary
_____ 6. Bookkeeper's salary
_____ 7. Maintenance cost for the store
_____ 8. Depreciation on sales equipment
_____ 9. Depreciation on bookkeeping computer
_____ 10. Sales clerks' salaries
_____ 11. Cost of shoes
_____ 12. Advertising cost for the chain

LO 1: Distinguish between Direct and Indirect Costs

2–13. Sue Lee is the president of Baby Care. The company operates a chain of four child care centers in southern Florida. In addition to the four Baby Care locations, the company rents office space which is used by the company's bookkeeper and Sue Lee.

REQUIRED:

a. List four costs that would be considered direct costs of one of the four child care centers.

b. List four costs that would be considered indirect costs of one of the four child care centers.

LO 1: Distinguish between Direct and Indirect Costs

2–14. Blue Water Travel operates a chain of travel agent offices in the eastern United States. Blue Water Travel's home office is in New York. There are six sales offices and a district office located in Florida.

REQUIRED:

If the cost object is one of the sales offices in Florida, indicate which of the following would describe a direct cost (D) and which would describe an indirect cost (I).

1. _____ Rent for the Florida district office building
2. _____ Rent for the home office building in New York
3. _____ Rent for the sales office
4. _____ The company president's salary
5. _____ The salary of the vice president in charge of the Florida division
6. _____ The salary of a sales office manager
7. _____ The salary of a sales associate

LO 2: Types of Cost for a Manufacturer

2–15. Following are several representative costs incurred in a typical manufacturing company. For each of the costs, indicate in the space provided whether the cost is a direct material (DM), direct labor (DL), manufacturing overhead (MO), selling (S), or administrative (A) cost.

1. _____ Material incorporated into products
2. _____ Sales supplies
3. _____ Supplies used in the factory
4. _____ Wages of plant security guard
5. _____ Wages of security guard for the sales office
6. _____ Depreciation on a file cabinet used in the factory
7. _____ Depreciation on a file cabinet used in the general accounting office
8. _____ President's salary
9. _____ President's secretary's salary
10. _____ Manufacturing vice president's salary
11. _____ Salary of the manufacturing vice president's secretary
12. _____ Wages paid to production-line workers
13. _____ Factory rent
14. _____ Accounting office rent
15. _____ Depreciation on a copy machine used in the sales department
16. _____ Depreciation on a copy machine used to copy work orders in the factory
17. _____ Salary of plant supervisor

LO 2: Types of Cost for a Manufacturer

2–16. Following are several representative costs incurred in a typical manufacturing company. For each of the costs, indicate in the space provided whether the cost is a product cost (PR) or a period cost (PE).

1. _____ Material incorporated into products
2. _____ Sales supplies
3. _____ Supplies used in the factory
4. _____ Wages of plant security guard
5. _____ Wages of security guard for the sales office
6. _____ Depreciation on a file cabinet used in the factory
7. _____ Depreciation on a file cabinet used in the general accounting office
8. _____ President's salary
9. _____ President's secretary's salary
10. _____ Manufacturing vice president's salary
11. _____ Salary of the manufacturing vice president's secretary
12. _____ Wages paid to production-line workers
13. _____ Factory rent
14. _____ Accounting office rent
15. _____ Depreciation on a copy machine used in the sales department
16. _____ Depreciation on a copy machine used to copy work orders in the factory
17. _____ Salary of plant supervisor

LO 5: Calculate Costs for a Manufacturer, No Inventories

2–17. The following data pertain to the Anderson Table Manufacturing Company for January 1997. The company made 1,000 tables during January, and there are no beginning or ending inventories.

Wood used in production	$25,000
Cleaning supplies used in the factory	300
Machine lubricants used in the factory	100
Factory rent	2,000
Rent on the sales office	3,000
Sales salaries	20,000
Production-line labor cost	50,000
Plant security guard cost	1,200
Plant supervision	2,500
Office supervision	3,000
Depreciation on production equipment	4,000
Depreciation on office equipment	1,000

REQUIRED:

a. What is the cost of direct material used in production during January 1997?
b. What is the cost of direct labor for January 1997?
c. What is the cost of manufacturing overhead for January 1997?
d. What is the total cost of tables manufactured in January 1997?
e. What is the cost of each table manufactured in January 1997?
f. Do you think the cost per table is valuable information for Carole Anderson, the company's owner? How might she use this information?

LO 5: Calculate Ending Inventory

2–18. Steinmann Window Company makes aluminum window units. At the beginning of November, the company's direct material inventory included 900 square feet of window glass. During November Steinmann purchased another 12,000 square feet of glass. Each completed window unit requires 9 square feet of glass. During November, 9,900 square feet of glass was transferred to the production line.

REQUIRED:

How many square feet of glass remain in the ending direct material inventory?

LO 4: Analyzing Inventory

2–19. Van Kirk Manufacturing Company has been in business for many years. Dottie Van Kirk, the company president, is concerned that the cost of raw material is skyrocketing. The production foreman assured Van Kirk that the use of direct material actually dropped in 2001.

Van Kirk has engaged your services to provide insight into what she thinks may be a sizable problem. Not only does it seem that the cost of direct material is increasing, but it also seems that her production foreman is being less than honest with her.

The following information is available:

VAN KIRK MANUFACTURING COMPANY
Direct Materials Schedule
For the Year Ending December 31, 2000

Beginning Direct Material Inventory	$ 25,000
Purchases during 2000	435,000
Materials Available during 2000	$460,000
Ending Direct Material Inventory	(30,000)
Direct Materials Used during 2000	430,000

VAN KIRK MANUFACTURING COMPANY
Direct Materials Schedule
For the Year Ending December 31, 2001

Beginning Direct Material Inventory	$ 30,000
Purchases during 2001	501,000
Materials Available during 2001	$531,000
Ending Direct Material Inventory	(103,000)
Direct Materials Used during 2001	428,000

REQUIRED:

Examine the information presented and write a brief report to Dottie Van Kirk detailing your findings relative to her concerns.

LO 3: Analyze Costs of a Merchandiser

2–20. Ralph Brito opened Brito Auto Sales several years ago. Since then, the company has grown and sales have steadily increased. In the last year, however, income has declined despite successful efforts to increase sales. In addition, the company is forced to borrow more and more money from the bank to finance the operation.

The following information is available:

BRITO AUTO SALES
Income Statement
For the Year Ending December 31, 2001

Sales		$758,000
Cost of Goods Sold		
Beginning Inventory	$ 66,000	
+ Cost of Goods Purchased	639,000	
= Goods Available for Sale	$705,000	
− Ending Inventory	85,000	
= Cost of Goods Sold		620,000
Gross Profit		138,000
Operating Expense:		
Selling Expense	$ 55,000	
Administrative Expense	60,000	(115,000)
Operating Income		$ 23,000

BRITO AUTO SALES
Income Statement
For the Year Ending December 31, 2002

Sales		$890,000
Cost of Goods Sold		
Beginning Inventory	$ 85,000	
+ Cost of Goods Purchased	799,000	
= Goods Available for Sale	$884,000	
− Ending Inventory	123,000	
= Cost of Goods Sold		761,000
Gross Profit		129,000
Operating Expense:		
Selling Expense	$ 66,000	
Administrative Expense	60,000	(126,000)
Operating Income		$ 3,000

REQUIRED:

Assume that you are hired by Mr. Brito as a consultant. Review the Brito income statement and write a report to Mr. Brito that addresses his concerns.

LO 4: Calculate Ending Direct Material Inventory for a Manufacturer

2–21. Matheis Designs, Inc. manufactures swimming suits. At the beginning of October 1999, the company had $1,450 worth of cloth on hand which was included in its direct material inventory. During October, Matheis purchased cloth costing $12,360 and used material costing $12,750 in production.

REQUIRED:

What is the cost of the ending direct material inventory of cloth for Matheis Designs, Inc.?

LO 4: Calculate Direct Material Used

2–22. The following information relates to the Penny Manufacturing Company.

Beginning direct material inventory	$ 540,000
Ending direct material inventory	$ 480,000
Direct material purchased	$4,680,000

REQUIRED:

    a. Compute the cost of direct material used in production.

    b. Appendix: Prepare a journal entry to record the use of direct material in production.

LO 4: Calculate Direct Material Used

2–23. The following information relates to the Montoya Manufacturing Company.

Beginning direct material inventory	$ 40,000
Ending direct material inventory	$ 48,000
Direct material purchased	$437,000

REQUIRED:

    a. Compute the cost of direct material used in production.

    b. Appendix: Prepare a journal entry to record the use of direct material used in production.

LO 4: Calculate the Cost of Supplies Used

2–24. The following information relates to Pons Maintenance Service.

Maintenance supplies at January 1, 2000	$ 4,210
Maintenance supplies at December 31, 2000	$ 3,840
Maintenance supplies purchased during 2000	$27,530

REQUIRED:

What was the cost of maintenance supplies consumed by Pons Maintenance Service during 2000?

LO 6: Calculate Cost of Materials Used by a Service Company

2–25. On January 1, 1999, Bowden Auto Repair had $3,560 worth of auto parts on hand. During the year, Bowden purchased auto parts costing $286,000. At the end of 1999, the company had parts on hand amounting to $4,260.

REQUIRED:

What was the cost of the auto parts used by Bowden Auto Repair during 1999.

LO 3: Calculate the Cost of Goods Sold for a Merchandiser

2–26. On January 1, 1997, the cost of merchandise on hand at Margaret's Fashions was $56,530. Purchases during the month amounted to $488,668 and the cost of merchandise on hand at the end of January was $52,849.

REQUIRED:

Determine January's cost of goods sold for Margaret's Fashions.

LO 5: Inventory and Production Costs for a Manufacturer

2–27. The following data pertain to the Hudik Manufacturing Company for the year ended December 31, 2000. The company made 115,000 light fixtures during 2000. There are no beginning or ending inventories.

Metal used in production	$750,000
Wire used in production	40,000
Factory supplies	5,200
Depreciation on the factory	48,000
Depreciation on the sales office	3,000
Sales salaries	90,000
Assembly-line labor cost	960,000
Factory security guard cost	8,200
Factory supervision	62,500
General accounting cost	43,000
Depreciation on production equipment	454,850
Depreciation on office equipment	9,200

REQUIRED:
a. What is the cost of direct material used during 2000?
b. What is the cost of direct labor during 2000?
c. What is the cost of manufacturing overhead during 2000?
d. What is the total product cost for 2000 production?
e. What is the cost per light fixture for 2000?

LO 5: Inventory and Production Costs Including Cost of Goods Manufactured and Cost of Goods Sold, No Inventories

2–28. The following data pertain to the Elsea Manufacturing Company for the year ended December 31, 2000. The company made 60,000 SW20 switching units during 2000.

Beginning direct material inventory	$ 42,000
Ending direct material inventory	48,000
Beginning work-in-process inventory	84,000
Ending work-in-process inventory	93,000
Beginning finished goods inventory	124,000
Ending finished goods inventory	133,000
Direct material purchased	850,000
Indirect material used in production	4,000
Factory supplies	6,200
Depreciation on the factory	60,000
Depreciation on the sales office	4,000
Depreciation on the administrative office	3,000
Sales salaries	120,000
Assembly-line labor cost	820,000
Factory security guard cost	12,000
Factory supervision	82,600
Depreciation on production equipment	560,000
Depreciation on office equipment	22,200

REQUIRED:
a. What is the cost of direct material used during 2000?
b. What is the cost of direct labor during 2000?
c. What is the cost of manufacturing overhead for 2000?

d. What is total manufacturing cost incurred during 2000?

e. What is the cost of goods manufactured for 2000?

f. What is the cost of goods sold for 2000?

LO 5: Inventory and Production Costs Including Cost of Goods Manufactured and Cost of Goods Sold

2–29. The following data pertain to the Miami Manufacturing Company for the year ended December 31, 2000.

Beginning finished goods inventory	$ 255,000
Ending finished goods inventory	270,000
Beginning direct material inventory	82,000
Ending direct material inventory	98,000
Beginning work-in-process inventory	164,000
Ending work-in-process inventory	184,000
Direct material purchased	1,740,000
Indirect material used in production	3,000
Factory supplies	12,500
Depreciation on the factory	134,000
Depreciation on the sales office	14,000
Depreciation on the administrative office	9,000
Sales salaries	350,000
Assembly-line labor cost	2,120,000
Factory security guard cost	22,000
Factory supervision	183,500
Depreciation on production equipment	1,340,000
Depreciation on office equipment	52,200

REQUIRED:

a. What is the cost of direct material used during 2000?

b. What is the cost of direct labor during 2000?

c. What is the cost of manufacturing overhead for 2000?

d. What is total manufacturing cost incurred during 2000?

e. What is the cost of goods manufactured for 2000?

f. What is the cost of goods sold for 2000?

LO 5: Inventory and Production Costs Including Cost of Goods Manufactured and Cost of Goods Sold

2–30. The following data pertain to the Mini Manufacturing Company for the year ended December 31, 2000.

Beginning direct material inventory	$ 2,000
Ending direct material inventory	3,000
Beginning work-in-process inventory	4,000
Ending work-in-process inventory	5,000
Beginning finished goods inventory	9,500
Ending finished goods inventory	8,000
Direct material purchased	22,000
Factory supplies	12,500
Depreciation on the factory	34,000
Assembly-line labor cost	120,000
Depreciation on production equipment	42,000
Other indirect factory costs	12,000

REQUIRED:

a. What is the cost of direct material used during 2000?
b. What is the cost of direct labor during 2000?
c. What is the cost of manufacturing overhead for 2000?
d. What is total manufacturing cost incurred during 2000?
e. What is the cost of goods manufactured for 2000?
f. What is the cost of goods sold for 2000?

LO 5: Inventory and Production Costs Including Cost of Goods Manufactured and Cost of Goods Sold

2–31. The following data pertain to the Ace Manufacturing Company for the year ended December 31, 2001.

Beginning direct material inventory	$ 22,000
Ending direct material inventory	28,000
Beginning finished goods inventory	30,000
Ending finished goods inventory	28,000
Beginning work-in-process inventory	16,000
Ending work-in-process inventory	15,000
Direct material purchased	280,000
Production worker labor cost	290,000
Depreciation on production equipment	80,000
Factory rent	24,000
Other indirect factory costs	36,000

REQUIRED:

a. What is the cost of direct material used during 2001?
b. What is the cost of direct labor during 2001?
c. What is the cost of manufacturing overhead for 2001?
d. What is total manufacturing cost incurred during 2001?
e. What is the cost of goods manufactured for 2001?
f. What is the cost of goods sold for 2001?

LO 5: Preparation of Cost of Goods Manufactured and Cost of Goods Sold Schedules

2–32. The following data pertain to the Adler Manufacturing Company for the year ended December 31, 2001.

Beginning direct material inventory	$ 12,000
Ending direct material inventory	13,000
Beginning work-in-process inventory	24,000
Ending work-in-process inventory	25,000
Beginning finished goods inventory	29,500
Ending finished goods inventory	28,000
Direct material purchased	122,000
Factory utilities	2,500
Rent on the factory	64,000
Assembly worker labor cost	86,000
Depreciation on production equipment	92,000
Other indirect factory costs	22,000

REQUIRED:

a. Prepare a cost of goods manufactured schedule for 2001.
b. Prepare a cost of goods sold schedule for 2001.

LO 5: Preparation of Cost of Goods Manufactured and Cost of Goods Sold Schedules

2–33. The following data pertain to the Clifford Manufacturing Company for the year ended December 31, 2001.

Beginning direct material inventory	$ 2,300
Ending direct material inventory	3,400
Beginning work-in-process inventory	5,500
Ending work-in-process inventory	4,100
Beginning finished goods inventory	6,500
Ending finished goods inventory	5,100
Direct material purchased	12,300
Factory supplies used	500
Depreciation on the factory	22,000
Assembly-line labor cost	48,600
Depreciation on production equipment	12,000
Other indirect factory costs	4,700

REQUIRED:

a. Prepare a cost of goods manufactured schedule for 2001.
b. Prepare a cost of goods sold schedule for 2001.

LO 5: Preparation of Cost of Goods Manufactured Schedule, Cost of Goods Sold Schedule, and Multistep Income Statement

2–34. The following data pertain to the Lowell Manufacturing Company for the year ended December 31, 2001.

Sales	$1,267,000
Beginning direct material inventory	40,000
Ending direct material inventory	50,000
Beginning work-in-process inventory	70,000
Ending work-in-process inventory	60,000
Beginning finished goods inventory	90,000
Ending finished goods inventory	80,000
Direct material purchased	350,000
Indirect material used in production	24,000
Factory supplies used	6,000
Depreciation on the factory	90,000
Depreciation on the sales office	24,000
Depreciation on the administrative office	36,000
Sales salaries	110,000
Assembly-line labor cost	220,000
Factory security guard cost	22,000
Factory supervision	42,000
Depreciation on production equipment	160,000
Depreciation on office equipment	16,000

REQUIRED:

a. Prepare a cost of goods manufactured schedule for 2001.
b. Prepare a cost of goods sold schedule for 2001.
c. Prepare a multistep income statement for 2001.

LO 5: Preparation of Cost of Goods Manufactured Schedule, Cost of Goods Sold Schedule, and Multistep Income Statement

2–35. The following data pertain to the Quintana Manufacturing Company for the year ended December 31, 2001.

Sales	$1,302,000
Beginning finished goods inventory	93,000
Ending finished goods inventory	86,000
Beginning direct material inventory	45,000
Ending direct material inventory	56,000
Beginning work-in-process inventory	72,000
Ending work-in-process inventory	77,000
Direct material purchased	370,000
Indirect material used in production	34,000
Depreciation on production equipment	145,000
Depreciation on office equipment	19,000
Factory supplies used	8,000
Depreciation on the factory	96,000
Depreciation on the sales office	34,000
Depreciation on the administrative office	30,000
Sales salaries	122,000
Assembly-line labor cost	240,000
Factory security guard cost	32,000
Factory supervision	48,000

REQUIRED:

a. Prepare a cost of goods manufactured schedule for 2001.
b. Prepare a cost of goods sold schedule for 2001.
c. Prepare a multistep income statement for 2001.

LO 5: Preparation of Cost of Goods Manufactured Schedule, Cost of Goods Sold Schedule, and Multistep Income Statement

2–36. The following data pertain to the Rodriguez Manufacturing Company for the year ended December 31, 2000.

Sales	$1,124,000
Beginning direct material inventory	55,000
Ending direct material inventory	56,000
Beginning finished goods inventory	83,000
Ending finished goods inventory	96,000
Beginning work-in-process inventory	62,000
Ending work-in-process inventory	67,000
Direct material purchased	290,000
Direct labor cost	220,000
Manufacturing overhead	286,000
Selling expense	122,000
Administrative expense	140,000

REQUIRED:

a. Prepare a cost of goods manufactured schedule for 2000.

b. Prepare a cost of goods sold schedule for 2000.

c. Prepare a multistep income statement for 2000.

LO 5: Preparation of Cost of Goods Manufactured Schedule, Cost of Goods Sold Schedule, and Multistep Income Statement

2–37. The following data pertain to the Avener Manufacturing Company for the year ended December 31, 2000.

Sales	$333,000
Beginning direct material inventory	5,000
Ending direct material inventory	4,000
Beginning work-in-process inventory	6,000
Ending work-in-process inventory	7,000
Beginning finished goods inventory	8,000
Ending finished goods inventory	10,000
Direct material purchased	56,000
Direct labor cost	96,000
Manufacturing overhead	86,000
Selling expense	46,000
Administrative expense	34,000

REQUIRED:

a. Prepare a cost of goods manufactured schedule for 2000.

b. Prepare a cost of goods sold schedule for 2000.

c. Prepare a multistep income statement for 2000.

LO 5: Preparation of Cost of Goods Manufactured Schedule

2–38. The following information is for Megan Hat Manufacturing Company.

Inventory information:

	January 1, 2001	December 31, 2001
Raw materials inventory	$ 9,000	$11,000
Work-in-process inventory	22,000	18,000
Finished goods inventory	42,000	38,000

Other information:

Direct materials purchases	$120,000
Direct labor cost	250,000
Manufacturing overhead	140,000

REQUIRED:

a. What is the cost of direct material used in production?

b. Prepare a cost of goods manufactured schedule in good form.

c. Prepare a cost of goods sold schedule.

d. Appendix: Prepare journal entries to record the following:
   1. The purchase of direct material
   2. The use of direct material in production
   3. Direct labor cost
   4. Manufacturing overhead cost (Use "various accounts" for the credit side of the entry.)
   5. The cost of goods manufactured
   6. The sale of finished goods assuming the sale price was $600,000

LO 5: Preparation of Cost of Goods Manufactured Schedule

2–39. The following information is for Friedman Shelving Manufacturing Company.

Inventory information:

	January 1, 2001	December 31, 2001
Raw materials inventory	$22,000	$24,000
Work-in-process inventory	42,000	43,000
Finished goods inventory	82,000	78,000

Other information:

Direct materials purchases	$280,000
Direct labor cost	540,000
Manufacturing overhead	240,000

REQUIRED:

a. What is the cost of direct material used in production?
b. Prepare a cost of goods manufactured schedule in good form.
c. Prepare a cost of goods sold schedule.
d. Appendix: Prepare journal entries to record the following:
　1. The purchase of direct material
　2. The use of direct material in production
　3. Direct labor cost
　4. Manufacturing overhead cost (Use "various accounts" for the credit side of the entry.)
　5. The cost of goods manufactured
　6. The sale of finished goods assuming the sale price was $1,400,000

LO 5: Preparation of Cost of Goods Manufactured Schedule

2–40. The following information is for Tatum Manufacturing Company.

Inventory information:

	January 1, 2001	December 31, 2001
Raw materials inventory	$2,000	$4,000
Work-in-process inventory	4,000	3,000
Finished goods inventory	8,000	6,000

Other information:

Direct materials purchases	$ 8,000
Direct labor cost	12,000
Manufacturing overhead	9,000

REQUIRED:

a. Prepare a cost of goods manufactured schedule in good form.
b. Appendix: Prepare journal entries to record the following:
　1. The purchase of direct material
　2. The use of direct material in production
　3. Direct labor cost
　4. Manufacturing overhead cost (Use "various accounts" for the credit side of the entry.)
　5. The cost of goods manufactured
　6. The sale of finished goods assuming the sale price was $40,000

LO 5: Preparation of Cost of Goods Manufactured Schedule

2–41. The following information is for Munter Manufacturing Company.

Inventory information:

	January 1, 2001	December 31, 2001
Raw materials inventory	$6,000	$5,000
Work-in-process inventory	3,000	4,000
Finished goods inventory	7,000	9,000

Other information:

Direct materials purchases	$ 9,000
Direct labor cost	10,000
Manufacturing overhead	11,000

REQUIRED:

a. Prepare a cost of goods manufactured schedule in good form.
b. Appendix: Prepare journal entries to record the following:
   1. The purchase of direct material
   2. The use of direct material in production
   3. Direct labor cost
   4. Manufacturing overhead cost (Use "various accounts" for the credit side of the entry.)
   5. The cost of goods manufactured
   6. The sale of finished goods assuming the sale price was $39,000

LO 5: Preparation of Cost of Goods Manufactured Schedule and Multistep Income Statement

2–42. The following information is for Collins Manufacturing Company.

Inventory information:

	January 1, 2001	December 31, 2001
Raw materials inventory	$16,000	$14,000
Work-in-process inventory	23,000	25,000
Finished goods inventory	33,000	36,000

Other information:

Sales	$760,000
Direct materials purchases	159,000
Direct labor cost	110,000
Manufacturing overhead	221,000
Selling expense	62,000
Administrative expense	47,000

REQUIRED:

a. Prepare a cost of goods manufactured schedule in good form.
b. Prepare a multistep income statement in good form.

LO 5: Preparation of Cost of Goods Manufactured Schedule and Multistep Income Statement

2–43. The following information is for Richard Manufacturing Company.

Inventory information:

	January 1, 2001	December 31, 2001
Raw materials inventory	$14,000	$16,000
Work-in-process inventory	25,000	28,000
Finished goods inventory	32,000	36,000

Other information:

Sales	$790,000
Direct materials purchases	162,000
Direct labor cost	140,000
Manufacturing overhead	234,000
Selling expense	72,000
Administrative expense	57,000

REQUIRED:

a. Prepare a cost of goods manufactured schedule in good form.

b. Prepare a multistep income statement in good form.

LO 3: Preparation of a Multistep Income Statement for a Merchandiser

2–44. Bonnie's Pet Cage Company has the following information for 2000:

Sales	$300,000
Cost of goods manufactured	200,000
Selling expense	30,000
Administrative expense	25,000
Beginning finished goods inventory	21,000
Ending finished goods inventory	28,000

REQUIRED:

Prepare a multistep income statement for Bonnie's Pet Cage Company.

LO 3: Preparation of a Multistep Income Statement for a Manufacturer

2–45. Albert's Manufacturing Company has the following information for 2000:

Beginning finished goods inventory	$ 41,000
Ending finished goods inventory	58,000
Sales	600,000
Cost of goods manufactured	400,000
Selling expense	90,000
Administrative expense	60,000

REQUIRED:

Prepare a multistep income statement for Albert's Manufacturing Company for 2000.

LO 5: Preparation of cost of a Multistep Income Statement for a Merchandiser

2–46. Phillips Merchandising Company has the following information for 2000:

Sales	$400,000
Cost of merchandise purchased	300,000
Selling expense	30,000
Administrative expense	20,000
Beginning finished goods inventory	40,000
Ending finished goods inventory	50,000

REQUIRED:

Prepare a multistep income statement for Phillips Merchandising Company for 2000.

LO 5: Preparation of Cost of a Multistep Income Statement for a Merchandiser

2–47. Robinson Merchandising Company has the following information for 2001:

Beginning finished goods inventory	$ 60,000
Ending finished goods inventory	50,000
Sales	840,000
Cost of merchandise purchased	630,000
Selling expense	90,000
Administrative expense	40,000

REQUIRED:

Prepare a multistep income statement for Robinson Merchandising Company for 2001.

LO 6: Determine the Cost of Services Provided and Preparation of a Single-Step Income Statement for a Service Company

2–48. Butterfield's Bookkeeping Service began operations on January 1, 2001. The following information is taken from its accounting records as of December 31, 2001.

Bookkeeping service revenue	$80,000
Bookkeeping salaries	42,000
Bookkeeping office rent	12,000
Depreciation on bookkeeping equipment	2,000
Bookkeeping supplies used	700
Advertising	800

REQUIRED:

a. What is the cost of services provided?
b. Prepare a single-step income statement for Butterfield's Bookkeeping Service.

LO 6: Determine the Cost of Services Provided and Preparation of a Single-Step Income Statement for a Service Company

2–49. Tony's Film Delivery Service began operations on January 1, 2001. The following information is taken from its accounting records as of December 31, 2001.

Delivery revenue	$40,000
Driver wages	22,000
Depreciation on truck	4,000

Fuel cost	2,700
Advertising	800
Bookkeeping cost	240

REQUIRED:

a. What is the cost of services provided?

b. Prepare a single-step income statement for Tony's Film Delivery Service.

LO 3: Preparation of a Multistep Income Statement for a Merchandiser

2–50. Cam's Swimsuit Shop provided the following information for 2001.

Merchandise inventory, January 1, 2001	$ 16,000
Merchandise inventory, December 31, 2001	19,000
Sales	190,000
Advertising	1,200
Store rent	2,400
Purchases of merchandise	82,000
Sales salaries	22,000
Store utilities	3,600
Sales supplies used during 2001	1,000
Sales supplies on hand, December 31, 2001	500
Office rent	800
Administrative salaries	18,000

REQUIRED:

Prepare a multistep income statement for Cam's Swimsuit Shop for 2001.

LO 3: Preparation of a Multistep Income Statement for a Merchandiser

2–51. Leroy's Auto Parts provided the following information for 2001.

Merchandise inventory, January 1, 2001	$ 19,000
Merchandise inventory, December 31, 2001	21,000
Sales	280,000
Advertising	2,200
Depreciation on the store	18,000
Purchases of merchandise	182,000
Sales salaries	21,000
Store utilities	1,200
Depreciation on office building	4,000
Administrative salaries	15,000
Office utilities	600

REQUIRED:

Prepare a multistep income statement for Leroy's Auto Parts for 2001.

LO 6: Preparation of a Single-Step Income Statement for a Service Company

2–52. Dan's Security Service provided the following information for 2001.

Security revenue	$480,000
Advertising	12,000

Depreciation on the home office building	12,000
Security guard wages	362,000
Administrative salaries	21,000
Sales salaries	24,000
Utilities	1,200

REQUIRED:

Prepare a single-step income statement for Dan's Security Service for 2001.

LO 3: Preparation of a Multistep Income Statement for a Merchandiser

2–53. Margaret's Flower Shop provided the following information for 2001.

Merchandise inventory, January 1, 2001	$ 1,000
Merchandise inventory, December 31, 2001	1,200
Sales	42,400
Advertising	3,200
Store rent	1,200
Purchases of merchandise	18,000
Sales salaries	21,000
Utilities	1,300
Sales supplies used during 2001	9,000
Sales supplies on hand, December 31, 2001	300

REQUIRED:

Prepare a multistep income statement for Margaret's Flower Shop for 2001.

LO 2, 3, & 4: Understanding Cost of Goods Sold

2–54. The management of Diversified Incorporated is concerned that few of its employees understand cost of goods sold. The company president has decided that a series of presentations will be made focusing on cost of goods sold.

Assume that the company has formed two teams, Team A and Team B. You and several of your classmates have been assigned to Team B.

Team A is given the responsibility of preparing a presentation detailing the cost of goods sold pertaining to a subsidiary that operates a chain of hardware stores. Team B, your team, has been given the responsibility of preparing a presentation detailing the cost of goods sold of a subsidiary that manufactures electronic calculators.

In short order, Team A has completed its assignment and is ready to make its presentation. Your team, however, is still working. Company executives question why Team A is so far ahead of your team's progress.

REQUIRED:

Working as a group, develop a response to the concerns relating to your teams slow progress. Explain why Team A could complete their assignment so quickly, and why your team will have to work longer.

LO 6: Understanding Service Company Costs

2–55. Assume that you are the manager of an accounting practice. You are concerned about billing your clients so that the company covers all costs and makes a reasonable profit.

REQUIRED:

a. What information might you desire to help develop a method of billing clients?

b. How would you use the information to ensure that costs are covered and profits result?

LO 1, 2, & 4: Understanding Inventory Cost Classifications

2–56. The inventory of a manufacturer is typically grouped into one of three classifications—raw material inventory, work-in-process inventory, and finished goods inventory.

REQUIRED:

Discuss why it provides more useful information to use three classifications of inventory rather than one for a manufacturer.

LO 1, 2, & 4: Understanding Inventory Costs

2–57. Assume that you work for the Acme Wire Manufacturing Company. Some employees in the company are unsure of which costs should be included in inventories and which costs should not. There is also some confusion regarding the logic of including some items while excluding others.

You have been assigned to a group that is responsible for making a presentation on which of Acme's costs would properly be classified as inventory costs and which would not.

REQUIRED:

Prepare a presentation describing the type of items that would be included in inventories and those that would not. Comment on the logic of including some cost items in inventory while excluding others.

LO 1, 2, & 3: General Inventory and Cost Analysis

2–58. One year ago, Herb Smith quit his job at Adcox Medical where he earned $28,000 a year as a health care technician to start the Super CD Store. He invested almost his entire life's savings in the venture and is now concerned. He notes that, when his money was in the bank, he earned about 4% interest. Now, when he compares his company profits to the amount invested in the store, the profits seem lower than what he could have earned if he had simply left the money in the bank. The following information is available for the company's first year of business:

Annual sales	$600,000
Cost of goods sold	450,000
Selling expense	90,000
Administrative expense	50,000
Inventory	300,000
Other assets	30,000
Total liabilities	50,000

The administrative expense includes $30,000 received by Herb in the form of salary. Herb's friend Bill has suggested that a simple $5,000 computer might help with company record keeping and ordering inventory. Herb has indicated that he does not mind the added work or ordering the merchandise without a computer. In fact, when it comes to ordering product, he seems quite proud of the job he is doing as he almost always has the CDs his customers want.

Herb has engaged your services as a consultant to determine whether his feelings are correct about the low earnings of the company and to suggest some possibilities to improve the situation. Also, Herb would like some input regarding the computer.

REQUIRED:
Prepare a report for Herb addressing each of his concerns.

LO 1, 2, & 3:   General Inventory and Cost Analysis

2–59. Alberto Manufacturing Company has been in business for many years. Toward the end of 2000, management began to notice that the company had to rely more and more on borrowing to support the cash flow needs of the operation. Although sales increased in 2001, profits declined and the cash flow problem worsened. The company president is very concerned that the cash shortfall is caused by mismanagement of the daily operation of the factory. Managers argue that the company's operations are quite satisfactory. They cite that expenses have increased only slightly as sales have risen, and that production levels have been dictated by customer demand.

The president has hired your team of consultants to review the situation and comment on the possible problems that exist. The following information is available for 2000 and 2001.

ALBERTO MANUFACTURING COMPANY
Schedule of Cost of Goods Manufactured
For the Year Ending December 31, 2000

Direct Materials:		
Beginning Direct Material Inventory	$ 15,000	
Purchases during 2000	420,000	
Materials Available during 2000	$435,000	
Ending Direct Material Inventory	(45,000)	
Direct Materials Used during 2000		$ 390,000
Direct Labor during 2000		225,000
Total Manufacturing Overhead Cost during 2000		415,000
Manufacturing Cost for Current Period		$1,030,000
Beginning Work-in-Process Inventory 1/1/00		40,000
Cost of Goods Available to be Finished		$1,070,000
Ending Work-in-Process Inventory 12/31/00		(82,000)
Cost of Goods Manufactured during 2000		$ 988,000

ALBERTO MANUFACTURING COMPANY
Income Statement
For the Year Ending December 31, 2000

Sales		$1,758,000
Cost of Goods Sold		
Beginning Finished Goods Inventory	$ 65,000	
+ Cost of Goods Manufactured	988,000	
= Goods Available for Sale in 2000	$1,053,000	
− Ending Finished Goods Inventory	(75,000)	
= Cost of Goods Sold for 2000		978,000
Gross Profit		780,000

Operating Expense:

Selling Expense	$ 355,000	
Administrative Expense	190,000	(545,000)
Operating Income		$ 235,000

ALBERTO MANUFACTURING COMPANY
Schedule of Cost of Goods Manufactured
For the Year Ending December 31, 2001

Direct Materials:

Beginning Direct Material Inventory	$ 45,000	
Purchases during 2001	457,000	
Materials Available during 2001	$502,000	
Ending Direct Material Inventory	(73,000)	
Direct Materials Used during 2001		$ 429,000
Direct Labor during 2001		263,000
Total Manufacturing Overhead Cost during 2001		450,000
Manufacturing Cost for Current Period		$1,142,000
Beginning Work-in-Process Inventory 1/1/01		82,000
Cost of Goods Available to be Finished		$1,224,000
Ending Work-in-Process Inventory 12/31/01		(154,000)
Cost of Goods Manufactured during 2001		$1,070,000

ALBERTO MANUFACTURING COMPANY
Income Statement
For the Year Ending December 31, 2001

Sales		$1,772,000
Cost of Goods Sold		
Beginning Finished Goods Inventory	$ 75,000	
+ Cost of Goods Manufactured during 2001	1,070,000	
= Goods Available for Sale in 2001	$1,143,000	
− Ending Finished Goods Inventory	(93,000)	
= Cost of Goods Sold for 2001		$1,052,000
Gross Profit		720,000
Operating Expense:		
Selling Expense	$ 365,000	
Administrative Expense	228,000	(593,000)
Operating Income		$ 127,000

REQUIRED:

Your team should review the provided information and comment on problems that exist. It may help to segment the statements into sections and assign group members to a particular area. For example, a group member might be assigned to review the purchase and use of direct material, another member might be assigned the direct labor and manufacturing overhead areas, and so forth. Each group member should comment on his or her assigned area as it pertains to cash flow and income.

Chapter 3

Determining Costs of Products

Every year *Fortune* magazine compiles a list of the top 500 publicly traded companies in the United States. This prestigious list is called the Fortune 500. Of the top 25 Fortune 500 companies, most are manufacturing companies demonstrating that manufacturing continues to play a pivotal role in our economy.

In recent years, however, manufacturing companies from outside the United States have begun to exert significant competitive pressure on U.S. manufacturers. The new global marketplace has forced U.S. manufacturers to take a hard look at both the way they operate and the way the results of their operations are measured and evaluated.

One area of vital importance to manufacturing companies is determining the cost of the products they manufacture. If you are the sales manager for IBM's laptop computer division, for example, you must be sure that the selling price you establish is high enough to earn a profit. To ensure that the selling price of each computer exceeds its cost, you need accurate product cost information.

Besides the product pricing decision are several other applications of information about product cost. First, a company must determine the cost of products to compute cost of goods sold on its income statement for a particular period. Second, a company must have product cost information to determine the value of inventories shown on its balance sheet. Third, product cost information helps managers evaluate the efficiency and productivity of a company's manufacturing facility.

In Chapter 2 we stated that the three elements of product cost for a manufacturer are direct material, direct labor, and manufacturing overhead. We also presented an overview of the product costing process. In this chapter we will delve more deeply into the methods that manufacturers use to determine the cost of the individual units of product they produce. ∎

After completing your work on this chapter, you should be able to do the following:

1. Compare and contrast process costing with job order costing.
2. Describe how process costing and job order costing work.
3. Describe the documents used to help control the costs of manufacturing products.
4. Describe how overhead costs are allocated to products.
5. Determine the cost of products using job order costing.
6. Determine the cost of products using process costing.

ACCUMULATING PRODUCT COST—COST ACCOUNTING

The process of assigning manufacturing costs to manufactured products is called *cost accounting.* When we first introduced this term in Chapter 1, we said that it is often used interchangeably with the terms *management accounting* and *managerial accounting,* but that cost accounting is a narrow application of management accounting dealing with costing products. Cost accounting information can help managers plan and control their operations; make decisions about investments in property, plant, and equipment; establish selling prices; and determine the value of inventories on the balance sheet. Cost accounting information also affects reported net income on the income statement, because the cost of the products sold during the income statement period is reported as cost of goods sold.

UNITS OF PRODUCT AS COST OBJECTS

Recall from Chapter 2 that a cost object is any activity or item for which a separate cost measurement is desired. For our purposes in this chapter, we will consider a unit of manufactured product as the cost object. As we said earlier, the cost of a unit of manufactured product includes the cost of the direct material, direct labor, and manufacturing overhead required to produce that unit of product. The amount of direct material included in each unit of production can actually be traced to finished products. Assigning the cost of direct material to production is relatively simple, as long as the company keeps track of the amount of material used to produce each unit of product. Similarly, if a company keeps track of the amount of direct labor used to produce each unit of product, it can readily assess the cost of direct labor used to produce each unit. Unlike direct material and direct labor, however, the amount of manufacturing overhead cost associated with particular units of production is quite abstract.

Manufacturing overhead cost includes all manufacturing cost except direct material or direct labor costs. Accordingly, it includes a wide assortment of factory-related items. Some examples are production design setup, plant security, supervisory salaries, raw materials storage, building maintenance, and factory supplies.

Even though their cost cannot easily be traced to individual units of production, the manufacturing overhead activities mentioned (and many others) are all necessary to produce products, and their cost should be included in the cost of products produced. The problem, of course, is that the cost of these activities cannot be traced directly to the units of product produced. Their cost, therefore, must be allocated to the units. Consider the cost of factory lighting, for example. The production facility has lights turned on so that those who are working on the product can see what they are doing. As units of product make their way through the production process the lights shine on them and lighting cost is incurred. Because the purpose of the lights is to enhance the production process, a certain amount of the cost of lighting should be included in the cost of each unit of product manufactured. Unfortunately, when the power company sends the bill at the end of the month, there is no breakdown as to how much lighting cost is to be included in each unit. The bill only shows the total cost of electricity used, say $10,000. The manufacturer has to determine how to assign some portion of the lighting cost to each unit produced. **Manufacturing overhead allocation** is a process of assigning or allotting an amount of manufacturing overhead cost to each unit of product produced based on some reasonable basis of distribution. This allocation has traditionally been a two-stage process.

manufacturing overhead allocation The process of assigning or allotting an amount of manufacturing overhead cost to each unit of product produced based on some reasonable basis of distribution.

TRADITIONAL MANUFACTURING OVERHEAD ALLOCATION

cost pool An accumulation of the costs associated with a specific cost object.

The first stage in the process of assigning manufacturing overhead costs to products is to gather overhead cost into a cost pool. A **cost pool** is an accumulation of the costs associated with a specific cost object. Traditionally, the cost of manufacturing overhead was gathered into one large cost pool, including all manufacturing costs except for direct material and direct labor.

The second stage is to assign the manufacturing overhead cost gathered in the pool to units of product manufactured. Manufacturers attempt to allocate the amount of manufacturing overhead cost that corresponds to the overhead resources consumed to make the product. In other words, if it seems likely that $1,000 worth of manufacturing overhead resources were consumed to manufacture a pool table, then $1,000 should be allocated to that pool table for overhead. Because it is impractical if not impossible for managers to estimate the amount of overhead associated with each unit of individual product produced, an equitable basis for cost allocation must be determined.

allocation base An amount associated with cost objects that can be used to proportionately distribute manufacturing overhead costs to each cost object.

An **allocation base** is an amount associated with cost objects that can be used to proportionately distribute manufacturing overhead costs to each cost object. The traditional approach to allocating manufacturing overhead cost to units produced is to identify some other cost or item to serve as an indicator of the relative amounts of indirect factory resources used to make each unit of production. This other cost or item is then used as the allocation base. Direct labor hours, direct labor cost, and machine hours are common traditional allocation bases.

It seems logical that a larger unit of production would require the use of more factory resources than a smaller unit of production, which may mean more direct labor, direct materials, machine time, or some combination of these. The idea behind using an allocation base such as direct labor dollars is that if a unit of product requires a large amount of direct labor cost, it follows that its manufacture would also consume a large amount of overhead resources.

As an example, assume Buck Slade Company uses direct labor cost as the allocation base for manufacturing overhead. Assume manufacturing overhead was $1,000,000 and direct labor cost totaled $100,000 for July 2000. Slade can express the relationship between these two costs by dividing the $1,000,000 manufacturing overhead by the $100,000 direct labor cost. Notice that we are dividing the cost we wish to allocate (the $1,000,000 manufacturing overhead) by the allocation base (the $100,000 direct labor cost). The result is the company's overhead application rate. Slade will allocate overhead cost to the units of manufactured product at a rate of $10 per direct labor dollar.

What this means is that every time $1 of direct labor cost is added to a unit of product, $10 of manufacturing overhead cost will be added to the product's cost, as well. A product that requires little direct labor will receive a small allocation for manufacturing overhead. The total direct material cost, direct labor cost, and the total allocated manufacturing overhead cost are then added together to determine the cost of the manufactured product.

For example, assume that Buck Slade Company produces a batch of 15,000 precision cutters. If 15,000 cutters required a total of 80 direct labor hours at $10 per hour, the manufacturing overhead allocation would be $8,000, calculated as follows:

Direct Labor Hours	×	Direct Labor Rate	=	Direct Labor Cost
80	×	$10	=	$800

Direct Labor Cost	×	Overhead Allocation Rate	=	Total Overhead Allocation
$800	×	$10	=	$8,000

This method uses a single manufacturing overhead cost pool and a single, plant-wide application rate. Virtually all manufacturers in the United States used this method until the mid-1980s, and many still do today.

During the mid-1980s, some companies realized that a plant-wide application rate has significant weaknesses. Whereas some manufacturing overhead costs may relate to the allocation base, many others do not. Manufacturing overhead costs are typically caused by (or related to) many different activities—the activity that drives one cost may be totally different from the activity that drives another cost. To use one activity (such as direct labor) as the allocation base for applying all manufacturing overhead cost to product will likely cause some products to be overcosted and others to be undercosted. For example, assume that a company uses direct labor hours to allocate all manufacturing overhead cost, and its factory has five machines, two of which use significant amounts of water for cooling. In this situation, the overhead cost per direct labor hour will include an amount for cooling water. The amount will be allocated to products whether they are produced on a machine that requires cooling water or not. Therefore, products that are produced on machines that do not require cooling water will be overcosted and, because some of the cost of cooling water is allocated to products produced on machines that do not require cooling water, products produced on machines that do require cooling water will be undercosted.

In the past decade, many companies have begun to study the cost incurred in their operations and are attempting to determine the activities that cause those costs. Great strides have been made and the result has been the development of a new costing method that provides more realistic and reasonable cost for units of manufactured product. This new method is activity-based costing.

MANUFACTURING OVERHEAD ALLOCATION USING ACTIVITY-BASED COSTING

activity-based costing
Allocating cost to products based on the activities that caused the cost to happen.

One way to increase the accuracy of product cost is to trace the cost of overhead activities to products based on activities that cause the cost. Allocating cost to products based on the activities that cause the cost is called **activity-based costing.**

This allocation process improves on traditional overhead allocation in two ways. First, an analysis of what causes cost to happen may result in the reclassification of certain costs from manufacturing overhead to direct material, direct labor, or some other direct cost classification. That is, some costs traditionally viewed as indirect can actually be traced directly to units of product and need not be allocated. This in and of itself contributes to a more accurate unit cost because less cost remains to be allocated.

Second, rather than using one giant cost pool and a single allocation base resulting in one plant-wide application rate, activity-based costing uses multiple cost pools to develop multiple application rates. Adding manufacturing overhead cost to the units of production based on the various activities that drive the costs leads to more accurate unit product cost.

For example, say Buck Slade Company has analyzed its $1,000,000 of manufacturing overhead cost and has classified the activities that cause that cost to happen. This analysis has led the company to reclassify $220,000 from manufacturing overhead to direct cost because it found that, using modern technology, it could readily trace those costs directly into units of product as they are produced. The remaining $780,000 manufacturing overhead cost consists of the items listed in Exhibit 3–1.

To implement activity-based costing, we begin by reviewing overhead to identify specific overhead activities and their cost. Once identified, the costs of a given overhead activity are removed from the general overhead pool and grouped together in a separate pool. This action results in costs being accumulated in several small cost pools within practical limits instead of a single large pool. For example, separate pools might be established for the cost of setup, materials handling, quality inspection, and so forth.

The second stage of manufacturing overhead allocation is to assign the cost accumulated in the pool to products. Manufacturers hope to find an activity associated with products that causes the cost and that can also be used as an allocation base. This cause is a **cost driver.** It differs from a traditional allocation base in that it actually *causes* the cost. Traditional allocation bases such as direct labor hours, direct labor cost, and machine hours do not cause cost. Rather, they are cost correlates that have historically been viewed as good indicators of the amount of overhead associated with particular products. The lack of a causal relationship between the cost and the allocation base is a significant weakness of traditional overhead allocation.

The estimated activities for the Buck Slade Company are listed in Exhibit 3–2.

Slade has separated the large $780,000 pool into various small pools and used cost drivers to allocate the manufacturing overhead to products. In other words, Slade allocates manufacturing overhead cost to products based on activities that cause the cost.

cost driver   A cost cause that is used as a cost allocation base.

Exhibit 3–1
Remaining Overhead for Buck Slade Company

Materials purchasing and handling cost	$ 75,000
Production engineering and design	60,000
Production machine setup	40,000
Production machine depreciation	300,000
Production machine maintenance	50,000
Quality testing	100,000
Plant security	25,000
Plant supervision	70,000
Building maintenance	10,000
Factory supplies	20,000
Factory insurance	30,000
Total manufacturing overhead	$780,000

Exhibit 3–2
Estimated Activities for
the Buck Slade
Company

Number of parts	750,000
Number of production runs	25
Number of machine hours	2,000
Number of components tested	25,000
Number of direct labor hours	10,000

Slade has separated the $780,000 manufacturing overhead pool into five smaller pools to be allocated as follows:

Pool 1—Materials purchasing and handling, allocated using the number of parts as the cost driver.

Pool 2—Production engineering and design cost, and production machine setup cost, allocated using the number of production runs as the cost driver.

Pool 3—Production machine depreciation and production machine maintenance, allocated using the number of machine hours as the cost driver.

Pool 4—Quality testing, allocated using the number of components tested as the cost driver.

Pool 5—Remaining manufacturing overhead costs. Because Slade is unable to determine cost drivers, or because it is impractical to determine cost drivers for these remaining costs, a traditional allocation base—direct labor hours—will be used.

To calculate the application rate, we divide the estimated cost from the cost pool by the estimated number of occurrences of the cost driver.

$$\frac{\text{Estimated Overhead Cost}}{\text{Cost Driver}} = \text{Overhead Application Rate}$$

Slade has developed the following applications rates:

Manufacturing Overhead Pool	Cost Driver (Allocation Base)	Application Based on Occurrence of the Cost Driver
Pool 1		
•Materials purchasing and handling cost	Number of parts	$75,000 ÷ 750,000= $0.10 per part
Pool 2		
•Production engineering and design	Number of production runs	$100,000 ÷ 25 = $4,000 per prod. run
•Production machine setup		
Pool 3		
•Production machine depreciation	Number of machine hours	$350,000 ÷ 2,000 = $175 per machine hour
•Production machine maintenance		
Pool 4		
•Quality testing	Number of components tested	$100,000 ÷ 25,000 = $4 per comp. tested
Pool 5		
•Plant security	Number of direct labor hours	$155,000 ÷ 10,000 = $15.50 per direct labor hour
•Plant supervision		
•Building maintenance		
•Factory supplies		
•Factory insurance		

For every part added to a unit of product, $0.10 of manufacturing overhead cost is added to the product as well (Pool 1). Every time a production run is made, $4,000 is added to the cost of the products in that production run (Pool 2). For every machine hour devoted to the unit of product, $175 of manufacturing overhead is added; and for every component tested, $4 of manufacturing overhead is added (Pools 3 and 4). For every hour of direct labor, $15.50 of manufacturing overhead is added to the cost of the product (Pool 5). The total direct material cost, direct labor cost, and total allocated manufacturing overhead cost are then added together to determine the cost of the product.

As an example, take another look at Slade's production run of 15,000 precision cutters. Each cutter is made of three parts. In addition, it takes 16 machine hours and 80 direct labor hours to produce the 15,000 cutters. Finally, during production, samples totaling 1,000 cutters are tested for sharpness. The manufacturing overhead cost for the cutters is calculated as follows:

Manufacturing Overhead Pool	Cost Allocation
Pool 1	
• Materials purchasing and handling cost	$15,000 \times 3 \times \$0.10 = \$ 4,500$
Pool 2	
• Production engineering and design	$1 \times \$4,000 = \$ 4,000$
• Production machine setup	
Pool 3	
• Production machine depreciation	$16 \times \$175 = \$ 2,800$
• Production machine maintenance	
Pool 4	
• Quality testing	$1,000 \times \$4 = \$ 4,000$
Pool 5	
• Plant security	$80 \times \$15.50 = \$ 1,240$
• Plant supervision	
• Building maintenance	
• Factory supplies	
• Factory insurance	
Total manufacturing overhead for the 15,000 cutters	$16,540
Manufacturing overhead per cutter ($16,540 ÷ 15,000)	$ 1.103

Notice that the $16,540 of overhead allocated to the precision cutters when activity-based costing is used is more than double the $8,000 allocated when a traditional allocation method is used. The cutters are not more expensive to make when activity-based costing is used; rather, the amount of overhead allocated to the cutters under activity-based costing is a more accurate representation of the cost attributable to the products produced.

PRODUCT COSTING METHODS

To make informed decisions about which products should be produced and what selling price should be charged, managers need accurate product cost information.

Users of accounting information generally rely on one of two methods for determining the cost of products, the job order cost method and the process cost method. Although both methods are used, they are not interchangeable. A company must select the method best suited to the type of products being made and to the manufacturing process itself.

Job Order Costing Basics

job order costing A costing method that accumulates cost by a single unit, or batch of units.

Job order costing is a method that accumulates the cost of production for each job, each individual unit of production, each order, or each product. This method is used to accumulate the cost of one-of-a-kind and custom-made goods such as custom furniture or custom cabinets, ships, airplanes, bridges, buildings, and advertising posters. For instance, when Boeing manufactured the five Boeing 777-200 passenger jets ordered by Air China in 1997, the airplane manufacturer used job order costing to determine how much each plane costs.

The key consideration for choosing between process costing and job order costing is whether the goods produced consumed similar enough amounts of factory resources (direct material, direct labor, and manufacturing overhead) that an average cost per unit would be an accurate reflection of the product's cost. If the units consumed very different amounts of factory resources, an average cost per unit is meaningless, and job order costing should be used.

Under job order costing, managers keep close track of the material and labor associated with each job. The "job" may consist of a single unit or a batch of units. For example, a job for Boeing would consist of a single airplane. For Perlmuter Printing, however, a job would consist of a batch of 20,000 advertising posters. In either case, the cost of direct material, direct labor, and overhead are accumulated and totaled for each job.

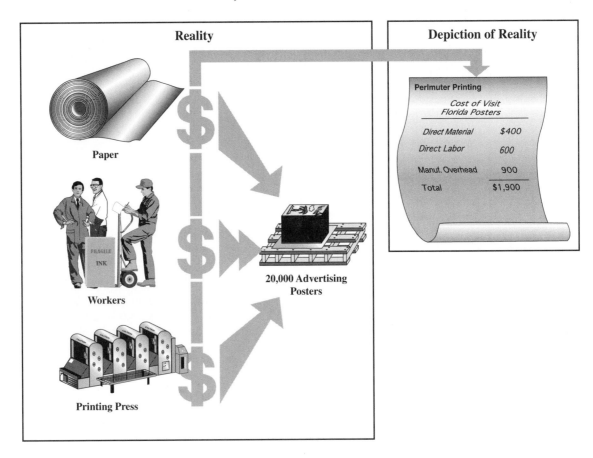

Process Costing Basics

process costing A method of allocating manufacturing cost to products to determine an average cost per unit.

Process costing is a method of allocating manufacturing cost to products to determine an average cost per unit. Process costing is used when units of production are identical, or nearly so, and each unit of production receives the same manufacturing input as the next. Examples of such products are milk, soda, canned goods, breakfast cereal, household cleaners, motor oil, and gasoline. For example, Eastman Kodak uses process costing to determine the cost of the color film it produces.

When process costing is used, total manufacturing cost is divided by the number of units produced to arrive at a per unit cost. For example, if a toothbrush factory makes 2 million toothbrushes and the total production cost is $400,000, then the cost per tooth brush is $0.20, computed as follows:

$$\frac{\text{Total Production Cost}}{\text{Number of Units Produced}} = \text{Cost Per Unit}$$

$$\frac{\$400,000}{2,000,000 \text{ Units Produced}} = \$0.20 \text{ Per Unit}$$

The reason this simple method is adequate for a product such as toothbrushes is that each toothbrush is identical to, and consumes the same amount of resources as, the next. Accordingly, an average cost per toothbrush provides an accurate indication of each unit's cost.

Discussion Questions

3-1. Name four products (other than those mentioned in the text) for which process costing would be appropriate.

3-2. Name four products (other than those mentioned in the text) for which job order costing would be appropriate.

3-3. Are any products difficult to classify? List some and explain the difficulty.

The first product costing method we will explore in detail is job order costing. As we cover job order costing, we will also look at the documents manufacturers use to control factory resources and accumulate the cost of products.

JOB ORDER COSTING

We have seen that in job order costing the job may be the production of a single unit, or a batch of units. The key is that the units produced for one job are dissimilar from the units produced for another job, and that cost information is gathered for each individual production job.

Keeping track of product cost is not as challenging as it may seem. Particular documents help keep track of the direct material, direct labor, and manufacturing overhead associated with each production job.

For example, a company that makes custom boats would keep a list of the direct material cost, direct labor hours, and direct labor cost used to make a boat. It would also need to keep track of the manufacturing overhead associated with each boat made. The firm would total the direct material, direct labor, and manufacturing overhead to determine the boat's cost.

Managers use a system of documents to track the cost of units produced and to control the costs incurred in the factory. We will review these documents—a critical part of a job order cost method—and explore the process of job order costing in the following sections.

The manufacturer in our example, Manta Power Boats, is a top-quality, custom boat manufacturer located in Hollywood, Florida. In contrast to production-line boats—boats made in large quantities that are nearly identical—Manta's boats are manufactured to the specifications of each customer. Customers select the boat style, interior, engines, construction material, and paint scheme they want. No two boats are alike. Let us look at how Manta calculates the cost of one power boat.

Documentation Relating to Job Order Costing

job cost sheet A document that tracks the costs of products and organizes and summarizes the cost information for each job.

When job order costing is used, a document called a **job cost sheet** simplifies tracking the costs of products because it organizes and summarizes the cost information for each job. An example of a job cost sheet is shown in Exhibit 3–3.

The job cost sheet in Exhibit 3–3 will list the manufacturing costs for job 97384. An entry will be made on the job cost sheet each time direct material, direct labor, and manufacturing overhead costs are incurred in connection with the job. Managers can refer to a job cost sheet any time they need information about the cost of producing a particular boat.

A job cost sheet is prepared for each individual unit produced. In Manta's case, the costs for each boat are placed on a separate job cost sheet. In Exhibit 3–3, job 97384 is for a 38-foot Open Fisherman. At any time, Tom Greco, owner of Manta Power Boats, can review the job cost sheet for job 97384 to determine its cost.

Job cost sheets not only help managers keep track of the costs of current production, but they also provide historical information that can help managers estimate the cost of future production. For example, if an order is received for a boat similar to one that Manta has made in the past, Tom Greco can look at the first boat's job cost sheet to help estimate how much the next boat will cost.

Let us now look at how these costs are monitored and measured. We begin with an analysis of direct material.

Exhibit 3–3
Job Cost Sheet for Manta Power Boats

Job Cost Sheet								

Job #: 97384   Date Promised: 7–11–99

Customer: Bill Hudik   Date Started: 6–2–99

Product Description: 38 Open Fisherman

Direct Materials			Direct Labor		Manufacturing Overhead			
Date	Req #	Amount	Date	Amount	Base	Rate	Amount	Total
		$		$			$	$
Total		$		$			$	$

Date Completed: _____

Cost Information for Raw Material   Manufacturers such as Manta generally keep close track of raw material costs because it is such an expensive part of the manufacturing process. The raw materials needed at Manta to build power boats include fiberglass cloth, polyester resin, wood, plastic, aluminum, engines, and much more. Because these materials are so costly, Manta, like other manufacturers, does not allow just any employee to buy raw material on behalf of the company. An unqualified employee might buy too much or too little, or they may buy the wrong raw material altogether. In most manufacturing companies, a request for material is made by the employee in charge of monitoring the raw material inventory levels. This person may be in charge of the materials store room or perhaps is the production supervisor. At Manta, Carl Bevans monitors the amount of material on hand, and when polyester resin is needed, Carl requests that more be purchased. This purchase request comes in the form of a purchase requisition.

purchase requisition
A request form that lists the quantity and description of the materials needed.

A **purchase requisition** is a request form that lists the quantity and description of the materials needed. This form helps to control and monitor all material requested to ensure that the company secures the right amount and quality. Copies of the completed purchase requisition are forwarded to Manta's purchasing department and to the accounts payable clerk in charge of paying the company's bills. Exhibit 3–4 shows the completed materials requisition for Manta Power Boats.

purchasing department
A specialized department that purchases all the goods required by a company.

The **purchasing department** is a specialized department that purchases all the goods required by the company. In the purchasing department, trained individuals called purchasing agents contact several competing vendors or suppliers to obtain the highest-quality material at the lowest price.

purchase order   A formal document used to order material from a vendor.

Once the purchasing agent has selected a vendor, the agent issues a **purchase order,** a formal document created to order material from a vendor. The purchase order specifies the quantity, type, and cost of the materials, payment terms, and method of delivery. Copies of the purchase order are distributed to the receiving department, the accounts payable department, and the vendor. A sample purchase order for Manta Power Boats is shown in Exhibit 3–5.

Exhibit 3–4
Purchase Requisition
for Manta Power Boats

Manta Power Boats Purchase Requisition	
	Number: 1001
Date: 6–4–99	
Name: Carl Bevans	
Department: Production Material Stores	

Quantity	Description
110 gal.	Polyester Resin

Signature: Carl Bevans

Exhibit 3–5
Purchase Order for
Manta Power Boats

Purchase Order

PO #: ___06059702___

Vendor:	_Pitman Sales Company_	**Order Date:**	_6-5-99_
Address:	_8650 SW 132 Street_	**Delivery Date:**	_6-7-99_
	Miami, FL 33156		
Phone:	_305_ – _555_ – _9558_		

Purchase Requisition #: ___1001___   **Department:** ___Prod. Mat. Stores___

Quantity	Description	Unit Cost	Total Cost
110 gal.	Polyester Resin	6.00	660.00

Purchasing Agent: ___Bob Pass___

receiving report A document that indicates the quantity of each item received.

When Manta's receiving department receives the material from the supplier, the receiving clerk compares the material received to the purchase order and completes a receiving report. The **receiving report** is a document that indicates the quantity of each item received. It is used to note any differences between the goods ordered and the goods received. Lauren Elsea, Manta's receiving clerk, completes a receiving report for each delivery received as shown in Exhibit 3–6.

A copy of the receiving report is sent to the accounts payable department. Manta's accounts payable clerk now has three documents related to the purchase: (1) the purchase requisition, (2) the purchase order, and (3) the receiving report. When the accounts payable clerk receives the vendor's invoice for the materials, information on the invoice is matched to the other three documents. If everything is correct, the invoice is paid according to the payment terms.

Exhibit 3–6
Receiving Report for
Manta Power Boats

Receiving Report

Vendor: _Pitman Sales Company_

Purchase Order #: _06059702_   **Date Received:** _6–7–99_

Quantity	Description
110 gal.	Polyester Resin

Receiving Clerk: _Lauren Elsea_

Discussion Question

3–4. The accounts payable department verifies that the information on the vendor's invoice matches the purchase requisition, the purchase order, and the receiving report. What would a discrepancy show if the information on the following documents conflicted?

a. The receiving report conflicts with the vendor's invoice.

b. The purchase order conflicts with the receiving report.

c. The purchase requisition conflicts with the purchase order.

Once the materials have been checked in, they are stored in the materials stores warehouse until they are needed for production. Generally, such storage space is quite secure to protect the raw material from damage and theft.

When the material is needed for production, Manta's production manager, Kevin Dunn, completes a materials requisition. The **materials requisition** is a formal request for material to be transferred from the raw materials storage area to production. The document lists the type of material and the quantity needed. To begin work on the 38-foot Open Fisherman boat for job 97384, fiberglass and polyester resin are needed, so Kevin Dunn has prepared the materials requisition shown in Exhibit 3–7 to transfer this material into production.

materials requisition A formal request for material to be transferred from the raw materials storage area to production.

Exhibit 3–7
Materials Requisition
for Manta Power Boats

Materials Requisition

Req #: 2002

Job #: ___97384___

Date: ___6–16–99___

Quantity	Item #	Description	Unit Cost	Total Cost
55 gal.	PR55X	Polyester Resin	6.00	330.00

Issued By: ___Carl Bevans___

Received By: ___Kevin Dunn___

Keep in mind that a materials requisition is different from a purchase requisition. The purchase requisition is a request to purchase material, whereas the materials requisition is a request by manufacturing personnel to transfer previously purchased material from the materials stores warehouse to production.

The materials requisition is a useful tool for accumulating the cost of products. Materials requisitions show how much material is being used, for what purpose, and at what cost. The information from the materials requisitions is transferred to the job cost sheets to show the quantity and cost of material used for each job.

For instance, Exhibit 3–8 shows how the accounting department at Manta Power Boats transfers information from the materials requisition to the job cost sheet for job 97384.

Materials requisitions are also valuable tools for controlling the movement of materials in the factory. Because the movement is documented, it is easier to monitor employees' use of material. This record helps prevent theft, waste, or other inappropriate use of material.

Cost Information for Direct Labor   Once raw material enters the production process, factory workers begin working with it, converting the material into finished product. Remember from Chapter 2 that the value of the goods in work-in-process inventory is enhanced by the cost of the raw material incorporated into the product *and* by the labor of production workers. Therefore, in accounting records, work-in-process inventory is increased not only by the cost of direct material, but also by the cost of direct labor.

Exhibit 3–8
Transfer of Information from a Materials Requisition Form to a Job Cost Sheet

labor time ticket   A document used to track the amount of time each employee works on a particular production job or a particular task in the factory.

A **labor time ticket** is used to track the amount of time each employee works on a particular production job or a particular task in the factory. Exhibit 3–9 shows a sample labor time ticket for Manta Power Boats.

Labor time tickets include a wealth of information regarding the amount of direct labor associated with each production job. As was the case with the materials requisitions, cost information is transferred from the labor time tickets to the job cost sheet for each job. Exhibit 3–10 shows how information is transferred from the labor time tickets to the job cost sheet for job number 97384 at Manta Power Boats.

Most companies now use computer technology to make entries on labor time tickets. Employees are issued identification cards that are scanned by a card

Exhibit 3–9
Labor Time Ticket for
Manta Power Boats

Labor Time Ticket

Employee: Edward Clark

Employee Number: 127   **Week Ending:** 6-8-99

Job #	M	T	W	T	F	S	S	Total
97384	8	8	4		8			28
97383			4	8				12

Supervisor: MLW   **Receiving Clerk:** E.C.

Exhibit 3–10
Transfer of Information
from Labor Time Tickets
to a Job Cost Sheet at
Manta Power Boats

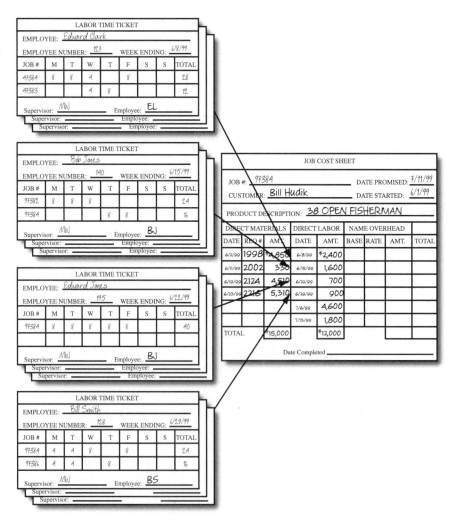

reader. The employee then enters codes to indicate the duties they are performing and the job to which these duties relate. Information from the electronic labor time tickets is stored in a computer file and transferred electronically to electronic job cost sheets.

Manufacturing Overhead

The information from the materials requisitions and labor time tickets makes it easy to trace direct material cost and direct labor cost to individual jobs. Tracing manufacturing overhead is not quite as straightforward.

As discussed, the cost of manufacturing overhead must be allocated to production. Accurate allocation is often difficult to achieve because the benefit of manufacturing overhead expenditures is difficult to trace to individual jobs or units of production. Manufacturing overhead generally benefits the factory as a whole and therefore all units produced. Because it cannot be traced to individual units, manufacturing overhead must be allocated to the individual units produced. As seen in Exhibit 3–11, generally the cost to be allocated is divided by the total allocation base to determine the amount to allocate per occurrence of the allocation base.

Exhibit 3–11
General Formula to Allocate a Cost

$$\frac{\text{Cost to Be Allocated}}{\text{Total Occurences of the Allocation Base}} = \text{Cost Per Occurrence of the Allocation Base}$$

When manufacturing overhead is allocated to production, the first step in the process is selecting an allocation base. One alternative is to use the number of units produced as the allocation base.

If we use the number of units produced as an allocation base, we divide the manufacturing overhead by the number of units to arrive at an amount of overhead per unit. This method of allocation provides an equal amount of manufacturing overhead cost for each unit of production. When the products produced are different from one another, such as Manta's, a uniform cost per unit is generally inadequate for job order costing.

For instance, if the overhead for Manta Power Boats is $75,000, and the company makes five boats, the overhead per boat would be $15,000 for each boat produced, as calculated in Exhibit 3–12.

However, this allocation of $15,000 per boat seems unfair because the boats are so different from one another. It stands to reason that a large boat would consume more factory resources and should receive a higher overhead cost allocation than a small boat. It would be more accurate to allocate according to the resources consumed instead of allocating the exact same manufacturing overhead cost to each boat produced.

In selecting an allocation base, we should strive to find one that will distribute cost fairly. The best allocation base would be one that causes the cost which is to be allocated; but, when a single cost pool is used for manufacturing overhead, it is impossible to find a single allocation base that causes all the cost in the pool. Instead, we attempt to find an allocation base that has the second-best attribute for cost allocation, an allocation base that is correlated to the incurrence of cost. Thus, we should try to find an allocation base that is correlated to the amount of manufacturing overhead resources consumed by each unit produced.

Exhibit 3–12
Allocating
Manufacturing
Overhead Based on
the Number of Units
Produced

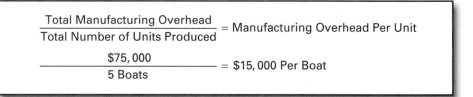

$$\frac{\text{Total Manufacturing Overhead}}{\text{Total Number of Units Produced}} = \text{Manufacturing Overhead Per Unit}$$

$$\frac{\$75,000}{5 \text{ Boats}} = \$15,000 \text{ Per Boat}$$

Manufacturing overhead cost

$15,000

$15,000

$15,000

$15,000

$15,000

Taking a closer look at our boat company example, we note that no two boats are identical, and manufacturing a larger or more complicated boat would, in all likelihood, consume more overhead than a smaller or less complicated boat. As a start, we should find an allocation base that would apportion more overhead to a larger or more complicated boat and less to a smaller, less complicated boat. To do this, the allocation base must increase as boat size or complexity increases.

It seems logical that the amount of factory resources consumed to make a large boat would be more than those consumed to make a small boat. It also seems reasonable that a correlation exists between the number of direct labor hours and the amount of manufacturing overhead resources consumed to make each boat.

As an example, let us use direct labor cost for Manta Power Boats as the allocation base for manufacturing overhead.

When we calculate product cost using actual amounts for direct material, direct labor, and manufacturing overhead, the system is called an actual cost system. Manufacturing overhead is allocated to production based on actual manufacturing overhead cost and the actual amount of the allocation base. For example, we use actual direct labor to allocate actual manufacturing overhead.

Unfortunately, when we do this, several problems emerge. First, managers must wait until the end of the accounting period for actual cost information to be known. Another problem with using actual amounts to allocate overhead is that the overhead application rate fluctuates as actual overhead and direct labor fluctuate.

The overhead application rate will be different for each period if it is calculated using these fluctuating actual amounts. This will result in identical products having different cost amounts unless they were made during the same months.

To eliminate these problems, we estimated annual amounts. In this approach, called a **normal cost system,** product cost reflects actual direct material cost, actual direct labor cost, and estimated overhead costs. Estimated annual manufacturing overhead cost and the annual estimated amount for the allocation base are used to calculate a **predetermined overhead application rate.**

Manta Power Boats allocates overhead using a normal cost system. Suppose, for example, that the estimated annual overhead for Manta Power Boats is $1,000,000 and estimated annual direct labor cost is $1,250,000. In this case, the predetermined overhead application rate is 80 percent ($1,000,000/$1,200,000) of direct labor cost. To determine the overhead cost for the 38-foot Open Fisherman boat for job 97384, we must know the direct labor cost. According to the job cost sheet in Exhibit 3–11, the direct labor cost for this job is $12,000. Using the predetermined overhead application rate of 80 percent of direct labor cost, we calculate the manufacturing overhead associated with job 97384 as follows: $12,000 × 80% = $9,600.

The total cost for job 97384 is $15,000 for direct material, $12,000 for direct labor, and $9,600 for manufacturing overhead. These costs are summarized in the job cost sheet in Exhibit 3–13.

A normal cost system generally is superior to an actual cost system because it smoothes out the fluctuations in product cost due to monthly differences in overhead cost and the allocation base. In addition, because the predetermined application rate is calculated at the very beginning of the year, there is no need to wait until month's end when actual overhead cost information is available to determine product cost.

normal cost system
System in which product cost reflects actual direct material cost, actual direct labor cost, and estimated overhead costs.

predetermined overhead application rate An overhead allocation rate calculated using estimated annual manufacturing overhead cost and the annual estimated amount for the allocation base.

Exhibit 3–13
Completed Job Cost Sheet for Job 97384

Job Cost Sheet

Job #: 97384   Date Promised: 7–11–99

Customer: Bill Hudik   Date Started: 6–2–99

Product Description: 38 Open Fisherman

Direct Materials			Direct Labor		Manufacturing Overhead			Total
Date	Req #	Amount	Date	Amount	Base	Rate	Amount	
6–2–99	1998	$ 4,850	6–8–99	$ 2,400	DL$	80%	$ 1,920	$
6–16–99	2002	330	6–15–99	1,600	DL$	80%	1,280	
6–19–99	2124	4,510	6–22–99	700	DL$	80%	560	
6–23–99	2216	5,310	6–29–99	900	DL$	80%	720	
			7–6–99	4,600	DL$	80%	3,680	
			7–13–99	1,800	DL$	80%	1,440	
Total		$ 15,000		$ 12,000			$ 9,600	$ 36,600

Date Completed: 7–11–99

Activity-Based Costing in Job Order Costing

Let us explore how activity-based costing works by revisiting our Manta Boats example. Manta boats are made of fiberglass and plastic resin formed in molds. A series of molds is used to make the necessary components of each boat. Before a mold can be used, it must be cleaned and waxed to keep the fiberglass and plastic resin from sticking. The process of preparing production equipment to produce a particular product, in this case preparing molds to make a boat, is called setup.

When activity-based costing is used, the cost of each manufacturing activity is accumulated in a dedicated cost pool. In the case of Manta Power Boats, overhead costs are examined and all costs associated with setup are separated out and grouped in a cost pool. Now setup cost can be allocated to products separately from other overhead costs. Assume the annual setup cost at Manta is $117,000.

Next a cost driver must be selected to allocate setup cost. Assume that Manta has decided to use the number of molds used as the cost driver. Preparing a single mold for use causes additional setup cost to occur. The number of molds required to make a single boat varies depending on each boat design. As shown in Exhibit 3–14, a basic Open Fisherman boat requires the use of 10 molds, but a basic sport boat requires the use of only five molds. The actual number of molds used to make a boat varies depending on the customer's specifications.

The effort and cost of setup varies from boat to boat depending on the number of molds required. By using the number of molds as the cost driver, we can reflect the differing amounts of setup effort in the costs of each boat produced. For example, the setup cost for a boat that requires 12 molds will be twice as much as the setup cost for a boat that requires six molds.

The calculations for allocating an overhead cost pool using a cost driver are similar to the calculations using a traditional allocation base. The total estimated annual cost for the cost pool is divided by the estimated annual activity of the cost

Exhibit 3–14
Number of Molds Used
for Each Basic Boat
Design

Number of Molds Used

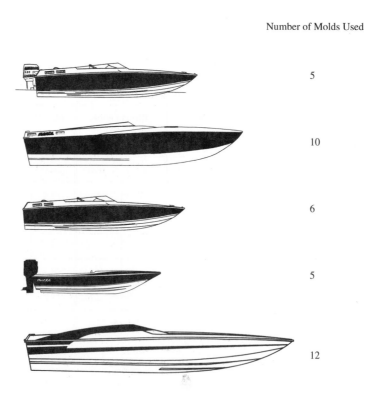

5

10

6

5

12

driver to arrive at an application rate per occurrence of the cost driver. The general formula is as follows:

$$\frac{\text{Total Cost to Be Allocated}}{\text{Total Occurrences of the Cost Driver}} = \text{Cost Per Occurrence of the Cost Driver}$$

Based on past experience, Manta estimates that it will need 360 mold preparations this year to produce 45 boats. Recall that Manta's estimated total annual setup cost is $117,000. With those two numbers, we can find Manta's application rate for setup. Manta divides the estimated total setup cost by the estimated number of mold preparations for the year to determine the application rate for setup cost.

$$\frac{\text{Total Setup Cost}}{\text{Total Number of Mold Preparations}} = \text{Cost Per Mold Preparation}$$

$$\frac{\$117,000}{360 \text{ Mold Preparations}} = \$325 \text{ Per Mold Preparation}$$

We find that with an estimated annual setup cost of $117,000 and a total number of mold preparations of 360, the application rate is $325 per mold used.

Discussion Questions

3-5. If you owned a factory, would you prefer that employees spend time setting up production equipment or producing product?

3-6. If the production manager was able to use one less mold when making a boat, would the cost allocated to that boat be less? Is it likely that the company's actual setup cost would also be less?

Using the activity-based costing application rate, we can now allocate setup cost to each boat based on the number of molds required. For example, boat 1 requires the use of five molds, so its setup cost would be $1,625 (5 × $325 = $1,625). The setup cost allocated to boat 2 would be $3,250 based on the use of 10 molds (10 × $325 = $3,250). The more molds required to make a boat, the higher the allocation for setup cost.

In a traditional cost system, a manager can reduce manufacturing overhead cost associated with a given product by reducing the allocation base used to allocate the cost. For example, if manufacturing overhead is allocated using machine hours, a manager could reduce the overhead allocated to his or her product by reducing the amount of machine time it takes to make the product. This process would reduce the manufacturing overhead cost allocated to the given product, but it would generally not affect the various overhead costs actually incurred by the company. Reducing machine hours has no significant effect on the amount the company spends for manufacturing overhead items such as property taxes, plant insurance, plant security, indirect material, indirect labor, and so forth. Even though accounting records would indicate a lower cost for that product's manufacturing overhead, the reduced machine hours would have little effect on the dollars the company spent for manufacturing overhead.

When activity-based costing is used to reduce the setup cost of a particular boat, a manager would try to decrease the number of molds used. For instance, if the number of molds used to make boat 2 were reduced by one mold, the cost allocated to that boat would be reduced by $325. With this cost reduction technique, the decrease in the allocation base (the cost driver) actually reduces the amount of cost incurred by the company. That is, reducing the number of molds used actually reduces the amount of work that must be done to make a boat. In general, this reduction in work contributes to true cost savings for the company.

We have seen how well job order costing works for custom-made, one-of-a-kind products, but tracking the cost of each unit would be impractical if hundreds or thousands of identical products are made on a dedicated production line. In such a case, a process costing method is preferred.

PROCESS COSTING

Recall that with process costing we allocate cost to products by dividing the total manufacturing cost of the period by the number of units produced to arrive at an average per unit cost. The basic method is simple—just total direct materials, direct labor, and manufacturing overhead; then divide by the number of units produced.

For example, to determine the cost of each tube of toothpaste made in a toothpaste factory, we first determine the total manufacturing cost and divide it by the number of units produced. Assume that the total manufacturing cost for toothpaste is $100,000 and the total number of units produced is 1 million. The cost per tube is 10 cents per tube ($100,000 / 1,000,000 = $0.10). Because each tube of toothpaste is identical to the next, the 10 cents per unit would be a reasonably accurate measure of the cost of each unit. This method only works well if all the units produced are the same—if each unit of production is identical to the next, with the exception of minor variations such as color.

Process costing presents some challenges, however, because some units are only partially completed at the end of the accounting period. To reflect reasonably accurate cost amounts, process costing calculations must accommodate situations when some units are only partially completed.

Like job order costing, process costing is simply a method to help managers determine the cost of products. It provides several key items of information:

1. The number of equivalent units of production
2. The cost per unit
3. The cost of the completed units
4. The cost of the units that remain in ending work-in-process inventory

An understanding of the basics of process costing is a necessary foundation to using product cost information wisely. Let us take a closer look at process costing and the complexities related to beginning and ending work-in-process inventories.

Assume that a company makes decorative pink flamingos. The process to make the decoration is simple. A two-part mold is pressed together and the inside coated with hot plastic. After the plastic has cooled and hardened, the mold is pulled apart and the animal figure drops out. It is finished except for painting the eyes and beaks and adding the legs.

Equivalent Units

The number of units produced must be established before a cost per unit can be determined. In our example, assume that 10,000 flamingos were completed and another 1,000 are still in production. The 1,000 units in production comprise the work-in-process inventory. Obviously the 10,000 units completed should be included in the number of units produced, but what about the other 1,000 units? By definition, units in ending work-in-process inventory are incomplete. Thus, it would be inaccurate to assign the same cost per unit to these units as to the completed units. However, they required expenditures for direct material, direct labor, and manufacturing overhead to bring them to their present state of completion. Thus, some cost should be assigned to these units. Let us see how we arrive at a cost.

The 1,000 flamingos in work-in-process inventory are at various stages of completion. It would be impractical to determine the percentage of completeness for each individual unit of production, so we use an average. In our example, on average, the flamingos in work-in-process inventory are approximately 40 percent complete.

Because the flamingos are only 40 percent complete, we should not include the entire 1,000 units in the number of units produced. Instead, we proportion the number of units by multiplying the number of units by their average completion percentage. Because the 1,000 flamingos are on average 40 percent complete, they are the equivalent of 400 completed flamingos (1,000 × 40% = 400 equivalent units).

Theoretically, if we had started only 400 flamingos into the production process, we could have concentrated our efforts on those 400 units and possibly completed them. However, we started 1,000 units into the production, and we ended up with 1,000 units that were 40 percent complete, which is equivalent to 400 completed units.

equivalent units The number of units that would have been completed if all production efforts resulted in only completed units.

In process costing, **equivalent units** are the number of units that would have been completed if all production efforts resulted in only completed units. The number of equivalent units is calculated by adding the number of completed units to the number of units in ending work-in-process inventory times their percentage complete. In our example the calculations for the number of equivalent units of production—10,400 units—is as follows:

	Number of Raw Units		Percent Complete		Equivalent Units
Units completed	10,000	×	100%	=	10,000
Ending work in process	1,000	×	40%	=	400
Total equivalent units					10,400

It is likely that the percentage of completion for direct material is different from that of direct labor or manufacturing overhead. Product costs would be more accurate if we used separate completion percentages for direct material, direct labor, and manufacturing overhead. Although necessary in practice, such precise calculations greatly complicate process costing. To keep our example simple and understandable, we will use a single percentage to represent the degree of completion for direct material, direct labor, and manufacturing overhead.

Cost Per Equivalent Unit

In our example, we also assume that the manufacturer uses the average inventory cost flow method. Generally acceptable accounting principals allow companies to use the first in first out (FIFO), last in first out (LIFO), or the average cost flow method. In process costing, the FIFO and average cost flow methods are popular.

The FIFO cost flow method assumes that the cost of the first units added to inventory is the first cost removed from inventory. Thus, the cost of units must be tracked through the inventory records so the first cost in is the first cost out. As you might expect, this complicates process costing calculations. To keep our example simple, we assume the average cost flow method is used.

Now let us examine the cost associated with producing the 10,400 equivalent units in our flamingo factory. Assume the production costs are $5,400 as summarized in Exhibit 3–15.

Exhibit 3–15
Summary of
Production Cost

Cost of beginning work in process	$ 500
Current month's cost	4,908
Total	$5,408

To compute cost per unit when the average cost flow method is used in process costing, we divide the total production cost by the number of equivalent units as follows:

$$\frac{\text{Total Production Cost}}{\text{Equivalent Units}} = \text{Cost Per Equivalent Unit}$$

$$\frac{\$5,408}{10,400 \text{ Equivalent Units}} = \$0.52 \text{ Per Equivalent Unit}$$

In our example we see that the cost per flamingo is $0.52. Now that we know the cost of each unit produced, we can determine the cost of the ending work-in-process inventory and the cost of the units completed. Barring theft or other losses, units of production are either completed and transferred to finished goods inventory, or they remain in ending work-in-process inventory. Therefore, it stands to reason that production costs are associated either with completed units or with units in ending work-in-process inventory.

Cost of Ending Work-in-Process Inventory

The cost of ending work-in-process inventory is shown as an asset on manufacturers' balance sheets. To determine this cost, the number of equivalent units (not raw units) in ending work-in-process inventory is multiplied by the cost per unit. For our flamingo example, 400 equivalent units are in ending work-in-process inventory and the cost per unit is $0.52. Therefore, the cost of the ending work-in-process inventory is $208 as follows:

Number of Equivalent Units		Cost Per Unit		Cost of Ending Work-in-Process Inventory
400	×	$0.52	=	$208

Cost of Completed Units

To determine the cost of completed units, we multiply the number of completed units by the cost per unit. For our flamingo example, 10,000 completed units is multiplied by the $0.52 cost per unit. The cost of the completed units then is $5,200, calculated as follows:

Number of Units		Per Unit Cost		Cost of Units Completed and Transferred to Finished Goods Inventory
10,000	×	$0.52	=	$5,200

The cost of completed units is important because initially it becomes part of finished goods inventory. Then, as products are sold, the cost of sold units becomes part of cost of goods sold on the income statement.

Assuming no units are spoiled, stolen, or otherwise lost, the cost of production is either transferred to finished goods inventory or remains as the cost of ending

Exhibit 3–16
Flow of
Manufacturing Cost

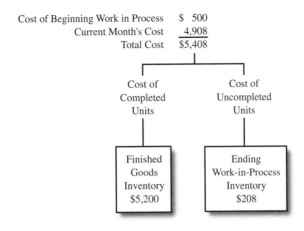

Cost of Beginning Work in Process $ 500
Current Month's Cost 4,908
Total Cost $5,408

Cost of Completed Units

Cost of Uncompleted Units

Finished Goods Inventory $5,200

Ending Work-in-Process Inventory $208

work-in-process inventory. In our example the total manufacturing cost was $5,408. If no units are lost or spoiled during production, the actual units are either completed and physically transferred to finished goods or they remain in ending work-in-process inventory. As we see in Exhibit 3–16, part of the $5,408 total manufacturing cost is transferred to finished goods inventory, and the remainder reflects the cost of the units that remain in ending work-in-process inventory.

As stated at the beginning of this chapter, it is important for managers, such as the sales manager for IBM's lap top computer division, to know how much products cost. Otherwise, how could managers know which products are profitable and which are not? Whether it is being used to determine the company's cost of goods sold, the cost of inventories shown on the balance sheet, or to help set selling prices and determine the profitability of individual products, accurate product cost information is essential.

SUMMARY

As American manufacturing companies experience increasing competition, both domestic and foreign, accurate costing of the products they produce becomes ever more important. Information about the cost of manufactured product is useful in establishing a selling price for the products, determining cost of goods sold on the income statement, and valuing of inventories on the balance sheet.

The cost of a manufactured product is composed of the cost of direct materials, direct labor, and manufacturing overhead associated with the units of product produced. Although accounting for the cost of direct materials and direct labor is relatively straightforward, determining the amount of manufacturing overhead that should be included in a unit of manufactured product is more difficult because these costs must be allocated to the units of product produced.

The traditional method of allocating manufacturing overhead to product uses a plant-wide application rate based on a single allocation base. Manufacturing overhead allocation using activity-based costing uses multiple application rates based on the various activities that cause costs to be incurred.

Job order costing is one of two main methods used to accumulate product costs and is most appropriate when units or batches of production are unique. Under this method, cost information is gathered for each production job. The second of the two main product costing methods is called process costing and is most appropriate when units of production are identical and each unit of production receives the same manufacturing input as the next.

Regardless of whether the job order costing method or the process costing method is used, the overall purpose of accumulating product costs is to provide managers with the information they need to make many of the decisions necessary to plan and control their operations.

APPENDIX

This appendix is intended to provide a basic overview of how costs are recorded for manufactured products.

After completing your work in this appendix, you should be able to record the following types of entries:

1. The use of direct material in production
2. The use of direct labor for production
3. The accumulation of manufacturing overhead
4. The allocation of manufacturing overhead to production
5. The transfer of the cost of a completed job to finished goods
6. The entry to close over or under applied manufacturing overhead
7. The transfer of the cost of completed products to finished goods when process costing is used

The following accounts will be used for the entries in this appendix:

1. Cash
2. Raw materials inventory
3. Work in process inventory
4. Manufacturing overhead incurred
5. Manufacturing overhead applied
6. Finished goods inventory
7. Accumulated depreciation
8. Utilities payable
9. Cost of goods sold

Recall that debits increase assets, expenses, and losses, while credits increase liabilities, equity, revenues, and gains. The dollar amount of the debits must equal that of the credits in each journal entry.

We will use the job cost sheet in Exhibit 3–13 for the 38 Open Fisherman job 97384 to provide information for the entries that follow. In practice, separate entries are made for each transfer of material, each payment of wages, and each application of manufacturing overhead. To simplify our example, we will make entries that summarize the amounts for each cost category.

1. The following entry records the $15,000 of direct material used to manufacture job 97384.

Work in process	15,000	
Raw material		15,000
To record the transfer of direct		
material to production for job 97384.		

2. The following entry records the $12,000 of direct labor cost incurred to manufacture job 97384.

Work in process	12,000	
Cash		12,000
To record direct labor for job 97384.		

3. The Manta Power Boats example indicates that the actual manufacturing overhead for the month is $75,000. We will assume that the manufacturing overhead is composed of the following items:

Factory rent	$33,000
Factory utilities	11,000
Factory supervision	23,000
Depreciation for production equipment	8,000
Total	$75,000

We will record the actual manufacturing overhead costs listed above in an account called manufacturing overhead incurred. Sometimes this account is called actual manufacturing overhead or simply manufacturing overhead.

The following entries would be made to record the actual overhead costs listed previously:

Manufacturing overhead incurred	33,000	
Cash		33,000
To record factory rent for June 1999.		

Manufacturing overhead incurred	11,000	
Cash (or utilities payable)		11,000
To record factory utilities for June 1999.		

Manufacturing overhead incurred	23,000	
Cash		23,000
To record factory supervision for June 1999.		

Manufacturing overhead incurred	8,000	
Accumulated depreciation		8,000
To record depreciation of production equipment June 1999.		

After the above entries have been posted, the manufacturing overhead incurred account has a balance of 75,000 as shown in the following T-account:

Manufacturing Overhead Incurred

33,000	
11,000	
23,000	
8,000	
75,000	

4. As you recall from the chapter, the actual costs of manufacturing overhead items is not generally assigned directly to particular products being manufactured. Rather, a predetermined overhead application rate is used to allocate manufacturing overhead to production. In our example, the overhead is allocated at 80 percent of direct labor cost. Therefore job 97384 was allocated overhead of $9,600.

Work in process	9,600	
Manufacturing overhead applied		9,600
To apply manufacturing overhead to job 97384.		

Note that the account used to record the application of manufacturing overhead to production is different from the one used to record the actual manufacturing overhead costs itself. The use of different accounts allows managers and accountants to keep track of both the actual overhead costs incurred and the overhead applied to production.

5. When job 97384 is completed, its cost is transferred to finished goods as follows:

Finished goods	36,600	
Work in process		36,600
To transfer the completed job from production to finished goods.		

6. As you might imagine, the actual amount of manufacturing overhead cost incurred will be different than the amount applied to production. In a given month, the actual amount of overhead may be more than the amount applied and in another month it may be less. The hope is that the differences will nearly balance out during the year. If the amount applied to production exceeds the actual overhead amount, overhead is over applied. If the amount applied to production is less than the actual overhead amount, overhead is under applied. The under or over application of overhead is monitored during the year but generally no accounting entries are made to dispense with the amount until the end of the year. In most cases, an accounting entry is made at year end to close the manufacturing overhead incurred, and manufacturing overhead is applied to cost of goods sold. Because the amount of under or over applied overhead is generally relatively small, and most product cost ends up in cost of goods sold by year end, closing the overhead accounts to cost of goods sold is adequate for most companies.

Assume that the year end balances in the manufacturing overhead incurred and manufacturing overhead applied accounts are as follows:

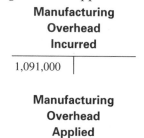

Manufacturing Overhead Incurred

1,091,000 |

Manufacturing Overhead Applied

| 1,072,000

In this case, manufacturing overhead is $19,000 under applied. The following entry closes the manufacturing overhead accounts to cost of goods sold.

Cost of goods sold	1,091,000	
Manufacturing overhead incurred		1,091,000
To close manufacturing overhead incurred to cost of goods sold.		

Manufacturing overhead applied	1,072,000	
Cost of goods sold		1,072,000
To close manufacturing overhead applied to cost of goods sold.		

7. The next entry is to transfer of the cost of completed products to finished goods when process costing is used.

You have already learned to record direct material, direct labor, and manufacturing overhead in the work-in-process account. Those entries are basically the same for job order and process costing. The purpose of the next section is to emphasize the fact that the cost calculated for the units completed in process costing is the same amount transferred from work in process to finished goods.

According to the information presented in the flamingo example, goods costing $5,200 were completed and transferred to finished goods. The entry to record this transaction is as follows:

Finished goods	5,200	
Work in process		5,200
To transfer completed goods from production to finished goods.		

The above entry is significant in arriving at appropriate ending balances in the inventory accounts. After the $5,200 is transferred to finished goods, the work-in-process account and finished goods have balances of $208 and $5,200, respectively, as shown below.

Work in Process

500	5,200
4,908	
5,408	5,208
208	

Finished Goods

5,200	

APPENDIX SUMMARY

Work in process is debited to record the transfer of direct material to production and the incurrence of direct labor. Manufacturing overhead incurred is debited to record the actual amount of manufacturing overhead cost incurred. To apply manufacturing overhead to production, work in process is debited and manufacturing overhead applied is credited. If the amount applied to production exceeds the actual overhead amount, overhead is over applied. If the amount applied to production is less than the actual overhead amount, overhead is under applied. Manufacturers generally make an accounting entry at year end to close the manufacturing overhead incurred and manufacturing overhead applied accounts to cost of goods sold. When products are completed, finished goods is debited and work in process is credited for the cost of those products.

KEY TERMS

activity-based costing   M-72
allocation base   M-71
cost driver   M-73
cost pool   M-71
equivalent units   M-91
job cost sheet   M-78
job order costing   M-76
labor time ticket   M-83
manufacturing overhead
  allocation   M-71

materials requisition   M-81
normal cost system   M-87
predetermined overhead
  application rate   M-87
process costing   M-76
purchase order   M-79
purchase requisition   M-79
purchasing department   M-79
receiving report   M-80

REVIEW THE FACTS

A. Describe a manufacturing overhead cost pool.
B. What are the two stages of assigning manufacturing overhead cost to products?
C. List three traditional manufacturing overhead allocation bases.
D. What is the significant weakness of a plant-wide allocation base?
E. What is activity-based costing?
F. In what two ways does activity-based costing improve upon the traditional approach to manufacturing overhead allocation?
G. Describe a cost driver.
H. What are the general characteristics of products for which process costing would be used?
I. What are the general characteristics of products for which job order costing would be used?
J. What is the purpose of a job cost sheet?
K. Which form is sent to a vendor to order materials and supplies?
L. What is the purpose of a receiving report?
M. What is the difference between a purchase requisition and a materials requisition?
N. Which type of form is used to track the amount of labor associated with various jobs?
O. List the four key items of information provided by process costing.
P. Define the term *equivalent units* as used in process costing.

APPLY WHAT YOU HAVE LEARNED

LO 1:   Compare Process Costing with Job Order Costing

3–7. Following is a list of several products.

1. _____ Commercial jetliners
2. _____ Hair spray
3. _____ Oil tankers
4. _____ Breakfast cereal
5. _____ Office buildings
6. _____ Aspirin
7. _____ Dog food
8. _____ Advertising posters
9. _____ Custom kitchen cabinets
10. _____ Gasoline

REQUIRED:
For each item, indicate whether job order costing (J) or process costing (P) would be the preferred costing method.

LO 4:   Calculate and Describe How Overhead Costs Are Allocated to Products

3–8. The Jessie Lynne Company manufactures playground equipment. For 2000, budgeted manufacturing overhead is $240,000. Budgeted direct labor is 30,000 hours at a cost of $384,000. Budgeted machine hours are 12,500.

REQUIRED:

a. When production begins on January 1, 2000, would it be a good idea for the managers to determine the cost of the manufacturing overhead associated with each swing set produced, or should managers wait for this information until actual overhead cost amounts are available at the end of the year?

b. If we assume that managers need to know the manufacturing overhead cost associated with the playground equipment as soon as the equipment is manufactured, would *actual* overhead cost information be available when the first few swing sets are made in January?

c. If we assume managers need to know the overhead cost associated with the playground equipment as soon as the equipment is made, and it is too early in the year to have actual overhead cost information, what overhead cost information must be used to allocate overhead cost to playground equipment produced by the company?

d. Determine the overhead application rates based on the following:
  (1) Direct labor hours
  (2) Direct labor cost
  (3) Machine hours

e. If you were asked to help select an allocation base for the Jessie Lynne Company, which of the three used in (d) would you recommend? Which would you not recommend? Why?

LO 4: Calculate Traditional Overhead Allocation

3–9. The Griswald Company allocates manufacturing overhead to production based on direct labor hours. The following information is available for Griswald:

Estimated manufacturing overhead	$403,200
Actual manufacturing overhead	$378,000
Estimated direct labor hours	21,000
Actual direct labor hours	20,000

REQUIRED:

a. Compute Griswald's overhead application rate.

b. Assuming that Griswald's overhead application rate is $19, calculate the amount of overhead that should be allocated to production.

c. Appendix: Prepare the following journal entries:
  (1) Record the actual manufacturing overhead. (Use "various accounts" for the credit side of the entry.)
  (2) Assuming that Griswald's overhead application rate is $19, record the overhead allocated to production.
  (3) Close the over or under application of overhead.

LO 4: Calculate Traditional Overhead Allocation

3–10. The Anderson Company allocates manufacturing overhead to production based on machine hours. The following information is available for Anderson:

Estimated manufacturing overhead	$2,000,000
Actual manufacturing overhead	$2,100,000
Estimated machine hours	125,000
Actual machine hours	140,000

REQUIRED:

a. Compute Anderson's overhead application rate.
b. Assume that Anderson's overhead application rate is $18. Calculate the amount of overhead that should be allocated to production.
c. Appendix: Prepare the following journal entries:
   (1) Record the actual manufacturing overhead. (Use "various accounts" for the credit side of the entry.)
   (2) Assuming that Anderson's overhead application rate is $18, record the overhead allocated to production.
   (3) Close the over or under application of overhead.

LO 4: Calculate Traditional and ABC Overhead Allocation

3–11. The president of Simple Products, Inc. is attending a management seminar and has just heard about activity-based costing. He wonders whether it would help his company.

Simple Products, Inc. uses common machinery to manufacture two simple products. Each year, there are two production runs for each product requiring similar setup effort. Manufacturing overhead includes setup cost of $50,400 per year. Total overhead for the company including the setup cost is $198,000 annually and direct labor hours are expected to total 18,000 for the year.

The following information is available for products A and B.

	Product A	Product B
Units produced	1,000	8,000
Direct material cost per unit	$14	$14
Direct labor cost per unit	$24	$24
Machine hours per unit	1	1
Direct labor hours per unit	2	2

REQUIRED:

a. Calculate the cost per unit for each product using traditional overhead allocation.
b. Calculate the cost per unit for each product using activity-based costing.
c. Do you believe activity-based costing would benefit Simple Products, Inc.? Explain your answer.

LO 4: Calculate Traditional and ABC Overhead Allocation

3–12. The president of Complex Products, Inc. is attending a management seminar and has just heard about activity-based costing. She wonders whether it would help her company.

Complex Products, Inc. uses common machinery to manufacture two complex products. Each year, there are two production runs for each product requiring similar setup effort. Manufacturing overhead includes setup cost totaling $52,000. To maintain a competitive edge, these products are updated periodically to conform to the latest technological advancements. These engineering changes are considered part of manufacturing overhead and cost $26,000 per year. Total overhead for the company including the cost of setup and engineering changes is $175,000 per year. Direct labor hours total 7,000 for the year.

The following information is available for products C and D.

	Product C	Product D
Units produced	1,000	1,000
Direct material cost per unit	$24	$24
Direct labor cost per unit	$36	$48
Machine hours per unit	6	8
Direct labor hours	3	4
Engineering changes per year	6	2

REQUIRED:

a. Calculate the cost per unit for each product using traditional overhead allocation.

b. Calculate the cost per unit for each product using activity-based costing.

c. Do you believe activity-based costing would benefit Complex Products, Inc.? Explain your answer.

LO 4: Calculate Traditional and ABC Overhead Allocation

3–13. The following estimates are available for Violette Manufacturing for 2000.

VIOLETTE MANUFACTURING
Estimated Manufacturing Overhead
For the Year Ended December 31, 2000

Materials handling cost	$ 50,000
Product engineering	110,000
Production machine setup	200,000
Production machine depreciation	450,000
Quality testing	100,000
Other overhead cost	250,000
Total manufacturing overhead	$1,160,000

VIOLETTE MANUFACTURING
Estimated Overhead Activities
For the Year Ended December 31, 2000

Number of material movements	200,000
Number of product engineering hours	4,400
Number of machine setups	100
Number of machine hours	18,000
Number of tests performed	125,000
Number of direct labor hours	25,000

The following information is available for production runs of two products, the FP111 and the FP222:

	FP111	FP222
Selling price	$ 23	$ 26
Number of units produced	5000	500
Direct material cost	$60,000	$6,000
Direct labor cost	$14,400	$1,440
Number of material movements	10,000	1,000
Number of product engineering hours	100	100
Number of machine setups	1	1
Number of machine hours	200	20
Number of tests performed	1,250	125
Number of direct labor hours	800	80

Violette Manufacturing uses a traditional overhead allocation system. Manufacturing overhead is allocated based on direct labor hours.

Violette Manufacturing's sales manager has submitted a proposal that would shift the marketing focus to low-volume products such as the FP222. The proposal is prompted by the higher markups that can be charged for these products without customer complaint. The company president is concerned that the company's cost per unit may be sending the wrong message. He recently learned of activity-based costing and wonders if it might help.

Assume that you are part of a group that has been assigned to review the situation.

REQUIRED:

a. Determine the per unit cost for FP111 and FP222 using direct labor hours as the allocation base for all manufacturing overhead cost.

b. Determine the per unit cost for FP111 and FP222 using activity-based costing to allocate manufacturing overhead cost. (Note: Allocate other overhead cost based on direct labor hours.)

c. Discuss the marketing manager's proposal in light of your findings. Discuss what would happen if the marketing manager's sales strategy was adopted.

LO 4: Calculate Traditional and ABC Overhead Allocation

3–14. The following estimates are available for George Manufacturing for 2000.

GEORGE MANUFACTURING
Estimated Manufacturing Overhead
For the Year Ended December 31, 2000

Production machine setup	$ 75,000
Production machine depreciation	240,000
Quality testing	25,000
Other overhead cost	150,000
Total manufacturing overhead	$490,000

GEORGE MANUFACTURING
Estimated Overhead Activities
For the Year Ended December 31, 2000

Number of machine setups	100
Number of machine hours	3,200
Number of tests performed	50,000
Number of direct labor hours	16,000

The following information is available for production of two products, the AA1 and the BB2:

	AA1	BB2
Selling price	$ 2.40	$3.25
Number of units produced	10,000	500
Direct material cost	$ 5,000	$ 250
Direct labor cost	$ 6,400	$ 320
Number of machine setups	1	1
Number of machine hours	100	5
Number of tests performed	100	50
Number of direct labor hours	400	20

George Manufacturing uses a traditional overhead allocation system. Manufacturing overhead is allocated based on direct labor hours. George Manufacturing's sales manager has submitted a proposal that would shift the marketing focus to low-volume products such as the BB2. The proposal is prompted by the higher markups and lack of competition, even at high selling prices.

The company president is concerned that the company's cost per unit may be sending the wrong message. He recently learned of activity-based costing and wonders if it might help.

Assume that you are a member of a work team that has been assigned to review the situation.

REQUIRED:

a. Determine the per unit cost for AA1 and BB2 using direct labor hours as the allocation base for all manufacturing overhead cost.
b. Determine the per unit cost for AA1 and BB2 using activity-based costing to allocate manufacturing overhead cost. (Note: Allocate other overhead cost based on direct labor hours.)
c. Discuss the marketing manager's proposal in light of your findings. Discuss what would happen if the marketing manager's sales strategy was adopted.

LO 4: Calculate Traditional Overhead Allocation

3–15. The Nunez Company allocates manufacturing overhead to production based on cost of direct labor. The following information is available for Nunez:

Estimated manufacturing overhead	$3,500,000
Actual manufacturing overhead	3,485,000
Estimated cost of direct labor	1,750,000
Actual cost of direct labor	1,700,000

REQUIRED:

a. Compute the overhead application rate for the Nunez Company.
b. Assume that the overhead application rate for Nunez is 190%. Calculate the amount of overhead that should be allocated to production.

LO 4 & 5: Calculate Traditional Overhead Allocation and Determine the Cost of Products Using Job Order Costing

3–16. LHE Custom Truck Bodies makes aluminum truck bodies for medium and large trucks. The estimated manufacturing overhead for 2001 is $40,000, and the estimated direct labor cost is $60,000. Manufacturing overhead is applied to production based on direct labor cost.

The following information pertains to truck bodies manufactured during February 2001.

Beginning work-in-process inventory:

Job 101	Direct material	$1,000
	Direct labor	2,000
Job 102	Direct material	750
	Direct labor	1,200

Cost for current month:

Direct material	Job 101	$ 500
	Job 102	1,100
	Job 103	2,300

Direct labor	Job 101	$ 800
	Job 102	1,300
	Job 103	3,200

Job 101 was completed and sold in February and job 102 was completed, but has not been sold. Job 103 remains in production.

REQUIRED:

a. What is the cost of LHE's beginning work-in-process inventory for February 2001?

b. What is the cost of LHE's ending work-in-process inventory for February 2001?

c. **(1)** What is the cost of job 101?
   (2) How would job 101 appear on LHE's financial statements?

d. **(1)** What is the cost of job 102?
   (2) How would job 102 appear on LHE's financial statements?

LO 4 & 5: Calculate Traditional Overhead Allocation and Determine the Cost of Products Using Job Order Costing

3–17. Williams Company began operations in June 2001. During that month, two jobs were started. The following costs were incurred:

	Job 101	Job 202
Direct material	$3,000	$4,000
Direct labor	6,000	7,000

Factory overhead is applied at 60% of direct labor cost. During the month, job 101 was completed but not sold. Job 202 is yet to be completed.

REQUIRED:

a. Calculate the cost of the ending work-in-process inventory as of June 30, 2001.

b. Calculate the cost of the finished goods inventory as of June 30, 2001.

LO 4 & 5: Calculate Traditional Overhead Allocation and Determine the Cost of Products Using Job Order Costing

3–18. Masa Manufacturing began operations in August 2001. During that month, two jobs were started. The following costs were incurred:

	Job 1	Job 2
Direct material	$5,400	$8,900
Direct labor	6,500	9,000

Factory overhead is applied at 50% of direct labor cost. During the month, job 1 was completed but not sold. Job 2 has not been completed.

REQUIRED:

a. Calculate the cost of the ending work-in-process inventory as of August 31, 2001.

b. Calculate the cost of the finished goods inventory as of August 31, 2001.

LO 4 & 5: Calculate Traditional Overhead Allocation and Determine the Cost of Products Using Job Order Costing

3–19. Northern Manufacturing began operations in September 2001. During that month, two jobs were started. The following costs were incurred:

	Job A	Job B
Direct material	$2,500	$5,000
Direct labor	7,000	9,500

Factory overhead is applied at 120% of direct labor cost. During the month, job A was completed but not sold. Job B has not been completed.

REQUIRED:

a. Calculate the cost of the ending work-in-process inventory as of September 30, 2001.
b. Calculate the cost of the finished goods inventory as of September 30, 2001.
c. Appendix: Prepare the following journal entries:
   (1) Record direct materials for each job.
   (2) Record direct labor for each job.
   (3) Record the allocation of manufacturing overhead for each job.
   (4) Record the transfer to finished goods of job A.

LO 4 & 5: Calculate Traditional Overhead Allocation and Determine the Cost of Products Using Job Order Costing

3–20. Southern Manufacturing began two jobs during the month of January 2001. There was no beginning inventory. The following costs were incurred:

	Job A	Job B
Direct material	$2,000	$3,000
Direct labor	4,000	5,000

Southern's estimated manufacturing overhead for 2001 is $117,000, and the estimated direct labor cost is $90,000. Southern applies overhead to production based on direct labor cost. During the month, job A was completed but not sold. Job B has not been completed.

REQUIRED:

a. Calculate the cost of the ending work-in-process inventory as of January 31, 2001.
b. Calculate the cost of the finished goods inventory as of January 31, 2001.
c. Appendix: Prepare the following journal entries:
   (1) Record direct materials for each job.
   (2) Record direct labor for each job.
   (3) Record the allocation of manufacturing overhead for each job.
   (4) Record the transfer to finished goods of job A.

LO 4 & 5: Calculate Traditional Overhead Allocation and Determine the Cost of Products Using Job Order Costing

3–21. Slater Industries makes custom optical glass equipment. The company began two jobs during January 2001. There was no beginning inventory. The following information is available:

	Job 7	Job 8
Direct material	$7,250	$3,640
Direct labor	$4,251	$5,125
Direct labor hours	212	234

Slater's estimated manufacturing overhead for 2001 is $110,400, and the company estimates that labor force will work 9,200 direct labor hours. Slater applies overhead to production based on direct labor hours.

REQUIRED:
a. Calculate the cost of job 7.
b. Calculate the cost of job 8.

LO 4 & 5: Calculate Traditional Overhead Allocation and Determine the Cost of Products Using Job Order Costing

3–22. Willig-Davis Cleaning Equipment began two jobs during March 2001. There was no beginning inventory. The following information is available:

	Job 10	Job 15
Direct material	$14,350	$23,530
Direct labor	$ 7,231	$15,125
Machine hours	124	236

The company estimated manufacturing overhead for 2001 is $307,200, and the company estimates that 4,800 machine hours will be used during the year. Willig-Davis applies overhead to production based on machine hours.

REQUIRED:
a. Calculate the cost of job 10.
b. Calculate the cost of job 15.

LO 5: Determine the Cost of Products Using Job Order Costing

3–23. Speace Automotive Security converts regular automobiles to armored cars. Each car is custom made to conform to the needs of each individual customer. Modifications may be as minor as the addition of bullet-resistant windows or as extravagant as full armor. The following information is presented for March 2001.

Beginning work-in-process inventory:

Job 2727	Direct material	$24,000
	Direct labor	9,000
	Manufacturing overhead	5,400

Cost for current month:

	Direct Material	Direct Labor	Manufacturing Overhead
Job 2727	$ 8,000	$4,000	$2,400
Job 2728	11,000	6,000	3,600

Job 2727 was completed and sold in March, and job 2728 was not complete as of March 31.

REQUIRED:
a. What is the cost of the beginning work-in-process inventory for March 2001?
b. What is the cost of the ending work-in-process inventory for March 2001?
c. (1) What is the cost of job 2727?
   (2) How would job 2727 appear on the financial statements?

LO 4 & 5: Calculate Traditional Overhead Allocation and Determine the Cost of Products Using Job Order Costing

3–24. Crespin Brothers Equipment Company began two jobs during March 2001. At the beginning of March, job 303 was the only job in work-in-process inventory. There was no finished goods inventory. The cost in beginning work-in-process inventory for job 303 consisted of $5,450 in direct material cost, $8,825 in direct labor cost, and manufacturing overhead cost of $7,354. The following information is available for costs added during March:

	Job 303	Job 304	Job 305
Direct material	$ 4,350	$12,650	$11,300
Direct labor	$ 8,400	$ 8,125	$ 6,750
Direct labor hours	560	520	480

Job 303 was completed and sold during March. Job 304 was completed but has yet to be sold, and job 305 remains in production.

Crespin's estimated manufacturing overhead for 2001 is $225,000, and the company estimates that the labor force will work 18,000 hours during the year. Crespin applies overhead to production based on direct labor hours.

REQUIRED:

a. Calculate the cost of the ending work-in-process inventory as of March 31, 2001.
b. Calculate the cost of the finished goods inventory as of March 31, 2001.
c. Calculate the cost of goods sold for March.

LO 4 & 5: Calculate Traditional Overhead Allocation and Determine the Cost of Products Using Job Order Costing

3–25. Greenberg and Son Manufacturing began two jobs during July 2001. At the beginning of July, job 227 was the only job in work-in-process inventory. There was no finished goods inventory. The cost in beginning work-in-process inventory for job 227 consisted of $1,500 in direct material cost, $2,000 in direct labor cost, and manufacturing overhead cost of $4,500. Total manufacturing overhead for the month was $16,054. The following information is available for costs added during July:

	Job 227	Job 228	Job 229
Direct material	$ 935	$ 2,850	$ 1,300
Direct labor	$ 1,840	$ 3,225	$ 1,975
Direct labor hours	184	310	204

Job 227 was completed and sold during July. Job 228 was completed but has yet to be sold, and job 229 remains in production.

Greenberg's estimated manufacturing overhead for 2001 is $180,000, and the company estimates that the labor force will work 8,000 hours during the year. Greenberg applies overhead to production based on direct labor hours.

REQUIRED:

a. Calculate the cost of the ending work-in-process inventory as of July 31, 2001.
b. Calculate the cost of the finished goods inventory as of July 31, 2001.
c. Calculate the cost of goods sold for July.

LO 4 & 5: Calculate Traditional Overhead Allocation and Determine the Cost of Products Using Job Order Costing

3–26. Baillie Manufacturing began two jobs during May 2001. At the beginning of May, job 411 was the only job in work-in-process inventory. There was no finished goods inventory. The cost in beginning work-in-process inventory for job 411 consisted of $4,000 in direct material cost, $6,000 in direct labor cost, and manufacturing overhead cost of $8,000. Total manufacturing overhead for the month was $22,050. The following information is available for costs added during May:

	Job 411	Job 412	Job 413
Direct material	$ 2,000	$ 4,000	$ 6,000
Direct labor	$ 2,500	$ 6,500	$ 8,500
Direct labor hours	225	570	780

Job 411 was completed and sold during May. Job 412 was completed but has yet to be sold, and job 413 remains in production.

Baillie's estimated manufacturing overhead for 2001 is $277,875, and the company estimates that the labor force will work 19,500 hours during the year. Baillie applies overhead to production based on direct labor hours.

REQUIRED:

a. Calculate the cost of the ending work-in-process inventory as of May 31, 2001.
b. Calculate the cost of the finished goods inventory as of May 31, 2001.
c. Calculate the cost of goods sold for May.

LO 4 & 5: Calculate Traditional and ABC Overhead Allocation and Determine the Cost of Products Using Job Order Costing

3–27. Salter Equipment Company began the following jobs during March 2001:

	Job 303	Job 304
Direct material	$2,000	$2,000
Direct labor	$3,120	$6,240
Direct labor hours	260	520
Machine hours machine A	5	30
Machine hours machine B	20	0
Machine setups	2	1
Engineering changes	22	9

Estimated overhead cost for 2001:

Depreciation machine A	$ 100,000
Depreciation machine B	500,000
Machine setup cost	50,000
Engineering cost	200,000
Other overhead cost	150,000
Total	$1,000,000

Estimated activities for 2001:

Machine hours machine A	1,000
Machine hours machine B	1,000
Number of setups	80
Number of engineering changes	800
Number of direct labor hours	20,000

REQUIRED:

a. Calculate the cost of each job using direct labor hours as the allocation base for all overhead.
b. Calculate the cost of each job using activity-based costing. Use direct labor hours as the allocation base for "other overhead cost."

LO 4 & 5: Calculate Traditional and ABC Overhead Allocation and Determine the Cost of Products Using Job Order Costing

3–28. Duskin Equipment Company began the following jobs during August 2001:

	Job 500	Job 600
Direct material	$1,000	$1,000
Direct labor	$1,800	$3,000
Direct labor hours	120	200
Machine hours machine A	10	50
Machine hours machine B	50	0
Machine setups	2	1
Material movements	200	75

Estimated overhead cost for 2001:

Depreciation machine A	$ 50,000
Depreciation machine B	300,000
Machine setup cost	75,000
Material handling cost	100,000
Other overhead cost	80,000
Total	$605,000

Estimated activities for 2001:

Machine hours machine A	500
Machine hours machine B	500
Number of setups	75
Number of material movements	5,000
Number of direct labor hours	10,000

REQUIRED:
a. Calculate the cost of each job using direct labor hours as the allocation base for all overhead.
b. Calculate the cost of each job using activity-based costing. Use direct labor hours as the allocation base for "other overhead cost."

LO 4 & 5: Calculate Traditional and ABC Overhead Allocation and Determine the Cost of Products Using Job Order Costing

3–29. Vazquez Manufacturing Company began the following jobs during July 2001:

	Job 901	Job 922
Direct material	$3,000	$3,000
Direct labor	$1,800	$3,000
Direct labor hours	250	100
Machine hours machine A	20	12
Machine hours machine B	0	8
Machine setups	1	2
Material movements	90	300

Estimated overhead cost for 2001:

Depreciation machine A	$ 150,000
Depreciation machine B	600,000
Machine setup cost	175,000
Material handling cost	150,000
Other overhead cost	180,000
Total	$1,255,000

Estimated activities for 2001:

Machine hours machine A	700
Machine hours machine B	700
Number of setups	100
Number of material movements	5,000
Number of direct labor hours	10,000

REQUIRED:

a. Calculate the cost of each job using direct labor hours as the allocation base for all overhead.

b. Calculate the cost of each job using activity-based costing. Use direct labor hours as the allocation base for "other overhead cost."

LO 6: Determine the Cost of Products Using Process Costing— No Beginning or Ending Inventory

3–30. Daysi's Specialty Food Company makes canned chili. The following cost information is available for March 2001:

Units produced	25,000 units
Direct material cost	$8,000
Direct labor cost	$3,000
Manufacturing overhead costs	$2,000

There were no beginning or ending inventories.

REQUIRED:

a. What is the total production cost for Daysi's Specialty Food Company?

b. What is the cost per unit?

c. If the chili sold for $0.82 per can, what is the gross profit for the company?

LO 6: Determine the Cost of Products Using Process Costing— With Beginning Inventory

3–31. Dunn Electronic Manufacturing Company makes low-cost calculators. The following information is available for January 2001:

	Units	Percent Complete	Cost
Beginning work-in-process inventory	700	40%	$224
Ending work-in-process inventory	900	60%	?
Units completed	12,000	calculators	

Manufacturing cost for January 2001 is $10,659.

REQUIRED:

a. What is the number of equivalent units of production for January 2001?

b. What is the cost per equivalent unit?

c. What is the cost of the 900 calculators in the ending work in process?

d. What is the cost of the calculators that were completed during January?

e. If 11,000 of the completed calculators were sold for $1.12 each, what is the gross profit for the Dunn Electronic Manufacturing Company?

f. **(1)** Do you think there is a benefit for Dunn's managers to know the cost of the calculators that are in ending work-in-process inventory? Explain.

    (2) Where would the cost of the ending inventory appear on the financial statements?

(3) Do you think there is a benefit for Dunn's managers to know the cost of the calculators completed during January? Explain.

(4) Where would the cost of the 11,000 sold calculators be found on the financial statements?

(5) Where would the cost of the calculators that were completed, but not yet sold be found on the financial statements?

LO 6: Determine the Cost of Products Using Process Costing— With Beginning Inventory

3–32. The following information is for Suzanne's Volleyball Manufacturing Company for February 2001:

	Units	Percent Complete	Cost
Beginning work-in-process inventory	2,400	80%	$2,304
Ending work-in-process inventory	3,200	50%	

64,000 volleyballs were completed in February. Manufacturing cost for February is $86,256.

REQUIRED:

a. What is the number of equivalent units of production for February?

b. What is the cost per equivalent unit for February?

c. What is the cost of the 3,200 volleyballs in the ending work-in-process inventory for February?

d. What is the cost of the volleyballs that were completed during February?

e. If 50,000 of the completed volleyballs were sold for $1.80 each, what is the gross profit for Suzanne's Volleyball Manufacturing Company?

LO 6: Determine the Cost of Products Using Process Costing— No Beginning Inventory

3–33. Valentine's Manufacturing makes candy. During 2001, the company's first year of operations, the company completed 200,000 boxes of candy and incurred direct material cost of $160,800, direct labor cost of $40,200, and manufacturing overhead cost of $60,300. There were 2,000 boxes of candy that were 50% in the production process at the end of the year.

REQUIRED:

a. What is the number of equivalent units of production for 2001?

b. What is the cost per equivalent unit of production for 2001?

c. What is the cost of the 2001 ending work-in-process inventory?

d. What is the cost of the boxes of candy that were completed in 2001?

LO 6: Determine the Number of Equivalent Units

3–34. The following information relates to the Collins Company for 2001:

	Units	Percent Complete
Work in process at January 1	10,000	75%
Units started into production	145,000	
Units completed	138,000	
Work in process at December 31	17,000	50%

REQUIRED:
Calculate the number of equivalent units of production.

LO 6: Determine the Number of Equivalent Units

3–35. The following information relates to the Munter Company for June 2001:

	Units	Percent Complete
Work in process at June 1	115,000	60%
Units started into production	1,800,000	
Units completed	1,850,000	
Work in process at June 30	65,000	30%

REQUIRED:
Calculate the number of equivalent units of production.

LO 6: Determine the Number of Equivalent Units

3–36. The following information relates to the Holder Company for July 2001:

	Units	Percent Complete
Work in process at July 1	5,000	90%
Units started into production	70,000	
Units completed	72,000	
Work in process at July 31	3,000	20%

REQUIRED:
Calculate the number of equivalent units of production.

LO 6: Determine the Number of Equivalent Units with Missing Information

3–37. The following information relates to the Mayber Company for May 2001:

	Units	Percent Complete
Work in process at May 1	5,000	45%
Units started into production	77,000	
Work in process at May 31	12,000	35%

REQUIRED:
a. Assuming no units of production were lost or spoiled, how many units were completed during May?
b. Calculate the number of equivalent units of production.

LO 6: Determine the Number of Equivalent Units with Missing Information

3–38. The following information relates to the Strayform Company for August 2001:

	Units	Percent Complete
Work in process at August 1	7,000	95%
Units started into production	87,000	
Work in process at August 31	6,500	25%

REQUIRED:

a. Assuming no units of production were lost or spoiled, how many units were completed during August?

b. Calculate the number of equivalent units of production.

LO 6: Determine the Number of Equivalent Units with Missing Information

3–39. The following information relates to the Golden Company for February 2001:

	Units	Percent Complete
Work in process at February 1	22,500	80%
Units started into production	185,000	
Work in process at February 28	14,500	25%

REQUIRED:

a. Assuming no units of production were lost or spoiled, how many units were completed during February?

b. Calculate the number of equivalent units of production.

LO 6: Determine the Cost of Products Using Process Costing— With Beginning Inventory

3–40. The following information relates to the Smithfield Company for July 2001:

	Units	Percent Complete
Work in process at July 1	19,500	50%
Units started into production	220,000	
Units completed in July	231,000	
Work in process at July 31	8,500	40%
Cost of the beginning work in process	$ 7,020	
Current month's production cost	166,436	

REQUIRED:

a. Calculate the number of equivalent units of production.

b. Calculate the cost per equivalent unit of production.

c. Calculate the cost of the ending work-in-process inventory.

d. Calculate the cost of the completed units.

LO 6: Determine the Cost of Products Using Process Costing— With Beginning Inventory

3–41. The following information relates to the Richard Renick Company for 2001:

	Units	Percent Complete
Work in process at January 1	42,000	50%
Units started into production	420,000	
Units completed in 2001	390,000	
Work in process at December 31	72,000	20%
Cost of the beginning work in process		$ 14,280
Current year's production cost		248,580

REQUIRED:

a. Calculate the number of equivalent units of production.
b. Calculate the cost per equivalent unit of production.
c. Calculate the cost of the ending work-in-process inventory.
d. Calculate the cost of the completed units.

LO 6: Determine the Cost of Products Using Process Costing—With Beginning Inventory

3–42. The following information relates to the Robert Lewis Manufacturing Company for 2001:

	Units	Percent Complete
Work in process at January 1	120,000	25%
Units started into production	1,300,000	
Units completed in 2001	1,290,000	
Work in process at December 31	130,000	70%
Cost of the beginning work in process		$ 40,200
Current year's production cost		1,768,910

REQUIRED:

a. Calculate the number of equivalent units of production.
b. Calculate the cost per equivalent unit of production.
c. Calculate the cost of the ending work-in-process inventory.
d. Calculate the cost of the completed units.

LO 6: Determine the Cost of Products Using Process Costing—With Beginning Inventory

3–43. The cost of the work-in-process inventory at January 1 for Ralph Robinson Manufacturing was $7,420, consisting of 10,000 units that were 35% complete. An additional 130,000 units were started into production during the year. The cost of material, labor, and overhead added during the year amounted to $280,680. The units completed and transferred to finished goods totaled 125,000. The ending work-in-process inventory consisted of 15,000 units which were 60% complete.

REQUIRED:

a. Calculate the number of equivalent units of production.
b. Calculate the cost per equivalent unit of production.
c. Calculate the cost of the ending work-in-process inventory.
d. Calculate the cost of the completed units.

LO 6: Determine the Cost of Products Using Process Costing—With Beginning Inventory

3–44. The cost of the work-in-process inventory at January 1 for Jim Mays Manufacturing was $61,875, consisting of 11,000 units that were 45% complete. An additional 150,000 units were started into production during the year. The cost of material, labor, and overhead added during the year amounted to $1,872,855. The units completed and transferred to finished goods totaled 145,000. The ending work-in-process inventory consisted of 16,000 units which were 65% complete.

REQUIRED:
a. Calculate the number of equivalent units of production.
b. Calculate the cost per equivalent unit of production.
c. Calculate the cost of the ending work-in-process inventory.
d. Calculate the cost of the completed units.

LO 6: Determine the Cost of Products Using Process Costing—With Beginning Inventory

3–45. The cost of the work-in-process inventory at January 1 for Hanamura Manufacturing was $119,805, consisting of 122,500 units that were 30% complete. An additional 750,000 units were started into production during the year. The cost of material, labor, and overhead added during the year amounted to $2,627,820. The units completed and transferred to finished goods totaled 790,000. The ending work-in-process inventory consisted of 72,500 units which were 25% complete.

REQUIRED:
a. Calculate the number of equivalent units of production.
b. Calculate the cost per equivalent unit of production.
c. Calculate the cost of the ending work-in-process inventory.
d. Calculate the cost of the completed units.
e. Appendix: Prepare a journal entry to transfer the cost of completed goods from work in process.

LO 6: Determine the Cost of Products Using Process Costing—With Beginning Inventory and Missing Information

3–46. The following information relates to the Robert Lewis Manufacturing Company for 2001:

	Units	Cost
Work in process at January 1	18,500	$ 35,668
Units started into production	190,000	
Units completed in 2001	187,000	
Current production cost		1,873,052

The beginning work-in-process inventory is 20% complete and the ending work-in-process inventory is 55% complete.

REQUIRED:
a. Calculate the number of equivalent units of production.
b. Calculate the cost per equivalent unit of production.
c. Calculate the cost of the ending work-in-process inventory.

d. Calculate the cost of the completed units.

e. Appendix: Prepare a journal entry to transfer the cost of completed goods from work in process.

LO 6: Determine the Cost of Products Using Process Costing—With Beginning Inventory and Missing Information

3–47. The following information relates to the Mathias Manufacturing Company for 2001:

	Units	Cost
Work in process at January 1	77,000	$ 107,415
Units started into production	602,500	
Work in process at December 31	92,000	
Current production cost		2,979,922

The beginning work-in-process inventory is 30% complete and the ending work-in-process inventory is 80% complete.

REQUIRED:

a. Calculate the number of equivalent units of production.

b. Calculate the cost per equivalent unit of production.

c. Calculate the cost of the ending work-in-process inventory.

d. Calculate the cost of the completed units.

e. Appendix: Prepare a journal entry to transfer the cost of completed goods from work in process.

LO 6: Determine the Cost of Products Using Process Costing—With Beginning Inventory and Missing Information

3–48. The following information relates to the Heromi Manufacturing Company for 2001:

	Units	Cost
Work in process at January 1	13,000	$ 4,368
Units started into production	83,500	
Work in process at December 31	7,500	
Current production cost		37,262

The beginning work-in-process inventory is 70% complete and the ending work-in-process inventory is 20% complete.

REQUIRED:

a. Calculate the number of equivalent units of production.

b. Calculate the cost per equivalent unit of production.

c. Calculate the cost of the ending work-in-process inventory.

d. Calculate the cost of the completed units.

e. Appendix: Prepare a journal entry to transfer the cost of completed goods from work in process.

Chapter 4

Cost Behavior

*L*aura Jorgensen is the newly elected social chairperson of her mountain climbing club. Her first duty is to plan the club's big kickoff party for the upcoming year. Of course funds are limited, so she must plan well and estimate costs carefully.

Laura's first step in estimating the total cost of the party is to identify the individual costs involved. As she begins the planning process, she identifies two major costs:

1. Entertainment—A live band is a must.

2. Food and drinks—Large amounts are essential.

When Laura checks the records of last year's social chairperson, she discovers he spent $3,650 on these two items for last year's party ($525 for entertainment and $3,125 for food and drinks). Assuming the prices for entertainment and food and drinks have remained the same, the club should be able to have this year's party for $3,650. In fact, Laura has money to spare because the spending limit for this year's event is $5,500.

But wait. . . . The mountain climbing club has grown, so about 175 guests are expected to attend this year's party, compared to 125 last year. Laura must estimate the party's cost for 175 guests, not 125. How should she begin?

To determine the total expected cost of the party, Laura needs to know which costs are and which costs are not affected by the number of guests attending. Let us examine Laura's two major costs for the party:

1. Entertainment: Will the band charge more if more guests attend? No.

2. Food and drinks: Will the caterer charge more if the number of guests increases? Yes.

How should Laura determine the cost of this year's party when the number of people attending is 175 rather than 125? Clearly, she knows her cost for the item that is unaffected by the activity level (the band), but what about the cost that is affected by a change in activity level (food and drinks)? This chapter will demonstrate how to determine these amounts.

As managers plan for business success, they must know which costs will vary with changes in business activity and which will remain constant. That is, managers must determine cost behavior. **Cost behavior** is the reaction of costs to changes in levels of business activity. ■

cost behavior   The reaction of costs to changes in levels of business activity.

LEARNING OBJECTIVES

After completing your work on this chapter, you should be able to do the following:

1. Describe the differences between fixed costs and variable costs.
2. Classify costs by cost behavior.
3. Explain the concept of relevant range and its effect on cost behavior information.
4. Describe the characteristics of a mixed cost and the four basic approaches to separating a mixed cost into its fixed and variable components.
5. Determine the fixed and variable components of a mixed cost using scatter graphs and the high-low method.

COMMON COST BEHAVIOR PATTERNS

Costs may react in various ways to changes in activity levels, creating many different cost behavior patterns. In this chapter we describe and compare the two most common patterns: fixed and variable.

Fixed Costs

fixed cost   A cost that remains constant in total regardless of the level of activity.

Fixed costs are costs that remain constant *in total* regardless of the level of activity. In our chapter-opening example, the entertainment cost is a fixed cost. As the number of guests increases, this cost does not change. The band will cost $525 for the night, regardless of how many guests attend the club's party.

Suppose Laura is interested in determining the fixed cost *per guest*. Would the fixed cost amount change per guest as the number of guests changes? Let us take a look.

	125 Guests	175 Guests
Total fixed cost	$525	$525
Cost per guest	$525 ÷ 125 = $4.20	$525 ÷ 175 = $3.00

As you can see, the fixed cost *per unit* (in this case, the entertainment cost per guest) changes as the activity level changes. A fixed cost, then, is a cost that remains constant in total, but changes per unit as the activity level changes. Fixed cost per unit decreases as activity increases.

Discussion Question

4-1. Consider the costs involved in operating a fast-food restaurant such as McDonald's. What are three examples of fixed costs?

Variable Costs

variable cost   A cost that changes in total proportionately with changes in the level of activity.

Variable costs are costs that change *in total* proportionately with changes in the level of activity. As activity increases, total variable cost also increases. In our party example, the variable cost is the catering cost of $25 per guest. We know this because the total cost for food and drinks last year was $3,125 for 125 guests, and $3,125 / 125 = $25. For each additional guest added to the party, the total cost for food and drinks will increase by $25.

If 175 guests attend, the total catering cost is as follows:

$$175 \text{ guests} \times \$25 = \$4,375$$

Variable cost per unit stays the same as activity changes. In our example, the catering cost per guest remains constant. Variable cost is a cost that increases in total, but remains constant per unit as activity increases.

Discussion Question

4-2. Consider the costs involved in operating a fast-food restaurant such as McDonald's. What are three examples of variable costs and the activity or activities that cause them to change?

Comparison of Cost Behaviors

Cost and activity can be plotted on a graph to yield a visual representation of cost behavior. When doing so, the activity is plotted on the horizontal axis (called the x-axis). The type of cost is plotted on the vertical axis (called the y-axis). You may recall from past math classes that x is the independent variable, and y is the dependent variable, which means that the item depicted on the x-axis (activity) affects the item shown on the y-axis (cost).

A graphical representation of a fixed cost is as follows:

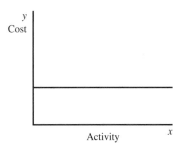

Examples of activities and fixed costs are shown in Exhibit 4–1. Notice that each example in Exhibit 4–1 suggests a cost that remains constant even if the level of the activity changes.

Exhibit 4–1
Examples of Fixed
Costs

Activity	Fixed Cost
Production	Rent on the factory building
Production	Depreciation on production equipment
Sales	Salary of vice president of sales
Delivery	Vehicle insurance

From our party example, we can graph the cost of the band as an example of a fixed cost, as shown in Exhibit 4–2.

Exhibit 4–2
Graph of Fixed Cost
Behavior Pattern of
Entertainment at the
Climbing Club Party

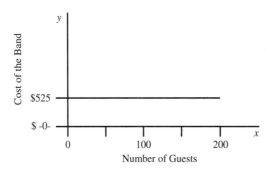

The horizontal line on the graph in Exhibit 4–2 shows that the fixed cost of entertainment stays constant no matter how the number of guests changes.

A graphical representation of variable cost is as follows:

Examples of activities and variable costs are shown in Exhibit 4–3. Notice that for each example in Exhibit 4–3, a change in the level of the activity results in a change in the total cost.

The cost of catering is a variable cost and can be graphically depicted as shown in Exhibit 4–4. The upward sloping line in Exhibit 4–4 shows us that as the number of guests increases from 125 to 175, the catering cost increases proportionately.

Exhibit 4–3
Examples of Variable
Costs

Activity	Variable Cost
Production	Direct material
Production	Direct labor
Sales	Sales commissions
Delivery	Gasoline

Exhibit 4–4
Graph of Variable Cost
Behavior Pattern for
Catering Cost at the
Climbing Club Party

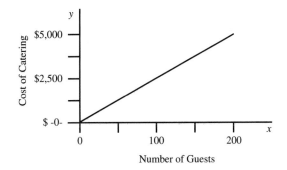

Discussion Question

4-3. Identify four additional costs of hosting the mountain climbing club party and describe the cost behavior of each if the number of guests changes.

In this section, we defined and compared the two most common types of cost behavior. Next, we see how to estimate the total cost of an activity.

Determining Total Cost

Once managers classify costs according to cost behavior, they can determine the total cost of an activity. The formula for finding total cost is as follows:

TOTAL COST = FIXED COST + VARIABLE COST

Recall from our example that we have $525 of fixed cost for the band, and $4,375 of variable cost for the food and drinks (based on 175 guests). Using this information, Laura can calculate the total cost of the party as $4,900, as follows:

$4,900 = $525 + $4,375

The total cost of the party is shown on the graph in Exhibit 4–5.

The graph in Exhibit 4–5 shows both the horizontal line depicting the fixed cost of the band and the upward sloping line representing the fixed cost plus the variable

Exhibit 4–5
Graph of Total Climbing
Party Cost

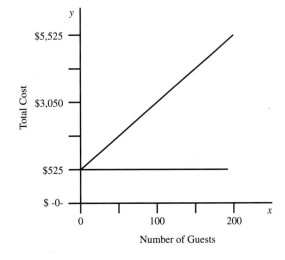

cost of the food and drinks. Exhibit 4–5, then, is actually a combination of the graphs in Exhibits 4–2 and 4–4. These graphs are consistent with the statement that total cost is equal to fixed cost plus variable cost.

Since the budget for the event was $5,500, and Laura plans to spend only $4,900, she must have planned well, right? Not necessarily. Keep in mind that the numbers only tell part of the story. As a decision maker, Laura must not be lulled into thinking that she has made the most effective spending choices just because she failed to spend every budgeted dollar. Is it wise to spend nearly $5,000 on one event? Could some costs be reduced? To make strong decisions, managers must consider all issues—not just whether the budget has been met. In this chapter, we examine cost behaviors to equip you with a cost estimation tool. Remember, however, that when making decisions the numbers tell part, not all, of a story.

Discussion Question

4-4. The total cost of $4,900 covers the cost of 175 guests. Based on the cost behavior information available, what is the largest possible number of guests that could attend the party within the $5,500 budget?

RELEVANT RANGE

relevant range The range of activity within which cost behavior assumptions are valid.

Are there any situations when a cost behavior might change? Let us reexamine the cost of entertainment in the party example to answer this question. We assumed the cost of the band would remain fixed if the number of guests attending the party increased; however, if the number of guests increased well outside normal expectations to 500 or 1,000, the guests could not be entertained with a single band. At least two bands would be needed. Once the number of guests exceeds a certain range, the entertainment cost does not remain fixed at $525.

The range of activity within which cost behavior assumptions are valid is the **relevant range.** In the party example, the relevant range might be up to 250 guests. If more than 250 guests attend, another band will be needed. For a business, relevant range is usually considered to be the normal range of activity for the company.

Activity that is outside the relevant range can affect costs in a business setting. For example, in Exhibit 4–1, we described rent for a factory building as a fixed cost relative to production. This fixed cost behavior holds true only within the relevant range. On the one hand, if production dropped to two units there would be no point in having a factory. Work could be contracted to an outside party. Conversely, if the factory building provided just enough space to produce 1,000 units per month, and production requirements increased to 1,500 units per month, a second factory would be needed. If the activity level were higher than the relevant range, factory rent would no longer be fixed at the original cost level.

Variable costs also have a relevant range. To illustrate, we return to the catering costs for the party example. The caterer charged the club $25 per guest for food and drinks for a party with 125 to 175 guests. Would the caterer offer the same service for $25 per guest if the event were a private evening with only six people attending? Probably not. The caterer's fee is based on a relatively large number of guests. Conversely, the caterer might be willing to provide food and drinks for a cost of less than $25 per guest if the crowd were significantly larger. For example, the caterer might offer a $25 per guest charge for groups of 50 to 200, and a $20 per guest charge for groups of more than 200. In such a case, the relevant range of the variable cost behavior would be from 50 to 200 guests.

In business settings, similar types of quantity discounts exist. For example, if IBM were to purchase just enough electrical wire to manufacture one computer, it would likely pay a higher price for the wire than if it were buying enough to make 1,000 computers. Buying enough electrical wire to make 1,000 computers allows IBM to get quantity discounts that would be unavailable otherwise. At the other extreme, if IBM were to make such a large number of computers that it outstripped its normal source for wire and had to resort to secondary, more expensive suppliers, the cost for electrical wire per computer could actually increase as production increased.

With these examples in mind, how can fixed cost be described as a cost that remains constant in total, and variable cost be described as cost that remains constant per unit regardless of activity? For most decision situations, the fixed and variable cost information provided to managers assumes activity will be within the relevant range, that is, the normal operating range for the company. The relevant range can be depicted graphically as shown in Exhibit 4–6.

Exhibit 4–6
Relevant Ranges of Fixed and Variable Costs

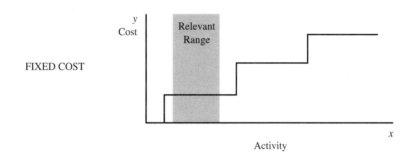

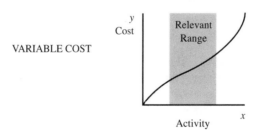

As shown in Exhibit 4–6, the fixed cost remains constant in total and the variable cost is constant per unit within the relevant range.

Decision makers usually assume activity levels will be within a company's relevant range. Activity levels may exceed or fall below the relevant range, such as when growth in production activity is significant. However, unless some evidence suggests the contrary, you should assume in our text discussion that the activity levels will be within the relevant range.

Mixed Costs

The costs we have looked at thus far have been either completely fixed (the cost of entertainment at the party) or completely variable (the cost of food and drinks at the party). Some costs, however, are actually a combination of fixed and variable

mixed cost An individual cost that has both a fixed cost and a variable cost component. It also describes a company's total cost structure.

cost, and are known as mixed costs. A **mixed cost** is an individual cost that has elements of both fixed and variable costs.

For decision-making purposes, it is useful to identify the fixed and variable components of a mixed cost. For example, consider the cost of electricity consumed in a manufacturing facility. When production lines are completely shut down on weekends, production is zero. Even without any production, however, the facility will still require minimal electricity to operate water heaters, refrigerators, and security lighting. This minimum cost of keeping the factory ready for use is the fixed portion of electricity cost. When production begins and production machinery cranks up, much more electric power is used. This incremental cost, which is driven by the actual use of the manufacturing facility, is the variable portion of electricity cost. Exhibit 4–7 shows a graph of a mixed cost.

Exhibit 4–7
Graph of a Mixed Cost

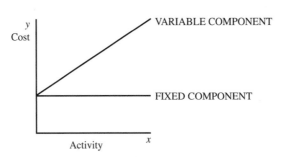

Exhibit 4–7 shows that even when the activity level is at zero (the intercept of the x-axis and the y-axis), cost is incurred. This cost is the fixed element of the mixed cost. As activity increases, the cost rises from that initial point. This cost is the variable component of the mixed cost.

You may have observed that the graph in Exhibit 4–7 is quite similar to that in Exhibit 4–5 depicting the total cost of the climbing club party. This similarity occurs because total cost (which is composed of its fixed costs and its variable costs) could be described as one giant mixed cost.

Discussion Questions

4–5. Consider the costs involved in operating a fast-food restaurant such as McDonald's. What are three examples of activities that would have mixed costs?

Assume you are the sales manager for the Hinds Wholesale Supply Company, and you are trying to estimate the cost of operating the fleet of delivery vehicles for the coming year. The only information you have is that $110,000 was spent last year to operate the fleet.

4–6. Would it help you to know which delivery vehicle costs are fixed and which are variable? Why?

4–7. What other information would you need to gather before being able to estimate next year's costs?

4–8. Why would the sales manager at Hinds Wholesale Supply Company be concerned about the cost of delivery vehicles?

IDENTIFYING THE FIXED AND VARIABLE ELEMENTS OF A MIXED COST

We often know that a cost has behavioral characteristics of both fixed and variable costs, but we have no information to tell us how much of the cost is unaffected by the level of activity (fixed) and how much of it will increase as activity increases (variable). Mixed cost information is much more useful for cost control, planning, and decision-making purposes if the manager can determine which part of the mixed cost is fixed and which is variable. In this section we will discuss four methods commonly used to identify the fixed and variable elements of a mixed cost: the engineering approach, scatter graphing, the high-low method, and regression analysis.

The Engineering Approach

engineering approach
A method used to separate a mixed cost into its fixed and variable components using experts who are familiar with the technical aspects of the activity and associated cost.

The **engineering approach** relies on engineers or other professionals who are familiar with the technical aspect of the activity and the associated cost to analyze the situation and determine which costs are fixed and which are variable. This approach may employ time-and-motion studies or other aspects of scientific management.

For example, experts in the field of aviation and aircraft operations could analyze the cost of operating a corporate aircraft to determine which portion of the operating cost increases as aircraft usage increases and which portion of the cost remains constant. Based on the experts' industry experience and evaluations, they would then separate the fixed and variable components of this mixed cost.

Analysts would be likely to use flying time as the activity level base because hours of use will affect costs. They would then classify the cost of insurance and of renting hangar space in which to store the plane as fixed costs. Why? The insurance and rental costs are unaffected by the number of hours the plane may be flown. The cost of the airplane's battery will likely be classified as a fixed cost because the deterioration of this item and the need for replacement are affected more by the passing of time and very little by the number of flight hours.

Aviation experts would probably classify fuel costs and expected maintenance and repair costs as variable costs, as both depend on usage. For example, experts may estimate that a plane's engines require an overhaul every 2,000 hours of flight time.

Discussion Questions

Again assume you are a sales manager for the Hinds Wholesale Supply Company trying to estimate the cost of operating the fleet of delivery vehicles for the coming year.

4–9. Would you engage the services of an automotive expert to help separate costs into fixed and variable? Why or why not?

4–10. List four costs you (or the automotive expert) would identify as part of the cost of operating the fleet of delivery trucks. Classify each by its cost behavior and the activity to which it relates.

4-11. If an expert determined that the fixed cost of operating each vehicle is $3,000 per year and the variable cost is $0.10 per mile, what would be the expected cost of operating the fleet? (Assume there are eight trucks, and they are driven an average of 25,000 miles each.)

The engineering approach to separating mixed cost relies on an expert's experience and judgment to classify costs as fixed or variable. It is often used when the company has no past experience concerning a cost's reaction to activity. In contrast, the other three methods we examine use historical data and mathematical computations to approximate the fixed and variable components of mixed cost.

Scatter Graphing

scatter graphing A method used to separate a mixed cost into its fixed and variable components by plotting historical activity and cost data to see how a cost relates to various levels of activity.

Scatter graphing plots historical activity and cost data on a graph to see how a cost relates to various levels of activity. The analyst places a straight line through the *visual center* of the points plotted on the graph, so roughly half the dots are above the line and half are below the line, as shown in Exhibit 4–8.

With some simple calculations, an analyst can now approximate the fixed and variable elements of the cost being analyzed.

Exhibit 4–8
A Scatter Graph

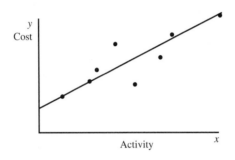

To demonstrate how scatter graphing is used, imagine you are again the sales manager for the Hinds Wholesale Supply Company with the task of estimating the expected delivery vehicle maintenance cost for 2001. Your first step is to obtain relevant historical cost data. At your request, the accounting department provides you with the following maintenance cost information about the company's delivery vehicles for 2000:

Truck Number	Maintenance Cost
202	$2,000
204	1,600
205	2,200
301	2,400
422	2,600
460	2,200
520	2,000

You now ask yourself a couple of questions. First, is vehicle maintenance cost a fixed cost? Clearly it is not a fixed cost, because the cost is not the same for all trucks. Second, is this cost a variable cost? Well, if it is a variable cost, it varies based on some activity. After careful consideration, you determine that activity might be either (1) the number of miles driven or (2) the number of packages delivered. On request, the accounting department provides you with the following expanded data for 2000:

Truck Number	Maintenance Cost	Miles Driven	Packages Delivered
202	$2,000	15,000	1,200
204	1,600	11,000	1,000
205	2,200	24,000	1,500
301	2,400	30,000	1,500
422	2,600	31,000	500
460	2,200	26,000	1,000
520	2,000	20,000	2,000

Remember, if a cost is truly variable, it changes proportionately as activity changes. Let us consider miles driven first and see whether there is a proportional change in total vehicle maintenance cost as activity changes. Compare trucks 202 and 301. The miles driven for truck 301 are exactly twice as many as for truck 202. If vehicle maintenance cost is variable based on miles driven, then the cost for truck 301 should be twice the cost for truck 202, but it is not.

Now we look at packages delivered as the activity. Compare truck 204 with truck 422. Truck 204 delivered twice as many packages as truck 422. If vehicle maintenance cost is variable based on the number of packages delivered, the cost for truck 204 should be exactly twice the cost for truck 422. Again, it is not.

If a cost is neither fixed nor variable, then it is mixed, meaning it has both a fixed element and a variable element. This is the case with Hinds' delivery vehicle maintenance cost. Therefore, you must find a way to estimate the amount of fixed and variable costs associated with the maintenance cost if you are to reasonably predict the vehicle maintenance cost for 2001.

You have decided to use the scatter graph method to determine the fixed and variable elements of the vehicle maintenance cost. The first step is to plot the information for each observation (in this case, each delivery vehicle) on a graph. Remember, the vertical axis on a graph is the y-axis (total cost), and the horizontal axis is the x-axis (activity). Recall also that the independent variable, shown as the x-axis, is not affected by a change in y. However, the dependent variable value, shown on the y-axis, depends on the numerical value of the x variable. The assumption is that a change in x will lead to a change in y.

If a truck driver travels 1,000 miles, for example, Hinds must spend money on gasoline. In our case, driving is the independent (x) variable and the company's gasoline cost is the dependent (y) variable. Driving affects the company's gasoline cost; however, the reverse does not hold true. The mere purchase of gasoline, which increases the dependent (y) variable, will not cause a change in the number of miles driven.

For mixed cost calculations, the y variable is the cost affected by the activity and it is the cost you are trying to estimate. The x variable represents the activity you believe will affect the cost behavior. Do not fall into the trap of thinking that the dependent variable (y) will be measured in dollars and the independent variable (x) will not. It is possible to predict a cost such as sales commissions, expressed in dollars, based on an activity such as sales, also expressed in dollars.

Recall the Hinds Wholesale Supply Company example. The data provided by the company's accounting department show two possible activity-cost pairs. The first pair is the number of miles driven and vehicle maintenance cost. The second pair is the number of packages delivered and vehicle maintenance cost.

We begin by graphing maintenance cost and miles driven. When we plot the data on a graph, we plot each observation as a pair of values. The maintenance cost for a particular vehicle, the dependent variable, is plotted using the index on the y-axis. The miles driven for the same vehicle, the independent variable, are plotted using the index on the x-axis. The position on the graph occupied by the plotted pair of numbers is called a *coordinate*. As the graph in Exhibit 4–9 indicates, each observation is represented by a dot.

Exhibit 4–9
Partial Scatter Graph for Hinds Company Vehicle Maintenance Cost and Miles Driven

DATA:

Truck Number	Maintenance Cost	Miles Driven
202	$2,000	15,000
204	1,600	11,000
205	2,200	24,000
301	2,400	30,000
422	2,600	31,000
460	2,200	26,000
520	2,000	20,000

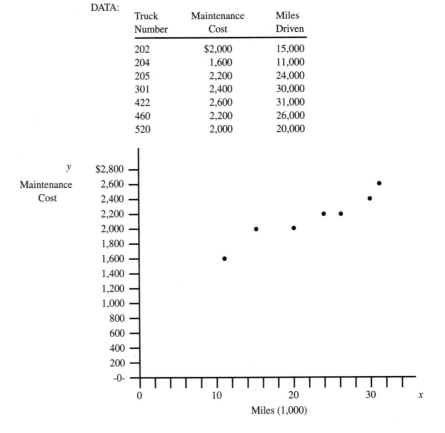

The next step is to place a straight line through the visual center of the plotted coordinates, which we have done in Exhibit 4–10.

In Exhibit 4–10 it is easy to place the straight line through the points on the graph because they seem to line up in a nearly straight line on their own. This straight line

Exhibit 4–10
Completed Scatter Graph for Vehicle Maintenance Cost and Miles Driven

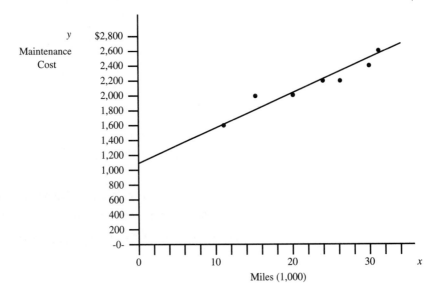

effect occurs when the relationship of the two variables is relatively constant, or linear. The graph in Exhibit 4–10 suggests a relatively constant relationship between the miles driven (x) and maintenance cost (y). The straight line represents the behavior of maintenance cost as it relates to the number of miles driven.

Now that we have a completed scatter graph for Hinds's vehicle maintenance cost, we can employ some simple calculations to approximate the fixed and variable portion of that cost. As you recall from earlier in the chapter:

Total Cost = Fixed Cost + Variable Cost

For total mixed costs we can modify the equation slightly as follows:

Total Mixed Cost = Fixed Cost Element + Variable Cost Element

When using the scatter graph method, we identify the fixed element of the maintenance cost first. Note that in Exhibit 4–10 the straight line that indicates the relationship of miles driven and maintenance cost intercepts the y-axis at $1,100. At this point, the x variable (miles) is zero, which suggests that when activity is zero, maintenance cost will still be $1,100. That $1,100 represents fixed cost. In the scatter graph method, fixed cost is determined simply by noting where the straight line intercepts the y-axis. Thus, in our example we now know the following information:

Total Mixed Cost = $1,100 + Variable Cost Element

Next, we find the variable cost per mile using simple mathematics. First we choose two points along the scatter graph line to determine the effect of the x variable on the y variable. Note: We select two points on the *scatter graph line*, not two points as plotted to represent our original data. Any two positions on the line are fine, but it is better to select points that are somewhat separated. That way, the error caused by our visual estimation in reading the graph will be small relative to the numerical difference between the two points selected.

As one coordinate for our variable cost per unit calculations, we select the point at which activity is zero and cost is $1,100. We then choose as our second point the coordinate at which the activity level is 34,000 miles and cost is $2,700. As the graph in Exhibit 4–11 indicates, we determined that coordinate by choosing a position on the line and following the lines to the x-axis and the y-axis. The locations on these axes indicate the cost and activity level represented by that position on the line.

Exhibit 4–11
Scatter Graph with
Activity Points Selected

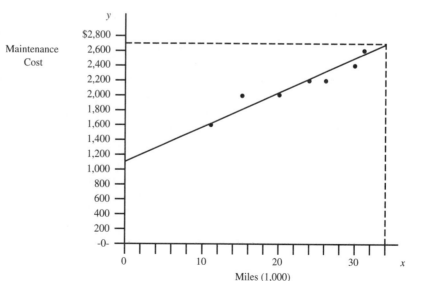

The next step is to determine the mathematical difference between the two coordinates.

Miles	Cost
34,000	$2,700
(-0-)	(1,100)
34,000	$1,600

We can see from our calculations that the maintenance cost at 34,000 miles is $1,600 higher than it is for zero miles. What do you think caused the $1,600 difference? We assume it is the change in the activity level that causes changes in the cost. That is, it cost an additional $1,600 in maintenance cost to drive the 34,000 extra miles.

Now we can calculate the average amount of maintenance cost per mile caused by the additional activity. We do this by dividing the 34,000 mileage difference into the $1,600 increased maintenance cost:

$$\$1,600 \div 34,000 = \$0.047059, \text{ or about 4.7 cents per mile}$$

The calculations show that each additional mile of driving causes maintenance cost to rise by $0.047. If we add this information to the fixed cost information determined earlier, we can create a cost formula for vehicle maintenance cost:

$$\text{Vehicle Maintenance Cost} = \$1,100 + (\$0.047 \text{ per mile driven})$$

We have now used scatter graphing to separate maintenance cost into its fixed and variable components. With this information, we can project maintenance cost at any level of activity. To do this, we add the fixed cost to the activity multiplied by the cost per unit of activity. For example, the estimated maintenance cost for a single delivery truck that is to be driven 28,000 miles is $2,416, calculated as follows:

$$\$1,100 + (\$0.047 \times 28,000) = \$2,416$$

Discussion Questions

4-12. Based on the information obtained from the scatter graph, what would be the maintenance cost of operating one delivery truck if we expected the truck to be driven 25,000 miles next year?

4-13. Based on the information obtained from the scatter graph, what would be the maintenance cost of operating a fleet of delivery trucks? (Assume there are eight trucks, and they are driven an average of 25,000 miles each.)

Now we turn to the information the accounting department provided about the number of packages delivered. Then we use the scatter graphing method to plot maintenance cost as the dependent (y) variable and packages delivered as the independent (x) variable. Exhibit 4–12 shows a partial scatter graph of the maintenance cost and packages delivered.

We draw a straight line through the points depicted by the observations, as in Exhibit 4–13.

Note in Exhibit 4–13 that placing a straight line through the points on this graph is considerably more challenging than in the previous scatter graph. This is because a straight line could take any one of several paths through the points on the graph. Each of the lines seems to depict the relationship between maintenance cost and packages delivered, but none does a very good job. The reason for the difficulty is

Exhibit 4–12
Partial Scatter Graph
for Vehicle
Maintenance Cost and
Packages Delivered

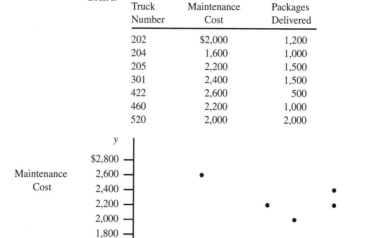

DATA:

Truck Number	Maintenance Cost	Packages Delivered
202	$2,000	1,200
204	1,600	1,000
205	2,200	1,500
301	2,400	1,500
422	2,600	500
460	2,200	1,000
520	2,000	2,000

Exhibit 4–13
Completed Scatter
Graph for Vehicle
Maintenance Cost and
Packages Delivered

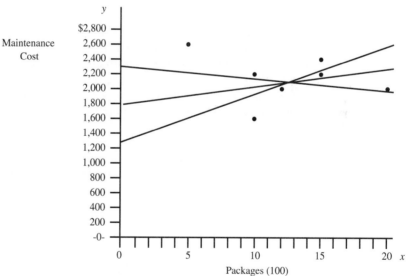

that the relationship between the variables is not linear. The question is, how do we use this method if the data do not have a clear linear relationship? The answer is, we don't. Before we employ the scatter graph method, we must be sure the activity we have chosen has a relatively linear relationship with the cost in question. If we plot points on a graph and the coordinates resemble a random pattern with little linearity, the data do not indicate a constant relationship between the activity and the cost. In the case of a random pattern, any conclusions drawn from the data will be useless for predicting future cost, and may cause trouble if used. Once we see that random pattern, then, we should not use the packages delivered data to estimate the fixed and variable elements of vehicle maintenance cost.

Even if a scatter graph appears to represent a linear relationship between an activity and a cost, we must be cautious to not imply relationships that do not exist. For instance, if we tried to determine cost behavior of vehicle maintenance cost by relating it to an activity such as the number of direct labor hours worked, we might possibly get mathematically reasonable results. However, common sense tells us that no relationship exists between direct labor hours and vehicle maintenance cost, so the results would be meaningless. A random guess would provide as good or better information. The activity and cost should have a clear, common sense relationship.

The High-Low Method

high-low method A method used to separate a mixed cost into its fixed and variable components using the mathematical differences between the highest and lowest levels of activity and cost.

Like the scatter graph approach, the **high-low method** uses historical data and mathematical computations to approximate the fixed and variable components of mixed cost. To illustrate the steps required by the high-low method, we review the following vehicle maintenance cost and activity data gathered for the Hinds Wholesale Supply Company:

Truck Number	Maintenance Cost	Miles Driven	
202	$2,000	15,000	
204	1,600	11,000	Low
205	2,200	24,000	
301	2,400	30,000	
422	2,600	31,000	High
460	2,200	26,000	
520	2,000	20,000	

The high-low method focuses on the mathematical differences between the highest and lowest observations. If we examine the data list, we see that the highest observation is 31,000 miles with a maintenance cost of $2,600. The lowest observation is 11,000 miles with a maintenance cost of $1,600.

Remember, our purpose is to find the amount of the fixed and variable elements of a mixed cost. With the high-low method, we focus on determining the variable component of the cost first. The calculations to determine variable cost per unit are similar to those used in scatter graphing. By comparing the differences in activity and cost between the highest observation and the lowest observation, we can calculate a per unit cost that describes the relationship shown by these differences as follows:

	Miles	Cost
High	31,000	$2,600
Low	(11,000)	(1,600)
Difference	20,000	$1,000

Notice the mileage difference of 20,000 miles is accompanied by a cost difference of $1,000. So, to drive the extra 20,000 miles, the company spent $1,000 more in maintenance cost. We assume that the $1,000 increase in maintenance cost was caused exclusively by the increase in the number of miles from 11,000 to 31,000 miles. The cost per mile, then, is simply the $1,000 increased cost divided by the 20,000 additional miles as shown here:

$$\$1,000 \div 20,000 = \$0.05, \text{ or 5 cents per mile}$$

Before we calculate the fixed cost element, recall that total mixed cost is total fixed cost plus total variable cost (Total Mixed Cost = Fixed Cost Element +

Variable Cost Element). The variable cost element can be calculated by multiplying the variable cost per unit by the activity. In this case we multiply the variable cost per mile by the number of miles. With what we have determined thus far, we can begin to construct a cost formula for vehicle maintenance cost as follows:

Total Mixed Cost = Fixed Cost Element + ($0.05 per mile driven)

For each of our observations (high and low), we know the total mixed cost and variable cost element. Therefore, we can easily determine the fixed cost element with simple calculations. Let us determine the fixed cost element associated with the high observation used in our example.

Total Mixed Cost = Fixed Cost Element + ($0.05 per mile driven)
$2,600 = ? + ($0.05 × 31,000)
$2,600 = ? + $1,550

To solve the equation, the fixed cost element must be $2,600–$1,550, or $1,050, shown as follows:

Total Mixed Cost = Fixed Cost Element + ($0.05 per mile driven)
$2,600 = $1,050 + $1,550

We now know both the variable cost per mile and the total fixed cost of operating one of the delivery vehicles. To check our math, we can do the same calculation for the low observation, as follows:

Total Mixed Cost = Fixed Cost Element + ($0.05 per mile driven)
$1,600 = ? + ($0.05 × 11,000)
$1,600 = ? + $550

For the low observation, to solve the equation, fixed cost must be $1,600–$550, or $1,050, as we see next.

Total Mixed Cost = Fixed Cost Element + ($0.05 per mile driven)
$1,600 = $1,050 + $550

The high-low method yields a fixed cost for maintenance of $1,050, and a variable cost of 5 cents per mile. As with scatter graphing, to estimate the mixed cost at a particular level of activity, we add the fixed cost to the activity multiplied by the cost per unit of activity. For example, the estimated maintenance cost for a single delivery truck that is to be driven 28,000 miles is $2,450, calculated as follows:

$1,050 + ($0.05 × 28,000) = $2,450

Discussion Questions

4-14. Using the high-low method and the data from our example, what would be the maintenance cost for operating one of the delivery trucks if we expected the truck to be driven 25,000 miles next year?

4-15. Using the high-low method and the information from our Hinds Company example, what would be the maintenance cost for operating the fleet of eight trucks, if each is to be driven 25,000 miles on average?

When we compare the scatter graph method with the high-low method, we find that the fixed and variable cost results are somewhat different. If you were going to present your cost estimates to the vice president of marketing, which method would you use? Which provides the most dependable information? The scatter graph method is based on visual estimation whereas the high-low method is based on hard mathematics with no visual estimation. Does that make the high-low method better? No, because the high-low method considers only two observations. What if these two observations are not representative of the data in general? Then the cost behavior conclusions will be flawed and possibly misleading.

Another drawback to the high-low method is that users cannot assess whether the data items have a linear relationship, which is necessary to find meaningful results. Because the scatter graph method considers all observations and indicates whether the data items have a linear relationship, practitioners regard it as superior to the high-low method, despite the fact that it is more time consuming to use and it is based on visual estimation.

Regression Analysis

regression analysis A method used to separate a mixed cost into its fixed and variable components using complex mathematical formulas.

least-squares method Another name for *regression analysis*.

linear regression analysis Another name for *regression analysis*.

Regression analysis, also called the **least-squares method** or **linear regression analysis,** is a mathematical approach to determining fixed and variable cost with statistical accuracy. The mathematical computations are complex and beyond the scope of this text; however, it is important to note that regression is a more reliable estimation technique than either the scatter graph method or the high-low method. Regression analysis uses the information contained in all the observations in a data set. That thoroughness makes it superior to the high-low method. Because it considers all these points of observation mathematically, rather than visually, regression analysis is also superior to the scatter graph method.

The basic mathematical equation for regression analysis follows:

$$Y = a + bX$$

When applying regression analysis to find the fixed and variable elements of a mixed cost, the variables in the regression equation are defined as follows:

$$Y = \text{total cost}$$
$$a = \text{fixed cost}$$
$$b = \text{unit variable cost}$$
$$X = \text{activity level}$$

Results of regression analysis would provide answers to the same questions that we posed for the scatter graph and the high-low methods. In fact, the results of regression analysis allow us to determine total cost, Y, for any given level of activity, X. Reexamine the basic regression analysis formula and compare it with the total cost equation.

$$Y = a + bX$$

Where: $Y = \text{total cost}$
$a = \text{fixed cost}$
$b = \text{unit variable cost}$
$X = \text{activity level}$

When we rewrite the equation, we see that it translates directly to our earlier total cost equation, as follows:

Total Cost = Fixed Cost + (Unit Variable Cost × Activity Level)

Although regression analysis is difficult to compute manually, most spreadsheet software packages provide easy-to-use regression functions. Also, almost all business calculators, such as the Hewlett-Packard 12c, are programmed to compute linear regression problems. By reading your calculator's instruction manual, and practicing a little, you can easily determine fixed and variable cost components of a mixed cost using linear regression.

No matter which of the methods a company uses to separate mixed costs into fixed and variable elements, the outcome of the mixed cost analysis is useful information for controlling costs, setting prices, and assessing profitability. Indeed, a variety of internal users of accounting information, from marketing managers to production managers, will want access to such cost behavior information.

Whether large or small, simple or complex, managers of all companies must understand cost behavior. Production managers at companies as diverse as Caterpillar Tractor and Campbell Soup Company need this information to plan and control their operations. Marketing managers at companies as different as General Motors and Gerber Baby Foods must know how costs react to activity if they are to do their jobs properly.

Once a determination has been made as to a cost's behavior, an appropriate notation can be made in the accounting records to designate it as fixed, variable, or mixed. Then, the accounting system can produce reports sorted by cost behavior. Internal reports providing cost behavior information are valuable in a variety of decision-making settings. We will explore several of these settings in more detail in the next chapter.

SUMMARY

If managers are to plan and control their operations effectively, they must understand cost behavior. Cost behavior is the reaction of costs to changes in levels of business activity.

The most common cost behavior patterns are fixed cost, variable cost, and mixed cost. A fixed cost is a cost that remains constant in total regardless of the level of activity within the relevant range. A variable cost is a cost that changes in total proportionately with changes in the level of activity within the relevant range. The relevant range is the range of activity within which fixed and variable cost assumptions are valid. A mixed cost is a cost that has both a fixed cost element and a variable cost element.

Over the years, several methods have been developed to separate a mixed cost into its fixed and variable components. The most commonly used methods are the engineering approach, scatter graphing, the high-low method, and regression analysis.

The engineering approach to separating a mixed cost into its fixed and variable components uses experts who are familiar with the technical aspects of the activity and associated cost. Scatter graphing separates a mixed cost into its fixed and variable components by plotting historical activity and cost data to see how a cost relates to various levels of activity. The high-low method uses the mathematical differences between the highest and lowest levels of activity and cost. Regression analysis uses complex mathematical formulas, but the results are more mathematically precise than those of the scatter graph or high-low method.

Regardless of the method that managers choose to separate mixed costs into fixed and variable elements, the analysis provides useful information for a myriad of business decisions.

KEY TERMS

cost behavior   M-120
engineering approach   M-127
fixed cost   M-120
high-low method   M-134
least-squares method   M-136
linear regression analysis   M-136

mixed cost   M-125
regression analysis   M-136
relevant range   M-124
scatter graphing   M-128
variable cost   M-121

REVIEW THE FACTS

A. What is cost behavior?
B. For fixed costs, what happens to total cost as activity increases?
C. For fixed costs, what happens to the cost per unit as activity increases?
D. For variable cost, what happens to total cost as activity increases?
E. For variable cost, what happens to the cost per unit as activity increases?
F. With respect to cost behavior, what is the relevant range?
G. Does the relevant range pertain to fixed costs, variable costs, or both fixed and variable costs?
H. What are the two elements of a mixed cost?
I. What are the four methods of separating a mixed cost into its two cost components?
J. Compare the high-low method to the scatter graph method. Which provides the more dependable information?
K. What is the major limitation of the high-low method?
L. What is another name for regression analysis?
M. If you desired the reliability of the regression analysis method but did not want to suffer through the difficulty of doing the mathematics manually, what would you do?

APPLY WHAT YOU HAVE LEARNED

LO 2: Classifying Cost by Cost Behavior

4–16. Indicate whether the following costs are more likely to be fixed (F), variable (V), or mixed (M) with respect to the number of units produced.

1. _____ Direct material
2. _____ Direct labor
3. _____ Cost of plant security guard
4. _____ Straight line depreciation on production equipment
5. _____ Maintenance on production equipment
6. _____ Maintenance on factory building
7. _____ Cost of cleaning supplies used in the factory
8. _____ Rent on the factory building
9. _____ Salary for the two factory supervisors
10. _____ Vice president of manufacturing's salary
11. _____ Cost of electricity used in the factory
12. _____ Cost of production machine lubricants

LO 2: Classifying Cost by Cost Behavior

4–17. Assume that you are trying to analyze the costs associated with driving your car. Indicate whether the following costs are more likely to be fixed (F), variable (V), or mixed (M) with respect to the number of miles driven.

1. _____ Cost of the car
2. _____ Insurance cost
3. _____ Maintenance cost
4. _____ Cost of gasoline
5. _____ The cost of a college parking permit
6. _____ AAA membership

LO 2: Classifying Cost by Cost Behavior

4–18. Assume that you are planning a large party. As you are trying to figure out how much the party will cost, you decide to separate the costs according to cost behavior. Indicate whether the following costs are more likely to be fixed (F), variable (V), or mixed (M) with respect to the number of guests attending the party.

    1. _____ Rent for the party hall
    2. _____ Cost of the band
    3. _____ Cost of cold drinks
    4. _____ Cost of food
    5. _____ Cost of party decorations
    6. _____ Cost of renting tables and chairs

LO 2: Classifying Cost by Cost Behavior

4–19. Assume that you have been assigned to analyze the costs associated with operating the law firm of Moore & Moore and Company. The law firm just moved into a new, large office building that it purchased last year. Indicate whether the following costs are more likely to be fixed (F), variable (V), or mixed (M) with respect to the number of attorneys working for the firm.

    1. _____ Cost of the new office building
    2. _____ Basic telephone service
    3. _____ Cost of attorney salaries
    4. _____ Cost of the receptionist's wages

LO 2: Classifying Cost by Cost Behavior

4–20. Assume that you have been assigned to analyze the costs of a retail merchandiser, Auto Parts City. Indicate whether the following costs are more likely fixed (F), variable (V), or mixed (M) with respect to the dollar amount of sales.

    1. _____ Cost of store rent
    2. _____ Basic telephone service
    3. _____ Cost of salaries for the two salespeople
    4. _____ Cost of advertising
    5. _____ Cost of store displays
    6. _____ Cost of electricity
    7. _____ Cost of merchandise sold

LO 4: Evaluating a Mixed Cost Situation

4–21. Assume that you work for Wilma Manufacturing Company and have been asked to review the cost of delivery truck maintenance. The company president, Wilma Hudik, is dissatisfied with the accounting department's reluctance to calculate the fixed and variable cost of truck maintenance as it pertains to the number of units produced in the factory.

The accounting department prepared the following scatter graph:

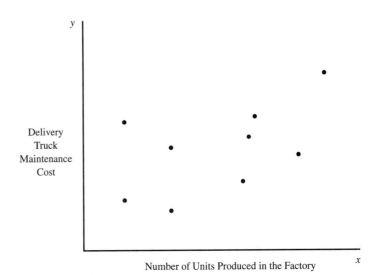

The accounting department personnel seem unable to use the graph to determine fixed and variable cost. The company president knows that regression analysis will provide mathematically accurate amounts for the fixed and variable truck maintenance cost, but no one in the accounting department seems to know how to do it.

REQUIRED:
Prepare a short memo to the president that details the feasibility of using the scatter graph and regression analysis to determine the fixed and variable components of delivery truck maintenance relative to the amount of factory production. In addition, your memo should recommend an alternative approach that could be used to evaluate the cost and cost behavior of truck maintenance.

LO 5: Use of a Scatter Graph for Separating Mixed Cost

4–22. Consider the following scatter graphs:

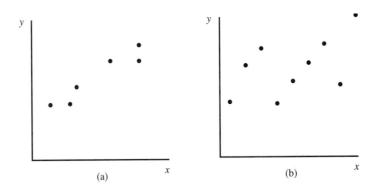

REQUIRED:
Which of the scatter graphs (a or b) do you think would be more appropriate for determining the fixed and variable portions of a mixed cost? Explain your reasoning.

LO 5: Separating Mixed Cost Using the High-Low Method

4–23. The following information pertains to Jacobs Incorporated:

2000	Information:	
	Sales	$2,300,000
	Selling expense	347,000
2001	Information:	
	Sales	$2,860,000
	Selling expense	369,400

REQUIRED:
Using the high-low method, determine the following:
a. The variable cost element for selling expense
b. The fixed selling expense
c. The selling expense that can be expected if sales are $2,500,000

LO 5: Separating Mixed Cost Using the High-Low Method

4–24. The following information pertains to the Robin Rappaport Company:

2000	Information:	
	Units packaged	14,500
	Packaging cost	$32,567
2001	Information:	
	Units packaged	15,300
	Packaging cost	$33,191

REQUIRED:
Using the high-low method, determine the following:
a. The variable cost element for packaging cost
b. The fixed packaging cost
c. The packaging cost that can be expected if 15,000 units are packaged

LO 5: Separating Mixed Cost Using the High-Low Method

4–25. The inspection department at the Rose Spiegel Company inspects every third unit produced. The following information is available for the inspection department:

2000	Information:	
	Number of inspections	41,950
	Inspection cost	$77,273
2001	Information:	
	Number of inspections	48,600
	Inspection cost	$83,790

REQUIRED:
Using the high-low method, determine the following:
a. The variable cost element for inspection cost
b. The fixed inspection cost
c. The inspection cost that can be expected if 45,000 units are inspected

LO 5: Separating Mixed Cost Using the High-Low Method

4–26. The plant manager has asked you to analyze the cost of electricity used in the manufacturing facility. Information for 2000 and 2001 follows:

	2000	2001
Machine hours	100,000	120,000
Cost of electricity	$188,000	$221,600

REQUIRED:

a. Determine the variable rate for electricity per machine hour.
b. Determine the total fixed cost of electricity.
c. Determine the estimated cost of electricity for next year if machine hours are expected to be 122,500.

LO 5: Separating Mixed Cost Using the High-Low Method

4–27. The office manager has asked you to analyze the cost of service and supplies for the office copy machines. Information for 2000 and 2001 follows:

	2000	2001
Number of copies produced	52,550	77,800
Cost of service and supplies	$1,961.57	$2,592.82

REQUIRED:

a. Determine the variable cost per copy.
b. Determine the total fixed cost for service and supplies for the copy machines.
c. Determine the estimated cost of service and supplies for next year if 75,000 copies are made.

LO 5: Separating Mixed Cost Using the High-Low Method

4–28. The production manager has asked you to analyze the cost of materials handling. Information for 2000 and 2001 follows:

	2000	2001
Number of parts handled	154,300	185,400
Materials handling cost	$9,244.77	$10,675.37

REQUIRED:

a. Determine the variable cost per part handled.
b. Determine the total fixed cost for materials handling.
c. Determine the estimated cost of materials handling if 160,000 parts are handled next year.

LO 5: Separating Mixed Cost Using the High-Low Method

4–29. The sales manager has asked you to estimate the shipping cost that can be expected for 2002. Following is information for 2000 and 2001:

	2000	2001
Sales in units	15,000	18,000
Shipping cost	$30,000	$35,400

REQUIRED:

Estimate 2002 shipping cost assuming sales of 16,500 units.

LO 5: Separating Mixed Cost Using the High-Low Method

4–30. The transportation manager has asked you to estimate the operating cost that can be expected for the company jet for 2002. Following is information for 2000 and 2001:

	2000	2001
Flight time in hours	1,250	1,875
Aircraft operating cost	$1,563,750	$2,148,125

REQUIRED:

Estimate the cost of operating the company jet for 2002 assuming that flight time will be 1,500 hours.

LO 5: Separating Mixed Cost Using the High-Low Method

4–31. Tom Robinson is the owner of Robinson Fishing Guide Service. He is trying to estimate the cost of operating his fishing service next year. He expects to have 185 charters during 2002. The following information is available:

	2000	2001
Number of charters	150	190
Operating cost	$7,741	$8,601

REQUIRED:

Determine the estimated operating cost for 2002.

LO 5: Separating Mixed Cost Using the High-Low Method

4–32. The following information pertains to Picon Manufacturing for 2000:

	Number of Purchase Orders Issued	Cost of Operating the Purchasing Department
Fourth quarter of 1999	2,500	$130,000
First quarter of 2000	1,000	80,000
Second quarter of 2000	1,500	110,000
Third quarter of 2000	2,000	115,000
Fourth quarter of 2000	3,000	140,000

REQUIRED:

Using the high-low method, determine the following:
a. The variable cost per purchase order
b. The fixed cost of operating the purchasing department for one quarter
c. The estimated cost of operating the purchasing department in 2001 assuming that 7,000 purchase orders will be issued. (Hint: Remember that the fixed cost for one year is four times the amount of fixed cost for one quarter.)

LO 5: Separating Mixed Cost Using the Scatter Graph Method

4–33. Refer to the information from problem 4–32.

REQUIRED:

Using the scatter graph method, determine the following:
a. The variable cost per purchase order
b. The fixed cost of operating the purchasing department for one quarter

c. The estimated cost of operating the purchasing department in 2001 assuming that 7,000 purchase orders will be issued. (Hint: Remember that the fixed cost for one year is four times the amount of fixed cost for one quarter.)

LO 5:   Separating Mixed Cost Using the High-Low Method

4–34. The following information pertains to Blue Glass Bottled Spring Water:

	Number of Sales Invoices Processed	Cost of Operating the Invoicing Department
Fourth quarter of 1999	10,500	$50,574.65
First quarter of 2000	11,000	52,711.12
Second quarter of 2000	15,000	58,231.51
Third quarter of 2000	12,000	59,439.73
Fourth quarter of 2000	9,000	46,299.73

REQUIRED:
Using the high-low method, determine the following:
a. The variable cost per invoice processed
b. The fixed cost of operating the invoicing department for one quarter
c. The estimated cost of operating the invoicing department in 2001 assuming that 45,000 invoices will be processed. (Hint: Remember that the fixed cost for one year is four times the amount of fixed cost for one quarter.)

LO 5:   Separating Mixed Cost Using the High-Low Method

4–35. The following information pertains to Jillian Munter & Associates:

	Number of Computers Repaired	Cost of Operating the Repair Department
Fourth quarter of 1999	125	$26,100.91
First quarter of 2000	130	26,529.16
Second quarter of 2000	110	25,400.65
Third quarter of 2000	105	25,212.91
Fourth quarter of 2000	115	25,799.88

REQUIRED:
Using the high-low method, determine the following:
a. The variable cost per computer repair
b. The fixed cost of operating the repair department for one quarter
c. The estimated cost of operating the repair department in 2001 assuming that 450 invoices will be processed. (Hint: Remember that the fixed cost for one year is four times the amount of fixed cost for one quarter.)

LO 5:   Separating Mixed Cost Using the High-Low Method

4–36. The following information is taken from Sweepy Broom Manufacturing Company:

	Number of Brooms Produced	Total Production Cost
January	9,800	$17,100
February	7,000	15,000

March	8,000	16,000
April	7,500	15,500
May	10,100	17,200
June	9,000	17,000
July	10,500	19,000
August	11,600	20,000
September	10,600	18,200
October	8,500	16,800
November	12,100	20,500
December	11,000	18,000

REQUIRED:
Using the high-low method, determine the following:
a. The variable production cost per unit
b. The total fixed production cost
c. The expected production cost to produce 12,000 brooms

LO 5: Separating Mixed Cost Using the Scatter Graph Method

4–37. Refer to the information in problem 4–36.

REQUIRED:
Using the scatter graph method, determine the following:
a. The variable production cost per unit
b. The total fixed production cost
c. The expected production cost to produce 12,000 brooms

LO 5: Separating Mixed Cost Using the High-Low Method

4–38. Ace Computer Training offers short computer courses. The number of course sessions offered depends on student demand. The following information pertains to 2001:

	Number of Sessions	Cost
First quarter	30	$ 75,000
Second quarter	35	78,000
Third quarter	15	42,000
Fourth quarter	20	48,000
Total	100	$243,000

REQUIRED:
Using the high-low method, determine the following:
a. The variable cost per session
b. The total fixed cost of operating the company
c. The expected cost for a quarter if 25 sessions are offered

LO 5: Separating Mixed Cost Using the Scatter Graph Method

4–39. Refer to the information in problem 4–38.

REQUIRED:
Using the scatter graph method, determine the following:
a. The variable cost per session
b. The total fixed cost of operating the company
c. The expected cost for a quarter if 25 sessions are offered

LO 5: Separating Mixed Cost Using the High-Low Method

4–40. The following information is taken from Miami Avionics Testing Service:

	Number of Tests Performed	Total Cost of Testing
January	61,000	$1,420,000
February	55,000	1,340,000
March	50,000	1,290,000
April	72,000	1,430,000
May	78,000	1,440,000
June	81,000	1,540,000
July	90,000	1,590,000
August	108,000	1,610,000
September	111,000	1,700,000
October	128,000	1,720,000
November	140,000	1,860,000
December	132,000	1,810,000

REQUIRED:
Using the high-low method, determine the following:
  a. The variable cost per test
  b. The total fixed cost of operating the testing facility
  c. The expected cost for a month if 125,000 tests are performed

LO 5: Separating Mixed Cost Using the Scatter Graph Method

4–41. Refer to the information in problem 4–40.

REQUIRED:
Using the scatter graph method, determine the following:
  a. The variable cost per test
  b. The total fixed cost of operating the testing facility
  c. The expected cost for a month if 125,000 tests are performed

LO 5: Separating Mixed Cost Using the High-Low Method

4–42. The following information is for the Valdez Supply Company:

	2001	2002
Sales	$1,000,000	$1,150,000
COSTS:		
Cost of goods sold	$ 800,000	$ 920,000
Sales commissions	15,000	17,250
Store rent	3,000	3,000
Depreciation	20,000	20,000
Maintenance cost	3,800	4,100
Office salaries	34,000	35,500

REQUIRED:
Assuming sales is the activity base, use the high-low method to determine the variable cost element and the fixed cost component of each of the costs just listed.

LO 5: Separating Mixed Cost Using the High-Low Method

4–43. The following information is for the General Production Company:

	2001	2002
Units produced	257,000	326,000
COSTS:		
Direct material	$ 611,660	$ 775,880
Direct labor	1,662,790	2,109,220
Manufacturing overhead	1,781,820	1,868,760

REQUIRED:

Assuming units produced is the activity base, use the high-low method to determine the variable cost element and fixed cost component of each of the costs just listed.

LO 5: Separating Mixed Cost Using the High-Low Method

4–44. The following information is for the Maupin Gift Shop:

	2001	2002
Sales	$100,000	$150,000
COSTS:		
Cost of goods sold	$ 75,000	$112,500
Sales commissions	5,000	7,500
Store rent	1,000	1,000
Depreciation	500	500
Maintenance cost	200	250
Office salaries	5,000	6,000

REQUIRED:

a. Assuming sales is the activity base, use the high-low method to determine the variable cost element and the fixed cost component of each of the costs just listed.

b. Why is it useful to know the information requested in requirement a?

LO 4: Components of Mixed Cost

4–45. Consider the following mathematical formula:

$$Y = a + bX$$

REQUIRED:

Match the variables to the correct descriptions. Some variables have two correct matches.

1. Y _____
2. a _____
3. b _____
4. X _____

   a. Independent variable
   b. Variable cost per unit
   c. Dependent variable
   d. Total fixed cost
   e. Activity
   f. Total cost

LO 4: Describing the Methods of Separating Mixed Cost

4–46. Besides the engineering approach, this chapter discussed three methods of separating a mixed cost into its variable and fixed components.

REQUIRED:

Write a brief memo outlining the relative advantages and disadvantages of the high-low method, the scatter graph method, and regression analysis in estimating the variable and fixed portions of a mixed cost.

LO 4: Describing the Methods of Separating Mixed Cost

4–47. Mr. Robinson, the director of Medical Diagnostics Clinic, is preparing a presentation to the clinic's board of directors about the fee charged for thallium stress tests. Part of the presentation will include information about the variable cost element and fixed costs associated with the tests. The accounting department has provided the director with a report which details the monthly costs associated with the thallium stress tests and the number of tests performed each month. Mr. Robinson is contemplating whether to use the scatter graph method, the high-low method, or regression analysis to separate the cost into its variable cost element and fixed cost. The director has asked your help in choosing an appropriate method.

REQUIRED:

Prepare a short report to Mr. Robinson providing insight into the strengths and weaknesses of the scatter graph method, the high-low method, and regression analysis. Your report should conclude with support for a final recommendation of one of the methods of separating mixed cost.

LO 1, 2, 4, and 5: Analyzing a Situation Using Cost Behavior

4–48. Accents Furniture Company has been in business for two years. When the business began, Accents established a delivery department with a small fleet of trucks. The delivery department was designed to be able to handle the substantial future growth of the company. As expected, sales for the first two years of business were low and activity in the delivery department was minimal.

In an effort to control costs, Accents Furniture Company's store manager is considering a proposal from a delivery company to deliver the furniture sold by Accents for a flat fee of $30 per delivery.

The following information is available regarding the cost of operating Accents's delivery department during its first two years of business.

	2000	2001
Number of deliveries	600	700
Cost of operating the delivery department	$25,480	$26,480

Sales and the number of deliveries are expected to increase greatly in the coming years. For example, sales next year will require an estimated 1,250 deliveries, while in 1999, it is expected that 1,775 deliveries will be required.

Due to the high growth rate, the store manager is concerned that the delivery cost will grow out of hand unless the proposal is accepted. He states that the cost per delivery was about $42.47 ($25,480/600) in 2000 and $37.83 ($26,480/700) in 2001. Even at the lower cost of $37.83, it seems the company can save about $7.83 ($30.00 - $37.83) per delivery. For 1999, the store manager believes the proposal can save the company about $13,898.25 (1,775 × $7.83).

REQUIRED:

Assume that you have been assigned to a group which has been formed to analyze the delivery cost of Accents Furniture Company. Your group should prepare a report and presentation that indicates the advantage or disadvantage of accepting the proposed delivery contract. Your report and presentation should not only include calculations to support your recommended course of action, but should also address the nonmonetary considerations of contracting with an outside source for delivery services.

LO 1, 2, 3, and 4: Addressing a Situation Using Cost Behavior Concepts

4–49. Mr. Reed is considering starting his own business. He has worked for a large corporation all his life and desires a change of pace. He is most interested in retail merchandising, but does not know what products his new business should sell. Mr. Reed is unsure about how to proceed with this major change in his life and has hired a consulting firm to help.

Assume that you have been assigned to the consulting group that will advise Mr. Reed.

REQUIRED:

Your group is to prepare a report that recommends a particular product line for Mr. Reed's new retail merchandising business. In addition, your report should recommend ways for Mr. Reed to gather information about the various costs associated with the merchandising business you have recommended. Finally, your report should explain how costs are classified as variable, fixed, and mixed costs, and why such classification by cost behavior is important.

LO 1, 2, and 4: Analyzing a Situation Using Cost Behavior

4–50. The Bowl-O-Mat operates a small chain of bowling alleys in southern Florida. Bowl-O-Mat's president, Al Palmer, is considering adding a supervised playground facility to each of the bowling alley properties. The playgrounds would require that a small addition be built onto each of the bowling alley buildings. Each playground would include a swing, a slide, climbing bars, and some other small-scale playground equipment. Each child would be charged an admission fee to use the facility. It is expected that parents will stay at the bowling alleys longer while their children are occupied in the playground area.

Mr. Palmer is interested in obtaining cost information relative to the proposed playground project. He understands that the more hours each playground area is open for business, the higher the cost of operating the playground will be. Beyond that, he knows nothing of cost behavior patterns.

REQUIRED:

Prepare a memorandum to Mr. Palmer that describes the following:
  a. The various variable, fixed, and mixed costs that are likely to be associated with the new playground facilities
  b. The concept of fixed costs, variable costs, and mixed costs
  c. Why an understanding of the methods available for estimating cost behavior patterns will help him to better plan and control his operations

Chapter 5

Business Decisions Using Cost Behavior

C laudia June is the owner of Upstart T-Shirt Shop, one of many souvenir shops located on Highway A1A in Daytona Beach, Florida. Upstart sold 3,000 T-shirts during 1997 (the company's first year of operation), and Claudia's accountant prepared the following multistep income statement for the year.

UPSTART T-SHIRT SHOP
Income Statement
For the Year Ended December 31, 1997

Sales		$36,000
Cost of Goods Sold		21,600
Gross Profit		$14,400
Operating Expense:		
Selling Expense	$9,500	
Administrative Expense	7,900	(17,400)
Operating Loss		$(3,000)

Frankly, Claudia was quite pleased with the results for 1997 because she did not expect the store to be profitable in its first year. As Claudia planned for 1998, she figured she needed to increase sales by only 625 T-shirts to break even for the year. Her reasoning was based on the fact that each T-shirt cost $7.20 and sold for $12, resulting in $4.80 gross profit on each T-shirt ($12.00 − $7.20 = $4.80). If the shop sold 3,625 T-shirts, it would earn a gross profit of $17,400 (3,625 × $4.80), which would be exactly enough to cover the selling and administrative expenses of $17,400. If Claudia met her sales goal, the store would break even in only its second year of operation.

As luck would have it, Upstart T-Shirt Shop sold exactly 3,625 T-shirts during the year ended December 31, 1998. Each T-shirt sold for exactly $12 and cost the company exactly

$7.20. Confident that the shop had broken even for the year, Claudia excitedly opened the envelope from her accountant and found the following multistep income statement for 1998.

UPSTART T-SHIRT SHOP
Income Statement
For the Year Ended December 31, 1998

Sales		$43,500
Cost of Goods Sold		26,100
Gross Profit		$17,400
Operating Expense:		
Selling Expense	$10,438	
Administrative Expense	8,897	(19,335)
Operating Loss		$(1,935)

Claudia was disappointed and discouraged when she saw an operating loss of $1,935 for the year. She rechecked the arithmetic and her assumptions about what it would take to break even for 1998 and could not understand why the store had an operating loss.

Claudia may not understand what happened, but after having studied Chapter 4 and its discussion of cost behavior, you should understand the problem. Claudia failed to consider that some costs are affected by changes in activity level and others are not. In this chapter, we explore cost-volume-profit analysis and see how business people use an understanding of this analytical technique to predict financial performance effectively. ■

LEARNING OBJECTIVES

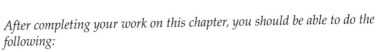

After completing your work on this chapter, you should be able to do the following:

1. Describe the differences between a functional income statement and a contribution income statement.
2. Determine per unit amounts for sales, variable cost, and the contribution margin.
3. Determine the contribution margin ratio and explain its importance as a management tool.
4. Prepare and analyze a contribution income statement for a merchandising firm.
5. Describe cost-volume-profit (CVP) analysis and explain its importance as a management tool.
6. Use CVP analysis to determine the amount of sales required to break even or to earn a targeted profit.
7. Use CVP to perform sensitivity analysis.

THE CONTRIBUTION INCOME STATEMENT

As discussed in Chapter 4, separating costs by means of cost behavior provides managers insight about forecasting cost at different levels of business activity. This valuable cost behavior information, however, is not presented in either the multistep or the single-step income statement used for financial reporting. The traditional income statement prepared for external parties separates costs (expenses) as either product costs or period costs.

functional income statement An income statement that classifies cost by function (product cost and period cost).

An income statement that separates product and period costs is called a **functional income statement.** Management accountants have developed a special income statement format for internal use that categorizes costs by behavior (fixed cost and variable cost) rather than by function (product cost and period cost). An income statement that classifies costs by behavior is a **contribution income statement.** Now, do not be alarmed, as this new format is no more complicated than the income statements you studied in earlier chapters. The main difference between the two is that the contribution income statements list variable costs first, followed by fixed costs. Note that the contribution income statement cannot be used for financial accounting information prepared for external decision makers; it is only used for internal decision-making purposes.

contribution income statement An income statement that classifies cost by behavior (fixed cost and variable cost).

Purpose of the Contribution Income Statement

Let us return to the Upstart T-Shirt Shop example to see how a contribution income statement could have helped Claudia better predict the future profitability of her merchandising company. The two income statements presented for Upstart (1997 and 1998) were functional income statements. Upstart's 1997 functional income statement is reproduced as Exhibit 5–1.

Exhibit 5–1
Upstart's 1997 Functional Income Statement

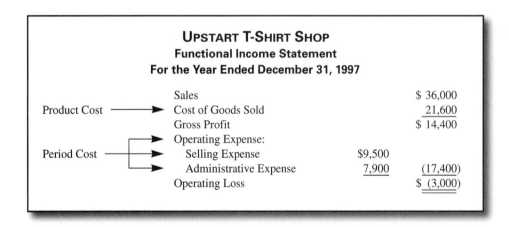

We see that the cost information in Exhibit 5–1 is separated into product cost (cost of goods sold) and period cost (selling expenses and administrative expenses). Next we will examine how Claudia can convert her functional income statement into a contribution income statement.

First, Claudia needs additional information about the cost behavior of the expenses in Upstart's 1997 functional income statement. On request, Claudia's accountant provides the following information:

Cost of goods sold	All variable
Selling expense	40% variable, so 60% must be fixed
Administrative expense	$6,300 Fixed, so $1,600 must be variable

Discussion Question

5-1. With the cost behavior information just presented, can you help Claudia determine how much her profit will change if she sells 5,000 shirts in 1999? (Remember to look at the 1998 income statement shown at the beginning of the chapter.)

Now that she has Upstart's cost behavior information, Claudia can prepare a contribution income statement for 1997. The contribution income statement lists sales first, as does the functional income statement, with variable costs listed next. These costs are subtracted from sales to arrive at the contribution margin. **Contribution margin** is defined as the amount remaining after all variable costs have been deducted from sales revenue. The contribution margin is an important piece of information for managers, because it tells them how much of their company's original sales dollars remain after deduction of variable costs. This remaining portion of the sales dollars contributes to fixed costs and, once fixed costs have been covered, to profit. The contribution margin, then, is the amount available to contribute to covering fixed costs and ultimately toward profits for the income statement period.

contribution margin The amount remaining after all variable costs have been deducted from sales revenue.

Upstart's 1997 contribution income statement (through the contribution margin) is presented as Exhibit 5–2.

Exhibit 5–2
Upstart's Partial 1997 Contribution Income Statement

UPSTART T-SHIRT SHOP Partial Contribution Income Statement For the Year Ended December 31, 1997		
Sales		$36,000
Variable Cost:		
Cost of Goods Sold	$21,600	
Variable Selling Expense ($9,500 × 40%)	3,800	
Variable Administrative		
Expense ($7,900 – $6,300)	1,600	
Total Variable Cost		(27,000)
Contribution Margin (Sales Less Total Variable Cost)		$ 9,000

Finally, fixed costs are listed and subtracted from the contribution margin to arrive at operating income, as shown in Exhibit 5–3.

Like a functional income statement, the contribution income statement can be detailed or condensed depending on the needs of the information users. It can also be prepared showing the per unit costs and percentage of sales calculations. A condensed version of Upstart's 1997 contribution income statement, including per unit and percentage of sales figures, is presented as Exhibit 5–4.

Throughout the rest of the chapter we will use a condensed version of the contribution income statement.

Discussion Questions

5–2. Why is the gross margin found on the functional income statement different from the contribution margin found on the contribution income statement?

5–3. Why is the operating loss shown on Upstart's 1997 contribution income statement exactly the same as the operating loss shown on the company's 1997 functional income statement?

Looking at the per unit column in Exhibit 5–4, we note that the contribution margin per unit is $3. We calculate this by dividing the total contribution margin of $9,000 by the number of units sold—in this case 3,000 ($9,000 / 3,000 = $3). The $3 per unit contribution margin means that for every T-shirt sold, the sale generates $3 to contribute toward fixed costs. Then, once fixed costs have been covered, $3 per T-shirt sold contributes to profit. That is, if Upstart sells one more shirt for $12, then the $12 selling price less the $9 variable cost leaves $3. The contribution margin contributes toward fixed cost first, then to profits.

Exhibit 5–3
Upstart's Completed 1997 Contribution Income Statement

UPSTART T-SHIRT SHOP
Contribution Income Statement
For the Year Ended December 31, 1997

Sales		$36,000
Variable Cost:		
Cost of Goods Sold	$21,600	
Variable Selling Expense ($9,500 × 40%)	3,800	
Variable Administrative		
Expense ($7,900 – $6,300)	1,600	
Total Variable Cost		(27,000)
Contribution Margin (Sales Less Total Variable Cost)		$ 9,000
Fixed Cost:		
Fixed Selling Expense ($9,500 × 60%)	$ 5,700	
Fixed Administrative		
Expense	6,300	
Total Fixed Cost		(12,000)
Operating Loss		$ (3,000)

Exhibit 5–4
Upstart's Condensed 1997 Contribution Income Statement

UPSTART T-SHIRT SHOP
Contribution Income Statement
For the Year Ended December 31, 1997

	Total	Per Unit	Sales (%)
Sales in Units	3,000	1	
Sales	$36,000	$12.00	100
Variable Cost	(27,000)	(9.00)	(75)
Contribution Margin	$9,000	$ 3.00	25
Fixed Cost	(12,000)		
Operating Loss	$ (3,000)		

contribution margin ratio
The contribution margin expressed as a percentage of sales.

Note in the percentage column of Exhibit 5–4 that the contribution margin is 25 percent of sales. When the contribution margin is expressed as a percentage of sales, it is called the **contribution margin ratio.**

The contribution margin ratio is calculated by dividing the total contribution margin by total sales, or by dividing the per unit contribution margin by per unit selling price, as follows:

$$\frac{\text{Total Contribution Margin}}{\text{Total Sales}} = \text{Contribution Margin Ratio}$$

or

$$\frac{\text{Per Unit Contribution Margin}}{\text{Per Unit Selling Price}} = \text{Contribution Margin Ratio}$$

In the case of Upstart T-Shirt Shop, the calculations are as follows:

$$\frac{\$9,000}{\$36,000} = 25\%$$

or

$$\frac{\$3}{\$12} = 25\%$$

The contribution margin ratio is the same whether it is computed using total figures or per unit figures, because the contribution margin is based on sales minus only variable costs. Thus, the variable costs and contribution margin change in direct proportion to sales. This proportional relationship holds true whether we are using per unit amounts or amounts in total.

In our example, the 25 percent contribution margin ratio means that, of each sales dollar, 25 percent (or 25 cents) is available to contribute toward fixed cost and then toward profit.

Discussion Question

5–4. If Upstart's sales increase by $20,000, and the contribution margin ratio is 25%, by how much will profits increase?

The contribution income statement is a wonderful management tool because it allows managers to see clearly the amounts of fixed and variable costs incurred by the company. Understanding which costs are variable and which are fixed is essential if managers are to reasonably predict future costs. More importantly, a solid understanding of the contribution income statement approach and the concept of the contribution margin and contribution margin ratio is the backbone of another important decision-making tool: cost-volume-profit analysis.

COST-VOLUME-PROFIT ANALYSIS

cost-volume-profit (CVP) analysis The analysis of the relationship between cost and volume and the effect of these relationships on profit.

As its name implies, **cost-volume-profit (CVP) analysis** is the analysis of the relationships between cost and volume (the level of sales), and the effect of those relationships on profit. In this section, we examine how managers can use CVP concepts to predict sales levels at which a firm will break even or attain target profits. CVP analysis is a useful tool for managers, business owners, and potential business owners for determining the profit potential of a new company or the profit impact of changes in selling price, cost, or volume on current businesses.

Thousands of businesses are started every day. Unfortunately, most of them fail a short time later, and the people who start these businesses suffer significant financial and emotional hardship. Such hardships might be avoided if new business owners used CVP analysis to evaluate the potential profit of their business ventures. With CVP analysis, a new business owner can discover potential disaster before starting the business, thereby preserving savings that could be used more productively elsewhere.

Breakeven

breakeven Occurs when a company generates neither a profit nor a loss.

break-even point The sales required to achieve breakeven. This can be expressed either in sales dollars or in the number of units sold.

We begin our coverage of CVP analysis with a discussion of breakeven. **Breakeven** occurs when a company generates neither a profit nor a loss. The sales volume required to achieve breakeven is called the **break-even point.** Because most businesses exist to earn a profit, why would managers be interested in calculating a break-even point? In at least two situations this kind of information is valuable. First, the break-even point will show a company how far product sales can decline before the company will incur a loss. This information could provide the encouragement to continue in business, or may provide an early warning of impending business failure. Second, owners and managers may use break-even analysis when starting a business, just as Claudia did with the Upstart T-Shirt Shop. Recall that Upstart experienced a $3,000 operating loss in its first year of operation, but Claudia expected the loss because she understood most businesses are not profitable in their first year. Her break-even prediction for Upstart's second year, however, failed to allow for certain cost increases as sales increased.

With our understanding of cost behavior and the contribution income statement, we can predict the level of sales that Upstart will need to break even for the year.

Let us look again at the 1997 contribution income statement for Upstart T-Shirt Shop, reproduced in Exhibit 5–5.

Exhibit 5–5
Upstart's Condensed 1997 Contribution Income Statement

	UPSTART T-SHIRT SHOP Contribution Income Statement For the Year Ended December 31, 1997		
	Total	**Per Unit**	**Sales (%)**
Sales in Units	3,000	1	
Sales	$36,000	$12.00	100
Variable Cost	(27,000)	(9.00)	(75)
Contribution Margin	$9,000	$ 3.00	25
Fixed Cost	(12,000)		
Operating Loss	$ (3,000)		

Managers who use CVP analysis must apply simple formulas to obtain useful information. Understanding and applying these formulas during this course should be relatively simple, but remembering them when you are actually working as a manager may be difficult. To make these formulas easier to remember, we will relate them to the most basic math used in an income statement, beginning with sales minus cost equals profit. Next, recall that cost can be broken down into variable and fixed cost. We use this information to derive a basic CVP equation, as shown in Exhibit 5–6.

Exhibit 5–6
Basic CVP Equation

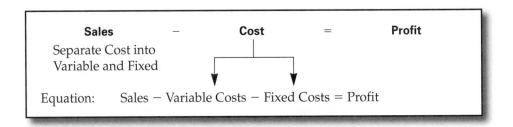

| Sales | − | Cost | = | Profit |

Separate Cost into
Variable and Fixed

Equation: Sales − Variable Costs − Fixed Costs = Profit

The basic equation for CVP analysis in Exhibit 5–6 requires that the costs be identified as fixed or variable, and that any mixed cost be separated into its fixed and variable components. In the examples that follow, we assume costs have been properly classified as fixed or variable.

Managers can calculate the break-even point based either on units or on sales dollars. We will demonstrate the process in units first, and then in sales dollars.

Break-Even Point in Units   To illustrate how to find the break-even point in units, we examine the Upstart T-Shirt Shop example. As shown in Exhibit 5–5, the selling price per T-shirt is $12, the variable cost is $9 per shirt, the contribution margin is $3 per T-shirt, and fixed costs total $12,000 per year. With this information, we can determine the number of T-shirts Upstart must sell to achieve a break-even point by dividing the contribution margin per unit into the total fixed cost, as shown in the following CVP formula:

CVP Formula 1—Break-Even Point in Units

$$\frac{\text{Total Fixed Cost}}{\text{Contribution Margin Per Unit}} = \text{Break-Even Point in Units}$$

Using the information from Upstart, we calculate the following:

$$\frac{\$12,000}{\$3} = 4,000 \text{ T-shirts}$$

By using this simple formula (and our knowledge of the cost behavior patterns associated with Upstart T-Shirt Shop), we see that if Upstart had sold exactly 4,000 T-shirts in 1998, the company would have broken even for the year. We can prove this fact if we use the equation from Exhibit 5–6 and the information from Upstart as follows:

Sales	−	Variable Costs	−	Fixed Costs	=	Profit
(4,000 × $12)	−	(4,000 × $9)	−	$12,000	=	Profit
$48,000	−	$36,000	−	$12,000	=	$ 0

We can also prove it by preparing a contribution income statement based on the results of our calculation, as shown in Exhibit 5–7.

Break-Even Point in Sales Dollars   Because business performance is measured in total dollar sales and in the number of units of product sold, managers also find it useful to have breakeven presented in both sales dollars and unit sales. To demonstrate the calculation of the break-even point in sales dollars, we once again use the information provided by Upstart T-Shirt Shop's contribution income statement in Exhibit 5–5.

When calculating the break-even point in sales dollars, we divide the contribution margin ratio into total fixed cost, as shown in the second of the CVP formulas.

Exhibit 5–7
Upstart's Condensed
1998 Contribution
Income Statement

UPSTART T-SHIRT SHOP
Projected Contribution Income Statement
For the Year Ended December 31, 1998

	Total	Per Unit	Sales (%)
Sales in Units	4,000	1	
Sales	$ 48,000	$12.00	100
Variable Cost	(36,000)	(9.00)	(75)
Contribution Margin	$ 12,000	$ 3.00	25
Fixed Cost	(12,000)		
Operating Income	$ -0-		

CVP Formula 2—Break-Even Point in Sales Dollars

$$\frac{\text{Total Fixed Cost}}{\text{Contribution Margin Ratio}} = \text{Break-Even Point in Sales Dollars}$$

Using the information from Upstart's contribution income statement, we know that total fixed cost is $12,000 and the contribution margin ratio is 25 percent. The break-even point calculation is

$$\frac{\$12,000}{25\%} = \$48,000 \text{ Sales Dollars}$$

A quick review of the contribution income statement in Exhibit 5–7 shows that our calculation of $48,000 sales at the break-even point is correct.

We have examined the calculation of a break-even point in required units and in sales dollars. As stated earlier, however, companies are not in business to break even. Rather, they are usually interested in earning profits. In the next section, we discuss how the break-even calculations are modified to predict a company's profitability.

Predicting Profits Using CVP Analysis

Claudia June now knows that her T-shirt business must sell 4,000 T-shirts to break even, assuming of course that the T-shirt selling price and the variable and fixed costs remain unchanged. Claudia can also use CVP analysis to predict Upstart's profit for any given level of sales above the break-even point. Assume, for example, that Upstart expects to sell 7,500 shirts in 1999. Claudia can quickly predict the expected profit at that sales level by preparing a contribution income statement, such as that in Exhibit 5–8.

UPSTART T-SHIRT SHOP
Projected Contribution Income Statement
For the Year Ended December 31, 1999

	Total	Per Unit	Sales (%)
Sales in Units	7,500	1	
Sales	$ 90,000	$12.00	100
Variable Cost	(67,500)	(9.00)	(75)
Contribution Margin	$ 22,500	$ 3.00	25
Fixed Cost	(12,000)		
Operating Income	$ 10,500		

If we did not want to take the time required to construct an actual contribution income statement, we could calculate the same operating income using the following basic CVP equation shown in Exhibit 5–6.

Sales	−	Variable Costs	−	Fixed Costs	=	Profit
(7,500 × $12)	−	(7,500 × $9)	−	$12,000	=	Profit
$90,000	−	$67,500	−	$12,000	=	$10,500

The sales figure in this calculation is the number of T-shirts multiplied by the selling price per unit (7,500 × $12 = $90,000). Variable cost is the number of T-shirts sold multiplied by the variable cost per unit (7,500 × $9 = $67,500). The fixed cost of $12,000 remains the same in total. With these three figures in place, simple arithmetic gave us the expected profit of $10,500 if 7,500 T-shirts are sold.

Projecting Sales Needed to Meet Target Profits Using CVP Analysis

Using CVP analysis to project profits at a given level of sales is only one application of this technique. Next we explore how to use CVP analysis when price and cost information are known, and a manager wants to determine the sales required to meet a specific target profit objective. As with the break-even point, we can apply CVP analysis to determine the sales needed to meet target profits in either units or sales dollars.

Projecting Required Sales in Units Assume Claudia targets $27,000 as Upstart's profit for 1999. By making a simple addition to the formula we used to calculate the break-even point, Claudia can determine how many T-shirts Upstart must sell to earn that target profit. The modified formula is as follows:

CVP Formula 3—Unit Sales Required to Achieve Target Profits

$$\frac{\left(\text{Total Fixed Cost + Target Profit}\right)}{\text{Contribution Margin Per Unit}} = \text{Required Unit Sales}$$

Recall that the contribution margin is the amount available to contribute to covering fixed cost first, and then profits. When considering the break-even point, we calculated the number of units required simply to cover the fixed cost. In our present discussion, we are looking for the number of units required not only to cover the fixed cost, but also to achieve a specific target profit. As shown in CVP formula 3, we simply add the target profit to the total fixed cost and then divide the sum by the contribution margin per unit. This equation will tell us how many units must be sold to cover all the fixed cost and to attain the target profit. Using the information from Upstart, the calculation is as follows:

$$\frac{\left(\$12,000 + \$27,000\right)}{\$3} = \text{Required Unit Sales}$$

or

$$\frac{\$39,000}{3} = 13,000 \text{ T-Shirts}$$

We see, then, that with a fixed cost of $12,000 and a contribution margin per unit of $3, Upstart will need to sell 13,000 T-shirts to earn $27,000 profit.

Discussion Question

5-5. How would you prove to Claudia that 13,000 T-shirts must be sold to earn a $27,000 profit?

Projecting Required Sales in Dollars To demonstrate the calculation of the sales dollars required to attain target profits, we once again use the information provided by Upstart T-Shirt Shop's contribution income statement in Exhibit 5–5.

We use the contribution margin ratio as the denominator in the CVP formula, instead of the unit contribution margin, as follows:

CVP Formula 4—Sales Dollars Required to Achieve Target Profits

$$\frac{(\text{Total Fixed Cost} + \text{Target Profit})}{\text{Contribution Margin Ratio}} = \text{Required Sales Dollars}$$

With the information from Upstart, the calculation is as follows:

$$\frac{(\$12,000 + \$27,000)}{25\%} = \text{Required Sales Dollars}$$

or

$$\frac{\$39,000}{25\%} = \$156,000 \text{ in Sales}$$

Discussion Question

5-6. How would you prove to Claudia that sales must total $156,000 to earn a $27,000 profit?

In this section we introduced you to four cost-volume-profit formulas, as summarized in Exhibit 5–9.

Exhibit 5-9
Cost-Volume-Profit Formulas

Formula	Calculation	Purpose
CVP Formula 1	$\dfrac{\text{Total Fixed Cost}}{\text{Contribution Margin Per Unit}}$	To determine the break-even point in units
CVP Formula 2	$\dfrac{\text{Total Fixed Cost}}{\text{Contribution Margin Ratio}}$	To determine the break-even point in sales dollars
CVP Formula 3	$\dfrac{(\text{Total Fixed Cost} + \text{Target Profit})}{\text{Contribution Margin Per Unit}}$	To determine the unit sales required to achieve a target profit
CVP Formula 4	$\dfrac{(\text{Total Fixed Cost} + \text{Target Profit})}{\text{Contribution Margin Ratio}}$	To determine the sales dollars required to achieve a target profit

These formulas are used daily by managers of manufacturing, merchandising, and service type companies as they attempt to predict the future performance of their firms. Regardless of the career you choose, if it involves business you will see these formulas again and will be using them much sooner than you might think.

Cost-Volume-Profit Graph

In addition to the calculations we have been studying, CVP analysis can also be depicted graphically. The graph used to present CVP analysis is similar to those used in the discussion of cost behavior in Chapter 4. A CVP graph for Upstart T-Shirt Shop is presented as Exhibit 5–10.

Exhibit 5–10
CVP Graph—Upstart
T-Shirt Shop

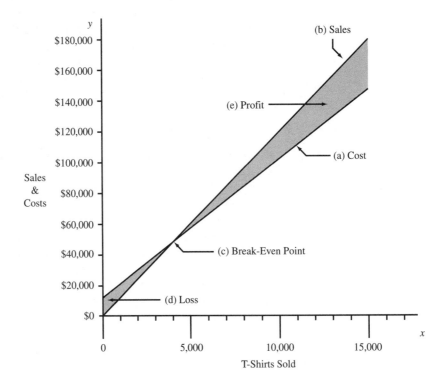

The main difference between the graph in Exhibit 5–10 and those in Chapter 4 is the graph in Exhibit 5–10 shows sales in addition to variable and fixed costs. The cost line (a) on the graph is exactly like those in Chapter 4. Note that this line intercepts the y-axis at $12,000, the total fixed cost for Upstart T-Shirt Shop. Thus, Upstart incurs $12,000 fixed cost even if the company sells no T-shirts. The cost line slopes upward at $9 for each T-shirt sold (variable cost).

Now consider the sales line (b) on the graph. If Upstart sells no T-shirts, there would obviously be no sales dollars, which explains why the sales line intercepts the y-axis at zero. The line slopes upward at $12 for every T-shirt sold. The point at which the cost line and the sales line cross (c) is Upstart's break-even point, which we know from our calculations in this chapter to be 4,000 T-shirts, or $48,000 in sales revenue. The loss area (d) on the graph and the profit area (e) represent a loss and profit, respectively, for Upstart. Thus, if Upstart sells fewer than 4,000 T-shirts, the company will experience a loss. If it sells more than 4,000 T-shirts, the company will earn a profit.

Discussion Question

5-7. Using the CVP graph in Exhibit 5–10, can you plot the level of sales (in units and dollars) where Upstart will earn a profit of

a. $10,500?

b. $27,000?

The CVP graph is a useful management tool. Although it should not take the place of the calculations we have demonstrated thus far in this chapter, it has a distinct advantage over the calculations in that it allows managers to view the entire cost-volume-profit picture. Claudia June can, for example, assess Upstart's profit potential at any level of business within the relevant range of activity.

Discussion Question

5-8. If Claudia is faced with competition from a new T-shirt shop in town, and is forced to lower her selling price to $11 per T-shirt, how much profit can she expect in 1998? (Assume that Claudia expects to sell 13,000 shirts and the cost information stays the same.)

To demonstrate the basics of CVP analysis, we have assumed that the selling price per unit, variable costs per unit, and total fixed cost all remained unchanged. Businesses, however, experience daily pressures that can cause each of these items to change. CVP analysis can adapt to any such change.

Now that we have covered the basics, we are ready to put CVP to perhaps its greatest use: sensitivity analysis.

Sensitivity Analysis—What If?

sensitivity analysis A technique used to determine the effect on cost-volume-profit when changes are made in the selling price, cost structure (variable and/or fixed), and volume used in the CVP calculations. Also called "what if" analysis.

Sensitivity analysis is a technique used to determine the effect on CVP when changes are made in the selling price, cost structure (variable and/or fixed), and volume used in the calculations. Sensitivity analysis is also called "what if?" analysis. Managers are often looking for answers to the following types of questions, in terms of the effect on projected profits: "What if we raised (or lowered) the selling price per unit?" "What if variable cost per unit increased (or decreased)?" and "What if fixed cost increased (or decreased)?" Sensitivity analysis can provide those answers.

One other item to note before we proceed with the discussion of sensitivity analysis is that we will be using only CVP formula 3 and CVP formula 4. Although sensitivity analysis can certainly be used to assess the effect of changes in selling price, variable cost, and fixed cost on breakeven, all our examples will include target profits.

To demonstrate how sensitivity analysis is used, we return to Claudia June and the Upstart T-Shirt Shop. Assume 1999 has now ended. Upstart's contribution income statement for the year is presented as Exhibit 5–11.

Exhibit 5–11
Upstart's Condensed
1999 Contribution
Income Statement

UPSTART T-SHIRT SHOP
Contribution Income Statement
For the Year Ended December 31, 1999

	Total	Per Unit	Sales (%)
Sales in Units	11,286	1	
Sales	$135,432	$12.00	100
Variable Cost	(101,574)	(9.00)	(75)
Contribution Margin	$ 33,858	$ 3.00	25
Fixed Cost	(12,000)		
Operating Income	$ 21,858		

Claudia is quite pleased with the $21,858 profit Upstart earned in 1999 and is aiming for a target profit of $27,000 in 2000 (the same target profit as 1999). The problem is that a new T-shirt shop just opened three doors from Upstart. Claudia feels she must lower her selling price to $11 due to competitive pressure and wants to know how many T-shirts Upstart must now sell to attain the $27,000 target profit. Claudia can use CVP analysis to determine the required sales level to achieve a targeted profit even if she changes her selling price.

Change in Selling Price

If the selling price changes but variable cost does not, the number of units required to attain a target profit is determined using CVP formula 3 and a recalculated contribution margin based on the new selling price. In the case of Upstart T-Shirt Shop, the new contribution margin is $2 (new selling price of $11 − variable cost of $9). We now apply this contribution margin to the formula. (Remember, the fixed cost is unchanged.)

$$\frac{(\$12,000 + \$27,000)}{\$2} = \text{Required Unit Sales}$$

or

$$\frac{\$39,000}{\$2} = 19,500 \text{ T-shirts}$$

Our calculations show that with a lower selling price, as reflected in the revised contribution margin per unit, Upstart must sell 19,500 T-shirts to attain the target profit of $27,000.

Discussion Question

5-9. How would you prove to Claudia that 19,500 T-shirts must be sold to earn a $27,000 profit if she reduces the selling price per T-shirt from $12 to $11?

We can also calculate the sales dollars required to attain the target profit of $27,000. To do this, we first calculate a new contribution margin ratio and then use CVP formula 4 to determine the sales dollars needed to earn the target profit. The new contribution margin ratio is 18.182 percent (rounded), which is calculated by dividing the new selling price ($11) into the new contribution margin ($2). We now apply this new information to CVP formula 4.

$$\frac{(\$12,000 + \$27,000)}{18.182\% \text{ (rounded)}} = \text{Required Sales Dollars}$$

or

$$\frac{\$39,000}{18.182\% \text{ (rounded)}} = \$214,498 \text{ Sales Dollars (rounded)}$$

By applying the revised contribution margin ratio to CVP formula 4, we see that Upstart will need $214,498 in sales to achieve the target profit of $27,000.

Discussion Questions

5-10. How would you prove to Claudia that sales must total $214,498 to earn a $27,000 profit if she reduces the selling price per T-shirt from $12 to $11?

5-11. Why must we calculate a new contribution margin ratio when the per unit selling price changes?

5-12. Under what other circumstances must we calculate a new contribution margin ratio?

If Claudia reduces her selling price to $11, then Upstart must sell 19,500 T-shirts in 2000 to earn the target profit of $27,000. Claudia believes it would be impossible to sell that many shirts, so she begins to consider alternative ways to earn a $27,000 profit in a competitive environment.

Notice that Claudia was able to determine by CVP analysis that her business may be in trouble. The analysis itself, however, does nothing whatever to solve the problem—that is up to Claudia. Management accounting can provide the informational tools to help managers and business owners spot problems, but it is ultimately up to the manager or owner to make the decisions and solve the problems.

Discussion Question

5-13. If Claudia must lower her selling price to $11 per shirt to be competitive, and it would be impossible to sell 19,500 T-shirts, what are some of the alternatives she might consider to attain the $27,000 profit?

Change in Variable Cost and Fixed Cost

Alternatives to changing the selling price include changing variable cost or fixed cost. Because Claudia believes the selling price per T-shirt must be $11, either the variable cost per unit or the total fixed cost must be reduced. We start with an analysis of possible changes in variable cost.

First, we must analyze how Upstart determined its original variable cost. We determine per unit variable cost by dividing the total variable cost by the number of units sold. Recall from the earlier discussion and Exhibit 5–4 that Upstart sold 3,000 T-shirts during 1997, and total variable cost was $27,000. Therefore, the variable cost per unit was calculated as $9 ($27,000 variable cost / 3,000 units sold).

Exhibit 5–12
Analysis of Upstart's
Variable Cost
Components

	Total Cost		Units Sold		Unit Cost
Cost of Goods Sold (T-shirts)	$21,600	÷	3,000	=	$7.20
Variable Selling Expenses	3,800	÷	3,000	=	1.27
Variable Administrative Expenses	1,600	÷	3,000	=	.53
Variable Cost	$27,000	Total			$9.00 Per Unit

To analyze how a change in variable cost will affect the variable cost per unit of $9, we must look at the three components of per unit variable cost: the cost of each T-shirt, the variable selling expenses, and the variable administrative expenses. We need to know what portion of the $9 variable unit cost relates to each component. We can determine these portions by dividing the 3,000 units sold into each of the three cost components. We use 3,000 because that number of units caused these costs to be incurred. We find the cost of each variable cost component in the contribution income statement presented in Exhibit 5–3. The cost and per unit calculation for each component are presented in Exhibit 5–12.

Claudia does not believe any change can be made in either the variable selling expenses or the variable administrative expenses. Any possible reduction in variable cost, then, must be in the cost of the T-shirts. Our calculations in Exhibit 5–12 show that the per unit cost of each T-shirt is $7.20.

Assume Claudia has contacted her shirt supplier which has agreed to lower its price from $7.20 to $6 per T-shirt. This reduction of $1.20 ($7.20 − $6.00 = $1.20) will reduce Upstart's variable cost from $9 per shirt to $7.80 per shirt ($9.00 − $1.20 = $7.80). The new contribution margin is $3.20 ($11 selling price − $7.80 variable cost = $3.20), and the new contribution margin ratio is 29.091 percent ($3.20 contribution margin / $11 selling price = 0.29091 or 29.091 percent rounded).

Now consider a change in Upstart's fixed cost. Recall that Upstart's total fixed cost is $12,000. Assume that Claudia has agreed to provide fellow businesswoman Susan Williams with space in her shop to sell bathing suits to Claudia's customers. Susan has agreed to pay Claudia $250 per month as rent on the space she will use. The $250 per month works out to be $3,000 per year ($250 per month × 12 months = $3,000). Thus, Upstart's total fixed cost decreases from $12,000 to $9,000.

With these proposed changes in Upstart T-Shirt Shop's variable cost and fixed cost, we can now do sensitivity analysis. Let us see what effect these changes would have on Claudia's company. To do this, again, we will use CVP formulas 3 and 4. We simply need to plug the new cost structures (variable and fixed) into the formulas as follows:

CVP Formula 3—Unit Sales Required to Achieve Target Profits

$$\frac{\left(\text{Total Fixed Cost} + \text{Target Profit}\right)}{\text{Contribution Margin Per Unit}} = \text{Required Unit Sales}$$

$$\frac{\left(\$9,000 + \$27,000\right)}{\$3.20} = 11,250 \text{ T-shirts}$$

By using CVP formula 3 (and Upstart's new variable and fixed cost structure), we found that if Upstart sells 11,250 T-shirts in 2000, the company will earn a profit of $27,000.

To calculate the sales dollars required to attain Upstart's target profit of $27,000, we use the company's new contribution ratio and CVP formula 4:

CVP Formula 4—Sales Dollars Required to Achieve Target Profits

$$\frac{\left(\text{Total Fixed Cost} + \text{Target Profit}\right)}{\text{Contribution Margin Ratio}} = \text{Required Sales Dollars}$$

$$\frac{\left(\$9,000 + \$27,000\right)}{29.091\% \text{ (rounded)}} = \$123,750 \text{ in Sales (rounded)}$$

With the changes in cost structure Claudia has negotiated, she will be able to earn $27,000 profit in 2000 even if her sales drop from 11,286 T-shirts (the 1999 sales level) to 11,250 T-shirts.

Discussion Questions

5–14. How would you prove to Claudia that sales must total $123,750 (11,250 T-shirts) to earn a $27,000 profit if she reduces the cost per T-shirt from $7.20 to $6 and reduces total fixed cost from $12,000 to $9,000?

5–15. If Claudia is more successful than anticipated in 2000 and sells 13,000 T-shirts by reducing her selling price to $11, and she also implements the variable and fixed cost changes described earlier, what will be Upstart's profits for 2000?

5–16. What complications do you foresee in using CVP analysis if Claudia begins selling a deluxe line of T-shirts that cost $11.50 each and sell for $17?

Multiple Products and CVP

In reality, most companies sell more than one product. Companies that sell multiple products often have information about total variable cost and total sales for a given income statement period, but have no one variable cost and selling price that can be easily determined and used for CVP.

When a company sells multiple products, managers may still use CVP analysis, but they must apply CVP formula 2 for break-even analysis and CVP formula 4 to determine the required level of sales to attain target profits. CVP formulas 1 and 3 are useless in a multiproduct situation if the various products sold have different unit contribution margins.

To demonstrate how managers use CVP analysis in a multiproduct situation when per unit information is unavailable, let us consider the example of Margaret's Frame Factory.

Margaret's Frame Factory makes and sells picture frames of various size and quality. Exhibit 5–13 presents Margaret's condensed contribution income statement for 1997.

There is a per unit variable cost and selling price for each of the frame models Margaret's manufactures and sells, but they are not included in Exhibit 5–13. All we have are the totals. The $185,000 contribution margin comes from the sale of several different products, each with its own contribution margin. The 37 percent contribution margin ratio, then, is an average contribution margin ratio based on the sales mix of these different products. Even with this limited information, however, we can use CVP analysis to both calculate a break-even point and predict target profits.

Exhibit 5–13
Margaret's Condensed
1997 Contribution
Income Statement

MARGARET'S FRAME FACTORY
Contribution Income Statement
For the Year Ended December 31, 1997

	Total	% of Sales
Sales	$ 500,000	100%
Variable Cost	(315,000)	(63%)
Contribution Margin	$ 185,000	37%
Fixed Cost	(143,000)	
Operating Income	$ 42,000	

Break-Even Point in a Multiproduct Situation

To calculate the break-even point in a multiproduct situation, we use CVP formula 2.

CVP Formula 2—Break-Even Point in Sales Dollars

$$\frac{\text{Total Fixed Cost}}{\text{Contribution Margin Ratio}} = \text{Break-Even in Sales Dollars}$$

Using the information from Margaret's, the calculation is as follows:

$$\frac{\$143,000}{37\%} = \$386,486 \text{ Sales Dollars (rounded)}$$

We know that Margaret's is well above the break-even point because the company earned a profit of $42,000 in 1997. The break-even calculation is still valuable to company management because it reveals how far sales could decline before the company would experience a loss. In this example, sales could decline by $113,514 ($500,000 1997 sales − $386,486 break-even point = $113,514 decline) before Margaret's would experience a loss.

Projecting Required Sales in a Multiproduct Situation

Assume that Margaret's is interested in increasing profits to $80,000 in 1998. Based on the information contained in the 1997 contribution income statement presented in Exhibit 5–13, what would be the required sales to earn this target profit of $80,000? To find out, we use CVP formula 4:

CVP Formula 4—Sales Dollars Required to Achieve Target Profits

$$\frac{\left(\text{Total Fixed Cost + Target Profit}\right)}{\text{Contribution Margin Ratio}} = \text{Required Sales Dollars}$$

Using the information from Margaret's Frame Factory's contribution income statement, we know that total fixed cost is $143,000, the target profit is $80,000, and the contribution margin ratio is 37 percent. The calculation of the required sales dollars is as follows:

$$\frac{\$143,000 + \$80,000}{37\%} = \$602,703 \text{ in Sales (rounded)}$$

Our calculations indicate that Margaret's Frame Factory will need $602,703 in sales to attain a target profit of $80,000.

Discussion Question

5-17. How would you prove to Margaret's that sales must total $602,703 to earn an $80,000 profit?

We have demonstrated how CVP analysis can provide useful information about how changes in selling price, variable cost, and fixed cost affect a company's break-even point. Managers can also use CVP analysis to see what sales (in either units or dollars) the company needs to attain target profits.

CVP analysis is highly adaptable. It works equally well when managers are trying to determine profit potential, whether of a small segment of a large business or of an entire company. Before a company expands an existing business market or makes the decision to enter new markets, management should invest some time in gathering revenue and cost data, separating the cost-by-cost behavior, developing a contribution income statement, and applying these simple CVP procedures.

CVP Assumptions

CVP analysis is a great "what if?" management tool because it is used by managers to estimate a company's profit performance under a variety of different scenarios. It is, however, an estimation technique only, and the following assumptions are made when this type of analysis is used.

1. All costs can be classified as either fixed or variable. Implicit in this assumption is that a mixed cost can be separated into its fixed and variable components.
2. Fixed costs remain fixed throughout the range of activity.
3. Variable cost per unit remains the same throughout the range of activity.
4. Selling price per unit remains the same throughout the range of activity.
5. The average contribution margin ratio in a multiproduct company remains the same throughout the range of activity.

These assumptions rarely, if ever, match reality. Market pressures, inflation, and a myriad of other factors cause revenue and cost structures to change in ways that place limitations on CVP analysis. Notwithstanding these limitations, however, CVP helps managers make more realistic estimates of future profit potential. It is a technique used every day by managers of large and small companies worldwide as they attempt to better manage their businesses.

SUMMARY

The functional income statement, which separates the costs shown into product cost and period cost, is limited in its usefulness to managers as they attempt to plan and control their operations. It does not take into account that some costs change as volume changes, and some do not. The contribution income statement is more useful to managers as a planning tool because it separates the costs presented into fixed costs and variable costs rather than into product costs and period costs.

An integral part of the contribution income statement is the contribution margin, which is the amount remaining after all variable costs have been deducted from sales revenue. When the contribution margin is presented as a percentage of sales, it is called the contribution margin ratio. Both the contribution margin and the contribution margin ratio are used in cost-volume-profit analysis.

Cost-volume-profit (CVP) analysis is the analysis of the relationships between cost and volume, and the effect of those relationships on profit. The first application of CVP analysis is the calculation of breakeven, which is the sales level resulting in neither a profit nor a loss. Breakeven can be calculated either in sales dollars or in the number of units of product that must be sold.

Cost-volume-profit analysis can also be used to calculate the sales level required to achieve a target profit. As was the case with breakeven, the sales level required to achieve a target profit can be calculated in both sales dollars and the number of units of product that must be sold.

Cost-volume-profit analysis can also be used to perform sensitivity analysis, which is a technique used to determine the effect on CVP when changes are made in the selling price, cost structure (variable and/or fixed), and volume used in the calculations.

Although CVP analysis is easier to perform in a single-product situation, it can also be used to calculate breakeven and sales required to achieve target profits in a multiple product situation.

KEY TERMS

breakeven   M-155
break-even point   M-155
contribution income statement   M-151
contribution margin   M-152
contribution margin ratio   M-154

cost-volume-profit (CVP)
  analysis   M-154
functional income statement   M-151
sensitivity analysis   M-161

REVIEW THE FACTS

A. What is the difference between a contribution income statement and a functional income statement?

B. What is the contribution margin?

C. What does the contribution margin "contribute toward"?

D. How does total contribution margin differ from contribution margin per unit?

E. What is the contribution margin ratio and how does it differ from the contribution margin?

F. What is cost-volume-profit (CVP) analysis?

G. What does the term *break-even point* mean?

H. In what ways does the calculation of the break-even point in units differ from the calculation of the break-even point in sales dollars?

I. How would you calculate the required sales in units to attain a target profit?

J. How would you calculate the required sales in dollars to attain a target profit?

K. What does the term *sensitivity analysis* mean in the context of CVP analysis?

L. What does the term *average contribution margin ratio* mean for a company that sells multiple products?

M. Which two of the four CVP formulas are used to calculate breakeven and sales required to attain target profits for a multiproduct company?

N. Why are two of the CVP formulas useless in a multiproduct situation when contribution margins for individual products are unknown?

APPLY WHAT YOU HAVE LEARNED

LO 4: Prepare a Contribution Income Statement

5–18. Fresh Baked Cookie Company sells cookies in a large shopping mall. The following multistep income statement was prepared for the year ending December 31, 2000.

FRESH BAKED COOKIE COMPANY
Income Statement
For the Year Ended December 31, 2000

Sales		$36,000
Cost of Goods Sold		4,000
Gross Profit		$32,000
Operating Expense:		
Selling Expense	$18,000	
Administrative Expense	10,000	28,000
Operating Income		$ 4,000

Cost of goods sold is a variable cost. Selling expense is 20% variable and 80% fixed, and administrative expense is 5% variable and 95% fixed.

REQUIRED:

Prepare a contribution income statement for the Fresh Baked Cookie Company.

LO 4: Prepare a Contribution Income Statement

5–19. The following multistep income statement was prepared for Steinmann's Bait Shop for the year ending December 31, 2000.

STEINMANN'S BAIT SHOP
Income Statement
For the Year Ended December 31, 2000

Sales		$98,000
Cost of Goods Sold		22,000
Gross Profit		$76,000
Operating Expense:		
Selling Expense	$27,000	
Administrative Expense	36,000	63,000
Operating Income		$13,000

Cost of goods sold is a variable cost. Selling expense is 30% variable and 70% fixed, and administrative expense is 10% variable and 90% fixed.

REQUIRED:

Prepare a contribution income statement for Steinmann's Bait Shop.

LO 4: Prepare a Contribution Income Statement

5–20. Quality Fishing Gear Company sells high-quality fiberglass fishing rods to retailers. The following multistep income statement was prepared for the year ending December 31, 2000.

QUALITY FISHING GEAR COMPANY
Income Statement
For the Year Ended December 31, 2000

Sales		$540,000
Cost of Goods Sold		360,000
Gross Profit		$180,000
Operating Expense:		
Selling Expense	$88,000	
Administrative Expense	72,000	160,000
Operating Income		$ 20,000

Cost of goods sold is a variable cost. Selling expense is 65% variable and 35% fixed, and administrative expense is 25% variable and 75% fixed.

REQUIRED:
Prepare a contribution income statement for Quality Fishing Gear Company.

LO 4:   Prepare a Contribution Income Statement

5–21. Ray Placid is considering opening a greeting card shop in a local mall. Ray contacted the mall manager and determined that the store rent will be $550 per month. In addition, he called the telephone company and based on the information from the telephone company representative, he estimates that the cost of telephone service will be about $95 per month. Based on the size of the store, Ray believes that cost of electricity will average about $200 per month. Ray will be able to buy the greeting cards for $0.50 each and plans to sell them for $2 each. Salaries are expected to be $1,200 per month regardless of the number of cards sold. Ray estimates that other miscellaneous fixed costs will total $150 per month and miscellaneous variable cost will be $0.10 per card. Ray anticipates that he will be able to sell about 3,000 greeting cards per month. If Ray opens the store, his first month of business will be November 2001.

REQUIRED:
Prepare a projected contribution approach income statement for November 2001.

LO 4:   Prepare a Contribution Income Statement

5–22. Joe's Pretzel Stand is located in the Orange Bowl stadium and sells pretzels during sporting events. The following information is available:

- Selling price per pretzel $2.00
- Cost of each pretzel $0.25
- Cost of renting the pretzel stand is $12,000 per year.
- Instead of an hourly wage, Joe pays college students $0.20 per pretzel sold to run the pretzel stand.

REQUIRED:
Prepare a contribution income statement for 2000 assuming that 8,000 pretzels are sold.

LO 4:   Prepare a Contribution Income Statement

5–23. The following information is available for Blaire's Snow Cone Stand:

- Selling price per snow cone $1.25
- Cost of each snow cone $0.30

- Rent paid for the stand, at a local flea market is $2,400 per year.
- Instead of an hourly wage, Blaire's pays high school students $0.40 per snow cone sold.

REQUIRED:

Prepare a contribution income statement for 2000 assuming that 6,000 snow cones are sold.

LO 4: Prepare a Condensed Contribution Income Statement

5–24. The following is the contribution income statement for The Bevens Company:

THE BEVENS COMPANY

Contribution Income Statement

For the Year Ended December 31, 2001

Sales		$800,000
Variable Cost:		
Cost of Goods Sold	$420,000	
Variable Selling Expense	75,000	
Variable Administrative Expense	33,000	
Total Variable Cost		528,000
Contribution Margin		$272,000
Fixed Cost:		
Fixed Selling Expense	$128,000	
Fixed Administrative Expense	53,000	
Total Fixed Cost		181,000
Operating Income		$ 91,000

REQUIRED:

Based on the contribution income statement for The Bevens Company, prepare a condensed contribution income statement.

LO 1: Prepare a Multistep Income Statement

5–25. Refer to the information presented in problem 5–24.

REQUIRED:

Prepare a multi-step income statement for the Bevens Company.

LO 4: Prepare a Condensed Contribution Income Statement

5–26. Following is the contribution income statement for The Lauren Company:

THE LAUREN COMPANY

Contribution Income Statement

For the Year Ended December 31, 2001

Sales		$4,800,000
Variable Cost:		
Cost of Goods Sold	$2,320,000	
Variable Selling Expense	265,000	
Variable Administrative Expense	484,000	
Total Variable Cost		3,069,000
Contribution Margin		$1,731,000
Fixed Cost:		
Fixed Selling Expense	$ 648,000	
Fixed Administrative Expense	973,000	
Total Fixed Cost		1,621,000
Operating Income		$ 110,000

REQUIRED:

Based on The Lauren Company's contribution income statement, prepare a condensed contribution income statement.

LO 1:   Prepare a Multistep Income Statement

5–27. Refer to the information presented in problem 5–26.

REQUIRED:

Prepare a multi-step income statement for The Lauren Company.

LO 4:   Prepare a Condensed Contribution Income Statement

5–28. The following is the contribution income statement for Carl's Athletic Shop:

CARL'S ATHLETIC SHOP

Contribution Income Statement

For the Year Ended December 31, 2001

Sales		$422,000
Variable Cost:		
Cost of Goods Sold	$205,000	
Variable Selling Expense	55,000	
Variable Administrative Expense	22,000	
Total Variable Cost		282,000
Contribution Margin		$140,000
Fixed Cost:		
Fixed Selling Expense	$ 75,000	
Fixed Administrative Expense	34,000	
Total Fixed Cost		109,000
Operating Income		$ 31,000

REQUIRED:

Based on this contribution income statement, prepare a condensed contribution income statement for Carl's Athletic Shop.

LO 1:   Prepare a Multistep Income Statement

5–29. Refer to the information presented in problem 5–28.

REQUIRED:

Prepare a multi-step income statement for Carl's Athletic Shop.

LO 4:   Prepare a Contribution Income Statement

5–30. Paradise Manufacturing makes weight-lifting equipment. During 2000, the following costs were incurred:

	Amount	Percent Fixed	Percent Variable
Direct material	$680,000	–	100
Direct labor	420,000	–	100
Variable manufacturing overhead	130,000	–	100
Fixed manufacturing overhead	900,000	100	–
Selling cost	300,000	20	80
Administrative cost	220,000	10	90

Sales for 2000 totaled $2,780,000 and there were no beginning or ending inventories.

REQUIRED:

Prepare a contribution income statement for the year ended December 31, 2000.

LO 4: Prepare a Contribution Income Statement

5–31. The following information is available for Nicole's Toy Manufacturing Company for 2000:

	Amount	Percent Fixed	Percent Variable
Direct material	$440,000	-	100
Direct labor	90,000	-	100
Variable manufacturing overhead	70,000	-	100
Fixed manufacturing overhead	800,000	100	-
Selling cost	950,000	45	55
Administrative cost	570,000	85	15

Sales for 2000 totaled $3,164,000 and there were no beginning or ending inventories.

REQUIRED:

Prepare a contribution income statement for the year ended December 31, 2000.

LO 4: Prepare a Contribution Income Statement

5–32. The following information is available for Rick's Watch Company for 2000:

	Amount	Percent Fixed	Percent Variable
Direct material	$534,000	-	100
Direct labor	129,000	-	100
Variable manufacturing overhead	397,000	-	100
Fixed manufacturing overhead	998,000	100	-
Selling cost	196,000	33	67
Administrative cost	243,000	78	22

Sales for 2000 totaled $2,745,000 and there were no beginning or ending inventories.

REQUIRED:

Prepare a contribution income statement for the year ended December 31, 2000.

LO 4: Prepare a Contribution Income Statement

5–33. Alumacraft Manufacturing makes aluminum serving carts for use in commercial jetliners. During 2001, the following costs were incurred:

	Amount	Percent Fixed	Percent Variable
Direct material	$2,600,000	-	100
Direct labor	1,820,000	-	100
Variable manufacturing overhead	540,000	-	100
Fixed manufacturing overhead	1,900,000	100	-
Selling cost	380,000	15	85
Administrative cost	230,000	5	95

Sales for 2001 totaled $7,900,000 and there were no beginning or ending inventories.

REQUIRED:

Prepare a contribution income statement for the year ended December 31, 2001.

LO 6: Determine Breakeven and Sales Required to Earn Target Profit Using Per Unit Amounts

5–34. The following information is available for Medical Testing Corporation.

Amount charged for each test performed	$ 90
Annual fixed cost	200,000
Variable cost per test	25

REQUIRED:

a. Calculate how many tests Medical Testing Corporation must perform each year to break even.

b. Calculate how many tests Medical Testing Corporation must perform each year to earn a profit of $25,000.

LO 6: Determine Breakeven and Sales Required to Earn Target Profit Using Per Unit Amounts

5–35. The following information is available for Dottie's Donut Shop.

Amount charged per dozen doughnuts	$ 0.99
Annual fixed cost	385,000.00
Variable cost per dozen doughnuts	0.22

REQUIRED:

a. Calculate how many dozen doughnuts Dottie must sell each year to break even.

b. Calculate how many dozen doughnuts Dottie must sell each year to earn a profit of $35,000.

LO 6: Determine Breakeven and Sales Required to Earn Target Profit Using Per Unit Amounts

5–36. Jim is considering starting a small company to paint driveways. The following information is available.

Amount charged per square yard painted	$ 5
Annual fixed cost	3,000
Variable cost per square yard painted	2

REQUIRED:

a. Calculate how many square yards of driveway Jim must paint each year to break even.

b. Calculate how many square yards of driveway Jim must paint each year to earn a profit of $5,000.

LO 6: Determine Breakeven and Sales Required to Earn Target Profit Using Per Unit Amounts

5–37. Carbonnel Calendar Company is considering adding a new calendar design to their line. The following information is available.

Selling price	$ 3.97
Additional annual fixed cost	4,558.00
Variable cost per calendar	3.11

REQUIRED:

a. Calculate how many calendars must be sold each year to break even.

b. Calculate how many calendars must be sold each year to earn a profit of $2,580.

LO 3 & 6:   Use Ratios to Determine Breakeven and Sales Required to Earn Target Profit

5–38. Melissa Valdez is planning to expand her clothing business by opening another store. In planning for the new store, Melissa believes that selling prices and costs of the various merchandise sold will be similar to that of the existing store. In fact, she thinks that variable and fixed costs for the new store will be similar to that of the existing store, except that rent for the new store will be $300 per month more than the rent paid for the existing store.

The following information is available for the existing store for the year ended December 31, 2000:

Sales	$200,000
Variable cost	130,000
Fixed cost	48,000

REQUIRED:

a. Determine the sales required for the new store to break even.

b. Determine the sales required for the new store to earn a profit of $20,000 per year. (Hint: Keep in mind that the $300 increase in rent is a monthly amount and the fixed cost of $48,000 is an annual amount.)

LO 3 & 6:   Use Ratios to Determine Breakeven and Sales Required to Earn Target Profit

5–39. Emergency Medical, Inc. is considering opening a new emergency care facility. The fees charged and costs of the new facility will be similar to that of the existing facility. The only exception is that the annual fixed cost for the new facility is expected to be $75,000 more than that of the existing facility.

The following information is available for Emergency Medical's existing facility for 2000:

Revenue	$1,250,000
Variable cost	600,000
Fixed cost	420,000

REQUIRED:

a. Determine the revenues required for the new emergency care facility to break even.

b. Determine the revenues required for the new emergency care facility to earn a profit of $120,000 per year.

LO 3 & 6:   Use Ratios to Determine Breakeven and Sales Required to Earn Target Profit

5–40. Wendt Industries is considering opening a second school supply store. The annual fixed cost of the new store is expected to be $225,000 per year. The following information is available for Wendt's first school supply store for 2000.

Revenue	$3,650,000
Variable cost	1,387,000

REQUIRED:

a. Based on this information, what is the required revenue for the second store to break even?

b. Based on this information, what is the required revenue for the second store to earn a profit of $125,000?

LO 2, 4, & 6:   Use Per Unit Amounts to Determine Breakeven and Sales Required to Earn Target Profit and Prepare a Contribution Income Statement

5–41. Richard Davenport owns a clothing store and is considering renting a soda vending machine for his store. He can rent the soda machine for $125 per month. Richard would supply the soda for the machine which he can buy for $3 per twelve pack. Richard plans to charge $0.75 per can.

REQUIRED:

a. List the fixed costs for renting and stocking the soda machine.

b. List the variable costs for renting and stocking the soda machine.

c. Calculate the contribution margin per can of soda.

d. (1) Calculate how many cans of soda Richard must sell each month to break even.

   (2) Prepare a contribution income statement that proves the answer you just calculated.

e. (1) Calculate how many cans of soda Richard must sell each month to earn a profit of $50.

   (2) Prepare a contribution income statement that proves your answer to the previous requirement.

LO 2, 4, & 6:   Use Per Unit Amounts to Determine Breakeven and Sales Required to Earn Target Profit and Prepare a Contribution Income Statement

5–42. Erich Traebeecke owns the Kenpo Karate School in Miami. He is considering renting a candy vending machine for his school lobby. He can rent the candy machine for $90 per month. Erich would supply the candy bars for the machine. He can buy a box of eight candy bars for $1 per box. Erich plans to sell each candy bar for $0.35.

REQUIRED:

a. List the fixed costs of renting and stocking the candy machine.

b. List the variable costs of renting and stocking the candy machine.

c. Calculate the contribution margin per candy bar.

d. (1) Calculate how many candy bars must be sold each month to break even.

   (2) Prepare a contribution income statement that proves the answer you just calculated.

e. (1) Calculate how many candy bars must be sold each month to earn a profit of $180.

   (2) Prepare a contribution income statement that proves your answer to the previous requirement.

LO 2, 4, and 6: Use Per Unit Amounts to Determine Breakeven and Sales Required to Earn Target Profit and Prepare a Contribution Income Statement

5–43. Monica Llobet owns Monica's School of Dance. She is considering installing a cappuccino machine in the school's dance studio. Monica can rent the cappuccino machine for $48.88 per month. Coffee and supplies would cost about $.12 per cup of cappuccino. Monica plans to sell each cup of cappuccino for $2.

REQUIRED:

a. List the fixed costs of renting and stocking the cappuccino machine.
b. List the variable costs of renting and stocking the cappuccino machine.
c. Calculate the contribution margin per cup of cappuccino.
d. **(1)** Calculate how many cups of cappuccino must be sold each month to break even.
   (2) Prepare a contribution income statement that proves the answer you just calculated.
e. **(1)** Calculate how many cups of cappuccino must be sold each month to earn a profit of $100. (Round your answer to the nearest unit.)
   (2) Prepare a contribution income statement that proves your answer to the previous requirement.

LO 2 & 6: Use Per Unit Amounts to Determine Breakeven and Sales Required to Earn Target Profit

5–44. Alberto Pons is interested in selling pin-on buttons at school pep rallies. The button machine will cost $200, and the material to produce each button costs $0.15. In exchange for the right to sell the buttons, Alberto has agreed to donate $300 per year and $0.20 per button to the school's booster club. Alberto plans to sell the buttons for $1 each and to operate the service for four years. By then it will be time to graduate, and the button machine will be worn out.

REQUIRED:

a. Assuming the button machine will be able to produce buttons for four years, calculate the cost per year for the button machine.
b. Calculate the total fixed cost per year for Alberto's button business.
c. Calculate the variable cost per button.
d. Calculate the annual break-even point
   (1) in units.
   (2) in dollars.
e. Calculate how many buttons must be sold to earn an annual profit of $800.
f. Calculate the sales in dollars required to earn an annual profit of $800.

LO 2 & 6: Use Per Unit Amounts to Determine Breakeven and Sales Required to Earn Target Profit

5–45. Betty Lopez is interested in setting up a stand to sell mylar helium balloons at a local roller rink. The stand would cost $250, and the material for each balloon would cost $0.75. In exchange for the right to sell the balloons, Betty has agreed to pay $500 per year and $0.50 per balloon to the roller rink's owner. Betty plans to sell the balloons $3 each. Betty thinks the stand will last four years.

REQUIRED:

a. Assuming the balloon stand has an estimated useful life of four years, with no salvage value, calculate the cost per year for the balloon stand.
b. Calculate the total fixed cost per year for Betty's balloon business.
c. Calculate the variable cost per balloon.
d. Calculate the annual break-even point
    (1) in units.
    (2) in dollars.
e. Calculate how many balloons must be sold to earn an annual profit of $2,000.
f. Calculate the sales in dollars required to earn an annual profit of $2,000.

LO 2 & 6: Use Per Unit Amounts to Determine Breakeven and Sales Required to Earn Target Profit

5–46. Bill Smith is interested in selling ice cream bars at school events. The vendor stand will cost $800, and the ice cream bars cost $0.65. In exchange for the right to sell the ice cream bars, Bill has agreed to donate $600 per year and $0.25 per ice cream bar to the school's booster club. Bill plans to sell the ice cream bars for $1.50 each. Bill intends to sell the ice cream bars and run the stand for four years. By then it will be time to graduate, and the vendor stand will be worn out.

REQUIRED:

a. Assuming the vendor stand can be used for four years, calculate the cost per year for the vendor stand.
b. Calculate the total fixed cost per year for Bill's ice cream business.
c. Calculate the variable cost per ice cream bar.
d. Calculate the annual break-even point.
    (1) in units.
    (2) in dollars.
e. Calculate how many ice cream bars must be sold to earn an annual profit of $3,000.
f. Calculate the sales in dollars required to earn an annual profit of $3,000.
g. Calculate Bill's profit if sales were $8,000 for this year.

LO 3 & 6: Determine the Contribution Margin Ratio and Determine Breakeven and Sales Required to Earn Target Profit

5–47. Amanda is considering opening a gift shop. She has collected the following information:

Monthly rent	$2,800
Monthly sales salaries	1,200

In addition to the sales salaries, Amanda intends to pay sales commissions of 5% of sales to her sales staff. The cost of the merchandise sold is expected to be 40% of sales.

REQUIRED:

a. Determine the following:
    (1) Amanda's break-even point in monthly sales dollars
    (2) The monthly sales dollars required to earn a profit of $2,000 per month
    (3) Amanda's break-even point if she is able to reduce rent by $200
b. Assume that Amanda has negotiated a 10% discount on all merchandise purchases. The new cost of merchandise will not change the selling price of product. Determine the following:

(1) The new contribution margin ratio

(2) The new break-even point in monthly sales dollars

LO 3 & 6: Determine the Contribution Margin Ratio and Determine Breakeven and Sales Required to Earn Target Profit

5–48. Noelle is considering opening a bookstore. She has collected the following information:

Monthly rent	$3,286
Monthly sales salaries	4,200

In addition to the sales salaries, Noelle intends to pay sales commissions of 10% of sales to her sales staff. The cost of the merchandise sold is expected to be 30% of sales.

REQUIRED:

a. Determine the following:

(1) Noelle's break-even point in monthly sales dollars

(2) The monthly sales dollars required to earn a profit of $1,500 per month

(3) Noelle's break-even point if she is able to reduce rent by $300

b. Assume that Noelle has negotiated a 5% discount on all merchandise purchases. The new cost of merchandise will not change the selling price of product. Determine the following:

(1) The new contribution margin ratio

(2) The new break-even point in monthly sales dollars

LO 2 & 6: Use Per Unit Amounts to Determine Breakeven and Sales Required to Earn Target Profit

5–49. Clarice is considering buying a video rental business. If she finances the entire purchase price, the payments will be $2,900 per month. Store rent would be $2,000 per month and cost of sales clerks, replacement tapes, and other expenses would be $1,200 per month. Clarice plans to rent the tapes for $2 each.

REQUIRED:

a. Calculate the variable cost (if any) per tape rental.

b. Calculate the total fixed cost per month.

c. Determine how many tapes Clarice must rent each month to break even.

d. Determine how many tapes Clarice must rent each month to earn a profit of $1,000 per month.

LO 3 & 6: Determine the Contribution Margin Ratio and Determine Breakeven and Sales Required to Earn Target Profit

5–50. Margaret Pitman is considering opening a gift shop. She has collected the following information:

Monthly rent	$1,800
Monthly sales salaries	1,200

The cost of the merchandise sold is expected to be 55% of sales.

REQUIRED:

a. What is the annual rent cost?

b. What is the annual sales salaries cost?

c. What is the contribution margin ratio?
d. What is the break-even point in dollars?
e. Determine the amount of sales needed to earn a profit of $12,000 for the year.

LO 3 & 6: Determine the Contribution Margin Ratio and Determine Breakeven and Sales Required to Earn Target Profit

5–51. Carol Jean is considering opening a frame shop. She has collected the following information:

Monthly rent	$ 600
Monthly sales salaries	1,100

The cost of the merchandise sold is expected to be 45% of sales.

REQUIRED:
a. What is the annual rent cost?
b. What is the annual sales salaries cost?
c. What is the contribution margin ratio?
d. What is the break-even point in dollars?
e. Determine the amount of sales needed to earn a profit of $18,000 for the year.

LO 3 & 6: Determine the Contribution Margin Ratio and Determine Breakeven and Sales Required to Earn Target Profit

5–52. Birdie Musicus is considering opening a beauty supply store. She has collected the following information:

Monthly rent	$3,400
Monthly sales salaries	2,800

The cost of the merchandise sold is expected to be 68% of sales.

REQUIRED:
a. What is the annual rent cost?
b. What is the annual sales salaries cost?
c. What is the contribution margin ratio?
d. What is the break-even point in dollars?
e. Determine the amount of sales needed to earn a profit of $36,000 for the year.

LO 3 & 6: Determine the Contribution Margin Ratio and Determine Breakeven and Sales Required to Earn Target Profit

5–53. Vivian Farias is considering opening a music store. She has collected the following information:

Monthly rent	$1,400
Monthly sales salaries	1,700

The cost of the merchandise sold is expected to be 52% of sales.

REQUIRED:
a. What is the annual rent cost?
b. What is the annual sales salaries cost?
c. What is the contribution margin ratio?
d. What is the break-even point in dollars?
e. Determine the amount of sales needed to earn a profit of $36,000 for the year.

LO 2, 3, 4, & 5: Analyze a Situation Using CVP

5–54. Quality Instrument Company manufactures various industrial thermometers. Last year the company sold 600 model QI-22 thermometers for $129 each. Managers are concerned that the profits from the QI-22 were only $7,740 last year. Fixed costs for this product are $50,000 per year. In an effort to increase profits, the company raised the price of the QI-22 to $148. Based on annual sales of 600 units, managers are confident that profits from the QI-22 will be increased to $19,140 next year.

The sales manager is concerned about the price increase. He believes the company should move a little slower in making the pricing decision and has suggested that a group be formed to explore the ramifications of such a pricing move.

REQUIRED:

Assume that you have been assigned to the group who will evaluate the proposed price change. The group is to create a report discussing the various ramifications of the price increase including its effect on projected sales and profits. Your report should make recommendations that are supported by calculations similar to those found in this chapter.

LO 2, 3, 4, & 5: Analyze a Situation Using CVP

5–55. Reuben Steinman's Sliding Glass Door Company manufactured and sold 1,000 model SD4896 doors for $88 each. Managers are concerned that the profits from the SD4896 doors were only $8,000 last year. In an effort to increase profits, the company raised the price of the SD4896 to $106. Based on annual sales of 1,000 units, managers are confident that profits from the SD4896 will increase to $26,000 next year. Fixed costs of $40,000 are allocated to the SD4896 based on the number of units produced.

The sales manager is concerned about the price increase. He believes the company should move a little slower in making the pricing decision and has suggested that a group be formed to explore the ramifications of such a pricing move.

REQUIRED:

Assume that you have been assigned to the group who will evaluate the proposed price change. The group is to create a report discussing the various ramifications of the price increase including its effect on projected sales and profits. Your report should make recommendations that are supported by calculations similar to those found in this chapter.

LO 2, 3, 4, & 5: Analyze a Situation Using CVP

5–56. Carol Juriet is considering the purchase of a hot dog vending cart to sell hot dogs in a busy parking lot. The city of Daytona Beach requires that the cart be licensed at a cost of $500 per year.

REQUIRED:

a. **(1)** How would Carol determine the cost to rent a small space in the parking lot to operate the hot dog cart?
(2) How much do you think the monthly rent would be?
(3) How much do you think the hourly wage would be for an employee to operate the stand?
(4) How many hours per day do you think the stand should be open?

      (5) Based on your answers to 3 and 4, what would you estimate monthly wage cost to be for the hot dog stand?

      (6) How much do you think Carol should charge for each hot dog?

  b. Answer the following questions using your answers to question 1.

      (1) What is the variable cost per hot dog?

      (2) What is the monthly fixed cost for operating the hot dog stand?

      (3) What is the contribution margin per hot dog?

      (4) What is the contribution ratio?

      (5) What is the variable cost ratio?

      (6) a) How many hot dogs must Carol sell each month to break even?

          b) Prepare a contribution income statement which proves your answer.

      (7) a) How many hot dogs must Carol sell each month to earn a profit of $300?

          b) Prepare a contribution income statement that proves your answer.

Chapter 6

Making Decisions Using Relevant Information

*F*inancial accounting information provided to external decision makers must be relevant to be useful. Not surprisingly, management accounting information provided to internal decision makers must also possess the characteristic of relevance. It is critically important that managers make their decisions based on relevant information and that they disregard all irrelevant information. To be relevant, the information must be pertinent to the decision at hand. In accounting, **relevant costing** is the process of determining which dollar inflows and outflows pertain to a particular management decision.

Determining which costs are relevant is not always an easy job. For instance, consider an actual example about a couple that went to Disney World with their three-year-old daughter, Jessica. The family stayed at a Disney hotel to be close to the Disney attractions, and to take advantage of the hotel's staff of baby-sitters. The baby-sitting service required payment of a 4-hour minimum at $11 per hour, or $44. Users must cancel 3 hours in advance to avoid the $44 minimum fee. Jessica's parents planned to take her to the Magic Kingdom early in the day and then leave her with a sitter in the late afternoon while they visited EPCOT on their own.

Jessica and her parents went to Disney's Magic Kingdom as they had planned and were having a wonderful time. As the day progressed, Jessica enjoyed the amusement park so much that Jessica's parents were having second thoughts about leaving her with the sitter. They had to make a decision: Should they take Jessica to EPCOT or leave her with the sitter as planned?

relevant costing The process of determining which dollar inflows and outflows pertain to a particular management decision.

Because the family's admission tickets permitted them to enter all the Disney parks, the main issue was the minimum $44 charge for the sitter, because it was too late to cancel. As Jessica's parents discussed the pros and cons of each alternative, they realized the $44 charge would have to be paid whether they took Jessica to EPCOT or not. The baby-sitter's fee, then, was an irrelevant cost in this decision, because Jessica's parents would have to pay the baby-sitting fee no matter which alternative they chose. Once Jessica's parents determined that the fee was irrelevant, they dismissed the sitter and Jessica was off to EPCOT with them.

In business, the issue of what is relevant often confuses even the most seasoned business executive. To make the best possible decisions, decision makers must learn to consider only relevant information. ■

LEARNING OBJECTIVES

After completing your work on this chapter, you should be able to do the following:

1. Identify the characteristics of a relevant cost.
2. Explain why sunk costs and costs that do not differ between alternatives are irrelevant costs.
3. Describe the qualitative factors that should be considered when making a business decision.
4. Use accounting information and determine the relevant cost of various decisions.
5. Explain the effects of fixed costs and opportunity costs on outsourcing decisions.

RELEVANT COSTS

You may wonder why an entire chapter of this text is devoted to determining which costs are relevant. Isn't it understood that decision makers should disregard superfluous information and concentrate on the facts that relate to the decision at hand? Yes, but with so many cost considerations to muddy the water, determining what information is relevant is not always as easy as it might seem.

relevant cost A dollar inflow or outflow that pertains to a particular management decision in that it has a bearing on which decision alternative is preferable.

A **relevant cost** is a cost that is pertinent to a particular decision in that it has a bearing on which decision alternative is preferable. A relevant cost possesses two important characteristics: (1) The cost must be a future cost, and (2) the cost must differ between decision alternatives.

A relevant cost must be a future cost because current decisions can have no effect on past expenditures. Expenditures that have already occurred are called **sunk costs** and they cannot be changed by current or future actions. Because sunk costs are unaffected by current decisions, they are irrelevant and should not be considered when evaluating current decision alternatives. For example, if your firm was deciding whether to replace an old printing press with a new, labor-saving model, the cost of the old press would be irrelevant. Why? The firm already bought the old

sunk cost A past cost that cannot be changed by current or future actions.

press. The purchase of the new printing press would not lessen or change the amount paid for the old press. Whether the company purchases the new press or not, the cost of the old press is a sunk cost: Nothing we can do now can change it. Sunk costs include both amounts paid in the past and past commitments to pay. That is, once there is a binding commitment to pay cash or otherwise transfer resources, the cost associated with that commitment is a sunk cost.

A relevant cost must differ between decision alternatives. If a cost remains the same regardless of the alternative we choose, it is irrelevant. Again, focus on the decision to buy a new printing press or to keep the old one. If the new printing press will use the same quantity and type of ink as the old one, the cost of ink is irrelevant no matter how large the dollar figure.

Discussion Questions

6–1. Refer back to the decision faced by Jessica's parents in Disney World. Which criteria of relevance did the $44 baby-sitting cost fail to meet? Explain your reasoning.

6–2. Have you ever made a decision and later found that you mistakenly let irrelevant factors sway your choice? Explain.

The term *relevant cost* is something of a misnomer. Perhaps a better description of this topic would be *relevant factors.* The reason for this is that the term relevant cost is used to describe not only changes in cost, but also changes in revenue. These cost and revenue changes often result in inflows of resources rather than outflows.

quantitative factors
Factors that can be measured by numbers.

Quantitative factors are those that can be represented by numbers. Almost all accounting information is quantitative, including relevant cost. However, managers often consider additional factors that cannot be quantified. **Qualitative factors** are factors that cannot be measured numerically—they must be described in words. Examples include customer satisfaction, product quality, employee morale, and customer perceptions.

qualitative factors Factors that cannot be measured by numbers—they must be described in words.

In addition to their financial impact, business decisions affect a multitude of nonfinancial areas. For example, closing an outdated factory may reduce production cost, but it will also adversely impact employee moral. The employees that remain after the plant closing may believe that the company's loyalty is to profits, not their well-being. Lower employee moral is likely to lead to less productivity. Qualitative factors should also be considered in smaller, routine decisions. For example, a furniture store manager considering a proposal to switch from company owned and operated delivery trucks to a delivery service should consider her lack of control if the delivery service is used. Even though it may be less expensive to use a delivery service, the furniture store's manager may not want to lose the ability to select the most responsible truck drivers and to schedule deliveries exactly as desired. When making a decision, managers should evaluate all relevant quantitative and qualitative factors.

Discussion Questions

Assume you are planning a trip from Miami to Texas to visit some friends. You have a job, but your boss will let you take off as many days as you wish for the trip. Your car is unreliable, so you compare two alternatives—take a bus or take an airplane.

6-3. What are the relevant quantitative factors you should consider in making your decision?

6-4. What are the relevant qualitative factors you should consider in making your decision?

Decision makers must question the relevance of accounting information. As discussed in Chapter 1, managers and engineers no longer specify accounting information requirements. Instead, accountants provide information to managers based on accepted accounting techniques, so its relevance to management decision makers has diminished. Although some businesses have taken steps to make management accounting information more relevant to internal decision makers, managers should be able to determine for themselves what is relevant so they can make sound, well-informed decisions (see Exhibit 6–1).

Exhibit 6–1
Determining
Relevant Cost

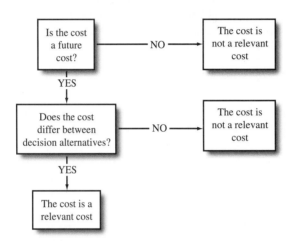

Throughout the remainder of this chapter, we will explore several common business situations to demonstrate how to determine relevant cost and its importance to good decision making. For each example, we will gather all costs associated with the decision. Next, we will determine the relevant cost of each decision alternative. Finally, we will compare the relevant costs of the alternative and determine the preferred alternative. The first example we will explore is an equipment replacement decision.

EQUIPMENT REPLACEMENT

To apply the concepts of relevant costing, we examine a proposed equipment replacement project. Our example highlights the treatment of depreciation, sunk costs, and costs that do not differ between alternatives.

Bill Smith & Partners, a local law firm, purchased and installed a sophisticated computer system two weeks ago at a cost of $35,500. Bill's brother, John, stops by the law office to say hello. While there, he notices the new system. He remarks that it is too bad the system is not the latest and quickest because, if it were, the data input time could be cut in half. John suggests that Bill consider updating. Bill responds, "I can't buy a new system. I just bought this one two weeks ago." John advises Bill to take a closer look before deciding.

Gather All Costs Associated with the Decision

Bill turns to you for advice. He explains that the recently installed computer system cost $35,500 to purchase, has an estimated useful life of five years, with a residual value of $500. He notes that the firm plans to use straight-line depreciation, so it will recognize $7,000 depreciation per year. The cost of operating the recently installed system, which we will call the "old" system, includes two operators at $18,000 per year, and a maintenance contract at $1,000 per year. The maintenance agreement, however, can be canceled at any time. After calling around, Bill informs you that he can sell the old system now, but he will get only $10,000 for it (everyone wants the new model). The new model would cost $76,000 and also has an estimated useful life of five years with a $1,000 residual value. Using the straight-line method, annual depreciation would be $15,000. Because data entry is twice as fast, the new computer system would require only one operator at $18,000 per year. The maintenance contract on the new machine would cost $1,000 per year and would be cancelable at any time.

A summary of the cost of each system is shown in Exhibit 6–2. These costs are generally classified as start-up costs, operating costs, and shutdown costs.

Exhibit 6–2
Computer System
Replacement
Cost Summary

	Old System	Replacement System
Start-up costs:		
Cost of system	$ 35,500	$76,000
Operating costs:		
Annual depreciation	$ 7,000	$15,000
Total depreciation	35,000	75,000
Annual labor cost	36,000	18,000
Total labor cost	180,000	90,000
Annual maintenance cost	1,000	1,000
Total maintenance cost	5,000	5,000
Shutdown costs:		
Residual value of system	$ 500	$ 1,000
Current sale price of old system	10,000	

To help Bill make a wise decision about the new computer system, you must first look at each cost and determine whether it is relevant. To make an informed decision, a manager must consider the total cost of each alternative, including all the costs incurred over the life of the alternative. For our computer replacement decision, the annual costs associated with each system are multiplied by the number of years the system will be used to determine the total cost of the system over its lifetime.

Determine the Relevant Cost of Each Alternative

Next we determine the relevant cost of each decision alternative. As you consider each cost, try to determine whether it is relevant to the equipment replacement decision. Ask yourself the following two questions: (1) Is the cost a future cost? and (2) Does the cost differ between alternatives? We will examine the cost associated with the old computer system first.

Relevant Cost of the Old Computer System The $35,500 cost of the old system is not relevant because it is a sunk cost. Bill's decision to purchase or not to purchase the new computer system cannot change the past expenditure for the old one.

Although it may appear that depreciation is a future cost, it is nothing more than an allocation of an asset's original cost. The cost of an asset purchased in the past is a sunk cost, and, therefore, depreciation simply allocates this sunk cost. If depreciation expense relates to an asset purchased in the past, it is irrelevant. In this situation, the depreciation for the old computer system is not relevant because the depreciation is an allocation of the purchase price, which is a sunk cost.

The total cost of $180,000 to pay for two operators is relevant, because it is a future cost and it differs between alternatives. The old system requires two operators, each costing $18,000 per year. Over the five-year expected life of the old system, that totals $180,000 (2 operators × $18,000 × 5 years).

The $5,000 total cost of the maintenance contract for the old system is irrelevant, because it does not differ between decision alternatives. The cost of the maintenance contract for the old system is the same as that for the new one. Therefore, although this is a future cost, it is irrelevant because it does not differ between alternatives.

The $500 residual value of the old system is relevant because it is a future cost and it differs between alternatives. If Bill stays with the old computer system, he will be able to sell it at the end of its useful life for $500. If, however, he buys the new one, he will sell the old one now for $10,000, and therefore he will be unable to sell it for its residual value in five years.

The $10,000 that Bill could get if he sells the old system now is a future cost that differs between alternatives, and therefore it is relevant. If Bill buys the new computer system, he can sell the old one for $10,000, but if he does not buy the new system, he will need the old one so he would not sell it.

Relevant Costs of the Replacement System   Next, we will analyze the start-up, operating, and shutdown costs of the replacement computer system. The only start-up cost for the replacement system is the $76,000 to purchase and install it. This cost is relevant because it is a future cost and it differs between alternatives.

The $75,000 in total depreciation on the new computer system is an allocation of the replacement system's cost. Because we have already considered the cost of the new computer system, we avoid double-counting by excluding its depreciation expense from our analysis of relevant costs.

The $90,000 ($18,000 × 5 years) total labor cost for the replacement system's one operator is relevant because it is a future cost that differs between alternatives. The labor cost for the old system is $180,000, whereas the labor cost for the replacement system is $90,000.

The total cost of the maintenance contract on the replacement system is $5,000. As it happens, the maintenance cost of the old system is also $5,000. In this situation, although maintenance cost is a future cost, it is irrelevant because it does not differ between alternatives.

The $1,000 residual value for the new computer system is relevant because it is a future cost that differs between alternatives. If Bill replaces his current system with a new one, then he can sell the new system for $1,000 at the end of its useful life (in the future). If he does not buy the new one, he obviously cannot sell it.

Compare the Relevant Costs and Select an Alternative

Now that you have determined which costs are relevant, you compare them to see which alternative is best for Bill's firm. It is important to differentiate between inflows and outflows. In Exhibit 6–3 we use parentheses to identify outflows.

As this analysis shows, Bill would save $24,500 over the next five years by buying the new computer system. So he should buy the new system to save money,

Exhibit 6-3
Relevant Cost
Comparison for Bill
Smith & Partners

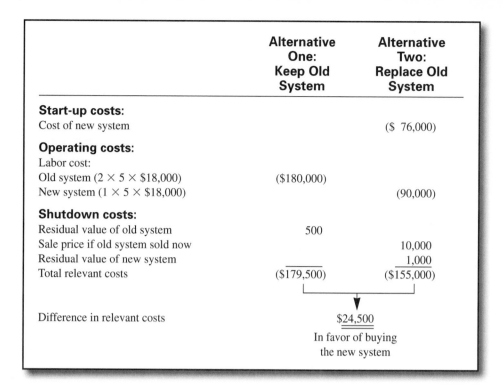

	Alternative One: Keep Old System	Alternative Two: Replace Old System
Start-up costs:		
Cost of new system		($ 76,000)
Operating costs:		
Labor cost:		
Old system (2 × 5 × $18,000)	($180,000)	
New system (1 × 5 × $18,000)		(90,000)
Shutdown costs:		
Residual value of old system	500	
Sale price if old system sold now		10,000
Residual value of new system		1,000
Total relevant costs	($179,500)	($155,000)
Difference in relevant costs		$24,500
		In favor of buying the new system

right? From a purely monetary point of view, he should. However, can he? The replacement system is not cheap. Often business decision makers determine the best alternative, only to learn the business does not have enough available cash to take advantage of a course of action that would save money in the long run. Considering only relevant costs in decision making will lead to better business decisions, but it will not necessarily enable a company to take advantage of what can be learned in the process.

Discussion Questions

6-5. Assuming all purchases and sales of computer systems are cash transactions, how much cash would Bill need to buy the new system?

6-6. Now that we know the relevant cost associated with the computer replacement, what qualitative factors should Bill consider before he makes his final decision?

Interest—The Time Value of Money

New equipment purchase decisions generally have long-term effects. Because of the long life of the equipment, the associated cash inflows and outflows will occur for many years. Therefore, decision makers should consider the interest-earning potential of the cash flows associated with equipment acquisitions. The interest earning potential of cash is sometimes called the **time value of money.** Chapter 7 covers special techniques developed to incorporate the effect of interest and the timing of cash flows.

time value of money The interest earning potential of cash.

SPECIAL ORDERS

special order An order that is outside a company's normal scope of business activity.

Manufacturing businesses must often consider whether to accept a **special order**—an order that is outside its normal scope of business activity. As we will see, proper treatment of fixed cost is critical in making sound special order decisions.

Assume that your company, Alumafloat, makes small aluminum boats. Alumafloat has been in operation for almost 10 years and sells boats to marine supply stores in southern Florida. One day, a Sears Roebuck and Company representative approaches you with an interesting proposition. Sears is interested in purchasing 1,000 of your boats for $125 each. The largest order your company has received to date was for 100 boats, so obviously, this huge order requires special consideration.

Gather All Costs Associated with the Decision

The $125 offer from Sears is considerably less than Alumafloat's normal selling price of $160 per boat. In fact, the boats cost $130 each to produce, so the company would lose $5 per boat if it accepts Sears's $125 offer.

As you discuss the order with the representative from Sears, you tell her that you would be willing to sell the boats to Sears at a discounted price of $140 each because of the large quantity of boats they need. Sears refuses your offer. The store will only pay $125 per boat, and the representative expects you to accept or reject the order within five days.

You gather all the information necessary to make a wise decision. First, you meet with your company's cost accountant, who confirms that your cost per unit is $130. You also request a report detailing production cost so you can see how the cost per unit figure was calculated. Using expected total sales (excluding the special order from Sears) and production costs for the year, the cost accountant prepares the report shown in Exhibit 6–4.

Exhibit 6–4
Per Unit Cost Report for Alumafloat

Expected sales (5,500 units at $160 each)		$880,000
Less: Cost of goods sold (see detail below)		(715,000)
Expected gross margin		$165,000

Detailed calculation for cost of goods sold:

	Per Unit	Total
Number of units	1	5,500
Direct material costs	$ 50	$275,000
Direct labor costs	55	302,500
Variable production costs	10	55,000
Fixed production costs	15	82,500
Total cost of goods sold	$130	$715,000

We must determine the potential effect on Alumafloat's revenues and expenses of accepting the order. Which costs shown in Exhibit 6–4 would be affected by the decision to accept the special order from Sears? To determine which costs are relevant, we will again ask the following two questions: (1) Is the cost a future cost? and (2) Does the cost differ between alternatives?

Determine the Relevant Cost of Each Alternative

Next you must determine which costs are relevant. In this situation, the alternatives are to accept the order or reject it. Generally speaking, because no cost is associated with rejecting the order, our analysis focuses on the alternative to accept.

If the order is accepted, sales will increase by $125,000 (1,000 boats × $125 per boat). The increase in sales due to the special order is relevant, because it is something that will happen in the future and it differs between alternatives.

All variable costs are relevant because they are future costs that differ between alternatives. If the special order is accepted, variable costs will be incurred to produce the 1,000 boats. In this example, variable cost includes direct material, direct labor, and variable production costs.

Depending on the decision situation, fixed cost may or may not be relevant. Often fixed production costs are not relevant costs because total fixed cost for the company will be unaffected by the increase in production volume. This fact holds true unless specific fixed cost increases occur due to the special order, or the order is so substantial that production would exceed the relevant range if the company accepts the order. As the report in Exhibit 6–4 indicates, the company expects total fixed costs to be $82,500. Assume in our example that the decision to accept or reject the special order from Sears would not affect total fixed cost. Therefore, in this case, fixed cost does not differ between alternatives and is irrelevant to the special order decision.

Compare the Relevant Costs and Select an Alternative

Armed with information about relevant cost, you can make an informed decision about the Sears order. Exhibit 6–5 presents a schedule of relevant costs for this special order. The schedule excludes fixed costs because they are irrelevant.

Exhibit 6–5
Relevant Costs for Special Order of 1,000 Boats

	Per Unit	Total
Sales from special order	$125	$125,000
Direct material costs	(50)	(50,000)
Direct labor costs	(55)	(55,000)
Variable production costs	(10)	(10,000)
Total relevant production costs	(115)	(115,000)
Total increase in income	$ 10	$ 10,000

Alumafloat's income would increase by $10,000 if it accepted the special order.

The reasoning in the Alumafloat example may seem logical, but companies often reject special orders that would increase profits, because managers do not understand the concept of relevant cost as it pertains to fixed cost. To avoid making poor decisions, managers must carefully consider how a special order will affect fixed cost.

An accountant for a Fortune 500 manufacturing company once remarked, "I can't believe that the product sales manager is selling below cost. He is disregarding fixed cost as he sets prices to move old stock." In fact, the manager may have made a good decision about the price of the product, depending on whether the fixed costs are relevant to the pricing decision. As a manager, you should know that routinely prepared accounting information cannot be relevant to every decision. Accounting information must be tailored, sometimes by the information user, to provide information that is relevant to the decision at hand.

Discussion Questions

6-7. What would happen if you treated every order as a special order and routinely disregarded fixed cost considerations from your pricing decisions?

6-8. Assume that the production manager at Alumafloat reminds you that four years ago sales skyrocketed for a while. Demand was so great that production increased to the limit of the company's capacity. Alumafloat produced 6,950 boats in a 12-month period. What implications does this information have on your decision to accept the special order from Sears?

6-9. What qualitative factors should you consider regarding accepting an order to sell Sears the boats for less than the price you charge your regular customers? For example, what would your regular customers think if they found that Sears was selling the same style boat they buy from you?

OUTSOURCING: THE MAKE OR BUY DECISION

Often companies purchase subcomponents used to manufacture their products instead of making them in their in-house manufacturing facilities. Buying services, products, or components of products from outside vendors instead of producing them is called **outsourcing.** Decision makers considering a make or buy decision must pay close attention to fixed costs and opportunity costs.

outsourcing Buying services, products, or components of products instead of producing them.

Assume you are a product manager at Microbake, a plant that manufactures microwave ovens. A vendor has approached you about supplying the timer assemblies for your ovens for $12 each. Currently, Microbake makes the timers in its own subassembly department. The subassembly department makes many of the small component parts for the various products manufactured at the plant. When you review the cost sheets for the timers, you discover that the company uses 80,000 timers each year and they cost $14 each to produce in-house.

Gather All Costs Associated with the Decision

You call a meeting with Microbake's cost accounting department to discuss the situation and confirm that the $14 in-house manufacturing cost is correct. Even when pressed, the cost accountants are confident their cost figures are carefully prepared and accurate. In fact, they are surprised the company can buy the timers from the outside vendor for only $12 each. At your request, the cost accounting department prepares the cost breakdown for the timers shown in Exhibit 6–6.

Exhibit 6–6
Cost of Producing Oven Timers In-House

Number of timers produced each year		80,000
	Per Unit	**Total**
Direct material	$ 5	$ 400,000
Direct labor	4	320,000
Variable manufacturing overhead	1	80,000
Fixed manufacturing overhead	4	320,000
Total	$14	$1,120,000

Exhibit 6–7
Selecting Relevant
Costs of Producing
Oven Timers

	Future?	Differs?	Relevant?
Direct material:	yes	yes	yes
Direct labor:	yes	yes	yes
Variable manufacturing overhead:	yes	yes	yes
Fixed manufacturing overhead:	yes	**no**	**no**

Determine the Relevant Cost of Each Alternative

Once again we assess whether each cost is relevant by asking the following questions: (1) Is the cost a future cost? and (2) Does the cost differ between alternatives? The answers follow in Exhibit 6–7.

By definition, *fixed* manufacturing overhead remains constant in total regardless of the level of activity (in this case "activity" is the number of units produced). The fixed cost presented by the cost accountants is an allocation of the total fixed overhead cost of the whole factory, or possibly of the subassembly department. If the company stops making the timers, the subassembly department will not go away and neither will its fixed cost, because the company needs the subassembly department to produce other components. Unless fixed cost changes based on management's decision to buy the timers, it is irrelevant.

Compare the Relevant Costs and Select an Alternative

We compare the relevant costs of the make or buy decision in Exhibit 6–8.

Exhibit 6–8
Relevant Cost of Make
or Buy Decision for
Oven Timers

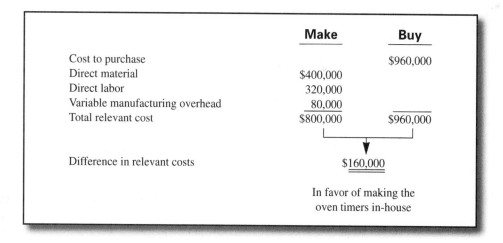

	Make	Buy
Cost to purchase		$960,000
Direct material	$400,000	
Direct labor	320,000	
Variable manufacturing overhead	80,000	
Total relevant cost	$800,000	$960,000
Difference in relevant costs		$160,000

In favor of making the
oven timers in-house

As Exhibit 6–8 indicates, once we have screened out the irrelevant fixed costs it becomes apparent that Microbake can save $160,000 per year by making the timers rather than buying them. Based on this relevant cost comparison, you decide to not purchase the timer assemblies from the outside vendor.

In a final effort to get the sale, the vendor contacts several people at Microbake informing them that you are squandering your company's money. The vendor points out to other Microbake managers that its price is $2 per unit less than your in-house production cost as determined by Microbake's highly trained cost accountants. Other managers are pressing to accept the outside vendor's proposal.

To settle the issue, you call a meeting of the managers and present your relevant cost findings. Several managers comment that your information disregards fixed manufacturing overhead. You explain that the fixed manufacturing overhead is irrelevant. The other managers argue that fixed manufacturing overhead is a very real part of business cost and that it should be included in your presentation. As it happens, this presents little problem. Including fixed manufacturing overhead, although irrelevant, may highlight how fixed costs are affected (or in this case, unaffected) by changes in production. You must demonstrate, however, that if the units are manufactured in-house, fixed manufacturing overhead cost will happen; and that if the units are purchased from the outside vendor, the fixed manufacturing overhead will still occur. The relevant cost comparison can include the irrelevant fixed cost as shown in Exhibit 6–9.

Exhibit 6–9
Relevant Cost of Make or Buy Decision for Oven Timers with Fixed Costs Shown

	Make	**Buy**
Cost to purchase		$ 960,000
Direct material	$ 400,000	
Direct labor	320,000	
Variable manufacturing overhead	80,000	
Fixed manufacturing overhead	320,000	320,000
Total cost	$1,120,000	$1,280,000
Difference in total costs		$160,000

In favor of making the
oven timers in-house

As Exhibit 6–9 shows, because fixed manufacturing overhead is the same for the two alternatives, the outcome of the comparison is the same as that in Exhibit 6–8. Microbake can save $160,000 by making the timers instead of buying them.

Discussion Question

6-10. What will happen to the cost of producing other Microbake products if your decision is overturned and the company outsources the timer assemblies?

Special Relevant Cost Considerations for Fixed Costs

In some situations, fixed costs are affected by the alternative selected. For example, suppose Microbake could eliminate an entire 8-hour production shift if it no longer made the timers. Eliminating that shift thus eliminates one line supervisor whose annual salary is $45,000 per year and reduces other fixed costs by $150,000. Therefore, fixed manufacturing overhead would decrease by 195,000 ($45,000 + $150,000). Exhibit 6–10 shows the relevant cost of the make or buy decision when the alternative to buy the timers enables the company to eliminate a production shift.

Exhibit 6–10
Relevant Cost of the
Make or Buy Decision
for Oven Timers with
Relevant Fixed Costs

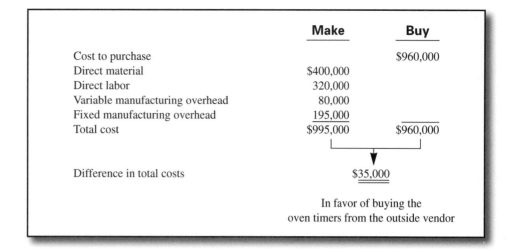

	Make	Buy
Cost to purchase		$960,000
Direct material	$400,000	
Direct labor	320,000	
Variable manufacturing overhead	80,000	
Fixed manufacturing overhead	195,000	
Total cost	$995,000	$960,000
Difference in total costs		$35,000

In favor of buying the
oven timers from the outside vendor

Exhibit 6–10 shows that the savings in fixed manufacturing overhead alters the cost comparison such that Microbake should opt to buy the timers. If the $195,000 reduction in fixed costs were realized, Microbake would save $35,000 by purchasing the timer assemblies from the vendor instead of making them.

Discussion Question

6–11. What qualitative factors should managers at Microbake consider with respect to their outsourcing decision?

Considering Opportunity Costs

opportunity cost The benefit foregone (given up) because one alternative is chosen over another.

Recall that an **opportunity cost** is the value of what is foregone (given up) because one alternative is chosen over another. For example, the opportunity cost of attending college rather than working full time is what you could have earned by working instead of going to college.

If Microbake buys the timer assemblies from an outside vendor, it may have an alternate use for the production capacity or assets used to make the timers—it may have an opportunity to enhance its earnings through an alternate use of the facilities. Assume that Microbake can use the production capacity freed up by purchasing the timers to make electronic alarm clocks. Assume further that the electronic alarm clocks would provide an annual contribution margin of $200,000 with no significant changes to fixed cost. If Microbake continues to make the timer assemblies, it would forego the opportunity to earn the $200,000. The foregone $200,000 contribution margin on the electronic alarm clocks is an opportunity cost.

Because opportunity cost is the cost of *not* doing something, it is not reflected in the accounting records of a business and is not reported in the company's external financial statements or internal management reports. This does not mean an opportunity cost is not real—remember, reality and the measurement of reality are not the same thing. Opportunity cost is an economic reality. Although it is not generally part of financial accounting measures, opportunity cost is a relevant consideration in business decisions.

Returning to the Microbake timer example, the relevant costs of making or buying the 80,000 timers, including the $200,000 opportunity, is presented in Exhibit 6–11.

Exhibit 6–11
Relevant Cost of Make or Buy Decision for Oven Timers with Opportunity Cost

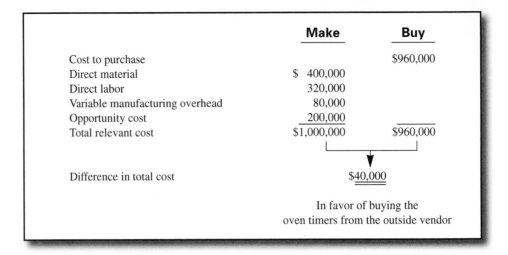

	Make	Buy
Cost to purchase		$960,000
Direct material	$ 400,000	
Direct labor	320,000	
Variable manufacturing overhead	80,000	
Opportunity cost	200,000	
Total relevant cost	$1,000,000	$960,000
Difference in total cost		$40,000

In favor of buying the oven timers from the outside vendor

Exhibit 6–11 suggests that if the $200,000 contribution margin from the production of alarm clocks could be realized, Microbake should buy the timer assemblies from the outside vendor. The production capacity no longer needed to produce the timers could then be used to produce the alarm clocks, resulting in a $40,000 difference in the relevant cost in favor of buying the timers.

Microbake's outsourcing problem is an example of a very real business dilemma. Managers cannot rely solely on the cost information from accountants. They themselves must have enough accounting knowledge to determine the relevant cost of each decision alternative.

A few years ago, an accounting instructor overheard some graduate students talking among themselves during a make or buy lecture. The students were engineers at a manufacturing plant that made sophisticated health care products. After some time, the instructor's curiosity prompted him to ask the students what they were discussing. They explained how their company had been outsourcing more and more components, and profits were declining. The problem had snowballed and production costs on the remaining in-house components seemed to rise as more components were outsourced. It seemed that outsiders found it progressively easier to sell components to the company for less than the in-house production cost. During the lecture, the students figured out that their company was treating fixed costs improperly in make or buy decisions. Oddly enough, the students had questioned company cost accountants, only to be told the product cost information provided was correct. Indeed, the product cost information probably was correct; however, was it all relevant? Probably not. The moral of the story: You cannot always rely on accountants to determine exactly what information is most useful to you in a given decision situation. As an economic decision maker, you need to be able to evaluate accounting information for yourself.

Although we have explored relevant cost using only three examples, you should understand that relevant cost concepts apply to almost every business decision. Relevant costing is even helpful with personal decisions such as whether to attend summer school at a local university or enroll in a student exchange program and study abroad. Business situations and life in general provide an array of quantitative and qualitative considerations for every decision alternative. As a decision maker, you must be able to seek out the relevant considerations and disregard the irrelevant ones.

SUMMARY

All management decision making entails choosing between or among alternatives. If managers are to have any chance of making the best decision in a given situation, they must attempt to consider only relevant information.

A relevant cost is a cost that makes a difference in a given decision situation. What is relevant in one situation may not be relevant in another. Relevant costs are also always future costs, because past costs cannot be changed by any current or future actions. Further, a future cost must differ between or among the alternatives to be considered relevant. Opportunity costs are often relevant and should be considered by managers making decisions. An opportunity cost is the value of benefits foregone because one alternative is chosen over another.

In addition to the quantitative information managers must consider in making decisions, qualitative information such as customer satisfaction, product quality, and employee morale must also be considered. Oftentimes the qualitative considerations should outweigh purely quantitative considerations.

There are many applications of relevant costing in management decision making. Careful application of relevant costing techniques can help managers to make appropriate decisions in various business situations.

KEY TERMS

opportunity cost   M-195
outsourcing   M-192
qualitative factors   M-185
quantitative factors   M-185
relevant cost   M-184

relevant costing   M-184
special order   M-190
sunk cost   M-184
time value of money   M-189

REVIEW THE FACTS

A. What is relevant costing?
B. What is a relevant cost?
C. What two important characteristics do all relevant costs possess?
D. What is a sunk cost?
E. Describe the difference between qualitative and quantitative factors.
F. When trying to determine whether a cost is relevant, what are the two questions the decision maker should ask?
G. Why is the depreciation for existing assets considered irrelevant for equipment replacement decisions?
H. What is the time value of money?
I. Why is the time value of money important for decisions involving the purchase of long-lived assets?
J. What would cause a fixed cost to be relevant for a special order decision?
K. What is outsourcing?
L. Define opportunity cost.
M. The concepts of relevant costing apply to what types of decisions?

APPLY WHAT YOU HAVE LEARNED

LO 1:   Determine Which Costs Are Relevant

6–12. The production manager at Ace Manufacturing is contemplating whether he should upgrade some old production equipment. He is considering the following factors:

1. _____ The cost of the old equipment
2. _____ The cost of the new equipment
3. _____ Depreciation on the old equipment
4. _____ Depreciation on the new equipment
5. _____ Trade-in value of the old equipment
6. _____ Salvage value of the old equipment
7. _____ Salvage value of the new equipment

REQUIRED:
For each item listed, indicate whether it is relevant (R) or irrelevant (I).

LO 3:   Quantitative and Qualitative Considerations

6–13. Tom Robinson is thinking about buying a portable computer. He has a computer at home, but the portable computer would allow him to work during his frequent business trips. Tom is trying to convince his boss that the computer would save the company some money. Tom hopes that his company will pay at least part of the computer's purchase price and the monthly fee for an e-mail service.

Tom has asked a group of friends to help him think of all the advantages of buying the computer. Assume you are part of the group.

GROUP REQUIREMENTS:
a. Prepare an informal schedule of the costs associated with the computer purchase.
b. List as many quantitative benefits as you can that the company will gain if Tom buys the portable computer.
c. List as many quantitative benefits as you can that Tom will gain if he buys the portable computer.
d. List as many qualitative benefits as you can that the company will gain if Tom buys the portable computer.
e. List as many qualitative benefits as you can that Tom will gain if he buys the portable computer.
f. How much of the computer's cost do you think Tom should pay? How much should Tom's employer pay?

LO 3 & 4:   Determine Relevant Cost Schedule and
Qualitative Factors

6–14. Tina Alberts is thinking about trading her car for a new one. Her present car is only three years old, completely paid for, but out of warranty. The car's original cost was $22,000. Lately, the car has been somewhat undependable and the repair bills have been quite high. In the last three months, Tina paid over $1,200 for repairs. Tina intends to use her trade-in as the down payment and then finance the balance. She is looking at a new Nissan which she can get for about $23,000, less her trade.

Tina has asked a group of close friends to help her think of all the relevant advantages and disadvantages of getting the new car. Assume you are part of this group.

GROUP REQUIREMENTS:

a. Prepare an informal schedule listing the relevant quantitative factors that Tina should consider. Do not limit your answer to the items found in the problem. Include all the factors you can think of. When possible, try to include estimated dollar amounts in your schedule.

b. Prepare an informal schedule listing the relevant qualitative factors that Tina should consider.

c. From a quantitative point of view, do you think Tina should buy the new car?

d. Considering both quantitative and qualitative factors, do you think Tina should buy the new car?

LO 1: Determine Which Costs Are Relevant

6–15. Jean Parks is a salesperson for Quality Food Products, Inc. She is considering a 250-mile trip to visit a potential customer, ByLots. Following are factors she is pondering.

1. _____ The cost of traveling the 250 miles to ByLots
2. _____ The time she will spend on the road
3. _____ The time she will spend visiting with ByLots's executives
4. _____ The amount of time already devoted to ByLots
5. _____ The revenue potential from ByLots
6. _____ The cost of her last visit to ByLots
7. _____ The probability that her visit will result in new sales
8. _____ The cost of lunch for herself if she visits ByLots
9. _____ The cost of the lunch she would buy for ByLots's executives

REQUIRED:

For each item listed, indicate whether it is relevant (R) or irrelevant (I).

LO 3: Determine Quantitative and Qualitative Factors

6–16. This question is based on the same situation as 6–15. Jean Parks is a salesperson for Quality Food Products, Inc. She is considering a 250-mile trip to visit a potential customer, ByLots. Following are factors she is pondering.

1. _____ The cost of traveling the 250 miles to ByLots
2. _____ The time she will spend on the road
3. _____ The time she will spend visiting with ByLots's executives
4. _____ The amount of time already devoted to ByLots
5. _____ The revenue potential from ByLots
6. _____ The cost of her last visit to ByLots
7. _____ The probability that her visit will result in new sales
8. _____ The cost of lunch for herself if she visits ByLots
9. _____ The cost of the lunch she would buy for ByLots's executives

REQUIRED:

For each item listed, indicate whether it is quantitative (A) or qualitative (B).

LO 3: Determine Quantitative and Qualitative Factors

6–17. Managers at Ace Manufacturing are considering upgrading some production equipment. They are considering the following factors:

1. _____ Maintenance cost
2. _____ Changes in product quality

3. _____ Salvage value of the old equipment
4. _____ Cost of new equipment
5. _____ Difficulty of training employees to use new equipment
6. _____ Salvage value of the new equipment
7. _____ The ill feelings due to the possible reduction in the labor force

REQUIRED:
For each item listed, indicate whether it is quantitative (A) or qualitative (B).

LO 1, 2, 3, & 5: List All Costs, Indicate Relevant Costs, Indicate Qualitative Factors

6–18. Assume that you are deciding whether to live in a campus dormitory room or an off-campus apartment.

REQUIRED:
a. List all the costs that come to mind as you think about this decision.
b. Review your list and indicate which costs are relevant and which are irrelevant to the decision.
c. What are some qualitative factors that you should consider when making this decision?

LO 1, 2, 3, & 5: List Costs, Indicate Relevant Costs, Indicate Qualitative Factors

6–19. Assume that you are deciding what to do next summer. You are considering two alternatives: Go to summer school, or tour Europe.

REQUIRED:
a. List all the costs that come to mind as you think about this decision.
b. Review your list and indicate which costs are relevant and which are irrelevant to your decision.
c. What are some qualitative factors that you should consider when making this decision?

LO 1, 2, 3, & 5: List Costs, Indicate Relevant Costs, Indicate Qualitative Factors

6–20. George Binkley's car is seven years old. The car is no longer under warranty and requires frequent repairs. George is trying to decide whether to buy a new car. He has asked you what you think about his idea.

REQUIRED:
a. List all the costs that come to mind as you think about his decision.
b. Review your list and indicate which costs are relevant and which are irrelevant to the decision.
c. What are some qualitative factors that he should consider when making this decision?

LO 4: Determine Relevant Cost for Equipment Replacement

6–21. The managers at Miami Manufacturing Company are considering replacing the industrial mixer used in the company's factory.

Information about the old mixer:

Cost	$28,000
Estimated useful life	10 years
Estimated salvage value	$0
Current age	5 years
Estimated current fair value	$8,000
Annual operating cost	$15,000

Information about the new mixer:

Cost	$34,000
Estimated useful life	5 years
Estimated salvage value	$0
Annual operating cost	$12,000

REQUIRED:

Prepare a relevant cost schedule showing the benefit of keeping the old mixer or buying the new one.

LO 4: Determine Relevant Cost for Equipment Replacement

6–22. The managers at General Manufacturing Company are considering replacing the industrial lathe used in the company's factory.

Information about the old lathe:

Cost	$57,000
Estimated useful life	8 years
Estimated salvage value	$0
Current age	2 years
Estimated current fair value	$32,000
Annual operating cost	$32,000

Information about the new lathe:

Cost	$61,000
Estimated useful life	6 years
Estimated salvage value	$0
Annual operating cost	$24,000

REQUIRED:

Prepare a relevant cost schedule showing the benefit of keeping the old lathe or buying the new one.

LO 4: Determine Relevant Cost for Equipment Replacement

6–23. John Paul Hudik, president of J. P. Hudik Boat Hauling, is considering replacing the company's industrial lift used to haul boats. The new lift would allow the company to lift larger boats out of the water.

Information about the old lift:

Cost	$94,000
Estimated useful life	12 years
Estimated salvage value	$10,000
Current age	4 years
Estimated current fair value	$48,000
Annual contribution margin	$50,000

Information about the new lift:

Cost	$128,000
Estimated useful life	8 years
Estimated salvage value	$ 25,000
Annual contribution margin	$ 65,000

REQUIRED:

Prepare a relevant cost schedule showing the benefit of keeping the old lift or buying the new one.

LO 4:   Determine Relevant Cost for Equipment Replacement

6-24. The managers at Wilma Manufacturing are considering replacing a printing press with a new, high-speed model.

Information about the old printing press:

Cost	$255,000
Estimated useful life	10 years
Estimated salvage value	$ 25,000
Annual depreciation	$ 23,000
Current age	3 years
Accumulated depreciation to date	$184,000
Estimated current fair value	$150,000
Annual contribution margin	$110,000

Information about the new printing press:

Cost	$535,000
Estimated useful life	7 years
Estimated salvage value	$ 45,000
Annual depreciation	$ 70,000
Annual contribution margin	$150,000

REQUIRED:

Prepare a relevant cost schedule showing the benefit of keeping the old printing press or buying the new one.

LO 4:   Determine Relevant Cost for New Business Segment

6-25. Photo Express operates a small camera store in Ft. Lauderdale, Florida. The store has two departments, camera sales and photo finishing. Rent, utilities, and other operating expenses are allocated to the departments based on the square footage occupied by the department. Currently, the camera sales department occupies 3,000 square feet and the photo finishing department occupies 2,000 square feet.

Photo Express president, Billy Clifford, is thinking about buying a computer system to produce poster prints. The poster print system would occupy 200 square feet of the store's floor space.

Budgeted monthly information for the store:

Store rent	$ 5,000
Salaries and wages	10,500
Utilities	750
Other operating expenses	3,000
Sales	125,000
Cost of goods sold	95,000

Information about the poster print system:

Cost of the poster system	$25,700
Estimated useful life	5 years
Estimated salvage value	$ 500
Floor space required	200 square feet
Monthly cost of electricity used by poster system	$ 50
Budgeted monthly amounts:	
Poster sales revenue	$ 1,200

Poster supplies	200
Wages for poster operation	250
Store rent	200
Utilities	32
Other operating expenses	120

Clifford believes the company should not buy the poster system because it will show a loss every month. Because he is not sure, he has contacted a small consulting group to seek advice. Assume you are part of the consulting group.

REQUIRED:

a. Would the poster system show a loss every month as Clifford suggests? Prepare a schedule to substantiate your answer.

b. Would the company's overall monthly profits increase or decrease as a result of buying the poster system? Prepare a schedule to substantiate your answer.

c. Prepare a relevant cost schedule showing the advantage or disadvantage of buying the poster system.

LO 4: Determine Relevant Cost for New Business Segment

6–26. The Largo Gift Hut operates a small souvenir shop in Key Largo, Florida. The shop has two departments, retail sales and mail order. Rent, utilities, and other operating expenses are allocated to the departments based on the square footage occupied by the department. Currently, the retail sales department occupies 5,000 square feet and the mail order department occupies 1,000 square feet.

Largo's president, Bobbye Kenyon, is thinking about buying a silk screen machine to make souvenir T-shirts. The silk screen machine would occupy 500 square feet of the souvenir shop's floor space.

Budgeted monthly information for the store:

Store rent	$ 5,100
Salaries and wages	8,500
Utilities	1,000
Other operating expenses	3,000
Sales	80,000
Cost of goods sold	57,000

Information about the silk screen machine:

Cost of the silk screen machine	$9,640
Estimated useful life	5 years
Estimated salvage value	$ 400
Floor space required	500 square feet
Monthly cost of electricity used by silk screen machine	$ 20
Budgeted monthly amounts:	
T-shirt sales revenue	$1,700
Cost of T-shirts	450
Cost of T-shirt supplies	100
Wages for the T-shirt operation	250
Store rent	425
Utilities	85
Other operating expenses	250

Kenyon believes she should not buy the silk screen machine because it will show a loss every month. Because she is not sure, she has contacted a small consulting group to seek advice. Assume you are part of the consulting group.

REQUIRED:

  a. Would the silk screen machine show a loss every month as Kenyon suggests? Prepare a schedule to substantiate your answer.

  b. Would the company's overall monthly profits increase or decrease as a result of buying the silk screen machine? Prepare a schedule to substantiate your answer.

  c. Prepare a relevant cost schedule showing the advantage or disadvantage of buying the silk screen machine.

LO 4: Determine Relevant Cost for Equipment Replacement

6–27. Frank's Marine Service purchased a forklift five years ago for $16,000. When it was purchased the forklift had an estimated useful life of 10 years and a salvage value of $4,000. The forklift can be sold now for $6,000. The operating cost for the forklift is $4,500 per year.

    Frank is thinking about buying a newer forklift for $17,000. The newer model would have an estimated useful life of five years and a salvage value of $7,000. The operating cost for the newer forklift would be $3,000 per year.

REQUIRED:

  a. What are the relevant costs associated with the decision to replace the forklift?

  b. Prepare a relevant cost schedule showing the advantage or disadvantage of buying the forklift.

LO 4: Determine Relevant Cost for Equipment Replacement

6–28. Al Hart of Hart Engineering is considering whether to purchase a new copy machine. He purchased the old machine two years ago for $8,500. When purchased, the old machine had an estimated useful life of eight years and a salvage value of $500. The operating cost of the old machine is $3,000 per year. The old machine can be sold today for $2,000. A new machine can be bought today for $10,000 and would have an estimated useful life of six years with a salvage value of $1,000. The operating cost of the new copy machine is expected to be $1,500 per year.

REQUIRED:

  a. Prepare a schedule showing all the costs associated with the current copy machine.

  b. Prepare a schedule showing all the costs associated with the new copy machine.

  c. Prepare a schedule showing the relevant cost of the copy machine replacement decision and the favored alternative.

  d. Discuss the qualitative factors that Hart should consider.

  e. Would you buy the newer copy machine?

LO 4: Determine Relevant Cost for Equipment Replacement

6–29. Mike Thomlinson is considering whether to replace one of his delivery trucks. He purchased the current delivery truck four years ago for $24,000, and it came with a three-year, 75,000-mile warranty. When purchased, the current truck had an estimated useful life of five years and a salvage value of $2,000. Thomlinson uses the straight-line method for depreciation. The new truck would be identical to the current truck, except it would be new and would have the new truck warranty. The operating cost for the current truck is $4,000 for fuel, $23,200 for the driver's salary, and maintenance cost is about $5,000 per year. If Thomlinson keeps the old truck, it will last another five years, but would require the $5,000 in maintenance each year. The current truck can be sold now for $4,000, or it can be sold in five years for $1,000. The new truck would cost $25,500, has an estimated useful life of five years, and can be sold at the end of the five years for $4,000. At the end of the warranty period, the new truck will require maintenance of $5,000 per year.

REQUIRED:

a. Prepare a schedule showing all the costs associated with the current truck.
b. Prepare a schedule showing all the costs associated with the new truck.
c. Prepare a schedule showing the relevant cost of the truck replacement decision and the favored alternative.
d. Discuss the qualitative factors that Thomlinson should consider.
e. If the old truck had an estimated useful life of five years when it was purchased, and it has already been used for four years, discuss the ramifications of using the truck for another five years.
f. Would you buy the new truck? Why or why not?

LO 4: Determine Relevant Cost for Equipment Replacement

6–30. Jack Owens is considering whether to replace a piece of production equipment with a new model. The new machine would cost $170,000, have an eight-year life, and have no salvage value. The variable cost of operating the machine would be $180,000 per year. The present machine was purchased one year ago, and could be used for the next eight years. When it was purchased, the present machine had an estimated useful life of nine years and a salvage value of zero. The present machine can be sold now for $28,000, but will have no salvage value in eight years. The variable cost of operating the present machine is $200,000 per year.

REQUIRED:

a. Prepare a schedule showing the costs associated with the present machine.
b. Prepare a schedule showing the costs associated with the new machine.
c. Prepare a schedule showing the relevant cost of the equipment replacement decision and the favored alternative.
d. Discuss the qualitative factors that Owens should consider.

LO 3 & 4: Determine the Relevant Cost of Buying a House and List Qualitative Factors

6–31. Lowell Elsea is in the process of buying a house. He is interested in two houses. One house is two miles from his work, the other is on the outskirts of town, 34 miles from work. Surprisingly, the two houses are nearly identical, except the closer house is much more expensive. The house that is two miles from Lowell's work is $127,000, whereas the other house is only $109,000. Maintenance, taxes, insurance, and other costs would be the same for both houses.

Lowell goes to work about 250 days each year. Lowell has just traded his old car for a new one. Each time his car reaches 80,000 miles, Lowell trades it for a new model. Generally, he expects to pay about $20,000 when he trades for a new car. His cars usually get about 20 miles per gallon of regular, $1.25-per-gallon gasoline. Maintenance on his car runs about 5 cents per mile on average. Other than driving to and from work,

Lowell drives about 15,000 miles each year.

Regardless of which house Lowell buys, he expects to be transferred to another area of the country in five years.

Lowell is about to buy the less expensive house when he asks your advice.

REQUIRED:

a. Which house should Lowell buy?

b. How much will Lowell save if he follows your advice? (Disregard the time value of money.)

c. What qualitative factors should Lowell consider?

LO 4: Relevant Cost of a Make or Buy Decision

6–32. Microline is considering buying computer cabinets from an outside vendor. Currently, Microline makes the cabinets in its own manufacturing facility. Microline can buy the cabinets for $15 each. The company uses 15,000 cabinets each year. Information about Microline's cost to manufacture the 15,000 cabinets follows:

	Per Unit	Total
Direct material	$ 4	$ 60,000
Direct labor	6	90,000
Variable overhead	7	105,000
Fixed overhead	5	75,000
Total	$22	$330,000

Fixed cost for Microline would not change if the company stopped making the cabinets.

REQUIRED:

Prepare a relevant cost schedule that indicates whether Microline should buy the cabinets or continue to make them.

LO 4: Relevant Cost of a Make or Buy Decision

6–33. Gem Products is considering buying the casters it uses in the manufacture of office chairs from an outside vendor. Currently, Gem Products makes the casters in its own manufacturing facility. Gem Products can buy the casters for $1.15 each. The company uses 450,000 casters each year.

Information about Gem Products' cost to manufacture the 450,000 casters follows:

	Per Unit	Total
Direct material	$ .50	$225,000
Direct labor	.10	45,000
Variable overhead	.40	180,000
Fixed overhead	.25	112,500
Total	$1.25	$562,500

Fixed cost for Gem Products would not change if the company stopped making the casters.

REQUIRED:

Prepare a relevant cost schedule that indicates whether Gem Products should buy the casters or continue to make them.

LO 4: Relevant Cost of a Make or Buy Decision

6–34. RJ Manufacturing is considering buying the mounting brackets it uses to make its fire extinguishers from an outside supplier. Currently, RJ Manufacturing makes the brackets in its own manufacturing facility. RJ Manufacturing can buy the brackets for $0.75 each. The company uses 700,000 brackets each year.

Information about RJ Manufacturing's cost to manufacture the 700,000 brackets follows:

	Per Unit	Total
Direct material	$.30	$210,000
Direct labor	.10	70,000
Variable overhead	.40	280,000
Fixed overhead	.14	98,000
Total	$.94	$658,000

Fixed cost for RJ Manufacturing would not change if the company stopped making the brackets.

REQUIRED:

Prepare a relevant cost schedule that indicates whether RJ Manufacturing should buy the brackets or continue to make them.

LO 4: Relevant Cost of an Outsourcing Decision

6–35. Jumbo Chinese Restaurant operates a small laundry facility to launder the uniforms, tablecloths, and other linens used by its restaurant chain. Jumbo's laundry operation occupies space in an industrial area close to the company's home office and its largest restaurant. Jumbo is considering using a laundry service to perform the laundering needed by the company.

Jumbo's $180,000 administrative expense is allocated based on the number of employees. Jumbo employs 90 people.

Information about the laundry facilities follows:

Direct cost information:	
Wages for two employees	$38,000
Cost of equipment	$ 7,500
Original estimated useful life of equipment	5 years
Estimated remaining useful life of equipment	1 year
Building rent per year	$ 3,000
Utilities	$ 2,000
Miscellaneous cost	$ 1,500
Indirect cost information:	
Administrative expense	$ 4,000

An outside laundry service has offered to provide Jumbo's laundering services for $50,000 per year. The fee is guaranteed for one year. If the offer is accepted, Jumbo will scrap the laundry equipment and close down its laundry operation completely.

REQUIRED:

The president of Jumbo has asked you to prepare a report that details the qualitative and quantitative factors that should be considered in making the decision about whether to close the laundry operation. Your report should discuss the relevant qualitative and quantitative factors for each alternative and include a relevant cost schedule. Your report should conclude with a well-supported recommended course of action.

LO 4: Relevant Cost of an Outsourcing Decision

6–36. Fast Track Delivery Service operates a small auto repair facility to service its fleet of 35 delivery vehicles. Fast Track's repair facility occupies space in an industrial area close to the company's home office. Fast Track is considering using a local repair shop to service its vehicles. Fast Track's $120,000 administrative expense is allocated based on the number of employees. Fast Track employs 50 people.

Information about the repair facility follows:

Direct cost information:	
Wages for three employees	$64,000
Cost of equipment used	$33,500
Original estimated useful life of equipment	12 years
Estimated remaining useful life of equipment	9 years
Building rent per year	$ 6,000
Utilities	$ 2,000
Cost of automobile parts	$30,000
Miscellaneous cost	$ 1,500
Indirect cost information:	
Administrative expense	$ 7,200

A dependable automotive service center has offered to provide maintenance contracts of each vehicle for $3,000 per vehicle. If Fast Track accepts the offer it would close the maintenance facility. The company estimates that it can sell the maintenance equipment for $10,000.

REQUIRED:

The president of Fast Track has asked you to prepare a report that details the qualitative and quantitative factors that should be considered in making the decision about whether to close the maintenance facility. Your report should discuss the relevant qualitative and quantitative factors for each alternative and include a relevant cost schedule. Your report should conclude with a well-supported recommendation.

LO 3 & 4: Relevant Cost and Qualitative Factors of a Special Order Decision

6–37. Abraham Manufacturing produces 22,000 rubber engine mounts each year for use in its electric cart manufacturing plant. Abraham's engine mounts have an excellent reputation for strength and durability. At a production level of 22,000, the cost per unit is as follows:

Direct material	$ .53
Direct labor	1.45
Variable overhead	.92
Fixed overhead	1.27
Total	$4.17

A competitor, Jenkins Cart Company, is interested in purchasing 14,000 rubber engine mounts from Abraham. Jenkins has offered to pay $4.17 each for the engine mounts. Abraham Manufacturing has the capacity and can easily manufacture the engine mounts for Jenkins.

Several managers at Abraham are concerned that there would be no financial benefit whatsoever for Abraham if the engine mounts are sold at cost.

REQUIRED:

a. Prepare a schedule that details the advantage or disadvantage of selling the 14,000 engine mounts to Jenkins.

b. Discuss the qualitative aspects of selling the parts to Jenkins.

LO 3 & 4: Relevant Cost and Qualitative Factors of a Special Order Decision

6–38. Kelly Gas Grill Company produces 200,000 RV22 propane gas regulator and valve assemblies each year for use in its gas grill factory. Kelly's gas grills are known for quality and have a reputation of lasting a lifetime.

At 200,000 units per year, the cost per unit is as follows:

Direct material	$ 3.02
Direct labor	2.44
Variable overhead	1.20
Fixed overhead	5.60
Total	$12.26

A competitor, Econo Grill, is interested in purchasing 80,000 RV22 assemblies from Kelly. Econo Grill has offered to pay $12.30 per unit. Kelly has the capacity and can easily manufacture the parts for Econo Grill.

Several managers at Kelly are concerned that there would be almost no financial benefit if the RV22 assemblies are sold for $12.30 each.

REQUIRED:

a. Prepare a schedule that details the advantage or disadvantage of selling the 80,000 RV22 assemblies to Econo Grill.

b. Discuss the qualitative aspects of selling the parts to Econo Grill.

LO 3 & 4: Relevant Cost and Qualitative Factors of a Special Order Decision

6–39. Eiroa Marine Cable Company produces 400,000 feet of SS316 cable each year. At 400,000 feet per year, the cost per foot is as follows:

Direct material	$.32
Direct labor	.14
Variable overhead	.08
Fixed overhead	.73
Total	$1.27

A competitor, Garcia Marine, is interested in purchasing 175,000 feet of SS316 cable from Eiroa. Garcia has offered to pay $0.92 per foot for the cable. Eiroa has the capacity and can easily manufacture the cable for Garcia Marine.

Frank Eiroa, president of Eiroa Marine Cable, is concerned that there is no financial benefit for the company if it sells the cable for only $0.92 per foot.

REQUIRED:

a. Prepare a schedule that details the advantage or disadvantage of selling the 175,000 feet of cable to Garcia Marine.

b. Discuss the qualitative aspects of selling the cable to Garcia.

LO 3 & 4: Relevant Cost and Qualitative Factors of a Special Order Decision

6–40. Gator Corporation manufactures camping equipment. One of the Gator's most popular product is its T1012 tent which the company sells for $28 each. Gator sells about 9,000 T1012 tents each year through its mail-order business. Another camping equipment company, TreeClimb Corporation has approached Gator about purchasing 2,000 T1012 tents. The tents would be the same as the T1012 except they would bear the TreeClimb brand. TreeClimb is willing to pay $20 per tent. Although Gator has plenty of plant capacity to produce the additional 2,000 tents, the company's manufacturing cost is $23 per unit, or $3 more per tent than TreeClimb is willing to pay.

The following per unit information pertains to Gator's cost to produce 9,000 T1012 tents.

Direct material	$ 9
Direct labor	4
Variable manufacturing overhead	2
Fixed manufacturing overhead	5
Total	$20

REQUIRED:

a. By what amount would Gator's operating income increase or decrease if the company accepts the special order?

b. Discuss the qualitative aspects of this special order decision.

LO 3 & 4: Relevant Cost and Qualitative Factors of a Special Order Decision

6–41. Refer to problem 6–40. Assume that Gator Corporation would have to purchase an additional sewing machine to accept the special order from TreeClimb. The cost of the new sewing machine is $2,500.

REQUIRED:

a. By what amount would Gator's operating income increase or decrease if the company accepts the special order under these circumstances?

b. Discuss the qualitative aspects of this special order decision.

LO 4: Relevant Cost of a Special Order Decision

6–42. Hi-Cast Corporation manufactures fishing rods. Part of Hi-Cast's sales success comes from a patented material, tuflex, used to make the fishing rods. Tuflex allows the fishing rods to be very flexible, yet nearly unbreakable. Hi-Cast sells about 150,000 fishing rods annually to wholesalers for $18 each. A major department store chain, Sale-Mart, is interested in purchasing 30,000 fishing rods that would bear the Sale-Mart's brand name. Sale-Mart is willing to pay only $9 per fishing rod, considerably less than Hi-Cast's normal selling price. Although Hi-Cast has plenty of plant capacity available to make the additional 30,000 fishing rods, the company's manufacturing cost is $11 per fishing rod, or $2 more per rod than Sale-Mart is willing to pay. Sale-Mart has indicated that the 30,000 fishing rods do not have to be as flexible and tough as the regular Hi-Cast rods.

The following per unit information pertains to Hi-Cast's cost to produce 150,000 fishing rods.

Direct material:	
Tuflex	$4
Other material	1
Direct labor	3
Variable manufacturing overhead	1
Fixed manufacturing overhead	2
Total	$11

If fiberglass is used in place of tuflex, the direct material cost can be reduced by $2 per rod.

REQUIRED:

By what amount would Hi-Cast's operating income increase or decrease if the company accepts the special order?

LO 3 & 4: Relevant Cost and Qualitative Factors of an Outsourcing Decision

6–43. Ace Equipment Company makes high-pressure pumps. Ace makes 10,000 V1 valve assembles per year for use in production. The manufacturing facilities used to make the V1 valves are also used to produce a variety of other subassemblies and products. Accordingly, no special production equipment is needed to make the V1 valves.

The production cost for V1 valve assembles is as follows:

Direct material	$ 55,000
Direct labor	140,000
Variable manufacturing overhead	70,000
Fixed manufacturing overhead	210,000
Total	$475,000

Sure Flow Valve Company has offered to supply the V1 valve assemblies to Ace for $32 each.

REQUIRED:

a. Prepare a schedule that shows whether Ace should buy the valves from Sure Flow or continue to make them.

b. Discuss the qualitative factors that Ace should consider in this make or buy decision.

LO 3 & 4: Relevant Cost and Qualitative Factors of an Outsourcing Decision

6–44. Refer to problem 6–43. Assume Ace could use the manufacturing facilities which are no longer needed to make the V1 valves to produce a new line of small pumps. The small pumps would provide a contribution margin of $60,000.

REQUIRED:

a. Prepare a schedule that shows whether Ace should buy the valves from Sure Flow or continue to make them.

b. Discuss the qualitative factors that Ace should consider in this make or buy decision.

LO 3 & 4:   Relevant Cost and Qualitative Factors of an Outsourcing Decision

6–45. General Manufacturing Company makes residential aluminum windows. A company has offered to supply General with the window crank assembly it needs for $3.50 each. General uses 50,000 crank assemblies each year. The machinery used to make the window cranks is used to produce a variety of other subassemblies and products.

The production cost for the window crank assemblies is as follows:

Direct material	$ 70,000
Direct labor	40,000
Variable manufacturing overhead	55,000
Fixed manufacturing overhead	35,000
Total	$200,000

REQUIRED:

a. Prepare a schedule that shows the relevant cost and the preferred alternative of this make or buy decision.

b. Discuss the qualitative factors that General should consider when deciding whether to buy the window cranks from the outside supplier.

LO 3 & 4:   Relevant Cost and Qualitative Factors of an Outsourcing Decision

6–46. Hutchens Electric produces electric fans. Hutchens manufactures 19,000 small electric fan motors each year. Dalta Motor Company has offered to supply Hutchens with the small electric motors for $12.50 each. The facilities that Hutchens uses to make the small motors is used to make larger motors and other components.

Hutchens's production cost for the small electric fan motors is as follows:

Direct material	$132,000
Direct labor	26,500
Variable manufacturing overhead	43,500
Fixed manufacturing overhead	77,500
Total	$279,500

REQUIRED:

a. Prepare a schedule that shows whether Hutchens Electric should buy the electric fans or continue to make them.

b. Discuss the qualitative factors that Hutchens should consider when making this make or buy decision.

LO 3 & 4:   Relevant Cost and Qualitative Factors of an Outsourcing Decision

6–47. Refer to problem 6–46. Assume that Hutchens Electric can use the facilities freed up by purchasing the electric motors from Dalta Motor Company to produce a new model fan that would have a contribution margin of $95,000.

REQUIRED:

a. Prepare a relevant cost schedule that shows whether Hutchens Electric should buy the electric fans or continue to make them.

b. Discuss the qualitative factors that Hutchens should consider when making this make or buy decision.

LO 3 & 4: Relevant Cost and Qualitative Factors of an Outsourcing Decision

6–48. Nunez Inc. requires 12,000 units of part X45 per year. At the current level of production, the cost per unit is as follows:

Direct material	$ 3
Direct labor	1
Variable overhead	2
Fixed overhead	4
Total	$10

JLW Inc. has offered to sell Nunez 12,000 units of X45 for $8 each. If Nunez is no longer required to produce the X45s, a supervisor can be eliminated. The supervisor's salary of $24,000 is part of fixed overhead cost. Other fixed overhead costs would remain the same.

REQUIRED:
a. Prepare a schedule that details the advantage or disadvantage of buying the 12,000 units of X45 from JLW Inc.
b. Discuss the qualitative aspects of purchasing the parts from JLW Inc.

LO 3 & 4: Relevant Cost and Qualitative Factors of an Outsourcing Decision

6–49. Cox Inc. requires 3,000 spindles per year. At the current level of production, the cost per unit is as follows:

Direct material	$ 38
Direct labor	12
Variable overhead	14
Fixed overhead	44
Total	$108

AMW Inc. has offered to sell Cox the 3,000 spindles for $100 each. If Cox is no longer required to produce the spindles, a supervisor can be eliminated. The supervisor's salary of $36,000 is part of fixed overhead cost. Other fixed overhead costs would remain the same.

REQUIRED:
a. Prepare a schedule that details the advantage or disadvantage of buying the 300 spindles from AMW Inc.
b. Discuss the qualitative aspects of purchasing the parts from AMW Inc.

LO 3 & 4: Relevant Cost and Qualitative Factors of an Outsourcing Decision

6–50. Adcox Inc. requires 4,000 switch assemblies per year. At the current level of production, the cost per unit is as follows:

Direct material	$ 3
Direct labor	3
Variable overhead	2
Fixed overhead	2
Total	$10

Camron Inc. has offered to sell Adcox Inc. the 4,000 switch assemblies for $9 each. If Adcox is no longer required to produce the switch assemblies, part of the building can be leased to another company for $10,000 per year. Other fixed overhead costs would remain the same.

REQUIRED:

a. Prepare a schedule that details the advantage or disadvantage of buying the 4,000 switch assemblies from Camron Inc.

b. Discuss the qualitative aspects of purchasing the parts from Camron Inc.

LO 1, 2, & 4: Prepare a Report for an Equipment Replacement Decision

6–51. The Sakura Company operates a chain of Japanese restaurants. Restaurant managers are paid bonuses based on the financial profits of their restaurants.

Last year, the manager of the South Miami Sakura Restaurant installed a new oven that cost $5,000. At the time, the oven had an estimated useful life of five years with no salvage value. Annual repair and maintenance on the oven is $900, and the cost of electricity used by the oven is $3,400 per year. The old oven can be sold now for $1,500.

A salesperson is trying to convince the store manager to replace the oven purchased last year with a new, energy-efficient model. The salesperson says the new oven will increase company profits. The new oven can be purchased for $6,000, and has an estimated useful life of four years with a salvage value of $1,000. The annual repair and maintenance would be the same as the old oven, or $900 per year, but the annual cost of electricity used by the oven would drop to $1,800.

The manager is not convinced by the salesperson. "If I buy this new oven, my financial income will drop and I'll never get my bonus. The loss in the first year will make me look like a fool!"

REQUIRED:

a. Prepare a report showing the relevant cost of keeping the old oven versus buying the new one.

b. Based on your report, what do you think of the restaurant manager's comments?

Chapter 7

The Capital Budget: Evaluating Capital Expenditures

*S*uppose for a moment that you are contemplating two very different kinds of purchases: a compact disc and a new automobile. You would probably devote different amounts of time and effort to each purchase. You probably would not spend time reviewing your long-term goals and annual budget for the compact disc purchase. Nor would you be likely to create a list of costs and benefits to decide which compact disc to buy. If you were in the market for a new car, however, you might spend considerable time deciding whether you needed a new car, and if you did, which car to buy. The purchase of an expensive item that will be used for a long time, such as a car, warrants careful planning. Such planning is needed because once you have bought the expensive item, it is usually costly to change your mind—in our example, you would have to sell or trade the new car, probably at a substantial discount.

What is true in your personal financial decisions is also true in business. Unlike personal expenditures made for comfort or convenience, business expenditures (large and small) are made to further the goals of the business. In fact, most business expenditures are made to increase a company's profits. For this reason, business expenditures are really investments, by which the company hopes to earn both a return *of* the investment and a return *on* the investment.

Business expenditures for acquiring expensive assets that will be used for more than one year are called **capital investments.** Because of the cost and extended useful life of these assets, companies devote tremendous time and energy to evaluating potential capital investments. For example, according to

capital investments
Business expenditures in acquiring expensive assets that will be used for more than one year.

capital projects   Another name for *capital investments*.

capital budgeting   The planning and decision process for making investments in capital projects.

information in its annual report, Motorola, Inc. invested more than $4.5 billion in capital expenditures during 1995. Certainly, this magnitude of investment required serious analysis on the part of this company before it committed to the various projects represented by those dollars.

Generally, capital investments, also known as **capital projects,** are investments in property, plant, and equipment. Examples include investments in computer equipment, production equipment, another factory, a new wing of a hospital, or a new campus dormitory. **Capital budgeting** is the planning and decision process for making investments in capital projects. Although we focus on business firms in our discussion, all types of organizations can use capital budgeting techniques: for-profit, nonprofit, and social organizations.

In this chapter, we explain how firms make capital budgeting decisions. Capital budgeting, however, is only part of a much more involved planning process, which we also discuss in this chapter.

Two of the evaluation techniques used to evaluate potential capital projects rely heavily on a knowledge of the time value of money. For this reason, we have included an appendix to the chapter that details the time value of money. ■

LEARNING OBJECTIVES

After completing your work on this chapter, you should be able to do the following:

1. Describe the overall business planning process and where the capital budget fits in that process.
2. Explain in your own words the process of capital budgeting.
3. Discuss the four shared characteristics of all capital projects.
4. Describe the cost of capital and the concept of scarce resources.
5. Determine the information relevant to the capital budgeting decision.
6. Evaluate potential capital investments using four capital budgeting decision models: net present value, internal rate of return, payback period method, and accounting rate of return.
7. Determine present and future values using present value tables and future value tables (chapter appendix).

THE BUSINESS PLANNING PROCESS

Managers use accounting information for two main types of business decisions, planning and control. In this section, we give an overview of how organizations plan for the future. We discuss the *why,* the *what,* the *how,* and the *who* of business planning. Though management accounting information is used in all steps in the planning process, it is especially important to the *what, how,* and *who* decisions.

Company Goals: The Why

People form an organization to accomplish a purpose or purposes—the organization's goals. These goals define why the organization exists. Setting goals, then, is the *why* of the business.

organizational goals The core beliefs and values of the company. They outline why the organization exists and are a combination of financial and nonfinancial goals.

Organizational goals constitute the core beliefs and values of the company, so those goals should not be subject to short-term economic pressures. Examples of some organizational goals might be to earn money, to save lives, or to improve communication among employees. Most companies' goals are stated in general terms that are not easily quantified, which means that although progress toward fulfillment can be measured, it is not really possible to determine when the goals have been attained. For instance, a firm with the goal of earning money usually does not specify exactly how much money it must earn to meet its goal.

The goals of a business organization are usually a combination of nonfinancial and financial aspirations. Whether nonfinancial or financial, however, almost all goals have either a direct or indirect effect on the company's financial well-being. Does this sound strange? The next section explains why almost all goals can affect the financial health of a business.

Nonfinancial Goals

Typically, nonfinancial goals do not mention money. Rather, they refer to activities that may or may not result in profits. A hospital's nonfinancial goals, for instance, might be to provide the best health care possible to its patients; to recruit and employ highly qualified workers; to provide a safe, pleasant environment for its employees and patients; and to create an atmosphere of caring for both the physical and the emotional concerns of its patients.

Discussion Questions

7–1. Consider the hospital's nonfinancial goals. What financial effect will occur if the hospital *does* work toward those goals?

7–2. What financial effect will result if the hospital *does not* work toward those goals?

7–3. Review the hospital's nonfinancial goals. How would you determine when those goals have been reached?

Note that the nonfinancial goals for the hospital are stated in very general language. More than specific results, these goals represent standards of conduct and performance toward which the hospital should always be striving. They are stated in such a way that it is very difficult, if not impossible, to determine when the goals have been attained.

Financial Goals

For most business organizations, the primary financial goal is to earn a profit. What this really means, of course, is that the goal is to earn a return on investment for the business owner or owners. This goal may be worded as "achieving superior financial performance," "earning a reasonable return for the stockholders," "maximizing shareholder value," or similar language. As was the case with the nonfinancial goals, it is difficult to determine when these financial goals have been attained.

Goal Awareness

mission statement A summary of the main goals of the organization.

Once goals have been set, the company should communicate them to every person in the organization. This communication maximizes the likelihood that a business will achieve its goals. Many companies use a **mission statement**—a summary of the main goals of the organization—to communicate the firm's goals to all employees. Exhibit 7–1 is a sample mission statement from Johnson & Johnson. This mission statement is representative of those of many large companies.

The goals in the Johnson & Johnson mission statement address the concerns of all parties who have a stake in how the company conducts its business. For instance, Johnson & Johnson's stakeholders include health care providers, consumers, suppliers, employees, the community, and stockholders. Johnson & Johnson's mission statement communicates the firm's goals and presents the image of a responsible, ethical business.

Exhibit 7–1
Johnson & Johnson
Mission Statement.
Copyright © Johnson &
Johnson, Inc.

Our Credo

We believe our first responsibility is to the doctors, nurses and patients, to mothers and fathers and all others who use our products and services. In meeting their needs everything we do must be of high quality. We must constantly strive to reduce our costs in order to maintain reasonable prices. Customers' orders must be serviced promptly and accurately. Our suppliers and distributors must have an opportunity to make a fair profit.

We are responsible to our employees, the men and women who work with us throughout the world. Everyone must be considered as an individual. We must respect their dignity and recognize their merit. They must have a sense of security in their jobs. Compensation must be fair and adequate, and working conditions clean, orderly and safe. We must be mindful of ways to help our employees fulfill their family responsibilities. Employees must feel free to make suggestions and complaints. There must be equal opportunity for employment, development and advancement for those qualified. We must provide competent management, and their actions must be just and ethical.

We are responsible to the communities in which we live and work and to the world community as well. We must be good citizens—support good works and charities and bear our fair share of taxes. We must encourage civic improvements and better health and education. We must maintain in good order the property we are privileged to use, protecting the environment and natural resources.

Our final responsibility is to our stockholders. Business must make a sound profit. We must experiment with new ideas. Research must be carried on, innovative programs developed and mistakes paid for. New equipment must be purchased, new facilities provided and new products launched. Reserves must be created to provide for adverse times. When we operate according to these principles, the stockholders should realize a fair return.

Johnson & Johnson

Merely stating lofty goals in a mission statement is not enough to reach the goals. Businesses must act consistently with their goals to ensure progress. Consider the following two examples. In 1982 Johnson & Johnson demonstrated the company's commitment to its goals after two fatalities occurred in the Chicago area when someone injected cyanide into six bottles of Tylenol. Once aware of these events, Johnson & Johnson immediately responded by recalling all Tylenol bottles. The company also instituted a nationwide advertising campaign advising consumers *not* to use Tylenol and provided full disclosure about the situation. In short, the company responded in a manner consistent with its goals.

Compare Johnson & Johnson's actions to Ford Motor Company's response to faulty ignition systems in some of its cars. These faulty ignition systems caught fire without warning and created a dangerous and potentially fatal situation. Ford's response was to wait for the federal government to tell the company which cars it had to recall. Legal? Certainly. A smart way to conduct business? In the short run, it cost Ford less than a total recall of the affected vehicles. In the long run, however, the company may not be conducting its business in a way consistent with its stated goal of total quality.

strategic plan A long-range plan that sets forth the actions a company will take to attain its organizational goals.

Once a business has set its goals, the firm must then create a **strategic plan**—a long-range plan that sets forth the actions the firm will take to attain its goals. In the following section, we explore briefly how firms develop strategic plans.

Strategic Plan: The What

The steps outlined in the strategic plan, sometimes referred to as a long-range budget, are the *what* of doing business. The actions specified in the strategic plan describe what actions a business must take to implement its goals. To be effective, then, strategic plans should support—not conflict with—the company's goals.

Companies make long-range plans so they are well positioned to reach their goals and benefit as the future unfolds. For example, it can take Dow Chemical Company five years or longer to build a production facility, so Dow managers must anticipate product demand accurately in advance, in order to build a plant of the appropriate size in time to produce enough to meet consumer demand.

A company's strategic plan tends to have objectives that are quantifiable, and a time frame for attainment of the objectives. A company might specify, for instance, that it plans to replace its four least-efficient production facilities over the next five years, reduce customer complaints by 20 percent over the next three years, or increase market share for its newest product by 25 percent within 10 years. As you can readily see, a firm can determine exactly when it has met all these objectives.

After an organization has developed a strategic plan that specifies the actions it will take to reach its goals, the company then decides how to allocate its monetary resources to implement its strategies, and who will be responsible for the day-to-day activities of the business. This step in the planning process is the preparation of budgets.

Preparation of the Capital Budget: The How

capital budget The budget that outlines how a company intends to allocate its scarce resources over a five-year, 10-year, or even longer time period.

The capital budget is the *how* of the planning process. The **capital budget** is the budget that outlines how a firm intends to allocate its scarce resources over a five-year, 10-year, or even longer time period.

The capital budget lays out plans for the acquisition and replacement of long-lived expensive assets such as land, buildings, machinery, and equipment. During the capital budgeting process, companies decide whether and what items should be purchased, how much should be spent, and how much profit can be generated from the items. In sum, capital budgeting decisions should further the strategic plan and goals of the business.

Operating Budget: The Who

operating budget The budget that plans a company's routine day-to-day business activities for one to five years.

Companies not only must budget for long-term activities, they also must plan and budget for day-to-day business activities. The budget that pertains to routine company operations for one to five years in the future is called the **operating budget.** The operating budget establishes who is responsible for the day-to-day operation of the organization, so we refer to it as the *who* of the planning process. The operating budget will be our focus in Chapter 8.

An important thing to understand about the planning process is the interrelationship among goals, strategic plan, capital budget, and operating budget. Exhibit 7–2 demonstrates that interrelationship.

Exhibit 7–2
Interrelationship among the Planning Elements

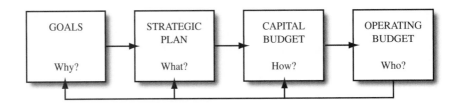

The overall function of management accounting is to provide a substantial portion of the information that company management needs not only to achieve the *what*, the *how*, and the *who*, but also to ensure that these functions are achieved within the context of the *why*.

THE CAPITAL BUDGET: WHAT IS IT?

capital assets Long-lived expensive items such as land, buildings, machinery, and equipment.

The capital budget plans for the acquisition and replacement of long-lived expensive items such as land, buildings, machinery, and equipment. These long-lived items are called **capital assets.** The capital budget focuses on the long-term operations of the company to determine how an organization intends to allocate its scarce resources over the next five, 10, or even 20 years. Thus, we refer to this part of the planning process as the *how* of being in business and doing business.

During the capital budgeting process, companies decide whether items should be purchased, how much should be spent, and how much profit the items promise to generate. No decisions made in the capital budgeting process, however, should conflict with the company's strategic plan or organizational goals.

Capitalizing Assets

Capital budgeting deals with decisions regarding investments that will benefit the company for many years, so most companies do not use capital budgeting techniques for small purchases or those that provide benefits for only the current year.

When an expenditure is made, the cost of the item purchased will be reflected either as an expense on the company's income statement for the year of purchase, or as an increase in the company's assets on its balance sheet. Theoretically, the distinction lies in whether the item purchased will provide economic value to the company beyond the year of purchase. If a purchased item is expected to provide economic benefits beyond the year in which it was purchased, it should be capitalized, which means that its cost has been recorded as an increase in long-term assets and will be depreciated (converted from asset to expense) over the item's estimated useful life. Conversely, if a purchased item is not expected to provide economic benefit to the company beyond the year of purchase, its cost should be reflected as an expense on the income statement for that year.

To illustrate, the cost of a delivery truck should be reflected as an increase in assets because the truck will likely be used for several years. In contrast, the cost of last month's lawn service does not provide any future value and therefore should be reflected as an expense immediately.

Judgment plays an important role in determining whether a purchased item should be capitalized or expensed. For example, how should the cost of a $3 wastebasket with an estimated useful life of three years be recorded? Because the wastebasket will be used for several years, the item should theoretically be capitalized—its cost should be added to long-term assets and depreciated over the wastebasket's estimated useful life.

From a practical standpoint, it is senseless to expend the additional accounting effort to capitalize and then depreciate the wastebasket. Why? Because, whether the wastebasket is capitalized and depreciated over its estimated useful life or expensed immediately, the effect on a company's financial statements would be so minimal that no economic decision maker will be influenced by the alternative selected. Thus, the cost of the wastebasket is immaterial, so due to the modifying convention of materiality discussed in financial accounting, the wastebasket is expensed when purchased.

Capitalization Amount

Generally, companies set a cost threshold that helps determine the appropriate accounting treatment for capitalizing long-lived items. For example, a company might say that any long-lived item costing less than $3,000 will be expensed when purchased, while those costing $3,000 or more will be capitalized. There are no hard and fast rules for setting the capitalization threshold, but most businesses choose an amount between $500 and $5,000 as their capitalization amount.

Characteristics of Capital Projects

Capital budgeting deals with planning for purchases of items that will be capitalized, meaning they will be classified as assets when purchased and then depreciated over their estimated useful lives. While the capitalization amount and the evaluation process for capital projects vary from company to company, all capital projects share certain characteristics. The four main shared characteristics include

1. *Long lives.* Capital projects are expected to benefit the company for at least two years, which is the whole idea behind capitalizing the cost of a purchased item. As discussed in the previous section, if a purchased item will benefit the company only in the year of purchase, the cost of the item is expensed immediately. If the item purchased is likely to benefit a company in years beyond the year of purchase, the cost of that item is capitalized. Usually the kinds of purchases we are discussing in this chapter benefit the company longer than two years, perhaps five, 10, or an even greater number of years.

2. *High cost.* Technically, the purchase of any long-lived item for which the cost exceeds a company's capitalization amount is considered a capital project. As stated earlier, this may be as low as $500 for some firms. As a practical matter, however, the capital budgeting techniques we consider in this chapter are used to evaluate high-cost projects. A good example is the cost of a new factory built by

Motorola or Intel. Such a factory may cost $500 million or more. Another example is the decision by Wal-Mart or KMart to open a new store in a particular location. Many millions of dollars are involved in opening a store for these companies.

3. *Quickly sunk costs.* Costs that cannot be recovered are called sunk costs. A capital project usually requires a firm to incur substantial cost in the early stages of the project. As new information about market size, technology, and so on becomes available, the company's management may decide the project should be abandoned. Unfortunately, much of the cost already incurred may not be able to be recouped. For example, consider the case of a manufacturer that begins construction on a new factory with an estimated cost of $500 million. After spending $200 million on construction, the company decides the new factory is not needed because the product it planned to manufacture in the facility has become obsolete. The company cannot sell the partially completed factory and has no other use for it. The $200 million is a sunk cost because it cannot be recovered.

4. *High degree of risk.* Capital projects have a high degree of business risk because they involve the future, which always entails uncertainty. Because of the long lives, high costs, and sunk costs of capital projects, companies must try to estimate the returns from those projects in future years. These characteristics increase the likelihood of erroneous estimates. The uncertainty of the future coupled with the high initial investment make capital projects quite risky.

Discussion Question

Consider these questions: "Will I be paid?" "How much will I be paid?" and "When will I be paid?"

7-4. Why do you think these questions were extremely difficult for Microsoft to answer as the company considered the development of Windows 98 as a potential capital project?

THE COST OF CAPITAL AND THE CONCEPT OF SCARCE RESOURCES

cost of capital The cost of obtaining financing from all available financing sources.

cost of capital rate Another name for *cost of capital.*

required rate of return Another name for *cost of capital.*

hurdle rate Another name for *cost of capital.*

When you put money into a savings account, you expect to earn interest. This interest is the return on your investment. Like most people, you would like the return to be as high as possible. If you were going to deposit $5,000 in a savings account, you would probably shop for a secure bank, with a return as high as or higher than that of competing banks.

Businesses shop for capital projects the same way you would shop for a bank in which to deposit your $5,000. If it appears that a capital project will be profitable, how does a company determine whether it will be profitable enough to warrant investing its money? A proposed project should promise a return that is equal to or exceeds the firm's cost of capital.

In evaluating potential capital projects, a company must determine a benchmark rate of return to help select which capital project or projects it will undertake. The benchmark return rate for selecting projects is usually the company's **cost of capital,** which is the cost of obtaining financing from all available financing sources. Cost of capital is also referred to as the **cost of capital rate,** the **required rate of return,** or the **hurdle rate.** For the sake of consistency, we use cost of capital throughout all our discussions in this chapter.

As you may recall from financial accounting, companies can obtain financing from two sources, borrowing from creditors (debt financing) and investments by owners (equity financing). When a company invests in a capital project, the money must come from one or both of these sources. Both creditors and owners require a return on the funding they provide to the company, and the company must seek investments that provide a return at least equal to the cost of obtaining funding from debt and equity sources. If a company borrows funds at an interest rate of 9 percent, then the expected return on a capital project must be at least 9 percent. Similarly, if a company's owners provide the financing and expect a return of 20 percent on their investment, then the expected return from a capital project should be at least 20 percent to be acceptable.

Blended Cost of Capital

blended cost of capital
The combined cost of debt financing and equity financing.

The funding for a company's capital projects usually comes from a combination of debt and equity financing. The combined cost of debt and equity financing is called the **blended cost of capital.** The rate for the blended cost of capital represents the combined rate of the cost of both debt and equity financing.

cost of debt capital The interest a company pays to its creditors.

The **cost of debt capital** is the interest a company pays to its creditors. The interest rate, say 8 percent, is agreed upon when a company borrows from either the bank or the bond market. The amount of interest a company pays is easy to determine because it is reported on the company's income statement as interest expense.

cost of equity capital
What equity investors give up when they invest in one company rather than another.

The cost of a company's equity financing is more challenging to determine than the cost of its debt financing, because the **cost of equity capital** is what equity investors relinquish when they invest in one company rather than another. To illustrate, assume Elizabeth Todd has $5,000 to invest and she is considering the purchase of either Boardman Company stock or Emry Company stock. The question is, what does Elizabeth give up if she invests her $5,000 in Boardman? She relinquishes what she would have earned had she invested in Emry. That is, she lost the opportunity to earn whatever she would have earned had she purchased Emry's stock rather than Boardman's.

The amount an equity investor earns is a combination of dividends received and the appreciation in the market value of the stock the investor owns. In Elizabeth's case, the amount earned if she buys the Boardman Company stock is a combination of the dividends she receives from Boardman, plus any increase in the market value of the Boardman stock she owns.

Discussion Question

Assume Elizabeth buys the Boardman stock and consistently earns an 8% return on her investment (dividends plus appreciation of the Boardman stock).

7-5. If Elizabeth could earn a 17% return on an investment in Emry Company stock (or some other company), what would you advise her to do? Explain your reasoning.

It's all well and good for us to discuss this topic from the investor's point of view (in this case Elizabeth Todd), but what has this to do with the cost of equity capital for Boardman Company? Well, if Boardman wants to keep Elizabeth as a stockholder, it must return to her an amount at least as great as she could earn by investing her money somewhere else. If Elizabeth can earn 17 percent from an investment in Emry, Boardman must give her that kind of return or she may sell her Boardman stock and invest in Emry (or some other company). Boardman, then, would use 17 percent as the cost of the equity capital it received from Elizabeth, because that is what she could earn elsewhere. In other words, that is what she gave up by investing in Boardman.

In a real-world situation, Boardman Company would not know about the alternatives being considered by Elizabeth Todd and her $5,000. Therefore, the company cannot determine the specific percentage return Elizabeth must earn to keep her happy. What Boardman must do is try to determine what percentage return equity investors can generally expect on their investments and use that percentage as the cost of equity capital.

Unlike debt financing costs (interest expense), the cost of equity financing is not reported in financial statements in its entirety. Firms do report profit distributions to stockholders in the form of dividends, but the larger part of the cost of equity capital is the appreciation in the market value of stockholders' ownership interest. This market value is not reported on financial statements.

To determine the full cost of equity capital, we must examine how stocks appreciate in value. We assume first that rational investors would desire a return on an investment in an individual company at least equal to the return they could receive from investing in other, similar publicly traded companies.

If all companies whose stocks are traded on recognized stock markets (NYSE, AMEX, NASDAQ, and so on) were separated based on the percentage return they provide their stockholders, the breakdown would appear as shown in Exhibit 7–3.

Exhibit 7–3
Returns Provided by
the Stock Market

| HIGH RETURN COMPANIES |
| 25% of Firms |

| MEDIUM RETURN COMPANIES |
| 50% of Firms |

| LOW RETURN COMPANIES |
| 25% of Firms |

The high return companies in Exhibit 7–3 represent one-fourth of all the companies whose stock is publicly traded. The medium return companies comprise one-half of the companies, and the low return companies represent one-fourth of the total.

Discussion Question

7-6. If you owned stock in a publicly traded company, in which group of companies in Exhibit 7–3 would you want your company to be?

Most equity investors desire to own stock in high return companies because they naturally want their investment to earn the highest possible return. Many high return companies in the stock market yield as high as 17 percent to 20 percent annually to their stockholders in the form of dividends and appreciation in stock value.

Discussion Questions

Assume you own stock in a publicly traded company and you consistently earn an 8% return on your investment (dividends plus appreciation of the company's stock).

7-7. If you are certain you could earn a 20% return on an investment in some other company's stock, what would you do? Explain your reasoning.

7-8. Because a publicly traded company receives money only when its stock is originally issued, why do you think it would care about the stock's market value in the stock market?

It is important to note here that the issue is not whether investors can, in fact, earn a 20 percent return by selling their stock in one company and investing in another. They only need to *think* they can earn the higher return.

If enough of a company's stockholders begin selling their stock, the market price of the stock will drop—the economic law of supply and demand at work. As the stock price drops, more stockholders may decide to sell their stock before the price drops even lower. This, of course, makes the stock price drop further.

Discussion Question

7-9. What would you think about a company whose stock was selling for $50 a share in January and $12 a share in December?

Stock analysts, customers, suppliers, and many other parties have a tendency to gauge a company's health by the market value of its stock. For this reason, companies have a vested interest in making sure the market value of their stock does not begin a downward spiral.

Because the investors in the stock market think they can earn a 17 to 20 percent return by investing in the top performing companies, a company must return 17 to 20 percent annual return to its stockholders to be considered one of the high performing companies. Publicly traded companies usually consider their cost of equity financing to be as high as 20 percent. This percentage is commonly used to compute the company's blended cost of capital.

To illustrate the calculation of the blended cost of capital, we consider the case of Adler Enterprises, which has $2,000,000 in assets. A total of $1,200,000 (60 percent) of these assets were obtained using debt financing with an interest rate of 7.5 percent. The remaining $800,000 (40 percent) was financed through equity capital and the company uses a 20 percent cost of equity financing. We find the blended cost of capital for Adler Enterprises using the following calculation.

Method of Financing	Proportion of Financing Provided		Cost of Financing		Weighted Cost of Financing
Debt	60%	×	7.5%	=	4.5%
Equity	40%	×	20.0%	=	8.0%
			Blended Cost of Capital		12.5%

We see that Adler's weighted cost of debt financing is the proportion of debt financing (60 percent) multiplied by the cost of that financing (7.5 percent). The company's weighted cost of equity financing is the proportion of equity financing (40 percent) times the cost of the equity financing (20 percent). Its blended cost of capital is the sum of the weighted cost of each type of financing—12.5 percent.

Firms use their blended cost of capital as a benchmark rate of return to evaluate capital projects. For example, suppose Adler Enterprises is considering a capital project that requires an investment of $200,000. If Adler decides to undertake this project, it must obtain $200,000 to fund it. Recall that Adler's blended cost of capital is 12.5 percent. Unless the expected rate of return on the project is 12.5 percent or higher, Adler's management will probably reject the project. Otherwise, it would cost more to fund the project than the project could earn.

Discussion Questions

7-10. When you consider that companies are generally in business to earn a profit, why might it be acceptable to select a capital project that promises a return that is just equal to the blended cost of capital?

7-11. Under what circumstances do you think a company might accept one capital project over another even though the project selected promises a lower return?

7-12. Do you think there would ever be a situation when a company should proceed with a capital project even though the project promises a return lower than the cost of capital? Explain your reasoning.

7-13. What do you think might cause a company to reject a proposed capital project even though it promises a return significantly higher than the cost of capital?

Scarce Resources

> *I'm so broke that if they was*
> *selling steamboats for a dime*
> *apiece, I could run up and down the*
> *bank saying 'ain't that cheap'.*
> —Roy Clark

In our personal lives, what we buy is usually not limited by how much we want, but rather by how much money we have available to spend. Well, what is true for individuals is also true for businesses. The number and size of capital projects a company undertakes is not limited by a lack of viable alternative projects. What limits companies is that they simply do not have access to enough money to take advantage of all the opportunities available to them. This limitation on the amount available to spend is commonly called **scarce resources.** Even huge multinational companies must select only investments they consider most favorable from a virtually unlimited pool of possible investment opportunities, because firms do not have access to enough money to invest in every good project that comes along. Managers must carefully evaluate the alternative capital projects available to their companies so they can select the projects that promise the highest return (as long as the projects are consistent with the company's goals and strategies).

scarce resources A term describing the limited amount of money a company has to invest in capital projects.

EVALUATING POTENTIAL CAPITAL PROJECTS

Because capital projects are usually long lived, costly, and high risk, managers must carefully evaluate capital expenditure decisions, especially in light of their financial limitations. The evaluation process generally includes the following four steps.

1. Identifying possible capital projects
2. Determining the relevant cash flows for alternative projects
3. Selecting a method of evaluating the alternatives
4. Evaluating the alternatives and selecting the capital project or projects to be funded

Let us investigate each of these steps from the manager's point of view.

Identifying Possible Capital Projects

Businesses usually make capital expenditures to maximize profits by either increasing revenue, reducing costs, or a combination of the two. A project that satisfies the company's desire to maximize profits will be identified as a potential capital expenditure.

Firms often generate revenue increases by investing in projects that increase capacity or draw more customers. For a hotel chain, an increase in available rooms might increase revenue. For a restaurant, revenue might be enhanced by investing in cooking equipment that prepares food more rapidly. For a hospital, the ability to provide additional services or an increased number of beds might be the key to added revenue.

To reduce operating costs a manufacturer might upgrade production equipment so less direct labor or less electricity is required. An airline catering company could invest in more energy-efficient ovens to reduce food preparation cost. Reducing cost has exactly the same effect as increasing revenue. As Benjamin Franklin said, "A penny saved is a penny earned." If you think about it, this really makes sense. If a company saves $1 by reducing costs by $1, the cost reduction has the same impact on profits as increasing selling price to increase revenue by $1.

Although the majority of potential capital projects are intended to either increase revenue or reduce costs, in certain instances a company must make a capital expenditure that will result in neither. These projects are usually concerned with safety or environmental issues and may come as a result of governmental regulation requirements; or, a company may simply determine such an expenditure is necessary given its goal of worker safety or good corporate citizenship.

In any event, capital projects that are deemed necessary but do not promise either to increase revenue or reduce costs are usually not evaluated using the same criteria as those projects that do promise increased profits. In this chapter, we restrict ourselves to the evaluation of potential capital projects that promise to either increase revenue or reduce costs.

As the need for increasing revenue or reducing costs presents itself, all alternative courses of action should be explored. Brainstorming sessions and input from multiple sources both within and outside a firm can help generate ideas for alternative options.

Determining Relevant Cash Flows for Alternative Projects

Throughout our discussion of capital budgeting, we have discussed capital projects that promise to increase a company's profits by either increasing revenue or reducing costs (expenses). Recall, however, that under accrual accounting, revenue is not the same as cash inflow and expense is not the same as cash outflow in the short run. Recall also that in the long run, revenue and expenses measured using accrual accounting *are* the same as cash inflow and cash outflow.

net cash flows Cash inflow less cash outflow.

Because capital projects usually are long lived, most business managers believe it is appropriate to analyze an alternative using cash inflow and cash outflow over the life of the project. They do this by determining the **net cash flow** of a project—the project's expected cash inflows minus its cash outflows for a specific time period. For example, if a manager estimates that investing in a new production machine will yield $40,000 in cash inflows during the useful life of the machine but will require spending $30,000 for the same period, the net cash flow would be $10,000 ($40,000 − $30,000).

relevant net cash flows Future net cash flows that differ between or among the alternatives being considered.

Only relevant net cash flows should be considered in a capital budgeting decision. **Relevant net cash flows** are future cash flows that differ between or among alternatives. Thus, a relevant cash flow must be one that will occur in the future, not one that has already occurred, and it must be affected by the investment decision. Past cash flows, or cash flows that will not change as a result of the investment decision, are irrelevant and should not be considered in the decision process. This concept should seem familiar because it follows the same reasoning as our discussion of relevant costs, the subject of Chapter 6.

Once a company obtains and assesses the relevant cash flows for each alternative project, the next step is to choose a method to measure the value of each project.

Selecting a Method of Evaluating the Alternatives

Over time, many capital budgeting decision methods have been developed to evaluate potential capital projects. In this chapter, we present four methods:

- Net present value
- Internal rate of return
- Payback period method
- Accounting rate of return

Each of these methods offers a different way to measure a project's value, and sometimes the different methods render conflicting rankings. In such a case, managers should be aware of the strengths and weaknesses of each capital budgeting method. In the next section we discuss each of the four methods and the advantages and disadvantages of each.

Selecting Capital Budgeting Projects

To select a capital budgeting project, firms decide first whether to accept or reject a project using one or more capital budgeting techniques to measure the project's value. If the project does not generate an acceptable rate of return, it will probably be rejected. Furthermore, any proposed capital project that is inconsistent with a company's goals and strategic plan should be rejected, even if the promised return on that project is higher than some other potential project.

Once a project has been accepted as viable, the project can then be ranked with other acceptable projects based on expected performance.

CAPITAL BUDGETING DECISION METHODS

In this section, we explain four capital budgeting methods: net present value, internal rate of return, payback period method, and accounting rate of return. The first two methods, which are discounted cash flow methods, are used more frequently in business because they include the concept of the time value of money.

A dollar received at some point in the future does not have the same value as a dollar received today. The reason for the difference in value is that if cash is available now, it can be invested now and earn a return as time passes. This increase in the value of cash over time due to investment income is referred to as the **time value of money**. The concept of the time value of money is used to determine either the future value of money invested today or the present value of money to be received at some point in the future.

In the following discussion of net present value and internal rate of return, we assume you have a working knowledge of the time value of money, discussed in detail in the appendix to this chapter. Refer to it now if you need to refresh your understanding.

Capital projects deal with cash flows that begin in the present and extend into the future, sometimes for many years. Therefore, the evaluation of these kinds of projects uses the concept of present value. Determining the present value of cash to be received in future periods is called **discounting cash flows.**

Discounted Cash Flow Methods

Business managers use two discounted cash flow methods to evaluate potential capital projects: net present value and internal rate of return.

Net Present Value The **net present value (NPV)** of a proposed capital project is the present value of cash inflows minus the present value of cash outflows associated with a capital budgeting project. Note that the net present value is different from the present value. The former is the difference between the present value of a capital project's net cash flows. The latter is the amount a future payment or series of payments is in today's dollars evaluated at the appropriate discount rate. The net present value method is used to determine whether a proposed capital project's return is higher or lower than the blended cost of capital.

A company calculates the NPV of a capital project by discounting the net cash flows for all years of the project using the company's blended cost of capital as the discount rate. A positive net present value indicates that the expected return on a proposed project is higher than the company's cost of capital. A negative net present value indicates that the expected return on a proposed project is lower than the company's cost of capital. A net present value of zero shows that the expected return on a project is exactly equal to the company's cost of capital.

To illustrate the net present value calculations, assume the Juan Rodriguez Company is considering a computer hardware upgrade that would require an investment of $100,000. Assume further that the enhanced speed of the computer is expected to save $31,000 annually in operator salaries. Remember, this reduction

time value of money The increase in the value of cash over time due to investment income.

discounting cash flows Determining the present value of cash to be received in the future.

net present value (NPV) The present value of all cash inflows associated with a proposed capital project minus the present value of all cash outflows associated with the proposed capital project.

of cash outflow is a cash inflow in net present value analysis. The computer has an estimated useful life of five years with no residual value.

The cash flows associated with the computer upgrade are shown in Exhibit 7–4.

Exhibit 7–4
Expected Cash Flows for Juan Rodriguez Company Computer Upgrade

Notice in Exhibit 7–4 that the initial cash outlay of $100,000 occurs at "time 0." When working with present values, time 0 is considered today, or the present. Unless otherwise specified, we assume all other cash flows for this project will occur at the end of each period.[1]

Juan Rodriguez Company has a 14 percent blended cost of capital, so we use 14 percent as the discount rate to evaluate whether the company should accept the computer upgrade project; that is, we use a 14 percent discount rate to calculate the present value of the project's cash outflows and cash inflows. In this case, the project's $100,000 cash outflow occurs today (time 0), so that amount is already stated in present value terms.

Next, we must find the present value of the project's cash inflows, which occur at the end of each of the next five years. Because the stream of $31,000 positive cash flows constitutes an annuity, we use the *Present Value of an Annuity of $1 Table*, found in the chapter appendix in Exhibit A7–10, to find the present value factor of a five-year annuity, with a discount rate of 14 percent. We have reproduced a portion of the table as Exhibit 7–5. As you can see from the highlighted portion in this exhibit, the factor for five years with a discount rate of 14 percent is 3.433.

Exhibit 7–5

Present Value of Annuity of $1

Period	4%	5%	6%	7%	8%	10%	12%	14%	16%
1	.962	0.952	0.943	.935	0.926	0.909	0.893	0.877	0.862
2	1.886	1.859	1.833	1.808	1.783	1.736	1.690	1.647	1.605
3	2.775	2.723	2.673	2.624	2.577	2.487	2.402	2.322	2.246
4	3.630	3.546	3.465	3.387	3.312	3.170	3.037	2.914	2.798
5	4.452	4.629	4.212	4.100	3.993	3.791	3.605	3.433	3.274
6	5.242	5.076	4.917	4.767	4.623	4.355	4.111	3.889	3.685
7	6.002	5.786	5.582	5.389	5.206	4.868	4.564	4.288	4.039

---

[1]We also ignore depreciation in our analysis because depreciation is a noncash expense under accrual accounting and the NPV method focuses on cash flow rather than accrual operating income.

We multiply $31,000, the amount of the annuity, by the 3.433 present value factor and find that the present value of the annuity is $106,423 ($31,000 × 3.433 = $106,423). Finally, we find the net present value of the project by subtracting the present value of cash outflows from the present value of cash inflows. In our example, the net present value calculations are presented in Exhibit 7–6.

Exhibit 7–6
Net Present
Value Calculations

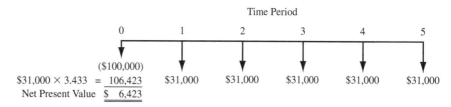

NPV = PV of project's expected returns - initial cash outlay

NPV = $106,423 - $100,000

NPV = $6,423

As Exhibit 7–6 shows, the positive net present value of $6,423 indicates that the project's expected return exceeds Juan Rodriguez Company's 14 percent blended cost of capital.

A word of caution here. A net present value of $6,423 does not mean that the project's return is only $6,423. Rather, it means that the project's return *exceeds* the company's 14 percent cost of capital by $6,423.

Discussion Questions

7-14. How would you explain the difference between present value and net present value?

7-15. Should a business accept or reject a project with an NPV of zero? Explain your reasoning.

The Juan Rodriguez Company example was relatively easy to calculate because the project's expected cash flows were the same each year (an annuity). When the expected cash flows are uneven, we find the present value of each year's cash flow and then add those amounts. To demonstrate, assume that the Juan Rodriguez Company's computer upgrade has expected annual returns of $31,000, but in year 3 the computer system will require $12,000 in maintenance fees (a cash outflow), and at the end of year 5, the system can be sold for $6,000 (a cash inflow). A time line depicting these additional cash flows is shown in Exhibit 7–7.

Exhibit 7–7
Uneven Expected Cash
Flows for Juan
Rodriguez Company
Computer Upgrade

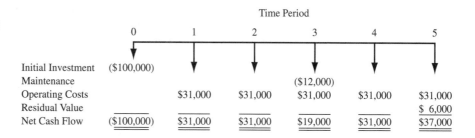

Each of the amounts for the five years shown in Exhibit 7–7 can be discounted to present value using the *Present Value of $1 Table,* found in the chapter appendix in Exhibit A7–5, a portion of which is reproduced as Exhibit 7–8.

Exhibit 7–8

Present Value of $1

Period	4%	5%	6%	7%	8%	10%	12%	14%	16%
1	0.962	0.952	0.943	0.935	0.926	0.909	0.893	0.877	0.862
2	0.925	0.907	0.890	0.873	0.857	0.826	0.797	0.769	0.743
3	0.889	0.864	0.840	0.816	0.794	0.751	0.712	0.675	0.641
4	0.855	0.823	0.792	0.763	0.735	0.683	0.636	0.592	0.552
5	0.882	0.784	0.747	0.713	0.681	0.621	0.567	0.519	0.476
6	0.790	0.746	0.705	0.666	0.630	0.564	0.507	0.456	0.410
7	0.760	0.711	0.665	0.623	0.583	0.513	0.452	0.400	0.354

The calculation of the present values, using the highlighted factors in the 14 percent discount rate column, are shown in Exhibit 7–9.

Exhibit 7–9
Net Present Value
Calculations with
Uneven Cash Flows

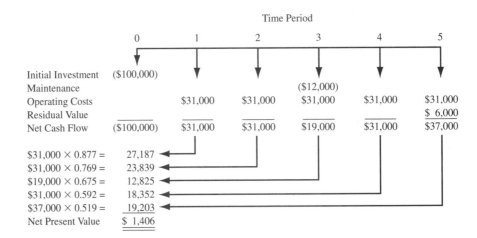

As Exhibit 7–9 demonstrates, the positive $1,406 net present value indicates that the computer upgrade exceeds the 14 percent blended cost of capital for the Juan Rodriguez Company. This positive NPV indicates that the project is acceptable for the company.

Although the net present value method indicates whether a proposed capital project is acceptable, it does have limitations as a ranking method to compare competing projects. A direct comparison of the net present values of various projects may lead to poor decisions regarding project selection, because NPV is measured in dollars rather than percentages. For example, assume that management intends to select one of two projects, Project A and Project B. Calculations indicate that the NPV of Project A is $5,000, whereas the NPV of Project B is $6,000.

Although choosing the project with the higher NPV seems wise, this is not always a good choice because NPV analysis does not consider the relative investments required by the projects. In our example, for instance, say the present value of Project A's cash inflows was $105,000 and the present value of its cash outflows was $100,000. Then suppose that the present value of Project B's cash inflows was

$206,000 and the present value of its cash outflows was $200,000. We see that Project A requires an investment of $100,000, whereas Project B requires double that investment amount. In firms with scarce funds, the relatively small increase in the NPV from $5,000 to $6,000 may not justify selecting a project that requires double the amount of investment. How then can the net present value method be used when ranking various projects? The problem of selecting among projects is solved by using a profitability index.

profitability index A method used to rank acceptable proposed capital projects.

Profitability Index The **profitability index** is an index of the values of alternative but acceptable capital budgeting projects, whose index values are calculated by dividing the present value of the project's cash inflows by the present value of its cash outflows. To illustrate, we return to our example. We know that both Projects A and B have positive NPVs and are acceptable projects. Suppose, however, we want to rank the projects in order of preference.

We find that the profitability index for Project A is 1.05 ($105,000/$100,000 = 1.05). The profitability index for Project B is 1.03 ($206,000/$200,000 = 1.03). We would rank Project A higher than Project B because Project A's index value is 1.05 compared to Project B's lower index value of 1.03. We see, then, how the profitability index is a tool that allows firms to rank competing projects.

Although the NPV method indicates whether a project's return is lower or higher than the required rate of return, it does not show the project's expected percentage return. Many managers find it helpful to know the expected rate of return of projects when making capital budgeting decisions. The internal rate of return method, discussed in the following section, is a capital budgeting method that provides this information.

internal rate of return (IRR) The calculated expected percentage return promised by a proposed capital project.

real rate of return Another name for *internal rate of return.*

time-adjusted rate of return Another name for *internal rate of return.*

Internal Rate of Return The **internal rate of return (IRR)** of a proposed capital project is the calculated expected percentage return promised by the project. Just like the net present value method, the internal rate of return method considers all cash flows for a proposed project and adjusts for the time value of money. However, the IRR results are expressed as a percentage, not a dollar amount. This method, also known as the **real rate of return,** or the **time-adjusted rate of return,** determines the discount rate that makes the present value of a project's cash inflows and the present value of a project's outflows exactly the same.

To calculate a project's IRR, we use the same present value tables we use to calculate net present value, but we interpret them differently. In this application, we consult the tables to determine a discount rate (a percentage), rather than present value amounts (expressed in dollars).

As an example, assume that Project C requires an initial investment of $300,000 and will provide cash inflows of $56,232 per year for eight years. Because this project is an annuity, to determine the IRR we use the *Present Value of an Annuity of $1 Table* found in the chapter appendix in Exhibit A7–10, a portion of which is reproduced as Exhibit 7–10.

First we calculate the present value factor for the project as follows:

$$\frac{\text{Initial Investment}}{\text{Expected Annual Return}} = \text{Present Value Factor}$$

In the case of Project C, the present value factor is

$$\frac{\$300,000 \text{ Initial Investment}}{\$56,232 \text{ Expected Annual Return}} = 5.335 \text{ Present Value Factor}$$

Now that we know the present value factor, we can find Project C's internal rate of return by moving down the time period column on the table in Exhibit 7–10 to eight periods, as that is the life of the project. Next we follow across the row corresponding to eight periods until we find a factor that is close to the one we calculated (5.335). As we follow across the row for eight periods, we find a factor that is not just close but matches exactly. The factor of 5.335 is in the 10 percent column, which indicates the internal rate of return for Project C is 10 percent. Thus, the actual rate of return promised by Project C is 10 percent.

Exhibit 7–10
Partial Present Value of an Annuity of $1 Table

Present Value of Annuity of $1

Period	4%	5%	6%	7%	8%	10%	12%
1	0.962	0.952	0.943	.935	0.926	0.909	0.893
2	1.886	1.859	1.833	1.808	1.783	1.736	1.690
3	2.775	2.723	2.673	2.624	2.577	2.487	2.402
4	3.630	3.546	3.465	3.387	3.312	3.170	3.037
5	4.452	4.629	4.212	4.100	3.993	3.791	3.605
6	5.242	5.076	4.917	4.767	4.623	4.355	4.111
7	6.002	5.786	5.582	5.389	5.206	4.868	4.564
8	6.733	6.463	6.210	5.971	5.747	5.335	4.968
9	7.435	7.108	6.802	6.515	6.247	5.759	5.328
10	8.111	7.722	7.360	7.024	6.710	6.145	5.650
11	8.760	8.306	7.877	7.499	7.139	6.495	5.938
12	9.382	8.863	8.384	7.943	7.536	6.814	6.194

Once determined, the internal rate of return is compared to the cost of capital to gauge the project's acceptability. An internal rate of return that exceeds the firm's cost of capital indicates an acceptable project. For example, if the company's cost of capital is nine percent, Project C's 10 percent internal rate of return shows that the firm would find the project acceptable.

In the example for Project C, we contrived the dollar amounts so that the factor we calculated exactly equaled one of the factors in the present value table. In a real-life situation, the calculated factor will usually fall between two factors on the present value table. For example, assume Project D would require an investment of $330,000 and would generate estimated annual returns of $64,900 for eight years. The present value factor for this project is 5.085, determined as follows:

$$\frac{\$330,000 \text{ Initial Investment}}{\$64,900 \text{ Annual Returns}} = 5.085 \text{ Present Value Factor}$$

Returning to the table in Exhibit 7–10 and following across the year 8 row, we find that our calculated 5.085 factor is between the factors 5.335 (the 10 percent column) and 4.968 (the 12 percent column), but is much closer to 4.968. Therefore, the project's return would fall between 10 and 12 percent, but would be much closer to 12 percent. We then estimate that the internal rate of return for Project D is slightly less than 12 percent.

Comparing Projects Using the IRR Method Managers can use the internal rate of return method to rank projects. For example, the internal rate of return of Project C (10 percent), can be compared to the approximate internal rate of return of Project D (almost 12 percent). Assuming both projects were acceptable, Project D would be ranked higher than Project C because it promises a higher IRR.

Comparing the NPV and IRR Methods Both the net present value method and the internal rate of return method are well-respected techniques used to determine the acceptability of a proposed capital project for two reasons. First, they are based on cash flows, not accounting income. Second, both methods consider the time value of money.

The net present value method is used to determine whether the promised return from a proposed capital project meets the minimum acceptable return requirements (cost of capital). A drawback of this method is that the calculated net present value is stated in dollars rather than percentages. Thus, comparison between projects is difficult. The profitability index overcomes this difficulty.

The internal rate of return method is used to calculate a proposed capital project's actual expected rate of return. Because this method is calculated using percentages rather than dollars, it can be used as a direct comparison of various proposed projects.

Nondiscounted Cash Flow Methods

The net present value and internal rate of return methods are generally considered the most reliable techniques available because they utilize the time value of money in their evaluation of potential capital projects. Other methods that ignore the time value of money exist, however, and are used to some degree by many companies. We now discuss two of them—the payback period method and the accounting rate of return method.

payback period method
A capital budgeting technique that measures the length of time a capital project must generate positive cash flows that equal the original investment in the project.

Payback Period Method As its name implies, the **payback period method** is a capital budgeting technique that measures the length of time a capital project must generate positive net cash flows that equal, or "pay back," the original investment in the project. For instance, assume that a project's estimated initial outlay is $40,000. Assume further that the project is expected to generate a net cash inflow of $12,500 per year. When net cash inflows are equal from one year to the next, we determine the payback period by dividing the required initial investment by the annual cash inflows. In our example, we find that the payback period is 3.2 years. The calculations follow:

$$\frac{\text{Required Initial Investment}}{\text{Annual Net Cash Inflow}} = \text{Payback Period in Years}$$

$$\frac{\$40,000}{\$12,500} = 3.2 \text{ Years}$$

If a project has uneven cash flows, we can determine the payback period by adding the cash inflows year by year until the total equals the required initial investment. For example, suppose a project requires an initial investment of $50,000 and is expected to generate the following net cash inflows:

2001	$12,000
2002	$15,000
2003	$18,000
2004	$15,000
2005	$12,000

We find the payback period by totaling the net cash inflows until we reach $50,000 as shown in Exhibit 7–11.

Exhibit 7–11
Payback Period with
Uneven Cash Flows

Year	Cash Received in Prior Years		Cash Received in Current Year		Accumulated Cash Received
1	0	+	$12,000	=	$12,000
2	$12,000	+	$15,000	=	$27,000
3	$27,000	+	$18,000	=	$45,000
4	$45,000	+	$15,000	=	$60,000
5	$60,000	+	$12,000	=	$72,000

As Exhibit 7–11 shows, the initial investment will be "paid back" after the third year, but before the end of the fourth year. At the end of the third year, it is anticipated that $45,000, or all but $5,000 of the initial $50,000 investment will be recouped. The remaining $5,000 will be received during the fourth year as part of the $15,000 net cash inflows anticipated for that year. It will take about 1/3 ($5,000/$15,000) of the fourth year to collect the final $5,000 to make up the $50,000 needed to payback the initial investment. Therefore the payback period is 3 1/3 years.

The payback period method highlights the liquidity of an investment and can be used as a screening device to reject projects with unreasonably low cash flow expectations. This method is simple to use, is easily understood, and offers some limited insight into a project's liquidity.

The payback period method is not often used to make final capital investment decisions because it does not consider three crucial elements: (1) the expected returns of a project after the payback period, (2) how the returns will compare to the firm's cost of capital, or (3) the time value of money.

Because the payback method ignores the firm's cost of capital, total cash flow, and time value of money concerns, managers do not normally accept or reject a project based solely on the payback period method. If used at all, the payback period method is usually a screening device only to eliminate potential projects from further evaluation. Companies often establish a maximum payback period for potential projects. If a proposed capital project promises a payback of longer than the established maximum period, that project would be eliminated from further consideration. For example, assume a company has established a maximum payback period of three years. Using this standard, the project presented in Exhibit 7–11 would be rejected because its payback period is longer than three years.

Accounting Rate of Return Method

In our discussion so far, we have emphasized that the focus in capital budgeting decisions should be on cash flows. Over time, however, the net cash flow associated with a capital project should approximate operating income as determined using accrual accounting revenue and expense recognition. The accounting rate of return method uses accrual accounting operating income, rather than net cash flow, as the basis for evaluating alternative capital budgeting projects.

The **accounting rate of return** is the rate of return for a capital project based on the anticipated increase in accounting operating income due to the project, relative to the amount of capital investment required.

accounting rate of return
The rate of return for a capital project based on the anticipated increase in accounting operating income due to the project, relative to the amount of capital investment required.

This method focuses on how the project changes a company's operating income and the company's required investment. As an example, we reexamine the computer hardware upgrade project for the Juan Rodriguez Company discussed earlier in the chapter. As you recall, the computer hardware upgrade required an initial investment of $100,000. Additionally, the upgrade would reduce operating expenses by $31,000 per year for five years. The computer has an estimated useful life of five years with no residual value. Accounting operating income would be affected in two ways by the computer upgrade. First, the reduced operating expenses would increase operating income by $31,000 each year. Second, depreciation for the computer upgrade would decrease operating income by $20,000 each year ($100,000/5 years). With this information, we can calculate the accounting rate of return as follows:

$$\frac{\text{Increase in Operating Income}}{\text{Required Investment}} = \text{Accounting Rate of Return}$$

$$\frac{\$31,000 - 20,000}{\$100,000} = 11\% \text{ Accounting Rate of Return}$$

The accounting rate of return is simple to calculate and provides some measure of a project's profitability; however, it has two major drawbacks. First, the accounting rate of return method focuses on accounting income rather than cash flow. In capital budgeting it is generally believed that a focus on cash flow is preferred to a focus on accounting income. Second, like the payback method, the accounting rate of return does not consider the time value of money.

The accounting rate of return method is generally considered to be superior to the payback period method because it offers at least a limited measure of a proposed capital project's rate of return. As with the payback period method, however, managers should not accept or reject a project based solely on the accounting rate of return. Both of these methods should be used only as screening devices or in conjunction with discounted cash flow methods of evaluating capital project alternatives.

FACTORS LEADING TO POOR CAPITAL PROJECT SELECTION

The process of determining which capital projects to select is serious business for any company. We mentioned earlier in the chapter that Motorola reported investment in capital projects of over $4.5 billion in 1995. If managers do not treat capital budgeting with the seriousness it deserves, they run the risk of making poor decisions as to the capital projects selected. At the very least, selecting the wrong capital projects is enormously costly. At worst, investing in the wrong projects can lead to financial ruin for any company, regardless of its size or past performance. The two main factors leading to poor capital project selection are natural optimism on the part of managers and the tendency of some managers to turn the capital project evaluation process into a game.

Natural Optimism

Human beings are essentially optimistic. As managers they estimate both the cash inflows and outflows associated with a proposed project they are sponsoring with an overly optimistic outlook. This means they will likely overstate the estimated cash inflows and understate the estimated cash outflows. At the very minimum, this natural optimism limits the effectiveness of any of the evaluation techniques we have discussed in this chapter, because all of them use inflow and outflow estimates as the basis of evaluation.

There is nothing wrong with thinking positively. Optimism is, in fact, a desirable trait. Managers must understand, however, that such optimism can cloud their judgment as they assess potential capital projects. Good managers attempt to be as realistic as possible as they prepare proposals for the evaluation of potential capital projects.

Capital Budgeting Games

The managers who propose potential capital projects understand that there is usually not enough money available to fund all projects, even if they all promise a return greater than the cost of capital. A manager who proposes a capital project is, in fact, competing with other managers' projects for a limited number of capital investment dollars. For this reason, the capital project evaluation process is sometimes treated like some sort of game with little consideration of the potentially disastrous consequences. Some managers manipulate the estimates of cash inflow and cash outflow to get "pet" projects approved, often at the expense of other, more deserving projects. Do not confuse this idea with the natural optimism we discussed a moment ago. The manipulation we are talking about here is an additional factor that can lead to selecting the wrong capital projects.

For example, consider the Electronics Division of Monolith Enterprises. This division has established a limit of $3 million for capital projects in 2002. Mary and Fred are the only two managers within the division who have potential capital projects to propose to division upper management. Both the potential projects will require an initial investment of $2 million, so only one of them is going to be approved.

Mary is in her office late one night putting the finishing touches on her proposal. She is reviewing the cash inflow and cash outflow estimates she has made for her project. As she goes over the estimates one last time, she is feeling a little guilty because she knows she has purposely overstated the inflows and understated the outflows to make her project look more favorable. She is convinced, however, that if she is totally realistic in her estimates, her project will stand no chance of being approved. Why? Because she knows Fred is in his office down the hall putting the finishing touches on his proposal, and she is sure he has manipulated the inflow and outflow estimates on his project to make it look better. To have any chance of approval, then, Mary must "play the game." The sad part of this situation is that Fred is down the hall in his office thinking exactly the same thing about Mary. He is certain she has manipulated her estimates, so he must also, or his project has no chance of being approved. Now we introduce one more person to our scenario—Bill, the division controller. Bill is the person who will evaluate the proposed projects submitted by Mary and Fred and will decide which of the two projects will be funded. He knows that both Mary and Fred have manipulated their estimates, so when he receives them, he compensates by arbitrarily revising their proposals or by using a higher cost of capital percentage in the NPV and IRR evaluations.

Does this seem to you to be an intelligent way to run a business? No, but this kind of game is played every day in many companies by otherwise bright and honest managers.

Discussion Question

Assume you have been hired as a consultant by Monolith Enterprises to help the company improve its capital project evaluation process.

7–16. What suggestions would you make to help Monolith eliminate the kind of "game" being played by Mary, Fred, and Bill?

How does a company make its capital project evaluation process more cooperative and less competitive? This question is difficult, if not impossible, to answer. What we do know, however, is that the global nature of business as we enter the 21st century will not allow these kinds of budget games to continue. U.S. companies are competing with companies from all over the world, and the kind of behavior we have been discussing does not seem to exist in many of these businesses. If U.S. firms are to compete in this worldwide market, they must eliminate dysfunctional business practices. The stakes are simply too high for managers of these companies to continue this approach to capital budgeting.

In a very short time, you will occupy the positions held by Mary, Fred, or Bill. Not at Monolith, of course, because it is a fictitious company. The company that employs you, however, may approach capital budgeting the same way Monolith does. If so, you must do all you can to help the company find a better, more constructive capital budgeting process.

SUMMARY

There are four elements in the overall planning process for any organization. These elements include the establishing of goals, the formulation of a strategic plan, the preparation of the capital budget, and the preparation of the operating budget.

The capital budgeting process has been described as the *how* of being in business and doing business, which means that the capital budget outlines how a company will allocate its scarce resources over the next five, 10, or even 20 years.

All capital projects have at least four shared characteristics. Such projects are usually long lived, carry with them high costs, have costs associated with the project that usually become sunk almost immediately, and usually involve a high degree of risk.

In the long run, the capital projects a company undertakes must cover at least the cost of the company's capital. The cost of capital is the cost of obtaining financing from both debt and equity sources. The combination of the cost of debt financing and equity financing is referred to as the blended cost of capital. If the capital project being considered does not at least cover the cost of capital, it makes no sense, from a purely financial standpoint, to undertake it.

Over time, several methods have been developed to evaluate potential capital projects. Among these are the net present value method, the internal rate of return method, the payback period method, and the accounting rate of return. Each of these four methods has certain advantages and disadvantages relative to the other methods. The NPV and IRR methods are generally considered to be superior to the payback and accounting rate of return methods because they incorporate the time value of money in their approach to evaluating potential capital projects.

APPENDIX: THE TIME VALUE OF MONEY

The Time Value of Money—The Concept of Interest

> *Interest is an interesting thing—*
> *Those who understand it, get it.*
> *Those who don't, pay it.*
>
> —Anonymous

A dollar received at some point in the future does not have the same value as a dollar received today. If you were asked why this is so, you might think the change in value is due to inflation. Even if inflation did not exist, a dollar received in the future would not have the same value as a dollar received today. The reason for the difference in value is that if cash is available now, it can be invested now and earn a return as time passes. This increase in the value of cash over time, due to investment income, is referred to as the time value of money. The concept of the time value of money is used to determine either the future value of money invested today or the present value of money to be received at some point in the future.

LEARNING OBJECTIVES

After completing your work in the appendix to this chapter, you should be able to do the following:

1. Explain the concept of simple interest and compound interest.
2. Determine the future value of a single amount invested today using a future value table.
3. Determine the present value of a single amount to be received at some point in the future using a present value table.
4. Describe the concept of an annuity.
5. Determine the future value of an annuity using a future value table.
6. Determine the present value of an annuity using a present value table.

Future Value

future value   The value of a payment, or series of payments, at some future point in time calculated at some interest rate.

Future value is the value of a payment, or series of payments, at some future point in time calculated at some interest rate. For example, if you were to invest $2,000 at an annual interest rate of 10 percent, your investment would grow to $2,200 in one year. How? The amount of the increase is calculated by multiplying the principal—the original investment—by the interest rate. In our case the principal is $2,000, the interest rate is 10 percent, so the total return on your investment is $200. The $200 is added to the $2,000 investment for a total of $2,200. So far, so good. But suppose you left the investment untouched for three years. What would be its total value at the end of the three years? The answer depends on whether the interest is calculated as simple interest or compound interest.

simple interest   Interest calculated on the original principal amount invested only

Simple interest is interest calculated only on the original principal. A calculation of interest earned at 10 percent per year for three years on a $2,000 principal using simple interest is presented in Exhibit A7–1.

Exhibit A7–1
Simple Interest Calculation

	Year 1	Year 2	Year 3
Principal	$2,000	$2,000	$2,000
Times the interest rate	× 10%	× 10%	× 10%
Equals interest earned	$ 200	$ 200	$ 200

Note in Exhibit A7–1 that interest for each of the three years is calculated only on the original investment of $2,000. At the end of three years you would receive your $2,000 (return of your principal) and $600 interest (return on your investment).

compound interest   Interest calculated on the original principal amount invested plus all previously earned interest.

Compound interest is interest calculated on the investment principal *plus* all previously earned interest. Continuing with our example, a principal of $2,000 that

	Year 1	Year 2	Year 3
Principal + Previously earned interest	$2,000	$2,200*	$2,420**
Times the interest rate	× 10%	× 10%	× 10%
Equals interest earned	$ 200	$ 220	$ 242

* Principal ($2,000) plus the interest earned in year 1 ($200) becomes the amount earning interest in year 2.

** Principal ($2,000) plus the interest earned in year 1 ($200) and the interest earned in year 2 ($220) becomes the amount earning interest in year 3.

earns a compounded rate of 10 percent interest per year for three years is shown in Exhibit A7–2.

Note in Exhibit A7–2 that interest for each of the three years is calculated not only on the original investment of $2,000, but also on the interest earned in previous years. At the end of three years you would receive your $2,000 back (return of principal) and $662 interest (return on your investment). The difference of $62 between the interest earned using compound interest ($662) and the interest earned using simple interest ($600) is interest earned on your previously earned interest.

The power of compounding is tremendous. To demonstrate, let us extend our example of the $2,000 investment. Suppose Dick Gustufson invests $2,000 at 10 percent annual interest when he is 18 years old and leaves it untouched until he is 38 years old. Using the simple interest calculation, Dick's investment will earn interest of $4,000 ($2,000 × 10% × 20 years). If, however, the interest over that same 20 years is compounded, the total interest earned would be $11,454. The $7,454 difference in interest earned is due entirely to interest earning interest on previously earned interest.

We could calculate the amount of compound interest on Dick's investment by extending the three-year example presented in Exhibit A7–2 for another 17 years. This, however, would be cumbersome, time consuming, and tiresome. Fortunately, future value tables greatly simplify the calculation of compound interest.

Future value tables are previously calculated values of $1 at various rates of interest and time periods. The tables are used to determine either the future value of a single payment or the future value of an annuity—that is, a stream of equal payments made at equal intervals.

The *Future Value of $1 Table* (Exhibit A7–3) is used to determine the future value of a single amount deposited today. With this information, we can quickly determine the future value of Dick Gustufson's $2,000 investment at a 10 percent interest rate compounded annually.

As we see in Exhibit A7–3, by moving across the interest rate column headings to the 10 percent column, and then down the time period row to the 20 time periods row, we find a number on the table at the point where the row and column intersect, at a value of 6.727. This number is called a future value factor. Because we are using the *Future Value of $1 Table*, the 6.727 factor tells us that the value of a single dollar 20 years into the future is $6.727, or about $6.73. That is to say that if $1 is invested today at 10 percent, it will be worth $6.73 in 20 years.

But Dick invested $2,000, not $1. To determine the future value of $2,000, we multiply $2,000 by the factor of 6.727 to determine that $2,000 invested today at 10 percent will be worth $13,454 after 20 years ($2,000 × 6.727 = $13,454). If you subtract his initial investment of $2,000, the amount of interest he will earn is $11,454.

A *Future Value of an Annuity of $1 Table*, presented as Exhibit A7–4, is used to determine the future value of a stream of cash flows when the stream of cash flows constitutes an annuity. An **annuity** is a stream of cash flows where the dollar amount of each payment and the time interval between each payment are uniform.

annuity   A stream of equal periodic cash flows.

Exhibit A7–3
Future Value of $1 Table

Future Value of $1

Period	4%	5%	6%	7%	8%	9%	10%	12%	14%	16%
1	1.040	1.050	1.060	1.070	1.080	1.090	1.100	1.120	1.140	1.160
2	1.082	1.103	1.124	1.145	1.166	1.188	1.210	1.254	1.300	1.346
3	1.125	1.158	1.191	1.225	1.260	1.295	1.331	1.405	1.482	1.561
4	1.170	1.216	1.262	1.311	1.360	1.412	1.464	1.574	1.689	1.811
5	1.217	1.276	1.338	1.403	1.469	1.539	1.611	1.762	1.925	2.100
6	1.265	1.340	1.419	1.501	1.587	1.677	1.772	1.974	2.195	2.436
7	1.316	1.407	1.501	1.606	1.714	1.828	1.949	2.211	2.502	2.826
8	1.369	1.477	1.594	1.718	1.851	1.993	2.144	2.476	2.853	3.278
9	1.423	1.551	1.689	1.838	1.999	2.172	2.358	2.773	3.252	3.803
10	1.480	1.629	1.791	1.967	2.159	2.367	2.594	3.106	3.707	4.411
11	1.539	1.710	1.898	2.105	2.332	2.580	2.853	3.479	4.226	5.117
12	1.601	1.796	2.012	2.252	2.518	2.813	3.138	3.896	4.818	5.936
13	1.665	1.886	2.113	2.410	2.720	3.066	3.452	4.363	5.492	6.886
14	1.732	1.980	2.261	2.579	2.937	3.342	3.797	4.887	6.261	7.988
15	1.801	2.079	2.397	2.759	3.172	3.642	4.177	5.474	7.138	9.266
16	1.873	2.183	2.540	2.952	3.426	3.970	4.595	6.130	8.137	10.748
17	1.948	2.292	2.693	3.159	3.700	4.328	5.054	6.866	9.276	12.468
18	2.026	2.407	2.854	3.380	3.996	4.717	5.560	7.690	10.575	14.463
19	2.107	2.527	3.026	3.617	4.316	5.142	6.116	8.613	12.056	16.777
20	2.191	2.653	3.207	3.870	4.661	5.604	6.727	9.646	13.743	19.461

Exhibit A7–4
Future Value of an Annuity of $1 Table

Future Value of Annuity of $1

Period	4%	5%	6%	7%	8%	9%	10%	12%	14%	16%
1	1.000	1.000	1.000	1.000	1.000	1.000	1.000	1.000	1.000	1.000
2	2.040	2.050	2.060	2.070	2.080	2.090	2.100	2.120	2.140	2.160
3	3.122	3.153	3.184	3.215	3.246	3.278	3.310	3.374	3.440	3.506
4	4.246	4.310	4.375	4.440	4.506	4.573	4.641	4.779	4.921	5.006
5	5.416	5.526	5.637	5.751	5.867	5.985	6.105	6.353	6.610	6.877
6	6.633	6.802	6.975	7.153	7.336	7.523	7.716	8.115	8.536	8.977
7	7.898	8.142	8.394	8.654	8.923	9.200	9.487	10.089	10.730	11.414
8	9.214	9.549	9.897	10.260	10.637	11.028	11.436	12.300	13.233	14.240
9	10.583	11.027	11.491	11.978	12.488	13.021	13.579	14.776	16.085	17.519
10	12.006	12.578	13.181	13.816	14.487	15.193	15.937	17.549	19.337	21.321
11	13.486	14.207	14.972	15.784	16.645	17.560	18.531	20.665	23.045	25.733
12	15.026	15.917	16.870	17.888	18.977	20.141	21.384	24.133	27.271	30.850
13	16.627	17.713	18.882	20.141	21.495	22.953	24.523	28.029	32.089	36.786
14	18.292	19.599	21.015	22.550	24.215	26.019	27.975	32.393	37.581	43.672
15	20.024	21.579	23.276	25.129	27.152	29.361	31.772	37.280	43.842	51.660
16	21.825	23.657	25.673	27.888	30.324	33.003	35.950	42.753	50.980	60.925
17	23.698	25.840	28.213	30.840	33.750	36.974	40.545	48.884	59.118	71.673
18	25.645	28.132	30.906	33.999	37.450	41.301	45.599	55.750	68.394	84.141
19	27.671	30.539	33.760	37.379	41.446	46.018	51.159	63.440	78.969	98.603
20	29.778	33.066	36.786	40.995	45.762	51.160	57.275	72.052	91.025	115.380

To see how the table in Exhibit A7–4 is used, assume Susan King intends to deposit $2,000 in an account at the end of each year for four years at a compound interest rate of 12 percent per year. Using the *Future Value of an Annuity of $1 Table* we determine that the factor for 4 years at 12 percent is 4.779. Accordingly, if Susan deposits $2,000 at the end of each year for four years at 12 percent, the account balance will be approximately $9,558 ($2,000 × 4.779).

Present Value (Discounting)

The basic premise of the present value of money is that it is more valuable to receive cash today (so it can be invested to receive interest) than to receive the cash later. The question is, just *how* valuable is it to receive cash sooner rather than later?

If we know the expected rate of return, it is possible to actually calculate the value of receiving cash sooner rather than later. For example, if you are offered the option of receiving $1,000 today or $1,000 one year from now, how much more valuable is it to receive the $1,000 today? If the $1,000 received today can be invested in a savings account earning six percent interest, then it will grow by $60 during the year. At the end of one year, it will be worth $1,060 and you would be $60 richer than if you had opted to receive the $1,000 one year from now. The $60 growth in value over time exemplifies the time value of money. Clearly, if money is available and invested, it grows as time passes.

If cash can be invested at six percent, $1,000 received today is equivalent to receiving $1,060 one year from now. The amount a future cash flow or stream of cash flows is worth today evaluated at the appropriate interest rate is the cash flow's **present value.** Determining the present value of an amount of cash to be received in the future is called *discounting*.

present value The amount future cash flows are worth today based on an appropriate interest rate.

Present value tables greatly simplify the calculation of discounting to find the present value of a single amount or an annuity. Present value tables are previously calculated values of $1 at various interest rates and time periods. The tables are used to determine either the present value of a single amount or the present value of an annuity.

A *Present Value of $1 Table*, presented as Exhibit A7–5, is used to determine the present value of a single amount to be received at some point in the future.

To see how we use the *Present Value of $1 Table,* suppose you visited your rich Aunt Hattie and helped her wash her dog. Your aunt was so touched by your kindness, she offers to give you a gift of $1,000. You are excited and hold out your hand for the money, but she informs you that she is not going to give you the money now. Rather she intends to give you the money one year from now. Her only request is that you tell her how much to deposit in a six percent savings account today so that the account will equal $1,000 one year from now.

In this case, you know that the future value of the amount is $1,000 one year from now. The amount your Aunt Hattie wants to know is the present value, the amount that must be deposited today at six percent so that the account will be worth $1,000 in one year. To find out how much Aunt Hattie must deposit, we use the *Present Value of $1 Table* in Exhibit A7–5. We quickly scan the table to find the point of intersection between the six percent interest rate column and the number of time periods row which is 1. The point of intersection, the present value factor, is 0.943. This factor indicates that the present value of one dollar discounted at six percent is $0.943, or about 94 cents. Thus, if $0.943 is invested today at six percent, it will be worth $1 one year from now.

But Aunt Hattie is going to give you $1,000, not $1. To determine the present value of $1,000, we simply multiply $1,000 by the factor of 0.943 to determine that $943 invested today at six percent will be worth $1,000 in one year, as shown by the time line presentation in Exhibit A7–6.

Exhibit A7-5
Present Value of $1 Table

Present Value of $1

Period	4%	5%	6%	7%	8%	10%	12%	14%	16%
1	0.962	0.952	0.943	0.935	0.926	0.909	0.893	0.877	0.862
2	0.925	0.907	0.890	0.873	0.857	0.826	0.797	0.769	0.743
3	0.889	0.864	0.840	0.816	0.794	0.751	0.712	0.675	0.641
4	0.855	0.823	0.792	0.763	0.735	0.683	0.636	0.592	0.552
5	0.882	0.784	0.747	0.713	0.681	0.621	0.567	0.519	0.476
6	0.790	0.746	0.705	0.666	0.630	0.564	0.507	0.456	0.410
7	0.760	0.711	0.665	0.623	0.583	0.513	0.452	0.400	0.354
8	0.731	0.677	0.627	0.582	0.540	0.467	0.404	0.351	0.305
9	0.703	0.645	0.592	0.544	0.500	0.424	0.361	0.308	0.263
10	0.676	0.614	0.558	0.508	0.463	0.386	0.322	0.270	0.227
11	0.650	0.585	0.527	0.475	0.429	0.350	0.287	0.237	0.195
12	0.625	0.557	0.497	0.444	0.397	0.319	0.257	0.208	0.168
13	0.601	0.530	0.469	0.415	0.368	0.290	0.229	0.182	0.145
14	0.557	0.505	0.442	0.388	0.340	0.263	0.205	0.160	0.125
15	0.555	0.481	0.417	0.362	0.315	0.239	0.183	0.140	0.108
16	0.534	0.458	0.394	0.339	0.292	0.218	0.163	0.123	0.093
17	0.513	0.436	0.371	0.317	0.270	0.198	0.146	0.108	0.080
18	0.494	0.416	0.350	0.296	0.250	0.180	0.130	0.095	0.069
19	0.475	0.396	0.331	0.277	0.232	0.164	0.116	0.083	0.060
20	0.456	0.377	0.312	0.258	0.215	0.149	0.104	0.073	0.051

Exhibit A7-6
Time Line Presentation
of Present Value of $1

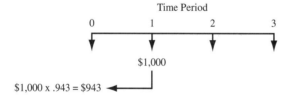

Exhibit A7–6 shows that to earn $1,000 a year from now, given an expected rate of interest of six percent per year, Aunt Hattie must deposit $943. So, the present value of $1,000 to be received one year from now at six percent is $943. The $943 will grow in value as it accumulates interest. This growth is the time value of money. You immediately inform your aunt Hattie that she must deposit $943 today at six percent to have the $1,000 gift ready for you one year from now.

Aunt Hattie is so happy with your quick response that she offers you an additional $1,000 gift. The second $1,000 gift, however, will be given two years from now, which means you will receive the first $1,000 gift at the end of year 1, and the second $1,000 gift at the end of year 2. You are thrilled, but again, your Aunt Hattie requests that you tell her exactly how much she must deposit today at six percent to have the additional $1,000 in two years. We use the *Present Value of $1 Table* in Exhibit A7–5 to find that the present value factor for a time period of two and an interest rate of six percent is 0.890. Accordingly, the present value of $1,000 to be received two years from now is $890 ($1,000 × 0.890). You quickly inform your aunt that she must deposit a total of $1,833 ($943 + $890) today to pay both the $1,000 at the end of year 1, and the $1,000 at the end of year 2. The time line and calculations are shown in Exhibit A7–7.

Exhibit A7–7
Time Line Presentation

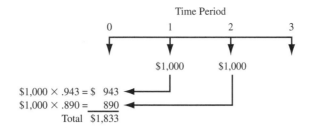

Now suppose your Aunt Hattie planned to give you a gift of $1,000 per year for the next three years. We could rely on the *Present Value of $1 Table* and add the totals for each year as shown in Exhibit A7–8.

Exhibit A7–8
Time Line Presentation

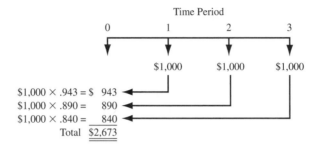

We can simplify the calculations, however, by multiplying the $1,000 by the sum of the three present value factors, which is 2.673. Accordingly, instead of multiplying $1,000 by 0.943, then $1,000 by 0.890, then $1,000 by 0.840, and summing the total, we simply multiply the $1,000 by the sum of the factors as shown in Exhibit A7–9.

Exhibit A7–9
Time Line Presentation

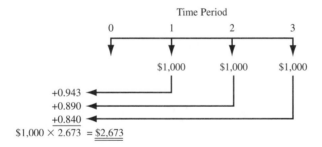

Because the stream of cash flows in our example is an annuity—three equal payments made at regular intervals of one year—we can use the *Present Value of an Annuity of $1 Table*, presented as Exhibit A7–10.

By examining the table in Exhibit A7–10, we find that the present value factor of an annuity for three periods at six percent is 2.673. Notice that the 2.673 equals the sum of the individual present value of $1 factors for each of the three years in Exhibit A7–9. Next, we multiply the $1,000 by the 2.673 factor to find that the present value of Aunt Hattie's $1,000, three-year annuity paid yearly is $2,673.

As you use the future value and present value tables provided in this book, note that the number of interest rates and time periods is limited. Although these smaller tables are useful for learning the basics, in business practice future value and present value tables include a much larger number of interest rates and time periods. If needed, comprehensive tables are available at bookstores and office supply stores.

Exhibit A7–10
Present Value of an Annuity of $1 Table

Present Value of Annuity of $1

Period	4%	5%	6%	7%	8%	10%	12%	14%	16%
1	0.962	0.952	0.943	0.935	0.926	0.909	0.893	0.877	0.862
2	1.886	1.859	1.833	1.808	1.783	1.736	1.690	1.647	1.605
3	2.775	2.723	2.673	2.624	2.577	2.487	2.402	2.322	2.246
4	3.630	3.546	3.465	3.387	3.312	3.170	3.037	2.914	2.798
5	4.452	4.629	4.212	4.100	3.993	3.791	3.605	3.433	3.274
6	5.242	5.076	4.917	4.767	4.623	4.355	4.111	3.889	3.685
7	6.002	5.786	5.582	5.389	5.206	4.868	4.564	4.288	4.039
8	6.733	6.463	6.210	5.971	5.747	5.335	4.968	4.639	4.344
9	7.435	7.108	6.802	6.515	6.247	5.759	5.328	4.946	4.607
10	8.111	7.722	7.360	7.024	6.710	6.145	5.650	5.216	4.833
11	8.760	8.306	7.877	7.499	7.139	6.495	5.938	5.453	5.029
12	9.382	8.863	8.384	7.943	7.536	6.814	6.194	5.660	5.179
13	9.986	9.394	8.853	8.358	7.904	7.103	6.424	5.842	5.342
14	10.563	9.899	9.295	8.745	8.244	7.367	6.628	6.002	5.468
15	11.118	10.380	9.712	9.108	8.559	7.606	6.811	6.142	5.575
16	11.652	10.838	10.106	9.447	8.851	7.824	6.974	6.265	5.669
17	12.166	11.274	10.477	9.763	9.122	8.022	7.120	6.373	5.749
18	12.659	11.690	10.828	10.059	9.372	8.201	7.250	6.467	5.818
19	13.134	12.085	11.158	10.336	9.604	8.365	7.366	6.550	5.877
20	13.590	12.462	11.470	10.594	9.818	8.514	7.469	6.623	5.929

As an alternative to using future and present value tables, we can compute future value and present value using nothing more than a somewhat sophisticated business handheld calculator. (It must be a business calculator. Engineering and scientific calculators generally do not have present value and future value functions.) In the business world, most managers rely on calculators and computers to calculate future and present values.

Most computers can also be used to solve present value and future value problems. Many software packages now include modules that can handle simple and advanced calculations dealing with the time value of money.

A working knowledge of present and future value concepts will be extremely important to you not only in your college course work but also in your professional career. Whether the task is the evaluation of potential capital projects, as in this chapter, or any of its many other applications, you will find these concepts invaluable throughout your life.

KEY TERMS

accounting rate of return   M-236
annuity   M-241
blended cost of capital   M-223
capital assets   M-220
capital budget   M-219
capital budgeting   M-216
capital investments   M-216
capital projects   M-216

compound interest   M-240
cost of capital   M-222
cost of capital rate   M-222
cost of debt capital   M-223
cost of equity capital   M-223
discounting cash flows   M-229
future value   M-240
hurdle rate   M-222

REVIEW THE FACTS

A. What constitutes a firm's goals?

B. What is a mission statement and how does it relate to a company's goals?

C. What is a strategic plan and how does it relate to a company's goals?

D. What is the purpose of a capital budget and how does it relate to the strategic plan and a company's goals?

E. What is the purpose of an operating budget and how does it relate to the capital budget, the strategic plan, and a company's goals?

F. What are capital investments?

G. What is the difference between a capital investment and a capital project?

H. What is the focus of the capital budget?

I. What does it mean when the cost of a purchased item is capitalized?

J. What does it mean when the cost of a purchased item is expensed?

K. What are the four shared characteristics of virtually all capital projects?

L. What are some other terms used to describe the cost of capital?

M. Describe what is meant by the net present value of an investment.

N. With respect to net present value calculations, what is the advantage of calculating the profitability index?

O. What is determined by the internal rate of return?

P. What is determined by the payback method?

Q. What is the accounting rate of return?

R. What are two factors that can lead to poor capital project selection?

S. What is the basic difference between simple interest and compound interest? (Appendix)

T. What is an annuity? (Appendix)

APPLY WHAT YOU HAVE LEARNED

LO 1:   Match Elements of Planning to Characteristics

7–17. Following are the elements of the planning process as discussed in this chapter, with some characteristics pertaining to those elements.

   a. Goals   **c.** Capital budget

   b. Strategic plan   **d.** Operating budget

   1. _____ Pertains to day-to-day activities

   2. _____ Pertains to the allocation of scarce resources

   3. _____ Consists of both financial and nonfinancial considerations

   4. _____ Stated in terms that are not easily quantified

   5. _____ Stated in terms that are easily quantified

   6. _____ Constitutes the *who* of business planning

7. _____ Constitutes the *why* of business planning
8. _____ Constitutes the *how* of business planning
9. _____ Constitutes the *what* of business planning
10. _____ Relates to long-lived, expensive assets

REQUIRED:

Match each element of the planning process with the appropriate characteristics. Each letter may be used more than once.

LO 4: Discuss and Calculate the Cost of Capital

7–18. The Marcus Company is in the process of determining a return rate to use for its cost of capital.

Upon review of the financial statements it was determined that the total interest bearing debt is $1,400,000 and total stockholders equity is $1,000,000. In addition, it was determined that the cost of debt financing is 8%, and the cost of equity financing is 18%.

REQUIRED:

a. What proportion of the Marcus Company's total financing comes from debt?
b. What proportion of the Marcus Company's total financing comes from equity?
c. Calculate the Marcus Company's blended cost of capital rate.

LO 4: Discuss and Calculate the Cost of Capital

7–19. The Byrne Company is in the process of determining a return rate to use for its cost of capital.

Upon review of the financial statements it was determined that the total interest bearing debt is $4,800,000 and total stockholders' equity is $14,400,000. In addition, it was determined that the cost of debt financing is 7%, and the cost of equity financing is 22%.

REQUIRED:

a. What proportion of The Byrne Company's total financing comes from debt?
b. What proportion of The Byrne Company's total financing comes from equity?
c. Calculate The Byrne Company's blended cost of capital rate.

LO 4: Discuss and Calculate the Cost of Capital

7–20. The Cunningham Company is in the process of determining a return rate to use for its cost of capital.

Upon review of the financial statements it was determined that the total interest bearing debt is $800,000 and total stockholders' equity is $1,700,000. In addition, it was determined that the cost of debt financing is 9%, and the cost of equity financing is 20%.

REQUIRED:

a. What proportion of The Cunningham Company's total financing comes from debt?
b. What proportion of The Cunningham Company's total financing comes from equity?
c. Calculate The Cunningham Company's blended cost of capital rate.

LO 2: Determine the Sequence of Evaluating Capital Expenditures

7–21. Following in random order are the five steps for evaluating a capital expenditure.

    a. _____ Identify alternative capital projects.
    b. _____ Identify the need for a capital expenditure.
    c. _____ Select a method for evaluating the alternatives.
    d. _____ Evaluate the alternatives and select the project or projects to be funded.
    e. _____ Determine relevant cash inflow and cash outflow information.

REQUIRED:
In the space provided, indicate a logical sequence of the steps for evaluating a capital expenditure.

LO 6 & 7: Determine Net Present Value, No Residual Value

7–22. Florence Kundrat owns Discount Fashions. She is contemplating the purchase of a soda machine which would be used to sell soft drinks to customers for $0.75 each. The following estimates are available:

Initial outlay	$3,500
Annual cash inflow	$1,000
Cost of capital	10%
Estimated life of the soda machine	5 years
Estimated residual value of the soda machine	$ -0-

REQUIRED:
Determine the net present value of the soda machine purchase.

LO 6 & 7: Determine Net Present Value, No Residual Value

7–23. Brianna Garcia is contemplating the purchase of an ice cream vending machine which would be used to sell ice cream to customers for $2 each. The following estimates are available.

Initial outlay	$4,000
Annual cash inflow	$1,200
Cost of capital	12%
Estimated life of the ice cream machine	5 years
Estimated residual value of the ice cream machine	$ -0-

REQUIRED:
Determine the net present value of the ice cream machine purchase.

LO 6 & 7: Determine Net Present Value, No Residual Value

7–24. Javier Cruz is contemplating the purchase of a machine which will automate the production of baseball bats in his factory. The following estimates are available.

Initial outlay	$97,000
Annual reduction in manufacturing labor cost	$22,500
Cost of capital	14%
Estimated life of the baseball bat machine	8 years
Estimated residual value of the bat machine	$ -0-

REQUIRED:
Determine the net present value of the baseball bat machine purchase.

LO 6 & 7:   Determine Net Present Value, No Residual Value

7–25. Dahlia Garcia is contemplating the purchase of a machine which will automate the production of hosiery in her factory. The following estimates are available.

Initial outlay	$112,000
Annual reduction in manufacturing labor cost	$ 22,500
Cost of capital	12%
Estimated life of the hosiery machine	8 years
Estimated residual value of the hosiery machine	$ -0-

REQUIRED:

Determine the net present value of the hosiery machine purchase.

LO 6 & 7:   Determine Net Present Value and Profitability Index, Various Rates, No Residual Value

7–26. Michael Diaz Sporting Goods is considering the purchase of a machine that is used to cut material to make baseball gloves. The cost of the machine is $265,000. The machine has an estimated useful life of eight years, with no residual value. Currently, the company leases a similar machine for $50,000 per year. If the new machine is purchased, the company's cost of labor would be reduced by $12,000 per year.

REQUIRED:

a. Determine the net present value of the machine under each of the following assumptions.
   1. The cost of capital is 12%
   2. The cost of capital is 14%
   3. The cost of capital is 16%
b. Determine the profitability index under each of the following assumptions.
   1. The cost of capital is 12%
   2. The cost of capital is 14%
   3. The cost of capital is 16%

LO 6 & 7:   Determine Net Present Value and Profitability Index, Various Rates, No Residual Value

7–27. Carlos Urriola Manufacturing is considering the purchase of a computer-controlled manufacturing machine that is used in its factory. The cost of the machine $3,600,000. The machine has an estimated useful life of 10 years, with no residual value. If the new machine is purchased, the company's cost of labor would be reduced by $650,000 per year.

REQUIRED:

a. Determine the net present value of the machine under each of the following assumptions.
   1. The cost of capital is 10%
   2. The cost of capital is 12%
   3. The cost of capital is 14%

b. Determine the profitability index under each of the following assumptions.
  1. The cost of capital is 10%
  2. The cost of capital is 12%
  3. The cost of capital is 14%

LO 6 & 7: Determine Net Present Value, No Residual Value

7–28. Frank Eiroa is considering the purchase of an engine lift for use in his marine repair business. He has determined that a used lift is available for $5,500. The engine lift has an estimated useful life of eight years and a residual value of zero. Currently, Frank rents engine lifts as needed. If the lift is purchased, annual rental payment of $1,400 would be saved. The cost of capital is 16%.

REQUIRED:
Calculate the net present value of the engine lift purchase.

LO 6 & 7: Determine Net Present Value, No Residual Value

7–29. Alfredo Lomando is considering the purchase of an industrial glass-cutting machine for use in his business. He has determined that a used glass cutter is available for $25,800. The cutter has an estimated useful life of 10 years and a residual value of zero. Currently, Alfredo rents an industrial cutter for $4,400 annually. The cost of capital is 14%.

REQUIRED:
Calculate the net present value of the industrial glass cutter.

LO 6 & 7: Determine Net Present Value, with Residual Value

7–30. The owner of Wynn Sports Cards is contemplating the purchase of a machine which will automate the production of baseball cards in her factory. The following estimates are available.

Initial outlay	$35,000
Annual reduction in manufacturing labor cost	$ 8,500
Cost of capital	14%
Estimated life of the card machine	5 years
Estimated residual value of the card machine	$ 2,000

REQUIRED:
Determine the net present value of the baseball card machine purchase.

LO 6 & 7: Determine Net Present Value, with Residual Value

7–31. Kevin Petty owns Discount Auto Parts. He is contemplating the purchase of a brake lathe that could be used to refurbish brake parts for customers. The following estimates are available.

Initial outlay	$6,500
Annual cash inflow	$1,500
Cost of capital	16%
Estimated life of the brake lathe	6 years
Estimated residual value of the brake lathe	$1,000

REQUIRED:
Determine the net present value of the brake lathe purchase.

LO 6 & 7:   Determine Net Present Value, with Residual Value

7–32. Paola Grillon owns Grillon Skin Care Products. She is contemplating the purchase of an industrial mixer that would be used to mix cosmetics in her factory. The following estimates are available.

Initial outlay	$78,500
Annual cash inflow	$19,500
Cost of capital	16%
Estimated life of the mixer	7 years
Estimated residual value of the mixer	$ 4,000

REQUIRED:

Determine the net present value of the industrial mixer purchase.

LO 6 & 7:   Determine Net Present Value, with Residual Value

7–33. Elianne Vinas owns Vinas Shoe Company. She is contemplating the purchase of a cutting machine that would be used to make shoes in her factory. The following estimates are available.

Initial outlay	$58,000
Annual cash inflow from reduced labor cost	$11,500
Cost of capital	12%
Estimated life of the cutter	8 years
Estimated residual value of the cutter	$ 2,000

REQUIRED:

Determine the net present value of the cutting machine purchase.

LO 6 & 7:   Determine Net Present Value and Profitability Index, Various Rates, with Residual Value

7–34. George Gonzalez Construction Company is considering the purchase of a new road grader. The cost of the road grader is $68,000. The road grader has an estimated useful life of seven years and an estimated residual value of $5,000. Currently, the company rents road graders as needed. If the road grader is purchased, annual rental payments of $17,000 would be saved.

REQUIRED:

a. Determine the net present value of the grader purchase under each of the following assumptions.
 1. The cost of capital is 12%
 2. The cost of capital is 14%
 3. The cost of capital is 16%
b. Determine the profitability index under each of the following assumptions.
 1. The cost of capital is 12%
 2. The cost of capital is 14%
 3. The cost of capital is 16%

LO 6 & 7:   Determine Net Present Value and Profitability Index, Various Rates, with Residual Value

7–35. Wesley Parks Pencil Company is considering the purchase of a new machine to make pencils. The cost of the machine is $248,000. The pencil machine has an estimated useful life of 10 years and an estimated residual value of $25,000. Currently, the company leases a similar machine for $45,000 per year.

REQUIRED:
a. Determine the net present value of the pencil machine purchase under each of the following assumptions.
   1. The cost of capital is 10%
   2. The cost of capital is 12%
   3. The cost of capital is 14%
b. Determine the profitability index under each of the following assumptions.
   1. The cost of capital is 10%
   2. The cost of capital is 12%
   3. The cost of capital is 14%

LO 6 & 7: Determine Net Present Value and Profitability Index, Various Rates, with Residual Value

7–36. Sylvia Heain's Catering Service is considering the purchase of new energy-efficient cooking equipment. The cost of the new equipment is $78,000. The equipment has a estimated useful life of eight years and an estimated residual value of $5,000. Currently, the company leases similar cooking equipment for $10,000 per year. If the new cooking equipment is purchased, the company's cost of electricity would be reduced by $8,000 per year.

REQUIRED:
a. Determine the net present value of the cooking equipment under each of the following assumptions.
   1. The cost of capital is 12%
   2. The cost of capital is 14%
   3. The cost of capital is 16%
b. Determine the profitability index under each of the following assumptions.
   1. The cost of capital is 12%
   2. The cost of capital is 14%
   3. The cost of capital is 16%

LO 6 & 7: Determine Internal Rate of Return, Various Rates, No Residual Value

7–37. Penny Williams is contemplating the purchase of a new computer system for her company, Williams Manufacturing. She has made the following estimates.

Initial outlay	$18,023.88
Annual cash savings	$ 5,000.00
Estimated life of the computer	5 years
Estimated residual value of the computer	$ -0-

REQUIRED:
a. Determine the internal rate of return for the computer purchase.
b. Indicate whether the computer purchase should be accepted under each of the following assumptions.
   1. The cost of capital is 9%
   2. The cost of capital is 11%
   3. The cost of capital is 13%
   4. The cost of capital is 15%

LO 6 & 7: Determine Internal Rate of Return, Various Rates, No Residual Value

7–38. Valdez Moving and Storage is contemplating the purchase of a new delivery truck. The following estimates are available.

Initial outlay	$ 51,590
Annual cash flow from the new truck	$14,000.00
Estimated life of the truck	6 years
Estimated residual value of the truck	$ -0-

REQUIRED:

a. Determine the internal rate of return for the truck purchase.

b. Indicate whether the truck purchase should be accepted under each of the following assumptions.
   1. The cost of capital is 14%
   2. The cost of capital is 16%
   3. The cost of capital is 18%

LO 6 & 7: Determine Internal Rate of Return for Three Projects, Select Project, No Residual Value

7–39. Hank Maupin & Company is in the process of replacing its existing computer system. The following three proposals are being considered.

	System A	System B	System C
Initial outlay	$18,023.88	$22,744.72	$24,031.57
Annual cash savings	$ 5,000.00	$ 6,000.00	$ 7,000.00
Estimated useful life	5 years	5 years	5 years

The estimated residual value of all computer systems under consideration is zero.

REQUIRED:

a. Determine the internal rate of return for each of the proposed computer systems.

b. Which computer system would you recommend? Explain your reasoning.

LO 6 & 7: Determine Internal Rate of Return for Three Projects, Select Project, No Residual Value

7–40. David Wilson Equipment Company is in the process of selecting some new manufacturing equipment. The following three proposals are being considered.

	Equipment A	Equipment B	Equipment C
Initial outlay	$14,902.92	$18,555.46	$26,674.63
Annual cash savings	$ 3,000.00	$ 4,000.00	$ 5,000.00
Estimated useful life	8 years	8 years	8 years

The estimated residual value of all equipment under consideration is zero.

REQUIRED:

a. Determine the internal rate of return for each of the proposed pieces of equipment.

b. Which piece of equipment would you recommend? Explain your reasoning.

LO 6 & 7: Determine Net Present Value, Profitability Index, and Internal Rate of Return, Various Rates, No Residual Value

7–41. Dunn Manufacturing Company is considering the purchase of a factory that makes valves. These valves would be used by Dunn to manufacture water pumps. The purchase would require an initial outlay of $1,564,800. The factory would have an estimated life of 10 years and no residual value. Currently, the company buys 500,000 valves per year at a cost of $1.50 each. If the factory were purchased, the valves could be manufactured for $0.90 each.

REQUIRED:

a. Determine the net present value of the proposed project and whether it should be accepted under each of the following assumptions.
   1. The cost of capital is 12%
   2. The cost of capital is 14%
   3. The cost of capital is 16%

b. Determine the profitability index under each of the following assumptions.
   1. The cost of capital is 12%
   2. The cost of capital is 14%
   3. The cost of capital is 16%

c. Determine the internal rate of return of the proposed project and indicate whether it should be accepted under each of the following assumptions.
   1. The cost of capital is 12%
   2. The cost of capital is 14%
   3. The cost of capital is 16%

LO 6: Determine Payback Period, Even Cash Flows

7–42. Tom Robinson owns Discount Hardware. He is contemplating the purchase of a copy machine which would be used to make copies to sell to customers for five cents each. The following estimates are available.

Initial outlay	$4,500
Annual cash inflow	$1,800

REQUIRED:
Determine the payback period for the copy machine purchase.

LO 6: Determine Payback Period, Even Cash Flows

7–43. Rebecca Pons owns Magic Makers Manufacturing. She is contemplating the purchase of a machine that would be used to manufacture various products that would be sold to magic shops. The following estimates are available.

Initial outlay	$23,539.20
Annual cash inflow	$ 7,356.00

REQUIRED:
Determine the payback period for the machine purchase.

LO 6: Determine Payback Period, Even Cash Flows

7–44. Claudia Vargas is contemplating the purchase of a machine that would be used in her business. The following estimates are available.

| Initial outlay | $5,826.50 |
| Annual cash inflow | $1,355.00 |

REQUIRED:

Determine the payback period for the machine purchase.

LO 6: Determine Payback Period, Even Cash Flows

7–45. Cesar Nieto is contemplating the purchase of a machine that would be used in his business. The following estimates are available.

| Initial outlay | $323,400.00 |
| Annual cash inflow | $ 33,000.00 |

REQUIRED:

Determine the payback period for the machine purchase.

LO 6: Determine Payback Period, Uneven Cash Flows

7–46. Junior Gonzales is considering the purchase of a fuel truck that he would use to sell gasoline at motor sport racing events in Puerto Rico. He has determined that a used truck is available for $11,000. He believes that the cash inflows would grow each year as he is able to sign fuel supply contracts at more and more events. He has made the following cash inflow estimates.

First year	$3,000
Second year	$4,500
Third and subsequent years	$5,000

REQUIRED:

Determine the payback period for the purchase of the fuel truck.

LO 6: Determine Payback Period, Uneven Cash Flows

7–47. Veronica Torres is considering opening a ceramic studio. She has determined that it would require an investment of $14,000 to open the store. She believes that the cash inflows would grow each year as more and more people learn of the store. She has made the following cash inflow estimates.

First year	$2,000
Second year	$4,000
Third and subsequent years	$5,000

REQUIRED:

Determine the payback period for the ceramic studio.

LO 6: Determine Payback Period, Uneven Cash Flows

7–48. Karen Calloway is considering adding a new style of gym shorts to her product line. She has determined that it would require an investment of $22,000 to add the new style shorts. She believes that the cash inflows would grow each year as the new style becomes more popular. She has made the following cash inflow estimates.

First year	$ 4,000
Second year	$ 6,000
Third and subsequent years	$10,000

REQUIRED:

Determine the payback period for the new style of gym shorts.

LO 6: Determine Accounting Rate of Return

7–49. BRV Construction Company is contemplating the purchase of scaffolding at the cost of $32,000. Currently, the company rents similar scaffolding for use at each of its construction sites. The scaffolding has an estimated useful life of five years and an estimated residual value of $2,000. By purchasing the scaffolding, BRV could save rental fees of $11,760 per year.

REQUIRED:

Determine the accounting rate of return for BRV's investment in the scaffolding.

LO 6: Determine Accounting Rate of Return

7–50. Smith and Smith & Associates is contemplating the purchase of equipment that would cost $196,600. Currently, the company rents similar equipment for $45,076 per year. The proposed new equipment has an estimated useful life of eight years and an estimated residual value of $9,000.

REQUIRED:

Determine the accounting rate of return for the Smith and Smith & Associates investment in the new equipment.

LO 6: Determine Accounting Rate of Return

7–51. Condore & Company is contemplating the purchase of a machine that would cost $142,790. The machine would provide an annual contribution margin of $47,262.55 each year. The proposed new machine has an estimated useful life of five years and an estimated residual value of $10,000.

REQUIRED:

Determine the accounting rate of return for Condore & Company's investment in the new machine.

LO 5, 6, & 7: Determine Relevant Information, Net Present Value, Screen Project, with Residual Value

7–52. Frank's Marine Service purchased a forklift five years ago for $16,000. When it was purchased, the forklift had an estimated useful life of 10 years and a salvage value of $4,000. The forklift can be sold now for $6,000. The operating cost for the forklift is $4,500 per year.

Frank is thinking about buying a newer forklift for $17,000. The newer forklift would have an estimated useful life of five years and a salvage value of $7,000. The operating cost for the newer forklift would be 3,000 per year.

The company's cost of capital is 10%.

REQUIRED:

a. Prepare a relevant cost schedule showing the benefits of buying the new forklift. (For this requirement, ignore the time value of money.)
b. How much must the company invest today to replace the old forklift?

c. If the company replaces the old forklift, what is the increase in the company's annual contribution margin?
d. If the company sells the old forklift now to make room for the new one, it will not receive the $4,000 salvage value at the end of its useful life. Instead, the company will receive the $7,000 salvage value from the new forklift. With this in mind, if the company buys the forklift, what is the change in the salvage value the company is to receive at the end of the five-year life of the equipment?
e. Calculate the net present value of replacing the old forklift.
f. Do you think the company should replace the old forklift?

LO 5, 6, & 7: Determine Relevant Information, Net Present Value, Screen Project, with Residual Value

7–53. Al Hart of Hart Engineering is considering the purchase of a new copy machine. He purchased the old machine two years ago for $8,500. When it was purchased the old machine had an estimated useful life of eight years and a salvage value of $500. The operating cost of the old machine is $3,000 per year. The old machine can be sold today for $2,000. A new machine can be bought today for $10,000 and would have an estimated useful life of six years with a salvage value of $1,000. The operating cost of the new copy machine is expected to be $1,500 per year.

The company's cost of capital is 8%.

REQUIRED:
a. Prepare a relevant cost schedule showing the benefit of buying the new copy machine. (For this requirement, ignore the time value of money.)
b. How much must the company invest today to replace the old copy machine?
c. If the company replaces the old copy machine, what is the increase in the company's annual contribution margin?
d. If the company sells the old copy machine now to make room for the new one, it will not receive the $500 salvage value at the end of its useful life. Instead, the company will receive the $1,000 salvage value from the new copy machine. With this in mind, if the company buys the copy machine, what is the change in the salvage value the company is to receive at the end of the six-year life of the equipment?
e. Calculate the net present value of replacing the old copy machine.
f. Do you think the company should replace the old copy machine?

LO 5, 6, & 7: Determine Relevant Information, Net Present Value, Screen Project, No Residual Value

7–54. The managers at AAA Manufacturing Company are considering replacing an industrial mixer used in the company's factory. The company's cost of capital is 10%.

Information about the old mixer:

Cost	$28,000
Estimated useful life	10 years
Estimated salvage value	$ 0
Current age	5 years
Estimated current fair value	$ 8,000
Annual operating cost	$18,000

Information about the new mixer:

Cost	$34,000
Estimated useful life	5 years
Estimated salvage value	$ 0
Annual operating cost	$12,000

REQUIRED:

a. Prepare a relevant cost schedule showing the benefit of buying the new mixer.

b. How much must the company invest today to replace the industrial mixer?

c. If the new mixer is purchased, how much would be saved in operating costs each year?

d. How much would the company receive at the end of the five-year useful life of the new mixer?

e. Calculate the net present value of replacing the old mixer.

f. Do you think the company should replace the old mixer?

LO 5, 6, & 7: Determine Relevant Information, Net Present Value, Screen Project, No Residual Value

7–55. The managers at General Manufacturing Company are considering replacing the industrial lathe used in the company's factory. The company's cost of capital is 12%.

Information about the old lathe:

Cost	$57,000
Estimated useful life	8 years
Estimated salvage value	$ 0
Current age	2 years
Estimated current fair value	$32,000
Annual operating cost	$32,000

Information about the new lathe:

Cost	$61,000
Estimated useful life	6 years
Estimated salvage value	$ 0
Annual operating cost	$24,000

REQUIRED:

a. Prepare a relevant cost schedule showing the benefit of buying the new lathe. (For this requirement, ignore the time value of money.)

b. How much must the company invest today to replace the old lathe?

c. If the company replaces the old lathe, how much will be saved in operating costs each year?

d. Calculate the net present value of replacing the old lathe.

e. Do you think the company should replace the old lathe?

LO 5, 6, & 7: Determine Relevant Information, Net Present Value, Screen Project, with Residual Value

7–56. John Paul Hudik, president of J.P. Hudik Boat Hauling, is considering replacing the company's industrial lift used to haul boats. The new lift would allow the company to lift larger boats out of the water. The company's cost of capital is 14%.

Information about the old lift:

Cost	$94,000
Estimated useful life	12 years
Estimated salvage value	$10,000
Current age	4 years
Estimated current fair value	$48,000
Annual contribution margin	$50,000

Information about the new lift:

Cost	$128,000
Estimated useful life	8 years
Estimated salvage value	$ 25,000
Annual contribution margin	$ 65,000

REQUIRED:

a. Prepare a relevant cost schedule showing the benefit of buying the new lift. (For this requirement, ignore the time value of money.)
b. How much must the company invest today to replace the old lift?
c. If the company replaces the old lift, what is the increase in the company's annual contribution margin?
d. If the company sells the old lift now to make room for the new one, it will not receive the $10,000 salvage value at the end of its useful life. Instead, the company will receive the $25,000 salvage value from the new lift. With this in mind, if the company buys the new lift, what is the change in the salvage value the company is to receive at the end of the eight-year life of the equipment?
e. Calculate the net present value of replacing the old lift.
f. Do you think the company should replace the old lift?

LO 5, 6, & 7: Determine Relevant Information, Net Present Value, Screen Project, with Residual Value

7–57. The managers at Wilma Manufacturing are considering replacing a printing press with a new, high-speed model. The company's cost of capital is 12%.

Information about the old printing press:

Cost	$255,000
Estimated useful life	10 years
Estimated salvage value	$ 25,000
Annual depreciation	$ 23,000
Current age	3 years
Accumulated depreciation to date	$184,000
Estimated current fair value	$150,000
Annual contribution margin	$110,000

Information about the new printing press:

Cost	$535,000
Estimated useful life	7 years
Estimated salvage value	$ 45,000
Annual depreciation	$ 70,000
Annual contribution margin	$150,000

REQUIRED:

a. Prepare a relevant cost schedule showing the benefit of buying the new printing press. (For this requirement, ignore the time value of money.)
b. How much must the company invest today to replace the old printing press?

c. If the company replaces the old printing press, what is the increase in the company's annual contribution margin?
d. If the company sells the old printing press now to make room for the new one, it will not receive the $25,000 salvage value at the end of its useful life. Instead, the company will receive the $45,000 salvage value from the new printing press. With this in mind, if the company buys the printing press, what is the change in the salvage value the company is to receive at the end of the seven-year life of the equipment?
e. Calculate the net present value of replacing the old printing press.
f. Do you think the company should replace the old printing press?

APPENDIX

LO 7:   Calculate Simple, Compound Interest, Full Years

7–58. Greg Gluck Marine borrowed $5,000 from National Bank on January 1, 2000.

REQUIRED:
a. Assuming 9% simple interest is charged, calculate interest for 2000, 2001, and 2002.
b. Assuming 9% compound interest is charged, calculate interest for 2000, 2001, and 2002.

LO 7:   Calculate Simple, Compound Interest, Full Years

7–59. Gary borrowed $8,000 from Orlando National Bank on January 1, 2000.

REQUIRED:
a. Assuming 8% simple interest is charged, calculate interest for 2000, 2001, and 2002.
b. Assuming 8% compound interest is charged, calculate interest for 2000, 2001, and 2002.

LO 7:   Calculate Simple, Compound Interest, Full Years

7–60. Cam borrowed $2,000 from Miami National Bank on January 1, 2000.

REQUIRED:
a. Assuming 6% simple interest is charged, calculate interest for 2000, 2001, and 2002.
b. Assuming 6% compound interest is charged, calculate interest for 2000, 2001, and 2002.

LO 7:   Calculate Future Value, Single Cash Flow, Various Rates and Maturities

7–61. Susan Jones made the following investments on January 1, 2000:
1. $ 2,000 at 10% for 5 years
2. $12,000 at 4% for 8 years
3. $ 9,000 at 14% for 15 years

Assume the interest on each investment is compounded annually.

REQUIRED:

Calculate the future value of each of the investments listed above at their maturity.

LO 7: Calculate Future Value, Single Cash Flow, Various Rates and Maturities

7–62. Ivan Zhang made the following investments on January 1, 2000:
1. $3,000 at 8% for 6 years
2. $4,000 at 6% for 8 years
3. $5,000 at 10% for 5 years

Assume the interest on each investment is compounded annually.

REQUIRED:

Calculate the future value of each of the investments listed above at their maturity.

LO 7: Calculate Future Value, Single Cash Flow, Various Rates and Maturities

7–63. Orlando Gonzalez made the following investments on January 1, 2000:
1. $1,000 at 14% for 3 years
2. $2,000 at 10% for 5 years
3. $4,000 at 8% for 8 years

Assume the interest on each investment is compounded annually.

REQUIRED:

Calculate the future value of each of the investments listed above at their maturity.

LO 7: Calculate Future Value, Yearly Cash Flows, Various Rates and Maturities

7–64. Consider the following investments:
1. $2,000 at the end of each of the next five years at 10% interest compounded annually.
2. $12,000 at the end of each of the next eight years at 4% interest compounded annually.
3. $9,000 at the end of each of the next 15 years at 14% interest compounded annually.

REQUIRED:

Calculate the future value of each of the investments listed above at their maturity.

LO 7: Calculate Future Value, Yearly Cash Flows, Various Rates and Maturities

7–65. Consider the following investments.
1. $12,000 at the end of each of the next three years at 12% interest compounded annually.
2. $16,000 at the end of each of the next five years at 10% interest compounded annually.
3. $20,000 at the end of each of the next 10 years at 8% interest compounded annually.

REQUIRED:

Calculate the future value of each of the investments listed above at their maturity.

LO 7: Calculate Future Value, Yearly Cash Flows, Various Rates and Maturities

7–66. Consider the following investments.

1. $1,000 at the end of each of the next five years at 6% interest compounded annually.
2. $1,000 at the end of each of the next five years at 8% interest compounded annually.
3. $1,000 at the end of each of the next five years at 10% interest compounded annually.

REQUIRED:

Calculate the future value of each of the investments listed above at their maturity.

LO 7: Calculate Present Value, Single Cash Flow, Single Rate

7–67. Jim Johnson is planning to buy a new car when he graduates from college in three years. He would like to invest a single amount now, in order to have the $24,000 he estimates the car will cost.

REQUIRED:

Calculate the amount Jim must invest today, to have enough to buy the new car assuming his investment will earn 4% compounded annually for the three-year investment.

LO 7: Calculate Present Value, Single Cash Flow, Single Rate

7–68. Lowell Pitman needs to have $50,000 at the end of five years. Lowell would like to invest a single amount now, to have the $50,000 in five years.

REQUIRED:

Calculate the amount Lowell must invest today, to have the amount of money he needs assuming his investment will earn 8% compounded annually for the five-year investment.

LO 7: Calculate Present Value, Single Cash Flow, Single Rate

7–69. Lauren Elsea is planning to buy a house when she graduates from college. She would like to have $20,000 for the down payment. Lauren would like to invest a single amount now, to have the $20,000 at the end of three years.

REQUIRED:

Calculate the amount Lauren must invest today, to have the amount of money she needs assuming her investment will earn 6% compounded annually for the three-year investment.

LO 7: Calculate Present Value, Yearly Cash Flows, Single Rate

7–70. Linda Chidister is planning to send her son, Edward, to college. While he is in college, Linda intends to give him $3,000 at the end of each year.

REQUIRED:

How much must Linda invest today so she will have enough to give Edward $3,000 at the end of each of the next four years assuming the investment will earn 6% interest.

LO 7: Calculate Present Value, Yearly Cash Flows, Single Rate

7–71. Alex Malpin is planning to spend the next three years doing research in China. An Asian studies research institute has agreed to pay Alex $20,000 at the end of each of the three years he is in China.

REQUIRED:

How much must be invested today to have enough to pay Alex $20,000 at the end of each of the next three years assuming the investment will earn 10% interest.

LO 7: Calculate Present Value, Yearly Cash Flows, Single Rate

7–72. Photo Factory is planning to purchase some photo processing equipment from Ace Equipment Company. The equipment will provide cash flow of $15,000 at the end of each of the next eight years.

REQUIRED:

How much should Photo Factory pay for the equipment assuming it will provide $15,000 at the end of each of the next eight years and Ace has promised that it will earn a return of exactly 14%?

Chapter 8

The Operating Budget

*I*magine for a moment that midway through your accounting class you and three of your classmates decide to go to Europe. You stand up, excuse yourself from class, and the four of you head for the airport. At the airport you discover that the next flight to Europe departs in four hours and there are only three seats available. You buy three tickets, send one friend back to class, and begin the long wait until boarding. After what seems like an eternity, you board the flight and are on your way.

When you arrive in Paris, your friends ask, "Well, we're here. What now?" You respond, "I don't know, this is a spontaneous thing. We have the freedom to do whatever we want." Your friends have many questions: "Where will we stay? Did you bring any money? Who has a French/English dictionary? Are the clothes we are wearing adequate for the weather in Paris? By the way, what *is* the weather in Paris? Now that we're here, how long will we stay? What will we do? Is there anything other than the Eiffel Tower here? Why did we go to Paris and not some other place? How will we get back home?"

What's wrong with this Paris trip? The obvious answer is a complete lack of planning. Thoughtful planning increases the possibility of success in almost anything we might do, whether business related or not.

Careful planning is in fact a key element of business success. Without such planning, business activities founder and a company almost certainly loses direction. In Chapter 7 we described planning as the *why,* the *what,* the *how,* and the *who* of being in business. Recall that the *why* is the process of setting company goals. The *what* is the development of a strategic plan to implement those goals in the long term. These two planning elements were discussed in some detail in Chapter 7. The *how* is the process of capital budgeting to allocate scarce resources and was the major topic of Chapter 7.

operating budget A budget for a specific period, usually one to five years, that establishes who is responsible for the day-to-day operation of a business during that time.

master operating budget Another name for *operating budget.*

master budget Another name for *operating budget.*

The *who* is the final step—the preparation of the operating budget. The **operating budget** is a budget for a specific time, usually one to five years, that establishes who is responsible for the day-to-day operation of the business during that time. This budget is also sometimes called the **master operating budget** or simply the **master budget.** For the sake of consistency, we will use the term *operating budget* throughout our discussions of this topic.

The operating budget will be an important part of your business life, regardless of your occupation or the type of company for which you choose to work. Whether the organization is profit or not for profit, and whether it is a service, merchandising, or manufacturing firm, budgeting has become increasingly more important in charting the success of today's organizations. Gone are the days when companies could succeed on simple luck and optimism. Gone, too, are the days when a select group of top managers prepared operating budgets with little input from others in the organization. Many companies today involve all managers and employees in the budgeting process. Fortune 500 companies such as Motorola, Honeywell, General Motors, and others have recognized that better budgeting is achieved when they involve those who actually work in the area or function for which the budget is being prepared. As you read the pages that follow, we hope you remember that budgets will be an important ingredient in your personal business success, and that you will very likely be involved in the budgeting process much earlier in your career than you may have expected.

The chapter is divided into two main parts. Part One contains an overview of the operating budget, its purpose, and where it fits into the overall management process. Part Two contains a detailed presentation of how the operating budget is actually prepared and how it should and should not be used by managers. ∎

LEARNING OBJECTIVES

After completing your work on this chapter, you should be able to do the following:

1. Describe some of the benefits of the operating budget.
2. Describe the three budgeted financial statements contained in the operating budget and the other budgets that support the budgeted financial statements.
3. Compare and contrast various approaches to the preparation and use of the operating budget.
4. Describe the role of the sales forecast in the budgeting process.
5. Prepare the budgets included in the operating budget.
6. Describe the appropriate use of the operating budget in the overall management process.

The Operating Budget: What Is It?

What exactly *is* an operating budget? We know it is the plan for a company's operating activities for some period of time, but what is in that plan? The operating budget includes a set of estimated financial statements.

Recall that the three main financial statements are the balance sheet, the income statement, and the statement of cash flows. Businesses prepare these statements at the end of a given time period to show the effects of past transactions and events. An operating budget contains those same three financial statements, except they are estimates—or forecasts—of future transactions and events. The forecasted financial statements in the operating budget are sometimes called pro forma financial statements. *Pro forma* is a Latin phrase meaning "provided in advance."

Because the operating budget is a set of estimated financial statements, much of what we will cover in this chapter will at least be familiar to you. The only difference between the financial statements businesses use to show the effects of past events and transactions, and the ones you will explore in this chapter, is that the budgeted financial statements are used to predict future events.

BENEFITS OF BUDGETING

A well-prepared operating budget can create many benefits for the company. In this section, we will explore four of them. First, budgeting serves as a guide. Second, it helps organizations allocate resources. Third, it encourages communication and coordination. Fourth, it sets performance standards, or *benchmarks*.

Serves as a Guide

The operating budget should serve as a guide for a company to follow during the budgeted period. Recall the hypothetical trip to Paris we described in the chapter opener. Suppose that while touring France, our travelers heard about a fantastic side trip (a terrific art show in Nice) not included in their original itinerary. Based on this new information, our travelers would probably adjust their original plan to allow for this side trip. And so it should be with a budget, because companies should adjust their budgets when desirable or necessary.

To illustrate, suppose the budget for Pam's Flower Shop forecasted sales revenue of $310,000 for the first three months of 2002. Business was better than expected and the flower shop had sales of $310,000 by the end of February. Should Pam close the flower shop until April 1 because she attained her budgeted sales figure for the quarter? Of course not. Or suppose Pam has the opportunity to purchase 20 dozen roses just before Valentine's Day at a bargain basement price. She can probably sell all of them for a whopping profit, but she didn't budget for this special purchase. What should she do? It may seem obvious that she should take advantage of this terrific opportunity, but a surprising number of businesses view the budget as "set in stone," so to speak, and meeting the budget becomes the primary business objective. An unwillingness to adjust a budget based on new information can be detrimental to a company because opportunities are missed and poor decisions made.

Assists in Resource Allocation

As discussed in Chapter 7, all organizations have scarce resources. No company can afford to do everything it desires, or even everything it needs to do within a given time period. A budget can help management decide where to allocate its limited resources.

The budgeting process may uncover potential bottlenecks and allow managers to address these issues in advance as the budget is being prepared, rather than as problems occur during the year. An example of a bottleneck in a manufacturing environment is presented for Montrose Manufacturing Company in Exhibit 8–1.

Exhibit 8–1
Example of Production
Bottleneck at Montrose
Manufacturing

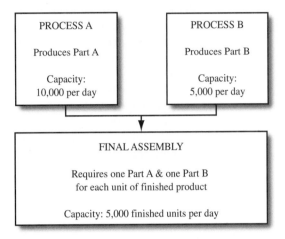

As you can see from Exhibit 8–1, each unit of finished product Montrose manufactures requires one Part A and one Part B. The maximum number of finished units of product the company can produce per day is 5,000. The limiting factor is Process B, which can produce only 5,000 parts per day. Montrose could increase the capacity of Process A from 10,000 parts per day to 100,000 parts per day and the company *still* could produce only 5,000 finished units per day because of the restriction caused by Process B. Process B is the bottleneck in this company's production process.

Assume Montrose Manufacturing Company moved some production machinery from Process A to Process B. This change reduces the capacity of Process A by 2,500 units per day, but the capacity of Process B was increased by 2,500 units per day as reflected in Exhibit 8–2.

Exhibit 8–2
Elimination of
Production Bottleneck
at Montrose
Manufacturing

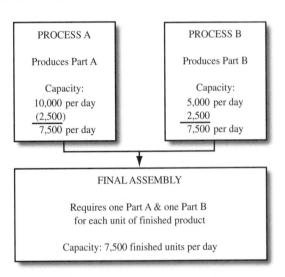

As you can see by looking at Exhibit 8–2, Montrose has increased its capacity to produce finished units by 50 percent (from 5,000 units to 7,500 units) without adding any additional machinery to its operation, which is a significant factor if you recall our discussion of capital expenditures in Chapter 7.

The issue of resource allocation is also important for a merchandising business. For example, February may be so busy for a Pam's Flower Shop that she will need extra workers. If Pam knows this in advance, she will have time to hire the needed workers at the least cost so she can offer quality service and sell more flowers. In contrast, if Pam did not plan for the February rush, she would find herself understaffed and unable to provide quality, timely service. She might lose customers before she could hire more workers, and sales could drop. Budgeting, then, helps Pam make good decisions about how to allocate her resources.

Fosters Communication and Coordination

As managers from different functional areas in an organization work together to prepare the budget, they gain a better understanding of the entire business. When managers from all areas learn of difficulties facing others and spot duplication of effort, the firm can then solve problems and coordinate efforts more effectively. Our previous example of Montrose Manufacturing Company and its production bottleneck points out the possibilities of increased communication and coordination through the budgeting process. In working to solve this production problem, the managers of Process A, Process B, and Final Assembly had the opportunity to view the production process from a broader perspective. Rather than concentrating only on their own part of the process, they were better able to understand the problems facing managers in other areas of the company's operations. They were forced to communicate with one another and to better coordinate their efforts.

Even for a small company like Pam's Flower Shop, success can depend on coordinating many activities. For example, Pam expects sales to increase in February because of Valentine's Day. She anticipates she will need more flowers to sell, and more labor to sell them. The number of extra workers, however, may depend on the amount of additional flowers ordered. When she prepares the budget, Pam speaks to the inventory manager and the personnel manager about the February rush to better coordinate their activities. Then the managers will know in advance exactly what needs to be done.

Establishes Performance Standards

The operating budget also sets performance standards for an organization. As managers prepare budgets for their companies, they must estimate performance levels they both want and can attain. If a company's actual sales, for example, are less than its budgeted sales for a particular period, the sales manager will review the deficit and ask why. Once she has learned why, she will probably budget more effectively next time. Without a budget she might not notice the sales shortfall and therefore would not learn from it.

These performance standards become benchmarks against which firms can compare the actual results. Differences between the actual results and the budget can be explored and improvements made. The improvements may focus on performance, the budgeting process, or both.

Discussion Question

8-1. In what other ways do you think a company might benefit from preparing an operating budget?

Many of us have had to prepare a personal cash budget, in which we compare the amount of cash coming in to the amount of cash going out. Because of this personal experience with budgeting, many people think that business budgeting focuses only on budgeting for cash inflows and outflows. This view, however, is far too narrow. Remember, the operating budget is a set of estimated financial statements that includes the balance sheet, income statement, and statement of cash flows, regardless of whether the business preparing the budget is a manufacturer, a merchandiser, or a service company.

Technically, the operating budget consists of only these three pro forma financial statements. In preparing the budget, however, several supporting schedules are included that, when completed, provide the information necessary to complete the three financial statements contained in the budget. These supporting schedules are also usually referred to as budgets, and we will refer to them as such in all our discussions.

Sales Budget

sales budget Details the expected sales revenue from a company's primary operating activities during a certain time period.

The sales budget is the first budget prepared and is based on a sales forecast. As the name implies, the **sales budget** details the expected sales revenue from a company's primary operating activities during a certain time period. Because manufacturers and merchandisers sell tangible, physical product, the sales budget is based on the number of units the firm expects to sell. The sales budget of a service business is based on the amount of services the firm expects to render.

Because sales revenue is an income statement item, the information provided by the sales budget is used to construct the budgeted income statement.

Production or Purchases Budget

production budget Details the cost and number of units that must be produced by a manufacturer to meet the sales forecast and the desired ending inventory.

purchases budget Details the cost and number of units that must be purchased by a merchandiser to meet the sales forecast and the desired ending inventory.

For manufacturers, the budget that plans for the cost and number of units that must be manufactured to meet the sales forecast and the desired quantity of ending finished goods inventory is known as the **production budget.** Although merchandisers call this budget the **purchases budget,** the two are functionally equivalent. Their names reflect the source of the item sold: Manufacturers produce the products they sell, and merchandisers purchase the products they sell.

The production budget and the purchases budget are simply pro forma versions of the cost of goods manufactured schedule and the cost of purchases schedule, as discussed in Chapter 2. A production budget is usually more complicated than a purchases budget because, as discussed in Chapter 2, costing manufactured product is more complicated than costing purchased product. A production budget includes schedules for materials, labor, and manufacturing overhead. An operating budget for a service business does not include a production budget or purchases budget because a service company does not sell tangible, physical product.

Only some of the product scheduled to be produced by a manufacturer or purchased by a merchandiser is intended to be sold during the period covered by the budget. The product not projected to be sold is called *ending finished goods inventory* for a manufacturer and *ending merchandise inventory* for a merchandiser. In either case, this projected ending inventory is classified as an asset. Therefore, some of the information provided by the production budget or purchases budget is used to construct the budgeted balance sheet.

The product that is projected to be sold during the period covered by the budget is classified as an expense item and will be shown on the budgeted income statement. As you recall, this expense item is called cost of goods sold. The cost of goods sold information needed to construct the budgeted income statement comes from the cost of goods sold budget.

Cost of Goods Sold or Cost of Services Budget

cost of goods sold budget
Calculates the total cost of all the product a manufacturing or merchandising company estimates it will sell during the period covered by the budget.

cost of services budget
Calculates the total cost of all the services a service type business estimates it will provide during the period covered by the budget.

A **cost of goods sold budget** calculates the total cost of all the product a company estimates it will sell during the period covered by the operating budget. This budget differs from the production (purchases) budget because of inventory requirements. Under accrual accounting, the cost of product is not recognized as an expense (cost of goods sold) on the income statement until it is sold. Until then, it is recorded as an asset (inventory) and is shown as such on the balance sheet. For a service type business, this budget is called the **cost of services budget.**

Whether we are talking about the cost of goods sold budget or the cost of services budget, they are similar to the schedules in Chapter 2 regarding the costing of products and services. The only difference is that the budgets discussed in this chapter pertain to the future.

Because cost of goods sold or cost of services is an income statement item, the information provided by the cost of goods sold budget or cost of services budget is used to construct the budgeted income statement.

Selling and Administrative Expense Budget

selling and administrative expense budget Calculates all costs other than the cost of product or services required to support a company's forecasted sales.

After a company makes its sales forecast and estimates its product (or service) cost, it can estimate all other costs needed to support that level of sales. A **selling and administrative expense budget** calculates all costs other than the cost of product or services required to support a company's forecasted sales. The kinds of items included in this budget are identical to those included in the income statements, as discussed throughout this text. They are what we described as period costs in Chapter 2 and include such items as advertising, administrative salaries, rent, and utilities.

Budgeted Income Statement

budgeted income statement
Shows the expected net income for the period covered by the operating budget.

A **budgeted income statement** shows the expected net income for the period covered by the operating budget. It subtracts all estimated product (or service) cost and period cost from estimated sales revenue. This budget is prepared using information from the sales budget, the cost of goods sold (or cost of services) budget, and the selling and administrative expense budget.

Cash Budget

cash budget Shows whether the expected amount of cash generated by operating activities will be sufficient to pay anticipated expenses during the period covered by the operating budget.

A **cash budget** shows whether the expected amount of cash generated by operating activities will be sufficient to pay anticipated expenses during the period covered by the operating budget. It also reveals whether a company should expect a need for short-term external financing during the budget period. Be careful not to confuse the cash budget with the budgeted statement of cash flows, as discussed later in the chapter. The budgeted statement of cash flows is more comprehensive than a simple cash budget.

Budgeted Balance Sheet

budgeted balance sheet
A presentation of estimated assets, liabilities, and owners' equity at the end of the budgeted period.

A **budgeted balance sheet** is a presentation of estimated assets, liabilities, and owners' equity at the end of the budgeted period. It is created exactly the way a balance sheet based on actual historical results is prepared. At the start of the period being budgeted, a company has a balance sheet that presents its assets, liabilities, and owners' equity. Most (if not all) of the company's asset, liability, and equity items will be changed by the estimated results of operations (budgeted income statement). The result is an estimated balance sheet at the end of the budget period.

The budgeted balance sheet for a manufacturer or a merchandiser is prepared using information from the actual balance sheet at the beginning of the period covered by the budget, the production (purchases) budget, and the budgeted income statement. A service type company has no production or purchases budget, so the budgeted balance sheet is prepared using information from the actual balance sheet at the beginning of the budget period and the budgeted income statement.

Budgeted Statement of Cash Flows

budgeted statement of cash flows A statement of a company's expected sources and uses of cash during the period covered by the operating budget.

A **budgeted statement of cash flows** is a statement of a company's expected sources and uses of cash during the period covered by the operating budget. Manufacturers, merchandisers, and service companies create the budgeted statement of cash flows in a manner similar to the way they create the budgeted balance sheet. At the start of the period being budgeted, they report their cash balance. Based on the estimated results of operations (budgeted income statement) and other business activities that either generate or use cash, they estimate the cash balance at the end of the budget period. The purpose of the budgeted statement of cash flows is to explain how that change in cash is to happen.

Discussion Question

8–2. In what ways do you think the cash budget described earlier differs from the budgeted statement of cash flows?

Interrelationship among the Budgets

The budgets we have discussed are closely interrelated. A change in any one of them will cause a ripple effect throughout all the others. Exhibit 8–3 shows the extent of this interrelationship.

To demonstrate the interrelationship among the budgets, we return to Pam's Flower Shop for a moment. Because Pam's company is a merchandiser, the operating budget she prepares will include a sales budget, a purchases budget, a cost of goods sold budget, a selling and administrative expense budget, a cash budget, a budgeted income statement, a budgeted balance sheet, and a budgeted statement of cash flows.

Pam prepared the various budgets described for the first three months of 2002 based on the following sales forecast.

PAM'S FLOWER SHOP
Sales Forecast
For the Three Months Ended March 31, 2002

	January	February	March	Total
Sales	$90,000	$120,000	$100,000	$310,000

Exhibit 8-3
Interrelationship
among the Budgets

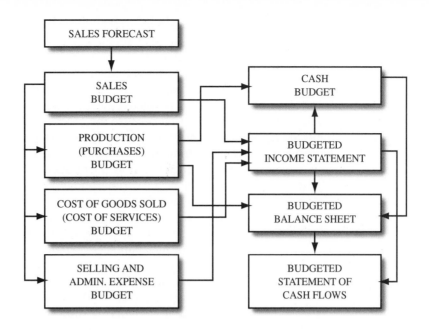

Discussion Question

8-3. From what you have learned so far about the operating budget, which of the budgets for Pam's Flower Shop will be affected by the amounts in this sales forecast? Explain how each is affected.

Now assume that a new flower shop opened just down the street from Pam's after she had prepared her operating budget. Pam believes that to be realistic in her planning, she needs to revise her sales forecast as follows:

PAM'S FLOWER SHOP
Revised Sales Forecast
For the Three Months Ended March 31, 2002

	January	February	March	Total
Sales	$75,000	$100,000	$90,000	$265,000

Discussion Question

8-4. Which of the budgets for Pam's Flower Shop will be affected by the changes in her sales forecast? Explain how each is affected.

Because sales revenue is changed in Pam's revised sales forecast, the sales budget will be different. Even without any information about purchases, you should intuitively recognize that lower sales probably means fewer flowers sold; therefore, fewer flowers will need to be purchased, meaning that the purchases budget must be revised. The same holds true for the cost of goods sold budget. The selling and administrative expense budget may need to be revised based on the new forecast, because lower sales probably means fewer sales clerks, at least. The cash budget will need to be revised because lower sales means less cash collected and lower purchases means less cash spent. The budgeted income statement must surely be revised, because the sales budget, the cost of goods sold budget, and the selling and administrative expense budget are used to construct the budgeted income statement. If those budgets must be revised, the budgeted income statement must also be revised. If the budgeted income statement is affected, the budgeted balance sheet must be revised because the results from the income statement are reflected in the balance sheet. If cash is affected in any way (and we already determined it would be), the budgeted statement of cash flows must be revised.

As you can see, a change in any of the budgets has a ripple effect throughout all the other budgets. Because the various budgets contained in the operating budget are so closely tied together, the preparation of the operating budget in most organizations is extremely time consuming and complicated. Depending on the size of the company, it may take several months to prepare the operating budget. For example, a manufacturer or merchandiser prepares a sales budget for each product the company sells. If the company sells 80 products, then 80 sales budgets must be prepared. If the company also has 80 sales territories, a whopping 6,400 sales budgets must be prepared (80 products × 80 sales territories). Companies must begin the budgeting process early enough to allow sufficient time for completion. If the budgeted period begins on January 1, 2002, for example, the budgeting process may begin in August or September 2001, or even earlier.

For some large, multinational companies, the process never ends. They work on the 2002 budget from January through December 2001. Then they turn right around in January 2002 and begin work on the 2003 budget, and so on. It takes so long to complete the process that by they time they finish one year, it is time to start again for the next year.

DIFFERENT APPROACHES TO BUDGETING

We now know what an operating budget is, but exactly how do businesses prepare one? The answer depends on the needs of the business and the approach it takes to the budgeting process. Next we investigate seven budgeting approaches: perpetual, incremental, zero-based, top-down, bottom-up, imposed, and participative approaches.

Firms may vary as to the maximum duration for the operating budget period. Because virtually all prepare it for at least one year, we focus on a one-year budget period in the following discussion.

Perpetual Budgeting

perpetual budgeting
The budgeting approach of updating the budget every month.

continual budgeting
Another name for *perpetual budgeting.*

Some companies continually update their operating budgets. As one month ends, another month's budget is added to the end of the budget. Therefore, at any given time, the budget projects 12 months into the future. This budgeting approach is called **perpetual budgeting,** or **continual budgeting.** Companies that use perpetual budgeting always budget 12 months in advance. At any given time, these companies have an operating budget that forecasts 12 months into the future.

The main advantage of perpetual budgeting is that it spreads the workload for budget preparation evenly over the year, which allows employees to incorporate the work required to prepare the budget into their routine work schedule. Another advantage of a perpetual budget is that the budget always extends 12 months into the future. In contrast, when perpetual budgeting is *not* used, the new operating budget is typically prepared when only a couple of months are left on the old budget. One disadvantage of perpetual budgeting may be that the budget preparation process becomes so routine that employees lose the motivation and creativity required to prepare an inovative operating budget. An important aspect of solid budgeting is looking for better ways to do things. Think back to the example we used earlier for Montrose Manufacturing Company, which was able to restructure its production process because its managers were serious about looking for a better way. If the preparation of the budget becomes routine (just another bunch of forms to fill out), managers may stop this critical evaluation and become satisfied with the status quo. Another disadvantage is that many managers believe they do not have sufficient time to do all that is asked of them in their regular day-to-day responsibilities. Adding the responsibility of preparing a perpetual budget to a heavy workload can lead to sloppy budgeting.

Incremental Budgeting

incremental budgeting
The process of using the prior year's budget or the company's actual results to build the new operating budget.

The process of using the prior year's budget or the company's actual results to build the new operating budget is called **incremental budgeting.** If, for example, a company's 2001 budget included $200,000 for maintenance and repairs on the machinery and equipment in its production facility, $200,000 becomes the starting point for this item in preparing the 2002 budget. The only question to be answered is whether the company needs to include more than $200,000 for repairs and maintenance in 2002. This budgeting approach is used by governmental entities such as the federal government and by many companies.

The trouble with the incremental budgeting approach is that if the prior year's budget includes unnecessary costs, or items that do not optimize performance, this waste may be simply rolled over into the next year's budget. The advantage to this approach is its simplicity. Some practitioners and many experts believe the disadvantages greatly outweigh the advantages.

Discussion Question

8–5. In what ways, if any, do you think the federal government's use of incremental budgeting contributes to the national debt?

Zero-Based Budgeting

zero-based budgeting
A process of budgeting in which managers start from scratch, or zero, when preparing a new budget.

An alternative to the incremental budgeting approach is zero-based budgeting. In **zero-based budgeting,** managers start from scratch, or zero, when preparing a new budget. Each item on the budget must be justified every year as though it were a new budget item. Zero-based budgeting is much more difficult and time consuming than incremental budgeting, but many organizations believe the results are worth that time and effort because managers are forced to reexamine the items included in the budget and justify their continuation.

Top-Down versus Bottom-Up Budgeting

Budgeted information can flow either from the upper levels of management in a company down to managers and employees at lower levels, or vice versa. For fairly obvious reasons, the former approach is known as the top-down approach and the latter as the bottom-up approach. Each has distinct advantages and disadvantages.

Top-Down Budgeting

When a budget is prepared by top managers in the company, the process is called **top-down budgeting.** The top executives prepare the budget, and lower-level managers and employees work to meet that budget.

The top-down approach has several advantages. First, a company's upper management is usually most knowledgeable about the company's overall operation. It makes sense (on the surface, at least) that upper managers be responsible for the information contained in the operating budget because they are the most experienced and knowledgeable individuals in the company. Second, top management is keenly aware of company goals, so they will prepare the budget with these goals in mind. Finally, the top-down budgeting approach involves fewer people, so it causes fewer disruptions, is more efficient, and is less time consuming than the bottom-up approach.

The top-down approach to budgeting has two major disadvantages. First, lower-level managers and employees are usually less accepting of budgets when they have no part in setting the standards. Second, top managers may be keenly aware of the big picture, but they do not have the working knowledge of daily activities needed to prepare the detailed budgets for all company activities.

Most large, publicly traded companies in the United States use some form of top-down budgeting. Why? If you recall our discussion of the cost of equity capital in Chapter 7, you know that a firm's top management fully understands the need to maximize returns for stockholders. Most of that return is in the form of stock appreciation (increase in the market price of the stock), rather than dividends. The greatest influence on the selling price of a company's stock price is company profits. So, to ensure maximum stock appreciation, a company must be as profitable as possible. The top management of these publicly traded companies generally have a better sense than lower-level managers and employees of how much profit the company must have in a given year to maintain (or attain) a high return for stockholders. In top-down budgeting, the target profit figures become the starting point of the budgeting process.

Traditionally, most firms that used top-down budgeting also used an imposed budgeting process. An **imposed budget** is a budget in which upper management sets figures for all operating activities that the rest of the company rarely, if ever, can negotiate. No matter how unreasonable the budget numbers, top management expects all other managers to "do whatever it takes to make it happen." This type of budgeting process can do more harm than good, because it can lead to business practices that conflict with the company's stated goals. Today, however, not all top-down budgets are imposed budgets, as we will see shortly.

Bottom-Up Budgeting

In **bottom-up budgeting,** the budget is initially prepared by lower-level managers and employees. For example, members of the sales force prepare the sales schedule for their own sales territories. The sales manager then reviews these sales schedules, makes any necessary changes, and combines them to form the overall company sales schedule. Likewise, employees in the production facility prepare schedules for production, including schedules for direct material, direct labor, and manufacturing overhead.

Bottom-up budgeting has three main advantages. First, the budget may be more realistic. Those who work in a functional area are usually better informed about what should be included in the budget than upper managers. If lower-level managers and employees take the budgeting process seriously, they are likely to

top-down budgeting A budget prepared by top managers in a company.

imposed budget A budget in which upper management sets figures for all operating activities that the rest of the company rarely, if ever, can negotiate.

bottom-up budgeting A budget initially prepared by lower-level managers and employees.

create an operating budget based on accurate, realistic information. Second, lower-level managers and employees are more likely to work toward budgeted performance standards because they helped to set those standards. Third, as employees prepare the budget, they learn to think about the company's goals, how various activities can affect the future, and how they personally will participate. In short, they begin to think about the work they will need to do in the coming year.

Bottom-up budgeting has two disadvantages. First, employees at every level must take time from their day-to-day responsibilities to work on the budget as it is prepared, reviewed, revised, and approved—all of which adds up to substantial time and effort. Second, some employees may be tempted to prepare a budget that is so generous they can effortlessly outperform it. For example, sales representatives may budget sales of $300,000, when they can achieve sales of $350,000 with little effort. Thus, their actual sales performance looks great compared with budgeted sales. Manipulating the budget to make certain that the actual performance exceeds budgeted performance is one example of a budget game. A *budget game* is the game of using the budget to do things it was never intended to do, such as ensuring a strong performance appraisal.

Bottom-up budgeting is always a participative budgeting process. A **participative budget** is one in which managers and employees at many levels of the company are involved in setting the performance standards and preparing the budget. Recent developments have expanded the use of participative budgeting to top-down budgeting, so it is beneficial to discuss imposed and participative budget philosophies a little further.

participative budget A budget in which managers and employees at many levels of the company are involved in setting the performance standards and preparing the budget.

Imposed versus Participative Budgets

A bottom-up budget will always be a participative budget. Managers and employees at all levels of the company participate in the preparation of a bottom-up budget. A top-down budget, however, can be either imposed or participative.

In recent years, companies have discovered that by allowing more participation, they empower their employees. To empower employees means to give employees the authority to make decisions concerning their job responsibilities, including decisions about items in the operating budget.

A company committed to both top-down budgeting and empowered employees must combine the top-down and bottom-up approaches to budgeting. Rather than having all budget information flow from the top of the company downward to lower levels, upper management provides profit targets to managers at lower levels. These lower level managers then prepare the operating budget for their functional areas, given the profit targets provided by upper management.

Discussion Questions

8–6. What possible positive results do you think can come from more empowerment:

   a. for the company? Explain your reasoning.
   b. for managers and employees? Explain your reasoning.

8–7. What possible negative results do you think can come from more empowerment:

   a. for the company? Explain your reasoning.
   b. for managers and employees? Explain your reasoning.

As an example of combining the top-down and bottom-up approaches to budgeting, we look at Preston Nydegger Company. Nydegger is a publicly traded company that wants to be one of the top-performing companies (in terms of dividends and stock appreciation) in the stock market. Upper management has determined that the company must earn a profit of $1 million in the upcoming year to reach that goal. The company has three divisions (A, B, & C), and each must earn some part of the targeted $1 million profit. Division C is the smallest of the three, and corporate headquarters has assigned this division a target profit of $150,000 for the next year.

Now that Division C has received its target profit (this is the top-down part), the division manager, Joenne Moss, and her managers and employees set about to prepare the operating budget for the year (this is the participative part). When they have completed their budgeting process, the result in summary form is as follows:

Sales	$500,000
Expenses	(450,000)
Net Income	$150,000

Wait a minute! Something's wrong. The numbers just don't add up. Well, what we see is a conflict between the top-down target profit ($150,000) and what Joenne and her people at Division C think they can accomplish in the upcoming year ($500,000 in sales and $450,000 in expenses). What happens next will determine whether this budget is imposed or participative.

If the upper management of Nydegger Company refuses to negotiate and compromise with Division C, the budget becomes imposed. Remember, there is little room for negotiation between upper management and the rest of the company as to the amounts included in an imposed operating budget. If, however, upper management is willing to yield somewhat on its profit targets, the budget becomes participative.

It is unrealistic to think Nydegger will simply adjust its target from $150,000 to $50,000, which would certainly make the arithmetic in the budgeted income statement work. More than likely, Nydegger's upper management will meet with Joenne and her staff to negotiate a compromise target profit. Let us say they did just that, and the negotiations led to a revised target profit of $90,000 for the division. The revised summary budgeted income statement, then, would be as follows:

Sales	$500,000
Expenses	(450,000)
Net Income	$ 90,000

The math still doesn't work! Management at the division level must now either forecast more sales or find some way to reduce expected expenses (or some combination of the two) to project an additional $40,000 in profit for the year.

The key to making a top-down budget a participative budget is the ability and willingness on the part of upper management to negotiate and compromise.

Discussion Questions

8-8. If you were the chief executive officer of your company, would you prefer a top-down or bottom-up budgeting process? Why?

8-9. If you were in middle management, would you prefer a top-down or bottom-up budgeting process? Why?

8-10. If you were the company CEO, do you think it would be wise for you to spend time tending to the details of the various budgets, given all your other responsibilities?

The overall approach a company takes to preparing its operating budget may actually be a combination of several of the approaches we have discussed here. For example, one company may have a top-down, participative, zero-based budgeting approach. Another company may be committed to an incremental, participative, bottom-up, perpetual budgeting philosophy. The object is not to select a particular approach from a laundry list. Rather, managers must approach the preparation of the operating budget in a way that makes sense in the circumstances.

THE SALES FORECAST

After analyzing all available data, the certified meteorologists at the U.S. Weather Service predicted sunny and warm weather for the next five days, with only a 10 percent chance of rain. It rained every day for the next five days.

What is true for predicting future weather conditions is also true for predicting the future sales performance of a business. Although technological advances over the past 30 years have improved financial forecasting methods, predicting future sales still remains largely an educated guess. The prediction of sales for the period covered by the operating budget is called the **sales forecast.**

sales forecast The prediction of sales for the period covered by the operating budget.

Cornerstone and Keystone of Budgeting

A solid, realistic sales forecast is perhaps the most critical feature of a solid, realistic operating budget. Why? Once the sales forecast has been developed, the business can prepare the sales budget, the production or purchases budget, the cost of goods or cost of services budget, the selling and administrative expense budget, the cash budget, and the three budgeted financial statements (income statement, balance sheet, and statement of cash flows).

The sales forecast is often called the cornerstone of budgeting. In the construction of a building, the first brick or stone laid is called the cornerstone. The remainder of the entire building is built off this cornerstone. In the construction of the operating budget, the sales forecast is the first step; all the budgets are built from the sales forecast. The sales forecast, then, is the cornerstone of the budgeting process, as depicted in Exhibit 8–4.

Exhibit 8–4
The Sales Forecast as the Cornerstone of Budgeting

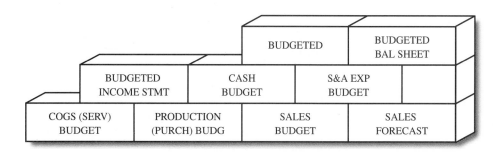

Exhibit 8–5
The Sales Forecast
as the Keystone
of Budgeting

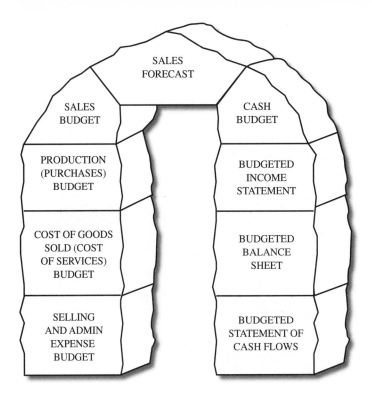

The sales forecast has also been called the keystone of budgeting. This description clearly reflects the importance of the forecast. In the building of a stone archway, the keystone is the stone placed at the exact center at the top of the arch. If this stone is strong and placed properly, the arch will last. In fact, some arches built without mortar in the Middle Ages are still standing. They are held together solely from the strength of the keystone. If the keystone is weak, however, or is improperly set, the arch will collapse; and so it is with budgeting. The quality of the entire master budget depends on the quality and accuracy of the sales forecast as depicted in Exhibit 8–5.

As an archway made of stones depends on the keystone for its strength, the reliability of the operating budget depends on the strength of the sales forecast. If the sales forecast does not reasonably reflect the actual sales during the operating budget period, the budget will not reasonably estimate the actual results for the period. Thus, there will be differences between the actual income statement, balance sheet, and statement of cash flows and the budgeted income statement, balance sheet, and statement of cash flows.

Factors Affecting the Accuracy of the Sales Forecast

Many factors influence the accuracy of the sales forecast. We have chosen four to discuss here: the economy, industry conditions, the competition, and technology.

General Economy   If the economy goes into a recession, consumer saving and spending patterns change. Sales forecasts are usually affected as a result. The problem is, most economists estimate that the economy can be entering or moving out of a recession for at least six to nine months before we realize it. Thus, when a firm creates its sales forecast for the next year's budget, it may be unaware of what the actual state of the economy will be throughout the period covered by the operating budget.

Industry Conditions It is possible for the general economy to be healthy and a particular industry to be in a recession or for the economy to be unhealthy and the industry quite healthy.

Actions of Competitors All companies take great pains to keep information about their plans from their competitors. Therefore, all companies make their sales forecasts without information that has a tremendous impact on the accuracy of the forecast. For example, imagine Intel is about to launch a revolutionary product that could absolutely blow its competitors away. Motorola does not know this, so it creates a sales forecast that is inaccurate because it is unaware of Intel's planned actions.

Technological Developments Technological developments can greatly influence the quality of the sales forecast. It is possible that the market for a particular product may not be as strong—or may not even exist—when the time the period being budgeted for arrives. When Microsoft introduced its Windows 95 program, the need for products compatible with Microsoft's old operating system sharply declined. Sales forecasts for software companies that did not expect the drop in demand for their products were rendered unreliable.

Discussion Question

8–11. What other factors can you think of that would influence the accuracy of a company's sales forecast?

We cannot overemphasize the importance of the sales forecast in the budgeting process, despite the difficulty of being completely accurate. It is worth the time and effort. Managers, however, must prepare and use the operating budget with a solid understanding of its limitations.

Part Two: Preparing and Using the Operating Budget

Preparing a Master Operating Budget

Marcy's Surf Shop is a retail store that sells only one product (surfboards) and deals in only one product model. The company's fiscal year ends June 30. At Marcy's request, we will prepare the operating budget for the first quarter of the fiscal year ending June 30, 2003. Thus, we will be budgeting for the quarter ending September 30, 2002.

We start with Marcy's budgeted income statement and the budgets that provide information used to construct that budgeted financial statement. We will then prepare the budgeted balance sheet along with all other budgets required to prepare the budgeted balance sheet. Finally, we will prepare the budgeted statement of cash flows.

Because we focus on a merchandising company rather than a manufacturer, we will work with a purchases budget rather than a production budget.

Budgeted Income Statement

To prepare the budgeted income statement, we need information about sales, cost of goods sold, and selling and administrative expenses for the period covered by the budget. Therefore, we must prepare a budget for each of those items before we can construct the budgeted income statement.

Sales Budget   The first information we need to build the budgeted income statement is found in the sales budget. Our first task, then, is to request that Marcy's marketing and sales personnel provide a sales forecast. They tell us that they will be happy to do so, but are not sure how. Should we suggest they take last year's sales numbers and increase them by, say, five percent? This would be incremental budgeting, and—without a critical look at market factors that affect sales—it is a poor approach to budgeting. If simply increasing last year's amounts by a constant percentage were adequate, a computer could easily be programmed to do the job.

Before Marcy's Surf Shop can forecast its sales realistically, sales management and the sales personnel must first consider the factors that influence market conditions. After much discussion, Marcy's staff decided to research the following items:

- Current customer spending patterns
- The ability to attract new customers through market promotions
- The introduction of any new products
- The discontinuation of any products
- The competition
- Price changes
- The general economy
- Technological changes

The sales department's recent customer satisfaction survey shows, for example, that 60 percent of all current customers plan to buy another product in the next quarter and that price is the number one consideration in surfboard purchases. Any increase in price is therefore likely to have a negative impact on repeat business. The market research done by the company indicates that thanks to planned market promotions, Marcy's can expect a 20 percent growth in first-time customer purchases.

You see, then, that each of the items chosen for evaluation by the company is researched and the results examined in an attempt to make the forecasting of sales something more than just a guessing game.

Once the sales team considers all its research, it develops a forecast of unit sales for each month in the quarter. The sales team forecasts sales for Marcy's Surf Shop of 30 units in July, 50 units in August, and 40 units in September, shown as Exhibit 8–6.

Exhibit 8–6
Sales Forecast for
Marcy's Surf Shop

MARCY'S SURF SHOP Sales Forecast For the Quarter Ended September 30, 2002				
	July	August	September	Total
Forecasted Sales in Units	30	50	40	120

Based on this forecast, we can prepare Marcy's sales budget for the quarter, as shown in Exhibit 8–7.

We simply used the sales forecast of unit sales and the projected selling price of $200 per surfboard to develop the sales budget.

A real sales budget for an actual company is no more complicated than this one. Of course, in our example, Marcy's sells only one product. Remember from our earlier discussion that if Marcy's sold 80 different products, the company would need to prepare 80 of these sales budgets. If Marcy's sold 80 different products in 80 different locations, the company would need to prepare 6,400 of these sales budgets (80 products × 80 locations).

Exhibit 8–7
Sales Budget for
Marcy's Surf Shop

MARCY'S SURF SHOP				
Sales Budget				
For the Quarter Ended September 30, 2002				
	July	August	September	Total
Forecasted Unit Sales	30	50	40	120
× Forecasted Sales Price	$ 200	$ 200	$ 200	$ 200
= Budgeted Sales Dollars	$6,000	$10,000	$8,000	$24,000

Discussion Question

8–12. What factors should Marcy's management consider when setting the $200 budgeted selling price for its surfboards?

Cost of Goods Sold Budget Once we know how many units Marcy's Surf Shop plans to sell, and the cost per unit, we can prepare a cost of goods sold budget. As its name implies, this budget is used to determine how much cost of goods sold should be based on forecasted sales. Preparing the cost of goods sold budget consists of multiplying forecasted unit sales by the cost per unit. The cost of goods sold budget for Marcy's Surf Shop is presented in Exhibit 8–8.

Exhibit 8–8
Cost of Goods Sold
Budget for Marcy's
Surf Shop

MARCY'S SURF SHOP				
Cost of Goods Sold Budget				
For the Quarter Ended September 30, 2002				
	July	August	September	Total
Forecasted Unit Sales	30	50	40	120
× Forecasted Unit Cost	$ 120	$ 120	$ 120	$ 120
= Budgeted COGS	$3,600	$6,000	$4,800	$14,400

Exhibit 8–8 shows that Marcy's forecasted cost of goods sold for the quarter is $14,400 ($3,600 + $6,000 + $4,800 = $14,400). The cost of goods sold budget provides the forecasted product cost information that is used to prepare the budgeted income statement. This product cost information helps Marcy's management determine whether the company will be profitable based on its budget, or whether changes should be planned now to ensure profits in the budget period.

Discussion Questions

Compare the sales budget in Exhibit 8–7 with the cost of goods sold budget in Exhibit 8–8.

8–13. What are the similarities?
8–14. What are the differences?

Realistically, Marcy's will need to purchase more units of product than just the ones it expects to sell in July, August, and September. Thus, in addition to the budgets required to prepare the budgeted income statement, Marcy's will need to prepare a purchases budget. For our demonstration purposes, however, we will wait until after we have prepared the budgeted income statement to present the purchases budget. The only additional budget we need to prepare before we can prepare the budgeted income statement is the selling and administrative expense budget.

Selling and Administrative Expense Budget   The various expenses associated with the selling and administrative functions are estimated and used to prepare this budget. Selling and administrative expenses include salaries, advertising, rent, utilities, etc. The selling and administrative expense budget for Marcy's Surf Shop is presented in Exhibit 8–9.

Exhibit 8–9
Selling and Administrative Expense Budget for Marcy's Surf Shop

MARCY'S SURF SHOP Selling and Administrative Expense Budget For the Quarter Ended September 30, 2002				
	July	August	September	Total
Salaries and Wages	$1,600	$2,000	$1,800	$5,400
Rent	200	200	200	600
Depreciation	100	100	104	304
Others	800	1,000	900	2,700
Total	$2,700	$3,300	$3,004	$9,004

The types of items and the amounts included in the selling and administrative expense budget vary from company to company. As we said earlier, the items included in this budget are determined by what is required to support the level of sales in the sales budget.

Discussion Questions

8–15. If you were preparing a selling and administrative expense budget, what are some of the things you would consider as you mapped out strategies to increase sales?

8–16. Besides those included in Exhibit 8–9, what are some other administrative costs you think would normally be included in a selling and administrative expense budget?

8–17. What do you think might explain the increase in anticipated depreciation expense in September from $100 to $104?

Building the Budgeted Income Statement

To prepare the budgeted income statement, we use information from the sales, cost of goods sold, and selling and administrative expense budgets. The budgeted income statement depicts the amount of profit or loss a business can expect from its budgeted operating activities. First, we take the total forecasted sales revenue from the sales budget and subtract the forecasted cost of goods sold from the cost of goods sold budget. The result is a forecasted gross profit. We then subtract the total selling and administrative expense which we get from the selling and administrative expense budget. The result is the company's budgeted net income for the period covered by the budget. The budgeted income statement for Marcy's Surf Shop is presented in Exhibit 8–10.

Exhibit 8–10
Budgeted Income
Statement for
Marcy's Surf Shop

MARCY'S SURF SHOP
Budgeted Income Statement
For the Quarter Ended September 30, 2002

	July	August	September	Total
Sales	$6,000	$10,000	$8,000	$24,000
− Cost of Goods Sold	3,600	6,000	4,800	14,400
= Gross Profit	2,400	4,000	3,200	9,600
− Selling and Admin. Expense	(2,700)	(3,300)	(3,004)	(9,004)
= Net Income	$(300)	$ 700	$ 196	$ 596

We see from Exhibit 8–10 that Marcy's Surf Shop is projecting a $300 net loss for July. In August Marcy's is projecting a net income of $700 and in September it is $196. The total net income for the quarter, then, is $596.

After the budgeted income statement has been prepared, Marcy's management team may want to change its plans so that it meets its profit goals more effectively. For instance, management may look at the budgeted income statement in Exhibit 8–10 and find the $300 loss in July unacceptable. If so, it would review all the information used to build the budgeted income statement and either adjust its expectations or adjust the assumptions used to prepare the budget.

Whatever the outcome of this evaluation, Marcy's Surf Shop has a better chance of planning for a successful future if management takes the budgeting process seriously. If budgets are used properly, managers will have an opportunity to see trouble spots in advance and make the required adjustments before it is too late.

Budgeted Balance Sheet

Now that we have prepared the budgeted income statement, we have much of the information we need to prepare the budgeted balance sheet. First, however, we must prepare two more budgets: the purchases budget, as mentioned when we were preparing the budgeted income statement, and the cash budget.

Purchases Budget

The cost of goods sold budget we prepared accounts only for the units projected to be sold during the period covered by the budget. If Marcy's planned to begin and end the period covered by the budget with no inventory on hand and planned to purchase only the amount of inventory during the budgeted period sufficient to support the level of projected sales, there would be no need for a separate purchases budget. Rather, the company could just use the information from the cost of goods sold budget. This plan is unrealistic, however, because a company like Marcy's must begin and end each period with a certain amount of merchandise on hand. These inventory requirements create the need for the purchases budget. Marcy's purchases budget for the three months ended September 30, 2002, is presented as Exhibit 8–11.

Exhibit 8–11
Purchases Budget for
Marcy's Surf Shop

MARCY'S SURF SHOP
Purchases Budget
For the Quarter Ended September 30, 2002

	July	August	September	Total	
Forecasted Unit Sales	30	50	40	120	(a)
+ Desired Ending Inventory*	20	16	24	24	(b)
= Total Units Needed	50	66	64	144	(c)
− Beginning Inventory	(8)	(20)	(16)	(8)	(d)
= Units to Be Purchased	42	46	48	136	(e)
× Cost Per Unit	$ 120	$ 120	$ 120	$ 120	(f)
= Cost of Purchases	$5,040	$ 5,520	$5,760	$16,320	(g)

*40% of the next month's sales requirements

As you can see by looking at Exhibit 8–11, the purchases budget, even for a small company like Marcy's Surf Shop, can seem rather complicated. A line-by-line analysis of this budget, however, reveals that much of the information it contains is already known, and the new information is basically straightforward.

(a) *Forecasted Unit Sales.* These numbers should look familiar to you because you have seen them three times already. They come directly from the sales forecast presented in Exhibit 8–6 and were used to construct the sales budget in Exhibit 8–7 and the cost of goods sold budget in Exhibit 8–8.

(b) *Desired Ending Inventory.* These numbers represent the number of units of product the company believes it needs on hand at the end of a given period to support sales in the early days of the next period. As the asterisk note in Exhibit 8–11 explains, Marcy's has decided it should have inventory of product on hand at the end of any given month equal to 40 percent of the next month's sales requirements. At the end of July, for example, Marcy's desires an ending inventory of 20 units, which is 40 percent of August's sales of 50 units (50 × 40% = 20 units).

The amount of desired ending inventory is determined by at least two factors. First, the company must consider how long it usually takes to get product from the company's supplier. This information is obtained from the purchasing records and discussions with the purchasing department. Second, the company must estimate the number of units of product it will sell in the early days of each month. This information comes from historical sales records and discussions with sales personnel.

The desired ending inventory amounts for July, August, and September will be important to us when we construct the budgeted balance sheet, but we will defer our discussion of how they are used until we actually prepare that budget.

Discussion Question

8-18. Can you tell by looking at the purchases budget in Exhibit 8–11 how many surfboards Marcy's has forecasted it will sell in October? Explain your reasoning.

(c) *Total Units Needed.* This figure is the sum of (a) and (b).

(d) *Beginning Inventory.* Because the purpose of the purchases budget is to determine how many units of inventory must be purchased during each of the months included in the budget period, any inventory forecasted to be on hand at the beginning of each month must be subtracted from the total units needed to determine how many units must be purchased during the month.

   The beginning inventory for any period is the ending inventory for the previous period. You will note in the purchases budget in Exhibit 8–11 that the beginning inventory for August (20 units) is the same as the desired ending inventory for July, and the beginning inventory for September (16 units) is the same as the desired ending inventory for August. You should also note that the beginning inventory in the total column (eight units) is the same as the beginning inventory for July, because the total column is for the entire quarter and the quarter begins in July.

Discussion Question

8-19. The purchases budget in Exhibit 8–11 indicates that Marcy's desires ending inventory equal to 40% of the next month's sales requirements. Because sales in July are expected to be 30 surfboards, the beginning inventory in July (which is the ending inventory for June) should be 12 units (30 × 40%). Why do you think the beginning inventory in July is only eight surfboards?

(e) *Units to Be Purchased.* This figure is simply (c) minus (d) and tells us the number of surfboards that must be purchased in each of the three months of the budget period and the total for the quarter.

(f) *Cost Per Unit.* The cost per unit is what Marcy's must pay for each surfboard it purchases. Note that this cost is the same as the cost per unit used when we prepared the cost of goods sold budget presented in Exhibit 8–8.

(g) *Cost of Purchases.* This figure is simply (e) multiplied by (f) and tells us what the purchase of surfboards will cost Marcy's in each of the three months of the budget period and the total for the quarter.

Cash Budget

When a company uses accrual accounting, revenue is recognized when it is earned rather than when the cash associated with that revenue is collected, and expenses are recognized when the benefit is received rather than when the cash associated with the expenses is paid. Meaning of course, that while the budgeted income statement (including the sales budget, cost of goods sold budget, and the selling and administrative expense budget) provides information about Marcy's projected earnings activities for the budget period, it does not provide direct information about what is projected to happen during that period in terms of cash. Also, unless Marcy's pays cash for its purchase of surfboards, the purchases budget suffers from the same limitation.

   Before we can prepare the budgeted balance sheet, we must determine the effect on cash of the budgets we have prepared so far. We do that by preparing a cash budget, which is composed of a cash receipts schedule and a cash payments schedule.

Cash Receipts Schedule   The **cash receipts schedule** presents the amount of cash a company expects to collect during the budget period from the sales of its product. Before we can prepare Marcy's cash receipts schedule, we must make certain estimates about the composition of the company's sales (cash or credit) and the pattern of collecting the accounts receivable created by the credit sales. We estimate that 25 percent of Marcy's sales are for cash and the remaining 75 percent are on account (credit sales). Of the sales on account, we estimate that 30 percent are collected in the month of the sale, 60 percent in the month following the sale, and 10 percent in the second month following the sale. Because of the lag between the time a credit sale is made and the time cash is collected, some of the cash for credit sales made in May and June will not have been collected by the end of June, which means that those amounts will be collected during the three months included in our budget period. Therefore, we need to know May credit sales were $4,500, and June credit sales were $6,000.

Using the credit sales figures from May and June, and our assumptions about when cash is collected, we can prepare Marcy's cash receipts schedule for the three months ended September 30, 2002 as shown in Exhibit 8–12.

Exhibit 8–12
Cash Receipts Schedule for Marcy's Surf Shop

MARCY'S SURF SHOP
Cash Receipts Schedule
For the Quarter Ended September 30, 2002

	Jul	Aug	Sep	Total	
Credit Sales Collected:					
From Accounts Receivable at 6/30/02:					
May Credit Sales ($4,500)					
Collected in July (10%)	$ 450			$ 450	
June Credit Sales ($6,000)					(a)
Collected in July (60%)	3,600			3,600	
Collected in August (10%)		$ 600		600	
From New Credit Sales:					
July Credit Sales ($4,500)					
Collected in July (30%)	1,350			1,350	
Collected in August (60%)		2,700		2,700	
Collected in September (10%)			$ 450	450	
August Credit Sales ($7,500)					(b)
Collected in August (30%)		2,250		2,250	
Collected in September (60%)			4,500	4,500	
September Credit Sales ($6,000)					
Collected in September (30%)			1,800	1,800	
Budgeted Receipts from Credit Sales	$5,400	$5,550	$6,750	$17,700	(c)
Cash Sales:					
July Cash Sales	1,500			1,500	
August Cash Sales		2,500		2,500	(d)
September Cash Sales			2,000	2,000	
Budgeted Cash Receipts	$6,900	$8,050	$8,750	$23,700	(e)

Although the cash receipts schedule presented in Exhibit 8–12 seems quite complex, it is more straightforward than it first appears. It is broken into two major parts. The first presents the amount of cash collected from credit sales during the period covered by the schedule (a through c) and the second part presents the amount of cash collected from cash sales during the budget period (d).

Let us take a few minutes to examine this schedule and see where the numbers came from and what they mean.

(a) *From Accounts Receivable at 6/30/02.* The accounts receivable balance at 6/30/02 is composed of receivables arising from sales in May and June. May's credit sales were $4,500. Based on our collection assumption, 30 percent of that amount was collected in May and 60 percent in June. If 90 percent had been collected by the end of June, the remaining $450 ($4,500 × 10%) had not and was included in the balance of accounts receivable at 6/30/02. Since July is the second month following the credit sales in May, the $450 balance is shown as a collection in July ($4,500 × 10%).

Credit sales in June totaled $6,000. Only $1,800 of that amount was collected in June ($6,000 × 30%). If 30 percent had been collected by the end of June, $4,200 ($6,000 × 70%) had not and was included in the balance of accounts receivable at 6/30/02. Since July is the month following the credit sales in June, $3,600 is shown as a collection in July ($6,000 × 60%); and because August is the second month following the credit sales in June, the remaining $600 balance is shown as a collection in August ($6,000 × 10%).

(b) *From New Sales.* Recall from the sales budget in Exhibit 8–7 that budgeted sales for the three months covered by our budget example were $6,000 in July, $10,000 in August, and $8,000 in September. One of the assumptions we made as we began our discussion of the cash receipts schedule was that 75 percent of Marcy's sales were credit sales. Therefore, the amounts we are dealing with in this section of the schedule are $4,500 for July ($6,000 × 75%), $7,500 for August ($10,000 × 75%), and $6,000 for September ($8,000 × 75%).

The collection pattern for each of the three months is the same: 30 percent of credit sales are collected in the month of sale, 60 percent in the month following the sale, and 10 percent in the second month following the sale. So for July's credit sales, for example, the schedule shows $1,350 will be collected in July ($4,500 × 30%), $2,700 will be collected in August ($4,500 × 60%), and $450 ($4,500 × 10%) in September. The amounts projected to be collected for August and September credit sales are calculated exactly the same way.

(c) *Budgeted Receipts from Credit Sales.* This figure is simply the sum of (a) and (b). It presents the total amount of cash Marcy's expects to collect during the period covered by the schedule from credit sales.

(d) *Cash Sales.* This section is the least complicated of the schedule. For the three months included in the schedule it presents the portion of sales that will be cash sales. If 75 percent of the sales made in a given month are credit sales, then 25 percent will be cash sales. Therefore, in July the cash sales will be $1,500 ($6,000 × 25%) and that amount is shown as a cash receipt in July. The amount for August is $2,500 ($10,000 × 25%), and for September $2,000 ($8,000 × 25%).

(e) *Budgeted Cash Receipts.* This figure is simply the sum of (c) and (d). As the description indicates, it presents the total amount of cash Marcy's plans to collect from the accounts receivable balance at 6/30/02, the credit sales it will have during the period covered by the schedule, and the cash sales made during the period.

Cash Payments Schedule The **cash payments schedule** presents the amount of cash a company expects to pay out during the budget period. Before we can prepare Marcy's cash payments schedule, we must make certain assumptions about the company's pattern of cash payments. We assume that payment for the purchase of surfboards is made in the month following the purchase. Because of the lag time between the time a purchase is made and the time cash is paid, the purchases made in June will not have been paid by the end of June, which means that this amount will be paid in July, one of the months included in our budget period. Therefore, we need to know that purchases of merchandise in June totaled $5,200. All cash selling and administrative expenses are paid in the month incurred.

Using these assumptions about when cash is paid and the purchases figure from June, we can prepare Marcy's cash payments schedule for the three months ended September 30, 2002, as shown in Exhibit 8–13.

Exhibit 8–13
Cash Payments Schedule for Marcy's Surf Shop

MARCY'S SURF SHOP
Cash Payments Schedule
For the Quarter Ended September 30, 2002

	July	August	September	Total	
Purchases	$5,200	$5,040	$5,520	$15,760	(a)
Selling and Admin. Expense:					
Salaries and Wages	1,600	2,000	1,800	5,400	
Rent	200	200	200	600	(b)
Other Selling and Admin. Expense	800	1,000	900	2,700	
Purchase of Display Case		240		240	(c)
Budgeted Cash Payments	$7,800	$8,480	$8,420	$24,700	(d)

As you can see from Exhibit 8–13, the cash payments schedule is not nearly as complex as either the purchases budget or the cash receipts schedule. There are a couple of tricky parts, however, so let us examine the items included.

(a) *Purchases.* These are payments for the purchase of surfboards. Recall our assumption that payment for the purchase of merchandise is made in the month following purchase. The projected payment of $5,200 in July, then, is for purchases made in June, the payment of $5,040 in August will be for July purchases, and the $5,520 payment in September will be for August purchases.

Discussion Question

8-20. In our assumptions about cash payments, we said that June purchases of merchandise totaled $5,200 so it is easy to see where the July payment originated. Where do you suppose the payment amounts ($5,040 and $5,520) originated for August and September?

(b) *Selling and Administrative Expense.* These are payments for the support costs Marcy's anticipates for each month of the budget period. The amounts come directly from the selling and administrative expense budget in Exhibit 8–9.

Discussion Question

8-21. Look back at the selling and administrative expense budget in Exhibit 8–9. All the expense items included in that budget are included in the cash payments schedule *except* depreciation. Why do you think depreciation expense was included in the selling and administrative expense budget but excluded from the cash payments schedule?

    (c) *Purchase of Display Case.* Evidently, Marcy's is planning to purchase a new display case for the showroom during the month of August. This purchase will be addition to Marcy's property, plant, and equipment and will be important to us when we prepare the budgeted balance sheet and the budgeted statement of cash flows. Incidently, the planned purchase of this display case is what caused depreciation expense in Exhibit 8–9 to increase by $4 in September.

    (d) *Budgeted Cash Payments.* This figure is simply the sum of (a), (b), and (c). As the description indicates, it presents the total amount of cash Marcy's plans to pay out during the period covered by the schedule.

Building the Cash Budget

Now that we have prepared the cash receipts schedule and the cash payments schedule, we can prepare Marcy's cash budget for the quarter ended September 30, 2002. As was the case with the schedules, we must make some assumptions for the cash budget. First, we estimate that Marcy's Surf Shop will have a cash balance of $2,170 on June 30, 2002. Second, Marcy's desires to maintain a cash balance of at least $1,900 at all times. If cash falls below $1,900, the company will borrow from a local bank. Finally, we ignore the interest Marcy's would be required to pay on any borrowings from the bank.

    Using the assumption about Marcy's desired minimum cash balance, and the information from the cash receipts schedule and the cash payments schedule, we can prepare the company's cash budget for the quarter ending September 30, 2002, as shown in Exhibit 8–14.

Exhibit 8–14
Cash Budget for
Marcy's Surf Shop

MARCY'S SURF SHOP
Cash Budget
For the Quarter Ended September 30, 2002

		July	August	September	Total	
	Beginning Cash Balance	$2,170	$ 1,900	$ 1,900	$ 2,170	(a)
+	Cash Receipts	6,900	8,050	8,750	23,700	(b)
=	Cash Available	$9,070	$ 9,950	$10,650	$25,870	(c)
−	Cash Payments	(7,800)	(8,480)	(8,420)	(24,700)	(d)
=	Balance before Borrowing	$1,270	$ 1,470	$ 2,230	$ 1,170	(e)
+/−	Borrowing/(Repayment)	630	$ 430	$ (330)	$ 730	(f)
=	Ending Cash Balance	$1,900	$ 1,900	$ 1,900	$ 1,900	(g)

The cash budget itself is not as seemingly complicated as the purchases budget, the cash receipts schedule, or the cash payments schedule. There are, however, some potential pitfalls in your understanding of the way this budget is constructed, so we will take a few minutes and discuss the items included.

(a) *Beginning Cash Balance.* Like all balance sheet items, the beginning cash balance for any period is the ending cash balance for the previous period. As mentioned earlier, the ending cash balance for June will be $2,170. Therefore, July's beginning cash balance will be June's ending cash balance. The same pattern holds true for the other months presented. August's beginning balance is July's ending balance and September's beginning balance is August's ending balance. Note, however, that the beginning balance in the total column ($2,170) is the same as the beginning balance for July. Likewise, the ending balance in the total column ($1,900) is the same as the ending balance for September, because the total column represents the entire quarter. The beginning balance for the quarter is July's beginning balance and the ending balance for the quarter is September's ending balance.

(b) *Cash Receipts.* The cash receipts amounts are taken directly from the budgeted cash receipts line of the cash receipts schedule shown in Exhibit 8–12.

(c) *Cash Available.* This figure is simply the sum of (a) and (b). This amount represents the total cash Marcy's expects to be available before deducting any payments.

(d) *Cash Payments.* The cash payments amounts are taken directly from the budgeted cash payments line of the cash payments schedule shown in Exhibit 8–13.

(e) *Balance before Borrowing.* This amount is calculated by simply subtracting (d) from (c). It represents the anticipated ending cash balance before any adjustments for borrowing or loan payments.

(f) *Borrowing/(Repayment).* Marcy's wants to maintain a cash balance of at least $1,900. If the balance before borrowing drops too low, Marcy's will borrow enough money from the bank to bring the balance up to the desired ending cash balance of $1,900. As you can see, July's balance before borrowing is expected to be only $1,270. Therefore, Marcy's can anticipate the need to borrow $630 to bring the balance up to $1,900. So, if the balance before borrowing is less than the desired ending cash balance, as it will be in July and again in August, the amount that must be borrowed to bring the cash balance to the desired amount can be easily calculated. If, on the other hand, the expected balance before borrowing is greater than $1,900, as is the case in September, any amount in excess of the desired ending cash balance will be used to repay the loan ($330 in this instance).

(g) *Ending Cash Balance.* This figure is simply (e) plus the borrowing or less the repayment shown in (f). As we said earlier, this ending cash amount also becomes the next month's beginning cash balance.

Now the information from the cash budget and other budgets can be used to prepare the budgeted balance sheet.

Building the Budgeted Balance Sheet

We assume that you already know the basics of how a balance sheet is constructed, so, for our presentation of the budgeted balance sheet, we focus on how to determine the various asset, liability, and equity items and dollar amounts for these items.

Although some of the amounts needed to prepare the budgeted balance sheet are taken directly from the budgets already prepared, many amounts are not specifically included in any of those budgets. For example, we have not prepared a budget or schedule that shows the ending balances for accounts receivable, inventory, property, plant, and equipment, accumulated depreciation, accounts payable, notes payable, common stock, additional paid-in capital, or retained earnings. For each of these items, we will present a brief discussion and a schedule to show how to calculate the amounts that should appear on the budgeted balance sheet. You will find as you examine each of these items that the budgeted ending balance is calculated by taking the beginning balance and adding or subtracting the changes that are expected to occur during the budget period. So, for each of these items, the beginning balance is our starting point. As discussed, the *beginning* balance of any balance sheet item is the prior month's *ending* balance. Therefore, all we need is the balance sheet for June 30 to determine the beginning balance for July. The balance sheet of June 30, 2002, for Marcy's Surf Shop is shown in Exhibit 8–15.

Exhibit 8–15
Balance Sheet as of June 30, 2002, for Marcy's Surf Shop

MARCY'S SURF SHOP
Balance Sheet
June 30, 2002

Assets	
Current Assets	
Cash	$ 2,170
Accounts Receivable	4,650
Inventory	960
Total Current Assets	$ 7,780
Property, Plant, and Equipment	
Equipment	6,000
Less Accumulated Depreciation	(1,200)
Equipment, Net	$ 4,800
Total Assets	$12,580
Liabilities	
Current Liabilities	
Accounts Payable	$ 5,200
Total Liabilities	$ 5,200
Owner's Equity	
Paid-in Capital	
Common Stock	$ 1,000
Additional Paid-in Capital	5,475
Total Paid-in Capital	$ 6,475
Retained Earnings	$ 905
Total Equity	$ 7,380
Total Liabilities and Equity	$12,580

Using the June 30, 2002, balance sheet in Exhibit 8–15 and information from the other budgets we have prepared so far, we can prepare a budgeted balance sheet for each of the three months included in our budget period, as shown in Exhibit 8–16.

The balance sheets presented in Exhibit 8–16 are much like the other balance sheets you have seen throughout your studies. The essential difference is not the format, but rather, the time frame. These are projected balance sheets whereas the others have presented past results. There is no total column for this budget, because the balance sheet is a financial snapshot of a business taken at the end of a period. Therefore, in a very real sense, the snapshot taken at the end of September is the total column.

Exhibit 8–16
Budgeted Balance
Sheets for Marcy's
Surf Shop

MARCY'S SURF SHOP
Budgeted Balance Sheet
For the Quarter Ended September 30, 2002

	July	August	September	
Assets				
Current Assets				
Cash	$ 1,900	$ 1,900	$ 1,900	(a)
Accounts Receivable, Net	3,750	5,700	4,950	(b)
Inventory	2,400	1,920	2,880	(c)
Total Current Assets	$ 8,050	$ 9,520	$ 9,730	
Property, Plant, and Equipment				
Equipment	$ 6,000	$ 6,240	$ 6,240	(d)
Less Accumulated Depreciation	(1,300)	(1,400)	(1,504)	(e)
Equipment, Net	$ 4,700	$ 4,840	$ 4,736	
Total Assets	$12,750	$14,360	$14,466	
Liabilities				
Current Liabilities				
Accounts Payable	$ 5,040	$ 5,520	$ 5,760	(f)
Bank Loan Payable	630	1,060	730	(g)
Total Liabilities	$ 5,670	$ 6,580	$ 6,490	
Owner's Equity				
Paid-in Capital				
Common Stock	$ 1,000	$ 1,000	$ 1,000	
Additional Paid-in Capital	5,475	5,475	5,475	(h)
Total Paid-in Capital	$ 6,475	$ 6,475	$ 6,475	
Retained Earnings	$ 605	$ 1,305	$ 1,501	(i)
Total Equity	$ 7,080	$ 7,780	$ 7,976	
Total Liabilities and Equity	$12,750	$14,360	$14,466	

As we have done with the other budgets prepared in this chapter, we will now take a few minutes and explain how the items on the budgeted balance sheet were determined.

(a) *Cash.* This amount is taken directly from the ending cash balance line of the cash budget shown in Exhibit 8–14. For example, the amount shown as the ending cash balance of $1,900 in the July column of the cash budget is shown as cash in the July column of the budgeted balance sheet.

(b) *Accounts Receivable.* To determine the ending accounts receivable balance for each month shown in Exhibit 8–16, we simply take the beginning accounts receivable balance, add budgeted credit sales for that month, and subtract budgeted collections for that month.

	Jul	Aug	Sep
Beginning Balance	$4,650	$3,750	$5,700
+ Credit sales	4,500	7,500	6,000
− Collections	(5,400)	(5,550)	(6,750)
Ending Balance	$3,750	$5,700	$4,950

The beginning accounts receivable balance of $4,650 for July is taken from the June 30, 2002, balance sheet shown in Exhibit 8–15. The cash receipts budget provides the rest of the information we need. The cash receipts budget shows the projected credit sales, and the total expected to be collected from credit sales. For July, the cash receipts budget shows credit sales of $4,500 and a total of $5,400 collected from credit sales. After adding the credit sales of $4,500 to the beginning balance of $4,650, we subtract the collections of $5,400 to arrive at the ending accounts receivable balance of $3,750. This amount is shown on the budgeted balance sheet for July. The ending accounts receivable amounts for other months are calculated the same way.

(c) *Inventory.* To determine the ending inventory balance for each month shown in Exhibit 8–16, we simply take the beginning inventory balance, add purchases made during the month, and subtract that month's cost of goods sold.

	Jul	Aug	Sep
Beginning Balance	$ 960	$2,400	$1,920
+ Purchases	5,040	5,520	5,760
− Cost of goods sold	(3,600)	(6,000)	(4,800)
Ending Balance	$2,400	$1,920	$2,880

The beginning inventory balance for July of $960 is taken from the June 30, 2002, balance sheet shown in Exhibit 8–15. By looking at the purchases budget in Exhibit 8–11 and the cost of goods sold budget in Exhibit 8–8, we find that expected purchases for July are $5,040 and cost of goods sold are expected be $3,600. After adding the purchases of $5,040 to the beginning balance of $960, we subtract the cost of goods sold of $3,600 to arrive at the ending inventory balance of $2,400. This amount is shown on the budgeted balance sheet for July. The ending inventory amounts for other months are calculated the same way.

(d) *Equipment.* To determine the ending balance in the equipment, we adjust the beginning balance by adding the cost of equipment purchased and subtracting the cost of any equipment sold. In our example, the only change in equipment is the $240 for the showcase the company is planning to buy in August. We add $240 to the $6,000 beginning balance to arrive at the budgeted ending balance of $6,240.

(e) *Accumulated Depreciation.* To determine the ending balance for accumulated depreciation, we adjust the beginning balance by adding the depreciation for the period and subtracting the accumulated depreciation associated with any assets that have been sold or scrapped. In our example, the company does not expect to sell or otherwise dispose of any equipment, so the only changes to accumulated depreciation are increases relating to the budgeted monthly depreciation. You might notice that the amount added to accumulated depreciation in September is slightly higher than that for July and August. This is so because of the added depreciation for the showcase the company expects to buy in August.

(f) *Accounts Payable.* To determine the ending accounts payable balance for each month shown in Exhibit 8–16, we simply take the beginning accounts payable balance, add budgeted purchases for that month, and subtract budgeted payments for that month.

	Jul	Aug	Sep
Beginning Balance	$5,200	$5,040	$5,520
+ Purchases	5,040	5,520	5,760
− Payments	(5,200)	(5,040)	(5,520)
Ending Balance	$5,040	$5,520	$5,760

The beginning accounts payable balance for July of $5,200 is taken from the June 30, 2002, balance sheet shown in Exhibit 8–15. By looking at the purchases budget in Exhibit 8–11 and the cash payments budget in Exhibit 8–13, we find that expected purchases for July are $5,040 and cash payments are expected be $5,200. After adding the purchases of $5,040 to the beginning balance of $5,200, we subtract the cash payments of $5,200 to arrive at the ending accounts payable balance of $5,040. This amount is shown on the budgeted balance sheet for July. The ending accounts payable amounts for other months are calculated the same way.

(g) *Bank Loan Payable.* To determine the ending notes payable balance for each month shown in Exhibit 8–16, we simply take the beginning notes payable balance, add the budgeted borrowing for that month, and subtract budgeted payments for that month.

	Jul	Aug	Sep
Beginning Balance	$ -0-	$ 630	$1,060
+ Borrowing	630	430	-0-
− Repayments	-0-	-0-	(330)
Ending Balance	$630	$1,060	$ 730

The beginning notes payable balance for July would normally come from the June 30, 2002, balance sheet shown in Exhibit 8–15; however, in this example the beginning balance for notes payable on June 30, 2002, is zero, so notes payable does not appear. By looking at the cash budget in Exhibit 8–14, we find that borrowing of $630 is expected in July, borrowing of $430 is expected in August, and a repayment of $330 is expected in September.

(h) *Common Stock and Additional Paid-in Capital.* In this example, no common stock or additional paid in capital transactions are expected during the budget period. Therefore, the beginning July balance for these items found on the June 30, 2002, balance sheet in Exhibit 8–15 remains unchanged during the budget period.

(i) *Retained Earnings.* To determine the ending retained earnings balance, we add the income for the period or, if the company has a loss, subtract the loss and deduct dividends, if they exist, from the beginning retained earnings balance.

	Jul	Aug	Sep
Beginning Balance	$ 905	$ 605	$1,305
+ Income/Loss	(300)	700	196
− Dividends	-0-	-0-	-0-
Ending Balance	$ 605	$1,305	$1,501

In our example, the $905 beginning balance of retained earnings is found on the June 30, 2002, balance sheet shown in Exhibit 8–15. To find the ending retained earnings that should appear on the budgeted balance sheet for July, we deduct the budgeted loss for that month of $300 from the beginning retained earnings balance of $905. That figure becomes the beginning balance in August. To determine the August ending balance of retained earnings we simply add August's budgeted net income. September's ending balance would be calculated the same way. There are no dividends in our example so the dividend amount is zero for each month presented.

Budgeted Statement of Cash Flows

Now that we have prepared all the other budgets, we can now prepare the budgeted statement of cash flows (SCF). This statement must be the final budget prepared because, as you recall from your earlier study of this financial statement, it is a form of financial statement analysis. An SCF prepared on historical results analyzes the income statement and the balance sheet to explain what caused cash to change from the beginning of a period to the end of the period. The budgeted statement of cash flows does exactly the same thing, except that it analyzes the budgeted income statement and the budgeted balance sheet to explain what will cause the projected change in cash from the start to the end of the budget period.

A budgeted statement of cash flows for Marcy's Surf Shop is presented as Exhibit 8–17.

Exhibit 8–17
Budgeted Statement
of Cash Flows for
Marcy's Surf Shop

MARCY'S SURF SHOP
Budgeted Statement of Cash Flows
For the Quarter Ended September 30, 2002

	July	August	September	Total
Cash Flows from				
Operating Activities:				
Net Income	($ 300)	$ 700	$ 196	$ 596
Add: Depreciation	100	100	104	304
Changes in CA & CL:				
Accounts Receivable	900	(1,950)	750	(300)
Inventory	(1,440)	480	(960)	(1,920)
Accounts Payable	(160)	480	240	560
Net Cash Flow from Op Act	($ 900)	($ 190)	330	($ 760)
Cash Flow From				
Investing Activities:				
Cash Paid for Showcase		(240)		(240)
Net Cash Flow from Inv Act		(240)		(240)
Cash Flow From				
Financing Activities:				
Borrowing	$ 630	$ 430		$1,060
Loan Payments			($ 330)	(330)
Net Cash Flow from Fin Act	$ 630	$ 430	($ 330)	$ 730
Increase/(Decrease) in Cash	($ 270)	$ -0-	$ 0	($ 270)
Budgeted Beginning Cash Balance	2,170	1,900	1,900	2,170
Budgeted Ending Cash Balance	$1,900	$1,900	$1,900	$1,900

We will not do a line-by-line analysis of the presentation in Exhibit 8–17 because we have explained all the items elsewhere in this chapter as we have constructed the other budgets. It is worthwhile, however, for us to discuss what this budget reveals in overall terms.

In the normal course of business, a company can obtain cash from only three sources: borrowing, owner contributions, and profitable operations. Ultimately, the only source of cash for any company, including Marcy's Surf Shop, is the profitable operation of the business. If a company does not generate enough cash from operations to run the business, it must seek outside financing (borrowing and owner contributions).

The budgeted statement of cash flows in Exhibit 8–17 reveals that for the three months covered by the budget, at least, Marcy's does not anticipate generating enough cash through operations to run the business and must, therefore, borrow the money. Three months is not a very long time, and all companies must obtain outside financing from time to time, but Marcy may not like what she sees when she looks at this budget. If she finds the prospects unacceptable, she may want to continue the budgeting process and make adjustments in how she plans to go about operating her business.

You will be delighted to know we are not going to do that for Marcy. We hope, however, that you have learned what a powerful tool the operating budget can be by going through the steps required to prepare one.

We have seen that the operating budget can serve as a guide for the company to follow, assist a company in allocating its scarce resources, and foster communication and coordination among managers from different functional areas within the company. It can also establish performance standards, or benchmarks, against which the company can compare the actual results. This fourth application presents some serious challenges to managers, however. Misunderstanding how to set and use performance standards can lead to behavior that is actually detrimental to the organization.

Once upon a time, in the United States at least, someone figured out that the operating budget could be used as a means of controlling a company's activities. It is really a pretty simple concept. Once the operating budget is established for the year, you keep one eye on the budget and one eye on the actual results. The idea is that if you prepare a solid budget and then perform to meet that budget, you will naturally keep control of your operation. Before long, this way of using the operating budget had become quite common among U.S. companies. As this practice became more popular, firms began evaluating the performance of their managers based on how they performed against the budget as well. This practice is known as the **performance to budget** evaluation. Salary increases, year-end bonuses, and promotions to senior management began to be dependent on a manager's ability to "meet or beat" the budget. By now, the operating budget had become the principal means used to control costs. It was felt that if managers performed well against the budget, they were doing a good job of controlling the operations they managed, which makes sense, right? Wrong! Unfortunately, that is not what happens when the budget is used as the primary control device in a company. What happens is that using the budget for this purpose actually encourages managers to make bad decisions and discourages them from making good decisions.

performance to budget
A process of evaluating managers and employees based on how they perform against the budget.

The Budget Performance Report

*If I get bigger pants,
does that mean I've lost weight?*

—Paul Valenzuela

As performance to budget became a popular way of measuring management performance, an instrument known as the **budget performance report** was developed to capture the information management thought was needed to perform the evaluation. A typical budget performance report has four columns as shown in Exhibit 8–18.

budget performance report
The evaluation instrument used to evaluate a manager's performance to budget.

Exhibit 8–18
Budget Performance Report

(a) Description	(b) Budget	(c) Actual	(d) Variance
Salaries and Wages	$25,000	$23,000	$2,000 F
Office Rent	10,000	10,000	-0-
Office Supplies	1,000	1,200	200 U

As you can see, the report is not terribly complicated. In the description column (a), the items for which the manager being evaluated is responsible are listed. In the budget column (b), the budgeted amount for each of those items is listed. In the actual column (c), the amount actually spent during the period covered by the

variance The difference between the amount budgeted and the actural amount

budget is listed. The difference between the amount bedgeted and the actual amount is called a **variance.** The variances in our example appear in column (d). The letter *F* indicates a favorable variance and the letter *U* indicates an unfavorable variance.

Discussion Question

8-22. What do the words *favorable* and *unfavorable* mean to you?

The major problem with the budget performance report is not the report itself but rather the way it is used. As an example, say that Brian Sedgwick is the sales manager at Pepperwood Furniture Company. Among other things, Brian is responsible for gas and oil expenditures for the fleet of delivery trucks his company owns. These trucks are used to deliver products to customers. Say further that Brian is responsible for establishing the budget for this item and he budgeted $50,000 for 2002. Now say that 2002 has ended and he spent $90,000 on gas and oil. Brian's budget performance report for this item would be as follows:

Description	Budget	Actual	Variance
Gas & Oil	$50,000	$90,000	$40,000 U

Now, what do you think might have caused this variance? Well, of the several possibilities, we will mention four.

1. Perhaps gas prices went through the roof. The budget was established based on what Brian *thought* gas and oil prices would be during the year. Maybe there was another gulf war in 2002 like there was in 1991. You may not remember but, during the Gulf War, gas prices went sky high.
2. Perhaps the budget Brian established was poorly done. Do not confuse this idea with the first possible explanation. In the first one, Brian did the best he could with the information he had—the information just turned out not to be reliable. This possibility comes from not taking the budgeting process seriously. Thus, for Brian, budgeting may mean filling out forms rather than being part of a real planning process.
3. Perhaps Brian was inefficient and wasted a lot of money. We would never want to forget this possibility. If he did waste money, he should be held accountable for his actions.
4. Perhaps business picked up significantly and the company had to make many more deliveries. This surely would have caused Brian to spend more money on gas and oil. Remember, the support costs in the budget are based on what is forecast to be sold.

Let us expand on the fourth possibility. Brian had an unfavorable variance caused by a good thing (greatly increased sales). This fact should help you understand that *unfavorable* in this context does not mean "bad," but rather "over budget."

Brian Sedgwick's performance evaluation will depend on his company's attitude about what performance to budget means. Unfortunately, in all too many companies in the United States today, the evaluation begins with the variance column. If there are unfavorable variances, regardless of cause, Brian's performance evaluation will not be good. He may not get his bonus, he may not get that raise he was anticipating, and he may not be promoted.

Before we talk about how to overcome the problem we just described, let us look at another example using the same essential facts. Brian budgeted $50,000 for gas and oil expenditures for 2002, but only spent $30,000. His budget performance report would be as follows:

Description	Budget	Actual	Variance
Gas & Oil	$50,000	$30,000	$20,000 F

We will not discuss what might have caused this variance, but with the exception of the poor budgeting possibility (which is the same in either case), the reasons are just the opposite of what caused the $40,000 unfavorable variance in our first example. If you think about the fourth possibility, then, this favorable variance could have been caused by a decline in the company's business. In other words, Brian has a favorable variance caused by a bad thing. That should help you understand that favorable in this context does not mean "good." It simply means "under budget."

What about Brian's performance evaluation? Once again, it depends greatly on how his company management views the performance to budget. In all too many companies, he would be rewarded in two ways. First, he would receive congratulations from everyone involved in the evaluation on what a great job he did of controlling gas and oil costs for the year. Second, his gas and oil budget for next year will be cut by $20,000. The reasoning is that if that's all he needed for this year, that's all he will need for next year, as well. This is called "use it or lose it" and is a practice that flourishes in many companies in the United States today.

If this is how Brian's company views the evaluation process, it is in his best interest to make sure he does not have actual expenditures that are too far under budget. If Brian is smart, he will make certain that his performance report on gas and oil costs looks something like the following:

Description	Budget	Actual	Variance
Gas & Oil	$50,000	$50,000	-0-

This item will probably not be examined in any great detail during Brian's performance review, because the usual practice is to concentrate on the variance column. If no variance exists, it is assumed that the amount spent on the item was what should have been spent. This interpretation indicates efficient management, which is what Paul Valenzuela meant in the quotation that opened this section. Buying bigger clothes makes it appear you have lost weight, when in fact you may not have lost any. The way this translates into the topic we are discussing is that if managers are able to secure a large budget for a particular item, they will appear to be efficient simply by spending less than, or exactly, the amount budgeted.

In many companies, then, the focus is only on items with large variances. Further, when these variances are investigated, the analysis usually focuses on the actual performance column of the performance report. If a large, unfavorable variance exists, managers are called on the carpet to explain why they spent more than the budget allowed. If a large, favorable variance exists, the item becomes a target for reducing costs next year, so the budget is cut.

What is bizarre about this method of using the budget performance report is that everybody knows budgets are established for the future. Everybody also knows that the future is to a great extent unknown to us. Yet, once the budget is established it becomes set in stone, so to speak, and any variance (favorable or unfavorable) between the budgeted cost and the actual cost is assumed to be because of the actual.

Are we suggesting that managers should be free to spend whatever amount they see fit on the cost items for which they are responsible? Absolutely not! This idea makes no sense, and it runs counter to everything we have said throughout this chapter, and indeed, throughout this book. Managers should be working every day to control costs and run their operations more efficiently. What we are saying is that this has very little to do with the operating budget. Cost control is an ongoing management process, of which the operating budget is only a part. Using the budget as the primary cost control device in a business is done in place of real control. Perhaps worse than that, using performance to budget as the evaluation instrument for managers encourages them to focus on the elimination of variances as their primary goal. As stated, because the budget is often considered to be set in stone, the only way to eliminate variances is to manipulate the actual performance to match the budget. This is what leads to silly budget games, such as the "use it or lose it" phenomenon we mentioned earlier.

If we lived in a perfect world where we could predict the future accurately, there would be no problem with the performance to budget evaluation technique. Unfortunately, we do not live in such a perfect world, and the future is largely unknown to us. When we prepare the operating budget we are attempting to predict the future. Differences are bound to exist between what we predict and what actually happens.

Earlier in the chapter we presented an exhibit that showed the interrelationship among all the budgets. We have reproduced that presentation as Exhibit 8–19.

Exhibit 8–19
Interrelationship among the Budgets

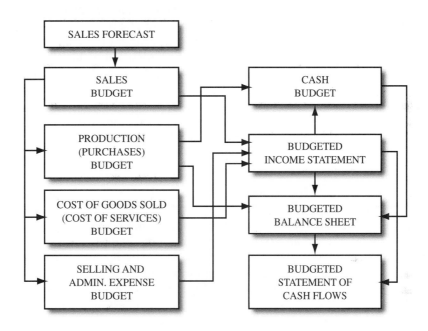

As discussed during this interrelationship topic earlier in the chapter, a change in any one of the budgets has a ripple effect throughout all the other budgets. A little logic tells us that if there are variances in any one of the budgets there will also be a ripple effect throughout all the other budgets.

Perhaps more important as a cause of variances than the interrelationship among the budgets is the role of the sales forecast in the budgeting process. Note in Exhibit 8–19 that all the budgets included in the operating budget are dependent upon the sales forecast, which explains why we described the sales forecast as both the cornerstone and the keystone of the operating budget in our earlier discussions.

The sales forecast is so critical in the budgeting process that we will end this section by sharing three truths with you about the sales forecast and the operating budget:

Truth 1: If the sales forecast is inaccurate, the operating budget will be inaccurate. Do not confuse *inaccurate* with *bad*. A bad sales forecast comes from lack of effort and attention. An inaccurate sales forecast comes about when the actual results are different from the operating budget because the future did not turn out the way company management predicted.

Truth 2: The sales forecast will be inaccurate. Recall the items we discussed earlier in the chapter that affect a company's ability to forecast sales. The state of the general economy, actions of competitors, technological developments, and many other factors make an accurate sales forecast literally impossible.

Truth 3: The operating budget will be inaccurate. Once again, do not confuse inaccurate with bad. Inaccurate simply means that the actual results are going to be different from what was budgeted, meaning, of course, that variances will always exist.

Some approaches to the budget performance report help overcome the variances caused by actual sales being different from budgeted sales. The most popular of these is the flexible budget performance report, which is covered in more advanced accounting courses. Note, however, that it does not eliminate the problem of using the budget in a way that was never intended, that is, as the primary control device in a business.

So, how do managers overcome the problems we have been discussing in this section? Well, they do it by using the budget as it was intended to be used—as a guide for the business. Just as prudent travelers would not hesitate to alter their plans during a trip as updated information becomes available, businesses should not hesitate to adjust their budgets when desirable or necessary. Further, when the period covered by the operating budget is over, an analysis should be performed to compare the actual results to the budget. The focus of this analysis, however, should be on how to improve the budgeting process rather than on the inevitable variances that have occurred.

SUMMARY

The operating budget is an integral part of the overall planning process for any company. Besides serving as a guide for the business throughout the period covered by the budget, the operating budget can assist management in the allocation of resources, foster communication and coordination among various segments of the company, and establish performance standards.

The operating budget is a set of estimated financial statements. These are the budgeted income statement, the budgeted balance sheet, and the budgeted statement of cash flows. Besides the budgeted financial statements, the operating budget includes several other budgets prepared to support the budgeted financial statements. These are the sales budget, the production (or purchases) budget, the cost of goods sold (or cost of services) budget, the selling and administrative expense budget, and the cash budget (including the cash receipts schedule and the cash payments schedule).

There are several different approaches to the preparation of the operating budget. Perpetual, incremental, zero-based, top-down, bottom-up, imposed, and participative approaches to budgeting are just some that have developed over time. Each approach has certain advantages and certain disadvantages relative to the other approaches.

All the budgets included in the operating budget are dependent on the sales forecast. Indeed, the accuracy of the entire budget is dependent on the accuracy of the forecast. Many factors, including the state of the general economy, the condition of the company's industry, the actions of competitors, and technological developments all influence a company's ability to forecast its sales reasonably.

The operating budget was never meant to be used as the principal cost control device in business. Using the budget for this purpose actually encourages managers to make decisions that are detrimental to the business. If used properly, however, as a guide and coordination instrument, the operating budget can be of tremendous benefit for any company.

KEY TERMS

bottom-up budgeting   M-276
budget performance report   M-298
budgeted balance sheet   M-271
budgeted income statement   M-271
budgeted statement of cash flows   M-272
cash budget   M-271
cash payments schedule   M-290
cash receipts schedule   M-288
continual budgeting   M-274
cost of goods sold budget   M-271
cost of services budget   M-271
imposed budget   M-276
incremental budgeting   M-275
master budget   M-266

master operating budget   M-266
operating budget   M-266
participative budget   M-277
performance to budget   M-298
perpetual budgeting   M-274
production budget   M-270
purchases budget   M-270
sales budget   M-270
sales forecast   M-279
selling and administrative
   expense budget   M-271
top-down budgeting   M-276
variance   M-299
zero-based budgeting   M-275

REVIEW THE FACTS

A. What is the operating budget?
B. What is the master budget?
C. Which financial statements are part of the operating budget?
D. What is the difference between the financial statements included in the operating budget and other financial statements you have learned about in this course?
E. List the main benefits of budgeting.
F. What is the basic difference between the production budget and the purchases budget?
G. What are two advantages of perpetual budgeting?
H. What is a disadvantage of perpetual budgeting?
I. What is incremental budgeting?
J. What problem is associated with incremental budgeting?
K. What is zero-based budgeting?
L. Describe the differences between top-down and bottom-up budgeting.
M. Describe the differences between an imposed budget and a participative budget.
N. Why is the sales forecast often called the cornerstone of budgeting?
O. Why is the sales forecast often called the keystone of budgeting?
P. List three factors that should be considered when preparing the sales forecast.
Q. Why does the number of units budgeted to be purchased differ from the number of units budgeted to be sold?
R. When preparing the purchases budget, what two factors should be considered when determining the budgeted ending inventory?
S. What is presented on the cash receipts schedule?

T. For a particular budget period, why doesn't the budgeted cash collections from customers equal budgeted sales?

U. What is the basic difference between a budgeted balance sheet and an historical balance sheet?

V. In the normal course of business, what are the three sources from which a company can obtain cash?

W. What is a *performance to budget* evaluation?

APPLY WHAT YOU HAVE LEARNED

LO 3 & 4:   Determine Order of Operating Budget Preparation

8–23. During the budgeting process, not all budgets are prepared at the same time. Following are several operating budgets.

    1. _____ Cash budget
    2. _____ Budgeted financial statements
    3. _____ Purchases budget
    4. _____ Sales budget
    5. _____ Administrative expense budget
    6. _____ Selling expense budget

REQUIRED:
Indicate a logical sequence for the preparation of the master budget.

LO 3:   Indicate Advantages and Disadvantages of Top-Down, Bottom-Up Approaches

8–24. The master budget can be prepared using either the top-down or bottom-up approach. Following in random order are several advantages and disadvantages of each approach.

Top-down Bottom-up	Advantage Disadvantage	
1. _____	_____	Budgeting process forces managers at various levels to think about future activities.
2. _____	_____	Top manager is more knowledgeable.
3. _____	_____	Employees at various levels must take time from their schedules to work on the budget.
4. _____	_____	Employees will be more eager to work toward goals they helped set.
5. _____	_____	Employees feel more like part of the company team.
6. _____	_____	Top manager is more aware of company goals.
7. _____	_____	Employees may try to pad the budget.
8. _____	_____	Employees are less accepting of budgeted goals if they had no part in setting them.
9. _____	_____	Top manager lacks detailed knowledge required to prepare budgets.

REQUIRED:
For each of these items, indicate whether it is associated with top-down (T) or bottom-up (B), and whether it is an advantage (A) or disadvantage (D).

LO 3: Indicate Budgeting Approaches

8–25. Following are approaches to budgeting, with a partial definition of those items in scrambled order.

a. Perpetual budgeting
b. Incremental budgeting
c. Zero-based budgeting
d. Top-down budgeting
e. Bottom-up budgeting

1. _____ Lower-level managers and employees initially prepare the budget.
2. _____ Each item on the budget must be justified each year.
3. _____ The budget is updated every month.
4. _____ Lower-level managers generally do not participate in budget preparation.
5. _____ Uses the prior year's budget to build the new budget.

REQUIRED:
For each partial definition, identify the budgeting approach to which it refers.

LO 5: Prepare a Sales Budget

8–26. For 2003, David's Computer Game Company expects to sell 6,000 games in the first quarter, 7,000 games in the second quarter, 9,000 games in the third quarter, and 12,000 games in the fourth quarter. Each game sells for $11.

REQUIRED:
Prepare the 2003 sales budget for David's Computer Game Company.

LO 5: Prepare a Sales Budget

8–27. For 2003, Paul Elsea's Barber Supply Company expects to sell 100 hair dryers in the first quarter, 90 hair dryers in the second quarter, 130 hair dryers in the third quarter, and 150 hair dryers in the fourth quarter. Each hair dryer sells for $67.

REQUIRED:
Prepare the 2003 sales budget for hair dryers for Paul Elsea's Barber Supply Company.

LO 5: Prepare a Sales Budget

8–28. For 2003, Taub Yo Yo Company expects to sell 20,000 units in January, 25,000 units in February, and 30,000 units in March. Each unit sells for $1.20.

REQUIRED:
Prepare the sales budget for Taub Yo Yo Company for the first quarter of 2003.

LO 5: Prepare a Sales Budget

8–29. The Golden Bird Cage Company intends to sell 11,500 bird cages during 2003. The budgeted selling price per cage is $88. The following sales forecast is available:

	Units
First quarter	2,500
Second quarter	2,100
Third quarter	3,800
Fourth quarter	3,100

REQUIRED:

Prepare the 2003 sales budget for Golden Bird Cage Company.

LO 5: Prepare a Sales Budget

8–30. Easy-Glide Strollers intends to sell 73,000 baby strollers in the first quarter of 2000. The budgeted selling price per stroller is $59. The following sales forecast is available:

	Units
January	22,500
February	22,500
March	28,000

REQUIRED:

Prepare the sales budget for Easy-Glide Strollers for the first quarter of 2000.

LO 5: Prepare a Purchases Budget

8–31. Florence Marie's Hat Shop plans to sell the following quantity of hats during the first four months of 2003.

	Units
January	200
February	250
March	300
April	320

Florence pays $6 for each hat which she sells for $15.

At the beginning of January, Florence plans to have 40 hats on hand, and hopes to maintain an ending inventory equal to 20% of next month's sales.

REQUIRED:

Prepare a purchases budget for the first quarter of 2003 for Florence Marie's Hat Shop. Remember, the first quarter is January, February, and March. April sales are only provided to help compute the ending inventory for March.

LO 5: Prepare a Sales Budget and Cost of Goods Sold Budget

8–32. Refer to the information in problem 8–31.

REQUIRED:

a. Prepare a sales budget for the first quarter of 2003 for Florence Marie's Hat Shop.

b. Prepare a cost of goods sold budget for the first quarter of 2003 for Florence Marie's Hat Shop.

LO 5: Prepare a Purchases Budget

8–33. Anahi's Art Supplies plans to sell the following quantity of model AB222 airbrush during the first four months of 2000.

	Units
January	400
February	26
March	22
April	20

Anahi's pays $44 for each airbrush and sells them for $65.

At the beginning of January, Anahi's Art Supplies plans to have six airbrushes on hand, and hopes to maintain an ending inventory equal to 15% of next month's sales.

REQUIRED:
Prepare a purchases budget for the first quarter of 2000 for Anahi's Art Supplies. Remember, the first quarter is January, February, and March. April sales are only provided to help compute the ending inventory for March.

LO 5: Prepare a Sales Budget and Cost of Goods Sold Budget

8–34. Refer to the information in problem 8–33.

REQUIRED:
a. Prepare a sales budget for the first quarter of 2000 for Anahi's Art Supplies.
b. Prepare a cost of goods sold budget for the first quarter of 2000 for Anahi's Art Supplies.

LO 5: Prepare a Sales Budget, Cost of Goods Sold Budget, and Purchases Budget

8–35. Diaz Lumber plans to sell the following quantity of BC Grade 1/2-inch plywood during the first four months of 2000.

January	220 sheets
February	250 sheets
March	200 sheets
April	300 sheets

Diaz pays $7 for each sheet of plywood and sells them for $12.

At the beginning of January, Diaz plans to have 66 sheets of plywood on hand, and hopes to maintain an ending inventory equal to 30% of next month's sales.

REQUIRED:
a. Prepare a sales budget for the first quarter of 2000 for Diaz Lumber.
b. Prepare a cost of goods sold budget for the first quarter of 2000 for Diaz Lumber.
c. Prepare a purchases budget for the first quarter of 2000 for Diaz Lumber.

LO 5: Prepare a Budgeted Income Statement Using Information Provided in Other Budgets

8–36. Smith Manufacturing has prepared the following budgeted information for January 2000.

SMITH MANUFACTURING
Sales Budget
For January 31, 2000

Budgeted Sales in Units	3,300
× Budgeted Sales Price	$ 200
= Budgeted Sales Dollars	$660,000

SMITH MANUFACTURING
Cost of Goods Sold Budget
For January 31, 2000

Budgeted Sales in Units		3,300
× Budgeted Cost Per Unit		$ 110
= Budgeted COGS		$363,000

SMITH MANUFACTURING
Selling and Administrative Expense Budget
For January 31, 2000

Salaries and Wages	$101,500
Rent	64,000
Depreciation	53,200
Other	2,300
Budgeted S & A Expense	$221,000

REQUIRED:

Prepare a budgeted income statement for January 2000 for Smith Manufacturing.

LO 5:   Prepare a Budgeted Income Statement Using Information Provided in Other Budgets

8–37. Gomez Sales Company has prepared the following budgeted information for March 2000.

GOMEZ SALES COMPANY
Sales Budget
For March 31, 2000

Budgeted Sales in Units		110,000
× Budgeted Sales Price		$ 4.95
= Budgeted Sales Dollars		$544,500

GOMEZ SALES COMPANY
Cost of Goods Sold Budget
For March 31, 2000

Budgeted Sales in Units		110,000
× Budgeted Cost Per Unit		$ 3.35
= Budgeted COGS		$368,500

GOMEZ SALES COMPANY
Selling and Administrative Expense Budget
For March 31, 2000

Sales Salaries	$ 51,500
Sales Commission	11,000
Other Salaries and Wages	35,000
Store Rent	24,000
Other Expenses	10,500
Budgeted S & A Expense	132,000

REQUIRED:

Prepare a budgeted income statement for March 2000 for Gomez Sales Company.

LO 5: Prepare a Budgeted Income Statement Using Information Provided in Other Budgets

8–38. Copas Company has prepared the following budgeted information for December 2000.

COPAS COMPANY
Sales Budget
For December 31, 2000

Budgeted Sales in Units		10,000
× Budgeted Sales Price		$ 1,200
= Budgeted Sales Dollars		$120,000

COPAS COMPANY
Cost of Goods Sold Budget
For December 31, 2000

Budgeted Sales in Units		10,000
× Budgeted Cost Per Unit		$ 800
= Budgeted COGS		$80,000

COPAS COMPANY
Selling and Administrative Expense Budget
For December 31, 2000

Sales Salaries	$18,500
Sales Commission	3,000
Store Rent	9,000
Other Expenses	1,500
Budgeted S & A Expense	32,000

REQUIRED:
Prepare a budgeted income statement for December 2000 for Copas Company.

LO 5: Prepare a Budgeted Income Statement

8–39. For the first quarter of 2000, Philip's Sales Corporation has budgeted sales of $390,000 and budgeted cost of goods sold of $280,000. In addition, the budget for the first quarter of 2000 includes wages and salaries of $42,000, rent of $9,000, utilities of $2,000, maintenance of $1,000, and other expenses of $3,000.

REQUIRED:
Prepare a budgeted income statement for the first quarter of 2000 for Philip's Sales Corporation.

LO 5: Prepare a Budgeted Income Statement

8–40. For January 2000, Edwardo Manufacturing has budgeted sales of $1,200,000 and budgeted cost of goods sold of $980,000. In addition, the budget for January 2000 includes sales salaries of $98,000, administrative salaries of $54,000, rent of $24,000, utilities of $8,000, and other expenses of $9,000.

REQUIRED:
Prepare a budgeted income statement for January 2000 for Edwardo Manufacturing.

LO 5: Prepare a Budgeted Income Statement

8–41. For the year 2000, Martin Sales Corporation has budgeted sales of $3,500,000 and budgeted cost of goods sold of $2,800,000. In addition, the budget for 2000 includes sales salaries of $220,000, administrative salaries of $130,000, depreciation of $180,000, utilities of $38,000, and other expenses of $22,000.

REQUIRED:

Prepare a budgeted income statement for 2000 for Martin Sales Corporation.

LO 5: Prepare a Budgeted Income Statement for One Quarter

8–42. The following budgets were prepared for Gary's Jean Store.

GARY'S JEAN STORE
Sales Budget
For the Quarter Ended June 30, 2003

	Apr	May	Jun	Total
Budgeted Sales in Units	300	350	400	1,050
× Budgeted Sales Price	$ 27	$ 27	$ 27	$ 27
= Budgeted Sales Dollars	$8,100	$9,450	$10,800	$28,350

GARY'S JEAN STORE
Cost of Goods Sold Budget
For the Quarter Ended June 30, 2003

	Apr	May	Jun	Total
Budgeted Sales in Units	300	350	400	1,050
× Budgeted Cost Per Unit	$ 14	$ 14	$ 14	$ 14
= Budgeted Cost of Goods Sold	$4,200	$ 4,900	$5,600	$14,700

GARY'S JEAN STORE
Selling and Administrative Expense Budget
For the Quarter Ended June 30, 2003

	Apr	May	Jun	Total
Salaries and Wages	$1,800	$2,200	$1,900	$ 5,900
Rent	500	500	500	1,500
Depreciation	100	100	100	300
Other	600	900	800	2,300
Budgeted Sales Dollars	$3,000	$3,700	$3,300	$10,000

REQUIRED:

Prepare a budgeted income statement for the second quarter of 2003 for Gary's Jean Store.

LO 5: Prepare a Budgeted Income Statement for One Quarter

8–43. Franco's Cart Company manufactures small carts that are designed to be pulled behind a small tractor or riding lawn mower. The following budgets were prepared for Franco's Cart Company.

FRANCO'S CART COMPANY
Sales Budget
For the Quarter Ended March 31, 2003

	Jan	Feb	Mar	Total
Budgeted Sales in Units	1,300	1,450	1,700	4,450
× Budgeted Sales Price	$ 186	$ 186	$ 186	$ 186
= Budgeted Sales Dollars	$241,800	$269,700	$316,200	$827,700

FRANCO'S CART COMPANY
Cost of Goods Sold Budget
For the Quarter Ended March 31, 2003

	Jan	Feb	Mar	Total
Budgeted Sales in Units	1,300	1,450	1,700	4,450
× Budgeted Cost Per Unit	$ 154	$ 154	$ 154	$ 154
= Budgeted COGS	$200,200	$223,300	$261,800	$685,300

FRANCO'S CART COMPANY
Selling and Administrative Expense Budget
For the Quarter Ended March 31, 2003

	Jan	Feb	Mar	Total
Salaries and Wages	$21,950	$22,200	$23,600	$67,750
Rent	4,000	4,500	4,500	13,000
Depreciation	3,200	3,200	3,200	9,600
Other	2,300	2,500	2,800	7,600
Budgeted S & A Expense	$31,450	$32,400	$34,100	$97,950

REQUIRED:

Prepare a budgeted income statement for the first quarter of 2003 for Franco's Cart Company.

LO 5: Prepare a Budgeted Income Statement for One Quarter

8–44. The following budgets were prepared for Byrne Manufacturing.

BYRNE MANUFACTURING
Sales Budget
For the Quarter Ended September 30, 2000

	Jul	Aug	Sep	Total
Budgeted Unit Sales	900	1,100	1,300	3,300
× Budgeted Sales Price	$ 225	$ 225	$ 225	$ 225
= Budgeted Sales Dollars	$202,500	$247,500	$292,500	$742,500

BYRNE MANUFACTURING
Cost of Goods Sold Budget
For the Quarter Ended September 30, 2000

	Jul	Aug	Sep	Total
Budgeted Unit Sales	900	1,100	1,300	3,300
× Budgeted Cost Per Unit	$ 204	$ 204	$ 204	$ 204
= Budgeted COGS	$183,600	$224,400	$265,200	$673,200

BYRNE MANUFACTURING
Selling and Administrative Expense Budget
For the Quarter Ended September 30, 2000

	Jul	Aug	Sep	Total
Salaries and Wages	$ 4,800	$ 5,200	$ 5,800	$15,800
Rent	2,400	2,400	2,400	7,200
Depreciation	1,150	1,150	1,150	3,450
Other	1,800	2,000	2,200	6,000
Budgeted S & A Expense	$10,150	$10,750	$11,550	$32,450

REQUIRED:

Prepare a budgeted income statement for the third quarter of 2000 for Byrne Manufacturing.

LO 5:   Prepare a Cash Receipts Schedule for One Quarter

8–45. The Deacon Company is preparing a cash receipts schedule for the first quarter of 2003. Sales for November and December of 2002 are expected to be $180,000 and $200,000, respectively. Budgeted sales for the first quarter of 2003 are presented here.

THE DEACON COMPANY
Sales Budget
For the Quarter Ended March 31, 2003

	Jan	Feb	Mar	Total
Budgeted Sales	$220,000	$240,000	$260,000	$720,000

Twenty percent of sales are for cash, the remaining 80% are on account. Ten percent of the sales on account are collected in the month of the sale, 60% in the month following the sale, and the remaining 30% in the second month following the sale. There are no uncollectible accounts receivable.

REQUIRED:

Prepare a cash receipts schedule for the first quarter of 2003.

LO 5:   Prepare a Cash Receipts Schedule for One Quarter

8–46. The V & A Velez Company is preparing a cash receipts schedule for the first quarter of 2003. Sales for November and December of 2002 are expected to be $300,000 and $310,000, respectively. Budgeted sales for the first quarter of 2003 are presented here.

THE V & A VELEZ COMPANY
Sales Budget
For the Quarter Ended March 31, 2003

	Jan	Feb	Mar	Total
Budgeted Sales	$220,000	$290,000	$340,000	$850,000

Ten percent of sales are for cash, the remaining 90% are on account. Twenty percent of the sales on account are collected in the month of the sale, 70% in the month following the sale, and the remaining 10% in the second month following the sale. There are no uncollectible accounts receivable.

REQUIRED:
Prepare a cash receipts schedule for the first quarter of 2003.

LO 5: Prepare a Cash Receipts Schedule for One Quarter

8–47. The Arauz Company is preparing a cash receipts schedule for the first quarter of 2000. Sales for November and December of 1999 are expected to be $30,000 and $50,000, respectively. Budgeted sales for the first quarter of 2000 are presented here.

THE ARAUZ COMPANY
Sales Budget
For the Quarter Ended March 31, 2000

	Jan	Feb	Mar	Total
Budgeted Sales	$20,000	$25,000	$40,000	$85,000

Fifteen percent of sales are for cash, the remaining 85% are on account. Twenty percent of the sales on account are collected in the month of the sale, 50% in the month following the sale, and the remaining 30% in the second month following the sale. There are no uncollectible accounts receivable.

REQUIRED:
Prepare a cash receipts schedule for the first quarter of 2000.

LO 5: Prepare a Cash Receipts Schedule for One Quarter

8–48. The Phillips Company is preparing a cash receipts schedule for the first quarter of 2000. Sales for November and December of 1999 are expected to be $33,000 and $55,000, respectively. Budgeted sales for the first quarter of 2000 are presented here.

THE PHILLIPS COMPANY
Sales Budget
For the Quarter Ended March 31, 2000

	Jan	Feb	Mar	Total
Budgeted Sales	$20,000	$30,000	$45,000	$95,000

Fifteen percent of sales are for cash, the remaining 85% are on account. Twenty percent of the sales on account are collected in the month of the sale, 50% in the month following the sale, 30% in the second month following the sale. There are no uncollectible accounts receivable.

REQUIRED:
Prepare a cash receipts schedule for the first quarter of 2000.

LO 5: Prepare a Cash Receipts Schedule for One Quarter

8–49. The Aimin Company is preparing a cash receipts schedule for the first quarter of 2000. Sales for November and December of 1999 are expected to be $40,000 and $80,000, respectively. Budgeted sales for the first quarter of 2000 are presented here.

THE AIMIN COMPANY
Sales Budget
For the Quarter Ended March 31, 2000

	Jan	Feb	Mar	Total
Budgeted Sales	$30,000	$40,000	$50,000	$120,000

Ten percent of sales are for cash, the remaining 90% are on account. Fifteen percent of the sales on account are collected in the month of the sale, 60% in the month following the sale, 25% in the second month following the sale. There are no uncollectible accounts receivable.

REQUIRED:
Prepare a cash receipts schedule for the first quarter of 2000.

LO 5: Prepare a Cash Receipts Schedule for One Quarter

8–50. The Gabriel Diaz Company is preparing a cash receipts schedule for the first quarter of 2003. Sales on account for November and December of 2002 are expected to be $500,000 and $750,000, respectively. Budgeted sales for the first quarter of 2003 are presented here.

THE GABRIEL DIAZ COMPANY
Sales Budget
For the Quarter Ended March 31, 2003

	Jan	Feb	Mar	Total
Budgeted Cash Sales	$ 40,000	$ 45,000	$ 55,000	$ 140,000
Budgeted Sales on Account	$400,000	$450,000	$550,000	$1,400,000
Total Sales	$440,000	$495,000	$605,000	$1,540,000

Expected collection pattern for sales on account:
　15% in the month of sale
　60% in the month following the sale
　25% in the second month following the sale
　0% uncollectible

REQUIRED:
Prepare a cash receipts schedule for the first quarter of 2003.

LO 5: Prepare a Cash Receipts Schedule for One Quarter

8–51. The Lila Steinman Company is preparing a cash receipts schedule for the first quarter of 2000. Sales on account for November and December of 1999 are expected to be $200,000 and $400,000, respectively. Budgeted sales for the first quarter of 2000 are presented here.

The Lila Steinman Company
Sales Budget
For the Quarter Ended March 31, 2000

	Jan	Feb	Mar	Total
Budgeted Cash Sales	$ 20,000	$ 25,000	$ 27,000	$ 72,000
Budgeted Sales on Account	$180,000	$210,000	$250,000	$640,000
Total Sales	$200,000	$235,000	$277,000	$712,000

Expected collection pattern for sales on account:
- 10% in the month of sale
- 70% in the month following the sale
- 20% in the second month following the sale
- 0% uncollectible

REQUIRED:

Prepare a cash receipts schedule for the first quarter of 2000.

LO 5:   Prepare a Cash Receipts Schedule for One Quarter

8–52. The Lowensohn Company is preparing a cash receipts schedule for the first quarter of 2000. Sales on account for November and December of 1999 are expected to be $320,000 and $550,000, respectively. Budgeted sales for the first quarter of 2000 are presented here.

THE LOWENSOHN COMPANY
Sales Budget
For the Quarter Ended March 31, 2000

	Jan	Feb	Mar	Total
Budgeted Cash Sales	$120,000	$150,000	$125,000	$395,000
Budgeted Sales on				
Account	$180,000	$225,000	$190,000	$595,000
Total Sales	$300,000	$375,000	$315,000	$990,000

Expected collection pattern for sales on account:
- 30% in the month of sale
- 50% in the month following the sale
- 20% in the second month following the sale
- 0% uncollectible

REQUIRED:

Prepare a cash receipts schedule for the first quarter of 2000.

LO 5:   Prepare a Cash Receipts Schedule for One Quarter

8–53. The S.R. Jackson Company is preparing a cash receipts schedule for the second quarter of 2003. Sales on account for February and March of 2003 are expected to be $50,000 and $60,000, respectively. Budgeted sales for the second quarter of 2003 are presented here.

THE S.R. JACKSON COMPANY
Sales Budget
For the Quarter Ended June 30, 2003

	Apr	May	Jun	Total
Budgeted Cash Sales	$15,000	$20,000	$25,000	$ 60,000
Budgeted Sales on				
Account	$30,000	$40,000	$50,000	$120,000
Total Sales	$45,000	$60,000	$75,000	$180,000

Expected collection pattern for sales on account:
25% in the month of sale
50% in the month following the sale
25% in the second month following the sale
0% uncollectible

REQUIRED:

Prepare a cash receipts schedule for the second quarter of 2003.

LO 5: Prepare a Cash Receipts Schedule for One Quarter

8–54. The Hodson Company is preparing a cash receipts schedule for the third quarter of 2003. Sales on account for May and June of 2003 are expected to be $100,000 and $120,000, respectively. Budgeted sales for the third quarter of 2003 are presented here.

THE HODSON COMPANY
Sales Budget
For the Quarter Ended September 30, 2003

	Jul	Aug	Sep	Total
Budgeted Cash Sales	$ 8,000	$ 9,000	$ 11,000	$ 28,000
Budgeted Sales on Account	$80,000	$90,000	$110,000	$280,000
Total Sales	$88,000	$99,000	$121,000	$308,000

Expected collection pattern for sales on account:
    10% in the month of sale
    60% in the month following the sale
    30% in the second month following the sale
    0% uncollectible

REQUIRED:

Prepare a cash receipts schedule for the third quarter of 2003.

LO 5: Prepare a Cash Receipts Schedule for One Quarter

8–55. The A.R. Oddo Company is preparing a cash receipts schedule for the fourth quarter of 2003. Sales on account for August and September of 2003 are expected to be $200,000 and $220,000, respectively. Budgeted sales for the fourth quarter of 2003 are presented here.

THE A.R. ODDO COMPANY
Sales Budget
For the Quarter Ended December 31, 2003

	Oct	Nov	Dec	Total
Budgeted Cash Sales	$ 42,000	$ 46,000	$ 60,000	$148,000
Budgeted Sales on Account	$210,000	$230,000	$300,000	$740,000
Total Sales	$252,000	$276,000	$360,000	$888,000

Expected collection pattern for sales on account:
    20% in the month of sale
    70% in the month following the sale
    10% in the second month following the sale
    0% uncollectible

REQUIRED:

Prepare a cash receipts schedule for the fourth quarter of 2003.

LO 5 Prepare a Cash Receipts Schedule for One Quarter

8–56. The law firm of Hendricks & Hendricks is preparing a cash receipts schedule for the first quarter of 2003. Service revenue for November and

December of 2002 are expected to be $90,000 and $50,000, respectively. All billings are on account. There are no "cash sales." Budgeted service revenue for the first quarter of 2003 is presented here.

HENDRICKS & HENDRICKS
Service Revenue Budget
For the Quarter Ended March 31, 2003

	Jan	Feb	Mar	Total
Budgeted Service Revenue	$40,000	$50,000	$65,000	$155,000

Expected collection pattern:
  30% in the month of sale
  60% in the month following the sale
  10% in the second month following the sale
  0% uncollectible

REQUIRED:
Prepare a cash receipts schedule for the first quarter of 2003.

LO 5: Prepare a Cash Receipts Schedule for One Quarter

8–57. The medical practice of Healit & Quick is preparing a cash receipts schedule for the first quarter of 2000. Service revenue for November and December of 1999 are expected to be $120,000 and $110,000, respectively. All billings are on account. There are no "cash sales." Budgeted service revenue for the first quarter of 2000 is presented here.

HEALIT & QUICK
Service Revenue Budget
For the Quarter Ended March 31, 2000

	Jan	Feb	Mar	Total
Budgeted Service Revenue	$120,000	$130,000	$140,000	$155,000

Expected collection pattern:
  20% in the month of sale
  60% in the month following the sale
  20% in the second month following the sale
  0% uncollectible

REQUIRED:
Prepare a cash receipts schedule for the first quarter of 2000.

LO 5: Prepare a Cash Payments Schedule for One Quarter

8–58. Marcy Steinmann and Company has prepared the following budgets for the first quarter of 2000.

MARCY STEINMANN AND COMPANY
Selling and Administrative Expense Budget
For the Quarter Ended March 31, 2000

	Jan	Feb	Mar	Total
Salaries and Wages	$1,700	$2,200	$1,900	$ 5,800
Rent	300	300	300	900
Depreciation	200	200	200	600
Other	900	1,200	1,000	3,100
Total	$3,100	$3,900	$3,400	$10,400

MARCY STEINMANN AND COMPANY
Purchases Budget
For the Quarter Ended March 31, 2000

	Jan	Feb	Mar	Total
Forecasted Unit Sales	50	60	70	180
+ Desired Ending Inventory	12	14	16	16
= Total Units Needed	62	74	86	196
− Beginning Inventory	(10)	(12)	(14)	(10)
= Units to Be Purchased	52	62	72	186
× Cost Per Unit	$ 220	$ 220	$ 220	$ 220
= Cost of Purchases	$11,440	$13,640	$15,840	$40,920

Selling and administrative expenses are paid in the month incurred and purchases are paid in the month following the purchase. Purchases for December 1999 are $10,500. No equipment purchases or additional expenditures are made during the quarter.

REQUIRED:
Prepare a cash payment schedule for the first quarter of 2000.

LO 5: Prepare a Cash Payments Schedule for One Quarter

8–59. Jackson Sales Company has prepared the following budgets for the second quarter of 2000.

JACKSON SALES COMPANY
Selling and Administrative Expense Budget
For the Quarter Ended June 30, 2000

	Apr	May	Jun	Total
Salaries	$1,000	$1,200	$1,300	$3,500
Rent	200	200	200	600
Utilities	120	180	220	520
Depreciation	80	80	80	240
Other	500	600	650	1,750
Total	$1,900	$2,260	$2,450	$6,610

JACKSON SALES COMPANY
Purchases Budget
For the Quarter Ended June 30, 2000

	Apr	May	Jun	Total
Forecasted Unit Sales	70	80	90	240
+ Desired Ending Inventory	16	18	19	19
= Total Units Needed	86	98	109	259
− Beginning Inventory	(15)	(16)	(18)	(15)
= Units to Be Purchased	71	82	91	244
× Cost Per Unit	$ 100	$ 100	$ 100	$ 100
= Cost of Purchases	$ 7,100	$ 8,200	$ 9,100	$24,400

Selling and administrative expenses are paid in the month incurred and purchases are paid in the month following the purchase. Purchases for March 2000 are $6,800. No equipment purchases or additional expenditures are made during the quarter.

REQUIRED:
Prepare a cash payment schedule for the second quarter of 2000.

LO 5: Prepare a Cash Payments Schedule for One Month

8–60. The following budgeted information is available for the Top Coat Clothing Company for January 2000.

Salaries	$120,000
Rent	9,000
Utilities	1,200
Depreciation	3,200
Others Expenses	1,500
Purchases	380,000

Selling and administrative expenses are paid in the month incurred and purchases are paid in the month following the purchase. Purchases for December 1999 are $350,000. No equipment purchases or additional expenditures are made during the month.

REQUIRED:

Prepare a cash payment schedule for January 2000.

LO 5: Prepare a Cash Payments Schedule for One Month

8–61. The following budgeted information is available for Jack's Feed Store in June 2000.

Salaries	$12,000
Rent	600
Electricity	140
Depreciation	800
Others Expenses	700
Purchases	80,000

Selling and administrative expenses are paid in the month incurred and purchases are paid in the month following the purchase. Purchases for May 2000 are $75,000. No equipment purchases or additional expenditures are made during the month.

REQUIRED:

Prepare a cash payment schedule for June 2000.

LO 5: Prepare a Cash Budget for One Quarter

8–62. The following information is available for the Art Kriner Company for the first quarter of 2000.

	Jan	Feb	Mar
Budgeted Receipts from Credit Sales	$5,000	$5,500	$5,800
Budgeted Cash Sales	1,200	1,250	1.300
Budgeted Cash Payments	6,300	7,185	6,520

Beginning cash balance for January 2000 is expected to be $1,500. The company intends to maintain a cash balance of at least $1,000. The company has made arrangements to borrow from a local bank if necessary.

REQUIRED:

Prepare a cash budget for the first quarter of 2000.

LO 5: Prepare a Cash Budget for One Quarter

8–63. The following information is available for the Dixon Company for the second quarter of 2000.

	Apr	May	Jun
Budgeted Receipts from Credit Sales	$500,000	$520,000	$550,000
Budgeted Cash Sales	100,000	105,000	112,000
Budgeted Cash Payments	670,000	615,000	627,000

Beginning cash balance for April 2000 is expected to be $90,000. The company intends to maintain a cash balance of at least $50,000. The company has made arrangements to borrow from a local bank if necessary.

REQUIRED:
Prepare a cash budget for the second quarter of 2000.

LO 5: Prepare a Cash Budget for One Quarter

8–64. The following information is available for the Ortega Company for the first quarter of 2000.

	Jan	Feb	Mar
Budgeted Receipts from Credit Sales	$100,000	$110,000	$115,000
Budgeted Cash Sales	80,000	95,000	98,000
Budgeted Cash Payments	178,000	215,000	206,000

Beginning cash balance for January 2000 is expected to be $20,000. The company intends to maintain a cash balance of at least $15,000. The company has made arrangements to borrow from a local bank if necessary.

REQUIRED:
Prepare a cash budget for the first quarter of 2000.

LO 5: Prepare a Cash Budget for One Month

8–65. The following information is available for November 2000.

Budgeted Receipts from Credit Sales	$25,100
Budgeted Cash Sales	5,900
Budgeted Cash Payments	32,600

Beginning cash balance for November is expected to be $5,800. The company intends to maintain a cash balance of at least $5,000. The company has made arrangements to borrow from a local bank if necessary.

REQUIRED:
Prepare a cash budget for November 2000.

LO 5: Prepare a Cash Budget for One Month

8–66. The following information is available for October 2000.

Budgeted Receipts from Credit Sales	$300,000
Budgeted Cash Sales	80,000
Budgeted Cash Payments	410,000

Beginning cash balance for October is expected to be $60,000. The company intends to maintain a cash balance of at least $50,000. The company has made arrangements to borrow from a local bank if necessary.

REQUIRED:
Prepare a cash budget for October 2000.

LO 5:   Prepare a Cash Budget for One Month

8-67. The following information is available for July 2000.

Budgeted Receipts from Credit Sales	$500,000
Budgeted Cash Sales	40,000
Budgeted Cash Payments	577,000

Beginning cash balance for July is expected to be $95,000. The company intends to maintain a cash balance of at least $75,000. The company has made arrangements to borrow from a local bank if necessary.

REQUIRED:
Prepare a cash budget for July 2000.

LO 5:   Prepare a Budgeted Balance Sheet and Budgeted Statement of Cash Flows for Three Months

8-68. The following information is available for the Perlmuter Printing Supply Company.

PERLMUTER PRINTING SUPPLY COMPANY
Sales Budget
For the Quarter Ended September 30, 2002

	July	August	September
Budgeted Sales Dollars	$90,000	$80,000	$70,000

PERLMUTER PRINTING SUPPLY COMPANY
Cost of Goods Sold Budget
For the Quarter Ended September 30, 2002

	July	August	September
Budgeted COGS	$54,000	$48,000	$42,000

PERLMUTER PRINTING SUPPLY COMPANY
Selling and Administrative Expense Budget
For the Quarter Ended September 30, 2002

	July	August	September
Salaries and Wages	$12,600	$12,000	$11,800
Rent	1,000	1,000	1,000
Depreciation	1,800	1,800	1,800
Other	3,800	3,000	2,900
Total	$19,200	$17,800	$17,500

PERLMUTER PRINTING SUPPLY COMPANY
Budgeted Income Statement
For the Quarter Ended September 30, 2002

	July	August	September
Sales	$90,000	$80,000	$70,000
Cost of Goods Sold	54,000	48,000	42,000
Gross Profit	36,000	32,000	28,000
Selling and Admin. Expense	19,200	17,800	17,500
Net Income	$16,800	$14,200	$10,500

PERLMUTER PRINTING SUPPLY COMPANY
Purchases Budget
For the Quarter Ended September 30, 2002

	July	August	September
Cost of Purchases	$52,000	$46,000	$41,000

PERLMUTER PRINTING SUPPLY COMPANY
Cash Receipts Schedule
For the Quarter Ended September 30, 2002

	July	August	September
Budgeted Receipts from Credit Sales	$78,000	$76,000	$68,000
Budgeted Cash Sales	9,000	8,000	7,000
Total Cash Receipts	$87,000	$84,000	$75,000

PERLMUTER PRINTING SUPPLY COMPANY
Cash Payments Schedule
For the Quarter Ended September 30, 2002

	July	August	September
Purchases	$56,000	$52,000	$46,000
Selling and Admin. Expense:			
Salaries and Wages	$12,600	$12,000	$11,800
Rent	1,000	1,000	1,000
Other	3,800	3,000	2,900
Budgeted Cash Payments	$73,400	$68,000	$61,700

PERLMUTER PRINTING SUPPLY COMPANY
Cash Budget
For the Quarter Ended September 30, 2002

		July	August	September
	Beginning Cash Balance	$ 18,500	$ 32,100	$ 48,100
+	Cash Receipts	87,000	84,000	75,000
=	Cash Available	$105,500	$116,100	$123,100
−	Cash Payments	(73,400)	(68,000)	(61,700)
=	Balance before Borrowing	$ 32,100	$ 48,100	$ 61,400
+/−	Borrowing/(Repayment)	-0-	$ -0-	$ -0-
=	Ending Cash Balance	$ 32,100	$ 48,100	$ 61,400

PERLMUTER PRINTING SUPPLY COMPANY
Balance Sheet
June 30, 2002

Assets		
Current Assets		
Cash		$ 18,500
Accounts Receivable		20,000
Inventory		16,000
Total Current Assets		$ 54,500
Property, Plant, and Equipment		
Equipment		108,000
Less Accumulated Depreciation		(43,200)
Equipment, Net		$ 64,800
Total Assets		$119,300
Liabilities		
Current Liabilities		
Accounts Payable		$ 56,000
Total Liabilities		$ 56,000
Owner's Equity		
Paid-in Capital		
Common Stock		$ 1,000
Additional Paid-in Capital		10,000
Total Paid-in Capital		$ 11,000
Retained Earnings		$ 52,300
Total Equity		$ 63,300
Total Liabilities and Equity		$119,300

REQUIRED:

a. Prepare budgeted balance sheets for July, August, and September of 2002.

b. Prepare budgeted statements of cash flows for July, August, and September of 2002.

LO 5: Determine Missing Budget Information

8–69. Following is a partial performance report.

Description	Budget	Actual	Variance
Wages	$5,000	$ 5,200	$?
Store Rent	6,000	?	200 F
Utilities Expense	?	1,200	50 U

REQUIRED:
Provide the missing information.

LO 5: Determine Budget Variances

8–70. Following is a partial performance report.

Description	Budget	Actual	Variance
Sales	$25,000	$22,000	$?
Cost of Goods Sold	20,000	17,600	?
Gross Profit	5,000	4,400	?

REQUIRED:
Calculate the variances for this information and indicate whether they are favorable (F) or unfavorable (U).

LO 5: Determine Budget Variances

8–71. Following is a partial performance report.

Description	Budget	Actual	Variance
Rent Revenue	$15,000	$14,000	$?
Interest Expense	15,000	14,000	?

REQUIRED:

Calculate the variances for this information and indicate whether they are favorable (F) or unfavorable (U).

LO 6: Discuss Variances

8–72. Robin Wince owns a small chain of frame shops. All the frames and other merchandise the company sells is purchased by the company's central purchasing department. A partial performance report showing the direct costs for one of Robin's stores appears as follows:.

	Budget	Actual	Variance
Sales	$200,000	$200,000	$ 0
Cost of Goods Sold	120,000	110,000	10,000 F
Selling and Admin. Expense	40,000	50,000	10,000 U
Income	$ 40,000	$ 40,000	$ 0

REQUIRED:

Robin is concerned even though the variance in income is zero. Because the total variance is zero, the store manager believes that there is no problem. Do you agree with the manager? Why?

LO 6: Prepare a Memo Regarding Variances

8–73. Matt Lehti owns the Zap Record Shop. He is in the process of examining the following performance report.

	Budget	Actual	Variance
Sales	$100,000	$120,000	$20,000 F
Cost of Goods Sold	60,000	72,000	12,000 U
Selling and Admin. Expense	10,000	9,000	1,000 F
Income	$ 30,000	$ 39,000	$ 9,000 F

Matt is very pleased that the company had favorable variances for sales and income. However, he finds the sizable unfavorable variance for cost of goods sold very disturbing. He is preparing himself for a serious discussion with the purchasing agent who is responsible for purchasing the merchandise sold.

REQUIRED:

Assume that Matt Lehti has asked you for assistance in preparing for the meeting with the purchasing agent. Prepare a memo to Matt that provides him with any information you think would be helpful.

Chapter 9

Standard Costing

How do managers know which problems are the most pressing ones? How do they know how much time to spend on such problems? Suppose, for example, that you are the production manager for Inline Skate Company. Your responsibilities include making sure that the plant produces high-quality skates at a relatively low cost. If the actual production cost for a pair of skates is $12.87, how would you know whether this amount is acceptable? In addition, how would you know which specific costs are too high, too low, or just right? You could focus on a selected cost area such as direct material, but you might be spending valuable time trying to control costs that are already under control.

Fortunately, standard costing can help overcome some of the guesswork inherent to operating a business. **Standard costing** is the process of setting cost performance goals that benchmark desirable performance and then using these cost goals to evaluate performance.

Under standard costing, employees work to establish performance goals that can be used as benchmarks for good performance. As these goals are being set, employees are planning how factory resources will be acquired and used. Then, once operations begin, employees strive to control costs so the goals can be met.

The goals also provide management with a basis for performance evaluation when actual results are compared to goals to help find areas of weakness.

If the Inline Skate Company used standard costing, you could evaluate the $12.87 cost per pair of skates by comparing it to the amount budgeted. In fact, standard costing would allow you to review each component of production cost. You

standard costing The process of setting cost performance goals that benchmark acceptable performance and then using these cost goals to evaluate performance.

would be able to detect cost overruns for direct material, direct labor, variable manufacturing overhead, or fixed manufacturing overhead. In short, standard costing provides managers with a means to quickly focus their attention on problem areas. ■

LEARNING OBJECTIVES

After completing your work on this chapter, you should be able to do the following:

1. Describe standard costing and indicate why standard costing is important.
2. Explain the concept of management by exception.
3. Contrast ideal and practical standards.
4. Identify and discuss the weaknesses of standard costing.
5. Compare standard costing, actual costing, and normal costing.
6. Determine standards for a manufacturing company.
7. Calculate standard cost variances for direct material, direct labor, variable manufacturing overhead, and fixed manufacturing overhead.
8. Describe the meaning of standard cost variances for direct material, direct labor, variable manufacturing overhead, and fixed manufacturing overhead.

WHY IS STANDARD COSTING USED?

standard A preestablished benchmark for desirable performance.

standard cost system A system in which cost standards are set after careful analysis and then used to evaluate actual performance.

In today's competitive environment, business success depends in large part on good planning, as discussed in Chapter 8. Standard costing is often a key planning tool. When a company uses standard costing, it establishes performance standards for the coming year. A **standard** is a preestablished benchmark for desirable performance. A **standard cost system** is one in which a company, after careful analysis, sets cost standards and then uses them to evaluate actual performance.

Standard costing is used to bolster business success. In general, the use of standard costing encourages planning, establishes performance targets, and provides a basis for evaluating actual performance.

Planning is a critical part of any standard cost system. Managers and other employees work to gather information and investigate ways of achieving acceptable performance at the lowest cost. With this information, standards are established. For example, standards are created for the amount and cost of direct material, and for the number of direct labor hours and their cost. The process of planning provides benefits to the company because, once employees have established standards during the planning process, they know what needs to be done and how to do it most efficiently.

Once standards have been set, they can be used as performance targets. Managers and employees are encouraged to act so that actual results meet the expectations established by the standards. For example, if the production cost standard (the cost goal) for a pair of skates made by the Inline Skate Company is $13, employees are encouraged to make the skates for $13 or less. In an ideal situation, every employee would work to make the highest-quality skates for less than the $13 standard cost.

variance The difference between actual performance and the standard.

To determine whether and where problems exist, managers compare actual results to the standards. A **variance** is the difference between actual performance and

unfavorable variance The difference between actual performance and standard performance when the actual performance falls below the standard.

the standard. Variances can be used to help determine where managers should focus their attention.

Actual performance that falls below standard results in an **unfavorable variance.** Essentially, an unfavorable variance reflects a situation in which the cost of actual performance is higher than planned performance. For example, if the standard direct labor time to manufacture a desk is 12 minutes and it actually takes 15 minutes, the three-minute difference constitutes an unfavorable variance of three minutes. Because it is more costly to the company when three minutes of additional labor is used than was planned, an unfavorable variance is an indication that a problem may exist and management attention is needed.

favorable variance The difference between actual performance and standard performance when the actual performance exceeds the standard.

When actual performance exceeds the expectations established by the standard, a **favorable variance** results. In our desk example, if it actually takes 11 minutes to make the desk instead of the standard 12 minutes, the difference constitutes a favorable variance of one minute because cost to the company is reduced if labor time is one minute less than planned.

It might seem that a favorable variance indicates that management attention is not needed, but such is not always the case. Managers should review all variances, favorable and unfavorable, and use judgment and additional information to prioritize problem-solving efforts. For example, if a purchasing agent is able to buy direct material for less than the standard price, a favorable variance will occur. If the lower price is the result of purchasing substandard material, the "favorable" variance may not actually be to the company's benefit at all. Another reason to look into the cause of favorable variances is to learn how performance was improved. If the favorable variance is the result of improved performance, management may be able to learn how to make similar performance improvements in other areas of the company.

Items that have no variance should also be investigated. As discussed in Chapter 8, the absence of a variance should not be construed as meaning that everything is as it should be with that particular item. Managers must also remember that the cause of a variance may be the standard and not the performance. Standard setting is not an exact science. Standards must be reviewed often and changed as circumstances warrant.

It is most helpful if managers are able to review related standard cost variances together. For this purpose, a performance report is often prepared that summarizes variances for a particular operation of the company and shows where attention is needed. The process of focusing management attention on areas where actual performance deviates from the preestablished standards is called **management by exception.**

management by exception The process of focusing management attention on areas where actual performance deviates from the preestablished standards.

Under management by exception, managers first tend to problems associated with large variances. Then, once the large problems have been addressed, managers can turn to areas associated with lesser variances. Finally, as time permits, items where no variances exist are examined.

STANDARDS—A CLOSER LOOK

Most companies set cost standards once each year. Even if variances occur, it is generally unwise to casually adjust standards during the year, because managers might be too quick to adjust them to eliminate unfavorable variance instead of working to improve performance. Also, if standards are often adjusted, performance becomes difficult to track. Performance that resulted in an unfavorable variance one month might result in a favorable variance the next month once the standard has been changed. Standards should be altered only if conditions change so significantly that the established standards lose their effectiveness as performance targets.

Cost and Quantity Standards

Performance standards can be set for almost any business activity. For example, standards can be set for the number of product returns, or for the amount of employee turnover. In practice, however, standards are used most often to help control costs.

Two things can cause cost to increase: the quantity used and the price paid. It is better to establish both a quantity standard and a separate price standard for each material used in production. For example, to say the direct material for product X should cost $3 per unit is not as helpful in controlling cost as saying that it should take 1.5 pounds of material at $2 per pound to make product X. Establishing a quantity and price standard provides performance targets for the amount of material used in production and a separate target for finding the material at the best purchase price.

Although it is also helpful to establish quantity and price standards for direct labor, we generally do not refer to labor in terms of "quantity" and "price." Instead we use the equivalent terms "hours" and "rate." The quantity standard for labor is the number of hours, and the price standard is the rate.

Ideal versus Practical Standards

During the planning process, managers and other employees work to set standards that will both help provide performance targets and provide a basis for performance evaluation. If we were setting a price standard for the purchase of gasoline, for example, we could set a cost goal of $0.50 per gallon, $5 per gallon, or any price in between. The object would be to select a standard that would challenge employees to find gasoline at the best price. If the standard is set at $0.50 per gallon, it is unlikely that employees will even try to achieve this impossible standard. On the other hand, if the standard is set at $5 per gallon, employees will be able to achieve the standard so easily that it will offer no incentive to find low-cost gasoline. Generally it is best to select a standard that offers a challenging, yet achievable, performance goal.

ideal standard A standard that is attainable only under perfect conditions.

Ideal Standards   A standard that is attainable only under perfect conditions is called an **ideal standard.** Under ideal standards, there is no room for substandard performance of any kind. In a manufacturing setting, for instance, ideal standards assume that the plant operates in a perfect world with no machine breakdowns, no waste of direct material for any reason, and no employee rest breaks. In the real world, ideal standards are nearly impossible to achieve. Such standards may frustrate employees because, no matter how hard they try, they will never be able to meet them. In time, employees may throw up their hands and stop trying to meet the standards altogether.

practical standard A standard that allows for normal, recurring inefficiencies.

Practical Standards   A standard that allows for normal, recurring inefficiencies is called a **practical standard.** For example, in manufacturing, a practical standard for the quantity of direct material would allow for waste due to expected defects in the material. For labor, a practical standard would provide for employees working at a normal pace with adequate rest periods. When compared to ideal standards, practical standards are more realistic and less likely to result in unreasonable unfavorable variances. In addition, when practical standards are used, an unfavorable variance indicates that a true problem exists. Accordingly, most companies use practical standards.

Setting Standards

Often, standards are based on past performance. For example, if material Y was purchased for $4.45 per pound last year, it is likely it can be purchased for about $4.45 the next year; but using last year's actual amounts as next year's standards is overly simplistic. When setting standards, it is best to use historical information, and then incorporate any anticipated changes in efficiency or price.

Often, it is best to use a team approach to evaluate each standard. Whether formal or informal, a team approach for gathering input from various knowledgeable employees will result in better, more appropriate standards. For example, when setting direct material standards for a manufacturer, a team approach would likely be better than a single employee setting the standards based solely on his or her own limited knowledge. The team might include an accountant, production-line workers, production supervisors, purchasing agents, and others who are knowledgeable about the quality, use, sources, and prices of direct material. Then, the historical information provided by the accountants, information about usage and quality requirements provided by production personnel, and information about sourcing and pricing from the purchasing agent can be analyzed. Once the team has examined all this information, appropriate direct material standards can be set.

Once reasonable standards have been established, actual performance has been measured and compared to the standards, and a system to provide performance reports has been put in place, standard costing can be a valuable management tool. A flowchart of how standard costing works is shown in Exhibit 9–1. Managers can then encourage employees to strive to meet the performance goals established by the standards, and can use performance reports and management by exception to help direct their attention to troubled areas. Unfortunately, standard costing is not the answer to all management's problems. When managers rely too heavily on standard costing, serious problems occur.

Exhibit 9–1
The Standard-Costing Process

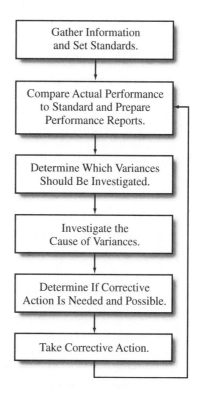

Problems with Standard Costing

To use standard costing as an effective management tool, managers must be aware of its drawbacks. The first problems may occur when standards are being set. Employees with expertise are often consulted to help establish an appropriate standard. Most of these employees are keenly aware that the standard will be used later to evaluate their performance. With lax standards, employees will not have to work as hard to meet the goals set by the standard, and unfavorable variances will be less likely. With stringent standards, employees will have to work much harder to meet targeted goals. Accordingly, employees often try to ensure that the standards adopted by the company are lax, resulting in suboptimal performance goals.

Another problem with standard costing stems from relying on historical information to set standards. If past performance was less than optimal, the new standards will call for performance that is less than optimal. The inefficiency of the past may be built into the new standards. Sometimes employees and lower-level managers deliberately manipulate actual performance so it appears that less stringent standards should be maintained. This way, employees are less likely to face the consequences of unfavorable performance variances in the future.

Still another serious problem associated with standard costing is that managers tend to manage everything "by the numbers." When a standard cost system is well established, managers often focus almost entirely on significant, unfavorable variances and overlook serious problems that do not give rise to unfavorable variances. For example, a manager may try desperately to reduce an unfavorable direct material variance while completely overlooking a significant product quality problem. Why? The product quality problem does not result in a variance; therefore, a manager whose attention is directed solely by management by exception would have no "exception" to direct him or her to the quality problem. Managers may get so engrossed in chasing down problems associated with unfavorable variance that they waste company time and resources as they try to rectify insignificant unfavorable variances.

In addition, managers who use management by exception may spend so much time on unfavorable variances that they fail to recognize employees who are responsible for favorable variances. By failing to recognize employees who do a good job, managers lose the benefit of positive reinforcement as a management tool.

Still another problem is that managers lose sight of the overall business operation as they focus on the multitude of details which have resulted in unfavorable variances. In time, managers focus so much on unfavorable variance details that they cannot see the forest for the trees. The overall performance of the company may suffer because managers are managing details while ignoring the big picture.

A summary of the problems associated with standard costing is presented in Exhibit 9–2. Take some time to become familiar with these problems.

Exhibit 9–2
Summary of Standard
Costing Problems

Problems with Standard Costing

1. Employees who help set standards try to avoid unfavorable variances by setting lax standards.
2. Reliance on historical information may perpetuate past inefficiencies in current standards.
3. Managers manage "by the numbers" and overlook significant problems that do not result in an unfavorable variance or waste time on insignificant unfavorable variances.
4. Managers focus so much on unfavorable variances that they fail to recognize employees who are doing a good job.
5. Managers focus so much on variances that they fail to see the big picture.

Who Uses Standard Costing?

Almost any business entity can use standard costing regardless of whether it is a for-profit or a not-for-profit organization. Service, merchandising, and manufacturing firms may use standard costing, although it is most often used by manufacturers. When it is appropriate to establish standards of performance for purposes of planning and control, standard costing can be used. For example, a tire store might establish a standard for the amount of time it should take to change a set of tires. An oil change center might establish a standard for the amount of time it should take to change the oil and service an automobile. An airline catering company could develop standards for the quantity and price of each food item, the labor hours and labor rate to prepare each item, and a standard for the amount of overhead cost associated with the preparation of each item it sells.

In a manufacturing environment, a standard cost system is used to budget the cost of producing each individual unit of product. In effect, standard costing is like preparing a budget for a single unit of production. Managers estimate the cost of direct material, direct labor, variable manufacturing overhead, and fixed manufacturing overhead required to produce each item.

In Chapter 3 we discussed two types of cost systems. In an *actual cost system* we compute actual direct material, direct labor, and manufacturing overhead costs. In a *normal cost system* we compute actual direct material and actual direct labor costs, and use a predetermined rate for manufacturing overhead. Standard costing goes one step further. In a standard cost system, estimated amounts are used for direct material, direct labor, and manufacturing overhead. Exhibit 9–3 compares the three cost systems.

In the sections that follow, we discuss the details of how standard costing is used in manufacturing.

Exhibit 9–3
Comparison of Actual, Normal, and Standard Cost Systems

Cost Classification	Actual Cost System	Normal Cost System	Standard Cost System
Direct Material	Actual	Actual	Estimated
Direct Labor	Actual	Actual	Estimated
Manufacturing Overhead	Actual	Estimated	Estimated

BASIC STANDARD COSTING FOR A MANUFACTURER

Standard costing is often used by manufacturing companies. Standards are set for direct material, direct labor, variable manufacturing overhead, and fixed manufacturing overhead. We will walk through the most commonly used standards and variances using the Tree Top Mail Box Company as an example. Tree Top is a small company that makes a single product.

Tree Top Mail Box Company was founded by three college sophomores, Ali, Maria, and Bill. They started the company to earn spending money while they attended college. The trio had done some market research and determined that they could sell decorative wooden mail boxes for $10 each. They each planned to work about 60 hours per month for $10 per hour. Any remaining profits would be left in the company to be divided equally at the end of their venture.

The three entrepreneurs rented a garage to house the small company for $200 per month plus utilities. They purchased equipment, a table saw and drill press, for $900. The estimated useful life of the equipment is three years.

Exhibit 9–4
Tree Top's October 2001
Income Statement

TREE TOP MAIL BOX COMPANY		
Income Statement		
For the Month Ended October 31, 2001		
Sales (300 mail boxes at $10 each)		$3,000
Less Expenses		
Direct Material	$ 600	
Direct Labor (180 hours at $10 per hour)	1,800	
Rent	200	
Utilities (all variable)	40	
Miscellaneous Variable Cost	30	
Depreciation	25	2,695
Net Income		$ 305

In October, Tree Top's first month of operation, the company was able to sell every mail box produced. By the end of October, they had made and sold 300 boxes. As shown on the income statement in Exhibit 9–4, the company's profits for October totaled $305.

Discussion Questions

9–1. How did Ali, Maria, and Bill calculate the depreciation expense of $25 per month?

9–2. Can you tell from Exhibit 9–4 whether the three Tree Top employees met their business goals in the month of October? Why or why not?

Ali, Maria, and Bill were thrilled that their equity in the company had grown by $305 in the first month. They felt that information for October's business activity could be used to develop a standard cost system to help manage their company.

SETTING DIRECT MATERIAL STANDARDS

As stated, setting direct material standards involves two important considerations: the quantity of material and the price paid. We now discuss each of these in some detail.

Direct Material Quantity Standard

direct material quantity standard The amount of direct material it should take to manufacture a single unit of product.

bill of materials A listing of the quantity and description of each item of direct material used to manufacture an individual product.

The amount of direct material it should take to make a single unit of production is called the **direct material quantity standard.** A bill of materials is often used to help establish the direct material quantity standard. A **bill of materials** is a listing of the quantity and description of each item of direct material used to manufacture an individual product. The bill of material for the 7ULTRA-A CB radio made by Cobra Electronics Corporation included just under 300 items, as shown in Exhibit 9–5.

Each item of direct material, from the speaker to the smallest resistor, is listed. With input from engineering, production, and other personnel, a bill of materials can be prepared and direct material quantity standards can be set. For the Tree Top

Exhibit 9–5

Bill of Materials for 7ULTRA-A CB Radio. © Cobra Electronics Corporation, Chicago, IL. Reprinted by permission.

BILL OF MATERIAL FOR 7ULTRA-A

COVER ASS'Y	
SPEAKER 8 OHM 0.3W 66MM P-250	
(+)TAPPING SCREW(BH)T3X6-2S (+)BH ZN-PLAT	SPK MTG:3
(+)TAPTITE SCREW(BH)T3X6 (+)BH BLK	UPPER.BOTTOM+ MAIN BODY:8
COVER UPPER ABS 94HB BLK	
COVER BOTTOM ABS 94HB BLK	
HOLDER(SPK)SPC 16X8XT1.2	SPK MTG:3
CUSHION 25X25XT5 RUBB.SP0.BLK STIC	
FELT &65XT0.3 FELT BLK	
FELT 10X110XT0.3 FELT STIC	
FELT 10X100XT0.3 FELT BLK	AIR VENT
ESCUTCHEON ASS'Y	
(+)MACHINE SCREW(FH)M2.6X4 (+)FH ZN-PLAT	
NUT M7 BSBM	
E.S.C ABS94 L153-S9001 BLK(7ULTRA-A)	
LENS ACRYL CLEAR	
KNOB(VOL.SQ) ABS 94HB BLK	95/08/18
KNOB(DOWN) ABS 94HB BLACK	95/08/18
KNOB(UP)ABS 94HB BLACK	
SPRING(COIL) SWP-3 &0.2	
FRONT BODY ASS'Y	
TRANSISTOR KTC2078(TO-220AB)	Q704
I.C KIA7217AP	IC401
P.C.B SUB 54X27X1.6	
JACK EARPHONE DHJ-3T	
CONNECTOR CH-239(A) SW-1229	
CONNECTOR SCN-16-4 PCB(R)	
MICA (FOR T.R 2SC2078)	
BUSHING(FOR T.R 2SC2078)	
VR10KB:15SK 161V	VR2
VR 50KA:RK16311116B153A	VR1
POWER CORD ASS'Y	
(+)MACHINE SCREW(BH)M3X10 (+)BH ZN-PLAT	TR:2
(+)TAPPING SCREW(BH)T3X6-2S (+)BH ZN-PLAT	M.P+MAIN BODY:4 HEAT SINK:1
NUT M3-1S SS41 ZN-PLAT	
WASHER SPRING M3 ZN-PLAT	TR:2
RIVET BLIND &3.2 ALB	NAME PLATE MTG:2
BODY MAIN EGI T1.0 US COATING	
HOLDER(ANT MTG)SPTE 29X35XT0.3 NI-PLAT	
CORD STOPPER P.P BLK	
ESD PROTECTOR CUP T0.05 (TRC-499)	
HEAT SINK ALP3 T2	IC MTG
HEAT SINK ALP3 T2	
SHIELD HOUSHING SPTE T0.3	
NAME PLATE ALP3 40X20XT0.4 (7ULTRA-A)	
MIC ASS'Y	
DISK CERAMIC 0.001UF DD330F102Z 50V	C959
MIC CONDENSER KUC4023-010010	
CURD CURLED 3CON 1SH 300MM BLK(KSK-23059)	
CONNECTOR PLUG SW-1461	
WIRE 1007 AWG 24 11/0.16 WHT	MIC(-)---SW
SW PUSH SPS-9522	
(-)SECURING SCREW M6X8 (P:1) ABS BLK	ACCESSORY
(+)TAPPING SCREW(PH)T3X8-2S (+)PH ZN-PLAT	ACCESSORY
(+)TAPPING SCREW(TH)T5X12-1S (+)TH ZN-PLAT	ACCESSORY
(+)WOOD SCREW (R+FH)2.7X18-1S (+)R+FH NI-PLAT	COVER MTG:3
WASHER 7X25X1.5T BLK RUBBER	ACCESSORY
WASHER(LOCK"B"TYPE) M3 "B"ZN-PLAT	ACCESSORY
ZN-PLAT	ACCESSORY
(+)PLUS SCREW(PH)3X10(+)PH ZN-PLAT	HOLDER MTG
COVER BOTTOM ABS 94HB BLK	
COVER UPPER(MIC)ABS 94HB BLK	
BRACKET (MIC)SPC 58X41XT1 CR-PLAT	
BRACKET(SET)SPC T1.5 BLK-SPRAY PICA	
HOLDER(MIC)PC BLK	
PLATE WEIGHT SPC 36X24XT3 ZN-PLAT	
KNOB(LEVER)ABS 94HB GRAY	
WIRE CLAMP (CORD)NYLON	
HOLDER(MIC) RUBB.(UL)BLK	
BOX MIC SW1S 222(W)X70(D)X52(H)	
POLYBAG P.P 100X100XT0.05	ACCESSORY
POLYBAG P.P 100X200XT0.05	
MAIN PCB AUTO ASS'Y	
FILM RESISTOR 100 1/ 8W 5% ST	R410.513.707.709
FILM RESISTOR 1K 1/ 8W 5% ST	R413.414.901
FILM RESISTOR 10K 1/ 8W 5% ST	R399.411.431. 502.508.515.964
FILM RESISTOR 100K 1/ 8W 5% ST	R404
FILM RESISTOR 1.2K 1/ 8W 5% ST	R518
FILM RESISTOR 150 1/ 8W 5% ST	R951-957
FILM RESISTOR 150K 1/ 8W 5% ST	R701
FILM RESISTOR 180 1/ 8W 5% ST	R962
FILM RESISTOR 1.8K 1/ 8W 5% ST	R420
FILM RESISTOR 22 1/ 8W 5% ST	R511
FILM RESISTOR 2.2K 1/ 8W 5% ST	R401.402.403.408.963
FILM RESISTOR 22K 1/ 8W 5% ST	R967
FILM RESISTOR 2.2 1/ 8W 5% ST	R711
FILM RESISTOR 270 1/ 8W 5% ST	R501
FILM RESISTOR 2.7K 1/ 8W 5% ST	R426.959
FILM RESISTOR 27K 1/ 8W 5% ST	R430
FILM RESISTOR 270K 1/ 8W 5% ST	R428.516
FILM RESISTOR 3.3K 1/ 8W 5% ST	R407.708
FILM RESISTOR 390 1/ 8W 5% ST	R510.702
FILM RESISTOR 3.9K 1/ 8W 5% ST	R406
FILM RESISTOR 47 1/ 8W 5% ST	R425.902
FILM RESISTOR 470 1/ 8W 5% ST	R512
FILM RESISTOR 4.7K 1/ 8W 5% ST	R503.703.704. 705.960
FILM RESISTOR 47K 1/ 8W 5% ST	R961
FILM RESISTOR 470K 1/ 8W 5% ST	R400
FILM RESISTOR 560 1/ 8W 5% ST	R504
FILM RESISTOR 5.6K 1/ 8W 5% ST	R405.409
FILM RESISTOR 68 1/ 8W 5% ST	R706
FILM RESISTOR 6.8K 1/ 8W 5% ST	R517
FILM RESISTOR 15K 1/ 8W 2% ST	R412
AXIAL CERAMIC 0.001UF UP050B102MK 50V	C404.426.427. 950.953.954
AXIAL CERAMIC 0.01UF EP050Y103MN 16V	C402.425.501. 504.508.518.520.
AXIAL CERAMIC 0.0022UF EP050X222MN 16V	C410
AXIAL CERAMIC 0.022UF RH050F 223Z 50V	C406.408.521.705.905
AXIAL CERAMIC 220PF UP050B221K 50V	C413.716
DIODE ZENER 1N5239B 9.1V 0.5W (DO-35)	D504
DIODE ZENER 1N5231B 5.1V 0.5W (DO-35)	D501
DIODE 1N4148(R.L)	D405.502.503.902.903
DIODE RECTIFIER 1N4004T/R 400V 1A (DO-41)	D404.701
COIL AXIAL 2.2UH:LAL03TB2R2M	RFC704
COIL AXIAL 6.8UH:LAL03TB6R8K	RFC509.706
COIL AXIAL 0.39UH:LAL02TBR39K	RFC701
MAIN PCB MANUAL ASSY	
METAL OXIDE RESISTOR15 2W 5% ST	R427
FILM RESISTOR 10 1/ 2W 5% ST MINI	R999
FILM RESISTOR 4.7K 1/ 2W 5% ST MINI	R712
RESISTOR SEMIFIXED 10KB RVM083H H 8DIA	RV1
RESISTOR SEMIFIXED 2K RVM083H	RV2
ELECT CAPACITOR 0.1UF 50V 20% 5X11	C403.956
ELECT CAPACITOR 10UF 16V 20% 5X11	C417.503.902
ELECT CAPACITOR 100UF 16V 20% 8X11	C424
ELECT CAPACITOR 10UF 16V 20% 4X7	C411
ELECT CAPACITOR 1000UF 16V 20% 12X16	C423
ELECT CAPACITOR 2.2UF 50V 20% 5X11	C707
ELECT CAPACITOR 220UF 16V 20% 10X12	C422.514
ELECT CAPACITOR 3.3UF 50V 20% 5X11	C416.421
ELECT CAPACITOR 33UF 16V 20% 5X11	C407.412.415
ELECT CAPACITOR 47UF 16V 20% 6X11	C430.515
ELECT CAPACITOR 470UF 16V 20% 10X12	C502.510
DISK CERAMIC 0.01UF HIK(B)F 103 50V	C721.722.723
DISK CERAMIC 0.022UF F 223Z 50V	C711.714
DISK CERAMIC 0.047UF X 473M 50V	C414.418
AXIAL CERAMIC 0.047UF SA105E473MAA 50V	C405
NPO100D 50V	
DISK CERAMIC 100PF NPO101K 50V	C712.718.999
DISK CERAMIC 12PF NPO120K 50V	C513.903
DISK CERAMIC 150PF SL 151K 50V	C715
DISK CERAMIC 270PF SL 271K 50V	C420
DISK CERAMIC 330PF SL 331K 50V	C717
DISK CERAMIC 39PF NPO390K 50V	C704
DISK CERAMIC 4PF NPO040D 50V	C706
DISK CERAMIC 470PF SL 471K 50V	C713
DISK CERAMIC 5PF NPO050D 50V	C506
DISK CERAMIC 82PF NPO820K 50V	C708
DIP TANTALUM 1UF 489D105X0025A125V	C957.958
DIP TRIMMER 20PF 6DIA CVN	CT1
TRANSISTOR KTC3194(O)	Q701.702
TRANSISTOR KTC3198(GR)	Q400.401.505.507
TRANSISTOR KTA1266(GR)	Q402.501.502. 503.506
TRANSISTOR KTC1006 (TO-92L)	Q703
I.C C5122A1P	IC501
DIODE GE 1N60	D402.403
CRYSTAL HC18U 10.240M 30PM	X1
FILTER CERAMIC LTU455HT	CF2
FILTER CERAMIC SK107M4-AC-20	CF1
TRASNFORMER CHOKE EI-19	CH1
TRANSFORMER POWER EI-24	T1
COIL RF CHOKE 0.8UH SPRING	RFC401
COIL SPRING 5X0.6X13.5T:R	RFC709
COIL SPRING 3.4X0.55X8.5T:R	RFC705
COIL RF CHOKE 10UH 10%	RFC707
COIL IFT 455KHZ-A	L902
COIL IFT 455KHZ-B	L903
COIL 27MHZ RX ANT	L901
COIL VCO	L501
COIL RF PRE AMP A TX27MHZ	L701.702
P.C.B MAIN 150 X121.5X1.6 94HB1/0	
MAIN PCB SMD ASS'Y	
F AMP MODULE ASS'Y	
CHIP RESISTOR 0 1/10W 5% T 2012	R200.219
CHIP RESISTOR 100 1/10W 5% T 2012	R203
CHIP RESISTOR 1K 1/10W 5% T 2012	R209
CHIP RESISTOR 10K 1/10W 5% T 2012	R207
CHIP RESISTOR 12K 1/10W 5% T 2012	R211
CHIP RESISTOR 15K 1/10W 5% T 2012	R218
CHIP RESISTOR 150K 1/10W 5% T 2012	R205
CHIP RESISTOR 1.8K 1/10W 5% T 2012	R206
CHIP RESISTOR 220 1/10W 5% T 2012	R212
CHIP RESISTOR 22K 1/10W 5% T 2012	R213
CHIP RESISTOR 3.3K 1/10W 5% T 2012	R210
CHIP RESISTOR 33K 1/10W 5% T 2012	R217
CHIP RESISTOR 3.9K 1/10W 5% T 2012	R202
CHIP RESISTOR 470 1/10W 5% T 2012	R204.208
CHIP RESISTOR 47K 1/10W 5% T 2012	R214.216
CHIP RESISTOR 560 1/10W 5% T 2012	R201
CHIP RESISTOR 82K 1/10W 5% T 2012	R215
ELECT CAPACITOR 1UF 50V 20% 4X7	C209
ELECT CAPACITOR 10UF 16V 20% 4X7	C204
CHIP CERAMIC 0.001UF CM21 X7R102K 50V AT	C206
CHIP CERAMIC 0.01UF CM21 X7R103K 50V AT	C201.203
CHIP CERAMIC 0.047UF CM21 X7R473K 50V AT	C202.205.207.208
TRANSISTOR KTA1504SY(SOT-23)	Q204
TRANSISTOR KTC3880SY(SOT-23)	Q201.202.203
DIODE GE 1N60	D201
P.C.B IF MODULE 44X16.88X1.6 94HB1/1	
VCO MODULE ASS'Y	
CHIP RESISTOR 0 1/10W 5% T 2012	R600.609
CHIP RESISTOR 10K 1/10W 5% T 2012	R606.607
CHIP RESISTOR 120K 1/10W 5% T 2012	R603
CHIP RESISTOR 22K 1/10W 5% T 2012	R608
CHIP RESISTOR 220K 1/10W 5% T 2012	R604
CHIP RESISTOR 2.7K 1/10W 5% T 2012	R605
CHIP RESISTOR 47 1/10W 5% T 2012	R601
CHIP RESISTOR 820 1/10W 5% T 2012	R602
CHIP CERAMIC 0.01UF CM21 X7R103K 50V AT	C601.610.611
CHIP CERAMIC 120PF CM21 CG 121J 50V AT	C608
CHIP CERAMIC 18PF CM21 CG 180J 50V AT	C602
CHIP CERAMIC 22PF CM21 CG 220J 50V AT	C603
CHIP CERAMIC 220PF CM21 CG 221J 50V AT	C607
CHIP CERAMIC 27PF CM21CG 270J 50V AT	C609
CHIP CERAMIC 33PF CM21 CG 330J 50V AT	C606
CHIP CERAMIC 47PF CM21 CG 470J 50V AT	C605
TRANSISTOR KTC3875SY	Q602
TRANSISTOR KTC3880SY(SOT-23)	Q601.603
DIODE VARICAP LV2209	D601
P.C.B VCO MODULE 30.7 X16.88X1.6 94HB1/1	
LOW PASS FILTER MODU	
CHIP CERAMIC 220PF CM21 CG 221J 50V AT	C801.805
CHIP CERAMIC 470PF CM21 CG 471J 50V AT	C802.803
COIL SPRING 3.4X0.55X6.5T:R	L802
COIL SPRING 3.4X0.55X7.5T:R	L803
COIL SPRING 3.4X0.55X8.5T:R	L804
P.C.B LPF MODULE 15.39X40.5 X1.6 94HB1/1	
4.5T SPRIN.COIL ASSY	L801
COIL SPRING 3.4X0.55X4.5T:R	
CORE 1108-KA-058 M9DTH3.7X6	
RF AMP H/H MODULE	
CHIP RESISTOR 0 1/10W 5% T 2012	
CHIP RESISTOR 100 1/10W 5% T 2012	R107
CHIP RESISTOR 10K 1/10W 5% T 2012	R106.108
CHIP RESISTOR 18 1/10W 5% T 2012	R104
CHIP RESISTOR 330 1/10W 5% T 2012	R103
CHIP RESISTOR 33K 1/10W 5% T 2012	R105
CHIP RESISTOR 470 1/10W 5% T 2012	R109.110
CHIP CERAMIC 0.01UF CM21 X7R103K 50V AT	C112
CHIP CERAMIC 150PF CM21 CG 151J 50V AT	C109
CHIP CERAMIC 220PF CM21 CG 221J 50V AT	C108
CHIP CERAMIC 33PF CM21 CG 330J 50V AT	C102
CHIP CERAMIC 47PF CM21 CG 470J 50V AT	C104
CHIP CERAMIC 680PF CM21 CG 681J 50V AT	C114
TRANSISTOR KTC3880SY (SOT-23)	Q102.103
DIODE SI CHIP KDS226 (SOT-23)	D101
P.C.B RF MODULE 39.25X16.88X1.6 94HB1/1	
6.5T SPRIN.COIL ASSY	L102.104
COIL SPRING 3.4X0.55X6.5T:R	
CORE 1108-KA-058 M9DTH3.7X6	
PACKING ASS'Y	
BOX TRAY SW1S 222(W)X127(D)X52(H)	
BOX INNER SW1S 224(W)X220(D)X54(H)	
BOX OUT DW1E 355(W)X238(D)X206(H)	
POLYBAG P.P 200X300XT0.05	SET:1 MANUAL:1
MANUAL OWNER'S MANUAL OWNER'S	
CARD REGISTRATION ARTPAPER 158X342	
CARD BOARD	
CB RULE	
SCHEMATIC DIAGRAM WOODFREEPAPER 420X297	
CARD INFORMATION WOODFREEPAPER 98.5X150	
LABEL CAUTION	
LABEL FCC POLYESTER 67X10XT0.05	
SUB PCB ASS'Y	
FILM RESISTOR 10K 1/ 8W 5% ST	R950
LED LAMP SLB55VR3 RED 3 V 60MW	LED1
LED DISPLAY UL-G233G-13 GRN	
SW TACT SAT-1102-2	SW3.4
SUB MATERIAL ASS'Y	
TUBE UL/CSA KEIT-30 AWG 12 (2&) CLEAR VINYL	
TUBE UL/CSA KEIT-30 AWG 2 (6.5&) CLEAR VINYL	
TUBE HIS 11M/M	
TUBE EMPIRE 1&	
PE SCOTCH 15M/M (0.015X20M)	
TAPE PACKING OPP (0.05X50M)	
TAPE PACKING O.P.P.(0.05X25M) IVORY	
SOLDER BAR 63:37	
SOLDER ROSIN CO.WIRE60:40 0.04"-0.05"	
FLUX ROSIN	
THINNER FOR FLUX	
SILICON GREASE YG-6111 OR XG-6111	
STAVILIZER MATERIAL	
BOND #201	
COMPOUND #1200 500GR	

Mail Box Company, the bill of materials would be quite simple. Basically it involves only one direct material—wood.

To determine the direct material quantity standard for the Tree Top Mail Box Company using practical standards, Ali measured the wood included in a single mail box. He determined that each mail box was made of 16 feet of $1/4 \times 2$ inch pine. Then he examined the scrap wood from the prior week's production and estimated that the amount of wood to make a single mail box should be increased by 35 percent to allow for scrap due to knots and other expected defects in the wood. Accordingly, Tree Top adopted a practical direct material quantity standard of 21.6 feet (16 feet $\times$ 1.35% = 21.6 feet) per mail box.

direct material price standard The anticipated cost for each item of direct material used in the manufacture of a product.

Direct Material Price Standard

In addition to the amount of direct material used, the price per measure of direct material will affect the total cost of direct material. The **direct material price standard** is the anticipated cost for each item of direct material used in the manufacture of a product. For the plastic used to make golf balls, the direct material price standard would be the cost per pound of plastic. For wire used in a CD player, the direct material price standard would be the cost per foot of wire. Notice that the direct material price standard reflects a price per measure of direct material (that is, per foot of wire), *not* per unit of production (such as, per CD player).

Because purchasing agents are generally knowledgeable about the price paid for direct material, they are likely to be key players in determining direct material price standards. Purchasing agents would also gather historical direct material price information, making necessary adjustments for any anticipated price changes.

As indicated, Tree Top uses wood that measures $1/4 \times 2$ inches. The direct material price standard is expressed as an amount per foot of this wood. The Tree Top Mail Box Company has no purchasing agent, so Ali shopped around and found that good-quality pine wood could be purchased for $0.70 per 8 foot length. Also, Ali determined that no price increases were expected during the year. Accordingly, Tree Top established a standard price per foot of wood of $0.0875 ($0.70 / 8 feet = $0.0875) per foot.

Although only a single direct material is used to make Tree Top's mail boxes, most products require the use of many different raw materials. Separate standards must be established for each direct material used in production. If production required the use of material A, material B, and material C, separate quantity and price standards must be prepared for each.

Once a manufacturer knows the direct material quantity standard and the direct material price standard, the standard cost for direct material per unit of production can be determined. For Tree Top, the standard cost for direct material of $1.89 is calculated by multiplying the standard quantity of 21.60 feet by the standard price of $0.0875, as shown.

Standard Quantity	$\times$	Standard Price	=	Standard Direct Material Cost Per Unit
21.60 Feet	$\times$	$0.0875	=	$1.89

SETTING DIRECT LABOR STANDARDS

As with direct material, setting direct labor standards involves two important considerations: the number of direct labor hours and the wage rate per hour.

Direct Labor Efficiency Standard

direct labor efficiency standard The estimated number of direct labor hours required to produce a single unit of product.

The estimated number of direct labor hours required to produce a single unit of product is called the **direct labor efficiency standard.** When the direct labor force works efficiently, labor hours are kept to a minimum. Conversely, too many hours of direct labor relative to production would indicate labor inefficiency. The standard for the number of direct labor hours could be called the direct labor quantity standard, or the direct labor hours standard, but neither of these terms sounds quite right, which explains why this standard has come to be known as the direct labor efficiency standard.

The production supervisors and other production employees are often key players in establishing direct labor efficiency standards. Historical information about direct labor and production volumes are used to help establish an appropriate standard for the number of direct labor hours per unit of production. Also, information from industrial engineers, such as the results of time-and-motion studies, may be helpful in determining the amount of direct labor time it should take to efficiently produce a unit of product.

Tree Top's founders wanted to select a standard that would help encourage them to make as many mail boxes as possible, but allow them to work at a quick, yet reasonable pace. After reviewing their activities for October, the three agreed that the standard hours allowed for a single unit of production should be 0.6 hours (36 minutes). This time, then, became Tree Top's labor efficiency standard.

Direct Labor Rate Standard

direct labor rate standard
The planned hourly wage paid to production workers.

The **direct labor rate standard** is the planned hourly wage paid to production workers. The personnel manager is often a key player in determining the direct labor rate standard. Sometimes direct labor rates are established through collective bargaining or other employment agreements. Other times a less formal procedure is used to set hourly pay rates. In either case, historical information coupled with information regarding anticipated pay rate changes establishes the direct labor rate standard. Often, companies compute an expected average hourly direct labor rate, which is used as the plant-wide direct labor rate standard. For Tree Top, Ali, Maria, and Bill agreed that, based on their original plan, the direct labor rate standard of $10 per hour should be used.

Once a company knows the direct labor efficiency standard and the direct labor rate standard, the standard labor cost per unit of production can be determined. In the case of Tree Top, based on the direct labor efficiency standard of 0.6 hours and the direct labor rate standard of $10 per direct labor hour, the standard labor cost to make a single mail box is $6, shown as follows:

$$
\begin{array}{ccccc}
\text{Direct Labor} & & \text{Direct Labor} & & \text{Standard} \\
\text{Efficiency} & \times & \text{Rate Standard} & = & \text{Direct Labor} \\
\text{Standard} & & \text{(Per Hour)} & & \text{Cost Per Unit} \\
\\
0.6 \text{ Hours} & \times & \$10 \text{ Per Hour} & = & \$6
\end{array}
$$

Setting Variable Manufacturing Overhead Standards

Recall that manufacturing overhead includes all production costs that are not part of direct materials or direct labor. Manufacturing overhead includes costs of operating the factory such as the cost of rent, insurance, depreciation, supplies, taxes, raw materials handling, and so forth. Recall also that costs can be classified as either fixed or variable. Fixed costs are those that remain constant in total, even as activity changes. Variable costs, in contrast, increase in total as activity changes. Therefore, variable manufacturing overhead would include those manufacturing overhead costs that increase in total as production increases.

In Chapter 3, we saw that manufacturing overhead was often allocated to production based on direct labor hours, direct labor cost, machine hours, or some other allocation base. In this section, we illustrate how a standard cost system works when manufacturing overhead is allocated using direct labor hours as the allocation base. Although the specific calculations would be somewhat different, standard costing can be used for other allocation bases as well.

To set standards for variable manufacturing overhead, managers must first estimate variable manufacturing overhead costs. Once they estimate total variable manufacturing overhead, they can then determine a cost per direct labor hour, or per unit of some other allocation base.

For Tree Top Mail Box Company, variable manufacturing overhead cost includes utilities and miscellaneous variable cost, as shown on October's income statement presented in Exhibit 9–4. The miscellaneous variable cost includes the cost of indirect material such as glue, small nails, and wood stain. Based on October's results, Ali, Maria, and Bill estimated that variable manufacturing overhead cost would be about $63. The $63 includes $33 for utilities and $30 for miscellaneous variable cost. Tree Top planned to allocate this variable overhead cost to production based on direct labor hours.

The Standard Variable Manufacturing Overhead Rate

standard variable manufacturing overhead rate The rate used to apply variable manufacturing overhead to units of manufactured product.

The rate used to apply variable manufacturing overhead to units of product is known as the **standard variable manufacturing overhead rate.** As stated, Ali, Maria, and Bill expected to work about 60 hours each, or a total of 180 direct labor hours per month. Based on the planned variable manufacturing overhead cost of $63 and 180 estimated direct labor hours, we compute a standard variable overhead rate of $0.35 by dividing the $63 budgeted variable manufacturing overhead by the 180 estimated direct labor hours, as follows:

Budgeted Variable Manufacturing Overhead	÷	Budgeted Direct Labor Hours	=	Standard Variable Manufacturing Overhead Rate
$63	÷	180 Hours	=	$0.35 Per Hour

When the variable manufacturing overhead allocation is based on direct labor hours, once the direct labor efficiency standard and the standard variable manufacturing overhead rate per direct labor hour have been determined, the standard variable manufacturing overhead cost per unit can be determined. The standard variable manufacturing overhead cost to build a single unit of production is calculated by multiplying the direct labor efficiency standard (the estimated direct labor hours per unit) by the standard variable manufacturing overhead rate. For Tree Top, standard cost per unit for variable manufacturing overhead is $0.21, determined as follows:

Standard Direct Labor Hours Allowed	×	Standard Variable Manufacturing Overhead Rate	=	Standard Variable Mfg Overhead Cost Per Unit
0.6 Hours	×	$0.35 Per Hour	=	$0.21

Fixed Manufacturing Overhead Standards

Unlike variable manufacturing overhead cost, which changes in total as production increases or decreases, fixed manufacturing overhead cost remains constant in total regardless of how many units are produced.

To set the fixed manufacturing overhead standards, manufacturers must first estimate the total cost of fixed manufacturing overhead. For Tree Top Mail Box Company, this amount consists of rent of $200 per month and monthly depreciation of $25 for the equipment used to make the mail boxes. Fixed manufacturing overhead then totals $225 per month ($200 + $25 = $225).

Standard Fixed Manufacturing Overhead Rate

standard fixed manufacturing overhead rate The rate used to apply fixed manufacturing overhead to units of manufactured product.

As with variable manufacturing overhead, fixed manufacturing overhead can be allocated to production based on units of production, direct labor hours, direct labor dollars, machine hours, or some other allocation base. The rate used to apply fixed manufacturing overhead to units of product is known as the **standard fixed manufacturing overhead rate.**

Our illustration assumes that fixed manufacturing overhead is allocated to production based on direct labor hours. In such a case, the standard fixed manufacturing overhead rate is determined by dividing the total estimated fixed manufacturing overhead cost by the total estimated direct labor hours. In the case of Tree Top Mail Box Company, the standard fixed manufacturing overhead rate of $1.25 per direct labor hour is calculated by dividing the budgeted fixed manufacturing overhead cost of $225 by the budgeted direct labor hours of 180 as shown here:

Budgeted Fixed Mfg Overhead	÷	Budgeted Direct Labor Hours	=	Standard Fixed Mfg Overhead Rate
$225	÷	180 Hours	=	$1.25

We calculate the standard fixed manufacturing overhead cost to build a single unit of product by multiplying the direct labor efficiency standard per unit by the standard fixed manufacturing overhead rate. For Tree Top, standard cost per unit for fixed manufacturing overhead is $0.75, determined as follows:

Standard Direct Labor Hours Allowed	×	Standard Fixed Mfg Overhead Rate	=	Standard Fixed Mfg Overhead Cost Per Unit
0.6 Hours	×	$1.25 Per Hour	=	$0.75

Total Standard Cost Per Unit   Once standards have been set for direct material, direct labor, variable manufacturing overhead, and fixed manufacturing overhead, the total standard cost per unit can be calculated. This amount reflects how much it *should* cost to produce a unit of product. The standard cost per unit represents a useful estimate that can be helpful for planning and setting selling prices. For Tree Top, the total standard cost per mail box is $8.85 as shown in Exhibit 9–6.

Exhibit 9–6
Total Standard Cost Per Mail Box Built

Standard Direct Material Cost Per Mail Box	$1.89
Standard Direct Labor Cost Per Mail Box	6.00
Standard Variable Manufacturing Overhead Cost Per Mail Box	.21
Standard Fixed Manufacturing Overhead Cost Per Mail Box	.75
Total Standard Cost Per Mail Box	$8.85

As you might imagine, the *actual* cost of producing an item is almost never exactly the same as the *standard* cost. When actual cost exceeds standard cost, management should take steps to determine the cause of the variance, and, if necessary, take corrective action.

Actual total production cost that exceeds the standard may indicate that a general problem exists, but it provides almost no information that can help managers focus on the true cause of the problem. Managers need access to information that can be used to isolate and address specific cost problems.

The next sections show how managers use standard costing to isolate specific problems for each production cost category.

VARIANCE ANALYSIS

Standard costs can help control costs by serving as benchmarks to compare with actual production costs. To use standard costing as a control device, managers compare *standard costs* to *actual costs* to see whether a variance exists. Instead of calculating a single variance for total production cost, they make variances specific enough to isolate a particular production process problem. In this section we examine how detailed standard costs variances are calculated for direct material, direct labor, variable manufacturing overhead, and fixed manufacturing overhead. We will walk through the calculations for each standard cost variance using Tree Top Mail Box Company as an example.

Unfortunately for Tree Top, November was not nearly as successful as October. The company produced and sold only 225 mail boxes in spite of demand for many more. The income statement for the month of November appears in Exhibit 9–7.

Exhibit 9–7
Tree Top's November 2001 Income Statement

TREE TOP MAIL BOX COMPANY		
Income Statement		
For the Month Ended November 30, 2001		
Sales (225 mail boxes at $10 each)		$2,250
Less Expenses		
Direct Material (6,000 feet of wood)	$ 477	
Direct Labor (162 hours at $10.50 per hr)	1,701	
Rent	200	
Utilities (all variable)	50	
Miscellaneous Variable Costs	90	
Depreciation	25	2,543
Net Income		$ (293)

November's loss disturbed Ali, Maria, and Bill because they had spent nearly as much time at the shop as in October, but produced far fewer mail boxes. The question is, what changes should Tree Top make to get the company back on track? We can answer this question once we have calculated the variances and examined their causes.

To calculate standard cost variances, we use the standard costs discussed in the preceding sections, and compare them with Tree Top's actual performance. Actual performance data are obtained from various sources, including company reports and files. In our Tree Top Mail Box Company example, we have included the key details in November's income statement, presented in Exhibit 9–7.

Direct Materials Variances

Direct material variances can be used to answer three important questions. (1) Did the company use more or less direct material than it should have, based on the standards set? (2) Did the company pay more or less than it should have when the direct material was purchased from the supplier based on the standards set? (3) What was the cost impact of these quantity and price differences?

Direct Material Quantity Variance

direct material quantity variance A measure of the over- or underconsumption of direct material for the number of units actually manufactured.

direct material usage variance Another name for the *direct material quantity variance.*

The **direct material quantity variance,** sometimes called the **direct material usage variance,** is a measure of the overconsumption or underconsumption of direct material for the number of units actually manufactured. It informs management whether too much or too little direct material is used in the manufacturing process based on the standards. The direct material quantity variance is the difference between the standard quantity and the actual quantity of direct materials used. We follow three steps to calculate the direct material quantity variances. First, we calculate the standard quantity of direct material allowed for actual production. Second, we calculate the variance in units of direct material. Finally, we calculate the variance in dollars.

Step 1: Calculate the standard quantity of direct material allowed for actual production.

The standard quantity of direct material allowed is the amount needed for actual production, according to the standard. It is the amount *allowed* for *actual* production. To calculate this amount, we determine how much direct material should have been used according to the standard to make the units actually produced.

Recall that Tree Top produced 225 mail boxes in November. To determine the quantity of the wood that *should* have been used to make 225 mail boxes, we multiply the direct material quantity standard (21.60 feet per unit) by the number of mail boxes produced (225). For Tree Top, the standard quantity of direct material allowed for the actual production of 225 mail boxes is 4,860 feet, as shown here:

Standard Quantity Per Unit		Number of Units Produced		Standard Quantity of Direct Material Allowed
21.60 Feet	×	225 Units	=	4,860 Feet

We see from the calculations that 4,860 feet of wood is the standard direct material quantity allowed for the units produced—the direct material quantity that *should* have been used based on the number of units *actually* produced.

Step 2: Calculate the direct material quantity variance in units of direct material.

We calculate the direct material quantity variance in units of direct material by subtracting the actual quantity of direct material used from the standard quantity of direct material allowed. For Tree Top Mail Box Company, the direct material quantity variance in feet is determined by comparing the quantity of wood it *should* have taken to make the 225 mail boxes (determined in step 1) to the quantity of wood it *actually* took to make the mail boxes (the actual quantity).

Discussion Question

9-3. If the actual amount of wood used was more than the standard quantity of wood, do you think the direct material quantity variance would be favorable or unfavorable? Explain your reasoning.

To use standard costing, a manufacturer must maintain a record of the quantity of direct material used in production. In the case of Tree Top, this information is found in the income statement as presented in Exhibit 9–7. A review of that income statement shows that the actual quantity of direct material Tree Top used to make the 225 mail boxes in November was 6,000 feet of wood. Often the quantity of material used in production differs from the quantity of material purchased. For this calculation it is important to remember to use the quantity of material used, not the quantity purchased.

Tree Top's direct material quantity variance is calculated by finding the difference between the standard quantity of direct material allowed and the quantity of direct material used in production. In this case the variance is 1,140 unfavorable, as calculated here:

Standard Quantity Allowed for Production		Actual Quantity Used		Quantity Variance in Feet
4,860 Feet	−	6,000 Feet	=	1,140 Unfavorable

We can see from the presentation that Ali, Maria, and Bill used 1,140 more feet of wood than the standard allowed to make the 225 mail boxes. Does this overuse of direct material really matter? Even if the direct material quantity variance in feet is 1,140 unfavorable, it *may* represent an insignificant dollar amount. To evaluate whether this variance is worthy of attention, we need to assign a dollar amount.

Step 3: Calculate the direct material quantity variance in dollars.

To avoid contaminating the quantity variance with problems relating to the actual price paid for material, the dollar amount assigned to the direct material quantity variance is based on the standard direct material price, not the actual price. Tree Top's direct material quantity variance in dollars is $99.75. This amount is calculated by multiplying the direct material quantity variance (1,140 feet) by the direct material standard price of $0.0875, as follows:

Quantity Variance in Units of Direct Material (Feet)		Standard Price Per Unit of Direct Material (Feet)		Quantity Variance in Dollars
1,140 Unfavorable	×	$0.0875	=	$99.75 Unfavorable

The direct materials quantity variance in dollars provides valuable information about the cost of using too much direct material to make the mail boxes. Now that a dollar amount has been assigned to the variance, we can evaluate its importance and devote the amount of management attention that is appropriate.

Discussion Questions

9-4. Based on Tree Top Mail Box Company's quantity variance, do you think that Ali, Maria, and Bill need to examine reasons for using so much wood? Explain your reasoning.

9-5. If the dollar amount of a variance is insignificant, does the variance information help Tree Top's management team determine where it should focus attention? Explain.

9-6. If there had been no variance, would this mean Tree Top used the appropriate amount of wood to build its mail boxes in November? Explain your reasoning.

We assume that only one direct material is used to make the mail boxes for Tree Top. In practice most products require several different direct materials, ranging from one to thousands, and a separate material quantity variance is computed for each direct material used. The logic and computations, however, are similar to those presented here.

Once the direct material quantity variance has been calculated, management can assess the situation and, if necessary, take corrective action. Generally, a quantity variance should be discussed with the individuals who are responsible for the amount of direct material used. The focus of the discussion should be on finding and eliminating the cause of the variance. In many companies, the person responsible for direct material consumption is the production supervisor, who would attempt to determine the cause of the variance and take steps to eliminate it.

Direct Material Price Variance

The **direct material price variance** is a measure of the difference between the amount the company *planned* to pay for direct material and the amount it *actually* paid. This variance provides an indication of whether the price paid to suppliers for direct material compares favorably to the standard price. To find the direct material price variance we use a two-step process. First, we determine the amount that should have been paid for the direct material. Second, we calculate the dollar amount of the direct material variance.

Step 1: Determine the amount that should have been paid for the direct material purchased according to the standard price.

According to the detailed information on November's income statement, Tree Top Mail Box Company purchased 6,000 feet of wood. How much should the company have paid for the 6,000 feet of wood if it had been able to purchase it at the standard price? We determine this amount by multiplying the actual quantity of direct material purchased by the standard price. Often the quantity of material purchased differs from the quantity of material used in production. Which amount should we use? For this calculation remember to use the quantity of material purchased, not the quantity used in production.

Actual Quantity Purchased	×	Direct Material Standard Price	=	Quantity Purchased Priced at Standard
6,000 Feet	×	$0.0875	=	$525

Our calculations show that, based on the standard price of $0.0875 per foot, the 6,000 feet of wood purchased should have cost $525.

Step 2: Calculate the dollar amount of the direct material price variance.

We calculate the dollar amount of the direct material price variance by subtracting the actual cost of direct material from the standard cost of the direct material purchased (determined in step 1). According to the detailed information on November's income statement, Tree Top purchased the 6,000 feet of wood for $477. By comparing the standard cost of $525 to the actual cost of $477, we determine that the price variance is $48 favorable.

Quantity Purchased Priced at Standard	−	Actual Direct Material Cost	=	Direct Material Price Variance
$525	−	$477	=	$48 Favorable

To review the calculations for the direct material price variance in dollars, we compare the amount the wood purchased *should* have cost, $525, to what the wood *actually* cost, $477, to determine the direct material price variance.

When a product requires the use of multiple direct materials, a separate material price variance is computed for each direct material used. The logic and computations, however, are similar to those presented here.

Once the direct material price variance has been calculated, management can assess the situation and, if necessary, take corrective action. In most manufacturing companies, direct material is purchased by purchasing agents working in the company's purchasing department. Therefore, direct material price variances are brought to the attention of the purchasing agent responsible for buying the particular direct material so that the price can be evaluated and corrective action taken when necessary.

In the case of Tree Top, the actual price paid for the wood was lower than the standard price, resulting in a favorable direct material price variance. It may seem that a favorable variance would not warrant investigation, but this is not always the case.

A significant favorable variance is worth examining for several reasons. First, repeated favorable variances may be an indication that the standard is too lax. Second, management should investigate the variance to see whether the techniques used to achieve the favorable variance can be used by other areas of the company to help reduce cost. Third, a favorable variance may have occurred because of a trade-off of some other value. For example, it might be achieved by purchasing direct material of a substandard quality.

Bill purchased the wood for Tree Top from the lumber company at a discounted price. The lumber company was able to offer the discount because another customer had refused the wood and the lumber company was overstocked. As it turned out, the wood had an unusually high number of knots and other blemishes. The substandard wood, then, may have caused the use of more direct material and direct labor than would have otherwise been required for production.

Discussion Questions

9-7. How might the purchase of wood at a discount affect the direct material quantity variance?

9-8. If there had been no variance, would this mean Tree Top paid what it should have for the wood used to build its mail boxes in November? Explain your reasoning.

Direct Labor Variances

Direct labor variances help managers answer three key questions. (1) Did it take more or fewer direct labor hours than it should have taken for the company to manufacture its products based on the standards set? (2) Was the company's hourly direct labor rate more or less than it should have been based on the standards set? (3) What was the cost impact of these differences in the number of direct labor hours and the hourly labor rate?

It may be helpful to consider some parallels between direct material and direct labor. Instead of using "quantities" and "prices" terms as for direct material, we use "hours" and "rates" with direct labor. In reality, only the descriptive words change, the meanings stay the same. The "quantity" of direct material is similar to the "hours" of direct labor. Likewise, the "price" per measure of direct material is similar to the "rate" per hour of direct labor. Because of these similarities, the steps and calculations of standard cost variances for direct labor are comparable to direct material variances.

direct labor efficiency variance A measure of the difference between the planned number of direct labor hours and the actual number of direct labor hours for the units actually manufactured.

Direct Labor Efficiency Variance

The **direct labor efficiency variance** is a measure of the over- or underconsumption of direct labor for the number of units actually manufactured. In other words, the direct labor efficiency variance informs management whether too much or too little direct labor is used in the manufacturing process based on the standards. This variance is comparable to the direct material quantity variance. Both are used to evaluate the quantity of something used. In the case of the direct material quantity variance, the focus is on the quantity of direct material used. In the case of the direct labor efficiency variance, the focus is on the quantity of direct labor hours used.

We use three steps to calculate this variance. First, we find the standard number of direct labor hours allowed for production. Second, we determine the variance in hours. Finally, we calculate the variance in dollars.

Step 1: Calculate the standard number of direct labor hours allowed for actual production.

In this first step we determine the amount of direct labor time it *should* have taken to make all the units that were *actually* made during the period. According to the direct labor efficiency standard for Tree Top, it should have taken 0.6 hours (36 minutes) to make each mail box. Because 225 mail boxes were made in November, the total amount of direct labor hours should have been 135 hours (225 × 0.6 = 135).

Step 2: Calculate the direct labor efficiency variance in hours.

We compute the direct labor efficiency variance in hours by subtracting the standard direct labor hours allowed from the actual number of direct labor hours worked. According to information taken from Tree Top's November income statement presented in Exhibit 9–7, the actual number of direct labor hours used in November was 162. By comparing the standard hours allowed for the 225 mail boxes, 135 hours, to the actual direct labor hours, 162 hours, we see that the direct labor efficiency variance in hours is 27 hours unfavorable.

Standard Direct Labor Hours Allowed		Actual Direct Labor Hours		Efficiency Variance in Hours
	−		=	
135 Hours	−	162 Hours	=	27 Hours Unfavorable

The variance between the standard and actual number of hours worked indicates that Tree Top's employees did not work very efficiently. If they had, they would have completed the 225 mail boxes in 135 hours, or maybe even less.

To grasp the true magnitude of the 27-hour unfavorable variance, we must assign a dollar amount.

Step 3: Calculate the direct labor efficiency variance in dollars.

To avoid contaminating the efficiency variance with problems relating to the actual labor rate, we calculate the direct labor efficiency variance in dollars by multiplying the variance in hours by the standard direct labor rate, not the actual labor rate. In the case of Tree Top, we multiply the 27 hour unfavorable direct labor efficiency variance by the standard direct labor rate of $10, shown as follows:

Direct Labor Efficiency Variance in Hours		Standard Direct Labor Rate		Direct Labor Efficiency Variance in Dollars
	×		=	
27 Hours	×	$10	=	$270 Unfavorable

Once the direct labor efficiency variance has been calculated, management can assess the variance and, if necessary, take corrective action. The plant manager would probably ask the production supervisor or production-line employees to help determine why the unfavorable variance occurred. Once the cause of the problem is found, corrective action can be taken.

Tree Top determined that substandard wood caused the unfavorable direct labor efficiency variance. To make mail boxes of sufficient quality, Ali, Maria, and Bill needed extra time to cut the knots and other blemishes from the wood. The solution to the variance problem is to purchase only good-quality wood in the future.

Direct Labor Rate Variance

direct labor rate variance
A measure of the difference between the actual wage rate paid to employees and the direct labor rate standard.

The **direct labor rate variance** is a measure of the difference between the actual wage rate paid to employees and the direct labor rate standard. This variance shows the effect of unanticipated wage rate changes. The direct labor rate standard for the company is $10 per hour. As you will note by looking at the November income statement in Exhibit 9–7, each of the three owners received a 50 cent raise during November. So, for Tree Top, the direct labor rate variance will indicate added cost caused by the pay raises. We use a two-step process to calculate the direct labor rate variance. First, we find the amount the company should have paid for direct labor for the hours worked. Second, we determine the dollar amount of the direct labor rate variance.

Step 1: Determine the amount that should have been paid for the actual direct labor hours worked according to the direct labor rate standard.

In this step we determine how much the company should have paid for the direct labor hours actually worked, based on the direct labor rate standard. For Tree Top, the actual direct labor hours totaled 162 for November. By multiplying the 162 actual direct labor hours by the direct labor rate standard of $10, we determine that the company should have paid $1,620.

Actual Direct Labor Hours	×	Direct Labor Rate Standard	=	Actual Direct Labor Hours at the Standard Rate
162 Hours	×	$10	=	$1,620

Once we determine what the company should have paid according to the standard, we can compare it to the amount actually paid to determine the direct labor rate variance.

Step 2: Calculate the dollar amount of the direct labor rate variance.

We compute the dollar amount of the direct labor rate variance by subtracting the actual cost of direct labor from the standard cost of the direct labor actually worked. The direct labor rate variance compares the amount the actual direct labor hours should have cost to the actual cost. In the case of Tree Top, we find that the actual direct labor cost for November was $1,701, as shown on the November income statement in Exhibit 9–7. Tree Top's labor hours at standard should have cost $1,620. When we compare actual labor cost ($1,701) to standard cost ($1,620), we find an unfavorable direct labor rate variance of $81, calculated as follows:

Actual Direct Labor Hours at the Standard Rate	−	Actual Direct Labor Cost	=	Direct Labor Rate Variance
$1,620	−	$1,701	=	$81 Unfavorable

The calculated variance is unfavorable because the actual labor cost is higher than the cost based on the standard rate. This $81 unfavorable variance provides useful information to Ali, Maria, and Bill about the effect of their $0.50 per hour raise.

Discussion Questions

9-9. What effect did the $0.50 per hour pay raise have on November's profits?

9-10. In light of the financial problems that occurred in November, do you think Tree Top's owners should roll back the wage rate to $10 per hour? Explain your reasoning.

As with other variances, once the direct labor rate variance has been calculated, management can assess the variance and, if necessary, take corrective action. Direct labor rate variances are caused by labor rate changes that are unanticipated. Generally, when labor rates are contractually set or a result of collective bargaining with labor unions, labor rate changes are not unexpected. Accordingly, these labor rates are factored into the labor rate standard. A labor rate variance can be caused by an unexpected rate change of some kind, or perhaps an unanticipated change in the makeup of the labor force. For example, if the company retains more experienced workers and has fewer new workers, an unfavorable rate variance is likely because new employees generally begin their employment at a lower hourly wage than experienced employees.

In the case of Tree Top Mail Box Company, the November income statement shows that Ali, Maria, and Bill gave themselves an unplanned 50 cent per hour raise. Although no corrective action will likely be taken, the trio now knows how the raise affected profits.

The direct labor variances reveal that Ali, Maria, and Bill had two important problems in November regarding direct labor cost. First, it took 27 extra hours to make the 225 mail boxes. The extra 27 hours increased labor cost by $270. Second, the hourly wage paid to Ali, Maria, and Bill was higher than the planned $10 standard wage rate. This higher wage rate increased labor cost by $81. The total effect of these two direct labor problems is $351 unfavorable.

Manufacturing Overhead Variances

Manufacturing overhead variances help managers answer two vital questions. (1) Did the company spend more or less on overhead items than it should have, based on the standards that were set? (2) Did the company utilize its production facility efficiently?

In this section we look at four different manufacturing overhead variances, two that deal with variable manufacturing overhead and two with fixed manufacturing overhead.

Variable Manufacturing Overhead Efficiency Variance

variable manufacturing overhead efficiency variance A measure of the variable manufacturing overhead cost attributable to the difference between the planned and actual direct labor hours worked.

The **variable manufacturing overhead efficiency variance** is a measure of the variable manufacturing overhead cost attributable to the difference between the planned and actual direct labor hours worked. Surprisingly, this variance relates more to the efficiency of direct labor than anything else. While production workers work in the factory, they consume electricity as they use lights and air conditioning and operate machinery. They also use supplies and other factory resources that all are part of manufacturing overhead. So, as workers work longer, they use more factory resources. How much more? The variable factory overhead efficiency variance helps answer this question.

An unfavorable variable manufacturing overhead efficiency variance is a measure of the variable manufacturing overhead cost associated with the extra hours worked by direct labor. A direct relationship exists between the direct labor efficiency variance and the variable manufacturing overhead efficiency variance. Accordingly, if the direct labor efficiency variance is unfavorable, the variable manufacturing overhead efficiency variance will also be unfavorable. Likewise, if the direct labor efficiency variance is favorable, the variable manufacturing overhead efficiency variance will also be favorable.

The first two steps for calculating the variable manufacturing overhead efficiency variance are the same as those for determining the direct labor efficiency variance. These steps are to find the standard number of direct labor hours allowed for actual production and then to calculate the direct labor efficiency variance in hours.

Assuming the direct labor efficiency variance has been calculated, we review the information learned from those calculations before moving to the third step of the calculations, which is determining the variable manufacturing overhead efficiency variance in dollars.

Recall that our calculation showed that Tree Top used an extra 27 direct labor hours to make the 225 mail boxes in November. The extra 27 direct labor hours not only increased direct labor cost, but it also increased other costs. While Ali, Maria, and Bill worked the extra 27 hours, they consumed electricity, supplies, and other factory resources. In sum, the inefficiency of the workforce increased variable manufacturing overhead cost. Had they not worked the extra 27 hours, Tree Top's owners would have saved not only the labor cost, but also the factory resources they consumed as they worked the extra time.

Step 3: Calculate the variable manufacturing overhead efficiency variance in dollars.

To calculate the variable manufacturing overhead efficiency variance in dollars, multiply the direct labor efficiency variance in hours by the standard variable manufacturing overhead rate.

For Tree Top, the direct labor efficiency variance in hours we calculated earlier is 27 hours. We multiply this amount by the standard variable manufacturing overhead rate we calculated earlier of $0.35. This results in an unfavorable variable manufacturing overhead efficiency variance of $9.45 as shown here:

Direct Labor Efficiency Variance in Hours		Standard Variable Mfg Overhead Rate		Variable Mfg Overhead Efficiency Variance
27 Hours	×	$0.35	=	$9.45 Unfavorable

Now that the $9.45 variance has been calculated, management can assess the variance and take corrective action if necessary. Because the variable manufacturing overhead efficiency variance is based on direct labor efficiency, improving the direct labor efficiency variance will solve the variable overhead efficiency variance problem.

Tree Top's variable manufacturing overhead efficiency variance is so small that it may warrant no management attention. Even so, as Ali, Maria, and Bill work to bring the direct labor efficiency variance under control, the variable manufacturing overhead variance will also improve.

Discussion Questions

9-11. If variable manufacturing overhead is allocated to production based on direct labor hours, will an unfavorable variable manufacturing overhead efficiency variance always accompany an unfavorable direct labor efficiency variance? Explain your reasoning.

9-12. If the direct labor efficiency variance is zero, will the variable manufacturing overhead efficiency variance also be zero? Explain your reasoning.

Variable Manufacturing Overhead Spending Variance

variable manufacturing overhead spending variance The difference between how much was actually spent on variable manufacturing overhead and the amount that should have been spent based on the actual direct labor hours worked.

The **variable manufacturing overhead spending variance** is the difference between what was actually spent on variable manufacturing overhead and what should have been spent, based on the actual direct labor hours worked. The question this variance answers is, based on the actual number of direct labor hours worked, is variable manufacturing overhead cost in line? In the case of Tree Top, given that production took 162 direct labor hours, was variable manufacturing overhead more or less than it should have been for that many direct labor hours? To find the answer, we must first determine the standard variable manufacturing overhead for the actual number of hours worked and then calculate the overhead spending variance in dollars. Let us look at the first step in this process.

Step 1: Determine the standard variable manufacturing overhead for the actual number of hours worked.

To determine the standard variable manufacturing overhead for the actual hours worked, we multiply the standard variable manufacturing overhead rate by the actual number of direct labor hours. This calculation shows us the amount that should have been spent for variable manufacturing overhead based on the actual labor hours worked. Based on Tree Top's standard variable manufacturing overhead rate of $0.35 per hour, the standard variable manufacturing overhead cost for the 162 actual direct labor hours is $56.70 as shown here:

Actual Direct Labor Hours		Standard Variable Mfg Overhead Rate		Standard Variable Mfg Overhead for Actual Direct Labor Hours
162 Hours	×	$0.35	=	$56.70

Now that we know how much Tree Top's variable manufacturing overhead should have been, we can compare it to the actual variable manufacturing overhead amount to determine the amount of the variance.

Step 2: Calculate the variable manufacturing overhead spending variance.

We calculate the variable manufacturing overhead spending variance by comparing standard variable manufacturing overhead for the actual number of hours worked (determined in step 1) to the amount actually spent for variable manufacturing overhead. This calculation compares *actual* variable manufacturing overhead cost to what it *should* have been for the actual hours worked. In the case of

Tree Top, the actual amount spent for variable manufacturing overhead in November was $140. By comparing this amount to the standard of $56.70, we determine that the variable manufacturing overhead spending variance is $83.30 unfavorable as shown here:

Standard Variable Mfg Overhead Cost for Actual Direct Labor Hours	–	Actual Variable Mfg Overhead Cost	=	Variable Mfg Overhead Spending Variance
$56.70	–	$140.00	=	$83.30 Unfavorable

Discussion Questions

9-13. What are some possible reasons why Tree Top Mail Box Company's variable manufacturing overhead spending was much higher than it should have been based on the standards?

9-14. If there had been no variance, would this mean Tree Top paid what it should have for variable manufacturing overhead in November? Explain your reasoning.

As managers assess the variable manufacturing overhead spending variance, they should keep in mind that it is a result of many different overhead expenditures. In practice, most companies break down the variable manufacturing overhead spending variance into separate variances for each variable manufacturing overhead item. For example, a manufacturer would have separate variance calculations for electricity, water, telephone, cleaning supplies, maintenance supplies, and so forth. The logic and calculations for each variance, however, would be similar to what we have presented here.

For Tree Top Mail Box Company, the trouble with variable manufacturing overhead cost is a combination of an unfavorable efficiency variance of $9.45 and an unfavorable spending variance of $83.30. Although the unfavorable efficiency variance will require little or no attention, the spending variance is sizeable and should be investigated. Each component of variable manufacturing overhead should be reviewed to see whether overhead spending can be reduced.

Fixed Manufacturing Overhead Budget Variance

fixed manufacturing overhead budget variance The difference between the actual amount of total fixed manufacturing overhead cost and the budgeted fixed manufacturing overhead cost.

The **fixed manufacturing overhead budget variance** is a measure of how actual total fixed manufacturing overhead compares to budgeted fixed manufacturing overhead. For example, if a company expects fixed manufacturing overhead cost to be $200,000 per month, the budget variance indicates whether the actual fixed manufacturing overhead is more or less than the $200,000.

We take only one step to compute the fixed manufacturing overhead budget variance. The dollar amount is calculated simply by subtracting actual fixed manufacturing overhead cost from the budgeted fixed manufacturing overhead. For Tree Top, the fixed manufacturing overhead budget variance for November is zero, because actual fixed manufacturing overhead cost exactly equals the amount budgeted, shown as follows:

Budget Fixed Mfg Overhead Cost	–	Actual Fixed Mfg Overhead Cost	=	Fixed Mfg Overhead Budget Variance
$225	–	$225	=	$0

The company has only two fixed overhead items, rent and depreciation, so the fact that actual cost equaled budgeted cost is not surprising. If Tree Top purchased additional production equipment resulting in higher depreciation cost, an unfavorable variance could occur.

Fixed manufacturing overhead costs are generally associated with long-term commitments for specific factory resources. Examples of fixed overhead include the cost of depreciation on factory equipment, factory rent, insurance, and property taxes. Unlike other factory costs, fixed overhead is less likely to be affected by the routine decisions that managers and employees make daily. Therefore, the variation between the amount budgeted and the actual fixed factory overhead incurred is just as likely to be caused by a flawed budget as it is by spending decisions made during the budgeted period. For example, if a company budgets $50,000 for property taxes but the taxes are actually $51,000, the $1,000 variance that results is caused by a flawed budget, not by uncontrolled spending. Accordingly, fixed manufacturing overhead budget variances should be closely scrutinized to determine whether the required corrective action is to improve the budgeting process or to modify spending during the period.

Like variable manufacturing overhead, fixed manufacturing overhead comprises many different items. In practice, separate budget variances are calculated for each fixed manufacturing overhead item.

Fixed Manufacturing Overhead Volume Variance

fixed manufacturing overhead volume variance A measure of the utilization of plant capacity. This variance is caused by manufacturing more or less product during a particular production period than planned.

The last standard cost variance we discuss is the **fixed manufacturing overhead volume variance,** which measures utilization of plant capacity. A variance is caused by the manufacture of more or less product during a particular production period than planned. When a manufacturer invests in expensive production machinery, it does so in anticipation of producing a given amount of product. If the company expects to produce only a small amount of product, it invests in inexpensive, low-volume equipment. If, however, the company expects to produce a large volume of product, it usually acquires more costly, high-volume equipment. If expensive, high-volume equipment is purchased but actual production is low, then it is likely that the company spent too much on production capacity. The fixed manufacturing overhead volume variance focuses on this relationship between production capacity and the actual volume produced.

When Ali, Maria, and Bill formed their manufacturing company, they could have set up shop to produce a very small number of mail boxes using hand tools; or they could have chosen to invest heavily in a building and automated equipment, thereby greatly increasing their plant capacity. They chose to rent a small garage and invest a small amount in power tools that gave them a capacity to produce about 300 mail boxes per month. If they produce more than 300 mail boxes, that's great, but if they produce fewer, they are underutilizing their capacity to produce. In November, they produced only 225 mail boxes. Tree Top Mail Box Company, then, underutilized its capacity to produce by 75 mail boxes. Is this a big problem? To evaluate the magnitude of the problem we need to assign a dollar amount to the underutilization.

In the case of Tree Top Mail Box Company, the monthly fixed cost of $225 provides a capacity to produce 300 mail boxes. We follow three steps to calculate the fixed manufacturing overhead volume variance. First, we find the difference between expected and actual production. Second, we determine the standard number of direct labor hours associated with the production. Finally, we calculate the dollar amount of the fixed manufacturing overhead volume variance. We examine these steps in detail next.

Step 1: Calculate the difference between expected (budgeted) production and actual production.

The budgeted production for Tree Top is 300 mail boxes per month. Tree Top's actual production was less than its budgeted production by 75 mail boxes, shown as follows:

Plant Production Capacity	−	Actual Number of Units Produced	=	Under- Or Overproduction in Units
300 Units	−	225 Units	=	75 Units Under

As you will see, when fixed manufacturing overhead is allocated to production based on direct labor hours, the direct labor efficiency standard, with the standard fixed manufacturing overhead rate per direct labor hour, is used to calculate the dollar amount of the fixed manufacturing overhead volume variance.

Step 2: Determine the standard number of direct labor hours associated with the under- or overproduction.

We determine the standard number of direct labor hours associated with the under- or overproduction by multiplying the under- or overproduction by the direct labor efficiency standard. In the case of Tree Top, the direct labor efficiency standard is 0.6 hours per unit. Accordingly, the standard direct labor hours associated with the underproduction of 75 mail boxes is 45 hours (75 units × 0.6 hours per unit), shown as follows:

Amount of Under- or Overproduction	×	Direct Labor Efficiency Standard	=	Standard Number of Hours Associated with Production
75 Units	×	0.6 Hours Per Unit	=	45 Hours

Now that we know the number of standard hours associated with the over- or underproduction, we can assign a dollar amount based on the standard fixed manufacturing overhead rate per hour.

Step 3: Calculate the dollar amount of the fixed manufacturing overhead volume variance.

The dollar amount of the fixed manufacturing volume variance is calculated by multiplying the standard number of direct labor hours associated with the under- or overproduction by the standard fixed manufacturing overhead rate per direct labor hour. In the case of Tree Top, the fixed manufacturing overhead volume variance is $56.25, calculated as follows:

Standard Direct Labor Hours for Under- or Overproduction	×	Standard Fixed Mfg Overhead Rate	=	Fixed Mfg Overhead Volume Variance
45 Hours	×	$1.25	=	$56.25 Unfavorable

Once the fixed manufacturing overhead volume variance has been calculated, management can attempt to determine what caused it. In the case of Tree Top, the variance resulted primarily from inefficiencies caused by substandard direct material. Surprisingly, however, fixed manufacturing overhead volume variances are often caused by marketing and sales activities, rather than by the production department. In general, production occurs in response to sales demand. If the product is selling poorly, production volume will be low because little product is needed to fulfill demand. Conversely, if sales demand is high, production volume is likely to be large to meet demand.

USING STANDARD COST VARIANCES TO MANAGE BY EXCEPTION

Once all the standard cost variances have been calculated, the accounting department prepares a performance report that lists each variance. Then managers can use management by exception to address the problems associated with the unfavorable variances, beginning with the largest. A performance report is presented in Exhibit 9–8 for Tree Top Mail Box Company.

As the Tree Top Mail Box Company example shows, sometimes relationships among standard cost variances can occur that help explain the cause of some variances. Also, managers must develop the skill to review the variances and then seek out their causes and possible remedies. Even though managers can use standard costing to spot pressing issues, they must be careful of its shortcomings. Standard costing is one management tool, but not the only tool.

Exhibit 9–8
Tree Top's November Performance Report

TREE TOP MAIL BOX COMPANY
Performance Report
For November 2001

Variance	Amount	Favorable/ Unfavorable
Direct material quantity variance	$ 99.75	Unfavorable
Direct material price variance	48.00	Favorable
Direct labor efficiency variance	270.00	Unfavorable
Direct labor rate variance	81.00	Unfavorable
Variable mfg overhead efficiency variance	9.45	Unfavorable
Variable mfg overhead spending variance	83.30	Unfavorable
Fixed mfg overhead budget variance	0	——
Fixed mfg overhead volume variance	56.25	Unfavorable
Total	$551.75	Unfavorable

SUMMARY

In the process of operating businesses, managers must focus their valuable time on areas that need to be improved. One area that requires constant attention is controlling the costs of operations. A process designed to help managers focus on cost items that need attention is standard costing, which sets cost performance goals and then uses these cost goals to evaluate performance.

Differences between the costs incurred by actual performance and what the costs should have been, based on the standards, are called variances. A favorable variance results when the cost of actual performance is lower than planned performance. An unfavorable variance results when the cost of actual performance is higher than planned performance. Managers can investigate all variances from standard, or they can focus their attention only on significant variances. Focusing only on significant variances is known as management by exception.

In establishing performance standards, managers can use either ideal standards, which can be attained only under perfect conditions, or practical standards, which allow for normal working conditions.

Although a standard costing system can be extremely helpful to managers, it has several potential problems. These include employees setting lax standards to avoid unfavorable variances, relying on historical information that may perpetuate past inefficiencies, and managing "by the numbers" thus overlooking significant problems that do not result in variances.

A standard cost system in a manufacturing environment uses estimates for the cost of direct materials, direct labor, and manufacturing overhead. This system is in contrast to both an actual cost system, which uses the actual cost for direct materials, direct labor, and manufacturing overhead, and a normal cost system, which uses actual costs for direct materials and direct labor, and estimates for manufacturing overhead.

The standards used in a manufacturing type company generally include a direct material quantity standard, a direct material price standard, a direct labor efficiency standard, a direct labor rate standard, a standard variable manufacturing overhead rate, and a standard fixed manufacturing overhead rate.

To use standard costing as a control device, managers compare standard costs to actual costs to see whether a variance exists. Then they investigate variances, as appropriate, which is known as variance analysis. The variances most commonly used are the direct material quantity variance, the direct material price variance, the direct labor efficiency variance, the direct labor rate variance, the variable manufacturing overhead efficiency variance, the variable manufacturing overhead spending variance, the fixed manufacturing overhead budget variance, and the fixed manufacturing overhead volume variance.

APPENDIX—RECORDING PRODUCT COST USING STANDARD COSTING

This appendix is intended to provide an overview of the accounting entries to record product costs using standard costing.

LEARNING OBJECTIVES

After completing your work in this appendix, you should be able to do the following:

1. Record the purchase of direct material and the direct material price variance.
2. Record the use of direct material and the direct material quantity variance.
3. Record the use of direct labor and the direct labor rate and efficiency variances.
4. Record actual variable manufacturing overhead cost incurred.
5. Record the application of variable manufacturing overhead to production.
6. Close the variable manufacturing overhead accounts and record the variable overhead variances.
7. Record actual fixed manufacturing overhead cost incurred.
8. Record the application of fixed manufacturing overhead to production.
9. Close the fixed manufacturing overhead accounts and record the variable overhead variances.
10. Close the standard cost variances to cost of goods sold.

The following accounts will be used for the entries in this appendix:

1. Cash
2. Raw materials inventory

3. Work-in-process inventory
4. Direct materials price variance
5. Direct materials quantity variance
6. Direct labor efficiency variance
7. Direct labor rate variance
8. Variable manufacturing overhead efficiency variance
9. Variable manufacturing overhead spending variance
10. Fixed manufacturing overhead budget variance
11. Fixed manufacturing overhead volume variance
12. Variable manufacturing overhead incurred
13. Variable manufacturing overhead applied
14. Fixed manufacturing overhead incurred
15. Fixed manufacturing overhead applied
16. Accumulated depreciation
17. Accounts payable
18. Cost of goods sold

Recall that debits increase assets, expenses, and losses, while credits increase liabilities, equity, revenues, and gains. Also, you will learn that if a variance is favorable, the variance account is credited and if a variance is unfavorable, the variance account is debit.

When standard costing is used, direct materials, work-in-process, and finished goods inventories are maintained at standard cost. The standard cost variances account for the difference between the standard cost maintained in inventory and actual costs.

Purchase of Direct Material

The following table presents the information needed to make the direct materials purchases entry for Tree Top Mail Box Company:

Actual Quantity × Actual Price
6,000 × $0.0795
$477.00

Actual Quantity × Standard Price
6,000 × $0.0875
$525.00

Direct Material Price Variance
$48.00 F

To record the purchase of raw material, raw materials inventory is debited for the actual quantity multiplied by the standard price. For Tree Top, the amount is $525. The amount credited to accounts payable or cash is the actual purchase price of the material. For Tree Top, the amount is $477. The difference between the amount debited to direct material and the amount credited to accounts payable is taken to the direct materials price variance account. If a credit to the variance account is required to balance the entry, the variance is favorable. Conversely, if a debit is required the variance is unfavorable. For Tree Top, the variance is $48 favorable so the direct material price variance account will be credited.

The entry for Tree Top appears as follows:

Raw Materials	525.00	
Accounts Payable		477.00
Direct Materials Price Variance		48.00

Use of Direct Material

The following table presents the information needed to make the entry for the direct materials used by Tree Top Mail Box Company:

Actual Quantity × Standard Price
6,000 × $0,0875
$525.00

Standard Quantity × Standard Price
225 × 21.6 Feet × $0.0875
4860 Feet × $.0875
$425.25

Quantity Variance
$99.75 U

To record the use of direct material, work-in-process inventory is debited for the standard quantity of material allowed for production multiplied by the standard price. For Tree Top, the amount is $425.25. The amount credited to raw materials is the actual quantity of material multiplied by the standard price. For Tree Top, the amount is $477. The difference between the amount debited to work in process and the amount credited to raw materials is taken to the direct material quantity variance account. If a credit to the variance account is required to balance the entry, the variance is favorable. Conversely, if a debit is required, the variance is unfavorable. For Tree Top, the variance is $99.75 unfavorable so the direct material quantity variance account will be debited.

The entry for Tree Top appears as follows:

Work-in-Process Inventory	425.25	
Direct Materials Quantity Variance	99.75	
Raw Materials Inventory		525.00

Recording Direct Labor

The following tables present the information needed to make the entry to record direct labor for Tree Top Mail Box Company:

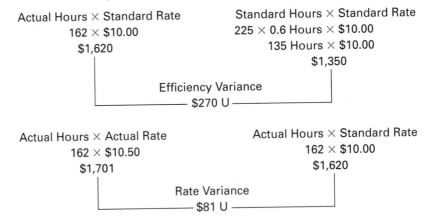

Actual Hours × Standard Rate
162 × $10.00
$1,620

Standard Hours × Standard Rate
225 × 0.6 Hours × $10.00
135 Hours × $10.00
$1,350

Efficiency Variance
$270 U

Actual Hours × Actual Rate
162 × $10.50
$1,701

Actual Hours × Standard Rate
162 × $10.00
$1,620

Rate Variance
$81 U

To record direct labor cost, work-in-process inventory is debited for the standard hours allowed for production multiplied by the standard direct labor rate. For Tree Top, the amount is $1,350. Cash or wages payable is credited for the actual amount of wages paid to employees. For Tree Top, the amount is $1,701. The difference between the amount debited to work in process and the amount credited to cash is equal to the direct labor efficiency and rate variances. If the variance is favorable, the variance account is credited. Conversely, if the variance is unfavorable, the variance account is debited. For Tree Top, the efficiency variance and the rate variance are unfavorable so both of these variance accounts will be debited.

The entry for Tree Top appears as follows:

Work-In-Process Inventory	1,350.00	
Direct Labor Efficiency Variance	270.00	
Direct Labor Rate Variance	81.00	
Cash		1,701.00

Recording Variable Manufacturing Overhead

The following tables present the information needed to make the entries for variable manufacturing overhead for Tree Top Mail Box Company:

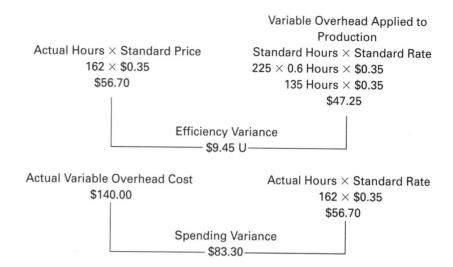

Actual Hours × Standard Price
162 × $0.35
$56.70

Variable Overhead Applied to Production
Standard Hours × Standard Rate
225 × 0.6 Hours × $0.35
135 Hours × $0.35
$47.25

Efficiency Variance
$9.45 U

Actual Variable Overhead Cost
$140.00

Actual Hours × Standard Rate
162 × $0.35
$56.70

Spending Variance
$83.30

The variable manufacturing overhead incurred account is debited for the actual cost of variable manufacturing overhead. For Tree Top, the amount is $140. Depending on whether the item was purchased on account or for cash, accounts payable or cash would be credited. We assume the items were purchased for cash.

The entry for Tree Top appears as follows:

Variable Manufacturing Overhead Incurred 140.00
    Cash   140.00

Work-in-process inventory is debited and variable manufacturing overhead applied is credited for the standard direct labor hours allowed for production multiplied by the standard variable overhead application rate. For Tree Top, the amount is $47.25.

The entry for Tree Top appears as follows:

Work-In-Process Inventory   47.25
    Variable Manufacturing Overhead Applied   47.25

The difference between the balance of the variable manufacturing overhead incurred account and the variable manufacturing overhead applied account is equal to the variable overhead efficiency and spending variances. These variance accounts are established when the variable manufacturing overhead incurred and the variable manufacturing overhead applied accounts are closed. This closing procedure is generally done only at year end. For demonstration purposes, we will assume that Tree Top has elected to close the overhead accounts to establish the variable overhead efficiency and spending variances at the end of November. As with the variance previously discussed, if the variance is favorable, the variance account is credited. Conversely, if the variance is unfavorable, the variance account is debited. For Tree Top, both the efficiency variance and the spending variance are unfavorable so the variance accounts will be debited as shown in the following entry.

Variable Manufacturing Overhead Applied   47.25
Variable Manufacturing Overhead Efficiency Variance   9.45
Variable Manufacturing Overhead Spending Variance   83.30
    Variable Manufacturing Overhead Incurred   140.00

Recording Fixed Manufacturing Overhead

The following tables present the information needed to make the entries for fixed manufacturing overhead for Tree Top Mail Box Company:

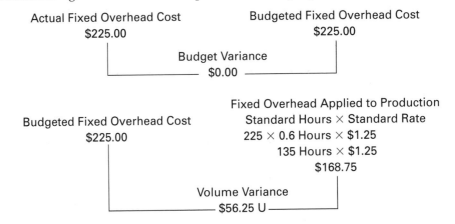

The fixed manufacturing overhead incurred account is debited for the actual cost of fixed manufacturing overhead. For Tree Top, the $225 actual fixed manufacturing overhead consists of $200 for rent and $25 for depreciation. Cash should be credited for the amount of rent paid and accumulated depreciation should be credited for the depreciation.

The entry for Tree Top appears as follows:

Fixed Manufacturing Overhead Incurred	225.00	
Cash		200.00
Accumulated Depreciation		25.00

Work-in-process inventory is debited and fixed manufacturing overhead applied is credited for the standard direct labor hours allowed for production multiplied by the standard fixed overhead application rate. For Tree Top, the amount is $168.75.

The entry for Tree Top appears as follows:

Work-In-Process Inventory	168.75	
Fixed Manufacturing Overhead Applied		168.75

The difference between the balance of the fixed manufacturing overhead incurred account and the fixed manufacturing overhead applied account is equal to the fixed overhead budget and volume spending variances. These variance accounts are established when the fixed manufacturing overhead incurred and the fixed manufacturing overhead applied accounts are closed. As with variable overhead, this closing procedure is generally done only at year end. For demonstration purposes, we will assume that Tree Top has elected to close the fixed manufacturing overhead accounts at the end of November. Once more, if the variance is favorable, the variance account is credited. Conversely, if the variance is unfavorable, the variance account is debited. Although entries for zero variances are not generally made in practice, we will show an entry for the budget variance for this demonstration. The volume variance will appear as a debit because it is an unfavorable variance.

The entry for Tree Top appears as follows:

Fixed Manufacturing Overhead Applied	168.75	
Fixed Manufacturing Overhead Budget Variance	0	
Fixed Manufacturing Overhead Volume Variance	56.25	
Fixed Manufacturing Overhead Incurred		225.00

Closing the Variance Accounts

The variance accounts are monitored during the year but generally no accounting entries are made to dispense with the amounts until the end of the year. For demonstration purposes, we will assume that Tree Top has elected to close the variance accounts at the end of November.

In most cases an accounting entry is made to close the standard cost variances to cost of goods sold. Because the amount of the variances is generally relatively small and most product cost ends up in cost of goods sold by year end, closing the variance accounts to cost of goods sold is adequate for most companies.

Tree Top's entry to close the standard cost variances to cost of goods sold follows:

Cost of Goods Sold	551.75	
Direct Material Price Variance	48.00	
Direct Material Quantity Variance		99.75
Direct Labor Efficiency Variance		270.00
Direct Labor Rate Variance		81.00
Variable Manufacturing Overhead Efficiency Variance		9.45
Variable Manufacturing Overhead Spending Variance		83.30
Fixed Manufacturing Overhead Budget Variance		0
Fixed Manufacturing Overhead Volume Variance		56.25

APPENDIX SUMMARY

When standard costing is used, direct materials, work-in-process, and finished goods inventories are maintained at standard cost. The standard cost variances account for the difference between the standard cost maintained in inventory and actual costs. If a variance is favorable, the variance account is credited. Conversely, if a variance is unfavorable, the variance account is debited.

To record the purchase of raw material, raw materials inventory is debited for the actual quantity multiplied by the standard price. The amount credited to accounts payable or cash is the actual purchase price of the material. The difference between the amount debited to direct material and the amount credited to accounts payable is taken to the direct materials price variance account.

To record the use of direct material, work-in-process inventory is debited for the standard quantity of material allowed for production multiplied by the standard price. The amount credited to raw materials is the actual quantity of material multiplied by the standard price. The difference between the amount debited to work in process and the amount credited to raw materials is taken to the direct material quantity variance account.

Work-in-process inventory is debited for the standard hours allowed for production multiplied by the standard direct labor rate. Cash or wages payable is credited for the actual amount of wages paid to employees. The difference between the amount debited to work in process and the amount credited to cash is equal to the direct labor efficiency and rate variances.

The variable manufacturing overhead incurred account is debited for the actual cost of variable manufacturing overhead. Work-in-process inventory is debited and variable manufacturing overhead applied is credited for the standard direct labor hours allowed for production multiplied by the standard variable overhead application rate. The difference between the balance of the variable manufacturing overhead incurred account and the variable manufacturing overhead applied account is equal to the variable overhead efficiency and spending variances. At year end, these variance accounts are established when the variable manufacturing overhead incurred and the variable manufacturing overhead applied accounts are closed.

The fixed manufacturing overhead incurred account is debited for the actual cost of fixed manufacturing overhead. Work-in-process inventory is debited and fixed manufacturing overhead applied is credited for the standard direct labor hours allowed for production multiplied by the standard fixed overhead application rate. The difference between the balance of the fixed manufacturing overhead incurred account and the fixed manufacturing overhead applied account is equal to the fixed overhead budget and volume spending variances. At year end, these variance accounts are established when the fixed manufacturing overhead incurred and the fixed manufacturing overhead applied accounts are closed.

The variance accounts are generally closed to cost of goods sold at year end. Because the amount of variances is generally relatively small and most product cost ends up in cost of goods sold by year end, closing the variance accounts to cost of goods sold is adequate for most companies.

KEY TERMS

bill of materials   M-332
direct labor efficiency standard   M-334
direct labor efficiency variance   M-342
direct labor rate standard   M-335
direct labor rate variance   M-344
direct material price standard   M-333
direct material price variance   M-341
direct material quantity standard   M-332
direct material quantity variance   M-338
direct material usage variance   M-338
favorable variance   M-327
fixed manufacturing overhead
 budget variance   M-348
fixed manufacturing overhead
 volume variance   M-349
ideal standard   M-328

management by exception   M-327
practical standard   M-328
standard   M-326
standard costing   M-326
standard cost system   M-326
standard fixed manufacturing
 overhead rate   M-336
standard variable manufacturing
 overhead rate   M-336
unfavorable variance   M-327
variable manufacturing overhead
 efficiency variance   M-345
variable manufacturing overhead
 spending variance   M-347
variance   M-326

REVIEW THE FACTS

A. What is standard costing?
B. What is a standard?
C. What is a variance?
D. Describe management by exception.
E. How often do most companies set cost standards?
F. What are the two things that can cause cost to increase?
G. What is the difference between an ideal standard and a practical standard?
H. Briefly describe five problems with standard costing.
I. What is a bill of material?
J. What are the two direct material standards?
K. What are the two direct labor standards?
L. How can standard costs be used to control cost?
M. What is measured by the direct material quantity variance?
N. What is measured by the direct material price variance?
O. What is measured by the direct labor efficiency variance?
P. What is measured by the direct labor rate variance?
Q. What is measured by the variable manufacturing overhead efficiency variance?

R. What is measured by the variable manufacturing overhead spending variance?

S. What is measured by the fixed manufacturing overhead budget variance?

T. What is measured by the fixed manufacturing overhead volume variance?

APPLY WHAT YOU HAVE LEARNED

LO 7: Determine Direct Material Variances

9–15. The Zhang Manufacturing Company purchased 4,000 pounds of direct material at $5.20 per pound. It used 2,700 pounds to make 5,000 finished units. The standard cost for direct material is $5.00 per pound and the quantity standard is 0.5 (one-half) pound per finished unit.

REQUIRED:

a. According to the appropriate standard, how much should the company have paid for the 4,000 pounds of direct material purchased?

b. Determine the direct material price variance based on the amount of direct material purchased.

c. According to the appropriate standard, how many pounds of direct material should have been used to make the 5,000 finished units?

d. Determine the direct material quantity variance in pounds of direct material.

e. Determine the direct material quantity variance in dollars.

f. Appendix: Prepare the following journal entries:
   (1) Record the purchase of direct material.
   (2) Record the use of direct material.

LO 7: Determine Direct Material Variances

9–16. The Carbonnell Manufacturing Company purchased 15,000 pounds of direct material at $1.30 per pound. It used 14,700 pounds to make 5,000 finished units. The standard cost for direct material is $1.35 per pound and the quantity standard is three pounds per finished unit.

REQUIRED:

a. According to the appropriate standard, how much should the company have paid for the 15,000 pounds of direct material purchased?

b. Determine the direct material price variance based on the amount of direct material purchased.

c. According to the appropriate standard, how many pounds of direct material should have been used to make the 5,000 finished units?

d. Determine the direct material quantity variance in pounds of direct material.

e. Determine the direct material quantity variance in dollars.

f. Appendix: Prepare the following journal entries:
   (1) Record the purchase of direct material.
   (2) Record the use of direct material.

LO 7: Determine Direct Material Variances

9–17. The Smithstone Company purchased 2,500 square feet of direct material at $6.30 per square foot. It used 2,055 square feet of material to make 500 finished units. The standard cost for direct material is $6.15 per square foot and the quantity standard is four pounds per finished unit.

REQUIRED:

a. According to the appropriate standard, how much should the company have paid for the 2,500 square feet of direct material purchased?

b. Determine the direct material price variance based on the amount of direct material purchased.

c. According to the appropriate standard, how many square feet of direct material should have been used to make the 500 finished units?

d. Determine the direct material quantity variance in square feet of direct material.

e. Determine the direct material quantity variance in dollars.

f. Appendix: Prepare the following journal entries:
   (1) Record the purchase of direct material.
   (2) Record the use of direct material.

LO 7: Determine Direct Material Variances

9–18. Econo Manufacturing purchased 20,000 square feet of direct material at $0.54 per square foot. It used 12,625 square feet to make 1,250 finished units. The standard cost for direct material is $0.55 per square foot and the quantity standard is 10 square feet per finished unit.

REQUIRED:

a. According to the appropriate standard, how much should the company have paid for the 20,000 square feet of direct material purchased?

b. Determine the direct material price variance based on the amount of direct material purchased.

c. According to the appropriate standard, how many square feet of direct material should have been used to make the 1,250 finished units?

d. Determine the direct material quantity variance in square feet of direct material.

e. Determine the direct material quantity variance in dollars.

LO 7: Determine Direct Material Variances

9–19. The following information is presented for the Scout Manufacturing Company.
- Direct material price standard is $1.55 per gallon.
- Direct material quantity standard is 2.5 gallons per finished unit.
- Budgeted production is 1,000 finished units.
- 4,000 gallons of direct material were purchased for $6,000.
- 2,800 gallons of direct material were used in production.
- 1,100 finished units of product were produced.

REQUIRED:

a. Determine the direct material price variance.

b. Determine the direct material quantity variance in dollars.

LO 7: Determine Direct Material Variances

9–20. The following information is presented for the Flowvalve Manufacturing Company.
- Direct material price standard is $15 per pound.
- Direct material quantity standard is 1/4 pound per finished unit.
- Budgeted production is 20,000 finished units.

- 6,000 pounds of direct material were purchased for $91,320.
- 4,650 pounds of direct material were used in production.
- 18,000 finished units of product were produced.

REQUIRED:
a. Determine the direct material price variance.
b. Determine the direct material quantity variance in dollars.

LO 7: Determine Direct Material Variances

9–21. The following information is presented for the Munter Manufacturing Company.

- Direct material price standard is $3.25 per pound.
- Direct material quantity standardis six pounds per finished unit.
- Budgeted production is 25,000 finished units.
- 175,000 pounds of direct material were purchased for $559,650.
- 155,200 pounds of direct material were used in production.
- 25,600 finished units of product were produced.

REQUIRED:
a. Determine the direct material price variance.
b. Determine the direct material quantity variance in dollars.

LO 7: Determine Direct Material Variances

9–22. Information from the Quincy Company is as follows:

Actual cost of 33,000 lbs of direct material purchased	$97,350
Direct material used in production	30,575 lbs
Actual production	2,980 units
Direct material price standard	$3.00 per lb
Direct material quantity standard per finished unit of production	10 lbs
Budgeted production	3,000 units

REQUIRED:
a. Determine the direct material price variance.
b. Determine the direct material quantity variance in dollars.

LO 7: Determine Direct Material Variances

9–23. Information from the Wayne Manufacturing is as follows:

Actual cost of 10,000 lbs of direct material purchased	$2,400
Direct material used in production	9,177 lbs
Actual production	980 units
Direct material price standard	$0.25 per lb
Direct material quantity standard per finished unit of production	9 lbs
Budgeted production	1,000 units

REQUIRED:
a. Determine the direct material price variance.
b. Determine the direct material quantity variance in dollars.

LO 7: Determine Direct Material Variances

9–24. Information from the Myco Manufacturing Company is as follows:

Actual cost of 120,000 feet of direct material purchased	$427,200
Direct material used in production	111,100 feet
Actual production	3,200 units
Direct material price standard	$3.50 per foot
Direct material quantity standard per finished unit of production	35 feet
Budgeted production	3,500 units

REQUIRED:

a. Determine the direct material price variance.

b. Determine the direct material quantity variance in dollars.

LO 7: Determine Direct Labor Variances

9–25. The direct labor rate standard for Amy Manufacturing is $12 per direct labor hour. The direct labor efficiency standard is two hours per finished unit. Last month, the company completed 8,000 units of product using 16,350 direct labor hours at an actual cost of $194,565.

REQUIRED:

a. According to the appropriate standard, how much should the company have paid for the 16,350 actual direct labor hours?

b. Determine the direct labor rate variance.

c. According to the appropriate standard, how many hours of direct labor should it have taken to produce the 8,000 units?

d. Determine the direct labor efficiency variance in hours.

e. Determine the direct labor efficiency variance in dollars.

f. Appendix: Prepare a journal entry to record the direct labor and the direct labor rate and efficiency variances.

LO 7: Determine Direct Labor Variances

9–26. The direct labor rate standard for Calspan Manufacturing is $18.50 per direct labor hour. The direct labor efficiency standard is six minutes or 1/10 of an hour per finished unit. Last month, the company completed 105,650 units of product using 10,400 direct labor hours at an actual cost of $191,360.

REQUIRED:

a. According to the appropriate standard, how much should the company have paid for the 10,400 actual direct labor hours?

b. Determine the direct labor rate variance.

c. According to the appropriate standard, how many hours of direct labor should it have taken to produce the 105,650 units?

d. Determine the direct labor efficiency variance in hours.

e. Determine the direct labor efficiency variance in dollars.

f. Appendix: Prepare a journal entry to record the direct labor and the direct labor rate and efficiency variances.

LO 7: Determine Direct Labor Variances

9–27. The direct labor rate standard for Key Largo Manufacturing is $10 per direct labor hour. The direct labor efficiency standard is three hours per finished unit. Last month, the company completed 2,800 units of product using 8,620 direct labor hours at an actual cost of $88,355.

REQUIRED:

a. According to the appropriate standard, how much should the company have paid for the 8,620 actual direct labor hours?
b. Determine the direct labor rate variance.
c. According to the appropriate standard, how many hours of direct labor should it have taken to produce the 2,800 units?
d. Determine the direct labor efficiency variance in hours.
e. Determine the direct labor efficiency variance in dollars.

LO 7: Determine Direct Labor Variances

9–28. The direct labor rate standard for Sakura Manufacturing is $15.25 per direct labor hour. The direct labor efficiency standard is 30 minutes or 1/2 of an hour per finished unit. Last month, the company completed 27,800 units of product using 14,050 direct labor hours at an actual cost of $215,246.

REQUIRED:

a. Determine the direct labor rate variance.
b. Determine the direct labor efficiency variance in dollars.
c. Appendix: Prepare a journal entry to record the direct labor and the direct labor rate and efficiency variances.

LO 7: Determine Direct Labor Variances

9–29. The direct labor rate standard for Melissa Valdez Manufacturing is $10 per direct labor hour. The direct labor efficiency standard is 0.25 (one-quarter) hour per finished unit. Last month, the company completed 38,000 units of product using 9,280 direct labor hours at an actual cost of $97,904.

REQUIRED:

a. Determine the direct labor rate variance.
b. Determine the direct labor efficiency variance in dollars.
c. Appendix: Prepare a journal entry to record the direct labor and the direct labor rate and efficiency variances.

LO 7: Determine Direct Labor Variances

9–30. The following information is presented for the Marathon Manufacturing Company.
- Direct labor rate standard is $11.55.
- Direct labor efficiency standard is 2.5 hours per finished unit.
- Budgeted production is 1,200 finished units.
- Production required 2,910 direct labor hours at a cost of $33,174.
- 1,150 finished units of product were produced.

REQUIRED:

a. Determine the direct labor rate variance.
b. Determine the direct labor efficiency variance in dollars.

LO 7:   Determine Direct Labor Variances

9–31. The following information is presented for the Picos Manufacturing Company.
- Direct labor rate standard is $12.
- Direct labor efficiency standard is two hours per finished unit.
- Budgeted production is 2,200 finished units.
- Production required 4,560 direct labor hours at a cost of $54,036.
- 2,250 finished units of product were produced.

REQUIRED:

a. Determine the direct labor rate variance.
b. Determine the direct labor efficiency variance in dollars.

LO 7:   Determine Direct Labor Variances

9–32. The following information is presented for the Lew Green Manufacturing Company.
- Direct labor rate standard is $24.
- Direct labor efficiency standard is three hours per finished unit.
- Budgeted production is 775 finished units.
- Production required 2,375 direct labor hours at a cost of $57,475.
- 810 finished units of product were produced.

REQUIRED:

a. Determine the direct labor rate variance.
b. Determine the direct labor efficiency variance in dollars.

LO 7:   Determine Direct Labor Variances

9–33. Information from the Spin Manufacturing Company is presented as follows:

Actual number of direct labor hours	275
Actual direct labor cost	$4,620
Actual number of units produced	800 units
Direct labor rate standard	$16.10
Direct labor efficiency standard	.3 hours per unit
Budgeted production	850 units

REQUIRED:

a. Determine the direct labor rate variance.
b. Determine the direct labor efficiency variance in dollars.

LO 7:   Determine Direct Labor Variances

9–34. Information from the Popular Manufacturing Company is as follows:

Actual number of direct labor hours	1,275
Actual direct labor cost	$16,065
Actual number of units produced	1,255 units
Direct labor rate standard	$12
Direct labor efficiency standard	1 hour per unit
Budgeted production	1,200 units

REQUIRED:

a. Determine the direct labor rate variance.
b. Determine the direct labor efficiency variance in dollars.

LO 7: Determine Direct Labor Variances

9–35. Information from the Electronic Manufacturing Company is as follows:

Actual number of direct labor hours	12,830
Actual direct labor cost	$292,524
Actual number of units produced	2,040 units
Direct labor rate standard	$23.10
Direct labor efficiency standard	6 hour per unit
Budgeted production	2,000 units

REQUIRED:

a. Determine the direct labor rate variance.
b. Determine the direct labor efficiency variance in dollars.

LO 7: Determine Direct Material and Direct Labor Variances

9–36. Information from the Atlantic Company is presented as follows:

Actual cost of 30,000 lbs of	
direct material purchased	$97,500
Direct material used in production	28,100 lbs
Actual number of direct labor hours	12,850
Actual direct labor cost	$165,765
Actual production	2,500 units
Direct material price standard	$3.30 per lb
Direct material quantity standard	
per finished unit of production	11 lbs
Direct labor rate standard	$13
Direct labor efficiency standard	5 hour per unit
Budgeted production	2,400 units

REQUIRED:

a. Determine the direct material price variance.
b. Determine the direct material quantity variance in dollars.
c. Determine the direct labor rate variance.
d. Determine the direct labor efficiency variance in dollars.

LO 7: Determine Direct Material and Direct Labor Variances

9–37. Information from the Progressive Company is presented as follows:

Actual cost of 9,000 lbs of	
direct material purchased	$2,200
Direct material used in production	7,800 lbs
Actual number of direct labor hours	980
Actual direct labor cost	$14,945
Actual production	240 units
Direct material price standard	$0.25 per lb
Direct material quantity standard	
per finished unit of production	30 lbs
Direct labor rate standard	$15
Direct labor efficiency standard	4 hour per unit
Budgeted production	250 units

REQUIRED:

a. Determine the direct material price variance.
b. Determine the direct material quantity variance in dollars.
c. Determine the direct labor rate variance.
d. Determine the direct labor efficiency variance in dollars.

LO 7: Determine Direct Material and Direct Labor Variances

9–38. Information from the Packard Company is presented as follows:

Actual cost of 1,000 lbs of direct material purchased	$10,300
Direct material used in production	830 lbs
Actual number of direct labor hours	1,220
Actual direct labor cost	$13,176
Actual production	400 units
Direct material price standard	$10 per lb
Direct material quantity standard per finished unit of production	2 lbs
Direct labor rate standard	$11
Direct labor efficiency standard	3 hour per unit
Budgeted production	450 units

REQUIRED:

a. Determine the direct material price variance.
b. Determine the direct material quantity variance in dollars.
c. Determine the direct labor rate variance.
d. Determine the direct labor efficiency variance in dollars.

LO 7: Determine Variable Manufacturing Overhead Variances

9–39. Billy Clifford Manufacturing applies variable manufacturing overhead to production on the basis of $15 per direct labor hour. The labor efficiency standard is five hours per finished unit. Last month the company produced 12,000 units and used 62,000 direct labor hours. Actual variable overhead cost incurred totaled $920,000.

REQUIRED:

a. Determine the variable manufacturing overhead spending variance.
b. According to the appropriate standard, how many direct labor hours should it have taken to produce the 12,000 units?
c. Determine the direct labor efficiency variance in hours.
d. Determine the variable manufacturing overhead efficiency variance in dollars.

LO 7: Determine Variable Manufacturing Overhead Variances

9–40. Clifford Knapp Manufacturing applies variable manufacturing overhead to production on the basis of $5 per direct labor hour. The labor efficiency standard is two hours per finished unit. Last month the company produced 11,000 units and used 22,400 direct labor hours. Actual variable overhead cost incurred totaled $111,700.

REQUIRED:

a. Determine the variable manufacturing overhead spending variance.
b. According to the appropriate standard, how many direct labor hours should it have taken to produce the 11,000 units?

c. Determine the direct labor efficiency variance in hours.

d. Determine the variable manufacturing overhead efficiency variance in dollars.

LO 7: Determine Variable Manufacturing Overhead Variances

9–41. Carlos Gonzalez Marine Manufacturing applies variable manufacturing overhead to production on the basis of $6 per direct labor hour. The labor efficiency standard is three hours per finished unit. Last month the company produced 15,000 units and used 45,650 direct labor hours. Actual variable overhead cost incurred totaled $277,800.

REQUIRED:

a. Determine the variable manufacturing overhead spending variance.

b. According to the appropriate standard, how many direct labor hours should it have taken to produce the 15,000 units?

c. Determine the direct labor efficiency variance in hours.

d. Determine the variable manufacturing overhead efficiency variance in dollars.

e. Appendix: Prepare the following journal entries:

(1) Record the actual variable manufacturing overhead. (Use "various accounts" for the credit side of the entry.)

(2) Record the variable manufacturing overhead applied to production.

(3) Close the variable manufacturing overhead accounts and establish the variable overhead variance accounts.

(4) Close the variance accounts to cost of goods sold.

LO 7: Determine Variable Manufacturing Overhead Variances

9–42. Alpine Manufacturing applies variable manufacturing overhead to production on the basis of $13 per direct labor hour. The labor efficiency standard is four hours per finished unit. Last month the company produced 3,000 units and used 11,700 direct labor hours. Actual variable overhead cost incurred totaled $157,200.

REQUIRED:

a. Determine the variable manufacturing overhead spending variance.

b. Determine the variable manufacturing overhead efficiency variance in dollars.

c. Appendix: Prepare the following journal entries:

(1) Record the actual variable manufacturing overhead. (Use "various accounts" for the credit side of the entry.)

(2) Record the variable manufacturing overhead applied to production.

(3) Close the variable manufacturing overhead accounts and establish the variable overhead variance accounts.

(4) Close the variance accounts to cost of goods sold.

LO 7: Determine Variable Manufacturing Overhead Variances

9–43. The Adler Manufacturing Company applies variable manufacturing overhead to production on the basis of $22 per direct labor hour. The labor efficiency standard is 0.5 hours per finished unit. Last month the company produced 14,500 units and used 7,300 direct labor hours. Actual variable overhead cost incurred totaled $162,000.

REQUIRED:

a. Determine the variable manufacturing overhead spending variance.

b. Determine the variable manufacturing overhead efficiency variance in dollars.

LO 7: Determine Variable Manufacturing Overhead Variances

9–44. The following information is presented for the Carol Green Manufacturing Company.

- Standard variable manufacturing overhead rate is $3.50 per direct labor hour.
- Direct labor efficiency standard is three hours per finished unit.
- Budgeted production is 810 finished units.
- Production required 2,370 direct labor hours.
- Variable manufacturing overhead cost was $8,500.
- 775 finished units of product were produced.

REQUIRED:

a. Determine the variable manufacturing overhead spending variance.
b. Determine the variable manufacturing overhead efficiency variance in dollars.

LO 7: Determine Variable Manufacturing Overhead Variances

9–45. The following information is presented for the Anne Reed Manufacturing Company.

- Standard variable manufacturing overhead rate is $7.00 per direct labor hour.
- Direct labor efficiency standard is six hours per finished unit.
- Budgeted production is 500 finished units.
- Production required 3,400 direct labor hours.
- Variable manufacturing overhead cost was $23,600.
- 550 finished units of product were produced.

REQUIRED:

a. Determine the variable manufacturing overhead spending variance.
b. Determine the variable manufacturing overhead efficiency variance in dollars.

LO 7: Determine Variable Manufacturing Overhead Variances

9–46. The following information is presented for the Willie Kemp Manufacturing Company.

- Standard variable manufacturing overhead rate is $2 per direct labor hour.
- Direct labor efficiency standard is four hours per finished unit.
- Budgeted production is 1,500 finished units.
- Production required 6,100 direct labor hours.
- Variable manufacturing overhead cost was $12,325.
- 1,550 finished units of product were produced.

REQUIRED:

a. Determine the variable manufacturing overhead spending variance.
b. Determine the variable manufacturing overhead efficiency variance in dollars.

LO 7: Determine Variable Manufacturing Overhead Variances

9–47. Information from the Systems Manufacturing Company is as follows:

Actual number of direct labor hours	12,000
Actual variable manufacturing overhead cost	$145,965
Actual number of units produced	2,440 units
Standard variable manufacturing overhead rate	$12.10 per direct labor hour
Direct labor efficiency standard	5 hours
Budgeted production	2,500 units

REQUIRED:
a. Determine the variable manufacturing overhead spending variance.
b. Determine the variable manufacturing overhead efficiency variance in dollars.

LO 7: Determine Variable Manufacturing Overhead Variances

9–48. Information from the Altos Manufacturing Company is as follows:

Actual number of direct labor hours	12,330
Actual variable manufacturing overhead cost	$74,490
Actual number of units produced	12,540 units
Standard variable manufacturing overhead rate	$6 per direct labor hour
Direct labor efficiency standard	1 hour
Budgeted production	12,000 units

REQUIRED:
a. Determine the variable manufacturing overhead spending variance.
b. Determine the variable manufacturing overhead efficiency variance in dollars.

LO 7: Determine Variable Manufacturing Overhead Variances

9–49. Information from the Aspen Manufacturing Company is as follows:

Actual number of direct labor hours	175,000
Actual variable manufacturing overhead cost	$2,400,000
Actual number of units produced	21,740 units
Standard variable manufacturing overhead rate	$14 per direct labor hour
Direct labor efficiency standard	8 hours
Budgeted production	20,000 units

REQUIRED:
a. Determine the variable manufacturing overhead spending variance.
b. Determine the variable manufacturing overhead efficiency variance in dollars.

LO 7: Determine Fixed Manufacturing Overhead Variances

9–50. The Hill Manufacturing Company applies fixed manufacturing overhead at the rate of $5.50 per direct labor hour. Fixed manufacturing overhead is budgeted to be $330,000 per month. The direct labor efficiency standard is five hours per finished unit. Although budgeted production for the month was 12,000, the company only produced 11,800 units. Production required actual direct labor hours of 60,000 and actual fixed manufacturing overhead cost incurred was $325,000.

REQUIRED:
a. Determine the fixed overhead budget variance.
b. What is the difference between the planned number of units and the number of units actually produced?
c. Determine the fixed manufacturing overhead volume variance.
d. Appendix: Prepare the following journal entries:
   (1) Record the actual fixed manufacturing overhead. (Use "various accounts" for the credit side of the entry.)
   (2) Record the fixed manufacturing overhead applied to production.
   (3) Close the fixed manufacturing overhead accounts and establish the fixed overhead variance accounts.
   (4) Close the variance accounts to cost of goods sold.

LO 7: Determine Fixed Manufacturing Overhead Variances

9–51. The Johnson Manufacturing Company applies fixed manufacturing overhead at the rate of $4.60 per direct labor hour. Fixed manufacturing overhead is budgeted to be $910,800 per month. The direct labor efficiency standard is three hours per finished unit. Although budgeted production for the month was 66,000, the company produced 67,800 units. Production required actual direct labor hours of 203,000 and actual fixed manufacturing overhead cost incurred was $920,000.

REQUIRED:
a. Determine the fixed manufacturing overhead budget variance.
b. What is the difference between the planned number of units and the number of units actually produced?
c. Determine the fixed manufacturing overhead volume variance.
d. Appendix: Prepare the following journal entries:
   (1) Record the actual fixed manufacturing overhead. (Use "various accounts" for the credit side of the entry.)
   (2) Record the fixed manufacturing overhead applied to production.
   (3) Close the fixed manufacturing overhead accounts and establish the fixed overhead variance accounts.
   (4) Close the variance accounts to cost of goods sold.

LO 7: Determine Fixed Manufacturing Overhead Variances

9–52. The Quality Manufacturing Company applies fixed manufacturing overhead at the rate of $7 per direct labor hour. Fixed manufacturing overhead is budgeted to be $336,000 per month. The direct labor efficiency standard is three hours per finished unit. Although budgeted production for the month was 16,000, the company only produced 15,500 units. Production required actual direct labor hours of 60,000 and actual fixed manufacturing overhead cost incurred was $344,000.

REQUIRED:
a. Determine the fixed manufacturing overhead budget variance.

b. Did the company produce as many units as it had planned? What is the difference between the planned number of units and the number of units actually produced?

c. Determine the fixed manufacturing overhead volume variance.

LO 7: Determine Fixed Manufacturing Overhead Variances

9–53. The following information is presented for the Oddo Manufacturing Company.
- Standard fixed manufacturing overhead rate is $2 per direct labor hour.
- Direct labor efficiency standard is four hours per finished unit.
- Budgeted production is 2,500 finished units.
- Budgeted fixed manufacturing overhead is $20,000.
- Actual fixed manufacturing overhead cost was $10,750.
- 2,150 finished units of product were produced.

REQUIRED:
a. Determine the fixed manufacturing overhead budget variance.
b. Determine the fixed manufacturing overhead volume variance in dollars.

LO 7: Determine Fixed Manufacturing Overhead Variances

9–54. The following information is presented for the Alexander Manufacturing Company.
- Standard fixed manufacturing overhead rate is $6.50 per direct labor hour.
- Direct labor efficiency standard is two hours per finished unit.
- Budgeted production is 5,000 finished units.
- Budgeted fixed manufacturing overhead is $65,000.
- Actual fixed manufacturing overhead cost was $66,100.
- 5,150 finished units of product were produced.

REQUIRED:
a. Determine the fixed manufacturing overhead budget variance.
b. Determine the fixed manufacturing overhead volume variance in dollars.

LO 7: Determine Fixed Manufacturing Overhead Variances

9–55. The following information is presented for the Adcox Manufacturing Company.
- Standard fixed manufacturing overhead rate is $9.50 per direct labor hour.
- Direct labor efficiency standard is nine hours per finished unit.
- Budgeted production is 9,000 finished units.
- Budgeted fixed manufacturing overhead is $769,500.
- Actual fixed manufacturing overhead cost was $755,360.
- 8,500 finished units of product were produced.

REQUIRED:
a. Determine the fixed manufacturing overhead budget variance.
b. Determine the fixed manufacturing overhead volume variance in dollars.

LO 7: Determine Fixed Manufacturing Overhead Variances

9–56. Information from the Michael Manufacturing Company is as follows:

Actual number of direct labor hours	12,200
Actual fixed manufacturing overhead cost	$145,900
Actual number of units produced	2,400 units
Standard fixed manufacturing overhead rate	$12 per direct labor hour
Direct labor efficiency standard	5 hours
Budgeted production	2,500 units
Budgeted fixed manufacturing overhead	$150,000

REQUIRED:
a. Determine the fixed manufacturing overhead budget variance.
b. Determine the fixed manufacturing overhead volume variance in dollars.

LO 7: Determine Fixed Manufacturing Overhead Variances

9–57. Information from the Jennings Manufacturing Company is as follows:

Actual number of direct labor hours	5,130
Actual fixed manufacturing overhead cost	$24,900
Actual number of units produced	5,400 units
Standard fixed manufacturing overhead rate	$5 per direct labor hour
Direct labor efficiency standard	1 hour
Budgeted production	5,000 units
Budgeted fixed manufacturing overhead	$25,000

REQUIRED:
a. Determine the fixed manufacturing overhead budget variance.
b. Determine the fixed manufacturing overhead volume variance in dollars.

LO 7: Determine Fixed Manufacturing Overhead Variances

9–58. Information from the Cathy Manufacturing Company is as follows:

Actual number of direct labor hours	5,200
Actual fixed manufacturing overhead cost	$88,960
Actual number of units produced	2,700 units
Standard fixed manufacturing overhead rate	$15 per direct labor hour
Direct labor efficiency standard	2 hours
Budgeted production	3,000 units
Budgeted fixed manufacturing overhead	$90,000

REQUIRED:
a. Determine the fixed manufacturing overhead budget variance.
b. Determine the fixed manufacturing overhead volume variance in dollars.

LO 7: Determine Fixed Manufacturing Overhead Variances

9–59. Todd Manufacturing Company's budgeted production is 200,000 units per month. Budgeted monthly fixed manufacturing overhead is $2,400,000 and is applied to production at a rate of $4 per direct labor hour. The direct labor efficiency standard is three direct labor hours per unit of production. Last month it took 520,000 actual direct labor hours to produce 175,000 units. Actual fixed manufacturing overhead for the month was $2,435,000.

REQUIRED:
a. Determine the fixed manufacturing overhead budget variance.
b. Determine the fixed manufacturing overhead volume variance.

LO 7: Determine Budgeted Production and Fixed Manufacturing Overhead Variances

9–60. The E. O. Mast Manufacturing Company applies fixed manufacturing overhead at the rate of $20 per direct labor hour. Fixed manufacturing overhead is budgeted to be $4,000,000 per month. The direct labor efficiency standard is two hours per finished unit. Last month the company produced 89,000 units using 180,000 direct labor hours and incurring fixed manufacturing overhead cost of $4,100,000.

REQUIRED:
a. Determine the fixed manufacturing overhead budget variance.
b. Did the company produce as many units as it had planned? What is the difference between the planned number of units and the number of units actually produced?
c. Determine the fixed manufacturing overhead volume variance.

LO 7: Determine Budgeted Production and Fixed Manufacturing Overhead Variances

9–61. The Annie Manufacturing Company applies fixed manufacturing overhead at the rate of $10 per direct labor hour. Fixed manufacturing overhead is budgeted to be $418,000 per month. The direct labor efficiency standard is four hours per finished unit. Last month the company produced 9,800 units using 36,500 direct labor hours and incurring fixed manufacturing overhead cost of $410,000.

REQUIRED:
a. Determine the fixed manufacturing overhead budget variance.
b. Did the company produce as many units as it had planned? What is the difference between the planned number of units and the number of units actually produced?
c. Determine the fixed manufacturing overhead volume variance.

LO 7: Determine Budgeted Production and Fixed Manufacturing Overhead Variances

9–62. The St. Hill Manufacturing Company applies fixed manufacturing overhead at the rate of $15 per direct labor hour. Fixed manufacturing overhead is budgeted to be $247,500 per month. The direct labor efficiency standard is six hours per finished unit. Last month the company produced 2,500 units using 15,500 direct labor hours and incurring fixed manufacturing overhead cost of $230,000.

REQUIRED:
a. Determine the fixed manufacturing overhead budget variance.

b. Did the company produce as many units as it had planned? What is the difference between the planned number of units and the number of units actually produced?
c. Determine the fixed manufacturing overhead volume variance.

LO 7: Determine Budgeted Fixed Factory Overhead and Fixed Manufacturing Overhead Variances

9–63. Information from the South Manufacturing Company is as follows:

Actual number of direct labor hours	32,500
Actual fixed manufacturing overhead cost	$428,000
Actual number of units produced	8,000 units
Standard fixed manufacturing overhead rate	$12 per direct labor hour
Direct labor efficiency standard	4 hours
Budgeted production	9,000 units
Budgeted fixed manufacturing overhead	$?

REQUIRED:
a. Determine the fixed manufacturing overhead budget variance.
b. Determine the fixed manufacturing overhead volume variance in dollars.

LO 7: Determine Fixed Manufacturing Overhead Variances

9–64. Information from the North Manufacturing Company is as follows:

Actual number of direct labor hours	13,000
Actual fixed manufacturing overhead cost	$50,000
Actual number of units produced	2,120 units
Standard fixed manufacturing overhead rate	$4 per direct labor hour
Direct labor efficiency standard	6 hours
Budgeted production	2,000 units
Budgeted fixed manufacturing overhead	$?

REQUIRED:
a. Determine the fixed manufacturing overhead budget variance.
b. Determine the fixed manufacturing overhead volume variance in dollars.

LO 7: Determine Fixed Manufacturing Overhead Variances

9–65. Information from the West Manufacturing Company is as follows:

Actual number of direct labor hours	27,000
Actual fixed manufacturing overhead cost	$260,000
Actual number of units produced	3,250 units
Standard fixed manufacturing overhead rate	$9 per direct labor hour
Direct labor efficiency standard	8 hours
Budgeted production	3,500 units
Budgeted fixed manufacturing overhead	$?

REQUIRED:
a. Determine the fixed manufacturing overhead budget variance.
b. Determine the fixed manufacturing overhead volume variance in dollars.

LO 7: Determine Direct Material, Direct Labor, Variable Manufacturing Overhead and Fixed Manufacturing Overhead Variances

9–66. Information from the Quintana Company is as follows:

Actual costs and amounts:

Actual production	3,800 units
Actual cost of 23,000 lbs of direct material purchased	$89,700
Actual amount of direct material used	22,950
Actual direct labor cost	$23,205
Actual direct labor hours	1,950 hours
Actual variable overhead cost	$12,000
Actual fixed overhead cost	$18,000

Standards and other budgeted amounts:

Budgeted production	4,000 units
Direct material price standard	$3.85
Direct material quantity standard	6 lbs per unit
Direct labor rate standard	$11 per hour
Direct labor efficiency standard per unit	0.5 hours
Standard variable mfg. overhead rate	$5.50 per direct labor hour
Standard fixed mfg. overhead rate	$10 per direct labor hour
Budgeted fixed manufacturing overhead	$20,000

REQUIRED:

Determine the following variances:
  a. Direct material price variance
  b. Direct material quantity variance in dollars
  c. Direct labor rate variance
  d. Direct labor efficiency variance in dollars
  e. Variable manufacturing overhead spending variance
  f. Variable manufacturing overhead efficiency variance in dollars
  g. Fixed manufacturing overhead budget variance
  h. Fixed manufacturing overhead volume variance in dollars

LO 7: Determine Direct Material, Direct Labor, Variable Factory Overhead and Fixed Factory Overhead Variances

9–67. Information from the Holzmann Company is as follows:

Actual costs and amounts:

Actual production	6,300 units
Actual cost of 20,000 lbs of direct material purchased	$40,000
Actual amount of direct material used	19,100
Actual direct labor cost	$386,100
Actual direct labor hours	26,000 hours
Actual variable overhead cost	$165,000
Actual fixed overhead cost	$310,000

Standards and other budgeted amounts:

Budgeted production	6,000	units
Direct material price standard	$2.10	
Direct material quantity standard	3	lbs per unit
Direct labor rate standard	$15	per hour
Direct labor efficiency standard per unit	4	hours
Standard variable mfg. overhead rate	$6.50	per direct labor hour
Standard fixed mfg. overhead rate	$12.75	per direct labor hour
Budgeted fixed manufacturing overhead	$306,000	

REQUIRED:

Determine the following variances:
  a. Direct material price variance
  b. Direct material quantity variance in dollars
  c. Direct labor rate variance
  d. Direct labor efficiency variance in dollars
  e. Variable manufacturing overhead spending variance
  f. Variable manufacturing overhead efficiency variance in dollars
  g. Fixed manufacturing overhead budget variance
  h. Fixed manufacturing overhead volume variance in dollars

LO 7: Determine Direct Material, Direct Labor, Variable Factory Overhead and Fixed Factory Overhead Variances

9–68. Information from the Collins Company is as follows:

Actual costs and amounts:

Actual production	2,300	units
Actual cost of 16,000 lbs of direct material purchased	$19,360	
Actual amount of direct material used	12,000	
Actual direct labor cost	$46,410	
Actual direct labor hours	4,750	hours
Actual variable overhead cost	$29,100	
Actual fixed overhead cost	$50,125	

Standards and other budgeted amounts:

Budgeted production	3,000	units
Direct material price standard	$1.10	
Direct material quantity standard	5	lbs per unit
Direct labor rate standard	$12	per hour
Direct labor efficiency standard per unit	2	hours
Standard variable mfg. overhead rate	$6	per direct labor hour
Standard fixed mfg. overhead rate	$8	per direct labor hour
Budgeted fixed manufacturing overhead	$48,000	

REQUIRED:

Determine the following variances:
  a. Direct material price variance
  b. Direct material quantity variance in dollars
  c. Direct labor rate variance
  d. Direct labor efficiency variance in dollars
  e. Variable manufacturing overhead spending variance
  f. Variable manufacturing overhead efficiency variance in dollars
  g. Fixed manufacturing overhead budget variance
  h. Fixed manufacturing overhead volume variance in dollars

Chapter 10

Evaluating Performance

*I*magine for a moment that you opened a shoe store in a local shopping center. After you have operated the store for some time, its success prompts you to open a second location. So you set up shop in the second location, select a manager, and open for business. The second store too does very well, and in time, your shoe store chain grows to five stores. Needless to say, it was a lot easier to manage the company when there was just a single location and you could oversee the entire operation personally. Unfortunately, it is impossible to give five separate stores the same personal, hands-on management attention. There are practical limits to how much a single manager can manage, especially when there are several different geographic locations. As a business grows, the diversity of knowledge required to effectively manage, combined with time constraints, adds to the inability of a single manager to manage the entire enterprise.

When a manager can no longer manage the whole company singlehandedly, management responsibility must be delegated to subordinate managers, each of whom is responsible for the performance of a part of the company. Evaluating the performance of these managers is the focus of this chapter. ■

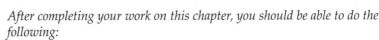

LEARNING OBJECTIVES

After completing your work on this chapter, you should be able to do the following:

1. Describe centralized and decentralized management styles.
2. Describe the different types of business segments and the problems associated with determining segment costs.
3. Prepare a segment income statement.
4. Describe and calculate the return on investment.
5. Describe and calculate residual income.
6. Describe nonfinancial performance measures.

BUSINESS SEGMENTS

business segment A part of a company managed by a particular individual or a part of a company about which separate information is needed.

To help make businesses more manageable, their owners often divide them into parts. A **business segment** represents a part of a company managed by a particular individual, or a part of a company about which separate information is needed, perhaps to evaluate management performance or to help managers make better management decisions.

Companies can be segmented by geographic area or location, business function, product, product line, or department. Examples of business segments include the Latin American Area of the Dow Chemical Company, an individual Sears department store, a Motorola manufacturing plant, and the Department of Accounting at the University of Miami. A segment can be described as a department, a division, an area, a region, a product line, or some other designation.

Obtaining detailed information about business segments is a vital part of the management decision process. Managers need information that relates to their business segment. Reports that provide information pertaining to a particular business segment are called **segment reports.** Segment reports should not be clouded by data that relate to other segments or by general information pertaining to the company as a whole. For example, if you were the manager of the Hard Rock Cafe in Orlando, Florida, and responsible for enhancing the restaurant's profits, you would benefit by having information about your particular restaurant. Although it might be somewhat helpful to know the overall profitability of the entire restaurant chain, specific information about the Orlando Hard Rock would be much more useful. You might want to know detailed sales information by product, by server, and by time of day. You would also want a comprehensive listing of your restaurant's expenses. Reports that include only revenues and expenses for your restaurant would help you to find opportunities to increase profits.

segment reports Reports that provide information pertaining to a particular business segment.

Discussion Question

10-1. If you were the manager of the Contemporary Hotel at Disney World, what information would you want to help maximize the performance of the hotel?

Segment Information

Depending on the needs of management and the availability of information, segment reports may be simple and include little detail, or they may be quite elaborate and include an abundance of detailed segment information. For example, it is possible for segment reports to consist simply of a listing of the segment's sales by product; or, segment reports may include sales, expenses, and other information. The extent of the information included in segment reports depends on management's need to know, balanced with the cost of providing the information.

THE SEGMENT INCOME STATEMENT

segment income statement
An income statement prepared for a business segment.

An income statement prepared for a business segment is called a **segment income statement.** When a segment income statement is prepared, either the functional income statement or the contribution income statement format can be used. Recall from our discussions in Chapter 5 that the functional income statement separates costs into product and period costs. The contribution income statement classifies costs by behavior, either variable or fixed. We know that a variable cost is one that changes in total based on some activity, whereas a fixed cost is one that remains unchanged regardless of the level activity. To be sure you remember these two income statement formats, we reproduce them in Exhibit 10–1.

Exhibit 10–1
Functional and Contribution Income Statement Formats

Functional Format	Contribution Income Format
Sales	Sales
− Cost of Goods Sold (Product Cost)	− All Variable Costs (Product and Period)
= Gross Profit	= Contribution Margin
− Selling and Admin. Expense (Period Cost)	− All Fixed Costs (Product and Period)
= Net Income	= Net Income

segment margin The amount of income that pertains to a particular segment.

To prepare a segment income statement, we gather revenue and expense information that pertains to the particular segment and then arrange it in the appropriate income statement format. The amount of income that pertains to a particular segment is called the **segment margin.** Because the contribution income format is particularly well-suited for our work in this chapter, we use that format in all our remaining presentations. A segment income statement for the Miami office of the Quintana Company appears in Exhibit 10–2.

It is important that the segment income statement for the Miami office of the Quintana Company include all the appropriate information for the Miami office, and no more. Often, this is easier said than done. Generally, revenue can easily be traced to individual business segments, therefore, obtaining detailed revenue information by segment is not too difficult. Unfortunately, however, the same cannot always be said for cost information.

Exhibit 10–2
Segment Income Statement for the Miami Office

QUINTANA COMPANY MIAMI OFFICE
Segment Income Statement
For the Year Ended December 31, 2001

Sales	$1,200,000
Variable cost	800,000
Contribution margin	400,000
Fixed cost for Miami office	300,000
Segment margin	$ 100,000

It is often difficult (if not impossible) to obtain cost information that includes all the costs for a particular segment and excludes costs associated with other segments. There are several reasons for this. First, it may be difficult to identify all the costs that relate to the segment. For example, say that the Norris Division of the NHL Company has three copiers. Certainly the cost of these copiers should be included in any evaluation of the Norris Division. These three copiers, however, are just three of the 27 copiers owned by the NHL Company (the other 24 copiers are in other segments). The problem is that all 27 copiers were purchased by the central company purchasing department and Norris has no record of the cost of its three copiers.

Discussion Question

10–2. What are three other costs that relate directly to the Norris Division, but for which the division probably does not have information?

The second reason it may be difficult to identify costs to particular segments is that costs are often mixed together in the accounting process. An example of this might be advertising purchased by the NHL Company, which benefits not only the Norris Division, but also the five other divisions of the company. The exact amount that should be charged to the Norris Division is virtually impossible to determine accurately.

Discussion Question

10–3. What are three other costs that benefit the Norris Division but benefit at least one other division as well?

To help manage a business segment, we should include all the costs associated with the segment on cost reports prepared for it. It is equally important that costs that do not pertain to the segment be excluded from the segment's cost reports. In the case of variable costs, this is fairly straightforward. Variable costs can be traced directly to the business segments to which they pertain and then be included on the appropriate segment reports.

Fixed cost are more difficult to trace to individual business segments and therefore present more of a challenge. One problem with tracing fixed costs to business segments is that some fixed costs pertain to a single business segment whereas others benefit several segments or perhaps the company as a whole. Fixed costs that arise to support a single segment are called **direct fixed costs** or **traceable fixed costs.** These fixed costs can be *traced* to an individual business segment. Direct fixed costs should be included on the cost reports for the segment to which they pertain. Fixed costs that arise to support more than one segment or the company as a whole are called **common fixed costs** or **indirect fixed costs.**

This discussion of direct and indirect costs should not seem entirely new. It is a subject we covered in some depth in Chapter 2 when we discussed the concept of a cost object. As you recall, a cost object is any activity or item for which a separate cost measurement is desired. A cost that can be traced directly to a cost object is a direct cost, whereas a cost that is incurred to support multiple cost objects is an indirect cost. In our present discussion, the cost object is the business segment.

direct fixed cost   Fixed costs incurred to support a single business segment.

traceable fixed cost Another name for *direct fixed cost.*

common fixed cost   Fixed costs incurred to support more than one business segment, or the company as a whole.

indirect fixed cost   Another name for *common fixed cost.*

Because common fixed costs benefit several segments or the company in general, segment managers often have little control over these costs. A simple question can be asked to determine whether a cost is a common cost or a direct cost:

Would the cost continue if the segment were to disappear?

If the cost will continue even if the segment disappeared, the cost is a common fixed cost. If, on the other hand, the cost would disappear if the segment disappears, the cost is a direct fixed cost. There are very few, if any, common variable costs; thus, in virtually all instances, the common costs we must consider are fixed.

For many years there has been debate as to whether cost reports prepared for an individual segment should include some allocated amount of common fixed costs. Proponents of allocation maintain that common fixed costs benefit the entire company and therefore each segment should be charged for its "fair share" of the common cost. Further, they argue that it is impossible to determine true segment profitability if common costs are excluded. Opponents of allocation argue just the opposite. They maintain that because segment managers have little or no authority to exercise control over common fixed costs, these costs should not be included in segment reports. These folks believe it is unfair to charge a manager's department for costs that are out of his or her control. In addition, common fixed costs are generally distributed to various business segments based on an arbitrary allocation scheme and can make a segment appear to be unprofitable when, in fact, that segment is contributing to the overall profitability of the company. Managers may attempt to "control" the common fixed costs allocated to their segment by manipulating the allocation base.

Discussion Question

10-4. Assume for a moment that you are a segment manager at Motorola. How would you react to a charge made to your department for a portion of the cost of the fleet of corporate aircraft, even though you have never even seen one of the planes?

Both the proponents and opponents of common fixed cost allocation to business segments feel strongly about their positions. There seems to be little question, however, that the practice of including common fixed costs in segment reports is losing popularity. This fact is not surprising when we consider that the main purpose of management accounting is to influence managers to act to benefit the company. It seems clear that including common fixed costs in segment reports can lead managers toward behavior that is counterproductive. Restricting a segment cost report to costs over which a manager has control makes it a more useful tool for supporting sound business decisions.

PITFALL OF ALLOCATING COMMON FIXED COSTS— A CLOSER LOOK

When common fixed costs are allocated to segments, segment information may be misleading and result in disastrous business decisions. As an example, consider the segmented income statement for Flandro Feed Stores presented in Exhibit 10–3.

Exhibit 10–3
Flandro Feed Stores
Segment Income
Statement

FLANDRO FEED STORES
Segment Income Statement
For the Year Ended December 31, 2002

	Company Total	North Store	South Store	Central Store
Sales	$500,000	$105,000	$225,000	$170,000
Variable cost	332,950	73,750	141,000	118,200
Contribution margin	167,050	31,250	84,000	51,800
Direct fixed cost	75,000	20,000	32,000	23,000
Segment margin	92,050	11,250	52,000	28,800
Common fixed cost	60,000	12,600*	27,000**	20,400***
Net income	$ 32,050	($ 1,350)	$ 25,000	$ 8,400

* $105,000/$500,000 = 21% × $60,000 = $12,600

** $225,000/$500,000 = 45% × $60,000 = $27,000

*** $170,000/$500,000 = 34% × $60,000 = $20,400

As you can see from Exhibit 10–3, the $60,000 common fixed cost has been allocated to the business segments based on relative sales volume, which means that because the South Store provided 45 percent of the company's sales ($225,000/$500,000 = 45%), this store is allocated 45 percent of the common fixed cost ($60,000 × 45% = $27,000). Of the common fixed cost, 34 percent was allocated to the Central Store based on its percentage of sales, and 21 percent was allocated to the North Store. As you can see, it appears that the North Store is unprofitable. Based on the information in Exhibit 10–3, it seems that profits could be increased if the unprofitable North Store is closed. By closing the North Store it appears that the $1,350 loss would be eliminated. Let us look at the results had the North Store been eliminated. The segment income statement for Flandro Feed Stores without the North Store is presented in Exhibit 10–4.

FLANDRO FEED STORES
Segment Income Statement
For the Year Ended December 31, 2002

	Company Total	South Store	Central Store
Sales	$395,000	$225,000	$170,000
Variable cost	259,200	141,000	118,200
Contribution margin	135,800	84,000	51,800
Direct fixed cost	55,000	32,000	23,000
Segment margin	80,800	52,000	28,800
Common fixed cost	60,000	34,200*	25,800**
Net income	$ 20,800	$ 17,800	$ 3,000

* $225,000/$395,000 = 57% (rounded) × $60,000 = $34,200

** $170,000/$395,000 = 43% (rounded) × $60,000 = $25,800

As Exhibit 10–4 shows, when the North Store is eliminated, Flandro's net income actually *declines* from $32,050 to $20,800. On the surface this seems to make no sense, because the results in Exhibit 10–3 showed the North Store with a net loss for the year of $1,350. So, how did eliminating the North Store cause profits to drop by $11,250 ($32,050 − $20,800)? The answer lies in the practice of allocating common fixed cost. Notice in Exhibit 10–4 that the common fixed cost of $60,000 did not change when the North Store was removed, because the common fixed cost is for items that are necessary to operate the company even if there are fewer stores. For example, even if the North Store closes, common costs for such items as accounting, finance, and the cost of operating the home office would continue. Therefore, the $60,000 common fixed cost would have to be distributed to the two remaining stores. Again, this configuration is done based on relative sales values.

In truth, the North Store is contributing to Flandro's overall profitability. When the North Store is eliminated, so is its segment margin. It is not a coincidence that the $11,250 decline in profits without the North Store is exactly equal to the North Store's segment margin in Exhibit 10–3. If the North Store is eliminated, its segment margin disappears, but the common fixed cost remains and must be allocated to the remaining segments.

To avoid such misleading information and the poor decisions that can result, many companies have stopped the practice of allocating common fixed costs to segments. The segmented income statement for Flandro Feed Stores without the allocation of common fixed cost is shown in Exhibit 10–5.

Exhibit 10–5
Flandro Feed Stores Segment Income Statement without Allocation of Common Fixed Cost

FLANDRO FEED STORES

Segment Income Statement

For the Year Ended December 31, 2002

	Company Total	North Store	South Store	Central Store
Sales	$500,000	$105,000	$225,000	$170,000
Variable cost	332,950	73,750	141,000	118,200
Contribution margin	167,050	31,250	84,000	51,800
Direct fixed cost	75,000	20,000	32,000	23,000
Segment margin	92,050	$ 11,250	$ 52,000	$ 28,800
Common fixed cost	60,000			
Net income	$ 32,050			

As shown in Exhibit 10–5, when common fixed costs are not allocated, the segment margin becomes the "bottom line" for each segment. This amount is a better indicator of segment profit performance because it considers direct costs, costs over which the segment manager has control.

To provide useful information to help evaluate segment performance and to help segment managers make informed decisions, all direct costs that pertain to a particular segment must be included in the management reports for that segment. If a direct cost is excluded, it is unlikely that the segment manager will work to reduce that cost. For example, assume that a leased copy machine is used exclusively by the finance department of a major corporation. Assume further that the rent for the copy machine, plus the rent for all the other copy machines used by the company, is included in a monthly bill from the Acme Copy Machine Company. If the rent cost included on this single bill is not distributed (charged) to user departments, the cost for each department is understated by the amount of the rent. If this happens, the rent for the copy machine would be excluded from the information used to help evaluate the finance department's performance. Therefore, it is unlikely that the finance department manager would work to reduce the rental cost by switching to a less expensive copy machine. In fact, once the manager finds that the cost of the copy machine is not charged to the department, he or she might even upgrade to an overly elaborate copy machine knowing that the department will not be penalized for such an expenditure. Thus, it is important to include all costs associated with a business segment in the segment's cost reports.

SERVICE DEPARTMENT COST ALLOCATION

service department A business segment responsible for secondary (support) functions. Service departments provide service to the main business operations and to other service departments.

The main operation of a merchandiser is selling products. For a manufacturer, the main operation is manufacturing and selling products. For a service business, the main operation is providing services to customers. In addition to any company's main business operation, however, secondary support operations also occur. Most companies, whether merchandisers, manufacturers, or service-type businesses, also have accounting departments, a personnel department, and other departments that provide support to the various functions of the company. Further, telephone service must be provided, and a facility (building) within which to operate. The business segments that handle these and other secondary operations are called **service departments.** These departments provide necessary services to the main business operations and other service departments.

Discussion Question

10–5. Besides the ones listed in the previous paragraph, what are five other service departments you think would be common to most companies?

The cost of operating a service department can be substantial. This cost is allocated to the departments that use the services provided. In other words, if a particular department receives benefit from a service department, that department should be charged for the cost of the service.

Determining the amount of service department cost to charge various user departments is not an exact science. For some kinds of service cost, a direct correlation can be found between the amount of service provided to a department and the cost charged to that department. In these instances, the manager of the user department rarely disputes the charge. For other types of service cost, however, no direct cause and effect can be found. In that event, the cost charged to departments for services is based on an allocation method that may or may not be accurate or even fair. This allocation is much like that of common fixed cost to segments, as discussed earlier. The allocation of service department cost when no correlation can be found between the service and the cost can actually cloud management's vision about the performance of a department.

As was the case with the allocation of fixed common cost to segments, certain managers believe that service department costs should be allocated whereas others believe the practice should be stopped. As usual, both sides hold strongly to their views. Although some companies have stopped allocating service department cost, the majority of companies still maintain this practice. The responsibility of department managers is to be vigilant in making certain that the costs charged to their departments reasonably reflect the amount of service received. Examples of service departments and possible allocation bases are shown in Exhibit 10–6.

Exhibit 10–6
Representative Service Departments and Possible Allocation Bases

Service Department	Allocation Basis
Personnel Department	• Number of employees
Telephone	• Number of phones • Number of lines • Long-distance charges

Copy Machine or Copy Center	• Quantity of services used:
	  • Number of single-sided copies
	  • Number of double-sided copies
	  • Number of bindings

Employee Cafeteria	• Number of employees • Number of meals served
Finance Department	• Amount of capital invested
Building Occupancy	• Square footage of building occupied
Computer Operations	• Computer mainframe time • Number of personal computers • Number of reports generated
Computer Programming	• Hours of programming
Office Services	• Square footage of office occupied • Number of offices
Engineering Department	• Number of engineering changes • Hours of engineering services
Maintenance	• Square footage of building occupied • Hours of maintenance
Aircraft Operations	• Number of passenger miles • Number of hours flown • Weight of load and distance flown

ACTIVITY-BASED SERVICE DEPARTMENT COST ALLOCATION

Activity-based costing is a topic we covered in Chapter 3 when we discussed alternative ways to allocate manufacturing overhead to units of product produced. Activity-based costing can also be a valuable tool for allocating service department cost to other departments. When possible, the allocation base used to allocate cost should be an activity that causes the cost. As stated in Chapter 3, an activity that causes cost to occur is called a *cost driver.* The two major benefits to using cost drivers to allocate service department cost are (1) this cost allocation method tends to be more fair and accurate, and (2) in attempting to control the cost allocated to their departments, managers will work to reduce the allocation base—the cost driver. Because the cost driver is also the cost cause, reducing the cost driver will actually reduce the amount paid by the company for goods and services. For example, when the cost driver used to allocate basic phone service is the number of phone lines, a reduction in the number of phone lines will not only reduce the allocation of phone cost, but it will also reduce the amount the company spends for phone service. This reduction results in true cost savings for the company.

Discussion Question

10-6. Refer to the list of five service departments you made in response to Discussion Question 10-5. What is a possible allocation base for each of the departments you listed?

It is important to know about service department cost allocation for several reasons. First, as a department manager, you will need to know how to control service department costs allocated to your department. Second, you should be able to discriminate between costs that are arbitrarily allocated to your department and those that are equitable. Third, as a high-level manager, you should be able to recognize when an allocation method should be modified or replaced, because it does not result in information that provides incentives for managers to act in fulfillment of company goals.

Sometimes the allocation method can cause managers to do counterproductive things, especially when activity-based costing is not used to allocate costs. For example, consider what happened to a major corporation when it changed the allocation base it used to distribute the cost of office space. From a charge for all the square footage the departments occupied, the firm changed to a charge for only the square footage of the enclosed office space occupied by the departments. Top managers felt that departments should not be charged for halls, elevator waiting areas, or other common areas but only for the office space dedicated entirely to the department's use. Some managers recognized that their department's allocation for office space could be cut if they were to reduce the square footage used for enclosed offices. Accordingly, they demolished several offices occupied by department secretaries and provided them with desks and work space in the "common" area. The result was an increase in the amount of common space, and a marked decrease in the amount of square footage used for enclosed offices. Because the departments were only charged for enclosed office space, their office space cost allocation was reduced.

The change worked to the detriment of the company as a whole, however, because managers were rewarded for remodeling their offices even though the cost of the remodeling was unnecessary. Interestingly, only managers who had a working knowledge of how service department costs were allocated knew how to take advantage of the situation.

Discussion Question

10-7. Do you think the cost previously described should even be allocated? If not, explain your reasoning. If yes, what would you suggest to the company to overcome the dysfunctional management behavior described?

Reducing the service cost allocated to a particular department is not a difficult task to accomplish. First, the department manager must determine what allocation base is being used. Second, the manager must reduce the amount of the allocation base consumed by the department. If the allocation base used is a cost driver, the actual cost involved will decrease. If the allocation base is arbitrary and unrelated to the actual cost, the amount allocated to the department will decrease, but the actual cost to the company will continue and simply be shifted to some other manager's department.

As an example of how to control service department cost allocation, assume that the cost of photocopies is allocated based on the number of copies made. A reduction in the number of copies made will reduce the copy cost allocated to the user department. An attempt to reduce the number of copies would include a review of department procedures to ensure that only necessary copies are made. It might also include a review of alternate imaging technology to find ways to reduce the need for photocopies. This same logic can be used to control the cost allocation for telephone use, which is often allocated to departments based on the number of phone lines used. To reduce the cost allocation, unnecessary telephones are eliminated.

In each of these two examples, because the allocation base is a cost driver, a reduction in the base would not only cause a reduction in the cost allocated to the department but would also cause a true reduction in cost to the company.

APPROACHES TO SEGMENT MANAGEMENT

The strategy used to manage business segments varies from company to company. Some companies prefer that top management make all but the most routine decisions, whereas other companies prefer that lower-level managers make most or all of the decisions within their area. When almost all decisions are made by the top managers and little is left to the discretion of lower-level managers, the company is said to have a centralized management style. Conversely, if management decisions are made at the lowest possible management level, the company is said to have a decentralized management style. These management styles have both advantages and disadvantages.

Centralized Management

centralized management
A management style in which top managers make most management decisions.

When a **centralized management** style is used, top management makes most management decisions. Middle- and lower-level managers are responsible only for routine decisions and supervisory functions. This management style ensures that the wishes of top management are incorporated into each management decision. Top managers often have the most experience, which could lead to wise business decisions. A centralized management style has certain disadvantages: (1) Top managers must spend their valuable time making routine, low-level business decisions. (2) Top managers may not have an intimate familiarity with the various routine aspects of the business. (3) Lower-level employees have little opportunity to gain experience in decision making.

Decentralized Management

decentralized management
A management style in which lower-level managers are responsible for decisions that relate to their segment of the company.

When a **decentralized management** style is used, lower-level managers are responsible for management decisions that relate to their segment of the business. When a highly decentralized management style is used, decisions are made at the lowest possible level in the organization.

A decentralized management style has several advantages. It helps spread the decision-making responsibilities among the various management levels of the company and allows lower-level managers greater control over their business segments. Another benefit is that a decentralized management style provides an opportunity for lower-level managers to sharpen their decision-making skills, thus providing the company with experienced managers to progress through the ranks to top management positions. Decentralization also means that decisions are made by the managers who are most familiar with the problems and opportunities occurring in the routine operations of the company. Top managers may be somewhat removed from the intimacies of the daily routine business operations and therefore would be hard pressed to make well-informed decisions. Another advantage is that it relieves top managers of the responsibility of routine decisions and allows them to focus on strategic decisions and the overall goals of the organization.

A disadvantage of decentralized management is that decisions may not entirely reflect the views of top managers. Also, decisions are made by managers who may be less experienced than the top managers.

Discussion Questions

10–8. If you were the chief executive officer of your company, would you prefer a centralized or decentralized management style? Why?

10–9. If you were a lower-level manager in your company, would you prefer a centralized or decentralized management style? Why?

10–10. What similarities do you see between our discussion here of centralized and decentralized management and our discussion in Chapter 8 of top-down and bottom-up budgeting?

EVALUATION OF BUSINESS SEGMENTS

To evaluate the performance of business segments, we must first determine just what constitutes good performance. To establish whether a manager is doing a good job, for example, we must first have some idea of just what a "good job" means. To evaluate segment performance, a standard must be developed that establishes just what constitutes "good performance."

The performance of a business segment can be evaluated based on a number of criteria. The most logical evaluation criteria match the scope of responsibility and authority afforded the segment's manager. That is, if a particular segment's manager has the responsibility and authority only to control costs, the segment performance should be evaluated based on criteria that focus on cost control. Conversely, if the segment manager has the responsibility to generate revenue and also to control costs, the segment's performance should be evaluated based on criteria that focus on profits. Segments may be categorized based on the criteria used for their evaluation. The most popular segment categories are revenue centers, cost centers, profit centers, and investment centers.

Revenue Centers

revenue center A business segment in which the manager has responsibility and authority to act to increase revenues but has little or no control over costs and the amount invested in the segment.

A **revenue center** is a business segment whose manager has responsibility and authority to act to increase revenues but has little control over costs and the amount invested in the segment. The performance of a revenue center is evaluated based on the amount of revenue generated by the segment, and the manager is evaluated based on his or her ability to generate sales revenue.

An example of a business segment properly designated a revenue center is a sales office whose segment manager has little or no control over costs. The results of the manager's actions would affect sales revenue but have minimal effect on cost.

Cost Centers

cost center   A business segment where the manager has responsibility and authority to act to decrease or at least control costs but has little or no control over the revenues generated or the amount invested in the segment.

A **cost center** is a business segment whose manager has responsibility and authority to decrease or at least control costs while keeping output high. Generally, cost center managers are not responsible for generating revenue, nor do they have control over the amount invested in the segment. The performance of a cost center is evaluated based on the amount of cost incurred by the segment and the manager is evaluated based on his or her ability to control these costs.

Business segments that provide service to the company or customers but do not contribute directly to revenues are good candidates to be designated as cost centers. Examples of cost centers include the accounting department of a hospital, a repair department that handles warranty repair work, an assembly department, and an inspection facility in a manufacturing plant.

Profit Centers

profit center   A business segment in which the manager has the responsibility and authority to act to increase revenue and decrease or at least control costs, but has little or no control over the amount invested in the segment.

A **profit center** is a business segment whose manager has the responsibility and authority to act to increase revenue and decrease or at least control costs but does not have control over the amount invested in the segment. The performance of a profit center is evaluated based on the amount of profits it generates. The manager of a profit center is evaluated based on his or her ability to increase revenue and control expenses, because profits are increased by increasing revenue and/or decreasing expenses.

Examples of profit centers include individual stores in a department store chain, a college bookstore, and a pathology testing center.

Measuring Performance of Revenue, Cost, and Profit Centers

The most commonly used method of evaluating the performance of revenue centers, cost centers, and profit centers is performance to budget. The sales goals established during the budgeting process can be used as a basis for evaluating the performance of revenue centers. If, for example, actual sales are higher than budgeted sales, this would be a favorable indication. If, on the other hand, actual sales are lower than budgeted sales, this would be an unfavorable indication. For a cost center, the goals established during the budgeting process for output and cost can be used as a basis for evaluating cost center performance. Actual production that exceeds budgeted production, for example, would be a favorable indication. Costs per unit of output that are lower than budgeted would also be a favorable indication. Obviously, favorable performance would be indicated by high output and low cost relative to output volume. For a profit center, the profit goals established during the budgeting process can be compared to actual profits to evaluate profit center performance. Favorable performance would be indicated by actual profits that meet or exceed budgeted profits.

It is often argued that having managers strive to meet budgeted performance targets is so simplistic that it leads to suboptimal performance. Managers may simply strive to meet the expectations established by the budget instead of trying to maximize sales. Another potential problem is that managers who are evaluated based on performance to budget can make themselves look good by negotiating relatively low budgeted sales and relatively high budgeted costs. Then when the actual sales are higher than budget, and the actual costs are lower than budgeted, the manager appears to have performed well. This information may seem familiar to you. Other chapters in the text included brief discussions of the problems associated with performance to budget as a way to measure managers' performance—a subject addressed in Chapter 8 when we presented the operating budget and again in Chapter 9 in the presentation of standard costing. Everything about the potential for counterproductive behavior inherent in the performance to budget evaluation technique applies to measuring the performance of revenue centers, cost centers, and profit centers.

If we move away from performance to budget as a means of evaluating revenue center managers, however, what do we put in its place? This topic has been a topic of debate for some time in management accounting circles. The answer, we suspect, is not to drop performance to budget as a performance measure entirely. Rather, it should be supplemented with other types of measures, some of which are presented near the end of this chapter. For now, just remember that a company runs a real risk of encouraging silly management behavior if it relies too heavily on performance to budget as a means of evaluating its managers.

Investment Centers

Does earning a profit of $100,000 constitute good performance? Before we can tell just how good it is, we should also consider the amount of investment required. Surely, almost any business segment can be profitable if there is an unlimited amount to invest in assets and technology. In business, the hope is to keep the profit high and the amount invested low.

investment center A business segment that is evaluated based on the amount of profit generated relative to the amount invested in the segment.

An **investment center** is a business segment that is evaluated on the amount of profit generated relative to the amount invested in the segment. An investment center manager should strive to maximize profit while minimizing the amount of investment used to earn the profit. Reducing the investment in a given segment allows the freed-up funds to be used by other segments. If the funds are not needed by the company elsewhere, financing can be reduced.

If a segment manager has responsibility and authority for revenues, costs, and capital investment in the segment, it should probably be designated an investment center. Examples of business segments that might be designated investment centers are individual stores in a department store chain, a college bookstore, and a pathology testing center. Note that these examples are the same as those given for segments designated as profit centers in our earlier discussion, because the classification of a business segment as a revenue center, profit center, cost center, or investment center depends not only on the operation of the segment but also, and as importantly, on the responsibility and authority afforded the segment's manager. If a manager's responsibility includes the generation of revenue, cost control, and control of the amount invested in the segment, then the business segment she or he manages should be designated an investment center.

As stated earlier, an investment center should be evaluated not only on the income generated by the segment, but also on the amount of investment required to earn the income. Obviously the higher the net income, the better, and the lower the investment required to generate that net income, the better. To evaluate the performance of an investment center we must be able to quantify the relationship between income earned and the investment required. For example, if you are about to invest in a savings account, it might be beneficial to know that a $5,245 deposit will earn interest of $183.57 in one year's time. Without knowing the percentage interest rate of return, however, the amounts have little meaning when evaluating the performance of the savings account. In business, the percentage return on an amount invested is called the return on investment.

RETURN ON INVESTMENT

In 1903, Pierre Du Pont and two cousins, Alfred and Coleman, formed the E.I. Du Pont de Nemours Powder Company by combining several gunpowder companies they had purchased from other Du Pont family members. When the cousins purchased the companies, they paid for them by issuing bonds equal in value to the expected future earnings potential of the companies acquired to form the new business. Pierre and his cousins could realize a profit only when the income from the new company exceeded the projected income of the companies they had purchased. Therefore, if income did not increase, there would only be enough profits to pay the bonds, leaving no profit for the cousins. This transaction is an early example of a leveraged buyout.

Knowing only the *amount* of income was not enough to monitor the success of the new organization. Accordingly, Pierre Du Pont devised the return on investment model to calculate the percentage return on the cousins investment. The return on investment could be used to assess whether the returns of the individual segments of the Du Pont Company exceeded the rate used to calculate the purchase price and interest payments on the bonds. Of course, the hope was that each of the segments of the Du Pont Company would have a return on investment that exceeded the rate used to determine the purchase price. The company went on to become the Du Pont Chemical Company we know today.

Discussion Question

10-11. What similarities do you see between our discussion here of return on investment and our discussion in Chapter 7 of capital expenditures?

return on investment (ROI)
The percentage return generated by an investment in a business or a business segment.

Since its inception, Du Pont's return on investment model has been a popular method of evaluating investment centers. **Return on investment (ROI)** is the percentage return generated by an investment in a business or business segment. The ROI is calculated by dividing the amount of income by the amount invested. For example, assume that the Eastern Division of the Lisa Company generated a segment margin of $896,750 for 2002 and the amount invested in the division was $10,550,000. This information is interesting, but it is probably more meaningful to know the percentage return that the investment generated. The ROI for the Lisa Company is 8.5 percent, determined as follows:

$$\frac{\text{Segment Income}}{\text{Investment in the Segment}} = \text{Return on Investment}$$

$$\frac{\$896,750}{\$10,550,000} = 8.5\%$$

After we determine the ROI for the division, the next question is, is the ROI adequate? If a company uses ROI as the measurement criterion for evaluating segment performance, it must establish a required rate for the ROI. The required rate of return that companies normally use is the blended cost of capital rate, as discussed in Chapter 7 concerning capital expenditures. Once established, the required ROI rate is used as a benchmark to evaluate the performance of the various investment centers in the company. A segment with an ROI that equals or exceeds the company's required rate will be viewed favorably, whereas a segment with an ROI that is lower than the required rate will be viewed as deficient. If we assume that the required rate for the ROI for the Lisa Company is eight percent, then the Eastern Division's performance is certainly adequate.

Discussion Question

10-12. What similarities do you see between our discussion here of the ROI calculation and our discussion in Chapter 7 of the internal rate of return?

In evaluating segment performance, we can rank segments by their return on investment. For example, if the Western Division of the Lisa Company has income of $857,500 with an investment on $9,800,000, how does the performance of the Western Division compare to that of the Eastern Division? The return on investment of both divisions is presented as Exhibit 10–7.

Exhibit 10–7
Return on Investment for Both Divisions of Lisa Company

Eastern Division	Western Division
$\dfrac{\text{Segment Income}}{\text{Investment in the Segment}} = \text{ROI}$	$\dfrac{\text{Segment Income}}{\text{Investment in the Segment}} = \text{ROI}$
$\dfrac{\$896,750}{\$10,550,00} = 8.5\%$	$\dfrac{\$857,500}{\$9,800,000} = 8.75\%$

Based on the ROI, the performance of the Western Division is superior to that of the Eastern Division because its ROI is greater. In this case, the Western Division's manager may be rewarded because of that division's better performance. As you might imagine, the use of ROI tends to encourage competition among segment managers, who strive to enhance performance evaluation by choosing investments that will work to increase their segment's ROI.

For the ROI to increase, the ROI of any new investment must exceed the segment's current ROI. If a new investment promises an ROI that is equal to the segment's current ROI, the segment's ROI will remain unchanged. However, if the new investment's ROI is less than the segment's current ROI, the segment's ROI will decrease. For example, assume that the manager of the Eastern Division is contemplating a new investment in the hope of improving his or her performance evaluation. An investment opportunity is available that promises additional income of $123,750 and requires an additional investment of $1,500,000. The ROI for this new investment opportunity is 8.25 percent calculated as follows:

$$\frac{\text{New Investment Income}}{\text{Investment in the New Project}} = \text{ROI}$$

$$\frac{\$123,750}{\$1,500,000} = 8.25\%$$

Based on the company's required rate of return of eight percent, it seems that the project should be accepted. Will the manager of the Eastern Division accept the project because it exceeds the company's required ROI and would benefit the company as a whole? Unfortunately, the answer is probably no. The manager of the Eastern Division may not select this project because it would work to reduce the *segment's* current ROI, as shown in Exhibit 10–8.

Although the Eastern Division's ROI would still be well above the required ROI rate of eight percent, the new investment would reduce the division's ROI from 8.5 percent to approximately 8.47 percent.

Exhibit 10–8
Effect of New Project
on Eastern Division's
Segment ROI

Eastern Division *Without* the New Investment Opportunity	Eastern Division *With* the New Investment Opportunity
$\dfrac{\text{Segment Income}}{\text{Investment in the Segment}} = \text{ROI}$	$\dfrac{\text{Segment Income}}{\text{Investment in the Segment}} = \text{ROI}$
$\dfrac{\$896,750}{\$10,550,000} = 8.5\%$	$\dfrac{\$896,750 + \$123,750}{\$10,550,000 + \$1,500,000} = \text{ROI}$
	$\dfrac{\$1,020,500}{\$12,050,000} = 8.47\%$

When ROI is used as the segment performance measure, the evaluation is usually based not only on how the segment's ROI compares to the company's required rate, but also on how segment's ROI compares to the ROI of other segments. Therefore, managers will only select projects that will enhance their current ROI. Unfortunately this often works to the detriment of the company as a whole, because projects that meet the company's required ROI rate are rejected simply because they will not increase the segment's ROI. Fortunately, another evaluation technique encourages managers to accept projects that have an ROI exceeding the company's required ROI rate. This evaluation technique is called residual income.

RESIDUAL INCOME

residual income The amount by which a segment's actual income exceeds the income needed to meet a company's required rate of return.

Residual income is a technique used to evaluate investment centers by focusing on the amount by which a segment's actual income exceeds the income needed to meet the company's required rate of return. As an example, let us take another look at the Lisa Company. Recall that the investment in the Eastern Division of the Lisa Company is $10,550,000 and that the company's required rate of return is eight percent. With that said, the Eastern Division must earn $844,000 ($10,550,000 × 8%) just to equal the eight percent required rate of return. This required earnings amount represents the dollar amount of earnings the segment must earn to equal the required rate of return for the company. Any earnings in excess of the required earnings (in this case $844,000) will constitute the segment's residual income. For the Eastern Division, the $896,750 actual income exceeds the $844,000 required income by $52,750. Therefore, the residual income for the Eastern Division is $52,750, calculated as follows:

Actual Income	$896,750
Less Required Income ($10,550,000 × 8%)	($844,000)
Equals Residual Income	$ 52,750

This is not to say that the Eastern Division only earned $52,750. Rather, the Eastern Division's income exceeded the company's required earnings by $52,750.

If the division's actual income were less than the income required to meet the company's required rate of return, the residual income amount would be a negative number. In our example, the positive residual income amount indicates that the segment's actual earnings exceed the company's required rate of return. In the unlikely event that residual income is zero, it would indicate that the actual income for the segment exactly equals the company's required rate of return.

Discussion Question

10–13. What similarities do you see between our discussion here of the residual income calculation and our discussion in Chapter 7 of net present value?

We now calculate the residual income for the Western Division so we can evaluate the relative performance of the two divisions. Using the amounts previously presented for the Western Division, we calculate residual income as $73,500:

Actual Income	$857,500
Less Required Income ($9,800,000 × 8%)	($784,000)
Equals Residual Income	$ 73,500

Notice that the residual income of the Western Division exceeds that of the Eastern Division. Accordingly, the performance of the Western Division would obviously be viewed more favorably than that of the Eastern Division. In an attempt to improve the Eastern Division's relative performance, managers would strive to increase revenue, decrease expenses, or seek new, high-return investment opportunities.

When ROI is used to evaluate potential investment opportunities, managers invest only in projects with an anticipated return that exceeds the segment's current ROI. Projects that exceed the company's required rate of return but did not exceed the segment's current ROI would likely be rejected. Look again at the investment opportunity proposed for the Eastern Division. Recall that the project would require an investment of $1,500,000 with anticipated additional income of $123,750. Therefore, the total investment of the Eastern Division would increase to $12,050,000 ($896,750 + $123,750), while total segment income would increase to $1,020,500 ($896,750 + $123,750).

If residual income were used to evaluate segment performance, management of the Eastern Division would tend to accept the proposed project if it worked to increase residual income. Look again at the residual income for the Eastern Division both with and without the proposed investment opportunity. The data are presented in Exhibit 10–9.

Exhibit 10–9
Residual Income for Eastern Division with and without Proposed Investment

Eastern Division *Without* the New Investment Opportunity		Eastern Division *With* the New Investment Opportunity	
Actual Income	$896,750	Actual Income	$1,020,000
Required Income		Required Income	
$10,550,000 × 8% =	$844,000	$12,050,000 × 8% =	$ 964,000
Residual Income	$ 52,750	Residual Income	$ 56,000

As you can see, the investment opportunity for the Eastern Division would increase residual income. Therefore, management of the Eastern Division would tend to favor the investment. Notice that the residual income method, unlike ROI, prompts managers to accept projects with return rates that exceed the company's required rate of return even if the project's rate of return falls short of the segment's current ROI.

In the past, business in the United States has focused almost exclusively on financial amounts to measure success. Success has been gauged by how much revenue can be generated, how much costs can be reduced, or how much profit can be earned. Recently, however, many companies have begun to also consider nonfinancial performance measures in evaluating business performance. Many managers are finding out that tracking the various flows of dollars and cents alone cannot ensure business success. Intense competition has prompted U.S. businesses to take a second look at nonfinancial performance measures in the hope that better performance on these will ultimately lead to greater financial rewards.

Quality

Today, many companies are calling for continuous quality improvement in every area of business. Today's quality-conscious companies are not only producing higher-quality products, but also demanding high-quality performance throughout every aspect of business. To remain competitive, U.S. companies must produce the high-quality products their customers have come to expect. Thus, they have begun to monitor product quality in a number of ways. Production reports are no longer limited to data pertaining to numbers of units and unit cost. Information about the number of defective products and the amount of rework is now prepared and used as a basis for measuring segment success. Product quality is also monitored by tabulating the amount and nature of customer complaints. Product warranty repair costs and the number of repairs or service calls are also useful tools in evaluating product quality.

The trend in business today is to establish extremely high goals for quality. For FedEx, 100 percent on-time deliveries is the goal. Imagine, not 90 percent or 95 percent, but 100 percent on-time deliveries. This goal may seem impossible to achieve, but FedEx has mobilized the company to achieve high-quality performance in every aspect of the delivery process. From delivery truck maintenance to the package tracking system, quality is the hallmark of the company.

Discussion Question

10–14. What, if any, are the potentially negative financial effects of focusing on quality?

Customer Satisfaction

In today's competitive business environment, customer satisfaction is often viewed as the most critical ingredient in achieving and maintaining success. Even if customer satisfaction is important, how can it be evaluated to measure segment performance? There are several ways. First, customer complaints can be monitored. At IBM, for example, detailed records are kept regarding each customer complaint. In addition to a simple count of the number of complaints, IBM records the nature and severity of each and follows up every compliant to ensure that the customer's needs have been reasonably met.

To satisfy customers, you must first know what customers want. Surveys can be used to identify what is important to customers and to help determine whether they are satisfied with products and services. For example, buyers of Infinity automobiles are surveyed each time their cars are serviced. This survey accomplishes at least two important things. First, it provides information that can be used to evaluate the performance of the service facilities. Second, it can alert the company to an unhappy customer so that reasonable action can be taken to remedy each customer complaint.

Discussion Question

10–15. What, if any, are the potentially negative financial effects of focusing on customer satisfaction?

Employee Morale

An increasing number of companies are targeting company morale as an almost certain road to higher profits. It stands to reason that employees who are happy with their jobs are more likely to work hard to benefit both themselves and the company. Without question, low morale leads to high turnover, which in turn leads to the enormous cost of hiring and training employees. It follows, then, that managers should work to keep employee morale high. Measuring employee morale can be challenging, but some useful indicators of employee morale are the amount of absenteeism, the rate of employee turnover, and recruiting success rates.

Discussion Question

10–16. What, if any, are the potentially negative financial effects of focusing on employee morale?

Employee Safety

In today's business world, it is critical that employees be provided with a safe work environment. The Dow Chemical Company, for example, has invested a great deal of money in promoting safety in the workplace. Employees are routinely reminded of the importance of safety through company-provided posters, safety seminars, and safety awareness contests. The information Dow provides to its people is not limited to safety on the job but also extends to automobile and home safety.

Dow Chemical is not alone in its campaign to promote safety. Many companies are using employee safety information to evaluate segment performance. Some measures that indicate the level of employee safety include the number of hours worked between injury accidents, the number of hours worked per injury accident, and the number of employees injured or killed in a given time period. Managers can be evaluated based on the number of safety seminars or other safety programs they hold per year.

Discussion Question

10–17. What, if any, are the potentially negative financial effects of focusing on employee safety?

Efficiency

In today's competitive environment, customers demand high-quality products at the lowest possible price. Accordingly, efficiency has become one of the cornerstones of success for many companies. Efficiency is the measure of output achieved versus the amount of resources required. To increase production efficiency relative to material, companies are attempting to produce the maximum number of units with the minimum amount of wasted material. This efficiency can be measured by the amount of scrap or the amount of material used per unit produced. For labor, efficiency can be measured by the relationship of production output to the direct labor required.

Many manufacturers are making major commitments to improve general plant efficiency. To be successful, these efforts must be supported by everyone from production-line workers to the chief executive officer. It is particularly important that top management be supportive. Typically, efficiency drives extend far beyond making minor changes and rallying the troops to work a little faster. Rather, they encompass major reorganizations of labor, new plant layouts, and innovative work flow philosophies. Many of the concepts that contribute to increased plant efficiency are part of the just-in-time philosophy.

Discussion Question

10–18. What, if any, are the potentially negative financial effects of focusing on efficiency?

JUST-IN-TIME PHILOSOPHY

just-in-time (JIT) A philosophy that eliminates all unnecessary inventory and limits the use of company resources until they are absolutely needed to fulfill customer demand.

The **just-in-time (JIT)** philosophy involves eliminating all unnecessary inventory and limiting the use of company resources until they are absolutely needed to fulfill customer demand. Expenditures are made only to fulfill the immediate customer demand. Products are "pulled" through the system. That is, products are made in response to the *pull* from customer demand, rather than to a *push* to have inventory to fill orders that may or may not materialize.

Often, JIT is described as a method of eliminating or greatly reducing inventory by delaying the purchase of raw material until it is needed for production. This narrow view is greatly flawed and prompts many managers to reject the whole JIT idea. Limiting the use of company resources until they are needed for production cannot be achieved by simply adopting a mind-set that purchases will be delayed until the last possible minute. Instead, the JIT philosophy focuses on delaying expenditures for inventory and reducing inventory levels to near zero by creating very efficient production processes that require only a minimal amount of inventory to successfully manufacture high-quality products.

One key component of JIT is that manufacturers must be able to depend on their suppliers for 100 percent on-time deliveries of 100 percent defect-free material. For JIT to work, manufacturers must develop close relationships with suppliers who can provide absolutely on-time deliveries and absolutely consistent high quality. When JIT is implemented, manufacturers defer quality inspections to suppliers and insist upon parts and components that are free of defects. **Zero defects** is a term that is often used to describe the concept of products that are completely free of imperfections. In a JIT environment, zero defects becomes the norm.

zero defects Describes the concept of products that are completely free of imperfections.

As part of the program to develop close relationships with their suppliers, firms greatly reduce that number of suppliers. By working with a core of carefully selected suppliers, the manufacturer is able to make substantial purchase commitments that help compensate suppliers for the added effort required to meet the manufacturer's demands. Also, the financial benefits they gain from receiving on-time deliveries of consistently high-quality products make it possible for manufacturers to justify paying a premium price for the goods they purchase.

In a JIT environment, setup times must be reduced to the lowest possible levels. As mentioned in Chapter 3, **setup time** is the time it takes to prepare manufacturing equipment for the production of a particular product. One major problem with long setup times is that while production equipment is being setup, it cannot be used to produce anything. The trouble does not end there, however. If setup time is substantial, fewer and longer production runs must be made to justify the substantial setup effort. It makes no sense to go through a long setup process to produce only a few units. The result of long production runs is higher inventory levels. This method is in direct conflict with the JIT philosophy. Conversely, if setup time is very short, running a short production run to produce fewer units of product is more feasible. With shorter production runs making fewer units, inventories can be reduced.

In JIT environments, setup time is now measured and average setup times are used to evaluate the performance of segment managers. In factories using just-it-time production, setup time is reduced from hours or days to minutes.

Another focus of the JIT philosophy is reduced throughput time. **Throughput time** is the time between the entrance of a unit of production into the production process and the time it emerges as a finished product. It is an important measure of plant efficiency because the amount of money invested in work-in-process inventory can be lowered by reducing the time products are in the production process. In addition to reducing inventories, shorter throughput time frees production equipment so it can be used to make other products. Throughput time can thus be measured and used as a basis for evaluating performance.

Another hallmark of the JIT philosophy is reduction in lead time. **Lead time** is the time between the receipt of an order and the completion of a product ready for shipment. Decreasing setup and throughput times can greatly reduce lead time. Many manufacturers that have adopted JIT have reduced lead time from months or years, to days or even hours. Lead time can be measured and used as a basis for evaluating plant performance.

In a further effort to increase efficiency, managers are working to reduce unscheduled downtime. **Unscheduled downtime** is the amount of time production equipment is out of service due to unscheduled repairs and maintenance. To keep this factor low, managers implement routine maintenance programs that not only keep unscheduled downtime to a minimum but also keep machinery running at peak performance. Companies are now tracking unscheduled downtime and using the information to evaluate plant performance.

By now, you may be wondering just how these JIT production improvements can be achieved. They do not come cheaply or easily. A great deal of time and money must be spent to achieve the added efficiency that comes with a JIT production environment. Some key factors are improved plant layout and product flow, mechanized procedures for machine setup, convenient storage and labeling of machine parts used in the setup process, and a formal plant maintenance program.

The production plant layout should be designed so that raw materials enter the production process with little or no need to be transported to work stations. For example, when a new Saturn automobile in made, the truck that transports the seats to the factory is literally connected to the production building, and the seats are fed

setup time The time it takes to prepare manufacturing equipment for the production of particular products.

throughput time The time that passes from the time a unit of product enters the production process until it emerges as a finished product.

lead time The time that passes from the time an order is received until the product is complete and ready for shipment.

unscheduled downtime The amount of time production equipment is out of service due to unscheduled repairs and maintenance.

to the production line, in the proper order, through conveyors in the truck to conveyers in the factory. The days of buying a bunch of seats of various colors and styles to be stored in a warehouse are gone at Saturn. Gone too are the days when materials handling personnel picked through massive inventories of seats to find the color and style they needed only to transport the selected seats to the production line. By cooperating with a seat manufacturer and a transportation company, Saturn can depend on the seats not only arriving on time but being received in the correct order by color and style with zero defects. A backup plan for shipment delays is the responsibility of the supplier and transportation company.

In addition to facilitating efficient handling of raw material, a JIT environment should also strive to streamline the movement of material from one production process to the next. For example, the Dunlop Golf Ball Factory in South Carolina has eliminated the use of hopper carts to transport golf balls from the painting process to the packaging process. This decision was achieved by changing the plant layout so that golf balls travel by conveyor from one process to the next. This production improvement saves time and eliminates the need for handling the golf balls between processes. An added feature of this change was the elimination of inspection stations between the painting department and the packaging department, as the golf balls were no longer subject to blemishes caused by rough treatment in the hopper carts. The production change worked to greatly increase plant efficiency and improve product quality.

Each manufacturing environment is unique. Managers and plant workers cooperate to continually reinvent the production environment. Old production techniques and strategies must be set aside in favor of new standards of production excellence, efficiency, and product quality. Company management and production personnel must work together to achieve the world-class production excellence required in today's competitive business environment. It takes a team effort characterized by an innovative spirit and a willingness to invest in grand-scale changes.

SUMMARY

As companies grow and the products and services they provide become more diversified, it becomes a virtual impossibility for one person to perform all management functions. More managers are required to operate and control the various facets of what we call management. A natural outgrowth of a company's evolution is the creation of business segments. A segment is any part of a company about which separate information is required to evaluate performance.

When a company is segmented, it will employ either a centralized management style or a decentralized management style. In a centralized company, upper management makes most of the important business decisions. In a decentralized company, lower-level managers are responsible for virtually all decisions that relate to their segment of the company.

Determining what costs should be charged to a particular business segment and the amount of those costs is sometimes very difficult. Some costs associated with operating a business segment are directly incurred by that segment. Others, however, are incurred to support more than one segment. These common costs must be allocated in some way to the segments receiving the benefit of the costs.

The four most commonly used designations of business segments are revenue centers, cost centers, profit centers, and investment centers. Revenue centers, cost centers, and profit centers are usually evaluated based on performance to budget.

The performance of investment centers is most often evaluated using the return on investment (ROI) technique or the residual income approach.

Although performance to budget and either return on investment or residual income are still commonly used to evaluate business segment performance, other nonfinancial measures have become popular in recent years. Many companies are now emphasizing such things as product quality, customer satisfaction, employee morale, safety in the workplace, and efficiency as ways to better measure and improve company performance.

KEY TERMS

business segment   M-378
centralized management   M-387
common fixed cost   M-380
cost center   M-389
decentralized management   M-387
direct fixed cost   M-380
just-in-time (JIT)   M-397
indirect fixed cost   M-380
investment center   M-390
lead time   M-398
profit center   M-389
residual income   M-393

return on investment (ROI)   M-391
revenue center   M-388
segment income statement   M-379
segment margin   M-379
segment reports   M-378
service department   M-384
setup time   M-398
throughput time   M-398
traceable fixed cost   M-380
unscheduled downtime   M-398
zero defects   M-397

REVIEW THE FACTS

A. Describe a business segment.
B. What is the difference between direct fixed cost and common fixed cost?
C. What is a service department?
D. Why is it important to know about service department cost allocation?
E. Describe the difference between centralized and decentralized management.
F. Describe a revenue center.
G. Describe a cost center.
H. What is the difference between a profit center and an investment center?
I. Why is residual income sometimes preferred to return on investment?
J. List five nonfinancial performance measures.
K. What is meant by the just-in-time philosophy?
L. How can companies achieve the very low inventory levels embraced by the just-in-time philosophy?

APPLY WHAT YOU HAVE LEARNED

LO 2 & 3:   Prepare a Segment Income Statement with and without the Allocation of Common Fixed Costs to Segments

10–19. The Almer Sales Company has two divisions. The following information is available for the year ended December 31, 2000.

   The sales for Almer are $300,000 for the Eastern Division and $200,000 for the Western Division. Variable costs for the Eastern Division are $250,000, whereas variable costs for the Western Division are $170,000. Direct fixed costs of the Eastern Division are $20,000 and direct fixed costs of the Western Division are $15,000. The Almer Company allocates common fixed costs to segments based on relative sales. Common fixed costs for the company are $25,000.

REQUIRED:
a. Prepare a segment income statement for the company which distributes common fixed costs to segments based on relative sales. Your answer should include a column for the total company and columns for each segment.
b. Do you think it is wise to evaluate the performance of a business segment based on income that includes an allocation for common fixed costs? Why or why not?
c. Prepare a segment income statement for the company which does not distribute common fixed cost to segments. Your answer should include a column for the total company and columns for each segment.

LO 2 & 3:   Prepare a Segment Income Statement with and without the Allocation of Common Fixed Costs to Segments

10–20. The Ted Green Sales Company has two divisions. The following information is available for the year ended December 31, 2000.

The sales for the company are $30,000 for the North Division, and $90,000 for the South Division. Variable costs for the North Division are $18,000, while variable costs for the South Division are $54,000. Direct fixed costs of the North Division are $5,000 and direct fixed costs of the South Division are $15,000. The company allocates common fixed costs to segments based on relative sales. Common fixed costs for the company are $10,000.

REQUIRED:
a. Prepare a segment income statement for the company which distributes common fixed costs to segments based on relative sales. Your answer should include a column for the total company and columns for each segment.
b. Do you think it is wise to evaluate the performance of a business segment based on income that includes an allocation for common fixed costs? Why or why not?
c. Prepare a segment income statement for the company which does not distribute common fixed cost to segments. Your answer should include a column for the total company and columns for each segment.

LO 2 & 3:   Prepare a Segment Income Statement with and without the Allocation of Common Fixed Costs to Segments

10–21. The Albert Pons Company has two divisions. The following information is available for the year ended December 31, 2000.

The sales for the company are $200,000 for the Central Division, and $400,000 for the South Division. Variable costs for the Central Division are $150,000, whereas variable costs for the South Division are $300,000. Direct fixed costs of the Central Division are $19,000 and direct fixed costs of the South Division are $54,000. The company allocates common fixed costs to segments based on relative sales. Common fixed costs for the company are $27,000.

REQUIRED:

a. Prepare a segment income statement for the company which distributes common fixed costs to segments based on relative sales. Your answer should include a column for the total company and columns for each segment.

b. Do you think it is wise to evaluate the performance of a business segment based on income that includes an allocation for common fixed costs? Why or why not?

c. Prepare a segment income statement for the company which does not distribute common fixed cost to segments. Your answer should include a column for the total company and columns for each segment.

LO 2 & 3: Prepare a Segment Income Statement with and without the Allocation of Common Fixed Costs to Segments

10–22. The Peppermill Company has three divisions. The following information is available for the year ended December 31, 2000.

The sales for the company are $200,000 for the Central Division, and $400,000 for the South Division, and $600,000 for the West Division. Variable costs for the Central Division are $150,000, variable costs for the South Division are $300,000, and variable costs for the West Division are 450,000. Direct fixed costs of the Central Division are $20,000, direct fixed costs of the South Division are $54,000, and direct fixed costs of the West Division are $100,000. The company allocates common fixed costs to segments based on relative sales. Common fixed costs for the company are $102,000.

REQUIRED:

a. Prepare a segment income statement for the company which distributes common fixed costs to segments based on relative sales. Your answer should include a column for the total company and columns for each segment.

b. Based on your answer for part a, which segment seems to have generated the least profit?

c. Prepare a segment income statement for the company which does not distribute common fixed cost to segments. Your answer should include a column for the total company and columns for each segment.

d. Based on your answer for part c, which segment seems to have generated the most profit?

LO 2 & 3: Prepare a Segment Income Statement with and without the Allocation of Common Fixed Costs to Segments

10–23. The Pitman Sales Company has three divisions. The following information is available for the year ended December 31, 2000.

The sales for the company are $100,000 for Division A, and $200,000 for Division B, and $300,000 for Division C. Variable costs for Division A are $50,000, variable costs for Division B are $100,000, and variable costs for Division C are $150,000. Direct fixed costs of Division A are $20,000, direct fixed costs of Division B are $30,000, and direct fixed costs of Division C are $60,000. The company allocates common fixed costs to segments based on relative sales. Common fixed costs for the company are $186,000.

REQUIRED:

a. Prepare a segment income statement for the company which distributes common fixed costs to segments based on relative sales. Your answer should include a column for the total company and columns for each segment.

b. Based on your answer for part a, which segment seems to have generated the least profit?

c. Prepare a segment income statement for the company which does not distribute common fixed cost to segments. Your answer should include a column for the total company and columns for each segment.

d. Based on your answer for part c, which segment seems to have generated the most profit?

LO 2 & 3: Prepare a Segment Income Statement with and without the Allocation of Common Fixed Costs to Segments

10–24. The Porter Sales Company has three divisions. The following information is available for the year ended December 31, 2000.

The sales for the company are $100,000 for Division 101, and $100,000 for Division 202, and $200,000 for Division 303. Variable costs for Division 101 are $50,000, variable costs for Division 202 are $60,000, and variable costs for Division 303 are $110,000. Direct fixed costs of Division 101 are $20,000, direct fixed costs of Division 202 are $30,000, and direct fixed costs of Division 303 are $50,000. The company allocates common fixed costs to segments based on relative sales. Common fixed costs for the company are $40,000.

REQUIRED:

a. Prepare a segment income statement for the company which distributes common fixed costs to segments based on relative sales. Your answer should include a column for the total company and columns for each segment.

b. Based on your answer for part a, does it appear that one of the segments should be closed?

c. Prepare a segment income statement for the company which does not distribute common fixed cost to segments. Your answer should include a column for the total company and columns for each segment.

d. Based on your answer for part c, does it still seem that one of the segments should be closed?

LO 2: Analyze Segment Cost and Prepare a Memo

10–25. The following segment income statement has been prepared for the Albertson Sales Company.

ALBERTSON SALES COMPANY
Segment Income Statement
For the Year Ended December 31, 2000

	Company Total	Medical Division	Industrial Division	Consumer Division
Sales	$750,000	$337,500	$157,500	$255,000
Variable cost	499,425	211,500	110,625	177,300
Contribution margin	250,575	126,000	46,875	77,700
Direct fixed cost	112,500	48,000	30,000	34,500
Segment margin	138,075	78,000	16,875	43,200
Common fixed cost	90,000	40,500[*]	18,900[**]	30,600[***]
Net income	$ 48,075	$ 37,500	($ 2,025)	$ 12,600

[*] $337,500/$750,000 = 45% × $90,000 = $40,500

[**] $157,500/$750,000 = 21% × $90,000 = $18,900

[***]$255,000/$750,000 = 34% × $90,000 = $30,600

The company President, Bob Albertson, is calling a management meeting to explore the idea of closing or selling the Industrial Division. Many managers are complaining that the division is "dragging the company down."

Assume that, in preparation for the meeting, Mr. Albertson has contacted you and asked that you explore the situation.

REQUIRED:
Based on the information presented for the Albertson Sales Company, prepare a memo to Mr. Albertson which includes a brief summary of the problem and a proposed solution.

LO 2: Identify the Area of Responsibility Associated with Different Types of Business Segments

10–26. Following are some popular segment classifications followed by three areas of management responsibility.

Segment Classification:

Revenue center	_____	_____	_____
Cost center	_____	_____	_____
Profit center	_____	_____	_____
Investment center	_____	_____	_____

R—Revenue
C—Cost
I—Amount invested

REQUIRED:
In the blank spaces provided, match the area or responsibility, revenue (R), cost (C), and amount invested (I) to the appropriate segment classification. Although not all the blank spaces will be used, some segment classifications will have more than one area of responsibility.

LO 4: Determine Return on Investment

10–27. The Chemical Division of CalChem Incorporated generated a segment margin of $220,680 for the year 2000 and the amount invested in the division was $1,226,000.

REQUIRED:
Determine the return on investment for the Chemical Division.

LO 4: Determine Return on Investment

10–28. The Southern Division of the Benson Sales Company generated a segment margin of $790,020 for the year 2000 and the amount invested in the division was $4,158,000.

REQUIRED:
Determine the return on investment for the Southern Division.

LO 4: Determine Return on Investment

10–29. The Automotive Division of the Bascom Company generated a segment margin of $1,916,800 for the year 2000 and the amount invested in the division was $11,980,000.

REQUIRED:
Determine the return on investment for the Automotive Division.

LO 4: Determine Return on Investment

10–30. The Alcad Farm Products Company generated income of $558,620 for the year 2000 and the amount invested in the division was $3,286,000.

REQUIRED:
Determine the return on investment for Alcad.

LO 2 & 4: Determine and Interpret Return on Investment

10–31. The following information is available for the three divisions of the Pompano Company.

Amount invested in each division:

Division A	$3,255,000
Division B	$2,145,000
Division C	$3,587,000

Segment margin of each division:

Division A	$553,350
Division B	$407,550
Division C	$573,920

The required rate of return for the company is 16%.

REQUIRED:
a. Determine the return on investment for each division.
b. Rank the three divisions assuming they are considered profit centers.
c. Rank the three divisions assuming they are considered investment centers and performance is evaluated based on return on investment.
d. Why do the rankings for parts b and c differ?

LO 2 & 4: Determine and Interpret Return on Investment

10–32. The following information is available for the three divisions of the Stevens Company.

Amount invested in each division:

Division 101	$1,225,000
Division 202	$2,445,000
Division 303	$3,697,000

Segment margin of each division:

Division 101	$198,450
Division 202	$371,640
Division 303	$569,338

The required rate of return for the company is 15%.

REQUIRED:
a. Determine the return on investment for each division.
b. Rank the three divisions assuming they are considered profit centers.
c. Rank the three divisions assuming they are considered investment centers and performance is evaluated based on return on investment.
d. Why do the rankings for parts b and c differ?

LO 2 & 4: Determine and Interpret Return on Investment

10–33. The following information is available for the three divisions of the Reed Company.

Amount invested in each division:

North Division	$7,225,000
South Division	$5,105,000
Central Division	$4,322,000

Segment margin of each division:

North Division	$1,336,625
South Division	$ 898,480
Central Division	$ 816,858

The required rate of return for the company is 14%.

REQUIRED:

a. Determine the return on investment for each division.
b. Rank the three divisions assuming they are considered profit centers.
c. Rank the three divisions assuming they are considered investment centers.
d. Why do the rankings for parts b and c differ?

LO 5: Determine Residual Income

10–34. The Eastern Division of the Key Largo Company generated a segment margin of $1,836,800 for the year 2000 and the amount invested in the division was $12,780,000.

  The company's required rate of return is 14%.

REQUIRED:
Determine the residual income for the Eastern Division.

LO 5: Determine Residual Income

10–35. Division A of the Emry Company generated a segment margin of $522,567 for the year 2000 and the amount invested in the division was $2,778,450.

  The company's required rate of return is 18%.

REQUIRED:
Determine the residual income for Division A.

LO 5: Determine Residual Income

10–36. Central Division of the Craft Company generated a segment margin of $244,765 for the year 2000 and the amount invested in the division was $1,335,500.

  The company's required rate of return is 17%.

REQUIRED:
Determine the residual income for the Central Division.

LO 2, 4, & 5: Determine and Interpret Return on Investment and Residual Income

10–37. The following information is available for the three divisions of the Top Company.

<table>
<tr><td colspan="2">**Amount invested in each division:**</td></tr>
<tr><td>Division D</td><td>$7,555,000</td></tr>
<tr><td>Division E</td><td>$5,995,000</td></tr>
<tr><td>Division F</td><td>$3,082,000</td></tr>
<tr><td colspan="2">**Segment margin of each division:**</td></tr>
<tr><td>Division D</td><td>$1,133,250</td></tr>
<tr><td>Division E</td><td>$ 911,240</td></tr>
<tr><td>Division F</td><td>$ 493,120</td></tr>
</table>

The required rate of return for the company is 14%.

REQUIRED:
a. Determine the return on investment for each division.
b. Determine the residual income for each division.
c. Rank the three divisions assuming they are considered profit centers.
d. Rank the three divisions assuming they are considered investment centers and performance is evaluated based on return on investment.
e. Rank the three divisions assuming they are considered investment centers and performance is evaluated based on residual income.
f. Why do some of the rankings for parts c, d, and e differ?

LO 2, 4, & 5: Determine and Interpret Return on Investment and Residual Income

10–38. The following information is available for the three divisions of the Slick Company.

<table>
<tr><td colspan="2">**Amount invested in each division:**</td></tr>
<tr><td>Division 1</td><td>$1,155,000</td></tr>
<tr><td>Division 2</td><td>$3,988,000</td></tr>
<tr><td>Division 3</td><td>$3,080,000</td></tr>
<tr><td colspan="2">**Segment margin of each division:**</td></tr>
<tr><td>Division 1</td><td>$196,350</td></tr>
<tr><td>Division 2</td><td>$634.092</td></tr>
<tr><td>Division 3</td><td>$492,800</td></tr>
</table>

The required rate of return for the company is 15%.

REQUIRED:
a. Determine the return on investment for each division.
b. Determine the residual income for each division.
c. Rank the three divisions assuming they are considered profit centers.
d. Rank the three divisions assuming they are considered investment centers and performance is evaluated based on return on investment.
e. Rank the three divisions assuming they are considered investment centers and performance is evaluated based on residual income.
f. Why do some of the rankings for parts c, d, and e differ?

LO 2, 4, & 5: Determine and Interpret Return on Investment and Residual Income

10–39. The following information is available for the three divisions of the Kenyon Company.

Amount invested in each division:

Division H	$5,188,000
Division I	$2,588,000
Division J	$6,386,000

Segment margin of each division:

Division H	$ 933,840
Division I	$ 491,720
Division J	$1,136,708

The required rate of return for the company is 16%.

REQUIRED:

a. Determine the return on investment for each division.
b. Determine the residual income for each division.
c. Rank the three divisions assuming they are considered profit centers.
d. Rank the three divisions assuming they are considered investment centers and performance is evaluated based on return on investment.
e. Rank the three divisions assuming they are considered investment centers and performance is evaluated based on residual income.
f. Why do some of the rankings for parts c, d, and e differ?

LO 2 & 4: Determine and Interpret Return on Investment

10–40. The following information is available for the three divisions of the Planet Company.

Amount invested in each division:

Automotive Division	$1,235,000
Industrial Division	$2,005,000
Consumer Division	$6,022,000

Segment margin of each division:

Automotive Division	$202,540
Industrial Division	$332,830
Consumer Division	$963,520

The required rate of return for the company is 14%.

The company uses return on investment to evaluate segment performance.

The company is considering acquiring an automotive parts manufacturing company that is expected to provide income of $36,450. The acquisition would require an investment of $225,000. Although the prospective acquisition would fit nicely into the Automotive Division's operation, the Automotive Division's manager has voiced considerable reservations. He believes it would not be in the company's best interest to acquire the new segment.

The manager of the Industrial Division concurs with the Automotive Division manager. Oddly enough, the Consumer Division manager not only thinks the acquisition is a good idea, but has volunteered to accept it in her division.

REQUIRED:

a. Determine the return on investment for each division.
b. Do you feel that it is in the company's best interest to acquire the automotive parts manufacturer? Explain your answer.
c. Why are the Automotive and Industrial Division managers reluctant to recommend the acquisition?
d. Why would the Consumer Division manager volunteer to accept the proposed acquisition into her division?

LO 2 & 5: Determine and Interpret Residual Income

10–41. Refer to the information in problem 10–40.

REQUIRED:

Explain how each of the managers' feelings about the acceptability of the proposed acquisition would differ if the company used residual income to evaluate segment performance instead of return on investment.

Glossary of Accounting Terms in IMA

accounting rate of return   The rate of return for a capital project based on the anticipated increase in accounting operating income due to the project, relative to the amount of capital investment required. (p. M-236)

activity-based costing   Allocating cost to products based on the activities that caused the cost to happen. (p. M-72)

administrative cost   All costs incurred by a company that are not product costs or selling costs. Includes the cost of accounting, finance, employee relations, and executive functions. (p. M-22)

allocation base   An amount associated with cost objects that can be used to proportionately distribute manufacturing overhead costs to each cost object. (p. M-71)

annuity   A stream of equal periodic cash flows. (p. M-241)

bill of materials   A listing of the quantity and description of each item of direct material used to manufacture an individual product. (p. M-332)

blended cost of capital   The combined cost of debt financing and equity financing. (p. M-223)

bottom-up budgeting   A budget initially prepared by lower-level managers and employees. (p. M-276)

breakeven   Occurs when a company generates neither a profit nor a loss. (p. M-155)

break-even point   The sales required to achieve breakeven. This can be expressed either in sales dollars or in the number of units sold. (p. M-155)

budget performance report   The evaluation instrument used to evaluate a manager's performance to budget. (p. M-298)

budgeted balance sheet   A presentation of estimated assets, liabilities, and owners' equity at the end of the budgeted period. (p. M-271)

budgeted income statement   Shows the expected net income for the period covered by the operating budget. (p. M-271)

budgeted statement of cash flows   A statement of a company's expected sources and uses of cash during the period covered by the operating budget. (p. M-272)

business segment   A part of a company managed by a particular individual or a part of a company about which separate information is needed. (p. M-378)

capital assets   Long-lived expensive items such as land, buildings, machinery, and equipment. (p. M-220)

capital budget   The budget that outlines how a company intends to allocate its scarce resources over a five-year, 10-year, or even longer time period. (p. M-219)

capital budgeting   The planning and decision process for making investments in capital projects. (p. M-216)

capital investments   Business expenditures in acquiring expensive assets that will be used for more than one year. (p. M-216)

capital projects   Another name for *capital expenditures.* (p. M-216)

cash budget   Shows whether the expected amount of cash generated by operating activities will be sufficient to pay anticipated expenses during the period covered by the operating budget. (p. M-271)

cash payments schedule   Presents the amount of cash a company expects to pay out during the budget period. (p. M-290)

cash receipts schedule   Presents the amount of cash a company expects to collect during the budget period. (p. M-288)

centralized management   A management style in which top managers make most management decisions. (p. M-387)

common cost   Another name for *indirect cost.* (p. M-21)

common fixed cost   Fixed costs incurred to support more than one business segment, or the company as a whole. (p. M-380)

compound interest   Interest calculated on the original principal amount invested plus all previously earned interest. (p. M-240)

continual budgeting   Another name for *perpetual budgeting*. (p. M-274)

contribution income statement   An income statement that classifies cost by behavior (fixed cost and variable cost). (p. M-151)

contribution margin   The amount remaining after all variable costs have been deducted from sales revenue. (p. M-152)

contribution margin ratio   The contribution margin expressed as a percentage of sales. (p. M-154)

controller   A company's chief accountant, who is responsible for the preparation of accounting reports for both external and internal decision makers. (p. M-8)

cost   The resources forfeited to receive some goods or services. (p. M-20)

cost accounting   A narrow application of management accounting dealing specifically with procedures designed to determine how much a particular item (usually a unit of manufactured product) costs. (p. M-5)

cost behavior   The reaction of costs to changes in levels of business activity. (p. M-118)

cost center   A business segment where the manager has responsibility and authority to act to decrease or at least control costs but has little or no control over the revenues generated or the amount invested in the segment. (p. M-389)

cost driver   A cost cause that is used as a cost allocation base. (p. M-73)

cost object   Any activity or item for which a separate cost measurement is desired. (p. M-21)

cost of capital   The cost of obtaining financing from all available financing sources. (p. M-222)

cost of capital rate   Another name for *cost of capital*. (p. M-222)

cost of debt capital   The interest a company pays to its creditors. (p. M-223)

cost of equity capital   What equity investors give up when they invest in one company rather than another. (p. M-223)

cost of goods sold budget   Calculates the total cost of all the product a manufacturing or merchandising company estimates it will sell during the period covered by the budget. (p. M-271)

cost of services budget   Calculates the total cost of all the services a service type business estimates it will provide during the period covered by the budget. (p. M-271)

cost pool   An accumulation of the costs associated with a specific cost object. (p. M-71)

cost-volume-profit (CVP) analysis   The analysis of the relationship between cost and volume and the effect of these relationships on profit. (p. M-154)

decentralized management   A management style in which lower-level managers are responsible for decisions that relate to their segment of the company. (p. M-387)

direct cost   A cost that can be easily traced to an individual cost object. (p. M-21)

direct fixed cost   Fixed costs incurred to support a single business segment. (p. M-380)

direct labor cost   The cost of all production labor that can be traced directly to a unit of manufactured product. (p. M-26)

direct labor efficiency standard   The estimated number of direct labor hours required to produce a single unit of product. (p. M-332)

direct labor efficiency variance   A measure of the difference between the planned number of direct labor hours and the actual number of direct labor hours for the units actually manufactured. (p. M-342)

direct labor hours   The time spent by production workers as they transform raw materials into units of finished products. (p. M-28)

direct labor rate standard   The planned hourly wage paid to production workers. (p. M-333)

direct labor rate variance   A measure of the difference between the actual wage rate paid to employees and the direct labor rate standard. (p. M-344)

direct material   The raw material that becomes a part of the final product and can be easily traced to the individual units produced. (p. M-28)

direct material price standard   The anticipated cost for each item of direct material used in the manufacture of a product. (p. M-332)

direct material price variance   A measure of the difference between the amount the company planned to pay for direct material purchased and the amount it actually paid for the direct material. (p. M-341)

direct material quantity standard   The amount of direct material it should take to manufacture a single unit of product. (p. M-332)

direct material quantity variance   A measure of the over- or underconsumption of direct material for the number of units actually manufactured. (p. M-338)

direct material usage variance   Another name for the *direct material quantity variance.* (p. M-338)

direct materials cost   The cost of all raw materials that can be traced directly to a unit of manufactured product. (p. M-26)

discounting cash flows   Determining the present value of cash to be received in the future. (p. M-229)

engineering approach   A method used to separate a mixed cost into its fixed and variable components using experts who are familiar with the technical aspects of the activity and associated cost. (p. M-125)

equivalent units   The number of units that would have been completed if all production efforts resulted in only completed units. (p. M-91)

factory burden   Another name for *manufacturing overhead cost.* (p. M-29)

factory overhead   Another name for *manufacturing overhead cost.* (p. M-29)

favorable variance   The difference between actual performance and standard performance when the actual performance exceeds standard. (p. M-327)

finished goods inventory   Products that have been completed and are ready to sell. (p. M-27)

fixed cost   A cost that remains constant in total regardless of the level of activity. (p. M-118)

fixed manufacturing overhead budget variance   The difference between the actual amount of total fixed manufacturing overhead cost and the budgeted fixed manufacturing overhead cost. (p. M-348)

fixed manufacturing overhead volume variance   A measure of the utilization of plant capacity. This variance is caused by manufacturing more or less product during a particular production period than planned. (p. M-349)

functional income statement   An income statement that classifies cost by function (product cost and period cost). (p. M-151)

future value   The value of a payment, or series of payments, at some future point in time calculated at some interest rate. (p. M-240)

high-low method   A method used to separate a mixed cost into its fixed and variable components using the mathematical differences between the highest and lowest levels of activity and cost. (p. M-132)

hurdle rate   Another name for *cost of capital.* (p. M-222)

hybrid firms   Companies that generate revenue from providing services and selling products. (p. M-39)

ideal standard   A standard that is attainable only under perfect conditions. (p. M-328)

imposed budget   A budget in which upper management sets figures for all operating activities that the rest of the company rarely, if ever, can negotiate. (p. M-276)

incremental budgeting   The process of using the prior year's budget or the company's actual results to build the new operating budget. (p. M-275)

indirect cost   A cost that supports more than one cost object. (p. M-21)

indirect fixed cost   Another name for *common fixed cost.* (p. M-380)

indirect labor   The labor incurred in support of multiple cost objects. (p. M-29)

indirect materials   Materials consumed in support of multiple cost objects. (p. M-29)

Industrial Revolution   A term used to describe the transition in the United States from an agricultural-based economy to a manufacturing-based economy. (p. M-9)

Institute of Management Accountants (IMA)   A professional association of management accountants comparable to the professional association of financial accountants (American Institute of Certified Public Accountants). (p. M-11)

internal rate of return (IRR)   The calculated expected percentage return promised by a proposed capital project. (p. M-233)

inventoriable cost   Another name for *product cost.* (p. M-22)

investment center   A business segment that is evaluated based on the amount of profit generated relative to the amount invested in the segment. (p. M-390)

job cost sheet   A document that tracks the costs of products and organizes and summarizes the cost information for each job. (p. M-78)

job order costing   A costing method that accumulates cost by a single unit, or batch of units. (p. M-76)

just-in-time (JIT)   A philosophy that eliminates all unnecessary inventory and limits the use of company resources until they are absolutely needed to fulfill customer demand. (p. M-397)

labor time ticket   A document used to track the amount of time each employee works on a particular production job or a particular task in the factory. (p. M-83)

lead time The time that passes from the time an order is received until the product is complete and ready for shipment. (p. M-398)

least-squares method Another name for *regression analysis.* (p. M-134)

linear regression analysis Another name for *regression analysis.* (p. M-134)

management accounting The branch of accounting designed to provide information to internal economic decision makers (managers). (p. M-5)

management by exception The process of focusing management attention on areas where actual performance deviates from the preestablished standards. (p. M-327)

managerial accounting Another name for management accounting. (p. M-5)

manufacturing overhead All activities involved in the manufacture of products besides direct materials or direct labor. (p. M-29)

manufacturing overhead allocation The process of assigning or allotting an amount of manufacturing overhead cost to each unit of product produced based on some reasonable basis of distribution. (p. M-71)

manufacturing overhead cost All costs associated with the operation of the manu-facturing facility besides direct materials cost and direct labor cost. It is composed entirely of indirect manufacturing cost—that incurred to support multiple cost objects. (p. M-26)

master budget Another name for *operating budget.* (p. M-266)

master operating budget Another name for *operating budget.* (p. M-266)

materials requisition A formal request for material to be transferred from the raw materials storage area to production. (p. M-81)

material stores Another name for *raw materials inventory.* (p. M-26)

mission statement A summary of the main goals of the organization. (p. M-218)

mixed cost An individual cost that has both a fixed cost and a variable cost component. It also describes a company's total cost structure.(p. M-124)

net cash flows Cash inflow less cash outflow. (p. M-228)

net present value (NPV) The present value of all cash inflows associated with a proposed capital project minus the present value of all

cash outflows associated with the proposed capital project. (p. M-229)

normal cost system System in which product cost reflects actual direct material cost, actual direct labor cost, and estimated overhead costs. (p. M-87)

operating budget The budget that plans a company's routine day-to-day business activities for one to five years. (p. M-220)

operating budget A budget for a specific period, usually one to five years, that establishes who is responsible for the day-to-day operation of a business during that time. (p. M-266)

opportunity cost The benefit foregone (given up) because one alternative is chosen over another. (p. M-195)

organizational goals The core beliefs and values of the company. They outline why the organization exists and are a combination of financial and nonfinancial goals. (p. M-217)

outsourcing Buying services, products, or components of products instead of producing them. (p. M-192)

overhead In a manufacturing company, another name for manufacturing overhead cost; in a service type business, the indirect service cost. (p. M-29)

participative budget A budget in which managers and employees at many levels of the company are involved in setting the performance standards and preparing the budget. (p. M-277)

payback period method A capital budgeting technique that measures the length of time a capital project must generate positive cash flows that equal the original investment in the project. (p. M-235)

performance to budget A process of evaluating managers and employees based on how they perform against the budget. (p. M-298)

period cost All costs incurred by a company that are not considered product cost. Includes selling and administrative cost. (p. M-22)

perpetual budgeting The budgeting approach of updating the budget every month. (p. M-274)

practical standard A standard that allows for normal, recurring inefficiencies. (p. M-328)

predetermined overhead application rate An overhead allocation rate calculated using estimated annual manufacturing overhead cost and the annual estimated amount for the allocation base. (p. M-87)

present value The amount future cash flows are worth today based on an appropriate interest rate (p. M-243)

process costing A method of allocating manufacturing cost to products to determine an average cost per unit. (p. M-76)

product cost The cost of the various products a company sells. (p. M-22)

production budget Details the cost and number of units that must be produced by a manufacturer to meet the sales forecast and the desired ending inventory. (p. M-270)

profit center A business segment in which the manager has the responsibility and authority to act to increase revenue and decrease or at least control costs, but has little or no control over the amount invested in the segment. (p. M-389)

profitability index A method used to rank acceptable proposed capital projects. (p. M-233)

purchase order A formal document used to order material from a vendor. (p. M-79)

purchase requisition A request form that lists the quantity and description of the materials needed. (p. M-79)

purchases budget Details the cost and number of units that must be purchased by a merchandiser to meet the sales forecast and the desired ending inventory. (p. M-270)

purchasing department A specialized department that purchases all the goods required by a company. (p. M-79)

qualitative factors Factors that cannot be measured by numbers—they must be described in words. (p. M-185)

raw materials inventory Materials that have been purchased but have not yet entered the production process. (p. M-26)

real rate of return Another name for *internal rate of return.* (p. M-233)

receiving report A document that indicates the quantity of each item received. (p. M-80)

regression analysis A method used to separate a mixed cost into its fixed and variable components using complex mathematical formulas. (p. M-134)

relevant cost A dollar inflow or outflow that pertains to a particular management decision in that it has a bearing on which decision alternative is preferable. (p. M-184)

relevant costing The process of determining which dollar inflows and outflows pertain to a particular management decision. (p. M-184)

relevant net cash flows Future net cash flows that differ between or among the alternatives being considered. (p. M-228)

relevant range The range of activity within which cost behavior assumptions are valid. (p. M-122)

required rate of return Another name for *cost of capital.* (p. M-222)

residual income The amount by which a segment's actual income exceeds the income needed to meet a company's required rate of return. (p. M-393)

return on investment (ROI) The percentage return generated by an investment in a business or a business segment. (p. M-391)

revenue center A business segment in which the manager has responsibility and authority to act to increase revenues but has little or no control over costs and the amount invested in the segment. (p. M-388)

sales budget Details the expected sales revenue from a company's primary operating activities during a certain time period. (p. M-270)

sales forecast The prediction of sales for the period covered by the operating budget. (p. M-279)

scarce resources A term describing the limited amount of money a company has to invest in capital projects. (p. M-227)

scatter graphing A method used to separate a mixed cost into its fixed and variable components by plotting historical activity and cost data to see how a cost relates to various levels of activity. (p. M-126)

scientific management A management philosophy based on the notion that factories were run by machines—some mechanical and some human. Scientific management experts believed they could improve production efficiency by establishing standards of performance for workers. (p. M-10)

segment income statement An income statement prepared for a business segment. (p. M-379)

segment margin The amount of income that pertains to a particular segment. (p. M-379)

segment reports Reports that provide information pertaining to a particular business segment. (p. M-378)

selling and administrative expense budget Calculates all costs other than the cost of product or services required to support a company's forecasted sales. (p. M-271)

selling cost   The cost of locating customers, attracting customers, convincing customers to buy, and the cost of necessary paperwork to document and record sales. (p. M-22)

sensitivity analysis   A technique used to determine the effect on cost-volume-profit when changes are made in the selling price, cost structure (variable and/or fixed), and volume used in the CVP calculations. Also called "what if" analysis. (p. M-161)

service department   A business segment responsible for secondary (support) functions. Service departments provide service to the main business operations and to other service departments. (p. M-384)

setup time   The time it takes to prepare manufacturing equipment for the production of particular products. (p. M-398)

simple interest   Interest calculated on the original principal amount invested only. (p. M-240)

special order   An order that is outside a company's normal scope of business activity. (p. M-190)

standard   A preestablished benchmark for desirable performance. (p. M-326)

standard cost system   A system in which cost standards are set after careful analysis and then used to evaluate actual performance. (p. M-326)

standard costing   The process of setting cost performance goals that benchmark acceptable performance and then using these cost goals to evaluate performance. (p. M-326)

standard fixed manufacturing overhead rate   The rate used to apply fixed manufacturing overhead to units of manufactured product. (p. M-334)

standard variable manufacturing overhead rate   The rate used to apply variable manufacturing overhead to units of manufactured product. (p. M-334)

strategic plan   A long-range plan that sets forth the actions a company will take to attain its organizational goals. (p. M-219)

sunk cost   A past cost that cannot be changed by current or future actions. (p. M-184)

throughput time   The time that passes from the time a unit of product enters the production process until it emerges as a finished product. (p. M-398)

time-adjusted rate of return   Another name for *internal rate of return.* (p. M-233)

time value of money   The interest earning potential of cash. (p. M-189)

time value of money   The increase in the value of cash over time due to investment income. (p. M-229)

top-down budgeting   A budget prepared by top managers in a company. (p. M-276)

traceable fixed cost   Another name for *direct fixed cost.* (p. M-380)

treasurer   The corporate officer who is responsible for cash and credit management and for planning activities, such as investment in long-lived property, plant, and equipment. (p. M-7)

unfavorable variance   The difference between actual performance and standard performance when the actual performance falls below standard. (p. M-324)

unscheduled down time   The amount of time production equipment is out of service due to unscheduled repairs and maintenance. (p. M-398)

variable cost   A cost that changes in total proportionately with changes in the level of activity. (p. M-119)

variable manufacturing overhead efficiency variance   A measure of the variable manufacturing overhead cost attributable to the difference between the planned and actual direct labor hours worked. (p. M-345)

variable manufacturing overhead spending variance   The difference between how much was actually spent on variable manufacturing overhead and the amount that should have been spent based on the actual direct labor hours worked. (p. M-347)

variance   The difference between actual performance and the budgeted or standard amount. (p. M-326)

work-in-process inventory   Products that have entered the production process but have not yet been completed. (p. M-27)

zero-based budgeting   A process of budgeting in which managers start from scratch, or zero, when preparing a new budget. (p. M-275)

zero defects   Describes the concept of products that are completely free of imperfections. (p. M-397)

Index: Financial and Management Accounting

H

High-low method, **M**-130–32
Historical cost, **F**-276
Hoover's Handbook of American Business, **F**-26
Hurdle rate, **M**-222–23
Hybrid companies, **F**-14
Hybrid firms, **M**-37

I

Ideal standards, **M**-328
Imposed budget, **M**-276
Income
　net, **F**-143, 144
　　as an increase in owners' equity, **F**-149
　operating, **F**-146
Income statements, **F**-142–49, **F**-373–95
　accrual basis, **F**-198–200
　budgeted, **M**-271, **M**-281–84
　　building, **M**-284–85
　cash basis, **F**-189–91
　changes in accounting principles, **F**-386–88
　contribution, **M**-149–65
　　CVP analysis, **M**-152–65
　　definition of, **M**-149
　　purpose of, **M**-149–52
　earnings per share, **F**-390–91
　effect of income taxes on, **F**-394–95
　expenses in, **F**-143
　functional, **M**-149
　history and development of, **F**-374–75
　multistep, **F**-146
　organization of, **F**-379–88
　　discontinued operations, **F**-384–85
　　extraordinary items, **F**-385–86
　　income tax disclosure, **F**-382–84
　　recurring and nonrecurring items, **F**-380–82
　revenues in, **F**-142
　segment, **M**-379–81
　single-step, **F**-145–46
Income tax disclosure, **F**-382–84
Income tax expense, recording, **F**-394–95
Incremental budgeting, **M**-275
Indenture, **F**-118
Indirect costs, **M**-19
Indirect fixed costs. *See* Common fixed costs
Indirect labor, **M**-27–28
Indirect manufacturing costs. *See* Manufacturing overhead
Indirect materials, **M**-27, **M**-28
Indirect method, **F**-415, **F**-423–27
Indirect service costs, **M**-35–36
Industrial Revolution, **M**-7–8
Industry averages, comparing ratios to, **F**-471–75
Industry comparisons, **F**-470–71
Industry Norms and Key Business Ratios, **F**-470
Industry outlook, **F**-452–54, **F**-477–78

Industry Surveys, **F**-478
Information. *See also* Accounting information
　definition of, **F**-57
Information-processing styles, **F**-47
Infotrac, **F**-24
Initial offerings, of bonds, **F**-121
Initial public offerings (IPOs), **F**-92
Institute of Management Accountants (IMA), **M**-9
Intangible assets, **F**-378
Integrated Disclosure System, **F**-26
Interest, **F**-114–15
　definition of, **F**-112
Interest rate(s)
　effective (yield rate or market interest rate),
　　F-116–19
　nominal, **F**-118
　secondary bond market and, **F**-122–23
Interest, time value of money and, **M**-187, **M**-239–46
Internal decision makers, **F**-53, **F**-54, **M**-3–4. *See also*
　　Managers
Internal financing, **F**-109
Internal rate of return (IRR), **M**-233–35
Internal Revenue Service, **F**-320, **F**-471
　depreciation methods prescribed by, **F**-277–78
Internet, the. *See* Web sites
Intrinsic rewards, **F**-45
Intuitive style, **F**-47
Inventoriable costs, **M**-20
Inventory. *See* Finished goods inventory; Merchandise
　　inventory; Raw materials inventory; Work-in-
　　process inventory
Inventory turnover ratio, **F**-462–63
Investing activities, **F**-413, **F**-414
　determining cash flow from, **F**-427
Investment bankers (underwriters), **F**-92
Investment centers, **M**-390–91
　residual income and, **M**-393–94
　return on investment and, **M**-390–91, **M**-394
Investments
　definition of, **F**-378
　by owner(s), **F**-79–80, **F**-81–83
Issued shares, **F**-86

J

Job cost sheets, **M**-76–77
Job order costing, **M**-74, **M**-75–88
　definition of, **M**-74
　documentation relating to, **M**-76–83
　manufacturing overhead, **M**-83–88
Journal entries, **F**-233–34
　compound, **F**-234
Journalizing transactions, **F**-226–27, **F**-235–37
Journals
　definition of, **F**-226
　general, **F**-226
　special, **F**-226
Just-in-time (JIT) philosophy, **M**-12, **M**-397–99

cash discounts, **F**-341–42
freight terms, **F**-342–43
Purchases budget, **M**-270–71
preparing, **M**-285–87
Purchasing departments, **M**-77

Q

Qualitative factors, **M**-183
Quality standards, **M**-395
Quantitative factors, **M**-183
Quantity standards, **M**-328
Quick ratio, **F**-460–61
Quotas, **F**-15

R

Rates of return
accounting, **M**-236–37
internal (IRR), **M**-233–35
real, **M**-233
required, **M**-222–23
time-adjusted, **M**-233
Ratio analysis, **F**-448, **F**-449, **F**-454–79
definition of, **F**-448
limitations of, **F**-479
measuring liquidity, **F**-459–63
measuring profitability, **F**-455–59
measuring solvency, **F**-463–66
summary of key ratios, **F**-466
using the ratios, **F**-466–79
industry comparisons, **F**-470–71
Standard Industrial Classification (SIC) system,
F-467–70
Raw materials inventory, **F**-318, **M**-24–25
Real accounts (permanent accounts), **F**-231
Realization, **F**-188
Real rate of return, **M**-233
Reasoned decision making, **F**-48–50
Receivable, **F**-192
Receivables turnover ratio, **F**-462
Receiving reports, **M**-78–79
Recognition
expense, **F**-187
accrual basis, **F**-193–94
cash basis, **F**-188
revenue, **F**-187
accrual basis, **F**-192–93
cash basis, **F**-188
Reconciling bank statements, **F**-229
Recording, **F**-187
income tax expense, **F**-394–95
long-lived assets and depreciation, **F**-296–99
merchandise inventory, **F**-343–50
Recurring items, **F**-380–82
Regression analysis, **M**-132–33
Regulation S-K, **F**-26
Regulation S-X, **F**-26

Relevance of accounting information, **F**-58, **F**-59
Relevant costing, **M**-181–94
definition of, **M**-182
determining relevant cost of each alternative,
M-185–86, **M**-189, **M**-190–91
equipment replacement, **M**-184–87
gathering all costs associated with decision, **M**-185,
M-188, **M**-190
interest and, **M**-187
outsourcing, **M**-190–94
selecting an alternative, **M**-186–87, **M**-189, **M**-191–92
special orders, **M**-188–90
Relevant costs, **M**-182–83
comparing, **M**-186–87, **M**-189, **M**-191–92
Relevant net cash flows, **M**-228
Relevant range, **M**-120–21
Reliability of accounting information, **F**-58, 59
Reporting, **F**-187
Representational faithfulness of accounting information,
F-59
Required rate of return, **M**-222–23
Residual income, **M**-393–94
Residual value, **F**-196
Resource allocation, **M**-267–69
Retailers, **F**-14, **M**-22. *See also* Merchandising firms
Retained earnings, **F**-86, **F**-151
cash dividends and, **F**-155–57
statement of, **F**-156
Return before interest on equity ratio, **F**-458–59
Return on assets ratio, **F**-456
Return on equity ratio, **F**-458
Return on investment (ROI), **M**-391–93, **M**-394
Revenue centers, **M**-388, **M**-389–90
Revenue(s). *See also* Gains
accrued, **F**-197
deferred, **F**-197
definition of, **F**-143
in income statement, **F**-142
owners' equity and, **F**-149
recognition of, **F**-187
accrual basis, **F**-192–93
cash basis, **F**-188
sales, **F**-146
Rewards, decision making and, **F**-44, **F**-45, **F**-46
Risk/reward trade-off, **F**-46
Robert Morris Associates' Annual Statement Studies, **F**-470
Routine decisions, **F**-46

S

Sales budget, **M**-270, **M**-281–82
Sales forecast, **M**-270, **M**-279–81, **M**-301–2
factors affecting accuracy of, **M**-280–81
Sales projection, using CVP analysis, **M**-156–58, **M**-164–65
Sales revenue, **F**-146
Salvage value, **F**-196
Savings and loan associations (S&Ls), **F**-111
Scarce resources, **M**-226–27
Scatter graphing, **M**-124–30, **M**-131–32

Stocks
  appreciation of, **F**-125–26, **F**-449
  common, **F**-86–89
  no-par, **F**-88
  preferred, **F**-89–91
  treasury, **F**-86
Straight-line depreciation, **F**-196, **F**-276–81, **F**-283–84, **F**-296–97
Strategic plans, **M**-219
Sunk costs, **M**-182–83
Supplemental schedule, **F**-428–29
Survey of Current Business, **F**-451
Syndicates, **F**-121
Systematic style, **F**-47

T

T-accounts, **F**-233
Tangible property, **F**-276
Tariffs, **F**-15
Technological change, **F**-452–53
Technological developments, sales forecast and, **M**-281
Technological obsolescence, **F**-284–85
Temporary accounts (nominal accounts), **F**-230–31
Throughput time, **M**-398
Time-adjusted rate of return, **M**-233
Timeliness, of information, **M**-5
Timeliness of accounting information, **F**-59
Times interest earned ratio, **F**-464–65
Time value of money, **M**-187, **M**-229, **M**-239–46
  future value, **M**-240–43
  present value (discounting), **M**-243–46
Top-down budgeting, **M**-275–76, **M**-277–78
Total asset turnover ratio, **F**-457–58
Total liabilities to net worth ratio, **F**-464
Traceable fixed costs. *See* Direct fixed costs
Tracking inventory costs, **F**-316–18
  manufacturing companies, **F**-318
  merchandising companies, **F**-316–18
Translation of currency, **F**-15
Treasurer, **F**-85
Treasurers, **M**-5, **M**-6
Treasury stock, **F**-86
Trend analysis, **F**-448
  definition of, **F**-448
Trends, in management accounting, **M**-12–13
Trial balance, **F**-228
  post-closing, **F**-231, **F**-251–52
  preparing the, **F**-228, **F**-237–42

U

U. S. Industry & Trade Outlook, **F**-454
Uncertainty, **F**-46

Underwriters, **F**-92, **F**-121–22
Unfavorable variance, **M**-327
Unqualified opinion, **F**-21–22
Unscheduled downtime, **M**-398
Useful life of an asset, **F**-195–96

V

Variable costs, **M**-117, **M**-118
  change in, **M**-161–63
  on contribution income statement, **M**-152
  identifying elements in mixed costs, **M**-123–33
  relevant range, **M**-120–21
Variable manufacturing overhead efficiency variance, **M**-345–47
Variable manufacturing overhead spending variance, **M**-346, **M**-347–48
Variable manufacturing overhead standards, **M**-335–36
Variance, definition of, **M**-326–27
Variance analysis, **M**-337–51
  direct labor variances, **M**-342–45
  direct materials variances, **M**-338–42
  manufacturing overhead variances, **M**-345–51
Verifiability of accounting information, **F**-59
Volume-profit analysis. *See* Cost-volume-profit analysis

W

Wage system, **M**-7
Wall Street Journal, The, Annual Report Service of, **F**-24
Web sites, annual reports available on, **F**-23–24
"What if?" analysis, **M**-159–60, **M**-165
Wholesalers, **F**-14, **M**-21–22. *See also* Merchandising firms
Withdrawals (drawings), **F**-153–54
Working capital, **F**-410
Work-in-process inventory, **F**-318, **M**-25
  cost of ending, **M**-90
Worksheets, **F**-228
  definition of, **F**-228
  preparing, **F**-228, **F**-237–42

Y

Yield rate. *See* Effective interest rate

Z

Zero-based budgeting, **M**-275
Zero defects, **M**-397